LUKE

LUKE

ZONDERVAN Exegetical Commentary

ON THE

New Testament

DAVID E. GARLAND

CLINTON E. ARNOLD
General Editor

ZONDERVAN.com/
AUTHORTRACKER
follow your favorite authors

*To the faculty and staff
of George W. Truett Theological Seminary,
Baylor University*

ZONDERVAN

Luke
Copyright © 2011 by David E. Garland

Requests for information should be addressed to:

Zondervan, *Grand Rapids, Michigan 49530*

Library of Congress Cataloging-in-Publication Data

Garland, David E.
    Luke / David Garland.
        p. cm.—(Zondervan exegetical commentary series on the New Testament; v. 3)
    Includes bibliographical references and index.
    ISBN 978-0-310-24359-5 (hardcover, printed)
    1. Bible N.T. Luke—Commentaries. I. Title.
BS2595.53.G37   2012
226.4'077—dc23
                                                                          2011018826

Cover design: *Tammy Johnson*
Interior design: *Beth Shagene*

Printed in the United States of America

11 12 13 14 15 16 17 18 /DCI/ 25 24 23 22 21 20 19 18 17 16 15 14 13 12 11 10 9 8 7 6 5 4 3 2 1

Contents

Series Introduction

This generation has been blessed with an abundance of excellent commentaries. Some are technical and do a good job of addressing issues that the critics have raised; other commentaries are long and provide extensive information about word usage and catalogue nearly every opinion expressed on the various interpretive issues; still other commentaries focus on providing cultural and historical background information; and then there are those commentaries that endeavor to draw out many applicational insights.

The key question to ask is: What are you looking for in a commentary? This commentary series might be for you if

- you have taken Greek and would like a commentary that helps you apply what you have learned without assuming you are a well-trained scholar.
- you would find it useful to see a concise, one- or two-sentence statement of what the commentator thinks the main point of each passage is.
- you would like help interpreting the words of Scripture without getting bogged down in scholarly issues that seem irrelevant to the life of the church.
- you would like to see a visual representation (a graphical display) of the flow of thought in each passage.
- you would like expert guidance from solid evangelical scholars who set out to explain the meaning of the original text in the clearest way possible and to help you navigate through the main interpretive issues.
- you want to benefit from the results of the latest and best scholarly studies and historical information that help to illuminate the meaning of the text.
- you would find it useful to see a brief summary of the key theological insights that can be gleaned from each passage and some discussion of the relevance of these for Christians today.

These are just some of the features that characterize the new Zondervan Exegetical Commentary on the New Testament series. The idea for this series was refined over time by an editorial board who listened to pastors and teachers express what they wanted to see in a commentary series based on the Greek text. That board consisted of myself, George H. Guthrie, William D. Mounce, Thomas R. Schreiner, and Mark L. Strauss along with Zondervan senior editor at large, Verlyn Verbrugge, and former Zondervan senior acquisitions editor, Jack Kuhatschek. We also enlisted a board of consulting editors who are active pastors, ministry leaders, and seminary professors to help in the process of designing a commentary series that will be useful to the church. Zondervan senior acquisitions editor David Frees has now been shepherding the process to completion.

We arrived at a design that includes seven components for the treatment of each biblical passage. What follows is a brief orientation to these primary components of the commentary.

Literary Context

In this section, you will find a concise discussion of how the passage functions in the broader literary context of the book. The commentator highlights connections with the preceding and following material in the book and makes observations on the key literary features of this text.

Main Idea

Many readers will find this to be an enormously helpful feature of this series. For each passage, the commentator carefully crafts a one- or two-sentence statement of the big idea or central thrust of the passage.

Translation and Graphical Layout

Another unique feature of this series is the presentation of each commentator's translation of the Greek text in a graphical layout. The purpose of this diagram is to help the reader visualize, and thus better understand, the flow of thought within the text. The translation itself reflects the interpretive decisions made by each commentator in the "Explanation" section of the commentary. Here are a few insights that will help you to understand the way these are put together:

1. On the far left side next to the verse numbers is a series of interpretive labels that indicate the function of each clause or phrase of the biblical text. The corresponding portion of the text is on the same line to the right of the label. We have not used technical linguistic jargon for these, so they should be easily understood.

2. In general, we place every clause (a group of words containing a subject and a predicate) on a separate line and identify how it is supporting the principal assertion of the text (namely, is it saying when the action occurred, how it took place, or why it took place?). We sometimes place longer phrases or a series of items on separate lines as well.

3. Subordinate (or dependent) clauses and phrases are indented and placed directly under the words that they modify. This helps the reader to more easily see the nature of the relationship of clauses and phrases in the flow of the text.

4. Every main clause has been placed in bold print and pushed to the left margin for clear identification.

5. Sometimes when the level of subordination moves too far to the right — as often happens with some of Paul's long, involved sentences! — we reposition the flow to the left of the diagram, but use an arrow to indicate that this has happened.

6. The overall process we have followed has been deeply informed by principles of discourse analysis and narrative criticism (for the Gospels and Acts).

Structure

Immediately following the translation, the commentator describes the flow of thought in the passage and explains how certain interpretive decisions regarding the relationship of the clauses were made in the passage.

Exegetical Outline

The overall structure of the passage is described in a detailed exegetical outline. This will be particularly helpful for those who are looking for a way to concisely explain the flow of thought in the passage in a teaching or preaching setting.

Explanation of the Text

As an exegetical commentary, this work makes use of the Greek language to interpret the meaning of the text. If your Greek is rather rusty (or even somewhat limited), don't be too concerned. All of the Greek words are cited in parentheses following an English translation. We have made every effort to make this commentary as readable and useful as possible even for the nonspecialist.

Those who will benefit the most from this commentary will have had the equivalent of two years of Greek in college or seminary. This would include a semester or two of working through an intermediate grammar (such as Wallace, Porter, Brooks and Winberry, or Dana and Mantey). The authors use the grammatical language that is found in these kinds of grammars. The details of the grammar of the passage, however, are only discussed when it has a bearing on the interpretation of the text.

The emphasis on this section of the text is to convey the meaning. Commentators examine words and images, grammatical details, relevant OT and Jewish background to a particular concept, historical and cultural context, important text-critical issues, and various interpretational issues that surface.

Theology in Application

This, too, is a unique feature for an exegetical commentary series. We felt it was important for each author not only to describe what the text meant in its various details, but also to take a moment and reflect on the theological contribution that it makes. In this section, the theological message of the passage is summarized. The authors discuss the theology of the text in terms of its place within the book and in a broader biblical-theological context. Finally, each commentator provides some suggestions on what the message of the passage is for the church today. At the conclusion of each volume in this series is a summary of the whole range of theological themes touched on by this book of the Bible.

Our sincere hope and prayer is that you find this series helpful not only for your own understanding of the text of the New Testament, but as you are actively engaged in teaching and preaching God's Word to people who are hungry to be fed on its truth.

CLINTON E. ARNOLD, general editor

Author's Preface

This commentary was written during a time of personal transition when I moved from Associate Dean to being the Dean of George W. Truett Theological Seminary and then, within a year, to become the interim President of Baylor University, an office I served in for almost two years. I wish to thank Dennis Tucker, who served as Acting Dean of the Seminary, and the members of the Executive Council of the Seminary, Jan Cason, Ron Cook, David Hardage, and Grear Howard, who carried on during my semi-absence. I am also grateful to the Executive Council of the University, Juan Alejandro, John Barry, Charlie Beckenhauer, Elizabeth Davis, Karla Leeper, Ian McCaw, Dennis Prescott, Pattie Orr, and Reagan Ramsower for helping to make the interim presidency so personally rewarding. I am appreciative of the administrative assistants in the Dean's and President's offices — Paula Autrey, Angela Bailey, Judy Carpenter, Rita Cox, and Laura Hendrix — for all they did to make coming to work every day an enjoyable experience and for scheduling time for me to do research as well as administration.

I am most grateful to the following students of George W. Truett Theological Seminary at Baylor University who served as my Teaching Fellows and read portions of the manuscript and offered insights and critique: Matt Vandagriff, Brad Arnold, Emily McGowan, Joey Pyle, Taylor Rogers, and Richard Villareal. Another student, Casey Ramirez, gave critical technical assistance in formatting the manuscript. Andrew and Tia Kim gave invaluable assistance in the final editing process. I also would like to thank the following doctoral students from the Department of Religion at Baylor University for reading parts of the manuscript and also offering their insights and critique: Alicia Myers, Josh Stigall, Jim Keener, and especially Eric Gilchrist, who read the entire manuscript. I appreciated their reactions, both positive and critical. All of these students are excellent readers of biblical texts and are not responsible for any of my errors and infelicities. I would be remiss in not thanking Clinton Arnold and the various editorial readers for their careful editing work. In particular, I would like to thank Verlyn Verbrugge, senior editor at large at Zondervan, for his valuable insights and corrections.

I am grateful to the Baylor Board of Regents, who granted me a research sabbatical leave at the end of my term of service as interim president to finish this commentary. I also cannot thank enough the many churches who invited me to preach and heard sermons from Luke over the past years. From my perspective, one of the major purposes of the careful study of Scripture is to lead to proclamation and witness.

I am eternally thankful to my wife, Diana, who offered significant encouragement while reading various editions of the manuscript despite her own heavy workload as Dean of the Baylor School of Social Work. Her partnership is a source of constant joy.

Abbreviations

AB	Anchor Bible
ABD	*Anchor Bible Dictionary*. Edited by D. N. Freedman. 6 vols. New York, 1992.
ʾAbot R. Nat.	ʾAbot de Rabbi Nathan
ACCS	Ancient Christian Commentary on Scripture
ACNT	Augsburg Commentaries on the New Testament
Ag. Ap.	*Against Apion* (Josephus)
Alleg. Interp.	*Allegorical Interpretation* (Philo)
AnBib	Analecta biblica
ANRW	*Aufstieg und Niedergang der römischen Welt: Geschichte und Kultur Roms im Spiegel der neueren Forschung.* Edited by H. Temporini and W. Haase. Berlin, 1972 – .
Ant.	*Jewish Antiquities* (Josephus)
Apoc. Ab.	*Apocalypse of Abraham*
As. Mos.	*Assumption of Moses*
ASV	American Standard Version
ASTI	Annual of the Swedish Theological Institute
AUSS	Andrews University Seminary Studies
AYB	Anchor Yale Bible
b. ʿAbod. Zar.	*ʿAbodah Zarah* (Babylonian Talmud)
b. B. Bat.	*Baba Batra* (Babylonian Talmud)
b. B. Meṣ.	*Baba Meṣiʿa* (Babylonian Talmud)
b. B. Qam.	*Baba Qamma* (Babylonian Talmud)
b. Ber.	*Berakot* (Babylonian Talmud)
b. ʿErub.	*ʿErubin* (Babylonian Talmud)
b. Giṭ.	*Gittin* (Babylonian Talmud)
b. Ḥag.	*Ḥagigah* (Babylonian Talmud)
b. Ker.	*Keritot* (Babylonian Talmud)
b. Ketub.	*Ketubbot* (Babylonian Talmud)
b. Meg.	*Megillah* (Babylonian Talmud)
b. Menaḥ.	*Menaḥot* (Babylonian Talmud)
b. Moʿed Qaṭ.	*Moʿed Qaṭan* (Babylonian Talmud)

b. Naz.	*Nazir* (Babylonian Talmud)
b. Ned.	*Nedarim* (Babylonian Talmud)
b. Nid.	*Niddah* (Babylonian Talmud)
b. Qidd.	*Qiddušin* (Babylonian Talmud)
b. Šabb.	*Šabbat* (Babylonian Talmud)
b. Sanh.	*Sanhedrin* (Babylonian Talmud)
b. Šeqal.	*Šeqalim* (Babylonian Talmud)
b. Soṭah	*Soṭah* (Babylonian Talmud)
b. Sukkah	*Sukkah* (Babylonian Talmud)
b. Yebam.	*Yebamot* (Babylonian Talmud)
b. Yoma	*Yoma* (Babylonian Talmud)
b. Zebaḥ.	*Zebaḥim* (Babylonian Talmud)
BAR	*Biblical Archaeology Review*
2 Bar.	*2 Baruch* (Syriac Apocalypse)
BDAG	Bauer, W., F. W. Danker, W. F. Arndt, and F. W. Gingrich, *Greek-English Lexicon of the New Testament and Other Early Christian Literature*. 3rd ed. Chicago, 2000.
BDF	Blass, F., A. Debrunner, and R. W. Funk. *A Greek Grammar of the New Testament and Other Early Christian Literature*. Chicago, 1961.
BECNT	Baker Exegetical Commentary on the New Testament
BETL	Bibliotheca ephemeridum theologicarum lovaniensium
Bib	*Biblica*
BibInt	*Biblical Interpretation*
BibTheol	*Biblical Theology*
BN	*Biblische Notizen*
BR	*Biblical Research*
BT	*The Bible Translator*
BTB	*Biblical Theology Bulletin*
BZ	*Biblische Zeitschrift*
BZNW	Beihefte zur Zeitschrift für die neutestamentliche Wissenschaft
CahRB	Cahiers de la Revue biblique
Cant. Rab.	*Canticles* (Song of Songs, Song of Solomon) *Rabbah*
CBQ	*Catholic Biblical Quarterly*
CC	Concordia Commentary
CIL	Corpus inscriptionum latinarum
ConBNT	Coniectanea neotestamentica or Coniectanea biblica: New Testament Series
Creation	*On the Creation of the World* (Philo)
CRINT	Compendia rerum iudaicarum ad Novum Testamentum
CSB	Holman Christian Standard Bible
CSR	*Christian Scholar's Review*

CurTM	*Currents in Theology and Mission*
DJG	*Dictionary of Jesus and the Gospels.* Edited by J. Green and S. McKnight. Downers Grove, IL:IVP, 1992.
DSD	*Dead Sea Discoveries*
EKK	Evangelisch-katholischer Kommentar zum Neuen Testament
1 En.	*1 Enoch*
2 En.	*2 Enoch*
ESV	English Standard Version
ETL	Ephemerides theologicae lovanienses
ETS	Erfurter theologische Studien
EvT	*Evangelische Theologie*
EvQ	*Evangelical Quarterly*
Exod. Rab.	*Exodus Rabbah*
ExpTim	*Expository Times*
Flaccus	*Against Flaccus* (Philo)
GELNT	*Greek-English Lexicon of the New Testament: Based on Semantic Domains.* Edited by Johannes P. Louw and Eugene A. Nida. New York: United Bible Societies, 1989.
Gen. Rab.	*Genesis Rabbah*
Good Person	*That Every Good Person Is Free* (Philo)
Gos. Thom.	*Gospel of Thomas* (Nag Hammadi)
GWT	God's Word Translation
HBT	*Horizons in Biblical Theology*
Heir	*Who Is the Heir?* (Philo)
HeyJ	*Heythrop Journal*
HNT	Handbuch zum Neuen Testament
HTKNT	Herders theologischer Kommentar zum Neuen Testament
HTR	*Harvard Theological Review*
HTS	Harvard Theological Studies
HvTSt	*Hervormde teologiese studies*
IBR	Institute for Biblical Research
IBS	*Irish Biblical Studies*
ICC	International Critical Commentary
IDB	*Interpreter's Dictionary of the Bible.* Edited by G. A. Buttrick and K. Crim. 4 vols. New York: Abingdon, 1962.
Int	*Interpretation*
ISBE	*International Standard Bible Encyclopedia.* Edited by G. W. Bromiley. 4 vols. Grand Rapids: Eerdmans, 1979 – 1988.
ITQ	*Irish Theological Quarterly*
j. Ber.	*Berakot* (Jerusalem Talmud)
j. Demai	*Demai* (Jerusalem Talmud)

j. Ḥag.	*Ḥagigah* (Jerusalem Talmud)
j. Šabb.	*Šabbat* (Jerusalem Talmud)
j. Sanh.	*Sanhedrin* (Jerusalem Talmud)
j. Šeb.	*Šebiʿit* (Jerusalem Talmud)
JB	Jerusalem Bible
JBL	*Journal of Biblical Literature*
JES	*Journal of Ecumenical Studies*
JETS	*Journal of the Evangelical Theological Society*
JJS	*Journal of Jewish Studies*
Jos. Asen.	*Joseph and Aseneth*
JPTSup	Journal of Pentecostal Theology Supplement
JRS	*Journal of Roman Studies*
JSNT	*Journal for the Study of the New Testament*
JSNTSup	Journal for the Study of the New Testament: Supplement Series
JSOTSup	Journal for the Study of the Old Testament: Supplement Series
JTS	*Journal of Theological Studies*
Jub.	*Jubilees*
J.W.	*Jewish War* (Josephus)
KEK	Kritisch-exegetischer Kommentar über das Neue Testament
KJV	King James Version
L.A.B.	*Liber Antiquitatum Biblicarum* (Pseudo-Philo)
Lam. Rab.	*Lamentations Rabbah*
Let. Aris.	*Letter of Aristeas*
Lev. Rab.	*Leviticus Rabbah*
Life	*The Life* (Josephus)
LNT	Library of New Testament Studies
LSJ	Liddell, H. G., R. Scott, H. S. Jones. *A Greek-English Lexicon.* 9th ed. with revised supplement. Oxford, 1996.
LTQ	*Lexington Theological Quarterly*
LXX	Septuagint
m. ʾAbot	*ʾAbot* (Mishnah)
m. ʿArak.	*ʿArakin* (Mishnah)
m. B. Bat.	*Baba Batra* (Mishnah)
m. B. Meṣ.	*Baba Meṣiʿa* (Mishnah)
m. B. Qam.	*Baba Qamma* (Mishnah)
m. Ber.	*Berakot* (Mishnah)
m. Demai	*Demai* (Mishnah)
m.ʿErub.	*ʿErubin* (Mishnah)
m. Giṭ.	*Giṭṭin* (Mishnah)
m. Ḥag.	*Ḥagigah* (Mishnah)
m. Ḥal.	*Ḥallah* (Mishnah)

m. Ketub.	*Ketubbot* (Mishnah)
m. Maʿaś.	*Maʿaśerot* (Mishnah)
m. Meg.	*Megillah* (Mishnah)
m. Menaḥ.	*Menaḥim* (Mishnah)
m. Mid.	*Middot* (Mishnah)
m. Miqw.	*Miqwaʾot* (Mishnah)
m. Naz.	*Nazir* (Mishnah)
m. Neg.	*Negaʿim* (Mishnah)
m. Nid.	*Niddah* (Mishnah)
m. ʾOhal.	*ʾOhalot* (Mishnah)
m. Peʾah	*Peʾah* (Mishnah)
m. Pesaḥ.	*Pesaḥim* (Mishnah)
m. Qidd.	*Qiddušin* (Mishnah)
m. Roš Haš.	*Roš Haššanah* (Mishnah)
m. Šabb.	*Šabbat* (Mishnah)
m. Sanh.	*Sanhedrin* (Mishnah)
m. Šeb.	*Šebiʿit* (Mishnah)
m. Šeqal.	*Šeqalim* (Mishnah)
m. Soṭah	*Soṭah* (Mishnah)
m. Tamid	*Tamid* (Mishnah)
m. Taʿan	*Taʿanit* (Mishnah)
m. Yad.	*Yadayim* (Mishnah)
m. Yoma	*Yoma* (Mishnah)
Mart. Isa.	*Martyrdom of Isaiah*
Mek. Amalek	*Mekilta Amalek*
Midr. Pss.	*Midrash on Psalms*
MM	Moulton, J. H., and G. Milligan. *The Vocabulary of the Greek Testament.* London, 1930. Reprint, Peabody, MA, 1997.
MNTC	Moffat New Testament Commentary
Moses	*On the Life of Moses* (Philo)
MT	Masoretic Text
NAB	New American Bible
NAC	New American Commentary
NASB	New American Standard Bible
NCB	New Century Bible
NEB	New English Bible
Neot	*Neotestamentica*
NET	New English Translation
NICNT	New International Commentary on the New Testament
NIGTC	New International Greek Testament Commentary
NIV	New International Version

NIVAC	NIV Application Commentary
NJB	New Jerusalem Bible
NLT	New Living Translation
NovT	*Novum Testamentum*
NovTSup	Novum Testamentum Supplements
NRSV	New Revised Standard Version
NRTh	*La nouvelle revue théologique*
NTAbh	Neutestamentliche Abhandlungen
NTS	*New Testament Studies*
NTTS	New Testament Tools and Studies
NV	*Nova et vetera*
OBT	Overtures to Biblical Theology
ÖTK	Ökumenischer Taschenbuch-Kommentar zum Neuen Testament
OTL	Old Testament Library
PBM	Paternoster Biblical Monographs
PEQ	*Palestine Exploration Quarterly*
Pesiq. Rab.	*Pesiqta Rabbati*
PNTC	Penguin New Testament Commentary
P. Oxy.	*Oxyrhynchus Papyri.* Edited by B. P. Grenfell, A. S. Hunt, et al. London, 1898 – .
PRSt	*Perspectives in Religious Studies*
PSB	*Princeton Seminary Bulletin*
PSBSup	Princeton Seminary Bulletin Supplements
Ps.-Phoc.	Pseudo-Phocylides
Pss. Sol.	*Psalms of Solomon*
Qoh. Rab.	*Qoheleth [Ecclesiastes] Rabbah*
RB	*Revue biblique*
REB	Revised English Bible
RevExp	*Review and Expositor*
Rewards	*On Rewards and Punishments* (Philo)
RNT	Regensburger Neues Testament
RSV	Revised Standard Version
Ruth Rab.	*Ruth Rabbah*
SBLDS	Society of Biblical Literature Dissertation Series
SBLMS	Society of Biblical Literature Monograph Series
SBLSP	*Society of Biblical Literature Seminar Papers*
SBS	Stuttgarter Bibelstudien
SBT	Studies in Biblical Theology
SE	*Studia evangelica*
Sib. Or.	*Sibylline Oracles*

SJ	Studia Judaica
SJT	*Scottish Journal of Theology*
SNT	Studien zum Neuen Testament
SNTSMS	Society for New Testament Studies Monograph Series
SP	Sacra Pagina
Spec. Laws	*On the Special Laws* (Philo)
SR	*Studies in Religion*
Str-B	Strack, H. L., and P. Billerbeck. *Kommentar zum Neuen Testament aus Talmud und Midrasch.* 6 vols. Munich, 1922 – 1961.
SwJT	*Southwestern Journal of Theology*
SymBU	Symbolae Biblicae Upsalienses
T. Ab.	*Testament of Abraham*
T. Ash.	*Testament of Asher*
T. Benj.	*Testament of Benjamin*
T. Gad	*Testament of Gad*
T. Iss.	*Testament of Issachar*
T. Jud.	*Testament of Judah*
T. Levi	*Testament of Levi*
T. Reu.	*Testament of Reuben*
T. Sol.	*Testament of Solomon*
t. Ber.	*Berakot* (Tosefta)
t. Demai	*Demai* (Tosefta)
t. Ketub.	*Ketubbot* (Tosefta)
t. Meg.	*Megillah* (Tosefta)
t. Neg.	*Negaʿim* (Tosefta)
t. Nid.	*Niddah* (Tosefta)
t. Parah	*Parah* (Tosefta)
t. Peʾah	*Peʾah* (Tosefta)
t. Qidd.	*Qiddušin* (Tosefta)
t. Soṭah	*Soṭah* (Tosefta)
t. Taʿan.	*Taʿanit* (Tosefta)
TBei	*Theologische Beiträge*
TBT	*The Bible Today*
TDNT	*Theological Dictionary of the New Testament.* Edited by G. Kittel and G. Friedrich. Translated by G. W. Bromiley. 10 vols. Grand Rapids, 1964 – 1976.
TEV	Today's English Version
THKNT	Theologischer Handkommentar zum Neuen Testament
TLG	Thesaurus linguae graecae: Canon of Greek Authors and Works
TJ	*Trinity Journal*

TJT	*Toronto Journal of Theology*
TLNT	*Theological Lexicon of the New Testament.* By Ceslas Spicq. Translated and edited by J. D. Ernest. 3 vols. Peabody, MA, 1994.
TNIV	Today's New International Version
TS	*Theological Studies*
TU	Texte und Untersuchungen
TynBul	*Tyndale Bulletin*
Virtues	*On the Virtues* (Philo)
WBC	Word Biblical Commentary
WTJ	*Westminster Theological Journal*
WUNT	Wissenschaftliche Untersuchungen zum Neuen Testament
WW	Word and World
ZNW	*Zeitschrift für die neutestamentliche Wissenschaft und die Kunde der älteren Kirche*

Introduction to Luke

Authorship of Luke-Acts

These works have long been ascribed to Luke, assumed to be Paul's loyal co-worker (Col 4:14; 2 Tim 4:11; Phlm 24).[1] Though Luke does not attach his name to the gospel or Acts, the author would have been known from the start since he includes a specific dedication to Theophilus (see comments on 1:3 that he is a real person). Complete anonymity would have been impossible.

Traditions external to the New Testament unanimously attribute the gospel to Luke from an early date. Hengel observes that "the strange uniformity and early attestation of the titles of the Gospels excludes the possibility that for a long time they had been circulating anonymously in the communities" or that they had received their titles "as a secondary addition."[2] A Western recension of Acts 20:13, which may date as early as AD 120, possibly includes the writer's name in the text, "But I Luke...."[3] "According to Luke" appears as the title at the end of $\mathfrak{P}^{75}$, the oldest extant copy of Luke dating from around AD 200. The gospel would have probably included the name of the author in the title or as an attached tag to be able to catalogue it.[4] Other attestations appear in the Muratorian Canon (c. AD 170 – 180), which attributes the gospel to Luke, a doctor, who is Paul's companion and a native of Antioch in Syria. The so-called Anti-Marcionite Prologue (c. AD 175) also describes Luke as a native of Antioch in Syria and claims that he lived to be eighty-four, was a doctor, was unmarried, wrote in Achaia, and died in Boeotia. Irenaeus (c. AD 175 – 195) claimed that Luke was an "inseparable companion" of Paul (*Haer.* 3.14.1; 3.1.1), though it is more accurate to say that he was a "sometime companion."[5] Perhaps under the

---

1. This assertion was questioned in the nineteenth century under the influence of F. C. Baur, whose model of dialectic history dated Acts in the second century so that the author could not have been a companion of Paul.

2. Martin Hengel, *The Four Gospels and the One Gospel of Jesus Christ* (trans. John Bowden; Harrisburg, PA: Trinity Press International, 2000), 54.

3. F. F. Bruce, *The Acts of the Apostles: The Greek Text with Introduction and Commentary* (Grand Rapids: Eerdmans, 1951), 5.

4. Martin Dibelius, *Studies in the Acts of the Apostles* (ed. H. Greeven; London: SCM, 1956), 148. See also R. F. Strout, *Toward a Better Cataloging Code* (Chicago: Univ. of Chicago, Press, 1956), 7.

5. Joseph A. Fitzmyer, *Luke the Theologian: Aspects of His Teaching* (New York: Paulist, 1983), 9, 22.

influence of this tradition, Tertullian (early third century) calls the gospel a digest of Paul's gospel (*Marc.* 4.2.2; 4.2.5; 4.5.3).

Were he not the actual author, Luke would have been an unlikely candidate to connect with the gospel. He was neither an apostle nor a prominent figure in the New Testament, and many others from Paul's lists of companions in his letters could have been chosen as the potential author of the we-passages in Acts. The traditions about Luke that derive from the late second century probably began with the gospel's ascription to Luke from an earlier time and prompted the scouring of New Testament texts to elaborate upon it. It is less likely that the texts were probed to contrive an author for the gospel.

It is possible that Luke was the unnamed brother Paul mentions as famous for proclaiming the gospel in all the churches (2 Cor 8:18). He was not an eyewitness to the events he records in the gospel, but, like a good historian, he relies on eyewitness testimony (Luke 1:2–4), and he presents himself as a companion of Paul in the we-passages of Acts (Acts 16:10–17; 20:5–16; 21:1–18; 27:1–28:16). There are three interpretations of these passages. (1) The traditional view is that the author of Acts was physically present at the events he records and a member of Paul's troupe. (2) A second view argues the author was using a source written by someone else who witnessed the events, and Luke merely retains its first-person narration. (3) A third view understands the "we" to be purely made-up to add verisimilitude and vividness to his account.

These sections begin at Troas on Paul's second missionary journey and appear and disappear in such an arbitrary manner that they cannot be attributed to some literary convention for making sea voyages more vivid.[6] The "we" reference does not occur in every sea journey and first appears when Paul is on land in Philippi, not at sea (Acts 16:10–17). Thornton's research on first-person narratives in ancient literature shows that if the author had completely fabricated the we-passages and was not present as an eyewitness, he would have been perceived in the ancient context as a liar.[7] The prima facie sense of the we-passages is that they are intended to convey to the readers the author's participation in the events.[8] They possibly derive from a "diary-like record" that the author himself kept.[9]

---

6. Ibid., 16–22. Contra Vernon K. Robbins, "The We-Passages in Acts and Ancient Sea Voyages," *BR* 20 (1975): 5–18; and "By Land and by Sea: The We-Passages and Ancient Sea Voyages," in *Perspectives on Luke-Acts* (ed. C. H. Talbert; Danville, VA: Association of Baptist Professors of Religion, 1978), 215–42. On Luke as the author of the we-passages, see Colin J. Hemer, *The Book of Acts in the Setting of Hellenistic History* (ed. C. H. Gempf; Winona Lake, IN: Eisenbrauns, 1990), 312–34.

7. Claus-Jürgen Thornton, *Der Zeuge des Zeugen. Lukas als Historiker des Paulusreisen* (WUNT 1/56; Tübingen: Mohr Siebeck, 1991), 200. J. B. Lightfoot (*St Paul's Epistles to the Colos-*

sians and to Philemon [1879; Grand Rapids: Zondervan, repr. 1959], 241–42), contends that the first we-passage in Acts 16:10 occurred near the time of Paul's malady mentioned in Gal. 4:13–14. He deduces from this that Luke may have joined Paul "in a professional capacity."

8. The biggest problem in regarding Luke as a companion of Paul is the estimation, common among scholars, that the portrayal of Paul in Acts differs significantly in theology and factual details, notably, the Jerusalem Council (Acts 15 and Gal 2), from the Paul revealed in his letters (see Philipp Vielhauer, "Zum 'Paulinismus' der Apostelgeschichte," *EvT* 10

Is Luke a Gentile or a Jew? Paul lists a series of persons who extend greetings to the Colossians and says, "These are the only Jews among my co-workers for the kingdom of God, and they have proved a comfort to me" (Col 4:11). He then mentions Epaphras, "who is one of you" (v.12), "our dear friend Luke, the doctor" (v.14),[10] and Demas (v.14). Most conclude that since Luke and Demas are not mentioned earlier, they are not Jews. I conclude, however:

> If it means that they are the *only* Jewish converts among his coworkers, it would appear to exclude Timothy, the coauthor of the letter. Possibly the phrase "of the circumcision" [lit. trans.] refers to the circumcision party (see Acts 10:45; 11:2; Gal. 2:12) and means: These are the only ones from that group who bring him comfort. If it refers to these three as Jews, it may be a lament (see Rom. 9:1 – 3) — these are the only ones. In the context of Jewish opposition in Colosse, however, it is more likely that Paul wants to remind them that some Jews, whom they know or know about, have been willing to throw aside their religious entitlements for the sake of the gospel in which there is no Jew nor Greek, circumcised or uncircumcised. They also serve with him in the mission among the Gentiles.[11]

It may well be that Luke was a Hellenistic Jewish Christian but not a member of "the circumcision group" (see Titus 1:10). If the we-passage in Acts 16:10 – 16 extends to 16:20, then the narrator is a Jew: "These men are Jews, and are throwing our city into an uproar." Luke may have escaped arrest, since only Paul and Silas are mentioned, but all the missionaries in Acts are Jews! When Paul wanted Timothy to accompany him on his mission, "he circumcised him because of the Jews who lived in that area, for they all knew that his father was a Greek" (Acts 16:3). Paul's coworker Titus, an uncircumcised Gentile (Gal 2:1 – 5), is never mentioned in Acts. The missionaries in Acts, like Paul, represent what is truly Jewish.

If Luke were a Jew, it would easily explain his extensive knowledge of the Greek Old Testament and why Fletcher-Louis could say that he is "thoroughly at home in Jewish culture and theology."[12] He adopts a Septuagintal style of Greek in the

[1950 – 51}: 1 – 15). This discussion is best left to a commentary on Acts, and Joseph A. Fitzmyer (*The Acts of the Apostles* [AB; New York: Doubleday, 1998], 145 – 47) and Jacob Jervell (*Die Apostelgeschichte* [KEK; Göttingen: Vandenhoeck & Ruprecht, 1998], 81 – 84) offer weighty counterarguments (see also Joseph A. Fitzmyer, *The Gospel According to Luke* [AB; Garden City, NY: Doubleday, 1981], 1:47 – 51).

9. Fitzmyer, *Luke the Theologian*, 22.

10. The arguments of William Kirk Hobart (*The Medical Language of St. Luke* [1882; repr. Grand Rapids: Baker, 1954]) and William M. Ramsay (*Luke the Physician and Other Studies in the History of Religion* [London: Hodder and Stoughton, 1908], 1 – 68) that Luke's vocabulary paralleled that found in Greek medical writings was refuted by Henry J. Cadbury (*The*

Style and Literary Method of Luke [Harvard Theological Studies 6; Cambridge: Harvard University Press, 1920], 39 – 72). W. G. Marx ("Luke the Physician, Re-examined," *ExpTim* 91 [1979 – 80], 168 – 72) seeks to revive the possibilities. The arguments of Loveday Alexander (*The Preface to Luke's Gospel: Literary Convention and Social Context in Luke 1.1 – 4 and Acts 1.1* [SNTSMS 78; Cambridge: Cambridge Univ. Press, 1993]) about Luke's affinities to the style of technical or scientific writing in his preface may add more evidence to the argument, but one must always guard against parallelomania.

11. David E. Garland, *Colossians/Philemon* (NIVAC; Grand Rapids: Zondervan, 1998), 278.

12. Crispin H. T. Fletcher-Louis, *Luke-Acts: Angels, Christology and Soteriology* (WUNT 2/94; Tübingen: Mohr Siebeck, 1997), 31.

opening chapters and makes allusions to the Scriptures without announcing that he is doing so. In addition to his knowledge of Scripture and his techniques in interpreting it that accord with contemporary Jewish methods, Strelan argues that his authority in offering foundational interpretation of the traditions of Jesus, Paul, and Christian history for the comparatively small Christian community, not just a local congregation but the more widespread community, would be greater if he were a Jewish teacher than a Gentile one.[13]

Luke also is at home in the Greco-Roman culture, and the preface indicates that he was aware of literary customs and self-consciously intended to enter the world of letters. The use of such a preface does not appear in the Jewish Apocrypha, Pseudepigrapha (with the exception of the *Letter of Aristeas* 1:1 – 8), or in the earliest Christian writings.[14] Jerome praised Luke's Greek (*Epist. ad Damasum* 20.4.4), and Luke avoids Hebraic expressions that might disconcert a Greek reader. He also tends to relate narrative details to fit a Greco-Roman context (e.g., compare Luke's tiled roof [Luke 5:19] with Mark's earthen roof [Mark 2:4]).

Luke's Sources

Luke mentions other narratives that were compiled before he undertook his project (1:1). He does not label them "gospels" but uses "a neutral historical-literary term [διήγησις] which appears both in Jewish-Hellenistic literature among Greek authors."[15] Mark appears to have been an important source, since almost 40 percent of Luke's gospel (around 410 verses) correlates with Mark. Bauckham asserts that Luke does so because he "takes Mark's Gospel to be substantially Peter's testimony," and Peter was an "eyewitness."[16] He includes all of Mark's healing miracles with the exception of a large omission of material from Mark 6:45 – 8:26.[17]

A few texts related to Mark also have added to them material from Q or L.[18] Q is a hypothetical source that consists of material shared by Matthew and Luke that does not appear in Mark.[19] Over 20 percent of Luke's gospel (around 250 verses) might be

13. Rick Strelan, *Luke the Priest: The Authority of the Third Gospel* (Aldershot, Eng.: Ashgate, 2008), 106. He goes perhaps too far in arguing that Luke was a priest (117 – 44).

14. Hengel, *The Four Gospels*, 101.

15. Ibid., 100. See, e.g., *Let. Aris.* 1:1; 2 Macc 2:32; 6:17; Sir 6:35; 9:15; 22:6; 27:11, 13; 38:25; 39:2; and Josephus, *J.W.* 7.3.2 §42; 7.8.1 §274; *Ant.* 9.10.2 §214; 11.3.10 §68; 12.3.3 §§136 – 37; 20.8.3 §157.

16. Richard Bauckham, *Jesus and the Eyewitnesses: The Gospels as Eyewitness Testimony* (Grand Rapids: Eerdmans, 2006), 146 – 47.

17. It is likely that Luke omitted this material to limit Jesus' mission to Galilee. Luke reserved the issue of food purity

(Mark 7:1 – 23) and the justification of the Gentile mission for the second volume (Acts 10:1 – 11:18) (so Gregory E. Sterling, "'Opening the Scriptures': The Legitimation of the Jewish Diaspora and the Early Christian Mission," in *Jesus and the Heritage of Israel: Luke's Narrative Claim upon Israel's Legacy* [ed. D. P. Moessner; Harrisburg, PA: Trinity Press International, 1999], 215).

18. See 3:7 – 14; 3:23 – 38; 4:2b – 13; 5:1 – 11; 19:1 – 10, 11 – 27; 22:28 – 33, 35 – 38; 23:6 – 16; 23:27 – 31; 23:39b – 43; 23:47b – 49.

19. Whether Matthew or Luke followed and had access to and used the other may be irresolvable and takes us beyond the purview of this commentary.

designated Q, but in the central section (9:51 – 19:44) much of this material is mixed with what is labeled L. L is material special to Luke and includes the unique portrait of Jesus in the infancy narrative and many sayings and parables of Jesus. Evans identifies 485 verses (over 40 percent of the gospel) as L material.[20]

Five miracles in Mark are absent from Luke: Jesus walking on water (Mark 6:45 – 52), the woman from Tyre (7:24 – 30), the deaf and mute man (7:31 – 37), the feeding of the four thousand (8:1 – 10), and the blind man who was touched twice (8:22 – 26). In addition, he omits the cursing of the fig tree (11:12 – 14, 20). Luke has eight miracles of his own: the catch of fish and the call of Peter (Luke 5:1 – 11), the healing of the centurion's slave (7:1 – 10; cf. Matt 8:5 – 13), the raising to life of the son of the woman from Nain (7:11 – 17), the casting out of a demon from a deaf man (11:14), the healing of the woman with the bent back (13:10 – 17), the healing of the man with dropsy (14:1 – 6), the healing of the ten lepers (17:11 – 19), and the healing of the ear of the high priest's slave (22:50 – 51). He also includes a number of memorable parables: the good Samaritan (10:29 – 37); the friend at midnight (11:5 – 8); the rich fool (12:13 – 21); the shepherd with a hundred sheep combined with the woman with ten coins, and the father who had two sons (15:1 – 32); the unrighteous agent (16:1 – 8); the rich man and Lazarus (16:19 – 31); the widow and the unrighteous judge (18:1 – 8); and the Pharisee and the tax collector (18:9 – 14). An additional four parables are similar to those found in Matthew: the faithful and unfaithful servants (12:35 – 48 = Matt 24:45 – 51), the great banquet (14:15 – 24 = Matt 22:1 – 14), the shepherd with a hundred sheep (15:1 – 7 = Matt 18:10 – 14), and the vengeful throne claimant (19:11 – 27 = Matt 25:14 – 30). These parables are cast in such a completely different light in Luke that it is likely that Luke preserves similar stories that Jesus used in other contexts to different effect.

Since Luke mentions that the events were handed down by eyewitnesses (1:1 – 2), it is plausible that some of these traditions came from disciples other than the Twelve (see Acts 1:21 – 22; 10:37; 13:31). Bauckham argues that the "whole of Luke's special material (so-called L) derives from a circle of women disciples, including Joanna, who were the eyewitnesses, traditioners, and custodians of a cycle of Gospel traditions."[21] Women figure prominently in this material.[22] He observes:

20. C. F. Evans, *St. Luke* (TPI New Testament Commentaries; London: SCM, 1990), 26 – 27, citing 1:5 – 2:52; 3:10 – 14; 3:23 – 38; 4:16 – 30 (possibly influenced by Mark, Q); 5:1 – 11; 5:39 (possibly influenced by Mark, Q); 7:11 – 17; 7:36 – 50 (possibly influenced by Mark, Q); 8:1 – 3; 9:51 – 55; 9:61 – 62; 10:1, 17 – 20; 10:25 – 28 (possibly influenced by Mark, Q); 10:29 – 37; 10:38 – 42; 11:5 – 8; 11:27 – 28; 12:1 (possibly influenced by Mark, Q); 12:13 – 21; 12:35 – 38 (possibly influenced by Mark, Q); 12:47 – 48; 12:49 – 50; 12:54 – 56; 13:1 – 9; 13:10 – 17; 13:31 – 33; 14:1 – 6; 14:7 – 14; 14:28 – 35; 15:1 – 10; 15:11 – 32; 16:1 – 15; 16:19 – 31; 17:7 – 10; 17:11 – 19; 17:20 – 21; 17:28 – 32

(possibly influenced by Mark, Q); 18:1 – 8; 18:9 – 14; 19:1 – 10; 19:41 – 44; 21:34 – 36; 22:15 – 18, 27, (31 – 33), 35 – 38; 23:6 – 16; 23:27 – 31; 23:39 – 43; 24:13 – 53.

21. Richard Bauckham, *Gospel Women: Studies in the Named Women in the Gospels* (Grand Rapids: Eerdmans, 2002), 190, noting the work of Thorlief Boman, *Die Jesus-Überlieferung in Lichte der neuen Volkskunde* (Göttingen: Vandenhoeck & Ruprecht, 1967), 122 – 37.

22. Luke mentions thirteen women not mentioned in the other gospels, and stories about men are frequently paralleled by stories about women: the angelic annunciation to Zechariah

Unlike Matthew and Mark, where it comes as something of a surprise to the reader to learn, during the passion narrative, that many women had accompanied Jesus from Galilee and had "provided" for him (Matt 27:55 – 56; Mark 15:40 – 41), Luke makes clear that these women disciples were constant companions of Jesus from an early stage of the Galilean ministry.[23]

The women listed in 8:1 – 3 "would surely have been sources and guarantors of traditions from the ministry of Jesus: stories and dominical sayings."[24] Luke may be playing up these sources by naming Joanna as a witness at the empty tomb (24:10, absent from Mark 16:1). He also mentions Cleopas, a male, as one of the two disciples on the road to Emmaus (24:18). Regarding Cleopas, Bauckham observes, "There is no narratological reason for Luke to name either of the travelers, and it is curious that he names only one." He concludes that this special tradition, which reached him in oral or written form, indirectly or directly through his firsthand acquaintance with the sources, derived from named persons who are not mentioned prominently in other gospels, Joanna, Susannah, and Cleopas.[25]

The Genre of Luke-Acts

Identifying the genre of a work can be important for understanding the expectations it might create in readers.[26] Hemer cautions, however:

Contemporary literature, in particular, was an aristocratic avocation pursued within the confines of a social and cultural élite, whereas the Christian movement seems to have been concerned from the outset with popular proclamation. It is wholly probable that their writers, especially one with the literary ability and aspiration of Luke, were influenced by their cultural environment and reflect their trends, but it is by no means certain how closely or consciously.[27]

(1:11 – 20) and to Mary (1:26 – 38); the praise of God in the temple for the child Jesus by Simeon (2:25 – 35) and Anna (2:36 – 38); mention of the widow of Zarephath (4:25 – 26) and Naaman the Syrian (4:27) in Jesus' first sermon; the first healings of a demoniac (4:31 – 37) and Peter's mother-in-law (4:38 – 39); the healing of a loved one, the centurion's slave (7:1 – 10) and the only son of the widow of Nain (7:11 – 17); the parable of the two debtors, representing Simon the Pharisee and the woman who was a sinner (7:36 – 50); the lesson on serving with the parable of the merciful Samaritan (10:25 – 37) and Mary and Martha (10:38 – 42); parables of the reign of God, the man who sowed a mustard seed (13:18 – 19) and the woman who hid leaven in some meal (13:20 – 21); those healed on the Sabbath, a daughter of Abraham (13:10 – 17) and a man with dropsy (14:1 – 6); parables about prayer, the urgent host and the reluctant neighbor (11:5 – 8) and the persistent widow and the wicked judge (18:1 – 8); parables of the last judgment,

two men in bed (17:34) and two women grinding meal at the same place (17:35); those Jesus encounters on the way to crucifixion, Simon of Cyrene (23:26) and the daughters of Jerusalem (23:27 – 31); and the resurrection announcement to the women at the tomb (23:55 – 24:11) and the appearance to the followers on the road to Emmaus (24:13 – 27).

23. Bauckham, *Gospel Women*, 112 – 13.

24. Ibid., 189.

25. Bauckham (ibid., 165 – 86) also argues that Joanna is the Junia mentioned by Paul (Rom 16:7) and that her husband Chuza (Luke 8:3) had either chosen the name Andronicus or she was widowed and he was her second husband.

26. Luke Timothy Johnson, *The Gospel of Luke* (SP; Collegeville, MN: Liturgical, 1991), 5.

27. Hemer, *The Book of Acts in the Setting of Hellenistic History*, 34.

The multiple proposals that attempt to identify the genre of Luke-Acts reveal that it is not immediately obvious.[28] According to Downing, there is a "flexibility and overlap between all the genres we or the ancients discern,"[29] which makes the confusion in precisely identifying the genre of Luke-Acts something that should not cause surprise.

For some time, it was thought that the Gospels were unique (*sui generis*).[30] Aune comments that this view is true "in the sense that no other ancient composition, Greco-Roman or Jewish, is precisely like them."[31] Knight observes, "The Gospel form was an innovation in first century Christianity but it is broadly related to another ancient literary type."[32] While Luke-Acts bears affinities with other genres, these can coexist and mingle to create something new. The noun for "gospel" (εὐαγγέλιον) does not appear in Luke and only twice in Acts 15:7 and 20:24, so Luke does not see himself as writing a gospel, even though he has Mark for a model, and possibly Matthew. Luke in particular has similarities with various types of Hellenistic literature, and an inordinate number of proposals have been made trying to connect Luke to one of them. The following elements deserve mention.

Some have made the case that the gospel is a biography, the life of Jesus, though this should not be confused with the modern genre of biographies.[33] Knight points out, however, that "the impression remains that Luke describes not so much the life of Jesus as such but what Acts 2:11 calls 'the mighty works of God' (R.S.V.)."[34] Luke says in his preface that he is writing about "*the events* [πραγμάτων or 'things'] that have been fulfilled among us" (1:1), which refer to divine acts (see Heb 2:3–4).[35] He is writing not simply about the life of Jesus but what Jesus inaugurated that continued in the deeds of his followers (Acts 1:1–8). That Luke begins with John's birth and continues the story after Jesus' death, resurrection, and ascension in Acts with an emphasis on the progress of the gospel in the world suggests that Luke's gospel cannot be classified simply as a biography of Jesus.

---

28. Hemer (ibid.) also cautions regarding genre criticism, "We can find almost whatever we seek, and we can see significance in what we find. In such a case the study of literary forms is a task to be pursued with special caution, with a care not to use categories which arise out of imposed, rather than inherent, classifications."

29. F. Gerald Downing, "Theophilus's First Reading of Luke-Acts," in *Luke's Literary Achievement: Collected Essays* (ed. C. M. Tuckett; JSNTSup 116; Sheffield: Sheffield Academic, 1995), 99.

30. See Rudolf Bultmann, *The History of the Synoptic Tradition* (trans. J. Marsh; New York: Harper & Row, 1963), 371; Robert A. Guelich, "The Gospel Genre," in *Das Evangelium und die Evangelien* (ed. P. Stuhlmacher; Tübingen: Mohr Siebeck, 1983), 183–219.

31. David E. Aune, *The Westminster Dictionary of New Testament and Early Christian Literature* (Louisville/London:

Westminster John Knox, 2003), 204.

32. Jonathan Knight, *Luke's Gospel* (New Testament Readings; New York: Routledge, 1998), 4.

33. Charles H. Talbert, *What Is a Gospel? The Genre of the Canonical Gospels* (Philadelphia: Fortress, 1977); Richard A. Burridge, *What Are the Gospels? A Comparison with Graeco-Roman Biography* (2nd ed.; Grand Rapids: Eerdmans, 2004).

34. Knight, *Luke's Gospel*, 6.

35. I. Howard Marshall ("Acts and the Former Treatise," in *The Book of Acts in Its First Century Setting*; vol. 1: *The Book of Acts in Its Ancient Literary Setting* [ed. B. W. Winter and A. D. Clarke; Grand Rapids: Eerdmans, 1993], 173), comments: "The use of 'things' in the plural is an odd way of referring simply to the life-story of one person. And the word 'fulfill' may also suggest more than simply the life of Jesus, the more especially since Jesus himself spoke of things that were yet to be fulfilled in the activity of his followers (Lk. 24:47–49)."

I take the position that Luke and Acts must be considered together when discussing genre. Aune asserts that Luke wrote his single literary work "in *two* 'books' (a 'book' was identical with the content of one papyrus roll, a convention preserved in the English word 'volume' from the Latin *volumen*, 'papyrus roll'), probably using one roll for Luke of ca. 35 feet, and another of ca. 32 feet (papyrus rolls came in stock sizes with maximum lengths of 35 to 40 feet)."[36] He cites a striking proportionality between the two books. Both cover approximately the same amount of time, a thirty-year period: the gospel from 4 BC to AD 30, and Acts from AD 30 to AD 60 or 62. The last 23 percent of Luke (19:28 – 24:53) deals with the arrest, trials, death, resurrection, and ascension of Jesus, and the last 24 percent of Acts deals with Paul's arrest, trials, and arrival in Rome.[37]

Such symmetry suggests that these are not two different works with two different genres but a single work. Johnson avers, "Luke-Acts must be read as a *single* story. Acts not only continues the story of the Gospel but provides Luke's own authoritative commentary on the first volume. Any discussion of Luke's purposes, or the development of his themes must take into account the entire two-volume work."[38] I would contend that this also applies to genre, despite recent attempts to remove the hyphen between Luke-Acts.[39]

The connection between Luke and Acts is important for understanding both writings fully, though they have been separated in the canon and can be read profitably independently of one another. Longenecker highlights "the chain-link interlock" at the Luke-Acts seam. Luke's ending looks forward to what is picked up in Acts. Jesus' citation of the promise of Scripture that "repentance for the forgiveness of sins be preached in his name to all the nations, beginning from Jerusalem" (Luke 24:47) correlates with what happens in the early chapters of Acts (Acts 2:38; 3:19; 5:31) and beyond (Acts 10:43; 11:18; 13:38; 20:21; 26:20). His instruction that the disciples are to "stay in the city" (Luke 24:49) is fulfilled through the first seven chapters of Acts, which describe the disciples' experiences there. The temporal qualification "until you are clothed with power from on high" (24:49) is fulfilled with the description of the coming of the Holy Spirit on Jesus' followers at Pentecost (Acts 2:1 – 41). The disciples' special role as "witnesses of these things" (Luke 24:48) is reemphasized in Acts 1:8 with the promise that their witness is to spread from Jerusalem, Judea, and Samaria to the ends of the earth. The emphasis on their testimony appears throughout the narrative (Acts 1:22; 2:32; 3:15; 4:33; 5:32; 10:39, 41; 13:31; 22:20; 26:16).[40]

36. Aune, *The Westminster Dictionary*, 280.

37. David E. Aune, *The New Testament in Its Literary Environment* (Philadelphia: Westminster, 1987), 119.

38. Johnson, *The Gospel of Luke*, 1.

39. Henry J. Cadbury (*The Making of Luke-Acts* [London: SPCK, 1927; repr. 1968]) gets credit for identifying the work as Luke-Acts with the hyphen. Patrick E. Spencer ("The Unity of Luke-Acts: A Four-Bolted Hermeneutical Hinge," *CSR* 5 [2007]: 341 – 66) dismantles the arguments that would dissolve the unity of Luke-Acts and confirms that the four bolts that keep Luke and Acts hinged together — genre, narrative, theology, and reception history — remain firmly in place.

40. Bruce W. Longenecker, *Rhetoric at the Boundaries: The Art and Theology of New Testament Chain-Link Transitions*

In addition, the beginning of Acts recounts the ascension of Jesus from a new and different perspective than what appears at the end of Luke.

Longenecker recognizes that thematic correlations are "not a sure foundation for demonstrating literary unity," and the links can be explained away as a later attempt by Luke to connect the two works when he set about to write Acts as an independent, supplementary volume.[41] Marguerat and Dunn, however, point to scenes that appear in Mark and are omitted in Luke but whose themes appear in Acts, where they seem to have a greater narrative impact.[42]

1. The quotation from Isa 6:9 – 10 in Mark 4:12 as the explanation for speaking in parables is abbreviated in Luke 8:10. It appears in a much lengthier form, however, in Acts 28:26 – 27 at the climax of that narrative.
2. The discourse on clean and unclean foods and what defiles a person in Mark 7:1 – 23 has Jesus declare all foods clean (Mark 7:19). It is omitted in Luke, but Peter's vision from God about unclean food in Acts 10 addresses the same issue, "Do not call anything impure that God has made clean" (Acts 10:15). Here it applies more transparently to the inception of the Gentile mission. Had Jesus already declared all food clean in the gospel of Luke, it would have been strange in the narrative for Peter to balk so adamantly at eating profane food (Acts 10:14).
3. The charge during Jesus' trial in Mark 14:58 that he said he would destroy the temple does not surface in Luke. It does appear in the charges against Stephen that he declared that Jesus of Nazareth will destroy this place (Acts 6:14). Since the disciples are said to be "regularly in the temple praising God" (Luke 24:53; see Acts 2:46; 5:21, 42), and teach, pray, and perform a miracle in the temple through the first five chapters of Acts, it would seem that Jesus' threat against the temple is more appropriate in Acts 6 – 7 after Luke has narrated these events. After the priestly hierarchy has so mistreated *both* Jesus *and* the disciples, rejected the message of his resurrection, and forbidden preaching in his name, the denunciation of the temple and the threat of its demise are more forceful and understandable. Longenecker concludes from these observations that Luke "made adjustments to the plot in volume one in view of the needs of the plot in volume two" and that Luke seems to have projected "one grand plot line running throughout the two volumes." The chain-link evidence would then support the view that Luke-Acts was intended to be one great work.[43]

(Waco, TX: Baylor Univ. Press, 2005), 166 – 70. Arie W. Zwiep (*The Ascension of the Messiah in Lukan Christology* [NovTSup 87; Leiden: Brill, 1997], 118) lists seventeen motifs shared by Luke 24:36 – 53 and Acts 1:1 – 14; see the Literary Context for 24:36 – 53.

41. Longenecker, *Rhetoric at the Boundaries*, 219.

42. Daniel Marguerat, *The First Christian Historian: Writing the "Acts of the Apostles"* (SNTSMS 121; trans. K. McKinney, G. J. Laughery, and R. Bauckham; Cambridge: Cambridge Univ. Press, 2002), 47 – 48; and James D. G. Dunn, *The Acts of the Apostles* (Valley Forge: Trinity Press International, 1996), xv.

43. Longenecker, *Rhetoric at the Boundaries*, 216.

Spencer identifies other narrative features that stitch the two works together. The trajectory prophesied by Simeon that Jesus would extend salvation to the Gentiles (Luke 2:25 – 35) does not come to fruition until the narrative in Acts, and the phrase "God's salvation" in Acts 28:28 forms an inclusio with Simeon's prophecy in 2:30 – 32. Moreover, Luke-Acts forms a beginning, middle, and end; "the progression from possibility (Luke-Acts 1), to realization (Acts 2 – 15), to result (Acts 16 – 28) is only complete when Acts is viewed as a whole."[44]

Schmidt comments that "the opening of Luke's gospel claims that it is passing along a reliable story about the past. Modern scholars continue to debate the status of this statement. Is Luke in fact making a historiographical claim?"[45] Alexander's analysis of Luke's preface notes how it varies from other historical writings. It is much shorter, does not identify the author, and offers a dedication. Its style, lofty as it is when compared to the rest of the gospel, falls short of the elevated style of the prefaces found in the Greek historians, and it also uses the first person as opposed to the normal third person.[46] She claims that the closest formal parallels to Luke's preface are to be found in writing that is characterized as technical or scientific writing (*Fachprosa*). The problem with this conclusion is that technical writing "is a level of language and not genre-specific"[47] (see comments on 1:1 – 4 for more on this).

In my view, Luke intends to write history, and Luke-Acts belongs within the broad spectrum of Hellenistic historiography.[48] Aune contends that Luke "adapted the genre of general history, one of the more eclectic genres of antiquity, as an appropriate literary vehicle for depicting the origins and development of Christianity."[49] Luke sets his account in the context of world history (1:5; 2:1 – 2; 3:1 – 2) and uses chronological references throughout Acts.

The imitation of the style of the Septuagint in the infancy narrative is a clue that he understood his history not just to be any history of any events but to be a continuation of biblical history. As O'Toole states it, "God who brought salvation to his

---

44. Spencer, "The Unity of Luke-Acts," 353, citing Joel B. Green, *The Gospel of Luke* (NICNT; Grand Rapids: Eerdmans, 1998), 8 – 10.

45. Daryl D. Schmidt, "Rhetorical Influences and Genre: Luke's Preface and the Rhetoric of Hellenistic Historiography," in *Jesus and the Heritage of Israel: Luke's Narrative Claim upon Israel's Legacy* (ed. D. P. Moessner; Harrisburg, PA: Trinity Press International, 1999), 27.

46. Alexander, *The Preface to Luke's Gospel*, 102.

47. Schmidt, "Rhetorical Influences and Genre," 32. "Its style is between that of vernacular spoken Greek and a more elevated prose found, for example, in Polybius and Diodorus." See Lars Rydbeck, "On the Question of Linguistic Levels and the Place of the New Testament in the Contemporary Language Milieu," in *The Language of the New Testament: Classic Essays* (ed. S. E. Porter; JSNTSup 60; Sheffield: Sheffield Academic, 1991), 177.

48. Aune (*The Westminster Dictionary*, 78) notes that "acts" (πράξεις) "was a term applied to entire historical works (Polybius 1.1.1; 9.1.5 – 6; Diodorus Siculus 1.1.1) or to portions of them (Xenophon, *Education of Cyrus* 1.2.16; Polybius 4.1.3; Josephus, *Ant.* 14.68; Diodorus Siculus 1.1.1; 16.1.1; Dio Cassius 62.29).

49. Aune, *The Westminster Dictionary*, 77. He also (ibid., 368) summarizes the conventions found in the prefaces of historiographical works: (1) emphasis on the importance of the subject; (2) inadequacy of previous treatments; (3) the author's circumstances and the reason for writing; (4) the author's impartiality and concern only with the truth; (5) the author's intensive research efforts; (6) the thesis of the author, including his view of the causes of the events he will narrate; (7) a brief outline of the work's contents. Luke adopts some of these conventions in his preface.

people in the Old Testament continues to do this, especially through Jesus Christ."[50] Luke was influenced by biblical Deuteronomistic and Hellenistic historiography.[51] Jervell asserts that for Luke the only meaningful and "normative" (*normativ*) and "compelling" (*verpflichtend*) history is that of the people of God because it alone is the history of God's interaction with the world.[52] It is to be expected, then, that his work would manifest differences from other secular histories. Luke affirms that these events really happened, but they signify the fulfillment of what God is doing in the world. He recounts God as acting in history to fulfill the divine plan despite human rebellion and wickedness.

I agree with Hengel that Luke "shows himself — far ahead of his time — to be the first Christian 'historian' and 'apologist.'"[53] The reader should expect that his work will provide a historically accurate account of the events surrounding Jesus and the founding of the church. The reader should also expect to discern the moral implications of the account and learn positive attitudes and behavior. Luke further expects the reader to learn and be persuaded of the truth and, since Luke is a Christian historian, to see God behind these events.

Date, Provenance, and the Readers of Luke-Acts

A perusal of recent commentaries reveals that the dating of Luke-Acts has not drawn much interest lately. It may be attributable to the fact that the evidence is so scanty and the interpretation of it so speculative. Also, the dating of these works may be significant for the reconstruction of early Christian history but not necessarily for the interpretation of the texts. While Blomberg argues for an early date for Luke-Acts, he concedes that an early date does not improve the credibility of their historical reliability: "Accurate information can be transmitted over long periods of time from one person to the next, while falsification of reports can occur relatively rapidly even among eyewitnesses of events."[54]

Traditionally, three dates have been proposed for Luke-Acts. At one extreme, Baur and his followers in the Tübingen school famously proposed a date far into

---

50. Robert F. O'Toole, *The Unity of Luke's Theology: An Analysis of Luke-Acts* (Good News Studies 9; Wilmington, DE: Michael Glazier, 1984), 17.

51. See Daryl D. Schmidt, "The Historiography of Acts: Deuteronomistic or Hellenistic?" SBLSP 24 (1985): 417–27; and Brian S. Rosner, "Acts and Biblical History," in *The Book of Acts in Its First Century Setting;* vol. 1: *The Book of Acts in Its Ancient Literary Setting* (ed. B. W. Winter and A. D. Clarke; Grand Rapids: Eerdmans, 1993), 65–82.

52. Jervell, *Die Apostelgeschichte*, 78–79.

53. Hengel, *The Four Gospels*, 100–101. Gregory E. Sterling (*Historiography and Self-Definition: Josephus, Luke-Acts and*

Apologetic Historiography [NovTSup 64; Leiden: Brill, 1992]) argues that the genre of Luke-Acts is apologetic historiography. Scott Shauf (*Theology as History, History as Theology: Paul in Ephesus in Acts 19* [BZNW 133; Berlin: de Gruyter, 2005], 60–61) lists ten subcategories of historical genre that various scholars have ascribed to Acts, which suggests that attempts at delimiting the historical subgenre are not fruitful.

54. Craig L. Blomberg, "Where Do We Start Studying Jesus?," in *Jesus Under Fire: Modern Scholarship Invents the Historical Jesus* (ed. M. J. Wilkins and J. P. Moreland; Grand Rapids: Zondervan, 1995), 30.

the second century.[55] The arguments are primarily based on interpretation of a presumed theological tendency of Acts. Acts was regarded as a harmonizing document intended to mend the rupture between Gentile and Jewish Christianity. The differences between Peter and Paul, for example, are papered over, and they are made to sound alike in their speeches in Acts. Baur believed that the canonical Luke was written as an anti-Marcionite text, which places it sometime between AD 140 – 150. Marcion, he thought, used an earlier version of Luke.

At the other extreme, many have argued for a date around AD 61 – 63, during the two-year confinement of Paul in Rome when his release was expected. Since Luke records no events in Acts after this date, it is assumed that Luke-Acts must have been composed prior to it. Acts ends abruptly without any resolution to what happened to Paul. If Luke knew of Paul's release or his martyrdom, would he not have reported it? The Pastoral Epistles suggest that Paul revisited Ephesus, but this contradicts his prophecy in Acts that he would not return (Acts 20:25, 38). Had Luke known of this later visit, would he not have altered or omitted Paul's prophecy? The Acts 28 ending that leaves Paul in limbo finally caused Adolf von Harnack to shift his own views on the date. He rejected his former dating of Luke-Acts in the mid 80s and accepted the earlier date, arguing that Luke would have been an "absolutely incomprehensible historian if he wrote in 80, 90, or 100 and did not include the dramatic events and seismic changes that occurred in the 60's and the year 70."[56]

It is pure conjecture, however, to impose on Luke what we think he would have or should have included in his narrative. It cannot be a decisive piece of evidence for dating the documents. Luke is not interested in recording the life of Paul but the progress of the gospel. One can also argue that Luke stopped at the right place. Had he continued with his history, he presumably would have needed to record the death of James, Peter, and Paul, the blistering persecution of the church in Rome, and the destruction of Jerusalem, the temple, and the church there. This series of dramatic calamities would seem to undermine his theme of the gospel advancing "without hindrance" (ἀκωλύτως), the last word in Acts (28:31).

More pertinent to Luke's purpose, Marguerat states that in Acts 28:16 – 31, Luke recounts "how Christianity freed itself from its birthplace, Jerusalem, in order to acquire its new place, the Empire, as concretized in its capital." Rome has now become "the new centre for the diffusion for the gospel."[57] The first half of Acts ends with

55. Ferdinand Christian Baur, *Paul, the Apostle of Jesus Christ, His Life and Work, His Epistles and His Doctrine: A Contribution to the Critical History of Primitive Christianity* (trans. A. Menzies; London: Williams & Norgate, 1876), 1:1 – 14. Joseph B. Tyson (*Marcion and Luke-Acts: A Defining Struggle* [Columbia, SC: Univ. of South Carolina Press, 2006]) seeks to revive this argument for a late date. This issue of a proto-Luke takes us far afield and offers little to help in the interpretation of the gospel.

56. Adolf von Harnack, *The Date of Acts and the Synoptic Gospels* (trans. J. R. Wilkinson; New York: Putnam, 1911), 97. Hemer (*The Book of Acts in the Setting of Hellenistic History*, 365 – 410) presents the arguments and believes their cumulative weight is compelling.

57. Marguerat, *The First Christian Historian*, 249.

Peter's arrest by Herod, but then he miraculously escapes. Herod sought for him, could not find him, and then put the sentries to death. We next find Herod in Caesarea in his royal robes sitting upon his throne and making an oration. The people shouted him down, yelling, "This is the voice of a god, not of a man." He was then struck down by an angel of the Lord "because Herod did not give praise to God … and he was eaten by worms and died" (Acts 12:21 – 23).[58]

Acts ends with Paul under house arrest in Rome, where the emperor, as all would know, made even more grandiose boasts. Readers can deduce what would happen next to an idolatrous empire that did not give glory to God. The ending of Acts is no less abrupt than the ending of Mark, and I would argue that it has a similar effect.[59] The readers know that the end of Acts is not the end. Christianity is not a closed book. Acts 28 is the latest chapter in a continuing story that Jesus began. The question for them and for modern readers is the same as it was for those early apostles, "Where will God's Spirit lead us from here?"

An intermediate date, a period of between AD 75 – 90, is most widely accepted, but the arguments in support of it are slight. Luke tells us that many have undertaken to compose an account of the events that have been fulfilled among us (1:1). If Mark is to be dated around 68 – 70,[60] and if Luke used Mark, then Luke would be written some time after this period. The argument based on the more detailed prophecy about Jerusalem being surrounded by armies that is sometimes used to support a date after the destruction of Jerusalem is specious. It does not serve as evidence that Luke fine-tuned the saying on the lips of Jesus to accord with what he knew to have happened. Setting up "siege works" (19:43) was part of the standard method in taking fortified cities. Falling by the edge of the sword, being taken captive among the nations, and the trampling of Jerusalem (21:24) may be more explicit details than the parallel prophecies in Matthew and Mark, but, again, these things happened in the normal course of war.[61]

Luke also omits Jesus' concern that those who live on the cusp of those perilous days should pray that it may not be in winter (Matt 24:20; Mark 13:18), but it need not be because he knew these events did not actually occur in winter. It is more likely that it was omitted because it requires a peculiar knowledge of Palestinian weather and geography to appreciate its significance. Others have noted that the mention of Theudas-Judas in Gamaliel's speech in Acts 5:36 – 37 oddly reverses their actual

58. Peter reappears briefly at the Jerusalem Council (Acts 15:7 – 11) but then disappears from the narrative without any explanation about what eventually happens to him.

59. See David E. Garland, *Mark* (NIVAC; Grand Rapids: Zondervan, 1996), 615 – 18, 625 – 30; Joel Marcus, *Mark 8 – 16* (AYB; New Haven: Yale Univ. Press, 2009), 1088 – 96.

60. See Martin Hengel, *Studies in the Gospel of Mark* (trans. John Bowden; London: SCM, 1985), 1 – 30.

61. C. H. Dodd ("The Fall of Jerusalem and the 'Abomination of Desolation,'" *JRS* 37 [1947]: 47 – 54) argues that the language derives from the LXX. Jesus' prophecy of Jerusalem's destruction looks rather nebulous compared to the statement in *Sib. Or.* 4.125 – 127: "A leader of Rome will come to Syria who will burn the temple with fire, at the same time slaughter many men and destroy the great land of the Jews with its broad roads," which is clearly *ex eventu*.

chronological order. Since Theudas is mentioned nowhere else, they take it as evidence of Luke's familiarity with Josephus's *Antiquities*. Josephus wrote about them in the same reverse order (*Ant.* 20.5.1 §§97–102).[62] Since Josephus wrote *Antiquities* around AD 93–94, and if Luke knew this work, it would require that he wrote after this time. Again, this evidence is not decisive. It may be coincidental, or it could suggest that Luke and Josephus shared a common tradition.

An intermediate date still seems to be the best alternative, though Cadbury advises that when facts cannot be demonstrated incontrovertibly it is best "to leave a wide margin for possibility of error."[63] Nevertheless, Luke's picture of Roman rule with proconsuls like Sergius Paulus, who became a believer (Acts 13:4–12), Gallio, who acted evenhandedly (Acts 18:12–17), and King Agrippa II, who was a prospect for conversion (Acts 26:27–28), reflects a calmer time when the gospel could be preached without hindrance. It suggests that Luke-Acts would not have been written much later than AD 75 to 85 before the persecution of Christians presumably carried out under the emperors Domitian and Trajan.[64]

Identifying Luke's provenance and community is no less difficult to pin down than the date of his writing. Form criticism assumed that there was a long period of oral tradition and that the material was shaped by tradents for their own communities and their own particular problems. The supposed rivalry among Christian camps is read into the texts from the rivalry of modern schools and professors who have assumed that diversity was a problem. This perspective rightly has been challenged.[65] Many of the first Christians traveled widely, as is evident from the greeting lists in Paul's letters, and one can surmise that they would have wanted to know all that they could about Jesus from one another. Allison argues that the term "the Lukan community" is devoid of meaning.[66] Luke may have been an itinerant with no permanent home as were the apostle Paul and Jesus before him. Therefore, like Paul, he would have not been bound up with only one local community for whom he wrote, but he would have written for the church universal.

An attempt to bring the provenance of Luke's gospel into some neat geographical alignment may be behind the tradition that Luke was written in Greece (Achaia) with Mark written in Rome, John in Asia Minor, and Matthew in Palestine.[67] Other options tie the gospel to Alexandria or Antioch, but these are based on conjecture. The elegant dedication to Theophilus, who seems to be a person of high rank (1:1–4), and the conclusion of Acts taking place in Rome suggest to some a Roman provenance.

62. Most recently, Richard Pervo, *Dating Acts: Between the Evangelists and the Apologists* (Santa Rosa, CA: Polebridge, 2006), 159.

63. Henry J. Cadbury, in *The Beginnings of Christianity, Part One: The Acts of the Apostles*; vol. II: *Prolegomena II: Criticism* (ed. F. J. Foakes Jackson and K. Lake; Grand Rapids: Baker, repr. 1979), 2:359.

64. Hengel, *The Four Gospels*, 202–3.

65. See the essays in Richard Bauckham, ed., *The Gospels for All Christians: Rethinking the Gospels' Audiences* (Grand Rapids: Eerdmans, 1998).

66. Dale C. Allison Jr., "Was There a 'Lukan Community'?" *IBS* 10 (1988): 62–70.

67. Hengel, *The Four Gospels*, 40.

The readers are assumed to be Christians (see comment on 1:4), and they also are assumed to have familiarity with Scripture and to accept its divine authority. As Roth points out, "Numerous passages contain unclarified references to historic characters in the drama of Israel's story."[68] For example, Luke mentions the following names without any elucidation: Abijah and the daughters of Aaron (1:5), Elijah (1:17), Gabriel (1:19), David (1:27, 32, 69), Jacob (1:33), Abraham (1:55; 3:8), Asher (2:36), the widow of Zarephath and Naaman and Elijah and Elisha (4:26–27), Noah (17:26–29), and Lot's wife (17:32). To those unfamiliar with Israel's biblical story, the names would be baffling, but Luke also does not explain the meaning of terms like the "Son of Man" or the "reign of God."[69]

Ancients did not read silently, and Luke was intended to be read aloud in a group. Its oral character aided memorization and recall. Writers therefore did not try to make reading easier so that one could read more quickly. Reading was done slowly so that one would not miss the catchwords and allusions. Hearers and readers attribute coherence and relevance to the text until they are forced not to do so,[70] and the approach of discourse analysis in this commentary assumes the coherence of the text. McComiskey argues, however, that the structural "design for the book has eluded scholarly detection."[71] He presents a new proposal for the structure of the narrative in 4:14–24:53 that consists of four cycles (4:14–9:50; 9:51–13:21; 13:22–19:27; 19:28–24:53) with a sequence of twelve strata that is successively repeated in each cycle.[72]

This complex proposal is based on the assumption that Luke borrowed an architectonic pattern that is found in the detailed repetitive structures of earlier and contemporary, biblical and secular, ancient literature.[73] To my mind, this theory with its several pages of charts best elucidates how Luke proceeded in composing his work, though I would only quibble about where the third panel ends and the last one begins. Where the central section (or travel narrative) beginning in 9:51 ends is disputed. Some contend it ends in 18:14, where Luke again picks up the Markan narrative in 18:15. Others, like McComiskey, contend that it ends in 19:27, with the conclusion of the parable of the vengeful throne claimant. The most logical ending point, however, is 19:44.

Baarlick sees a cyclical structure for the central section (which he thinks begins

---

68. S. John Roth, *The Blind, the Lame, and the Poor: Character Types in Luke-Acts* (JSNTSup 144; Sheffield: JSOT Press, 1997), 84.

69. William S. Kurz (*Reading Luke-Acts* [Louisville: Westminster John Knox, 1993], 16) observes: "Many other Lukan gaps presuppose readers with a knowledge of the Greek Old Testament. Luke-Acts is permeated with indirect allusions to persons, events and teachings of the Greek Old Testament. Luke generally alludes to the Old Testament without announcing that he is doing so. This indirect approach presumes an ability on the part of the intended readers to understand the allusions and to make the connections."

70. Gillian Brown and George Yule, *Discourse Analysis* (Cambridge: Cambridge Univ. Press, 1983), 66.

71. Douglas S. McComiskey, *Lukan Theology in the Light of the Gospel's Literary Structure* (Paternoster Biblical Monographs; Carlisle: Paternoster, 2004), 204.

72. Ibid., 27–29, 206–8.

73. Ibid., 163–203.

in 9:43b) that revolves around the statement in 13:33, "Nevertheless, it is necessary for me to go today, tomorrow, and the next day, because it is impossible for a prophet to be killed outside of Jerusalem."[74] The various proposals for a chiastic structure to this section are unconvincing, and their number and variations confirm that this pattern is in the eye of the beholder.[75] Baarlick sees fourteen matching units (e.g., 9:43b – 45/18:31 – 34; 9:46 – 50/18:15 – 17; 9:51/19:28) that rather may be attributable to the parallels resulting from a panel assembly than to an elaborate chiasm. What is crucial in this section is the stated intention that Jesus' destination is Jerusalem (9:51, 53; 13:22, 33 – 34; 17:11; 18:31; 19:11, 28). In 19:28 he is still going up to Jerusalem, and 19:29 – 44 serves as a kind of hinge that describes his preparation for entry into Jerusalem and his descent from the Mount of Olives. In the next scene (19:45 – 48), Jesus enters the temple and engages in prophetic actions that will precipitate his death.

Luke's Purpose

Conzelmann's view that Luke wrote in order to explain why Jesus had not returned held sway for some years. He argues that the first Christians expected the imminent end of the world and return of Christ, and Luke wrote in a time when that hope was fading. Luke recognized that the church had come to stay and must settle down in the world. Why else write a history? Luke emerged as a theologian of church history and addressed the problem of disillusionment by reinterpreting eschatology. He divided salvation history into distinct successive epochs: the period of Israel recorded in the Old Testament, the period of Jesus' ministry in the center of time, and the period of the church.[76]

Stagg scathingly dismisses this view, "How a theory so poorly based exegetically, so forced, so arbitrary, and so dogmatic could so capture so many scholars is a modern marvel!"[77] Two important points, however, can be drawn from Conzelmann's hypothesis. Luke's presentation of the kingdom of God and eschatology is highly complex. I translate the phrase dynamically as "God's reign," referring to God's kingship, but there are passages where it clearly refers to a "kingdom" (13:28 – 29). Luke's teaching here is paradoxical. In the Lord's Prayer, Jesus tells his disciples to pray, "Your reign come" (11:2), but in 11:20, he warns his adversaries, "If I cast out demons by the finger of God, then the reign of God has come upon you." In 17:20 – 21, he tells the Pharisees, "The reign of God does not come with observable [signs]," but it

74. Heinrich Baarlink, "Die zyklische Struktur von Lukas 9.43b – 19.28," *NTS* 38 (1992): 481 – 506.

75. Johnson, *The Gospel of Luke*, 163, disputes those who see a "great chiasm" radiating out from a central point: "There are such points of balance to be discovered, obviously, otherwise such theories would be impossible. But the points of re-

semblance often result as much from the definitions given by scholars as from the stories themselves."

76. Hans Conzelmann, *The Theology of St. Luke* (trans. G. Buswell; New York: Harper & Row, 1960), 95 – 97.

77. Frank Stagg, "The Unhindered Gospel," *RevExp* 71 (1974): 457.

"is in your midst." Jesus also tells his disciples, "certain ones standing here ... will not taste death until they see the reign of God" (9:27). In 21:31 – 32, he warns, "when you see these things taking place, know that the reign of God is near," and "this genera- tion will not pass away until all things take place." Yet, at the Last Supper, knowing the proximity of his death, he says that he will not drink the fruit of the vine until the reign of God comes (22:18). Luke has not abandoned a belief in the nearness of the end,[78] but God's reign is both present in the person of Jesus and also to be con- summated in the future.

A second point is that Luke "does not divide God's dealings with his people into three distinct epochs; he thinks rather of 'one unfolding divine plan.'" He "empha- sizes the *continuity* of salvation history."[79] If Luke thinks in terms of epochs, they are only two, the time of prophecy (1:70; 10:24; 16:16, 31; 18:31; 24:25, 27, 44; Acts 3:18, 21, 24; 10:43; 15:15 – 18; 26:22 – 23; 28:23) and the time when it has been fulfilled (1:1; 4:21; 22:37; 24:44; Acts 1:16; 3:18; 13:26 – 40). Luke does not regard the new as discontinuous with the past. His narrative shows "how Jesus represents the con- tinuation of the biblical story."[80] Smith tentatively allows "that the intention to write scripture should not be excluded from a consideration of the purpose as well as the result of the composition of the Gospels."[81] I would argue this point more positively. Luke presents the scriptural story and its themes as culminating in Jesus.

Why write church history? Luke states in the preface that he wished to reassure the readers about the truth of the gospel. His work is an apology for the Christian movement that is valuable to Christian insiders since it seeks to relieve any potential incertitude and also help them understand who they are, where they came from, and where they are ultimately headed. Why was this necessary? When Luke wote, the Christian community had largely separated from its Jewish roots, and the Jewish rejection of Jesus was overwhelming. That split forced the question: Who are the real people of God?

Paul raised this concern much earlier in Rom 9 – 11. His answer is that not all Israelites belong to Israel and not all of Abraham's children are his true descendants (Rom 9:6 – 7). As Paul explains via a lengthy argument in Rom 9 – 11, Luke-Acts explains via a lengthy narrative that God sanctions the inclusion of Gentiles in the people of God and that the rejection of Jesus as the Messiah by some in Israel is part of a long, sad story in which many have opposed God's purposes. For Gentile believers, Luke's narrative legitimizes their decision to convert to this faith. Brown concludes:

---

78. I. Howard Marshall, *The Gospel of Luke: A Commentary on the Greek Text* (NIGTC; Grand Rapids: Eerdmans, 1978), 676 – 77, 754.

79. Charles H. H. Scobie, "A Canonical Approach to Inter- preting Luke: The Journey Motif as a Hermeneutical Key," in *Reading Luke: Interpretation, Reflections, Formation* (ed. Craig Bartholomew, Joel B. Green, Anthony C. Thiselton; Grand Rapids: Zondervan, 2005), 340.

80. D. Moody Smith, "When Did the Gospels Become Scripture?" *JBL* 119 (2000): 10.

81. Ibid., 19.

By divine providence a Gospel that had its beginning in Jerusalem, the capital of Judaism, ultimately came to Rome, the capital of the Gentile world. The Gentiles addressed by Luke-Acts could thus be assured that their acceptance of Jesus was no accident or aberration but part of God's plan reaching back to creation, a plan that ultimately includes the conversion of the whole Roman world.[82]

As the preface makes clear, Luke's purpose is to assure believers: "in order that you may recognize in full the certainty of the teachings in which you have been instructed" (1:4). The Christian community was not a reclusive fringe group that broke off from Judaism. The promise was to Israel (1:14–17, 67–79; 2:29–35; Acts 2:39; 3:25–26; 5:31; 7:5, 17; 10:36; 13:23, 32–34; 26:6–7), and many in Israel, but not all, did respond to God's initiative to gather them. God's visitation, however, created a divided response (Luke 2:34), and those who did not listen "will be completely cut off from their people" (Acts 3:23). Those who did listen and submit to God's plan fulfilled the Scripture that God intended Israel to become a light to the nations (Gen 12:3; Isa 12:4; 42:6; 49:6; Ezek 47:22–23). Through their mission to the world Gentiles will come to Christ and be included in the people of God.

Luke wrote with the assurance that the Gentile Christians "will listen" (Acts 28:28). Squires highlights the parallels between the beginning of Luke's gospel and the conclusion of Acts 28:28.[83] Luke's work ends with the fulfillment of the predictions with which it began. Salvation came to the Gentiles as a result of the direct intervention of God. It was validated by Scripture, Jesus' ministry that prefigured the inclusion of Gentiles, the certification of the Spirit, and visions and dreams that followers experienced in Acts, which reveal that this is God's way.

Structure

    I. Prologue and Infancy Narrative (1:1 – 2:52)

        A. Prologue (1:1 – 4)

        B. The Annunciation to Zechariah (1:5 – 25)

        C. The Annunciation to Mary (1:26 – 38)

        D. The Meeting of Mary and Elizabeth and Mary's Thanksgiving Psalm (1:39 – 56)

        E. The Birth of John and Zechariah's Thanksgiving Psalm (1:57 – 80)

        F. The Birth of the Messiah (2:1 – 21)

        G. The Presentation of Jesus in the Temple (2:22 – 40)

        H. Jesus' Pronouncement in the Temple (2:41 – 52)

82. Raymond E. Brown, *Introduction to the New Testament* (New York: Doubleday, 1997), 272 – 73.

83. John T. Squires, *The Plan of God in Luke-Acts* (SNTSMS 76; Cambridge: Cambridge Univ. Press, 1993), 151. The vocabulary of Acts 28:28 echoes words from Luke 1 – 2: "known" appears in Luke 1:18; "salvation/Savior" in Luke 1:47, 69, 71; 2:11, 30; "sent" in Luke 1:19, 26; "Gentiles" in Luke 2:31 – 32; and "hear/listen" in Luke 1:41, 58, 66; 2:18, 20, 47.

Select Bibliography

Alexander, Loveday. *The Preface to Luke's Gospel: Literary Convention and Social Context in Luke 1.1–4 and Acts 1.1.* Society for New Testament Studies Monograph Series 78. Cambridge: Cambridge University Press, 1993.

Bailey, Kenneth E. *Poet and Peasant: A Literary-Cultural Approach to the Parables in Luke.* Grand Rapids: Eerdmans, 1976.

———. *Through Peasant Eyes.* Grand Rapids: Eerdmans, 1980.

———. *Jesus through Middle Eastern Eyes: Cultural Studies in the Gospels.* Downers Grove, IL: IVP, 2008.

Bartholomew, Craig, Joel B. Green, and Anthony C. Thiselton, eds. *Reading Luke: Interpretation, Reflections, Formation.* Scripture and Hermeneutics 6. Grand Rapids: Zondervan, 2005.

Bauckham, Richard. *Gospel Women: Studies in the Named Women in the Gospels.* Grand Rapids: Eerdmans, 2002.

Bendemann, Reinhard von. *Zwischen Δόξα und Σταυρός: Eine exegetische Undersuchungen der Texte des sogenannten Reiseberichts im Lukasevangelium.* Beiheft zur Zeitschrift für die neutestamentliche Wissenschaft 2/101. Berlin/New York: Walter de Gruyter, 2001.

Betz, Hans Dieter. *The Sermon on the Mount: A Commentary on the Sermon on the Mount, including the Sermon on the Plain (Matthew 5:3–7:27 and Luke 6:20–49).* Hermeneia. Minneapolis: Fortress, 1995.

Bock, Darrell. *Luke.* 2 volumes. Baker Exegetical Commentary on the New Testament. Grand Rapids: Baker, 1994.

———. *Luke.* NIV Application Commentary. Grand Rapids: Zondervan, 1996.

Bornkamm, Günther. *Jesus of Nazareth.* Translated by I. McCluskey, F. McCluskey, and J. M. Robinson. New York: Harper & Row, 1960.

Bovon, François. *Luke 1:1–9:50.* Hermeneia. Translated by Christine M. Thomas. Minneapolis: Fortress, 2002.

———. *Das Evangelism nach Lucas (Lk 9,51–14,35).* Evangelisch-katholisch Kommentar zum Neuen Testament. Zürich and Düsseldorf: Bendier/Neukirchener, 1996.

———. *Luke the Theologian.* Second revised edition. Waco, TX: Baylor University Press, 2006.

Braun, Willi. *Feasting and Social Rhetoric in Luke 14.* Society for New Testament Studies Monograph Series 85. New York: Cambridge University Press, 1995.

Brawley, Robert L. *Luke-Acts and the Jews: Conflict, Apology, and Conciliation.* Society of Biblical Literature Monograph Series 33. Atlanta: Scholars Press, 1987.

Bridge, Steven L. *Where the Eagles Are Gathered: The Deliverance of the Elect in Lukan Eschatology.* Journal for the Study of the New Testament Supplement Series 240. London/New York: Sheffield Academic, 2003.

Brown, Raymond E. *The Birth of the Messiah: A Commentary on the Infancy Narratives in Matthew and Luke*. New York: Doubleday, 1977.

————. *The Death of the Messiah*. 2 volumes. New York: Doubleday, 1994.

Brown, Schuyler. *Apostasy and Perseverance in the Theology of Luke*. Analecta biblica 36. Rome: Pontifical Biblical Institute, 1969.

Buckwalter, H. Douglas. *The Character and Purpose of Luke's Christology*. Society for New Testament Studies Monograph Series 89. Cambridge/New York: Cambridge University Press, 1996.

Bultmann, Rudolf. *The History of the Synoptic Tradition*. Translated by John Marsh. New York: Harper & Row, 1963.

Byrne, Brendan. *The Hospitality of God: A Reading of Luke's Gospel*. Collegeville, MN: Liturgical, 2000.

Caird, G. B. *Saint Luke*. Penguin New Testament Commentary. London: Penguin, 1963.

Chance, J. Bradley. *Jerusalem, the Temple and the New Age in Luke-Acts*. Macon, GA: Mercer University Press, 1988.

Coleridge, Mark. *The Birth of the Lukan Narrative: Narrative as Christology in Luke 1–2*. Journal for the Study of the New Testament Supplement Series 88. Sheffield: Sheffield Academic, 1993.

Conzelmann, Hans. *The Theology of St. Luke*. Translated by G. Buswell. New York: Harper & Row, 1960.

Craddock, Fred B. *Luke*. Interpretation. Louisville: Westminster/John Knox, 1990.

Creed, John Martin. *The Gospel According to St. Luke*. London: Macmillan, 1930.

Crump, David. *Jesus the Intercessor*. Wissenschaftliche Untersuchungen zum Neuen Testament 2/49. Tübingen: Mohr Siebeck, 1992.

Culpepper, R. Alan, "The Gospel of Luke." Pages 3–490 in volume 9, *The New Interpreter's Bible*. Edited by Leander E. Keck. Nashville: Abingdon, 2003.

Danker, Frederick W. *Jesus and the New Age*. Philadelphia: Fortress, 1988.

Darr, John A. *Herod the Fox: Audience Criticism and Lukan Characterization*. Journal for the Study of the New Testament Supplement Series 163. Sheffield: Sheffield Academic, 1998.

Dillon. Richard J. *From Eye-Witnesses to Ministers of the Word: Tradition and Composition in Luke 24*. Analecta biblica 82. Rome: Pontifical Biblical Institute, 1978.

Doble, Peter. *The Paradox of Salvation: Luke's Theology of the Cross*. Society for New Testament Studies Monograph Series 87. Cambridge: Cambridge University Press, 1996.

Donahue, John R. *The Gospel in Parable: Metaphor, Narrative and Theology in the Synoptic Gospels*. Philadelphia: Fortress, 1988.

Dunn, James D. G. *Jesus Remembered*. Grand Rapids: Eerdmans, 2003.

Ellis, E. Earle. *The Gospel of Luke*. New Century Bible. Grand Rapids: Eerdmans, 1983.

Esler, Philip F. *Community and Gospel in Luke-Acts: The Social and Political Motivations of Lukan Theology*. Society for New Testament Studies Monograph Series 57. Cambridge: Cambridge University Press, 1987.

Evans, C. F. *St. Luke*. Trinity Press International New Testament Commentaries. London, SCM, 1990.

Evans, Craig A. *Luke*. New International Biblical Commentary. Peabody, MA: Hendrickson, 1990.

Farrar, F. W. *St. Luke*. Cambridge Bible for Schools and Colleges. Cambridge: Cambridge University Press, 1895.

Farris, Stephen. *The Hymns of Luke's Infancy Narratives: Their Origin, Meaning and Significance*. Journal for the Study of the New Testament Supplement Series 9. Sheffield: JSOT, 1985.

Fitzmyer, Joseph A. *The Gospel According to Luke.* 2 volumes. Anchor Bible. Garden City, NY: Doubleday, 1981.

———. *Luke the Theologian: Aspects of His Teaching.* New York/Malwah: Paulist, 1983.

Fletcher-Louis, Crispin H. T. *Luke-Acts: Angels, Christology and Soteriology.* Wissenschaftliche Untersuchungen zum Neuen Testatment 2/94. Tübingen: Mohr Siebeck, 1997.

Garland, David E. *Mark.* NIVAC. Grand Rapids: Zondervan, 1996.

———. *1 Corinthians.* Baker Exegetical Commentary on the New Testament. Grand Rapids: Baker, 2003.

Garrett, Susan R. *The Demise of the Devil: Magic and the Demonic in Luke's Writings.* Minneapolis: Fortress, 1989.

Giblin, Charles H. *The Destruction of Jerusalem according to Luke's Gospel: A Historical-Typological Moral.* Analecta biblica 107. Rome: Pontifical Biblical Institute, 1985.

Gibson, Jeffrey B. *The Temptations of Jesus in Early Christianity.* Journal for the Study of the New Testament Supplement Series 112. Sheffield: Sheffield Academic, 1995.

Godet, Frederic L. *A Commentary on the Gospel of St. Luke.* 2 volumes. Translated by E. W. Shalders and M. D. Cusin. New York: I. K. Funk, 1881.

Grangaard, Blake, R. *Conflict and Authority in Luke 19:47 to 21:4.* Studies in Biblical Literature 8. New York: Peter Lang, 1999.

Green, Joel B. *The Gospel of Luke.* New International Commentary on the New Testament. Grand Rapids: Eerdmans, 1998.

Grundmann, Walter. *Das Evangelium nach Lucas.* Theologischer Handkommentar zum Neuen Testament. Fourth edition. Berlin: Evangelische Verlaganstalt, 1966.

Hamel, Gildas. *Poverty and Charity in Roman Palestine, First Three Centuries CE.* Berkeley: University of California Press, 1990.

Harrington, Jay M. *The Lukan Passion Narrative: The Markan Material in Luke 22,54 – 23,25: A Historical Survey, 1891 – 1997.* New Testament Tools and Studies 30. Leiden: Brill, 2000.

Hays, Christopher M. *Luke's Wealth Ethics: A Study in Their Coherence and Character.* Wissenschaftliche Untersuchungen zum Neuen Testatment 2/275. Tübingen: Mohr Siebeck, 2010.

Heil, John Paul. *The Meal Scenes in Luke-Acts: An Audience-Oriented Approach.* Society of Biblical Literature Monograph Series 52. Atlanta: Society of Biblical Literature, 1999.

Hendrickx. Herman. *The Third Gospel for the Third World.* 5 volumes. Collegeville, MN: Liturgical, 1996.

Hengel, Martin. *The Four Gospels and the One Gospel of Jesus Christ.* Translated by John Bowden. Harrisburg, PA: Trinity Press International, 2000.

Hultgren, Arland J. *The Parables of Jesus: A Commentary.* Grand Rapids: Eerdmans, 2000.

Jeremias, Joachim. *The Parables of Jesus.* Translated by S. H. Hooks. New York: Scribner's, 1963.

———. *The Eucharistic Words of Jesus.* Translated by Norman Perrin. London: SCM; 1966.

Johnson, Luke Timothy. *The Gospel of Luke.* Sacra Pagina. Collegeville, MN: Liturgical, 1991.

Just, Arthur A., Jr. *Luke.* Concordia Commentary. St. Louis: Concordia, 1996.

Karris, Robert J. *Luke: Artist and Theologian.* New York: Paulist, 1985.

Kimball, Charles A. *Jesus' Exposition of the Old Testament in Luke's Gospel.* Journal for the Study of the New Testament Supplement Series 94. Sheffield: JSOT, 1994.

Klutz, Todd. *The Exorcism Stories in Luke Acts: A Sociostylistic Reading.* Society for New Testament Studies Monograph Series 129. Cambridge: Cambridge University Press, 2004.

Knight, Jonathan. *Luke's Gospel.* New Testament Readings. London/New York: Routledge, 1998.

Liefeld, Walter L., and David W. Pao. "Luke." Pages 9–355 in *The Expositor's Bible Commentary.* Volume 10, revised edition. Edited by Tremper Longman and David E. Garland. Grand Rapids: Zondervan, 2007.

Linnemann, Eta. *Parables of Jesus: Introduction and Exposition.* London: SPCK, 1975.

Litwak, Kenneth D. *Echoes of Scripture in Luke-Acts: Telling the History of God's People Intertextually.* New York: T&T Clark, 2005.

Manson, T. W. *The Sayings of Jesus.* London: SCM, 1949.

Manson, William. *The Gospel of Luke.* Moffat New Testament Commentary. New York: Harper, 1930.

Marguerat, Daniel. *The First Christian Historian: Writing the "Acts of the Apostles."* Society for New Testament Studies Monograph Series 121. Translated by K. McKinney, G. J. Laughery, and R. Bauckham. Cambridge: Cambridge University Press, 2002.

Marshall, I. Howard. *The Gospel of Luke: A Commentary on the Greek Text.* New International Greek Testament Commentary. Grand Rapids: Eerdmans, 1978.

Matera, Frank J. *Passion Narratives and Gospel Theologies: Interpreting the Synoptics through Their Passion Stories.* New York: Paulist, 1986.

McComiskey, Douglas S. *Lukan Theology in the Light of the Gospel's Literary Structure.* Paternoster Biblical Monographs. Carlisle: Paternoster, 2004.

Méndez-Moratella, Fernando. *The Paradigm of Conversion in Luke.* Journal for the Study of the New Testament Supplement Series 252. London/New York: T & T Clark, 2004.

Menzies, Robert P. *The Development of Early Christian Pneumatology with Special Reference to Luke-Acts.* Journal for the Study of the New Testament Supplement Series 54. Sheffield: Sheffield Academic, 1991.

Minear, Paul S. *To Heal and to Reveal: The Prophetic Vocation According to Luke.* New York: Seabury, 1976.

Miura, Yuzuru. *David in Luke-Acts.* Wissenschaftliche Untersuchungen zum Neuen Testament 2/232. Tübingen: Mohr Siebeck, 2007.

Moessner, David P. *Lord of the Banquet: The Literary and Theological Significance of the Lukan Travel Narrative.* Minneapolis: Fortress, 1989; repr., Harrisburg, PA: Trinity Press International, 1998.

——, ed. *Jesus and the Heritage of Israel: Luke's Narrative Claim upon Israel's Legacy.* Harrisburg, PA: Trinity Press International, 1999.

Montefiore, Claude G. *The Synoptic Gospels.* Second edition. New York: Ktav, 1927 (repr. 1968).

Moxnes, Halvor. *The Economy of the Kingdom: Social Conflict and Economic Relations in Luke's Gospel.* Philadelphia: Fortress, 1988.

Nave, Guy D., Jr. *The Role and Function of Repentance in Luke-Acts.* Academia Biblica. Atlanta: Society of Biblical Literature, 2002.

Neagoe, Alexandru. *The Trial of the Gospel: An Apologetic Reading of Luke's Trial Narratives.* Society for New Testament Studies Monograph Series 116. Cambridge: Cambridge University Press, 2002.

Neale, David A. *None but the Sinners: Religious Categories in the Gospel of Luke.* Journal for the Study of the New Testament Supplement Series 58. Sheffield: JSOT, 1991.

Nelson, Peter K. *Leadership and Discipleship: A Study of Luke 22:24–30.* Society of Biblical Literature Dissertation Series 138. Atlanta: Scholars, 1994.

Neyrey, Jerome. *The Passion According to Luke: A Redaction Study of Luke's Soteriology.* New York/Mahwah: Paulist, 1985.

———, ed. *Social World of Luke-Acts*. Peabody, MA: Hendrickson, 1991.

Nielsen, Anders E. *Until It Is Fulfilled: Lukan Eschatology according to Luke 22 and Acts 20*. Wissenschaftliche Untersuchungen zum Neuen Testament 2/126. Tübingen: Mohr Siebeck, 2000.

Nolland, John. *Luke 1–9:20. Luke 9:21–18:34. Luke 18:35–24:53*. 3 volumes. Word Biblical Commentary. Dallas: Word, 1993.

O'Toole, Robert F. *The Unity of Luke's Theology: An Analysis of Luke-Acts*. Good News Studies 9. Wilmington, DE: Michael Glazier, 1984.

Parsons, Mikeal. *Body and Character in Luke and Acts: The Subversion of Physiognomy in Early Christianity*. Grand Rapids: Baker, 2006.

Patella, Michael. *The Death of Jesus: The Diabolical Force and the Ministering Angel: Luke 23,44–49*. Cahiers de la Revue Biblique 43. Paris: J. Gabalda, 1999.

Plummer, Alfred. *A Critical and Exegetical Commentary on the Gospel According to St. Luke*. International Critical Commentary. Edinburgh: T&T Clark, 1922.

Ravens, David. *Luke and the Restoration of Israel*. Journal for the Study of the New Testament Supplement Series 119. Sheffield: Sheffield Academic, 1995.

Resseguie, James L. *Spiritual Landscape: Images of the Spiritual Life in the Gospel of Luke*. Peabody, MA: Hendrickson, 2004.

Roth, S. John. *The Blind, the Lame, and the Poor: Character Types in Luke-Acts*. Journal for the Study of the New Testament Supplement Series 144. Sheffield: JSOT, 1997.

Rowe, C. Kavin. *Early Narrative Christology: The Lord in the Gospel of Luke*. Beiheft zur Zeitschrift für die neutestamentliche Wissenschaft 2/139. Berlin/New York: de Gruyter, 2006.

Sanders, James A., and Craig A. Evans, eds. *Luke and Scripture: The Function of Sacred Tradition in Luke-Acts*. Eugene, OR: Wipf & Stock, 2001.

Scaer, Peter J. *The Lukan Passion and the Praiseworthy Death*. New Testament Monographs 10. Sheffield: Sheffield Phoenix, 2005.

Schneider, Gerhard. *Das Evangelium nach Lukas*. Ökumenischer Taschenbuchkommentar zum Neuen Testament. Gütersloh: Mohn, 1977.

Schürmann, Heinz. *Das Lukasevangelium*. Fourth edition. Herders Theologischer Kommentar zum Neuen Testament. Freiburg: Herder, 1990.

Schweizer, Eduard. *The Good News According to Luke*. Translated by David E. Green. Atlanta: John Knox, 1984.

———. *Jesus, the Parable of God: What Do We Really Know about Jesus?* Princeton Theological Monographs 37. Allison Park, PA: Pickwick, 1994.

Scott, Bernard Brandon. *Hear Then the Parable: A Commentary on the Parables of Jesus*. Minneapolis: Fortress, 1989.

Senior, Donald. *The Passion of Jesus in the Gospel of Luke*. Wilmington, DE: Michael Glazier, 1989.

Snodgrass, Klyne R. *Stories with Intent: A Comprehensive Guide to the Parables of Jesus*. Grand Rapids: Eerdmans, 2008.

Stein, Robert. *Luke*. New American Commentary 24. Nashville: Broadman, 1992.

Strauss, Mark L. *The Davidic Messiah in Luke-Acts: The Promise and Its Fulfillment in Lukan Christology*. Journal for the Study of the New Testament Supplement Series 110. Sheffield: Sheffield Academic, 1995.

Summers, Ray. *Commentary on Luke*. Word Biblical Commentary. Waco, TX: Word, 1972.

Talbert, Charles H. *Reading Luke: A Literary and Theological Commentary on the Third Gospel*. Macon, GA: Smyth & Helwys, 2002.

Tannehill, Robert C. *The Narrative Unity of Luke-Acts: A Literary Interpretation*. Philadelphia: Fortress, 1986.

———. *The Shape of Luke's Story: Essays in Luke-Acts*. Eugene, OR: Cascade, 2005.

Tiede, David L. *Prophecy and History in Luke-Acts*. Philadelphia: Fortress, 1980.

———. *Luke*. Augsburg Commentary on the New Testament. Minneapolis: Fortress, 1988.

Tilborg, Sjef van, and Patrick Chatelion Counet. *Jesus' Appearances and Disappearances in Luke 24*. Biblical Interpretation Series. Leiden: Brill, 2000.

Tolbert, Malcolm. "Luke." Pages 1–187 in *The Broadman Bible Commentary: Luke-John*. Volume 9. Edited by Clifton J. Allen. Nashville: Broadman, 1970.

Turner, Max. *Power from on High: The Spirit in Israel's Restoration and Witness in Luke/Acts*. Journal of Pentecostal Theology Supplement Series 9. Sheffield: Sheffield Academic, 2000.

Twelftree, Graham H. *Jesus the Exorcist: A Contribution to the Study of the Historical Jesus*. Wissenschaftliche Untersuchungen zum Neuen Testatment 2/54. Tübingen: Mohr Siebeck, 1993.

Wallace, Daniel B. *Greek Grammar beyond the Basics: An Exegetical Syntax of the New Testament*. Grand Rapids: Zondervan, 1996.

Weatherly, Jon A. *Jewish Responsibility for the Death of Jesus in Luke-Acts*. Journal for the Study of the New Testament Supplement Series 106. Sheffield: Sheffield Academic, 1994.

Wengst, Klaus. *Pax Romana and the Peace of Jesus Christ*. Translated by John Bowden. Philadelphia: Fortress, 1987.

Wilson, Stephen G. *Luke and the Law*. Society for New Testament Studies Monograph Series 50. Cambridge: Cambridge University Press, 1983.

Woods, Edward J. *The "Finger of God" and Pneumatology in Luke-Acts*. Journal for the Study of the New Testament Supplement Series 205. Sheffield: Sheffield Academic, 2001.

Wright, N. T. *Jesus and the Victory of God*. Minneapolis: Fortress: 1997.

Zwiep, Arie W. *The Ascension of the Messiah in Lukan Christology*. Novum Testamentum Supplements 87. Leiden: Brill, 1997.

CHAPTER 1

Luke 1:1 – 4

Literary Context

Luke is the only gospel to include a preface in which the author addresses the one to whom the work is dedicated. He composes these opening verses in elegant Greek with a carefully balanced structure and employs current literary conventions used in opening dedications. This care and skill would reassure an educated Greek reader.[1] It signals that the author was aware of the customs used in the non-Christian world and that he self-consciously intended for his work to be read widely and by those familiar with these literary conventions.

Luke's use of secular models for his preface does not mean that the Bible is not also his model. Du Plessis comments that while Luke writes as a historian of the Christian movement, "we must guard against the temptation to consider Luke as a mere imitator of classical conventions. He was writing independently although using conventional form, and uses his own terminology when it suits him.... He is not just writing ordinary history and thus the differences should be considered in the same way as the similarities!"[2] He establishes his authority as one who has "followed everything closely" and as a result compiled an improved "orderly account," which leads the auditor to "full … certainty" about the teachings received from the tradition.

➡ **I. Prologue and Infancy Narrative (1:1 – 2:52)**
   A. Prologue (1:1 – 4)
   B. The Annunciation to Zechariah (1:5 – 25)

Main Idea

This gospel's narrative is intended to persuade readers of the full certainty of the truth of the traditions about Jesus and their significance for salvation.

---

1. George A. Kennedy, *New Testament Interpretation through Rhetorical Criticism* (Chapel Hill, NC: Univ. of North Carolina Press, 1984), 107.

2. I. J. du Plessis, "Once More: The Purpose of Luke's Prologue (Luke I. 1 – 4)," *NovT* 16 (1974): 262.

Translation

Luke 1:1–4

1:1	Cause	Inasmuch as many have set their hands to compile a narrative concerning the events that have been fulfilled among us,
2	Explanation	just as they were delivered to us by those who were eyewitnesses from the beginning and became ministers of the word,
3a	Decision	**it seemed good also to me,** **having followed everything closely back to the beginning, to write an orderly account for you,**
b	Address	most excellent Theophilus,
4	Purpose	in order that you may recognize in full the certainty of the teachings in which you have been instructed.

Structure and Literary Form

Luke composes a carefully balanced period (a single sentence) for his preface. This preface has been conventionally linked to historiographical works[3] that typically include mention of any predecessors (sometimes with criticism), the subject, the qualifications of the writer, the purpose of the work, its organization, and often a dedication to a patron or friend.[4] This formal preface has traditionally, and I think rightly, been taken as an indication that Luke intended to write history.

Alexander has seriously challenged this view and argues that "Luke's preface-style seems to be more closely related to that of the 'scientific' tradition than it is to that of the hellenistic Jewish literature or any other Greek literary tradition."[5] In a review of her work, Marshall argues that her conclusions strengthen the assumptions about the historical reliability of Luke's work since readers would expect accuracy from a scientific writing, and it would suit the tradition that Luke was a medical doctor who would have been familiar with these kinds of works.[6] The problem is that Alexander compares style, which is not genre specific.

Aune offers these other criticisms of Alexander's conclusions. (1) Few historical works survive, and those that do often cover a millennium of historical writing and are missing the preface. This fact impairs any statistical comparison to determine what is normative or rare. (2) Those histories that have survived come from authors of much higher social status than Luke, whose preface may have been more comparable to the hundreds of histories (see Lucian, *Hist.* 2) that have been lost and would have been considered pedestrian and lacking taste and ability by the educated (see Lucian's satirical critique of examples of such a preface in contemporary historians [*Hist.* 16]). (3) In trying to demonstrate what Luke's preface is not, a historical preface, Alexander does not demonstrate, beyond citing the parallels, how scientific prefaces functioned. (4) Luke's writing does not strike anyone as a scientific or technical treatise. It has biographical and historical content with a plotted narrative. It is not an explicatory discourse that is characteristic of a scientific treatise.[7] Alexander's work has not completely derailed the premise that Luke intends to write history.[8]

Aune compares Luke's preface to Plutarch's essay "The Dinner of the Seven Wise Men" (*Mor.* 146B – 164D). He characterizes its preface as "a cliché" in that it "adopts

3. See Henry J. Cadbury, "Commentary on the Preface to Luke-Acts," in *The Beginnings of Christianity, Part One: The Acts of the Apostles*; vol II; *Prolegomena II: Criticism* (ed. F. J. Foakes Jackson and K. Lake; Grand Rapids: Baker, repr. 1979), 489 – 510.

4. Aune, *The Westminster Dictionary*, 368.

5. Alexander, *The Preface to Luke's Gospel*, 167.

6. I. Howard Marshall, "The Preface to Luke's Gospel by L. Alexander," *EvQ* 66 (1994): 373 – 76.

7. David E. Aune, "Luke 1:1 – 4: Historical or Scientific

Prooimion?" in *Paul, Luke and the Graeco-Roman World: Essays in Honour of Alexander J. M. Wedderburn* (ed. A. Christopherson et al.; JSNTSup 217; Sheffield: Sheffield Academic, 2002), 142 – 44.

8. For other arguments that Luke intended to write history, not biography or a novel, see Terence Callan, "The Preface of Luke-Acts and Historiography," *NTS* 31 (1985): 576 – 81; and David L. Balch, "The Genre of Luke-Acts: Individual Biography, Adventure Novel, or Political History?" *SwJT* 33 (1990): 5 – 19.

a pastiche of elements that the ancient reader would reflexively recognize as an explanatory *prooimion* whose primary function would be to bolster the claim that the following account is the truth and nothing but the truth."[9] Plutarch's work has numerous parallels with Luke's preface, which suggests that Luke's intention with his preface is also to bolster the claim that what follows is the truth and nothing but the truth.[10]

The structure divides into two balanced segments:

Inasmuch as many ...
     to compile a narrative ...
          just as they were delivered to us ...
It seemed good also to me
     to write an orderly account for you ...
          ... the certainty of the teachings in which you have been instructed.

Exegetical Outline

→ I. Previous endeavors to relate the events that have been fulfilled among us (1:1 – 2)
   II. Qualifications for undertaking the task anew (1:3)
   III. Purpose of the task: to establish the reliability of the tradition and the certainty of faith (1:4)

Explanation of the Text

1:1 Inasmuch as many have set their hands to compile a narrative concerning the events that have been fulfilled among us (Ἐπειδήπερ πολλοὶ ἐπεχείρησαν ἀνατάξασθαι διήγησιν περὶ τῶν πεπληροφορημένων ἐν ἡμῖν πραγμάτων). Luke was not the first to undertake the audacious task of committing to writing the oral traditions about Jesus, and he explains why he tackles this comprehensive project. It is a literary convention among historians to refer to one's predecessors when writing on the same topic. Marincola says that ancient historiography did not attempt "to strike out boldly in a radical departure from one's predecessors, but rather to be incrementally innovative within a tradition, by embracing the best in previous performers and adding something of one's own marked with an individual stamp."[11] "Inasmuch as" expresses cause so that Luke associates his work with these predecessors and thereby justifies it.

The verb "set their hands" underscores the difficulty of the task. "To compile [ἀνατάξασθαι, an uncommon verb] a narrative [διήγησιν]" means that Luke's predecessors have arranged the events sequentially.[12] The "events" are not simply occurrences; they are matters that concern salvation

9. Aune, "Luke 1:1 – 4: Historical or Scientific *Prooimion*?" 147.

10. It must be pointed out that Plutarch's essay is an imaginary account, so using this kind of preface does not guarantee historical veracity. Historical accuracy must be judged on other

grounds. The point is that Luke's preface serves as an aside that expresses his intention to write a trustworthy account.

11. John Marincola, *Authority and Tradition in Ancient Historiography* (Cambridge: Cambridge Univ. Press, 1997), 14.

12. Cadbury, "Commentary on the Preface to Luke-Acts," 494.

history. The passive participle translated "that have been fulfilled" (τῶν πεπληροφορημένων) can simply mean "happened" or "taken place," but here it refers to divine acts (see Heb 2:3 – 4), and Luke customarily refers to God's action with the passive voice (4:21; 22:37; 24:44; Acts 1:16; [3:18 has God as the subject]). The perfect tense used here suggests that these are not only events "in which God is active" but those "which He brings to completion."[13]

1:2 Just as they were delivered to us by those who were eyewitnesses from the beginning and became ministers of the word (καθὼς παρέδοσαν ἡμῖν οἱ ἀπ᾽ ἀρχῆς αὐτόπται καὶ ὑπηρέται γενόμενοι τοῦ λόγου). Hellenistic historians believed that writing history required either being an eyewitness or having access to eyewitnesses (Polybius, 3.4.13; Josephus, *Ag. Ap.* 1.10 §55; Eusebius, *Hist. eccl.* 3.39).[14] Luke was not an eyewitness to the first events, but he had access to eyewitnesses of what happened and to those who had conducted close inquiries. They were present "from the beginning" (ἀπ᾽ ἀρχῆς; see Acts 1:21 – 22;

John 15:27), and Luke records the tradition that has been delivered[15] by them "just as" (καθώς) it was delivered.

Some translate "eyewitnesses" and "ministers of the word" as two separate groups, which fits the criteria laid out for Judas's replacement in Acts 1:21 – 22. Those who accompanied Jesus during his ministry as eyewitnesses are distinguished from the Twelve, who are witnesses to his resurrection. In Acts 13:31 – 32, Paul differentiates himself, as one who proclaims the gospel, from the eyewitnesses of the resurrection.[16] The relative pronoun (οἵτινες) that governs the construction, however, suggests that Luke refers to one group. In Acts 26:16, Paul records his commissioning by Jesus on the road to Damascus to appoint him "as a servant [ὑπηρέτην] and as a witness of what you have seen and will see of me." The participle γενόμενοι separates "ministers" from "the word" and has its primary sense "becoming."[17] It suggests that the eyewitnesses of the events recorded in the gospel "became" the ministers of the word. Acts records this transformation. Since the infancy narrative immediately follows this statement, might

---

13. du Plessis, "Once More: The Purpose of Luke's Prologue (Luke I. 1 – 4)," 263 – 64.

14. In his *Against Apion*, Josephus bitterly counters those who disparaged the veracity of his previous histories, *Jewish War* and *Antiquities of the Jews*, and defends his historical accuracy with language that appears in Luke's preface: "Surely they ought to recognize that it is the duty of one who promises to present his readers with actual facts first to obtain an exact knowledge (ἐπίτασθαι ἀκριβῶς) of them himself, either through having close touch with the events, or by inquiry from those who knew them" (*Ag. Ap.* 1.10 §53).

He also asserts that he was an "actor" in many of the events and an "eyewitness" of most. Alexander (*The Preface to Luke's Gospel*, 123) claims that the term "eyewitness" (αὐτόπτης) does not always have the same meaning in Greek historical writing as it does in English, in which it tends to mean someone who was physically present at an event. It is related to "autopsy." Daryl D. Schmidt ("Rhetorical Influences and Genre: Luke's Preface and the Rhetoric of Hellenistic Historiography," in *Jesus*

and the Heritage of Israel: Luke's Narrative Claim upon Israel's Legacy [ed. D. P. Moessner; Harrisburg, PA: Trinity Press International, 1999], 29) explains, "The implications are more of having traveled to the original site of the event, after the fact, than actually having experienced the event first hand." But Josephus's use of the term reveals that it also refers to someone who actually witnessed events.

15. Paul uses the same verb "delivered/passed on" (παρέδοσαν) for his source for the Last Supper account (1 Cor 11:23) and the resurrection (1 Cor 15:1 – 3).

16. The terminology is slippery. John (Mark) is identified as an "assistant" or "helper" (ὑπηρέτης) to Paul and Barnabas in Acts 13:5. In Acts 26:16, Paul recounts his call when Jesus commissioned him as "a minister and witness" (ὑπηρέτην καὶ μάτυρα). In 1 Cor 4:1, Paul describes himself as a "servant" (ὑπηρέτης) of Christ and a steward of the mysteries.

17. Richard J. Dillon, "Previewing Luke's Project from His Prologue," *CBQ* 43 (1981): 215 – 16.

one also assume that it represents an eyewitness report? Kuhn believes so.[18] The proclamation of the gospel events was not limited to the apostles. Women were also with Jesus in Galilee (8:1 – 3) and were witnesses of his crucifixion, burial, and resurrection (23:55 – 24:10).

The term "word" (τοῦ λόγου) can also be translated "report" ("matter"). In 5:15 and 7:17, it has the neutral meaning, but to any insider it would refer to the Christian proclamation of what God has done in Christ. In Acts 1:1, the whole gospel of Luke is referred to as (lit.) "the first word." In Acts 6:2 – 4, "word" is equated with the "word of God." Both are used interchangeably for the message God sent to the people of Israel (see Acts 4:4, 29, 31; 6:2, 4; 8:4, 14, 25; 10:36 – 38, 44; 11:1, 19; 13:48) and for the Christian movement (Acts 6:7; 12:24; 13:49; 19:10, 20). Here the "word" refers to the traditions about Jesus and the proclamation of what it means.[19]

1:3 It seemed good also to me, having followed everything closely back to the beginning, to write an orderly account for you, most excellent Theophilus (ἔδοξε κἀμοὶ παρηκολουθηκότι ἄνωθεν πᾶσιν ἀκριβῶς καθεξῆς σοι γράψαι, κράτιστε Θεόφιλε). Luke presents his qualifications to write the account. "It seemed good also to me" (ἔδοξε κἀμοί) indicates that Luke does not wish to criticize his predecessors. They belong to the "us" (1:1) and had the same tradition (1:3).

What Luke does differently from his predecessors is write a " 'continuous' account — one that tells the story from the beginning to Rome."[20] The verb ἔδοξε(ν) is used in Acts 15:22, 25, 28 for a decision that is prompted by the Holy Spirit.

Luke prepared himself to write the account by following everything with care as befits a historian. The verb "followed" (παρηκολουθηκότι) means he "brought himself abreast of" events.[21] He did so, first, by consulting "everything" (πᾶσιν), which, if neuter, refers to sources and other independent traditions, but, if masculine, may also include people. Second, he went "back to the beginning" (ἄνωθεν). This word can mean "for some time," referring to the length of research, but more likely refers to the scope of his investigations. He traced the events back to their starting point (see Acts 26:5) and probably refers to the infancy narrative that immediately follows (absent from Mark). The rich allusions to the Old Testament in chs. 1 – 2, however, suggest that Luke follows the interpretative approach used by Jesus at Emmaus when he began with Moses and all the prophets to interpret the things about himself in the Scriptures (24:27). The beginning, then, may extend back beyond the recent historical events surrounding Jesus' birth and John's appearance in the wilderness to God's purposes outlined by Moses and reaffirmed by the prophets. What happens in this story is a fulfillment of the Scriptures.[22]

---

18. Karl A. Kuhn, "Beginning the Witness: The αὐτόπται καὶ ὑπηρέται of Luke's Infancy Narrative," NTS 49 (2003): 237 – 55.

19. Wayne A. Meeks ("Assisting the Word Making [Up] History: Luke's Project and Ours," Int 57 [2003]: 159) notes that in John, the word became "flesh"; in Luke, the word became the story of Jesus.

20. Vernon K. Robbins, "The Claims of the Prologues and Greco-Roman Rhetoric," in Jesus and the Heritage of Israel: Luke's Narrative Claim upon Israel's Legacy (ed. D. P. Moessner; Harrisburg, PA: Trinity Press International, 1999), 83.

21. Alfred Plummer, A Critical and Exegetical Commen-

tary on the Gospel According to St. Luke (ICC; Edinburgh: T&T Clark, 1922), 4. David P. Moessner ("'Eyewitnesses,' 'Informed Contemporaries,' and 'Unknowing Inquirers': Josephus' Criteria for Authentic Historiography and the Meaning of ΠΑΡΑΚΟΛΟΥΘΕΩ," NovT 38 [1996]: 105 – 22) argues that the verb does not mean "investigate" but to "follow with the mind." He interprets it to mean that he "stayed actively informed" about events.

22. John Gillman, "The Emmaus Story in Luke-Acts Revisited," in Resurrection in the New Testament: Festschrift Jan Lambrecht (ed. R. Bieringer, V. Koperski, and P. B. Latare; BETL 165; Leuven: Leuven Univ. Press, 2002), 172 – 73.

Third, Luke followed things "closely" (ἀκριβῶς). This term appears frequently in Greek prefaces, and Luke uses it in connection to his following things carefully and accurately (see Acts 18:26).[23] It results in enabling him to do more than "compile" but to write "an orderly account" (καθεξῆς).[24] "Orderly" modifies the infinitive "to write" rather than the phrase that precedes it. It does not refer to a chronological sequence of what happened but to a coherent, sequential arrangement of the material so that the reader has clear impressions.[25] Luke will articulate his theological vision through narrative, and he fashions the narrative's unity "by the display of major developments and patterns."[26]

Moessner points out that "in Hellenistic poetics the meaning of any incident or event (πρᾶξις ἢ πρᾶγμα) is conferred by the movement of the plot; any event is 'figured' by its relation to all the other events and characters and their causally configured interactions according to the 'thoughts' of the author."[27] The objective is to present the reader with the truth in a plotted narrative and to convince the reader of that truth, not to present just

the facts.[28] The orderly account discloses "why these events are seen as having reached their fulfillment (πεπληροφορημένων, 1:1)."[29] The order is designed to be persuasive, and one can compare Peter's justification for preaching to Gentiles before the circumcised believers who raised questions (Acts 11:1 – 17). He gave them a point by point (καθεξῆς; Acts 11:4) account, but his telling of the story does not follow a chronological order.[30] Peter's account is considered "orderly" not because of its accurate chronology "but in retelling the incident from a 'narratival' perspective, that is, with the larger sequence and purpose of the narrative."[31]

The phrase "most excellent Theophilus" (κράτιστε Θεόφιλε) can be translated "your Excellency" and refer to a high official of some kind. It has this meaning in Acts in the tribune Claudius Lysius's letter to the governor Felix (Acts 23:26), in Tertullus's address to the governor (Acts 24:3), and in Paul's address to the governor Festus (Acts 26:25). Some infer from these instances that Theophilus is also a Roman official and that Luke writes a defense of

23. David L. Balch ("ἀκριβῶς … γράψαι [Luke 1:3]: To Write the *Full* History of God's Receiving All Nations," in *Jesus and the Heritage of Israel: Luke's Narrative Claim upon Israel's Legacy* [ed. D. P. Moessner; Harrisburg, PA: Trinity Press International, 1999], 229 – 50) argues that the adverb "closely" is governed by the verb "to write" and it has the connotation of "fully." Luke is not claiming to write an accurate account so much as he is compiling a full narrative that includes the speeches. Mark Janse ("L'importance de la position d'un mot 'accessoire' [à propos de Lc 1,3]," *Bib* 77 [1996]: 93 – 97) provides strong arguments, however, that the adverb is governed by the participle "followed."

24. Josephus uses it to refer to "exact knowledge" and "accuracy" in reporting actual facts (*Ag. Ap.* 1.53 §10; *J.W.* 1.1.6 §1; 1.1.17 §6).

25. Richard Longenecker, "Acts," in *The Expositor's Bible Commentary: Luke-Acts* (rev. ed.; ed. T. Longman and D. E. Garland; Grand Rapids: Zondervan, 2007), 10:672.

26. Robert C. Tannehill, *The Narrative Unity of Luke-Acts: A Literary Interpretation* (Philadelphia: Fortress, 1986), 10.

27. David P. Moessner, "Reading Luke's Gospel as Ancient

Hellenistic Narrative: Luke's Narrative Plan of Israel's Suffering Messiah as God's Saving 'Plan' for the World," in *Reading Luke: Interpretation, Reflections, Formation* (ed. Craig Bartholomew, Joel B. Green, and Anthony C. Thiselton; Grand Rapids: Zondervan, 2005), 134.

28. If Luke had access to the theoretical Q as a written source, it was perhaps only an amorphous collection of Jesus' sayings and incidents from his ministry. If he also had Mark, Papias is said to have complained about that gospel's lack of order. David P. Moessner ("The Appeal and Power of Poetics [Luke 1:1 – 4]," in *Jesus and the Heritage of Israel: Luke's Narrative Claim upon Israel's Legacy* [ed. D. P. Moessner; Harrisburg, PA: Trinity Press International, 1999], 118) notes that three key terms ("to compile," "followed," and "closely") in Luke's preface appear in Papias's comparison of Mark and Matthew (Eusebius, *Eccl. hist.* 3.39.15 – 16). He contends that Luke's "'proper' narrative … has set the standard for the critique."

29. Schmidt, "Rhetorical Influences and Genre," 32.

30. Martin Völkel, "Exegetisches Verständnis des Begriffs καθεξής im lukanischen Prolog," *NTS* 20 (1973 – 74): 293.

31. Schmidt, "Rhetorical Influences and Genre," 31.

the Christian movement to appeal for help. While Theophilus may be an official and certainly has high status, it is improbable that Luke writes an official defense of Christianity or of Paul. Though the opening paragraph is directed to Theophilus, the rest of the gospel is directed to the general reader. Luke explicitly states that his purpose is not to provide "definite information about a story" but to convey "the certainty or trustworthiness of a story" that Theophilus has been taught.[32] Why would a disinterested Roman official want to wade through two volumes to find out about Christians unless he already was one himself?

It is more likely that this phrase is a polite form of address that means "most excellent."[33] Josephus uses the same term in his preface to *Against Apion* 1.1 §1 ("most excellent Epaphroditus"; see *Life* 430 §76) to salute his patron who enabled him to write and publicly distribute the work. Theophilus, a common name that appears for real persons in the papyri,[34] is addressed as if he were the sole recipient according to ancient dedicatory custom, but the work is meant for all who are interested in learning the truth of Christianity. I do not think that he is a fictitious person (so Epiphanius, *Pan.* 51.429) because the epithet "most excellent" would be unsuitable. It is a happy coincidence that his name means "friend of God" and is applicable to any faithful reader.[35] Acts 1:1 has a short rededication to Theophilus, omitting the epithet, "most excellent," with a brief reference to the preceding volume.

In my view, Theophilus is the patron who provided funds to publish and distribute Luke-Acts. I assume, then, that he is a Christian, and the gospel and Acts will convince him (and others) of the reliability of what he has been taught and believed. It is possible that Theophilus, the friend of God, is an alias for a prominent Roman who needed to remain incognito.[36] Hengel points out, "He was certainly not an ordinary man. It is his rank in society that requires the preface, which is extremely strange for the earliest church."[37] It may explain the warnings in Luke about the dangers of wealth that is not used rightly.

1:4 In order that you may recognize in full the certainty of the teachings in which you have been instructed (ἵνα ἐπιγνῷς περὶ ὧν κατηχήθης λόγων τὴν ἀσφάλειαν). "Recognize in full" (ἐπιγνῷς) is a stronger verb than simply "know" (γνῷς). Luke uses this verb when the disciples in Emmaus finally recognize that they were breaking bread with the resurrected Jesus (24:30 – 31). "The certainty" (ἀσφάλειαν) is placed in the emphatic position at the end of this period. It may be translated "truth," which can imply that Theophilus does not know the truth, and Luke's work compares with Josephus's *Against Apion*, to whom he wrote to combat "mendacious and scurrilous statements" about the Jews (*Ag. Ap.* 1.3 – 4 §1). Luke also may seek to counter falsehoods about the Christian movement (Acts 28:22). The adverbial form of the word (ἀσφαλῶς), however, appears in Acts 2:36

---

32. F. H. Colson, "Notes on St. Luke's Preface," *JTS* 24 (1923): 304.

33. See Peter M. Head, "Papyrological Perspectives on Luke's Predecessors (Luke 1:1)," in *The New Testament in Its First Century Setting: Essays on Context in Honour of B. W. Winter on His 65th Birthday* (ed. P. J. Williams et al.; Grand Rapids: Eerdmans, 2004), 30 – 71.

34. Ibid., 34.

35. Origen (*Hom. Luc.* 1) believed that the name symbolically represented the addressees who are or would become "lovers of God." While this assumption that Luke expected that

the readers would become "friends of God" as Moses did (Exod 33:11; Philo, *Moses* 1.156) is true, ancient writers addressed a specific recipient in their dedication while assuming that their work would receive a wider readership.

36. B. H. Streeter (*The Four Gospels* [London: Macmillan, 1930], 559) suggests that it was the secret name of Titus Flavius Clemens, a great nephew of the Emperor Vespasian, who along with his wife, Domitilla, Vespasian's granddaughter, may have converted.

37. Hengel, *The Four Gospels*, 102.

and means to know "with certainty," and it is connected to the certain knowledge that God made Jesus Messiah and Lord.[38] It supports the translation "certainty" here and implies that Luke writes to instill confidence in the reliability of the teaching (see the adjectival form in Phil 3:1; Heb 6:9).

In Acts 18:25, the verb "instructed" (κατηχήθης) refers to Apollos's instruction in "the way of the Lord" (see 1 Cor 14:19). It can also mean "informed" (Acts 21:21, 24), but in that passage it is connected to reports. Here it refers to the teaching and preaching of the words of Jesus and the events of his life by the ministers of the word (1:2; see Acts 2:22, "listen to this").

Theology in Application

1. Saving Events That Occurred in History

Luke self-consciously adopts a literary style and uses the contemporary techniques of historical method to convey the gospel to his culture.[39] For Luke, it is not enough to receive the tradition about Jesus; he wants to set it in a historical framework to convey its truth, as the Scriptures do, and to transmit that truth from one generation to another. The preface moves from the past to the future, that is, from the saving events — the institution of witnesses, the handing down of their tradition, previous accounts, Luke's own literary aspiration to write an account — to the assurance of faith.[40]

History for Luke is not merely one thing after another but has a purpose and is moving somewhere. The events he records are not mere occurrences but are things that have filled up or fulfilled something. They are momentous and epoch-making (see 16:16) and attain a goal. The reader, then, needs to be aware of a larger context to understand the story. It is a continuation of God's long history of dealing with Israel and the world since "the foundation of the world" (11:50). These events fulfill Scripture (24:27, 44) and lead to salvation.

Luke's history is, therefore, wholly different from other histories. Du Plessis writes: "His purpose was not to draw important lessons from history, as it was the case with other Greek historians, but to serve Christianity with a true report of *God acting in history*."[41] These are sacred events that manifest and fulfill God's plan for the salvation of the world. They remain relevant. That is why people today use the

---

38. du Plessis, "Once More: The Purpose of Luke's Prologue (Luke I. 1 – 4)," 270. Steve Mason (*Josephus and the New Testament* [Peabody, MA: Hendrickson, 1992], 216) notes that philosophers used this term to describe their efforts: "Their goal was to provide a sure basis for ethical action." Plutarch (*Superst.* 171E) "distinguishes philosophy from superstition on the ground that only philosophy offers a way of seeing the world that is 'secure.'"

39. See Aune, "Luke 1:1 – 4: Historical or Scientific *Prooimion*?" 142. Comparisons with other historical prefaces reveals

that Luke intended to write history not biography nor a novel (see Terence Callan, "The Preface of Luke-Acts and Historiography," 576 – 81; and David L. Balch, "The Genre of Luke-Acts: Individual Biography, Adventure Novel, or Political History?" 5 – 19).

40. Eduard Schweizer, *The Good News According to Luke* (trans. David E. Green; Atlanta, John Knox, 1984), 10.

41. Du Plessis, "Once More: The Purpose of Luke's Prologue (Luke I. 1 – 4)," 271.

present tense in asking, "Who is Jesus?" By contrast, they use the past tense when asking, "Who was Augustus?"[42] Unlike the emperor Augustus, this Jesus still influences and commands his subjects.

2. Saving Events That Create a Community of Faith

By referring to "eyewitnesses," Luke affirms the Christian faith is rooted in historical reliability and not the imagined speculations or myths that characterized the contemporary mystery religions.[43] They are historically verified and are made public to all, not just to initiates. But mere historical research is insufficient to bring certainty of the truth. It also requires *"theological understanding."*[44] That these events occurred "among us" (1:1) and were delivered "to us" (1:2) indicates that a community is created by these events and is the framework for understanding them. The community is the place where they have saving significance and power. There can be no relationship to the saving God outside the witness of a faithful community. We cannot establish a relationship to God on our own.

The purpose of the gospel is to give not information but certainty that will change lives. Erudition about Jesus is not the same as insight into Jesus. The history of Jesus is not to be divorced from the proclamation about Jesus, as if the two were somehow incompatible.

Since Luke does not indicate that he is compiling his narrative for a particular community or that he is responding to a particular community crisis, it is best to understand the "us" to refer to all Christians. This story cannot be consigned to the distant past as if it has nothing to do with us.

---

42. George W. MacRae, "'Whom Heaven Must Receive Until the Time': Reflections on the Christology of Acts," *Int* 27 (1973): 151.

43. E. Earle Ellis, *The Gospel of Luke* (NCB; Grand Rapids: Eerdmans, 1983), 65.

44. du Plessis, "Once More: The Purpose of Luke's Prologue (Luke I. 1 – 4)," 271.

Luke 1:5 – 25

Literary Context

Luke presents the infancy narrative in interlocking panels with the double an-nunciations and the double birth accounts of John and Jesus. The narrative contains seven episodes:

1. The announcement of John's coming birth to Zechariah (1:5 – 25)
2. The announcement of Jesus' coming birth to Mary (1:26 – 38)
3. The meeting of the two mothers and Mary's thanksgiving praise to God (1:39 – 56)
4. The birth of John and Zechariah's thanksgiving praise to God (1:57 – 80)
5. The birth of Jesus (2:1 – 21)
6. Religious ritual: circumcision/naming and praise/prophecy (2:22 – 40)
7. Religious ritual: Passover in the temple (2:41 – 52)

Each scene ends with a refrain noting a departure (1:23, 38, 56, 80; 2:20, 39, 51). The infancy narrative primarily "forms a bridge between the Old Testament age of promise and the age of fulfillment, structurally setting the stage for the theme of promise-fulfilment which will run as a connecting thread throughout the whole of Luke-Acts."[1] The allusions to Scripture make it clear that the action does not really start when the angel Gabriel comes to Zechariah in the temple but is a continuation of God's activity in Israel's history. It is now entering a climactic stage, however, which is bringing about something different and unforeseen. In each of these epi-sodes, "something new, challenging, threatening even, takes place, causing wonder, disturbance, and surprise."[2] The various scenes introduce John and Jesus and what their coming means for Israel: the fulfillment of prophetic expectations and the stupefying accomplishment of the unexpected.

1. Mark L. Strauss, *The Davidic Messiah in Luke-Acts: The Promise and Its Fulfillment in Lukan Christology* (JSNTSup 110; Sheffield: Sheffield Academic, 1995), 86.

2. Brendan J. Byrne, *The Hospitality of God: A Reading of Luke's Gospel* (Collegeville, MN: Liturgical, 2000), 18.

I. Prologue and Infancy Narrative (1:1 – 2:52)

A. Prologue (1:1 – 4)

➡ **B. The Annunciation to Zechariah (1:5 – 25)**

C. The Annunciation to Mary (1:26 – 38)

Main Idea

Remembering what God has done in the past as recorded in the Scripture is a prerequisite for believing that God acts to fulfill promises in the present even in surprising ways.

Translation

(See pages 62 – 63.)

Structure and Literary Form

Brodie notes the diptych structure (a bifold structure of two matching panels) of Luke's infancy narrative:[3]

Panel A	Panel B
John's birth foretold (1:5 – 25)	John's birth (1:57 – 80)
Jesus' birth foretold (1:26 – 38)	Jesus' birth (2:1 – 14)
Journey and visit of Mary to Elizabeth (1:39 – 56)	Journey and visit of shepherds to the family and journey and visit of family to Jerusalem (2:15 – 52)

The structure of the present episode forms a chiastic pattern:

A Introduction of Zechariah and Elizabeth as righteous yet childless (1:5 – 7)

   B Zechariah chosen by lot to serve as a priest in the sanctuary (1:8 – 9)

      C The people praying outside the sanctuary (1:10)

         D Reaction of fear to the appearance of the angel (1:11 – 12)

            E Reassurance by the angel (1:13a)

               F Announcement of good news (1:13b – 17)

3. Thomas L. Brodie, *The Birthing of the New Testament: The Intertextual Development of the New Testament Writings* (Sheffield: Sheffield Phoenix, 2004), 101.

D′ Reaction of doubt to the announcement of the angel (1:18)

    E′ Rebuke by the angel (1:19 – 20)

  C′ The suspense of the people waiting outside (1:21)

 B′ Zechariah stricken by silence and leaving the sanctuary (1:22)

A′ Zechariah and Elizabeth conceive a child and acknowledge God's favor (1:23 – 25)

Mention of Elizabeth's barrenness, her "disgrace" (vv. 7, 25), frames the account and underscores God's intervention. She changes from one who is "barren" (v. 7) to one who conceives (v. 24).

Brown contends that the announcement of John's birth follows a pattern of birth annunciations in the Old Testament: (1) the appearance of an angel of the Lord (or the Lord himself); (2) response of fear or prostration; (3) the divine message (birth, name giving, and child's future role); (4) objection or request for a sign; (5) the giving of a sign.[4] Conrad simplifies the structure to include more biblical examples: (1) the announcement of the birth; (2) the designation of the name; (3) the specification of the child's destiny.[5]

Exegetical Outline

➡ **I. Introduction of a righteous, childless couple of priestly heritage (1:5 – 7)**

II. Priestly service in the temple (1:8 – 10)

    A. Zechariah serving by burning the incense (1:8 – 9)

    B. The people at prayer (1:10)

III. Appearance of the angel Gabriel (1:11 – 20)

    A. Gabriel's appearance (1:11 – 12)

    B. Announcement of good news (1:13 – 17)

        1. Announcement of conception and name of the child (1:13 – 14)

        2. Announcement of the role of the child (1:15 – 17)

    C. Zechariah's reaction (1:18 – 20)

IV. Completion of the priestly service (1:21 – 23)

    A. The people waiting anxiously (1:21)

    B. Zechariah emerges from the sanctuary mute as a sign (1:22 – 23)

V. Barren Elizabeth conceives and acknowledges God's blessing (1:24 – 25)

---

4. Raymond E. Brown, *The Birth of the Messiah: A Commentary on the Infancy Narratives in Matthew and Luke* (New York: Doubleday, 1977), 156. See Gen 16:7 – 12; 17:1 – 21; 18:1 – 15; Judg 13:3 – 21.

5. Edgar W. Conrad, "The Annunciation of Birth and the Birth of the Messiah," *CBQ* 47 (1985): 656 – 63. The form takes the reader back to the patriarchal narratives.

Luke 1:5–25

1:5a	Chronological note	**And it happened**
		in the days of Herod, king of Judea,
b	Character introductions	**there was a priest by the name of Zechariah of the division of Abijah, and**
		his wife was of the daughters of Aaron
		and her name was Elizabeth.
6	Characterization	**They were both righteous before God,** walking in all of the commandments and statutes of the Lord blamelessly.
7	Complication	And **they did not have a child because Elizabeth was barren,**
		and both were advanced in their days.
8		**It happened**
	Time reference	while he was serving as priest before God in the appointed order of his division,
9	Circumstance	according to the custom of the priestly service,
		he was selected by lot to enter the sanctuary of the Lord to offer the incense.
10		And **the whole multitude of the people was praying outside**
		at the hour of the incense offering.
11	Appearance of an angel	And **an angel of the Lord appeared to** him, standing on the right side of the incense altar.
12	Reaction of distress	And when he saw him,
		Zechariah was troubled and fear fell upon him.
13a	Reassurance	**The angel said to him,**
		"Fear not, Zechariah, for your supplication has been heard,
b	Birth announcement	*and your wife Elizabeth will bear a son to you*
		and you will call his name John.
14	Promise	*And he will be joy and exultation to you,*
		and many will rejoice at this birth.
15a	Reason	*For he will be great before the Lord,*
b	Prophecy	*and he must never drink wine or an intoxicating drink,*
c		*and he will be full of the Holy Spirit while yet in his mother's womb.*

16		And he will turn many of the sons of Israel to the Lord their God.
17a		And he will go before him in the spirit and power of Elijah,
b		to turn the hearts of the fathers to their children and
c		the disobedient to [walk] in the ways of the thinking of the righteous,
d		to prepare a people made ready for the Lord."
18a	Doubting request for a sign	And Zechariah said to the angel, "On what basis will I know this?
b	Reason for doubt	For I am old and my wife is advanced in her days."
19	Rebuke	And the angel answered him, "I am Gabriel who stands before God, and I have been sent to speak to you and to proclaim this good news to you!
20	Giving of a sign/ punishment	And behold, you will be silent and not be able to speak until the days these things happen because you did not believe my words, which will be fulfilled in their fixed time!"
21	Suspense	And the people were waiting for Zechariah and wondered while he continued to stay in the sanctuary.
22	Sign	When he came out, he was unable to speak to them, and they knew that he had seen a vision in the sanctuary. And he was motioning to them and remained mute.
23a	Chronological note	When the days of his service came to an end,
b	Departure	he went back to his house.
24	Fulfillment of promise	After these days, Elizabeth conceived, and hid herself entirely for five months, saying,
25	Acknowledgment	"The Lord has done this to me in the days in which he looked favorably upon me and removed my disgrace among men."

Explanation of the Text

1:5 And it happened in the days of Herod, king of Judea, there was a priest by the name of Zechariah of the division of Abijah, and his wife was of the daughters of Aaron and her name was Elizabeth (Ἐγένετο ἐν ταῖς ἡμέραις Ἡρῴδου βασιλέως τῆς Ἰουδαίας ἱερεύς τις ὀνόματι Ζαχαρίας ἐξ ἐφημερίας Ἀβιά, καὶ γυνὴ αὐτῷ ἐκ τῶν θυγατέρων Ἀαρὼν καὶ τὸ ὄνομα αὐτῆς Ἐλισάβετ). This beginning of the narrative sets the account in history, as do many of the prophetic books (Isa 1:1; Jer 1:2 – 3; Hos 1:1; Amos 1:1; Mic 1:1; Zeph 1:1). The plan and purpose of God, embedded in the long-foretold prophecies, will unfold in human history and are not acted out on the stage of a cosmogonic myth.

In Luke's account, the kings and governors play no direct role in the story's action and serve only as chronological ciphers (see 3:1 – 2) or as those issuing decrees from afar (2:1). Busy with their own affairs, they take no note of the birth of John or of Jesus that will turn their world upside down. The vital characters in the story are unknowns: an ordinary priest and his aging wife; a young peasant girl and a Jewish man, who has to register to pay his taxes; shepherds, a despised class; and two prophets, male and female, who hang out in the temple waiting for God's intervention.

"Herod" is Herod the Great, an Edomite, a people not highly favored in Scripture (Obad 1 – 14; Mal 1:2 – 5). He was granted the title "king of Judea" by the Roman senate as the client ruler of a native land on the outskirts of the empire (Josephus, *Ant.* 14.14.4 §384 – 85). "Judea" refers to the land of the Jews (see 4:44; 7:17; 23:5; Acts 10:37). Herod may hold the title "king of Judea" (βασιλέως τῆς Ἰουδαίας), but Jesus will be crucified as "*the*

king of the Jews" (ὁ βασιλεὺς τῶν Ἰουδαίων, 23:37 – 38). Herod's meager kingdom is fragile. Upon his death, it will shrink, parceled out to three heirs. Judea will soon come under the direct rule of a Roman governor. By contrast, Jesus will receive a kingdom conferred on him by God (22:29), and he "will reign over the house of Jacob forever, and of his reign there will be no end" (1:33).

Zechariah is identified as a priest serving in the division of Abijah. The divisions were named for Aaron's twenty-four descendants (1 Chr 24:1 – 19) and were reconstituted after the return from exile (Neh 12:1 – 7). Zechariah's wife, Elizabeth, also comes from a priestly family and is identified as a "daughter of Aaron," the first of great figures in Israel's history whose names pepper the infancy narrative.[6]

1:6 – 7 They were both righteous before God, walking in all of the commandments and statutes of the Lord blamelessly. And they did not have a child because Elizabeth was barren, and both were advanced in their days (ἦσαν δὲ δίκαιοι ἀμφότεροι ἐναντίον τοῦ θεοῦ, πορευόμενοι ἐν πάσαις ταῖς ἐντολαῖς καὶ δικαιώμασιν τοῦ κυρίου ἄμεμπτοι. καὶ οὐκ ἦν αὐτοῖς τέκνον, καθότι ἦν ἡ Ἐλισάβετ στεῖρα, καὶ ἀμφότεροι προβεβηκότες ἐν ταῖς ἡμέραις αὐτῶν ἦσαν). Zechariah and Elizabeth are further characterized as "righteous before God." They do not have an imitation righteousness that can fool humans (see 18:9) but are truly righteous in God's eyes. They also "walk in all of the commandments and statutes [ταῖς ἐντολαῖς καὶ δικαιώμασιν] of the Lord" and are described as "blameless" (ἄμεμπτοι, see Phil 3:6). This last adjective stands in the emphatic position at the end of the clause.

6. Abraham (1:55, 73); Moses (2:22); David (1:27, 32, 69; 2:4, 11). Elizabeth is the name of Aaron's wife (Exod 6:23), and Mary (Miriam) is the name of his sister (Exod 15:20).

This characterization recalls the Abraham saga. Abraham was to be "blameless" (Gen 17:1) before God. When his son Isaac moved to Gerar, God told him to stay in the land and promised that he and his descendants would be blessed and his offspring would be as numerous as the stars of heaven "because Abraham your father obeyed my voice and kept my charge, my commandments, my statutes [τὰς ἐντολάς μου καὶ τὰ δικαιώματά μου], and my laws" (Gen 26:5 LXX). Also like Abraham and Sarah, Zechariah and Elizabeth are childless and advanced in their days, making the birth of a child unlikely, if not impossible.

The assertion that they are righteous and blameless makes clear that their childlessness is not a punishment for some sin. But it does introduce an incongruity. According to Deut 7:14, if Israel heeds the "laws" (δικαιώματα, 7:12 LXX), "you will be the blessed more than any other people; none of your men or women will be childless, nor will any of your livestock be without young." Something is wrong. The oracle against Babylon in Isaiah 47 declares that "in a moment … loss of children and widowhood. They will come upon you in full measure" (Isa 47:9). In the infancy narratives, we encounter a righteous, childless woman, Elizabeth, and a righteous, husbandless woman, Anna (Luke 2:36 – 37). It is as if the curse against Babylon has fallen on Israel. The barrenness of this righteous couple is not simply a private misfortune but symbolizes that Israel is under a curse worse than Herod's tyranny and Rome's overlordship and is in need of deliverance and rescue. Elizabeth and Zechariah represent God's people, seemingly without hope for the future. Elizabeth's disgrace (1:25) is symptomatic of Israel's disgrace of spiritual barrenness. It explains why the miraculous birth of John does not simply bring private joy to a bereft couple but promises to be good news for a comfortless nation.[7]

The first two characters introduced in the gospel, therefore, take on the guise of biblical figures who reprise the familiar story of a righteous, barren couple. If readers remember other stories of righteous, childless couples in the Old Testament (Abraham and Sarah, Jacob and Rachel [Gen 30:22 – 24], Manoah and his wife [Judg 13:3 – 25], and Elkanah and Hannah [1 Sam 1:1 – 20]), they are primed to expect God to step in to bring the pain of barrenness to an end.

1:8 – 9 It happened while he was serving as priest before God in the appointed order of his division, according to the custom of the priestly service, he was selected by lot to enter the sanctuary of the Lord to offer the incense (Ἐγένετο δὲ ἐν τῷ ἱερατεύειν αὐτὸν ἐν τῇ τάξει τῆς ἐφημερίας αὐτοῦ ἔναντι τοῦ θεοῦ, κατὰ τὸ ἔθος τῆς ἱερατείας ἔλαχε τοῦ θυμιᾶσαι εἰσελθὼν εἰς τὸν ναὸν τοῦ κυρίου). The twenty-four divisions of priests alternated by performing their duties in the temple for one week twice a year.[8] Zechariah serves during the afternoon (the ninth hour) public offering, the *Tamid* (cf. Exod 29:38 – 42; Num 28:1 – 10; *m. Tamid* 6.3 – 7.3), which took place twice a day. All of the necessary duties to carry out the various tasks for the sacrifices were assigned by lot, and Zechariah has a once-in-a-lifetime opportunity to be in charge of the incense portion.[9]

In the afternoon sacrifice, the incense was last, and the assigned priest and two assistants carried

---

7. Because Jerusalem did not recognize her visitation from God, the story that begins on a note of hope and joy will end ominously. The rejection of Jesus casts a wintry pall of looming disaster on the nation as Jesus predicts, "The days are coming when they will say, 'Blessed are the barren and the wombs that did not give birth and the breasts that did not nurse'" (23:29).

8. The term "division" (ἐφημερία) literally means "daily" and

refers to their daily duties in the temple ritual (see Heb 9:6).

9. Dennis Hamm, "The Tamid Service in Luke-Acts: The Cultic Background behind Luke's Theology of Worship (Luke 1:5 – 25; 18:9 – 14; 24:50 – 53; Acts 3:1; 10:3, 30)," *CBQ* 65 (2003): 22. On the preparation of the incense, which would have been done by other priests, see Exod 30:34 – 38.

burning coals from the great altar into the chamber of the Holy Place to burn the incense on the altar of incense, made of gold-plated wood and located in the center of the room before the veil separating the Holy Place from the Most Holy Place (Exod 30:1 – 10). The assistants then withdrew, leaving the priest alone in the sanctuary, when he would lay the incense on the coals at the signal of the presiding priest and prostrate himself in prayer (*m. Tamid* 3:6, 9; 6:3; *b. Ker.* 6b; *b. Zebaḥ.* 59a; *b. Menaḥ* 26b). Coleridge suggests, "The cultic action is never narrated, since, as the narrator has it, it is not through the Temple cult that God visits his people."[10]

1:10 And the whole multitude of the people was praying outside at the hour of the incense offering (καὶ πᾶν τὸ πλῆθος ἦν τοῦ λαοῦ προσευχόμενον ἔξω τῇ ὥρᾳ τοῦ θυμιάματος). "The people" (τοῦ λαοῦ) in Luke usually refers to Israel as the elect nation. Incense was a symbol of prayer (Ps 141:2; Rev 5:8; 8:3 – 4). The whole assembly appropriately prays outside during the Tamid service. Significant things happen in Luke-Acts during times of prayer.

1:11 – 12 And an angel of the Lord appeared to him, standing on the right side of the incense altar. And when he saw him, Zechariah was troubled and fear fell upon him (ὤφθη δὲ αὐτῷ ἄγγελος κυρίου ἑστὼς ἐκ δεξιῶν τοῦ θυσιαστηρίου τοῦ θυμιάματος. καὶ ἐταράχθη Ζαχαρίας ἰδὼν καὶ φόβος ἐπέπεσεν ἐπ᾽ αὐτόν). Angels were believed to occupy the sanctuary (see Isa 6:1 – 3; Zech 3), but according to a legend in the *Lives of the Prophets* 23:1 – 2, when Joash killed Zechariah, son of Jehoiada the priest, near the altar, "the priests were not able to see a vision of angels of God" in the temple from that time. Thus,

something new is happening as an angel now stands by the altar ready to deliver a message from God. The visitation is hidden from the gathering of worshipers outside. What God is now doing will be made manifest only to a select few. The angel's appearance causes Zechariah to quake in fear, a common reaction when humans are confronted by the numinous (2:9).

1:13 The angel said to him, "Fear not, Zechariah, for your supplication has been heard, and your wife Elizabeth will bear a son to you and you will call his name John (εἶπεν δὲ πρὸς αὐτὸν ὁ ἄγγελος· μὴ φοβοῦ, Ζαχαρία, διότι εἰσηκούσθη ἡ δέησίς σου, καὶ ἡ γυνή σου Ἐλισάβετ γεννήσει υἱόν σοι καὶ καλέσεις τὸ ὄνομα αὐτοῦ Ἰωάννην). The first words from God in the gospel are, "Fear not." Zechariah's prayer has been heard, and God is taking action. That Zechariah had prayed for a child (as Isaac had for the barren Rebekah, Gen 25:21) is implied by the personal announcement, "your wife Elizabeth will bear a son." This announcement echoes the one made to Abraham long ago (Gen 17:19).

At the end of the gospel, Luke also characterizes Joseph of Arimathea as a "good and righteous man" and notes that he "was waiting [expectantly] for the reign of God" (23:50 – 51). One may assume that this righteous priest did not pray only for his own needs but, like Joseph, also prayed expectantly for the deliverance of Israel. The description of the child's role that follows reveals that God is answering not only the prayers of a desperate couple but also those of a desperate people. Divine intervention in the lives of this couple is divine intervention for Israel.[11] Their personal prayers have meshed with God's plans in the drama of redemption to restore Israel to God.[12]

10. Mark Coleridge, *The Birth of the Lukan Narrative: Narrative as Christology in Luke 1 – 2* (JSNTSup 88; Sheffield: Sheffield Academic, 1993), 33.

11. Green, *The Gospel of Luke*, 62.

12. François Bovon, *Luke 1:1 – 9:50* (Hermeneia; trans. Christine M. Thomas; Minneapolis: Fortress, 2002), 34, notes

Name giving is the right of the father, but God takes over that right because God is the one who gives the child and will claim and shape his life. The name is not picked for its pleasant ring. In Hebrew, John (*Yoḥanan*) means "Yahweh is gracious (or merciful)," though this etymology would have been lost on Greek readers and is not developed by Luke.

1:14 And he will be joy and exultation to you, and many will rejoice at this birth (καὶ ἔσται χαρά σοι καὶ ἀγαλλίασις, καὶ πολλοὶ ἐπὶ τῇ γενέσει αὐτοῦ χαρήσονται). Coleridge suggests, "As far as Zechariah is concerned, the angel can stop right there, but he goes on to reveal a greater role."[13] The parent's joy will be shared by others who will be affected by his ministry. But the reference to "the many" (1:16) sounds an ominous note (see 2:34). Not all will respond to him with joy (3:7, 20; 7:29 – 30; 9:7 – 9; 20:4 – 6).

1:15 – 17 For he will be great before the Lord, and he must never drink wine or an intoxicating drink, and he shall be full of the Holy Spirit while yet in his mother's womb. And he will turn many of the sons of Israel to the Lord their God. And he will go before him in the spirit and power of Elijah, to turn the hearts of the fathers to their children and the disobedient to [walk] in the ways of thinking of the righteous, to prepare a people made ready for the Lord." (ἔσται γὰρ μέγας ἐνώπιον [τοῦ] κυρίου, καὶ οἶνον καὶ σίκερα οὐ μὴ πίῃ, καὶ πνεύματος ἁγίου πλησθήσεται ἔτι ἐκ κοιλίας μητρὸς αὐτοῦ, καὶ πολλοὺς τῶν υἱῶν Ἰσραὴλ ἐπιστρέψει ἐπὶ κύριον τὸν θεὸν αὐτῶν. καὶ αὐτὸς προελεύσεται ἐνώπιον αὐτοῦ ἐν πνεύματι καὶ δυνάμει Ἡλίου, ἐπιστρέψαι καρδίας πατέρων ἐπὶ τέκνα καὶ

ἀπειθεῖς ἐν φρονήσει δικαίων, ἑτοιμάσαι κυρίῳ λαὸν κατεσκευασμένον). The prediction about John's role (vv. 13 – 17) reveals a pattern: "God first announces what he intends doing and then does it."[14] The angel announces what John will be and do.

(1) John will be "great before the Lord," which has nothing to do with his personal status (see 7:28) but refers to his doing what is pleasing to the Lord (see Sir 48:22).

(2) That he must "never" (οὐ μή, emphatic negation) "drink wine or an intoxicating drink" does not refer to a temporary vow but means that his entire life is to be set apart to fulfill his divine calling, as significant figures in Israel's past were (see Judg 13:4 – 5, 7; 1 Sam 1:11). The Holy Spirit is to control him, so he must not lose control from intoxication (Eph 5:18).

(3) Being filled with the Holy Spirit "from his mother's womb" prepares for the child leaping in his mother's womb when Elizabeth hears Mary's greeting (1:44). His prophetic role, therefore, will begin even before his birth (see Isa 49:1; Jer 1:5; Sir 49:7; Gal 1:15). Luke's infancy narrative highlights an outbreak of the prophetic Spirit as each of the main characters bursts forth with prophetic utterances and praise.

(4) "He will turn many of the sons of Israel to the Lord their God" is connected to turning "the hearts of the fathers to their children and the disobedient to [walk] in the ways of thinking of the righteous." Turning the hearts of the fathers to the children suggests that the fathers are the ones who have disrupted the relationship with God. This prediction does not simply refer to the creation of family harmony but to an image of repentance and conversion.

(5) "He will go before him in the spirit and

---

that in each case the announcement of births in the Old Testament "happened for the good not only of individuals but of the whole nation."

13. Coleridge, *The Birth of the Lukan Narrative*, 36.
14. Ibid., 35.

power of Elijah" refers to going before God, since the Messiah has not been mentioned. Luke's narrative makes clear, however, that "God's coming was realized" in Jesus.[15] John is no competitor to Jesus (see John 3:25 – 30) "but an instrument of God's climactic purpose, which finds its highest expression in Jesus."[16] Like Elijah, he will bring a message of judgment and warning to reprobate Israel, but he also has eschatological significance. He will sound the final warning. The last of the prophetic books, Malachi, prophesies that God will send "the prophet Elijah ... before that great and terrible day of the LORD comes. He will turn the hearts of the parents to their children, and the hearts of the children to their parents; or else I will come and strike the land with total destruction" (Mal 4:5 – 6).[17] Bovon comments, "The prophet's message is the last chance for the nation in view of the coming day of the Lord with its consuming judgment (Mal 4:1, 6 [MT/LXX 3:19, 23])…. The Baptist's future activity thus receives an eschatological apocalyptic significance."[18]

(6) His ultimate goal is "to prepare a people made ready for the Lord." They are not simply to be made ready for the Lord's coming (1:76; 3:4) but to be prepared to become what the Lord created them to be and to do. They are to be ready for action.

1:18 And Zechariah said to the angel, "On what basis will I know this? For I am old and my wife is advanced in her days." (καὶ εἶπεν Ζαχαρίας πρὸς τὸν ἄγγελον· κατὰ τί γνώσομαι τοῦτο; ἐγὼ γάρ εἰμι πρεσβύτης καὶ ἡ γυνή μου προβεβηκυῖα ἐν ταῖς ἡμέραις αὐτῆς). Zechariah's question begins with κατὰ τί, which literally means "according to what," and I translate it to show that

he is asking for proof, "on what basis?" His question differs from Mary's in 1:34, which begins with "how?" (πῶς). Many versions translate both questions identically as "how?" This rendering obscures the distinction between the two questions. Unlike Mary, Zechariah will not trust the angel's word *until* he receives a sign (see 11:16, 29). By contrast, Mary asks in what way her pregnancy will happen, assuming that it will happen. She trusts first before she is given a sign.

Zechariah's question differs little from Abraham's in Genesis 15:8, "But Abram said, 'Sovereign LORD, how can I know that I will gain possession of it?'" Unlike Abraham, Zechariah cannot be said to have trusted God and it was counted to him as righteousness (Gen 15:6). Zechariah's righteousness derives from his obedience to the commandments and statutes. He had been praying all these years for a child, but his response reveals that he did not expect his prayers to be answered. Even when an angel announces to him that they will be granted, he wants more definitive proof. The name Zechariah means "God has remembered," but Zechariah does not remember what God has done in the past with Abraham and does not trust the word from the angel. By contrast, two other righteous people, Anna and Simeon (2:25 – 38), had also been praying and fasting faithfully for years, and they immediately rejoiced when they saw the answer to their prayers.

1:19 And the angel answered him, "I am Gabriel who stands before God, and I have been sent to speak to you and to proclaim this good news to you!" (καὶ ἀποκριθεὶς ὁ ἄγγελος εἶπεν αὐτῷ, Ἐγώ εἰμι Γαβριὴλ ὁ παρεστηκὼς ἐνώπιον τοῦ θεοῦ, καὶ ἀπεστάλην λαλῆσαι πρὸς σὲ καὶ εὐαγγελίσασθαι

---

15. Schweizer, *Luke*, 23.

16. Frederick W. Danker, *Jesus and the New Age* (Philadelphia: Fortress, 1988), 27.

17. Sirach 48:10 interprets this final role more positively, "At the appointed time, it is written, you [Elijah] are destined

to calm the wrath of God before it breaks out in fury, to turn the hearts of parents to their children, and to restore the tribes of Jacob."

18. Bovon, *Luke 1:1 – 9:50*, 37.

σοι ταῦτα). His veracity challenged, the angel of the Lord now identifies himself as Gabriel. It is an assertion of his divine authority in the face of this human's doubt. To the "I" of Zechariah, "How will *I* know this? *I* am an old man," Gabriel responds imperiously, "*I* am Gabriel, *I* stand in the presence of God, and *I* have been sent to speak to you."

Gabriel is one of only two angels mentioned by name in the Bible; he appeared to Daniel as he was praying at the time of the evening sacrifice (Dan 8:15 – 16; 9:21 – 27) to help him interpret eschatological visions. Brown contends, "The eschatological atmosphere evoked from Daniel is echoed in the tone of the message that follows."[19]

1:20 "And behold, you will be silent and not able to speak until the days these things happen because you did not believe my words, which will be fulfilled in their fixed time!" (καὶ ἰδοὺ ἔσῃ σιωπῶν καὶ μὴ δυνάμενος λαλῆσαι ἄχρι ἧς ἡμέρας γένηται ταῦτα, ἀνθ' ὧν οὐκ ἐπίστευσας τοῖς λόγοις μου, οἵτινες πληρωθήσονται εἰς τὸν καιρὸν αὐτῶν). Sometimes signs are given unasked; sometimes they are given when they are requested (Exod 4:2 – 6; Judg 6:36 – 39; 2 Kgs 20:8). Zechariah asks for a sign (see Luke 11:16, 29) but receives a punitive sign. He will become speechless because he cannot bring himself to believe. Gabriel assures him that his divine message will be fulfilled despite human doubt. His response reads literally that these things "will be filled into their time" (πληρωθήσονται εἰς τὸν καιρὸν αὐτῶν), which refers to a preordained time, a "fixed time" set by God. Coleridge argues, "The silence is also a sign that the initiative does not pass to Zechariah, but remains firmly with heaven."[20] The chronological details that placed the events during Herod's reign are now overruled by the special moment of

God's saving action. The one who reigns over the universe and history makes the ones who reign on earth forgettable.

1:21 – 23 And the people were waiting for Zechariah and wondered while he continued to stay in the sanctuary. When he came out, he was unable to speak to them, and they knew that he had seen a vision in the sanctuary. And he was motioning to them and remained mute. When the days of his service came to an end, he went back to his house (καὶ ἦν ὁ λαὸς προσδοκῶν τὸν Ζαχαρίαν, καὶ ἐθαύμαζον ἐν τῷ χρονίζειν ἐν τῷ ναῷ αὐτόν. ἐξελθὼν δὲ οὐκ ἐδύνατο λαλῆσαι αὐτοῖς, καὶ ἐπέγνωσαν ὅτι ὀπτασίαν ἑώρακεν ἐν τῷ ναῷ· καὶ αὐτὸς ἦν διανεύων αὐτοῖς καὶ διέμενεν κωφός. καὶ ἐγένετο ὡς ἐπλήσθησαν αἱ ἡμέραι τῆς λειτουργίας αὐτοῦ, ἀπῆλθεν εἰς τὸν οἶκον αὐτοῦ). Because Zechariah delayed so long in the sanctuary, the people in the temple court may have despaired that something disastrous had happened. Coming so close to the Most Holy Place was fraught with danger, like coming close to a spiritual nuclear reactor core (see 1 Macc 9:54 – 56; Josephus, *Ant.* 12.10.6 §413).

When Zechariah exits, the people immediately assume that he has been struck dumb from seeing a vision (see Dan 10:15). They remain in the dark about what really happened, and his waving his arms in sign language is inadequate to proclaim the truth. He has been struck dumb because he did not believe Gabriel's promise.[21] Consequently, the angel's announcement will be hidden from the people. When he does speak, his prophecy and praise are not delivered in the sacred confines of the temple. Prophecy does not emanate from a dysfunctional temple (19:45), and God's salvation plan ultimately will make it obsolete.[22]

19. Brown, *The Birth of the Messiah*, 271.
20. Coleridge, *The Birth of the Lukan Narrative*, 44.
21. Ibid., 45.

22. Brown (*The Birth of the Messiah*, 280) claims that his inability to speak also means that he cannot join in uttering the priestly blessing (Num 6:24 – 26). Jesus does so in 24:50 – 52.

1:24 – 25 After these days, Elizabeth conceived, and hid herself entirely for five months, saying, "The Lord has done this to me in the days in which he looked favorably upon me and removed my disgrace among men" (μετὰ δὲ ταύτας τὰς ἡμέρας συνέλαβεν Ἐλισάβετ ἡ γυνὴ αὐτοῦ καὶ περιέκρυβεν ἑαυτὴν μῆνας πέντε λέγουσα ὅτι Οὕτως μοι πεποίηκεν κύριος ἐν ἡμέραις αἷς ἐπεῖδεν ἀφελεῖν ὄνειδός μου ἐν ἀνθρώποις). Zechariah leaves Jerusalem at the end of his week of service for home, an unnamed Judean town in the hill country (1:39). This detail discreetly implies that John's conception will take place in the normal way.[23]

God is true to his word, and his wife conceives. Elizabeth then goes into deep seclusion ("she hid herself all around," "on all sides," περιέκρυβεν) for five months. No motive is given for her action. Again, mysterious silence shrouds what has happened. The good news is not proclaimed to the public. In the narrative, it means that Mary is the first to learn of the pregnancy as it becomes a sign for her from the angel Gabriel (1:36).

When Elizabeth speaks, she speaks only to God. She gives thanks that God has removed her disgrace among the people (see Rachel's cry, Gen 30:23). Rachel's lament, "Give me children, or I'll die!" (Gen 30:1), was the basis for the widespread assumption that the childless were accounted as dead (*b. Ned.* 64b). Elizabeth's piety had not spared her from the shame of being childless. Her culture told her, daughter of a priest or not, that the number of children that she bore, particularly sons, set her value as a wife and a person. A barren woman was assumed to have sinned in some way to bring this desolation upon herself.[24] Without a visitation from an angel or an explanation from her speechless husband, Elizabeth recognizes that God has intervened in her life. Her understanding, however, is limited. As Coleridge notes, she thinks that "God has intervened primarily to vindicate her."[25] Her interpretation of her pregnancy is incomplete. She cannot imagine now its wider implications for the people of Israel or how it fits in the fulfillment of God's plan.

Theology in Application

1. The Continuation of the Biblical Story

The opening chapters of this gospel are filled with hints of the divine promises from long ago and with "angelic appearances, psalms, and biblical phrases." They "transport the reader back to the world of the Jewish Scriptures."[26] The echoes of scriptural stories from Israel's hallowed past reveal Luke's basic theological assumption: the same God who made promises and acted in surprising ways in Israel's history is now acting in the present in surprising ways to bring those promises to fulfillment.[27] In these opening scenes, Luke lays the scriptural subflooring of promise and fulfillment that forms the basis for understanding the story of Jesus.

23. It also reveals that Zechariah is not a member of the priestly establishment in Jerusalem but on the periphery and shared the struggle of ordinary people living in small villages and struggling for survival.

24. Tal Ilan, *Jewish Women in Greco-Roman Palestine* (Pea-

body MA: Hendrickson, 1996), 111.

25. Coleridge, *The Birth of the Lukan Narrative*, 48.

26. Helen K. Bond, *Caiaphas: Friend of Rome and Judge of Jesus?* (Louisville/London: Westminster John Knox, 2004), 109.

27. See C. Kavin Rowe, *Early Narrative Christology: The*

In addition, Luke abruptly changes from the elegant Greek syntax in the preface to a Septuagintal style, which is like shifting to King James English in public prayer. It gives the narrative an archaic, holy resonance. These scriptural reverberations help those familiar with the LXX to recognize that this story of the events "fulfilled among us" (1:1) continues the divine history of salvation and marks its fulfillment.[28] The abundance of Old Testament allusions means that Luke's account is "no narrative for beginners" because it cannot "be rightly understood unless seen as the fulfillment of past promises; and the assumption is that the reader knows the OT well enough to recognize the echoes that the narrator now brings."[29]

The identification of Israel as the people of God is prominent. The promise is to Israel (1:16 – 17, 54, 68, 77), and Israel's messianic hope figures prominently (1:32 – 33, 69, 78; 2:11, 25 – 26, 29 – 30, 38). The story introduces faithful Jews who are waiting: Zechariah and Elizabeth, Mary, Simeon and Anna. Nouwen writes, "Waiting finally became the attitude of only the remnant of Israel, of that small group of Israelites that had remained faithful."[30] Zephaniah 3:12 – 13 aptly describes this group waiting for God:

> But I will leave within you
>> the meek and humble.
> The remnant of Israel
>> will trust in the name of the Lord.
> They will do no wrong;
>> they will tell no lies.
> A deceitful tongue
>> will not be found in their mouths.
> They will eat and lie down
>> and no one will make them afraid.

2. Moving beyond the Temple Cult

Throughout the infancy narrative cultic moments are conspicuous. The story opens in the temple during the Tamid service (1:8 – 10), the twice-daily sacrifice for the forgiveness of the sins of the people. Circumcision is mentioned twice (1:59; 2:21), and the rite of purification and a sacrifice after a birth are mentioned once (2:22 – 39). The Passover festival appears in 2:41 – 43. These references show that the Christian way was cradled in pietistic Judaism and is not some newfangled

---

Lord in the Gospel of Luke (BZNW 2/139; Berlin/New York: de Gruyter, 2006), 34 – 35.

28. Daryl D. Schmidt, "Rhetorical Influences and Genre," 52. Nils A. Dahl ("The Story of Abraham in Luke-Acts," in *Studies in Luke-Acts* [ed. L. E. Keck and J. L. Martyn; Philadelphia: Fortress, 1966], 153) claims that Luke intends to "write

the continuation of the biblical history."

29. Coleridge, *The Birth of the Lukan Narrative*, 30.

30. Henri Nouwen, "The Path of Waiting," in *Finding My Way Home: Pathways to Life and the Spirit* (New York: Crossroad, 2001), 95.

eccentricity. What is striking, however, is that these rituals are not described. For this new movement, they do not serve to mark the identity of Christ followers.

3. Moving beyond Knowledge to Faith

The opening encounter with the angel reveals that God is directing this story. He overcomes seemingly insurmountable barriers to accomplish his purposes. This includes human questioning. Zechariah is pious though still afflicted by doubt. Note the contrast between Zechariah's demand *to know* (v. 18) and Gabriel's emphasis on *belief* (v. 20). Knowledge provides the illusion of certainty, which then becomes a poor substitute for the more vital confidence of faith. Knowledge would also provide Zechariah with the illusion that he has some measure of control over what happens. But only One is in control — God. Zechariah's silence, which I interpret as a punishment and not simply the aftereffects of a vision, makes a theological point: "God looks to the human being to accept his plan, but does not depend on the human being for its implementation."[31]

Having all the facts does not automatically lead to faith. One never has all the facts. The decision to believe requires trust in God's faithfulness. Mary becomes a positive example of this trust in the next scene. Having made that decision, she will learn from the incidents that follow that there is much to be discovered, and some of that may prove daunting. There is much pondering to be done as the accomplishment of God's will unfolds.

4. Hope against Hope

For all his righteousness, Zechariah does not believe when his prayers and deepest hopes are about to be fulfilled, because he felt it was an impossible dream. He stands in contrast to Abraham who, in the same situation, hoped against hope (Rom 4:18). Zechariah had been praying faithfully but apparently did not believe that his prayers would be answered. He was faithfully carrying out the ritual perilously near the Most Holy Place in the temple, where God's presence was believed to emanate, yet he could not quite bring himself to believe the angel who appeared to him in this Holy Place was on the up and up. Instead of the joy and exultation one might expect Zechariah to exude at the news, he expressed doubt and consternation. His reaction reveals that his hope for a child was all but dead even though it kept itching like a scab. He went through the motions of religious activity, prayer, and priestly service, but after all these years he could not bring himself to believe that God would ever really do anything.

---

31. Coleridge, *The Birth of the Lukan Narrative*, 41.

Perhaps his hopes had been raised so many times in the past and then dashed that he could not bring himself to dare to believe. He did not want to go through the pain of disappointment again. Perhaps the routine of all his priestly activity caused him to forget that God remembers and fulfills promises. If it is true that hope is like oxygen for the soul, then Zechariah needed an oxygen tank and respirator.

His doubting in the face of the fulfillment of hopes is not a foreign experience for Christians through the ages. When Peter escaped from his shackles and passed by the guards and through an impregnable iron gate that miraculously opened by itself and then made his way to the room where the believers had gathered and were fervently praying for his release, the reaction is almost comical (Acts 12:1 – 17). The young maid Rhoda met him at the gate but forgot to open it for him. When she announced that Peter was at the gate, the people chided her for interrupting the prayer meeting for his release and basically told her, "You are mad. How could Peter ever get free? You are seeing ghosts." It is easy to be caught off guard when God answers prayer. Frequently, the church is dumbfounded in the face of liberation.

It is possible that in praying Christians only go through the motions without faith that God will answer. There may be little interest in seeing how God might answer prayers. A lack of anticipation that anything will ever change can lead to spiritual languor, which, in turn, leads to a voice that is mute about the hope that God's promises awaken. How can Christians "always be prepared to give an answer to everyone who asks you to give the reason for the hope that you have" (1 Pet 3:15), if they have no hope in them?

There is another danger that our hopes can become domesticated and self-centered. We as Christians can become so wrapped up in our own little world that we fail to lift up our eyes to see the unimaginable things God has planned and promised. The bold challenge in Heb 13:13 – 14 ("Let us, then, go to him outside the camp, bearing the disgrace he bore. For here we do not have an enduring city, but we are looking for the city that is to come") cannot be answered if our hopes are centered only in this world and its possibilities. Bauckham and Hart write, "Most readers of this book live in a society where the fear of death and loss holds the majority subconsciously in its grip, and where ideologies of self-advancement and the artificially stimulated appetite for 'more of everything good now' dominates our view of the world, our practical priorities, and our understanding of life's ultimate meaning and goal."[32]

---

32. Richard Bauckham and Trevor Hart, *Hope against Hope: Christian Eschatology at the Turn of the Millennium* (Grand Rapids: Eerdmans, 1999), 203.

We as Christians should measure our hopes for today and tomorrow in a despairing world by the promises that God has unfolded in Scripture that extend far beyond the materiality of this orb. Mostert writes:

> To live in hope is to adopt a basic stance or direction, like iron filings in a magnetic field. It is to be drawn to something beyond the immediate concerns of the everyday, to look to the horizon and to see more than a limit to our vision, and our own possibilities. In short, it is to be oriented to the future, understood as a gift with God, with new divinely imagined possibilities, not just the outcome of events and actions in the past and present. To live in hope is to live in the energy field of the future.[33]

33. Christiaan Mostert, "Living in Hope," in *Hope: Challenging the Culture of Despair* (ed. C. Mostert; Hindmarsh: ATF, 2004), 62.

Luke 1:26–38

Literary Context

The birth announcement by the angel Gabriel to Mary parallels the announcement he made to Zechariah in the previous episode. Luke intends for Jesus and John to be compared in these two panels and for the reader to see that Jesus is demonstrably greater than John. The step-parallelism of the two annunciations, therefore, serves a christological purpose. John's conception is remarkable, but Jesus' conception through the creative power of the Holy Spirit is miraculous. The angel announced to Zechariah that John's role is "to prepare a people made ready for the Lord" (1:17). The announcement to Mary reveals that John will prepare the way *for Jesus*, who is the Son of the Most High and embodies the Lord in his mission and person.[1] John's significance in salvation history is tied solely to his connection to Jesus. The themes of mercy, showing favor (1:25, 28, 30, 48, 50, 54), the power of God to do the impossible (1:35, 37, 49), and God who brings salvation (1:47, 69, 71, 77; 2:11) run through the passages.

The step-parallelism of the two annunciations also marks a paradoxical downward trend. The scene shifts from the temple to a nontemple setting, from the holy city to a village of no consequence. The prestige of the character the angel visits shifts from an elderly male with high status to a young female with no status. The contrasts portend that the reign of God will turn everything topsy-turvy. In the immediate context of the infancy narratives, they foreshadow the surprising developments that the Son of God will be born in a manger and acclaimed by shepherds.

---

1. Karl A. Kuhn, "The Point of the Step-Parallelism in Luke 1 – 2," *NTS* 47 (2001): 49.

Main Idea

The life of Jesus that Luke records, beginning in 4:1, is possible because his conception was the result of God's direct, creative intervention so that Jesus shares in both the divine and the human sphere. Mary's response to this divine intervention shows that God's action requires human submission to the divine will.[2]

Translation

Luke 1:26–38

1:26a	Chronological note	In the sixth month,
b	Character reintroduction	**the angel Gabriel was sent from God to a town of Galilee**
c	Location	named Nazareth,
27a	Character introduction	to a virgin
b		betrothed to a man by the name of Joseph from the house of David,
c		**and the name of the virgin was Mary.**
28	Greeting	And when he came to her, **he said:** "Hail, highly favored one, the Lord is with you."
29	Reaction of consternation	But **she was vexed by this word** and **was considering what sort of greeting ↻ this might be.**
30a	Assurance	**The angel said to her,** "Fear not, Mary,
b	Reason	*for you have found grace with God.*
31	Birth announcement	*And behold you will conceive in your womb and will bear a son and ↻ will call his name Jesus.*
32a	Announcement of the child's future role	*This one will be great and will be called Son of the Most High,*
b		*and the Lord God will give to him the throne of David his father.*
33a		*He will reign over the house of Jacob forever,*
b		*and of his reign there will be no end.*"

Continued on next page.

2. Charles H. Talbert, "Jesus' Birth in Luke and the Nature of Religious Language," *HeyJ* 35 (1994): 397 – 98.

34	Reaction of questioning	**And Mary said to the angel,**

And **Mary said to the angel,**
 "How will this be, since I have not had sexual relations with a man?"

| 35a | Explanation | **The angel answered and said to her,** |

The angel answered and said to her,
 "The Holy Spirit will come upon you
 and the power of the Most High will overshadow you;

   and   *for this reason*
 the one who will be born is holy and
        will be called the Son of God.

| 36 | Giving of a sign | |

And behold, Elizabeth your kinswoman has conceived a son herself in ↵
                her advanced age
 and this is the sixth month for her who is called barren,

| 37 | Reason | *because nothing is impossible with God.* |
| 38a | Reaction of submissive faith | **Mary said,** |

Mary said,
 "Behold, [I am] a slave of the Lord.
 Let it happen to me according to your word."

| b | Departure | **And the angel left her.** |

Structure and Literary Form

Like 1:5 – 25, this unit contains a birth oracle, but it modifies the form more heavily.[3] The structure also forms a chiastic pattern:

A The angel's appearance and greeting and the introduction of Mary,
 a virgin espoused to Joseph (1:26 – 28)

 B Mary's consternation over the angel's greeting and the angel's reassurance
  not to fear (1:29 – 30a)

  C Announcement that she has found favor with God and will conceive
   and bear a son who will be called the Son of the Most High
   (1:30b – 33)

 B′ Mary's questioning about how this will occur and the angel's reassuring
  explanation (1:34 – 37)

A′ Mary's submissive response to the angel's announcement and the angel's
 departure (1:38)

---

3. John Nolland, *Luke 3* (vol 5. WBC; Dallas: Word, 1993), 1:41.

Exegetical Outline

➡ **I. Setting and introduction of Mary (1:26 – 27)**
   A. The town of Nazareth in Galilee (1:26)
   B. Mary, a virgin, espoused to Joseph of the house of David (1:27)

II. The angel's greeting of Mary (1:28 – 30)
   A. Greeting as a favored one (1:28)
   B. Mary's perplexity over this greeting (1:29)
   C. Reassurance as favored by God (1:30)

III. The angel's announcement of the conception and role of the child (1:31 – 33)
   A. Announcement of conception and name of the child Jesus (1:31)
   B. Role of the child (1:32 – 33)

IV. Mary's objection that she is a virgin (1:34)

V. The angel's explanation and giving of a sign (1:35 – 37)
   A. The Holy Spirit will come upon her and the power of the Most High will overshadow her (1:35)
   B. Elizabeth, her barren relative, has conceived and is in her sixth month (1:36)
   C. Nothing is impossible with God (1:37)

VI. Mary's humble submission to God's plan of salvation (1:38)

Explanation of the Text

1:26 – 27 In the sixth month, the angel Gabriel was sent from God to a town of Galilee named Nazareth, to a virgin betrothed to a man by the name of Joseph from the house of David, and the name of the virgin was Mary (Ἐν δὲ τῷ μηνὶ τῷ ἕκτῳ ἀπεστάλη ὁ ἄγγελος Γαβριὴλ ἀπὸ τοῦ θεοῦ εἰς πόλιν τῆς Γαλιλαίας ᾗ ὄνομα Ναζαρὲθ πρὸς παρθένον ἐμνηστευμένην ἀνδρὶ ᾧ ὄνομα Ἰωσὴφ ἐξ οἴκου Δαυίδ, καὶ τὸ ὄνομα τῆς παρθένου Μαριάμ). The "sixth month" refers to the sixth month of Elizabeth's pregnancy (1:36), which along with the reappearance of the angel Gabriel announcing another conception connects this episode to the previous one. Gabriel is sent by God, and Coleridge observes that this sending underscores "the heavenly initiative" in which "God does not so much enter a story as make a story."[4]

The town of Nazareth receives no notice in Scripture, intertestamental literature, Josephus, or rabbinic literature. This means that the story moves from sacred temple space and Judea to far-flung nowheresville in Galilee. The continuation of the clause reveals that Gabriel is sent to a virgin named Mary, so that "the goal of the divine action is not a place but a person."[5] She is referred to as "a virgin" twice before being named. The emphasis on her virginity sets up the miracle of the child's genesis. Barren wombs, like Elizabeth's, had been opened before, but a virginal conception was an unprecedented act of God.

Luke assumes the marriage customs without explaining that Mary's father has given his consent for her to marry Joseph and the bride price has been paid, but Joseph has not yet taken her

---

4. Coleridge, *The Birth of the Lukan Narrative*, 52.   5. Ibid., 53.

to live with him in his household (see Matt 1:18; 25:1 – 13; *m. Ketub.* 4:4 – 5). Her betrothal to Joseph, who plays no role in this episode, sets up the child's connection to David (1:32, 69; 2:4, 11; 3:31) with those messianic reverberations.

1:28 And when he came to her, he said: "Hail, highly favored one, the Lord is with you" (καὶ εἰσελθὼν πρὸς αὐτὴν εἶπεν, Χαῖρε, κεχαριτωμένη, ὁ κύριος μετὰ σοῦ). Gabriel does not announce to Mary who he is as he did to Zechariah, and then only as an angry response to Zechariah's unbelief, "I am Gabriel who stands before God" (1:19). The angel never reveals his identity or status to Mary. The greeting "hail" (χαῖρε) is a normal one but contains a play on words with the address "highly favored one" (κεχαριτωμένη). The passive voice of the participle is a divine passive: God is the one who shows her favor. She is greeted in terms of God's relationship to her as a recipient of grace. The angel has yet to explain how she has been graced.

The phrase "the Lord is with you" (ὁ κύριος μετὰ σοῦ) does not have a verb in Greek and expresses a reality, not a wish that "the Lord *be* with you" (see Judg 6:12; Ruth 2:4). It comes without any qualification. That is, the Lord is with her now. Bovon notes that in the Old Testament, "when God is 'with' Israel or a chosen individual, this alludes not only to his protection but also to the task to come."[6]

1:29 But she was vexed by this word and was considering what sort of greeting this might be (ἡ δὲ ἐπὶ τῷ λόγῳ διεταράχθη καὶ διελογίζετο ποταπὸς εἴη ὁ ἀσπασμὸς οὗτος). Luke has no interest in the extraordinary aspects of the visit. It is the angel's word, not his appearance, that causes Mary's consternation.[7] Fitzmyer argues from the Jewish tradition that males extended no greetings to women (*b. Qidd.* 70a), and therefore she would be perplexed that someone who was not a woman greets her.[8] While that may be true, her vexation may simply confirm that God's direct intervention is always unexpected, perplexing, and potentially disturbing.

In this scene, the angel will clarify what this visitation means, but he does not disclose everything that will happen to her. Mary will spend most of the infancy narrative in a state of wonderment and must ponder the stupendous events without an angelic interpreter (2:19, 51). The angel also does not unveil the full picture of what this child will do or what will be done to him. That would have been too overwhelming.[9]

1:30 The angel said to her, "Fear not, Mary, for you have found grace with God (καὶ εἶπεν ὁ ἄγγελος αὐτῇ· μὴ φοβοῦ, Μαριάμ, εὗρες γὰρ χάριν παρὰ τῷ θεῷ). The angel reiterates that she is an object of God's grace. That a young girl of such humble circumstances receives such special favor reinforces the moral adage that "God opposes the proud but gives grace to the humble" (Jas 4:6; 1 Pet 5:5, citing Prov 3:34 LXX). Mary acknowledges this explicitly in 1:48, 52. Grace is not limited simply to receiving mercy and forgiveness. Finding grace with God means that God entrusts her with something great to do and to bear.

1:31 – 33 And behold you will conceive in your womb and will bear a son and will call his

---

6. Bovon, *Luke 1:1 – 9:50*, 50.

7. Zechariah was "troubled" (ἐταράχθη) when the angel appeared (1:12). With the addition of the preposition to the verb (διεταράχθη), Mary's reaction is more intense: she is "vexed."

8. Fitzmyer, *Luke*, 1:346.

9. Visitations from supernatural beings could bring tragedy in their wake. For example, according to Tob 3:7 – 8, Sarah "had been married to seven husbands, and the wicked demon Asmodeus had killed each of them before they had been with her as is customary for wives."

name Jesus. **This one will be great and will be called Son of the Most High, and the Lord God will give to him the throne of David his father. He will reign over the house of Jacob forever, and of his reign there will be no end** (καὶ ἰδοὺ συλλήμψῃ ἐν γαστρὶ καὶ τέξῃ υἱόν, καὶ καλέσεις τὸ ὄνομα αὐτοῦ Ἰησοῦν. οὗτος ἔσται μέγας καὶ υἱὸς ὑψίστου κληθήσεται, καὶ δώσει αὐτῷ κύριος ὁ θεὸς τὸν θρόνον Δαυὶδ τοῦ πατρὸς αὐτοῦ, καὶ βασιλεύσει ἐπὶ τὸν οἶκον Ἰακὼβ εἰς τοὺς αἰῶνας, καὶ τῆς βασιλείας αὐτοῦ οὐκ ἔσται τέλος). The grace Mary receives from God is the gift of a son. Gabriel makes seven predictions about him in vv. 31 – 33 that unfold the identity of a divinely conceived Messiah who will bring God's grace to a nation and many others. The first four relate to the unique conception of her son. The next three evoke messianic themes: Davidic descent and reigning forever on the Davidic throne.[10] The result is that the ideas associated with a Davidic Messiah must be modified by the divine nature of this child's conception.

(1) Gabriel announces that Mary, an unwed virgin, will conceive (v. 31a). The language differs from the announcement to Zechariah in 1:13, "and your wife Elizabeth will bear a son to you." Mary has no husband and therefore she does not bear a son for him.

(2) You "will call his name Jesus" (v. 31b). Unlike Matt 1:21, Luke does not explain the etymology of the name. Instead, the emphasis falls on the divine initiative that both creates the child and gives the name.

(3) "This one will be great" (v. 32a). This epithet is used for God (Deut 10:17) and is applied to Christ in Titus 2:13. In contrast, John will be "great *before* the Lord" (1:15). At the Last Supper, Jesus

clarifies that greatness comes from serving others (22:26 – 27). For Jesus, it is his self-giving death on the cross in obedience to God's great plan that "all flesh shall see the salvation of God" (3:6).

(4) He "will be called Son of the Most High" (v.32a). "Most High" is a description of God (1:76; 6:35; 8:28; Acts 7:48; 16:17). This identity is equivalent to "Son of God" in v. 35, where its meaning is clarified. It is not simply another messianic title but a reference to his divinity. Strauss points out that Jesus' divine sonship is not "merely 'functional' — a special relationship with God by virtue of his role as king. He is rather the Son of God from the point of conception, before he has taken on any of the functions of kingship."[11]

(5) "The Lord God will give to him the throne of David his father" (v. 32b). This promise recalls one of the two major covenant promises in the Old Testament (2 Sam 7:12 – 16; Pss 2:7; 89:27 – 29; Isa 9:6; 55:3 – 5) and emphasizes the child's future ruling function, not his suffering.

(6) and (7) The previous theme accords with the parallel last promises, "he will reign over the house of Jacob forever," "and of his reign there will be no end" (v. 33), which apply the Lord's reign to Jesus as king of Israel (see Dan 7:14; Mic 4:7). The covenant promise that the prophet Samuel delivered to David envisioned a Davidic dynasty, but Jesus will be the only one ever to ascend this promised throne. The continuation of the narrative will also reveal that his reign is not limited to "the house of Jacob" (Israel). These promises clearly identify Jesus as the awaited Messiah, but his miraculous conception reveals "that he is uniquely related to God in filial terms vastly outstripping any conventional expectation concerning the Davidic Messiah and that this drastically transforms the nature of his messianic mission and behavior."[12]

---

10. The theme of the fulfillment of the Davidic promise is developed further in 1:69 – 71 and 2:11. See also Acts 2:30 – 31; 13:22 – 23, 32 – 35; 15:16 – 17.

11. Strauss, *The Davidic Messiah in Luke-Acts*, 93.

1:34 And Mary said to the angel, "How will this be, since I have not had sexual relations with a man?" (εἶπεν δὲ Μαριὰμ πρὸς τὸν ἄγγελον· πῶς ἔσται τοῦτο, ἐπεὶ ἄνδρα οὐ γινώσκω;). Mary's question differs from Zechariah's. She asks, "How will this be?" not "How *can* this be?" She is not asking for confirmation through a sign. Instead, she asks in what manner the prediction of the angel will happen, assuming that it will happen. Zechariah asked his question incredulously, ignoring or forgetting that there was biblical precedent for older, barren women to conceive. There is no precedent for a virgin to conceive. Mary simply reminds the angel that her circumstances, as one who has not and does not have sexual relations with a man (the meaning of the euphemism "know" [γινώσκω], see Matt 1:25), makes this promise physically impossible.[13]

Since betrothal typically lasted only about a year and the angel speaks of the conception in the future tense, one might reasonably ask, why does Mary not assume that she would conceive in the normal fashion after she came to live with Joseph? The answer is that she must interpret the angel's promise to mean that the conception will occur immediately while she is still a virgin.[14] The other birth annunciations in Scripture were given to those who were already married. Mary questions how someone who is a virgin can conceive and give birth to a child. Luke does not stress Mary's virginity to exalt her as one who is a pure and holy vessel and worthy to give birth to such a child.[15] Her virginity is presented as an obstacle to conception that can only be overcome by the miraculous, creative power of God.

The pattern in the two annunciations reveals Jesus' superiority over John. John's conception is extraordinary; Jesus' conception is beyond extraordinary. As Coleridge describes it, "rather than demanding to see, Mary simply states her inability to see."[16] Her question sets up the angel's answer, which takes the concept of a Davidic Messiah beyond all current expectations. Gabriel's answer means that Jesus exceeds any previous understanding about the Messiah as the Son of God. He is to be divinely conceived, not simply divinely anointed.

Mary also might have asked, "How will this be that his reign will have no end?" Again, the answer would be that this child is uniquely related to God. His reign coincides with God's.

1:35 The angel answered and said to her, "The Holy Spirit will come upon you and the power of the Most High will overshadow you; and for this reason the one who will be born is holy and will be called the Son of God" (καὶ ἀποκριθεὶς ὁ ἄγγελος εἶπεν αὐτῇ· πνεῦμα ἅγιον ἐπελεύσεται ἐπὶ σὲ καὶ δύναμις ὑψίστου ἐπισκιάσει σοι· διὸ καὶ τὸ γεννώμενον ἅγιον κληθήσεται υἱὸς θεοῦ). The Holy Spirit has a divinely active, creative function here (as in Gen 1:2; Ps 33:6; Ezek 37:14) that differs from the Spirit of prophecy that causes inspired speech.[17] As God created the world out of nothing through the Spirit, so he will create this unique child.

---

12. Brendan Byrne, "Jesus as Messiah in the Gospel of Luke: Discerning a Pattern of Correction," *CBQ* 65 (2003): 85.

13. The translation "have not had" interprets the verb (γινώσκω) as a perfective present that emphasizes "that the results of a past action are still continuing" (see Daniel B. Wallace, *Greek Grammar beyond the Basics: An Exegetical Syntax of the New Testament* [Grand Rapids: Zondervan, 1996], 532 – 33).

14. David L. Landry, "Narrative Logic in the Annunciation to Mary (Luke 1:26 – 38), *JBL* 114 (1995): 74 – 75.

15. Some have seized on Luke's ambiguity regarding Mary's virginity to argue that she conceives in the normal way any young woman would conceive. Herman Hendrickx, *The Third Gospel for the Third World* (Collegeville, MN: Liturgical, 1996), 1:84 – 96, refutes this view in an excellent excursus.

16. Coleridge, *The Birth of the Lukan Narrative*, 64 – 65.

17. W. Barnes Tatum, "The Epoch of Israel: Luke I-II and the Theological Plan of Luke-Acts," *NTS* 13 (1967): 187.

Mary is a passive recipient of the divine initiative. The verb "to come upon" (ἐπελεύσεται) occurs seven times in Luke-Acts, and the parallel in Isa 32:15, where the verb occurs in the LXX, makes it clear that the image has no sexual connotation.[18] The same is true for the verb "to overshadow" (ἐπισκιάσει), which is a figure of speech for the presence (Exod 40:35) and miraculous activity of God. Neither of the terms is the normal language for conception. As Nolland states it, "God is not father as Mary is mother."[19]

Luke does not narrate the conception, as he does not narrate the resurrection of Jesus. This mysterious action is hidden from the gaze of curious humans. The angel depicts the presence of God descending on Mary, which explains how the one who will be born is holy and why he will be called the Son of God.[20] "The Holy Spirit" and "the power of the Most High" are in synonymous parallelism, but this divine action has distinguishable results.

The Greek allows the adjective "holy" (ἅγιον) to modify the child to be born, "the one born to you is holy," or it can be part of a double predicate, "the one born to you will be called holy, the Son of God."[21] The latter is the reading more commonly chosen since it parallels the description in v. 32, he "will be great and will be called Son of the Most High" (see also 2:23). I agree with Kilgallen, however, who takes the adjective "holy" with the participle "being born" (γεννώμενον) that immediately precedes it. The angel separates in a literary balance "the Holy Spirit" and "the power of the Most High." The theological result is that the child who will be generated will be holy because "the Holy Spirit's act creates holiness." The power of the Most High, God's presence, will effect "divinity."[22] To be holy means to be consecrated to God, but here it can mean more than that. The one consecrated to God is divine. Paul's statement in Rom 7:12 that "the law is holy," implies that it is perfect and pure. This usage of the adjective "holy" also applies to Jesus.

To be God's Son does not imply that Jesus has "'divine blood' running through his veins,'" as Nolland characterizes the "history of religions" view.[23] Nolland shows how this title fits in a Jewish matrix where the term does not refer to physical origin. Instead, in the Old Testament it expresses "election to a special relationship with God," "God's formation of the nation," and, applied to a supernatural being, those belonging to "the heavenly order, not the earthly," and possibly "moral likeness to God."[24] In this context, however, the title marks Jesus out as having a special relationship to God that is greater than some messianic title or role. He "will be called" suggests that others will come to recognize at a later point what the readers of the gospel know is true from his conception — he is the Son of God.

1:36 – 37 And behold, Elizabeth your kinswoman has conceived a son herself in her advanced age and this is the sixth month for her who is called barren, because nothing is impossible with God (καὶ ἰδοὺ Ἐλισάβετ ἡ συγγενίς σου καὶ αὐτὴ συνείληφεν υἱὸν ἐν γήρει αὐτῆς, καὶ οὗτος μὴν ἕκτος ἐστὶν αὐτῇ τῇ καλουμένῃ στείρᾳ ὅτι οὐκ ἀδυνατήσει παρὰ τοῦ θεοῦ πᾶν ῥῆμα). Since Elizabeth has sequestered herself, Mary would not have known of her pregnancy. It therefore becomes a sign to her that God's power

---

18. Brown, *The Birth of the Messiah*, 290.

19. Nolland, *Luke*, 1:58.

20. The verb "overshadow" appears in the transfiguration when the cloud overshadows the disciples (9:34).

21. Nolland, *Luke*, 1:55. In 4:34, Jesus is called "the Holy One of God," but this is the shriek of a demonic spirit.

22. John J. Kilgallen, "The Conception of Jesus (Luke 1,35)," *Bib* 78 (1992): 231.

23. Nolland, *Luke*, 1:45.

24. Ibid., 1:45 – 46 with references.

is moving in her relative's life and that the angel's announcement about her conception will be fulfilled. The assertion "because nothing is impossible with God" (see Gen 18:14 LXX) further confirms the certainty of this promise but also reinforces that this conception is beyond human potentiality.[25]

Mentioning again Elizabeth's old age and barrenness, traditional obstacles to conception, highlights the difference between Elizabeth and Mary. Mary is an unmarried virgin! Conception for her without a husband is "impossible," but this state presents no obstacle to God in accomplishing the divine plan. The offer of salvation to all (18:27) that this child will bring will seem no less impossible to many in Israel. Raising him from the dead after his crucifixion is also seemingly impossible. The beginning and end of Jesus' story, his conception and his death, reveal God's miraculous power to do the impossible.

1:38 Mary said, "Behold, [I am] a slave of the Lord. Let it happen to me according to your word." And the angel left her (εἶπεν δὲ Μαριάμ· ἰδοὺ ἡ δούλη κυρίου· γένοιτό μοι κατὰ τὸ ῥῆμά σου. καὶ ἀπῆλθεν ἀπ᾽ αὐτῆς ὁ ἄγγελος). Mary's

humble response of faith basically conveys, "I do not know what all of this means, but I trust God to do what is good." She does not say, "Wait, let me see if this is true, and then I will be a maidservant of the Lord." She gracefully accepts what the angel tells her and does not request more information. She accepts as true that nothing is impossible with God.

Mary also accepts her role as God's instrument to be used as the sovereign God sees fit.[26] The term slave (δούλη) is not degrading as if she were only a domestic drudge. As "a slave of the Lord" she has an exalted status as one close to the Lord and willing to perform the humblest service out of loyalty and love. The term is applied to Joshua (Judg 2:8) and David (Ps 35:1 LXX). Most importantly, God chose Israel to be his servant (Isa 41:8 – 9; 44:21; see 49:1 – 7). The compliant and faithful Mary represents what God called Israel to become.

With this confession, the angel departs. Brown comments, "such a heavenly presence has to be temporary."[27] But it also means that no angel hovers over her to ease the pathway, to comfort her, or to explain the perplexing things that will continue to happen.

Theology in Application

1. Promise and Fulfillment

The infancy narrative highlights a pattern of promise and fulfillment. What God has promised to people of old, which is brought out by the collage of Old Testament allusions, is now being fulfilled. Sobosan comments, "Every promise fulfilled 'overspills,' so to speak, into a new promise with the possibility of an even greater fulfillment."[28] The annunciations by the angel Gabriel also contain predictions that

25. Luke uses "word" (ῥῆμα) for "thing," an event that can be spoken about (see 1:65; 2:15, 19, 51; Acts 5:32; 10:37; 13:42).

26. Landry ("Narrative Logic," 77) makes the important observation that Mary *consents to her situation*. Against those who have argued that the pregnancy was caused by natural

human means, it is impossible to consent to rape or seduction."

27. Brown, *The Birth of the Messiah*, 292.

28. Jeffrey G. Sobosan, "Completion of Prophecy, Jesus in Luke 1:32 – 33," *BTB* 4 (1974): 320.

are immediately fulfilled. According to Frein, these predictions set "the stage for immediately upcoming events (births)," provide "an interpretive framework in which to view the ministries of John and Jesus in the more distant future," and emphasize "the continuity between the fulfillment of recent prophecies made in the past." The immediate fulfillment of prophecies in the narrative serves "to increase readers' confidence that the rest of the angelic announcement will prove to be true."[29]

This fulfillment of the promise to Mary is brought about by the Holy Spirit. This fact reveals a fundamental theological perspective: "Luke sees the whole Christian movement, from its earliest beginning in John and from the conception of Jesus in the womb, to the ascension and afterwards, as inspired, governed, and empowered by the Holy Spirit."[30]

2. The Theological Message of the Contrasts between the Annunciations

The contrasts between the annunciations to Zechariah and Mary reveal salient theological issues for Luke.

1. John's parents both belong to a priestly line (1:5).	1. Nothing is said of Mary's family background. She has no inherited status. Only at the end of the scene do we learn that she is kin to Elizabeth (1:36). The degree of kinship is unspecified. Elizabeth is mentioned only as a sign for Mary — she has conceived and is in her sixth month — not to exalt Mary's heritage.
2. John's parents are righteous and blameless in the law (1:6).	2. Nothing is said of Mary's obedience or righteousness. She is the object of unasked, unmerited grace (1:28, 30).
3. Devout prayer occasions the appearance to Zechariah: "Your prayer has been heard" (1:13).	3. The visit to Mary comes completely at the divine initiative (1:26, 30) and not as the result of her fervent prayers.
4. Zechariah is addressed by name when the angel first greets him (1:13)	4. Mary is not addressed by name when the angel greets her but only in terms of how God has bestowed grace on her, "Hail, highly favored one" (1:28). God's grace is highlighted.

29. Brigid C. Frein, "Narrative Predictions, Old Testament Prophecies and Luke's Sense of Fulfillment," *NTS* 40 (1994): 26.

30. R. E. O. White, *The Answer Is the Spirit* (Philadelphia: Westminster, 1979), 34 – 35.

5. Zechariah is in Jerusalem, the holy city of David, and serving as a priest in the holy sanctuary of the temple, where one might expect to encounter God.	5. Mary is a young woman in a village of no reputation (see John 1:46). As a lowly woman, she is a type for those who will respond properly to the good news that God's reign inaugurates.
6. Zechariah's wife, Elizabeth, is barren and past the age of childbearing. The conception of a child to them is beyond hope.	6. Mary is an unmarried virgin. The conception of a child to her is beyond human possibility.
7. Zechariah is asked to believe that God will do again what the biblical record reveals he has done for other elderly, barren couples. Zechariah, however, responds to the announcement with doubt: "How shall I *know* this?"	7. Mary is asked to believe that God will do what he has never done before. She responds with submissive faith: "Let it happen to me according to your word" (1:38). As a result, she "who believed that there will be a fulfillment of the things that were spoken to her" will be pronounced "blessed" (1:45).
8. Zechariah demands some sort of sign, and the sign he receives is punitive for not believing (1:18, 20). He remains mute for many months and then praises God.	8. The sign Mary receives is a blessing from her kinswoman for believing (1:45).
9. John is to be great before the Lord (1:15).	9. Jesus is identified as great without the qualification "before the Lord." He is conceived of the Spirit and is the Son of the Most High (1:32, 35).
10. John's mission is preparatory and therefore temporary. He is to be a prophet (1:14 – 17) who will eventually pass off the scene.	10. Jesus' mission is eternal and messianic. He is to reign forever (1:32 – 33).
11. John will "be filled with the Holy Spirit" even prior to his birth (1:15), but it is a prophetic Spirit.	11. Jesus' conception will come directly from the creative and miraculous intervention of the Holy Spirit and the power of the Most High (1:35).
12. John will turn many in Israel to God (1:16).	12. Jesus will be the Son of God and the messianic king who will reign over the house of Jacob (1:32 – 33).

Coleridge notes three other elements in the account that have theological significance. The angel's announcement makes these things clear. (1) God's power is not something belonging only to past history; it is at work in the present. (2) God's power is "mysterious, but not distant." (3) God's power "empowers the powerless."[31] I would add two more elements. (4) As Cosgrove observes, "Where human possibilities fail, there God's action stands out in bold relief."[32] (5) God requires cooperation

---

31. Coleridge, *The Birth of the Lukan Narrative*, 68.

32. Charles H. Cosgrove, "The Divine ΔΕΙ in Luke-Acts: Investigations into the Lukan Understanding of God's Providence," *NovT* 26 (1984): 188.

from humans to accomplish the divine plan. Mary "will conceive, bear, and name the child."[33] To do so, she must submit in faith. God works through faithful humans who trust his power to bring his promises to fulfillment and who yield themselves to his control.

3. Jesus as the Messiah

The infancy narrative emphasizes that Jesus is the fulfillment of the promises to David that were construed to refer to the coming Messiah. That Jesus came to a shameful end on a cross, however, would seem to preclude that he could be that Messiah. As Byrne comments, the Gospels convey "the impression that this 'messianic issue' was a confounded nuisance with which the authors had to deal rather than a helpful lens through which to view Jesus." Jesus did not win military victories but hung on a cross where his messianic claims became a subject of mockery. His ministry seemed to be a sad parody of the royal status and authority associated with a messianic deliverer. Byrne shows, however, that throughout the narrative Luke qualifies, redefines, and corrects any messianic assumptions that might be attached to the role. Messianic categories may not be imposed on Jesus. His public career, death, and resurrection essentially define what Davidic messiahship means.[34] Brown understands this well:

> The action of the Holy Spirit and the power of the Most High do not come upon the Davidic king but upon his mother. We are not dealing with the adoption of a Davidide by coronation as God's son or representative; we are dealing with the begetting of God's Son through God's creative Spirit.[35]

Consequently, Jesus is preeminent over all earthly kings and powers. His role preempts any selfish dreams, no matter the religious dressing that might cloak them, of an earthly, messianic kingdom exercising earthly power. His coming was prophesied in Scriptures; his birth was announced by an angel who ranks highest in the hierarchy of angels; his conception was enabled by the creative power of the divine Spirit. He will be uniquely powerful and will fulfill God's plans for Israel's and the world's salvation.

---

33. Green, *The Gospel of Luke*, 88.
34. Byrne, "Jesus as Messiah in the Gospel of Luke," 95. See also Christopher M. Tuckett, "The Christology of Luke-Acts," in *The Unity of Luke-Acts* (ed. Jozef Verheyden; BETL 142; Leuven: Peeters, 1999), 164.
35. Brown, *The Birth of the Messiah*, 312. See also Strauss, *The Davidic Messiah in Luke-Acts*, 93.

Luke 1:39 – 56

Literary Context

The story lines of the two separate annunciations to Zechariah and Mary now converge when Mary goes to stay with Zechariah's wife, Elizabeth. This section containing the beautiful hymn known as the Magnificat (a term derived from the first word in the Latin version of Mary's response) marks the first human interpretation of the angelic annunciations. The angel simply announced what God was going to do. Humans are left to respond and to interpret it for others. Mary's ode praises God for bringing salvation to Israel and recognizes that the conception of the child in her womb and his coming into the world are the fulfillment of ancient prophecies.

Many have commented that the Lukan canticles "fit awkwardly in their present context; in fact, the narrative would read more smoothly without them."[1] Dillon summarizes the common view:

> The canticles are often "patronized" as vagrant psalms that were taken over from somewhere — who can be certain where? — and decorously placed on the lips of Mary, Zechariah, the angel host, and Simeon. To many exegetes they do not seem to add anything except decoration or gilding to those ageless narratives, which have fascinated interpreters and beguiled the Christian faithful for centuries.[2]

Tannehill corrects this view by comparing them to an operatic aria.[3] As Dillon explains it, the aria allows

> the composer to stop the action at any point so that, through a poetic and musical development exceeding the possibilities of ordinary life, a deeper awareness of what is happening may be achieved. A similar deep participation in the meaning of an event is made possible by the placement of this poem [the Magnificat] in Luke's narrative.[4]

The hymns inset in Hebrew narrative have been given the same negative

1. Brown, *The Birth of the Messiah*, 347.
2. Richard J. Dillon, "The Benedictus in Micro- and Macro-context," *CBQ* 68 (2006): 457.

3. Robert C. Tannehill, "The Magnificat as Poem," *JBL* 93 (1974): 265.
4. Dillon, "Benedictus," 459 – 60.

assessment since they too play no role in plot development.[5] Watts helpfully compares the function of these hymns to "Broadway-style musical theater." He writes:

> In contrast to the prose dialogue, which is spoken between characters and passively observed by the audience, the songs are often performed facing the spectators and addressed to them, establishing a more direct rapport between actors and audience. The most successful numbers may elicit such a positive reaction from the spectators that they become "show-stoppers," literally bringing the action to a momentary halt while the audience registers its approval, and occasionally, prompts a repetition of the song.[6]

The hymns in the infancy narrative poetically interpret what is going on and directly engage the audience to join in the celebration. They have a show-stopping quality. Luke, therefore, does not include this hymn and the ones to follow as an extra frill to garnish the narrative. Instead, it highlights a major theme that stages "a meeting of faith and interpretation."[7] God has acted, and now a believer responds and interprets what it means from the stance of faith. The effect has been that for centuries the audience has joined to rejoice with Mary, Zechariah, and Simeon and in some cases to sing along.

Main Idea

The miraculous conception of the child Jesus evokes joy and signals that God is fulfilling the covenant promises made to David and Abraham long ago.

---

5. See Exod 15:1 – 21; Deut 32:1 – 43; Judg 5; 1 Sam 2:1 – 10; 2 Sam 22; 1 Chr 16:8 – 36; Isa 38:9 – 20; Dan 2:20 – 23; Jonah 2:2 – 9.

6. James W. Watts, *Psalm and Story: Inset Hymns in Hebrew Narrative* (JSOTSup 139; Sheffield: JSOT, 1992), 187.

7. Coleridge, *The Birth of the Lukan Narrative*, 75. Many have sought to trace the origins of the canticles, a speculative exercise that produces little help for their interpretation.

Translation

Luke 1:39–56

1:39	Circumstance	**And Mary** **arose in these days** and **went eagerly to the hill country to a**⤴
		town of Judah
40a		and **entered into the house of Zechariah**
b	Greeting	and **greeted Elizabeth.**
41a	Response of joy	**And it happened**
		when Elizabeth heard the greeting of Mary,
b		**the babe in her womb leaped,**
c		**and Elizabeth was filled with the Holy Spirit** and
42a	Beatitude	**cried out with a loud shout and said,**
		"Blessed are you among women and
		blessed is the fruit of your womb!
43	Confessional question	*And why is this [granted] to me that the mother of my Lord comes to me?*
44a	Explanation	*For behold,*
		as the sound of your greeting reached my ears,
b		*the babe leaped for joy in my womb.*
45	Beatitude	*And blessed is she who believed that there will be a fulfillment of the things* ⤴
		that were spoken to her from the Lord."
46	Response of joy (synonymous parallelism)	**And Mary said,**
		"My soul exalts the Lord
47		*and my spirit has rejoiced*
		because of God my Savior
48a	Motive for joy	*because he looked upon the humble station of his* ⤴
		maidservant.
b		*For behold from now on all the generations will count me blessed*
49	Motive for joy	*because the Mighty* ⤴
		One has done great things for me,
		and holy is his name.
50	Amplification of motive (1)	*His mercy [extends] from generation to generation to those who fear him.*
51a	Amplification of motive (2)	*He did a mighty deed with his arm,*
b	(synonymous parallelism)	*he scattered [those who were] haughty in the thoughts of their hearts.*
52a	Amplification of	*He took down the mighty from their thrones* and
b	motive (3) (antithetical parallelism)	*exalted the humble.*

Continued on next page.

Continued from previous page.		
53a	(antithetical parallelism)	*He filled the hungry with good things and*
b		*sent the rich away empty.*
54a	Amplification of motive (4)	*He has come to the aid of his servant Israel,*
b		*[to prove] he has not forgotten mercy*
55a	(synonymous parallelism)	*to Abraham and his seed⟳ forever,*
b		*just as he spoke to our fathers."*
56	Circumstance	**And Mary stayed with her about three months and then returned to her house.**

Structure and Literary Form

The hymn that Mary sings is a personal psalm of praise that parallels traditions in the Old Testament where persons sang hymns of praise in response to God's mighty deeds (e.g., Moses, Exod 15:1 – 18; Miriam, Exod 15:19 – 21; Deborah, Judg 5:1 – 31; Hannah, 1 Sam 2:1 – 10; the Song of Asaph, 1 Chr 16:7 – 36; see also Pss 33; 47; 136). It conforms to Hebrew poetry using synonymous parallelism, where the second line advances the first line in different words (x is the case, and moreover, so is y), and antithetical parallelism, where the idea of the second line is the converse of the first.

The structure begins with a narrated encounter between Elizabeth and Mary. Elizabeth's response to Mary's greeting implies that the divine conception promised by the angel has occurred. This response evokes Mary's ode praising God. The hymn has a bipartite structure. Mary first sings about God's gracious action toward her in this miraculous conception (1:46b – 50). Then she sings about what it means for Israel and all generations, depicting it as God's fulfillment of his promises in the present and as a great turnabout in circumstances of the mighty and the lowly (1:51 – 55). The section ends with a return to the narrative and Mary's departure to her home (1:56).

Exegetical Outline

→ **I. Departure to Elizabeth's home with eagerness (1:39)**

II. Mary's greeting of Elizabeth and her response (1:40 – 45)

    A. Mary's greeting (1:40)

    B. The babe's leap in Elizabeth's womb (1:41a-b)

    C. Filling with the Holy Spirit (1:41c – 45)

        1. Announcement that Mary is blessed (1:41c)

        2. Acknowledgment of Mary's superiority as the mother of the Lord (1:42 – 43)

        3. Interpretation of the babe's leap as for joy (1:44)

        4. Announcement that Mary is blessed for her faith (1:45)

III. Mary's praise of God for her miraculous conception (1:46 – 51)

    A. God's saving power acting in behalf of Mary (1:46 – 49a)

    B. God's saving power governed by mercy (1:49b – 51)

IV. Mary's praise of God for his mighty intervention for Israel (1:52 – 55)

    A. God's reversal of the status of the powerful and the lowly (1:52 – 53)

    B. God's mercy to Israel and fidelity to his promises (1:54 – 55)

V. Mary's departure to her home (1:56)

Explanation of the Text

1:39 And Mary arose in these days and went eagerly to the hill country to a town of Judah (Ἀναστᾶσα δὲ Μαριὰμ ἐν ταῖς ἡμέραις ταύταις ἐπορεύθη εἰς τὴν ὀρεινὴν μετὰ σπουδῆς εἰς πόλιν Ἰούδα). Mary departs without delay after hearing the news of Elizabeth's pregnancy. Translations often render it that she leaves "with haste" (μετὰ σπουδῆς), but that phrase can also mean "eagerly" (3 Macc 5:24, 27),[8] "with fervor," or "with earnest commitment." Her faith in the promise spurs her speedy departure to witness its fulfillment, as the shepherds will later hasten to the manger (2:16). The "hill country" (τὴν ὀρεινήν) probably refers to the area around Jerusalem (Pliny, *Nat.* 5.15; Josephus, *J. W.* 4.8.2 §451).

In contrast to Zechariah, who goes home to his wife after the angel's announcement (1:23), Mary goes away. Luke has no interest in any psychological explanation for her trip, for example, that she might want to wait with Elizabeth rather than wait alone. Her journey shows her acting on her faith as a humble servant of the Lord (1:38). The angel pointed to Elizabeth's pregnancy as a sign of the fulfillment of the promise to Mary. But most important, her leaving means that she has no contact with her betrothed during the time that she conceives.

1:40 – 41 And entered into the house of Zechariah and greeted Elizabeth. And it happened when Elizabeth heard the greeting of Mary, the babe in her womb leaped, and Elizabeth was filled with the Holy Spirit (καὶ εἰσῆλθεν εἰς τὸν οἶκον Ζαχαρίου καὶ ἠσπάσατο τὴν Ἐλισάβετ. καὶ ἐγένετο ὡς ἤκουσεν τὸν ἀσπασμὸν τῆς

---

8. Nolland, *Luke*, 1:65.

Μαρίας ἡ Ἐλισάβετ, ἐσκίρτησεν τὸ βρέφος ἐν τῇ κοιλίᾳ αὐτῆς, καὶ ἐπλήσθη πνεύματος ἁγίου ἡ Ἐλισάβετ). Mary's greeting of her kinswoman on entering the house of Zechariah (1:40) ends Elizabeth's seclusion. Her husband remains mute offstage. The greeting is mentioned three times for emphasis, and it creates three effects: the child leaps in Elizabeth's womb, Elizabeth is filled with the Holy Spirit, and she announces twice that Mary is blessed and interprets the meaning of the child's leap in her womb theologically.

Elizabeth interprets the babe leaping in her womb at the sound of Mary's voice as a leap for joy (1:44). Since her husband is mute, she would not know Gabriel's prophecy that the babe would be filled with the Holy Spirit before his birth (1:15), but the auditors would know and are likely to interpret this stirring as joy inspired by the Spirit and confirmation of Jesus' divine identity. The verb "leap" (ἐσκίρτησεν) appears in 6:23 ("jump for joy") in an eschatological context "in that day." This leap appropriately represents "a gladness that hails the advent of the messianic age."[9]

Being filled with the Holy Spirit leads Elizabeth to the immediate recognition that God has intervened in Mary's life, and she opens her mouth to proclaim her blessedness and to prophesy. The Spirit takes center stage in Acts after Pentecost and prompts Jesus' followers in various breakthroughs in taking the gospel to the world. The Spirit does something new, but the Spirit is not something new. The Spirit always has been the messenger of God's truth and guidance to humans and came upon various persons in the Old Testament to lead them to prophesy (see Num 11:16–25; 24:2; 2 Sam 23:2; 1 Chr 12:18; Neh 9:30; Isa 61:1; Mic 3:8; Ezek 2:2; 3:12, 14, 24; 8:3; 11:1, 5, 24; 37:1; 43:5; Zech 7:12). David spoke through the Spirit (Acts 1:16; 4:25) as did Isaiah (Acts 28:25).

If any Jews in Luke's day believed that the Spirit had somehow passed from the scene and been replaced by a distant echo of God's voice (see _t. Soṭah_ 13:2; _b. Soṭah_ 48b; _b. Yoma_ 9b; _b. Sanh._ 11a; see also 1 Macc 4:46, 9:27, 14:41) and the tradition and reason of scribes, the prominence of the Holy Spirit in Luke's infancy narrative contradicts that view absolutely. Elizabeth, Zechariah (1:67), and Simeon (2:25, 27) are filled with the Spirit of prophecy, and the angel Gabriel prophesies that John will be filled with the Holy Spirit _even before_ his birth (1:15).

1:42 And cried out with a loud shout and said, "Blessed are you among women and blessed is the fruit of your womb!" (καὶ ἀνεφώνησεν κραυγῇ μεγάλῃ καὶ εἶπεν· εὐλογημένη σὺ ἐν γυναιξὶν καὶ εὐλογημένος ὁ καρπὸς τῆς κοιλίας σου). Elizabeth humbles herself in the presence of Mary, and from Elizabeth's exclamation, we learn that Mary is pregnant. The text gives no indication how she knows that Mary is pregnant except that she is full of the Holy Spirit and presumably has divine insight. She is the first human to recognize that the angel's announcement to Mary has come to fruition.

What is most important is that she discerns that God's salvation is being carried out through this pregnancy. She does not see Mary as her rival and therefore does not selfishly compete with her to have her son come out on top. Her joy anticipates the future cooperation of John and Jesus even though Jesus will supersede John in fulfilling God's plan of salvation. But they will not be engaged in some power struggle. She pronounces that both the mother and her child are blessed. The passive participles "blessed" (εὐλογημένη and εὐλογημένος) refer to what God has done and reinforce that Mary is a recipient of God's favor (1:28).

9. Brown, _The Birth of the Messiah_, 341.

In the Old Testament, Jael was pronounced blessed among women in the song of Deborah for killing Sisera, the commander of the Canaanite armies (Judg 5:24; cf. 4:17 – 22). In the Apocrypha, Judith was pronounced blessed among all women on earth (Jdt 13:18) for cutting off the head of the drunken Holofernes, Nebuchadnezzar's general. These assassins were regarded as models of piety, pluck, and patriotism. Mary, by contrast, is blessed because she "believed that there will be a fulfillment of the things that were spoken to her from the Lord" (1:45)! She believes that she has received God's grace and that God will accomplish salvation through the child that has been miraculously conceived.

Later in this gospel, a woman cries out to Jesus from the crowd, "Blessed is the womb that carried you and the breasts from which you nursed!" He responds, "But blessed are those who hear the word of God and keep it!" (11:27 – 28). This reply clarifies that Mary is not blessed simply because she is the mother who brings this special child into the world. It is because Mary has heard, believed, and obeyed (see Deut 28:1, 4), and she becomes a model of faith.

1:43 – 44 And why is this [granted] to me that the mother of my Lord comes to me?" For behold, as the sound of your greeting reached my ears, the babe leaped for joy in my womb (καὶ πόθεν μοι τοῦτο ἵνα ἔλθῃ ἡ μήτηρ τοῦ κυρίου μου πρὸς ἐμέ; ἰδοὺ γὰρ ὡς ἐγένετο ἡ φωνὴ τοῦ ἀσπασμοῦ σου εἰς τὰ ὦτά μου, ἐσκίρτησεν ἐν ἀγαλλιάσει τὸ βρέφος ἐν τῇ κοιλίᾳ μου). Under the inspiration of the Holy Spirit, Elizabeth also acknowledges the lordship of the embryonic Jesus.

Her greeting is the first time that "Lord" is applied to Jesus in this gospel (see 2:11), a term that occurs twenty-three times in the birth narrative to refer to the God of Israel. It highlights the continuity between Jesus and the Lord God of Israel, whose mighty acts of deliverance in Israel's past are recalled in Mary's hymn of praise. This recognition also confirms that he is Lord "from the inception of his life."[10] The greeting further highlights the contrast between Jesus and John; Jesus is Lord.

1:45 And blessed is she who believed that there will be a fulfillment of the things that were spoken to her from the Lord (καὶ μακαρία ἡ πιστεύσασα ὅτι ἔσται τελείωσις τοῖς λελαλημένοις αὐτῇ παρὰ κυρίου). The ὅτι can refer to the content of what Mary believed ("that") or express cause, "because" she believed. The translation renders it as referring to the content of her belief — that she would conceive as a virgin (cf. Acts 27:25). This rendering does not exclude the truth that Mary is in a state of blessedness because she believed what she has been told.

1:46 – 47 And Mary said, "My soul exalts the Lord and my spirit has rejoiced because of God my Savior (καὶ εἶπεν Μαριάμ· Μεγαλύνει ἡ ψυχή μου τὸν κύριον καὶ ἠγαλλίασεν τὸ πνεῦμά μου ἐπὶ τῷ θεῷ τῷ σωτῆρί μου). The narrative stops to reflect on what all this means and to exalt God through a hymn.[11] The external evidence for reading "and Mary said" is overwhelming. The internal evidence also supports this reading. Dibelius pointed out that it would be most strange for Elizabeth to praise God for her own pregnancy immediately after hailing Mary as "the mother of my Lord" and pronouncing her "blessed."[12]

---

10. Rowe, *Early Narrative Christology*, 44.

11. A textual variant appears in three Old Latin manuscripts that reads, "and Elizabeth said." It appears in three Latin versions: a, b, and ms. 1, which was corrected. It also appears in Irenaeus, Niceta, and Jerome's account of a remark

in Origen (see Bruce M. Metzger, *A Textual Commentary on the Greek New Testament* (New York: American Bible Society, 1994), 130 – 31).

12. Martin Dibelius, "Jesu in Lukasevangelium," in *Botschaft und Geschichte* (Tübingen: J. C. B. Mohr, 1953), 14.

One would expect Mary to respond to this unrestrained praise. Farris notes that it fits a promise — evidence of fulfillment — and response of praise progression that occurs in Luke 1–2. He concludes, "Just as Luke attributes a hymn to Zechariah when the word of the angelic annunciation is first fulfilled, so he would have attributed a hymn to Mary in similar circumstances."[13] Elizabeth's exclamation of joy, therefore, sparks Mary's hymn of joy. Both women recognize God's action in their lives and exhibit the proper human reaction to God's miraculous intervention.

Luke does not tell us that Mary is full of the Holy Spirit as Elizabeth was, perhaps because the Holy Spirit has come upon her in such a unique way to cause her to conceive that it is assumed. Her celebration of the miraculous conception of the baby in her womb draws on the Old Testament as if it were a palette from which to mix together the various hues of her praise to God.[14] In declaring God to be great,[15] she resonates with Hannah's exultation at the birth of her son (1 Sam 2:1–2), the psalmist's expectation that God will contend against his enemies for him (Ps 35:9), and Habakkuk's prayer that God will act mightily to save his people (Hab 3:18). It casts her as a model of piety. Elizabeth is the first to hint that Jesus is Lord as God is Lord; Mary is the first to hint that Jesus' birth will bring salvation. This truth will resound throughout the infancy narrative (1:69, 71, 77; 2:11, 30).

1:48–50 Because he looked upon the humble station of his maidservant. For behold from now on all the generations will count me blessed because the Mighty One has done great things for me, and holy is his name. His mercy [extends] **from generation to generation to those who fear him** (ὅτι ἐπέβλεψεν ἐπὶ τὴν ταπείνωσιν τῆς δούλης αὐτοῦ. ἰδοὺ γὰρ ἀπὸ τοῦ νῦν μακαριοῦσίν με πᾶσαι αἱ γενεαί ὅτι ἐποίησέν μοι μεγάλα ὁ δυνατός, καὶ ἅγιον τὸ ὄνομα αὐτοῦ. καὶ τὸ ἔλεος αὐτοῦ εἰς γενεὰς καὶ γενεὰς τοῖς φοβουμένοις αὐτόν). Mary offers the motive for her praise because of what God has done for her. Her "humble station" (ταπείνωσιν) does not refer to her humility but to her "low estate" (cf. Gen 29:32; 1 Sam 1:11; 2 Esd 9:45). She belongs to "the little people, of modest circumstances," in contrast to the lofty rulers and the arrogant (v. 52). Mary the humble maidservant (1:48) parallels the humble people (1:52). Though she rejoices because of what God has done for her, she does not simply speak "as an individual." Farris contends:

> What God does for her, he does for the whole people. That Mary speaks for the people is also shown by the change from the first-person singular self-reference of the first part of the hymns (vv. 48–49) to the first-person plural of the conclusion, "our fathers" (v. 55). The "I" who speaks in the hymn is both a particular individual, Mary, and the representative of God's people.[16]

Mary is one of the lowly in Israel, but that situation has been reversed so that she has become the most blessed among women. But God's mercy extends beyond her person to generation after generation. This is what God does for those who are low on the totem pole, and it foreshadows what Jesus will do in his ministry: healing the sick, exorcizing demons from the demonized, reaching out to and restoring the discredited sinners and friendless pariahs, and preaching good news to the poor.

---

13. Stephen Farris, *The Hymns of Luke's Infancy Narratives: Their Origin, Meaning and Significance* (JSNTSup 9; Sheffield: JSOT, 1985), 112.

14. For a chart of all the allusions, see Brown, *The Birth of the Messiah,* 358–60.

15. The verb μεγαλύνει means here to "declare great" rather than "make great" (see Ps 69:30; Hendrickx, *The Third Gospel,* 1:124).

16. Farris, *The Hymns of Luke's Infancy Narratives,* 118.

When Mary says that "from now on all the generations will count me blessed," it is not a mandate to venerate her. Instead, she points to God, who poured out this particular grace on her, and declares that God is holy and merciful and pours out grace on all from generation to generation. What God has done for Mary is an expression of God's mercy on the people (2:10). It is the holy and merciful God who is to be venerated. To regard Mary as blessed is to praise God for what he has done for her because of what it means for us.

1:51 He did a mighty deed with his arm, he scattered [those who were] haughty in the thoughts of their hearts (ἐποίησεν κράτος ἐν βραχίονι αὐτοῦ, διεσκόρπισεν ὑπερηφάνους διανοίᾳ καρδίας αὐτῶν). The hymn shifts appropriately to praising God for his mighty deeds done on behalf of Israel. The two verbs in this verse are in the aorist tense (the simple past tense, as are the six verbs that follow in vv. 52–55) and refer to God's redemptive acts on behalf of Israel in the past. The image of God's arm is of one who is mighty in battle. It particularly harkens back to the exodus and God's redemption of the people from their slavery in Egypt: "The God of the people of Israel chose our ancestors; he made the people prosper during their stay in Egypt; with mighty power he led them out of that country" (Acts 13:17).[17] Israel's first creed is not, "I believe in one God who created heaven and earth," but "I believe in one God who freed us from slavery."[18]

But the use of the aorist tense may also reveal the perspective of Luke and the reader and include, in retrospect, the events related to Christ's ministry, death, and resurrection. The joy flies in

the face of the current circumstances of Israel, still under the thumb of oppressive rulers, but it implies that God is bringing about a new exodus. The mighty, divine Warrior will lift his arm against his enemies in a disarming way, however — through a miraculous conception, through the births of infants in arms, through favor toward the weak, lowly, and powerless, and through death on a cross.

God scatters the proud who are self-sufficient. Brown writes, "The proud look down on others because they do not look up to God, and so, in the Bible, the proud are constantly presented as God's enemies (Isa 13:11)."[19] Spicq avers, "Their understanding and their will are oriented against God; they usurp the divine prerogatives."[20] They do not have any sense of divine transcendence and scorn both God's divine sovereignty and the needs of other humans because of their exaggerated opinions of themselves.

1:52–53 He took down the mighty from their thrones and exalted the humble. He filled the hungry with good things and sent the rich away empty (καθεῖλεν δυνάστας ἀπὸ θρόνων καὶ ὕψωσεν ταπεινούς, πεινῶντας ἐνέπλησεν ἀγαθῶν καὶ πλουτοῦντας ἐξαπέστειλεν κενούς). This reversal motif is expressed in a chiasm and is a familiar theme in Scripture.[21] "The mighty" rule to serve their own self-interests, and "the rich" are violent and deprive others of their fair share of what they need to survive. God exalts the humble who fear God, and the hungry who look only to God to supply their need. Toppling the mighty from their thrones[22] does not mean that God turns the tables so that the weak and lowly can now reign over the

17. Exod 6:6; Deut 4:34; 5:15; 7:19; 9:29; 11:2; 26:8; 2 Kgs 17:36; Pss 77:15; 136:12; Isa 63:12.
18. Christian L. Mhagama, "God Does the Unexpected," *International Review of Mission* 77 (1988): 210.
19. Brown, *The Birth of the Messiah*, 337.
20. Ceslas Spicq, "ὑπερηφανία, ὑπερήφανος," *TLNT*, 3:394.
21. See 1 Sam 2:7–8; Job 5:8–11; Isa 2:11; 5:15–16; Ezek 17:24; 21:25–26
22. See Job 12:19; Ezek 21:26; Sir 10:14.

great and mighty and subject them to the same humiliations. Instead, it means that God levels the playing field so that both are equal and that the high and mighty might humble themselves before God and others to become part of God's redemptive plan in the world. Kodell comments:

> To be "mighty" here means to be self-sufficient, in no need of salvation. God raises the lowly, but the mighty do not recognize their lowliness; they desire to raise themselves up. This spirit of self-exaltation is the key to sinfulness for Luke.[23]

The same verb "took down" (καθεῖλεν) appears in 23:53 (see also Acts 13:29) when Joseph of Arimathea takes Jesus down from the cross. The contrast between the mighty being taken down from their thrones is striking. Jesus is taken down as "King of the Jews" from a throne of degradation only to be exalted to an eternal throne because of his obedience.

1:54–55 He has come to the aid of his servant Israel, [to prove] he has not forgotten mercy to Abraham and his seed forever, just as he spoke to our fathers (ἀντελάβετο Ἰσραὴλ παιδὸς αὐτοῦ, μνησθῆναι ἐλέους καθὼς ἐλάλησεν πρὸς τοὺς πατέρας ἡμῶν, τῷ Ἀβραὰμ καὶ τῷ σπέρματι αὐτοῦ εἰς τὸν αἰῶνα). As did the first half (1:50), the second half of the hymn ends in a reference to God's mercy. It specifically recalls the promise to Abraham (Gen 22:16–24; Acts 3:25) and takes the story back to the beginning of Israel. The present and the future must be understood in light of God's merciful intervention and faithfulness in

the past (see also 2 Sam 22:51; Ps 98:3; Mic 7:20) as revealed in Scripture. Coleridge asserts, "Mary finds her way to faith because she reads the signs of the past aright."[24] The same will be true of Zechariah, who also interprets the birth of his son in terms of the promises to David (1:69) and Abraham (1:72–73). The covenant with Abraham is a reminder that God's mercy will extend not only to every generation but to all people.

1:56 And Mary stayed with her about three months and then returned to her house (ἔμεινεν δὲ Μαριὰμ σὺν αὐτῇ ὡς μῆνας τρεῖς, καὶ ὑπέστρεψεν εἰς τὸν οἶκον αὐτῆς). Mary goes to her home because she is still not married to Joseph. It underscores the virginal conception. She left immediately after the angel's announcement for Judea, stayed there for three months (until the time Elizabeth's baby was due), and then returns to her own house.

Luke's usage of panels to narrate the story explains her disappearance at this juncture. He presents the material in interlocking panels (or diptych)[25] to deal with one topic at a time and to shine the spotlight on a particular character in each panel. When the next panel starts, he resets the chronology.[26] Mary may have been present, as the reference to the relatives in 1:58 suggests, but she has faded into the scenery hung at the back of the stage. She perhaps stays until shortly after the baby is born, but the reference to her departure here in 1:56 fast-forwards the action, so to speak, to the time when she departs.

---

23. Jerome Kodell, "Luke's Theology of the Death of Jesus," in *Sin, Salvation, and the Spirit* (ed. D. Durkin; Collegeville, MN: Liturgical, 1979), 226.

24. Coleridge, *The Birth of the Lukan Narrative*, 93.

25. From a two-leaved, hinged, wax writing tablet that

folded together to protect the wax.

26. See Stanislas Giet, "Un procédé littéraire d'exposition: l'anticipation chronologique," *Revue des Études Augustiniennes* (1956): 243–49, particularly 248.

Theology in Application

Including a psalm like this in the narrative is theologically significant. It does not simply function as part of the text to be read, but because it is poetic, it encourages readers to claim the text as their own. This psalm reveals that the gospel story to be narrated is more than "history" to be read, but a story to be appropriated.

1. The Promise to Israel

During troubled times, it is hard to believe that God will actually return to save and guide his people as he did in the past. Schweizer alludes to the problem of God's seeming absence: "Centuries of silence in which Israel had only the record of God's word from the past ... do not mean that God had forgotten Israel."[27] The canticles affirm that God has now acted but in an unexpected manner. Byrne comments, "God has been faithful to the promises but exercised that faithfulness in a challenging, open-ended way."[28]

God has demonstrated throughout Israel's history that he can make an exalted instrument out of human nothingness to accomplish his purposes. Mary represents those of "low estate" whom God has consistently chosen. She also represents the poor on whose behalf God acts. Remarkably, she is the first to interpret how God is moving and the first to express her faith in what she cannot see but knows will happen because she believes that nothing is impossible with God. All three of the infancy hymns "emphasize strongly that God has done something for Israel" (1:54, 68; 2:32). The references to Scripture reveal that "the present salvation is the fulfillment of ancient promise."[29] The promise to Abraham and the promise to David are "part of the same unified plan and purpose of God."[30] The coming of the promised Davidic Messiah will fulfill the promise to Abraham.

Mary interprets God's grace toward her as representative of God's acts of salvation toward all Israel from Abraham on. The predominance of the aorist tenses in her hymn reveals that what God is doing now is a continuation of what God has done for the Israelites throughout their history. It is in this sense that some see Mary as "Israel personified."[31] As Coleridge frames it, "Salvation ... is understood not only as an isolated act of power in favour of a particular person, but as a manifestation of God's transcendent holiness which reaches beyond this act of power and this particular person to touch all generations with an enduring mercy."[32]

27. Schweizer, *Luke*, 42–43.
28. Byrne, *The Hospitality of God*, 18.
29. Farris, *The Hymns of Luke's Infancy Narratives*, 125.
30. Strauss, *The Davidic Messiah in Luke-Acts*, 97.

31. John T. Carroll, *Response to the End of History: Eschatology and Situation in Luke-Acts* (SBLDS 92; Atlanta: Scholars Press, 1988), 43.
32. Coleridge, *The Birth of the Lukan Narrative*, 91.

2. Jesus as the Lord

Elizabeth's response to Mary's greeting is the first time that "Lord" is applied to Jesus in Luke's gospel (see 1:76; 2:11). It is startling since the title occurs twenty-three times in the birth narrative to refer to the God of Israel. The subsequent narrative will clarify the ambiguity whether it refers to God or Jesus, but the ambiguity has christological significance. Rowe explains:

> … unlike John, Luke does not write anything that approaches a propositional statement that posits a unity of identity between Jesus and the God of Israel. Nor does Luke seem to think in these terms. Instead, by means of a single word variously set within the flow of the narrative, he creates a space where an overlap cannot help but take place, and this overlap results in a doubleness in the referent κύριος [Lord].[33]

Since the term does not require identity with God, Rowe contends, "in the immediate context of Luke 1, Luke speaks of the κύριος [Lord] of Israel and the Old Testament with the aim or purpose of presenting a strong theological continuity between the events surrounding Jesus and those of the Old Testament."[34] He shows that this continuity plays out in the rest of the narrative. Luke prepares the reader to recognize the divinely conceived Jesus as the human presence of the heavenly Lord God of Israel. Minear rightly contends that Luke does not discriminate precisely between "the various christological titles and images." He contends that Luke "speaks of the prophetic work of Christ; of his links to Abraham, to Moses, to Elijah, to David; of his priestly intercession; of his kingship and kingdom" without regard to the superiority of one over the other. But I would contend that all christological titles and images are to be subsumed under Luke's fundamental conviction that Jesus is the incarnation of God's visitation to Israel for her consolation on the way to bringing "light … to the Gentiles" (2:32; Acts 28:28).[35]

3. Liberation

The pregnant Mary anticipates Christ's birth with some fiery political theology — potentates tossed from thrones, the haughty humbled, the rich made bankrupt, the lowly exalted, and the hungry fed. These words from Jesus' mother should keep this baby from simply being gazed upon and adored. They create disturbing ripples that rock the placid waters of the comfortable who think all is right with the world, with God safely tucked away in heaven and oblivious to injustice on earth. Through Mary we hear the insistent voice of the marginalized ringing out a challenge from on high to those entrenched in their seemingly impregnable seats of temporal power.

---

33. Rowe, _Early Narrative Christology_, 45.

34. Ibid., 46–47.

35. Paul S. Minear, "Luke's Use of the Birth Stories," in _Studies in Luke-Acts: Essays Presented in Honor of Paul Schubert_ (ed. L. E. Keck and J. L. Martyn; Nashville: Abingdon, 1966), 117–18.

Mary's words prepare for Jesus' announcement of good news for the poor (4:18 – 19) and his beatitudes for the poor, hungry, and weeping (6:20 – 21) and the woes on the rich, well-fed, and laughing (6:24 – 25). They make clear that God opposes the powerful who set themselves up as lords and the status quo that grinds the faces of the poor in the dust. As Gail O'Day states, "These songs can only be sung with full impact by people who are not part of the dominant social structure, by people who know what it is to be oppressed and who know that the present social systems are bankrupt of hope … these songs are songs of *defiance* and *thanksgiving*."[36] Farris comments, "Only 'he who is down need fear no fall,' and only he who is objectively of 'low estate' will rejoice that God has reversed human fortunes." But he notes that interpreting the song as referring "only to the political and economic revolution of the oppressed masses … ignores the stereotyped OT nature of the language."[37]

Mary's words should not be taken as warrant for the more radical approaches found in contemporary liberation theology that puts the spiritual message second to economic and political upheaval and sanctions violence. Yet neither are these verses simply to be spiritualized. Farris remarks, "These verses are meaningful not only because they reverberate with the language of the revered tradition."[38] The oppressed expect their lot to be bettered. In the Old Testament narrative, Israel's liberation from captivity in Egypt is followed by the imperative to root out injustice in all its forms. God's purpose is not to kick out the rogues and replace them with a new set of rogues, as if to replace one "-archy" with another (e.g., patriarchy with matriarchy, etc.). It is to transform rogues into those who do good to their neighbors.

As Green correctly recognizes, Mary's hymn of praise has God as the subject of the verbs. It is therefore not "a revolutionary call to human action but a celebration of God's action. Indeed, God's dramatic work is *against* those who would take power into their own hands."[39] This does not mean that God's actions do not require human response. Mary responds with faith to the announcement that God is acting, and then she follows through with obedience.

---

36. Gail R. O'Day, "Singing Woman's Song: A Hermeneutic of Liberation," *CurTM* 12 (1985): 210.

37. Farris, *The Hymns of Luke's Infancy Narratives*, 124.

38. Ibid.

39. Green, *The Gospel of Luke*, 100.

5

Luke 1:57 – 80

Literary Context

This section completes the story begun in 1:5 – 25 by recording the birth of John as predicted by the angel Gabriel. Zechariah had not responded to that announcement with faith and consequently became mute. After the birth and the confirmation of the child's name, his mouth is opened and he erupts with praise to God for the divine intervention in his life and the life of Israel. Like his wife, Elizabeth, in the previous panel, he prophesies through the Holy Spirit (vv. 67, 76 – 79). Like Mary, he utters a thanksgiving psalm that interprets what it means (vv. 68 – 75).

As Mary celebrated in her hymn the national implications of what would seem to be a private affair, so does Zechariah. The focus of his praise is the coming of the Messiah to reverse the fortunes of Israel. Farris is correct:

> It is only because John's birth is so closely connected with the coming of Jesus, the Davidic Messiah, and is, indeed, a sign of that coming, that Zechariah can praise God so triumphantly. The gift of John to the aged couple is a sign of the certainty of the coming of the Messiah, Jesus. It is not at all surprising, therefore, that the figure in view in most of the Benedictus is not John but Jesus the Messiah.[1]

---

1. Farris, *The Hymns of Luke's Infancy Narratives*, 134.

Main Idea

The age of salvation has begun. Zechariah's perfected faith and the Holy Spirit help him to interpret the significance of John's birth with prophetic insight. God fulfills the promise to Abraham and visits Israel to bring salvation through the coming of the Davidic Messiah, and his son will prepare the way for the Lord.

Translation

(See next two pages.)

Structure and Literary Form

After the birth and naming of John at the ritual of his circumcision, Zechariah thanks God for keeping his promises and saving his people by raising up the Messiah (1:68 – 75). All of the finite verbs are in the aorist tense. Then in 1:76 – 79, he answers the question of the chorus of bystanders, "What then will this child become?" (1:66). All of these verbs are future.

The literary form is a thanksgiving psalm, which, like Mary's song, has a bipartite structure. Zechariah's song (*Benedictus*), however, reverses the structure of Mary's song. She sang first of God's gracious action toward her in her miraculous conception (1:46b – 50) and then applied this divine action to all Israel and lauded the great reversal of fortunes between the mighty and the lowly (1:51 – 55). Zechariah begins with "generalized praise of God" pertaining to God's faithfulness in his covenants to David and Abraham (1:68 – 75) and then celebrates the birth in a direct address to the newborn about his role to go before the Lord (1:76 – 79).[2]

Exegetical Outline

→ **I. The birth of the child (1:57 – 58)**

    A. The birth of the child to Elizabeth (1:57)

    B. The reaction of the bystanders to the birth (1:58)

        1. Praising God's mercy (1:58a)

        2. Rejoicing (1:58b)

II. The naming of the child (1:59 – 66)

    A. Circumcision of the child and naming him after his father (1:59)

    B. The conflict of the name (1:60 – 66a)

        1. Objection of the mother and naming him John (1:60)

---

2. Dillon, "Benedictus," 466 – 67.

Luke 1:57–80

57a	Circumstance	Now for Elizabeth the time of her bearing was fulfilled
b	Birth notice	and she bore a son.
58	Reaction of rejoicing	Her neighbors and relatives heard that the Lord had magnified his mercy with her, and they rejoiced with her.
59a	Circumstance	And it happened on the eighth day that they came to circumcise the child, and they were calling him Zechariah after the name of his father.
60	Objection	His mother responded, saying, "No! He will be called John!"
61	Counterobjection	They said to her, "No one of your relatives is called by this name."
62		Then they were making signs to his father to find out what he would want him to be called.
63a	Confirmation and naming	He asked for a little wax writing tablet and wrote, "John is to be his name."
b	Reaction: marveling	They all marveled [at this].
64a	Removal of the punishment	Immediately, his mouth was opened and his tongue [was loosed],
b	Blessing	and he began to speak blessing God.
65a	Reaction to the events: (1) Fear	And fear came upon all their neighbors,
b	(2) Spreading of the news	and all these events were talked about throughout the hill country of Judea.
66a	(3) Pondering the meaning	All who heard [these things] stored [them] in their hearts, saying, "What then will this child become?"
b	Narrative aside	For the hand of the Lord was with him.
67	Prophetic interpretation and praise	And Zechariah, his father, was full of the Holy Spirit and prophesied, saying,
68a	Beatitude	"Blessed be the Lord God of Israel,
b	Cause	because he has visited and brought about redemption for his people,

Verse	Function	Text
69	Amplification of cause	*and* he raised a horn of salvation for us in the house of David his servant.
70	Reiteration of 68b	Just as he spoke through the mouth of his holy prophets from ages gone by,
71a		salvation from our enemies and
b		from the hand of all who hate us,
72		to show mercy to our fathers *and* to remember his holy covenant,
73		the oath that he swore to Abraham our father, to give to us
74–75		to serve him without fear in holiness and righteousness before him all our days, having been rescued from our enemies.
76a-b	Direct address: prophetic interpretation of John's role	*And you, child,* will be called the prophet of the Most High;
c		*for you* will go before the Lord to prepare his ways
77		to give knowledge of salvation to his people in the forgiveness of their sins
78a		by the compassionate mercy of our God,
b	Prophetic interpretation of the Messiah's role	upon whom the dawn from on high will visit us,
79		to shine light for those who sit in darkness and in the shadow of death, to direct our feet into the path of peace."
80a	Summary refrain	**The child grew and became strong in spirit,**
b	Departure	**and he was in the wilderness until the time he was made known to Israel.**

Explanation of the Text

1:57 – 58 Now for Elizabeth the time of her bearing was fulfilled and she bore a son. Her neighbors and relatives heard that the Lord had magnified his mercy with her, and they rejoiced with her (τῇ δὲ Ἐλισάβετ ἐπλήσθη ὁ χρόνος τοῦ τεκεῖν αὐτήν καὶ ἐγέννησεν υἱόν. καὶ ἤκουσαν οἱ περίοικοι καὶ οἱ συγγενεῖς αὐτῆς ὅτι ἐμεγάλυνεν κύριος τὸ ἔλεος αὐτοῦ μετ᾿ αὐτῆς καὶ συνέχαιρον αὐτῇ). Luke concentrates on the reaction to the birth of the child rather than the actual birth. Since Elizabeth had hidden herself and Zechariah was mute, the news of the birth comes as a sudden surprise for the neighbors and kin. They react appropriately, rejoicing in God's remarkable demonstration of mercy, knowing that God has done such things in the past. Their rejoicing is a fulfillment of the angel's prediction in 1:14. Joy and praise are strains that run through the infancy narrative (1:14, 64; 2:10, 14, 28), and rejoicing with others in community is a theme that runs throughout the gospel. That God "magnified" (ἐμεγάλυνεν) his mercy recalls the verb in 1:46 where Mary "magnifies" (μεγαλύνει) the Lord. As humans magnify the Lord, the Lord magnifies his

mercy. The reference to God's mercy recalls 1:50, 54 (see 1:72).

1:59 – 60 And it happened on the eighth day that they came to circumcise the child, and they were calling him Zechariah after the name of his father. His mother responded, saying, "No! He will be called John!" (καὶ ἐγένετο ἐν τῇ ἡμέρᾳ τῇ ὀγδόῃ ἦλθον περιτεμεῖν τὸ παιδίον καὶ ἐκάλουν αὐτὸ ἐπὶ τῷ ὀνόματι τοῦ πατρὸς αὐτοῦ Ζαχαρίαν. καὶ ἀποκριθεῖσα ἡ μήτηρ αὐτοῦ εἶπεν· οὐχί, ἀλλὰ κληθήσεται Ἰωάννης). Circumcision on the eighth day reflects conformity to traditional Jewish piety (Gen 17:12; 21:4; Phil 3:5). The rite is mentioned but not narrated. The anonymous "they" who gather for the custom of the circumcision assume that the parents will follow tradition and name the son after the father. With the father mute, they "were calling" (ἐκάλουν) him "Zechariah," which is not to be taken as a conative imperfect (i.e., "they were trying to call him Zechariah"). They actually are doing so until they are brusquely corrected by the mother.

"He will be called" (κληθήσεται) reminds the reader that God is the one "who has chosen the name" (1:13).[3] Luke does not narrate how Elizabeth knows this, but it confirms that God's plans are being worked out. Zechariah does not figure in this decision, and neither do the family and friends. They object that she violates what was customarily done in naming a child. But Elizabeth will not submit to the pressure of the community, which hints that traditional expectations will be overturned by God's new work. The conflict over the name underscores that just as this child's birth is extraordinary, he will play an extraordinary role in God's plan.

1:61–62 They said to her, "No one of your relatives is called by this name." Then they were making signs to his father to find out what he would want him to be called (καὶ εἶπαν πρὸς αὐτὴν ὅτι οὐδείς ἐστιν ἐκ τῆς συγγενείας σου ὃς καλεῖται τῷ ὀνόματι τούτῳ. ἐνένευον δὲ τῷ πατρὶ αὐτοῦ τὸ τί ἂν θέλοι καλεῖσθαι αὐτό). The bystanders reject this announcement from the mother and turn to the father, expecting him to follow normal conventions and overturn her decision. The optative "what he would want him to be called" (θέλοι) ties it to a human decision. That they need to make signs to communicate with him assumes that he is deaf as well as mute.

1:63 He asked for a little wax writing tablet and wrote, "John is to be his name." They all marveled [at this] (καὶ αἰτήσας πινακίδιον ἔγραψεν λέγων· Ἰωάννης ἐστὶν ὄνομα αὐτοῦ. καὶ ἐθαύμασαν πάντες). Zechariah, still speechless, must communicate on a writing tablet. The bystanders may be amazed that he substantiates what his wife said independently, because he could not have heard her insistence that the child be called John. Since "John" was not an uncommon name for priests, their amazement may signal instead that they

realize that something numinous is happening. Zechariah's confirmation of the name means that "he has read rightly the signs of God's action and that he reads the larger promise differently in the light of the fulfillment he has witnessed." He now understands and accepts "the divine plan at which he baulked in the first episode."[4]

1:64–65 Immediately, his mouth was opened and his tongue [was loosed] and he began to speak blessing God. And fear came upon all their neighbors, and all these events were talked about throughout the hill country of Judea (ἀνεῴχθη δὲ τὸ στόμα αὐτοῦ παραχρῆμα καὶ ἡ γλῶσσα αὐτοῦ, καὶ ἐλάλει εὐλογῶν τὸν θεόν. Καὶ ἐγένετο ἐπὶ πάντας φόβος τοὺς περιοικοῦντας αὐτούς, καὶ ἐν ὅλῃ τῇ ὀρεινῇ τῆς Ἰουδαίας διελαλεῖτο πάντα τὰ ῥήματα ταῦτα). Belief opens Zechariah's mouth (cf. 24:31), and praise is the proper response when one understands what God has done. Byrne remarks, "What is so consoling about Zechariah is that he got a second chance — and, in the end, is given the best lines (the *Benedictus*)."[5] This event evokes fear in the crowd, and it is a normal response to evidence that something transcendent has touched their lives (1:12, 30). The bystanders spread the news of these events far and wide, which prepares for the report on John's celebrated ministry (3:1–18).

1:66 All who heard [these things] stored [them] in their hearts, saying, "What then will this child become?" For the hand of the Lord was with him (καὶ ἔθεντο πάντες οἱ ἀκούσαντες ἐν τῇ καρδίᾳ αὐτῶν λέγοντες· τί ἄρα τὸ παιδίον τοῦτο ἔσται; καὶ γὰρ χεὶρ κυρίου ἦν μετ᾽ αὐτοῦ). Coleridge contends, "The act of storing in the heart implies not only incomprehension, but also an openness to clarification in the future, a preparedness to live

---

3. Coleridge, *The Birth of the Lukan Narrative*, 107.
4. Ibid., 110.

5. Byrne, *The Hospitality of God*, 38.

with unclarity in the hope that there will come a time when the puzzling signs will disclose their true meaning."[6] The people do not ask *who* the child will be but *what* (τί) he will become. They have only an inkling that he is a child of destiny, but little more. To their question Luke adds a rare narrative aside that shifts the perspective with the use of the imperfect tense, "For the hand of the Lord was [ἦν] with him" (see Acts 11:21). This divine hand will be most evident when John reappears preaching and baptizing in the wilderness (3:3).

1:67 – 68 And Zechariah, his father, was full of the Holy Spirit and prophesied, saying, "Blessed be the Lord God of Israel, because he has visited and brought about redemption for his people" (Καὶ Ζαχαρίας ὁ πατὴρ αὐτοῦ ἐπλήσθη πνεύματος ἁγίου καὶ ἐπροφήτευσεν λέγων· Εὐλογητὸς κύριος ὁ θεὸς τοῦ Ἰσραήλ, ὅτι ἐπεσκέψατο καὶ ἐποίησεν λύτρωσιν τῷ λαῷ αὐτοῦ). Attention turns back to Zechariah, who moves from dead silence to praise. Luke characterizes his speech as prophecy, which is always directed to others, not God.[7] It is guidance for those gathered for the circumcision.[8]

Jewish intertestamental literature suggests that Spirit-inspired prophecy had waned in this era. Prophets became apocalyptic seers, mystics, and scribes. Greenspahn argues that the later rabbis relegated the Spirit to the past because their legitimacy was based on the interpretation of a previous revelation, and they wanted to protect themselves from those claiming a more direct link to the divine while undermining the theological basis for such figures' antiestablishment activities.[9] Scribes do not depend on direct inspiration by the Holy Spirit as the prophets did. Luke reveals, however, that the Holy Spirit is active, moving Elizabeth, Zechariah, and Simeon to prophetic speech.[10]

Zechariah answers more than the question raised in v. 66, "What then will this child become?" He declares what this child's birth reveals about God's faithfulness to the promises made to Abraham and David, but, surprisingly, he also declares that it signals the advent of the Messiah to deliver Israel.

The verb "visit" (ἐπεσκέψατο) forms an inclusio around Zechariah's ode (1:68, 78). It refers here to God's action in saving or helping his people (see 7:16; Acts 15:14). Zechariah declares that God has "brought about redemption" (ἐποίησεν λύτρωσιν; lit., "made redemption").[11] He looks to the past to what God has done, and from that memory of God's fidelity and power he celebrates a victory yet to be narrated. Bock contends that political redemption is in view, but that it "is delayed, because of the failure of much of the nation to respond (13:31 – 35; 19:44)."[12] I would argue instead that Zechariah's hope for political redemption for the nation is mistaken. After Jesus' crucifixion, the disciples dejectedly travel to Emmaus and tell their fellow traveler that they "were hoping" that Jesus "was about to redeem Israel" (24:21). The

---

6. Coleridge, *The Birth of the Lukan Narrative*, 114.

7. The opening words, "Blessed be the Lord God of Israel," match lines from Pss 41:13; 72:18; 106:48.

8. Hendrickx, *The Third Gospel*, 1:149.

9. Frederick E. Greenspahn, "Why Prophecy Ceased," *JBL* 108 (1989): 37 – 49.

10. According to Robert P. Menzies (*The Development of Early Christian Pneumatology with Special Reference to Luke-Acts* [JSNTSup 54; Sheffield: Sheffield Academic, 1991], 121), for Luke, "the Spirit is inextricably related to prophetic phenomena."

11. The aorist tenses used in vv. 68 – 69 ("visited," "brought about redemption," "raised a horn of salvation") are "prophetic aorists," which describe what will happen as if it had already happened. Dillon ("Benedictus," 468 – 69) comments that the use of verbs in the aorist tense does not "disqualify the first part of the song from the genre of prophecy. God's action is complete in the prophet's idiom even when humans have yet to see it."

12. Darrell Bock, *Luke* (2 vols.; BECNT; Grand Rapids: Baker, 1994), 1:179.

truth is, he has, but it was not the redemption they were expecting, limited as it was by their narrow, self-centered worldview.

1:69 – 71 And he raised a horn of salvation for us in the house of David his servant. Just as he spoke through the mouth of his holy prophets from ages gone by, salvation from our enemies and from the hand of all who hate us (καὶ ἤγειρεν κέρας σωτηρίας ἡμῖν ἐν οἴκῳ Δαυὶδ παιδὸς αὐτοῦ, καθὼς ἐλάλησεν διὰ στόματος τῶν ἁγίων ἀπ᾽ αἰῶνος προφητῶν αὐτοῦ, σωτηρίαν ἐξ ἐχθρῶν ἡμῶν καὶ ἐκ χειρὸς πάντων τῶν μισούντων ἡμᾶς). What follows in vv. 69 – 75 amplifies why God is to be blessed. Zechariah does not refer to his son but to the coming of the Davidic Messiah ("the house of David"). To accomplish his purpose, God raised up "a horn of salvation," an image that denotes power and strength and is applied to the royal descendant of David (Pss 89:17 – 24; 132:17; 148:14). That the prophets are "from ages gone by" reminds the reader that God fulfills the promises of the past and that the present and future must be understood in terms of what God has said and done in the past (see Acts 3:21). God is not finished speaking, however, because a new outbreak of prophecy is occurring.

The language "salvation from our enemies and from the hand of all who hate us" resonates with a militaristic understanding of national redemption (Ps 106:10, a reference to the deliverance at the Red Sea). But Zechariah understands that the purpose of this "salvation" is to enable Israel to serve God unceasingly and assiduously without the distraction of external conflict or persecution (vv. 74 – 75; see 4:8; Acts 24:14; 26:7).

1:72 – 75 To show mercy to our fathers and to remember his holy covenant, the oath that he swore to Abraham our father, to give to us to serve him without fear in holiness and righteousness before him all our days, having been rescued from our enemies (ποιῆσαι ἔλεος μετὰ τῶν πατέρων ἡμῶν καὶ μνησθῆναι διαθήκης ἁγίας αὐτοῦ, ὅρκον ὃν ὤμοσεν πρὸς Ἀβραὰμ τὸν πατέρα ἡμῶν, τοῦ δοῦναι ἡμῖν ἀφόβως ἐκ χειρὸς ἐχθρῶν ῥυσθέντας λατρεύειν αὐτῷ ἐν ὁσιότητι καὶ δικαιοσύνῃ ἐνώπιον αὐτοῦ πάσαις ταῖς ἡμέραις ἡμῶν). The string of infinitives here defines further how God has helped and reveals the purposes and future results of God's action. God shows mercy by remembering his holy covenant, which he made in an oath to Abraham. The content of that oath is expressed in an infinitival clause: "to serve him without fear in holiness and righteousness before him all our days."

In Gen 17 and 22, God specifically promised to make Abraham's offspring as numerous as the stars and required him to circumcise every male among them, a command that both John's and Jesus' parents obey. In Gen 26:3 – 5, however, God promised Isaac to fulfill the oath to Abraham because "Abraham obeyed me and did everything I required of him, keeping my commands, my decrees and my instructions." Zechariah is a model of one who is righteous and who serves God in the temple. But the narrative will redefine what it means to keep God's statutes and laws. The verb "to serve" (λατρεύειν) will mean more than carrying out cultic religious duties (see Phil 3:3).

"Having been rescued from our enemies" recalls the defining event in Israel's history when God freed his people from the shackles of slavery in Egypt. The biblical account of what happened after that liberation reveals God's concern to establish a spiritual relationship with the people and concern for social justice. These twin concerns will manifest themselves in the gospel's narrative of the new liberation brought about through Jesus.

Who "the enemies" are is not specified and need not be limited to the Roman overlords. Hendrickx observes, "To a peasant, enemies are all those who try to get what is rightfully his."[13] The identity of the enemies will be expanded beyond earthly foes to include the far more deadly demonic powers opposed to God.

1:76 – 77   And you, child, will be called the prophet of the Most High; for you will go before the Lord to prepare his ways to give knowledge of salvation to his people in the forgiveness of their sins (καὶ σὺ δέ, παιδίον, προφήτης ὑψίστου κληθήσῃ· προπορεύσῃ γὰρ ἐνώπιον κυρίου ἑτοιμάσαι ὁδοὺς αὐτοῦ, τοῦ δοῦναι γνῶσιν σωτηρίας τῷ λαῷ αὐτοῦ ἐν ἀφέσει ἁμαρτιῶν αὐτῶν). Zechariah now directly addresses his own son, and the finite verbs switch from the aorist to the future tense. The angel Gabriel announced John's future role (1:14 – 17), and Zechariah's recapitulation of that promise reveals that he both remembers and believes it. John's role is therefore announced by a heavenly messenger and by his father prophesying under the inspiration of the Holy Spirit.[14] The prophet Malachi (4:1 – 6) had also prophesied his role. He will go before the Lord (1:17, 76; 7:27), which is synonymous with preparing the way (1:76; 3:4; 7:27). He will lead the people to repent for the forgiveness of sins (1:17, 77; 3:3), and he will herald the coming of salvation (1:77; 3:6).[15]

1:78 – 79   By the compassionate mercy of our God, upon whom the dawn from on high will visit us, to shine light for those who sit in darkness and in the shadow of death, to direct our feet into the path of peace (διὰ σπλάγχνα ἐλέους θεοῦ ἡμῶν, ἐν οἷς ἐπισκέψεται ἡμᾶς ἀνατολὴ ἐξ ὕψους, ἐπιφᾶναι τοῖς ἐν σκότει καὶ σκιᾷ θανάτου καθημένοις, τοῦ κατευθῦναι τοὺς πόδας ἡμῶν εἰς ὁδὸν εἰρήνης). God's "compassionate mercy" (σπλάγχνα ἐλέους, lit., "the bowels [vital organs] of mercy") drives the action. The future tense "will visit" (ἐπισκέψεται) finds support among widespread early witnesses and is to be preferred over the aorist tense "visited," which also has strong, but later, textual support. It is plausible that a scribe changed the future to an aorist to make it conform to the aorist in v. 68. The future tense refers to the expected coming of the Messiah.

The messianic metaphor changes from "a horn of salvation" to "the dawn from on high." The word translated "dawn" (ἀνατολή) can refer to the sprouting up of a plant and the rising of a star, and its usage gave it a messianic connotation of "branch" (Jer 23:5; Zech 3:8; 6:12). The image of shining a light for those sitting in darkness suggests that it should be interpreted "as a light metaphor" (see Isa 58:8; 60:1; Rev 22:16).[16] Coleridge shows that this image transforms the association of ideas evoked by the messianic "horn of salvation":

> The messiah appears as a presence (light) which drives out an absence (darkness) rather than a presence (power) which drives out another presence (enemies). A new depth of mercy is revealed as God's new and more spectacular display of power. It is this which will be the fulfillment

13. Hendrickx, *The Third Gospel*, 1:155. He goes on to say, "They are those who destroy his honor, take his land, undermine his family, and threaten his women."

14. Frein, "Narrative Predictions," *NTS* 40 (1994): 24.

15. John gives specific instructions about what repentance requires (3:10 – 14). Dillon ("Benedictus," 474) comments: The connection between the restoration of a righteous community of Israel, the forgiveness of sins, and the fulfillment of the divine promise to Abraham was furnished by Micah 7. The connection to the mission of God's precursor, Elijah; the preparation of a people well suited for God's final coming; and the "rising" of the "sun of righteousness" over the elect was given by Malachi 4. Both texts envision God's final saving action as the completion of all prophecy, and Malachi casts the returning Elijah as the last of the prophets.

16. Strauss, *The Davidic Messiah in Luke-Acts*, 104. See also Mic 7:8 – 9.

of the promise made to Abraham; and it is this which will be the new and final visitation of God which demands recognition.[17]

The "path of peace" is not simply the path that leads to peace but is itself a peaceful path: "Peace will characterize the walk along this road."[18]

1:80 The child grew and became strong in spirit, and he was in the wilderness until the time he was made known to Israel (τὸ δὲ παιδίον ηὔξανεν καὶ ἐκραταιοῦτο πνεύματι, καὶ ἦν ἐν ταῖς ἐρήμοις ἕως ἡμέρας ἀναδείξεως αὐτοῦ πρὸς τὸν Ἰσραήλ). In a transitional summary, Luke describes John's maturity into manhood (see 1 Sam 2:21, 26; 3:19) and his departure for the wilderness before he describes the birth of Jesus. This jump in the chronological sequence is again to be explained by Luke's use of interlocking panels to tell the story (see 1:56). When the next panel starts, he resets the clock. "He was made known" (ἀναδείξεως αὐτοῦ; lit., "his showing forth") refers to John's, not Jesus', public manifestation. Since the noun can refer to an installation into an office, I have used the passive voice to render the phrase in order to reinforce that God is behind his public appearance.

John waxes strong in spirit (πνεύματι), which refers here to "the source and seat of insight, feeling, and will."[19] It means that he develops the "inner resources for the understanding and performance of God's will."[20] In the infancy narratives, the Holy Spirit fills people so that they can make prophetic utterances, but the power of the Holy Spirit is tied solely to Jesus in the gospel.

"The word of God" comes to John in the wilderness (3:2), but the Holy Spirit comes upon Jesus at his baptism (3:22; 4:1, 18).

The surface similarities between elements in the Dead Sea Scrolls and John's ministry in the wilderness[21] have caused some to speculate that John was in some way connected to the community at Qumran. Some suggest that since John's parents were elderly, he may have been orphaned, and the community took him in to raise and mold him, as Josephus attests that they did with orphaned children (*J.W.* 2.8.2 §120). Bovon comments, however, "The theological distance between the historical Baptist and the sect at Qumran seems too large to make a sojourn there probable."[22] Any parallels between John and Qumran do not necessarily indicate a direct association but may only reflect the fact that they shared a similar Scripture and similar expectations that were in the religious air at that time.

John's connection to Qumran is unlikely for a number of reasons.[23] Both John and the Qumran covenanters dwelt in the Judean wilderness and appealed to Isa 40:3, "a voice of one calling" in the wilderness (1QS 8:13 – 14, 9:19 – 20), but this verse sounded a common eschatological hope that imagined the desert to be "the staging ground for Yahweh's future victory over the power of evil."[24] John and the community at Qumran both had an ascetic bent, but the purpose of the asceticism at Qumran was self-purification, which was linked to a rigid exclusivism. The members set themselves apart from a people they considered to be

---

17. Coleridge, *The Birth of the Lukan Narrative*, 122. The image of shining a light on those who sit in darkness derives from Isa 9:2.

18. Hendrickx, *The Third Gospel*, 1:162.

19. BDAG, 833.

20. Hendrickx, *The Third Gospel*, 1:164.

21. Marshall, *The Gospel of Luke*, 95, notes that the plural "wilderness" in the Greek (ταῖς ἐρήμοις; here; 5:16; 8:29) is a

Septuagintalism (see Gen 21:20).

22. Bovon, *Luke 1:1 – 9:50*, 77.

23. See Hartmut Stegemann, *The Library of Qumran: On the Essenes, Qumran, John the Baptist, and Jesus* (Grand Rapids: Eerdmans/Leiden: Brill, 1998), 221 – 25.

24. Joel Marcus, *The Way of the Lord: Christological Exegesis of the Old Testament in the Gospel of Mark* (Louisville: Westminster John Knox, 1992), 22.

unclean. By contrast, John expressed no interest in creating an exclusive, priestly dominated sect. While both were interested in water rites, the ritual baths at Qumran were limited to members of the sect and were repeated daily to achieve Levitical purity. It was not associated with repentance or the forgiveness of sins. John's immersion was open to *everyone* who repented, had nothing to do with Levitical cleansing, and was not recurring. It was a proleptic experience of the divine judgment and forgiveness that prepared one for the coming judgment of God.

Theology in Application

1. The Visitation of God for Salvation

Jesus will affirm that John is more than a prophet (7:26) and the last of the prophets (16:16), but Zechariah makes clear that "the prophet of the Most High" is subordinate to the "Son of the Most High" (1:32). His prophetic hymn has a christological slant, and it becomes clear that "the main reason for blessing the God of Israel is what He has done for His people in Jesus the Messiah."[25]

In that regard, Zechariah says more than he knows. To "go before the Lord" from Zechariah's point of view would not be the Lord Jesus but the Lord God. Elizabeth's greeting in 1:43, however, introduces another Lord, and the narrative makes clear that John will prepare the way for Jesus. The ambiguity has theological consequences and is deliberate. John does not prepare the way for either the God of Abraham or Jesus but for both.[26] Schweizer scores the point: "the eschatological coming of God is thus identified with the coming of Jesus."[27] The meaning of "the Lord" is therefore transformed to include Jesus, whose mission and person is the incarnation of God's visitation.

It is remarkable to note how theological terms in Scripture have lost their meaning in contemporary American culture. For example, the term *redemption* (1:68) is now more often connected with sports than with Christianity. Whatever the sport, if a player has flubbed something that cost his or her team the game and the championship, he or she may live in infamy and have their error played and replayed on TV and in the minds of the fans. Then, that player may do something in another game or season that "atones" for the poor performance and wins "redemption." This concept of "redemption" requires that one must *do* something that makes amends for previous mistakes. Redemption in a far more profound sense, the biblical sense, cannot be won by our better performance that makes up for past letdowns, flops, and humiliations. It is brought by God and God alone to persons who are unworthy to receive it except that they have placed their hope exclusively in God. God delivers

---

25. Brown, *The Birth of the Messiah*, 383.
26. Rowe, *Early Narrative Christology*, 70, 74 n. 134.

27. Schweizer, *Luke*, 65.

us from evil, provides the atonement for our sins, and saves us from our seemingly irreversible corrupted state.

2. Salvation as the Forgiveness of Sins

When Zechariah praises God for "rais[ing] up a horn of salvation," readers familiar with the story know that God does more than cause Jesus to come into existence but will raise him up triumphantly from death (Acts 4:10). The result is that the word will go out to all the world, as Jesus commissions Paul "to open their eyes and turn them from darkness to light, and from the power of Satan to God, so that they may receive forgiveness of sins and a place among those who are sanctified by faith in me" (Acts 26:18).

When Zechariah first mentions "salvation," which he ties to God's fidelity to his covenant promises, mercy, and power, it refers to rescue from enemies (1:71, 74). But in 1:77, he connects "salvation" to the forgiveness of sins, a key theme in Luke-Acts.[28] It means more than the defeat of physical enemies. "The redemption of his people" (1:68) will also entail forgiveness of sins and the reestablishment of something more than a political state.

The reference to the "darkness" and to the "shadow of death" are images of ignorance and sin, the existential plight of every human being. Humans cannot save themselves from this predicament because they live in darkness. Living in darkness means that one makes all the wrong choices that inevitably lead to spiritual and physical death. Hendrickx says that these images bring us "face to face … with human existence itself—an existence which knows its own bitter fatality; the destruction of its very self contained in itself, for it neither knows the way to happiness nor can it put off forever the return to dust."[29] The coming of Jesus promises to cast light into the darkness and banish the shadow of death.

3. Salvation as Reconciliation

The hymn lauds God for showing mercy to Elizabeth and Zechariah (1:58) and to Israel (1:72). Israel's external enemies would seem to be left out (see *Pss. Sol.* 17; 4QpIsa^a D 1–8; 1Qsb 5:20–29). This limited view will be corrected in the narrative through Jesus' ministry as the gospel of repentance and the forgiveness of sins are to be proclaimed to all nations (24:47) through the apostles' ministry. The real enemy is revealed to be Satan (cf. Acts 13:10). Green comments, "When it is recognized that Luke identifies 'the enemy' as the cosmic power of evil resident and active behind all forms of opposition to God and God's people, it is plain that Zechariah's hope has not been dashed but clarified and, indeed, radicalized."[30] Coleridge avers, "That

28. The "forgiveness of sins" is a favorite phrase in Luke (3:3; 24:47; Acts 2:38; 5:31; 10:43; 13:38; 26:18).

29. Hendrickx, *The Third Gospel*, 1:161.

30. Green, *The Gospel of Luke*, 420.

the 'horn of salvation' will bring salvation through forgiveness implies that the real enemy is not the aggressive neighbor whose military pressure disallows peace, but the sin which disallows peace of another kind."[31]

The narrative reveals that this forgiveness will come not through John's baptism of water but through Jesus. Paul stresses that peace with God only comes through Jesus Christ, through whom we are reconciled to God (Rom 5:1 – 11). One of the unexpected ways of saving the people from their enemies is to turn the enemies into friends rather than seeking to have them destroyed. This is the paradigm of how God works, reconciling enemies through the death of his Son (Rom 5:10), not the through the deaths of the enemies.

4. Salvation as a Call to be a Blessing to Others

God frees Israel from the shackles of slavery and oppression. The goal is not simply to save the people so that they can live in tranquility but so they can serve God "in holiness and righteousness." They are not to serve God in serene isolation but to make God known to the world and so become a blessing to the nations.

Paul expresses this reality in Eph 3:1 – 2. He reminds the readers of his commission of "God's grace that was given to me for you." The grace bestowed on every Christian is always intended by God to be on its way to someone else. One is saved if one is spreading this grace to others. If one sees oneself as being saved without the obligation to be saving, then clearly one needs to grow in salvation. The evidence of salvation — that God's grace has taken effect in one's life — is to be found in one's participation in bringing salvation to others.

31. Coleridge, *The Birth of the Lukan Narrative*, 121.

Luke 2:1 – 21

Literary Context

The prophecy and praise of God's visitation in the coming of the promised Messiah are now fulfilled with an account of his birth. In contrast to the brief description of John's birth and the lengthy description of his circumcision and naming, Jesus' birth is described at length and his circumcision and naming are recounted in one verse. It is then followed by a lengthy description of his presentation in the temple and worshipful reactions to his presence. The response of wonder and praise in John's story is evoked by his circumcision and naming. In Jesus' story, it is evoked by his birth and presentation in the temple.

> I. Prologue and Infancy Narrative (1:1 – 2:52)
>   E. The Birth of John and Zechariah's Thanksgiving Psalm (1:57 – 80)
> → **F. The Birth of the Messiah (2:1 – 21)**
>   G. The Presentation of Jesus in the Temple (2:22 – 40)

Main Idea

"God chooses to visit his people in the midst of poverty and powerlessness, in a manger and among shepherds."[1]

Translation

(See next two pages.)

---

1. Coleridge, *The Birth of the Lukan Narrative*, 152.

Luke 2:1–21

Ref	Label	Text
2:1	Chronological note	**It happened in those days**
		that a decree went out from Caesar Augustus
		that the entire world should be registered [on tax lists].
2	Circumstance	**This registration was before Quirinius governed Syria.**
3		**And all went to be registered, each one to his own town.**
4a	Journey	**Joseph went up from Galilee**
		from the town of Nazareth
		to Judea to the town of David
		called Bethlehem,
b	Cause	because he was from the house and family line of David
5a		to be registered
b	Character introduction	with Mary,
c		who was betrothed to him and pregnant.
6	Chronological note	**It happened**
		that while they were there, the days for her to give birth were fulfilled;
7a	Birth	**she** **gave birth to her firstborn son and**
b		**wrapped him in bands of cloth and**
c		**laid him in a feeding trough**
d	Cause	because there was no place for them in the guest room.
8	Character introduction	**There were shepherds in the same region** **living outdoors and**
		keeping the night watch over their flock.
9a	Appearance of an angel	**Then an angel of the Lord stood before them,**
		and the glory of the Lord shone around them,
b	Reaction of fear	**and they were filled with great fear.**

Verse	Label	Text
10a	Assurance	**The angel said to them,** *"Fear not,*
b	Cause	*for behold, I bring good news of great joy which will be for all the people,*
11	Cause	*because to you is born today in the town of David a Savior, who is Christ and Lord.*
12	Sign	*This will be a sign to you.* *You will find a babe wrapped in bands of cloth and lying in a feeding trough."*
13	Praise	And suddenly **there was with the angel a multitude of the heavenly army praising God** and **saying,**
14a		*"Glory to God in the highest [heaven] and*
b		*upon earth peace among those favored by God!"*
15a	Departure of angels	When the angels went from them into heaven,
b	Obedience	**the shepherds were speaking to one another,** *"Indeed, let us go to Bethlehem and see this thing that has happened, which the Lord has made known to us."*
16a	Departure	Then they **went hurriedly**
b	Fulfillment of sign	and **found both Mary and Joseph, and the babe lying in the feeding trough.**
17	Announcement	When they saw [this], **they made known the word that had been told them about this child.**
18	Reaction: marveling	**Everyone who heard it marveled about what was told them by the shepherds.**
19	Reaction: pondering	**But Mary was treasuring all these words and pondered them in her heart.**
20	Departure	**The shepherds then returned glorifying and praising God for all that they had heard and seen,** just as it had been told them.
21a	Chronological note	When eight days were fulfilled [and the time came] to circumcise him,
b	Naming	**he was called Jesus, which the angel called him before he was conceived in the womb.**

Structure and Literary Form

The structure matches that of the previous account of John's birth: "A birth is followed by an announcement made concerning the child's identity; those to whom the announcement is made spread the news; and this in turn prompts amazement in those who hear."[2] This reflects Luke's technique of reprising an earlier pattern.

Exegetical Outline

→ **I. The political context of the birth (2:1 – 5)**

   A. The decree of Caesar Augustus to tax the world (2:1)

   B. The infamous tax registration under Quirinius (2:2)

   C. The obedience of Joseph, who travels with Mary to Bethlehem (2:3 – 5)

II. The birth (2:6 – 7)

   A. Wrapped in bands of cloth (2:6 – 7b)

   B. Cradled in a feeding trough (2:7c)

III. The heavenly interpretation of the birth to shepherds (2:8 – 14)

   A. The appearance of an angel of the Lord (2:8 – 9)

   B. The angel's announcement (2:10 – 12)

      1. Great joy is to replace fear (2:10)

      2. The birth of the Savior, who is Christ and Lord (2:11)

      3. The sign: a baby wrapped in bands of cloth and lying in a feeding trough (2:12)

   C. The chorus of the heavenly host: heaven and earth intersect in praise of this birth (2:13 – 14)

      1. Glory in the highest heaven (2:13 – 14a)

      2. Peace on earth (2:14b)

IV. The earthly reaction to the birth (2:15 – 20)

   A. The shepherds' reaction of faith in seeking the child (2:15 – 17)

   B. The shepherds' announcement to others of what had happened (2:18)

   C. Mary's reaction of treasuring what had happened (2:19)

   D. The shepherds' reaction of giving glory and praise to God (2:20)

V. The circumcision and naming of Jesus (2:21)

---

2. Ibid., 129.

Explanation of the Text

2:1 It happened in those days that a decree went out from Caesar Augustus that the entire world should be registered [on tax lists] (Ἐγένετο δὲ ἐν ταῖς ἡμέραις ἐκείναις ἐξῆλθεν δόγμα παρὰ Καίσαρος Αὐγούστου ἀπογράφεσθαι πᾶσαν τὴν οἰκουμένην). Herod's reign served as the chronological marker for John's birth (1:5); so now Caesar Augustus's reign is the chronological marker for Jesus' birth. The mention of these rulers is a painful reminder that Israel was still in captivity even in their own land. Herod's heir, Herod Antipas (identified by Luke only as "Herod the tetrarch" in the narrative) will put John to death (3:19–20; 9:7–9). Caesar's governor, Pontius Pilate, will put Jesus to death (23:24). At the beginning and end of the gospel, the Romans are introduced doing the two things most hated by their subjects: taxation and crucifixion.

The census is mentioned four times. This imperial decree need not mean that it refers to a specific census that Augustus ordered. It is simply "part of a coordinated empire-wide policy of Augustus."[3] The statement sets up a comparison between the presumption of Caesar's worldwide authority and that of the newborn child laid in an animal's feeding trough but declared by an angel from highest heaven to be Savior, Christ, and Lord. It also shows how God uses an unwitting Caesar to accomplish divine purposes so that the child is born in the town of David.

The emperor mentioned here was born Gaius Octavius. Julius Caesar adopted his grandnephew and made him his heir. After Octavius defeated Mark Antony at Actium and brought an end to civil war, the senate honored him in 27 BC with the title "Augustus" ("majestic"). Luke uses the Latin title as if it were a personal name, even though he knows and uses the Greek translation "his majesty the emperor" (Σεβαστός; Acts 25:21, 25). "Augustus" avoids the Greek term that had a sacred connotation for a Greek audience.[4]

2:2 This registration was before Quirinius governed Syria (αὕτη ἀπογραφὴ πρώτη ἐγένετο ἡγεμονεύοντος τῆς Συρίας Κυρηνίου). This statement is often translated, "This was the first registration and was taken while Quirinius was governor of Syria" (NRSV), which raises questions about Luke's historical accuracy. Josephus (*Ant.* 18.1.1 §§2–4) reports that when Herod's son Archelaus was deposed in AD 6, the Romans decided to rule Judea directly instead of through another Herodian client king. They sent their own governor, Publius Sulpicius Quirinius, to administer the province directly. He was legate to Syria for only a short time in AD 6–7. He administered a census, since direct rule necessitated direct taxation, and it also symbolized Judea's subjugation to Rome. To avoid the chronological discrepancy, some argue that Quirinius had served as legate earlier during the time of Herod the Great.[5] The

3. Nolland, *Luke*, 1:99.

4. Royce L. B. Morris, "Why Αὔγουστος? A Note to Luke 2.1," *NTS* 38 (1992): 142–44. He argues that as a result, Luke "created, probably inadvertently, a proper name by this peculiar use of the word."

5. William Mitchell Ramsay (*Was Christ Born in Bethlehem?: A Study on the Credibility of St. Luke* [2nd ed.; London: Hodder and Stoughton, 1898], 227–48; and *The Bearing of Recent Discovery on the Trustworthiness of the New Testament* [2nd ed.; London: Hodder and Stoughton, 1915], 222–300) provides a thorough history of Quirinius and argues that Luke,

as a writer of good Greek, referred to the first enrollment of many in a series. He contends that Quirinius previously governed Syria alongside Saturninus as military governor when a census was conducted and finds support in an inscription, *Lapis Tiburtinus* (CIL XIV, 3613). The census was ordered in 8–7 BC but delayed until 6 BC. The interpretation of the inscription is in doubt and does not offer incontrovertible proof, but others assume that Quirinius may have exercised some kind of special, wide-scale command of the East during this time. Tertullian (*Marc.* 4.19) substitutes "Saturninus," who governed Syria from 9 to 6 BC, for "Quirinius" in reading Luke 2:2.

evidence, however, is inconclusive. Also, the census ordered by Quirinius in AD 6 registered only those in Judea, not Galilee, which remained under the control of Herod Antipas.[6]

The translation offered here avoids this historical problem by rendering the superlative adjective "first" with a comparative sense "before."[7] Fitzmyer dismisses this view as a "last ditch solution to save the historicity involved,"[8] but valid arguments commend it. The translation "first" is odd because no sequence of other known censuses follows. Why does it need to be identified as the first? The structure of the phrase is also similar to the usage in John 1:15, 30 with the adjective "first"/"before" (πρῶτος) followed by the genitive — in this case, the genitive absolute (ἡγεμονεύοντος ... Κυρηνίου).[9]

This translation fits historically. Pearson shows that the census under Quirinius was not the first that the Jews had undergone. Herod, whose charge as a client king of Rome was to Romanize his territory, had a "well-organized system of taxation and ... he needed to, and did, exercise social control over his people."[10] This census would have been one of many conducted by Herod according to the Roman example.

Why, then, would Luke cite the census of Quirinius that occurred later? Pearson answers, because it was "more memorable than the continual process of census and taxation that Herod practiced, if for no other reason than because it caused a rebellion!"[11]

Josephus considered the census of Quirinius to be a watershed event that was the impetus for the rebellion led by Judas of Galilee. That rebellion sowed the seeds for the Zealot movement that burgeoned into a pattern of sedition and conflict and culminated in the revolt against Rome and Jerusalem's destruction (Josephus, *J.W.* 2.8.1 §§117 – 18; 2.9.1 §167; *Ant.* 17.3.5 §§354 – 55; 18.1.1 §§1 – 9).

Pearson makes the case that the censuses and taxation under Herod, hated as they were, at least appeared to be under the auspices of a Jewish state even though they were in the Roman style. The census under Quirinius, however, was "the first taste of direct, immediate rule by the Romans." What stirred Judas and Saddok to foment revolt was not that God's people were being assessed and taxed but was driven by "the *status* which such an assessment carried with it." They were under indirect Roman rule before under Herod, but this census made it crystal clear that they "were now under direct Roman rule."[12] Luke knows of the connection of the revolt led by Judas and the census and cites it in Acts 5:37 as a memorable event.

Luke connects this earlier census under Herod involving Jesus' family to the more infamous one conducted by Quirinius as a "prominent chronological signpost." Pearson explains, "Time keeping in cultures with limited literacy is accomplished not necessarily by reference to a calendar on the wall or a watch on the wrist, but rather by significant events."[13] It also serves other purposes. First,

---

6. For bibliography and abstracts of the numerous proposals to explain the census as a historical problem, see Joel B. Green and Michael C. McKeever, *Luke-Acts and New Testament Historiography* (IBR Bibliographies 8; Grand Rapids: Baker, 1994), 112 – 17.

7. A. J. B. Higgins, "Sidelights on Christian Beginnings in the Graeco-Roman World," *EvQ* 41 (1969): 200 – 201, argues from the use of πρῶτος in John 15:18 that it is equivalent to πρό and it governs the participial phrase here to mean: "This census took place before Quirinius was governor." See also W. Brindle, "The Census and Quirinius: Luke 2:2," *JETS* 27 (1984):

48 – 50; Nigel Turner, *Grammatical Insights into the Greek New Testament* (Edinburgh: T&T Clark, 1965), 23 – 24.

8. Fitzmyer, *Luke*, 1:401. Marshall, *The Gospel of Luke*, 104, allows it as a possibility: "Luke does write loose sentences on occasion, and this may be an example of such."

9. Brook W. R. Pearson, "The Lucan Censuses, Revisited," *CBQ* 61 (1999): 281.

10. Ibid., 268 – 69.

11. Ibid., 277.

12. Ibid., 269 – 73.

13. Ibid, 277.

Jesus' family, like Judas the Galilean (Acts 5:37), was also from Galilee, but they peaceably complied with the requirement to be registered rather than rebelled (see 23:2). Second, a census was not simply a means of organizing the tax rolls but was also "a means of demonstrating control of the world."[14] Luke's mention of the infamous census sets up the opposition between the proud, formidable empire of Caesar and God's eternal reign. The child born in Bethlehem to parents subjected to Roman tyranny will ultimately challenge the existing political order and create an astonishing reversal of authority and power, not through violence but through obedience to God and the giving of his life.

2:3 – 5 And all went to be registered, each one to his own town. Joseph went up from Galilee from the town of Nazareth to Judea to the town of David called Bethlehem, because he was from the house and family line of David, to be registered with Mary, who was betrothed to him and pregnant (καὶ ἐπορεύοντο πάντες ἀπογράφεσθαι, ἕκαστος εἰς τὴν ἑαυτοῦ πόλιν. ἀνέβη δὲ καὶ Ἰωσὴφ ἀπὸ τῆς Γαλιλαίας ἐκ πόλεως Ναζαρὲθ εἰς τὴν Ἰουδαίαν εἰς πόλιν Δαυὶδ ἥτις καλεῖται Βηθλέεμ, διὰ τὸ εἶναι αὐτὸν ἐξ οἴκου καὶ πατριᾶς Δαυίδ, ἀπογράψασθαι σὺν Μαριὰμ τῇ ἐμνηστευμένῃ αὐτῷ, οὔσῃ ἐγκύῳ). We need

not envision a mass movement of people. Pearson cites the historical observation of Ramsay:

> We in modern time make the census for one fixed and universal moment, catching our migratory population at the given instant, as if by an instantaneous photograph. The Romans tried to cope in another way with the difficulty of numbering people who might be far from home, viz., by bringing them at some time during the enrolment-year to their proper and original home; and they permitted them to come for enrollment at any time during the year.[15]

What is important for Luke is Jesus' connection to the house of David through Joseph and Bethlehem, the town of David, which was prophesied to be the birthplace of the "one who will be ruler over Israel," the Messiah (Mic 5:2).[16] It keeps in the forefront the promise to Mary that "the Lord God will give to him the throne of David his father" (1:32). Augustus's decree causes Jesus to be born in Bethlehem. His reign will end with his death in AD 14. Jesus' reign will have no end (1:33).

The reversal theme emerges subtly in this verse. The word order of the sentence has Joseph rising from Galilee to go to Judea and the "town [πόλις] of David"; this expression would lead those familiar with Scripture and with the prevailing identification of Jerusalem as the πόλις of David[17] to

14. R. S. Bagnall and B. W. Frier, *The Demography of Roman Egypt* (Cambridge Studies in Population, Economy, and Past Time 23; Cambridge: Cambridge Univ. Press, 1994), 229 – 30 (cited by Pearson, "The Lucan Censuses, Revisited," 266).

15. Pearson, "The Lucan Censuses, Revisited," 275, citing W. M. Ramsay, "Luke's Narrative of the Birth of Christ," *ExpTim* 4 (1912): 385 – 407, 481 – 501.

16. Of the 164 instances of the word "city" (πόλις) in the New Testament, half of them appear in Luke-Acts (39 in Luke and 43 in Acts). It may seem to be a misnomer to call Bethlehem and Nazareth "cities." "Village" or "town" would be more appropriate. But Luke opts for this term over the word for village (κώμη; cf. Mark 8:23; Luke 9:16, 12; John 7:42). Richard Rohrbaugh ("The Pre-Industrial City," in *The Social Sciences and New Testament Interpretation* [ed. R. Rohrbaugh; Pea-

body, MA: Hendrickson, 1996], 108) notes that scholars have attributed this misdesignation to Luke's unfamiliarity with the actual situation in Roman Palestine. There is no suggestion, however, that Luke's usage refers to a political organization. The term seems to refer to a populated center, " 'an enclosed place of human habitation' as distinct from uninhabited areas, pastures, villages, and single houses" (Hermann Strathmann, "πόλις," *TDNT*, 6:528). I have opted to translate it "town" so as not to confuse it with the modern understanding of the nature of a city.

17. 2 Sam 5:7, 9; 6:10, 12, 16; 1 Kgs 2:10; 8:1; 9:24; 11:43; 14:31; 15:8, 24; 22:50; 2 Kgs 8:24; 9:28; 12:21; 14:20; 15:7, 38; 16:20; 1 Chr 11:7; 13:13; 15:1, 29; 2 Chr 5:2; 8:11; 9:31; 12:16; 14:1; 16:14; 21:1, 20; 24:16, 25; 25:28; 27:9; 32:5, 30; 33:14; Neh 3:15, 12:37; Isa 22:9; 1 Macc 2:31; 7:32; 14:36.

expect that Joseph travels to Jerusalem. "Bethlehem" as the πόλις of David would come as a surprise. The πόλις of David one would expect to be the center of Israel politically and religiously, but there is a deliberate contrast with Bethlehem.

Jesus is the legitimate Davidic ruler of Israel who comes out of lowly Bethlehem, the town of David, in fulfillment of Mic 5:1 – 2; he stands in contrast to the Davidic kings in the great city of Jerusalem. This Micah prophecy itself contrasts the present Davidic king who relies on military power and is subsequently defeated with the coming Davidic ruler from Bethlehem, who will rely on God and will triumph and "his greatness will reach to the ends of the earth" (Mic 5:4).[18]

Mentioning again Mary's betrothal to Joseph suggests that the marriage has not yet been consummated and underscores that she has not become pregnant in the normal way.[19] The unit's conclusion (2:21) reinforces the virginal conception by harking back to the angel's visit to Mary and the announcement of the child's conception and name (1:31). Luke is silent about why Mary went with Joseph, but one might presume that she needed to be registered with him as part of a poll tax or that with the birth at hand they wanted to be together. Luke does not share their personal feelings or thoughts about this imposed journey.

2:6 – 7 It happened that while they were there, the days for her to give birth were fulfilled; she gave birth to her firstborn son and wrapped him in bands of cloth and laid him in a feeding trough because there was no place for them in the guest room (ἐγένετο δὲ ἐν τῷ εἶναι αὐτοὺς ἐκεῖ ἐπλήσθησαν αἱ ἡμέραι τοῦ τεκεῖν αὐτήν, καὶ ἔτεκεν τὸν υἱὸν αὐτῆς τὸν πρωτότοκον·

καὶ ἐσπαργάνωσεν αὐτὸν καὶ ἀνέκλινεν αὐτὸν ἐν φάτνη, διότι οὐκ ἦν αὐτοῖς τόπος ἐν τῷ καταλύματι). Noting that Jesus is "the firstborn" (τὸν πρωτότοκον) recalls God's claim on those who open the womb (Exod 13:2) and the right of inheritance (Deut 21:15 – 17). Being the firstborn may reinforce the idea that Jesus is to be the heir to David's throne (2 Chr 21:3).[20]

At birth, a baby was normally wrapped in bandage-like strips to keep the legs and arms still. It provided some warmth and may have been presumed to provide the newborn a sense of security. Since it is mentioned three times, what is its significance? First, it reveals parental care for the child (see Ezek 16:4 – 5). Second, though Jesus has been divinely conceived, it reveals that he shares the lot of all mortals. Solomon says: "I was nursed with care in swaddling cloths. For no king has had a different beginning of existence; there is for all one entrance into life, and one way out" (Wis 7:4 – 6). At the end of his life, Jesus will be wrapped in a linen death shroud (23:53).

I translate the familiar "manger" (φάτνη) as "feeding trough."[21] The word could refer to a stall (13:15), but it makes more sense that Mary wrapped her baby and "laid" him in something that can function as a crib. The trough would be in a stall. The point is, "the child lies outside the human dwelling in an unusual place where there are only animals."[22] The "manger" has been sanctified and glorified over the many years of Christmas celebrations, and this stark translation deliberately diminishes that aura of dignity. No one sings "Away in a feeding trough," which is just the point. The Savior who dies on a shameful cross was placed in a lowly trough for barn animals when he was born: "his head rests where cattle have fed."[23]

---

18. Yuzuru Miura, *David in Luke-Acts* (WUNT 2/232; Tübingen: Mohr Siebeck, 2007), 202 – 3.

19. Marshall, *The Gospel of Luke*, 105.

20. Danker, *Jesus and the New Age*, 55.

21. Martin Hengel, "φάτνη," *TDNT*, 9:54.

22. Ibid.

23. Ibid., 9:55.

The text is unclear whether this takes place in a separate stall attached to a house, an enclosure in the open, or a cave.[24] It is more likely that the stall was part of the dwelling. Luke uses that same word that is frequently translated "inn" (κατάλυμα) in 22:11 (Mark 14:14) to refer to "the guest room" where Jesus and his disciples eat the Last Supper. Luke does not use here the word for "inn" (πανδοχεῖον), which appears in 10:34 in the parable of the good Samaritan. Peasant homes normally consisted of two rooms, with one used exclusively for guests (see Matt 5:15, where the lamp on the lampstand gives light to all in the house; cf. also Luke 15:8).

The family "cooked, ate, slept, and lived" in the main room, and any animals were also brought in for the night and kept at the lower level of the living room, where the feeding trough would be.[25] The picture in 13:15 of the synagogue audience untying an ox or donkey from the stall on the Sabbath to lead it away to water implies leading them *out of* the house. Bailey observes, "Were animals kept in a separate stable, the head of the synagogue could have saved face by asserting firmly, 'I never touch the animals on the Sabbath.' But if he tried to claim that he leaves the animals in the house all day, the people in the synagogue would ridicule him with laughter!"[26]

The noun translated "guest room" (κατάλυμα) refers to a guest chamber attached to the home. Jesus' family stayed in an ordinary home, as would be expected. Because of his lineage, Joseph "belonged" in this village, and room would have been made for him and his wife. Bailey notes that Joseph could have announced, " 'I am Joseph, son of Heli, son of Matthat, the son of Levi' and most homes in town would have been open to him."[27] It would have been shameful for the entire community had the couple been turned out (see the discussion on expected Oriental hospitality in the commentary on 11:5 – 8).[28] The couple stayed in the animal quarters of the home of a relative or acquaintance because someone who "outranked" them occupied the upper room in an overcrowded home.[29]

This view is confirmed by the chronological note in 2:6. They were already in Judea and "while they were there" Mary gave birth. They did not arrive late at night so that they had to accept whatever emergency shelter might be available. Joseph would have made arrangements by then for lodging his pregnant wife, even if it meant going to the home of her cousin, Elizabeth, in the Judean hill country (1:39). The fiction of a heartless innkeeper who turns them away is not only a fantasy, it leads away from Luke's point.

Finding the child wrapped in bands of cloth and lying in a feeding trough is to be a sign for the shepherds (2:12).[30] Since every baby was wrapped in bands of cloth, this detail is incidental as part of the sign. What is primary is that this baby's crib is a feeding trough. But it is no less ambiguous than the sign of an empty tomb at the end of the gospel. Given the importance in the infancy narrative of remembering and interpreting the events through the lens of Scripture, it requires remembering Scripture to interpret its meaning, as the empty

---

24. Hengel (ibid., 9:52) notes that "caves were limited to big estates," which makes this traditional view less likely.

25. Kenneth E. Bailey, *Jesus through Middle Eastern Eyes: Cultural Studies in the Gospels* (Downers Grove, IL: InterVarsity Press, 2008), 28 – 29.

26. Ibid., 31.

27. Ibid., 26.

28. For a somewhat different view, see Verlyn D. Verbrugge, *A Not-So-Silent Night: The Unheard Story of Christmas and Why It Matters* (Grand Rapids: Kregel, 2009), 53 – 57.

29. Bruce J. Malina and Richard L. Rohrbaugh, *Social-Science Commentary on the Synoptic Gospels* (Minneapolis: Fortress, 1992), 297. See also Plummer, *Luke*, 54; Nolland, *Luke*, 1:105 – 6. The verb form of the noun "guest room" appears in 19:7, where it clearly means that Jesus will lodge with Zacchaeus as his guest (see also 9:12).

30. The sign is not a virgin giving birth — how would they know?

tomb will require remembering the words of Jesus (24:6–8).

Its sign value is likely connected to Isaiah 1:3: "The ox knows its master, the donkey its owner's manger, but Israel does not know, my people do not understand."[31] Isaiah laments that Israel did not know God as their "manger," who nourished his people. Heil, among others, interprets "the feeding trough" in which Jesus lies (2:12, 16) to be "the sign by which God makes known to lowly shepherds (2:15) and through them to all the people (2:10, 17) the birth of their Savior, Christ and Lord (2:11), through whom God will feed his hungry people."[32] In Luke's subtle symbolism, the feeding trough *is* now made known. Angels announce to the shepherds the news of the birth, but they do not direct them to the place. On their own, the shepherds find their way to "the manger" of the Lord (2:16). They see Jesus, tell others, and then glorify God for what he has done.

2:8–9 There were shepherds in the same region living outdoors and keeping the night watch over their flock. Then an angel of the Lord stood before them, and the glory of the Lord shone around them, and they were filled with great fear (καὶ ποιμένες ἦσαν ἐν τῇ χώρᾳ τῇ αὐτῇ ἀγραυλοῦντες καὶ φυλάσσοντες φυλακὰς τῆς νυκτὸς ἐπὶ τὴν ποίμνην αὐτῶν. καὶ ἄγγελος κυρίου ἐπέστη αὐτοῖς καὶ δόξα κυρίου περιέλαμψεν αὐτούς, καὶ ἐφοβήθησαν φόβον μέγαν). Heaven's glory (see Acts 7:55) comes to earth, filling the night sky with light for a gallery of shepherds who were sitting in darkness. The "glory of the Lord" is God's visible presence in creation and is associated with awesome events in Israel's past: the giving of manna (Exod 16:10) and the covenant at Sinai (Exod 24:16–17). For Isaiah,

the revealing of the glory of the Lord is associated with the restoration of Israel (Isa 40:3–5). For Habakkuk, the earth will be filled with the glory of the Lord in the end time (Hab 2:14).

The glory of the Lord is also associated with the tabernacle and, later, the temple (Exod 40:34–35; 1 Kgs 8:11; 2 Chr 5:7; Ps 63:2). Surprisingly, that glory does not appear in the temple in nearby Jerusalem. Nor does it shine around the manger and the newborn child. Instead, it appears in an open field to lowly shepherds faithfully keeping watch over their sheep. Does this incident allude to the attacks on the false shepherds of Israel that appear in the Prophets (Jer 23:1–6; Ezek 34)?

2:10–12 The angel said to them, "Fear not, for behold, I bring good news of great joy which will be for all the people, because to you is born today in the town of David a Savior, who is Christ and Lord. This will be a sign to you. You will find a babe wrapped in bands of cloth and lying in a feeding trough" (καὶ εἶπεν αὐτοῖς ὁ ἄγγελος, μὴ φοβεῖσθε, ἰδοὺ γὰρ εὐαγγελίζομαι ὑμῖν χαρὰν μεγάλην ἥτις ἔσται παντὶ τῷ λαῷ, ὅτι ἐτέχθη ὑμῖν σήμερον σωτὴρ ὅς ἐστιν Χριστὸς κύριος ἐν πόλει Δαυίδ. καὶ τοῦτο ὑμῖν τὸ σημεῖον, εὑρήσετε βρέφος ἐσπαργανωμένον καὶ κείμενον ἐν φάτνῃ). The angel remains anonymous since only the message matters. The shepherds' great fear will be overcome by great joy, and that joy will extend to "all the people" (παντὶ τῷ λαῷ), a term that refers to "all the people of Israel" (3:21; 24:19). The announcement of good news (εὐαγγελίζομαι) was a term familiar to the ancient audience from Roman propaganda. It was used for the glad tidings related to the birth of an heir to the emperor, his coming of age, and his accession to the throne.

---

31. In the LXX, it is the φάτνη of its owner.

32. John Paul Heil, *The Meal Scenes in Luke-Acts: An Audience-Oriented Approach* (SBLMS 52; Atlanta: Society of Biblical Literature, 1999), 15. So also Hendrickx, *The Third Gospel*, 1:185.

The term will be completely redefined by the gospel story of Jesus.

The prophecy is fulfilled "today," an emphasis throughout Luke (4:21; 5:26; 19:5, 9; 23:43). "Today" connects to the yesterday of God's promises and Old Testament prophecies, which are now being fulfilled.

The "town of David" is identified as Jerusalem in 2 Sam 5:7, 9, but Bethlehem is closely associated with David (1 Sam 17:12 – 16; 17:58; 20:6, 28 – 29; John 7:42). According to Mic 5:2, it is one of the little clans of Judah, but this birth suggests that things are being reversed.

The heavenly messenger next identifies the "horn of salvation," whom Zechariah prophesied was being raised by God (1:69), as Jesus. This Savior is a swaddled babe in a manger. The juxtaposition of the nominatives "Christ Lord" (Χριστὸς κύριος) is striking and should be read as in apposition.[33] The terms clarify that Jesus is not "just another deliverer like one of the judges of Israel" but *the Savior*.[34] The term was applied to God in 1:47 and now it is applied to Jesus, who is also the Lord (1:43). Paul will proclaim him to be the Lord Jesus Christ in the very capital of the Roman Empire (Acts 28:31).

2:13 – 14   And suddenly there was with the angel a multitude of the heavenly army praising God and saying, "Glory to God in the highest [heaven] and upon earth peace among those favored by God!" (καὶ ἐξαίφνης ἐγένετο σὺν τῷ ἀγγέλῳ πλῆθος στρατιᾶς οὐρανίου αἰνούντων τὸν θεὸν καὶ λεγόντων· δόξα ἐν ὑψίστοις θεῷ καὶ ἐπὶ γῆς εἰρήνη ἐν ἀνθρώποις εὐδοκίας). The term often translated "host" (στρατιᾶς) is a military term applied to God's attendants. This heavenly army does not come to wreak desolation and terror but to announce good tidings and peace and to give glory to God (Ps 148). "Peace" was mentioned in 1:79 and again in 2:29, but here it refers to a spiritual peace between God and humanity. It is not a peace wish but "a proclamation of the divine event."[35] The term evokes both the *Pax Romana* and the Hebrew *šālôm*.

Wengst cites an inscription from Asia Minor that reveals the Romans were praised as "the saviors of all" and that peace and concord meant submission to Roman rule and showing goodwill to the Romans through obedience in all things.[36] For Luke, God is the only source of true peace.

"Those favored by God" (ἀνθρώποις εὐδοκίας) translates a difficult phrase. A textual variant has the nominative form (εὐδοκία), which would be rendered "goodwill among humans." The more difficult reading is the genitive (εὐδοκίας), and its ambiguity allows for the "goodwill" or "favor" to be God's or humans': "among humans of goodwill" or "among humans of (his) goodwill."[37] This translation interprets the phrase to refer to God's divine favor in his gracious visitation of humans (see the verb form in 12:32, where the disciples are the recipients of divine favor: "It is the Father's good pleasure to give to you his reign").

The movement is from heaven to earth, but it requires a response from those so favored so that it moves back from earth to heaven. This is quite different from the goodwill of Caesar Augustus. First, Caesar's goodwill has to be won. Second, it only ensured victory for a political office. God's goodwill is not won by anything that humans have done, and it ensures the grace that leads to salvation. As Metzger notes, "The meaning seems to be, not that divine peace can be bestowed only

33. Bock, *Luke*, 1:217.
34. Nolland, *Luke*, 1:107.
35. Gotlob Schrenk, "εὐδοκέω, εὐδοκία," *TDNT*, 2:748.
36. Klaus Wengst, *Pax Romana and the Peace of Jesus Christ*

(trans. John Bowden; Philadelphia: Fortress, 1987), 21.
37. The nominative form may be explained by the accidental deletion of the small elevated half-circle (ᶜ) that scribes used for the final genitive sigma.

where human good will is already present, but that at the birth of the Saviour God's peace rests on those whom he has chosen in accord with his good pleasure."[38]

2:15 – 18 When the angels went from them into heaven, the shepherds were speaking to one another, "Indeed, let us go to Bethlehem and see this thing that has happened, which the Lord has made known to us." Then they went hurriedly and found both Mary and Joseph, and the babe lying in the feeding trough. When they saw [this], they made known the word that had been told them about this child. Everyone who heard it marveled about what was told them by the shepherds (καὶ ἐγένετο ὡς ἀπῆλθον ἀπ᾽ αὐτῶν εἰς τὸν οὐρανὸν οἱ ἄγγελοι, οἱ ποιμένες ἐλάλουν πρὸς ἀλλήλους· διέλθωμεν δὴ ἕως Βηθλέεμ καὶ ἴδωμεν τὸ ῥῆμα τοῦτο τὸ γεγονὸς ὃ ὁ κύριος ἐγνώρισεν ἡμῖν. καὶ ἦλθαν σπεύσαντες καὶ ἀνεῦρον τήν τε Μαριὰμ καὶ τὸν Ἰωσὴφ καὶ τὸ βρέφος κείμενον ἐν τῇ φάτνῃ· ἰδόντες δὲ ἐγνώρισαν περὶ τοῦ ῥήματος τοῦ λαληθέντος αὐτοῖς περὶ τοῦ παιδίου τούτου. καὶ πάντες οἱ ἀκούσαντες ἐθαύμασαν περὶ τῶν λαληθέντων ὑπὸ τῶν ποιμένων πρὸς αὐτούς). After making the announcement and singing praise to God, the angels leave. They do not stick around to goad the shepherds to go, to guide them where to go, or to guard them along their way. God's initiative now is transferred to humans. Three reactions occur. The shepherds go, see, and rejoice. They tell others, who then marvel. Mary treasures and ponders these things in her heart.

The shepherds confess that the Lord (through the angel) has made known to them what has happened, and they understand that it requires a response. Though the angel does not order them to go, they make haste (see 1:39) to find the babe.

As Coleridge recognizes, they do not go "in order to believe, but because they believe."[39] When they see, they glorify God and become interpreters who proclaim to others what has happened. The amazement of those who hear the news may be caused by the surprise that the Savior actually has been born to fulfill God's promises, that a child who is Christ and Lord was born in such circumstances, and/or that the angels would deliver such stupendous news to persons of such low estate. The communal response of marveling, however, is not quite to the level of faith and exultation that God expects.

2:19 – 20 But Mary was treasuring all these words and pondered them in her heart. The shepherds then returned glorifying and praising God for all that they had heard and seen, just as it had been told them (ἡ δὲ Μαριὰμ πάντα συνετήρει τὰ ῥήματα ταῦτα συμβάλλουσα ἐν τῇ καρδίᾳ αὐτῆς. καὶ ὑπέστρεψαν οἱ ποιμένες δοξάζοντες καὶ αἰνοῦντες τὸν θεὸν ἐπὶ πᾶσιν οἷς ἤκουσαν καὶ εἶδον καθὼς ἐλαλήθη πρὸς αὐτούς). The Holy Spirit does not overshadow Mary to give her divine insight to understand what everything means. It is sometimes hard to see what God is doing when one is living in the midst of the events. She learns more information from the shepherds who come to see her child. They tell her about the angels and the announcement that the child is the Savior, the Christ, and the Lord. The imperfect "was treasuring" (συνετήρει) and the participle "pondered" (συμβάλλουσα) imply that she continued to try "to put the pieces together" to see the whole picture (see 2:51).[40]

Mary reveals that spirituality includes the intellectual activity of moral reasoning, wondering about things and trying to figure them out. Brown suggests that the interpretation of the parable of

38. Metzger, *A Textual Commentary*, 133.
39. Coleridge, *The Birth of the Lukan Narrative*, 146.
40. Ibid., 151.

the sower might apply to Mary. She represents those who, "when they hear the word, hold it fast in a good and honest heart and bear fruit with endurance" (8:15).[41] Her continuing contemplation of what has happened, therefore, contrasts with the hearers who only marvel (2:18).[42]

2:21 When eight days were fulfilled [and the time came] to circumcise him, he was called Jesus, which the angel called him before he was conceived in the womb (καὶ ὅτε ἐπλήσθησαν ἡμέραι ὀκτὼ τοῦ περιτεμεῖν αὐτὸν καὶ ἐκλήθη τὸ ὄνομα αὐτοῦ Ἰησοῦς, τὸ κληθὲν ὑπὸ τοῦ ἀγγέλου πρὸ τοῦ συλλημφθῆναι αὐτὸν ἐν τῇ κοιλίᾳ). Like John the son of Zechariah and Elizabeth (1:59), Jesus is also circumcised on the eighth day by his pious parents in obedience to the law (Gen 17:12; 21:4; Lev 12:3; see Phil 3:5). This rite was the sign of the covenant between God and Abraham (Gen 17:1 – 27), and it would have been witnessed by friends and relatives. As a physical mark of the covenant, it was considered to be a seal of the election, a confession of faith, and an act of obedience to God's holy law. It also marked off Jews from the heathen people around them, as God had commanded them to be separate. Circumcision was considered to be one of the most important commands because it superseded even the Sabbath laws; that is, one could break the Sabbath to circumcise a boy on the eighth day (John 7:22 – 23; *b. Šabb.* 132a).

Luke's narrative of Paul having Timothy circumcised (Acts 16:1 – 3) affirms that circumcision was fine for Jews even though it could not be required for Gentiles to be saved (Acts 15:1 – 29). It exposes the mendacity of the charge against Paul that he encouraged Diaspora Jews to forsake Moses and not to circumcise their children (Acts 21:21). Jesus is the circumcised Jewish Messiah, and it is all part of Luke's picture in the infancy narrative that the Christian movement was cradled in pietistic Judaism.[43]

Theology in Application

1. The World Ruler versus the World's Redeemer

The hymns in the infancy narrative herald God's visitation, and the birth narrative reveals that "God visits his people in ways more surprising than ever."[44] The account of Jesus' birth "is set against the background of imperial authority."[45] I argue that Luke did not get "his facts wrong," as Johnson asserts,[46] but he uses the facts of Augustus's taxation and Quirinius's census to make ironic political/theological points. Luke's description of the birth of Jesus in the time of the *Pax Augusta* challenges imperial propaganda and proclaims that Jesus is the real Savior, the real Lord, and the real bearer of peace for the whole world. Caesar flexed his political muscle

---

41. Brown, *The Birth of the Messiah*, 428.

42. Bock, *Luke*, 1:222.

43. Some in popular piety may have regarded that the blood shed in circumcision moves God to atone sin (see Shaye J. D. Cohen, "A Brief History of Circumcision Blood," in *The Covenant of Circumcision: New Perspectives on an Ancient Jewish Rite* [ed. E. W. Mark; Lebanon, NH: Brandeis Univ. Press,

2003], 30 – 40). At the Last Supper, Jesus instead identifies the pouring out of his own life's blood as the new covenant in his blood (22:20).

44. Hendrickx, *The Third Gospel*, 1:167.

45. Ibid., 1:214.

46. Johnson, *The Gospel of Luke*, 49, agreeing with many others.

with the decree that the entire world had to register to be taxed with the arrogance of one who ruled the world. His purpose was to fill his coffers and to enforce the subjugation of the vassal kingdoms. God outflanks Caesar's decree, however, to accomplish divine ends. Luke provides an example of how God works through the events of history and uses the emperor's decree to get Joseph and Mary to Bethlehem and to fulfill the Jewish expectation that the Messiah would be born there (Mic 5:1 – 2; Matt 2:5).

Augustus reigned in the lap of luxury from all the taxes his subjects supplied him. Jesus, by contrast, lies in a feeding trough. Hengel comments, "For Luke, the manger expresses the contrast between the world-ruler Augustus and the hidden and lowly birth of the world-redeemer (Lk. 2:1, 11, 14). It points forward to the way of humility and suffering which is taken by the Son of God who 'hath not where to lay his head,' Lk. 9:58."[47] Luke links the Messiah's birth to the lowly and the outcast. Caesar's decree was worldwide, but the announcement of Jesus' birth comes to those who live out under the stars at night with rocks for pillows and hovels for homes. The good news of Jesus Christ, however, will spread "without hindrance" (the last word in Acts 28:31) to the entire world not through autocratic decrees but through witness of transformed lives giving themselves to others (see Acts 20:18 – 24).

Jesus says that the rulers of this world want to be acclaimed benefactors (22:25). They also want to be hailed as "peacemakers," and Augustus was renowned for pacifying the world. A great altar to the peace brought by him was erected in Rome (13 – 9 BC) to honor him. An inscription from Halicarnassus in Asia Minor calls him the savior of the whole human race because "land and sea have peace, the cities flourish under a good legal system, in harmony and with an abundance of food, there is an abundance of all good things, people are filled with happy hopes for the future and with delight at the present."[48]

A frequently cited inscription from the Roman province of Asia decreed that the birthday of the emperor Augustus (September 23) would mark the beginning of the year when persons assumed civil office. It was filled with exaggerated praise:

> … it is a day which we may justly count as equivalent to the beginning of everything — if not in itself and in its own nature, at any rate in the benefits it brings — inasmuch as it has restored the shape of everything that was failing and turning into misfortune, and has given a new look to the Universe at a time when it would gladly have welcomed destruction if Caesar had not been born to be the common blessing of all men.

The decree resolves that:

> Whereas the Providence which has ordered the whole of our life, showing concern

---

47. Hengel, "φάτνη," 9:54.
48. Cited by Wengst (*Pax Romana*, 9), from *The Collection* *of Ancient Greek Inscriptions in the British Museum IV* (ed. G. Hirschfeld, London, 1893), no. 894.

and zeal has ordained the most perfect consummation for human life by giving to it Augustus, by filling him with virtue for doing the work of a benefactor among men, and by sending in him, as it were, a saviour for us and those who come after us, to make war to cease, to create order everywhere … and whereas the birthday of the God [Augustus] was the beginning for the world of the *glad tidings* [italics mine] that have come to men through him … Paulus Fabius Maximus, the proconsul of the province … has devised a way of honouring Augustus hitherto unknown to the Greeks, which is that the reckoning of time for the course of human life should begin with his birth.[49]

Again, God works through historical circumstances to accomplish his will. The Christian mission will indeed benefit from the *Pax Romana*, which created peaceful conditions to spread the gospel around the world. But Luke knows that peace dictated by an imperial government is a false peace. Only the God of peace brings peace. Virgil refers to the rule of Augustus as the beginning of a golden age of pastoral rule (*Aen.* 6.791 – 95; *Ecl.* 4.4 – 10). Angels from the heavenly host come to another bucolic scene to announce to shepherds the birth of the one true Lord who brings real peace.

The reality is that the Roman peace, like that promised by many earthly ruling powers through the ages, was an armed peace with the Roman foot planted squarely on the necks of the vanquished foes.[50] It was won on the battlefield at the cost of an enormous amount of bloodshed (Tacitus, *Ann.* 1.10.4). Tacitus has the British general Calgacus attempt to rally his troops before battle with the Romans by saying: " 'To plunder, butcher, steal these things they misname empire: they make a desolation and call it peace' " (*Agr.* 30.5).[51] Roman peace was simply forced pacification that brought the cessation of war through war. Tacitus said Augustus "seduced everyone with the sweetness of peace" (*Ann.* 1.2.1). It was intended to produce goodwill toward the Romans, but it required servility and produced terror, slavery, and taxation. Most feared it (Tacitus, *Ann.* 12.33). Even their lackeys who benefitted from Roman patronage feared Roman reprisals (see John 11:48; Acts 19:40).

The peace that God brings through the Messiah is proclaimed by a heavenly host of angels. It is a peace offered to all people, and the cost of this peace is borne by God alone through the death of his Son. As Talbert notes, God is the source of peace in "(a) the relation of persons and God, (b) the relation of persons with one another, (c) the relations of persons with the natural world, and (d) one's relation with oneself."[52] Jesus comes to incarnate and teach the way of peace (1:79), and ignoring it will bring inevitable destruction (19:42 – 44).

49. Ernest Barker, *From Alexander to Constantine: Passages and Documents Illustrating the History of the Social and Political Ideas 336 B.C. — A.D. 337* (Oxford: Clarendon, 1956), 211 – 12.

50. Wengst, *Pax Romana*, 12.

51. Ibid., 52.

52. Charles H. Talbert, *Reading Luke: A Literary and Theological Commentary on the Third Gospel* (Macon, GA: Smyth & Helwys, 2002), 34.

Tannehill also helpfully outlines how Jesus' reign will differ from that of the world's current superpower and the world of *Realpolitik*:

1. It will extend to "all flesh" (3:6) and include people who are excluded and on the margins for whatever reasons: purity, economic, or ethnic.
2. It will require "a new economy" that excludes the accumulation of wealth to eat, drink, and be merry while others starve. It is based on care for the poor.
3. It will require a different kind of leadership. "The leader is to have no more honor in the community than those who perform the lowliest functions."
4. It will require a new way of relating to others. It forbids vengeance and is controlled by the love of enemies instead of their subjugation or destruction (6:27 – 36).[53]

This is why the angels can announce "good news of great joy ... for all the people" (2:10).

Divine peace comes into the world filled with darkness to humans who are morally corrupt. It is evidence of God's goodwill toward humans. Goodwill is not a prerequisite to receive God's blessing, but divine peace can rest only on those who allow themselves to be transformed by God's blessing into humans of goodwill.

2. Christmas Fantasy versus the True Christmas

It may be unpopular to trespass on popular images associated with Christ's birth and to debunk myths, but it is theologically dangerous to allow the account of his birth to be hijacked by fiction. Christmas fables lure us to seasonal sentimentality and away from the year-round task of discipleship in which we are to deny ourselves and take up our crosses daily (9:23). They yield only superficial spirituality.

The fictional Christmas has been a long time in the making. It has been said that whoever (it is debated) wrote "'Twas the Night before Christmas" in 1822 changed the way Americans celebrate the holiday of Christmas. The poem manufactured the character who became Santa Claus by combining St. Nicholas Day (Dec. 6) with Christmas. In 1863, Thomas H. Nast drew a cartoon of Santa as a fat, jolly man with a white beard, who became the standard image. A Coca-Cola advertising campaign from the 1930s dressed Santa in red and white clothing.

The same kind of fictional development happened centuries ago in the popular conception of what happened at Christ's birth. *The Protevangelium of James*, an apocryphal, fictional account of Mary's and Jesus' birth, contributed mythical details. For example, it has Joseph as an older widower, Jesus' birth in a cave, and the midwife's astonishment that the Virgin Mary's hymen remained miraculously intact even after the birth.

53. Robert C. Tannehill, *The Shape of Luke's Story: Essays on Luke-Acts* (Eugene, OR: Cascade, 2005), 52 – 54.

The traditional date for the nativity may have been set to coincide with the celebration of the winter solstice in the pagan calendar set by the emperor Aurelean in AD 274, the day of the birth of "Sol Invictus," the "Unconquerable Sun."[54] It is possible that Christians, who identified Jesus as "the sun of righteousness" (Mal 4:2; Luke 1:78 – 79), may have been influenced by this dating. It is also possible, however, that a growing number of Christians celebrating the birth of Christ on this date may have influenced Aurelian to attempt to coopt the festival.[55] The straw and gentle animals surrounding the stall were an addition by St. Francis of Assisi.[56] We have since joined wise men (three) with the shepherds as visitors to the manger. The carol "The First Noel" has shepherds looking up and seeing a star "shining in the East beyond them far." We have since added a little drummer boy along with an assortment of angels.

The sentimental Christmas may be popular as a religious holiday for some because it can come off as celebrating the birth of a helpless baby. Jesus lies in a manger to be gazed upon and adored, but not to be heard and heeded. A speechless babe wrapped tightly in swaddling cloths seems more obliging in allowing people to tailor their religious beliefs however they see fit.

The commercial Christmas has been decried by many. Upton Sinclair wrote:

Or consider Christmas — could Satan in his most malignant mood have devised a worse combination of graft plus bunkum than the system whereby several hundred million people get a billion or so gifts for which they have no use, and some thousands of shop clerks die of exhaustion while selling them, and every other child in the Western world is made ill from overeating — all in the name of the lowly Jesus?[57]

True, many hear only the Christmas bells of cash registers ringing, accompanied by mawkish seasonal, secular music. Churches do not always help by competing for the entertainment spotlight. One church I know of boasts of their Christmas program's "pageantry, marvel, magic, and awe," and emphasizes that they have been "entertaining and inspiring audiences ... for more than 25 years."

The story of Christmas celebrates the fulfillment of God's promises and the incarnation of God in human flesh. That meaning is memorably captured by John 3:16. God loves, and God gives in order to save. Luke's birth narrative portrays the nature of divine power that gives itself to save. God does not appear as an all-powerful despot but as a vulnerable child. Paul blazons this profound paradox in Phil 2:6 – 8. For Christ, equality with God meant emptying himself, taking the form of a slave, who

54. See Oscar Cullmann, "The Origin of Christmas," in *The Early Church* (Philadelphia: Westminster, 1956), 21 – 36; and Susan K. Roll, *Toward the Origins of Christmas* (Kampen: Kok Pharos, 1995).

55. J. Neil Alexander, *Waiting for the Coming: The Liturgical Meaning of Advent, Christmas, Epiphany* (Washington, DC: Pastoral, 1993), 46 – 51.

56. Ben Witherington III, *The Indelible Image: The Theological and Ethical Thought World of the New Testament;* Vol. 1: *The Individual Witnesses* (Downers Grove, IL: InterVarsity Press, 2009), 687.

57. Upton Sinclair, *Money Writes!* (New York: Albert and Charles Boni, 1927), 23.

had no rights and owed obedience, humbling himself and dying a slave's death on the cross. It meant giving rather than getting, and Christ gave until he was empty; but his obedience led to an empty tomb and ultimate vindication that will culminate when throngs in heaven and on earth and under the earth, not just a host of angels, will bow down and sing glory in the highest to the One whose name is above every name.

The story of this poor couple subject to an oppressive empire prepares for Jesus' care for the poor and outcast. Christians express the true spirit of Christmas when they stop thinking only of themselves and instead reach out to others and relieve their loneliness, shine light in their darkness, and radiate the warmth of God's love to defrost their wintry existence. Christmas lives throughout the year when followers share the gift of the knowledge of salvation with others (1:77), give to those who beg out of their need (6:30; 11:41; 19:8), give the hungry something to eat (9:13), and proclaim that it is the Father's good pleasure to give the kingdom to those who believe and follow Christ (12:32).

Luke 2:22–40

Literary Context

The movement of Jesus' story is from Galilee to Jerusalem and the temple. In establishing the setting, the law is mentioned three times in 2:22–24, and Jesus' family's obedience to the law frames the unit (2:22, 39). As the birth was set against the background of imperial authority (2:1–2), the presentation of Jesus in the temple is set against the background of the law's authority.[1] Caesar's authority brings the family to Bethlehem (2:4); the law's authority brings them to Jerusalem, the first time the city is mentioned in the narrative. Following the pattern of step parallelism, Luke conveys his conviction that God's law is higher than the law of the emperor. What is first introduced as the law of Moses is referred to as "the law of the Lord" (2:23, 24, 39).

Main Idea

Jesus' coming into the world to fulfill God's promises to Israel will also bring salvation to Gentiles, but it will evoke a divided response in Israel and will result in their falling or rising.

Translation

(See next two pages.)

---

1. Coleridge, *The Birth of the Lukan Narrative*, 158; Hendrickx, *The Third Gospel*, 1:214.

Luke 2:22–40

Verse	Label	Text
2:22a	Circumstance	And when the days for their purification according to the law of Moses were fulfilled,
b		they brought him to Jerusalem to present him to the Lord,
23	Scriptural basis for the presentation	just as it stands written in the law of the Lord,
		"Every male opening the womb shall be called holy to the Lord"; (Exod 13:2, 12, 15) and
24	Scriptural basis for the purification	to give a sacrifice according to what is said in the law of the Lord,
		"a pair of doves or two young pigeons." (Lev 12:8)
25	Character introduction	And behold, a man by the name of Simeon was in Jerusalem,
		and this man was righteous and devout, waiting for the consolation of Israel,
		and the Holy Spirit was upon him.
26	Promise by the Holy Spirit	It had been made known to him by the Holy Spirit
		that he would not see death before he had seen the Lord's Christ.
27a	Direction by the Holy Spirit	He came in the Spirit into the temple complex,
b		and when the parents brought in the child Jesus
		to perform for him what was customary according to the law,
28	Blessing	he himself took him in his arms and blessed God and said,
29	Praise	*"Now, Master, you are dismissing your servant,*
		according to your word, in peace,
30	Cause	*because my eyes have seen your salvation,*
31	Amplification of cause	*which you have prepared in the presence of all peoples,*
32a		*a light for revelation to the Gentiles and*
b		*glory for your people Israel."*
33	Reaction: marveling	His father and mother were marveling over what was being spoken about him.

34a	Oracle	**And Simeon** **blessed them** and **said to Mary his mother,**
b		*"Behold, this one is set*
c		*for the falling and*
d		*rising of many in Israel and*
e		*[to be] a sign that is refused—*
35a		*and of yourself also, a sword will pierce the soul—*
b		*in order that the secret thoughts might be revealed out of many hearts."*
36	Character introduction	**And Anna a prophetess, the daughter of Phanuel from the tribe of Asher, was there.** **She was getting on in years,** having lived with her husband seven years from marriage and then
37		as a widow since then for eighty-four years. **She** **never left the temple** but **served [God] night and day fasting and praying.**
38	Chronological note / Praise	At that very hour, **she** **stood by** and **began** **to praise God publicly and** **to speak about [the child]** to all those waiting for the redemption of Jerusalem.
39a	Circumstance	When they had completed everything required by the law of the Lord,
b	Departure	**they returned to Galilee to their own town of Nazareth.**
40	Summary refrain	**The child grew and became strong, filled with wisdom, and the grace of God was upon him.**

Structure and Literary Form

The structure of the text presents a journey to the Jerusalem temple (2:22 – 24) that sets up an encounter with two witnesses, male (2:25 – 35) and female (2:36 – 38), declaring Jesus' special destiny. It concludes with a return journey and a summary of Jesus' maturation. It includes a mixture of forms, a hymnic oracle, and a prophecy.

Exegetical Outline

→ **I. Setting in the temple: obedience to the law of the Lord (2:22 – 24)**
 II. Greeting by Simeon (2:25 – 35)
  A. Introduction of Simeon (2:25 – 27)
   1. Righteous and devout and waiting for the consolation of Israel (2:25)
   2. Assured by the Holy Spirit to see the Messiah (2:26)
   3. Guided by the Holy Spirit (2:27)
  B. Hymn of praise (2:28 – 32)
   1. Jesus as the instrument of God's salvation (2:28 – 30)
   2. Universal reach of salvation (2:31 – 32)
    a. Light for the Gentiles (2:31 – 32a)
    b. Glory to Israel (2:32b)
  C. The parents' reaction of wonder (2:33)
  D. A divided response in Israel to God's salvation (2:34 – 35)
 III. Greeting by Anna (2:36 – 38)
  A. Introduction of Anna (2:36 – 37)
   1. A prophetess (2:36a)
   2. A devout, aged widow (2:36b – 37)
  B. Praise to God for the child to all looking for the redemption of Jerusalem (2:38)
 IV. Return to Nazareth (2:39)
 V. Refrain on the child's growth (2:40)

Explanation of the Text

2:22 – 24 And when the days for their purification according to the law of Moses were fulfilled, they brought him to Jerusalem to present him to the Lord, just as it stands written in the law of the Lord, "Every male opening the womb is holy to the Lord"; and to give a sacrifice according to what is said in the law of the Lord, "a pair of doves or two young pigeons" (καὶ ὅτε ἐπλήσθησαν αἱ ἡμέραι τοῦ καθαρισμοῦ αὐτῶν κατὰ τὸν νόμον Μωϋσέως, ἀνήγαγον αὐτὸν εἰς Ἰεροσόλυμα παραστῆσαι τῷ κυρίῳ, καθὼς γέγραπται ἐν νόμῳ κυρίου ὅτι πᾶν ἄρσεν διανοῖγον μήτραν ἅγιον τῷ κυρίῳ κληθήσεται, καὶ τοῦ δοῦναι θυσίαν κατὰ τὸ εἰρημένον ἐν τῷ νόμῳ κυρίου, ζεῦγος τρυγόνων ἢ δύο νοσσοὺς περιστερῶν). The infancy story is filled with evidence of the pious observance of the law, and Jesus' parents are shown to be as obedient to the authority of Moses as they were to the authority of Augustus.[2] The family travels to Jerusalem to fulfill religious obligations that are presented chiastically:

A Mary's purification (v. 22a)

   B Jesus' presentation as the firstborn
     to God (v. 22b)

   B´ Scriptural basis for the presentation (v. 23)

A´ Scriptural basis for the purification (v. 24)

Since only the mother had to undergo rites of purification (Lev 12:1 – 8), why mention that it was for "their" (αὐτῶν) purification?[3] Luke presents it as "a family matter"[4] probably because he does not want the spotlight to fall solely on Mary. What is of key importance in this account is the reaction to the presence of Jesus in the temple. The actual rites have little significance, so Luke does not feel it is incumbent on him to be pedantically precise in explaining the rites to his readers.

The law is mentioned, though it did not require the presentation of the child in the temple. The basis for the presentation of Jesus as the firstborn is found in Exod 13:2, 12, 15. The point is driven home again that they are obedient, and it does not matter what command they obey. Luke identifies the sacrifice for Mary's purification, a "pair of doves or two young pigeons," which derives from Lev 12:8 (see Lev 5:11). One can infer from this option that Joseph cannot afford a lamb. But Luke says nothing about the parents paying for the redemption of the firstborn (Num 18:15 – 16). Bovon asserts it is because Jesus is already "holy" (Luke 1:35) and belongs to God: "He has no need to be redeemed. Thus he can fulfill the λύτρωσις ('redemption') of Israel."[5]

2:25 And behold, a man by the name of Simeon was in Jerusalem, and this man was righteous and devout waiting for the consolation of Israel, and the Holy Spirit was upon him (καὶ ἰδοὺ ἄνθρωπος ἦν ἐν Ἰερουσαλὴμ ᾧ ὄνομα Συμεών, καὶ ὁ ἄνθρωπος οὗτος δίκαιος καὶ εὐλαβής, προσδεχόμενος παράκλησιν τοῦ Ἰσραήλ, καὶ πνεῦμα ἦν ἅγιον ἐπ᾽ αὐτόν). Simeon is another of God's faithful servants (1:38). Luke highlights his piety and then mentions that the power of the Spirit was (ἦν, imperfect tense) upon him. "Holy Spirit" (πνεῦμα … ἅγιον) is anarthrous, but for Luke it is *the* Holy Spirit who gives Simeon divine direction.[6] Zechariah and Elizabeth were identified for being righteous. Only later did the Holy Spirit come upon them so that they could prophesy and praise God. Simeon is able to prophesy now because of the Holy Spirit.

There were many other pious people in the temple, but piety alone is not enough to bring recognition of the nature of this child. What is new is that Luke presents the Holy Spirit directing Simeon's actions, not just his speech. The old man has not been parked in the temple on a lookout for the Messiah. The Spirit is the impetus leading him to the temple at this particular moment (v. 27, "he came in the Spirit into the temple complex" (ἦλθεν ἐν τῷ πνεύματι εἰς τὸ ἱερόν).

"The consolation of Israel" (παράκλησιν τοῦ Ἰσραήλ) is grounded in the images of comfort for forlorn Israel in Isa 40:1; 49:13; 51:3; 61:2; 66:13. Israel would find comfort from "glory for … Israel" (Luke 2:32), the restoration of the kingdom to Israel (Acts 1:6), and the repentance and forgiveness of sins of Israel (Acts 5:31). It foreshadows Paul's statement in Acts 28:20 near the conclusion

---

2. Coleridge, *The Birth of the Lukan Narrative*, 158.

3. The variant reading "hers" (αὐτῆς) apparently is a scribal attempt to make the text conform to the ritual purification prescribed in the law.

4. Nolland, *Luke*, 1:117.

5. Bovon, *Luke 1:1 – 9:50*, 107.

6. Brown, *The Birth of the Messiah*, 438.

of Luke's work: "because of the hope of Israel ... I am bound with this chain."

2:26 – 29 It had been made known to him by the Holy Spirit that he would not see death before he had seen the Lord's Christ. He came in the Spirit into the temple complex, and when the parents brought in the child Jesus to perform for him what was customary according to the law, he himself took him in his arms and blessed God and said, "Now, Master, you are dismissing your servant, according to your word, in peace" (καὶ ἦν αὐτῷ κεχρηματισμένον ὑπὸ τοῦ πνεύματος τοῦ ἁγίου μὴ ἰδεῖν θάνατον πρὶν [ἢ] ἂν ἴδῃ τὸν Χριστὸν κυρίου. καὶ ἦλθεν ἐν τῷ πνεύματι εἰς τὸ ἱερόν· καὶ ἐν τῷ εἰσαγαγεῖν τοὺς γονεῖς τὸ παιδίον Ἰησοῦν τοῦ ποιῆσαι αὐτοὺς κατὰ τὸ εἰθισμένον τοῦ νόμου περὶ αὐτοῦ καὶ αὐτὸς ἐδέξατο αὐτὸ εἰς τὰς ἀγκάλας καὶ εὐλόγησεν τὸν θεὸν καὶ εἶπεν· νῦν ἀπολύεις τὸν δοῦλόν σου, δέσποτα, κατὰ τὸ ῥῆμά σου ἐν εἰρήνῃ). Unlike the previous hymns of Mary and Zechariah that refer to God in the third person, Simeon addresses God directly in the second person. His outburst of praise to God begins with "now" (νῦν), placed first in the clause for emphasis, and Luke again sounds the note that the day that God's people have longed for has now arrived (1:48; 2:11). God has fulfilled the promise made to him personally that he would not see death before seeing the Messiah. The Holy Spirit made a promise and "effects its fulfillment."[7] More importantly, God has fulfilled the promise made to *Israel* that will engage *all* people, another *leitmotif* in the infancy narrative.

"You are dismissing your servant ... in peace" (ἀπολύεις τὸν δοῦλόν σου ... ἐν εἰρήνῃ) is a euphemism for Simeon's death (see Gen 15:15; Tob 3:6, 13; 2 Macc 7:9). Simeon is so overjoyed by the presence of God's salvation that he is now ready to

die. Or, he may refer to his dismissal from watchful service.[8] Whichever it is, he fulfills his role as one who can interpret for others what this child means in God's salvation plan even though he will not live to see it carried out.

2:30 – 32 "Because my eyes have seen your salvation, which you have prepared in the presence of all peoples, a light for revelation to the Gentiles and glory for the people of Israel" (ὅτι εἶδον οἱ ὀφθαλμοί μου τὸ σωτήριόν σου, ὃ ἡτοίμασας κατὰ πρόσωπον πάντων τῶν λαῶν, φῶς εἰς ἀποκάλυψιν ἐθνῶν καὶ δόξαν λαοῦ σου Ἰσραήλ). Simeon does not praise the child but what God will do through the child he holds in his arms. Through Jesus, God will bring salvation. Under the impulse of the Holy Spirit, Simeon sees salvation extending beyond the nation of Israel to include Gentiles. The citation from Isa 49:6 that follows picks up on the themes in Isaiah promising salvation (see also Isa 40:5; 42:6; 52:9 – 10).

2:33 – 35 His father and mother were marveling over what was being spoken about him. And Simeon blessed them and said to Mary his mother, "Behold, this one is set for the falling and rising of many in Israel and [to be] a sign that is refused — and of yourself also, a sword will pierce the soul — in order that the secret thoughts might be revealed out of many hearts" (καὶ ἦν ὁ πατὴρ αὐτοῦ καὶ ἡ μήτηρ θαυμάζοντες ἐπὶ τοῖς λαλουμένοις περὶ αὐτοῦ. καὶ εὐλόγησεν αὐτοὺς Συμεὼν καὶ εἶπεν πρὸς Μαριὰμ τὴν μητέρα αὐτοῦ· ἰδοὺ οὗτος κεῖται εἰς πτῶσιν καὶ ἀνάστασιν πολλῶν ἐν τῷ Ἰσραὴλ καὶ εἰς σημεῖον ἀντιλεγόμενον — καὶ σοῦ [δὲ] αὐτῆς τὴν ψυχὴν διελεύσεται ῥομφαία — ὅπως ἂν ἀποκαλυφθῶσιν ἐκ πολλῶν καρδιῶν διαλογισμοί). Simeon rains on the parade of messianic exultation that has pulsed through the narrative thus far. He provides

---

7. Bovon, *Luke 1:1 – 9:50*, 100.   8. Green, *The Gospel of Luke*, 147.

the first ominous hint that opposition will arise against Jesus and there will be judgment against Israel. When Jesus reveals the "secret thoughts," the people will be narrow-minded and intolerant. One particularly sore point that will evoke hostility will be the "breadth of the hospitality God" offered to sinners, outcasts, Samaritans, and Gentiles.[9]

The metaphor of a sword piercing through Mary's soul is difficult to decipher. It may refer to the pain of witnessing her son's rejection. Others draw on the image of the sword in Ezekiel used for judgment (Ezek 5:1–2, 6:8–9; 12:14–16; 14:17) and interpret it to mean that Mary will be tested like the rest of Israel.[10] As one aligned with Jesus, who will be opposed, Mary will also be opposed (Ps 22:20; Zech 12:10; 13:7).[11] Bovon comments, "The Messiah, now present (vv. 26, 30), will be a suffering Messiah (Luke 9:22; Acts 26:23), and his mother will partake of his sorrows."[12] Luke does not report the parents' reaction to Simeon's words. It allows the readers to ponder their significance as Mary pondered the shepherds' words (2:19).

2:36–38 And Anna a prophetess, the daughter of Phanuel from the tribe of Asher, was there. She was getting on in years, having lived with her husband seven years from her marriage and then as a widow since then for eighty-four years. She never left the temple but served [God] night and day fasting and praying. At that very hour, she stood by and began to praise God publicly and to speak about [the child] to all those waiting for the redemption of Jerusalem (καὶ ἦν Ἄννα προφῆτις, θυγάτηρ Φανουήλ, ἐκ φυλῆς Ἀσήρ· αὕτη προβεβηκυῖα ἐν ἡμέραις πολλαῖς, ζήσασα μετὰ ἀνδρὸς ἔτη ἑπτὰ ἀπὸ τῆς παρθενίας αὐτῆς

καὶ αὐτὴ χήρα ἕως ἐτῶν ὀγδοήκοντα τεσσάρων, ἣ οὐκ ἀφίστατο τοῦ ἱεροῦ νηστείαις καὶ δεήσεσιν λατρεύουσα νύκτα καὶ ἡμέραν. καὶ αὐτῇ τῇ ὥρᾳ ἐπιστᾶσα ἀνθωμολογεῖτο τῷ θεῷ καὶ ἐλάλει περὶ αὐτοῦ πᾶσιν τοῖς προσδεχομένοις λύτρωσιν Ἰερουσαλήμ). The testimony of Simeon and Anna comprise a complimentary pair of witnesses. Anna's name is spelled the same in Greek as Hannah, the mother of Samuel (1 Sam 1:2). The Scripture identifies Miriam (Exod 15:20), Deborah (Judg 4:4), Huldah (2 Kgs 22:14), and Isaiah's wife (Isa 8:3) as female prophets, but the rabbis add to the list Sarah, Hannah, Abigail, and Esther (*b. Meg.* 16a).

If Anna were married at age twelve or fourteen, plus the seven years of marriage and the eighty-four years lived as a widow, she would be one hundred three to one hundred five years old. The latter is the age of Judith (Jdt 16:23), who also served God night and day as a widow (Jdt 8:1–8; 11:17).

Green states, "Fasting constitutes a form of protest, an assertion that all is not well."[13] Combined with constant prayer, they are supplications for God to bring about the redemption of Jerusalem (see Ps 130:5–8). Anna represents the physically and spiritually hungry whom God promises to fill with good things (1:53).[14] God speaks through her to proclaim the messianic role of Jesus to all those "waiting for the redemption of Jerusalem." This phrase is synonymous with "the consolation of Israel" (2:25). Jerusalem gets special attention in Luke, "thirty references to Jerusalem by name, more than the sum of those in Matthew (twelve) and Mark (eleven) together," and sixty more in Acts.[15] Jerusalem's consolation is tied to its reception of Jesus (19:41–44).

---

9. Byrne, *The Hospitality of God*, 36.

10. Brown, *The Birth of the Messiah*, 463–65.

11. Nolland, *Luke*, 1:121.

12. Bovon, *Luke 1:1–9:50*, 105.

13. Green, *The Gospel of Luke*, 151.

14. Heil, *The Meal Scenes in Luke-Acts*, 16.

15. Peter Doble, *The Paradox of Salvation: Luke's Theology of the Cross* (SNTSMS 87; Cambridge: Cambridge Univ. Press, 1996), 216.

2:39 – 40 When they had completed everything required by the law of the Lord, they returned to Galilee to their own town of Nazareth. The child grew and became strong, filled with wisdom, and the grace of God was upon him (καὶ ὡς ἐτέλεσαν πάντα τὰ κατὰ τὸν νόμον κυρίου, ἐπέστρεψαν εἰς τὴν Γαλιλαίαν εἰς πόλιν ἑαυτῶν Ναζαρέθ. τὸ δὲ παιδίον ηὔξανεν καὶ ἐκραταιοῦτο πληρούμενον σοφίᾳ, καὶ χάρις θεοῦ ἦν ἐπʼ αὐτό). The family returns home to resume their lives, and Luke provides the briefest summary of Jesus' maturation in a refrain that will be repeated in 2:52. The unit began with an emphasis on obedience to the law of Moses (2:22) and ends with a note that "the grace of God was upon him [Jesus]."

Luke's summary refrain is not as bold as John's, "For the law was given through Moses; grace and truth came through Jesus Christ" (John 1:17), but it does establish a similar tone from the outset of the narrative. The grace of God upon Jesus will be poured out into the lives of others as he bestows on them the forgiveness, renewal, freedom, power, healing, peace, and hope that the law of Moses could not provide. The grace of God was upon Jesus, but his sacrifice in giving his life will make it possible for all of his followers to enjoy God's favor (Rom 5:1 – 2; 1 Cor 1:4). This grace is the fulfillment of what the prophets prophesied and angels longed to see (1 Pet 1:10 – 12).

Theology in Application

1. The Transition from the Law to Christ

The obedience of Jesus' family to the law is mentioned three times in this passage. The Holy Spirit is mentioned three times in directing Simeon's meeting with the family, which is followed by his hymn of praise and prophecy. Luke goes out of his way to show the continuity between the old and the new — the law, prophecy, and the gospel. This narrative illustrates Paul's statement: "But when the set time had fully come, God sent his Son, born of a woman, born under the law, to redeem those under the law, that we might receive adoption to sonship" (Gal 4:4 – 5).

This undercurrent in the infancy narrative that shows Jesus' family as being obedient to Caesar and faithful to the Mosaic law fits the defense of Christianity personified in the trials of Paul in Acts. Paul was accused of being a rabble-rouser, intent on causing social unrest throughout the world as an enemy of Roman law and order (Acts 18:6; 21:38; 22:25 – 29; 25:8). As with one voice, the officials ruled that Paul had done nothing to merit prison or death under Roman law (18:14 – 15; 19:37; 23:28 – 29; 25:25; 26:31 – 32; 28:18). Paul also was charged with religious disloyalty: teaching against the law (18:13; 21:21, 28), the Jewish people (21:28), Jewish customs (21:21), and the temple (21:28). These charges were proven false. He was not a renegade Jew but was in chains because of his dedication to "the hope of Israel" (28:20). Christianity and its first followers were rooted in God's law (see 22:12; 24:14), but the coming of Jesus brings a transition to something new. As Songer avers:

> The reality of this revelation is causing the regularity of the cult and the significance of the law to pale into subordinance before the loftier divine plan; yet there remains

those who are unable to perceive the new reality and who will in their devotion to the old patterns ultimately oppose the new as irregular and even destructive. Luke points out, however, that the old patterns are carefully observed because it is out of the divinely appointed cult and law that the new movement emerges; and this emergence is God's will — a circumstance which implies that the old has served its function and is fulfilled by the new which should replace it.[16]

The law required that the firstborn must be redeemed, and Jesus' parents present him in the temple to fulfill that obligation. Moessner draws out the theological significance that will result in a transition from the temple cult to Paul's view that Christ's sacrifice redeems those under the law: "in the opening of the third gospel, Jesus is presented to the Lord with a sacrifice of redemption as the firstborn of Israel; in the 'end,' Jesus presents himself to the Lord as a sacrifice for the redemption of Israel and all the nations."[17]

While obedience to the ceremonial law is not denigrated in this passage, it can lead to a tendency to focus on outer forms, proper performance of rites, proper religious attire, proper oversight, and the proper people with whom to associate. That can lead to a spiritless formalism, cold smugness, and indifference to the welfare of others, and the narrative in Luke offers many examples of how this plays out. An emphasis on the ethical and spiritual, which characterizes Jesus' teaching, leads to growth in grace and love for God and others.

2. The Falling and Rising of Many in Israel

Simeon's oracle foreshadows threatening and promising developments: the fall and rise of many in Israel. Bovon claims that "the falling" applies to the first of Luke's two volumes; the rising, to the second.[18] In the first volume, the people rejected Christ and crucified him (23:13 – 25; Acts 2:23, 36; 4:10). In the second volume, Israel is restored (Acts 15:15 – 17). That restoration will include Gentiles. Both Israel and the Gentiles are "parallel beneficiaries of the salvation which is offered in the name of Jesus" (Acts 9:15; 11:15; 14:1; 15:9, 16 – 18; 18:4, 20; 19:10, 17; 26:17 – 18, 23).[19]

But in Acts, every time the gospel is preached to Jews, it creates a divided response. It does not meet with wholesale repentance or wholesale rejection. They fall if they trip over the stone of stumbling (Isa 8:14; Luke 20:17 – 18; Acts 4:11; Rom 9:32 – 33; 1 Cor 1:23; 1 Pet 2:7 – 8). They rise if they receive him as Simeon does, and if they come to him and "like living stones" allow themselves to be "built into a spiritual house to be a holy priesthood, offering spiritual sacrifices acceptable to God through Jesus Christ" (1 Pet 2:4 – 5). The story in Luke and Acts is not about

16. Harold S. Songer, "Luke's Portrayal of the Origins of Jesus," *RevExp* 64 (1967): 463.

17. Moessner, "Reading Luke's Gospel as Ancient Hellenis-

tic Narrative," 151.

18. Bovon, *Luke 1:1 – 9:50*, 104.

19. Nolland, *Luke*, 1:120.

the tragedy of Israel's rejection as the people of God, although some Jews do reject the hope of Israel and thereby cast themselves off from the people. But many Jews do respond and become the light to the Gentiles that God created them to be.

This is how this salvation brings glory to Israel. Israel will serve as the mediator of the promise and its fulfillment. The tragedy is that Israel became a light to the nations with an intensity that sometimes blinded those who were nearest to it. The result is that "those who reject Jesus fall from the people of salvation history who form the true Israel."[20]

Caird makes a valid observation that everyone will fall, even Jesus' closest, most devoted followers, before they can or will rise.[21] Jesus' disciples will be humbled by their failure. Falling then can be interpreted as the condition from which one can be raised. Examples of this are the fallen Zacchaeus, the fallen thief on the cross next to Jesus, and the fallen Peter. In their recognition of their fallen condition, they are most ready to be raised up by their Lord. Conversion is often the deepest when we are at our lowest.

---

20. O'Toole, *The Unity of Luke's Theology*, 18.

21. G. B. Caird, *Saint Luke* (PNTC; London: Penguin, 1963), 64.

Luke 2:41 – 52

Literary Context

From angels and from humans Luke has presented testimony about who Jesus is and what his future role is — from Mary and Zechariah, lowly shepherds, and the godly Israelites Simeon and Anna. In this episode, the revelation comes directly from Jesus. It contains the first words spoken by him in the gospel. He announces and accepts his divine vocation as one placed under a divine necessity.

Main Idea

Because of his scripturally defined messianic consciousness and his special relationship to the Father, Jesus understands his life as framed by divine mandates, which he must obey.

Translation

(See next page.)

Luke 2:41–52

| 2:41 | Circumstance | Now **his parents went every year to Jerusalem to the Feast of Passover.** |

2:41 Circumstance Now **his parents went every year to Jerusalem to the Feast of Passover.**

42 Circumstance And   when he was twelve years old,
they went up according to the feast's custom.

43 When they completed the days, while they returned,
the boy Jesus remained in Jerusalem
and his parents did not know it.

44a Supposition Thinking that he was in the caravan,
b Action based on supposition **they   went a day's journey** and
began searching for him among their relatives and acquaintances.

45a Circumstance When they did not find him,
b Action based on realization **they returned to Jerusalem to search for him.**

46a Circumstance After three days,
they found him in the temple,
b sitting in the midst of the teachers and
listening to them and
asking them questions.

47 Reaction: astonishment **All those who heard him were astounded by his understanding and his ↵ answers.**

48 Exclamation When his parents saw him,
they were shocked,
and his mother said to him,
"Child, why did you do this to us?
Look, your father and I have been in anguish searching for you!"

49 Response with a question **And he said to them,**
"Why were you searching for me?
Did you not know that it is necessary for me to be in my Father's house?"

50 Lack of understanding But **they did not understand this word that he spoke to them.**

51 Circumstance **Then he went down with them and came to Nazareth and was obedient to ↵ them.**

His mother was treasuring all these events in her heart.
52 Summary refrain And **Jesus continued to advance in wisdom and in stature and in favor with ↵ God and humans.**

Structure and Literary Form

The episode is framed by two journeys from Nazareth to Jerusalem and back. In between, the supposition of Jesus' parents that he was with their traveling party when they first returned home left Jesus in Jerusalem for three days. The subsequent search finds him among the teachers in the temple. His parents' distress leads to Jesus' climactic pronouncement in 2:49, making this a pronouncement story. The episode and the infancy narrative conclude with a summary refrain about Jesus' maturation into manhood.

Exegetical Outline

➡ **I. Journey to Jerusalem for the Passover (2:41 – 42)**

  II. Losing Jesus on the way home (2:43 – 45)

  III. Finding Jesus in the temple (2:45 – 50)

    A. Search for Jesus (2:45)

    B. Jesus as a young sensation among teachers (2:46 – 47)

    C. Jesus' disclosure of his self-understanding of his divine calling (2:48 – 50)

  IV. Journey back to Nazareth (2:51)

  V. Summary of Jesus' growth in wisdom, maturity, and favor (2:52)

Explanation of the Text

2:41 Now his parents went every year to Jerusalem to the Feast of Passover (καὶ ἐπορεύοντο οἱ γονεῖς αὐτοῦ κατ᾽ ἔτος εἰς Ἰερουσαλὴμ τῇ ἑορτῇ τοῦ πάσχα). Luke again emphasizes the piety of Jesus' family, who trekked every year to Jerusalem to celebrate the Passover. The law required the attendance of adult males at three feasts a year (Exod 23:14 – 17; 34:23; Deut 16:16), but the poor could not always go. The Passover Feast was most apropos as the setting for this event. It commemorated God's deliverance of Israel from Egypt when the angel of death "struck down all the firstborn in Egypt" (Exod 12:29) but passed over the congregation of Israel, who had smeared the blood of a sacrificed lamb on their doorposts (Exod 12; Heb 11:28). Jesus has been identified and presented as the firstborn (2:7, 23), but in the next recorded celebration of Passover at the end of the gospel,

the destroyer will not pass over this firstborn Son, who will die on a cross. His death will lead to a greater liberation.

2:42 And when he was twelve years old, they went up according to the feast's custom (καὶ ὅτε ἐγένετο ἐτῶν δώδεκα, ἀναβαινόντων αὐτῶν κατὰ τὸ ἔθος τῆς ἑορτῆς). The age of twelve was regarded as the age of discernment. In the Jewish tradition a boy became a man at age thirteen and was fully responsible for keeping the law.[1] By portraying the young Jesus making his way from Nazareth in Galilee to Jerusalem, Luke anticipates the journey motif in Jesus' public ministry when he sets his face to go to Jerusalem, which ends when he arrives for the Passover and spends several days teaching in the temple to enthralled crowds (9:51 – 22:38).

---

1. Schweizer, *Luke*, 63. According to Josephus, Samuel began to act as a prophet at age twelve and was called by God (*Ant.* 5.10.4 §348), and Josiah began his reform when he was twelve, showing his "piety" and "wisdom and discernment" (*Ant.* 10.4.1 §§50 – 51).

2:43 – 44 When they completed the days, while they returned, the boy Jesus remained in Jerusalem and his parents did not know it. Thinking that he was in the caravan, they went a day's journey and began searching for him among their relatives and acquaintances (καὶ τελειωσάντων τὰς ἡμέρας, ἐν τῷ ὑποστρέφειν αὐτοὺς ὑπέμεινεν Ἰησοῦς ὁ παῖς ἐν Ἰερουσαλήμ, καὶ οὐκ ἔγνωσαν οἱ γονεῖς αὐτοῦ. νομίσαντες δὲ αὐτὸν εἶναι ἐν τῇ συνοδίᾳ ἦλθον ἡμέρας ὁδὸν καὶ ἀνεζήτουν αὐτὸν ἐν τοῖς συγγενεῦσιν καὶ τοῖς γνωστοῖς). The family mistakenly assumed that Jesus was with their traveling party because they took for granted that he would be taken care of by the community, which became an extended family. The time lapse before they discovered his absence allowed Jesus time to make an impression in the temple. Luke does not tell us why Jesus tarried in Jerusalem until he utters his climactic pronouncement to his parents.

2:45 – 46 When they did not find him, they returned to Jerusalem to search for him. After three days, they found him in the temple, sitting in the midst of the teachers and listening to them and asking them questions (καὶ μὴ εὑρόντες ὑπέστρεψαν εἰς Ἰερουσαλὴμ ἀναζητοῦντες αὐτόν. καὶ ἐγένετο μετὰ ἡμέρας τρεῖς εὗρον αὐτὸν ἐν τῷ ἱερῷ καθεζόμενον ἐν μέσῳ τῶν διδασκάλων καὶ ἀκούοντα αὐτῶν καὶ ἐπερωτῶντα αὐτούς). "After three days" (μετὰ ἡμέρας τρεῖς) would include travel from Jerusalem on the first day and not finding Jesus that night, returning back to Jerusalem on the second, and finding him on the third day. Discovering him in this setting reveals his devotion to learning. Jesus is perhaps joining the teachers on the temple terrace that bordered the sanctuary. The anxious parents are hit with a double surprise: that he did not leave with them but stayed in the temple precincts, and that he is not only soaking up the teaching of these sages but engaged in dialogue with them. One may presume that Jesus and the teachers are absorbed with the task of discerning God's will by discussing matters of Scripture and tradition.[2]

2:47 All those who heard him were astounded by his understanding and his answers (ἐξίσταντο δὲ πάντες οἱ ἀκούοντες αὐτοῦ ἐπὶ τῇ συνέσει καὶ ταῖς ἀποκρίσεσιν αὐτοῦ). Jesus' understanding is demonstrated by his answers, which reveal "insight nourished by religious faith."[3] Early on, Jesus is demonstrated to be an insightful interpreter of Scripture. This prowess is vital to his besting the devil in the wilderness, his refutation of the Pharisees and Sadducees in each of his confrontations with them, and his interpretation of his ministry and death after his resurrection (24:25 – 27, 44 – 49). The readers will recognize that his understanding comes from being more than simply a precocious child; he is the Son of God.

2:48 When his parents saw him, they were shocked, and his mother said to him, "Child, why did you do this to us? Look, your father and I have been in anguish searching for you!" (καὶ ἰδόντες αὐτὸν ἐξεπλάγησαν, καὶ εἶπεν πρὸς αὐτὸν ἡ μήτηρ αὐτοῦ, τέκνον, τί ἐποίησας ἡμῖν οὕτως; ἰδοὺ ὁ πατήρ σου κἀγὼ ὀδυνώμενοι ἐζητοῦμέν σε). As a natural reaction to the trauma they have undergone in searching for their missing child, his mother rebukes him for breaching his filial responsibility to them. They may have been shocked to see him huddling with this learned assembly of teachers. He is not sitting on the sidelines in awed silence but in the thick of the conversation, presumably about the interpretation of Scripture. Their distress at the loss of Jesus and

---

2. Pieter W. van der Horst, "Notes on the Aramaic Background of Luke II 41 – 52," *JSNT* 7 (1980): 63 – 64.

3. Bovon, *Luke 1:1 – 9:50*, 112.

their discovery of him on the third day in his Father's house may hint of the resurrection. Wright argues:

> Luke intends the reader to understand the whole gospel, not just the final chapter, as the story of the resurrection, so that when Easter actually happens there will be a rightness, an appropriateness about it. It will not be a strange "happy ending" tacked on to the end of the story about something else, but the god-given [sic], scripture-fulfilling completion of what had been true all along.[4]

2:49 – 50 And he said to them, "Why were you searching for me? Did you not know that it is necessary for me to be in my Father's house?" But they did not understand this word that he spoke to them (καὶ εἶπεν πρὸς αὐτούς· τί ὅτι ἐζητεῖτέ με; οὐκ ᾔδειτε ὅτι ἐν τοῖς τοῦ πατρός μου δεῖ εἶναί με; καὶ αὐτοὶ οὐ συνῆκαν τὸ ῥῆμα ὃ ἐλάλησεν αὐτοῖς). The question "Why were you searching for me?" is a strange one. The phrasing of the question "Did you not know?" in Greek (with οὐκ) expects the answer "Yes," they did know. Previously, others have interpreted the meaning of events concerning Jesus. From now on, he will interpret what they mean.

The phrase "in my Father's house" (ἐν τοῖς τοῦ πατρός μου) reads literally "in the ... of my Father" with no corresponding noun for the definite article (τοῖς). The translation "in my Father's house" (see 6:4; 19:46) is chosen because it makes best sense of the temple context: "You should have known where to find me — where God my Father lives."[5] Brown cites biblical examples of such phrasing in Job 18:19 (LXX), "Strangers will dwell in his place" [ἐν τοῖς αὐτοῦ]," and Esth 7:9, "A gallows have been set up in the premises of Aman [ἐν τοῖς Ἀμαν]." Josephus also has a parallel, "in the place [temple] of Zeus [ἐν τοῖς τοῦ Διός]" (Ag. Ap. 1.18 §118). This interpretation also has the support of the Syriac, Armenian, and Persian versions, and the Greek and Latin church fathers.[6]

Another option is to interpret the "missing noun" as a noun of activity, which would be translated, "In [or about] the things [affairs] of my Father" (see 20:25 for similar usage). Jesus' response implies that his parents should have known he would be involved in discussing the law.[7] This translation is supported by the Ethiopic, Arabic, Coptic, and Latin versions. Nolland rejects this interpretation because being "involved in the affairs of God provides little basis for finding him, nor is it carried through in terms of a continuing independence for Jesus from this point on."[8]

Luke may have chosen deliberately ambiguous language.[9] It makes sense that his parents should have looked for him in the most likely locale in Jerusalem, the temple. But the verb "it is necessary" (δεῖ) in Luke applies to the unfolding of God's plan (4:43; 9:22; 13:33; 17:25; 22:37; 24:7, 26, 44), to which Jesus submits. While it makes most sense in the context of this episode for Jesus to be referring to the temple, it leaves itself open to a more subtle application. His teaching in the temple prefigures the teaching ministry of Jesus. The next time he teaches in the temple (19:45 – 21:38), his teaching will precipitate his death.

After all the events that have occurred — his conception, his birth, his presentation in the temple — his parents should know that as God's Son he would begin to play out his role in the

4. N. T. Wright, *The Resurrection of the Son of God* (Minneapolis: Fortress, 2003), 436.

5. Evans, *St. Luke*, 426.

6. Brown, *The Birth of the Messiah*, 475 – 76.

7. Henk J. De Jonge, ""Sonship, Wisdom, Infancy: Luke II.41 – 51a," *NTS* 24 (1977 – 78): 331 – 37.

8. Nolland, *Luke*, 1:132.

9. Dennis D. Sylva, "The Cryptic Clause *en tois tou patros mou dei einai me* in Lk 2:49b," *ZNW* 78 (1987): 132 – 40.

divine plan for which he was sent. It is this aspect that his parents do not yet comprehend. The short comment about their lack of understanding shows how difficult it is to grasp who Jesus is. Even those who experienced firsthand the miraculous events surrounding his birth cannot get their minds completely around it. His rejection and crucifixion will be even harder to penetrate.

2:51 – 52   Then he went down with them and came to Nazareth and was obedient to them. His mother was treasuring all these events in her heart. And Jesus continued to advance in wisdom and in stature and in favor with God and humans (καὶ κατέβη μετ᾿ αὐτῶν καὶ ἦλθεν εἰς Ναζαρέθ, καὶ ἦν ὑποτασσόμενος αὐτοῖς. καὶ ἡ μήτηρ αὐτοῦ διετήρει πάντα τὰ ῥήματα ἐν τῇ καρδίᾳ αὐτῆς. καὶ Ἰησοῦς προέκοπτεν [ἐν τῇ] σοφίᾳ καὶ ἡλικίᾳ καὶ χάριτι παρὰ θεῷ καὶ ἀνθρώποις). Jesus' obedience to his parents makes it clear that this previous incident was not a case of adolescent rebellion. Again, Luke informs us that Mary treasures these things in her heart (see 2:19). She is open to understanding what it all means, but full comprehension has not yet been given to her.

The noun translated "stature" (ἡλικίᾳ) can apply to age (12:25) or stature (19:3). Luke is summarizing Jesus' growth into manhood (see 1 Sam 2:21, 26). Jesus knows himself to be God's Son, but advancing in wisdom suggests that he must grow in his understanding of his role. This understanding and commitment will be put to a severe test by the devil (4:1 – 13).

Theology in Application

1. God as Jesus' Father

The focus of this episode is Jesus' response to his distressed parents as they discover him among the learned teachers in the temple. In this encounter, Luke unpacks "something of the complexity of the relationships between his identity as the Son of God and as son in the family of Joseph."[10] Coleridge notes, "The initiative in the interpretative task passes at this point from angels and inspired human characters to Jesus. This is another way of saying that it passes from God to Jesus, since though he has chosen to work through angels and the Holy Spirit it has been God who held the initiative."[11]

Jesus reveals his unique relationship to God as his Father long before he begins his ministry. He also reveals that his life requires obedience to more than earthly parents. "The grace of God ... upon him" (2:40) brings the task that God gives to him. Jesus understands his life to be controlled by divine mandates, which he will obey. His obedience to his heavenly Father must come before obedience to earthly parents or earthly authorities. As Nave recognizes, "From the very beginning Jesus indicated that there was a divine necessity compelling his every action, and nothing would get

---

10. Nolland, *Luke*, 1:131.   11. Coleridge, *The Birth of the Lukan Narrative*, 208.

in the way of his submitting to that divine necessity."[12] This incident makes clear that Jesus has a Father other than Joseph whom he must obey, even if it will cause pain to his parents. Mary will have to lose the child given to her by God to gain him as her Savior. This obedience to his heavenly Father will be put to the test and exhibited in the temptation story.

2. Jesus as Fully Human

The concluding verse of the infancy narrative (2:52) balances the special importance given to Jesus' miraculous divine conception in the previous episodes by emphasizing his full humanity. He did not come into the world with a brain fully programmed, as if he were a divine robot. He must develop and reach maturity as any other human must do. He will grow physically, mentally, and spiritually and will need to pray, as the psalmist did, to know God's ways, to be led by God, and to be taught God's truth.

The danger in church history has been to go to extremes in Christology by either elevating the divine dimension of Jesus' nature to the exclusion of his human nature or discounting the divine dimension to make him only human. The *Infancy Gospel of Thomas* is guilty of the first error with its pious fiction about Jesus' lost childhood years. It depicts him as a wonder boy who imparts knowledge to his teachers about the mysteries of the alphabet and stuns his family and playmates with miracles that are more like a sorcerer's tricks. This fanciful portrayal reflects how difficult it is for humans to accept Jesus' full humanity.

Modern scholars have gone to the opposite extreme by presenting Jesus in purely human terms as a political revolutionary, a Galilean charismatic holy man, a wandering peasant, among many other views that usually simply reflect their own values and ideals that they project onto Jesus. The church has wrestled with the mystery of the incarnation, and an image might be helpful to clarify the orthodox view. Jesus' nature is like an ellipse with two foci, divine and human. What is important from Luke's summary statement is that the life of Jesus reveals what a human life full of God's Spirit and wisdom looks like.

---

12. Guy D. Nave Jr., *The Role and Function of Repentance in Luke-Acts* (Academia Biblica; Atlanta: Society of Biblical Literature, 2002), 17.

Luke 3:1 – 20

Literary Context

The appearance of John and the description of his ministry and preaching fulfill the prophecy spoken by Zechariah and the prophecy found in Scripture (1:67 – 79). John's preaching is interpreted in light of Isaiah and reiterates the theme sounded in the infancy narrative that "all flesh shall see the salvation of God" (3:6). John confronts the people and the powers that be and calls them to repentance.

> I. Prologue and Infancy Narrative (1:1 – 2:52)
> → **II. Preparing for Ministry (3:1 – 4:13)**
>   **A. The Preparatory Ministry of John (3:1 – 20)**
>   B. Jesus as the Son of God (3:21 – 38)

Main Idea

John prepares the crowds for the coming judgment through their repentance, expressed by their immersion and ethical transformation, and testifies that the One who comes after him is the fulfillment of God's promises to Israel.

Translation

(See next two pages.)

Luke 3:1–20

3:1	Chronological note	In the fifteenth year of the reign of Tiberius Caesar,

3:1   Chronological note

In the fifteenth year of the reign of Tiberius Caesar,
when Pontius Pilate was governor of Judea,
    Herod tetrarch of Galilee,
    his brother Philip tetrarch of the territories of Ituraea⤴
        and Trachonitus, **and**
    Lysanias tetrarch of Abilene,

2a   during the high priesthood of Annas and Caiaphas,
b   **the word of God came to John, son of Zechariah, in the wilderness.**

3a   Geographical transition   **He went into all the region around the Jordan**

b   proclaiming an immersion of repentance for the forgiveness of sins.

4a   Scriptural foundation   **As it stands written in the book of the words of Isaiah the prophet:**

b   *"The voice of one crying out in the wilderness:*
c   *'Prepare the way of the Lord,*
d   *make straight his paths;*
5a   *every valley shall be filled,*
b   *and every mountain and hill shall be brought low,*
c   *and the crooked [roads] will be made straight,*
d   *and the rough roads smooth;*
6   *and all flesh shall see the salvation of God.'"* (Isa 40:3-5)

7   Rebuke   **Therefore, he began to say to the crowds coming out to be immersed by him,**
"You sons of snakes! Who showed you how to flee the coming wrath?

8a   Admonition   *Bear fruits therefore worthy of repentance*
b   Warning   *and do not begin to say to yourselves, 'We have Abraham as our father,'*
c   Cause   *for I say to you that God is able to raise up children to Abraham from⤴ these stones.*

9   Warning   *Already the ax is being laid at the root of the trees;*
every tree that does not bear good fruit is cut down and thrown into the fire."

10   Question (1)   **The crowds asked him,**
"What then should we do?"

11   Answer (1)   **He answered them,**
"Let the one who has two undergarments give one to another who has none,
and let the one who has food do likewise."

12   Question (2)   **Even the tax collectors came to be immersed and said to him,**
"Teacher, what should we do?"

13   Answer (2)   **He said to them,**
"Collect no more taxes than has been authorized for you."

14a   Question (3)   **Soldiers asked him,**
"What should we do?"

b   Answer (3)   **He said to them,**
"Do not engage in extortion or false accusations,
and be content with your wages."

Continued on next page.

Continued from previous page.

15	Circumstance	As the people were filled with eager expectation,
		they were all questioning in their hearts about John,
		whether perhaps he himself might be the Messiah.

16a	Answer (4)	**John answered them all,**
		"I immerse you with water.
b		*The one who comes is stronger than me.*
		I am not worthy to loose the straps of his sandals.
c		*He will immerse you in the Holy Spirit and fire.*
17	Warning	*His winnowing shovel is in his hand* to clean out the threshing floor and
		to gather the wheat into his ↵
		storehouse;
		but the chaff he will burn up with an unquenchable fire."

18	Summary	**Then,** with many other strong appeals,
		he proclaimed the good news to the people.
19	Reaction	But **Herod the tetrarch, . . .**
		who had been reproved by him concerning Herodias,
		his brother's wife, and
		all the [other] evil things Herod ↵
		had done,

| 20 | | **. . . added to them all this: He locked John away in prison.** |

Structure and Literary Form

The text merges various forms: a historical note to establish the political context (3:1 – 2), a long scriptural quotation to establish that John's ministry was anticipated by Isaiah (3:4 – 6), prophetic warnings to stir the people to repentance (3:7 – 9), ethical exhortations describing the consequences of repentance (3:10 – 14), and a prophecy that contrasts John with the One who will soon come (3:15 – 17). It ends with a summary of John's ministry (3:18) and a historical note about his imprisonment (3:19 – 20). The reference to Herod the tetrarch in 3:1 and 3:19 – 20 forms an inclusio and marks off the section on John's ministry.

Exegetical Outline

➡ **I. Introduction of John as a prophet (3:1 – 6)**

     A. Political context (3:1 – 2)

     B. John's preaching of a repentance immersion (3:3)

     C. Fulfillment of Scripture (3:4 – 6)

II. Example of the preaching of John (3:7 – 17)

   A. Bear fruits worthy of repentance to avoid the coming judgment (3:7 – 9)

   B. The nature of those fruits (3:10 – 14)

      1. The crowds, "What then should we do?" (3:10 – 11)

      2. The tax collectors, "What should we do?" (3:12 – 13)

      3. The soldiers, "What should we do?" (3:14)

   C. Question about the coming Christ, who will immerse with the Holy Spirit and fire (3:15 – 17)

III. Summary (3:18)

IV. John's imprisonment by Herod (3:19 – 20)

Explanation of the Text

3:1 In the fifteenth year of the reign of Tiberius Caesar, when Pontius Pilate was governor of Judea, Herod tetrarch of Galilee, his brother Philip tetrarch of the territories of Ituraea and Trachonitus, and Lysanias tetrarch of Abilene (Ἐν ἔτει δὲ πεντεκαιδεκάτῳ τῆς ἡγεμονίας Τιβερίου Καίσαρος, ἡγεμονεύοντος Ποντίου Πιλάτου τῆς Ἰουδαίας, καὶ τετρααρχοῦντος τῆς Γαλιλαίας Ἡρῴδου, Φιλίππου δὲ τοῦ ἀδελφοῦ αὐτοῦ τετρααρχοῦντος τῆς Ἰτουραίας καὶ Τραχωνίτιδος χώρας, καὶ Λυσανίου τῆς Ἀβιληνῆς τετρααρχοῦντος). Placing the events in a fresh historical context marks a new beginning in the story and ties salvation history to world history.[1] "The events that have been fulfilled among us" (1:1) happen on the world stage and will have an effect on the world that will escape the notice of these rulers and many more who come after them.

Luke's reference to the fifteenth year of the reign of Tiberius is calculated from the time of the coregency with Augustus (AD 11/12). According to Strobel, this interpretation is confirmed by the proclamation of "the acceptable year of the Lord" (4:19), which refers to a clearly established Jubilee

year in the Jewish chronology of the time, dated to AD 26/27.[2]

The list of names cited here brings up the Roman Empire that looms in the background. The various echelons of power interlock much like a Russian nested doll. The list also reveals how fleeting earthly rule is. Tiberius, the emperor, will be dead in a few years (AD 37). He had withdrawn from public life to the isle of Capri, and his name would be vilified by the later Roman historians who claim that he spent his days in dissipation (Tacitus, *Ann.* 1 – 4; Dio Cassius, *Hist.* 46 – 48; Suetonius, *Tib.*).

Today, millions of children have never heard the name of Tiberius, second emperor of Rome, but they know the name of John the Baptist. I imagine that Tiberius would have been galled to know that they might also know the name of his petty underling Pilate. Pilate was forced from office in AD 37. As governor of Judea, Pilate was responsible for all aspects of the Roman administration of the province. But when he used violence to stop an armed demonstration by Samaritans near Mount Gerizim and had executed a number of their leaders, a

---

1. O'Toole (*The Unity of Luke's Theology*, 12) points out that Luke presents the salvation God brings to Israel as happening in history, and the mention of the names and years of an emperor or king and other officials appears in the introduction of the reign of each king in the books of Kings and in other biblical passages (Ezra 1:1; 4:6 – 7; 7:1 – 9; Neh 2:1; 5:14; Dan 1:1; 2:1; 7:1; 8:1; 9:1 – 2).

2. August Strobel, "Plädoyer für Lukas: Zur Stimmigkeit des chronistischen Rahmens von Lk 3.1," *NTS* 41 (1995): 466 – 69.

Samaritan delegation complained to Vitellius, the legate of Syria. Vitellius responded by suspending Pilate from office and sending him off to Emperor Tiberius, who died before Pilate arrived (Josephus, *Ant.* 18.4.1 – 2 §§85 – 89). Pilate then disappears into the mist of history.

Herod Antipas was deposed in AD 39. When Caligula became emperor after the death of Tiberias, he gave his friend Agrippa I, the brother of Herodias and nephew of Antipas, the land of Herod Philip the tetrarch. He also gave him the title "king." Herod Antipas had never received that coveted title, although he had ruled as a loyal puppet of Rome since 4 BC. His wife Herodias nagged him to go to the emperor to make his case that he too should be named a king. Agrippa did not want any other kings in the family and sent an envoy to Rome to bring accusations against Antipas. This action resulted in the banishment of Antipas and Herodias into exile in the foothills of the Pyrenees (Josephus, *Ant.* 18.7.1 – 2 §§240 – 55). Herod Philip died in AD 34 after an undistinguished reign, and Lysanius was out of office by AD 37; he was so insignificant that most commentators are mystified why he was included in this list.

These rulers may appear to have far more influence than John, but they have no inkling that the foundations that supported their thrones and murderous ideologies would be shaken to the core because of what would happen in an obscure corner of the empire beginning with an obscure prophet. This list reveals that Roman political dominance over the world does not control the story but a transcendent power does — God's eternal will. God was moving in ways that would dethrone them.

3:2a During the high priesthood of Annas and Caiaphas (ἐπὶ ἀρχιερέως Ἄννα καὶ Καϊάφα). Jewish high priests were now appointed by the Romans as political pawns, which profaned their holy status in the eyes of many and also meant that they had to appease their patrons to keep their power. "During the high priesthood of Annas and Caiaphas" implies that both were high priest at the same time, an odd statement. In Acts 4:6, Annas, not Caiaphas, is identified as the high priest. Annas served as high priest from AD 6 – 15 and was then deposed by the Romans. He remained a powerful influence as head of a priestly dynasty with five sons and his son-in-law, Caiaphas, serving as high priests. He may have kept the title of high priest and played the role akin to that of a "godfather" in the Mafia (Josephus, *Life* 38).[3] The reference may convey how the high priesthood has been degraded in the political context.

Caiaphas was deposed as high priest in AD 37. When Luke wrote his gospel, all of these worldly leaders had long since departed from the world. They were the high and mighty in their day when John came preaching. Luke records Jesus being tried before the high priest Caiaphas, Herod Antipas, and Pilate and sentenced to his death. But he was resurrected. The rule of these earthly rulers was short-lived, and new rulers took their place.

The story continues in Acts, and the apostles' mission took place during the reign of "King" Herod Agrippa I (Acts 12:1 – 23), during the reign of the emperor Claudius (Acts 11:28; 18:2), during the proconsulship of Sergius Paulus in Cyprus (Acts 13:7), during the proconsulship of Gallio in Achaia (Acts 18:12 – 17), during the governorships of Felix and Festus in Judea (Acts 24 – 25), and

---

3. Helen K. Bond (*Caiaphas: Friend of Rome and Judge of Jesus?* [Louisville: Westminster John Knox, 2004], 189, n. 7) notes: "A man like Annas, who had held the office for some time himself and still retained influence through his family, might well have continued to enjoy the title high priest well after he had technically been deposed by a Roman governor (some people, indeed, may have refused to recognize such a deposition)."

during the reign of "King" Herod Agrippa II (Acts 25:13 – 26:32). Paul winds up in Rome because he appealed to a new Caesar, the unnamed Nero, who reigns over the empire in that city. There seems to be an endless supply of new Lord High Poobahs wearing the crowns, wielding the scepters, holding the reins, calling the tunes, and ruling the roost — or so they think. Their reign is ephemeral.

The list here comprises an impressive bunch, but not an admirable bunch. They appear to have far more influence than John. Little did they know that in Judea, with an unacclaimed prophet, God was moving in ways that would shake their rule and have ultimate consequences on the history of humankind. The coming of God's word brings the empire one step closer to the oblivion it deserves.

3:2b The word of God came to John, son of Zechariah, in the wilderness (ἐγένετο ῥῆμα θεοῦ ἐπὶ Ἰωάννην τὸν Ζαχαρίου υἱὸν ἐν τῇ ἐρήμῳ). John was last mentioned going into the wilderness (1:80), and now his ministry is described. Prophets are commonly introduced in Scripture by listing the current rulers as the chronological setting for their career.[4] The mention of the rulers provides the political context and opposition that will ultimately bring about John's undoing. Prophets are also frequently introduced as "the son of" someone. The mention of "Zechariah" takes us back to the infancy narrative and the prophecies about John's future role. The prophet's vocation was also launched in Scripture by noting that the "the word of God" came to him.[5]

Luke's language, therefore, casts John "in the

role of Old Testament prophet (as predicted in 1:76)."[6] Readers familiar with the Old Testament narrative would know that prophets clash with the potentates in power who would try to squelch their message if it were unwelcomed news. Informed readers also know that when God is about to do something or is angry about something, a prophet shows up. John is not a scribe, interpreting indirectly the word of God, but a prophet who speaks directly for God and announces God's impending judgment.

The wilderness refers to an uninhabited region, not necessarily a sandy wasteland. Murphy-O'Connor raises the question as to why John chose such a place. It was "a place difficult for individuals, impossible for mass baptisms, and virtually inaccessible during the one season in the year when he could expect people to come to him, namely, the relatively cool winter months." The area also lacked a permanent population; how could he expect to convert all Israel there? He therefore contends that John did not choose this area simply because it had an available water supply or because of the symbolism of the wilderness but because he wanted to make a "deliberate prophetic gesture."[7]

This episode recalls Israel's wilderness sojourn (Jer 2:2; Hos 13:5; Amos 2:10; Acts 7:36). It was perceived as a region where God would begin the renewal of the people (Hos 2:14 – 15; 12:9). The wilderness was also the place where other prophets went, expecting the coming activity of God (Matt 24:26; Acts 21:38). According to 2 Kgs 2:4 – 11, Elijah was taken up in the wilderness beyond

---

4. See Isa 6:1; Jer 1:1 – 4; Ezek 1:1 – 3; Dan 1:1; Hag 1:1; Zech 1:1.

5. See 1 Sam 15:20; 2 Sam 7:4; 24:11; 1 Kgs 12:22; 13:20; 16:1; 17:2, 8; 18:1; 20:28; 2 Kgs 20:4; Jer 1:2; Ezek 1:3; Mic 1:1; Joel 1:1; Jonah 1:1; Hag 1:1; 2:1, 10; Zech 1:1, 7; 7:1. Christoph Burchard ("A Note on ῬHMA in JosAs 17:1f.; Luke 2:15, 17; Acts 10:37," *NovT* 27 [1985]: 281 – 95) shows that the word "word" (ῥῆμα) is used to stress the actual words spoken. Luke

uses another word for "word" (λόγος) more broadly to refer to the gospel message or God's revelatory acts.

6. John A. Darr, *Herod the Fox: Audience Criticism and Lukan Characterization* (JSNTSup 163; Sheffield; Sheffield Academic, 1998), 144.

7. Jerome Murphy-O'Connor, "John the Baptist and Jesus: History and Hypothesis," *NTS* 36 (1990): 359 – 74.

Jericho, across the Jordan. This may be why John retreats to the wilderness to proclaim the coming eschatological judgment that would be preceded by the coming of Elijah.[8] He did not understand himself to be Elijah redivivus, let alone the coming Messiah.

3:3 He went into all the region around the Jordan proclaiming an immersion of repentance for the forgiveness of sins (καὶ ἦλθεν εἰς πᾶσαν [τὴν] περίχωρον τοῦ Ἰορδάνου κηρύσσων βάπτισμα μετανοίας εἰς ἄφεσιν ἁμαρτιῶν). Only Luke tells us that John engaged in an itinerant preaching ministry. Whereas in Matt 3:5 and Mark 1:5 people came to him from all over Jerusalem and Judea, in Luke, John goes to them. Nave explains that in Luke it is the immersion connected to repentance, not John himself, that is central.[9] This message cannot be confined to the wilderness but is to be proclaimed everywhere in the region around the Jordan. The quotation from Isa 40 in Mark 1:2 – 4 would seem to make John "the object of prophetic fulfillment," but in Luke it is the message, the immersion as a sign of repentance, that is the object.[10] What is important is not the prophet but his divine message. Preaching that the people must urgently repent is part of God's plan to renew and deliver Israel.

John is "the voice" proclaiming "the word of God." "Preaching" (κηρύσσων) means to "herald" or "announce." Announcing an "immersion" is an "uncommon expression,"[11] but it is even more unusual to call all Israel to be immersed. Brownlee argues that John's preaching implies that "the whole nation was apostate and sinful and if it was to become the people of God, it must enter the society of God's people through repentance and baptism. Proselytes became members of God's people through baptism."[12] But it is incorrect to regard John's immersion as a derivative form of proselyte immersion, since the latter was not related to repentance.[13] The prophets connected repentance and renewal with washing (Isa 1:16 – 17; 4:4; Ezek 36:25 – 26; Zech 13:1), and this is the closest antecedent to what John was doing.

3:4 – 6 As it stands written in the book of the words of Isaiah the prophet: "The voice of one crying out in the wilderness: 'Prepare the way of the Lord, make straight his paths; every valley shall be filled, and every mountain and hill shall be brought low, and the crooked [roads] will be made straight, and the rough roads smooth; and all flesh shall see the salvation of God'" (ὡς γέγραπται ἐν βίβλῳ λόγων Ἠσαΐου τοῦ προφήτου· φωνὴ βοῶντος ἐν τῇ ἐρήμῳ,

---

8. Unlike Mark (Mark 1:6), Luke does not mention John's unusual garb and diet that is intended to evoke the image of Elijah, perhaps because his readers might interpret him to be a wild man intent on something subversive. The mention of the Roman overlords and their underlings, however, is reminiscent of the context in which Elijah appears out of the blue (1 Kgs 16:1 – 34; 17:1).

9. Nave, *Repentance in Luke-Acts*, 30. I have chosen to use the translation "immersion" (βάπτισμα) and "immerse" (βαπτίζω) rather than to transliterate the noun and verb as "baptism" and "baptize" (as is commonly done). The terms were used in Judaism for the immersion required in ritual washing (see 4 Kgdms 5:14; Jdt 12:7; Sir 34:25, 30; Mark 7:4). The description of Jesus coming up *out of the water* in Mark 1:10 and Matt 3:16 clearly depicts immersion. Josephus used

the term for plunging a sword into a throat (*J.W.* 2.18.4 §476). He also used it for "sinking" (*J.W.* 2.20.1 §556; 3.8.5 §368; 3.9.2 §423; 3.10.9 §§525, 527; *Ant.* 9.10. 2 §212; *Life* §15) and for "drowning" or "holding under water" (*J.W.* 1.22.2 §437; *Ant.* 15.3.4 §55). This usage explains how it could be employed metaphorically for being "overwhelmed." Jesus uses the metaphor for his passion (Mark 10:38 – 39; Luke 12:50). The outer sign of being submerged conveys the image of the drowning of the old life.

10. Nave, *Repentance in Luke-Acts*, 31.

11. Evans, *St. Luke*, 235.

12. William H. Brownlee, "John the Baptist in the New Light of Ancient Scrolls," *Int* 9 (1955): 75.

13. Nolland, *Luke*, 1:141.

Ἐτοιμάσατε τὴν ὁδὸν κυρίου, εὐθείας ποιεῖτε τὰς τρίβους αὐτοῦ· πᾶσα φάραγξ πληρωθήσεται καὶ πᾶν ὄρος καὶ βουνὸς ταπεινωθήσεται, καὶ ἔσται τὰ σκολιὰ εἰς εὐθείαν καὶ αἱ τραχεῖαι εἰς ὁδοὺς λείας· καὶ ὄψεται πᾶσα σὰρξ τὸ σωτήριον τοῦ θεοῦ). Luke reported John going into the wilderness in 1:80 without any explanation as to why he did so. Now, the citation from Isa 40:3 – 5 explains it. John's ministry is to be the fulfillment of Isaiah's prophecy.

"The way of the Lord"[14] is an apt title for Luke-Acts, since Luke views "the continuity of salvation history as a journey or a way."[15] "The way of the Lord" is heading to the Gentiles, and many seemingly insurmountable obstacles will hamper its progress. Rough terrain that obstructs travel is a symbol of the roadblocks presented by unrepentant hearts. The image of road building applies to repentance. It requires transforming the rocky terrain, removing obstructions, and leveling as the crooked ways of humans are turned into the straight ways of God. In Peter's first sermon in Acts, repentance saves one from "this corrupt generation" (Acts 2:38 – 40; see 8:21; 13:10).

Isaiah 40:3 (LXX) has "make straight the paths *of our God*," which Luke omits and substitutes the pronoun "his." The verse then unambiguously refers to Jesus, who already has been identified as "the Lord" in the narrative. Luke also omits the phrase in Isa 40:5 about seeing "the glory of the Lᴏʀᴅ." He does not present the earthly ministry of Jesus as characterized by glory, and only Peter, James, and John saw Jesus' glory for a brief moment at the transfiguration and then without

understanding its significance. The final line of the quote, "all flesh shall see the salvation of God" foreshadows the conclusion to Acts 28:28. Isaiah is quoted again in Acts 28:25 – 28, after which Paul declares: "Therefore I want you to know that God's salvation has been sent to the Gentiles, and they will listen!" Nave well summarizes its significance:

> … despite the separation and unfair treatment of people on the basis of ethnic identity, economic status, occupation, power, gender, and all other social barriers, the extension of salvation to and the inclusion of all people within the family of God has been and continues to be the plan of God. This universal saving purpose of God is the chief moving force behind the entire narrative.[16]

3:7 Therefore, he began to say to the crowds coming out to be immersed by him, "You sons of snakes! Who showed you how to flee the coming wrath?" (ἔλεγεν οὖν τοῖς ἐκπορευομένοις ὄχλοις βαπτισθῆναι ὑπ' αὐτοῦ· γεννήματα ἐχιδνῶν, τίς ὑπέδειξεν ὑμῖν φυγεῖν ἀπὸ τῆς μελλούσης ὀργῆς;). The people throng to heed John's call for immersion, but he harshly rebukes them by characterizing them as "sons of snakes."[17] This may be intended as a wake-up call to drive home the gravity of their situation. It will not be remedied by a solemn dip in the Jordan River.

The epithet also reveals that John is not after cheap success with a host of followers whose hearts have not been renewed. He also does not believe that this immersion rite has any saving efficacy in itself. The implied answer to the question "Who showed you how to flee from the coming

---

14. The ambiguity of "the Lord" (κύριος), which Luke has used to refer to both Jesus and God in the infancy narrative "creates a shared identity, and the structure and movement of the story prepares us to follow the way of the Lord of Israel as his coming is embodied in the life and person of the Lord Jesus" (Rowe, *Early Narrative Christology*, 77).

15. John Navone, "The Way and the Journey in Luke-Acts,"

TBT 44 (2006): 99. David W. Pao (*Acts and the Isaianic New Exodus* [WUNT 2/130; Tübingen: Mohr Siebeck, 2000], 45 – 68) shows that the description of the church as "the Way" (Acts 9:2; 19:9, 23; 22:4; 24:14, 22) derives from Isa 40:3.

16. Nave, *Repentance in Luke-Acts*, 25.

17. The poisonous asps are a threat to the people in Isa 11:8; 14:29; 30:6, but John identifies them *with* some of the people.

wrath?" is, "Certainly not I, since it is impossible to escape."[18] If they want to escape, they will need to bear the necessary fruit associated with repentance. If their repentance is fruitless (i.e., fake), any attempt to escape the coming wrath through immersion will fail. This threat implies once again that a separation will take place within Israel. All people, including those written off by the religious gatekeepers, are presumed able to produce these fruits, but not all will do so, including the religious rulers. These will be cut off and destroyed. John's preaching debunks the pretensions of outwardly religious people who try to pass themselves off to God and others as virtuous.

3:8 "Bear fruits therefore worthy of repentance and do not begin to say to yourselves, 'We have Abraham as our father,' for I say to you that God is able to raise up children to Abraham from these stones" (ποιήσατε οὖν καρποὺς ἀξίους τῆς μετανοίας· καὶ μὴ ἄρξησθε λέγειν ἐν ἑαυτοῖς· πατέρα ἔχομεν τὸν Ἀβραάμ. λέγω γὰρ ὑμῖν ὅτι δύναται ὁ θεὸς ἐκ τῶν λίθων τούτων ἐγεῖραι τέκνα τῷ Ἀβραάμ). "Fruit" refers to deeds consistent with repentance that proceed naturally from a changed heart and mind. Jews commonly understood themselves to be the "sons of Abraham" (see *m. B. Meṣ.* 8:1; *m. ʾAbot* 5:19; *b. B. Qam.* 32b; *Gen. Rab.* 53:12). They were deluding themselves if they thought that their ancestral connections to God through a forefather would shield them from the wrath to come. God's choice of Abraham did not guarantee the eternal security of his descendants. The image of stones may come from Isa 51:1 – 2, where Abraham's descendants are compared to stones hewn out of Abraham, the rock.[19]

In Depth: A Different View

A completely different view from John's is found in *b.ʿErub.* 19a:

> Resh Lakish stated: The fire of Gehenna has no power over the transgressors of Israel, as may be inferred *qal wa homer* from the golden altar: If the golden altar on which was only the thickness of a denar lasted for many years and the fire has no power over it, how much more would that be the case with the transgressors of Israel who are full of good deeds as a pomegranate, as it is said in Scripture, "thy temples are like a pomegranate" (Cant 6:7), and R. Simeon b. Lakish remarked, "Read not, The temples but Thy empty ones [signifying] that even the worthless among you are as full of good deeds as a pomegranate [with seed]."
>
> What, however, about what is written, Passing through the valley of Baca [Ps 84:7]? That [refers to the fact] that [the wicked] are at that time under sentence to suffer in Gehenna, but our father Abraham comes, brings them up, and receives them, except such an Israelite as had immoral intercourse with the daughter of an idolater, since his foreskin is drawn and so he cannot be discovered.

Jesus' parable of the rich man and Lazarus (16:19 – 31) shows the error of this assumption.

---

18. Marshall, *The Gospel of Luke*, 139.

19. Joachim Jeremias, "λίθος, λίθινος," *TDNT*, 4:270 – 71.

3:9 **"Already the ax is being laid at the root of the trees; every tree that does not bear good fruit is cut down and thrown into the fire"** (ἤδη δὲ καὶ ἡ ἀξίνη πρὸς τὴν ῥίζαν τῶν δένδρων κεῖται· πᾶν οὖν δένδρον μὴ ποιοῦν καρπὸν καλὸν ἐκκόπτεται καὶ εἰς πῦρ βάλλεται). John's fire-and-brimstone message takes for granted that the wicked in Israel will be judged, so he does not pray for them to be spared.[20] He reflects the deep pessimism of the apocalyptist toward this present, evil age. The hope of God's intervention on behalf of the faithful will bring blistering destruction to those opposed to God. What is astounding is that the divine ax is raised to hack down the trees of Israel (13:1 – 9), not the majestic trees of Lebanon (Isa 10:33 – 34). But the decision to side with God or against God will determine each individual's, not the nation's, fate.

3:10 **The crowds asked him, "What then should we do?"** (καὶ ἐπηρώτων αὐτὸν οἱ ὄχλοι λέγοντες· τί οὖν ποιήσωμεν;). John's dire warnings put fear into the hearts of his listeners, and three representative groups — the crowds, the tax collectors, and the soldiers — ask the same question, "What should we do?" Under different circumstances, Jesus is asked a similar question (10:25; 18:18), as are the apostles (Acts 2:37; 16:30; 22:10).

3:11 **He answered them, "Let the one who has two undergarments give one to another who has none, and let the one who has food do likewise"** (ἀποκριθεὶς δὲ ἔλεγεν αὐτοῖς· ὁ ἔχων δύο χιτῶνας μεταδότω τῷ μὴ ἔχοντι, καὶ ὁ ἔχων βρώματα ὁμοίως ποιείτω). John's answer to the question posed by the crowds about how to prepare for the coming judgment is that they must surrender all false securities that keep them from depending entirely on God. He claims that if repentance is real, it will show up in the first-century equivalent of the bank balance, and they will show care for the needs of others. Darr comments:

> Disregard for the welfare of others can be rooted in religious elitism ("we are descendants of Abraham" vv. 7 – 11), or a bureaucratic system that encourages tax collectors to gouge a vulnerable populace (vv. 12 – 13), or a military that condones the extortion of civilians by soldiers (v. 14). Like the prophets of old, Luke's Baptist defines true righteousness in terms of social justice rather than in terms of religious affiliation, social status or wealth.[21]

God demands generosity of his people, and almsgiving among the Jews became the highest virtue. Covering the naked was vital (see Job 31:16 – 22; Isa 58:7; Ezek 18:7, 16; Tob 1:17; 2 Esd 2:20; Matt 25:36, 38, 43 – 44; Jas 2:14 – 17). When confronted with another human who has nothing, John expects them to give that person their other undergarment or food. The undergarment (χιτών) is a short undershirt worn by both sexes under an outer garment (6:29). He does not say, "If you have *extra* food, share with another who has nothing," but if you have "food." Tobit contains more conventional advice: "If you have many possessions, make your gift from them in proportion; if few, do not be afraid to give according to the little you have" (Tob 4:8). John is not addressing people who have "many possessions" — they have only two undergarments — and he does not expect them to give "in proportion" but even beyond reasonable limits. If they cannot give a shirt away, they do not own the shirt; it owns them.

20. Pss 3:7; 7:9; 9:16 – 17; 10:15; 34:21; 37:10, 12 – 13, 20 – 22, 34; 50:22; 91:8; 92:7; 94:2, 3, 13; 101:8; 104:35; 129:4; 141:5 – 7; 145:20; 146:9; 147:6.

21. Darr, *Herod the Fox*, 154.

3:12 – 13 Even the tax collectors came to be immersed and said to him, "Teacher, what should we do?" He said to them, "Collect no more taxes than has been authorized for you." (ἦλθον δὲ καὶ τελῶναι βαπτισθῆναι καὶ εἶπαν πρὸς αὐτόν· διδάσκαλε, τί ποιήσωμεν; ὁ δὲ εἶπεν πρὸς αὐτούς· μηδὲν πλέον παρὰ τὸ διατεταγμένον ὑμῖν πράσσετε). Tax collectors worked for those who were the highest bidders for the contract with the Romans to take in the taxes levied on a province. The winner set the tax rates to recoup his costs and make a profit. The contractors made their profit from collecting more than was levied, particularly from the indirect taxes, such as tolls and custom duties. With no "supervisory bureaucracy," there were no restraints against cheaters among the agents, and it was assumed that they used their office to engage in theft.[22]

John does not call for them to give up their profession, regarded by most as dishonorable, but to carry it out honorably. Farmer argues, however, that "once the prospect of becoming rich has been removed, few would want to continue the onerous duties of collecting unpopular taxes from a resentful people."[23] Zacchaeus becomes an exemplar of a truly repentant tax collector (19:1 – 10).

3:14 Soldiers asked him, "What should we do?" He said to them, "Do not engage in extortion or false accusations, and be content with your wages" (ἐπηρώτων δὲ αὐτὸν καὶ στρατευόμενοι λέγοντες· τί ποιήσωμεν καὶ ἡμεῖς; καὶ εἶπεν αὐτοῖς· μηδένα διασείσητε μηδὲ συκοφαντήσητε καὶ ἀρκεῖσθε τοῖς ὀψωνίοις ὑμῶν). The soldiers are assumed to belong to the corrupt system that tyrannized the people rather than fighting to defend them. With their weaponry and authority, they could bully others and confiscate property to supplement their meager provisions or salaries. To have these military underlings treating others justly would certainly be a shock to the system.[24] The centurion in Capernaum is an exemplar of an honorable and generous soldier (7:1 – 10; see also Cornelius, Acts 10).

3:15 As the people were filled with eager expectation, they were all questioning in their hearts about John, whether perhaps he himself might be the Messiah (προσδοκῶντος δὲ τοῦ λαοῦ καὶ διαλογιζομένων πάντων ἐν ταῖς καρδίαις αὐτῶν περὶ τοῦ Ἰωάννου, μήποτε αὐτὸς εἴη ὁ χριστός). John's preaching stirred messianic expectations, and some in the crowd thought he might be the Messiah.[25] The New Testament contains a corrective to this view that apparently was fostered by his followers even after his death (see John 1:20; Acts 13:25; 19:4). The miserable oppression of Israel, represented by the crushing taxation and strong-arm intimidation by its rulers, sparked a desperate longing for God's intervention. Josephus mentions how susceptible the people were to deceivers who held out false hopes of deliverance (J.W. 2.13.4 §§258 – 60; 6.5.1 §§285 – 86), as does Luke (Acts 5:36 – 37). John is not a deceiver. He is simply a herald who points them to the One who is coming. The theme of the Coming One recurs in 7:19 – 20; 13:35; and 19:38.

3:16 – 18 John answered them all, "I immerse you with water. The one who comes is stronger than me. I am not worthy to loose the straps of his sandals. He will immerse you in the Holy Spirit and fire. His winnowing shovel is in his hand to clean out the threshing floor and to gather the wheat into his storehouse; but the chaff he

22. Schweizer, Luke, 74.
23. W. R. Farmer, "John the Baptist," IDB, 2:960.
24. See Paul Hollenbach, "Social Aspects of John the Baptizer's Preaching Mission in the Context of Palestinian Judaism," ANRW II.19.1 (1979): 850 – 75.
25. "Whether perhaps he himself might be" translates the rare optative (εἴη) and the intensive pronoun (αὐτός).

will burn up with an unquenchable fire." Then, with many other strong appeals, he proclaimed the good news to the people (ἀπεκρίνατο λέγων πᾶσιν ὁ Ἰωάννης· ἐγὼ μὲν ὕδατι βαπτίζω ὑμᾶς· ἔρχεται δὲ ὁ ἰσχυρότερός μου, οὗ οὐκ εἰμὶ ἱκανὸς λῦσαι τὸν ἱμάντα τῶν ὑποδημάτων αὐτοῦ· αὐτὸς ὑμᾶς βαπτίσει ἐν πνεύματι ἁγίῳ καὶ πυρί· οὗ τὸ πτύον ἐν τῇ χειρὶ αὐτοῦ διακαθᾶραι τὴν ἅλωνα αὐτοῦ καὶ συναγαγεῖν τὸν σῖτον εἰς τὴν ἀποθήκην αὐτοῦ, τὸ δὲ ἄχυρον κατακαύσει πυρὶ ἀσβέστῳ. Πολλὰ μὲν οὖν καὶ ἕτερα παρακαλῶν εὐηγγελίζετο τὸν λαόν). John speaks to "all" to correct their confused messianic expectations. His water immersion is only a shadow of what is to come. Marshall identifies it as a "prophetic sign" in "anticipation of this future cleansing and forgiveness."[26] All that John is doing is only preparatory.[27]

John identifies the One, not by the title "the Christ," but as the "one stronger than me" (ὁ ἰσχυρότερός μου). Since he confesses that he is unfit to perform even the lowliest task — "loose the straps of his sandals" — he also makes clear that Jesus is not a disciple of John who now rises above him. A Hebrew slave was not supposed to perform this act, according to a rabbinic commentary on Lev 25:39 (*Mekilta Nezikin* 1 to Exod 21:2). John's sense of his overwhelming unworthiness is striking.

John's image of an immersion of fire and Spirit is vivid: "He envisaged the one to come as immersing people into the river of God's fiery breath as it (probably) flowed from heaven."[28] "Fire" is used as an image of the exalted, powerful otherness of God in Jewish literature (Exod 24:17). Uncontrolled, it devours everything in its path (Isa 66:15; Dan 7:10; Amos 1:14; 7:4; Mal 4:1; 2 Esd 13:10), yet it can function as a purifier of anything that can hold up under its heat (Num 31:21 – 23; Zech 13:9; Mal 3:2 – 3). In combination with the Holy Spirit ("holy wind"; see Isa 4:4), it represents a blast of messianic judgment that all will experience.

In the next image, the coming judge is like a farmer who harvests his grain (see Jer 15:7). The unrighteous, portrayed as chaff that has been winnowed from the grain, will be incinerated (3:17). The righteous, portrayed as grain, will be gathered. If the word translated as "winnowing shovel" (τὸ πτύον) refers to a winnowing fork, the picture is of a thresher who does not individually separate the chaff from the grain but rather uses the fork to toss threshed grain to the wind to separate the light chaff from the heavy kernels. The very natures of the chaff and grain cause them to be separated. The lightweight chaff is carried off by the wind, while the heavier grain falls back to the threshing floor. Their true character is revealed in the threshing process.

But if τὸ πτύον refers to a "shovel," then the attention is on what happens on the threshing floor. The verb "clean out" (διακαθᾶραι) and the direct object "the threshing floor" (τὴν ἅλωνα) point to this meaning as the thresher cleanses it thoroughly after winnowing the harvest with the fork.[29] The farmer gathers the grain into the storeroom and the useless chaff (often identified with

26. Marshall, *The Gospel of Luke*, 135.
27. Walter Wink (*John the Baptist in the Gospel Tradition* [SNTSMS 7; Cambridge: Cambridge Univ. Press, 1968], 55) contends that Luke does not identify him as the one who comes "*after me*" (Matt 3:11; Mark 1:7) because he uses this phrase almost as a technical term for discipleship (Luke 9:23; 14:27; 21:8), and it might imply that Jesus was John's disciple. In Acts 13:25, the phrase is more clearly chronological. Both it and Acts 19:4 affirm that Jesus is the one about whom John prophesied.
28. James D. G. Dunn, *Jesus Remembered* (Grand Rapids: Eerdmans, 2003), 367.
29. Robert L. Webb, "The Activity of John the Baptist's Expected Figure at the Threshing Floor (Matthew 3.12 = Luke 3.17)," *JSNT* 43 (1991): 103 – 11; but see the objections of Menzies, *The Development of Early Christian Pneumatology*, 95.

the wicked, Ps 1:4; Isa 17:13) is then burnt. Luke emphasizes "the positive aspect of the prophecy: the sifting out of the righteous remnant," which continues in the mission of the church after Pentecost.[30] John, therefore, does not refer to an end-of-time scenario but confirms with more fearsome imagery what Simeon predicted. The child Jesus, who is the One to come, is destined "for the falling and rising of many in Israel" (2:34). The separation will occur during John's ministry as people respond or do not respond to his call to repentance (see 7:29 – 30; 20:3 – 7).

Luke's narrative will show how this promised spiritual transformation will reach beyond Israel to the Gentiles. In justifying the conversion of Cornelius and other Gentiles to the circumcised in Jerusalem, Peter remembers "what the Lord had said" (Acts 11:16), namely, that "John baptized with water, but you will be baptized with the Holy Spirit."

3:19 – 20 But Herod the tetrarch, who had been reproved by him concerning Herodias, his brother's wife, and all the [other] evil things Herod had done, added to them all this: He locked John away in prison (ὁ δὲ Ἡρῴδης ὁ τετραάρχης, ἐλεγχόμενος ὑπ᾽ αὐτοῦ περὶ Ἡρῳδιάδος τῆς γυναικὸς τοῦ ἀδελφοῦ αὐτοῦ καὶ περὶ πάντων ὧν ἐποίησεν πονηρῶν ὁ Ἡρῴδης, προσέθηκεν καὶ τοῦτο ἐπὶ πᾶσιν, καὶ κατέκλεισεν τὸν Ἰωάννην ἐν φυλακῇ). As God's prophet, John is no respecter of persons, and he takes on Herod, as Elijah took on Ahab and Jezebel. Rebuking the powerful for their evil normally has deadly consequences for a prophet.

Luke does not go into the complicated details behind Herod's imprisonment of John except to say that he had reproved Herod concerning his wife. It may be that he did not want to burden the reader with the mazy interrelationships of the various Herods that require some kind of scorecard to keep them straight.[31] Or, the problem of Herod's divorcing his wife in order to marry the daughter of his half brother, married to another half brother, which so offended pious Jewish sensibilities (see Lev 18:16), may not have seemed as heinous to his Gentile audience.[32] He is content to state, "This Herod is evil," and leave the details to the readers' imagination. Luke does not mention John's death at Herod's hands here; later, John reappears in 7:18 – 23 when he dispatches his disciples to Jesus to ask if he is the One who is to come.

Herod is an example of those who are wicked chaff. He is the persecutor of John the Baptist and his executioner (cf. 9:7 – 9). He will be the persecutor of Jesus (13:31 – 33) and will add to the mockery of him during his trial (23:8 – 12). Darr writes, "Herod is among those, who because of their abuse of power and lack of repentance, are never able truly to see and hear the revelation of God in Jesus."[33]

---

30. Menzies, *The Development of Early Christian Pneumatology*, 144.

31. Herod Antipas was the son of Herod the Great and Malthace and was tetrarch of Galilee and Perea from 4 BC to AD 39.

32. See further, Josephus, *Ant.* 18.5.1 §§109 – 15. Josephus attributes John's arrest to Herod's fear that he was fomenting unrest among the people (*Ant.* 18.5.2 §118).

33. Darr, *Herod the Fox*, 212. For an historical analysis of this minor client ruler, see Morton Hørning Jensen, *Herod Antipas in Galilee* (WUNT 2/215; Tübingen: Mohr Siebeck, 2006).

Theology in Application

1. God Overruling the Rulers

Christianity is not a mystery religion with mythical, fantastical stories. It happened in history. Luke fixes his story firmly in the context of world history. According to Bovon, the opening list of rulers suggests that "Luke seems to accept Roman rule without hesitation, as the given framework of divine intervention."[34] But Green contends that it "may be read within the interpretive matrix of earlier material, such as the critique of 'the powerful' and 'the rich' in Mary's Song (1:52 – 53); having read the preceding narrative we now have a bias against rulers who enter the narrative."[35] It reminds the reader that the world is under the thrall of evil. Four of these leaders in the list will have direct roles in Jesus' death. When the gospel begins, the situation is desperate for God's people.

Those wearing the crowns and holding the reins of power fool themselves into believing that they determine the course of history. But the narrative makes clear that God's plan is not controlled by the laws of kings, the machinations of politicians, or the solemn rituals of priests. History is directed by a transcendent power leading to an appointed time that is not in the appointment books of any of these rulers. It is a time only God controls. The Word of God bypasses the halls of power with their royal trappings and comes to a lone prophet in the wilderness. The potentates get footnotes in the secular histories, but God's purposes are manifest in persons who were largely unknown to the historians of the age.

Those who hold great political, economic, and/or spiritual power are often guilty of pride against God and of injustice against the poor and the weak. But Jesus and his followers will not seek to make a concordat with these political powers or to stir up a violent revolution against the tyrants. They will simply proclaim God's Word and the truth of the gospel, as John did, in weakness. Jesus' followers have no temporal power. They know that those who take the physical sword will perish by the sword (Matt 26:52). They have only "the sword of the Spirit, which is the word of God" (Eph 6:17), and the seeming weakness of God (1 Cor 1:25) will bring down not only the earthly powers but the cosmic powers that stand in opposition.

The list of rulers in Luke 3 reveals that two ways of ruling the world will come head-to-head. They rule through violence and fear; Jesus' way shows the power of powerlessness and love. He will rebuke James and John, who would have him incinerate stubborn Samaritans with a divine fireball (9:51 – 56). He will rebuke the disciples who think they can do God's will by wielding their two swords (22:38) and will undo one of his follower's swordplay by healing an injured man's ear (22:49 – 51). He will not take up arms against his enemies but instead insist that if there is any killing to be done, it will be done *to* him, not *by* him.

34. Bovon, *Luke 1:1 – 9:50*, 120.   35. Green, *The Gospel of Luke*, 168.

The pagan kings may lord it over others through violence, but the truly great, who will ultimately rule, are to serve and to give their lives for others. They will sit on thrones in an *eternal* kingdom (22:25 – 30). As the state should not be allowed to commandeer the church for its political ends, so the church should not seek to achieve its spiritual goals through political power or violence. That strategy is destined to fail. Only the plainspoken proclamation of the Word of God to the powerful and the powerless, even when it is just a lonely voice in a wilderness, will win the day.

2. Repentance and the Forgiveness of Sins

John is to prepare the way of the Lord. Like the morning star heralding the sun, he was the glimmer of light that betokened the coming of the day that was about to shed its rays on Israel and the world. He was a voice crying out before the coming of the Word. Tannehill notes that this task of preparing the way is continued by Jesus' followers in the narrative (9:52; 10:1), and they preach the same message as John (Acts 2:37 – 38, 40; 26:20). Since they continue what John began, calling for repentance and offering forgiveness of sins, he may be regarded as a "prototype of the Christian evangelist."[36]

Prophets give voice to the primary demand from God that the people repent. The angel declared to his father that this was John's primary destiny (1:16 – 17), and this is what John is remembered for doing (Acts 13:24; 19:4). Repentance becomes a central theme in Luke-Acts. It entails changing "one's attitude and orientation that results in a new relation to God and fellow humans."[37] Half of the New Testament uses of the noun "repentance" (μετάνοια) appear in Luke-Acts (3:3, 8; 5:32; 15:7; 24:47; Acts 5:31; 11:18; 13:24; 19:4; 20:21; 26:20). The verb "repent" (μετανοέω) appears nine times in Luke (10:13; 11:32; 13:3, 5; 15:7, 10; 16:30; 17:3, 4) and five times in Acts (2:38; 3:19; 8:22; 17:30; 26:20) compared with seven times in Matthew and Mark combined. Luke also uses the verb "to turn" (ἐπιστρέφω) as a synonym for the verb "repent."

In the context of preaching to Jews, repentance refers to turning around and returning to the already given covenant and the relationship that covenant entails (1 Sam 7:3, 1 Kgs 18:37). In the context of the coming judgment, they must turn around if they "are to meet God from the right direction."[38] For Gentiles, it will entail turning from idols to the one true God. The theme of repentance in Luke is not limited to the use of verbs or nouns, but it is also described narratively without the verb, as, for example, in the woman's loving response to Jesus (7:36 – 50), the prodigal

---

36. Talbert, *Reading Luke*, 31. Tannehill, *Unity of Luke-Acts*, 52, notes that the similar way the narrator introduces the missions of John the Baptist, Jesus (4:18 – 19), Peter and the apostles (Acts 2:17 – 21), and Paul (Acts 13:47) with a sermon at the beginning, accompanied by a scriptural quotation "which reveals the divine purpose behind the mission which is beginning"; this indicates a continuity between them. They are not separated into different epochs.

37. Tannehill, *The Shape of Luke's Story*, 85. It is often completed by the phrase "to the Lord," or "to God" in 1:16, 17; and in Acts 9:35; 11:21; 14:15; 15:19; 26:18, 20.

38. Frederick Dale Bruner, *The Christbook: A Historical/ Theological Commentary: Matthew 1 – 12* (Waco: Word, 1987), 71.

son's return home (15:11 – 32), and Zacchaeus's intention to compensate those he had cheated (19:1 – 10).

(1) The repentance John called for did not require going to the temple to offer a sacrifice for sins, or fasting, or putting on sackcloth and ashes, or any other self-mortifying measures, nor did one have to withdraw to some desert hermitage.[39] The divinely sanctioned way of repentance took one "down by the Jordan instead of up in Jerusalem."[40] John therefore bucked the idea that forgiveness was obtained through participation in the sacrificial cult as prescribed in the law. Dunn notes that a priest

> was an indispensable intermediary in the offering of the sacrifice. But John's preaching gives no indication that a sacrifice or act of atonement was necessary. In a sense, baptism took the place of the sin-offering. That was the really distinctive feature of John's baptism: not that he rejected the Temple ritual on the grounds that repentance alone was sufficient, but that he offered his own ritual as an alternative to the Temple ritual. Perhaps we should even say that John the Baptist in baptizing played the role of the priest.[41]

John came from a priestly family but did not act as a priest. Josephus, who also hailed from a priestly family, gives a favorable review of John in his history but probably reflects his sacerdotal bias in rejecting the efficacy of John's repentance immersion for the forgiveness of sins: "They must not employ it to gain pardon for whatever sins they committed, but as a consecration of the body implying that the soul was thoroughly cleansed by right behavior" (*Ant.* 18.5.2 §117). John's ministry reveals that God was now bypassing the temple and its cult.

(2) Real repentance requires a change in one's inward attitude and outward actions — as it always has (see 1QS 3.3 – 12) — to be efficacious. Keck draws out the contemporary application of John's warning to those who refuse to repent:

> Somehow we have come to think that we can save souls without repentance. We have come to think that repentance is feeling sorry for not being religious sooner, that repentance is something sinners go through on the way to salvation. But repentance is turning one's whole life toward the will and way of God, and so repentance is not the preliminary step to something else but the name of the game. Repentance is the discipline of rebuilding life in alignment with the will of God.[42]

(3) Because we are embodied creatures, repentance is not simply a cerebral exercise but something that affects daily living. For John, it directly affects one's finances. Danker states it boldly:

> The ax is heading downstroke in any society that thinks these words are an invitation merely to distribute Christmas food baskets, handouts of castoff clothes, or money.

---

39. Fitzmyer, *Luke*, 1:469.

40. N. T. Wright, *Jesus and the Victory of God* (Minneapolis: Augsburg Fortress, 1997), 257.

41. Dunn, *Jesus Remembered*, 359.

42. Leander E. Keck, "Listen to and Listen For: From Text to Sermon (Acts 1:8)," *Int* 27 (1973): 198.

Anyone who is insensitive to the broadening gulf between the prosperous and the economically disadvantaged deserves to know that the prophets did not risk their necks for petty moralizing of that sort.[43]

Spiritual reform, according to John, will lead to economic reform that produces "justice, equity, and humanity."[44]

(4) John's call for repentance redrew the religious boundaries. Those who repented would be included in the restored Israel; those who did not would be excluded. The restored Israel would even include uncircumcised Gentiles (Acts 11:18). As a result, the New Testament will redefine what it means to be a "son of Abraham." It has nothing to do with physical descent and does not exclude women (see Rom 9:6 – 9; 2 Cor 11:22; Gal 3:7; 4:31). John's radical views prepare the way for Paul's radical assertion that one becomes a child of Abraham by faith.

(5) In Luke-Acts, repentance is something people can be summoned to do, but it also comes as a gift from God (Acts 5:31; 11:18). The promise of immersion in the Holy Spirit means that God will not simply hold persons accountable and judge them but will give them access to divine power beyond themselves. The paradox is reflected in Ezekiel's prophecy. The prophet demanded that the people "get a new heart and a new spirit" (Ezek 18:31) but later recorded God's promise: "I will give you a new heart and put a new spirit in you; I will remove from you your heart of stone and give you a heart of flesh. And I will put my Spirit in you and move you to follow my decrees and be careful to keep my laws" (Ezek 36:26 – 27).

(6) Those who do not repent will not see. Darr correctly contends that the repentance John calls for "is not an end in itself, but, rather, is the necessary precondition for perceiving the 'salvation of God' when it/he confronts them."[45] John's function is to adjust and "reorient the spiritual vision of the people so that they will be able to recognize and respond to 'the salvation of God' when it appears."[46] Consequently, John does not point out the Coming One for the people but gets them ready to recognize him through their repentance. This is why John's question to Jesus through his disciples, "Are you the one who is to come or should we expect another?" (7:19), is one of dawning recognition, not doubt.

(7) John announces that Israel must repent or be laid waste. Israel's long-term, special relationship with God does not exempt them from God's judgment. In fact, the winnowing process begins with them. The church also is not exempt from the judgment, and unless it is shaped by the repentance John describes, it too will be cut down and destroyed. The image suggests that there will be no universal salvation even among those who count themselves as part of the people of God.

43. Danker, *Jesus and the New Age*, 88.
44. Frederic L. Godet, *A Commentary on the Gospel of St. Luke* (2 vols.; trans. E. W. Shalders and M. D. Cusin; New York: I. K. Funk, 1881), 1:176.
45. Darr, *Herod the Fox*, 153.
46. Ibid., 155.

Luke 3:21 – 38

Literary Context

Luke continues the pattern of the infancy narrative by treating John and Jesus in parallel scenes. After the adult John is introduced beginning his ministry, the adult Jesus is introduced beginning his. Luke continues to show John as subordinate to Jesus, the Son of God. Jesus' immersion and the heavenly manifestations that occur afterward while he is praying (3:21 – 22) should not be read as part of the account of John's ministry (3:1 – 20) but constitute a single unit that includes the genealogy.[1]

Luke is not pulling off a "literary *tour de force*" by having John imprisoned before he baptizes Jesus, as Wink would have it.[2] Instead, by using panels (diptychs) to construct the narrative, he resets the chronology in the story when he introduces a new subject (see 1:56 – 57; 1:80 – 2:4). Verse 20 does *not* mean that John's ministry was completed before that of Jesus began. By bringing the account of John's preaching to a close with his imprisonment, John goes offstage so that the spotlight falls only on Jesus. Bovon is correct that the sequence is rooted in Luke's literary style: he "does not want to turn to Jesus until he has finished his account of the Baptist. For him, Jesus' baptism belongs in the life of Jesus, no longer to the story of the Baptist."[3]

The sequence of baptism, genealogy, and testing by the devil that immediately follows (4:1 – 13) has theological significance that will be discussed in the Theology in Application section. The sequence focuses on what it means for Jesus to be the Son of God.

---

1. Schweizer, *Luke*, 75; Josep Rius-Camps ("Constituye Lc 3,21 – 38 un solo período? Propuesta de un cambio de puntuación," *Bib* 65 [1984]: 189 – 209) contends that 3:21 – 22 is the protasis and 3:23 – 38 the apodosis.

2. Wink, *John the Baptist*, 46. Wink draws this conclusion

by misguidedly following Conzelmann's schematization of Luke's salvation history in which John is the last of the prophets in the period of Israel's law and the prophets.

3. Bovon, *Luke 1:1 – 9:50*, 127.

I. Prologue and Infancy Narrative (1:1 – 2:52)

II. Preparing for Ministry (3:1 – 4:13)

   A. The Preparatory Ministry of John (3:1 – 20)

➡   **B. Jesus as the Son of God (3:21 – 38)**

     1. Jesus' Baptism (3:21 – 23a)

     2. Jesus' Genealogy (3:23b – 38)

   C. The Testing of Jesus in the Wilderness (4:1 – 13)

Main Idea

Jesus is declared to be the Son of God by a heavenly voice, and the Holy Spirit rests on him to empower him to be perfectly obedient to God in fulfilling his ministry.

Translation

(See next page.)

Structure and Literary Form

The unit introduces the adult Jesus by combining a revelatory testimony about him from heaven (3:21 – 22) with a genealogy (3:23 – 38). They are linked by the reference to Jesus as Son of God in the heavenly declaration and Adam as son of God in the genealogy.

Exegetical Outline

➡ **I. Setting: after Jesus' baptism with the people (3:21a-b)**

II. Setting: as he was praying (3:21c)

III. Heavenly manifestations (3:21d – 22)

   A. Heaven opened (3:21d)

   B. The Holy Spirit descended (3:22a)

   C. A voice from heaven declared Jesus to be "my Son, the beloved" (3:22b)

IV. Jesus begins his ministry around thirty years of age (3:23a)

V. The genealogy from Joseph to Adam, the son of God (3:23b – 38)

Luke 3:21–38

3:21a	Circumstance	**Now it happened when all the people had been immersed**
b		**and Jesus also had been immersed,**
c		and as he was praying,
d	Heavenly manifestations	**heaven was opened**
22a		and **the Holy Spirit descended upon him**
		in bodily form like a dove.
b		**And a voice came from heaven,**
		"You are my Son, the beloved; with you I am well pleased."
23a		When Jesus himself was beginning his ministry,
		he was about thirty years of age.
b	Genealogy	**He was the son,**
		as was thought,
		of Joseph the son of Heli,
24	List	the son of Matthat, the son of Levi, the son of Melchi, the son of Jannai, the son of Joseph,
25		the son of Mattathias, the son of Amos, the son of Nahum, the son of Esli, the son of Naggai,
26		the son of Maath, the son of Mattathias, the son of Semein, the son of Josech, the son of Joda,
27		the son of Joanan, the son of Rhesa, the son of Zerubbabel, the son of Shealtiel, the son of Neri,
28		the son of Melchi, the son of Addi, the son of Cosam, the son of Elmadam, the son of Er,
29		the son of Joshua, the son of Eliezer, the son of Jorim, the son of Matthat, the son of Levi,
30		the son of Simeon, the son of Judah, the son of Joseph, the son of Jonam, the son of Eliakim,
31		the son of Melea, the son of Menna, the son of Mattatha, the son of Nathan, the son of David,
32		the son of Jesse, the son of Obed, the son of Boaz, the son of Sala, the son of Nahshon,
33		the son of Amminadab, the son of Admin, the son of Arni, the son of Hezron, the son of Perez, the son of Judah,
34		the son of Jacob, the son of Isaac, the son of Abraham, the son of Terah, the son of Nahor,
35		the son of Serug, the son of Reu, the son of Peleg, the son of Eber, the son of Shelah,
36		the son of Cainan, the son of Arphaxad, the son of Shem, the son of Noah, the son of Lamech,
37		the son of Methuselah, the son of Enoch, the son of Jared, the son of Malaleel, the son of Cainan,
38		the son of Enosh, the son of Seth, the son of Adam, the son of God.

Explanation of the Text

3:21a-b Now it happened when all the people had been immersed and Jesus also had been immersed (ἐγένετο δὲ ἐν τῷ βαπτισθῆναι ἅπαντα τὸν λαὸν καὶ Ἰησοῦ βαπτισθέντος). Luke's literary technique of bringing a story to a close (John's ministry) only to start the next panel by going back to what happened before leaves ambiguous who immersed Jesus (note the passive voices here). It must be assumed that John immersed him as he did "all the people." There is no need to argue that the passive voice of the participle "had been immersed" (βαπτισθέντος) should be translated as the middle voice and that Jesus baptized himself.[4] Luke ties Jesus' immersion to that of "all the people" so that it is clear that he submits to the same obedience and conditions required of all Israel. The description of his immersion is subordinate to the heavenly events that occur after it and serves only as the setting for them.

The sentence begins with an introductory formula ("now it happened"), two time indicators ("when all the people … and Jesus also had been immersed"; "and as he was praying"), which is then followed by the main clause that notes heaven opening, the Holy Spirit coming down, and a voice from heaven speaking.[5]

3:21c-d And as he was praying, heaven was opened (καὶ προσευχομένου ἀνεῳχθῆναι τὸν οὐρανόν). Jesus' immersion is described with an aorist participle, but his prayer is described with a present participle (προσευχομένου), suggesting that he continued in prayer.[6] The emphasis falls on what God does as Jesus prays, not as he

is immersed.[7] In comparison with Mark 1:10, Luke describes heaven opening during Jesus' prayer rather than as he was coming up out of the water. He also describes heaven as "being opened" (ἀνεῳχθῆναι) rather than being "rent" or "split asunder" (σχιζομένους), which is more apt as an image of God responding to prayer (see Acts 7:56, where heaven opens before Stephen's prayer).

Crump maintains that "prayer opens up a doorway between earth and heaven." Through prayer Jesus "not only spoke with the Father, but also made himself susceptible to the communication of the divine will, whatever that might entail."[8] Luke therefore presents Jesus as beginning his ministry in prayer, and he will cite him praying at crucial moments so that it becomes clear that this was his habitual practice.

3:22 And the Holy Spirit descended upon him in bodily form like a dove. And a voice came from heaven, "You are my Son, the beloved; with you I am well pleased" (καὶ καταβῆναι τὸ πνεῦμα τὸ ἅγιον σωματικῷ εἴδει ὡς περιστερὰν ἐπ᾽ αὐτόν, καὶ φωνὴν ἐξ οὐρανοῦ γενέσθαι· σὺ εἶ ὁ υἱός μου ὁ ἀγαπητός, ἐν σοὶ εὐδόκησα). Luke describes the Holy Spirit coming down in "bodily form" (σωματικῷ) in outward appearance (εἴδει) as a dove *upon* (ἐπί) him rather than "into" (εἰς) him, as in Mark 1:10. The image of the Spirit resting on him may derive from Isa 11:2; 42:1.

Picturing the Holy Spirit descending bodily conveys that this experience is "not to be confused with thought or feeling alone" but was an objective reality.[9] For the same reason, Luke uses the image

---

4. Contra Wink, *John the Baptist*, 83, n. 1, citing 11:38.

5. Hendrickx, *The Third Gospel*, IIA:55.

6. Prayer precedes receiving of the Spirit in the early Christian community in Acts 4:31.

7. Hendrickx, *The Third Gospel*, IIA:55.

8. David Crump, *Jesus the Intercessor* (WUNT 2/49; Tübingen: Mohr Siebeck, 1992), 115.

9. Fred B. Craddock, *Luke* (Interpretation; Lousville: Westminster John Knox, 1990), 51. See Fritzleo Lentzen-Deis, *Die Taufe Jesu nach den Synoptikern: literarkritische und gattungsge-*

of tongues of fire to describe the phenomenon of the Spirit's coming to rest on the disciples at Pentecost (Acts 2:3 – 4). Schweizer makes the case that the Spirit comes as "an objective divine reality which encounters and claims man.... The decisive thing is that man stands here before a reality which comes from God, which in some sense represents the presence of God, and yet which is not identical with God."[10] For Jesus, the Spirit comes to empower him for his ministry. In this sense, he is no different from the disciples in Acts and serves as the model for them. Prayer and the Holy Spirit unleash the power of God in their lives to engage in their mission effectively (see Acts 1:14; 2:3 – 4).

Why the Spirit appears as a dove is difficult to discern. Dove imagery was multivalent, and numerous explanations have been proposed.[11] The dove could represent "a herald or trustworthy messenger (so *b. Giṭ.* 45a; *b. Sanh.* 95a) and bearer of good tidings (cf. Gen 8:11), and so further interprets the Spirit on Jesus as the power to proclaim the messianic 'good news.'"[12] Or, it may connote the gentleness of Jesus' ministry of restoration as opposed to John's grim vision of the Spirit conducting "a fiery purging."[13] According to 2 Esd 5:23 – 27, God chose the dove above all other birds, and it, along with the vine, the lily, the river Jordan, Zion, and sheep, are linked to Israel's special election over all others. The dove descending on Jesus may signify that he is specially chosen to be God's unique instrument. But Luke and the other gospel writers (Matt 3:13 – 17; Mark 1:9 – 11; John 1:32 – 34) do not explain the symbolism or develop

it. It is part of a momentous event that becomes a signal to Jesus to begin his ministry.

Angels declared Jesus to be the Son of God (see 1:32, 35). Satan appealed to Jesus' status as the Son of God for argument's sake, "if you are the Son of God ... " (4:3, 9), and demons cried out their recognition of him as the Son of God and flinched in his presence (4:41; 8:28). Here, however, the voice from heaven (see also 9:35) makes the definitive pronouncement: "You are my Son, the beloved; with you I am well pleased." "Beloved" (ὁ ἀγαπητός) appears to be synonymous with "chosen" for Luke (9:35; see Matt 17:5; Mark 9:7; Acts 15:25).

This heavenly testimony echoes two Old Testament texts and joins them together. Psalm 2:7, "You are my son; today I have become your father," is an enthronement psalm that points to the figure of the Davidic Messiah. Isaiah 42:1, "Here is my servant, whom I uphold, my chosen one in whom I delight; I will put my Spirit on him, and he will bring justice to the nations," refers to the Servant. In combination, they present the divine perspective that Jesus is the Servant-Messiah.[14]

This event signals "the beginning of Jesus' messianic ministry, but not of messiahship."[15] It represents "divine empowering, not divine adoption."[16] At the commencement of Jesus' ministry, he is praying, the heavens open, the Spirit descends on him, and God announces that he is the beloved Son. At the end of his earthly ministry, Jesus prays, the temple veil splits, he commits his spirit to his Father (23:34, 45 – 46), and a centurion

schichtliche Untersuchungen (Frankfurter Theologische Studien 4; Frankfurt: Knecht, 1970), 44, 285.

10. Eduard Schweizer, "πνεῦμα, πνευματικός," *TDNT*, 6:387 – 88.

11. W. D. Davies and Dale C. Allison Jr. (*The Gospel According to Saint Matthew* [ICC; Edinburgh: T&T Clark, 1988], 1:331 – 35) list sixteen proposals for the origin of the dove symbolism. Joy Palachuvattil (*He Saw: The Significance of Jesus' Seeing Denoted by the Verb* εἶδεν *in the Gospel of Mark* [Tesi

Gregoriana 84; Rome: Pontificia Univesità Gregoriana, 2002], 71 – 75) adds others.

12. M. M. B. Turner, "Holy Spirit," *DJG*, 345.

13. Nolland, *Luke*, 1:161.

14. Menzies, *The Development of Early Christian Pneumatology*, 151.

15. Ibid., 152.

16. Ibid., 153.

acknowledges that he is righteous (23:47). In Acts, this term becomes a messianic title for Jesus, "the Righteous One" (Acts 3:14 – 15; 7:52; 22:14). He is "the Righteous One" because he did not seek to serve or save himself but was completely obedient to his Father.

3:23a   When Jesus himself was beginning his ministry, he was about thirty years of age (καὶ αὐτὸς ἦν Ἰησοῦς ἀρχόμενος ὡσεὶ ἐτῶν τριάκοντα). Thirty years old marks a "threshold age" in the ancient sources.[17] Joseph was thirty when he entered the service of the Pharaoh (Gen 41:46), and David was thirty years old when he began to reign (2 Sam 5:4). The age signals to the reader that Jesus is now a mature, responsible man ready for his public career. After the extraordinary events surrounding his conception and birth, Jesus has apparently lived for thirty years as an ordinary, anonymous man. Luke has no interest in fantasies of Jesus' youth that appear in some apocryphal gospels.

3:23b – 38   He was the son, as was thought, of Joseph the son of Heli, the son of Matthat, the son of Levi, the son of Melchi, the son of Jannai, the son of Joseph, the son of Mattathias, the son of Amos, the son of Nahum, the son of Esli, the son of Naggai, the son of Maath, the son of Mattathias, the son of Semein, the son of Josech, the son of Joda, the son of Joanan, the son of Rhesa, the son of Zerubbabel, the son of Shealtiel, the son of Neri, the son of Melchi, the son of Addi, the son of Cosam, the son of Elmadam, the son of Er, the son of Joshua, the son of Eliezer, the son of Jorim, the son of Matthat, the son of Levi, the son of Simeon, the son of Judah, the son of Joseph, the son of Jonam, the son of Eliakim, the son of Melea, the son of Menna, the son of Mattatha, the son of Nathan, the son of David, the son of Jesse, the son of Obed, the son of Boaz, the son of Sala, the son of Nahshon, the son of Amminadab, the son of Admin, the son of Arni, the son of Hezron, the son of Perez, the son of Judah, the son of Jacob, the son of Isaac, the son of Abraham, the son of Terah, the son of Nahor, the son of Serug, the son of Reu, the son of Peleg, the son of Eber, the son of Shelah, the son of Cainan, the son of Arphaxad, the son of Shem, the son of Noah, the son of Lamech, the son of Methuselah, the son of Enoch, the son of Jared, the son of Malaleel, the son of Cainan, the son of Enosh, the son of Seth, the son of Adam, the son of God (ὢν υἱός, ὡς ἐνομίζετο, Ἰωσὴφ τοῦ Ἠλὶ τοῦ Μαθθὰτ τοῦ Λευὶ τοῦ Μελχὶ τοῦ Ἰανναὶ τοῦ Ἰωσὴφ τοῦ Ματταθίου τοῦ Ἀμὼς τοῦ Ναοὺμ τοῦ Ἐσλὶ τοῦ Ναγγαὶ τοῦ Μάαθ τοῦ Ματταθίου τοῦ Σεμεῒν τοῦ Ἰωσὴχ τοῦ Ἰωδὰ τοῦ Ἰωανὰν τοῦ Ῥησὰ τοῦ Ζοροβαβὲλ τοῦ Σαλαθιὴλ τοῦ Νηρὶ τοῦ Μελχὶ τοῦ Ἀδδὶ τοῦ Κωσὰμ τοῦ Ἐλμαδὰμ τοῦ Ἢρ τοῦ Ἰησοῦ τοῦ Ἐλιέζερ τοῦ Ἰωρὶμ τοῦ Μαθθὰτ τοῦ Λευὶ τοῦ Συμεὼν τοῦ Ἰούδα τοῦ Ἰωσὴφ τοῦ Ἰωνὰμ τοῦ Ἐλιακὶμ τοῦ Μελεὰ τοῦ Μεννὰ τοῦ Ματταθὰ τοῦ Ναθὰμ τοῦ Δαυὶδ τοῦ Ἰεσσαὶ τοῦ Ἰωβὴδ τοῦ Βόος τοῦ Σαλὰ τοῦ Ναασσὼν τοῦ Ἀμιναδὰβ τοῦ Ἀδμὶν τοῦ Ἀρνὶ τοῦ Ἐσρὼμ τοῦ Φάρες τοῦ Ἰούδα τοῦ Ἰακὼβ τοῦ Ἰσαὰκ τοῦ Ἀβραὰμ τοῦ Θάρα τοῦ Ναχὼρ τοῦ Σεροὺχ τοῦ Ῥαγαὺ τοῦ Φάλεκ τοῦ Ἔβερ τοῦ Σαλὰ τοῦ Καϊνὰμ τοῦ Ἀρφαξὰδ τοῦ Σὴμ τοῦ Νῶε τοῦ Λάμεχ τοῦ Μαθουσαλὰ τοῦ Ἐνὼχ τοῦ Ἰάρετ τοῦ Μαλελεὴλ τοῦ Καϊνὰμ τοῦ Ἐνὼς τοῦ Σὴθ τοῦ Ἀδὰμ τοῦ θεοῦ).

Since Luke inserts the genealogy after God declares him to be his Son, Jesus' physical lineage

---

17. C. G. Mueller, " 'Ungefähr 30': Anmerkungen zur Altersangabe Jesu in Lukasevangelium (Lk. 3:23)," *NTS* 49 (2003): 489 – 504.

becomes less important, as is clear from the parenthetical phrase "as was thought" (ὡς ἐνομίζετο). This phrase reminds the reader that Joseph was not the biological father of Jesus, for Jesus was conceived of a virgin. Joseph did assume parental responsibilities, and as Joseph's presumed firstborn son, Jesus has the status of heir in Joseph's family.[18]

Luke's genealogy begins with Jesus and works back to Adam, while Matthew begins with Abraham and works up to Jesus (Matt 1:1 – 17).[19] Matthew divides the list into three periods of fourteen generations; Luke's list is less clearly structured. [20] Some scholars may be right in counting "seventy-seven generations, so that Jesus' activity starts at the end of the eleventh and the beginning twelfth (and last!) period of seven generations."[21]

It seems that Luke has simply taken over the list from a source to underscore two things. First, and most obviously, it provides proof of Jesus' royal, messianic identity.[22] But the list of names avoids the kingly line of David, beginning with David's little known son Nathan (1 Chr 3:5) rather than King Solomon (Matt 1:6 – 7), and with a list of mostly unknown persons rather than the royal personages listed in Matt 1:7 – 12.

The kingly line was filled with scandalous behavior, but it may be that Luke deliberately chose this version of the genealogy to stress a more humble Davidic status, like that of David's own origins. He stands in contrast to the Davidic kings who reigned in Jerusalem (see the comments on "the town of David" in 2:4).[23] Bauckham links it to the prophecy in Isa 11:1, "A shoot will come up from the stump of Jesse." He notes that the image portrays a tree cut down to the stump, which applies to the royal house of David cut down in judgment (Isa 10:33 – 34). Just as Jesus is not born in a palace in Jerusalem but in a manger in insignificant

18. Nolland, *Luke*, 1:171.

19. Speculation about the source of Luke's list is just that, speculation. William S. Kurz ("Luke 3:23 – 38 and Greco-Roman and Biblical Genealogies," in *Luke-Acts: New Perspectives* [ed. C. H. Talbert; New York: Crossroad, 1984], 169 – 87) argues that the list is based on LXX 1 Chr 1 – 9. Gert J. Steyn ("The Occurrence of 'Kainam' in Luke's Genealogy: Evidence of Septuagint Influence," *ETL* 65 [1989]: 409 – 11) contends that the list in 3:34 – 38 derives from LXX Gen 11:10 – 32 and 5:1 – 32. Fitzmyer, *Luke*, 1:491, challenges that the list of names derives from any of these passages. James M. Scott ("Acts 2:9 – 11 as an Anticipation of the Mission to the Nations," in *The Mission of the Early Church to the Jews and Gentiles* [ed. J. Ådna and H. Kvalbein; WUNT 127; Tübingen: Mohr Siebeck, 2000], 88 – 97) contends that the original text contained seventy-two names and Luke composed this list "representing the nations of the world" from *Jubilees*.

20. Where the list overlaps with Matthew's from Abraham to Jesus, Luke has fifty-six names and Matthew forty-two. From Adam to Shem (3:36b – 38) the names are drawn from the list of names in Gen 5; from Shem to Abraham (3:34 – 36a), from Gen 11:10 – 32; from Abraham to David, from 1 Chr and Ruth. From David to Jesus the two lists diverge completely. Matthew traces the line from David through Solomon; Luke through David's insignificant son Nathan, who was not part of the ruling dynasty.

Several attempts have been made to explain the differences. Codex Bezae eliminated them altogether by substituting the Matthean genealogy, which it copies in reverse order. Julius Africanus distinguished between biological descent, represented by Luke, and adoptive, legal descent (via levirate marriage) represented by Matthew (cf. Eusebius, *Hist. eccl.* 1.7). Some adopt this solution but reverse the functions of the genealogies. Annius of Viterbo claimed that Matthew gives Joseph's line while Luke gives Mary's line. Arthur C. Hervey (*The Genealogies of Our Lord and Saviour Jesus Christ* (London: Hatchard, 1853) argued that Matthew gives the legal line of descent from David, and Luke gives the actual descendants of David in Joseph's branch of the family. None of these proposals solve the problem.

21. Bovon, *Luke 1:1 – 9:50*, 135. See also 2 Esd 14:11. George J. Brooke (*The Dead Sea Scrolls and the New Testament* [Minneapolis: Fortress, 2004], 129) notes, "The organization of history into 11 weeks of seven generations is to be found in *1 Enoch* 10.12, now extant in 4QEnoch[b] 1 IV, 10: Michael is there instructed to bind the Watchers for 70 generations." He also observes (139): "For Luke's genealogy, as Enoch is the seventh, so Jesus is the ultimate seventy-seventh, and Jesus' only namesake in the list is not surprisingly the forty-ninth."

22. Strauss, *The Davidic Messiah in Luke-Acts*, 209 – 15.

23. Miura, *David in Luke-Acts*, 212.

Bethlehem, so the genealogy represents "a return to the authentic source of David's line among the ordinary people."[24]

Second, it shows Jesus' connection to the human race. Tracing the genealogy beyond Abraham, the father of the Jews, to Adam, the father of all nations, takes the genealogy beyond a Jewish perspective to encompass "the entire human race."[25] Jesus is not only heir to Jewish hopes; he is "heir to human destiny."[26] It foreshadows the universal scope of God's salvation that comes through Jesus (see Acts 17:24 – 31).

Theology in Application

1. The Holy Spirit Coming through Prayer

In some contexts, people talk about "getting" the Holy Spirit. How terribly small the Spirit would be if we could get hold of him. The issue is not that we get the Holy Spirit but that the Holy Spirit takes possession of us. Barth complains:

> But theology now supposes it can deal with the Spirit as though it had hired him or even attained possession of him. It imagines that he is a power of nature that can be discovered, harnessed, and put to use like water, fire, electricity or atomic energy. As a foolish church presupposes his presence and action in its own existence, in its offices and sacraments, ordinations, consecrations and absolutions, so a foolish theology presupposes the Spirit as the premise of its own declarations. The Spirit is thought to be one whom it knows and over whom it disposes. But a presupposed spirit is certainly not the Holy Spirit, and a theology that presumes to have it under control can only be unspiritual theology.[27]

Jesus' experience in his baptism counters this attitude that we can control the Spirit's coming and going and direction. The Holy Spirit comes on Jesus when he is in the passive state of submitting himself to God's will in baptism and while he is praying. The Holy Spirit is poured out on the disciples in Acts in the same way. They were constantly devoting themselves to prayer (Acts 1:14), and then, unexpectedly, the Spirit came roaring into their lives (Acts 2:1 – 4), driving them from the passive state to fiery activity.

The effects of the Spirit in the life of Jesus are evident in what follows: the power to resist the wiles of Satan, the power to recall and apply Scripture, the power to see God's plan and purposes and to proclaim the Word boldly, the power to withstand hostility, and the power to minister to and heal the oppressed. The Spirit in the lives of believers can do the same things.

24. Bauckham, *Gospel Women*, 74. See Richard Bauckham, *Jude and the Relatives of Jesus in the Early Church* (Edinburgh: T&T Clark, 1990), 315 – 73.

25. Bovon, *Luke 1:1 – 9:50*, 134.

26. Stephen I. Wright, "Luke, Book of," in *The Dictionary for the Theological Interpretation of Scripture* (ed. K. Vanhoozer, C. Bartholomew, and N. T. Wright; Grand Rapids: Baker, 2005), 468.

27. Karl Barth, *Evangelical Theology: An Introduction* (trans. G. Foley; New York: Holt, Rinehart, and Winston, 1963), 58.

2. God's Purposes Hidden in a Family Tree

Family trees, other than our own, may strike us as only a boring list of unpronounceable names, but they have significance in Scripture. Genealogies in Scripture are not simply a record of human fertility. They undergird the status of one for a particular office where lineage is important. In Neh 7:5, 64 – 65, those who sought to be registered as priests and were not found among those enrolled in the genealogies were excluded. The Messiah was believed to be of the lineage of David, and Jesus must be demonstrated to belong to that lineage. Jesus belongs to the royal line of Judah. But a person's genealogy conveyed more in the ancient world. Jesus' genealogy establishes continuity over those periods of time not covered by Luke's narrative. The story of Jesus goes back to Adam. It reminds us that God keeps promises, and it demonstrates God's providence across the ages directing the traffic of history to the climactic birth of Jesus.

Many people in this list are completely unknown, and, unknown to them, they were playing a part in salvation history. John W. Gardner said, "History never looks like history when you are living through it. It always looks confusing and messy, and it always feels uncomfortable."[28] Our lives may seem to be a series of disappointments, our hopes in disarray, and our future desperate. Did those who lived in the days of Melchi and Addi have a clue what God was preparing? One knows what God is doing during this time only when one looks back and sees what God has done. All along God secretly ordered the economy of salvation so that all of Israel's history moved toward the Messiah. It gives hope for the future. God continues to work to bring all things to a final glorious culmination.

3. Jesus and Adam

As Jesus prays after his immersion, a voice from heaven declares: "You are my Son, the beloved; with you I am well pleased" (3:22). Jesus' genealogy is then traced through Joseph, beginning with the statement, "He was the son, as was thought, of Joseph the son of Heli" (3:23). This parenthetical note suggests that the genealogy does not really apply to Jesus. Luke knows Jesus to be the son of David (18:38 – 39; 20:41 – 44), but he does not use the genealogy to establish that point as Matthew does (1:1 – 25). Instead, he connects Jesus to the whole human race. Matthew seeks to answer the question how one born of a virgin could be the son of David. The answer is that Joseph, son of David, adopted him. Luke's genealogy confirms Jesus' Davidic descent, but it also serves to contrast Jesus with Adam, who is also identified as "son of God" (3:38). How is Jesus different from Adam as *the* Son of God?

---

28. As cited by Joseph R. Conlin, *The American Past: A Survey of American History* (Belmont, CA: Thomson Wadsworth, 2009), 834.

Jesus was conceived by the Holy Spirit. Philo states that Adam, "the first and earthborn man," was not conceived in the normal way. His body was molded "by the hand of God, the Master Sculptor and judged worthy to receive his soul not from any other thing already created, but through the breath of God imparting of His own power such measure as mortal nature could receive.... His father was no mortal but the eternal God" (*Virtues* 203 – 204). But Jesus redefines what it means to be the Son of God. Adam disobeyed God and sinned and as a result was excluded from paradise. The temptation scene that immediately follows has the devil test Jesus as the Son of God, "If you are the Son of God ..." (4:3, 9), and Jesus successfully vanquishes the devil at every turn. Neyrey concludes: "The genealogy provides the link between assertion and question; it provides the context in which to assess the meaning of 'son of God.' While Jesus is not the first to be so named, Luke suggests that he is the one most fittingly called 'son of God.'"[29]

Paul's comments in Rom 5:12 – 21 develop ideas that are latent in Luke's sequence of the heavenly testimony that Jesus is the Son of God, the genealogy, and Jesus' testing by Satan in the wilderness. Christ's victory over Satan in the wilderness, the cross, and the resurrection brought a new life that counters the death brought into the world by Adam and his sin. Adam's transgression was one of deliberate disobedience to God, "I'm better off doing what God told me not to do." Jesus was obedient unto death, "Let your will, not mine, be done" (22:42). Adam started a plague of sin in which all humans share. Starting a contagion is easy to do. Jesus came when the plague was in full swing to reverse its effects, which is far more difficult.

---

29. Jerome Neyrey, *The Passion According to Luke: A Redaction Study of Luke's Soteriology* (Mahwah, NJ: Paulist, 1985), 166.

CHAPTER 11

Luke 4:1 – 13

Literary Context

Jesus' baptism and the genealogy reinforce the fact conveyed in the infancy narratives that Jesus is the Son of God (3:22, 23, 38). The sequel that shows Jesus' being tested in the wilderness adds a new dimension for understanding his identity. In 3:38 Jesus was identified as "the son of Adam." The temptation incident is only the second time in Scripture in which a human comes face-to-face with the devil. Unlike Adam and Eve in paradise, Jesus does not succumb to the devil's enticements. The testing reveals that "being God's son ... entails a mission which must be fulfilled."[1] Jesus shows that he is committed to accomplishing this mission according to God's marching orders and means. Sonship requires obedience. Jesus demonstrates that as God's Son (4:3, 9), he is faithful and will not serve his own needs and desires. The worshipers in the Nazareth synagogue are mistaken when they ask, "Is this not the son of Joseph?" (4:22), and therefore they cannot appraise Jesus correctly. Understanding Jesus as God's Son and what that entails is crucial for interpreting what happens to Jesus in the rest of the narrative and the climax at the cross, when blasphemers taunt him to save himself (23:35 – 37).

This temptation incident also reinforces Jesus' unique relation to the Holy Spirit. He was conceived through the creative power of the Holy Spirit (1:35), and the Spirit came down on him in his baptism (3:21 – 22). Jesus, now full of the Holy Spirit, is led by the Spirit in the wilderness (4:1). When he begins his public ministry, he is filled with the power of the Spirit (4:14) and anointed by the Spirit to accomplish his messianic program (4:18). Through the power of the Spirit, Jesus drives out demons and heals the sick (4:31 – 44).

This incident also shows that Jesus resists and overturns evil as he engages in a toe-to-toe face-off with the devil. In the next incident, Jesus encounters evil in the religious setting of a synagogue. He then takes on various kinds of evil, sickness, and demonic possession that twist and deform human lives. This conflict will be waged throughout the story until it reaches its climax at the cross.

---

1. Tannehill, *Unity of Luke-Acts*, 58.

Main Idea

Jesus, led by the Spirit, overcomes Satan's temptations and demonstrates both his fidelity to God's purposes and his knowledge of Scripture, which reveals God's will for him as God's Son.

Translation

Luke 4:1–13

4:1a	Circumstance	**And Jesus, full of the Holy Spirit, returned from the Jordan,**
b		**and he was being led by the Spirit**
c		in the wilderness,
2a		where he was tested for forty days by the devil.
b		**He ate nothing during those days,**
c		and when they were completed,
		he was hungry.
3a	Temptation	**The devil said to him,**
b	Concession	*"If you are the Son of God,*
c	Command	*tell this stone to become a piece of bread."*
4a	Answer from Scripture	**Jesus answered him,**
b		*"It stands written, 'Man shall not live by bread alone!'"* (Deut 8:3)
5	Transition of location	When he led him up,
		he showed him in an instant all the kingdoms of the inhabited world.
6a	Promise	**The devil said to him,**
		"I will give you all this authority over them and
		all the glory that comes with it
b		*because it has been handed over to me and*
		I can give it to whomever I want.

Continued on next page.

7	Indirect command by a conditional clause	*If therefore you bow down before me,* *it all will be yours.*"
8a	Answer from Scripture	**Jesus answered him,**
b		*"It stands written, 'You shall worship the Lord your God* *and him alone shall you serve!'"* (Deut 6:13)
9a	Transition of location	**He then led him to Jerusalem and stood him on the wingtip of the temple⤸ and said to him,**
b	Concession	*"If you are the Son of God,*
c	Command	*throw yourself down from here.*
10	Promise (from Scripture)	*For it stands written,* *'Concerning you he will charge his angels to protect you,'*
11		*and, 'They will catch you up in their hands* *to prevent your foot from striking a⤸ stone.'"* (Ps 91:11-12)
12a	Answer from Scripture	**Jesus answered him,**
b		*"It also says, 'You shall not tempt the Lord your God!'"* (Deut 6:16)
13	Departure	And when the devil finished every test, **he departed from him** for a while.

Structure and Literary Form

The order of the temptations in Luke varies from that recorded in Matthew. The devil's offer of all the kingdoms of the world appears last in Matthew as the climax. That temptation scene, therefore, concludes with the emphasis on worshiping and serving only God, which connects to the conclusion of Matthew when the disciples worship Jesus on a mountain (Matt 28:16 – 20). Satan pledged to give Jesus "all the kingdoms of the world" if he would worship him and adopt his malevolent way to power, but Jesus grasped after nothing, accepted his death, and received much more than earthly power through this faithful obedience to God: he is given all authority in heaven and earth (Matt 28:18). Matthew's temptation order also has Jesus quoting passages from Deuteronomy (Deut 8:3; 6:16, 13).

According to Luke's sequence, the last temptation occurs in the temple in Jerusalem.[2] In Luke's extensive travel narrative beginning in 9:51, Jerusalem is the goal of

---

2. Jesus' responses to the devil's bait, therefore, do not follow any sequential order from Deuteronomy.

Jesus' ministry and his "exodus" (9:31; 9:53; 13:22; 17:11; 18:31; 19:11, 28). He knows this will be the place of his death (13:31 – 35; 18:31). When he finally arrives in the city, he faces his greatest temptation and prays that God might, if possible, rescue him from his impending death (22:42). Buoyed by prayer and strengthened by an angel (22:39 – 46), he remains obedient to God's will. God rescues him *out of* death instead of *from* death, and he uses Jesus' death to displace the temple sacrificial cult as a means of atonement.

The order of the temptations in Luke follows Psalm 106.[3] The first temptation about bread matches Ps 106:14 – 15, which recaps the manna and quails incident in Exod 16 and Num 11:4: "In the desert they gave in to their craving; in the wilderness they put God to the test. So he gave them what they asked for, but sent a wasting disease among them." The temptation to worship the devil matches Ps 106:19 – 20, which recaps Exod 32, "At Horeb they made a calf and worshiped an idol cast from metal. They exchanged their glorious God for an image of a bull, which eats grass." The third temptation matches Ps 106:32 – 33, which recaps the episode at Meribah; when the people complained that God has brought them into the wilderness to die, they angered the Lord, and rash words came from Moses' mouth (cf. Num 20:2 – 13; Ps 78:12 – 22).[4]

Exegetical Outline

→ **I. Setting: Jesus being led by the Spirit in the wilderness and fasting forty days (4:1 – 2)**

II. The devil's testing him as the Son of God (4:3 – 12)

    A. To turn stones into bread to satisfy his hunger (4:3 – 4)

    B. To rule the kingdoms of this world through obedience to the devil (4:5 – 8)

    C. To test God's faithfulness to protect him from injury (4:9 – 12)

III. The devil's departure until an opportune time (4:13)

Explanation of the Text

4:1a And Jesus, full of the Holy Spirit, returned from the Jordan (Ἰησοῦς δὲ πλήρης πνεύματος ἁγίου ὑπέστρεψεν ἀπὸ τοῦ Ἰορδάνου). The "spontaneous outburst of the prophetic Spirit" in the lives and utterances of Elizabeth (1:41), Zechariah (1:67), John (1:15, 80), and Simeon (2:25 – 27) is now "stilled."[5] The Spirit's relationship to Jesus is different from these representatives of Israel. Luke uses the passive form of the verb "to fill" (πίμπλημι) to describe persons filled with the Spirit (e.g., John, Elizabeth, and Zechariah; see also Acts 2:4; 4:8, 31; 13:9), but he never uses it for Jesus. Luke tells us that in Jesus' baptism the Spirit came upon him (3:22), and the adjectival phrase

---

3. Hamish Swanston, "The Lukan Temptation Narrative," *JTS* 17 (1966): 71; Brooke, *The Dead Sea Scrolls and the New Testament*, 131, n. 50.

4. The pattern also fits Paul's account of Israel's failings in the wilderness in 1 Cor 10:6 – 9: craving (v. 6), idolatry (v. 7), and putting to the test (v. 9).

5. W. Barnes Tatum, "The Epoch of Israel: Luke I–II and the Theological Plan of Luke-Acts," *NTS* 13 (1967): 190 – 91.

"full [πλήρης] of the Holy Spirit" suggests that he is not "seized by an external power" but appears as the bearer of the Spirit and is anointed by the Spirit.[6] Other characters are described in Acts as full of the Holy Spirit (Acts 6:3, 5; 7:55; 11:24), and all are given special tasks to fulfill. In Jesus' case, it means that the Spirit directs his actions and that he is empowered "to carry out his divinely appointed task."[7]

4:1b – 2a And he was being led by the Spirit in the wilderness, where he was tested for forty days by the devil (καὶ ἤγετο ἐν τῷ πνεύματι ἐν τῇ ἐρήμῳ ἡμέρας τεσσαράκοντα πειραζόμενος ὑπὸ τοῦ διαβόλου). Luke's wording differs from the harsher language of Mark, who has the Spirit "sent [Jesus] out into the wilderness" (ἐκβάλλει εἰς τὴν ἔρημον, Mark 1:12), and from Matthew, who has Jesus "led by the Spirit into the wilderness" (ἀνήχθη εἰς τὴν ἔρημον ὑπὸ τοῦ πνεύματος, Matt 4:1) by the Spirit. In these other accounts, the Spirit directs Jesus to the wilderness, but Luke's phrase that "he was being led … in the wilderness," using an imperfect tense (ἤγετο) and the preposition "in" (ἐν) rather than "into" (εἰς), may suggest that while he was in the wilderness the Spirit was directing him.

Luke's account, then, depicts the Spirit's role more as an inward inspiration than as an external compulsive force. It reinforces the point that Jesus will be guided in his ministry by the Holy Spirit rather than by Satan, who seeks to preempt the Spirit's role.[8] It also means that Jesus' experience more closely echoes the wilderness experience of Israel. As God led the people in the wilderness (Deut 8:2, 15), so the Spirit, as God's presence, leads Jesus. The "wilderness" evokes the image of "the vast and dreadful wilderness, that thirsty and waterless land, with its venomous snakes and scorpions" (Deut 8:15), rather than some idyllic retreat.[9]

The wilderness is uninhabited by humans and a haunt of evil (see 11:24) where demons — hairy satyrs, storm devils, howling dragons and monsters, the winged night monsters, and Azazel — prowl.[10] "*The* wilderness" (τῇ ἐρήμῳ) recalls "the wilderness of Israel's post-Exodus sojourn."[11] It represents the proverbial place of testing Israel's covenant loyalty to God, since it was there that the wilderness generation continually questioned God's presence, rebelled against his leadership, and toyed with idolatry (see Exod 16 – 20; 24; 33 – 35). Like Israel in the wilderness, Jesus is there under divine direction, and his loyalty to God is put to the test.

The number "forty" is a familiar one in Old Testament lore and may be a biblical round number for a long time.[12] In the context of being tested, however, the reference to forty days can

---

6. Ibid., 191. In Acts, the prophetic Spirit is again active, but in contrast to the infancy narrative "where only a *few* chosen individuals receive the Spirit, within the Church everyone is a recipient (Acts 2:4,17; 4:31; 5:32; 8:17; 9:44 – 45; 13:52; 15:8; 19:2, 6)." The adjectival phrase "full of the Holy Spirit" can now be used of Christians.

7. Menzies, *The Development of Early Christian Pneumatology*, 157.

8. Note the contrast with John, who is guided to the Jordan region by "the word of God" (Luke 3:2).

9. The wilderness was first mentioned in the gospel in connection to the word of God: the word of God bypassed the halls of power to come to John in the wilderness (1:80; 3:2).

10. W. D. Davies, *The Gospel and the Land* (Berkeley: Univ. of California Press, 1974), 86 – 88. See *1 En.* 10:4 – 5; 4 Macc 18:8; *2 Bar.* 10:8.

11. Jeffrey B. Gibson, *The Temptations of Jesus in Early Christianity* (JSNTSup 112; Sheffield: Sheffield Academic, 1995), 60 – 61.

12. Forty is the number of the days of rain during the flood (Gen 7:4, 12, 17), the time that the people were handed over to the Philistines for their disobedience (Judg 13:1), the amount of time before the judgment of Nineveh (Jonah 3:2), the time Ezekiel lay on his side to symbolize the judgment of Israel (Ezek 4:6), the time Abraham fasted (*Apoc. Ab.* 12:1 – 2), and the time Jesus spent with the disciples after the resurrection (Acts 1:3). It also matches the time Moses spent on the mountain when he received the stone tablets of the covenant from

bring to mind Israel's wilderness sojourn under Moses when they were tested by God (Deut 2:7; 8:2; Neh 9:21; Ps 95:10; Amos 2:10; Acts 7:30, 36). Forty days is specifically equated with the forty years of wandering in Num 14:34 (see Ezek 4:6). As was Israel, so Jesus is tempted by hunger (Exod 16:1 – 8), tempted to worship something other than God (Exod 32), and tempted to put God to the test (Exod 17:1 – 3). Appropriately, his responses come from Deut 6:13, 16 and 8:3, texts directly connected to the testing of Israel in the wilderness.

The present participle of the verb "to test" (πειράζω) following a main, controlling verb (in this case, "was being led") indicates the purpose of the action in every other usage in the New Testament (Matt 16:1; 19:3; 22:35; Mark 8:11; 10:2; Luke 11:16; John 6:6; 8:6) except one (Heb 11:17). It probably has that function here.[13] It explains the purpose of Jesus' wilderness sojourn; he was being led in order to be tested. If "forty days" is to be linked to the participle "being tested," then Jesus is tempted for forty days as in Mark 1:13. The three temptations could epitomize the temptations the devil offered, or they could represent the devil launching a last-ditch effort when these days were completed, pulling out all stops to get Jesus to give homage to him as his supreme patron.

"The devil" (ὁ διάβολος) is the one who both puts the faithful to the test and who opposes divine interests. In particular, the devil "tries to disrupt the relation between God and man, and especially between God and Israel."[14] Garrett concludes: "When Satan tests the righteous, he hopes that they will fail the tests (by disobeying, or even cursing, God), and so lose their rightful place in God's realm."[15] When the righteous endure Satan's tests, Satan is put to shame. He seeks to get Jesus to act in a way that would spurn God's predetermined pathway but will fail.

4:2b-c He ate nothing during those days, and when they were completed, he was hungry (καὶ οὐκ ἔφαγεν οὐδὲν ἐν ταῖς ἡμέραις ἐκείναις καὶ συντελεσθεισῶν αὐτῶν ἐπείνασεν). In the Bible, fasting is an act of humility and a means to open oneself up to God.

Since Luke records that Jesus "ate nothing" instead of using the verb for "fasting" (see Matt 4:2), he recalls the wording in Exod 34:28 and Deut 9:9, where Moses "ate no bread and drank no water" prior to receiving the law. Philo assumes that during this time Moses received communications from God (*Alleg. Interp.* 3.142). The allusion suggests that as Jesus is poised to begin his ministry, his abstinence from food is not an act of penitence but part of his preparation to receive God's guidance. The devil seeks to take over that role and times his big tests at the end of a long period when Jesus is famished. Like Amalek attacking Israel on the way when they were faint and weary (Deut 25:18), the devil attacks Jesus when he is faint and weary.[16] The devil cleverly varies his attack and probes for weak spots to secure his tentacles.

4:3 The devil said to him, "If you are the Son of God, tell this stone to become a piece of bread" (εἶπεν δὲ αὐτῷ ὁ διάβολος, εἰ υἱὸς εἶ τοῦ θεοῦ, εἰπὲ τῷ λίθῳ τούτῳ ἵνα γένηται ἄρτος). In Luke's Greek, the devil uses the first class condition, "if you are the Son of God," for the sake of argument. Assuming that the statement is true (see 1:32, 35;

God (Exod 24:18; Deut 9:11), when he pleaded for God not to destroy the people for their disobedience (Deut 9:25; 10:10), and when he fasted for forty days and nights before receiving the Ten Commandments (Exod 34:28; Deut 9:9; see also Deut 9:18). Elijah fasted for forty days and forty nights on Horeb, the mount of God (1 Kgs 19:8).

13. Wallace, *Greek Grammar*, 635 – 36.
14. Werner Foerster, "διαβάλλω, διάβολος," *TDNT*, 2:76.
15. Susan R. Garrett, *The Temptations of Jesus in Mark's Gospel* (Grand Rapids: Eerdmans, 1998), 49.
16. At the end of his ministry during the Last Supper, Jesus announces that he will refrain from eating it (22:16).

3:22, 23 – 38), it naturally follows that the Son of God need not deny himself and go hungry and has the power to turn stones into bread. It is not a request to prove that he is the Son of God by performing a miracle. Prove it to whom? There are no witnesses. The focus lies on what it means to be the Son of God.

Luke has shown in the infancy narratives that Jesus is God's Son conceived through the Holy Spirit, and now it becomes clear that being God's Son brings with it a divinely mandated mission to accomplish God's will and to reveal to the world the true nature of God. What the devil attempts to do is to turn Jesus away "from a particular and God-ordained pattern of sonship with which he is already familiar and to which he has already been called."[17] He bases his appeal on Jesus' being the exalted Son of God who should not suffer. Jesus responds that his sonship requires obedience even if it leads to suffering and humiliation.

This is not a temptation to become a Messiah who gives out physical bread to all those who are hungry, but a temptation to satisfy his own present hunger and use his close relation to God to meet his own needs.[18] He is the one who is hungry; others are not in view. Jesus will have no qualms later about miraculously providing bread for the hungering multitudes (14:13 – 21).

4:4 Jesus answered him, "It stands written, 'Man shall not live by bread alone!'" (καὶ ἀπεκρίθη πρὸς αὐτὸν ὁ Ἰησοῦς, γέγραπται ὅτι οὐκ ἐπ' ἄρτῳ μόνῳ ζήσεται ὁ ἄνθρωπος). Jesus resists the temptation by resorting to Scripture and citing Deut 8:3a. "It stands written" (γέγραπται) basically means "God has said it."[19] He responds as a human, as a "man" (ὁ ἄνθρωπος), not as someone with superpowers. What applies to all humans

applies to himself. He too cannot live by bread alone. But he will not allow the legitimate desire to assuage his physical hunger to take priority over his relationship to God.

Jesus is not at the point of utter starvation, so the temptation is the same as that which plagued Israel in their wilderness sojourn: *"to be dissatisfied with what God appoints as the means appropriate for sustaining and attaining 'life.'"*[20] As the Son of God, he cannot succumb to "a wanton craving" and make getting "bread" the center of his life. Instead, he devotes himself to God and will become known as the "author of life" (Acts 3:15). His three rejoinders from Scripture to the different temptations reveal that he lives "on every word that comes from the mouth of the LORD" (Deut 8:3).

4:5 – 7 When he led him up, he showed him in an instant all the kingdoms of the inhabited world. The devil said to him, "I will give you all this authority over them and all the glory that comes with it because it has been handed over to me and I can give it to whomever I want. If therefore you bow down before me, it all will be yours" (καὶ ἀναγαγὼν αὐτὸν ἔδειξεν αὐτῷ πάσας τὰς βασιλείας τῆς οἰκουμένης ἐν στιγμῇ χρόνου καὶ εἶπεν αὐτῷ ὁ διάβολος· σοὶ δώσω τὴν ἐξουσίαν ταύτην ἅπασαν καὶ τὴν δόξαν αὐτῶν, ὅτι ἐμοὶ παραδέδοται καὶ ᾧ ἐὰν θέλω δίδωμι αὐτήν. σὺ οὖν ἐὰν προσκυνήσῃς ἐνώπιον ἐμοῦ, ἔσται σοῦ πᾶσα). The devil tries to lure Jesus to forsake God through the human hunger for power and to achieve it by any means. He "led him up" (ἀναγαγών) to view all the kingdoms of the world, but Luke does not identify where this "up" is. He does not describe it as "a very high mountain" (Matt 4:8), so that this spot does not eclipse the temple as the highest point. The kingdoms flash

---

17. Gibson, *The Temptations of Jesus*, 108.
18. Gibson (ibid., 99) contends that the wording does not mean that Jesus is to perform a miracle but that he is to "give the command [to God] so that he will provide bread."
19. Evans, *St. Luke*, 258.
20. Gibson, *The Temptations of Jesus*, 113.

across the screen, as it were, like a commercial trying to entice his interest with a dashing display of their glory and allures.

The scenario parallels something imagined by Dio Chrysostom: what "if someone should raise me aloft and transport me through the sky, either, as it were, on the back of some Pegasus or in some winged car of Pelops, offering me the whole earth and its cities?" (*2 Fort.* 64:14). The difference is that for Jesus that "someone" is the devil. The scene has resonances with Deut 34:1 – 4, when Moses went up from the plains of Moab to the top of Pisgah and the Lord showed him the whole land. The Lord said that the land would be given to Moses' descendants but he would not be allowed to cross over there. The devil expands the promise to include the entire world and promises that it can all belong to Jesus. The catch: Jesus must worship him. As Bovon puts it, "the devil demands nothing less than a change of command."[21]

The devil tempts Jesus to do what redounds to his own glory rather than to God's. It is a temptation to accelerate the access to power by bypassing the path of suffering and service, to achieve power for power's sake, giving no thought to justice, to adopt satanic means of attaining power by exploiting, dominating, and crushing others. The angel Gabriel announced to Mary that God would give to her divinely conceived son the throne of David and that there would be no end to his kingdom (1:31 – 33). The devil offers "a shabby substitute" to replace "an everlasting kingdom."[22]

It is striking that Jesus does not challenge the devil's claim to have authority over all of the kingdoms of the world (see the decree of Cyrus in Ezra

1:2). Luke gives the devil his due. It would not have been a real temptation if the devil did not have this authority.[23] Bovon remarks that this "pessimistic view of the world that lies behind this statement may be peculiar to Luke."[24] Supposedly, the entire world is ruled currently by Caesar, who, for example, can decree that "the entire world should be registered" (2:1). This assertion subtly implies that the Roman rule over the world is diabolic (see Rev 13:1 – 18). Since the devil will be overthrown (see John 12:31), all these kingdoms are on shaky ground. They will soon become irrelevant footnotes of history.[25] What truly matters and will last eternally is God's kingdom. And it is the Father's good pleasure to give *this* kingdom to his "little flock" of worshipers (12:32).

4:8 Jesus answered him, "It stands written, 'You shall worship the Lord your God and him alone shall you serve!'" (καὶ ἀποκριθεὶς ὁ Ἰησοῦς εἶπεν αὐτῷ· γέγραπται, κύριον τὸν θεόν σου προσκυνήσεις καὶ αὐτῷ μόνῳ λατρεύσεις). Jesus' answer comes from Deut 6:13 – 15. Israel was to worship God alone but became entangled in idolatry in the wilderness (see Acts 7:43), and the anger of the Lord was kindled against them. The result was disastrous. When Israel entered the Promised Land, they did exactly what God forbade them to do and again became mired in idolatry (see Deut 7:1 – 5; Judg 3:5 – 7). Again, the results were disastrous. By contrast, Jesus stands firm in his allegiance to serve God alone.

4:9 – 10 He then led him to Jerusalem and stood him on the wingtip of the temple and said to him, "If you are the Son of God, throw yourself

21. Bovon, *Luke 1:1 – 9:50*, 144.

22. Green, *The Gospel of Luke*, 194 – 95.

23. Dominic Rudman, "Authority and Right of Disposal in Luke 4:6," *NTS* 50 (2004): 79.

24. Bovon, *Luke 1:1 – 9:50*, 144.

25. The wording of the temptation harkens back to the

coronation language used in Ps 2:8 regarding the Davidic monarchy: "Ask me, and I will make the nations your inheritance, the ends of the earth your possession." Might this be an implicit rejection of the traditional vision of a restored Davidic monarchy?

down from here. For it stands written, 'Concerning you he will charge his angels to protect you,' and, 'They will catch you up in their hands to prevent your foot from striking a stone'" (ἤγαγεν δὲ αὐτὸν εἰς Ἰερουσαλὴμ καὶ ἔστησεν ἐπὶ τὸ πτερύγιον τοῦ ἱεροῦ καὶ εἶπεν αὐτῷ· εἰ υἱὸς εἶ τοῦ θεοῦ, βάλε σεαυτὸν ἐντεῦθεν κάτω· γέγραπται γὰρ ὅτι τοῖς ἀγγέλοις αὐτοῦ ἐντελεῖται περὶ σοῦ τοῦ διαφυλάξαι σε καὶ ὅτι ἐπὶ χειρῶν ἀροῦσίν σε μήποτε προσκόψῃς πρὸς λίθον τὸν πόδα σου). His parents brought Jesus to the temple in Jerusalem to present him to the Lord (2:22); the devil brings him to the wingtip of the temple to have him test the Lord. The "wingtip" (τὸ πτερύγιον) probably refers to the pinnacle of a tower at the top of the royal colonnade that overlooked the deep ravine on the south side. Josephus refers to its dizzying height (*Ant.*15.11.5 §§411 – 12).

Jesus is not tempted to pull off some miraculous feat. The text mentions no onlookers who would witness and be impressed by such an exploit. The devil shifts the temptation to the temple because it is the place where God's protection is particularly effective, as the psalm quoted by Satan attests. The temple is a "refuge," a "fortress," the place where God gives shelter (Ps 91:1 – 2). The devil quotes a psalm of blessed assurance, saying in effect: "You will find safety under God's wing. God's angels will protect you and no evil will befall you."

The devil would have Jesus believe that this should be true especially for the Son of God. Johnson unpacks the basic argument: "If God commands the angels to protect David (Ps 90:11 – 12, LXX) from stubbing his foot, how much more would God protect the Messiah who is 'God's Son' if he throws himself headlong from the Temple height?"[26] As Nolland puts it, "By the devil's logic, there should be no martyrs."[27] Jesus makes

a different kind of leap of faith. He chooses radical obedience to God, knowing that this obedience will lead him to the cross (9:22; 17:25; 24:7, 26; Acts 17:3; see 14:22). An angel from heaven does appear — not to protect him from a violent death but rather to strengthen him for the struggle (22:43). It will be the essence of his messianic task, and his last act of obedience will occur in Jerusalem.

This account becomes a defense for Jesus' death on the cross. Bovon argues that to question, "Why did God not spare his son this death (Luke 23:35, 37, 39)? The Christian answer runs this way: It is because of faith, not powerlessness, that Jesus did not save himself. Again, this is not only the answer of a believer, but also of the Messiah of the Christians, who is under attack."[28] Jesus' power is given to him by God to be used for others, not for his own interests.

4:12 Jesus answered him, "It also says, 'You shall not tempt the Lord your God!'" (καὶ ἀποκριθεὶς εἶπεν αὐτῷ ὁ Ἰησοῦς ὅτι εἴρηται· οὐκ ἐκπειράσεις κύριον τὸν θεόν σου). Jesus understands that the devil wants him to put God to the test. Will God keep his word? To test God basically means that one fails to acknowledge his power or take seriously his will to save. To test God is to impugn God's power and faithfulness to fulfill the covenant promises. Such an attitude is a serious offense in Scripture (see Exod 17:1 – 7; Num 14:22; Pss 78:40 – 41; 95:9; 106:6 – 7; Heb 3:7 – 19). Jesus knows that God's power and love do not have to be proven at every turn.

4:13 And when the devil finished every test, he departed from him for a while (καὶ συντελέσας πάντα πειρασμὸν ὁ διάβολος ἀπέστη ἀπ' αὐτοῦ ἄχρι καιροῦ). The phrase "every test" suggests that Jesus faced "the whole gamut of temptation" and

---

26. Johnson, *The Gospel of Luke*, 74.
27. Nolland, *Luke*, 1:183.

28. Bovon, *Luke 1:1 – 9:50*, 145.

not just these three.[29] It also does not mean that the devil is now finished. His withdrawal is simply the conclusion to the testing narrative and a temporary concession of defeat.[30] Luke does not have the sharp command, "Away from me, Satan!" (Matt 4:10). Instead, the devil departs "for a while" (ἄχρι καιροῦ). This note is ominous, and it could also mean "until an opportune time."

Luke does not mean to imply that "the life of Jesus is one long series of temptations."[31] The devil is vanquished here and "forced for a while to use indirect maneuvers (see, for example Luke 8:12)."[32] When Satan reenters the story, Judas collaborates with the high priests and scribes and looks for a "good occasion" (εὐκαιρίαν) to hand Jesus over (22:6).

The devil's stratagems are derailed by Jesus' humble faith and staunch allegiance to God. Leivestad comments, *"As the tormentor he is overcome by miraculous power, as the tempter by humble faith and obedient surrender to God's will."*[33] Jesus will now go on the attack against this tormenter of humankind, raiding the devil's stronghold as the Stronger One with his miraculous power. But Satan is not yet routed. Satan ensnares Judas (22:3), sifts Simon (22:31), and is behind Jesus' arrest and death (22:53). The passion becomes the final proving ground of Jesus' obedience as God's Son.

Theology in Application

1. The Reality of the Devil

Whether one believes in God or not, Satan or not, evil is a fact of human experience. No simple solution can explain it, and it is particularly difficult to explain when one believes that God created all things and is perfectly good, omniscient, and omnipotent. Many credit God for good things that happen and blame Satan for bad things, but this approach is too simplistic. Things can get confusing. For example, Zechariah's muteness was caused by an angel as punishment for not believing (1:19 – 20), but another's muteness is attributed to a demon (11:14). How does one distinguish?

Some may throw up their hands in trying to understand and attribute everything that happens to impersonal luck or to human causes, which are more easily classified and understood. The cause of evil from a secular perspective has been variously attributed to genetics, mental illnesses, social environment, brain chemistry, class distinctions, oppression, and the like. These may all be contributing factors to wicked human behavior, but a refusal to acknowledge that transhuman evil exists that cannot be eradicated by human means or power is dangerous. Albert Einstein said, "It is easier to change the nature of plutonium than man's evil spirit."[34] It may be true, but that does not mean that the only problem is in the hearts of humans.

29. Evans, *St. Luke*, 260.

30. Susan R. Garrett, *The Demise of the Devil: Magic and the Demonic in Luke's Writings* (Minneapolis: Fortress, 1989), 42 – 43.

31. Heinrich Seesemann, "πεῖρα ...," *TDNT*, 6:35.

32. Garrett, *The Demise of the Devil*, 43.

33. Ragnar Leivestad, *Christ the Conqueror: Ideas of Conflict and Victory in the New Testament* (London: SPCK, 1954), 52.

34. Antonina Vallentin, *The Drama of Albert Einstein* (trans. Moura Budberg; Garden City, NY: Doubleday, 1954), 291.

A recent analysis by the Baylor Religion Survey (2005) shows that "roughly 58 percent of Americans absolutely believe in Satan while slightly fewer (48%) believe in demons."[35] Belief in Satan has fallen by the wayside. It may be that some who believe in Satan have only a trivial, cartoonish view shaped by popular fables. Those who do not believe in Satan may simply be turned off by the bizarre caricatures and then reject the whole subject as an out-and-out fabrication. The survey also shows that "among those who believe that the devil is the source of most evil, 84 percent also attribute most evil to mankind. In short, *most* people believe that mankind is responsible for evil in the world," yet "most people do not believe that human nature is basically evil."[36]

Russell shows that a single personification of evil in Greco-Roman religions did not exist.[37] The New Testament, however, presents a view of evil caused by an anthropomorphized Satan who stands in opposition to God. In another study, Russell writes, "The devil is the personification of the principle of evil."[38] He wills and directs evil, and his basic function is to say, "My will, not yours, be done."[39] "The devil is the prince of this world of space (*kosmos*) and time (*aiôn*), as opposed to Jesus Christ, whose kingdom is not of this world."[40] Russell concludes from his historical studies: "If the devil does not exist, then Christianity has been dead wrong on a central point right from the beginning."[41] After the ravages of World War II, Barth wrote that modern Christians pass over the reality of the devil too lightly:

> There exists a superior, ineluctable enemy whom we cannot resist unless God comes to our aid. I do not care for demonology, nor for the manner in which it is treated in Germany today and perhaps elsewhere. Ask me no questions about the Demon, for I am not an authority on the subject! However, it is necessary for us to know that the Devil exists, but then we must hasten to get away from him.[42]

Paul's words are pertinent: "For we do not wrestle against flesh and blood, but against the rulers, against the authorities, against the cosmic powers over this present darkness, against the spiritual forces of evil in the heavenly places" (Eph 6:12 ESV).

Jesus faces down the enemy that haunts all of us and that vies with God's will through lying words that sound religious. Luke's temptation scene reveals at least four things about the devil. First, he rarely appears as manifestly evil. The devil makes his approach with deference, and to hook the pious, he cloaks himself with piety. He can quote Scripture or appear decked out as an angel of light (2 Cor 11:14)

35. Rodney Stark, *What Americans Really Believe* (Waco, TX: Baylor Univ. Press, 2008), 81.

36. Ibid.

37. Jeffrey Burton Russell, *The Devil: Perceptions of Evil from Antiquity to Primitive Christianity* (Ithaca, NY: Cornell Univ. Press, 1977), 122 – 73.

38. Jeffrey Burton Russell, *Satan: The Early Christian Tradi-tion* (Ithaca, NY: Cornell Univ. Press, 1981), 23.

39. Ibid., 25.

40. Ibid., 27.

41. Ibid., 25.

42. Karl Barth, *Prayer According to the Catechisms of the Reformation* (trans. S. F. Terrien; Philadelphia: Westminster, 1952), 73 – 74.

to deceive. This idea is captured in the novel *The Portage to San Cristóbal of A.H.* by George Steiner, when a character holds forth:

> When He made the Word, God made possible also its contrary. Silence is not the contrary of the Word, but its guardian. No, He created on the night side of language a speech for hell. Whose words mean hatred and vomit of life. Few men can learn that speech or speak it for long. It burns in their mouths. It draws them into death. But there shall come a man whose mouth shall be as a furnace and whose tongue shall be as a sword laying waste. He will know the grammar of hell and teach it to others. He will know the sounds of madness and loathing and make them seem music.[43]

The "whisky priest" in Graham Greene's novel *The Power and the Glory* says, "I know — from experience — how much beauty Satan carried down with him when he fell. Nobody ever said the fallen angels were the ugly ones. Oh, no, they were just as quick and light and ..."[44]

It is important to note as well that those who already belong to the devil do not get tested by him. When the devil comes to test, he is not in control or all-powerful. He can be resisted, and Christians have a far more powerful ally in the Holy Spirit to fend him off. Sometimes, as the case with Jesus, the testing can serve God's purposes. Stuhlmueller's comment on Isa 45:6c – 7 is apt: "Evil is no giant staggering through the world at his own whim; somehow, it accomplishes God's will for purifying and disciplining his chosen ones."[45]

Third, since the devil declares that these kingdoms have "been handed over" (παραδέδοται, 4:6) to him, he unintentionally lets slip that he is God's subordinate. Rudman points out the subtle irony. Jesus' rejoinder "operates not just as a statement of where Jesus' own loyalties lie, but also as a rebuke to the chaotic power that refuses to recognize God as the ultimate source of its authority over the world." This "diabolical middleman" expects fealty because of "the power he gives but does not offer the same fealty to the one who has given him this power in the first place."[46]

Jesus recognizes that all power is God's, that all authority operates within God's will, and that nothing on earth could even remotely threaten divine supremacy. What is crucial is the source of his authority — he receives it from God (22:29) — and how he exercises this authority — by giving his life, not by taking life. Christ's way of rule is to be different from the norm: "The kings of the Gentiles lord it over them," but Jesus comes among us as one who serves (22:25 – 27). Jesus took the preferential option to be poor and to have solidarity with the poor (4:18 – 20; see Phil 2:7) as God intended for him. Had Jesus submitted to the devil's program, he would have been

43. George Steiner, *The Portage to San Cristóbal of A.H.* (Chicago: Univ. of Chicago Press, 1999), 45.

44. Graham Greene, *The Power and the Glory* (New York: Bantam, 1954), 123.

45. Carroll Stuhlmueller, "Deutero-Isaiah," in *Jerome Bib-* *lical Commentary* (ed. R. E. Brown, J. A. Fitzmyer, and R. E. Murphy; Englewood Cliffs, NJ: Prentice Hall, 1968), 1:373.

46. Rudman, "Authority and Right of Disposal in Luke 4:6," 85.

another failed, dead revolutionary. Shortly after this encounter, Jesus speaks with authority (4:32) and exercises power over unclean spirits, the devil's minions, driving them out (4:36). After the crucifixion and resurrection, Jesus is declared Lord of all (Acts 10:36).

Fourth, the confrontation with the devil reveals that proclaiming the reign of God (4:43) will be done in the context of satanic resistance. It will take many forms. The devil may be fawning and wily to break one's commitment to God, or he may be hostile and deadly. He appeals to the innate selfishness of humans to get us to disobey God: "You desire things, you deserve them, and you will get them." The word that we can gain anything we want in life — wealth, health, the perfect mate, business success, respect from others — is irresistible to those who are obsessed with themselves.

The devil can quote Scripture and tell lies about God so that evil masquerades as something good. He can get persons to believe that their personal interests are indistinguishable from God's interests. When we do not get what we want, the devil uses a snake-headed bitterness that rears up from the caverns of the heart to destroy others and ourselves. Satan also tries to lead us to mistrust God and so to put God to the test.

2. Jesus, Fully Human, Fully Divine

Jesus was divinely conceived, but he was also fully human. He came into the world in the likeness of sinful flesh (Rom 8:3). Paul uses "flesh" (σάρξ) to represent our creatureliness, and he does not disparage it. The problem with the flesh, however, is that it is "highly combustible material."[47] Temptation is powerless unless there is something to respond to it, and the flesh is the normal responder. It is susceptible to temptation and is easily inflamed.

As our Savior, Jesus was sufficiently like us to reach us. He was not invulnerable to sin and temptation. He is shown here to be fully human, and he faced fully human temptations and overcame them. He was sufficiently different from us to save us. He was not under the power of the flesh, which warps human nature. He was led by the Spirit, which enabled him to checkmate Satan. The same Spirit was given to his disciples to empower them. If they too were filled with the Spirit, they too could resist temptation (see 22:28, 40, 46).

From a biblical point of view, the tests Jesus faced are not simply those common to humanity. They applied specifically to his vocation as the Son of God. The devil sought to entice "Jesus to a selfish misuse of his filial prerogative and thus to a compromise of his Messianic vocation."[48] Gibson states, "What the Devil is trying to win from Jesus with his challenges to Jesus is a denial that the particular pattern of

47. John A. T. Robinson, *The Body* (London: SCM, 1963), 37.

48. Alexandru Neagoe, *The Trial of the Gospel: An Apologetic Reading of Luke's Trial Narratives* (SNTSMS 116; Cambridge: Cambridge Univ. Press, 2002), 44.

Sonship to which Jesus has committed himself is truly what God has in mind for his Son."[49] The devil tried to convince Jesus that God wanted something better for him than what self-denial would bring: "You need to serve yourself, take power, claim the promises as someone who is special!"

Since Luke traces Jesus' genealogy back to Adam, who is identified as the son of God in 3:38, the parallels with the temptation of Adam that led to the fall are evident.[50]

- Jesus obeys God and remains faithful to God whereas Adam, and later Israel, failed. The human fall was caused by disobedience.
- Adam yielded to the temptation to eat certain foods that he and his wife were forbidden to eat (Gen 2:15 – 17; 3:1 – 5). Jesus as the Son of God prized obedience to God over satisfying his hunger and remained a faithful son by not eating.
- Adam was given dominion over the world (Gen 1:26 – 28) but was tempted to seize even more and become like God (Gen 3:5). Jesus did not seek power or a kingdom for himself.
- Adam risked disobeying the command of God because of the promise that he and his wife would not die. Jesus refused the devil's challenge to test his promised invulnerability by jumping off the pinnacle of the temple and put God to the test. He will accept his mission that brings death.
- Adam lost paradise. Jesus can tell a repentant sinner that he will share paradise with him (23:43).

3. Jesus, A Paragon of Virtue

From the viewpoint of the Greco-Roman world, overcoming the temptations establishes Jesus as a paragon of virtue. Cicero (*Verr.* 1.16.46), for example, contends, "Integrity deserves no praise if no one has either the power or the will to corrupt it." Jesus withstood temptations to infidelity and knew the full force of the struggle of a life committed to God. Westcott writes that only the sinless can know the full power of temptation "in its full intensity."[51] Similarly, Caird says: "The man who turns back at his garden gate knows nothing of the strength of the gale in comparison with the man who battles his way through to his destination."[52]

One resists Satan when one is more concerned with serving others than serving oneself. One defeats Satan when one knows and accepts one's place in the order of creation and trusts God's promise to save. One conquers Satan when one conquers fear of reprisals and death.

---

49. Gibson, *The Temptations of Jesus*, 116.
50. Neyrey, *The Passion According to Luke*, 172 – 77.

51. B. F. Westcott, *The Epistle to the Hebrews* (2nd ed; London: Macmillan, 1892), 59.
52. Caird, *Saint Luke*, 79.

Luke 4:14 – 30

Literary Context

Luke's prelude to Jesus' ministry in 3:21 – 4:13 attests that he is the Son of God, as pronounced by the divine voice at his baptism, (3:22); that he is the Davidic Messiah, as traced in the genealogy (3:23 – 38); and that he is the faithful Son of God, as demonstrated in his triumph over the devil (4:1 – 13). Now Luke shows that Jesus is the prophet on whom the Spirit of God rests (4:16 – 30).

This section begins with a summary of Jesus' teaching in the synagogues and the impact that he has (4:14 – 15); it ends with a summary of his continued teaching in the synagogues (4:44). He sets this passage as the frontispiece to Jesus' public ministry as the first recorded public utterance, and it introduces several programmatic themes in Luke-Acts. Jesus consciously embarks on fulfilling the Scripture, which unfolds God's foundational plan. Announcing that God intends for him to bring good news not only to the poor but also to those who are not a part of Israel provokes rejection. The service begins with the people smiling and applauding and ends with them breathing threats and murder. This hostility foreshadows his suffering, and his escape from death at their hands foreshadows the resurrection.

It is possible that Luke has deliberately shifted and edited the incident he found in Mark 6:1 – 6a to make it Jesus' maiden sermon. In this passage (and in Matt 13:53 – 58), the visit to Nazareth and his subsequent rejection occurs after an extended period of ministry, and Luke does not have this incident in his parallel section. Mark and Matthew do not record the synagogue's initial approbation of Jesus that turns into disapproval, only their repudiation of him. Mark concludes the incident by commenting that Jesus was unable to do any mighty work there, except heal a few people, and he marveled at their lack of faith (Mark 6:6a). Matthew's account also concludes that Jesus did not do many mighty works there because of a lack of faith (Matt 13:58). Luke records fuller details of his sermon, including the Scripture he reads. The only mighty works mentioned are those that he will do in Capernaum that will spark the jealousy of Nazareth.

Whether Luke used Mark or an independent source, the Nazareth incident is a programmatic text for his gospel. It reveals what kind of Messiah Jesus will be. His mission brings good news and deliverance to the outcasts and oppressed. He emphasizes his role as the anointed eschatological prophet filled with the Spirit. God's purposes for Israel as promised by the prophets are being fulfilled. The recipients of his ministry will not be Jews alone; God will include Gentiles in the blessing of Israel (see 2:32; 3:6, citing Isaiah).[1]

The word of God sent to Israel (Acts 10:34 – 38) brings healing (Acts 13:26), but it also creates a crisis because it is to be sent to the Gentiles as well as to Jews (Acts 28:28). The inclusion of Gentiles will become the sticking point for some Jews as the story develops in Acts. As Jesus' ministry meets with rejection in Israel, the same pattern will be found in Paul's first experience of preaching in the Diaspora synagogue in Antioch of Pisidia (Acts 13:13 – 52; see 17:2 – 9).[2] The incident foreshadows Jesus' lament that predicts Jerusalem's rejection of him as it has rejected all the prophets sent to her (13:31 – 35). It also foreshadows the ominous lament that Jerusalem did not recognize the time of her visitation, which is the occasion of salvation that Jesus proclaims (19:41 – 44). Their rejection will become the grounds for their judgment.

Main Idea

Anointed by the Spirit of the Lord, Jesus proclaims that his mission will be to bring good news to the poor and to proclaim God's acceptance of those whom others may want to write off as unacceptable.

Translation

(See pages 192 – 93.)

---

1. The message is the same that came to Simeon in the temple. The Holy Spirit rested on him and he recognized in Jesus that God had prepared a salvation that would be a "light for revelation to the Gentiles" (2:25 – 35).

2. Nave (*Repentance in Luke-Acts*, 24) notes that it is "the first of six pericopes in Luke-Acts having a common pattern and theme of confrontation and rejection." See 20:9 – 19; Acts 3:1 – 4:31; 5:12 – 42; 13:13 – 52; 18:1 – 18.

Structure and Literary Form

The section of 4:14 – 44 divides into two parts: Jesus' teaching in the synagogue in Nazareth (4:14 – 30) and the continuation of his teaching in the synagogues (4:31 – 44). The Nazareth episode divides into three parts: the introduction as Jesus returns to Galilee and enters the synagogue in Nazareth and is asked to read in the service (4:14 – 17); the presentation of Jesus' reading of the Scripture, his teaching (4:18 – 21), and the positive reaction to it (4:22); Jesus' elaboration (4:23 – 27) and the violent reaction to it (4:28 – 30).

The structure highlights Jesus' anointing and sending. Unlike John, who referred to someone else who was coming, Jesus refers to himself ("the Spirit of the Lord is upon *me* because he anointed *me* to announce good news to the poor. He has sent *me*," 4:18). The verb "to herald" and the noun "release" capture the purpose of his being sent. Proclaiming good news to the poor is the principal statement outlining his primary mission followed by three subordinate infinitive phrases, which say the same thing in different and expanding ways. The structure also provides a preview of how Jesus will be received in his ministry: cheering acceptance and then violent rejection from which he will ultimately escape through the resurrection.

Exegetical Outline

➡ **I. Jesus' return to Galilee (4:14 – 15)**
  A. Empowered by the Spirit (4:14)
  B. Praised in the synagogues for his teaching (4:15)
II. Jesus' reading from Isaiah at the synagogue in Nazareth (4:16 – 20)
III. Pronouncement that the Scripture has been fulfilled today in their hearing (4:21)
IV. Elated reaction of the Nazareth gathering (4:22)
V. Jesus' prophetic response (4:23 – 27)
  A. Prediction of complaints from his hometown (4:23)
    1. Proverb: "Physician, heal yourself" (4:23a-b)
    2. Do here what you have done at Capernaum (4:23c-d)
  B. Pronouncement that prophets are unwelcome in their hometown (4:24)
  C. Examples of ministry to Gentiles (4:25 – 27)
    1. Elijah and the widow of Zarephath (4:25 – 26)
    2. Elisha and Naaman the Syrian leper (4:27)
VI. Irate reaction of the Nazareth gathering (4:28 – 30)
  A. Attempt to kill Jesus (4:28 – 29)
  B. Jesus' escape, passing through their midst (4:30)

Luke 4:14–30

4:14a	Circumstance	**Jesus returned to Galilee in the power of the Spirit.**
b	Summary	**And a report about him spread throughout the whole region.**
15		**And he began teaching in their synagogues and was being glorified by all.**
16a	Circumstance	**And he came to Nazareth where he had been raised,**
b		**and he entered the synagogue as was his custom on the Sabbath day**
c		**and he rose to read.**
17a		**And the scroll of the prophet Isaiah was handed to him,**
b		**and when he unrolled the scroll, he found the place where it was written:**
18a	Scripture	*"The Spirit of the Lord is upon me*
b		*because* *he anointed me*
c		*to announce good news to the poor.*
d		*He has sent me*
e		*to herald release* *to the captives and*
f		*to the blind* *recovery of sight,*
g		*to send in release for those who are oppressed,*
19		*to herald the acceptable year of the Lord."* (Isa 61:1-2)
20a	Circumstance	*When* he rolled up the scroll,
b		he handed it back to the attendant
c		**and sat down.**
d		**Every eye in the synagogue was staring intently at him.**
21	Pronouncement	**He began to speak to them:** *"Today this Scripture has been fulfilled in your hearing."*
22	Response (positive)	**All** began to testify well of him **and** marvel at the gracious words that came from his mouth, **and** **they were saying,** *"Is this not the son of Joseph?"*

23a	Challenge	**He said to them,**
b		"You will certainly quote this old saying to me,
c		'Physician, heal yourself!'
d		*and* will say to me,
		'Do also here in your own hometown what we heard happened in Capernaum.'"
24	Proverb	**He said,**
		"Amen, I say to you that no prophet is acceptable in his own hometown.
25a	Scriptural precursor (1)	To tell you the truth,
b		there were many widows in Israel in the days of Elijah,
c		when the heavens were shut up for three years and six months and
		a terrible famine gripped the entire land.
26a		*But Elijah* was not sent to a single one of them but instead
b		[was sent] to the widow of Zarephath,
		a town in the region of Sidon."
27a	Scriptural precursor (2)	There were also many with skin diseases in Israel
		in the time of Elisha the prophet
b		*and* not one of them was cleansed except Naaman the Syrian."
28	Reaction (negative)	As they heard these things,
		those in the synagogue boiled over with rage.
29	Violence	When they arose,
		they drove him out of the town
		and led him to the edge of a hill on which the town was built so that they might hurl him off the cliff.
30	Escape	**But he slipped through their midst and left.**

Explanation of the Text

4:14 Jesus returned to Galilee in the power of the Spirit. And a report about him spread throughout the whole region (Καὶ ὑπέστρεψεν ὁ Ἰησοῦς ἐν τῇ δυνάμει τοῦ πνεύματος εἰς τὴν Γαλιλαίαν. καὶ φήμη ἐξῆλθεν καθ' ὅλης τῆς περιχώρου περὶ αὐτοῦ). As the curtain is raised on his public ministry, it is not surprising that Jesus, who was conceived by the Spirit (1:35), anointed by the Spirit at his baptism (3:22), and led by the Spirit in his face-off with the devil in the wilderness (4:1), should appear empowered by the Spirit to begin his ministry. It will not be conflict-free as it shifts from the cosmic level, after the confrontation with the devil, to the human level, with members from his hometown synagogue taking umbrage at his teaching and trying to do him in.[3] When Jesus takes the center stage, the Spirit's power is evident in his teaching and the working of miracles.[4]

Jesus' repute spreads throughout the region, but Luke has yet to record Jesus doing anything publicly that would be reported (contrast Matt 9:26). The rumors about Jesus may have mysterious origins, but this detail establishes that his fame precedes his arrival in Nazareth and sets up their anticipation. His provocation of the gathering in Nazareth makes clear, however, that he is not a publicity hound looking for splashy headlines to further his popular appeal but one who is engaged in a divine mission.

4:15 And he began teaching in their synagogues and was being glorified by all (καὶ αὐτὸς ἐδίδασκεν ἐν ταῖς συναγωγαῖς αὐτῶν, δοξαζόμενος ὑπὸ πάντων). The use of the imperfect of the verb "to teach" (ἐδίδασκεν) stresses the

beginning of the action and implies that it continued. "Their synagogues" has no antecedent but in the context refers to Galilean synagogues and does not reflect Luke's sense of alienation, as if he were saying "theirs," not "ours." The "synagogue" need not be a distinct building. Synagogues were generally gatherings of people, not buildings. It is where the villages or towns assembled and is sometimes translated "meeting place" (as in *The Message*). In Jesus' time, most village synagogues were probably modified rooms in private homes. Some towns, like Capernaum (see 7:5), would be able to afford special buildings for communal gatherings and for the reading of Scripture and prayer.[5]

Both Mark (1:21, 39) and Matthew (4:23; 9:35) report that Jesus taught in the synagogues but never give a description of what he taught. From this one example in Luke, we can infer that his teaching centered on the reading and explication of the Jewish Scriptures. "Teaching" aptly summarizes Jesus' public ministry and matches Paul's ministry of teaching in the Diaspora synagogues (Acts 13:5, 14 – 16; 14:1; 17:10; 18:4, 26; 19:8).[6]

Luke emphasizes that Jesus' teaching aroused general acclaim, and the present tense of the verb "being glorified [δοξαζόμενος] by all" indicates a continuing response. His miracles of healing later will give more cause for praise (5:25 – 26; 7:16; 13:13; 17:15; 18:43). The verb "glorify" and the corresponding noun "glory" (δόξα) call to mind the angelic host giving glory to God at Jesus' birth (2:13 – 14), the shepherds glorifying and praising God after their visit to the babe in the manger (2:20), and Simeon prophesying that

3. Neagoe, *The Trial of the Gospel*, 44.
4. See the debate between Max Turner, "The Spirit of Prophecy and the Power of Authoritative Preaching in Luke-Acts: A Question of Origins," *NTS* 38 (1992): 66 – 88, and Robert P. Menzies, "Spirit and Power in Luke-Acts: A Response to Max Turner," *JSNT* 49 (1993): 11 – 20.
5. Dunn, *Jesus Remembered*, 304.
6. Bovon, *Luke 1:1 – 9:50*, 152.

Jesus' appearance on the scene will yield glory for "the people of Israel" (2:32). It also brackets Jesus' earthly ministry. All those glorifying him in Galilee for his teaching may be paired with the centurion who "began to glorify God" when he saw what happened in his death on the cross (23:47). The glory that ultimately counts is not the fickle hero worship bestowed by humans. It is the glory that comes from the giving of his life, which is tied to the eternal glory that is to come (9:26; 21:27; 24:26).

Simeon prophesied that his coming will bring "a light for revelation to the Gentiles" (2:32), but its fulfillment will meet with unexpected resistance by some in Israel, which will cause their own downfall. The hostility at Nazareth contrasts with what was happening in the synagogues elsewhere in Galilee, according to the summary, but it prepares the reader for the intransigence that Jesus will encounter from many quarters. Jesus' application of Scripture to Gentiles reveals that this aspect of the fulfillment of God's plan will provoke open hostility instead of lyrical praise. The issue of Gentiles being included as recipients of God's grace (and their inclusion in the people of God) will be one of the major sources of difficulties for Jesus' apostles in their mission beyond Judea and Galilee.

4:16 And he came to Nazareth, where he had been raised, and he entered the synagogue as was his custom on the Sabbath day and he rose to read (καὶ ἦλθεν εἰς Ναζαρά, οὖ ἦν τεθραμμένος, καὶ εἰσῆλθεν κατὰ τὸ εἰωθὸς αὐτῷ ἐν τῇ ἡμέρᾳ

τῶν σαββάτων εἰς τὴν συναγωγὴν καὶ ἀνέστη ἀναγνῶναι). Nazareth was mentioned in 2:51 – 52 as the home of Jesus' parents. The village is estimated to have had a population of less than four hundred and to have been quite poor since excavations have uncovered no paved streets, public structures and inscriptions, or fine pottery.[7]

His parents were observant of the law (2:41), and Jesus faithfully attended the synagogue on the Sabbath. Josephus explains the reason for such gatherings:

> He [Moses] appointed the Law to be the most excellent and necessary form of instruction, ordaining, not that it should be heard once for all or twice or on several occasions, but that every week men should desert their other occupations and assemble to listen to the Law and to obtain a thorough and accurate knowledge of it, a practice which all other legislators seem to have neglected (*Ag. Ap.* 2.17 §175).

Luke's note, however, describes Jesus attending not as an auditor but as a teacher.[8] The narrative begins with Jesus' rising up to read (4:16), and it ends with the synagogue rising up to throw him out of the town and throw him off a cliff (4:29).[9]

4:17 And the scroll of the prophet Isaiah was handed to him, and when he unrolled the scroll, he found the place where it was written (καὶ ἐπεδόθη αὐτῷ βιβλίον τοῦ προφήτου Ἡσαΐου καὶ ἀναπτύξας τὸ βιβλίον εὖρεν τὸν τόπον οὖ ἦν γεγραμμένον). Luke is not interested in outlining the details of synagogal worship order. It

---

7. Jonathan L. Reed, *Archaeology and the Galilean Jesus* (Harrisburg, PA: Trinity Press International, 2000), 131 – 32. Nazareth was approximately four miles southeast from the comparatively opulent city of Sepphoris (see James F. Strange, "Sepphoris," *ABD*, 5:1090 – 93). When Herod Antipas inherited Galilee and Perea after his father's death, his first project was to rebuild Sepphoris's wall and make it the metropolis of the country and the center of his rule (Josephus, *Ant.* 18.2.1 §27) until he rebuilt Tiberias in AD 25 (Josephus, *Ant.* 18.2.3 §§36 – 38).

8. So Marshall, *The Gospel of Luke*, 181; Nolland, *Luke*, 1:195; Charles A. Kimball, *Jesus' Exposition of the Old Testament in Luke's Gospel* (JSNTSup 94; Sheffield: JSOT, 1994) 101.

9. The same is said of Paul, who went to the synagogue, as was his custom, and taught (Acts 17:2; see 18:4; 19:8). Paul also had brushes with those who were vexed by what he said and threatened his life (13:44 – 52; 14:19 – 20; 17:5, 13; 18:5 – 7, 12; 19:9).

varied from era to era and from region to region. We can assume that an ordinary service consisted of prayers and the reading and exposition of Scripture, and Luke boils it down to focus only on the extraordinary role Jesus plays in this service.

The Nazareth synagogue, like most others, would have been unable to afford numerous scrolls of Scripture, but they did have an Isaiah scroll. Since Luke relates that Jesus took the scroll of Isaiah after it was given to him and unfolded the two cylinders until the column of text that he wanted to read became visible,[10] he is portrayed as choosing his text. The text implies that the Spirit of the Lord was upon him to read this particular text. Finding a specific text in a scroll without chapter and verse divisions is difficult, and it suggests that Jesus was so familiar with the Scriptures that he knew where to turn.

In Depth: Synagogue Worship

The synagogue worship order may be similar to Philo's description of the Essenes (*Good Person* 81 – 82):

In these [the ethical parts of Scripture] they are instructed at all other times, but particularly on the seventh days. For that day has been set apart to be kept holy and on it they abstain from all other work and proceed to sacred spots which they call synagogues. There, arranged in rows according to their ages, the younger below the elder, they sit decorously as befits the occasion with attentive ears. Then one takes the books and reads aloud and another of especial proficiency comes forward and expounds what is not understood. For most of their philosophical study takes the form of allegory, and in this they emulate the tradition of the past.

Luke cites the LXX text of Isaiah, his readers' Bible.[11] Several differences stand out from the passage that is quoted in Luke and in the LXX.

(1) The phrase "to bind up the brokenhearted" (Isa 61:1c) is absent. Its absence is surprising since it would provide an apt segue into the response, "Physician, heal yourself" (4:23). Perhaps Luke wanted to use the verb "heal" (ἰάομαι) only "for cases of physical healing,"[12] or the phrase could have been absent from his copy of the LXX.[13] Whatever the reason, the result is that preaching becomes

---

10. See Peter Van Minnen, "Luke 4:17 – 20 and the Handling of Ancient Books," *JTS* 52 (2001): 689 – 90, against Roger S. Bagnall ("Jesus Reads a Book," *JTS* 51 [2000]: 577 – 88), who thinks Luke refers anachronistically to unfolding a codex.

11. Kimball (*Jesus' Exposition of the Old Testament in Luke's Gospel*, 100) notes that Luke has one agreement with the MT against the LXX ("proclaim" instead of "call") and four agreements with the LXX against the MT. The Hebrew text, for example, has "the opening of the prison house to those who are bound" rather than "recovering the sight of the blind.

12. Marshall, *The Gospel of Luke*, 182.

13. Martin Rese (*Alttestamentliche Motive in der Christologie des Lukas* [SNT 1; Gütersloh: Gütersloher Verlagshaus, 1969], 214; cf. 144 – 45, 151 – 52) believes it is stricken because Luke presents the Spirit as a prophetic Spirit and not as a miracle-working power. He has been criticized by M. Turner ("The Spirit of Prophecy," 60 – 67), but Turner has been refuted by Menzies (*The Development of Early Christian Pneumatology*,

the most prominent dimension of Jesus' mission, according to the text, and this could also be the reason that Luke omitted it. Healings are ephemeral and bring ephemeral praise. Preaching "cut[s] to the heart" (Acts 2:37) and leads to repentance that runs deeper than healing.

(2) The passage is a composite of Isa 61:1; 58:6; and 61:2a. Kimball suggests that Jesus employed the exegetical technique of *gezerah shawah*, which connects two texts based on a common catchword.[14] It is not likely that Jesus paused to roll the scroll back to Isa 58. Such a move is specifically forbidden in the Mishnah — albeit a later tradition (*m. Meg.* 4:4; *t. Meg.* 4:19). It is an oddity that is difficult to explain as something that Jesus is doing and not something a later editor has done. Luke may have deliberately inserted Isa 58:6 into the quotation because the word "release" (ἄφεσις) is a key word in the gospel.[15] The omission of Isa 61:1c and the insertion of Isa 58:6 does create a parallelism in the text by repeating "release" and emphasizing it.[16] Isaiah 58 and 61 may have been linked already in Jesus' time because the same words "today" (ἡμέρα) and "acceptable" or "welcome" (δεκτήν) appear in both texts (Isa 58:5; 61:2).[17] While this citation may not be a verbatim quote of what was read at this particular synagogue service, the cross-fertilization of the two texts enriches their meaning. Their fusion may derive from the teaching of Jesus and was probably central in his homiletic exposition of Scripture.

(3) Isaiah's "to call [καλέσαι] the acceptable year of the Lord" has been replaced with the verb "to proclaim" (κηρύξαι). Menzies claims that the change "reflects his [Luke's] emphasis on preaching as the pre-eminent activity inspired by the Spirit."[18]

(4) The reference to the day of vengeance in Isa 61:2b is absent. If the Nazareth audience is intimately aware of the Isaiah text, this omission might signal to them that Jesus will not be "an avenging agent of God." Roth notes, however, that the text contains no clues "that any of the three departures from the LXX should be unsettling to Luke's authorial audience."[19] Luke does not narrate that the Nazareth audience picked up on this omission and demanded a note of

---

166 – 71). Spirit-inspired speech is related to prophetic activity (see the infancy narratives and Acts 2:17).

14. See Kimball, *Jesus' Exposition of the Old Testament in Luke's Gospel*, 108 – 10.

15. James A. Sanders, "From Isaiah 61 to Luke 4," in *Christianity, Judaism and Other Graeco-Roman Cults: Festschrift for Morton Smith* (ed. Jacob Neusner; New York: Columbia Univ. Press, 1975), 89 – 90. The noun "release" (ἄφεσις) appears five times in Luke and five times in Acts and only twice in Mark and once in Matthew.

16. Kimball, *Jesus' Exposition of the Old Testament in Luke's Gospel*, 107.

17. Bovon, *Luke 1:1 – 9:50*, 153, contends: "Texts such as Isa 57:15 – 58:14 and Isa 61:1 – 11 became associated with each other on the occasion of the celebration of Yom Kippur, the first because of fasting and contrition, the second because of the beginning of the Year of Jubilee."

18. Menzies, *The Development of Early Christian Pneumatology*, 173.

19. Roth, *The Blind, the Lame, and the Poor*, 156 – 57.

vengeance. The effect of the omission is that the emphasis falls on the year of release, not vengeance.

A note of vengeance is sounded in 21:22, "because these are [the] days of vengeance, so that all that has been written may be fulfilled"; thus, Luke does not shun this message. It is more likely that Luke intends to present the outset of Jesus' ministry as one marked by grace and release. John stridently harangued the crowd, who all had better repent or face a fiery judgment. By contrast, Jesus heralds that now is the time when God's long-awaited promises are being fulfilled. Now is the time of salvation when God is acting to redeem his people.

4:18 **"The Spirit of the Lord is upon me because he anointed me to announce good news to the poor. He has sent me to herald release to the captives and to the blind recovery of sight, to send in release for those who are oppressed"** (πνεῦμα κυρίου ἐπ᾽ ἐμέ, οὗ εἵνεκεν ἔχρισέν με εὐαγγελίσασθαι πτωχοῖς, ἀπέσταλκέν με κηρύξαι αἰχμαλώτοις ἄφεσιν καὶ τυφλοῖς ἀνάβλεψιν, ἀποστεῖλαι τεθραυσμένους ἐν ἀφέσει). The preposition "upon" (ἐπί) "implies a compelling force rather than an indwelling."[20] Isaiah 42:1 provides an apt parallel from the heavenly voice when Jesus was praying after his immersion: "Here is my servant, whom I uphold, my chosen one in whom I delight; I will put my Spirit on him, and he will bring justice to the nations."

The title "Christ" (Χριστός) derives from the verb "to anoint" (χρίω), and the verb here alludes to Jesus as "the anointed one," the Christ (see Acts 4:25 – 27, 10:38). This anointing is narrated after his immersion when the Holy Spirit descended on him in bodily form like a dove and a voice from heaven declared, "You are my Son, the beloved; with you I am well pleased" (3:22). The anointing is causally connected to the task of preaching.

Proclaiming the good news of the reign of God summarizes the essence of Jesus' ministry (see 4:43; 7:22 – 23).

The "poor" who are the recipients of this good news are "not only the economically impoverished but all those who are marginal or excluded from human fellowship, the outcast."[21] They are the losers in the competitive race for scarce resources, economic security, honor, and power. Their only recourse is to "look to God for help."[22] They include the disciples. Jesus' Beatitudes begin with a blessing on the poor (6:20) that is specifically addressed to the disciples. They have left home and livelihood to follow Jesus (5:11, 28; 18:28 – 30), and he will instruct them to sell their possessions and give alms (12:33). Jesus does not promise relief to the poor but the reversal of the structures of victimization.

Since Luke's account of Jesus' ministry does not have him setting free literal prisoners, the image is metaphorical. John, for example, will remain locked up. "Release" (ἄφεσις, "setting free, liberty") is synonymous with salvation. Those who are captive are those shackled by Satan. The exorcisms mark the release of the victims from Satan's

20. Evans, *St. Luke*, 269.
21. Johnson, *The Gospel of Luke*, 79.

22. Danker, *Jesus and the New Age*, 106.

stranglehold. The healing of the bent woman, for example, marks her release from Satan's bondage (13:16; see Acts 10:36 – 38). The captives are also those imprisoned by sin (see 1:77; 3:3). The chains of iniquity (Acts 8:23) incarcerate sinners, and the noun "release" is primarily tied to the forgiveness of sins in Luke-Acts (1:77; 3:3; 24:47; Acts 2:38; 5:31; 10:43; 13:38; 26:18).

It is not a stretch to assume that the later rabbis' belief that Israel's failure to observe the sabbatical year (see Jer 34:8, 15, 17) and other requirements brought exile, poverty, pestilence (*b. Šabb.* 33a; *b. Sukkah* 40b; *m. ʾAbot* 5:9) was current in the time of Jesus. When Israel is in captivity, she is "helplessly dependent on the Lord for salvation."[23] Jesus announces that their salvation is at hand.

Blindness was a common disease in Palestine, and "the blind" may refer to those who are literally blind (see 7:21 – 22; 18:35 – 43). They belonged to a class of persons excluded from the temple (Lev 21:17 – 23; 2 Sam 5:8). Blindness is also attributed to sin in the Old Testament (Deut 28:29; Zeph 1:17), and Luke uses blindness metaphorically in the parable about a blind person guiding another blind person and both falling into a pit (Luke 6:39). It is also a Lukan theme that Jesus will open the eyes and bring sight to those imprisoned in darkness (1:79; 3:6; Acts 26:17 – 18). "To open the eyes" in these passages means to lead someone to salvation.[24]

Opening the eyes is also related to seeing God's salvation plan being accomplished in Jesus. The disciples on the Emmaus road, for example, had their eyes opened (24:31). When Paul encountered Christ on the Damascus road, his eyes were blinded and then later opened, literally and spiritually (Acts 9:1 – 19). He is then sent out to open the eyes of others. Many who belong to Israel, however, will shut their eyes and go blind (Acts 28:27, citing Isa 6:10).

This literal and awkward rendering "to send in release for those who are oppressed" seeks to allow the auditor to hear the repetition of key words "to send" (ἀποστεῖλαι) and "release" (ἄφεσις), which is lost in more paraphrastic translations (e.g., "to let the oppressed go free," NRSV). Whether this quotation from Isa 58:6 was intentionally added to do so, as Green surmises, it does "draw special attention to the word 'release' as a characteristic activity of Jesus' ministry."[25]

Roth regards the perfect participle "oppressed" (τεθραυσμένους) as primarily a warfare image — those who are at the mercy of others — and translates it as the "shattered."[26] It may well fit the perception that Israel remains shattered by its idolatrous oppressors even after returning from the Babylonian exile.

4:19 "To herald the acceptable year of the Lord" (κηρύξαι ἐνιαυτὸν κυρίου δεκτόν). The acceptable year of the Lord is closely connected to the reign of God, and *The Message* aptly paraphrases it: "This is God's year to act!" In 4:43, Jesus uses similar language about being sent to proclaim the good news, except that he uses the term "the reign of God" rather than "the acceptable year of the Lord."

Isaiah 61:1 – 2 develops themes from the Jubilee year, which is also called "the year of release" in Lev 25:10 (LXX): "And you shall sanctify the year,

23. Roth, *The Blind, the Lame, and the Poor*, 101.
24. Robert F. O'Toole, "Does Luke Also Portray Jesus as the Christ in Luke 4,16 – 30?" *Bib* 76 (1995): 511. See also Dennis Hamm, "Sight to the Blind: Vision as Metaphor in Luke," *Bib* 67 (1986): 431 – 37.
25. Green, *The Gospel of Luke*, 210. Menzies (*The Development of Early Christian Pneumatology*, 172 – 73) claims that Luke linked the two texts because of his interest in "the liberating power of Jesus' preaching, of which an important aspect was forgiveness of sins.
26. Roth, *The Blind, the Lame, and the Poor*, 101.

the fiftieth year, and you shall proclaim *a release* upon the land to all that inhabit it; it shall be given *a year of release*, a jubilee for you; and each one shall depart to his possession, and ye shall go each to his family." Jesus' manifesto, however, is not a literal reference to the Jubilee year and the forgiveness of debts.[27] Though many in Israel drowned in debt,[28] Jesus' agenda is not simply social reform. Instead, "Luke portrays his liberating work in terms of personal exorcisms, healings, and the teaching of the people."[29]

Since Jesus quotes from Isaiah, not Leviticus, it is more likely that he is drawing on Jubilee *imagery* to refer to the day of salvation. Paul uses the imagery in 2 Cor 6:2, quoting Isa 49:8, "In the time of my favor [καιρῷ δεκτῷ] I heard you, and in the day of salvation I helped you" and declaring, "Now is the time of God's favor, now is the day of salvation." The Jubilee imagery is therefore intended to evoke images of eschatological redemption rather than temporal social and political reform. Jesus announces the dawn of salvation with deliverance from Satan and the forgiveness of sins.

11QMelchizedek highlights the Sabbath and Jubilee year motifs by interlacing Lev 25; Deut 15:2; Isa 52:7 (referring to the messianic herald of the "good tidings"); Isa 61:1 – 3; and Pss 7:8 – 9; 82:1 – 2. It provides first-century evidence of an eschatological interpretation of the Jubilee motif that is related to a Messiah figure. Brooke contends that Luke shares the same set of messianic

expectations found in 4Q521 2 II, which refers to the anointed one and the Lord's Spirit hovering upon the poor, "freeing prisoners, giving sight to the blind, straightening out the twisted. The Lord will perform [presumably through the anointed] marvelous acts, healing the badly wounded, make the dead alive, and proclaim good news to the poor."[30]

Social and political reform is not excluded, however, but follow from this redemption. Wright observes:

> … although Jesus did not envisage that he would persuade Israel as a whole to keep the Jubilee year *he expected his followers to live out the Jubilee principle among themselves.* He expected, and taught, that they should forgive one another not only "sins" but also debts. This may help to explain the remarkable practice within the early church whereby resources were pooled, in a fashion not unlike the Essene community of goods. Luke's description of this in Acts 4:34 echoes the description of the sabbatical year in Deuteronomy 15:4.[31]

4:20 – 21 When he rolled up the scroll, he handed it back to the attendant and sat down. Every eye in the synagogue was staring intently at him. He began to speak to them: "Today this Scripture has been fulfilled in your hearing" (καὶ πτύξας τὸ βιβλίον ἀποδοὺς τῷ ὑπηρέτῃ ἐκάθισεν· καὶ πάντων οἱ ὀφθαλμοὶ ἐν τῇ συναγωγῇ ἦσαν

---

27. Contra Sharon H. Ringe, *Jesus, Liberation, and the Biblical Jubilee* (OBT 19; Philadelphia: Fortress, 1985). Against those who assume that Luke would recognize the jubilary connections in Isa 61:1 – 2, Tannehill, *Unity of Luke-Acts*, 68, argues that "it is not so clear that the author of Luke-Acts was aware of the connection between this passage and the law of Jubilee." It is unlikely that the Jubilee year was ever celebrated in Israel. It is not mentioned in the Old Testament, and the discussion of it in the Mishnah is idealized (*m. Roš. Haš.* 1:1; 3:5; *m. ʿArak.* 7:1 – 5).

28. According to Josephus (*J.W.* 2.17.6 §§426 – 27) one of

the first things the rebels did at the start of the war was to burn the treasury where the debt records were kept.

29. Johnson, *The Gospel of Luke*, 81.

30. Brooke, *The Dead Sea Scrolls and the New Testament*, 162. T. H. Lim, ("11QMelch, Luke 4 and the Dying Messiah," *JJS* 43 [1992]: 90 – 92) argues: "11QMelch provides the exegetical link between Daniel 9:25 – 26 and Luke 4:16 – 21, allowing for the early Christian development of the motif of a dying Messiah."

31. Wright, *Jesus and the Victory of God*, 295.

ἀτενίζοντες αὐτῷ. ἤρξατο δὲ λέγειν πρὸς αὐτοὺς ὅτι σήμερον πεπλήρωται ἡ γραφὴ αὕτη ἐν τοῖς ὠσὶν ὑμῶν). When Jesus hands the scroll back to the attendant and sits down, the normal position for teaching, the audience fixes their eyes on him in anticipation of his exposition of this Scripture. He does not disappoint.

In Luke 3:4 – 6, Isa 40:3 – 5 was cited as being fulfilled in John's ministry. Now Jesus declares the prophecies of Isaiah are being fulfilled in his own ministry. "Someday" has become "today" as the emphasis falls on salvation happening now. It recalls 2:11, "To you is born today in the town of David a Savior, who is Christ and Lord."

"In your hearing" is a vital component of the fulfillment. Jesus is not speaking in the air but speaking in community (see 1:1). It requires hearing, and the people are witnesses of the plan that God has embedded in Old Testament prophecy. "This Scripture" gives divine authorization for what Jesus is doing to fulfill that plan. The problem, which will soon become evident, is that God's plan does not match the plan that the audience has in mind, which would vouchsafe them their special privilege and status.

"Has been fulfilled" (πεπλήρωται) is in the perfect tense, denoting completed action in past time with continuing results. Frein, however, notes that the actual fulfillment does not occur until later in the narrative. Jesus answers the query from John's disciples that the blind receive their sight, the lame walk, the lepers are cleansed, the deaf hear, the dead are raised, and the poor have good news brought to them (in 7:21 – 22), which fulfills prophecies in Isa 28:18 – 19; 35:5 – 6; 61:1 – 2. Frein comments: "These two pericopes are keys in the development of Luke's theme of prophecy and

fulfillment, and they show that when Jesus fulfills his own predictions of his ministry, he also fulfills the promises of the prophets of old."[32]

4:22 All began to testify well of him and marvel at the gracious words that came from his mouth, and they were saying, "Is this not the son of Joseph?" (καὶ πάντες ἐμαρτύρουν αὐτῷ καὶ ἐθαύμαζον ἐπὶ τοῖς λόγοις τῆς χάριτος τοῖς ἐκπορευομένοις ἐκ τοῦ στόματος αὐτοῦ καὶ ἔλεγον· οὐχὶ υἱός ἐστιν Ἰωσὴφ οὗτος;). Jeremias claims that the synagogue did not respond positively to Jesus' words and argues that they witnessed *against* him and marveled at his bravado in making such a bold assertion about the fulfillment of Scripture.[33] This view is driven by a mistaken attempt to explain how the synagogue's attitude toward Jesus suddenly turns from admiration to violent hostility. The verb "to testify" (ἐμαρτύρουν) has only a positive connotation in Acts (see Acts 6:3; 10:22; 16:2; 22:12), and since it is combined here with the verb "marvel," it should be understood positively in this context: "All began to testify well of him." His initial words won their approval and excited their wonder.

Their positive reaction is further confirmation of his spiritual power. Nolland contends that their pleasant amazement serves as

> evidence (witness) for the authenticity of this Christ and his message precisely because they are about to be revealed as implacably opposed to Jesus. Their very rejection of him underlies the impartiality of their witness to him. And in Luke's understanding such "impartial" witness — the objective, visible-in-history impact of Jesus — has a not insignificant contribution to make to that witness through which Luke means to bring Theophilus to faith in Christ.[34]

32. Frein, "Narrative Predictions," 28.
33. Joachim Jeremias, *Jesus' Promise to the Nations* (SBT 24; London: SCM, 1958), 44 – 46.
34. See John Nolland, "Impressed Unbelievers as Witnesses to Christ," *JBL* 98 (1979): 228.

Their astonished testimony has an apologetic function that confirms Jesus' identity. They receive him with enthusiasm because he appealed to deeply rooted hopes of the restoration of Israel and of his clan as the offshoot of David.

The "gracious words" (οἱ λόγοι τῆς χάριτος) do not refer to his winsome oratorical skill that keeps them spellbound but are a technical reference to the message of grace (see Acts 14:3; 20:24, 32). The words can confer grace, however, only if one listens in obedience.

The phrase "that came from his mouth" (τοῖς ἐκπορευομένοις ἐκ τοῦ στόματος) recalls the temptation scene and Jesus' retort to Satan from Deut 8:3: "Man does not live on bread alone" (cf. 4:4). Luke omits the continuation of the quote, "but on every word that comes from the mouth of the Lord," but the biblical resonance of the phrase is so common that it implies that Jesus' words are like the Word of God in bringing life and salvation.[35]

Their question about Jesus' relationship to Joseph should not be read as dismissive, as if they were saying, "This is merely Joseph's son!" It is not a case where "familiarity breeds contempt," which leads the hometown crowd to discount such enormous claims coming from a common man's son.[36] No grammatical indicator, such as an adversative ("but"), is present to indicate that they wheel from being aglow with admiration to being hot with indignation. The question contains no hint of hostility. When someone is identified as the son of his father in the Old Testament, it is never intended to diminish the individual's status.[37] Instead, this question should be taken as an exclamation that happily points out that he is a local boy. Implicit with this recognition is the expectation that they will reap special favors from him. That is the way of the world; one's own clan always comes first.

An inscription shows that Natzareth was spelled in Hebrew with a ṣade (Naṣaret).[38] The clan members who settled there after returning from the Babylonian exile presumably regarded themselves as descendants of David and gave the place an intentionally messianic name, Little-Netzer ("offshoot [of David]"), under the influence of Isa 11:1–2. They would not have shared the prejudice against Nazareth that was voiced by Nathanael ("Can anything good come from [Nazareth]?" John 1:46).

Jesus' Davidic lineage has been emphasized with specific references to Joseph as one who was descended from the house and family of David (1:27; 2:4), and in the genealogy the Davidic line (3:31) is traced through Joseph (3:23). The hometown crowd may be presumed to know this connection along with the reader. This Davidic clan was impoverished but retained the messianic hopes of restoration. If the messianic promises are fulfilled in the Spirit-anointed Jesus, they can only take for granted that it bodes well for them. Through his honor, they will be honored, and the proverb Jesus cites in 4:23 assumes that they believe he has power to work mighty works.

The excited question also exposes their limited understanding of Jesus. The reader knows from the infancy narrative that Jesus is not simply Joseph's son but the Son of God. He is not merely a local boy speaking of the wondrous fulfillment of promises that would be a boon to this destitute community and exalt their lowly estate. Only when it dawns on them that this is not in the plan do they begin to turn on Jesus.

---

35. Heinz Schürmann, *Das Lukasevangelium* (4th ed.; HTKNT; Freiburg: Herder, 1990), 1:234–35.

36. Contra Bock, *Luke*, 1:415. The reaction recorded in John 6:42 should not be imposed on Luke's text.

37. Prophets are regularly introduced as the sons of their fathers (Isa 1:1; 2:1; 13:1; 20:2; 22:20; 36:3, 22; 37:2, 21; 38:1; Jer 1:1; 36:4, 8, 32; 45:1; Ezek 1:3; Hos 1:1; Joel 1:1; Jonah 1:1; Zeph 1:1; Zech 1:1).

38. Bargil Pixner, *With Jesus through Galilee according to the Fifth Gospel* (Collegeville, MN: Liturgical, 1992), 15.

4:23 He said to them, "You will certainly quote this old saying to me, 'Physician, heal yourself!' and will say to me, 'Do also here in your own hometown what we heard happened in Capernaum'" (καὶ εἶπεν πρὸς αὐτούς· πάντως ἐρεῖτέ μοι τὴν παραβολὴν ταύτην· ἰατρέ, θεράπευσον σεαυτόν· ὅσα ἠκούσαμεν γενόμενα εἰς τὴν Καφαρναοὺμ ποίησον καὶ ὧδε ἐν τῇ πατρίδι σου). Jesus splashes cold water on their eager anticipation that his local family connections will mean special advantages for them. There will be no nepotism in the reign of God.

Some do not see how there could be such a sudden turnaround in the attitude of the residents of Nazareth — from wonder in v. 22 to complaint in v. 23. The negative response, however, is caused by Jesus' intentional provocation. Simeon prophesied that he would reveal the secret thoughts of many hearts (2:35), and Jesus does so here (see also 5:21 – 22; 6:7 – 8; 7:39 – 40; 9:47; 11:17; 24:38). He reveals that they will become resentful because he will do no mighty work in their midst, and he rebukes them in advance for rejecting him. John also met the crowd's favorable reception of his preaching with a surly rebuff (3:7) and warnings of a fiery judgment (3:8 – 9).[39] As John rejected any appeal to their common father Abraham (3:8), so Jesus rejects any implicit assumptions about some messianic largesse based on a common hometown.[40]

The difference is that the crowds asked John, "What then should we do?" (3:10 – 14). The Nazareth assembly instead seethes with rage. As Tannehill describes it, "Hidden in the hearts of his townfolk are attitudes of which they, perhaps, are not yet conscious: resistance to God's purpose combined with jealous possessiveness. When

they come to understand more fully the nature of Jesus' mission, he will not be acceptable to them."[41] The people in Nazareth will want to see the same display of power that Jesus will unleash in other places and may even want him to restrict it to their own, limited circle. Though he may be perceived as a hometown boy, he is not; and his mission is not to be restricted to his hometown.

Luke does not explain why Jesus does not do mighty works in Nazareth. The reader will learn, however, that doing such things in Capernaum will not create the desired repentance. In commissioning his disciples for mission, he pronounces reproachful woes on Chorazin, Bethsaida, and Capernaum for their failure to repent after witnessing the deeds of power he performed there (10:12 – 16).

The proverb "Physician, heal yourself!" and variations of it were used with a wide assortment of meanings, such as a jeering retort to one who gives directives to others but who does not follow them himself.[42] Context determines the meaning. Nolland likens it to the taunt in 23:35, "He saved others; let him save himself, if this one is God's Messiah, the elect one." He thinks the force is: "Who do you think you are to offer to us what you do not have for yourself?"[43] This retort would be most appropriate when Jesus begins to meet stiff resistance during his ministry and is dismissed as "a glutton and a drunkard, a friend of tax collectors and sinners" (7:34). But this meaning does not fit well in this context. It more likely means that healing should begin at home. If one is to benefit others, one ought to extend the same benefits to one's own.[44] The proverb is explained by the next

39. Tannehill, *Unity of Luke-Acts*, 69 – 70.
40. Ibid., 70.
41. Ibid., 69.
42. John Nolland, "Classical and Rabbinic Parallels to 'Physician, Heal Yourself,' (Lk. IV 23)," *NovT* 21 (1979): 193 – 209.

43. Nolland, *Luke*, 1:199.
44. Sijbolt Jan Noorda, "'Cure Yourself, Doctor' (Luke 4,23): Classical Parallels to an Alleged Saying of Jesus," in *Logia: Les paroles de Jésus* (ed. Joel Delobel; Leuven: Leuven Univ. Press, 1982), 459 – 67.

statement: "Do also here in your own hometown what we heard happened in Capernaum."

Luke reports that Jesus returned to Galilee in the power of the Spirit and his fame spread widely throughout the region, but he has not yet narrated what Jesus will do in Capernaum (4:31; 7:1; 10:15). Some conclude that this reference is a smoking gun that reveals that the passage originally belonged at a later juncture in the story and has been moved forward. While Luke has made this sermon serve as Jesus' inaugural address for his Galilean ministry, he is not a clumsy author. In the context, Jesus anticipates with prophetic foresight his hometown's bitterness when they learn of his mighty works in Capernaum and refers to future, not previous, events.

4:24 He said, "Amen, I say to you that no prophet is acceptable in his own hometown" (εἶπεν δέ, ἀμὴν λέγω ὑμῖν ὅτι οὐδεὶς προφήτης δεκτός ἐστιν ἐν τῇ πατρίδι αὐτοῦ). In the context of the Jubilee imagery, the irony is that the instructions for observing it require that the people return to their homeland (πατρίς; Lev 25:10).[45] It is therefore appropriate that Jesus would proclaim the year of release in his hometown, but his call will not be welcomed.[46] This rejection does not catch him by surprise. He anticipates their rejection with another adage: prophets with their exhortations, warnings, and jeremiads are never warmly received (see 11:47 – 50; 13:34; Acts 7:52). With this adage, Jesus identifies himself as a prophet with a divine mission.

The introduction to his declaration, "Amen" (ἀμήν), is the only Hebrew word retained in the gospel (12:37; 18:17, 29; 21:32; 23:43). It normally functioned as a response to another's statement, often as a liturgical response, that meant "so be it." Jesus uses it to precede and validate his solemn declarations before any response. Jeremias claims it was unique to Jesus and that it reflected his sense of divine authority, replacing the prophetic "Thus saith the Lord."[47] Since the Greek preserves this distinctive speech by transliterating the term, it is perhaps best to preserve it also in English rather than translating it "truly." Jesus' use of the term reveals his prophetic consciousness,[48] and this statement foreshadows his ultimate rejection as a prophet.

4:25 To tell you the truth, there were many widows in Israel in the days of Elijah, when the heavens were shut up for three years and six months and a terrible famine gripped the entire land (ἐπ᾽ ἀληθείας δὲ λέγω ὑμῖν, πολλαὶ χῆραι ἦσαν ἐν ταῖς ἡμέραις Ἠλίου ἐν τῷ Ἰσραήλ, ὅτε ἐκλείσθη ὁ οὐρανὸς ἐπὶ ἔτη τρία καὶ μῆνας ἕξ, ὡς ἐγένετο λιμὸς μέγας ἐπὶ πᾶσαν τὴν γῆν). Two Old Testament illustrations further define the meaning of the poor, captives, blind, and oppressed who will receive good news and release. It will also include desolate widows, unclean lepers, and Gentiles. The phrase "the heavens were shut up," leading to a severe drought, is, in biblical parlance, an expression of the Lord's anger at sin (Deut 11:17; 1 Kgs 8:35 – 36). The land was under divine judgment because King Ahab, presumably under the influence of his wife, Jezebel, had erected altars to Baal, and the result was that the whole land suffered.

45. Bovon, *Luke 1:1 – 9:50*, 156.

46. The play on the acceptable/welcome (δεκτός) year of the Lord in 4:19 and the acceptable/welcomed (δεκτός) prophet is retained in the translation.

47. Joachim Jeremias, *The Prayers of Jesus* (SBT 6; London: SCM, 1967), 112 – 13; John Strugnell ("'Amen, I say to you' in the Sayings of Jesus in Early Christian Literature," *HTR* 67 [1974]:

180, n. 6) argues, however, that it was not unknown before Jesus. Luke does not consistently take it over from his sources elsewhere in the gospel and often substitutes other phrases (see 9:27 / Mark 9:1; 12:44 / Matt 24:47; 21:3 / Mark 12:43; 22:18 / Mark 14:25; 11:51 / Matt 23:36; 10:12 / Matt 10:15; 10:24 / Matt 13:17).

48. Johnson, *The Gospel of Luke*, 80.

4:26 But Elijah was not sent to a single one of them but instead [was sent] to the widow of Zarephath, a town in the region of Sidon (καὶ πρὸς οὐδεμίαν αὐτῶν ἐπέμφθη Ἠλίας εἰ μὴ εἰς Σάρεπτα τῆς Σιδωνίας πρὸς γυναῖκα χήραν). During the famine, Elijah, a prophet of Israel, only came to the aid of a Gentile widow in Zarephath. She hailed from Sidon, the same region as the infamous Jezebel, the daughter of the king of the Sidonians (1 Kgs 16:31). Elijah prevented the certain death of the widow and her son through a miraculous supply of meal and oil and later resuscitated her dead son (1 Kgs 17; Jas 5:17).

The "famine serves to bring together disparate peoples."[49] Both Jew and Gentile were saved together. Elijah, this Gentile widow, and her son lived and ate together, which betokened the fellowship between Jews and Gentiles that would come through Christ (see Acts 11:1 – 18).

4:27 There were also many with skin diseases in Israel in the time of Elisha the prophet and not one of them was cleansed except Naaman the Syrian (καὶ πολλοὶ λεπροὶ ἦσαν ἐν τῷ Ἰσραὴλ ἐπὶ Ἐλισαίου τοῦ προφήτου, καὶ οὐδεὶς αὐτῶν ἐκαθαρίσθη εἰ μὴ Ναιμὰν ὁ Σύρος). It is significant that Naaman is "cleansed" and not healed of his skin disease. A Gentile might be cured of his leprosy but, according to Jewish understanding of clean and unclean, he could never become "clean." Yet the Scripture is clear that he became clean (2 Kgs 5:14). This recollection of the "cleansing" of a Gentile leper in Scripture prepares for the cleansing of a Samaritan leper (17:11 – 19) and the vision Peter received in Acts 10:9 – 16, 28. Elisha's encounter with Naaman, a Syrian commander, is also similar to Peter's encounter with Cornelius, a

Roman commander (Acts 10). Both Gentiles took the initiative.

The two illustrations link Jesus' ministry with that of Elijah and Elisha. Jesus' healing of the centurion's slave (7:1 – 10) recalls Elisha's encounter with Naaman, and his raising of the son of the widow of Nain from the dead (7:11 – 17) recalls Elijah's raising of the son of the widow of Zarephath.

4:28 As they heard these things, those in the synagogue boiled over with rage (καὶ ἐπλήσθησαν πάντες θυμοῦ ἐν τῇ συναγωγῇ ἀκούοντες ταῦτα). The synagogue immediately fulfills Jesus' prophecy about a prophet being unwelcome in his homeland as things suddenly turn ugly. Initial delight changes into bloody-minded rage. If they are astute, they may be upset for "being implicitly cast in the role of apostate Israel in this analogy to the Old Testament."[50] Jesus' prophetic application of the Scripture implies that recalcitrant, unrepentant Israel may be judged and passed over and that Gentiles might be the recipients of God's blessing instead.

4:29 When they arose, they drove him out of the town and led him to the edge of a hill on which the town was built so that they might hurl him off the cliff (καὶ ἀναστάντες ἐξέβαλον αὐτὸν ἔξω τῆς πόλεως καὶ ἤγαγον αὐτὸν ἕως ὀφρύος τοῦ ὄρους ἐφ᾽ οὗ ἡ πόλις ᾠκοδόμητο αὐτῶν ὥστε κατακρημνίσαι αὐτόν). The assembly does not simply drive him out of town but tries to kill him by throwing him off a cliff. Presumably, they then want to stone him as a false prophet (Acts 7:58).[51] This violent rejection harks back to what happened to Moses, as Stephen sketches it in Acts 7:22 – 30.

This episode at the beginning of Jesus' ministry foreshadows what will happen to him in Jerusalem

---

49. Larrimore C. Crockett, "Luke 4:25 – 27 and Jewish-Gentile Relations in Luke-Acts," *JBL* 88 (1969): 178.

50. Cosgrove, "The Divine ΔΕΙ in Luke-Acts," 180.

51. Evans, *St. Luke*, 275. *M. Sanh.* 6:4 prescribes the place of stoning to be "twice the height of a man," and they would roll stones down on the victim.

at the end and may be intended "to create a typological connection between Nazareth and Jerusalem, between the first and last attempted murder 'outside the city' (cf. Heb 13:12 – 13, as well as Acts 7:58 in the case of Stephen)."[52] This incident also parallels the parable of the vineyard tenants (20:9 – 19), which stands at the beginning of Jesus' ministry in Jerusalem.[53] The line, "Then they cast him outside the vineyard and killed him" (20:15), echoes the attempted murder described here. This rejection in Nazareth also sounds a theme throughout Acts that Christians did not voluntarily disassociate themselves from the Jewish synagogues across the Roman world. They were thrown out and persecuted.

4:30 But he slipped through their midst and left (αὐτὸς δὲ διελθὼν διὰ μέσου αὐτῶν ἐπορεύετο). Jesus escapes the crowd unscathed, which testifies to his power and parallels John 7:30, "At this they tried to seize him, but no one laid a hand on him, because his hour had not yet come" (see also John 8:59; 10:39; 18:6). Luke does not dwell on the precise manner of his escape but "is content to let the readers wonder about this."[54] By doing so, this escape can also prefigure his end — death and escape through resurrection. He does not need the protection of angels promised in Ps 91:11 – 13, a promise that Satan seized upon (Luke 4:9 – 11). It also reveals a theme in Acts that the Word of God is unstoppable (see Acts 5:38 – 39; 28:28).

Theology in Application

Major theological themes in Luke-Acts emerge in this account of the beginning of Jesus' public ministry.

1. The Fulfillment of Isaianic Prophecy

Jesus' application of one of the Servant Songs in Isaiah to himself does more than announce good news to beleaguered people. He implies that he is the Anointed One, the Messiah, and the Servant of the Lord, who is to fulfill the program outlined in Isaiah. The sermon does not go further than announcing, "Today this Scripture has been fulfilled in your hearing," because the "'content' of the sermon lies in the phrases of the text outlining various ways in which Jesus will bring salvation."[55]

Jesus' presence alters the meaning of the present. Jesus announces good news for the poor, not because God is about to do something, but because God is already acting to forgive sins and release the oppressed from Satan's thraldom. It implicitly calls for repentance — a call that was central to the preaching of John the Baptist. Tannehill writes: "God is powerfully at work in the world changing things, and this provides a special opportunity in which you, too, can change. In this context, repentance is not an isolated human action. It is human action, which, theologically discerned, is also divine action in individuals and societies."[56]

52. Bovon, *Luke 1:1 – 9:50*, 156.

53. Judette Kolasny, "An Example of Rhetorical Criticism: Luke 4:16 – 30," in *New Views on Luke and Acts* (ed. Earl Richard; Collegeville, MN: Michael Glazier, 1990), 72 – 73.

54. Tannehill, *Unity of Luke-Acts*, 73.

55. Byrne, *The Hospitality of God*, 47 – 48.

56. Tannehill, *The Shape of Luke's Story*, 89.

What shortcircuits that divine action is the "we first" mentality that Jesus' encounters in the audience, who turns a deaf ear to what God is doing for the world. It assumes that "our" Messiah must serve our needs and must do so first. The Nazareth assembly apparently understood the fulfillment of the Isaiah prophecy to mean that something wonderful would happen to them. True. The Isaian context talks about the glory of the Lord rising upon Israel (Isa 60:1 – 2), accompanied by material abundance (60:5 – 7) and the submission of the nations (60:10 – 14). They wanted their Messiah to fulfill the golden words, "I will make you the everlasting pride and the joy of all generations" (60:15). Consequently, they expected to be especially favored in the year of the Lord's favor.

But Jesus lives under a divine "must" and was not sent just to serve the people of Nazareth or just to do their bidding. When he makes that clear, their admiring wonderment hardens into venomous hatred. The evident selfishness and provincialism of the Nazareth gathering disqualifies them, because "those who stand upon their rights and insist on preferential treatment are not likely to appreciate one who offers the chance to spend and be spent in the service of others and a Gospel which leaves no room for privilege."[57]

Jesus has resisted Satan's demands; he will resist any demands to please a hometown crowd. He does not do miracles on call. The real miracle, as Mark's and Matthew's account of Jesus' visit to Nazareth make clear, is the response of belief followed by repentance (see Matt 13:54 – 58; Mark 6:1 – 6). Repentance is not produced simply by witnessing the performance of mighty deeds. Kilgallen observes, "as one does not live by bread alone, so one does not live by miracle alone, but rather by every teaching word, every word of grace which proceeds from the mouth of God and His Messiah."[58]

2. Jesus as a Rejected Prophet

Jesus' lionization throughout Galilee (4:14 – 15) and the synagogue's keyed-up excitement over his gracious words (4:22) might lead readers to expect an account of Jesus' continuing success. Instead, he is confronted with violent rejection, and this sets the pattern for his ministry in the gospel and the ministry of his apostles in Acts. He is a prophet (4:24), and like Elijah and Elisha, he will be rejected and persecuted as were the prophets of old (6:22 – 23; 13:31 – 33). Tannehill comments, "Elijah and Elisha provide scriptural witness to the inevitable conflict between God's purpose and the human desire to make special claims to God's salvation or place limits on its scope."[59]

This rejection in Nazareth answers the question, "Can he be the divinely appointed agent for the restoration and salvation of God's people when he appears to bypass those who 'deserve' attention and to focus on those who cannot even hope

---

57. Caird, *Saint Luke*, 86 – 87.
58. John J. Kilgallen, "Provocation in Luke 4,23 – 24," *Bib*
70 (1989): 516.
59. Tannehill, *Unity of Luke-Acts*, 71.

for it?"[60] Hill comments, "Jesus, by refusing to do miracles for his own people and by his words, is affirming that his acceptability to God, his place in God's purpose, requires him to bring relief and release to those outside Israel, and it was this that really created the resentment and antagonism."[61]

What happens in Nazareth prepares for what will happen in Jerusalem. Prophets do not preach to those who already agree with them and do not deal in flattery and soft-soap to win high ratings. They declare what God will do and what God requires. They speak the truth that people often do not want to hear. This rubs against the grain of a culture that treats religion as a consumer item. Those who adjust the Word of God to meet market trends, assuming the consumer is always right, are simply peddlers (2 Cor 2:17). Those who come to religion assuming that the chief goal of God is to glorify humankind and asking, "What will it all get me?" receive only spiritual chaff. Like the Nazareth gathering, people of any culture are tempted to focus only on themselves rather than on God. Prophets speaking the truth will as often meet with misunderstanding, staggering hardships, and bloody violence as with a warm welcome. They may be crushed, but the message will not.

3. Release for the Poor, Captives, Blind, and Oppressed.

One could find the poor on every corner throughout the empire. Helping the poor in the Greco-Roman world was not done out of any altruistic, humanitarian concern but out of self-concern — to forestall them plundering the storehouses of the elite in times of famine. Jesus proclaims that God is acting through him to bring good news and deliverance to the poor. The backdrop of the Jubilee theme (Lev 25) recalls the ethical thrust of the Sabbath and sabbatical and Jubilee legislation and underscores "that God's reign and humankind's liberation go hand in hand."[62] Harrington draws out the relations of these themes:

> First, employees cannot be forced to work for days on end. Everyone, even animals, must be given a rest for one full day in the week as well as during other holy times. Second, the laws releasing debts in the seventh year provide a safeguard against enslaving fellow Israelites, who, due to unfortunate circumstances, might not be able to repay a large loan. Finally, the reversal of land back to its original, tribal owner during the jubilee year was, at least in theory if not in practice, a preventive measure against the monopoly of wealthy landowners who might otherwise remove a poor farmer from his land. According to the principles of holiness, every Jew has a divine right to a piece of the holy land.[63]

60. Neagoe, *The Trial of the Gospel*, 45.

61. David Hill, "The Rejection of Jesus at Nazareth (Luke IV 16 – 30)," in *The Composition of Luke's Gospel: Selected Studies from Novum Testamentum* (ed. David E. Orton; Leiden: Brill, 1999), 29.

62. Ringe, *Jesus, Liberation, and the Biblical Jubilee*, 32.

63. Hannah K. Harrington, *Holiness: Rabbinic Judaism and the Graeco-Roman World* (Religion in the First Christian Centuries; London and New York: Routledge, 2001), 102 – 3.

Holiness and social justice work together. In continuing the work of Christ, his church feeds the poor, cares for the sick, ministers to the imprisoned, rescues orphans, and reaches out to the oppressed. Celsus jeered at the results of this ministry. Instead of the clean and worthy, Christ "is followed about with the rag, tag, and bobtail of humanity trailing behind him" (Origen, *Cels.* 3.59). Origen countered, "Yes, but he does not leave them the rag, tag, and bobtail of humanity; but out of the material you would have thrown away as useless, he fashions men, giving them back their self-respect, enabling them to stand up on their feet and look God in the eyes. They were cowed, cringing, broken things. But the Son of God has made them free."[64]

4. The Salvation of Israel and Outsiders

God's saving purpose includes the Gentiles (2:30 – 32; 3:6). Wright's interpretation of the parable of the mustard seed (Matt 13:31 – 32; Mark 4:30 – 32; Luke 13:18 – 19) argues, "when the tree has grown to full height — when Israel becomes what her God intends her to become — others, presumably Gentiles, will come to share in her blessing."[65] What he dubs "the Nazareth Manifesto" declares the same thing. The illustrations from the ministries of Elijah and Elisha underscore that God shows no partiality. Neediness abounds everywhere, and God wills to save all, not just a holy few. But these incidents remind readers that "those who appear to be the least entitled to taste the benefits of 'the year of the Lord's favour' are the most likely to do so."[66] This reminder is galling to any who consider themselves to be most entitled to God's blessings.

All are undeserving, but Jesus announces that this is the year of the Lord's acceptance. Byrne interprets this to mean:

> The "acceptable year of the Lord" is the season of God's hospitality to the human race, which it is Jesus' mission to proclaim and enact. It is a time when people are simply accepted, not judged. True, it is a summons to conversion — an urgent and insistent summons to a deep and transforming conversion. But before conversion there is acceptance, welcome, a hand held out to the afflicted, the trapped and the bound.[67]

This welcome is extended with the offer of release, because "sin is not so much a situation of guilt that has to be forgiven as a plight from which one needs to be set free."[68] Stenschke captures the thrust of Luke-Acts in concluding that "people need to be saved because of their alienation from God, which shows itself in their attitude towards him, towards themselves and their fellow people, and which culminated

---

64. Cited by Arthur John Gossip, "The Gospel according to St. John, Exposition," in *The Interpreter's Bible* (ed. G. A. Buttrick; New York/Nashville: Abingdon, 1952), 8:603.

65. Wright, *Jesus and the Victory of God*, 241.

66. Neagoe, *The Trial of the Gospel*, 45.

67. Byrne, *The Hospitality of God*, 50.

68. Ibid., 48.

in the rejection of Jesus."[69] All, both Jew and Gentile, high and low, rich and poor, religious and irreligious, are mired in the same plight.

These references to grace extended to Gentiles in the Old Testament foreshadow the development of the Gentile mission in Acts. Tannehill notes: "At the point in Acts where the mission begins to spread to the Gentiles, the Nazareth scene is recalled" (Acts 10:36 – 38).[70] They do not foreshadow the movement of the gospel from Jew to Gentile, as if the Jews were to be rejected. God intends "to save and heal both together."[71] Crockett contends, "For Luke, God's spirit and power are fully manifested when Jew and gentile are brought together within the divine purpose."[72]

Jesus uses Scripture to announce the fulfillment of God's promises but also to redefine the mission of the community of God in light of that fulfillment. He seeks to insert a wide-angle lens on their perspective of the world so that they will focus on more than their narrow self-interest. He does more than speak gracious words, but by his words and his ensuing actions, he intends to give them a vision so that they can get beyond wanting God to do something only for themselves and see what God is doing for the world through him.

69. Christoph Stenschke, "The Need for Salvation," in *Witness to the Gospel: The Theology of Acts* (ed. I. H. Marshall and D. G. Peterson; Grand Rapids: Eerdmans, 1998), 144.

70. Tannehill, *Unity of Luke-Acts*, 71.
71. Crockett, "Luke 4:25 – 27," 183.
72. Ibid., 179.

13

Luke 4:31 – 44

Literary Context

Jesus continues to teach with awe-inspiring authority (4:14 – 15), but he also performs multiple exorcisms and healings. Jesus predicted that the people in Nazareth would complain that he had not done there the deeds he had done in Capernaum (4:23). Luke now gives examples of Jesus' mighty deeds in Capernaum — healing all the sick and casting out demons. The incidents emphasize the unity of Jesus' word and deed as empowered by the Spirit. His clash with the devil now takes a different tack. He no longer fires Scripture verses at the devil (4:3 – 12) but raids his outposts, routs his demonic legions, and sets free their captives.

His preaching in the synagogues in Nazareth and Capernaum is bracketed by a notice of his teaching in the synagogues throughout Galilee (4:14 – 15) and proclaiming the reign of God in the synagogues of Judea (4:43 – 44). His fame spreads throughout the land of the Jews, and these incidents prepare for the accounts of his calling of disciples, examples of his teaching, further healings and exorcisms, and rising opposition to counter his rising popularity.

I. Prologue and Infancy Narrative (1:1 – 2:52)

II. Preparing for Ministry (3:1 – 4:13)

III. Jesus' Ministry in Galilee (4:14 – 9:50)

    A. Jesus in Nazareth and Capernaum (4:14 – 44)

       1. Jesus' Nazareth Manifesto (4:14 – 30)

➡   **2. Illustrations of Jesus' Teaching, Healing, and Exorcisms (4:31 – 44)**

    B. Calling and Controversy (5:1 – 6:49)

Main Idea

Jesus acts with power and authority to set persons free from captivity of demon possession and sickness as part of the proclamation of the good news of God's reign.

Translation

Luke 4:31–44

4:31	Circumstance	**Then he went down to Capernaum, a town of Galilee,** **and he began teaching them on the Sabbath.**
32a	Reaction of astonishment	**They were astounded at his teaching,**
b	Cause	because his word carried authority.
33	Character introduction	**A man who had a spirit, an unclean demon, was in the synagogue** **and he began to cry out at the top of his lungs,**
34a	Recognition	*"Hey! Why are you bothering us, Jesus the Nazarene?*
b		*Have you come to destroy us?*
c		*I know who you are, the Holy One of God!"*
35a	Exorcism	**Jesus rebuked it, saying,** *"Shut up and come out from him!"*
b		After the demon hurled the man into the middle, **it came out from him without harming him.**
36a	Reaction of amazement	**Amazement came over all of them** **and they were discussing with one another,**
b		*"What is this word?*
		Because *with authority and power* *he commands unclean spirits and they come out!"*
37	Result	**The news about him swept everywhere through the surrounding countryside.**
38a	Circumstance	When he left the synagogue, **he entered Simon's house.**
b	Character introduction	**Simon's mother-in-law was racked by a severe fever,** **and they conferred with him about her.**
39a	Healing	When he stood over her, **he rebuked the fever and it released her.**
b		**Immediately,** **she rose and began to serve them.**
40a	Circumstance	As the sun was setting, **all those who had people who were sick with diseases of all sorts led them** **to him.**
b		**He laid his hands on each one and healed them.**
41a	Multiple exorcisms	Moreover, **demons were coming out from many people, shrieking,** *"You are the Son of God!"*
b		**He rebuked them and refused to let them speak**

Continued on next page.

		because they had known all along that he was the Christ.
42a	Circumstance	At sunup, **he went out to a deserted place.**
b		**The crowds were searching for him,**
		and when they came up to him, **they tried to hold him fast to prevent him from going away from them.**
43	Pronouncement	**He told them,** *"It is necessary for me to proclaim the good news of the reign of God in ⌘ other cities.* *I have been sent for this purpose."*
44	Summary	**He continued preaching in the synagogues of Judea.**

Structure and Literary Form

Luke depicts Jesus as teaching and preaching but does not describe here what he taught, only its impact. He narrates two mighty deeds, an exorcism of a demon and the healing of fever. The phrase "with authority" (ἐν ἐξουσίᾳ) brackets the exorcism in the synagogue (4:32, 36). The statement about authority becomes the "topical preview of all four of the pericopes that directly follow it (i.e., 4:33 – 37, 38 – 39, 40 – 41, 42 – 44), with the motif of Jesus' authoritative word in 4:32 being echoed not only in 4:33 – 37 but also in each of the next three units (4:35 – 36, 39, 41)."[1] The verb "rebuke" (ἐπιτιμάω) appears in 4:35, 39, 41 and shows Jesus putting his divine authority to use.

The exorcism story follows the form that normally contains the recognition of the exorcist by the demon, a defensive maneuver by the demons, the command for the demons to leave by the exorcist, the departure of the demon (usually with a commotion), and the reaction of the spectators.[2]

Exegetical Outline

➡ I. **Summary transition: teaching with authority in the Capernaum synagogue (4:31 – 32)**

  II. **Release of a man captive to a demon (4:33 – 36)**

  III. **Summary of increasing fame in the region (4:37)**

  IV. **Release of a woman from a fever (4:38 – 39)**

  V. **Multiple exorcisms and healing of townspeople (4:40 – 41)**

  VI. **Attempt to retain Jesus locally and the announcement of his divine mission to go to all (4:42 – 43)**

  VII. **Summary transition: proclaiming the good news of God's reign in the synagogues of Judea (4:44)**

---

1. Todd Klutz, *The Exorcism Stories in Luke-Acts: A Socio-stylistic Reading* (SNTSMS 129; Cambridge: Cambridge Univ. Press, 2004), 58.

2. Bultmann, *The History of the Synoptic Tradition*, 210.

Explanation of the Text

4:31 – 32 Then he went down to Capernaum, a town of Galilee, and he began teaching them on the Sabbath. They were astounded at his teaching, because his word carried authority (καὶ κατῆλθεν εἰς Καφαρναοὺμ πόλιν τῆς Γαλιλαίας. καὶ ἦν διδάσκων αὐτοὺς ἐν τοῖς σάββασιν· καὶ ἐξεπλήσσοντο ἐπὶ τῇ διδαχῇ αὐτοῦ, ὅτι ἐν ἐξουσίᾳ ἦν ὁ λόγος αὐτοῦ). This summary transition recalls the report that Jesus was teaching in the synagogues in Galilee and creating a buzz (4:14 – 15) and that he entered the Nazareth synagogue on the Sabbath (4:16). Since he has not yet called disciples, he travels alone as he descends from the hills of Nazareth to the seaside.

Capernaum was one of the larger Galilean villages (around 600 to 1,500 residents) and the main fishing village of the area. It is never mentioned in literature prior to the Gospels. There is no archaeological evidence of any public buildings (theaters, administrative buildings, shops, storage facilities, or public inscriptions denoting benefactions).[3] The home construction was of low quality with no evidence of "elite houses" and no evidence of wealth ("no fine pottery or even simple glass, no mosaics, no frescoes, no marble").[4]

4:33 A man who had a spirit, an unclean demon, was in the synagogue and he began to cry out at the top of his lungs (καὶ ἐν τῇ συναγωγῇ ἦν ἄνθρωπος ἔχων πνεῦμα δαιμονίου ἀκαθάρτου καὶ ἀνέκραξεν φωνῇ μεγάλῃ). As Jesus had predicted (4:23), Capernaum will experience both his mighty word and his mighty deeds. The phrase that reads literally "a spirit of an unclean demon" (πνεῦμα δαιμονίου ἀκαθάρτου) has been rendered as an appositional (epexegetical) genitive, "a spirit, an unclean demon." In this first encounter with the demonic, Luke needs to clarify for his audience the phenomenon that he is describing.[5]

"Spirit" (πνεῦμα) has occurred fourteen times previously to refer to the Holy Spirit, and the term "spirit" also did not carry the sense of "evil spirit" in the Greco-Roman world that it did in Jewish sources.[6] In the Jewish context, these kinds of "spirits," as *1 Enoch* explicates the evil influence of the "giants" in Gen 6:1 – 4, "afflict, oppress, destroy, attack, do battle and work destruction on the earth and cause trouble" (*1 En.* 7:3 – 4; 15:9 – 11). The word "demon" (δαιμόνιον) also could be applied to a lesser deity in the Greco-Roman context, as it does in Acts 17:18.

Luke's readers might not immediately associate "demons" with a bad thing. In the LXX, the word "demon" "has associations with foreign deities and idolatry" (see Deut 32:17; Pss 95:5; 105:37; Isa 13:21; 34:14; 65:3; Bar 4:7, 35).[7] In the first century, they have become personal powers. Josephus explains parenthetically that "the so-called demons" are "the spirits of wicked men who enter the living and kill them unless aid is forthcoming" (*J.W.* 7.6.3 §185). What is "unclean" in the Old Testament has "evaded the control of the divine holiness."[8] Luke makes clear at the outset that all three terms, "spirit," "unclean," and "demon," refer to evil phenomena that attempt to corrupt God's good purposes in the world.[9]

---

3. Reed, *Archaeology and the Galilean Jesus*, 149 – 52.

4. Dunn, *Jesus Remembered*, 318.

5. Klutz, *The Exorcism Stories in Luke-Acts*, 44.

6. Marshall, *The Gospel of Luke*, 192; citing Werner Foerster, "δαίμων …," *TDNT*, 2:9; Herman Kleinknecht, "πνεῦμα …," *TDNT*, 6:339. See *1 En.* 19:1; *Jub.* 10:5; *T. Benj.* 5:2.

7. Klutz, *The Exorcism Stories in Luke-Acts*, 44 – 45.

8. G. B. Caird, *New Testament Theology* (ed. L. D. Hurst; Oxford: Clarendon, 1994), 109.

9. Green, *The Gospel of Luke*, 222. See the references to "demons" (4:41; 8:36); "unclean spirits"(6:18); "evil spirits" (7:21); "spirit" (9:39; 13:11).

4:34 Hey! Why are you bothering us, Jesus the Nazarene? Have you come to destroy us? I know who you are, the Holy One of God! (ἔα, τί ἡμῖν καὶ σοί, Ἰησοῦ Ναζαρηνέ; ἦλθες ἀπολέσαι ἡμᾶς; οἶδά σε τίς εἶ, ὁ ἅγιος τοῦ θεοῦ). Only demons and angels can fathom the mysteries of the unseen world, though the demons have a perverted perspective. Consequently, Jesus' presence always ruffles demons, and they usually howl their alarm. In this case, his teaching with authority specifically agitates them. Their initial response is surprise and annoyance, expressed in the interrogative "hey" (ἔα). It could also be taken as the imperative of the verb ἐάω and would mean "stop!" or "That is enough!" (see 22:51).[10]

The phrase translated, "Why are you bothering us?" (τί ἡμῖν καὶ σοί) reads literally, "What to us and to you?" Similar language appears in the LXX (Josh 22:24; Judg 11:12; 2 Sam 16:10; 19:22; 1 Kgs 17:18; 2 Chr 35:21) to mean, "What is there between you and me?" "What do you have to do with us?" "Why do you interfere?" They know very well why Jesus has come and why he is intervening, and they try to ward off the impending exorcism. The ancient magical papyri assume that knowledge is power, and names were used as incantations because it was believed that knowing the name of the power or enemy gave one the upper hand in defeating them. The demons do not ask a sincere question but are taking evasive action, "We know what you are up to. You have come to try to destroy us." The Greco-Roman audience may assume that they have gained a tactical advantage by pronouncing his name, and it would mean, "We've got your number."

It is more likely, however, that Luke intends to present the demons as conceding Jesus' deity and submitting to him, more out of fear than reverence. They flinch in startled alarm with an interjection, "Hey," knowing that they have met their match (see Jas 2:19).[11] The verb "cry out" in v. 33 reflects "extreme consternation."[12] Ironically, their panicked question confirms Jesus' preeminence. He is more than Jesus the Nazarene; he is "the Holy One of God" (see 1:35), who is uniquely close to God (see John 6:69). They also declare his purpose in coming, the destruction of the whole demonic realm.[13] By acknowledging the antagonism between Jesus and the demonic realm, their testimony prepares the reader for the slander against Jesus that he is an ally with Satan (11:15) and makes that accusation patently ridiculous. After years of an arms buildup, Satan's forces are now being disarmed one by one by God's Holy One. That is why he cannot stay confined to Capernaum (4:44).

4:35 Jesus rebuked it, saying, "Shut up and come out from him!" After the demon hurled the man into the middle, it came out from him without harming him (καὶ ἐπετίμησεν αὐτῷ ὁ Ἰησοῦς λέγων· φιμώθητι καὶ ἔξελθε ἀπ᾽ αὐτοῦ. καὶ ῥῖψαν αὐτὸν τὸ δαιμόνιον εἰς τὸ μέσον ἐξῆλθεν ἀπ᾽ αὐτοῦ μηδὲν βλάψαν αὐτόν). Jesus does not call on God to drive the demons out and employs no incantations or rituals. His rebuke is a commanding utterance of authority and power that must be obeyed.[14] Its significance will be clarified in 11:20,

10. So NRSV; Schürmann, *Das Lukasevangelium*, 247 – 48; Green, *The Gospel of Luke*, 223.

11. Compare the response of the advisors to Pharaoh in Exod 10:7.

12. Graham H. Twelftree, *Christ Triumphant: Exorcism Then and Now* (London: Hodder and Stoughton, 1985), 60.

13. Twelftree (ibid., 63) aptly renders the phrase τί ἡμῖν καὶ σοί as "Why are you bothering us?" (see 1 Kgs 17:18; Judg 11:12).

14. Howard Clark Kee ("The Terminology of Mark's Exorcism Stories," *NTS* 14 [1967 – 68]: 233 – 38, 245) contends that its use in the LXX and the Hebrew equivalent (*gāʿar*) refers to "the sovereign word of command by the Lord [that] asserts the Holy Spirit's rule and brings the forces of chaos into subjection."

"But if I cast out demons by the finger of God, then the reign of God has come upon you."

In Mark's gospel, the demons usually put up a struggle and cause some kind of damage, harm, or noise when they leave (see Mark 1:26; 5:13; 9:26).[15] In Luke's account, the demon shrieks its recognition *before* the exorcism and leaves silently. After being gagged by Jesus, the demon immediately gives up the man without any further harm. Nolland interprets the phrase "hurled the man into the middle" (ῥῖψαν αὐτὸν ... εἰς τὸ μέσον) to mean that the demon "handed him over to Jesus."[16] Jesus is clearly the "Stronger One" whom John proclaimed was coming (3:16).[17]

4:36 Amazement came over all of them and they were discussing with one another, "What is this word? Because with authority and power he commands unclean spirits and they come out!" (καὶ ἐγένετο θάμβος ἐπὶ πάντας, καὶ συνελάλουν πρὸς ἀλλήλους λέγοντες· τίς ὁ λόγος οὗτος ὅτι ἐν ἐξουσίᾳ καὶ δυνάμει ἐπιτάσσει τοῖς ἀκαθάρτοις πνεύμασιν, καὶ ἐξέρχονται;). The crowd's amazement underscores that this event was not a normal occurrence every Sabbath in the synagogue. The audience did not wonder at what the unclean spirit proclaimed about Jesus. Did they hear it? Or was it simply too overwhelming for them to comprehend? Unlike the demons, they remain unknowing about the source of Jesus' power or his mission.

It is significant that these people use the present tense instead of the aorist to describe what Jesus does: "He *commands* unclean spirits and they *come* out!" (ἐπιτάσσει τοῖς ἀκαθάρτοις πνεύμασιν καὶ ἐξέρχονται). This is not a onetime fluke but a characteristic of his ministry. The emphasis is on his "word," which makes it clear that Jesus is

not simply an exorcist, as he is known in the Talmud (*b. Sanh.* 107b), but one who overthrows the power of demons as part of his proclamation of God's reign. Klutz maintains that Luke does not intend for this episode to be merely "as an account of Jesus' expulsion of a demon from a possessed man in the Jewish assembly but rather as a demonstration of the cosmic authority and power which Jesus embodies over the whole demonic realm and its impure schemes."[18] This incident belies the devil's assertion that he has authority over all of "the kingdoms of the inhabited world" (4:5 – 6).

4:37 The news about him swept everywhere through the surrounding countryside (καὶ ἐξεπορεύετο ἦχος περὶ αὐτοῦ εἰς πάντα τόπον τῆς περιχώρου). Jesus' spreading fame for performing deeds of power is mentioned again in 7:17 (throughout Judea; see 9:43; 13:17; 19:2 – 3, 37) and is presumed in Acts 2:22 and 10:37 – 38.

4:38 – 39 When he left the synagogue, he entered Simon's house. Simon's mother-in-law was racked by a severe fever, and they conferred with him about her. When he stood over her, he rebuked the fever and it released her. Immediately, she rose and began to serve them (ἀναστὰς δὲ ἀπὸ τῆς συναγωγῆς εἰσῆλθεν εἰς τὴν οἰκίαν Σίμωνος. πενθερὰ δὲ τοῦ Σίμωνος ἦν συνεχομένη πυρετῷ μεγάλῳ καὶ ἠρώτησαν αὐτὸν περὶ αὐτῆς. καὶ ἐπιστὰς ἐπάνω αὐτῆς ἐπετίμησεν τῷ πυρετῷ καὶ ἀφῆκεν αὐτήν, παραχρῆμα δὲ ἀναστᾶσα διηκόνει αὐτοῖς). Luke assumes that the reader would already know who Simon is because he is not introduced. "Fever" was considered to be an illness in and of itself and not simply a symptom of a disease (see John 4:52; Acts 28:8).[19] Views about

---

15. See Twelftree, *Christ Triumphant*, 71.

16. Nolland, *Luke*, 1:207.

17. Johnson, *The Gospel of Luke*, 84.

18. Klutz, *The Exorcism Stories in Luke-Acts*, 50.

19. Julius Preuss, *Biblical and Talmudic Medicine* (trans. F. Rosner; New York: Sanhedrin, 1978), 160.

what caused it varied.[20] According to *T. Sol.* 18:20, 23, it could be caused by a demon.

In Lev 26:16 and Deut 28:22, fever is listed as a punishment sent by God to those who violate the covenant (see also Philo, *Rewards* 143). Luke does not identify the cause, but his language that she "was racked" (ἦν συνεχομένη) by this fever, which literally means that she "was held fast" (was "in the grip of," NJB), suggests that he understands the fever to be a force that had taken her captive.[21] Given Jewish understanding of the disease, a great fever requires a great feat to vanquish it. Jesus "rebuked" (ἐπετίμησεν) it and forces it to "release" (ἀφῆκεν) its hold of her. This incident illustrates the theme of Jesus' release of the captives (4:18).

The service of Simon's mother-in-law is a sign of gratitude to Jesus for his service to her. It also represents her restoration to wholeness, both physical and mental. In Luke, serving at a meal becomes a "paradigm for Christian service in general" (see 8:3; 10:40; 17:8; 22:26 – 27).[22]

4:40 As the sun was setting, all those who had people who were sick with diseases of all sorts led them to him. He laid his hands on each one and healed them (δύνοντος δὲ τοῦ ἡλίου ἅπαντες ὅσοι εἶχον ἀσθενοῦντας νόσοις ποικίλαις ἤγαγον αὐτοὺς πρὸς αὐτόν· ὁ δὲ ἑνὶ ἑκάστῳ αὐτῶν τὰς χεῖρας ἐπιτιθεὶς ἐθεράπευεν αὐτούς). The setting of the sun marks the end of the day and the end of Sabbath restrictions on movement and carrying burdens. The present tense of the participle should be rendered "as the sun was setting" (δύνοντος δὲ τοῦ ἡλίου) and suggests the townspeople's impatience to get their sick to Jesus without delay. Jesus responds to the onslaught with patience, giving each one individual attention.

4:41 Moreover, demons were coming out from many people, shrieking, "You are the Son of God!" He rebuked them and refused to let them speak because they had known all along that he was the Christ (ἐξήρχετο δὲ καὶ δαιμόνια ἀπὸ πολλῶν κραυγάζοντα καὶ λέγοντα ὅτι σὺ εἶ ὁ υἱὸς τοῦ θεοῦ. καὶ ἐπιτιμῶν οὐκ εἴα αὐτὰ λαλεῖν, ὅτι ᾔδεισαν τὸν χριστὸν αὐτὸν εἶναι). Jesus' presence again causes demons to shriek as they clear out from their victims. "Known all along" (ᾔδεισαν) renders the pluperfect. Jesus' identity as the Son of God had been voiced by God's angel (1:32, 35) and by God (3:22). The devil tested Jesus as the Son of God (4:3, 9) in a failed attempt to break him, and now the devil's minions concede his authority as the Son of God. Jesus rebukes (ἐπιτιμῶν) and suppresses their confession because he does not want or need demonic testimony.

4:42 At sunup, he went out to a deserted place. The crowds were searching for him, and when they came up to him, they tried to hold him fast to prevent him from going away from them (γενομένης δὲ ἡμέρας ἐξελθὼν ἐπορεύθη εἰς ἔρημον τόπον· καὶ οἱ ὄχλοι ἐπεζήτουν αὐτόν, καὶ ἦλθον ἕως αὐτοῦ καὶ κατεῖχον αὐτὸν τοῦ μὴ πορεύεσθαι ἀπ᾽ αὐτῶν). Mark has Jesus retreating to a deserted place to pray, and it is surprising that Luke does not include this detail since Jesus' prayer life is highlighted in this gospel (see 5:16; 6:12). In Mark, the disciples hunt Jesus down, but in Luke "the crowds" pursue him, since the disciples have not yet been called.

Bovon observes, "In Mark they look for him to request more miracles; in Luke they detain him in order not to lose him."[23] This desire would seem to be positive compared with the violent reaction

---

20. These varied from natural physical phenomena, to demons, divine beings, curses, or astrological phenomena. See John Granger Cook, "In Defense of Ambiguity: Is There a Hidden Demon in Mark 1.29 – 31?" *NTS* 43 (1997): 184 – 208.

21. The verb συνέχω is used in 19:43 to mean "to hem in" and in 22:63 "to hold [prisoner]."

22. Heil, *The Meal Scenes in Luke-Acts*, 19.

23. Bovon, *Luke*, 1:1 – 9:50, 1:160.

in Nazareth. The people of Nazareth tried to destroy their own prophet who would not favor them above all others; the people of Capernaum now try to keep him (κατεῖχον, a conative imperfect) for their own. But the motivation behind these actions is similar. They both want a miracle man to serve their selfish ends. Jesus' harsh judgment on Capernaum in 10:13 – 15 should not be surprising. Their enthusiasm for him is exuberance for the miraculous, and it is insufficient for the long haul since it wanes over time.

4:43 He told them, "It is necessary for me to proclaim the good news of the reign of God in other cities. I was sent for this purpose" (ὁ δὲ εἶπεν πρὸς αὐτοὺς ὅτι καὶ ταῖς ἑτέραις πόλεσιν εὐαγγελίσασθαί με δεῖ τὴν βασιλείαν τοῦ θεοῦ, ὅτι ἐπὶ τοῦτο ἀπεστάλην). Nave notes that the noun "good news" (εὐαγγέλιον) occurs twelve times in Matthew and Mark but never in Luke. The verb "to proclaim good news" (εὐαγγελίσασθαι) appears twenty-five times in Luke-Acts, never appears in Mark, and occurs only once in Matthew. He explains that Luke "is more concerned with emphasizing the *preaching* of the good news than with emphasizing the *goodness* of the news. It is the act of preaching good news that is according to God's plan, and it is the act of preaching that indicates that there is a divine plan at work."[24] God speaks through his preaching (see Acts 10:36).

The term "the reign of God" (ἡ βασιλεία τοῦ θεοῦ) appears for the first time, and it begins and ends the book of Acts (1:3; 28:31). It characterizes the preaching of Jesus and that of Philip (Acts 8:12) and Paul (Acts 20:25; 28:23). It basically

means that God is king (see Ps 97:1 – 2), and Jesus announces that God's rule will be concretely embodied in the world. The translation "reign" is chosen because it is more dynamic and active than "kingdom." While its proclamation may be good news for some, it implies the overthrow of the rulers of this world and is bad news for them, unless they are willing to submit to God.[25] It is also related to preaching good news to the poor, which entails that God will bring justice (4:18; 6:20).

Again, Luke makes clear that Jesus is not a local Messiah but has been sent to others. The passive voice, "I was sent" (ἀπεστάλην, aorist tense) reveals Jesus' sense of his divine commission and that God is behind his words and mighty deeds. He thereby grounds his authority in God's authority, not his own initiative. God exercises his authority over a fallen world through Jesus to bring order from the chaos.

4:44 He continued preaching in the synagogues of Judea (καὶ ἦν κηρύσσων εἰς τὰς συναγωγὰς τῆς Ἰουδαίας). As a consequence of his calling to preach to all Israel, he does not confine himself to one locale where he has met with enormous success but continues to preach in synagogues spreading across Judea. Mark 1:39 (Matt 4:23) has Jesus going around in "Galilee," which seems to fit the context better. Dalman thinks Luke uses the general expression to refer to "the Jewish land" and refers to "the great extent of Jesus' activity."[26] "Judea" also would be better known to readers as a Roman province, and Luke uses it as a general term for the land of the Jews (1:5; 6:17; 7:17; Acts 10:37; 26:20).

24. Nave, *Repentance in Luke-Acts*, 20.

25. See Norman Perrin, *Jesus and the Language of the Kingdom: Symbol and Metaphor in New Testament Interpretation*

(Philadelphia: Fortress, 1976), 15 – 32.

26. Gustaf Dalman, *Sacred Sites and Ways* (trans. Paul P. Levertoff; New York: Macmillan, 1935), 109.

Theology in Application

1. Demons and Illness

Jesus repulsed the devil's false promise to give him authority (4:6 – 8) and now is shown exercising authority given him by God to expel the devil's minions. Later, he will give that authority to his disciples (9:1; 10:19). In this episode, his authority is connected to his "word." The teaching of the Jewish sages during this time was primarily exposition of the text and argument with others over its proper application, often by making appeals to authority. Jesus' teaching is clearly different. It is prophetic and powerful in effecting deliverance from both demonic powers and sickness. His preaching shows that God's reign is replacing the reign of the devil in humans' lives.

Most people in Western cultures today fear viruses more than they do demons. Foerster comments, "In the great reduction of fear of demons, however, we are to see an effect of the NT faith in God as the Guardian of His people. In the light of this faith all fear of demons necessarily yields to steadfast assurance."[27] He goes on to say that sickness belongs to the character of this age "of which Satan is the prince" (see 13:11, 16; Acts 10:38). While sicknesses need not be "the work of demons, they may all be seen as the work of Satan." He concludes, "in most of the stories of possession what is at issue is not merely sickness but a destruction and distortion of the divine likeness of man according to creation. The centre of personality, the volitional and active ego, is impaired by alien powers which seek to ruin the man and sometimes drive him to self-destruction (Mk. 5:5)."[28] When one interprets these incidents of healing and exorcism, what is crucial is that Jesus restores what Satan seeks to warp, brutalize, and cripple.

Luke differentiates between healing the sick and exorcizing demons. Having "a spirit, an unclean demon" is not some primitive medical diagnosis. As Caird recognizes, "It is rather a spiritual diagnosis, which says of an affliction, 'An enemy has done this' (Matt 13:28)."[29] That is why it is called an "unclean demon." What is "unclean" has not come under God's control. The exorcisms are not just cures of human physical maladies; they represent an assault against demonic forces that deface humans. One might wonder why Jesus only plucks individuals from the fire. Why not put out the fire? The scope of the opposition is overwhelming and the entire world is broken and wounded, languishing in bondage to forces alien to God. God intends to attack the problem at the source. Its defeat must await the crucifixion, and its final defeat, the parousia. That is why Jesus silences demonic testimony about himself: "a right knowledge of Jesus as Christ and redeemer is only to be had in connection with the cross."[30]

---

27. Foerster, "δαίμων …," *TDNT*, 2:17.
28. Ibid., 2:18 – 19.

29. Caird, *New Testament Theology*, 109.
30. Nolland, *Luke*, 1:214.

The possession is treated as evil and not as sinful. Jesus does not offer the victims forgiveness, as if they were in some way at fault for being demonized.[31] We distinguish between the evil of what we call a natural disaster, such as an earthquake, monsoon, or tornado, and the evil that lies behind personal sin. Those who suffer from unclean demons are victims who are completely helpless. Unlike the sick in body, they are too helpless even to ask for aid. It is the demon, who knows the full truth about Jesus and sees him as a threat, that speaks.

2. The Reign of God

Lowery addresses the issue of the king image that might not speak to democratic societies:

> While the monarchist metaphor hardly fits today's more egalitarian and democratic theologies, the notion of divine and human sovereignty … provides a helpful corrective to the more destructive forms of individualist ideology pervasive in American culture. Sovereignty, in the ancient view, was rooted in a strong sense of responsibility to the collective welfare of the nation. Kings may have been despots but, at least ideally, they operated out of concern for the well-being of the whole.[32]

Caird adds further insight about the use of this metaphor:

> When the Bible calls God judge, king, father or husband it is, in the first instance, using the human known to throw light on the divine unknown, and particularly God's attitude toward his worshippers. But no sooner has the metaphor travelled from earth to heaven than it begins the return journey to earth bearing with it an ideal standard by which the conduct of human judges, kings, fathers and husbands is to be assessed.[33]

It means that God is king, not _____ (whoever might be enthroned temporally, whether a literal ruler or some cultural phenomenon). Since kings go to battle, it also means that God takes to the battlefield against hostile powers that threaten the people. In this case, God takes on the forces of evil and chaos (see Ps 89:9 – 12). God brings final victory and deliverance to the people. It also means that as sovereign, God imposes special demands on the subjects. They must be obedient and loyal.

The proclamation of God's reign may have sounded like a summons to rally round the flag since it raised Jewish nationalist hopes. Ladd asserts that the idea of the kingdom of God

31. Ernest Best, "Exorcism in the New Testament and Today," *BibTheol* 27 (1977): 3.

32. Richard H. Lowery, "Sabbath and Survival: Abundance and Self-Restraint in a Culture of Excess," *Encounter* 54.2

(1993): 153.

33. G. B. Caird, *The Language and Imagery of the Bible* (Philadelphia: Westminster, 1980), 19.

was a dynamic concept expressing the frustrated hopes of a people who felt that they had met all the conditions required to enjoy God's Kingdom and yet continued to experience the sufferings and oppressions of an evil order. The coming of the Kingdom of God always meant some sort of a mighty manifestation of God's power to destroy evil, smite the wicked and the enemies of God's people, and exalt Israel to her promised salvation. Ideas of growth, gradual transformation, evolutionary development and the like were alien to the Jewish mind.[34]

It becomes clear as Jesus' ministry unfolds that he is not simply a liberationist bent on inaugurating a program of social reform, though social reform follows directly from submitting to God as sovereign ruler. Nor will there be dramatic displays of glory and violent disruptions of society as he purges evil from the world. God's reign manifests itself in preaching and healing and can be compared to a seed sowed in the ground (8:5 – 15). It requires patient endurance (8:15) to see its full effect. Humans do not bring in God's reign, build God's kingdom, hasten its final consummation, or hinder its advance. Jesus' preaching announces that God is in action and that one's ultimate well-being is tied to what God is doing, not what they are doing. They can only receive it and enter it or reject it and be swept away in judgment.

3. Avoiding Publicity

Not only is Jesus shown to be able to refuse the enticements of Satan; he is also shown to be able to refuse the cocktail of privilege, fame, and applause from others. He will not allow his ministry to become a variety show that plays to the audience. He resists the pressures from the crowds, and later from his own disciples, to do their bidding and to bring more fame to himself. He is able to resist them because through prayer he is centered on God's calling and purpose for his life.

34. G. E. Ladd, "The *Sitz im Leben* of the Parables of Matthew 13: the Soils," *SE II* (TU 87; Berlin: Akademie Verlag, 1962), 205 – 6.

14

Luke 5:1 – 11

Literary Context

The call of Simon is the first of six units introduced by the phrase "it happened" (ἐγένετο; see 5:1, 12, 17; 6:1, 6, 12).[1] This section introduces the disciples and others and sounds the themes of hearing Jesus' word and leaving everything to follow him. It also introduces the response of sinners to Jesus' call and the indignant carping of the Pharisees over Jesus' lack of discrimination in extending that call to all. They are even more upset over his audacity to announce the forgiveness of sins and to violate Sabbath rules (5:17, 21, 30, 33; 6:2, 7). In this section, sinners hear the offer of forgiveness, the apostles receive a "special call to join Jesus in the task" of mission, and the Pharisees have their righteousness exposed as hollow.[2]

Mark presents Jesus' calling of his disciples (Simon and Andrew; James and John) to follow him at the very beginning of his ministry when he suddenly appears by the sea as they are cleaning their nets. He gives no motivation as to why they should leave everything to follow him, which serves to underscore the divine force of Jesus' call: he commands as God commands and creates obedience (Mark 1:16 – 20).[3] Luke's account focuses only on Simon and provides a context and motivation for him to leave everything to follow him.

Luke notes that Jesus' fame has spread far and wide and he is already known to Simon. He has cast out a demon in the synagogue in Capernaum, amazing the crowd, and followed that up by healing Simon's mother-in-law. Jesus is not simply passing by, as in Mark, but teaching a huge crowd by the shore that forces him to commandeer Simon's boat and to teach them from a better vantage point on the lake. Simon, therefore, has already witnessed Jesus' power, heard his teaching, and joined the enthusiasm of the crowds pressing around him. After a futile night of fishing, when he and his partners have caught nothing, it makes sense that they will obey Jesus' command, even though it may seem an exercise in futility. Obedience results in an overwhelming catch of fish that almost swamps their boats.

The crowd seeks to hear the "word of God," but Luke does not present his teach-

---

1. The exception occurs in 5:27, which is introduced by the phrase "after this" (καὶ μετὰ ταῦτα). See Michael Theobald, "Die Anfänge der Kirche: Zur Struktur von Lk 5.1 – 6.19," *NTS* 30 (1984): 91 – 108.

2. Nolland, *Luke*, 1:221.

3. See Garland, *Mark*, 78 – 79.

ing to the crowd. Instead, we hear the word of God that comes directly to Simon in Jesus' command ("at your word," v. 5), and the assurance and promise that commission Simon with a missionary task ("you will be," v. 10). His obedience to Jesus' commands determines the new direction of his life and the lives of his partners, who leave everything to follow him.

I. Prologue and Infancy Narrative (1:1 – 2:52)

II. Preparing for Ministry (3:1 – 4:13)

III. Jesus' Ministry in Galilee (4:14 – 9:50)

    A. Jesus in Nazareth and Capernaum (4:14 – 44)

➡   **B. Calling and Controversy (5:1 – 6:49)**

       1. Peter's Confession and Calling (5:1 – 11)

       2. Four Controversy Stories (5:12 – 6:11)

Main Idea

Jesus' divine glory and power is manifested in the miraculous catch of fish. He overcomes Peter's deep sense of fear and unworthiness in the presence of the divine with a call to service. Jesus does not flee sinners but seeks them. He does not simply offer sinners forgiveness but recruits them to gain other sinners.

Translation

(See next page.)

Structure and Literary Form

The structure contains two dialogues between Jesus and Simon (5:4 – 5, 8, 10b-c), with Jesus speaking first and then last. The emphasis falls on Jesus' word and Simon's response to it. Others are present, but Simon is singled out. Jesus chooses his boat and orders him to put out into the deep. Simon responds to this command and reacts to the miracle of fish by begging Jesus to leave, and Jesus tells him not to fear and promises him he will have a new role catching people. Talbert identifies it as a commission story rather than a call story: "the dominant thrust is that of a commissioning of Simon for his role of catching people (i.e. mission)."[4]

---

4. Talbert, *Reading Luke*, 63.

Luke 5:1–11

5:1a	Circumstance	Now it happened

                                               while the crowd was swarming around him to hear the word of God,

b   **he was standing beside the Lake of Gennesaret,**

2a   **and he saw two boats by the lake's edge.**

b   Character introduction   **The fishermen from the boats had disembarked and were scrubbing their nets.**

3a   And   getting into one of the boats,
                                         which was Simon's,

b   Request   **[Jesus] asked him to put out a little way from the shore,**

                            and   when he sat in the boat,
he began to teach the crowd.

4   Command   When he stopped speaking,
he told Simon,
       "Put out into the deep water
       and [have the crew] let down your nets for a catch."

5a   Objection   **Simon responded,**
       "Master, after laboring through the whole night, we did not catch a thing,

b   Obedience   *but at your word I will let down the nets."*

6   Miracle   Now   when they had done this,
they captured such a huge haul of fish that their nets were beginning to tear.

7   **They signaled their partners on the other boat to come to help with the catch.**
They came and filled both boats so full that they were on the verge of sinking.

8a   Submission   When Simon Peter saw this,
he fell down at Jesus' knees, saying,

b   Confession   *"Depart from me, because I am a sinful man, Lord."*

9   Cause   **For he and all those with him were seized with awe over the catch of fish** ⌒
                              that they had taken together,

10a   Character introduction   as were both   James and John,
                                  the sons of Zebedee, who ⌒
                                  were partners with Simon.

b   Assurance   **Jesus said to Simon,**
       "Do not fear!

c   Prophecy/ commission   *From now on you will be catching alive people."*

11   Obedience   When the boats put in to shore,
they left everything and followed him.

Exegetical Outline

➡ **I. Setting: crowds swarming to hear the word of God from Jesus (5:1 – 2)**

II. First command to Simon (5:3)

   A. Command: "Put out a little way from the shore" (5:3a)

   B. Obedience (5:3b)

III. Second command to Simon (5:4 – 7)

   A. Command: "Put out into the deep water and let down your nets for a catch" (5:4)

   B. Protesting obedience (5:5)

   C. Results: spectacular catch of fish (5:6 – 7)

IV. Response of awe (5:8 – 10a)

   A. Simon's submission and confession: "Depart from me, because I am a sinful man, Lord" (5:8)

   B. Response of other witnesses (5:9 – 10a)

V. Jesus' assurance and commissioning promise (5:10b – 11)

   A. Commission: "From now on you will be catching alive people" (5:10b)

   B. Obedience: leaving everything to follow Jesus (5:11)

Explanation of the Text

5:1 Now it happened while the crowd was swarming around him to hear the word of God, he was standing beside the Lake of Gennesaret (ἐγένετο δὲ ἐν τῷ τὸν ὄχλον ἐπικεῖσθαι αὐτῷ καὶ ἀκούειν τὸν λόγον τοῦ θεοῦ καὶ αὐτὸς ἦν ἑστὼς παρὰ τὴν λίμνην Γεννησαρέτ). Because Jesus spoke and performed deeds of power with authority (4:32), the crowds press around to hear "the word of God" from his mouth (the καί has a final sense, "in order to"). Luke equates Jesus' message with the word of God, and it is equivalent to the good news of the kingdom (4:43). Simply hearing the word, however, is not enough. In Luke's gospel many gather to hear Jesus (2:47; 5:15; 6:18; 10:39; 15:1; 19:48; 21:38), but hearing his word must call forth repentance and action (6:47 – 49; 8:12 – 14, 18; 11:28). The appropriate response is demonstrated by Simon's obedience to Jesus' word.

Luke uses the term "the Lake of Gennesaret" (ἡ λίμνη Γεννησαρέτ) instead of Sea of Galilee, which is more familiar to readers of the New Testament, but the latter name is not found outside the New Testament (see 1 Macc 11:67; Josephus, *J.W.* 3.506). Luke uses "sea" properly for the larger body of water, the Mediterranean Sea, and "lake" for Gennesaret, a name that derives from the fertile area west of the lake.

5:2 And he saw two boats by the lake's edge. The fishermen from the boats had disembarked and were scrubbing their nets (καὶ εἶδεν δύο πλοῖα ἑστῶτα παρὰ τὴν λίμνην· οἱ δὲ ἁλιεῖς ἀπ᾽ αὐτῶν ἀποβάντες ἔπλυνον τὰ δίκτυα). The two boats suggest the partnership mentioned below in 5:7, 10. Cleaning their nets indicates that they have finished their fishing from the previous night ("through the whole night," 5:5), but Luke does not give a time indicator.

In Depth: A Galilean Fishing Boat

A boat that was discovered buried in the silt of the lake after a prolonged dry season in modern-day Israel when the sea level had receded, and carbon-dated from 120 BC to AD 40, may be similar to the boats these fishermen used. It measured 25.5 feet long, 7.5 feet wide, and 4.5 feet in depth. It had a deck in the bow and the stern and could be powered by sails or by four oars. It normally had a crew of five with a capacity for ten passengers or an excess of a ton of cargo.[5] Three types of nets were used: the seine net (Matt 13:47 – 48), the cast net (Mark 1:16), and the trammel net, which could stretch to five hundred feet and required two boats working together to pull it.

5:3 And getting into one the boats, which was Simon's, [Jesus] asked him to put out a little way from the shore, and when he sat in the boat, he began to teach the crowd (ἐμβὰς δὲ εἰς ἓν τῶν πλοίων, ὃ ἦν Σίμωνος, ἠρώτησεν αὐτὸν ἀπὸ τῆς γῆς ἐπαναγαγεῖν ὀλίγον· καθίσας δὲ ἐκ τοῦ πλοίου ἐδίδασκεν τοὺς ὄχλους). Simon grants a small favor by giving Jesus the use of his boat to teach the crowd. A sloping amphitheater-like inlet lies halfway between Capernaum and Tabgha and has excellent natural acoustics, and Jesus may have used this cove in teaching the crowds from the boat. Sitting is the normal posture for teaching (4:20). What Jesus teaches is left unreported because the focus is on the commands given to Simon.

5:4 When he stopped speaking, he told Simon, "Put out into the deep water and [have the crew] let down your nets for a catch" (ὡς δὲ ἐπαύσατο λαλῶν, εἶπεν πρὸς τὸν Σίμωνα· ἐπανάγαγε εἰς τὸ βάθος καὶ χαλάσατε τὰ δίκτυα ὑμῶν εἰς ἄγραν). Jesus commands Peter to put out beyond the shallows into the deep. "Put out" (ἐπανάγαγε) is singular and given to the captain of the boat, while "let down" (χαλάσατε) is plural, suggesting a crew in the boat. Jesus does not suggest that they try fishing again in hopes of catching something. It is a command coupled with an assurance.

5:5 Simon responded, "Master, after laboring through the whole night, we did not catch a thing, but at your word I will let down the nets" (καὶ ἀποκριθεὶς Σίμων εἶπεν· ἐπιστάτα, δι᾿ ὅλης νυκτὸς κοπιάσαντες οὐδὲν ἐλάβομεν· ἐπὶ δὲ τῷ ῥήματί σου χαλάσω τὰ δίκτυα). Jesus does not need to be informed that they were fishing all night. It is evident from the scrubbing of their nets. Consequently, since this response appears on the lips of Simon and not the narrator, it must be a weak protest.[6] It will not be the last time that disciples protest to Jesus (8:24, 45; 9:13; 18:28). Here, it serves to highlight failure when they are on their own and the promise of success when they obey his word.[7] They may be master fishermen, but Jesus is the Master of every situation.

5. See Shelley Wachsmann, *The Sea of Galilee Boat: An Extraordinary 2000 Year Old Discovery* (New York: Plenum, 1995), 349; K. C. Hanson, "The Galilean Fishing Economy and the Jesus Tradition," *BTB* 27 (1997): 106.

6. Timothy Wiarda, *Peter in the Gospels: Pattern, Personal-*ity and Relationship* (WUNT 2/127; Tübingen: Mohr Siebeck, 2000), 101.

7. Paul S. Minear, *To Heal and to Reveal: The Prophetic Vocation according to Luke* (New York: Seabury, 1976), 114.

"Master" (ἐπιστάτα) is Luke's equivalent for rabbi (9:33 = Mark 9:5), which he does not use, and this term was more understandable to a Hellenistic audience, emphasizing authority ("one who stands over") and could be used for a great teacher. Only the disciples (8:24, 45; 9:33, 49) and the lepers seeking help (17:13) address Jesus with this term.

The directive to put out again into the deep comes when the fishermen are exhausted from their night's labor and discouraged by their failure, and when the traditionally optimum time for fishing with nets has passed. During the daytime, the fish can see and evade the nets. The newly washed nets will have to be washed all over again, and rest from their previous night's toil will be put off for hours.

Despite the hint of reluctance, Simon obeys (see 6:46; 11:28). It need not imply that Simon was already a disciple.[8] "At your word" matches the emphasis in Mark's calling incident of the disciples — they follow immediately at Jesus' word (Mark 1:16 – 20) — and is the key point. Jesus' word (see 4:36) requires the response of obedience. Peter's obedience recalls Mary's submission to the divine word (1:34 – 38). Unlike the angel who explains to Mary how she will become pregnant, Jesus gives no explanation about how this catch will occur.

5:6 – 7 Now when they had done this, they captured such a huge haul of fish that their nets were beginning to tear. They signaled their partners on the other boat to come to help with the catch. They came and filled both boats so full that they were on the verge of sinking (καὶ τοῦτο ποιήσαντες συνέκλεισαν πλῆθος ἰχθύων πολύ, διερρήσσετο δὲ τὰ δίκτυα αὐτῶν. καὶ κατένευσαν τοῖς μετόχοις ἐν τῷ ἑτέρῳ πλοίῳ τοῦ ἐλθόντας συλλαβέσθαι αὐτοῖς· καὶ ἦλθον καὶ ἔπλησαν ἀμφότερα τὰ πλοῖα ὥστε βυθίζεσθαι αὐτά). As Jesus promised, they do make a catch, but it is a catch so large that it strains all of their resources. The glut of fish in their nets is almost more than they can handle. In the similar account in John 21:11, the wonder is that the nets do not break with the catch of fish, numbered at 153.[9] Luke employs the imperfect tense (διερρήσσετο) to portray something in progress but not completed, "their nets were beginning to tear." They have not broken or it would be pointless to signal the other boat for help.[10]

Luke does not mine the symbolic, allegorical potential of all of these details, and studies that do so mislead. What is important for Luke is that (1) Jesus has prophetic powers to know what will happen; (2) obedience to his word leads to success; and (3) the catch becomes a symbol of the mission that he will call Simon to engage in and a symbol

---

8. Contra Evans, *St. Luke*, 290.

9. Raymond E. Brown (*The Gospel According to John 13 – 21* [AB; New York: Doubleday, 1970], 1090) identifies ten similarities with John 21:1 – 11, but John's account contains at least twelve differences from Luke's: (1) The six fishermen are identified already as Jesus' disciples, and four are named. (2) They are already fishing from their boat and are not cleaning their nets. (3) Jesus remains on shore and does not get into the boat with them. (4) Jesus is not recognized initially. (5) Jesus specifically instructs them to cast their nets on the *right* side of the boat. (6) The miracle is that the net is not torn by the huge haul of fish. (7) The Beloved Disciple is mentioned and is in the same boat with Peter and is the first one to recognize Jesus. (8) They

are not in the deep but much closer to shore. (9) Simon Peter rushes to the Lord rather than begs him to depart from him. He is naked, puts on clothes, and jumps into the sea, leaving the task of bringing in the haul of fish to the other fishermen. (10) Jesus has a charcoal fire going and cooks a breakfast of fish for them. (11) The scene is identified as the third resurrection appearance to the disciples. (12) A long discussion between Jesus and Peter about feeding sheep and the status of the Beloved Disciple occurs afterward.

10. The present infinitive "to sink" (βυθίζεσθαι) in 5:7 also has a conative import: the boats are at the point of sinking, with the connotation that the action will not be completed ("on the verge of sinking").

of its great success. As Green puts it, the key is "the nexus between catching fish and proclaiming the word: success in fishing, under Jesus' authority, is a prophetic symbol for the mission in which Simon and the others will participate, which Jesus himself, in his word and miraculous deed, is engaged in 'catching.'"[11]

5:8 When Simon Peter saw this, he fell down at Jesus' knees, saying, "Depart from me, because I am a sinful man, Lord" (ἰδὼν δὲ Σίμων Πέτρος προσέπεσεν τοῖς γόνασιν Ἰησοῦ λέγων· ἔξελθε ἀπ᾽ ἐμοῦ, ὅτι ἀνὴρ ἁμαρτωλός εἰμι, κύριε). Simon Peter is called both these names together only here in Luke-Acts. The name Peter is anachronistic at this point, since Jesus has yet to give him that name (6:14).

One may presume that when the dangerous situation was brought under control—they did not capsize—and they could take a breather from their physical exertion, Simon takes a moment to reflect on what happened. He does not wonder how a non-fisherman would know where the fish were while he, a professional, did not. He deems it a miracle and recognizes that he is in the presence of one who is holy. It may seem unusual for a miracle to elicit the conviction of one's sin.[12] One might expect it to call forth gratitude rather than confession, and the latter would seem to be more apt in John's account of a great catch of fish (John 21:1 – 13) after Peter had denied Jesus three times (John 18:15 – 18, 25 – 27). Peter's bowing down before Jesus and exclaiming he is a sinner from whom Jesus should take leave has three implications.

First, it turns this incident into an epiphany, a manifestation of Jesus as someone with divine powers. Peter is the first person in the gospel to address Jesus as "Lord." Luke has used the title primarily to refer to the God of Israel with hints along the way that Jesus is also the "Lord" (1:43; 2:11). Standing in the presence of the Holy naturally evokes a response of unworthiness. John had already announced that he was unworthy to untie the sandals of the more powerful one who is to come (3:16), and Simon feels no differently. A holy presence brings destruction to those who are unholy (Exod 20:19; Judg 13:22; 1 Sam 6:20), and Simon's plea for him to depart acknowledges this reality. His confession "I am a sinful man" is a confession that Jesus represents the divine presence.

Second, the term "sinner" (ἁμαρτωλός) appears here for the first time in Luke,[13] and the reader will soon learn that the Pharisees' definition of a sinner is someone who is distant from God and not entitled to God's favor.[14] Evans's comment is on target: "the conviction of sin in the one who was to be the chief apostle is appropriate at the opening of a section where the dominant note is that Jesus calls not the righteous but sinners to repentance (5:32), and Luke has used the story for this purpose (cf. 22:32)."[15] Good news and forgiveness for sinners is a Lukan emphasis (5:30, 32; 7:34, 39; 15:1 – 2, 7, 10; 18:13; 19:7). Those who know themselves to be sinners are the most responsive to Jesus, while those who regard themselves as religiously virtuous and look down their noses on sinners regard him with antagonism.

Third, Simon's response echoes the commissioning of the prophets Isaiah (Isa 6:5) and Ezekiel (Ezek 1:28; see also Exod 3:5 – 6) when they were

---

11. Green, *The Gospel of Luke*, 233.

12. Evans, *St. Luke*, 290.

13. The noun "sinner" occurs eighteen times in the gospel (five times in Matthew, six in Mark, and four in John).

14. In the LXX it denotes the impious as opposed to the righteous. The term "sinner," however, did not have a religious connotation in ordinary Greek but denoted someone who had "opposed or disrupted law, order or custom" (Evans, *St. Luke*, 291).

15. Ibid., 291.

met by God. At Jesus' knees, it is almost as if Peter clings to him while at the same time asking him to depart.

5:9 For he and all those with him were seized with awe over the catch of fish that they had taken together (θάμβος γὰρ περιέσχεν αὐτὸν καὶ πάντας τοὺς σὺν αὐτῷ ἐπὶ τῇ ἄγρᾳ τῶν ἰχθύων ὧν συνέλαβον). The word for awe (θάμβος) appears only in Luke-Acts. The other usages reveal that it refers to religious awe in response to demonstrations of power (see 4:36, an exorcism; Acts 3:10, healing of a blind man).

Rendering their action as "they had taken together" (συνέλαβον) may be overtranslation, but it seeks to emphasize the preposition "with" (σύν) to make clear that the catch is a group effort. While the incident focuses almost entirely on the commissioning of Simon for a greater mission, the Christian mission requires group effort and cooperation and is not to be a one-man show.

5:10 As were both James and John, the sons of Zebedee, who were partners with Simon. Jesus said to Simon, "Do not fear! From now on you will be catching alive people" (ὁμοίως δὲ καὶ Ἰάκωβον καὶ Ἰωάννην υἱοὺς Ζεβεδαίου, οἳ ἦσαν κοινωνοὶ τῷ Σίμωνι. καὶ εἶπεν πρὸς τὸν Σίμωνα ὁ Ἰησοῦς· μὴ φοβοῦ· ἀπὸ τοῦ νῦν ἀνθρώπους ἔσῃ ζωγρῶν). The story began with two boats and assumes the presence of another boat to help with the overwhelming catch of fish, but only Simon and Jesus take center stage and are in the spotlight. In Mark's account, James and John are called in the same way and after Peter's and Andrew's calls. Luke does not mention Andrew, who only appears in the traditional listing of disciples (6:14; Acts 1:13), and James and John appear only incidentally. They make a cameo appearance with Peter (8:51; 9:28) and a less than flattering showing when they

ask Jesus if he wanted *them* to command that fire from heaven engulf an inhospitable Samaritan town (9:54). Luke does not include an account of their (or their mother's) request for seats of power on his right and his left (see Matt 20:20 – 28; Mark 10:35 – 45).

Peter and John serve as partners of a different kind when they are dispatched to prepare for the Passover meal (22:8), and they work as mission partners in Acts (3:1, 3, 11; 4:1, 13, 19; 8:14, 17, 25); but John never gets an individual speaking part. James's death by sword on the orders of Herod is briefly mentioned (Acts 12:1 – 3) as a lead-in to an account of Peter's imprisonment and miraculous deliverance.

Jesus gives Simon the same assurance, "Do not fear" (μὴ φοβοῦ; see 8:50; 12:32), that the angel gave in the infancy narrative (1:13, 30; 2:10; see Acts 18:9; 27:23 – 24; see Gen 21:17; 26:24; 28:13). In Jesus' presence, Simon need not fear the Holy. After his confession, Jesus does not speak of forgiveness but of his "future service."[16] Jesus does not flee from sinners but seeks them out (19:10), recruits them (5:27), and saves them (19:9). Simon remains a sinner but one who is commissioned to gain other sinners.

The fishing metaphor for mission is apropos, given the setting, and it makes clear that the miraculous catch of fish symbolically relates to the promise of catching humans in the net of God's grace. Simon has been in the business of catching fish and selling their flesh, and so the image can have negative connotations. Fishing is fatal for fish. Luke, however, plays with this image by choosing the phrase "catching people alive" (ἀνθρώπους ἔσῃ ζωγρῶν), an unusual expression and different from Mark's "fishers of people" (ἁλιεῖς ἀνθρώπων, Mark 1:17).

The verb "to catch alive" (ζωγρέω) was used

in the context of hunting and war (see Herodotus, *Hist.* 1.211.3; Thucydides 7.41.4) for capturing and sparing the life of the one captured. In a military context, prisoners of war were taken alive only to be tortured, paraded about, and then put to death, enslaved, or, rarely, liberated. Hengel claims that the word had "a predominantly negative ring, meaning more or less 'those who trap men' or 'slave stealers.'"[17] The verb aptly describes the devil ensnaring people (2 Tim 2:26). When applied to Simon's mission enterprise, however, it turns things upside down. Those captured by Simon (and others) do not meet literal death but are treated mercifully and restored to life. Theirs is to be a rescue operation to recapture those kidnapped by the devil. Spicq comments, "He will no longer catch dead fish, in order to eat them; rather, he will catch living people, not to reduce them to servitude, after the fashion of prisoners, but to give them liberty and true life."[18]

This prophecy "has the effect of a command"[19] and emphasizes the permanency of the task. It will not be accomplished in one miraculous casting of the nets. Simon cannot put up a temporary "Gone Fishing" sign on his door; this will become his permanent vocation. "From now on" means that Simon's "now" has been forever changed. This task of the apostles is reiterated in Acts 1:8.

We see only brief glimpses of the disciples fulfilling this role in the gospel because "in the interim, their primary role is to learn, and this is the major focus of 6:12–49 and the central, journey section of Luke (9:51–19:27)."[20] Here, they serve as "exemplars of appropriate response to Jesus and his message (5:11, 28)." Simon is now the "amateur fisherman" who must learn from the Master.[21]

5:11 When the boats put in to shore, they left everything and followed him (καὶ καταγαγόντες τὰ πλοῖα ἐπὶ τὴν γῆν ἀφέντες πάντα ἠκολούθησαν αὐτῷ). The boats did not sink but made it to shore with their catch. What did they do with their bounty? Geldenhuys thinks that the huge catch of fish will tide the families over during their absence,[22] but the emphasis is on these new disciples leaving everything at the height of their success as fishermen. Instead of having his wish granted that Jesus depart from him, Simon ends up following him. Craddock asserts: "The same power that prompted Simon to fall at Jesus' knees now lifts him into God's service."[23]

Marshall claims that "leaving everything" is perhaps a "more complex process" than narrated, which may be true; but Luke stresses that disciples must leave everything to follow Jesus (5:28; 14:33; 18:22–23, 28). Luke does not report that they sold their boats, fishing nets, and homes. Hays notes that "everything" (πάντα) is "Luke's catchword for abandoning possessions to follow Jesus." It frequently functions hyperbolically and does not mean all without exception.[24] In this case, it means that they walk out on their livelihoods.[25]

This meaning of "everything" is clear from the account of Levi leaving everything (5:28). He leaves his custom booth, but he still has a home and has the means to throw a banquet (5:29). Leaving their occupations is required because disciples are to share Jesus' mission and fate and cannot be encumbered by business interests. Peter must

17. Martin Hengel, *The Charismatic Leader and His Followers* (trans. J. Greig; New York: Crossroad, 1981), 78.
18. Ceslas Spicq, "ζωγρέω," *TLNT*, 2:162.
19. Marshall, *The Gospel of Luke*, 205.
20. Green, *The Gospel of Luke*, 228.
21. Danker, *Jesus and the New Age*, 117.
22. Norval Geldenhuys, *Commentary on the Gospel of Luke* (Grand Rapids: Eerdmans, 1952), 182.
23. Craddock, *Luke*, 79.
24. Christopher M. Hays, *Luke's Wealth Ethics: A Study in Their Coherence and Character* (WUNT 2/275; Tübingen: Mohr Siebeck, 2010), 82.
25. Ibid., 83.

"share the total insecurity, exposure to danger, and slander which were the fate of his master."[26] The prosperity promised by such a lucrative catch is ephemeral. The money will soon run out. The blessing Simon will impart to others by following Christ is eternal. Leaving everything will result in a new fellowship of sharing, and they will gain everything (18:28 – 30).

Theology in Application

1. Miracles and Faith

Jesus does not perform miracles to give economic assistance to beleaguered fishermen. Luke believes that miracles can evoke faith, which can lead to discipleship. Achtemeier shows that Luke understood the miracles "to have the capacity to validate Jesus, and show the source of his power." He points out that in Acts miracles "were an effective device for turning people to faith" (Acts 9:35, 42; 13:12; 16:30, 33; 19:17). [27] Origen (*Cels.*1.46) claims that without such wonders the apostles "would not have persuaded those who heard new doctrines and new teachings to leave their traditional religion and to accept the apostles' teaching at the risk of their lives."

The key is to see God's power at work behind the miracle. Before his calling, Simon witnessed the healing of his mother-in-law, the first recorded healing in the gospel (4:38 – 39), and in the present incident he witnesses the great haul of fish. He will witness the raising of the little girl from the dead (8:51 – 56) and the transfiguration (9:28 – 36). He is also the first to confess that Jesus is the Messiah of God (9:20) and the first of the Twelve to witness the empty tomb (24:12). It is understandable why he is the first on any list of disciples (6:14). He demonstrates the right response to a miracle: God has sent Jesus to do his mighty work and he is worthy of being followed at all costs.

2. Jesus and Sinners

Peter's plea to Jesus, "Depart from me," differs from the Capernaum crowd's demand, "Please stay" (4:42). It reveals that Peter has no interest in using "Jesus' power for his own ongoing benefit but asserts his lack of claim on Jesus (cf. 7:6 – 7)."[28] The message is that Jesus has not come to drive sinners away from his holy presence but to draw them into the net of his embracing grace. Those who fish for meaning in their lives and come up with only dirty, empty nets can be particularly receptive to this calling from Jesus that gives purpose and peace in life.

Jesus' recruits were not tried, tested, and true; they will prove to be rather shaky in spots. But he takes them as they are. Following Jesus is not the path to privilege, success, and a higher standard of living. If they hope by following him that they will

26. Hengel, *The Charismatic Leader*, 78.
27. Paul J. Achtemeier, "The Lucan Perspective on the Miracles of Jesus: A Preliminary Sketch," *JBL* 94 (1975): 553.
28. Green, *The Gospel of Luke*, 233.

get ahead in the world, they will be disappointed. Following Jesus means to learn from him a way of life — a special way of thinking, speaking, and acting. It means learning from what he says and does and allowing oneself to be formed by it. It involves engaging the feet along with their minds and ears. They do not know where he is going and must allow him to pick the destination and the way and to set the timetable.

3. The Call to Mission

The call to follow Jesus is also a call to missionary work. Jesus commands mission. The church is the church sent out. Blauw writes:

> … the great prime mover of preaching the gospel does not come from outside (the "need of the world") and not from within either (the "religious impulse") but from above, as a divine coercion — "woe unto me, if I preach not the gospel!" (1 Cor. 9:16), as a matter of life and death, not for the world, but for the Church itself – "And this I do for the gospel's sake, that I might be partaker thereof with you" (1 Cor. 9:23).[29]

Jesus' command concerning the fishing nets seems absurdly optimistic and a waste of time and energy, when there is little energy left. Success is unexpected and almost spells disaster. The new disciples move from nets about to rip, which means that they would lose their catch, to boats about to sink, which means they were in danger of losing everything — the fish, the boats, and their lives. Then, they leave everything anyway. The experience with the fishing nets and their success anticipates the church's experience in mission. But it also suggests that the church can have as much, if not more, trouble handling its successes as it does failures.

The clue for how to handle success occurs at the end of the narrative. They cannot have it all. They must leave everything behind to follow Jesus faithfully. Luke does not explain why this is necessary, but it is an obvious inference (5:28; 14:33; 18:22). The disciples cannot be effective in their mission calling if they want to use this miracle to establish themselves also as well-heeled fishing magnates. Discipleship requires forfeiting everything for Christ (Phil 3:7 – 10). The first disciples will get only the provisions that they need to carry out their mission, nothing more (9:1 – 4; 10:1 – 9). It helps to know that they are on a divine mission with eternal consequences and that they are working through a divine power far greater than themselves.

The incident makes clear that mission requires teamwork (see 1 Cor 3:5 – 9). No one will be able to carry out their mission calling alone. Everyone needs partners. Paul's lengthy greeting in Rom 16 gives evidence of how he relied on an extensive network of coworkers. He greets twenty-six people plus two who are unnamed but

29. Johannes Blauw, *The Missionary Nature of the Church: A Survey of the Biblical Theology of Mission* (New York / Toronto / London: McGraw-Hill, 1962), 126.

are related to those named. The list reveals striking diversity. The names represent Greek, Roman, and Jewish backgrounds and reveals that the church's mission is not carried out by a homogeneous group from one nation. They all are engaged in a joint enterprise throughout the world that binds them together. They share the same work and the same struggles, which gives them a sense of shared purpose. There is no clear evidence of rank among these persons listed. No one is an overlord, and the organizational structure seems quite flexible. The sole concern is how together they might bring about obedience of faith in the whole world.

The initial call sends out Jewish disciples on mission to their own people, to Israel. One would think that the pagan world required more urgent attention, but a similar phenomenon is occurring today as the center of gravity for Christianity has shifted from the Northern Hemisphere to the Southern, where Christianity is growing fast. European Christianity, which gave birth to so many mission initiatives, is now seen as a prime target for reevangelization. The same is true for many parts of the United States as Christians continue to give in to theological atrophy and to buy in to pseudo-evangelical kitsch and lose their missionary zeal. Missionaries from the third world will carry on the mission to cultures sapped by materialism, skepticism, and secular schools of thought.

Luke 5:12 – 26

Literary Context

In the previous episode, Simon Peter confesses he is a sinner and implores Jesus to depart from him. Instead, Jesus draws Simon closer to him by commanding him to follow him. Implicit in this command is the forgiveness of his sins and divine acceptance. For the leper to be healed of his skin disease, his sins must be forgiven. While Jesus does not state specifically that the leper's sins are forgiven, the widespread assumption that sin and sickness are directly connected — particularly in the case of leprosy — means that if he has been cleansed of his leprosy, his sins have been forgiven.

The forgiveness of sins becomes explicit in the healing of the paralytic. These are the first words Jesus speaks to the man. It is confirmed by the healing when he is able to walk away carrying his mat.

The calling of Levi, the tax collector, in the next incident (5:27 – 29) serves as a bookend to the calling of Simon. All tax collectors were automatically assumed to be sinners. Jesus not only calls him to follow as he did Simon, but he dines with him and those whom the Pharisees judge to be a confederacy of unsavory sinners. Calling and eating with sinners implicitly announces the forgiveness of sins. The two inner episodes, the cleansing of the leper and the healing of the paralytic, are discussed together here rather than as separate pericopes to highlight the primary issue of the forgiveness of sins.

Jesus' redemptive preaching is combined with healing, which illustrates that he has been anointed by God's Spirit to bring liberation from sin, disease, and the demonic. The Pharisees enter the picture as those who are more concerned with religious observances than liberation. The forgiveness of sins and the acceptance of sinners will be the sticking point for them. Though the healing of the paralytic presents unexpected but undeniable evidence that the power of God was with Jesus to heal, they balk at the implication that he has the authority also to announce God's forgiveness to all.

The healing of the paralytic is the first in a series of four controversy stories in which Jesus offends the sensibilities of the teachers of the law and the Pharisees, who silently or directly challenge him or his disciples. Each anecdote contains a concluding dramatic saying of Jesus. In each controversy, Jesus provides a fuller understanding of the gospel and the difference his authoritative presence makes. In this first story, Jesus forgives a paralytic his sins, and the scribes and the Pharisees silently challenge his claim to be able to forgive sins. Jesus responds by announcing "the Son of Man has authority on earth to forgive sins" (5:24) and commanding the paralytic to get up and walk away.

In the next controversy story (5:27 – 39), Jesus calls a tax collector, Levi, to be his disciple and accepts the invitation to a great feast in his house together with a large company of tax collectors and sinners. This celebration causes the teachers of the law and the Pharisees to challenge Jesus' principles. Jesus retorts, "The healthy do not need a physician but the sick do. I have not come to call the righteous to repentance but sinners" (5:31 – 32).

In the third story (6:1 – 5), some of Jesus' disciples pluck grain on the Sabbath, which meets with the objections from Pharisees. Jesus declares, "The Son of Man is Lord of the Sabbath" (6:5).

In the fourth story (6:6 – 11), the teachers of the law and the Pharisees keep their eyes glued on Jesus as he enters a synagogue to see whether he will heal on the Sabbath. Jesus challenges them with the question, "Is it lawful to do good on the Sabbath or to do harm, to save a life or to destroy it?" (6:9), and he heals a man with a withered hand. These stories end with Jesus' enemies discussing together what they might do to get rid of Jesus.

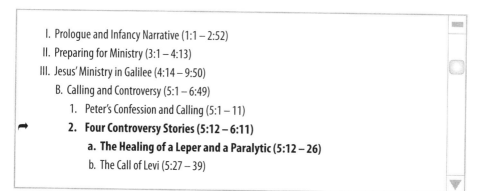

Main Idea

Jesus has the power to heal and the authority to forgive sins — and the two are intertwined.

Translation

Luke 5:12–26

12a Character introduction/

When he was
in one of the cities,

Entreaty

behold, a man covered with a skin disease, upon seeing Jesus, fell on his face
and **begged him, saying,**

b

"Lord, if you will it, you are able to cleanse me."

13 Healing

Stretching out his hand,
he touched him and **said,**
"I do will it. Be cleansed!"

14 Command

Immediately, **the skin disease vanished.**
He charged him to tell no one,
"But go,   be examined by the priest, and
bring the offering Moses required in relation to your cleansing
as evidence for them."

15 Summary

The word about him spread all the more,
and **large crowds would gather round to hear him** and **to be healed of their**
illnesses.

16 Summary

But he would often withdraw to deserted places to pray.

17a Character introduction

It happened on one of these days when he was teaching,
Pharisees and law scholars . . .
who had come from every town in Galilee and Judea and from Jerusalem

. . . were sitting there [to listen].

b Assertion

The power of the Lord was with him to heal.

18 Character introduction

Behold, some men . . .   **carrying on a sleeping mat a man who was**
paralyzed
. . . were trying to find a way to   **bring him in and**
set him down before him.

19

When they could not find a way to bring him in
because the crowd was so thick,

they climbed up on the roof and **lowered him with his mat through the tiles**
into the middle before Jesus.

20 Pronouncement

When he saw their faith,
he said,
"Man, your sins have been forgiven you."

Continued on next page.

21a	Reaction	**The scribes and the Pharisees began to think to themselves, saying,**
		"Who does he think he is speaking such blasphemy?
b	Conflict	*Who is able to forgive sins except God alone?"*
22	Confrontation	**Jesus, knowing their thoughts, answered them and said,**
		"Why are you thinking these things in your hearts?
23	Provocative question	*Which is easier, to say, 'Your sins have been forgiven,' or*
		to say, 'Rise and walk'?"
24a	Pronouncement	*"So that you might know that the Son of Man has authority on earth* & *to forgive sins,"*
		(he said to the paralyzed man),
b	Healing	*"I say to you, rise and take your mat and go to your house."*
25	Results: glorifying God	**Immediately, he rose before them,**
		picked up what he had been lying on,
		and he went to his house glorifying God.
26	Response: wonder	**Amazement gripped them all**
		and they were glorifying God and were filled with awe, saying again and again,
		"We have seen strange things today!"

Structure and Literary Form

The healing of the leper and the paralytic may seem to be miracles that follow one another randomly, but together they underscore Jesus' authority to forgive sins. In the biblical worldview, sickness and suffering were punishment for sin, and leprosy could be healed only by God with the forgiveness of the sin that caused this particular punishment.[1] The healing of the paralytic makes this clear with Jesus' pronouncement that the man's sins have been forgiven, followed by the healing miracle. The form of the healing of the paralytic is that of a *chreia* (from the Greek, meaning "advantage"), in which an event from Jesus' life is narrated and punctuated by a dramatic pronouncement. It occurs in an objection story, but both accounts are in the form of a quest for healing. The ailment is described, a request is made, the manner of healing is depicted, and the healing is attested by witnesses.

---

1. See David E. Garland, " 'I Am the Lord Your Healer':
Mark 1:21 – 2:12," *RevExp* 85 (1988): 327 – 43.

Exegetical Outline

→ **I. An encounter with a leper (5:12 – 14)**

    A. Request: If you will, you can cleanse me (5:12)

    B. Cleansing of the leper (5:13)

    C. Commands (5:14)

        1. To remain silent (5:14a)

        2. To show himself to the priest (5:14b)

II. Healing of many and withdrawal for prayer (5:15 – 16)

III. Healing of a paralytic (5:17 – 26)

    A. Setting: teaching amidst Pharisees and teachers of the law from all over (5:17a)

    B. The power was with him to heal (5:17b)

    C. The encounter with a paralytic (5:18 – 20)

        1. The audacious measures of his friends to bring him to Jesus (5:18 – 19)

        2. Pronouncement: "Your sins have been forgiven" (5:20)

    D. Secret dissent of the scribes and Pharisees (5:21)

    E. Jesus' public response (5:22 – 25)

        1. Question: "Which is easier . . . ?" (5:22 – 23)

        2. An audacious command: "Take your mat and go to your house" (5:24)

        3. Obedience and healing (5:25)

    F. Reaction of amazement from the crowd (5:26)

Explanation of the Text

5:12 When he was in one of the cities, behold, a man covered with a skin disease, upon seeing Jesus, fell on his face and begged him, saying, "Lord, if you will it, you are able to cleanse me" (καὶ ἐγένετο ἐν τῷ εἶναι αὐτὸν ἐν μιᾷ τῶν πόλεων καὶ ἰδοὺ ἀνὴρ πλήρης λέπρας· ἰδὼν δὲ τὸν Ἰησοῦν, πεσὼν ἐπὶ πρόσωπον ἐδεήθη αὐτοῦ λέγων· κύριε, ἐὰν θέλῃς δύνασαί με καθαρίσαι). The term translated "skin disease" (λέπρας) is transliterated as "leprosy" in most translations. This is misleading since many equate it with Hansen's disease (named after the nineteenth-century Norwegian who identified the microorganism that causes it). It was not. The biblical background for understanding the condition is Lev 13 – 14.[2] The same Hebrew term for leprosy (ṣâraʿat) was applied to something affecting clothes (Lev 13:47 – 48) and houses (Lev 14:34 – 53). It covered various kinds of skin ailments. In the Mishnah, some authorities identified "leprosy" as covering as many as seventy-two kinds of skin disease.

To understand the magnitude of the miracle,

2. Jacob Milgrom (*Leviticus 1 – 16* [AB; New York: Doubleday, 1991], 816 – 20) translates the Hebrew as "scale disease."

According to Leviticus, the basic features of the disease were: "(1) bright white spots or patches on the skin the hair on which also was white; (2) the depression of the patches below the level of the surrounding skin; (3) the existence of 'quick raw flesh'; (4) the spreading of the scab or scall" ("Leprosy," in *The Jewish Encyclopedia*, 8:9 – 11). Were this disease the same as modern leprosy, which is immediately conspicuous by the facial deformity and rotting of the members, it would not need the several examinations by the priest at intervals of seven days to note its progress as the instruction in Leviticus prescribes.

one must understand the severity of this "skin disease" in Judaism. The sufferer was cut off from the community by divine decree (Lev 13:45 – 52; Num 5:2 – 4; see 1Qsa 2:3 – 10; 11QTemple 46:16 – 18; 48:14 – 17), because the affliction could impart impurity to persons and objects found within the same enclosure to the same degree that a corpse would. The leper was thus like a walking corpse, and his cure was likened to raising the dead (b. Sanh. 47a-b). Isolating the victim was not intended to prevent the spread of the disease but the spread of the impurity. What was feared was not catching the disease but the impurity.[3] That fear is why the verb used to describe the cure is not "to heal" but "to cleanse."

Passages on leprosy in the Old Testament imply that God caused this disease as punishment for sin and that he alone could heal it (see Lev 14:34; Num 12:1 – 15; Deut 24:8 – 9; 28:27; 2 Sam 3:29; 2 Kgs 5:20 – 27; 15:5; 2 Chr 26:20). According to a Qumran fragment on purification, the leper "shall lie down in a bed of sorrows, and in a residence of lamentation he shall reside" (4Q 274), which is a sign of his penitence for his sin that brought on the ailment.

Nega'im, the title of the Mishnaic tractate that expounds the law of the leper, means "smitings," which assumes that the disease is a smiting by God, since this is what God does when extremely displeased. When King Uzziah flaunted God's law, the Lord smote him so that he was a leper to the day of his death (2 Kgs 15:5; 2 Chr 26:16–21; see Exod 4:6). When the king of Syria asked the king of Israel to heal Naaman, the leprous commander of the Syrian army (2 Kgs 5:1–27; see Luke 4:27), the king of Israel thought he simply wanted to start a fight: "Am I God? Can I kill and bring back

to life? Why does this fellow send someone to me to be cured of his leprosy?" (2 Kgs 5:7). This statement, possibly alluding to Deut 32:39, assumes that only God could heal this disease. Elisha intervened, "Have the man come to me and he will know that there is a prophet in Israel" (2 Kgs. 5:8). Elisha could not heal him either, but as a prophet of God he could intercede so that God would provide the cure. When the cure took place, Naaman confessed: "Now I know that there is no God in all the world except in Israel" (5:15). No god could cure leprosy except the God of Israel. When Elisha refused any payment from Naaman after he was cured, Elisha's servant Gehazi tried to collect money on the sly and became leprous forever as punishment (5:25–27).

Two points arise from this background. First, since this skin disease was believed to have no medical remedy and could only be healed by God, Jesus is portrayed as something more than a prophet close to God, like Moses and Elisha, who could intercede for God to remove the disease. Unlike Elisha with Naaman, Jesus gives no instructions about how to become clean, like washing in the Jordan. His word and touch can cleanse the man. Second, since the disease is associated with sin and shame, Jesus' intercession removes the shame and betokens the forgiveness of the sin.

Because of his defilement, the leper is not brought to Jesus as others were (4:40). He must bring himself, and he breaks through the religious barrier that fenced him off from contact with others to beg Jesus to make him clean. Moses cried to the Lord for Miriam to be cleansed of her leprosy (Num 12:13), but this man does not beg Jesus to ask God for his cleansing. Instead he says, "If you will it." He is the second person in the gospel to

---

3. In Josephus's discussion of leprosy (Ant. 3.11.3 §§261, 263 – 64), he distinguishes between lepers and those having a contagious disease!

address Jesus as "Lord" (5:8), and it means more than just "Sir" (contra NJB). He attributes to Jesus the power and grace of God to do as he wills (Wis 12:18), to forgive his sins and to cleanse him.

5:13 Stretching out his hand, he touched him and said, "I do will it. Be cleansed!" Immediately, the skin disease vanished (καὶ ἐκτείνας τὴν χεῖρα ἥψατο αὐτοῦ λέγων· θέλω, καθαρίσθητι· καὶ εὐθέως ἡ λέπρα ἀπῆλθεν ἀπ᾿ αὐτοῦ). Jesus does not call on the name of God to cleanse the man. He merely stretches out his own hand with divine power. God worked by stretching out his hand (see Exod 3:20; 6:6; 7:5; 9:15; 15:12; Deut 4:34; 5:15; 7:19; 9:29; 11:2; 2 Kgs 17:36; Ps 136:12; Jer 32:21). Moses also was vested with the authority to stretch out his hand and work mighty works (Exod 4:4, 7:19, 8:1; 9:22; 14:16, 21, 26). Jesus touches the one who was untouchable and cleanses even the worst impurity.

5:14 He charged him to tell no one, "But go, be examined by the priest, and bring the offering Moses required in relation to your cleansing as evidence for them" (καὶ αὐτὸς παρήγγειλεν αὐτῷ μηδενὶ εἰπεῖν, ἀλλὰ ἀπελθὼν δεῖξον σεαυτὸν τῷ ἱερεῖ καὶ προσένεγκε περὶ τοῦ καθαρισμοῦ σου καθὼς προσέταξεν Μωϋσῆς, εἰς μαρτύριον αὐτοῖς). To understand this command one must understand the regulations in Lev 13 – 14. In Israel's religion, the priests had the responsibility to identify the presence or absence of particular physical signs such as skin color change, hair color, infiltration, extension, or ulceration of the skin. They alone could declare whether the man had been cleansed of the affliction.[4] Even though Jesus had cleansed this man, he remained in social limbo until a priest examined him and declared

him clean, and the man had made the appropriate offerings in the temple (see Lev 14:1 – 32). Only a priest, not a doctor or holy man, could give him a clean bill of health so that he could rejoin his family.

The procedures of purification in the temple begin after the cure. When his gratitude to God is completed through appropriate sacrifices, he is certified so that he may be reinstated in the community. The "evidence for them" (εἰς μαρτύριον αὐτοῖς) refers to the proof to be shown to the priests or to the community into which the leper is being restored. The NCV is completely wrong in rendering it: "This will show the people what I have done." Jesus is not concerned about broadcasting his prowess to do miracles. He is as concerned about the man's full reintegration into society as he is his physical healing.

5:15 The word about him spread all the more, and large crowds would gather round to hear him and to be healed of their illnesses (διήρχετο δὲ μᾶλλον ὁ λόγος περὶ αὐτοῦ, καὶ συνήρχοντο ὄχλοι πολλοὶ ἀκούειν καὶ θεραπεύεσθαι ἀπὸ τῶν ἀσθενειῶν αὐτῶν). Luke does not record that the man disobeyed Jesus' command to silence (see Mark 1:45). The summary reiterates the theme sounded in 4:14 and 37 about Jesus' spreading fame. It provides a rationale why Jesus might need to withdraw into the wilderness.

5:16 But he would often withdraw to deserted places to pray (αὐτὸς δὲ ἦν ὑποχωρῶν ἐν ταῖς ἐρήμοις καὶ προσευχόμενος). The two imperfect periphrastic constructions, "he was withdrawing" (ἦν ὑποχωρῶν) and "he was praying" (ἦν ... προσευχόμενος) indicate that it was Jesus' regular practice to retire to pray.[5] It is conveyed

---

4. For this reason Lev 13 – 14 goes into extensive detail describing the cases so that the priest can identify the particular physical signs.

5. Crump, *Jesus the Intercessor*, 143.

in the translation by "often" (cf. 4:42). His regular, intensive prayer life explains how the power to heal was with Jesus (5:17). He spent hours with God in prayer. Luke notes Jesus as praying at key moments, and this prayer occurs before his first conflict with the Pharisees.

5:17 It happened on one of these days when he was teaching, Pharisees and law scholars who had come from every town in Galilee and Judea and from Jerusalem were sitting there [to listen]. The power of the Lord was with him to heal (καὶ ἐγένετο ἐν μιᾷ τῶν ἡμερῶν καὶ αὐτὸς ἦν διδάσκων, καὶ ἦσαν καθήμενοι Φαρισαῖοι καὶ νομοδιδάσκαλοι οἳ ἦσαν ἐληλυθότες ἐκ πάσης κώμης τῆς Γαλιλαίας καὶ Ἰουδαίας καὶ Ἰερουσαλήμ· καὶ δύναμις κυρίου ἦν εἰς τὸ ἰᾶσθαι αὐτόν). As Jesus' fame spreads everywhere, the Pharisees come from all over in response. Luke does not say why they come. Possibly, they are worried that his teaching with authority might erode their limited influence with the people.

Luke also does not describe who the Pharisees are. He assumes that the reader will soon learn who they are from their controversies with Jesus. In many ways, the gospel writers portray the Pharisees as a cast of nonunion cutout characters. The Pharisees were laypersons (mostly nonpriests) interested in the practical understanding of Scripture to enable the community to remain faithful to the covenant with God in their differing historical contexts.

The scribes of the Pharisees (or "law scholars") are learned interpreters of the law who apply it to Jewish life. They attempted to fend off Hellenization and its anti-Jewish values by rallying the people around renewed obedience to the law. They took seriously God's demand that Israel be holy (Lev 19:2) and tried to make that attainable in everyday life through their applications of the law. They were known for their strict piety and

observance but were also quite liberal in their application, for example, by reducing the biblical requirement of bathing the whole body (Lev 15; 16:26, 28; 17:15 – 16; 22:1 – 7) to the simple act of washing hands. They tried to maintain Israel's distinctiveness among the nations through strict adherence to laws, such as Sabbath observance, which clearly separated them from others. They believed the law applied to all of life and gave everyday acts holy significance, which became constant reminders of God and continual demonstrations of their devotion to God. Since they believed that God created order and that Israel prospered only when the nation conformed to that order, they sought to erect and maintain fences that would ensure that the people would stay within the divinely established borders of what God required the people to do and not to do.

The statement that "the power of the Lord was with him to heal" (δύναμις κυρίου ἦν εἰς τὸ ἰᾶσθαι αὐτόν) makes clear that Jesus' authority and power derives entirely from God (the anarthrous "Lord"), not from any skill in the black arts or association with Satan (11:15). It prepares for the challenge that will follow.

5:18 Behold, some men carrying on a sleeping mat a man who was paralyzed were trying to find a way to bring him in and set him down before him (καὶ ἰδοὺ ἄνδρες φέροντες ἐπὶ κλίνης ἄνθρωπον ὃς ἦν παραλελυμένος, καὶ ἐζήτουν αὐτὸν εἰσενεγκεῖν καὶ θεῖναι [αὐτὸν] ἐνώπιον αὐτοῦ). People have been bringing the sick to Jesus all along, but this is the first such case that Luke fully narrates because it features both an exhibition of resourcefulness driven by faith and the beginning of theological controversy with the Pharisees.

5:19 When they could not find a way to bring him in because the crowd was so thick, they climbed up on the roof and lowered him with

his mat through the tiles into the middle before Jesus (καὶ μὴ εὑρόντες ποίας εἰσενέγκωσιν αὐτὸν διὰ τὸν ὄχλον, ἀναβάντες ἐπὶ τὸ δῶμα διὰ τῶν κεράμων καθῆκαν αὐτὸν σὺν τῷ κλινιδίῳ εἰς τὸ μέσον ἔμπροσθεν τοῦ Ἰησοῦ). Luke envisions for his readers a Mediterranean house with a tiled roof rather than the one depicted in Mark 2:4, which would have been the norm in Capernaum. It would have consisted of wooden cross beams overlaid with a matting of reeds, branches, and dried mud. The friends demonstrate a tenacious faith and determination that the homeowner might not appreciate but that Jesus affirms.

5:20 When he saw their faith, he said, "Man, your sins have been forgiven you" (καὶ ἰδὼν τὴν πίστιν αὐτῶν εἶπεν· ἄνθρωπε, ἀφέωνταί σοι αἱ ἁμαρτίαι σου). Jesus knows the secrets in the hearts of those who encounter him; he knows this man's heart and announces God's verdict. The friends have not gone to all this trouble to bring the paralyzed man to receive absolution for his sins, however welcomed that might be, but for him to be healed. The story presupposes, however, a direct connection between sin and sickness, which most everyone assumed was true. Jesus is not asserting that forgiveness of sins is more important than physical healing, or that the man only suffered from a guilt-ridden psychological paralysis from which he could be set free through positive thinking. His announcement is grounded in Ps 103:3, praising God "who forgives all your sins and heals all your diseases" (see Isa 33:24).

In a Jewish context, the paralysis would have been viewed as a consequence of sin. To forgive the sin is to remove its consequences. This perspective was deep-seated and reflected in the later rabbis: "R. Alexandri said in the name of R. Chiyya

b. Abba: 'A sick man does not recover from his sickness until all his sins are forgiven him, as it is written, "Who forgiveth all thine iniquities, who healeth all thy diseases"' [Ps 103:3]" (b. Ned. 41a; see b. Meg. 17b). The 4Q242 fragment records the prayer of Nabonides, king of Babylon, who was smitten seven years with a malignant inflammation until a Jewish exorcist forgave his sin, and he was healed.

5:21 The scribes and the Pharisees began to think to themselves, saying, "Who does he think he is speaking such blasphemy? Who is able to forgive sins except God alone?" (καὶ ἤρξαντο διαλογίζεσθαι οἱ γραμματεῖς καὶ οἱ Φαρισαῖοι λέγοντες· τίς ἐστιν οὗτος ὃς λαλεῖ βλασφημίας; τίς δύναται ἁμαρτίας ἀφεῖναι εἰ μὴ μόνος ὁ θεός;). The "law scholars" (νομοδιδάσκαλοι) are now identified as "scribes" (γραμματεῖς). They are not separate from the Pharisees but would be better described as the law scholars among the Pharisees. They took it upon themselves to create sets of rules from their interpretation of Scripture that established what was acceptable and unacceptable to God in all spheres of life. They thus find Jesus' announcement of forgiveness unacceptable, which is understandable: "In Israel's history forgiveness was brought about by cultic acts and priestly pronouncements. Sins could only be forgiven by God on the strength of an atoning ritual — thus a transference of guilt in a ritual act."[6]

Their unspoken objection underlines the theological point for Luke. Jesus acts with the power and authority of God to heal and with the power and authority of God to announce the forgiveness of sins. The perfect passive form of the verb "have been forgiven you" (ἀφέωνται) indicates what God has done. This forgiveness is not connected to any

---

6. I. J. du Plessis, "The Saving Significance of Jesus and His Death on the Cross in Luke's Gospel — Focusing on Luke 22:19b – 20," *Neot* 28 (1994): 537.

atoning rituals and circumvents the temple cult. It helps clarify that the leper's return to the priests was simply a requirement for him to be reintegrated into society and not a theological necessity.

Blasphemy takes many forms in the Scripture, but basically it refers to mocking, reviling, or "lifting up one's eyes haughtily" against God (see Lev 24:10 – 11; 2 Kgs 19:4, 6, 22). What is labeled blasphemy, however, is in the eye of the beholder. These theological watchdogs obviously regard Jesus' announcement as making himself equal to God. Jesus' announcement, however, is no different from Nathan's announcement to David: "The LORD has taken away your sin. You are not going to die" (2 Sam 12:13). But the charges against Jesus are serious because the law prescribes that a blasphemer be taken outside the camp and stoned to death (Lev 24:14 – 16, 23). The opponents frame their objections in religious language, but they are driven by self-interest. Jesus' power to heal is eroding their influence.

5:22 – 23 Jesus, knowing their thoughts, answered them and said, "Why are you thinking these things in your hearts? Which is easier, to say, 'Your sins have been forgiven,' or to say, 'Rise and walk'?" (ἐπιγνοὺς δὲ ὁ Ἰησοῦς τοὺς διαλογισμοὺς αὐτῶν ἀποκριθεὶς εἶπεν πρὸς αὐτούς· τί διαλογίζεσθε ἐν ταῖς καρδίαις ὑμῶν; τί ἐστιν εὐκοπώτερον, εἰπεῖν· ἀφέωνταί σοι αἱ ἁμαρτίαι σου, ἢ εἰπεῖν· ἔγειρε καὶ περιπάτει;). Jesus exposes the secrets in the hearts of the Pharisees (see 2:35) and answers their question with a

question. They may believe that only God forgives sins, but they also believe that God must work through the proper channels, which they want to oversee. His response does not mean that one is easier than the other; the two are interconnected. The riddle allows him "to confirm his fundamental claim to divine authority and yet, by doing so indirectly, to avoid immediate indictment for blasphemy."[7] His answer also fits the criteria for verifying a true prophet and exposing a false one who presumes to utter in God's name what the Lord has not uttered (Deut 18:15 – 22). If what the prophet says does not take place, that person is a false prophet.

5:24 "So that you might know that the Son of Man has authority on earth to forgive sins" (he said to the paralyzed man), "I say to you, rise and take your mat and go to your house" (ἵνα δὲ εἰδῆτε ὅτι ὁ υἱὸς τοῦ ἀνθρώπου ἐξουσίαν ἔχει ἐπὶ τῆς γῆς ἀφιέναι ἁμαρτίας – εἶπεν τῷ παραλελυμένῳ· σοὶ λέγω, ἔγειρε καὶ ἄρας τὸ κλινίδιόν σου πορεύου εἰς τὸν οἶκόν σου). The Son of Man title is ambiguous, as the widely differing views among scholars about its meaning reveals.[8] Evans claims that the "special value of this title … may have been for Luke, that, more than any other, it had the capacity to span heaven and earth, and to encompass the whole career of Jesus as a man — his earthly ministry, his rejection by men, and his vindication by, and co-operation with, God."[9] Jesus asserts that he has the authority to act on God's behalf. He can pronounce forgiveness because God had already

---

7. Christopher D. Marshall, *Faith as a Theme in Mark's Narrative* (SNTSMS 64; Cambridge: Cambridge Univ. Press, 1989), 185 – 86.

8. For an exhaustive survey of the history of scholarship on the expression "son of man," see Mogens Müller, *The Expression 'Son of Man' and the Development of Christology: A History of Interpretation* (London: Equinox, 2008). He represents the view that in Aramaic, in everyday usage, it was a "colourless circumlocution" having no special meaning. It received its spe-

cial significance from the contexts in which it is used in the gospels. In my opinion, the term was innocuous enough for Jesus to use it without it being tainted by any preconceived notions his audience might have entertained, but its use in Dan 7:13 and *1 En.* 46 – 53 also made it suitably mysterious. Jesus could and did fill it with his own meaning.

9. Evans, *St. Luke*, 92. The "Son of Man" is capitalized throughout the commentary as a title of a heavenly figure.

done so. He could also associate with sinners to convey that God had forgiven their sins.

5:25 Immediately, he rose before them, picked up what he had been lying on, and he went to his house glorifying God (καὶ παραχρῆμα ἀναστὰς ἐνώπιον αὐτῶν, ἄρας ἐφ᾽ ὃ κατέκειτο, ἀπῆλθεν εἰς τὸν οἶκον αὐτοῦ δοξάζων τὸν θεόν). Like the leper who went to the priest to be certified that he was cleansed, the paralytic rises and carries his sleeping mat as a sign that his healing is fully accomplished. Presumably, the crowd now makes way to allow him to leave. Recognizing that God's power is working through Jesus, the man glorifies God, which is the appropriate response to a miracle.

5:26 Amazement gripped them all and they were glorifying God and were filled with awe, saying again and again, "We have seen strange things today!" (καὶ ἔκστασις ἔλαβεν ἅπαντας καὶ ἐδόξαζον τὸν θεὸν καὶ ἐπλήσθησαν φόβου λέγοντες ὅτι εἴδομεν παράδοξα σήμερον). The crowd is amazed and also glorifies God (see the similar reaction after the healing of the man born lame at the Beautiful Gate in the temple in Acts 3:1 – 10). They may not know, however, the significance of "today." "Today" may only mean this present twenty-four-hour day that will soon pass into another day (see 12:28). In Luke, it refers to the time of liberation and salvation from God that is dawning on the world (2:11, 4:21; 19:9; 23:43).

The term "strange things" (παράδοξα) appears only here in the New Testament. It refers to something unexpected, unbelievable, uncommon, or marvelous.[10] The Pharisees did not expect this demonstration of power when they came to examine Jesus to see if the reports were true, but the evidence was undeniable.

Theology in Application

1. The Problem of Sin

These two miracles manifest that God wills our physical and spiritual wholeness and that God's power working through Jesus can effect it. They also reveal that though humans may be beleaguered by various physical maladies that dominate their concern, the principal problem plaguing humans is sin. We see many people trying to raise awareness, joining forces in rallies and marches, seeking donations, and lobbying legislators to find cures for various diseases, with remarkable success. But few pay any attention to the sinful human condition whose only solution is the forgiveness of sin offered by God through Jesus (see Isa 43:18 – 25; Acts 13:38 – 39). Physical health does not make for an abundant life. Spiritual health can endure all things, including physical distress. It is possible for one to be forgiven and not healed, and to be healed and not forgiven. Luke's narrative affirms that forgiveness is the most important thing in life.

Jesus forgives a paralytic of sin, and it seems that this word loosens psychological

---

10. See Jdt 13:13; 2 Macc 9:24; 3 Macc 6:33; 4 Macc 2:14; Wis 5:2; 16:17; 19:5; Sir 43:25.

shackles that have bound his limbs. But sin is more than some psychological dissolution. Dunlap summarizes the Augustinian worldview of sin:

> The moral order is absolute, woven into the very fabric of creation. Personal sin, therefore, is never merely a private psychological event; owing to ignorance or stupidity or an idiotized upbringing, the sinner may be subjectively without blame, but the sin itself has objective consequences that claw at the well-being of the sinner and of others around him and of still others yet to be after him.[11]

All sin begins with lies told to oneself. Sin has a capacity to deceive so that persons do not recognize the product of their action for what it is. The consequences of sin, however, follow the sinner like a string of cans attached to a car. Sinful acts put one in the clutches of sin from which one cannot escape, like a fly caught in a spider's web. The forgiveness that Jesus offers not only sets one free but also allows one to face up to the truth about oneself. Walker Percy wrote, "We love those who know the worst of us and don't turn their faces away."[12] This statement applies even more to God, who knows more about us than any human can possibly know and not only does not turn away but atones for our sins.

2. Caring for Pariahs

Jesus is not horrified by the approach of a leper. He is not afraid of his disease. When the leper begs for help, he does not have to convince Jesus that he is worth the effort. He is someone who needs cleansing, and what commends him is that he comes to Jesus for help. The church should follow the model of Jesus in its care for the emotionally wounded outcasts of society who are leprous with visible and sometimes invisible sores. Too often, they are blocked off from access to God's power and healing, as the paralytic was blocked off from Jesus by the crowd (see also Zacchaeus). Legalists are concerned with being contaminated by lepers but do not care about lepers. If Christ followers care about the physically sick and the sin-sick, they must risk contact with them to bring them healing of the good news.

Healing trumps potential contamination. Divine power overcomes human illness. With the leper, Jesus does what a priest in the temple could not do, cleanse him of his disease and impurity. The priest could only examine persons to see if they had the disease or had been cured. Jesus does what even the law could not do, namely, forgive sins on the basis of grace. The consequences of past sin have been wiped out with a word. Can sin be dismissed so effortlessly? No. The crucifixion will clarify this matter. It is at Golgotha, the place of the skull, not at the temple, that the ultimate sacrifice for the forgiveness of sins will occur.

---

11. John R. Dunlap, "Identity Crisis," see www.catholiceducation.org/articles/education/ed0435.htm.

12. Walker Percy, *Love in the Ruins* (New York: Picador, 1971), 106.

Luke 5:27 – 39

Literary Context

This incident is the second in a series of four controversy stories in which Jesus offends the sensibilities of the scribes and the Pharisees who silently or directly challenge him (on this issue, see the Literary Context for 5:12 – 26). Including Levi among Jesus' followers reinforces his agenda to release captives from their sins and overtly signals the inauguration of this mission to "sinners."[1]

Main Idea

Jesus invites even "sinners" who are judged by others to be beyond the pale to follow him. His call to discipleship rewrites the conventional social maps that draw lines to segregate people according to purity and status.

---

1. David A. Neale, *None but the Sinners: Religious Categories in the Gospel of Luke* (JSNTSup 58; Sheffield: JSOT, 1991), 101.

Translation

Luke 5:27–39

27a	Circumstance	After this, **he left and observed a tax collector by the name of Levi sitting at the customs** ⤴ **post,**
b	Calling	**and he said to him,** *"Follow me!"*
28	Obedience	So leaving everything behind, **he rose up and began to follow him.**
29a	Celebratory meal	**Levi gave a great celebrative feast for him in his house**
b		with a large crowd of tax collectors and others who were reclining at table ⤴ with them.
30a	Objection	**The Pharisees and their scribes began grumbling to his disciples, saying,**
b		*"Why do you eat and drink with tax collectors and sinners?"*
31	Pronouncement	**Jesus answered them,** *"The healthy do not need a physician but the sick do.*
32		*I have not come to call the righteous to repentance but sinners."*
33	Objection	**They responded to him,** *"John's disciples often fast and make supplications and so also do Pharisees' disciples,* *but yours eat and drink!"*
34	Pronouncement	**Jesus said to them,** *"You cannot make the bridegroom's attendants fast while the bridegroom* ⤴ *is with them, can you?*
35	Clarification	*The days will come [soon enough] when the bridegroom will be taken* ⤴ *away from them.* *Then, in those days, they will fast."*
36a	Parable (1)	**He also told them a parable:** *"No one tears a piece from a new garment to patch an old garment.*
b	Rationale	*If one does,* *not only will one tear up the new garment,* *but the patch from it will also not match the old.*
37a	Parable (2)	*And no one puts new wine into old wineskins.*
b	Rationale	*If one does,* *not only will the new wine burst the skins and spill out,* *but the skins also will be ruined.*
38	Pronouncement	*New wine must be poured into new skins.*
39	Contrast	*No one who drinks old wine wants new wine.* *For he says,* *'The old is pleasing.'"*

Structure and Literary Form

Luke continues the *chreia* form (see the Structure and Literary Form for 5:12 – 26) in this next incident that is also a call story and a confrontation story. The beginning and ending of the call of Levi has similarities with the call of Peter (5:1 – 2). Jesus appears and Levi is busy at his work, just as Peter was. When Jesus called Peter, he left everything to follow Jesus (5:11). Here the calling of a tax collector and the subsequent celebratory banquet give religious opponents an opportunity to express their objections. Jesus' responds with two pointed aphorisms (5:31, 34), follows with two pronouncements (5:32, 35), and concludes with two parables.

Exegetical Outline

➡ **I. Call of Levi (5:27 – 29)**

    A. Call to follow (5:27)

    B. Response (5:28 – 29)

        1. Leaving everything (5:28)

        2. Rejoicing with a banquet (5:29)

II. Jesus' response to objections of the scribes and Pharisees (5:30 – 39)

    A. Eating with sinners (5:30 – 32)

        1. Aphorism about the sick (5:30 – 31)

        2. Pronouncement: I have come to call sinners to repentance (5:32)

    B. Eating and drinking rather than fasting and praying (5:33 – 35)

        1. Aphorism about the bridegroom and wedding guests (5:33 – 34)

        2. Pronouncement: fasting will occur when the bridegroom is taken away (5:35)

    C. Parables about new and old garments, new and old wineskins (5:36 – 39)

Explanation of the Text

5:27 After this, he left and observed a tax collector by the name of Levi sitting at the customs post, and he said to him, "Follow me!" (καὶ μετὰ ταῦτα ἐξῆλθεν καὶ ἐθεάσατο τελώνην ὀνόματι Λευὶν καθήμενον ἐπὶ τὸ τελώνιον, καὶ εἶπεν αὐτῷ· ἀκολούθει μοι). Capernaum was the last village on the road running northeast across the Jordan from Herod Antipas's territory, Galilee, to Herod Philip's territory, Gaulinitus, and on to Damascus.[2] Consequently, it was admirably situated for one of Herod Antipas's customs posts.

Levi's name does not appear in the list of disciples in 6:14 – 18. One identified as Matthew is called from his toll booth in Matt 9:9, and his name appears in all four lists of the Twelve (Matt 10:2 – 4; Mark 3:16 – 19; Luke 6:13 – 16; Acts 1:13). Levi may have been known by two names, Levi and Matthew, in the same way that Simon Peter is

---

2. Dunn, *Jesus Remembered*, 318 – 19.

identified as Simon or Peter (Cephas). Levi would reflect his tribal origins as a Levite (1 Chr 15:18, 21, where the name "Mattaniah" occurs).

Levi not only sits at the toll booth, as in Mark; rather, Luke specifically identifies him as a tax collector. He is not a chief tax collector, like Zacchaeus, but a minor functionary. Luke describes Jesus observing (ἐθεάσατο) him, which implies something more than simply spotting him at his post (as in Matt 9:9; Mark 2:14 ["he saw," εἶδεν]). He paid careful, thoughtful attention to him (see 7:24; 23:55). Jesus' own observation, not some preconceived notions about tax gatherers, guides his judgment about Levi.

Jesus takes the initiative in enlisting a follower from a member of a class that his society despised.[3] The call is no different from that extended to Peter except that there is no evidence of a previous relationship between Levi and Jesus. Giles comments, "Whereas the Rabbis pointed away from themselves and demanded allegiance to the Torah, the Jesus of Luke's Gospel (and the other Gospels) points to himself and says, 'follow me' (5:27; 9:59; 14:27) and demands that men obey his Word."[4]

5:28 So leaving everything behind, he rose up and began to follow him (καὶ καταλιπὼν πάντα ἀναστὰς ἠκολούθει αὐτῷ). Culpepper aptly comments, "The same call which lifted the paralytic from his mat now lifts Levi from his toll station."[5] Luke includes the phrase that Levi leaves everything behind (καταλιπὼν πάντα), which is absent in the Markan and Matthean accounts. This call is not to join the special band of the Twelve — they have not been chosen yet (6:13 – 16) — but to become a follower of Christ.[6] That he leaves

everything behind illustrates that such sacrifice is not something expected only of the elite band of apostles (18:28) but applies to all who follow Christ (see 14:33; 18:22).

While Levi may not have left the most lucrative or worthwhile position, "leaving everything" means walking away from any loyalties that would compete with loyalty to Christ. In so doing he does more than what the fishermen disciples did (5:11, where the phrase is ἀφέντες πάντα). They could always go back to fishing. After abandoning his post, Levi is unlikely to be welcomed back with open arms. His economic expectations have changed dramatically, and he must now live out the new economics of the reign of God. The imperfect tense of the verb "to follow" (ἠκολούθει) is inceptive: "he began to follow." He does not yet know where the path will lead. His willingness to give up everything at the start shows his readiness to stick it out to the end even when the going gets rough.

Nave points out, "In Luke, Jesus is not simply calling sinners to follow him; he is calling them to repentance," which entails "an abandonment of [their] former ways of thinking and living" and a "complete break with [their] occupation."[7] No longer could Levi be centered around his own needs and securities, particularly when they were secured at the expense of others.

5:29 Levi gave a great celebrative feast for him in his house with a large crowd of tax collectors and others who were reclining at table with them (καὶ ἐποίησεν δοχὴν μεγάλην Λευὶς αὐτῷ ἐν τῇ οἰκίᾳ αὐτοῦ, καὶ ἦν ὄχλος πολὺς τελωνῶν καὶ ἄλλων οἳ ἦσαν μετ᾽ αὐτῶν κατακείμενοι). Celebration

---

3. Minear, *To Heal and to Reveal*, 114.

4. K. N. Giles, "The Church in the Gospel of Luke," *SJT* 34 (1981): 127.

5. R. Alan Culpepper, "The Gospel of Luke," in *The New Interpreter's Bible* (ed. L. E. Keck; Nashville: Abingdon, 2003), 9:127.

6. A distinction is made when the Pharisees complain about Jesus' "disciples" (5:30), which is the first time that word appears in the gospel.

7. Nave, *Repentance in Luke-Acts*, 168.

is associated with repentance (see 15:1 – 32), and Levi celebrates the grace that comes in Jesus' call. That call extends salvation to persons who have normally been barred from the club by the pious elites. He leaves the camp of sinners but does not ignore the sinners. His first act of following Jesus is to throw a banquet with Jesus as the honored guest in the midst of reprobates.

The banquet reveals that "leaving everything" does not entail abandoning all of one's property, but Luke makes it clear that those who have the means to throw banquets are to invite one and all. The same noun for feast (δοχή) appears in 14:13, where Jesus instructs his host and fellow guests to invite the poor, maimed, lame and blind, who cannot repay the favor, whenever they give a banquet. Presumably, these are the "others" whom Levi has invited to his feast.

5:30 The Pharisees and their scribes began grumbling to his disciples, saying, "Why do you eat and drink with tax collectors and sinners?" (καὶ ἐγόγγυζον οἱ Φαρισαῖοι καὶ οἱ γραμματεῖς αὐτῶν πρὸς τοὺς μαθητὰς αὐτοῦ λέγοντες· διὰ τί μετὰ τῶν τελωνῶν καὶ ἁμαρτωλῶν ἐσθίετε καὶ πίνετε;). We must visualize meals in homes in Jesus' time differently from our normal experience. They are more public events, and the Pharisees are able to observe all that is going on. The contrast between the reaction of a woman sinner observing a dinner in Simon the Pharisee's house, where Jesus is deliberately slighted (7:36 – 50), and the Pharisees observing this dinner at a sinner's house is striking. Among sinners and outcasts Jesus is an honored guest.

The question "Why do you eat … with tax collectors and sinners?" is based on the assumption that eating with others symbolized religious

compatibility. The term "Pharisee" derives from the Hebrew *pârûš*, meaning "the separated one." It may not have been a name they chose for themselves but one given to them as a term of contempt (see, e.g., the origins of the names for Lutherans, Anabaptists, Methodists, etc.). They would have called themselves *hâberîm* ("neighbors, associates"), that is, observant Jews. They may have received the moniker "Separatists" because they believed that they should separate themselves from sinners to protect themselves from the contagion of their sin in the same way that moderns want to guard against the dangers of e-coli bacteria in mishandled food. They resonated with Solomon's prayer, "For you have separated them from among all the peoples of the earth, to be your heritage, just as you promised through Moses, your servant, when you brought our ancestors out of Egypt, O LORD God" (1 Kgs 8:53, NRSV).

In the face of ever-changing political and cultural circumstances in Palestine, many groups sought to carve out their own ways of how to live so as to preserve their identity as Jews. Each group competed for power, influence, and identity. [8] The Pharisees were a collection of factions consisting of Torah-concerned laymen who sought to renew Judaism according to the divinely revealed precepts found in the Torah. Even though they were not priests, they sought to extend the laws of ritual purity, associated in the Scriptures only with the priests and the temple, into the lives of ordinary Jews. What Cohen wrote about the rabbis of a later period applies to the Pharisees in Jesus' day: "The underlying motive was not exclusiveness or unsociability, but racial and spiritual self-preservation."[9] Spencer trenchantly observes: "People, animals, and things were 'set apart' from

---

8. Anthony J. Saldarini, *Pharisees, Scribes and Sadducees in Jewish Society: A Sociological Approach* (Wilmington, DE: Michael Glazier, 1988), 122.

9. A. Cohen, "Introduction to *Abodah Zarah*," in *The Babylonian Talmud: Seder Nezikin* (London: Soncino, 1935), xii.

one another in distinct compartments befitting their appropriate places in the created order. Purity depended on rigorous conformity within the respective cultural boxes. Variety was not the spice of life, but the stench of pollution."[10]

The Pharisees have unfairly gone down in history as those who thrive on hairsplitting arguments over arcane points of law and proper behavior, but they were interested in saving "their people from the ravages of paganism." They "were convinced that they were fighting for ethical purity as well as religious truth. In a world of debased standards of conduct they waged a resolute contest for the preservation of the higher and noble concepts of human behaviour which reflected the will of the God of Israel; and in so doing they rendered a conspicuous service to their own community and also to the advancement of civilisation."[11] Consequently, they believed in "salvation by segregation" versus "salvation by association" to fend off the heathens at the gate.[12] They also believed that the impiety of the sinners in Israel had brought catastrophe on the nation, and they needed to repent or be purged. They were of the opinion that God should condemn the guilty and vindicate the righteous by rewarding them according to their righteousness (1 Kgs 8:32).

Pharisees did not have hereditary ties to positions of power as the priests and village elders did, and therefore their social status was unstable. Their standing in society derived from their knowledge of Jewish law and traditions. They constantly struggled to exert their influence in society and to recruit new members. Their rules built up social boundaries and kept members united to one another. The throngs of people drawn to Jesus by his authority and power and the good news of his

message threatened their own power to affect persons. Their grumbling may be attributable to their fear that they were in danger of losing influence.

The narrator refers to those with Levi as simply "the tax collectors and others." The Pharisees referred to "the others" as "sinners," betraying their derisive attitude toward them. "Sinners" is not defined, but from Jesus' perspective, they represented a broad category of persons who needed forgiveness, which brought repentance in its wake. Peter has already identified himself as a sinner (5:8), so it is clear that Jesus had no fear of bonding with sinners.

Tax collectors were regarded as "gangsters and also as traitors."[13] They are not portrayed negatively in Luke's gospel, however. They came to John for immersion (3:12) and were not turned away, and they are later singled out as those who, unlike the Pharisees, "justified God because they were immersed with John's immersion" (7:29). From the Pharisees' perspective, however, they were beyond the pale and beyond repentance because of their constant contact with Gentiles, their collaboration with those who charged the people with extortionate tax rates, and their notorious dishonesty (see 3:12 – 13; 19:8 – 9).

The Pharisees view the gathering in Levi's house as a menagerie of crooks and sinners, and Luke alone notes that they direct their objections to the disciples. While seemingly an innocent question, it is accusatory and corresponds to their negative scrutiny of Jesus' supposed violation of Sabbath laws. In adopting this indirect tactic of addressing Jesus' disciples instead of Jesus himself, they reveal that they are intimidated by him. In Luke's context, it may suggest that the church continued to have to defend criticism of a ministry to

10. F. Scott Spencer, "The Ethiopian Eunuch and His Bible: A Social-Science Analysis," *BTB* 22 (1992): 159.

11. Bovon, *Luke 1:1 – 9:50*, 190.

12. William Manson, *The Gospel of Luke* (MNTC; New York: Harper, 1930), 55.

13. Hyam Maccoby, *Early Rabbinic Writings* (Cambridge: Cambridge Univ. Press, 1988), 132.

the entire spectrum of society and included in its membership those from the fringes of society and other so-called undesirables. The question, for example, continued to be relevant in the Christian community as disputes emerged over meal fellowship with Gentiles (Acts 11:3; Gal 2:11–14).

5:31 Jesus answered them, "The healthy do not need a physician but the sick do" (καὶ ἀποκριθεὶς ὁ Ἰησοῦς εἶπεν πρὸς αὐτούς· οὐ χρείαν ἔχουσιν οἱ ὑγιαίνοντες ἰατροῦ ἀλλὰ οἱ κακῶς ἔχοντες). Jesus responds with a pronouncement: Those who are well do not need a physician because they believe that they are well. The sick will usually call a physician to attend to them. In this case, however, Jesus as the physician does not wait for the sick to come to him to be restored to health; he goes hunting for them.

5:32 "I have not come to call the righteous to repentance but sinners" (οὐκ ἐλήλυθα καλέσαι δικαίους ἀλλὰ ἁμαρτωλοὺς εἰς μετάνοιαν). There is no irony in this response, as if the righteous are only those who think they are righteous. The issue is about the sinners, not the righteous. "I have come" expresses his sense of purpose (see 7:34, 48–49; 15:1–2, 7, 10; 19:7, 10). What Jesus is doing is perfectly natural and to be expected in light of Ezek 34:1–16. As the proper role of the physician is to tend to the sick, the proper role of the shepherd is to rescue scattered sheep and bind up the injured and strengthen the weak.[14] Eating with sinners is "part of his ministry of bringing God's healing and forgiveness to those who are sick and sinful."[15]

Luke has the additional phrase "to call ... *to repentance*," which is absent from Mark 2:17. This makes clear that Jesus is not a reveler. Eating with

these people is a means of calling them to repentance. Unlike the more strident message of John, who shouted that the people had better repent or they would be consumed by fire, Jesus calls them to repentance by communing with them, which symbolically conveys their acceptance by God. He places an emphasis on what God is already doing in proclaiming the good news that now is the time of salvation.[16]

5:33 They responded to him, "John's disciples often fast and make supplications and so also do Pharisees' disciples, but yours eat and drink!" (οἱ δὲ εἶπαν πρὸς αὐτόν· οἱ μαθηταὶ Ἰωάννου νηστεύουσιν πυκνὰ καὶ δεήσεις ποιοῦνται, ὁμοίως καὶ οἱ τῶν Φαρισαίων, οἱ δὲ σοὶ ἐσθίουσιν καὶ πίνουσιν). One can imagine the Pharisees frowning at Jesus' answer, and they try to vindicate themselves and their objections. The mention of repentance harks back to the hallmark of the preaching of John. His disciples, they recall, did things associated with repentance, and so did the Pharisees (see 18:12). Jesus seeks to call sinners to repentance. So did John. The difference is that John's followers showed evidence of their repentance by their fasting and prayer. Fasting was a sign of repentance and was attended by prayers for forgiveness (see Joel 2:12–17; Jonah 3:5–9; *Jos. Asen.* 10:14–17). Those whom Jesus calls show no traditional evidence of repentance. They eat and drink rather than fast and pray. Where is the mourning over sins, the sackcloth and ashes (see Joel 1:13–16)?

5:34 Jesus said to them, "You cannot make the bridegroom's attendants fast while the bridegroom is with them, can you?" (ὁ δὲ Ἰησοῦς εἶπεν πρὸς αὐτούς· μὴ δύνασθε τοὺς υἱοὺς τοῦ

---

14. Neale, *None but the Sinners*, 132.

15. Heil, *The Meal Scenes in Luke-Acts*, 25.

16. Tannehill, "Repentance in the Context of Lukan Soteriology," 90. In the journey to Jerusalem "it becomes clear that

the people in general (not just the 'sinners') must repent and that failure to repent in response to the mission of Jesus will bring condemnation in the judgment."

νυμφῶνος ἐν ᾧ ὁ νυμφίος μετ᾽ αὐτῶν ἐστιν ποιῆσαι νηστεῦσαι;). For Jesus, repentance is associated more with joy than with tears of remorse (19:6; Acts 8:8, 39; 13:48, 52), and he uses wedding imagery to make the point. The assumption is that weddings are a time to feast, not to fast, to loosen the belt rather than to tighten the belt. Jesus had cited Isa 61:1 – 2 as the theme of his ministry (4:18 – 19) and announced that this Scripture was being fulfilled in him. Isaiah 61:10 is no less appropriate for what is happening:

> I delight greatly in the LORD;
>> my soul rejoices in my God.
> For he has clothed me with garments of salvation
>> and arrayed me in a robe of his righteousness,
> as a bridegroom adorns his head like a priest,
>> and as a bride adorns herself with her jewels.
> (see also Isa 62:4 – 5)

The figure assumes that Jesus is the bridegroom, and it has christological implications. The bridegroom image is related to the eschatological banquet as wedding feast, and God is portrayed as the bridegroom of his people. Feasting is a recognition that "God's salvation has already arrived in the person of Jesus as the bridegroom of God's wedding banquet."[17] Anna spent her life praying and fasting night and day in the temple (2:37). She belonged to the time of expectancy and waiting. With Jesus' presence and the advent of the reign of God, "fasting represents the wrong form of spirituality at the wrong time."[18] If the Pharisees are fasting, they are out of step with what God is doing. Resseguie goes on to write:

> While fasting is appropriate as a plea for God to

usher in the messianic age, in this passage fasting represents a stubborn refusal to acknowledge that God has done so. Yet the problem is deeper than whether one should fast. Jesus recognizes that comfortable, familiar forms of spirituality exert a narcotic effect that blurs perception to new revelation. Even though Jesus brings "new wine," those accustomed to the "old" find the "new" inferior.[19]

5:35 "The days will come [soon enough] when the bridegroom will be taken away from them. Then, in those days, they will fast" (ἐλεύσονται δὲ ἡμέραι, καὶ ὅταν ἀπαρθῇ ἀπ᾽ αὐτῶν ὁ νυμφίος, τότε νηστεύσουσιν ἐν ἐκείναις ταῖς ἡμέραις). Green contends that Jesus refers to his death as the "taking away" of the bridegroom and that fasting will be appropriate then — *not only* as mourning *but also* in anticipation of Jesus' return.[20] Stein limits the time to the period between Jesus' arrest and his resurrection, citing 24:17 – 20 and John 16:20; 20:11 – 13. He notes that the period after the resurrection is a time of joy, not mourning (24:41, 52).[21] This interpretation makes the best sense and is supported by Jesus' own conduct. He fasts at the Last Supper (22:14 – 16), but after the resurrection he eats with the disciples who are filled with joy (24:41 – 43). Stein sums it up: "Jesus brought with him the 'new' (Jer 31:31 – 33). God's kingdom has been realized. The Anointed One has brought with him the fulfillment of the OT promises (Luke 4:18), and the joy of the awaited age has come."[22]

5:36 He also told them a parable: "No one tears a piece from a new garment to patch an old garment. If one does, not only will one tear up the

---

17. Heil, *The Meal Scenes in Luke-Acts*, 30. Danker, *Jesus and the New Age*, 127, explains the absence of women in the image: "At oriental weddings the bridegroom and his relatives are the chief participants. Hence there is no mention of the bride in this account (nor in John 2:1 – 10)."

18. James L. Resseguie, *Spiritual Landscape: Images of the*

Spiratal Life in the Gospel of Luke (Peabody, MA: Hendrickson, 2004), 83.

19. Ibid.

20. Green, *The Gospel of Luke*, 249.

21. Robert Stein, *Luke* (NAC; Nashville: Broadman, 1992), 185.

22. Ibid., 186.

new garment, but the patch from it will also not match the old" (ἔλεγεν δὲ καὶ παραβολὴν πρὸς αὐτοὺς ὅτι οὐδεὶς ἐπίβλημα ἀπὸ ἱματίου καινοῦ σχίσας ἐπιβάλλει ἐπὶ ἱμάτιον παλαιόν· εἰ δὲ μή γε, καὶ τὸ καινὸν σχίσει καὶ τῷ παλαιῷ οὐ συμφωνήσει τὸ ἐπίβλημα τὸ ἀπὸ τοῦ καινοῦ). The term "parable" (παραβολή) applies to a wide range of images, sayings, and stories that have some kind of comparative function. One must interpret this and the following parable as having allegorical significance; otherwise, it just offers the kind of wisdom that might be found in *Good Housekeeping* magazine.

What the "old" and the "new" represent, however, is not precisely clear. Set in the context of controversies with the Pharisees (5:17 – 6:11), the "old" would seem to represent the Judaism of the Pharisees and the "new" what Jesus brings. The comparison esteems both the old and the new garments, since it warns that *both* will be destroyed if the new were used to repair the old. The two garments are fundamentally incompatible, and the image does present the old garment as needing repair. If it needs a patch, something is wrong. Only a fool would cut up a new garment to repair an old one, particularly if the patch worsens the problem. The obvious solution is to replace the old one with the new.

This solution does not mean that one cannot live simultaneously as a Jew and a Christian, as Bovon surmises.[23] Paul, for example, is accused in Acts of teaching against the law (Acts 18:13; 21:21, 28), the Jewish people (21:28), Jewish customs (21:21), and the temple (21:28), but he also takes a

vow and shaves his hair as a pious Jew who follows the customs of the fathers (18:18), calls Jews his brothers (13:26, 38; 22:1; 23:6; 28:17), specifically identifies himself as a Jew (21:39; 22:3), talks about "our fathers" (24:14; 26:6), refers to "my nation" to whom he brought alms (26:4; 28:19), and claims to be in chains because of the hope of Israel (28:20). The continuation of the story in Acts makes it evident that it is only an exclusionary Judaism that focuses only on preserving the old, that is at odds with the new. Jesus' emphasis on inclusion and growth stretches the fiber of Judaism to its limits until it rips.[24]

What is "new" needs to be carefully defined. Since Luke grounds Christianity in the antiquity of Judaism, he is not presenting the Christian way as the new.[25] In the ancient world, unlike our contemporary culture, what is good is old! Our culture leads us too readily to assume that "new" implies "improved" and "better." Luke does not present Christianity as the latest thing but as the fulfillment of the ancient promises to Israel. In the context, however, the issue is about repentance and the traditional signs of repentance, not the relative age of the Christian movement. The parable makes the case "that it is impossible and destructive to mix new ways of thinking and living with old ways of thinking and living."[26] The "new" is the renewal of the old, in which God fulfills what he has promised. Old ways of thinking that cannot accommodate Jesus' offer of forgiveness to sinners and the reinstatement of the outcasts in God's covenant people needs to be replaced.[27] The new ways of thinking are created by the "new covenant" that

---

23. Bovon, *Luke 1:1 – 9:50*, 193.

24. Heil (*The Meal Scenes in Luke-Acts*, 30) argues that "the disciples of Jesus preserve both the new garment by appropriately feasting and the old garment by appropriately fasting in supplication and preparation for God's future salvific activity they have already tasted." The issue is not about the forms of

religious practice, fasting or feasting, but about the conceptual thinking behind such practice.

25. Green, *The Gospel of Luke*, 249 – 50.

26. Nave, *Repentance in Luke-Acts*, 172.

27. In Acts, this old way of thinking resists the inclusion of the Gentiles into the covenant people of God.

was announced by Jeremiah to be written on the heart, and it entails the forgiveness of sins (Jer 31:31 – 34; see 2 Cor 3:1 – 18).[28]

5:37 – 38 And no one puts new wine into old wineskins. If one does, not only will the new wine burst the skins and spill out, but the skins also will be ruined. New wine must be poured into new skins (καὶ οὐδεὶς βάλλει οἶνον νέον εἰς ἀσκοὺς παλαιούς· εἰ δὲ μή γε, ῥήξει ὁ οἶνος ὁ νέος τοὺς ἀσκούς, καὶ αὐτὸς ἐκχυθήσεται καὶ οἱ ἀσκοὶ ἀπολοῦνται. ἀλλὰ οἶνον νέον εἰς ἀσκοὺς καινοὺς βλητέον). In the second analogy, new wine bursts the old wineskins because their stiff and weakened fibers are unable to hold the new wine that continues to ferment. One always needs wineskins (traditions) to contain the wine, but they must be appropriate wineskins, strong enough to handle the power of fermenting new wine. The "new" that Jesus brings threatens to destroy the old forms. The concern, however, is to save the old wineskins from being ruined and to preserve the new wine.

When fermentation was finished and the wine ready for storing, it was important to protect it from the oxygen to avoid ruining it. The wine was poured into old wineskins that had a protective, sealing film inside.

5:39 "No one who drinks old wine wants new wine. For he says, 'The old is pleasing'" ([καὶ] οὐδεὶς πιὼν παλαιὸν θέλει νέον· λέγει γάρ· ὁ παλαιὸς χρηστός ἐστιν). This proverb about preferring the aged wine seems to contradict the argument about the superiority of the new vintage that Jesus brings.[29] The image, however, does not endorse the old over the new but alludes to "the difficulties those who cling to old ways of thinking and living have with accepting new ways of thinking and living."[30] Such preferences hamper acceptance of the new. This saying explains why the Pharisees criticize Jesus. They are mired in a mind-set that clings to the old and rejects the unexpected, new things that God is working through Jesus "today" (22:20).

Theology in Application

1. Breaking Down Artificial Boundaries

Jesus did not mind hobnobbing with conspicuous sinners, but the Pharisees are portrayed as having no sympathy for them. A cartoon by Engleman pictures a marquee outside a church announcing: "No shirt, no shoes, no salvation." This makes perfect sense to many who would find it inappropriate for persons to come to their worship service improperly attired.

The concern about such things is similar to the Pharisees' concerns. It is a matter of "purity." Purity has to do with the ways persons, things, and times are ordered and classified. Something becomes "impure" or "dirty" when "it is the wrong *thing*

---

28. Roland Meynet, "Le vin de la nouvelle alliance: la parabole du vieux et du neuf (Lc 5,36 – 39) dans son contexte," *Gregorianum* 86 (2005): 5 – 27.

29. The verse is omitted in D (so also Marcion, Irenaeus, Eusebius) perhaps because it could be taken to mean that Judaism is superior. The adjective νέος ("new") is used to describe

the wine three times and means "new" in terms of time. The adjective καινός ("new") is also used to describe the wineskins and means "new" in terms of quality or type, "fresh" as opposed to "worn out" (Plummer, *Luke*, 164).

30. Nave, *Repentance in Luke-Acts*, 173.

appearing in the wrong *place* at the wrong *time*."[31] The Pharisees' attention to purity derived from God's command that Israel was to be a holy people (Lev 19:2) and from the many biblical directives about holiness. The Levitical system regarded defilement as anything that could cut one off from fellowship with God. Impurity belonged to the realm of death and demons. The Pharisees' religious posture was basically defensive: How do we protect ourselves from contagion?

It is not simply that Jesus ignored purity restrictions, but he had a new concept of holiness. His open acceptance of those labeled sinners reflected his belief that holiness, not just impurity, was transferable (see Exod 29:37; 30:26 – 29; Ezek 44:19; 46:20). In the Old Testament, it was generally the impure that contaminated the holy. According to Stettler, Jesus believed that "through him and in him, the Holy One of God, God's holiness has come. His transferable holiness destroys the impurity so that it no longer has the capacity to render others impure. Those he touches he restores to communion with God."[32] She regards this concept of "contagious holiness" as "the fulfilment of the eschatological victory of the holy over the unholy as it is envisaged in Zech 14,20."[33] She concludes:

> In healing those whom the law would have expelled, Jesus indicates that he has come to fulfil the Torah with messianic authority. The Torah expelled the impure in order to witness to God as the God of life, wholeness and purity. Jesus witnessed to the same God by healing people, thus fulfilling the ultimate purpose of the Torah.[34]

As Jesus' opponents, the Pharisees have been vilified for being guilty of a smug self-righteousness. That attitude can beset any religious group, and the behaviors associated with it are not limited to religious people. For example, Wuthnow notes that university professors engage in boundary-maintenance behavior to maintain their significance, their distinctiveness. They define themselves over against "the other," and it prevents them from opening up to others and accepting them because it destroys their identity. They mark territory by identifying outsiders and shunning them. They tend to be dismissive of other views. Such behavior reflects their own insecurity that their own identity is shaky.[35]

Perhaps it is an overstatement to say that Jesus "got himself crucified because of the way he ate."[36] But what his eating with sinners entailed — God's grace and the forgiveness of sins offered to all — did create a sizeable, negative reaction. The Pharisees' middling imagination about what God's grace and power can do in people's lives is

31. Jerome Neyrey, "The Idea of Purity in Mark's Gospel," *Semeia* 35 (1986): 92.

32. Hanna Stettler, "Sanctification in the Jesus Tradition," *Bib* 85 (2004): 160.

33. Ibid., 161.

34. Ibid.

35. Robert Wuthnow, "Science and the Sacred," in *The Sacred in a Secular Age* (ed. P. E. Hammond; Berkeley: Univ. of California Press, 1985), 197.

36. Robert J. Karris, *Luke: Artist and Theologian* (New York: Paulist, 1985), 70.

not unique to them. Many Christians would place the same kinds of limitations on whom God can save and what God can do through them.

2. God's Indiscriminate Goodness to Sinners

In Jesus' culture, leprosy and paralysis would have been interpreted as the deserved repercussions of some unknown sin. Jesus does not address this particular theological perspective, nor does he identify any particular sins. The coming of the reign of God does not belabor the past but focuses on the present and the future. Focusing on the sins only reinforces their marginalization. From the perspective of the Pharisees, sinners must verbalize their guilt to God and to those whom they have injured to be forgiven (*m. Yoma* 8:9; *t. Taʿan.* 1:8; Lev 5:5; Philo, *Spec. Laws* 1.235). They must also demonstrate their repentance by changing their lifestyle to one that conforms to their rules and offer the appropriate sacrifices in the temple. There must first be evidence that the penitent are truly remorseful and have turned away from wrongdoing before there can be forgiveness, because they assume that God is not and cannot be "indiscriminately good."

Jesus' eating with tax collectors and sinners implies that God indeed is indiscriminately good. These sinners have done nothing required — no evidence of reformation, no confession, no temple sacrifice. But Jesus did not come to reward the deserving but to serve the needy with reckless abandon. This approach irritates the righteous, because they show themselves to be righteous by comparing themselves favorably to the sinner — in these cases, the sufferers.

3. The Response of Repentance

Nave defines repentance in Luke as "a fundamental change in thinking that permanently and radically alters the way things use [sic] to be."[37] It requires "an abandonment of his former ways of thinking and living," and for Levi it also required a "complete break with his occupation."[38] No longer could he center his life around his own needs and securities, particularly when they were secured at the expense of others. The incident with Levi makes it clear that Jesus is calling sinners to repentance. To follow Jesus means more than being a hanger-on, admiring his mighty works or giving superficial assent to his teaching (7:9; 9:11; 23:27 – 30). It demands that one "abandon one's present way of thinking and living."[39] It requires "a radical conversion from all that is evil and an absolute commitment to God."[40]

Tannehill identifies "noteworthy emphases related to repentance that differ from common assumptions." He argues:

---

37. Nave, *Repentance in Luke-Acts*, 146.
38. Ibid., 167.
39. Ibid., 169.

40. Dennis M. Sweetland, "Following Jesus: Discipleship in Luke-Acts," in *New Views on Luke and Acts* (ed. E. Richard; Collegeville, MN: Liturgical, 1990), 112.

human repentance should be understood as both divine and human action. The assumption that repentance is the human contribution to salvation and forgiveness is the divine contribution is not only theologically shallow but also ignores indications in Luke-Acts that God's saving purpose and action are manifest in the act of repentance itself. The same act of repentance can be viewed as God's saving action in a person's life and as a human decision. Luke-Acts is a narrative, not a systematic theology, and does not try to explain this puzzle, but there is evidence that both perspectives are important in this two-volume work.[41]

For example, in the parables of the shepherd who searched for a lost sheep and the woman who searched for a lost coin, the sheep and coin are passive figures (15:1 – 10). The shepherd combs the countryside looking for the sheep, and the woman looks in every nook and cranny in her house to find the coin. These two parables "suggest that the experience of repentance may be more like being found by someone who searches with great determination than like achieving something through our own determination." The third parable in Luke 15 about the father with two sons gives a different slant. It highlights "the human decision to return" (15:11 – 24). The incident with Levi reveals both aspects. Jesus takes the initiative in finding Levi, and the power of his call draws him from his tax booth. But Levi makes the decision to abandon everything to follow Jesus, to change his ways of thinking about what God is doing and what is vital in life. God is acting in this world through Jesus to change things, and Jesus offers the opportunity for Levi and "the others," whether they are to be classified as sinners or not, to change as well.[42]

---

41. Tannehill, "Repentance in the Context of Lukan Soteriology," 91. Nave (*Repentance in Luke-Acts*, 38) also argues that in Luke-Acts "it is God who gives repentance" (see Acts 5:32; 11:18; 13:48).

42. Tannehill, "Repentance in the Context of Lukan Soteriology," 89.

Luke 6:1 – 11

Literary Context

This unit contains the third and fourth controversy stories in which the scribes and Pharisees object to something Jesus does, and he responds with a startling claim (for more on this, see the Literary Context for 5:12 – 26). In the final dispute (6:6 – 11), Jesus' enemies are again bested in argument and left silent, but they proceed to plot how to undo Jesus. This action exposes their spiritual unfitness and irrelevancy to what God is doing, and it sets up Jesus' choice of the twelve apostles to become the replacement leaders of Israel (6:12 – 16).

Main Idea

Jesus has the authority to interpret the divine intention behind the Sabbath law; he makes the Sabbath subordinate to him and as something given for the benefit of humans.

Translation

Luke 6:1–11

6:1a	Circumstance	**It happened that he passed through some grainfields on the Sabbath.**
b	Controversial action	**His disciples were plucking the heads of grain, rubbing the husks off with their hands, and eating.**
2	Challenging question	**Certain ones from the Pharisees said,** *"Why do you do what is not lawful to do on the Sabbath?"*
3	Response from biblical precedent	**Jesus answered them and said,** *"Have you not read what David did when he was hungry and his companions with him?*
4a		*He went into the house of God, and taking the consecrated loaves he ate and gave some to his companions.*
b	Explanatory declaration	*It is only lawful for priests to eat consecrated loaves."*
5	Pronouncement	**He was saying to them,** *"The Son of Man is Lord of the Sabbath."*
6	Circumstance	**It happened on another Sabbath,** **that he entered into the synagogue to teach,** **and there was a man whose right hand was withered.**

7	Hostile inspection	**The scribes and the Pharisees were keeping an eye on him**
		                        so that they might find some charge to bring against him and
		
		            [were waiting to see] if he would heal on the Sabbath.

8	Setup for healing	**He knew their thoughts and said to the man with the withered hand,** *"Rise and stand in the middle!"* **He arose and stood there.**
9	Challenging question	**Jesus said to them,** *"I ask you, is it lawful to do good on the Sabbath or to do harm,* *to save a life or to destroy it?"*
10	Healing/ substantiation	*After looking around at them all,* **he said to him,** *"Stretch out your hand!"* **He did so and his hand was restored.**
11a	Reaction	**They were filled with rage and**
b	Escalation	**were talking it over with one another about what they might do to Jesus.**

Structure and Literary Form

Luke combines two accounts about Jesus' and his disciples' apparent violations of the Sabbath commandment. Jesus' adversaries object to the behavior of his disciples or manifest a suspicious attitude about what he will do. Jesus responds to the first objection with scriptural precedence from David and a pronouncement that he is Lord of the Sabbath. He responds to the second objection with a question that implies that doing good and saving a life are lawful on the Sabbath; he then follows that with a healing. The form is that of a *chreia*.

Exegetical Outline

➡ **I. Controversial action on the Sabbath: disciples plucking grain while traveling (6:1)**

II. Complaint about the disciples' action from the Pharisees (6:2)

III. Jesus' reply (6:3 – 5)

   A. The biblical precedent of David and his men (6:3 – 4)

   B. The declaration that Jesus is Lord of the Sabbath (6:5)

IV. Setting: Jesus teaching in the synagogue on the Sabbath (6:6)

V. The scrutiny of the scribes and Pharisees watching for infractions of the Sabbath law (6:7)

VI. Jesus' reply (6:8 – 10)

   A. The creation of a controversial situation by calling a man with a withered hand to the center (6:8)

   B. A challenging question: "Is it lawful to good on the Sabbath?" (6:9)

   C. The controversial healing of the man on the Sabbath (6:10)

VII. The reaction of the scribes and Pharisees: rage and plotting Jesus' demise (6:11)

Explanation of the Text

6:1 – 2 It happened that he passed through some grainfields on the Sabbath. His disciples were plucking the heads of grain, rubbing the husks off with their hands, and eating. Certain ones from the Pharisees said, "Why do you do what is not lawful to do on the Sabbath?" (ἐγένετο δὲ ἐν σαββάτῳ διαπορεύεσθαι αὐτὸν διὰ σπορίμων, καὶ ἔτιλλον οἱ μαθηταὶ αὐτοῦ καὶ ἤσθιον τοὺς στάχυας ψώχοντες ταῖς χερσίν. τινὲς δὲ τῶν Φαρισαίων εἶπαν· τί ποιεῖτε ὃ οὐκ ἔξεστιν τοῖς σάββασιν;). The law permitted one to pass through a neighbor's field and pluck grain as long as one did not attempt to harvest it (put a sickle to it, Deut 23:25). Picking grain and rubbing it on the Sabbath could be construed as harvesting (Exod 34:21), and that is how the Pharisees saw it (*m. Šabb.* 7:2). Therefore, they declare that the disciples are doing "what is not lawful to do on the Sabbath." God commanded that the Sabbath be kept holy. How does one keep the Sabbath holy? By not working.[1] This leads to the next question: What qualifies as work? The Pharisees sought to

---

1. Josephus (*Ag. Ap.* 2:27 §3) states that the word "sabbath" "in the Jew's language denotes cessation from all work.

give precise classifications of work to create habits of normalcy that prevented violations of the law.

The Pharisees set up what they described as a "fence around the law" (*m. ʾAbot* 1:1). Their interpretative decisions on how to apply the law (*halakah*) were designed to set up precautions that would prevent the actual breaking of the law. Two tractates in the Mishnah are devoted to Sabbath regulations,[2] and in it the rabbis admit, "The rules about the sabbath, festal offerings and sacrilege are as mountains hanging by a hair, for Scripture is scanty and the rules many" (*m. Ḥag.* 1:8).

The Pharisees' objections to the disciples' apparent violation of the Sabbath should not be dismissed as an obsession with trifles. The Sabbath was a sign of Israel's sanctification among all the nations and made them distinct. Careful observance was regarded as a bulwark against assimilation to pagan culture as well as a way to honor the holiness of Yahweh (Exod 20:8 – 11; Deut 5:12 – 15). Their concern over Sabbath violations would be similar to that voiced by Josephus at the beginning of his *Antiquities*.

> The main lesson to be learned from this history by any who cares to peruse it is that men who conform to the will of God, and do not venture to transgress laws excellently laid down, prosper in all things beyond belief and are rewarded by God with felicity; whereas, in proportion as they depart from the strict observances of these laws, things else practicable become impracticable, and whatever imaginary good they strive to do ends in irretrievable disasters. (*Ant.* 1. 1.3 §§14 – 15)

The shared assumption was that those who obey the law prosper; those who disobey "come to grief" (*Ant.* 1.1.2 – 3 §§5 – 13). But individuals disobeying the law did not bring grief to themselves

alone; they brought it to the whole nation of Israel (see Deut 28:15 – 68; 29:20 – 28). Sabbath infractions, the Pharisees believed, landed Israel in her current state of wretchedness under Roman oppression. Flaunting Sabbath law would only bring further disaster on the land and people.

6:3 – 4 Jesus answered them and said, "Have you not read what David did when he was hungry and his companions with him? He went into the house of God, and taking the consecrated loaves he ate and gave some to his companions. It is only lawful for priests to eat consecrated loaves" (καὶ ἀποκριθεὶς πρὸς αὐτοὺς εἶπεν ὁ Ἰησοῦς· οὐδὲ τοῦτο ἀνέγνωτε ὃ ἐποίησεν Δαυὶδ ὅτε ἐπείνασεν αὐτὸς καὶ οἱ μετ᾽ αὐτοῦ [ὄντες], [ὡς] εἰσῆλθεν εἰς τὸν οἶκον τοῦ θεοῦ καὶ τοὺς ἄρτους τῆς προθέσεως λαβὼν ἔφαγεν καὶ ἔδωκεν τοῖς μετ᾽ αὐτοῦ, οὓς οὐκ ἔξεστιν φαγεῖν εἰ μὴ μόνους τοὺς ἱερεῖς;). Jesus does not defend his disciples and himself as their teacher, who is held responsible for their behavior, by arguing the fine points of Sabbath law. Instead, he seems to concede that there was a violation.

But then he goes on to cite an even more egregious violation of the law by David (1 Sam 21:1 – 6).[3] Fleeing from the wrath of Saul, the famished David and his men demanded that the priest Ahimelech give them bread to eat. The priest said he had only the sanctified bread of the Presence, which was forbidden to all except priests (Lev 24:5 – 9). David's response is the key: "Indeed women have been kept from us, as usual whenever I set out. The men's bodies are holy even on missions that are not holy. How much more so today!" (1 Sam 21:5).

David was not just a hungry man but the one chosen by God to be king and the ancestor and type

---

2. Mishnah *Šabbat* seeks to define what constitutes a burden and *ʿErubin* seeks to define what constitutes a Sabbath resting place and how to expand it.

3. Josephus's account of this story does not mention David and his men eating the showbread, which reveals his sensitivity to such a violation (*Ant.* 6:12.1 §243).

of the Messiah to come. It was his urgent mission and his authority that overrode legal restrictions and also covered his followers. Jesus' emphasis is on those "companions with him" (οἱ μετ᾽ αὐτοῦ), which connects to the reference in 5:34: Jesus as the bridegroom who is with the bridegroom's attendants (μετ᾽ αὐτῶν), his disciples. His point is made from the lesser to the greater: if the law could be set aside by David and his men in their urgent situation, how much more so for Jesus and his disciples in a situation of greater urgency, the necessity of proclaiming the reign of God?

6:5 He was saying to them, "The Son of Man is Lord of the Sabbath" (καὶ ἔλεγεν αὐτοῖς· κύριός ἐστιν τοῦ σαββάτου ὁ υἱὸς τοῦ ἀνθρώπου). The controversy does not lead to a statement about the humanitarian purpose of the Sabbath. Instead, it results in a pronouncement that Jesus, as the enigmatic Son of Man, is Lord of the Sabbath. The conclusion is that he has the authority to set aside the Sabbath laws for the benefit of his disciples.[4] He can decree what is lawful and unlawful. He, not the Sabbath commandment (cf. Rom 7:1), is the Lord who rules over his disciples. Consequently, his disciples need not concern themselves about appearing irreligious or pay any attention to criticism when they are with him and are carrying out their urgent task for God. The Sabbath conflict becomes an opportunity to make a christological point.

6:6 – 7 It happened on another Sabbath that he entered into the synagogue to teach, and there was a man whose right hand was withered. The scribes and the Pharisees were keeping an eye on him so that they might find some charge to bring against him and [were waiting to see] if he would heal on the Sabbath (ἐγένετο δὲ ἐν ἑτέρῳ σαββάτῳ εἰσελθεῖν αὐτὸν εἰς τὴν συναγωγὴν καὶ διδάσκειν. καὶ ἦν ἄνθρωπος ἐκεῖ καὶ ἡ χεὶρ αὐτοῦ ἡ δεξιὰ ἦν ξηρά. παρετηροῦντο δὲ αὐτὸν οἱ γραμματεῖς καὶ οἱ Φαρισαῖοι εἰ ἐν τῷ σαββάτῳ θεραπεύει, ἵνα εὕρωσιν κατηγορεῖν αὐτοῦ). A withered hand is frequently understood to be the punishment of God (Ps 137:5; Zech 11:17). Jeroboam's hand "shriveled up," for example, when he tried to take action against the rebellious prophets (1 Kgs 13:4 – 6). Again, Jesus encounters a person who needs liberation from the captivity of his infirmity and his sins.

The Holy Spirit promised Simon (Luke 2:26) that he would not see death before he had seen the Lord's Messiah. Isaiah proclaimed, "All flesh shall see the salvation of God" (3:6), but all the scribes and the Pharisees care to see is whether Jesus would heal on the Sabbath. They are only interested in saddling him with the charge of Sabbath-breaker, an offense worthy of death (Exod 31:14). In their zeal to protect the law, they do not use it to set captives free but to bind them ever tighter. They have no power to heal, only to deal out death.

6:8 – 10 He knew their thoughts and said to the man with the withered hand, "Rise and stand in the middle!" He arose and stood there. Jesus said to them, "I ask you, is it lawful to do good on the Sabbath or to do harm, to save a life or to destroy it?" After looking around at them all, he said to him, "Stretch out your hand!" He did so and his hand was restored (αὐτὸς δὲ ᾔδει τοὺς διαλογισμοὺς αὐτῶν, εἶπεν δὲ τῷ ἀνδρὶ τῷ ξηρὰν ἔχοντι τὴν χεῖρα· ἔγειρε καὶ στῆθι εἰς τὸ μέσον. καὶ ἀναστὰς ἔστη. εἶπεν δὲ ὁ Ἰησοῦς πρὸς αὐτούς· ἐπερωτῶ ὑμᾶς, εἰ ἔξεστιν τῷ σαββάτῳ ἀγαθοποιῆσαι ἢ κακοποιῆσαι, ψυχὴν σῶσαι ἢ ἀπολέσαι; καὶ περιβλεψάμενος πάντας

---

4. Sven-Olaf Back, *Jesus of Nazareth and the Sabbath Commandment* (Åbo: Åbo Akademi Univ. Press, 1995), 84 – 85.

αὐτοὺς εἶπεν αὐτῷ· ἔκτεινον τὴν χεῖρά σου. ὁ δὲ ἐποίησεν καὶ ἀπεκατεστάθη ἡ χεὶρ αὐτοῦ).

Jesus knows the thoughts of his adversaries and provocatively makes the man stand in the center. He does not wait for the Sabbath to pass and avoid any misunderstanding and conflict but intends to drive home a point. Liberating captives is not to be limited only to certain days of the week. The Sabbath can become an occasion to do good rather than simply a time to refrain from work. The criterion is whether or not it helps those who are in need. These Pharisees are interested only in making sure that the law is well-defended, and, as a result, they barricade themselves and others in a stockade of their own making. They would be satisfied for the man to remain withered. Jesus came to set the withered free.

As Jesus asked a paralyzed man to stand up and walk (5:23 – 24), so he asks the man with a withered arm to stretch out his immobile limb. Jesus' word brings healing, but the healing takes effect when the person responds in faith. He does not reply, "I can't! My hand is withered!" As he obeys, he is healed.

6:11 They were filled with rage and were talking it over with one another about what they might do to Jesus (αὐτοὶ δὲ ἐπλήσθησαν ἀνοίας καὶ διελάλουν πρὸς ἀλλήλους τί ἂν ποιήσαιεν τῷ Ἰησοῦ). Jesus does not act independently of God. Luke has made it clear that "the power of the Lord was with him to heal" (5:17). The Pharisees do not consider the possibility that if this man's healing were not in accord with the will of God, he would not have been healed. They are imprisoned by their own inflexibility that blinds them to the coming of God's reign. Jesus brings healing on the Sabbath; the Pharisees plot destruction. This ominous note that the Pharisees were scrutinizing Jesus and then plotting how to get him recalls Ps 37:30 – 33, with its promise of ultimate vindication by God.

Theology in Application

1. Sabbath Consciousness

Kalas claims, "The gift of the Sabbath looks too good to be true; why would God want to do something so utterly kind? So we look for some meanness in the graciousness of God, and finding none, we impose … our own."[5] The legalistic extension and application of rules related to keeping the Sabbath promotes a fondness for negatives that always looks for others' shortcomings in conforming to those rules and harshly condemning them for any lapse. God intends for the Sabbath to free humans, but this negative approach makes the Sabbath burdensome. It becomes a deadweight the soul has to bear, not wings to lift up the soul. It also imports a mercenary spirit into religious behavior and fosters the idea that one can redeem oneself through one's own effort and resources — in this case, by obeying the rules to the letter.

The Pharisees' carping about Jesus' violations of the Sabbath has tended to result in a modern justification for ignoring the Sabbath. Those interested in preserving its

---

5. J. Ellsworth Kalas, *The Ten Commandments from the Back Side* (Nashville: Abingdon, 1998), 45 – 46.

sanctity are dismissed as overly sanctimonious. Jesus never disparages the Sabbath law and does not encourage his disciples to abandon it. In these Sabbath incidents, he argues that something new from God has broken into the present. One need not worry about supposed Sabbath transgressions when one is absorbed in the greater purposes of God and doing good. Rigorous observance of the Sabbath no less than the neglect of the Sabbath can both be rooted in self-centered pursuits.

Moderns have tended to lose the sense of the Sabbath as a gift from God. Wirzba notes that we tend to be obsessed with our "frantic schedules," "with speed and control," with seizing every opportunity to make more money. Many measure success by "the extent or pace of our own striving."[6] It is said of someone with pride: "This person works 24/7." It reflects our attempt to keep an anxious grip on the world and prevents people from experiencing a time to rejoice, refocus, and give gratitude. It also forecloses on the opportunity for God to do God's work in them. Lowery writes:

> Sabbath consciousness is grounded in the fundamental conviction that God is willing and able to provide enough for humans to survive and thrive. It is based on the belief that life and well-being ultimately are gifts from God, not products of human effort, though these gifts are channeled through human labor. Sabbath consciousness thus is grounded in humility, recognizing and respective of the limits of being human. In a nutshell, sabbath consciousness is grateful confidence in the abundant life given by God and humble self-restraint as the appropriate response to the God who unselfishly sustains all creation.[7]

2. The Dangers of a Coldhearted Legalism

Jesus places greater emphasis on the ethical-spiritual aspect of religion rather on than the ceremonial. Emphasis on the ceremonial leads invariably to formalism, cold smugness, and indifference to the welfare of others. Emphasis on the ethical-spiritual leads to growth in grace and in love for God and others. The bitter Pharisees in this incident reveal the tendency of some religious persons toward strict conformity to outer forms, proper religious rites, proper religious attire, and proper religious behavior to the neglect of mercy and compassion. This tendency imports a mercenary spirit into religion, a fondness for negatives, and a jaundiced view toward others. The Pharisees in plotting to destroy Jesus illustrate Pascal's adage, "Men never do evil so completely and cheerfully as when they do it from religious conviction."[8]

Consciousness of the goodness of God in giving the Sabbath should counter this mean-spirited outlook. Jesus' understanding of how Sabbath observance is to be lived out reveals God's ultimate love for humans, and those who know God manifest love of their fellow humans (1 John 4:7 – 8).

---

6. Norman Wirzba, "Time Out," *Christian Century* (July 12, 2005), 24.

7. Richard H. Lowery, "Sabbath and Survival," 158.

8. Blaise Pascal, *Pascal's Pensees* (trans. W. F. Trotter; New York: Dutton, 1958), 265 (no. 894).

18

Luke 6:12 – 49

Literary Context

Luke's setting for the Sermon on the Plain has Jesus ascending a mountain, where he prays and chooses twelve apostles, and then he descends to a level place where large crowds from all over have come to hear him and to be healed (cf. Mark 3:7 – 19). The result is that "Jesus is located with respect to the mountain upon which he has recently been praying; and, he is accompanied by the men for whom he has prayed"; his prayer also applies to the people who are attracted by his teaching and power.[1] This teaching applies to anyone who determines to call Jesus "Lord" (6:46), not just an elite class of disciple. It offers both an "invitation and challenge.... Having new leadership for God's people (6:12 – 16)," he also lays the foundation for "new practices, perceptions, and attitudes" that are to be distinctive features of the community.[2]

Luke's Sermon on the Plain is much shorter than the more familiar Sermon on the Mount in Matthew (Matt 5 – 7). One can debate that it is shorter because Matthew included more material from Q in his sermon or that they had different versions of Jesus' preaching.[3] Jesus would have "frequently repeated himself" in various settings.[4] The two discourses are similar yet different. Both begin with beatitudes, but Matthew's sermon is set near the beginning of Jesus' ministry in Galilee, while Luke's occurs well after the curtain has rung up on his ministry.

The emphasis on the law and righteousness and the practice of piety in Matthew's sermon is absent from Luke's. The distinctively Jewish background of Matthew's sermon is less obvious in Luke's sermon. Luke does not link the moral commands to the Mosaic law and, in fact, makes no mention of the law, which may make the sermon more accessible to a Gentile audience. In Luke, the emphasis falls on the reversal of fortunes for the poor and rich, love of enemies, and doing good. Both sermons stress the necessity of obeying Jesus' authoritative teaching at the conclusion. Jesus' sermon at Nazareth announced his campaign to bring good news to the poor (4:18 – 19); the Sermon on the Plain provides an example of that good news.

1. Crump, *Jesus the Intercessor*, 146.
2. Green, *The Gospel of Luke*, 261.
3. L. John Topel ("The Lukan Version of the Lord's Sermon," *BTB* 11 [1981]: 48 – 49) regards attempts to separate tradition from redaction in the sermon to be a "fruitless enterprise."
4. Kennedy, *New Testament Interpretation through Rhetorical Criticism*, 68.

Kennedy observes the "persistent polarization" running throughout the sermon: "Some are blessed and some cursed, some will hearken and some not, some build on a rock, and some without a foundation."[5] Luke's version offers no explanation for this state of affairs, but it prepares for the division in Israel that will become increasingly apparent as some will joyously respond to Jesus' ministry while others will sullenly reject him.

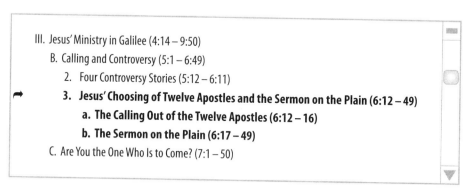

III. Jesus' Ministry in Galilee (4:14 – 9:50)

    B. Calling and Controversy (5:1 – 6:49)

        2. Four Controversy Stories (5:12 – 6:11)

➡   **3. Jesus' Choosing of Twelve Apostles and the Sermon on the Plain (6:12 – 49)**

           a. The Calling Out of the Twelve Apostles (6:12 – 16)

           b. The Sermon on the Plain (6:17 – 49)

    C. Are You the One Who Is to Come? (7:1 – 50)

Main Idea

Christ followers are to be defined by their characteristic behavior of loving enemies and doing good to others without any expectation of reciprocity.

Translation

Luke 6:12–49

6:12	Circumstance	**It happened in these days that**
		he departed to the mountain to pray and **spent the whole night in prayer with God.**
13	Selection of apostles	When day came,
		he summoned his disciples and **picked out twelve of them,**
		whom he also named apostles.
14	List	Simon,
		whom he named Peter,
		and Andrew, his brother,

Continued on next page.

5. Ibid., 66.

Continued from previous page.

          and James,
          and John,
          and Philip,
          and Bartholomew,

15   and Matthew,
          and Thomas,
          and James,
             son of Alphaeus,

          and Simon,
             who is called the zealot,

16   and Judas,
             son of James,

          and Judas Iscariot,
             who became a traitor.

17   Circumstance   When he came down with them,
          he stood upon a level place,
          and a large crowd of his disciples [were there]
               with a large multitude of the people
                    from   all Judea and↵
                            Jerusalem and
                            as far away as the↵
                            seacoast of Tyre and Sidon.

18   Circumstance   **They came to hear him and to be healed of their illnesses,**
          and those unhinged by unclean spirits were healed.

19   **The crowd was seeking to touch him**
     Explanation   for power was coming from him

          and he healed them all.

20a   **He raised his eyes toward his disciples and began to say,**
   b   Beatitude (1)   *"Blessed are the poor,*
   c   Reason   *because yours is the reign of God.*
21a   Beatitude (2)   *Blessed are those who hunger now,*
   b   Reason   *because they will be filled.*
   c   Beatitude (3)   *Blessed are those who weep now,*
   d   Reason   *because they will laugh.*
22   Beatitude (4)   *Blessed are you*
              when people will hate you, ostracize you, revile you, and↵
                  defame your name as evil
                 on account of the Son of Man.

23a   Command   *Rejoice in that day and jump for joy,*
   b   Reason   *for behold, your reward [will be] great in heaven.*
   c   Reason   *Their fathers were doing the same things to the prophets.*
24a   Woe (1)   But *woe to you who are rich,*
   b   Reason   *because you have cashed in on your consolation.*

25a	Woe (2)	Woe to you who are full now,
b	Reason	because you will go hungry.
c	Woe (3)	Woe to you who laugh now,
d	Reason	because you will mourn and weep.
26a	Woe (4)	Woe to you when all speak well of you,
b	Reason	for their fathers were doing the same things to the false prophets.
27a	Audience transition	But I say to you who are listening:
b	Command (1)	Love your enemies
		and do good to those who hate you.
28a	Command (2)	Bless those who curse you;
b	Command (3)	pray for those who abuse you.
29a	Command (4)	To the one who strikes you on the cheek offer him the other,
b	Command (5)	and from the one who takes your cloak do not hold back your shirt.
30a	Command (6)	Give to everyone who asks of you,
b	Command (7)	and do not demand your possessions back from the one who takes them.
31	Command (8)	And just as you want persons to do to you, do likewise to them.
32a	Conditional clause (1)	If you love those who love you,
b	Question	what credit is that to you?
c	Statement	For even the sinners love those who love them.
33a	Conditional clause (2)	And if you do good to those who do good to you,
b	Question	what credit is that to you?
c	Statement	For even the sinners do the same.
34a	Conditional clause (3)	For if you lend to those who you hope will pay you back,
b	Question	what credit is that to you?
c	Statement	Even the sinners loan to sinners so that they get back the same amount.
35a	Command (1)	But love your enemies,
b	Command (2)	do good [to them],
c	Command (3)	and lend [money] expecting nothing back
d	Reason (1)	and your reward will be great,
e	Reason (2)	and you will be sons of the Most High because he is kind to the ungrateful and selfish.
36	Summary command	Be merciful just as your Father is merciful.
37a	Command (1)	And do not judge,
b	Reason	and you will certainly not be judged.
c	Command (2)	Do not condemn,
d	Reason	and you will certainly not be condemned.

Continued on next page.

Continued from previous page.

e	Command (3)	*Pardon,*
f	Reason	*and you will be pardoned.*
38a	Command (4)	*Give,*
b	Reason	*and it will be given to you,*
c	Amplification	*a good measure, pressed down, shaken together, and overflowing ⌁*
		—they will give it in your lap.
d	Reason	*For the measure you give will be the measure you get back."*

39	Parable	**He also told a parable to them:**
		"Can a blind person guide the blind?
		Will they not both fall into a pit?
40	Proverb	*A disciple is not above the teacher;*
		but everyone who is fully trained will be like the teacher.
41	Parable	*Why do you look for the speck in your brother's eye*
		but do not notice the wooden beam in your own eye?
42a		*How are you able to say to your brother,*
		'Brother, let me take out the speck that is in your eye,'
		when you yourself do not see the wooden beam in your eye?
b		*Hypocrite, first take out the wooden beam from your own eye*
		and then you will see clearly to take the speck from your brother's eye.
43	Parable	*For a good tree does not bear worthless fruit,*
		nor again does a worthless tree bear good fruit.
44a	Proverb	*For each tree is known from its fruit.*
b		*For they do not gather figs from a thornbush, nor do they gather grapes ⌁*
		from a briar patch.
45		*The good person produces good from the good treasure [stored] in the heart,*
		and the evil produces evil from the evil [treasure stored in the heart];
		for the mouth speaks what overflows from the heart.
46	Challenging question	*Why do you call me, 'Lord, Lord,' and do not do what I say?*
47	Parable	*I will show you what this person is like who comes to me, hears my words, ⌁*
		and does them,
48		*This one is like a man who builds a house and excavates deeply and lays a ⌁*
		foundation upon the bedrock.
		When floodwaters rise, the river bursts against that house,
		and it is not powerful enough to shake it [from its foundations]
		because it was built well.
49		*The one who hears and does not do [what I say] is like a man who builds ⌁*
		a house without laying a foundation,
		and the river bursts against it,
		and immediately it falls in,
		and the collapse of that house is great."

Structure and Literary Form

An abbreviated call and then listing of disciples serves as an introductory transition to Jesus' teaching both his disciples and the crowds, who gather to listen and to be healed (6:12 – 19). The sermon divides into three sections. The first section (6:20 – 26) addresses two types of persons, the poor and the rich, with four beatitudes (with an amplification of the fourth) coordinated with four woes (with an amplification of the fourth). The beatitudes and the woes follow a pattern in which the causal clauses refer to a present, future, future, and then a present condition.

The second section (6:27 – 36) gives instructions on how to respond to mistreatment; these are bracketed between the command to love enemies, which is to be the distinctive characteristic of Christians (6:27, 35). The imperatives illustrate what loving enemies entails. The section concludes with contrasts between the standards of sinners and those expected of Christ's followers (6:32 – 34) and a final call to mercy (6:36).

The third section (6:37 – 49) includes rules for the community using various analogies: measure for measure, the blind leading the blind, the speck and the log, the good and the useless trees, and building a house with or without a foundation.

Exegetical Outline

→ **I. The calling out of the twelve apostles (6:12 – 16)**

    A. Jesus' ascent of the mountain to pray (6:12)

    B. Jesus' choice of twelve apostles from his disciples (6:13)

    C. Names of the twelve apostles (6:14 – 16)

II. The audience for the Sermon on the Plain (6:17 – 19)

    A. Jesus' descent from the mountain with his disciples (6:17)

    B. The approach of crowds to listen and to be healed by his power (6:18 – 19)

III. Beatitudes and woes (6:20 – 26)

    A. Beatitudes (6:20 – 23)

        1. Poor (6:20)

        2. Hungry (6:21a-b)

        3. Weeping (6:21c-d)

        4. Persecuted (6:22 – 23)

    B. Woes (6:24 – 26)

        1. Rich (6:24)

        2. Full (6:25a-b)

        3. Laughing (6:25c-d)

        4. Honored (6:26)

IV. Loving the enemy (6:27 – 36)

  A. Command to love enemies (6:27 – 34)

    1. Examples (6:27 – 29)

      a. Those who hate and curse you (6:27 – 28)

      b. Those who strike you (6:29a)

      c. Those who rob you (6:29b)

    2. Principles (6:30 – 31)

      a. Giving without expectations (6:30)

      b. Doing unto others as you want them to do to you (6:31)

    3. Contrasts with the reciprocity that governs the ways of sinners (6:32 – 34)

      a. Loving those who love you (6:32)

      b. Doing good to those who do good to you (6:33)

      c. Lending to those who pay back (6:34)

  B. Command to love enemies as God's way (6:35 – 36)

    1. Turning loans into gracious gifts (6:35)

    2. Being merciful (6:36)

V. Rules for the community (6:37 – 49)

  A. Not being judgmental (6:37 – 39)

    1. Principle of measure for measure (6:37 – 38)

    2. Principle of the blind leading the blind (6:39)

  B. Becoming fully trained by the teacher (Christ) (6:40 – 49)

    1. The speck and the log: judging oneself first before trying to help others (6:40 – 42)

    2. The good and the bad trees: watching what one says (6:43 – 45)

    3. Building a deep foundation: doing what Jesus says (6:46 – 49)

Explanation of the Text

6:12 It happened in these days that he departed to the mountain to pray and spent the whole night in prayer with God (ἐγένετο δὲ ἐν ταῖς ἡμέραις ταύταις ἐξελθεῖν αὐτὸν εἰς τὸ ὄρος προσεύξασθαι, καὶ ἦν διανυκτερεύων ἐν τῇ προσευχῇ τοῦ θεοῦ). Jesus spends time in intense prayer before singling out the Twelve from among his followers as his disciples. He prays regularly (5:16), but Luke highlights his prayer before important events as an example to his readers (see 9:28; 22:39 – 46). Bovon notes that he does not pray "for secular goods but for the unfolding plan of salvation by means of obedient faith in response to the revealed Word of God."[6] He does not pray for the magical conversion of the people but recognizes that reaching Israel will require new leadership for Israel and a lengthy mission.

The phrase "in prayer with God" (ἐν τῇ προσευχῇ τοῦ θεοῦ, lit., "in the prayer of God") is an objective genitive and implies that Jesus "speaks to God not for the sake of talking but to listen."[7] As the people come to listen to him, he listens to

6. Bovon, *Luke 1:1 – 9:50*, 208.   7. Ibid., 209.

God, and tying his choice of the Twelve to prayer means that this decision has a "divine impetus" and purpose.[8] They have not applied for the job.

6:13 When day came, he summoned his disciples and picked out twelve of them, whom he also named apostles (καὶ ὅτε ἐγένετο ἡμέρα, προσεφώνησεν τοὺς μαθητὰς αὐτοῦ, καὶ ἐκλεξάμενος ἀπ᾽ αὐτῶν δώδεκα, οὓς καὶ ἀποστόλους ὠνόμασεν). Luke does not explain why Jesus chooses these particular persons. The number "twelve" is what is significant because it anchors this choice in Israel's salvation history. It recalls how God ordered the community of Israel. As God gave Jacob twelve sons and ordered the community of Israel around the twelve tribes, so Jesus chooses twelve who will ultimately judge the twelve tribes of Israel (22:30).[9] Choosing "twelve" also "made visible to everyone His claim upon Israel, and He did so in such a way that it was evident that He did not merely claim a select group but the whole people in all its divisions."[10]

The term "apostles" (ἀποστόλους) is a functional one, referring not to an office but to their role as messengers who are sent with a commission and who will extend his ministry. In Acts, Peter becomes the "spearhead" of the mission. But in Luke the seventy-two are also sent out on mission to Israel (10:1 – 16), and Acts highlights the extension of the mission by others, such as Stephen, Philip, Paul, and Barnabas, who do not belong to the Twelve. For Luke, the key role of the Twelve is to serve as eyewitnesses (Acts 1:21 – 22; see 1 Cor 15:5). In Acts, they do not exercise any administrative authority, and Barrett argues, "They were important because they had accompanied Jesus during his ministry and thus served as a

guarantee — or perhaps a symbol — of the fact that the actions of the post-resurrection church were a valid continuation of the work of Jesus." This importance is unique and "cannot be transmitted to a succession."[11]

6:14 – 16 Simon, whom he named Peter, and Andrew, his brother, and James, and John, and Philip, and Bartholomew, and Matthew, and Thomas, and James, son of Alphaeus, and Simon, who is called the zealot, and Judas, son of James, and Judas Iscariot, who became a traitor (Σίμωνα ὃν καὶ ὠνόμασεν Πέτρον, καὶ Ἀνδρέαν τὸν ἀδελφὸν αὐτοῦ, καὶ Ἰάκωβον καὶ Ἰωάννην καὶ Φίλιππον καὶ Βαρθολομαῖον καὶ Μαθθαῖον καὶ Θωμᾶν καὶ Ἰάκωβον Ἀλφαίου καὶ Σίμωνα τὸν καλούμενον Ζηλωτὴν καὶ Ἰούδαν Ἰακώβου καὶ Ἰούδαν Ἰσκαριώθ, ὃς ἐγένετο προδότης). The list of disciples reappears in a different order in Acts 1:13 (e.g., John and Andrew switch the second and fourth places; see also the lists with different names in Matt 10:2 – 4; Mark 3:18). Peter always heads the lists, and Judas is always named last.

No explanation is given for renaming Simon as "Peter" (Πέτρον). At the end of the discourse, Jesus compares those who hear his words and do them to those who build a foundation on the "rock" (τὴν πέτραν, "bedrock," 6:48). The nickname becomes an enigmatic prediction of a solid future for Peter, though he will also have rocky moments when he fails.

James and John make cameo appearances in Luke as fishermen who left everything to follow Jesus (5:10 – 11), as witnesses of the restoration of the daughter of Jairus to life (8:51), as witnesses of the transfiguration (9:28), and as the militants who urge Jesus to call down fire on a disobliging

8. Green, *The Gospel of Luke*, 258.
9. See Num 1:1 – 19, 44, where God commands Moses to take a man from each tribe "to help you" (1:4) as representatives of "the heads of the clans of Israel" (1:16).

10. Karl Rengstorf, "δώδεκα," *TDNT*, 2:325.
11. C. K. Barrett, *Acts Volume II: XV-XXVIII* (ICC; Edinburgh: T&T Clark, 1998), xcv.

Samaritan town (9:54). In Acts, John joins Peter in the healing of the crippled beggar at the Beautiful Gate of the temple (Acts 3:1 – 11); he is arrested with Peter for speaking to the people and is hauled in to stand before the council, and they amaze the priestly hierarchy with their boldness despite their lack of learning (4:1 – 23).

Peter and John also team up to examine the converts in Samaria, laying hands on them to receive the Holy Spirit and preaching to them (Acts 8:14 – 25). John has no separate speaking part in Acts, and after this last incident he drops out of the picture. His brother James's martyrdom at the hands of Herod Agrippa I is narrated briefly in Acts 12:1 – 3. Luke gives no reason why Herod would take such murderous action except to say that "it met with approval among the Jews." We can only guess what James was doing to fan the flames of this opposition.

Matthew's name appears in all four lists of the Twelve. In Matt 9:9, "Matthew" is summoned from his toll booth, and he is specifically identified as "the tax collector" (Matt 10:3). In Mark 2:14 and Luke 5:27, the tax collector whom Jesus calls to follow him is named Levi. One explanation for the variation in names is that this toll collector may have been known by two names, Levi and Matthew, in the same way that Simon Peter is identified as Simon or Peter (Cephas). Another possibility is that Mark identifies Levi the tax collector as "the son of Alphaeus" (Mark 2:14), and the "James" who appears in all four lists is also identified as the son of Alphaeus, presumably to distinguish him from James the son of Zebedee. Could it be that James and Levi were two names for the same person or that they were brothers?[12]

The description of another Simon as "the zealot" probably means that he was "zealous" in a religious sense and not a subversive provocateur against Rome.[13] Josephus had not yet written his history of the Jewish war against Rome that identified "the zealots" as a revolutionary party (the "fourth philosophy") responsible for starting the insurrection against Rome. Luke does not identify Theudas and Judas, who led uprisings (Acts 5:36 – 37), as "zealots," but he does use the adjective to describe those zealous for the law (Acts 21:20; 22:3; cf. Rom 10:2; Gal 1:14).

The other disciples, except for Judas, receive no other notice. The Greek names (Philip, Andrew) reveal how hellenized Palestine had become, and they are striking beside the names of Jewish patriarchs and Maccabean military heroes (Simon, Jacob [James]). Andrew has a role in the Fourth Gospel for bringing his brother Simon to Jesus (John 1:35 – 42), and Philip's call and his reaching out to Nathanael is also narrated (John 1:43 – 51; see also 6:5; 12:20 – 22; 14:8). Some identify the Bartholomew, which means "son of Thalmai," in this list with the Nathaniel in John. Bartholomew would be a patronymic and Nathanael would be his given name, and this would explain why an important figure in John was not mentioned in the Synoptic Gospels and why his name appears after Philip's in the different lists. Thomas, identified as the "twin" (John 11:16; 20:24; 21:2), is infamous for articulating doubt about the resurrection (20:24 – 29). What we know about the other disciples derives from later traditions.

Judas Iscariot's future role as the betrayer is the first hint of the passion in the gospel. What "Iscariot' means has prompted numerous proposals. Most assume that it means "man of Kerioth," which would make him come from possibly Judea

---

12. Some ancient texts (D, Θ, 565, f¹³ [except 346], Tatian) solve the discrepancy by reading the name of James instead of Levi in Mark 2:14.

13. Christophe Mézange, "Simon le Zélote était-il un revolutionaire?" *Bib* 81 (2000): 489 – 506.

or Idumea and not from Galilee. Others have connected it to the Latin name for the dagger (*sicarius*) and the moniker of the Jewish assassins before the war. Also it has been connected to Aramaic for the "false one," "the man of Issachar," the man from Sychar, redhead, purse-bearer, and dyer. Variations in ancient transliterations make this issue almost impossible to solve.

6:17 – 19 When he came down with them, he stood upon a level place, and a large crowd of his disciples [were there] with a large multitude of the people from all Judea and Jerusalem and as far away as the seacoast of Tyre and Sidon. They came to hear him and to be healed of their illnesses, and those unhinged by unclean spirits were healed. The crowd was seeking to touch him for power was coming from him and he healed them all (καὶ καταβὰς μετ' αὐτῶν ἔστη ἐπὶ τόπου πεδινοῦ, καὶ ὄχλος πολὺς μαθητῶν αὐτοῦ, καὶ πλῆθος πολὺ τοῦ λαοῦ ἀπὸ πάσης τῆς Ἰουδαίας καὶ Ἰερουσαλὴμ καὶ τῆς παραλίου Τύρου καὶ Σιδῶνος. οἳ ἦλθον ἀκοῦσαι αὐτοῦ καὶ ἰαθῆναι ἀπὸ τῶν νόσων αὐτῶν· καὶ οἱ ἐνοχλούμενοι ἀπὸ πνευμάτων ἀκαθάρτων ἐθεραπεύοντο, καὶ πᾶς ὁ ὄχλος ἐζήτουν ἅπτεσθαι αὐτοῦ, ὅτι δύναμις παρ' αὐτοῦ ἐξήρχετο καὶ ἰᾶτο πάντας). Jesus descends with the disciples to "a level place." The mountain is a place of prayer and retreat. The level ground, where the people are, is the place of teaching.[14] The audience consists of the uncommitted and those fully committed. The crowds hail from the areas where Jesus will send out his witnesses (Acts 1:8), but the specific mention of "Tyre and Sidon" is surprising. The Old Testament deems this land to be a wealthy and godless oppressor of Israel (see Isa 23; Jer 47:4; Ezek 26 – 28; Joel 3:4; Amos 1:9 – 10; Zech 9:2 – 4). Josephus calls them "our bitterest enemies" (*Ag.*

Ap. 1 §70). Their presence sets the tone for Jesus' demand that his disciples love their enemies.

Like the men who brought their paralytic friend to Jesus to be healed only to hear a surprising announcement of the forgiveness of sins, the crowds come for one thing and receive far more. They come for physical healing and are given it, but then they are given teaching that will heal their lives and those of others around them.

Jesus does not impart secret teaching behind closed doors but out in the open — plain speech in plain view on the plain. If one wants to become a disciple and call him Lord, this is what is required. Before the demands that come in his teaching, Jesus exhibits God's grace and power by healing all without discrimination. He combines deed and word.

6:20 He raised his eyes toward his disciples and began to say, "Blessed are the poor, because yours is the reign of God" (καὶ αὐτὸς ἐπάρας τοὺς ὀφθαλμοὺς αὐτοῦ εἰς τοὺς μαθητὰς αὐτοῦ ἔλεγεν· Μακάριοι οἱ πτωχοί, ὅτι ὑμετέρα ἐστὶν ἡ βασιλεία τοῦ θεοῦ). The audience consists of the twelve apostles, the wider group of disciples, and the crowds, but the beatitudes that follow are aimed at disciples. The disciples do not fall into the category of the rich, to whom the woes are directed, so the audience extends beyond them.[15]

"Blessed" (μακάριοι) was a familiar ascription in the Greek world that was usually ascribed to those who had the things that were judged to make for earthly happiness. The emphasis was on worldly well-being. Beatitudes that appear in intertestamental literature reflect a change of focus from how to be happy in this life to how to be happy in the life to come. Jesus' beatitudes, combined with the woes, assume that happiness has nothing to do with one's external circumstances

14. Craddock, *Luke*, 86.

15. See Tannehill, *Unity of Luke-Acts*, 207 – 8.

in this present evil age but is to be found only in the sphere of God. Jesus addresses those in distress, whose present and future seem hopeless. The emphasis falls more on assurance that God sees their plight and will intervene to bring consolation rather than on ethical exhortation — be poor, be hungry, weep, be persecuted.

These beatitudes, so at odds with conventional wisdom, raise the questions: What is reality? Who is really well-off? Who is a good person? They challenge a perspective that thinks we are what we have accomplished or have accumulated. Jesus' beatitudes challenge conventional wisdom regarding political power and wealth. The world values the winners, but Jesus pronounces the losers, the marginal in Galilee, as blessed because God is "for them, not against them."[16] The beatitudes imply that their blessedness applies to the present, not to some distant future. The poor, deprived of the basic necessities of life, had little to be happy about in this world, but the arrival of God's reign in the person of Jesus heralds a change.

Jesus' first recorded sermon opens with the announcement of good news for the poor (4:17 – 19) because God is the God of the poor (1:46 – 55; see Pss 68:5; 109:31; 140:12; Isa 41:17). Matthew's parallel beatitude has "poor in spirit" (Matt 5:3). In Jesus' context, the poor are not simply those who are despoiled and in need, but the term can also apply to the humble pious who are beloved by God (Isa 61:1 – 2). Luke, however, does not spiritualize the meaning of poor to refer to the humble pious. They are the economically poor.

This was a broad category of people. MacMullen observes that a large percentage of the people in the Roman Empire would not have "lived their lives without at least once wondering where their next meal was coming from."[17] Two individuals are described as "poor" in Luke: Lazarus, who died from hunger and sores at the rich man's gate (16:20 – 22), and the widow who had only two mites to her name (21:2 – 3). The "poor" are those who are in desperate need of alms (18:22; 19:8).

Poverty is not blessed in itself, but the poor's extreme vulnerability may make them more likely than the rich to place their lives in the hands of God and respond to Jesus' preaching and healing. But even the poor can succumb to the tyranny of possessions. The possessive pronoun "yours," however, makes clear that Jesus addresses this beatitude to a particular audience and is not referring to the poor in the entire world. As those who are crushed and destitute, they developed an attitude of total dependence on God, like the poor widow (21:2 – 3). They can be happy because they trust that God is on their side, that they belong to God, and that God will act on their behalf to bring justice. But both John's and Jesus' teaching make it clear that those who repent and submit to God's reign will share their worldly goods to alleviate the suffering of the poor in this life.[18] Pronouncing the poor blessed, therefore, becomes an exhortation to those who have the means to help them.

6:21 Blessed are those who hunger now, because they will be filled. Blessed are those who weep now, because they will laugh (μακάριοι οἱ πεινῶντες νῦν, ὅτι χορτασθήσεσθε. μακάριοι οἱ κλαίοντες νῦν, ὅτι γελάσετε). The hungry and those beset by grief are subgroups of the poor. The adverb "now" (νῦν) indicates that their plight is in the present from the current oppression. The specter of hunger stalked many who lived in Jesus' day. The passive voice of "will be filled" is a divine

---

16. Danker, *Jesus and the New Age*, 138.

17. Ramsay MacMullen, *Enemies of the Roman Order: Treason, Unrest, and Alienation in the Empire* (Cambridge, MA: Harvard Univ. Press, 1967), 249.

18. L. John Topel, *Children of a Compassionate God: A Theological Exegesis of Luke 6:20 – 49* (Collegeville, MN: Liturgical, 2001), 85.

passive: God will fill them. Fitzmyer states that the consolation offered to the hungry alludes to the eschatological banquet that appears in Old Testament texts such as Pss 107:3–9; 132:15; 146:7; Isa 55:1–2 (see also Isa 25:6; Luke 22:18). A foretaste of what is to come occurs in the feeding of the five thousand (Luke 9:11–17). The conclusion to the parable of the rich man and Lazarus (16:21) reveals that this promise may not be fulfilled literally in this life, but that is no excuse for anyone to leave another hungry.

6:22–23 Blessed are you when people will hate you, ostracize you, revile you, and defame your name as evil on account of the Son of Man. Rejoice in that day and jump for joy, for behold, your reward [will be] great in heaven. Their fathers were doing the same things to the prophets (μακάριοί ἐστε ὅταν μισήσωσιν ὑμᾶς οἱ ἄνθρωποι καὶ ὅταν ἀφορίσωσιν ὑμᾶς καὶ ὀνειδίσωσιν καὶ ἐκβάλωσιν τὸ ὄνομα ὑμῶν ὡς πονηρὸν ἕνεκα τοῦ υἱοῦ τοῦ ἀνθρώπου. χάρητε ἐν ἐκείνῃ τῇ ἡμέρᾳ καὶ σκιρτήσατε, ἰδοὺ γὰρ ὁ μισθὸς ὑμῶν πολὺς ἐν τῷ οὐρανῷ· κατὰ τὰ αὐτὰ γὰρ ἐποίουν τοῖς προφήταις οἱ πατέρες αὐτῶν). The fourth beatitude marks a shift. It expands to four verbs to describe the present and includes a lengthier conclusion with two imperatives. The state of blessedness is tied to a close relationship to the Son of Man despite social ostracism. Those following the one who suffered and died are themselves experiencing oppression because of their faithfulness and association with him (see 1 Pet 4:12–14). "Your name" (τὸ ὄνομα ὑμῶν) is singular, suggesting that it does not refer to their personal names but to the name they bear as followers of Christ. Acts reports that they were first called "Christians" in Antioch (Acts 11:26; see 26:28). It was a derogatory term used to deride them as Christ lackeys (Jas 2:7; 1 Pet 4:14).

The disciple is no different from the teacher, and this rejection confirms "one's identification with God's purpose."[19] This principle is not intended to motivate them to seek out rejection to receive a reward but rather to comfort them. The present suffering comes because of "devotion to Christ, the happiness to come is bound up with this decision for Christ."[20] Paul applies Ps 69:9 to Christ: "The insults of those who insult you have fallen on me" (Rom 15:3). Whatever reproach one might suffer for being a follower of Christ in this world has already been borne by him. His crucifixion and resurrection bear away the shame. The promise of reward remains in heaven, but the joy of anticipation can be experienced now on earth (see 1:41, 44).

6:24 But woe to you who are rich, because you have cashed in on your consolation (πλὴν οὐαὶ ὑμῖν τοῖς πλουσίοις, ὅτι ἀπέχετε τὴν παράκλησιν ὑμῶν). Good news to the poor can mean bad news for the rich. Concern for the poor went hand in hand with opposition to those in the halls of power who trampled them down. These woes are not addressed to disciples but to the crowd from Judea, Jerusalem, Tyre, and Sidon, who came to be healed of their diseases and unclean spirits (6:17–18). In Luke's own context, however, wealthy Christians who were members of the community must also heed these threats.

The beatitudes combined with woes emphasize a reversal of circumstances that will occur in God's future. The woe form that appears here is not a malediction such as comes against the Galilean cities of Chorazin and Bethsaida, which stubbornly refused to respond to Jesus' mighty works (10:13–14). Instead, it is "an expression of pity for those who stand under divine judgment."[21] These woes pertain to any to whom these circumstances

19. Green, _The Gospel of Luke_, 268.
20. Bovon, _Luke 1:1–9:50_, 228, n. 56.
21. Marshall, _The Gospel of Luke_, 255.

apply: the rich, the full, the content, and the ex-tolled, which are four separate descriptions of the same group.

What most consider advantages in life and something to aim for turn out to be disadvantages that can lead to exclusion from the reign of God. The rich are not urged here to share with the poor to alleviate their hunger and pain. Jesus simply pronounces woes on them. They have to infer for themselves what they should do to extricate them-selves from their predicament, but more direct in-structions appear elsewhere in Luke.

The parables of the rich fool (12:13 – 21) and of the rich man and Lazarus (16:19 – 31) illustrate why the rich will be judged. They find security in their riches (12:13 – 21), selfishly serve themselves to perpetuate their status, and neglect or trample the poor (Jas 2:6 – 7). They have all the consola-tion they can ever hope to receive. The rich live under the awful burden of their riches. The ulti-mate question for them is whether they will share or sacrifice their comfort to bring consolation to others. Tiede presumes, "Luke's own commu-nity probably included some people of sufficient means and prosperity and illustrious reputation so that these words were understood as warnings to insiders."[22]

6:25 – 26 Woe to you who are full now, because you will go hungry. Woe to you who laugh now, because you will mourn and weep. Woe to you when all speak well of you, for their fa-thers were doing the same things to the false prophets (οὐαὶ ὑμῖν, οἱ ἐμπεπλησμένοι νῦν, ὅτι πεινάσετε. οὐαί, οἱ γελῶντες νῦν, ὅτι πενθήσετε καὶ κλαύσετε. οὐαὶ ὅταν ὑμᾶς καλῶς εἴπωσιν

πάντες οἱ ἄνθρωποι, κατὰ τὰ αὐτὰ γὰρ ἐποίουν τοῖς ψευδοπροφήταις οἱ πατέρες αὐτῶν). Disci-ples are not deliberately to seek a bad reputation; the abuse that comes to them is the natural result of society's hardened opposition to God. The real problem with others speaking well of them is that they are "attracting flattery toward themselves" rather than directing praise toward God (see Matt 5:16).[23]

Danker adds a biting contemporary applica-tion: "They operate under the guise of established tradition and are highly respected in their reli-gious communities for maintaining the status quo. They make no waves and rock no boats."[24] They may gain popularity by claiming to be God's mouthpieces, but they speak only what people want to hear so as to further their own careers (see Jer 5:12 – 13; 6:13 – 15; Mic 2:11).

6:27 But I say to you who are listening: Love your enemies and do good to those who hate you (ἀλλὰ ὑμῖν λέγω τοῖς ἀκούουσιν· ἀγαπᾶτε τοὺς ἐχθροὺς ὑμῶν, καλῶς ποιεῖτε τοῖς μισοῦσιν ὑμᾶς). The crowds came to listen to him (6:18). Whether they truly listen will be determined by their obedi-ence (7:1). Addressing these commands to all who listen means that this teaching is not only instruc-tion on what is obligatory for disciples but an "in-vitation and challenge to those who might become disciples."[25]

"Love" (ἀγαπᾶτε) is further defined as "do[ing] good" (cf. Matt 5:44). Bovon explains that it "is an explanatory paraphrase for Greek listeners, who did not understand the originally Semitic idiom."[26] This assertion may seem strange, but the verb ἀγαπάω was a neutral one that received its

22. David L. Tiede, "Luke 6:17 – 26: Things Are Not as They Seem," *Int* 40 (1986): 67.

23. Hans Dieter Betz, *The Sermon on the Mount: A Com-mentary on the Sermon on the Mount, including the Sermon on the Plain (Matthew 5:3 – 7:27 and Luke 6:20 – 49)* (Hermeneia;

Minneapolis: Fortress, 1995), 589.

24. Danker, *Jesus and the New Age*, 143.

25. Tannehill, *Unity of Luke-Acts*, 207.

26. Bovon, *Luke 1:1 – 9:50*, 236 – 37.

meaning from its usage in a context. Its choice in the LXX as the translation for אהב (*'hb*) was wise and gave it new meaning.[27] Since "love" is something commanded, it has little to do with a feeling or emotion. It is action, "doing good": "If you come across your enemy's ox or donkey wandering off, be sure to return it" (Exod 23:4); "If your enemy is hungry, give him food to eat; if he is thirsty, give him water to drink" (Prov 25:21).

Jesus defines what he means by love in the concrete examples that follow. This is what it does and does not do. It does not count the cost or calculate the reward. The "enemies" are "not limited to certain category of enemies."[28] It applies to enemies of all stripes — personal, religious, and political. Love is unselfish, hopeful that the enemies will change and not resentful if they do not.

6:28 Bless those who curse you; pray for those who abuse you (εὐλογεῖτε τοὺς καταρωμένους ὑμᾶς, προσεύχεσθε περὶ τῶν ἐπηρεαζόντων ὑμᾶς). Those who curse want to bring misfortune, evil, and doom on others; in a religious context, they want them to be accursed by God (see Matt 25:41). It usually evokes a countercurse. To bless means that one asks God to confer physical and spiritual well-being on another (see Rom 12:14; Jas 3:9). Retaliation is ruled out. Graphic examples of those praying for those who abuse them (verbally and physically) are found in 23:34 and Acts 7:60 (Luke 13:34; 19:41; 1 Pet 3:16). "To bless" (εὐλογεῖτε) and "to pray" (προσεύχεσθε) are plural

verbs and may refer not only to private intercession but also to corporate worship. Reacting to earthly abuse in this way is grounded in the recognition that no one in Christ can ever be truly accursed.

6:29 To the one who strikes you on the cheek offer him the other, and from the one who takes your cloak do not hold back your shirt (τῷ τύπτοντί σε ἐπὶ τὴν σιαγόνα πάρεχε καὶ τὴν ἄλλην, καὶ ἀπὸ τοῦ αἴροντός σου τὸ ἱμάτιον καὶ τὸν χιτῶνα μὴ κωλύσῃς). The detail of being struck on the *right* cheek included in Matt 5:39, which implies the insulting violence of a backhanded slap in the face, is omitted by Luke.[29] Nevertheless, the blow is intended to cheapen another (see 22:63 – 64; Acts 23:2 – 5). According to Tacitus (*Ann.* 4.3), Sejanus destroyed Drusus because the latter had once slapped him on the face. Barton asserts, "Turning the other cheek requires the aggressor to acknowledge you as a man, to credit you with dignity, capable of playing the game of honor and playing it well. The challenge confers honor."[30]

The "cloak" is a robe; the "shirt" is worn next to the skin. The parallel saying in Matt 5:40 contains an allusion to the Jewish law related to taking a cloak in pledge (Exod 22:25 – 27; Deut 24:10 – 13).[31] It is absent from Luke's version, probably because his Hellenistic readers did not understand this background. The order of the clothing taken is also reversed from that in Matt 5:40. Luke's saying therefore envisions one who is a victim of banditry. The robber first takes the outer garment.[32] The

---

27. Bovon (ibid., 236) notes that the verb "to treasure" (στέργω) seemed too emotional, "to love" (φιλέω) was confined to a group of friends, and another verb "to love" (ἐράω) was related to "irrational and passionate love." Luke's Greek readers who were unfamiliar with the LXX would need further explanation of what the verb meant, "to do good."

28. Wolfgang Schrage, *The Ethics of the New Testament* (trans. David Green; Philadelphia: Fortress, 1988), 76.

29. Such a calculated indignity is considered to be at least four times as injurious in a Mishnaic discussion on indemnities

for violence (*m. B. Qam.* 8:6), reflecting the values of an honor/shame society.

30. Carlin A. Barton, *Roman Honor: The Fire in the Bones* (Berkeley: Univ. of California Press, 2001), 86.

31. The law forbids a plaintiff from claiming the cloak that covered one's nakedness and kept the poor warm in the cool of the night.

32. In a contemporary, urban context, it would be akin to someone being robbed of expensive athletic shoes and giving the mugger the socks as well.

command becomes an example of how to respond to this violence and fits the context of traveling missionaries (see 2 Cor 11:26). Betz comments, "If the robber proves to be 'generous,' in that he is only after the victim's overcoat, he is outdone by the ever greater generosity of the victim."[33] It turns an act of violence intended to do harm into an act of charity intended to do good. The victim is thereby empowered.

6:30 Give to everyone who asks of you, and do not demand your possessions back from the one who takes them (παντὶ αἰτοῦντί σε δίδου, καὶ ἀπὸ τοῦ αἴροντος τὰ σὰ μὴ ἀπαίτει). In both the Jewish and Greco-Roman contexts, poverty was a constant, and many could survive only if others helped in a time a crisis. The benefactor became a patron and the recipient became a client who had to reciprocate in some way. Many were overwhelmed by the whirlpool of debt. Showing sympathy for poor "was alien to Greco-Roman ways of thinking, as was the notion of private or public assistance to the disadvantaged."[34]

A social *quid pro quo* ("one thing in return for another") governed all gift giving (see Seneca, *On Benefits* 5.11.5; *Epistles* 81.23). Anyone who received a gift was obligated to respond in kind. "I give so that you give" (*do ut des*) was the basic rule directing relationships. Consequently, benefactors gave to those deemed worthy to receive a gift and who could reciprocate. Those who outgave the other gained status as the superior while the other moved down a rung in the status ladder. Gifts were always business deals used to cement friendships among social equals or to gain or assert power over social inferiors. The benefactor became the patron and the recipient the client who must reciprocate through service or public praise.

Jesus' command about giving would have struck the listeners as bizarre. He makes no mention about the worthiness of the recipient and effectively erases the social distinctions between the giver and receiver. To Jesus, the true benefactor is a patron who gives without expecting any return from the one who receives. The benefactor will be repaid by a third party, who is an even greater benefactor as the source of all gifts, God. The early Christian community lived this ethic out (Acts 2:44 – 45; 4:32, 34 – 35), essentially becoming "fools for Christ" (1 Cor 4:10) from the perspective of the world's value system.

6:31 And just as you want persons to do to you, do likewise to them (καὶ καθὼς θέλετε ἵνα ποιῶσιν ὑμῖν οἱ ἄνθρωποι ποιεῖτε αὐτοῖς ὁμοίως). Crosby notes that Jesus challenges the conventional wisdom about reciprocity that governed most relationships. "Negative reciprocity" means "doing to others what one would *not* want done to one's self." Jesus rejects this entirely for his disciples. "Balanced reciprocity" means doing to others what they do to one's self, returning good for good. "General reciprocity" means doing good to all regardless of what they have done to one's self "because all are to be part of God's household."[35] The negative form of the so-called Golden Rule ("what you hate, do not do to anyone") can be found in Tob 4:15 and *b. Šabb.* 31a.[36] Danker contends, however, that this version permits "the priest and the Levite to pass by the wounded man (Luke 10:25 – 37)" and the rich man to ignore Lazarus.[37]

33. Betz, *The Sermon on the Mount*, 597.

34. Mary Ann Beavis, "'Expecting Nothing in Return': Luke's Picture of the Marginalized," *Int* 48 (1994): 363.

35. Michael H. Crosby, *House of Disciples: Church, Econom-*

ics and Justice in Matthew (Maryknoll, NY: Orbis, 1988), 184.

36. See further examples from Jewish and Greco-Roman traditions in Bock, *Luke*, 1:596 – 97.

37. Danker, *Jesus and the New Age*, 146.

6:32–33 If you love those who love you, what credit is that to you? For even the sinners love those who love them. And if you do good to those who do good to you, what credit is that to you? For even the sinners do the same (καὶ εἰ ἀγαπᾶτε τοὺς ἀγαπῶντας ὑμᾶς, ποία ὑμῖν χάρις ἐστίν; καὶ γὰρ οἱ ἁμαρτωλοὶ τοὺς ἀγαπῶντας αὐτοὺς ἀγαπῶσιν. καὶ [γὰρ] ἐὰν ἀγαθοποιῆτε τοὺς ἀγαθοποιοῦντας ὑμᾶς, ποία ὑμῖν χάρις ἐστίν; καὶ οἱ ἁμαρτωλοὶ τὸ αὐτὸ ποιοῦσιν). Three sayings challenge the norm of loving, doing good, or paying back only those who will do so in return. According to Matthew's version of these sayings, this is what the "tax collectors" and "the pagans" do (Matt 5:46–47). Luke chooses a less culturally specific term, "sinners," that his readers would know. Every age can identify persons who fall into the category of sinner, but "sinners" are surprisingly redefined as those who operate on the basis of *quid pro quo*. The problem is that this kind of behavior that acts only out of some ulterior motive always expects some return, pays off obligations to some while ignoring the needs of others, and creates closed groups.

The noun translated "credit" (χάρις) is normally translated "grace." Spicq writes, "Any gift, present, pardon, or concession that is granted freely, out of one's goodness, is called a *charis*."[38] None of these actions stems from one's goodness and do not qualify as "grace." Also, it only establishes "credit" with people as a business deal and "not with God."[39] Jesus expects disciples to be "gracious" at every level of life.

6:34 For if you lend to those who you hope will pay you back, what credit is that to you? Even the sinners loan to sinners so that they get back the same amount (καὶ ἐὰν δανίσητε παρ᾽ ὧν ἐλπίζετε λαβεῖν, ποία ὑμῖν χάρις [ἐστίν]; καὶ ἁμαρτωλοὶ ἁμαρτωλοῖς δανίζουσιν ἵνα ἀπολάβωσιν τὰ ἴσα). Most people loan money to get back more in return, not the same amount. It is possible that Jesus, ingrained in the scriptural prohibition of charging interest (Deut 23:19–20), takes for granted that one can expect only the same sum in return. It is also possible that the "same amount" includes any accrued interest. The amount received in return, however, is irrelevant. Jesus rejects the principle of reciprocity that underlies the lending. Benefactors normally gave to those deemed worthy to receive and with the means to pay back. Disciples will lend with no expectation of receiving *anything* back (6:35).

6:35 But love your enemies, do good [to them], and lend [money] expecting nothing back and your reward will be great, and you will be sons of the Most High because he is kind to the ungrateful and selfish (πλὴν ἀγαπᾶτε τοὺς ἐχθροὺς ὑμῶν καὶ ἀγαθοποιεῖτε καὶ δανείζετε μηδὲν ἀπελπίζοντες· καὶ ἔσται ὁ μισθὸς ὑμῶν πολύς, καὶ ἔσεσθε υἱοὶ ὑψίστου, ὅτι αὐτὸς χρηστός ἐστιν ἐπὶ τοὺς ἀχαρίστους καὶ πονηρούς). The command to love one's enemies is reiterated (v. 27) because it is the basis of every other command in this section and is what distinguishes disciples from "sinners." Sinners return enmity for enmity. Disciples of Christ are to return love for enmity.

The phrase "expecting nothing back" (μηδὲν ἀπελπίζοντες) translates a verb that means "to lose hope" — "hoping nothing from it." A textual variant reads "no one" (μηδένα), which can mean "disappointing no one" or "despairing of no one."[40] Bovon renders it, "in no way doubting."

---

38. Ceslas Spicq, "χάρις," *TLNT*, 3:503.

39. Betz, *The Sermon on the Mount*, 601.

40. The alpha between the two words (μηδὲν[α] ἀπελπίζοντες) could have been omitted (haplography) or added (dittography). Betz (*The Sermon on the Mount*, 604–5) argues that the problem "seems insoluble on merely textual or lexicographical grounds."

He interprets it to refer to not having any doubts about "the future of the person thus supported."[41] Most people lend on the basis of their judgment about the person's future prospects. In a culture where most lived on the margins and were one bad harvest away from total ruin, for a relatively poor person to lend to another could be risky. The question, "Will they lose what I have lent?" would have been uppermost in most lenders' minds.

It is unlikely that Jesus addresses wealthy creditors in Palestine. With their surplus, the rich were glad to lend out money because failure to pay off the debt could lead to the debtor becoming a debt slave (Matt 18:25) or, more usually, the loss of his land (see Neh 5:1 – 5). Wresting land from the peasants through their failure to pay debt was one of the ways that the rich became richer and the poor became poorer and resulted in a marked increase in large holdings during the time of Roman control of Palestine.[42]

Jesus envisions that his disciples will live out of egalitarian principles and lend with no strings attached and with no intention of capitalizing on another's need. Mutual assistance was one way to forestall the "avalanche of defaults through indebtedness" to rich predators. Nevertheless, the command applies to all. Expecting nothing in return changes a loan into a gift, and then it becomes an act of grace (χάρις).[43] When it comes to money, Jesus commands that one should use it to serve the needs of others and not for one's own material self-interest.

The "ungrateful and selfish" (τοὺς ἀχαρίστους καὶ πονηρούς [lit., "evil"]) is a common combination in Stoic texts. In this context it implies that a lack of gratitude toward God is evinced by a lack of gratitude toward others, which leads to the evils of selfishness and ruthlessness (see Matt 18:23 – 35).

"Sons of the Most High" (υἱοὶ ὑψίστου) preserves the Semitic idiom. The one who reproduces or expresses in his own way of life that of another is called a "son of" that one. A person's character is revealed in what is produced: "father of lies" (John 8:44), "mother of prostitutes" (Rev 17:5). A person's actions betray his or her origins (lit. trans.): "sons of this age" (Luke 16:8; 20:34); "[sons] of those who murdered the prophets" (Matt 23:31); "[sons] of light" (John 12:36; 1 Thess 5:5); "[sons] of Abraham" (Gal 3:7). Since God acts with grace toward those who do not deserve it, those who do likewise are "chips off the old block," so to speak, and will bear witness to God in the midst of a crooked and perverse generation (Phil 2:15).

Jesus overturns the normal way of relating to others through negative or balanced reciprocity. If there is to be any reciprocity in one's relationships, it is to be reciprocity with God. Relationships with others are not to be understood as bipolar but as always involving God. They are triangular. Jesus applies the principle that one who receives a benefit must return it in some form and the one who gives a benefit rightfully expects some return to our relationship to God. In this case, since God can never be repaid, it requires that we deal with others the way God has dealt with us. Giving to others and treating them graciously is praiseworthy behavior that imitates God, and God will reward it (see 14:13 – 14).

6:36 Be merciful just as your Father is merciful
(γίνεσθε οἰκτίρμονες καθὼς [καὶ] ὁ πατὴρ ὑμῶν οἰκτίρμων ἐστίν). Mercy is the inward disposition that leads one to spare or to help another. It is not simply an inward sentiment but an action. Mercy

---

41. Bovon, *Luke 1:1 – 9:50*, 238.

42. See Richard A. Horsley, *Jesus and the Spiral of Violence* (San Francisco: Harper & Row, 1987), 11 – 15.

43. Betz, *The Sermon on the Mount*, 605 – 6.

or compassion reflects Israel's earliest experience of God and was assumed to be one of God's essential characteristics (Exod 20:6; 33:19; 34:6 – 7; Ps 103:13; Mic 7:18, 20). God's mercy knows no bounds. As God is bound by the covenant of mercy with his people (Deut 30:3), so the people are bound to act mercifully to the oppressed, alien, orphan, and widow.

6:37 And do not judge, and you will certainly not be judged. Do not condemn, and you will certainly not be condemned. Pardon, and you will be pardoned (καὶ μὴ κρίνετε, καὶ οὐ μὴ κριθῆτε· καὶ μὴ καταδικάζετε, καὶ οὐ μὴ καταδικασθῆτε. ἀπολύετε, καὶ ἀπολυθήσεσθε). The present imperative (μὴ κρίνετε) may mean "stop judging," "stop condemning." It does not mean that Jesus expects us to suspend the faculty of judgment and never find fault with others. It refers to "condemnatory judgment."[44] It is a teaching device to hook the listeners' attention, since it is an everyday, taken-for-granted activity of most people. Only after reading the entire passage does it become clear what Jesus means.

Nor does Jesus mean that if we overlook the sins of others, God will do likewise with us. Craddock rightly notes that "without justice and fairness, grace degenerates into permissiveness, just as justice without grace hardens into cruelty."[45] The figure of the speck and the log (vv. 41 – 42) clarifies that he does not expect his followers to do away with discernment. He warns them not to condemn others heedlessly. The fault is judging others without *first* judging oneself using the same measuring stick. The order is judge yourself first, then you can move to help, rather than judge, another. Harsh judgment obstructs mercy (Jas 2:13) and destroys relationships.

6:38 "Give, and it will be given to you, a good measure, pressed down, shaken together, and overflowing — they will give it in your lap. For the measure you give will be the measure you get back" (δίδοτε, καὶ δοθήσεται ὑμῖν· μέτρον καλὸν πεπιεσμένον σεσαλευμένον ὑπερεκχυννόμενον δώσουσιν εἰς τὸν κόλπον ὑμῶν· ᾧ γὰρ μέτρῳ μετρεῖτε ἀντιμετρηθήσεται ὑμῖν). The concept of measure for measure was widespread in the ancient world and referred to fairness — an honest day's wage for an honest day's work. The "lap" refers to "the bosom of a garment," "the hollow formed by the upper forepart of a rather loose garment bound by a girdle, used for keeping and carrying things."[46]

The three passive participles present an image for a container filled with grain and refer to what God will repay. The third person plural "they will give" (δώσουσιν) refers to God (see 12:20, 48; 16:9), not humans. Those who imitate God's benevolence will receive even greater benevolence from God. This verse has nothing to do with receiving fabulous economic benefits on earth for being generous. Jesus does not encourage his disciples to give of their wealth in order to get more wealth. They give because their nature has been transformed.

6:39 He also told a parable to them: "Can a blind person guide the blind? Will they not both fall into a pit?" (εἶπεν δὲ καὶ παραβολὴν αὐτοῖς· μήτι δύναται τυφλὸς τυφλὸν ὁδηγεῖν; οὐχὶ ἀμφότεροι εἰς βόθυνον ἐμπεσοῦνται;). The term "parable" (παραβολή) applies to figurative speech and wisdom sayings. In the context, the blind guides refer to the scribes and Pharisees, who are blind to who Jesus is, what God is doing through him, and what their own faults are. They would be unable to lead someone like the Ethiopian eunuch to understand

44. Topel, *Children of a Compassionate God*, 184.
45. Craddock, *Luke*, 91.
46. Joseph Henry Thayer, *A Greek-English Lexicon of the*

New Testament (1889; repr. Grand Rapids, Zondervan, 1963), 354.

what he was reading from Isaiah (Acts 8:30 – 39). Disciples also may be blind — to the need to heed Jesus words, to the necessity of his suffering, to the reality of the resurrection (24:31) — and need to have their eyes opened.

The pit refers obviously to misfortune (Ps 7:15; Prov 22:14; 26:27; Eccl 10:8; Isa 24:18), but in a Jewish context it may refer to something far more serious, the pit of Sheol (Job 17:1, 13; Pss 16:10; 31:17; 141:7; Prov 1:12; Isa 38:18; Ezek 32:21 – 27). Blindness is associated with "the power of Satan" (Acts 26:17 – 18), and if those who live in darkness are led by the blind, they will perish (Rom 2:17 – 25).

In the immediate context, blindness must apply to ignoring Jesus' teaching on loving one's enemies, showing mercy, and withholding harmful judgment of others. If disciples who become leaders disregard this teaching (see 9:51 – 56), they will lead their charges to destruction since the pupil cannot tell if the teacher is blind.[47]

6:40 A disciple is not above the teacher; but everyone who is fully trained will be like the teacher (οὐκ ἔστιν μαθητὴς ὑπὲρ τὸν διδάσκαλον· κατηρτισμένος δὲ πᾶς ἔσται ὡς ὁ διδάσκαλος αὐτοῦ). As blind people cannot guide blind people, students do not know all that their teachers know and still have deficiencies in their education. It would be absurd for those in either situation to arrogate to themselves some sort of power over others. This prepares for the image of judging others that follows.

The verb "fully trained" (κατηρτισμένος) means "restored" (Gal 6:1; 1 Pet 5:10) or "perfectly united" (1 Cor 1:10). The term is used for mending

nets (Mark 1:19), and "Christian discipleship implies mending one's ways."[48] In the context of education, it refers to training and correction.[49] The training in the framework of the sermon has to do with reordering one's personal and spiritual life and how one relates to others. It will require continuous spiritual formation (see Phil 3:12 – 16).

The context also determines the referent for the "teacher." It is Jesus: "There is no authority besides Jesus, only the complete conformity with him establishes a teacher's authority in the community."[50] Bovon notes that one chooses a teacher to become like that teacher. For Luke,

> only the analogy with the ethical behavior of Jesus is important. But there is also no exemplary christology without a soteriological christology. To become like Jesus the teacher is possible only through the work of Christ and a relationship of faith with him. For this reason to become like him means to enter into service for those who suffer.[51]

6:41 – 42 Why do you look for the speck in your brother's eye but do not notice the wooden beam in your own eye? How are you able to say to your brother, "Brother, let me take out the speck that is in your eye," when you yourself do not see the wooden beam in your eye? Hypocrite, first take out the wooden beam from your own eye and then you will see clearly to take a speck from your brother's eye (τί δὲ βλέπεις τὸ κάρφος τὸ ἐν τῷ ὀφθαλμῷ τοῦ ἀδελφοῦ σου, τὴν δὲ δοκὸν τὴν ἐν τῷ ἰδίῳ ὀφθαλμῷ οὐ κατανοεῖς; πῶς δύνασαι λέγειν τῷ ἀδελφῷ σου· ἀδελφέ, ἄφες ἐκβάλω τὸ κάρφος τὸ ἐν τῷ ὀφθαλμῷ σου, αὐτὸς τὴν ἐν

47. Marshall, *The Gospel of Luke*, 269 – 70.
48. Ceslas Spicq, "καταρτίζω," *TLNT*, 2:274.
49. Betz, *The Sermon on the Mount*, 624 – 25.
50. Julius Wellhausen (*Das Evangelium Lucae* [Berlin: Reimer, 1904], 25, cited by Betz, *The Sermon on the Mount*, 624). Betz disagrees with this view and thinks it reflects a general maxim that corresponds roughly to "the modern distinction of

before and after graduation" (625). What follows in vv. 46 – 49, however, reveals that Luke would understand it christologically.
51. Bovon, *Luke 1:1 – 9:50*, 249. This is certainly how Paul understood his relationship to Christ as a teacher in the church (1 Cor 11:1; 4:6; 1 Thess 1:6).

τῷ ὀφθαλμῷ σοῦ δοκὸν οὐ βλέπων; ὑποκριτά, ἔκβαλε πρῶτον τὴν δοκὸν ἐκ τοῦ ὀφθαλμοῦ σοῦ, καὶ τότε διαβλέψεις τὸ κάρφος τὸ ἐν τῷ ὀφθαλμῷ τοῦ ἀδελφοῦ σου ἐκβαλεῖν).

This cartoon image pokes fun at those who seek to reform others when they are unreformed. The wooden beam is "the load-carrying beam in the room or floor of a house."[52] The disciples' first responsibility is to purify themselves and not to set themselves up as moral watchdogs over others (see Rom 2:1 – 3; Jas 5:9). Failure to come to terms with our own limitations and shortcomings warps our judgments of others. One first needs to do the logging on oneself before attending to another. Then one is able to recognize that the brother's sliver is just that, a sliver.

Also, the one who is to be corrected is identified three times as "your brother." Jesus assumes a communal bond. The expectation is that disciples, who are not blind to their own faults, deal with their brothers and sisters with the same love and hope that Jesus deals with them.[53] Persons should not expect to receive from God what they are not prepared to bestow on others.

The hypocrite is an inauthentic person, who, in this case, deceives himself more than he deceives others. The classic example of smugly judging others appears in the parable of the Pharisee and the tax collector (18:9 – 14). Caird labels it "pseudo-religion," which "is forever trying to make other people better; and the cure for it is a mirror."[54]

6:43 – 45 For a good tree does not bear worthless fruit, nor again does a worthless tree bear good fruit. For each tree is known from its fruit. For they do not gather figs from a thornbush, nor do they gather grapes from a briar patch. The good person produces good from the good treasure [stored] in the heart, and the evil produces evil from the evil [treasure stored in the heart]; for the mouth speaks what overflows from the heart (οὐ γάρ ἐστιν δένδρον καλὸν ποιοῦν καρπὸν σαπρόν, οὐδὲ πάλιν δένδρον σαπρὸν ποιοῦν καρπὸν καλόν. ἕκαστον γὰρ δένδρον ἐκ τοῦ ἰδίου καρποῦ γινώσκεται· οὐ γὰρ ἐξ ἀκανθῶν συλλέγουσιν σῦκα οὐδὲ ἐκ βάτου σταφυλὴν τρυγῶσιν. ὁ ἀγαθὸς ἄνθρωπος ἐκ τοῦ ἀγαθοῦ θησαυροῦ τῆς καρδίας προφέρει τὸ ἀγαθόν, καὶ ὁ πονηρὸς ἐκ τοῦ πονηροῦ προφέρει τὸ πονηρόν· ἐκ γὰρ περισσεύματος καρδίας λαλεῖ τὸ στόμα αὐτοῦ).

The metaphor of the good tree and the worthless tree leads to the point that the fruit a person bears grows out of his or her inner existence. From a vile heart comes villainy; from a good heart comes goodness. The assumption is that the mouth is a spigot from which flows what is hidden away in the heart (see Jas 3:1 – 18).[55] Speech reveals the person.

6:46 – 47 Why do you call me, "Lord, Lord," and do not do what I say? I will show you what this person is like who comes to me, hears my words, and does them (τί δέ με καλεῖτε· κύριε κύριε, καὶ οὐ ποιεῖτε ἃ λέγω; πᾶς ὁ ἐρχόμενος πρός με καὶ ἀκούων μου τῶν λόγων καὶ ποιῶν αὐτούς, ὑποδείξω ὑμῖν τίνι ἐστὶν ὅμοιος). The question and the parable that follows place an emphasis on obedience to Jesus' words. The great catch of fish experienced by Peter and his colleagues has already demonstrated the benefits of obedience to Jesus' word (5:1 – 11). Jesus now offers a warning

---

52. Topel, *Children of a Compassionate God*, 195.

53. Bovon, *Luke 1:1 – 9:50*, 250.

54. Caird, *Saint Luke*, 106.

55. Betz (*The Sermon on the Mount*, 630 – 35) shows that the New Testament "changed the language of its environment"

in talking about what it means to be a good human being. "The innermost life of a human being concerns the mortal heart rather than the immortal soul" (634), and that is revealed by one's words.

about disobedience. John had warned the people that the way to protect themselves from the coming inferno of judgment was to repent. Jesus now uses a different image, the conflagration caused by a flood. The only way to withstand it is to be obedient to his teaching. Simply calling him "Lord" will avail nothing (see 13:23 – 27). Token acknowledgment of Christ as Lord will not pass for radical obedience to his teaching.

6:48 – 49 This one is like a man who builds a house and excavates deeply and lays a foundation upon the bedrock. When floodwaters rise, the river bursts against that house, and it is not powerful enough to shake it [from its foundations] because it was built well. The one who hears and does not do [what I say] is like a man who builds a house without laying a foundation, and the river bursts against it, and immediately it falls in, and the collapse of that house is great (ὅμοιός ἐστιν ἀνθρώπῳ οἰκοδομοῦντι οἰκίαν ὃς ἔσκαψεν καὶ ἐβάθυνεν καὶ ἔθηκεν θεμέλιον ἐπὶ τὴν πέτραν· πλημμύρης δὲ γενομένης προσέρηξεν ὁ ποταμὸς τῇ οἰκίᾳ ἐκείνῃ, καὶ οὐκ ἴσχυσεν σαλεῦσαι αὐτὴν διὰ τὸ καλῶς οἰκοδομῆσθαι αὐτήν. ὁ δὲ ἀκούσας καὶ μὴ ποιήσας ὅμοιός ἐστιν ἀνθρώπῳ οἰκοδομήσαντι οἰκίαν ἐπὶ τὴν γῆν χωρὶς θεμελίου, ᾗ προσέρηξεν ὁ ποταμός, καὶ εὐθὺς συνέπεσεν καὶ ἐγένετο τὸ ῥῆγμα τῆς οἰκίας ἐκείνης μέγα). Jesus' sermon ends as it began (with the beatitudes and woes), with a contrast between two different types of persons. Those who call Jesus "Lord" (v. 46) are expected to heed his words (v. 48); otherwise, he is not truly their Lord. This truth is illustrated with an example of houses built on two different foundations and hit by a flood's destructive forces. It is impossible to schedule calamities; and when they come, those who ignore his teaching will be swept away because they are like the house with no solid foundation. The flood may refer to the "flood of mortal ills" that beset human life (see Job 22:11, 16; 27:13 – 23). But the image is also used for God's wrath and the judgment (Isa 8:7 – 8; 2 Pet 3:5 – 7).

The participles "coming" (ἐρχόμενος, v. 47), "hearing" (ἀκούων, v. 47), and "building a house" (οἰκοδομοῦντι) are in the present tense and suggest "the ongoing process of discipleship." The participles describing the failure in v. 49 are in the aorist tense and view the person's failure "as already accomplished."[56]

The issue is not where the house is built but how — whether one takes shortcuts or digs down to bedrock. The builder who is deceived by the appearance of solid ground takes no precautions. Schweizer notes that the value of the structure "lies in its foundation on the rock, not in its beauty, its turrets and terraces and swimming pools."[57] The image requires the hearer who comes to Jesus to take action, to lay a foundation, and not simply to be a passive listener.

56. Klyne Snodgrass, *Stories with Intent: A Comprehensive Guide to the Parables of Jesus* (Grand Rapids: Eerdmans, 2008), 332.

57. Eduard Schweizer, *Jesus, the Parable of God: What Do We Really Know about Jesus?* (Princeton Theological Monographs 37; Allison Park, PA: Pickwick, 1994), 42.

Theology in Application

1. The Disciple Register

What might the register of the disciples' names convey to readers? (1) Nothing in this list suggests that they have any special religious pedigree or qualifications. Danker comments:

> The innovativeness of Jesus in choosing a cast of totally nonclerical people for his mission puts heavily bureaucratized forms of institutional Christianity under scrutiny. Blunt is Luke's message: when holders of traditional offices obstruct paths to the future, the Lord of the churches directs his people to carry on through other channels.[58]

They are special not because of their special qualifications but because they accepted the call.

(2) The initiative in naming them belongs to Jesus, who decides who the Twelve will be. They do not volunteer. They may want to be the greatest among them (22:24), but their position depends entirely on Jesus' sovereign call and not on anything they are or have done.

(3) Judas is always identified as the betrayer. Did he slip through some kind of screening process? Was he chosen for his role to turn traitor? Both are unlikely. The object of the verb "picked out" in 6:13 is the number "twelve" (δώδεκα). Jesus chooses the number twelve as a foundation because of its symbolic significance. The specific individuals, as the differing names in the lists of the disciples may reveal, are not crucial. They fill slots, and Judas's slot must be filled after he is guilty of treason (Acts 1:17, 20, 24–26). The reality is that many other followers will fall by the wayside, and Jesus will explain this phenomenon with the parable of the sower (8:4–15). What makes Judas's treachery so poignant and frightening is that this failure can happen even to Jesus' closest associates.

2. The Radical Demands of Discipleship

Will Bakke, as a Baylor University student, directed and produced a 2010 documentary that was intended to raise consciousness about what radical commitment to Christ really means. It has a provocative title, "Beware of Christians."[59] It centers on four college guys who grew up in Texas seeking answers to their own questions about what being a Christian means. They grew up imbued with a superficial culture religion, and the idea behind the documentary is "to beware of Christians like us who never really have known what it means to follow Christ." Jesus' teaching brings with it blessing and demand. It requires a complete overhaul of one's life, and superficial Christianity may pass muster in some churches, but it will not endure God's judgment.

---

58. Danker, *Jesus and the New Age*, 136. 59. See www.bewareofchristians.com.

Jesus is not interested in giving his disciples a new system of morals but in transforming lives so that they will live out a higher standard of morals that emulates God's dealings with the world. The love of enemies, actively seeking to do good to them, is the heart of this sermon. It may seem naive, but its opposite has a proven track record of producing only chaos and perpetuating hostility and evil. The rough-and-ready ethic of those who refuse to hear says, "Do in all those who hate you, damn those who curse you, pray that those who harm you meet with immediate destruction." It leads to its own destruction by feeding a spiral of violence. It mutates into fiercer standards of conduct, "If they slap you, nuke them"; "if they try to take what is yours, blow them away."

The book of Esther describes the people doing unto their enemies as they had done to them: "The Jews struck down all their enemies with the sword, killing and destroying them, and they did what they pleased to those who hated them" (Esth 9:5). Later history reveals how ephemeral these victories were, and when the tables were turned, once again they suffered pogrom after pogrom. In Jesus' time, the Jews were under the thumb of the Romans, who were driven by the principle of military preparation and courage. Livy traces it back to Romulus, who stresses: "Declare to the Romans the will of Heaven that my Rome shall be the capital of the world; so let them cherish the art of war" (1.16.7).

This secular ethic presumes to be based on enlightened self-interest and common sense and is driven by the natural disposition to protect one's own rights and to have power over others. Juvenal wrote, "Even those who do not want to kill anyone want to have the power to do so" (*Sat.* 10.96 – 97). Those who adopt this ethic offer various rationalizations for doing so. Doing otherwise leaves one open for more abuse. Enemies only respect strength. Jesus did not really mean that this is what we are supposed to do in real life; it is too radical, too impossible, too foolishly lacking in worldly wisdom.

Jesus breaks down the natural division between friends and enemies and the normal way one relates to those classified as enemies. The command would have been jarring to Jesus' hearers who lived in enemy-occupied territory, and Luke's Christian audience also experienced social and religious persecution (cf. 1 Pet 3:16). How does one respond to abuse, hatred, cursing, maltreatment, being struck, or being swindled? In a culture of violence, enemies who do such things are never to be restored, prayed for, or redeemed, only destroyed. By contrast, "Jesus seeks an end of enmity, but not the end of the enemy."[60] Disciples are not to regard themselves as victims,[61] but are to be aggressive in a loving response. Wengst explains:

> Loving one's enemy does not leave the enemy as he is: it wants him not to go on being an enemy for ever, but to change him. By contrast hatred does not seek the end of

---

60. Wengst, *Pax Romana*, 71.   61. Craddock, *Luke*, 90.

enmity. It needs a picture of the enemy and must constantly keep it in full view: it wants the enemy as an enemy — but in order finally to make an end of him.[62]

Such loving aggression carries with it a high risk as is evident by Jesus' death on the cross.

Jesus' ethic assumes that evil spreads by contagion. It can be stopped only when the hatred is absorbed and neutralized by love — creative nonviolence. One overcomes evil only with good (Rom 12:21). A person should respond not on the basis of how one is treated but on the basis of how one wants to be treated. Maybe nothing happens to enemies. They may hate one all the more, but incredible things happen within the one who lives this ethic out. Hate has nowhere to go except inside. Love frees up energy. Consequently, the love of enemies and the Golden Rule are explicated by three points:

> (1) We should not do good based on our expectation that we will be treated well (vv. 32 – 35a); (2) we have to act in light of our future hope and relationship with God (v. 35b); and (3) the ultimate basis for our behavior is the nature and deeds of God (v. 36).[63]

The Golden Rule is, therefore, not given as good advice on how to succeed in the world. It contrasts with the counsel found in Sir 12:1 – 6: "If you do good, know to whom you do it, and you will be thanked for your good deeds. Do good to the devout, and you will be repaid — if not by them, certainly by the Most High." Jesus rejects a system in which winning is built on the defeat of another human being and a system in which one exchanges good for good. If people love only those who love them in return, it is simply a business deal, tit for tat. This is what sinners do. It is good enough for sinners, but it is not good enough for Christians, who must do more. Why should one expect congratulations from God for simply doing what the average sinner does? This is God's way and therefore it is to be the way of God's people. This sermon is directed to those who have experienced the love and power of God and have received God's gifts (vv. 18 – 19). We are to imitate God. A character in Iain Pears' *An Instance of the Fingerpost* assesses his life and his guilty involvement in an innocent girl's hanging:

> All is known to the highest Judge of all and Him I must entrust my soul, knowing that I have served him to the best of my ability in all my acts. But often now, late at night when I lie sleepless in my bed once more, or when I am deep in the frustration of prayers which no longer come, I fear my only hope of salvation is that His mercy will prove greater than was mine. I no longer believe it will.[64]

---

62. Wengst, *Pax Romana*, 71.

63. Walter L. Liefield and David W. Pao, "Luke," in *The Expositor's Bible Commentary: Revised Edition* (ed. Tremper Longman III and David E. Garland; Grand Rapids: Zondervan, 2007), 10:137.

64. Iain Pears, *An Instance of the Fingerpost* (New York: Riverhead Books, 1998), 525.

3. The Christocentric Beatitudes

The basis for this ethic is Jesus' redefinition of reality from God's perspective in the beatitudes and woes. The beatitudes are christocentric. They are associated with the religious joy that is directly related to the presence and activity of Jesus. The blessing is conditioned by his presence, not by anything that these persons may have accomplished. The end time is breaking into the present. For Jesus to pronounce people as blessed is to announce implicitly that the world to come (see 14:15) is at hand. Although the poor may remain poor, they are to live as if the blessings of the future age are so near at hand that they should determine the present. Wengst comments, "He does not wage armed warfare against the powerful authorities but raises up the helpless and lives out with them an alternative to the existing order."[65]

The beatitudes and the woes are consequently paradoxical. They "stress a reversal of values that people put on earthly things in view of the kingdom now being preached by Jesus."[66] They challenge the conventional wisdom of the world that prizes earthly security and well-being. Jesus proclaims those whom the world would identify as losers destined for the compost pile as blessed and maintains that they should be fully conscious of this divine blessing and favor. Appearances to the contrary, congratulations are in order because of what God is doing and will do. The blessings God's people will receive assure them that God is the one who will comfort, fill, and have mercy on them (cf. the divine passives in Matt 5:3–4, 6, 7, 9).

The beatitudes have power because they transform the situation of the hearer. It is not pie-in-the-sky by-and-by. Blauw notes that "while the gospel is the fulfillment of the expectation of salvation, that fulfillment still bears a tentative character, and becomes in itself the source of a new expectation."[67] But that new expectation changes everything in the here and now—how one views material possessions, earthly status, suffering, and other people (the downtrodden, the rich, and the enemy)—by changing how one views oneself as rescued by God from one's own wretchedness and impoverishment.

4. Who Are the Poor and Who Are the Rich Today?

Most persons would define the rich as anyone who has more money than they do. A precise definition that classifies the poor, those who have an annual income and a net worth less than a certain amount, is usually done by governments. They define what poverty-level income is and also who belongs in the top tax bracket. But what happens when one compares people in a prosperous country with those who live in comparative destitution in other parts of the world? Defining who is poor and who

65. Wengst, *Pax Romana*, 68.
66. Fitzmyer, *Luke*, 1:633.
67. Blauw, *The Missionary Nature of the Church*, 73.

is rich in this framework is more difficult. Many people earn no wages at all. We can always find someone who is worse off and someone much better off than ourselves.

Across all cultures, the poor are those who have no home or no security in their home, no way to care properly for their children, no access to affordable medical care, no guarantee that they can feed themselves from day to day, no power to change their lives — all the things that contribute to a loss of human dignity. The list can go on and on. They often are the ignored because their presence is an embarrassing reminder that we are more fortunate than we deserve and we have not done anything to relieve their suffering. Many want more specifics in the interpretation of the verses that talk about poor and rich primarily to find loopholes to assuage their consciences and so to receive some assurance that Jesus' warnings do not fully apply to them. Alas, they apply to all of us who can afford to write a commentary on these verses and to buy a copy, check it out of a library, or download it to a computer and read it.

Some general things can be said. Poverty is not something that Jesus considers blessed in itself, nor does it necessarily create greater spiritual depth. Poverty does not allow the poor the arrogance and the egotistical aggressiveness of the wealthy, but the poor can be just as mean-spirited and evil. Nevertheless, the poor may be better able to view the present in light of their redemption in the future (compare the many Negro spirituals by the enslaved African people in America). It may be easier for them to be free from the tyranny of possessions. They can more readily place their lives in the hands of God, who "raises the poor from the dust and lifts the needy from the ash heap" (Ps 113:7).

The lifestyle of the rich and famous, by contrast, feeds arrogance and self-sufficiency, which are dangerous for their spiritual health and eternal future. The rich fail to recognize that what they value (the list can go on and on) is of no value to God (16:15). Johnson goes too far in arguing that possessions and money function as symbols in Luke's narrative for one's attitude toward God and Jesus,[68] but this conclusion has contemporary application. Those who put a premium on their possessions will pay little heed to Jesus and his teaching and will find it prevents them from participating in God's reign and inheriting eternal life (18:18 – 24).

The rest of the gospel makes it clear that as one relates to the poor, one relates to God. God is like the father of the two sons who says to the eldest, "Everything that is mine is yours" (15:31), but few people and fewer churches adopt this radical attitude in their own lives (see 6:30) so that it can be said, "There were no needy persons among them" (Acts 4:34). Topel writes that it is God's nature "to provide abundance and respond to the outcry of the oppressed (Ps 103:6), as he has shown in his first revelation to Israel (Exod 2:23). His people are to be like Him, and if they are, 'there will be no poor in the land' (Deut 15:4)."[69]

68. Luke Timothy Johnson, *Literary Function of Possessions in Luke-Acts* (SBLDS 39; Missoula: Scholars, 1977), 140.

69. Topel, *Children of a Compassionate God*, 75.

Luke 7:1 – 10

Literary Context

Bovon states, "The overarching theme of chap. 7 is the saving visitation of God, and also the identity of the mediating messengers (cf. 7:49). Whereas chaps. 6 and 8 transmit Jesus' message, chap. 7 treats this double theme with the help of short narratives."[1] The healing of the centurion's slave occurs after references to Jesus' power to heal in 6:19. Crowds tried to touch him because "power was coming from him and he healed them all." Luke reports that it was "the crowd," and the present incident makes clear that Gentiles will not be excluded. This healing of a man at death's door along with the account of the raising of the widow's son (7:11 – 17) point forward to 7:23, where Jesus reports to the messengers from John the Baptist that the dead are raised. The two episodes in 7:1 – 17 reconfirm the Son of Man's authority to heal, and the final episode (7:36 – 50), the Son of Man's authority to forgive sins (5:24).

The surprising appearance of the centurion in this story is the first of three who exhibit exemplary faith (7:9). A centurion confesses that Jesus is righteous at the cross (23:47), and a centurion named Cornelius exhibits exemplary faith as a God-fearer who prays, gives alms, and receives the Holy Spirit in response to Peter's preaching (Acts 10). The introduction of this "chain of centurions" across Luke-Acts "prepares for the shock of the opening up of salvation to the Gentiles."[2]

---

1. Bovon, *Luke 1:1 – 9:50*, 290.   2. Marguerat, *The First Christian Historian*, 53.

Main Idea

Jesus acts graciously toward humans on the basis of their trust in him and recognition of their own unworthiness. Receiving benefits from him does not depend on one's social status, rank, religious affiliation, or good works.

Translation

Luke 7:1–10

7:1	Circumstance	When he finished all his words in the hearing of the people, **he entered Capernaum.**
2	Crisis	**A centurion's slave, who was valuable to him, was very ill and about to die.**
3	Character introduction	When he heard about Jesus, **he sent elders from the Jews to him to ask him to come that he might save ⮌ his slave.**
4	Petition	When they came to Jesus, **they were pleading with him earnestly [to come], saying,** "He is worthy for you to grant this for him
5a	Rationale (1)	because he loves our nation,
b	Rationale (2)	and he is the one who built the synagogue for us."
6a	Compliance with the petition	**Jesus was going with them;**
b	Interruption by other brokers	and when they were not far from the house, **the centurion sent friends who said to him,**
c	Petition	"Lord, do not trouble yourself,
d	Rationale (1)	for I am not deserving for you to come under my roof.
7a	Rationale (2)	That is why I did not deem myself fit to come to you,
b	Petition	but just give the word and my servant will be healed.
8	Rationale (3)	For I am a man placed under authority with soldiers under me, and I say to one, 'Go!' and he goes, and to another, 'Come!' and he comes, and to my slave, 'Do this!' and he does it."
9	Response	When Jesus heard these things, **he was astounded and turning to the crowd following him, he said,** "I tell you, not even in Israel have I found such faith."
10	Discovery of healing	When those who had been sent returned to the house, **they found the slave in good health.**

Structure and Literary Form

The account divides into two halves. The first half records Jewish intermediaries imploring Jesus to heal a centurion's slave because he is worthy. The second half records the centurion's protest that he is not worthy and his acknowledgment of Jesus' power to heal with only a word. It is punctuated by Jesus' pronouncement that he has not found faith like this in Israel. The miracle itself is almost an afterthought.

Exegetical Outline

→ **I. Jesus enters Capernaum (7:1)**

II. Jewish intermediaries appeal to Jesus on behalf of a worthy centurion (7:2 – 5)

    A. A centurion recruits Jewish elders to intercede with Jesus to heal his slave (7:2 – 3)

    B. Their appeal to Jesus: he is worthy to receive miraculous intervention (7:4 – 5)

III. Jesus' consent to go with them (7:6a)

IV. The centurion's second thoughts about Jesus' coming to him because he is unworthy (7:6b – 8)

    A. He is not worthy (7:6b-d)

    B. Appeal for Jesus only to speak the word and his slave will be healed (7:7)

    C. Confession of Jesus' authority and power (7:8)

IV. Jesus' amazement (7:9 – 10)

    A. Faith like this has not been found in Israel (7:9)

    B. Healing of the slave (7:10)

Explanation of the Text

7:1 When he finished all his words in the hearing of the people, he entered Capernaum (ἐπειδὴ ἐπλήρωσεν πάντα τὰ ῥήματα αὐτοῦ εἰς τὰς ἀκοὰς τοῦ λαοῦ, εἰσῆλθεν εἰς Καφαρναούμ). The verb "finished" (ἐπλήρωσεν) can also mean "fulfilled," and this summary statement marks a transition to a new stage of Jesus' mission in his first encounter with a Gentile recorded in Luke. The phrase "in the hearing of the people" picks up on 6:27 and reminds the reader that Luke is writing down what was passed on by eyewitnesses and servants of the word (1:2).

7:2 A centurion's slave, who was valuable to him, was very ill and about to die (ἑκατοντάρχου δέ τινος δοῦλος κακῶς ἔχων ἤμελλεν τελευτᾶν, ὃς ἦν αὐτῷ ἔντιμος). This favorable encounter with a centurion foreshadows the conversion of Cornelius in Acts 10.[3] He is not a Jew since the Jewish elders affirm that "he loves our nation" (7:5), but

---

3. According to A. N. Sherwin-White (*Roman Society and Roman Law in the New Testament* [Grand Rapids: Baker, repr. 1978], 123 – 24), no Roman forces were in Galilee before AD 44 because it did not become a Roman province until after the death of Agrippa I. The centurion may have been an officer in Herod Antipas's armed forces serving at the border post of Capernaum. Luke's Greco-Roman readers, however, are unlikely to know the history of Galilee and would probably regard him as a Roman officer.

he must have been attracted to Judaism since he built their synagogue.

Slaves were regarded as disposable by many owners, but this centurion appears to have regarded his slave differently — not as an animate tool but as a human being worth taking the trouble to save from a terminal illness.[4] The slave was "valuable" (ἔντιμος, 1 Pet 2:4, 6) to him, but it could mean that he was "honored" or "respected" (Luke 14:8; Phil 2:29) or that he was "valuable" or "precious" (1 Pet 2:4, 6).[5]

7:3 When he heard about Jesus, he sent elders from the Jews to him to ask him to come that he might save his slave (ἀκούσας δὲ περὶ τοῦ Ἰησοῦ ἀπέστειλεν πρὸς αὐτὸν πρεσβυτέρους τῶν Ἰουδαίων ἐρωτῶν αὐτὸν ὅπως ἐλθὼν διασώσῃ τὸν δοῦλον αὐτοῦ). Since reports about Jesus have reached every place in the region (4:37), he has heard about Jesus.

As an uncircumcised Gentile in the employ of a hostile oppressor, he decides to enlist Jewish brokers, leaders in the local community, to plead his case with Jesus. A go-between was used in this culture when social disparity prevented one of inferior status from dealing directly with a superior. Despite his rank and power as a commander, he must assume that he feels too inferior to appeal himself to Jesus. Unlike the woman with the flow of blood who wields no influence with anyone and thinks that she must steal up behind Jesus to purloin her healing (8:43 – 48), the centurion can cash in on the indebtedness of the local elders to beg a favor from a fellow Jew.

7:4 – 5 When they came to Jesus, they were pleading with him earnestly [to come], saying,

"He is worthy for you to grant this for him because he loves our nation, and he is the one who built the synagogue for us" (οἱ δὲ παραγενόμενοι πρὸς τὸν Ἰησοῦν παρεκάλουν αὐτὸν σπουδαίως λέγοντες ὅτι ἄξιός ἐστιν ᾧ παρέξῃ τοῦτο· ἀγαπᾷ γὰρ τὸ ἔθνος ἡμῶν καὶ τὴν συναγωγὴν αὐτὸς ᾠκοδόμησεν ἡμῖν). That they pled with Jesus earnestly (παρεκάλουν … σπουδαίως) presumes that he might not heed the request to help a Gentile. They cite the man's merits to show that he has proved himself worthy to receive a good turn. First, he loves their nation; second, he built their synagogue.[6] Crockett observes, "When Luke portrays the ideal gentile, he stresses the mutuality between gentiles and Jews" (see Acts 10:2).[7] The request with a summary of his benefactions assumes that reciprocity is required. Jesus needs to do his duty for the community by repaying such a generous patron.

7:6 Jesus was going with them; and when they were not far from the house, the centurion sent friends who said to him, "Lord, do not trouble yourself, for I am not deserving for you to come under my roof" (ὁ δὲ Ἰησοῦς ἐπορεύετο σὺν αὐτοῖς. ἤδη δὲ αὐτοῦ οὐ μακρὰν ἀπέχοντος ἀπὸ τῆς οἰκίας ἔπεμψεν φίλους ὁ ἑκατοντάρχης λέγων αὐτῷ· κύριε, μὴ σκύλλου, οὐ γὰρ ἱκανός εἰμι ἵνα ὑπὸ τὴν στέγην μου εἰσέλθῃς). For his own reasons, Jesus goes with the elders. The account has parallels with the story of Naaman and Elisha in 2 Kgs 5:1 – 27 (Luke 4:27). Both accounts involve a highly respected Gentile officer regarded as worthy, a report about a Jewish miracle worker (2 Kgs 5:2 – 3), an appeal to influential Israelite intermediaries (5:5 – 6), and healing without the

---

4. In Matthew's parallel (Matt 8:5 – 13), the slave is paralyzed and suffering greatly (8:6), but in Luke he is on his deathbed.

5. Bovon, *Luke 1:1 – 9:50*, 261, n. 29, claims that the tradition read παῖς (Matt 8:6), which was interpreted by Luke as

"slave" and by John as "son" (John 4:47).

6. Gentiles gave money for the upkeep of synagogues (*t. Meg.* 2:16; 3:5). See also inscriptions cited by Danker, *Jesus and the New Age*, 158 – 59; Nolland, *Luke*, 1:316 – 17.

7. Crockett, "Luke 4:25 – 27," 182.

afflicted person ever coming into direct contact with the healer (5:10). The differences, however, are striking and highlight this centurion's humility and faith:

- Naaman had commanded army raids against Israel; the centurion did things demonstrating his love for Israel ("our nation").
- Naaman comes to Elisha's doorstep with "horses and chariots" (2 Kgs 5:9); the centurion humbly sends intermediaries to Jesus.
- Elisha sends a message with instructions to Naaman (2 Kgs 5:10); Jesus leaves to go to the centurion.
- Naaman storms off in a pout when Elisha fails to meet his expectations, and he must be coaxed to obey Elisha's instructions (2 Kgs 5:11 – 14); the centurion's attitude is not one of entitlement and demand, and he sends messengers saying he is unworthy for Jesus to come under his roof.
- Naaman believes he needs to carry off two mule-loads of holy turf to worship the Lord (2 Kgs 5:17); the centurion humbly sends intermediaries with a statement of his faith in Jesus' power to heal by only uttering the word.

More emissaries come from the centurion to report that he has had second thoughts about Jesus' coming under his roof. The Jewish elders claim he is "worthy" (ἄξιος), but these other friends twice report his protest of unworthiness. They report him saying "I am not deserving" (οὐ … ἱκανός εἰμι) and "I did not deem myself fit" (ἠξίωσα). His unworthiness for Jesus to enter his house has nothing to do with issues of Jewish purity.[8] He believes that Jesus is someone sent from God who acts by God's authority. He feels the same as John the Baptist, who did not think himself worthy to unlace the sandals of the Messiah (3:16), and as

Simon Peter, who wanted Jesus to depart from his sinful presence (5:8).

7:7 "That is why I did not deem myself fit to come to you, but just give the word and my servant will be healed" (διὸ οὐδὲ ἐμαυτὸν ἠξίωσα πρὸς σὲ ἐλθεῖν· ἀλλὰ εἰπὲ λόγῳ· καὶ ἰαθήτω ὁ παῖς μου). The centurion still wants his slave to be healed but believes that someone with Jesus' authority and power need only say the word for it to happen. He need not attend to him in person. Bovon claims that "in antiquity, miraculous healings were thought to be possible only through direct contact (cf. Luke 5:17 and 6:19)."[9] God, however, is able to heal by his word (Ps 107:20), and the centurion's faith assumes that Jesus has the same power as God.

7:8 "For I am a man placed under authority with soldiers under me, and I say to one, 'Go!' and he goes, and to another, 'Come!' and he comes, and to my slave, 'Do this!' and he does it" (καὶ γὰρ ἐγὼ ἄνθρωπός εἰμι ὑπὸ ἐξουσίαν τασσόμενος, ἔχων ὑπ' ἐμαυτὸν στρατιώτας, καὶ λέγω τούτῳ πορεύθητι, καὶ πορεύεται, καὶ ἄλλῳ· ἔρχου, καὶ ἔρχεται, καὶ τῷ δούλῳ μου· ποίησον τοῦτο, καὶ ποιεῖ). The centurion explains that he knows something about authority. He is under orders, and he gives orders to his subordinates. His command has power because of whom he serves; how much more will Jesus' word have power? As the soldiers obey the centurion, so the sickness (or demons) will obey Jesus. He acknowledges, however, that his authority is totally useless when it comes to healing a sick loved one or overcoming death.

If the term "centurion" would have evoked for Luke's readers, not a soldier in Herod Antipas's police force but a Roman officer, it would have called to mind the image of Roman military

---

8. The houses of Gentiles are unclean to Jews (see John 18:28; Acts 10:28; 11:1 – 4; *m. ʾOhal.* 18:7).

9. Bovon, *Luke 1:1 – 9:50*, 262.

might and its iron discipline.[10] As conquered peoples were helpless before the power of Roman domination, this centurion is helpless before the power of death. To have this soldier both acknowledge and bow to Jesus' divine authority subverts the authority of his masters and Roman imperial propaganda.

7:9 When Jesus heard these things, he was astounded and turning to the crowd following him, he said, "I tell you, not even in Israel have I found such faith" (ἀκούσας δὲ ταῦτα ὁ Ἰησοῦς ἐθαύμασεν αὐτόν καὶ στραφεὶς τῷ ἀκολουθοῦντι αὐτῷ ὄχλῳ εἶπεν· λέγω ὑμῖν, οὐδὲ ἐν τῷ Ἰσραὴλ τοσαύτην πίστιν εὗρον). Jesus, the teller of parables, catches the drift of the centurion's parable and reacts with astonishment.[11] The statement "I tell you, not even in Israel have I found such faith" marks the climax of the story rather than the healing, which is mentioned almost as an afterthought.

Jesus has and will encounter those in Israel who challenge his authority (5:21; 20:2), but he also has encountered faith in Israel (see the example of the men who dropped the paralytic through the roof, 5:20). The Jewish elders came believing that Jesus could perform a miracle. They expected it because of the centurion's good works, because he had earned it. They commended his works; Jesus commended his faith. Jesus had not found such faith in Israel, a faith not based on works, a faith that does not think that God will help if one has done something to earn it, but that God will help despite who one is or what one has done or not done.

7:10 When those who had been sent returned to the house, they found the slave in good health (καὶ ὑποστρέψαντες εἰς τὸν οἶκον οἱ πεμφθέντες εὗρον τὸν δοῦλον ὑγιαίνοντα). The centurion says, "Just give the word," but Luke does not record any word of healing spoken by Jesus. The slave was healed through faith.

Theology in Application

1. Merit versus Grace

This incident sets up a contrast between merit and grace. First, the elders say that the centurion is worthy. Then, the centurion says he is not worthy. He is like the prodigal son who comes home from the far country and says to his father, "I am no longer worthy to be called your son" (15:19, 21). The centurion does not come in person because he believes himself to be so unworthy, and he makes his appeal as a beggar for grace. He is like the toll collector in the temple who stands afar off and cannot lift his eyes up to heaven but beats his breast and cries out, "God, make atonement for me, the sinner!" (18:13). He too confesses his unworthiness. The centurion voices the theological truth that applies to all. His hope is based on the goodness and power of Jesus, not on his own goodness and power. He knows himself to be unworthy, but he does not need to be worthy to seek Christ's help. He also recognizes his desperate need for help and his complete helplessness to do anything himself.

---

10. Danker, *Jesus and the New Age*, 157. The phrase "he is worthy for you to grant this for him" (ἄξιός ἐστιν ᾧ παρέξῃ τοῦτο, 7:4) is identified as a Latinism that appears rarely but "in connection with Roman authorities," according to BDF §5 [3b].

11. Bovon, *Luke 1:1–9:50*, 262.

The elders, therefore, are wrong.[12] This incident illustrates that there is no distinction; all are unworthy (Rom 3:9 – 20). No one can say to God, "I am worthy to receive your grace," or "You owe me" (cf. Eph 2:8). This message makes it possible for Gentiles to become members of God's people and beneficiaries of the promise by faith, not by works or by circumcision.[13] The story prepares for the message that Paul declares, we "all are justified freely by his grace through the redemption that came by Christ Jesus" (Rom 3:24). Grace is not something that one earns or gets; it is something that one can only receive. And it is given to prodigals, publicans, prostitutes, and Gentile troopers.

2. The Nature of Faith

The healing reveals several things about faith. (1) Like the believers who read Luke's gospel, the centurion trusts Jesus without having ever met him in person. He has only heard the reports (7:3) but believes and acts on his faith (see John 20:29; 1 Pet 1:8).

(2) The centurion shows love for another by being willing to humble himself that his servant might receive healing. The reason one built buildings like synagogues was to accrue honor in the community. He casts aside this earthly honor as worthless in his humble appeal to Jesus. Humility was not a virtue among the Greeks and Romans. In the biblical context, however, it refers to seeing oneself in one's rightful condition as a creature of God. Shedding the desire to be great or distinguished opens up the way for him to receive God's gifts (14:11; 18:14). He is on the same level as other suppliants for Jesus' healing — the lepers (5:12 – 14; 17:11 – 19), the woman with a hemorrhage (8:43 – 48), the blind man in Jericho (18:35 – 43).

(3) The centurion does not believe that he is so unworthy that he cannot boldly make an appeal to Jesus for healing.

(4) The centurion understands Jesus' authority and relation to God and trusts that for him space and time make no difference for his great power. Jesus could speak the word right where he was and his servant would be healed.

(5) As a commander, the centurion is used to being in charge, but grace comes when he gives up trying to be in control.

(6) The healing of the servant reveals that there is no partiality with God (Rom 2:11). It shows that a Gentile can demonstrate greater faith (and spiritual discernment) than God's people and portends that the promise that "all flesh shall see the salvation of God" (3:6) will come true.

---

12. Green, *The Gospel of Luke*, 287, comments, "Their words betray their captivity to a world system whose basis and practices run counter to the mercy of God."
13. Bovon, *Luke 1:1 – 9:50*, 260.

Luke 7:11 – 17

Literary Context

This incident on Jesus' raising to life a widow's son is a twin to the preceding healing of the centurion's slave (7:1 – 10). The main theme is laid out in the preceding episode: Jesus' word is authoritative and he has dominion over life and death. In the previous event, the crisis revolved around a centurion whose deathly ill slave was precious to him. The pathos in the present story is heightened by the plight of the widow whose only son has died. She is bereft of all hope, but Jesus can do more than heal with a word; he can raise the dead with a word.

These two accounts reflect Luke's pattern of alternating complementary episodes with male and female characters. The gap between the two could not be greater. The centurion was wealthy and had influence and power; he had a deathly sick slave. The woman, by contrast, is a poor and powerless widow whose only son is dead. She has no one to fend for her and no hope for her future. The raising of her son also matches up with the raising of the daughter of Jairus, the ruler of a synagogue (8:41 – 42, 49 – 56). Jesus shows equal compassion and concern over the loss of a daughter as well as a son, and he not only ministers to the poor and disenfranchised but to the well-to-do and empowered.

This miracle sets up an important piece of Jesus' answer to John's query in the next episode, "Are you the one who is to come or should we expect another?" (7:19 – 20). The dead are raised (7:22). The incident begins unfolding the central issue of Jesus' identity and role. The crowd's exultation at the conclusion that "a great prophet has been raised among us" (7:16) will be qualified in the next unit when Jesus declares John to be "much more than a prophet" (7:26; see 1:15, 17) and that "among those born of women none is greater than John" (7:28). If "the most insignificant person in the reign of God is greater than he [John]" (7:28), then is Jesus merely "a great prophet"? Luke's point of view is clear from 7:13: Jesus is "the Lord," not simply a great prophet mighty in deed and word (24:19).

Main Idea

Jesus combines compassion with power, and the authority of his word extends even to the realm of the dead.

Translation

(See next page.)

Structure and Literary Form

This incident begins with two crowds. A crowd with Jesus meets a crowd with a widow solemnly leading her son out to be buried. At the end the entire group raises a chorus of praise to God so that deep sorrow turns to immense joy. In between Jesus shows compassion and performs a miracle of resurrection with a word.

Exegetical Outline

➡ **I. Encountering a funeral procession at the gates of a town (7:11 – 12)**

II. The Lord's compassion on the mother (7:13)

III. Raising the boy from the dead by Jesus' word (7:14 – 15)

IV. The chorus of exultation (7:16 – 17)

   A. A great prophet has been raised among us (7:16a)

   B. God has visited his people (7:16b)

   C. Spread of the report (7:17)

Luke 7:11–17

| 7:11 | Circumstance | **It happened soon afterward that he went to a town called Nain,** and **his disciples and a large crowd went along with him.** |

12a
b — Character introduction

As they neared the gate of the town,
behold, a dead man was being carried out [to be buried],
his mother's only son,

and **she was also a widow.**
A considerable crowd from the town was with her.

13 — Response of compassion

When the Lord saw her,
he felt compassion for her and **said to her,**
"Do not weep."

14 — Miracle

He approached and
touched the bier,
and **the pallbearers stood still.**
He said,
"Young man, I say to you, arise!"

15

The dead man sat up and **began to speak,**
and **Jesus gave him to his mother.**

16a — Response

Fear gripped all and **they were glorifying God, saying,**
"A great prophet has been raised among us!"

b

and *"God has visited his people."*

17 — Summary

This report about him spread throughout the whole of Judea and all the ↵ surrounding region.

Explanation of the Text

7:11 It happened soon afterward that he went to a town called Nain, and his disciples and a large crowd went along with him (καὶ ἐγένετο ἐν τῷ ἑξῆς ἐπορεύθη εἰς πόλιν καλουμένην Ναΐν καὶ συνεπορεύοντο αὐτῷ οἱ μαθηταὶ αὐτοῦ καὶ ὄχλος πολύς). Nain was twenty-five miles south of Capernaum and six miles southeast of Nazareth. Luke tends to identify the villages in Galilee and Judea as cities (πόλις). The disciples are now distinguished from the crowd. The great crowd following Jesus meets the "crowd from the town"

carrying the corpse of a young man outside the town for burial, as was the custom.

7:12 As they neared the gate of the town, behold, a dead man was being carried out [to be buried], his mother's only son, and she was also a widow. A considerable crowd from the town was with her (ὡς δὲ ἤγγισεν τῇ πύλῃ τῆς πόλεως, καὶ ἰδοὺ ἐξεκομίζετο τεθνηκὼς μονογενὴς υἱὸς τῇ μητρὶ αὐτοῦ καὶ αὐτὴ ἦν χήρα, καὶ ὄχλος τῆς πόλεως ἱκανὸς ἦν σὺν αὐτῇ). This widow is the first of three parents whom Jesus meets whose "only" child has died, is near death (8:42, 52), or is plagued by demons and in danger of death (9:38). Burial was prompt in the biblical world (see Acts 5:1 – 11), and the sadness of a parent burying a child is heightened by the note that she is a widow and that this was her "only" son. It is a bitter day (Amos 8:10; Jer 6:26; Zech 12:10). As a widow, she will have no one to support her or to fend for her.

Many translations render the adjective describing the crowd's size as "large" (ἱκανός), though it can mean "sufficient in degree, adequate, large enough."[1] The crowd consisting of the men carrying the body and the mourners simply may have been sufficient for the task at hand.[2] Accompanying a funeral procession was considered to be virtuous, and the crowd may also have been "considerable." This magnifies the impact of their glorifying God after the miracle. Its size should not be taken to imply, however, that the widow had a huge support network to help her survive in the days to come.

7:13 When the Lord saw her, he felt compassion for her and said to her, "Do not weep" (καὶ ἰδὼν αὐτὴν ὁ κύριος ἐσπλαγχνίσθη ἐπ᾽ αὐτῇ καὶ εἶπεν αὐτῇ· μὴ κλαῖε). Jesus has compassion not simply because this woman has lost a child but because of the desperate predicament faced by widows with no means of support. For the first time the narrator describes Jesus as "the Lord" (see 7:19; 10:1, 39, 41; 11:39; 12:42; 13:15; 16:8; 17:5 – 6; 18:6). It reflects the Christian confession that Jesus is more than a great prophet and he has been exalted Lord (Acts 2:36; Rom 1:4). As the Lord, Jesus does not utter some vacuous cliché, such as, "He is in a better

place," to someone facing intense personal loss.[3] His command not to weep (see 8:52) is backed up with the divine power to turn weeping into joy (see Isa 25:8; 30:15 – 21; Rev 7:17; 21:4).

7:14 He approached and touched the bier, and the pallbearers stood still. He said, "Young man, I say to you, arise!" (καὶ προσελθὼν ἥψατο τῆς σοροῦ, οἱ δὲ βαστάζοντες ἔστησαν, καὶ εἶπεν· νεανίσκε, σοὶ λέγω, ἐγέρθητι). Jesus touches the bier to stop the procession. He does not notice a spark of life in the young man that others have missed. The young man is really dead, and Jesus' authoritative command for this dead young man to rise (see 8:54) revokes death's claim on him. The use of the passive voice of the verb ἐγέρθητι (aorist passive imperative) is normal to describe someone moving from a sitting or reclining position to a standing one (11:8; 13:25; Acts 9:8), and the English idiom requires translating it "rise" rather than "be raised."[4] Here it means to rise from the dead, not simply from the stretcher.

7:15 The dead man sat up and began to speak, and Jesus gave him to his mother (καὶ ἀνεκάθισεν ὁ νεκρὸς καὶ ἤρξατο λαλεῖν, καὶ ἔδωκεν αὐτὸν τῇ μητρὶ αὐτοῦ). At Jesus' command the corpse becomes a living person again who speaks. This poignant detail of Jesus' giving the boy to his mother underscores the purpose of his intervention. It is a dramatic example of bringing good news to the poor and release to the captives (4:18).

7:16 – 17 Fear gripped all and they were glorifying God, saying, "A great prophet has been raised among us!" and "God has visited his

---

1. BDAG, 472.

2. Ray Summers, *Commentary on Luke* (WBC; Waco, TX: Word, 1972), 84.

3. Martin Marty (*Martin Luther* [New York: Viking, 2004], 11) describes Martin Luther's devastation at the death of his daughter: "When in her early adolescence his favorite, Mag-

dalena, died, he was inconsolable and almost lost the ability to sustain the life of faith. He even spoke of losing his faith for a time, something he never did when he faced and had to fear the hatred of popes, emperors, and princes."

4. Luke uses the active voice of the imperative, however, in 5:23 – 24 and 8:54.

people." This report about him spread throughout the whole of Judea and all the surrounding region (ἔλαβεν δὲ φόβος πάντας καὶ ἐδόξαζον τὸν θεὸν λέγοντες ὅτι προφήτης μέγας ἠγέρθη ἐν ἡμῖν, καὶ ὅτι ἐπεσκέψατο ὁ θεὸς τὸν λαὸν αὐτοῦ. καὶ ἐξῆλθεν ὁ λόγος οὗτος ἐν ὅλῃ τῇ Ἰουδαίᾳ περὶ αὐτοῦ καὶ πάσῃ τῇ περιχώρῳ). This miracle is not done behind closed doors as is the raising of Jairus's daughter (8:49 – 56); it occurs before a crowd of witnesses. They attribute the miracle to the authority of God: God has visited his people (see 1:68, 78; Deut 18:18). Fear gripped the people, but this "visitation" is evidence of God's compassion. Refusing to recognize that God has visited the people through Jesus will result in desolation truly to be feared (19:44).

According to McComiskey, Jesus' ability to work miracles is "founded on the authority and power of God." Linking Jesus' power to God prevents readers from drawing "the conclusion that this wonder worker possessed his own independent authority or that he occasionally overstepped the bounds of his authority in confrontation with the Jewish leaders."[5]

Theology in Application

1. The Power of Jesus' Word

Urbach remarks: "An outstanding feature of the miracle stories in the Rabbinic literature is the fact that the personality of the miracle worker is not emphasized. The sages were careful not to turn the person himself, who performed the miracle, into a wonder and marvel."[6] In the Gospels, the opposite is true. Jesus' might and power is accentuated. The chorus of joy from the crowd, "A great prophet has been raised among us!" and "God has visited his people," affirms that they believe that God is back. The crowd is thinking in terms of a great prophet like Elijah, but Jesus is greater than Elijah.

Brodie argues that Luke has utilized the Greco-Roman composition method of *imitatio* and shapes the telling of this story by utilizing the great texts from the past.[7] The parallel is the story of Elijah's encounter with the widow of Zarephath in 1 Kgs 17. Elijah meets the widow at the gate of the town (1 Kgs 17:10), just as Jesus meets the widow at the gate. Both have sons who die, and both sons are brought back to life and given to the mother (17:23). The contrasts are striking, however. Elijah carries the dead child upstairs, lays him on his bed, remonstrates with God, asking why this calamity was brought upon her, and pleads that his life be restored (17:19 – 21). Jesus feels compassion as soon as he meets the widow and immediately commands the boy to rise. No mention is made of God bringing the widow's sin to remembrance as the cause of the child's death (cf. 1 Kgs 17:18), and Jesus does not appeal to God or

---

5. McComiskey, *Lukan Theology in the Light of the Gospel's Literary Structure*, 308.

6. Ephraim E. Urbach, *The Sages: Their Concepts and Beliefs* (trans. Israel Abrahams; Jerusalem: Magnes), 116 – 17.

7. Thomas L. Brodie, "Towards Unraveling Luke's Use of the Old: Luke 7:11 – 17 as an *Imitatio* of 1 Kings 17:17 – 24," *NTS* 32 (1986): 247 – 67.

perform any action (like stretching himself across the body three times [17:21; see 2 Kgs 4:34]). The contrast is clear from Sirach's praise of Elijah:

> How glorious you were, Elijah, in your wondrous deeds!
> Whose glory is equal to yours?
> You raised a corpse from death
> and from Hades, by the word of the Most High. (Sir 48:4–5)

Jesus' ministry is reminiscent of Elijah and Elisha, but Jesus raises a corpse by the power of his own authoritative word, which is emphasized in the previous incident (7:7). The word of the Lord "now penetrates to the sphere of death."[8] God is the one who raises the dead (Acts 26:8; John 5:21; 2 Cor 1:9), and Jesus has authority over death.

2. Modern Mourning and the Promise of the Resurrection

Death's door is always ajar. Many try to keep death at bay with power diets, wrinkle removal operations, and tummy tucks, but the nasty riposte, "I hope you rot in your grave," is a wish destined to come true. Until the second coming of Christ, we are not going to make it through life alive. Most do not take this fact of life well.

Gilbert has analyzed how the twentieth century reshaped dying and mourning. The corpse is camouflaged by the cosmetologist's brush or is simply absent, replaced by a memorial collage or a DVD playing highlights from a life gone by.[9] Sometimes friends speak as if it were open-mike night by sharing smarmy sentiments and awkward jokes that drown out the words of sacred Scriptures, if they are read at all. By contrast, the stark reality of death was driven home to all in Jesus' world since they had to carry the dead the arduous distance to the grave. Death seems less real in our culture when there is a company that creates synthetic gemstones from the carbon captured from the cremation of a loved one's remains.

But death is no less feared. A poignant poem by inner-city students expresses that dread:

> I fear death because I don't know.
> What will happen when I go?
> It is something I can't face.
> When I die, will I be thought about?
> Will my name be shouted out?[10]

If one does not want to be turned into a "synthetic diamond," some who are wealthy enough opt to build mausoleums of pharaonic proportions to memorial-

---

8. Evans, *St. Luke*, 348.

9. Sandra M. Gilbert, *Death's Door: Modern Dying and the Ways We Grieve* (New York: Norton, 2007).

10. Stephen O'Connor, *Will My Name Be Shouted Out?: Teaching Inner City Students through the Power of Writing* (New York: Simon & Schuster 1996), 292.

ize themselves or their loved ones. Such grandiose monuments with pillars, patios, hand-cast bronze doors, and chandeliers try to shout out to the world, "I think I was really significant." "I deserve better than to be covered with dirt and weeds." But this feeble stab at terrestrial immortality is also synthetic and ultimately no less hopeless. Others who only find solace for the loss of their loved ones from tokens of nature — a flower poking up through snow, a sunset, light shining through the trees — settle for a perishable, sentimental moment that offers no real hope.

The promise of the resurrection is the core of Christian faith. Death is the last enemy that God will permanently defeat through Christ (1 Cor 15). Malcolm Muggeridge poetically captures this Christian hope:

> For myself, as I approach my end, I find Jesus' outrageous claim ever more captivating and meaningful. Quite often, waking up in the night as the old do, and feeling myself to be half out of my body, that it is a mere chance whether I go back into it to live through another day, or fully disengage and make off; hovering thus between life and death,... Jesus's words ring triumphantly through the universe, spanning my two existences, the one in Time drawing to a close and the one in Eternity at its glorious beginning. So at last I may understand, and understanding, believe; see my ancient carcass, prone between the sheets, stained and worn like a scrap of paper dropped in the gutter, muddy and marred with being trodden underfoot, and, hovering over it, myself, like a butterfly released from its chrysalis stage and ready to fly away. Are caterpillars told of their impending resurrection? How in dying they will be transformed from poor earth-crawlers into creatures of the air, with exquisitely painted wings? If told, do they believe it? Is it conceivable to them that so constricted an existence as theirs should burgeon into so gay and lightsome as a butterfly's? I imagine the wise old caterpillars shaking their heads — no, it can't be; it's a fantasy, self deception, a dream. Similarly, our wise ones. Yet in the limbo between living and dying, as the night clocks tick remorselessly on, and the black sky implacably shows not one single streak or scratch of gray, I hear those words: "*I am the resurrection, and the life,*" and feel myself to be carried along on a great tide of joy and peace.[11]

---

11. Malcolm Muggeridge, *Jesus, the Man Who Lives* (New York: Harper & Row, 1975), 99 – 100.

Luke 7:18 – 35

Literary Context

The healing of the centurion's slave (7:1 – 10) and the raising of the widow's son at Nain (7:11 – 17) prepare for Jesus' response to the question from John in 7:22, which mentions Jesus' healing and raising the dead. They are signs that identify who Jesus is, and Luke continues to describe Jesus doing both in 8:40 – 56: healing the woman with the flow of blood and raising Jairus's daughter from the dead. Luke concludes the previous incident with the statement that word about Jesus spread into Judea (7:17), the area where John had ministered. This sets up his disciples' reporting "all these things" to John, which ties the following account to the preceding events (7:1 – 17). Jesus' answer to John's question "Are you the one who is to come?" (7:19 – 20) confirms the crowd's pronouncement that he is a great prophet who represents the visitation of God (7:16). Jesus' evaluation of John, however, raises new questions about how he will fulfill his role and how people should respond to him.

Main Idea

Jesus is the one who is to come, whom John prepared the people to receive, but this generation will turn a deaf ear and blind eye to him because of their stubbornness.

Translation

Luke 7:18–35

7:18a	Report	**John's disciples reported to him the news about all these things.**
b		**John summoned two of his disciples.**
19	Commission	**He sent them to the Lord, saying,**
		"Are you the one who is to come or should we expect another?"
20	Question	When the men came to him,
		they said,
		"John the Baptist sent us to you, saying,
		'Are you the one who is to come or should we expect another?'"
21	Substantiating healings	At that very moment,
		he healed many people of diseases, plagues, and evil spirits, and he gave ⮌ sight to many blind persons.
22	Commission	**He answered them,**
		"Go report to John the things you have seen and heard:
		the blind see again,
		the lame walk,
		those with skin diseases are cleansed,
		the deaf hear,
		the dead are raised,
		and good news is being proclaimed to the poor.
23	Beatitude	*And blessed is the one who is not offended by me."*
24a	Departure	When John's messengers left,
		he began to speak to the crowds about John.
b	Questions about John (1)	*"What did you go out into the wilderness to observe?*
c		*A reed fluttering in the wind?*
25a	Answer	*No.*
b	Question about John (2)	*Then what did you go out to see?*
c	Answer	*A man attired in soft finery?*
d		*Look, those decked out in such splendid finery who live in luxury are ⮌ found in royal palaces.*
26a	Question about John (3)	*What did you really go out to see?*
b	Answer	*A prophet.*
		Yes, I tell you, and much more than a prophet.
27	Scriptural fulfillment	*This is the one about whom it is written:*
		'Behold, I send my messenger ahead of you,
		who will prepare the way before you.' ⮌
		(Exod 23:20; Mal 3:1)

Continued on next page.

	Continued from previous page.	
28a	Pronouncement	*I tell you, among those born of women none is greater than John,*
b	Pronouncement	*yet the most insignificant person in the reign of God is greater than he is.”*
29	Acceptance of John	**All the people and even the tax collectors who had heard justified God because they were immersed with John's immersion.**
30	Rejection of John	**But the Pharisees and the law experts rejected the purpose of God for themselves because they had not been immersed by him.**
31	Parable	*“To what shall I compare the people of this generation? What are they like?*
32a		*They are like children who sit in the marketplace and yell out to one another:*
b		*'We played the pipes for you and you did not dance.*
c		*We sang dirges and you did not weep.'*
33	Application to John	*For John the Baptist has come and did not eat bread nor drink wine, and you say, 'He has a demon.'*
34	Application to Jesus	*The Son of Man has come eating and drinking, and you say, 'Look, a glutton and a drunkard, a friend of tax collectors and sinners.'*
35	Concluding proverb	*And yet Wisdom is justified by all of her children.”*

Structure and Literary Form

This section mixes pronouncement (7:18 – 23), discourse (7:24 – 30), and parable (7:31 – 35).[1] It divides into three units. The first unit (7:18 – 23) raises the question from John about Jesus' ministry. The question "Are you the one who is to come?" is repeated twice (7:19, 20) and is therefore vital. It is answered by Jesus' pronouncement about the testimony of his deeds. The question about John's role and identity is raised in the second scene (7:24 – 30). He is not "the one who is to come," but his ministry is both a culmination of the Old Testament prophets and a bridge to the new eschatological era that begins with Jesus. Consequently, he is the greatest of all the prophets. The third scene (7:31 – 35) reflects on the negative reaction of this generation to the different ministries of John and Jesus.

---

1. Bock, *Luke*, 1:661.

Exegetical Outline

→ I. **John's inquiry about Jesus (7:18 – 23)**

    A. John's disciples report Jesus' deeds (7:18)

    B. John commissions his disciples to ask Jesus if he is the one who is to come (7:19)

    C. John's disciples ask Jesus if he is the One who is to come (7:20)

    D. Jesus performs miracles as evidence (7:21)

    E. Jesus tells John's disciples to report to him what they have seen and heard (7:22)

    F. Beatitude for those who take no offense at how he fulfills his role (7:23)

II. **Jesus' evaluation of John (7:24 – 28)**

    A. Jesus' inquiry about the people's attraction to John (7:24 – 26)

        1. He was not a reed shaken by the wind (7:24 – 25a)

        2. He was not a man arrayed in soft raiment (7:25b-d)

        3. He was a prophet (7:26)

    B. Scriptural proof text (7:27)

    C. Pronouncement about John (7:28)

        1. John is the greatest prophet (7:28a)

        2. The least in the reign of God is greater than he (7:28b)

    D. Contrasting evaluations of John (7:29 – 30)

        1. The people and the tax collectors accept John and his immersion (7:29)

        2. The Pharisees and lawyers reject John and his immersion (7:30)

III. **The condemnation of this generation's response to John and Jesus (7:31 – 35)**

    A. Parable of the children in the marketplace (7:31 – 32)

    B. Negative response to John as an ascetic killjoy (7:33)

    C. Negative response to Jesus as a guzzling reveler (7:34)

    D. Proverb about Wisdom's children (7:35)

Explanation of the Text

7:18 John's disciples reported to him the news about all these things. John summoned two of his disciples (καὶ ἀπήγγειλαν Ἰωάννῃ οἱ μαθηταὶ αὐτοῦ περὶ πάντων τούτων. καὶ προσκαλεσάμενος δύο τινὰς τῶν μαθητῶν αὐτοῦ ὁ Ἰωάννης). The centurion, apparently informed about Jesus' power, sent two deputations asking for help and expressing his faith in Jesus. John, informed about Jesus' activity, sends a deputation to Jesus to see if faith in him is warranted. John's disciples were mentioned in 5:33, and he still had a significant following even after he was in prison and later killed (see Acts 18:25).

7:19 He sent them to the Lord, saying, "Are you the one who is to come or should we expect another?" (ἔπεμψεν πρὸς τὸν κύριον λέγων· σὺ εἶ ὁ ἐρχόμενος ἢ ἄλλον προσδοκῶμεν;). The question "Are you the one who is to come?" is repeated twice (7:19, 20) and is the vital question that Luke wants the reader to be able to answer with assured "certainty" (ἀσφάλεια, 1:4).[2] Luke inserts his point of view by writing that John sends them "to the Lord" (πρὸς τὸν κύριον).

John's inquiry recalls the question that the buoyant crowds earlier asked themselves about himself, whether he could be the Messiah (3:15). Now the shoe is on the other foot, and John puts the same expectant query to Jesus. In Luke's context, "the one who is to come" (ὁ ἐρχόμενος) is the Messiah. It recalls John's promise that a more powerful one was "coming" (3:16); the alarmed cry of demons about to be thrashed, "Have you come to destroy us?" (4:34); and Jesus' own statement of his mission, "I have not come to call the righteous to repentance but sinners" (5:32).[3]

Does John's question disclose "the rise of doubt or the dawn of faith"?[4] Fitzmyer claims, "John's hesitation stems, not from a failing faith in Jesus' messianic role, but from his failure to see Jesus playing the role of fiery reformer."[5] The inference from John's preaching is that he expected something along the lines of "The Battle Hymn of the Republic": "Mine eyes have seen the glory of the coming of the Lord; He is trampling out the vintage where the grapes of wrath are stored; He has loosed the fateful lightning of His terrible swift sword" (cf. 3:9, 17). The terrible swift sword that was to be laid at the root of the trees is turning out to be terribly slow. The only trampling that

was getting done was on John's head. He was one captive who was not being set free (4:18). Dupont infers that John was embarrassed to have declared that the day of judgment and the avenging judge were coming, only to learn that the Messiah was far kinder and gentler.[6]

I contend that John's question should be viewed instead as the dawning of recognition. As Luke presents it, the one who has been plowing ahead to make the paths straight to prepare the way of the Lord (3:4) hears what has been happening and stops to take a look back to see Jesus coming along with power. Caird states, "It was quite natural, then, that John should not have begun to think of Jesus as Messiah until he heard about the impression he was making wherever he went."[7] Even Jesus' own disciples did not grasp immediately his full identity. Peter's confession about Jesus (9:20) does not come until after John's death (9:7).

In Luke, John has not previously acknowledged that Jesus is the one who is to come (contrast John 1:29 – 37). Had he done so, he would have persuaded his disciples "to transfer their allegiance" to Jesus.[8] Luke makes no mention of John's imprisonment (contrast Matt 11:2) though it may be presumed from 3:20 and necessitates that he send word to Jesus through emissaries. Since Luke does not present John floundering in prison, John's question is not motivated by discouragement or

---

2. The question of Jesus' identity will be raised by the guests in the home of Simon the Pharisee (7:49), Jesus' disciples (8:25), Herod (9:9), the Sanhedrin (22:67, 70), and Pilate (23:3).

3. Johnson, *The Gospel of Luke*, 122; see also 19:38. In the Old Testament, the "coming one" could refer to the religious pilgrim coming to Jerusalem (Ps 118:26), to the coming prophet (Deut 18:15 – 18; see John 6:14), to Elijah (Mal 4:5; see Matt 11:14), to God (Zech 14:5; see Rev 1:4, 8; 4:8), or to a messianic figure (Hab 2:3; Mal 3:1; Dan 7:13). A key messianic link is the LXX version of Gen 49:10, "A ruler shall not cease from Judah, nor a ruler from his loins, until there come the things reserved for him; and he is the expectation of nations" (author's translation). See Jacques Dupont, "L'ambassade de Jean-Baptiste (Matthieu 11,2 – 6; Luc 7,18 – 23)," *NRTh* 83

(1961): 805 – 21, 943 – 59.

4. Caird, *Saint Luke*, 111.

5. Fitzmyer, *Luke*, 1:665. Green, *The Gospel of Luke*, 296, claims that Jesus is engaged in the work of sifting that John had prophesied, but it "had apparently proceeded along unanticipated lines."

6. Dupont, "L'ambassade de Jean-Baptiste (Matthieu 11,2 – 6; Luc 7,18 – 23)." The woes in 6:24 – 26; 10:13 – 15; and 11:42 – 53, however, reveal that Jesus does not reject John's expectations of judgment.

7. Caird, *Saint Luke*, 111. Herod also will hear about Jesus' works, and it will prompt him to wonder who he is (9:7 – 9).

8. Ibid.

impatience. Nor is John dismayed that Jesus kept company with the "chaff" that he thought was destined to be burned in the fire (3:17),[9] or that God's Messiah was giving "attention to the dead, the very poor, the outcast, the acknowledged violator of the law, and the diseased," rather than destroying Israel's oppressors.[10] Luke has no interest in what has prompted the question, only the answer to it. He does not report John's response when his disciples return with Jesus' answer because either it is irrelevant, or the answer to the question should now be self-evident to anyone who has prophetic discernment.

A theological reason shapes the construction of the narrative. Luke does not have John validate Jesus' credentials; only God does that (3:21 – 22).[11] John has simply foretold the coming of an anonymous eschatological Mighty One. Readers learn that it is Jesus from the narrative. John himself learns that it is Jesus from the reports of what Jesus has been doing.

7:20 – 21 When the men came to him, they said, "John the Baptist sent us to you, saying, 'Are you the one who is to come or should we expect another?'" At that very moment, he healed many people of diseases, plagues, and evil spirits, and he gave sight to many blind persons (παραγενόμενοι δὲ πρὸς αὐτὸν οἱ ἄνδρες εἶπαν· Ἰωάννης ὁ βαπτιστὴς ἀπέστειλεν ἡμᾶς πρὸς σὲ λέγων· σὺ εἶ ὁ ἐρχόμενος ἢ ἄλλον προσδοκῶμεν; ἐν ἐκείνῃ τῇ ὥρᾳ ἐθεράπευσεν πολλοὺς ἀπὸ νόσων καὶ μαστίγων καὶ πνευμάτων πονηρῶν καὶ τυφλοῖς πολλοῖς ἐχαρίσατο βλέπειν). John's disciples do exactly as they are told and ask Jesus the pointed question. Jesus does not answer the question with a defensive argument but with action. The miracles are not simply deeds of compassion that reveal that he is a more gentle Messiah than

was expected but point to his power and status as Messiah. They correspond to the program he announced in Nazareth that the Spirit had anointed him to do "today" (4:16 – 30).

7:22 He answered them, "Go report to John the things you have seen and heard: the blind see again, the lame walk, those with skin diseases are cleansed, the deaf hear, the dead are raised, and good news is being proclaimed to the poor" (καὶ ἀποκριθεὶς εἶπεν αὐτοῖς· πορευθέντες ἀπαγγείλατε Ἰωάννῃ ἃ εἴδετε καὶ ἠκούσατε· τυφλοὶ ἀναβλέπουσιν, χωλοὶ περιπατοῦσιν, λεπροὶ καθαρίζονται καὶ κωφοὶ ἀκούουσιν, νεκροὶ ἐγείρονται, πτωχοὶ εὐαγγελίζονται). Jesus' answer matches what Luke has narrated or will narrate. It also echoes prophecy in Isa 29 and 35: "the blind see again" (Luke 18:35 – 43; Isa 29:18; 35:5 – 6), "the lame walk" (Luke 5:17 – 26), and "those with skin diseases are cleansed" (Luke 5:12 – 16; 17:11 – 19). This miracle does not appear in Isaiah but it is akin to raising the dead and has other consequences. Stettler comments:

> Demons, scale disease, continuous blood discharges and death, all involved severe impurity and therefore excluded the people concerned from Israel. By cleansing and healing the sick, Jesus overcomes what separates them from God and reintegrates them in the holy people of God.[12]

Luke does not narrate a miracle where physical hearing is restored ("the deaf hear"), but the reference to the deaf in Isa 29:18 ("the deaf will hear the words of a scroll"; see Isa 35:5 – 6) may apply to the spiritually deaf. "The dead are raised" is recounted in the preceding episode (Luke 7:11 – 17; cf. Isa 26:19).

Jesus' answer shares the same set of messianic expectations found in the Dead Sea Scrolls

9. Contra Caird, ibid., 112.
10. Contra Craddock, *Luke*, 100.
11. Danker, *Jesus and the New Age*, 45.
12. Stettler, "Sanctification in the Jesus Tradition," 159.

fragment 4Q521 (frag 2 col. II), which applies Isa
29:18; 35:5 – 6; 26:19; and 61:1 – 2 to "the anointed
one" or the Messiah. This fragment reveals shared
expectations, current in Judaism, that derived
from a common core of Old Testament texts about
the signs of the Messiah:[13]

> 1 [for the heav]ens and the earth will listen to
> his Messiah, 2 [and all] that is in them will not
> turn away from the holy precepts. 3 Be encour-
> aged, you who are seeking the Lord in his service!
> 4 Will you not, perhaps, encounter the Lord in
> it, all those who hope in their heart? 5 For the
> Lord will observe the devout, and call the just by
> name, 6 and upon the poor he will place his spirit,
> and the faithful he will renew with his strength.
> 7 For he will honour the devout upon the throne
> of the eternal royalty, 8 freeing prisoners, giving
> sight to the blind, straightening out the twisted.
> 9 Ever shall I cling to those who hope. In his
> mercy he will jud[ge,] 10 and from no-one shall
> the fruit [of] good [deeds] be delayed, 11 and the
> Lord will perform marvellous acts such as have
> not existed, just as he sa[id] 12 for he will heal
> the badly wounded and will make the dead live,
> he will proclaim good news to the meek, 13 give
> lavishly [to the need]y, lead the exiled and enrich
> the hungry.[14]

Jesus, in effect, tells John, "What the Scripture says
about what is to come is being fulfilled. Yes, I am
he."

It may seem surprising that preaching good
news to the poor (see 4:18; 6:20; 14:13, 21) is the
capstone of his messianic activity because it seems
anticlimactic after the more pyrotechnic miracle
of raising the dead. Jesus' activity as Messiah,

however, marks the intervention of God's empire
on the world that inverts the categories of life and
death, disease and health, and rich and poor. In the
exorcisms, the house of Satan is being plundered;
in proclaiming good news to the poor, the structures of the Roman Empire are being overthrown.

**7:23 "And blessed is the one who is not of-
fended by me"** (καὶ μακάριός ἐστιν ὃς ἐὰν μὴ
σκανδαλισθῇ ἐν ἐμοί). This beatitude is the only
one in which Jesus issues a challenge rather than
a proclamation.[15] Blessedness is based on one's response to Jesus. If what he is doing is what one
hoped for from the Messiah, then one is fortunate
because he will not disappoint. If it is not what one
hoped for, Jesus blesses all who are willing to "undergo conversion in their views of God's purpose,
the inbreaking eschatological salvation, and, so, of
Jesus' mission."[16] This beatitude reveals Jesus' acknowledgment that barriers exist that can prevent
people from recognizing God's reign in his person and ministry. Preconceived ideas about what
the Messiah is supposed to do may lead them to
be shocked and dismayed by what Jesus does, and
worse, what is ultimately done to him.

**7:24 – 25 When John's messengers left, he began
to speak to the crowds about John. "What did
you go out into the wilderness to observe? A
reed fluttering in the wind? No. Then what
did you go out to see? A man attired in soft
finery? Look, those decked out in such splendid finery who live in luxury are found in
royal palaces"** (ἀπελθόντων δὲ τῶν ἀγγέλων
Ἰωάννου ἤρξατο λέγειν πρὸς τοὺς ὄχλους περὶ
Ἰωάννου· τί ἐξήλθατε εἰς τὴν ἔρημον θεάσασθαι;

---

13. John J. Collins ("The Works of the Messiah," *DSD* 1 [1994]: 98 – 112) calls it a remarkable parallel to Jesus' answer to John's disciples and concludes that "the actions described in Isa 61 were already viewed as 'works of the messiah' in some Jewish circles before the career of Jesus. They were indicative, however, of a prophetic messiah of the Elijah type rather than

of the royal messiah who was expected to restore the kingdom of David" (112).
14. Florentino García Martinez, *The Dead Sea Scrolls Trans-lated* (Leiden: Brill, 1994), 394.
15. Nolland, *Luke*, 1:331.
16. Green, *The Gospel of Luke*, 297.

κάλαμον ὑπὸ ἀνέμου σαλευόμενον; ἀλλὰ τί ἐξήλθατε ἰδεῖν; ἄνθρωπον ἐν μαλακοῖς ἱματίοις ἠμφιεσμένον; ἰδοὺ οἱ ἐν ἱματισμῷ ἐνδόξῳ καὶ τρυφῇ ὑπάρχοντες ἐν τοῖς βασιλείοις εἰσίν). The shaking reed may be a metaphor for someone "frail and fickle,"[17] or it may refer to something "commonplace," something no one would make a special effort to see.[18] The wilderness is the traditional place of God's revelation (Isa 40:3; 1QS 8:12 – 14; Josephus, *J.W.* 2.13.4 §259; 7.10.1 §438), and the people did not venture there to see something trivial but to meet a steadfast prophet. The man attired in "soft finery" (μαλακοῖς ἱματίοις) evokes the image of a frivolous dandy. The fashion plate does not wander about in the wilderness but instead lounges around in the comfortable confines of a palace.

Dunn reminds us that "Jesus' teaching could have a sharp political edge."[19] The combination of images suggests a possible gibe at Herod Antipas, whom Jesus later brands as "this fox" (13:32). The reed appeared on his coins celebrating the foundation of his new capital at Tiberias in AD 20 on the west coast of the Sea of Galilee with its plenteous reeds (identified as the "Sea of Tiberias" in John 6:1; 21:1).[20] The shaking reed "may refer to Antipas' bending with the wind to survive politically, or to his cowardice," and the two images hark back "to the biblical motif of the conflict between prince and prophet." Jesus is saying that they did not go out to see Herod Antipas, their oppressor, "but his prophetic nemesis; and they were not mistaken in their impression that John was someone worth going out to see in the wilderness."[21]

Contemporary allusions to political figures or events quickly lose their currency and relevance. As Luke understands it, Jesus is asking about John's purpose. Was he just an inconsequential passing craze? The attraction to fads are to be found in palaces where people are consumed by the beauty of their clothing, their estates, and their luxurious lifestyle. The contrast with John could not be greater.

7:26 – 27 "What did you really go out to see? A prophet. Yes, I tell you, and much more than a prophet. This is the one about whom it is written: 'Behold I send my messenger ahead of you, who will prepare the way before you'" (ἀλλὰ τί ἐξήλθατε ἰδεῖν; προφήτην· ναί, λέγω ὑμῖν, καὶ περισσότερον προφήτου. οὗτός ἐστιν περὶ οὗ γέγραπται· ἰδοὺ ἀποστέλλω τὸν ἄγγελόν μου πρὸ προσώπου σου, ὃς κατασκευάσει τὴν ὁδόν σου ἔμπροσθέν σου). Describing John as a prophet and more than a prophet recalls his father Zechariah's Spirit-filled word: "And you, child, will be called the prophet of the Most High" (1:76). The crowd's attention to John testifies that they regarded him as a prophet (20:3 – 6), but Jesus recasts their understanding of his role in salvation history. He was more than another prophetic voice crying in the wilderness for the people to repent. The scriptural quotation clarifies his greater significance.

The citation Jesus uses conflates two Old Testament (LXX) texts (Exod 23:20 and Mal 3:1). In Malachi the function of the messenger is to prepare the way of the Lord, whereas in Exodus his function is to guard Israel on the way to the Promised Land.[22] Whose way is being prepared in this

17. Fitzmyer, *Luke*, 1:674.

18. Nolland, *Luke*, 1:336.

19. Dunn, *Jesus Remembered*, 451.

20. Gerd Theissen, *The Gospels in Context: Social and Political History in the Synoptic Tradition* (trans. L. M. Maloney; Edinburgh: T&T Clark, 1992), 26 – 42.

21. David E. Garland, *Reading Matthew: A Literary and Theological Commentary on the First Gospel* (New York: Crossroad, 1992), 126. Herod sends Jesus back to Pilate arrayed in "shining raiment" (23:11) to mock him.

22. David Ravens, *Luke and the Restoration of Israel* (JSNT-Sup 119; Sheffield: Sheffield Academic, 1995), 288.

new context, Jesus' way or Israel's way? The use of the verb "prepare" (κατασκευάζω) in 1:17 suggests that it could refer to Israel, but the context requires that it refer to Jesus as an eschatological figure who is heralded by John.[23] Caird asserts that the hybrid Scripture fuses two messianic traditions, "one which said that Elijah would appear as herald of the day of the Lord, and one which said that God would raise up a prophet, a second Moses (Deut 18:15 – 19; cf. John 1:21; 6:14; 7:40). John has inherited both the staff of Moses and the mantle of Elijah."[24] Note how Moses and Elijah appear together as forerunners of Jesus in the transfiguration (9:30).

7:28 "I tell you, among those born of women none is greater than John, yet the most insignificant person in the reign of God is greater than he is" (λέγω ὑμῖν, μείζων ἐν γεννητοῖς γυναικῶν Ἰωάννου οὐδείς ἐστιν· ὁ δὲ μικρότερος ἐν τῇ βασιλείᾳ τοῦ θεοῦ μείζων αὐτοῦ ἐστιν). This high praise is hardly the creation of Christian tradition, since Jesus was also born of a woman.[25] John's birth was proof that with God nothing is impossible (1:37). He was commissioned as a prophet of the Most High (1:76), called great before the Lord, and would fulfill his mission in the spirit and power of Elijah (1:14 – 17), but his work was only preparatory. Jesus does not exclude John from a place in God's reign, since the patriarchs and all the prophets are also included (13:28). John had two functions: to prepare Israel for the reign of God and to prepare the way for Jesus.

7:29 All the people and even the tax collectors who had heard justified God because they were immersed with John's immersion (καὶ πᾶς ὁ λαὸς ἀκούσας καὶ οἱ τελῶναι ἐδικαίωσαν τὸν θεὸν βαπτισθέντες τὸ βάπτισμα Ἰωάννου). Luke interrupts the narration of Jesus' remarks with a parenthetical comment to describe who responded to John's message and who did not. It prepares for the reception that Jesus will also get from the same groups. As Johnson observes, this interjection, absent from the Matthean parallel, enables "the reader to put together diverse strands in the story up to this point."[26] It confirms that those considered sinners and outcasts, like the tax collectors, have been and will continue to be more receptive to God's message than the Pharisees with all their punctilious attention to religious regulations.

The emphasis on "hear[ing]" (ἀκούσας; see Rom 10:17) implies listening that produced the decision to submit to John's immersion. Their obedience is interpreted as "justify[ing] God" (ἐδικαίωσαν τὸν θεόν). This literal translation is preserved to reveal the parallel with 7:35, "And yet Wisdom is justified by … her children." But what does it mean "to justify God"?

Elsewhere in Luke, the verb "to justify" relates to the justification of human beings (Luke 10:29; 16:15; 18:14; Acts 13:38 – 39). Here and in 7:35 it means something else. In the paragraph's structure, those who "rejected the purpose of God for themselves" are the opposite of those who "justified God." Most translations understand it to mean that they acknowledged or deemed right something about God: "God's justice" (NASB; NRSV; NJB, "God's saving justice"); "God's way" (TNIV); "God's way of righteousness" (CSB). Louw and Nida render it: "all the people and the tax collectors heard him, and they obeyed God's righteous commands."[27]

John warned of God's judgment, proclaimed an immersion of repentance for the forgiveness of

23. Nolland, *Luke*, 1:337.

24. Caird, *Saint Luke*, 113, who believes that the synthesis originated "in the creative mind of Jesus."

25. The phrase is found in Job 14:1; 15:14; 25:4; Gal 4:4;

1QS 11.21; 1QH 13.14.

26. Johnson, *The Gospel of Luke*, 125.

27. *GELNT*, 36.22.

sins — bypassing the normal channels for obtaining forgiveness through the temple sacrifices — and pointed to the coming of the more powerful one who would immerse them with the Holy Spirit and fire (3:1 – 17). Those who submitted to his repentance immersion accepted as righteous God's judgment upon them and submitted to God's plan for Israel's redemption.[28] This sense of the verb "justify" is confirmed by its use in Ps 51:4 (LXX 50:6) and *Ps. Sol.* 2:15: "I shall prove you right, O God, in uprightness of heart; for your judgments are right, O God" (see also Ps 119:7, 9; Rom 3:4 – 5).[29]

7:30 But the Pharisees and the law experts rejected the purpose of God for themselves because they had not been immersed by him (οἱ δὲ Φαρισαῖοι καὶ οἱ νομικοὶ τὴν βουλὴν τοῦ θεοῦ ἠθέτησαν εἰς ἑαυτούς μὴ βαπτισθέντες ὑπ' αὐτοῦ). The word "law experts" (or "lawyers," νομικοί) occurs six times in Luke and is equivalent to the "scribes" (γραμματεῖς). Luke may have used this term because it was the nearest equivalent in Greco-Roman society to the Jewish scribe, i.e., an exegete of the (religious) law. It is shorthand for "law scholars" (νομοδιδάσκαλοι, 5:17; Acts 5:34).

The noun "purpose" (βουλή) is used in Acts to refer to a plan or purpose (Acts 4:28; 13:36; 20:27); in Acts 2:23 it refers specifically to God's plan and foreknowledge for Jesus to be crucified. Mary bears witness to God's plan to exalt the lowly and bring low the mighty (1:52). This purpose is bad news for those who despise the lowly and instead exalt themselves (18:14). The Pharisees seek to justify themselves (10:29; 16:15; see 18:9) and reject God's justification of others. They are overscrupulous about such matters as immersing before eating (ἐβαπτίσθη, 11:38) and express shock that Jesus does not follow suit, but they have refused to submit to John's repentance immersion, an immersion of far greater importance. Their refusal means that they are unwilling to repent and reveals that they are a brood of vipers, not sons of Abraham; they will not escape the coming wrath (3:7).

7:31 "To what shall I compare the people of this generation? What are they like?" (τίνι οὖν ὁμοιώσω τοὺς ἀνθρώπους τῆς γενεᾶς ταύτης καὶ τίνι εἰσὶν ὅμοιοι;). Jesus comments further on this situation. In the context, "this generation" must refer to the Pharisees and legal experts and persons of their ilk who failed to respond to John and Jesus and thereby rejected the purpose of God. "This generation" (τῆς γενεᾶς ταύτης) has a pejorative sense that recalls to mind the proverbial evil "generation" of the wilderness (Deut 1:35; 32:5, 20). Like the wilderness generation, this generation too is "faithless and crooked" (9:41) and "evil" (11:29 – 32; see Acts 2:40); but worse, it is destined to be damned for all the innocent blood that has been shed (11:50 – 51) and to reject the Son of Man (17:25). As God's mighty acts of salvation did not forestall the grumbling and rebellion of the wilderness generation, so Jesus' mighty acts of salvation do not prevent grumbling and rebellion in his generation.[30] The Pharisees grumble and bare their teeth throughout Jesus' ministry (5:30; 15:2; 19:7).

28. The aorist participle "immersed" (βαπτισθέντες) follows the primary verb and describes antecedent action as contemporaneous. Here it can express cause behind the statement that they "justified God" (Marshall, *The Gospel of Luke*, 299).

29. See also Prov 8:8 – 9: "All the words of my mouth are just; none of them is crooked or perverse. To the discerning all of them are right; they are upright to those who have found

knowledge." See also *Pss. Sol.* 4:8; 8:7, 26; 9:2 "that your righteousness might be proven right."

30. Evald Lövestam, "The ἡ γενεὰ αὕτη Eschatology in Mk 13:30 parr.," in *L'Apocalypse johanique et l'apocalyptique dans le Nouveau Testament* (ed. J. Lambrecht; Gembloux: Duculot, 1980), 403 – 13.

7:32 **"They are like children who sit in the marketplace and yell out to one another: 'We played the pipes for you and you did not dance. We sang dirges and you did not weep'"** (ὅμοιοί εἰσιν παιδίοις τοῖς ἐν ἀγορᾷ καθημένοις καὶ προσφωνοῦσιν ἀλλήλοις ἃ λέγει· ηὐλήσαμεν ὑμῖν καὶ οὐκ ὠρχήσασθε, ἐθρηνήσαμεν καὶ οὐκ ἐκλαύσατε). Jesus draws on the world of children's play to illustrate this generation's nature. They are like petulant children squabbling over playing the marriage game, piping and dancing, and the funeral game, wailing and mourning. The use of the third person, "they are like," shows that Jesus does not lump his audience together with "this generation" even though he uses the second person, "you say," in 7:33 – 34 (Matt 11:18 – 19 has "they say"). But the change in person offers a warning to the listeners: Do not become like them!

If this image functions as an allegory, to which group of children is this generation compared and how do John and Jesus figure in? (1) Are they the children who want to call the shots and demand that others play first "wedding" and then "funeral"? If so, Jesus and John become the children who refuse to join in their games. It pictures the Pharisees and legal experts wanting these prophets to dance to their tune. Like spoiled brats, who accuse their playmates of being the spoilsports because they will not do their bidding, they condemn John and Jesus for their refusal to defer to their wishes. This reading would assume that they not only reject the plan of God for themselves, they attempt to substitute their own plan. They want to direct God's prophets, demanding that John dance and then that Jesus mourn.

(2) Are John and Jesus the ones who pipe and wail, and this generation the ones who refuse to dance or weep? Jesus invites them to a joyous wedding with his announcement of the forgiveness of sins (7:33 – 34).[31] John invited them to a funeral with his demand of radical repentance and the prediction of certain doom for those who failed to heed his call. This generation will not be moved by the wailing of John's call to repentance or by the piping of Jesus' joyous announcement of God's forgiveness. They sit sulking on the sidelines. This reading lends itself to a chiastic pattern:

A Piping the wedding
   B wailing the funeral
   B′ John came
A′ The Son of Man came

This interpretation reverses the chronological order of John's and Jesus' appeals and, like the first interpretation, requires that John and Jesus be identified with one of the groups of children, who both seem to be portrayed in a negative light. The question asks, "What is this generation like?" The answer is, "They are like children." Are John and Jesus not to be distinguished from this puerile lot?

(3) Possibly, then, Jesus intends for the parable to present both the active and passive children as disagreeable. The one group wants to choose and control the game; the other refuses to join in any game. The children's play is paralyzed by their individual selfishness and ill-natured insistence on having their way. The image illustrates the cranky nature of this bunch who gives thumbs-down to whomever God sends to them. No matter who comes or what they do, this generation will complain.[32] "This generation" turns a deaf ear to God's eschatological prophets and ignores the crisis of God's reign breaking in on them. As a result, calamity awaits them (see Prov 1:24 – 32) because the reign of God is not child's play.

---

31. Jesus has identified himself as the bridegroom and his followers as wedding guests (5:34).

32. Neale, *None but the Sinners*, 138.

7:33 "For John the Baptist has come and did not eat bread nor drink wine, and you say, 'He has a demon'" (ἐλήλυθεν γὰρ Ἰωάννης ὁ βαπτιστὴς μὴ ἐσθίων ἄρτον μήτε πίνων οἶνον, καὶ λέγετε· δαιμόνιον ἔχει). The "for" (γάρ) introduces the application of the parable to the ministries of John and Jesus. John came neither eating nor drinking (see 1:15; 5:33), and they say he has a demon, perhaps because only supernatural beings can exist without food or water.

7:34 "The Son of Man has come eating and drinking, and you say, 'Look, a glutton and a drunkard, a friend of tax collectors and sinners'" (ἐλήλυθεν ὁ υἱὸς τοῦ ἀνθρώπου ἐσθίων καὶ πίνων, καὶ λέγετε· ἰδοὺ ἄνθρωπος φάγος καὶ οἰνοπότης, φίλος τελωνῶν καὶ ἁμαρτωλῶν). Jesus is found dining throughout Luke's narrative (5:29; 7:36; 10:38; 11:37; 13:26; 14:1, 12; 19:5 – 7), and it is part of his campaign to restore sinners. If the charge of being "a glutton and a drunkard" (see 5:33) is related to the stubborn and rebellious son of Deut 21:18 – 21, it is a serious one that prescribes stoning to death to purge the evil from their midst. If it echoes Prov 23:20 – 21, it simply characterizes Jesus as a fool who will come to poverty.[33]

"This generation" baits both messengers with their barbs. John is a churlish killjoy shrieking "Repent!" all of the time. He should be less austere, more congenial, and more open to the world. Jesus is too worldly and joyful. Being a friend of tax collectors and sinners (5:29 – 30) assumes that a reciprocal relationship exists and that he joins in their dissipation. He should demonstrate greater solemnity and more conformity to conventional, that is,

pharisaic, piety. As Findlay says, "These people find John too unsociable with the right people, and Jesus too sociable with the wrong people."[34]

7:35 "And yet Wisdom is justified by all of her children" (καὶ ἐδικαιώθη ἡ σοφία ἀπὸ πάντων τῶν τέκνων αὐτῆς). The καί has a constrastive force here that means "and yet."

"Wisdom" (ἡ σοφία) is a personification of God's counsel and means "God in his wisdom." In the context of Christian faith, it represents the divine plan manifested in Christ and the gospel (see 11:49; 1 Cor 1:24, 30; 2:7). John and Jesus have been sent to carry out the divine plan, but this childish generation rejects them and therefore also God's wisdom.

The phrase translated "is justified by" (ἐδικαιώθη … ἀπό) is difficult. The verb "justified" retains the basic meaning "to prove right" before any adversaries or accusers that is derived from its metaphorical roots in legal language. The preposition ἀπό plus the genitive has the meaning "by" in this context (see Acts 2:22; 15:4, 33; 2 Cor 7:13; Jas 1:13).[35] Matthew's parallel has "Wisdom is proved right by her deeds" (Matt 11:19), and "deeds" forms an inclusio with Matt 11:2. In Matthew's context, when John heard about the "works of the Messiah," Jesus' mighty deeds, it triggered his question to Jesus (Matt 11:2). Luke's phrase, "Wisdom is justified by … her children," is not as clear. The appearance of the verb "justify" in 7:29 suggests that it should bear upon the interpretation of 7:35, and this statement contrasts what precedes in 7:30 – 34. Green identifies an "inverted parallelism" in the sequence:

33. Howard Clark Kee, "Jesus: A Glutton and a Drunkard," *NTS* 42 (1996): 374 – 93.

34. J. Alexander Findlay, *The Gospel according to St. Luke: A Commentary* (London: SCM, 1937), 93.

35. Simon J. Gathercole ("The Justification of Wisdom [Matt 11.19b/Luke 7.35]," *NTS* 49 [2003]: 476 – 88) argues that the preposition ἀπό means "acquitted of," "not held responsible

for," "set free from" (citing Acts 13:38 – 39; Rom 6:7; Sir 26:29; 1 Esd 4:39). He concludes (480) that it means, "Wisdom has been dissociated from her children" and that this statement explains the bitter complaint about this generation rather than offering a contrast: "This generation has placed itself in the position of judge and given its verdict that Lady Wisdom has nothing to do with the Baptist or the Son of Man."

v. 29 All the people ... justified God

    v. 30 the Pharisees and lawyers reject God's purpose for themselves

    vv. 31 – 34 the people of this generation reject John and Jesus

v. 35 Wisdom is justified by all her children.[36]

According to Prov 1:20 – 33, scoffers refuse to listen because they hate knowledge and do not choose the fear of the Lord: "But those who listen to me will be secure and will live at ease, without dread of disaster" (Prov 1:33 NRSV). In Luke 7:35, the children of divine Wisdom are those who listen to the message of John and Jesus, recognize in it the plan of God, and align themselves with God's purpose by heeding their directives.[37] The following story in 7:36 – 50 illustrates the statement with a concrete example of a scoffing Pharisee and one of Wisdom's children, a female sinner in the town. Wisdom's children, who accept God's will and do it (8:21), comprise the most unlikely people — tax collectors and sinners.

Theology in Application

1. Confirming Truth

Jesus provides an example on how to respond to questions and doubts about whether the claims made about him are true. Instead of engaging in a disputation with his questioners, he acts. In response to a world that often questions the truth of Christianity, Christians often engage in aggressive polemical attacks, special pleading, or withdrawal from the arena. Jesus knows that he is dealing with an honest, sympathetic inquirer who is open to belief. In response, he engages in serving others. How does one know that Christianity is true? It is action, mercy-filled ministry in people's lives that speaks the loudest and confirms its truth.

2. John as the Greatest and the Least

The statement that John is "more than a prophet" is enigmatic. Does it mean that he is "the last prophet"? The declaration that none born of women is greater than John, yet the most insignificant person in the reign of God is greater than he is (7:28), is even more enigmatic. Bovon explains:

> Since he is the first to break the path into the eschatological fulfillment, he can be considered the greatest among humankind (v. 28a). But since he also has one foot in the old age, any full member of the kingdom of God is greater than he. The metaphorical comparison ("greater" and "smaller") refers to persons not as individuals

---

36. Green, *The Gospel of Luke*, 304.

37. M. Jack Suggs (*Wisdom, Christology, and Law in Matthew's Gospel* [Cambridge, MA: Harvard Univ. Press, 1970] 34 – 36) argues that in the original saying Wisdom's children referred to Wisdom's prophets, John and Jesus, but that Luke adapted it to apply to those who accept these prophets to fit the unit's theme of the proper response to John and Jesus. In Luke 11:49 – 51, Jesus warns that the Wisdom of God will send prophets and apostles, and "this generation" will kill and persecute some of them. In keeping with Luke's understanding, Lady Wisdom's "children" would refer to those who accept the prophets and apostles.

but as members of a community: humanity ... "among those born of women" versus the reign of God, in which they have found their new home and their new identity.[38]

John's greatness is "assigned to him by God" and has nothing to do with any "personal achievement or incredible personality." Nolland concludes,

> John stood at the pinnacle of all that was possible prior to the ministry of Jesus, but now the anticipated in-breaking of the kingdom has begun. In this new situation greatness has a now [sic] meaning and comes as the gift of the kingdom of God to the little ones.[39]

John, the greatest man who ever lived before the advent of God's reign (16:16), belongs to and represents the old order (the Aaronic priesthood), who pointed the way to the new. Ravens claims, "Like Moses, John prepares the way into the promised land and, like Moses, he does not enter it himself (7:28)."[40]

Jesus is not engaged in an abstract seminar discussion about the significance of John. His point is a summons to his audience to enter the reign of God. The disclosure about John's role from Scripture assumes that God's reign arrived with Jesus, and one can enter it now only by becoming *his* disciple. John himself acknowledged the difference between those who are immersed by him with water and those immersed by Spirit and fire by the coming one. The contrast is between those "born of women" and those born of the Spirit.[41]

3. The Rejection of God's Plan

Craddock maintains that a true prophet does not echo "public opinion" and is not "the spokesman for the wealthy and powerful."[42] Nor is a prophet a cheerleader for nationalistic ambitions. Neither John nor Jesus, who are both Elijah-like, will be welcomed by everyone in Israel. The parable about "this generation" is a partial fulfillment of what Simeon said would happen, "Behold, this one is set for the falling and rising of many in Israel and [to be] a sign that is refused" (2:34). The contrast between Jesus' followers and disciples and the obduracy of "this generation" marks the beginning of the unfolding of the division in Israel.

Those who resist John's call for repentance and Jesus' announcement about the presence of God's reign find fault with God's messengers. What they really attempt to do is make God's will conform to their own. They do not acknowledge the sovereign will of God but want to dictate the orders. They err in their judgments, and their judgments are meaningless anyway. They may reject God's plan for Israel and themselves, but they have not scuttled it. Interestingly, they would probably be even

---

38. Bovon, *Luke 1:1 – 9:50*, 284.

39. Nolland, *Luke*, 1:338.

40. Ravens, *Luke and the Restoration of Israel*, 289.

41. Minear, *To Heal and to Reveal*, 118 – 19.

42. Craddock, *Luke*, 101.

more aggrieved to see the gospel extend to Gentiles. The two very different lifestyles of John and Jesus, however, prepare for the mission into the Gentile world, where persons living in different cultures will have fellowship under the lordship of Christ.

Many members of Christian churches reading this parable would not automatically connect the ill-humored, obstinate children with those outside the church. They have witnessed this same kind of faultfinding and foot-dragging among Christians within the church. Such people always want their way and either force their will onto others or quit to join some other church. The petty bickering that afflicts many Christian communities causes nonbelievers to turn away from or to poke fun at the church. If the parable does its work, readers should be able to see themselves mirrored in the headstrong squabbling children. It is easy to slip into the role of those who hinder God's plan for the world with our power struggles and backbiting.

Luke 7:36 – 50

Literary Context

This dramatic narrative of Jesus' confrontation with a Pharisee in his home is the climax of the double theme in chap. 7 on the saving visitation of God and the identity of the mediating messengers. It demonstrates that sinners "justify God" and that the Pharisees feel no need to repent and reject God's plan both for themselves and for others (7:29 – 35). Here a repentant sinner responds to forgiveness, while a Pharisee rejects God's verdict that he too is a sinner who needs forgiveness and hence rejects God's mercy on others. The focus, however, is on Jesus, not the Pharisee or the woman, and it highlights the difference between Jesus and John the Baptist, who both preached the same message of repentance. Jesus is a prophet but more than a prophet. He is the messianic prophet, who brings the forgiveness of sins.

The story follows immediately after the charge that Jesus is a foolish glutton and drunkard and a friend of the moral riffraff, tax collectors, and sinners.[1] Neale comments, "The story appears to be a way to demonstrate and confirm, by means of a specific example, the ludicrousness of the complaints about Jesus' table-fellowship."[2] Jesus chooses to be reckoned with the transgressors that also include Pharisees because he brings God's forgiveness. The goal is to bring all to repentance.

1. No temporal phrases introduce this story as a new unit, which Luke uses elsewhere to introduce a new pericope (see 5:17, 27; 6:1, 6, 12, 17; 7:1, 11).

2. Neale, *None but the Sinners*, 140.

Main Idea

Those who recognize their need for forgiveness and have received it through Jesus will respond with overwhelming love for him.

Translation

Luke 7:36–50

7:36	Circumstance	**A certain Pharisee asked him to eat with him,**
		and when he entered the Pharisee's house, **he reclined at table.**

37a	Character introduction	Behold,
		      when a woman, who was a sinner in the town, found out that he was ↵
		                              reclining at dinner in the Pharisee's house,

b	Introduction of point of tension	**she brought an alabaster jar filled with perfumed ointment.**
38a	Provocative actions	**She stood behind his feet weeping, and her tears began to rain down on his feet**
b		and **she dried them with her hair.**
c		**She continued kissing his feet**
d		and **anointing them with the perfumed ointment.**

39	Disdainful judgment	When the Pharisee who invited him saw it,
		 he said to himself,
		      "If this one were a prophet, he would know who and what sort of woman ↵
		                              this is who is touching him.
		      She is a sinner!"

40	Response	**Jesus answering [his thoughts] said to him,**
		      "Simon, I have something to say to you."
		 He replied,
		      "Teacher, go ahead and say it."

41	Parable	*"Two persons were indebted to a certain moneylender.* *One owed the equivalent of five hundred days' wages;* *the other, the equivalent of fifty.*
42a		* Since they did not have the means to repay him,* *he graciously forgave both the debt.*
b	Request for response	*Now which of them will love him more?"*
43a	Response	**Simon answered,** *"I suppose that it is the one who was graciously forgiven the more."*

Continued on next page.

b	Affirmation	**He said,**
		"You judged rightly."
44a	Comparison of the different responses to Jesus	**Turning to the woman, he said to Simon,**
		"Do you see this woman?
b		*I entered your house,*
		and you gave me no water for my feet.
c		*This woman has rained down tears on my feet*
		and dried them with her hair.
45a		*You gave me no kiss [of greeting].*
b		*From the time I entered, this woman has not ceased kissing my feet.*
46a		*You did not anoint my head with oil.*
b		*This woman anointed my feet with perfumed ointment.*
47a	Pronouncement	*Therefore, I tell you, her many sins have been forgiven*
		and for this reason she has shown so much love.
b	Aphorism	*But the one to whom little is forgiven shows little love."*
48	Pronouncement	**He said to her,**
		"Your sins have been forgiven."
49	Reaction to the pronouncements	**Those who reclined at table with him began to say among themselves,**
		"Who is this one who forgives sins?"
50	Pronouncement	**He said to the woman,**
		"Your faith has saved you.
		Go in peace."

Structure and Literary Form

The narrative's drama recalls the healing of the paralytic (5:17 – 26). A female intruder appears out of nowhere and demonstrates faith in Jesus by an extraordinary gesture. This woman also demonstrates extraordinary love for Jesus. Jesus announces the forgiveness of sins, and Pharisees object in their hearts and question his authority to forgive sins. Jesus reads the minds of his detractors, confronts them, and then directs for the person involved (the paralytic, the woman) to go.[3] This incident includes a parable to reinforce the point, and the announcement of salvation and peace.

This account is the first of three instances unique to Luke in which Jesus accepts a Pharisee's invitation to share a meal (see also 11:37 – 54; 14:1 – 24). In all three scenes, Jesus confronts his host and triumphs over him with his greater divine wisdom. Some regard the meal scenes as conforming to literary genre of the Hellenistic symposium that developed after Plato.[4] In a symposium "guests are expected to make speeches — whether humorous or serious — as part of the entertainment after dinner."[5] Talbert argues "that it is better not to claim that these Lukan texts belong to the

---

3. Johnson, *The Gospel of Luke*, 129.

4. Originally proposed by Xavier de Meeûs, "Composition de Lc. XIV et genre symposiaque," *ETL* 37 (1961): 847 – 70.

5. Robert C. Tannehill, "The Lukan Discourse on Invitations (Luke 14,7 – 24)," in *The Four Gospels, 1992* (ed. F. Van Segbroeck et. al.; Leuven: Leuven Univ. Press, 1992), 1604.

symposium genre as such." He points out that in this literary genre "the entire writing is devoted to the banquet"; "the two parts of the meal, the eating part and the drinking part, are clearly marked out"; and "all guests speak."[6] These do not apply to Luke. Here we have a monologue by Jesus, not a lively dialogue with other participants. Luke simply employs the motif of a meal as a setting for teaching.

Exegetical Outline

→ **I. Setting: a Pharisee's home (7:36)**

II. A woman's intrusion at a meal (7:37 – 38)

    A. Identification of her as a sinner (7:37a)

    B. Gestures of love (7:37b – 38)

III. Pharisee's response: negative judgment (7:39)

IV. Jesus' response: parable of the two debtors (7:40 – 43)

V. Application of the parable to the woman and the Pharisee (7:44 – 47)

VI. Demonstration of Jesus' authority to forgive sins (7:48 – 50)

Explanation of the Text

7:36 A certain Pharisee asked him to eat with him, and when he entered the Pharisee's house, he reclined at table (ἠρώτα δέ τις αὐτὸν τῶν Φαρισαίων ἵνα φάγῃ μετ᾽ αὐτοῦ, καὶ εἰσελθὼν εἰς τὸν οἶκον τοῦ Φαρισαίου κατεκλίθη). The reader has been introduced to Pharisees as having high status as influential leaders in a particularly rigorous interpretation of the law. All of Jesus' previous contacts with them (5:17 – 6:11) have led to stern opposition. Why a religious leading light would invite a reputed glutton and winebibber (7:34) to his home can only be inferred. Since Simon says, "If this one were a prophet" (7:39), which recalls the crowd's judgment that "a great prophet has been raised among us!" (7:16), presumably he is interested in judging Jesus for himself. He is not spoiling for a fight, but the Pharisees' previous conflicts with Jesus would lead the reader to expect his hostility to surface.

7:37 Behold, when a woman, who was a sinner in the town, found out that he was reclining at dinner in the Pharisee's house, she brought an alabaster jar filled with perfumed ointment (καὶ ἰδοὺ γυνὴ ἥτις ἦν ἐν τῇ πόλει ἁμαρτωλός, καὶ ἐπιγνοῦσα ὅτι κατάκειται ἐν τῇ οἰκίᾳ τοῦ Φαρισαίου, κομίσασα ἀλάβαστρον μύρου). Some Middle Eastern cultural details assumed in the text need to be clarified for us to comprehend what is happening in the story. Ancient life was lived in public, not behind walls. A large home would have a courtyard with rooms surrounding it and opening onto it, and perhaps a small dining room. Entertainment was a public affair and the doors of the house would be wide open; those not invited to the meal were free to wander in.[7] This context explains the somewhat surprising appearance of the woman at the meal. The text does not say that she "entered the house," and they could be dining in a

---

6. Talbert, *Reading Luke*, 170.

7. Kenneth E. Bailey, *Through Peasant Eyes* (Grand Rapids: Eerdmans, 1980), 3 – 4.

courtyard. Her unexpected presence is stressed by the introduction "Behold" (καὶ ἰδού).[8]

The narrator identifies the woman as a sinner and known as such by everyone in the town, including this host. Readers are left in the dark about the nature of her sin. Is she guilty of adultery or prostitution, or is she simply married to a notorious sinner? Her unrestrained expression of emotion might lead the modern reader to think the worst.[9] What kind of sinner she is, however, is irrelevant. Peter identifies himself as a "sinful man" (5:8), and a paralytic has his sins forgiven (5:23), but Luke has no interest in identifying the nature of their sins. We should not try to guess the nature of her guilt. Jesus' parable makes clear that it makes no difference.

Somehow this woman learns that Jesus is dining in Simon's home. Presumably she has had prior contact with Jesus (as had the women listed in 8:1–3 and Mary and Martha in 10:38–42). Luke makes no mention of the value of the perfumed oil in the alabaster jar (vial or box) that she brings.[10] Bringing the jar suggests her action is premeditated. It is the woman's humble, loving actions that are key rather than the cost of the perfume she pours out.

7:38 She stood behind his feet weeping, and her tears began to rain down on his feet and she dried them with her hair. She continued kissing his feet and anointing them with the perfumed ointment (καὶ στᾶσα ὀπίσω παρὰ τοὺς πόδας αὐτοῦ κλαίουσα τοῖς δάκρυσιν ἤρξατο βρέχειν τοὺς πόδας αὐτοῦ καὶ ταῖς θριξὶν τῆς κεφαλῆς αὐτῆς ἐξέμασσεν καὶ κατεφίλει τοὺς πόδας αὐτοῦ καὶ ἤλειφεν τῷ μύρῳ). Jesus is reclining at table with his legs outstretched behind him. The imperfect verbs "was kissing" (κατεφίλει) and "was anointing" (ἤλειφεν) and Jesus' comment that she had not stopped kissing his feet since he entered (7:45) warrant the translation "she continued kissing his feet and anointing them." It indicates that from the time she appeared she was doing this. Her tears drip down on Jesus' feet. Why is she crying? Are they tears of repentance or tears of thanksgiving and relief?[11] She has no towel with which to dry them. In a gesture of abject devotion, she stoops and lets down her hair, her crown and glory (1 Cor 11:15), to wipe the dirt-caked feet, now soaked with oil and tears.

The woman's low reputation makes her unwelcome, and her remarkable actions in hostile company could be easily misinterpreted. The offensive nature of feet in this society makes her actions even more significant. The ultimate insult to a vanquished enemy is to make him a "footstool" (Ps 110:1). John the Baptist asserts that he is unworthy even to untie the sandals of the one who is to come after him (3:16). Kilgallen, however, points out that this woman's actions toward Jesus' feet, mentioned six times in this passage, resonate with Isa 52:7: "How beautiful upon the mountains are the feet of the messenger who announces peace,

8. Bovon, *Luke 1:1–9:50*, 293.

9. Neale, *None but the Sinners*, 142.

10. The perfume does not indicate that she was of ill-repute (contra Bailey, *Through Peasant Eyes*, 8), since Mary of Bethany in John 12:1–8 is not suspect for pouring out precious ointment, nor is the anonymous woman in Matt 26:6–13 and Mark 14:3–9. It might strike a Greco-Roman audience, familiar with banquet courtesans, as odd, however, since a woman's presence at a banquet usually meant that she was less than reputable.

11. Bailey (*Through Peasant Eyes*, 8–9) paints a more volatile scene by imagining that they are tears of rage after she had

observed the deliberate affront to one who had deeply touched her life. He imagines that she says to herself: "They have not even extended the kiss of greeting to him! They have offered no water for his feet!" In a mixture of devotion to Jesus and anger at his calloused host who had so abused him, she impulsively offers him an expression of love and devotion in an attempt to compensate for the insult that he has received. Against this reconstruction is the fact that she brought the alabaster jar for the purpose of demonstrating her affection and thanksgiving, and Jesus notes that she has been kissing his feet since he entered (7:45).

who brings good news, who announces salvation, who says to Zion, 'Your God reigns' " (NRSV).[12] Note how in Matt 28:9, when the women encounter the resurrected Jesus, they "clasped his feet and worshiped him."

Her actions have been unfortunately eroticized by interpreters. Letting down hair in public was a disgraceful act for a proper Jewish woman.[13] Green puts it on par with going out in public topless,[14] while Bock simply labels it "immodest."[15] But a woman's loosened hair did not always connote that the woman had loose morals. Cosgrove provides numerous examples that show that in certain social situations it would not have been indecorous for a woman to unbind her hair in public.[16] Since no one at the table condemns her actions with outrage, it is unlikely that they understand them to be unseemly.

Cosgrove shows that "unbound hair on a weeping woman is naturally associated with grief, supplication, and gratitude."[17] He cites an incident in the popular Greek novel *Chaereas and Callirhoe*, in which Callirhoe (after being reunited with her husband) enters the shrine of Aphrodite, "places her hands and face on the goddess's feet, lets down her hair, and kisses the feet of the goddess" (8.8.15). In this setting, loving attention to the feet and letting down her hair are clearly acts of thankful veneration."[18] In the setting of the parable, this woman's actions imply that she is seeking something from Jesus or expressing gratitude to him. She is either weighed down by her guilt and pleading for forgiveness with a gesture of grief and humility; or, unburdened of her guilt, she expresses her immense gratitude by venerating him. Jesus' pronouncement in 7:47 clarifies that she has been forgiven and expresses her devotion to him.

7:39 When the Pharisee who invited him saw it, he said to himself, "If this one were a prophet, he would know who and what sort of woman this is who is touching him. She is a sinner!" (ἰδὼν δὲ ὁ Φαρισαῖος ὁ καλέσας αὐτὸν εἶπεν ἐν ἑαυτῷ λέγων· οὗτος εἰ ἦν προφήτης, ἐγίνωσκεν ἂν τίς καὶ ποταπὴ ἡ γυνὴ ἥτις ἅπτεται αὐτοῦ, ὅτι ἁμαρτωλός ἐστιν). We are let in on the private thoughts of the host, now identified simply as "the Pharisee." Green notes that those persons who engage in soliloquy in the narrative are those who lack "insight into Jesus' divine commission or even are opponents of God's purpose (cf. 5:21–22; 6:8)."[19] What Simon sees is what he is disposed to see. A woman like this should not be touching Jesus.

Simon is unmoved by the woman's tears, and based on her reputation that precedes her, she could do nothing to save herself from the Pharisee's scathing judgment. He haughtily assumes that God shares the same judgment, and if Jesus has anything to do with God, he should also judge her. His ruminations focus the issue on whether Jesus is a prophet (see 7:16; 24:19). The second class conditional sentence assumes the answer is no, and referring to him as "this one" (οὗτος) expresses his contempt for Jesus. Nothing in the woman's appearance or actions necessarily gives her away as a sinner because Simon assumes that Jesus should know what she was from prophetic clairvoyance. Prophets can sniff sin's odor from

---

12. John J. Kilgallen, "Forgiveness of Sins (Luke 7:36–50)," *NovT* 40 (1998): 108.

13. Women were not to go out uncovered: see 3 Macc. 4:6. It was grounds for divorce (*m. Ketub.* 7:6; *t. Ketub.* 7:6); it was equivalent to acting without shame. See *t. Soṭah* 5:9.

14. Green, *The Gospel of Luke*, 310. See also Bovon, *Luke 1:1–9:50*, 294–95.

15. Bock, *Luke*, 1:696–97.

16. Charles H. Cosgrove, "A Woman's Unbound Hair in the Greco-Roman World with Special Reference to the Story of the 'Sinful Woman' in Luke 7:36–50," *JBL* 124 (2005): 675–92.

17. Ibid., 689.

18. Ibid., 679.

19. Green, *The Gospel of Luke*, 310.

miles away (see John 4:16 – 19). Since he does not denounce her or shoo her away, Simon concludes that Jesus could not be a true prophet.

7:40 Jesus answering [his thoughts] said to him, "Simon, I have something to say to you." He replied, "Teacher, go ahead and say it" (καὶ ἀποκριθεὶς ὁ Ἰησοῦς εἶπεν πρὸς αὐτόν· Σίμων, ἔχω σοί τι εἰπεῖν. ὁ δέ· διδάσκαλε, εἰπέ, φησίν). Jesus is able to read Simon's thoughts (see 5:21 – 22; 6:8). Jesus' opening gambit, "Simon, I have something to say to you," according to Bailey, was a phrase used in the Middle East "to introduce a blunt speech the listener may not want to hear."[20] It creates a moment of supercharged tension. Jesus takes a position of superiority. Simon acknowledges that Jesus is a teacher. Teachers ask questions and grade students' answers. Whether he will accept Jesus' teaching or not is up in the air.

7:41 – 42 "Two persons were indebted to a certain moneylender. One owed the equivalent of five hundred days' wages; the other, the equivalent of fifty. Since they did not have the means to repay him, he graciously forgave both the debt. Now which of them will love him more?" (δύο χρεοφειλέται ἦσαν δανιστῇ τινι· ὁ εἷς ὤφειλεν δηνάρια πεντακόσια, ὁ δὲ ἕτερος πεντήκοντα. μὴ ἐχόντων αὐτῶν ἀποδοῦναι ἀμφοτέροις ἐχαρίσατο. τίς οὖν αὐτῶν πλεῖον ἀγαπήσει αὐτόν;). Jesus does not immediately condemn Simon for being a self-righteous bigot but wishes to lead him to self-awareness through a simple parable. Parables are indirect and can more easily persuade than a direct rebuke. The parable's details are spare, which means that Jesus' application of it to the context is its key for understanding it.

While one of the debtors owes ten times more than the other, both are on the same level because both are unable to pay. Both could wind up in debtor's prison or worse, but both receive grace instead. The verb translated "graciously forgive" (ἐχαρίσατο) literally means he "graced" them.

A similar parable about debtors in *b. ʿAbod. Zar.* 4a offers a striking contrast. When a rabbi is asked to explain to hostile questioners the meaning of the verse, "You only have I chosen [or loved] of all the families of the earth; therefore I will punish you all your sins" (Amos 3:2), he explains it with a parable:

> "To what may it be compared? To a man who is the creditor of two persons, one of them a friend, the other an enemy; of his friend he will accept payment little by little, whereas of his enemy he will exact payment in one sum!"

Explanation: God punishes Israel with intermittent visitations of judgment. This rabbinic parable assumes that God always exacts punishment for sins. God simply gives his friends better terms for repayment, but repay they must. In Jesus' parable, the debt is cancelled because the debtors cannot repay it themselves.

Jesus draws the point sharply in a question: Both are released from their debts but both owe different amounts. Which one will love him more? According to Jeremias, this means, who will be the most grateful?[21] Fitzmyer claims, however, that "love" means much more than gratitude.[22] It is love that acknowledges indebtedness and forgiveness and that publicly showers the one loved with devotion.

7:43 Simon answered, "I suppose that it is the one who was graciously forgiven the more." He said, "You judged rightly" (ἀποκριθεὶς Σίμων εἶπεν· ὑπολαμβάνω ὅτι ᾧ τὸ πλεῖον ἐχαρίσατο. ὁ δὲ εἶπεν αὐτῷ· ὀρθῶς ἔκρινας). Simon responds

---

20. Bailey, *Through Peasant Eyes*, 12.
21. Joachim Jeremias, *The Parables of Jesus* (trans. S. H. Hooks; New York: Scribner's, 1963), 126 – 27.
22. Fitzmyer, *Luke*, 1:690.

cautiously with "I suppose" (ὑπολαμβάνω). Perhaps he is aware that in some cases it might not be so; or, more likely, he realizes that he is about to walk into a trap. Jesus commends his answer. The general rule is: One who is forgiven more is more likely to show the greater love.

This parable is colorless compared to the parable of the two debtors in Matt 18. What gives it its electricity is how it applies to this amazing scene of an indignant Pharisee trying to keep his composure and a teary-eyed woman with loosened hair showing unrestrained devotion.

7:44a Turning to the woman, he said to Simon, "Do you see this woman?" (καὶ στραφεὶς πρὸς τὴν γυναῖκα τῷ Σίμωνι ἔφη· βλέπεις ταύτην τὴν γυναῖκα;). The question, "Do you see this woman?" can be quickly answered. Of course, he sees her; but he does not see her as Jesus sees her. Simon judged "rightly" (ὀρθῶς), but his prejudgment of Jesus and this woman was wrong. Can Simon the Pharisee accept the implications of unmerited favor for others and for himself? The problem is not figuring out the point of the parable but applying it to life, the human scene before him. Jesus does not wait for Simon to do this but makes the connection for him.

7:44b-c "I entered your house, and you gave me no water for my feet. This woman has rained down tears on my feet and dried them with her hair" (εἰσῆλθόν σου εἰς τὴν οἰκίαν, ὕδωρ μοι ἐπὶ πόδας οὐκ ἔδωκας· αὕτη δὲ τοῖς δάκρυσιν ἔβρεξέν μου τοὺς πόδας καὶ ταῖς θριξὶν αὐτῆς ἐξέμαξεν). Offering water for the feet was a common courtesy (Gen 18:2–8; 19:2; 24:32; 43:24; Judg 19:21; see also 1 Sam 25:41; John 13:3–12; 1 Tim 5:10). According to the "Rules" found in

a Pompeian dining room from the *House of the Moralist*: "The slave shall wash and dry the feet of the guests; and let him be sure to spread a linen cloth on the cushions of the couches."[23]

In Jesus' world, hospitality was not simply a matter of entertaining family and friends. Hospitality had to do with the process of "receiving" outsiders and changing them from strangers to guests. Showing hospitality to strangers served as a means of attaining and preserving honor.[24] All guests were to be treated with deference. The host was to refrain from insulting the guest in any way or to show any signs of hostility or rivalry. The host was to protect the honor of the guest, show concern for their needs, and grant them precedence. The stranger who comes as a guest never leaves with the same status as when he entered. He departs either as an enemy who will get revenge (3 John) or as a friend who will sing the praises of the host, as Paul so often did (Phil 4:15; 1 Thess 1:9).

As the scene develops, we learn that Simon as host failed to provide Jesus with the basic amenities of hospitality. In this world, every gesture is freighted with meaning, and these omissions may be taken as a deliberate slight. Why did Simon neglect Jesus? The immediate context (7:29–35) provides a clue. The Pharisees were those who had rejected God's purposes, and they stood in contrast to sinners who acknowledged the justice of God, because the Pharisees rejected John's immersion. They disallowed the novel concept that sinners can find forgiveness, whether through John's immersion or through association with Jesus. The Pharisee expressed subtle contempt for Jesus.

Fitzmyer maintains: "The Pharisee's omissions should not be emphasized as impoliteness," but he offers no grounds as to why not.[25] Why

23. Michael Grant, *Cities of Vesuvius* (New York: Penguin, 1978), 117.
24. Bruce J. Malina, *Biblical and Social Values and Their*

Meanings: A Handbook (Peabody, MA: Hendrickson, 1993), 104.
25. Fitzmyer, *Luke*, 1:691; so also Nolland, *Luke*, 1:357.

would Jesus mention in detail Simon's failures of hospitality unless his intent was to contrast the *extraordinary* behavior of the woman with the *extraordinary* behavior of the host? In the context of expected good manners in the American South, for example, these omissions would be akin to failing to offer to take a guest's coat, or to offer him a seat or a glass of iced tea, and then directing him to eat on the card table set up in the kitchen with all the children.

Jesus breaches Oriental etiquette himself by pointing out all of the host's failures, something one never did. The guest was always expected to show appreciation for the hospitality offered to him no matter how meager it might be by saying such things as: "Oh, what trouble you have taken for my sake." Never does a proper guest point out the host's shortcomings. According to Ben Zoma in the Babylonian Talmud:

> What does a good guest say? How much trouble my host has taken for me! How much meat he has set before me! How much wine he has set before me! How many cakes he has set before me! And all the trouble he has taken was only for my sake! But what does a bad guest say? How much after all has mine host put himself out? I have eaten one piece of bread. I have eaten one slice of meat. I have drunk one cup of wine! All the trouble which my host has taken was only for the sake of his wife and his children! (*b. Ber.* 58a)

Simon deliberately slighted Jesus, and Jesus interprets the behavior of the intruding woman as taking over the role of host by welcoming him with loving gestures of hospitality. Cosgrove thinks it "surprising and ironic" for Jesus to interpret this woman's "actions as gestures of hospitality" since this is what one does for a person of high status or to venerate a deity.[26] According to Bovon, "The result of the comparison is not: she did what

you did not do, but rather, she did *more* than that which you did *not* do. Simon thus descends one level further. He has nothing more to say, and thus Luke has him stand speechless at this verdict (cf. vv. 29 – 30)."[27] Jesus is not being vindictive because he was slighted. He seeks to crack the armor of Simon's self-righteousness that prevents the proper response to him.

7:45 "You gave me no kiss [of greeting]. From the time I entered, this woman has not ceased kissing my feet" (φίλημά μοι οὐκ ἔδωκας· αὕτη δὲ ἀφ᾽ ἧς εἰσῆλθον οὐ διέλιπεν καταφιλοῦσά μου τοὺς πόδας). Students or disciples kiss the hands of their teacher in greeting (see *m. Roš Haš.* 2:9; Matt 26:49; Mark 14:45; Luke 22:47 – 48). If they are equals, they kiss on the cheek.

7:46 "You did not anoint my head with oil. This woman anointed my feet with perfumed ointment" (ἐλαίῳ τὴν κεφαλήν μου οὐκ ἤλειψας· αὕτη δὲ μύρῳ ἤλειψεν τοὺς πόδας μου). The oil would be to refresh the face. In Petronius's story of the excessive feast put on by Trimalchio, the guests are surprised when their eccentric and extravagant host has their feet anointed with ointment midway through the meal (*Sat.* 70).

7:47 "Therefore, I tell you, her many sins have been forgiven and for this reason she has shown so much love. But the one to whom little is forgiven shows little love" (οὗ χάριν, λέγω σοι, ἀφέωνται αἱ ἁμαρτίαι αὐτῆς αἱ πολλαί, ὅτι ἠγάπησεν πολύ· ᾧ δὲ ὀλίγον ἀφίεται, ὀλίγον ἀγαπᾷ). Is the woman's love a consequence of divine forgiveness or the cause of it? Is she forgiven after her gestures, which are interpreted as gestures of repentance, or has she been forgiven before and her gestures are interpreted as acts of thanksgiving for forgiveness she received?

---

26. Cosgrove, "A Woman's Unbound Hair," 690.

27. Bovon, *Luke 1:1 – 9:50*, 291.

If her demonstration of love precedes forgiveness, it may explain what immediately follows: Jesus' declaration, "Your sins have been forgiven"; the stunned question, "Who is this one who forgives sins?" and Jesus' words, "Your faith has saved you. Go in peace." The problem is that if her acts of love preceded her forgiveness, it would imply that she is saved by her works. It is more likely that this woman did not enter Simon's house on a quest for forgiveness but because she was conscious that her many sins already had been forgiven. The ὅτι clause ("for this reason") is evidential, not causal, and to be taken with the verb "I tell."[28] It is a statement of assurance: "Her great love proves that her many sins have been forgiven" (NEB).

This interpretation fits the point of the parable that love follows as the response to the forgiveness of debt. The woman's actions are to be viewed as her reaction in accepting divine forgiveness. The point would also counter the Pharisees' complaints about Jesus' fellowship with sinners (5:30; 7:34; 15:1 – 2). That association brings penitence and forgiveness.[29] This woman is not forgiven because she treated Jesus better than the Pharisee did. She treated Jesus better because she knew that it was through him that she had been forgiven. Jesus' question therefore asks Simon: Do you not recognize that this woman's behavior is a sign of one who has been forgiven many debts and is showing enormous love and gratitude?

7:48 He said to her, "Your sins have been forgiven" (εἶπεν δὲ αὐτῇ· ἀφέωνταί σου αἱ ἁμαρτίαι). The woman is twice identified as a sinner: by the town (7:37) and by the Pharisee (7:39). The perfect tense "have been forgiven" (ἀφέωνται) implies that her sins had been forgiven prior to this scene and contradicts the opinions about her. Jesus'

announcement serves as a public confirmation of what she already knew and which prompted her actions. She is no longer to be classified as an unforgiven sinner.

7:49 Those who reclined at table with him began to say among themselves, "Who is this one who forgives sins?" (καὶ ἤρξαντο οἱ συνανακείμενοι λέγειν ἐν ἑαυτοῖς· τίς οὗτός ἐστιν ὃς καὶ ἁμαρτίας ἀφίησιν;). The bystanders act as a chorus with their question. It goes unanswered. There is no indication that it is hostile, as in 5:21, where the question is coupled with the charge of blasphemy. It therefore underscores the theme of the saving visitation of God and the identity of the mediating messengers of God's purposes in this section. It challenges Simon's judgment that Jesus could not be a prophet. Besides priests, prophets also had the authority to announce forgiveness (see 2 Sam 12:13; Isa 40:1 – 2), and Jesus is indeed a prophet (7:16), but more than a prophet. Readers know the answer that is gradually being unfolded in the narrative.

7:50 He said to the woman, "Your faith has saved you. Go in peace" (εἶπεν δὲ πρὸς τὴν γυναῖκα· ἡ πίστις σου σέσωκέν σε· πορεύου εἰς εἰρήνην). Faith was linked to the healing of the centurion's slave (7:9) and now is related to the salvation, the forgiveness of sins, of a woman who showed faith. It is not her courage, devotion, or humility that makes her worthy of being saved. Jesus commends her faith that leads to the forgiveness of her debt, and that forgiveness inspires her courage, devotion, and humility. Her actions reveal that she has accepted by faith that this forgiveness is real. As a result, she is filled with an overwhelming sense of love and gratitude. Jesus' reactions prove that the

28. C. F. D. Moule (*An Idiom Book of New Testament Greek* [2nd ed.; Cambridge: Cambridge Univ. Press, 1959], 147) translates it: "I can say with confidence that her sins are forgiven, *because* her love is evidence of it."

29. Neale, *None but the Sinners*, 144.

slur directed against him as a "friend of tax collectors and sinners" (7:34) is true. The woman is not a welcomed guest in Simon's home and will need to leave, so Jesus sends her away in peace (see 1:79; 2:14; 2:29 – 30).

The episode is open-ended, as is the encounter with the scribes and Pharisees in chap. 15 after the parable of the prodigal son. What will Simon do? Will he repent too and show his overwhelming love for the forgiveness of his sins, or will he seethe because Jesus implies that he is on the same level before God as this scarlet woman?

Theology in Application

1. The Sin of Judgmentalism

Jesus eats with sinners, but he also eats with Pharisees (11:37; 14:1). God is not for one brand of sinners over against others, but for all sinners. The problem is that Simon does not recognize himself to be a sinner in need of forgiveness. By pigeonholing the woman as a sinner, Simon assumes that he is not to be classified as such. The Pharisees in Luke consistently misjudge their own and other persons' standing before God (see 18:9 – 14). This Pharisee believes himself to be morally superior to the likes of this woman.

The parable of the two debtors challenges that assumption. It blurs the line between sinners and the righteous. Both are debtors, and both are hopelessly bankrupt. Käsemann declares, "God's dealings are with the ungodly; always with the ungodly, and most of all when he is dealing with the pious." He goes on to say, "The Gospel does not establish a new religion for those who want to be pious, but salvation for the ungodly; and Christians are not pious people resting safely on grace but ungodly people standing under grace."[30]

Simon, however, wishes to preserve the distinction between righteous and sinner that sets him apart from this woman. He therefore presumes to know more than Jesus and to know the mind of God better than Jesus. He wants to call the tune to which Jesus must dance, and the name of that tune is "Sinners Begone."

Simon does know the role of the prophet, however. The prophet is to make plain the secrets hidden in a person's heart. The prophet is also one who knows and reveals the mind of God. Jesus clearly assumes the role of the prophet because both of these things happen (see 2:34 – 35). He knows the woman's heart and announces God's verdict: her sins have been forgiven. He also knows the Pharisee's heart. He exposes his inner thoughts and implies God's verdict. If he were to acknowledge his debt, seek forgiveness, and accept other sinners whom God has accepted, he would find the same welcoming forgiveness as the woman.

---

30. Ernst Käsemann, "Thoughts on the Present Controversy about Scriptural Interpretation," in *New Testament Questions of Today* (trans. by W. J. Montague; Philadelphia: Fortress, 1969), 271 – 72.

Kierkegaard's insight into the opposite of sin is apt and elucidates the Pharisee's problem:

> But too often it has been overlooked that the opposite of sin is not *virtue*, not by any manner or means. This is in part a pagan view which is content with a merely human measure and properly does not know what *sin* is, that all sin is before God. No, *the opposite of sin is faith*, as is affirmed in Rom. 14:23, "whatsoever is not of faith is sin."[31]

The Pharisee must assume that the antonym of sin is virtue. From his perspective, he exudes virtue; the woman oozes sin. The problem with setting up virtue as sin's opposite number is that one then tries to avoid the sinner category by being virtuous. This effort leads to a lifetime of trying to maintain a report card of good works that demonstrates one's virtue to God. The irony is that this effort stokes the attitudinal sins of self-righteousness and reproachful faultfinding in others. The reality is that we all start out with an F and work it into an F-. The only remedy is divine grace and the response of faith that trusts God's salvation through Christ.

2. The Social Nature of Justification

This incident reveals how the gospel applies to human relationships, and it corresponds to what Paul says about justification by faith in Gal 2:11 – 21. Barth writes:

> Justification in Christ is ... not an individual miracle happening to this person or that person, which each person may seek or possess for himself. Rather, justification by grace is a joining together of this and that person, of the near and the far, of the good and the bad, of the high and the low, liberal and fundamentalist. It is a social event. No one is joined to Christ except together with a neighbor.[32]

Simon the Pharisee depends on his "works of the law" that reassure him of his status with God and prove his superiority over his fellow humans who do not measure up. If he does not accept God's forgiveness (and justification) of this woman, it reveals that he loves only himself and expects salvation from his own resources. The gist of this concept is captured in Paul's exhortation to "accept one another ... just as Christ accepted you" (Rom 15:7).

3. Forgiveness and Gratitude

"The one to whom little is forgiven shows little love" is a sly reference to Simon. The woman would not act this way if she had not felt overwhelming gratitude for being forgiven. Simon would not think and act this way if he has not convinced himself that he has little need of forgiveness. One can recall another Pharisee, Paul, who

---

31. S. Kierkegaard, *The Sickness unto Death* (trans. W. Lowrie; Princeton, NJ: Princeton Univ. Press, 1941), 132.

32. Markus Barth, "Jews and Gentiles: The Social Character of Justification in Paul," *JES* 5 (1968): 259.

could boast of his religious heritage and his blameless righteousness derived from his obedience to the law (Phil 3:5 – 6). Consequently, Simon has no motivation to show love to Jesus or this woman.

The implication is that Simon too is a sinner in the town, but his sins are more socially respectable: the sins of pride, arrogance, hard-heartedness, insensitivity, and a judgmental spirit — things that religious people rarely identify as sin. Because he has no consciousness of his totally irretrievable sinful condition before God, he has no sense of absolute indebtedness to God or of unmerited grace. He has never had the experience of having an IOU torn up. He could boast in his uprightness attained through his own achievements and could look down on all others who have not achieved the same spiritual level that he had. The result is that he has no real love for God and no real love for others.

Being religious can often be a great cover for sin lurking in the depths of one's being. The parable combined with the incident seems to say that there are two kinds of sinners, overt and covert — those who know that they have been forgiven much and exude love and devotion, and those who think that their misdemeanors are so minor that they feel little compulsion to show love to God or others. Jesus loves both kinds of sinners and announces that God stands ready to forgive them their debt. The problem is that repentance comes hardest for the righteous sinners who feel no need to cast themselves on the mercy of God. It is also harder for them to discover grace, to grow in grace, and to live gracefully.

In the preceding unit, the theme of Jesus as the eschatological prophet has been in the forefront. Jesus is a prophet but more than a prophet. He represents God fully and is the forgiver of sins.[33] While the announcement "your sins have been forgiven" (7:48) may be a divine passive, Kilgallen asserts, "Luke wants Jesus to be understood as centrally involved in the forgiveness of the woman's sins and it touches on the mystery of the interrelated roles of God and Jesus involved in this forgiveness."[34] If the large debtor in the parable applies to the woman, then her elaborate expression of love to Jesus means that he is the one who forgives sins.[35] The statements in 5:21, 24 and 7:49 "are clear authorial affirmations that Jesus has the power to forgive sins."[36] Faith in him marks the moment of forgiveness that cleansed the woman's heart. As the story unfolds, it will become clearer that this forgiveness does not come cheap. The one who is forgiven much should love much because it cost so much to the one who forgives so much.

The woman responds with gratitude to Jesus. Her gratitude differs from that of the Pharisee in Jesus' parable who is thankful to God because he is so much better than others: the robbers, rogues, adulterers, and tax collectors (18:11). This woman's

---

33. Josef Ernst, *Das Evangelium nach Lukas* (4th ed.; RNT; Regensburg: Friedrich Pustet, 1977), 259.

34. John J. Kilgallen, "A Proposal for Interpreting Luke 7:36 – 50," *Bib* 72 (1991): 322 – 23.

35. Ibid.

36. Kilgallen, "Forgiveness of Sins," 112, n. 17.

thankful spirit recognizes how God's grace has saved her in spite of herself. This kind of gratitude should fill the lives of Christ followers. It reminds us that we are not self-sufficient but totally dependent on God. It directs our feelings outward in showing love toward others rather than inward, where it congeals into viscous lumps of self-pity. It stifles that ugly competitive spirit that looks down on others who do not measure up to our standards. They are judged to be less accomplished in life than we are, less dedicated, less worthy, and just plain less than us. When we measure ourselves against others, we always come out head and shoulders above them and become smug. A thankful spirit recognizes that all we are and can become is a result of God's grace.

Luke 8:1 – 21

Literary Context

Jesus' censure of "this generation" for its refusal to respond to John or to him (7:31 – 35) led to the account of the woman intruding on a dinner party hosted by Simon the Pharisee and lavishing loving attention on Jesus (7:36 – 50). Her demonstration of love for Jesus contrasted dramatically with Simon's censorious aloofness. It revealed that those who responded to Jesus' preaching are not those one might expect to respond favorably. Tax collectors and sinners, who "justify God" (7:29), humble themselves at Jesus' feet in gratitude (7:37 – 38) and provide for him from their resources (8:2 – 3). Disgruntled Pharisees, who reject God's purpose (7:30), sit on the sidelines in stonyhearted silence. This theme of a divided response is illustrated in the present section with the parable of the sower. It is framed by references to the sacrificial ministry of women to Jesus and his disciples (8:1 – 3) and Jesus' redefinition of his family as those who "hear and do the word of God" (8:19 – 21).

The parable of the sower provides the explanation for this varied response to Jesus' sowing of the word (8:5 – 15). The title, "the parable of the sower," is partly misleading. It is perhaps better titled "the parable of four types of ground." Its meaning cannot be confined to one point. France maintains, "To argue, as has been done, that the parable is all about the assurance of an ultimate harvest despite disappointments is to do scant justice to the careful way in which the unproductive areas are sketched and to the differentiation of the yields."[1] The emphasis is on *hearing* (8:8, 10, 12, 13, 14, 15, 18, 21), beginning with the warning at the conclusion of the parable (8:8), and people have heard and responded to Jesus' message differently and will continue to do so. It recalls the reason why the people and the tax collectors submitted to John's preaching: they "heard" (7:29) and apparently heard well. The parable of the lamp (8:16 – 17) introduces the element of *seeing*. John and others are to respond to what they have *heard* and *seen* about Jesus (7:22). Demonstrations of Jesus' miraculous power continue in 8:22 – 9:50 and provide further proof that Jesus is the one who is to come.

The previous incident of the woman anointing Jesus' feet with her tears and

---

1. R. T. France, *The Gospel of Matthew* (NICNT; Grand Rapids: Eerdmans, 2007), 503 – 4.

ointment (7:36–50) prepares for the account of the women followers of Jesus, who provide for him and his disciples out of their means. The women also heard well. Witherington comments: "The women are the living embodiments of what happens when the sower sows his seed in the soil that can receive and nurture it."[2] Like the woman who was judged to be a sinner (7:37), they were formerly marginalized as victims of "evil spirits and illnesses" (8:2). Jesus has set them free, and they respond with loving gratitude and service.

This service should be linked to Jesus' declaration about who constitutes his family. Having women followers was something unheard of in Jesus' context. Danker wryly observes, "Prophetic ministry does not permanently, if indeed ever, enjoy institutional support, and Jesus' enemies would counter, as at Luke 23:5, that it was poor judgment to flaunt custom in this way."[3] Jesus' pronouncement that those "who hear and do the word of God" are his mother and brothers (8:21) means that these women are not to be regarded simply as groupies or attendants but as family members. The scandal is removed. Their financial support is what one would expect of family. Their sacrificial ministry is also what one expects of all who hear the Word, are liberated, and determine to follow Jesus whatever the cost (9:57–62; 14:25–35).

III. Jesus' Ministry in Galilee (4:14–9:50)
   C. Are You the One Who Is to Come? (7:1–50)
➡   **D. Responding to Jesus and the Word of God (8:1–21)**
     1. Jesus' Itinerant Teaching (8:1–4a)
     2. The Parable of the Sower (8:4b–8)
     3. Interpretation of the Parable (8:9–18)
     4. Statement about Jesus' Expanded Family (8:19–21)
   E. Jesus' Power over Creation, Demons, Sickness, and Death (8:22–56)

Main Idea

The ministry of Jesus has met with abundant success, but those who do not hear and do not respond to the Word of God fail to bear fruit.

Translation

(See next three pages.)

2. Ben Witherington III, "On the Road with Mary Magdalene, Joanna, Susanna, and Other Disciples — Luke 8, 1–3," *ZNW* 70 (1979): 243.

3. Danker, *Jesus and the New Age*, 172–73.

Luke 8:1–21

8:1a	Circumstance	**And it happened**
		that afterward he went about from town to village
		preaching and
		proclaiming the good news of the reign of God,
b		**and the Twelve were with him.**
2a	Character introduction	**And certain women . . .**
		who had been healed from evil spirits and illnesses,
b	List	Mary
		who is called Magdalene,
		from whom seven demons had gone out, and
3a		Joanna
		the wife of Chuza,
		a steward of Herod, and
b		Susanna, and
		many others,
c	Description	**. . . helped to support them**
		out of their means.
4a	Circumstance	When a large crowd came together and those from every town journeyed ↵
		to him,
b		**he said in a parable,**
5a	Parable	*"The sower went out to sow his seed.*
		While he was sowing,
b	Location of the seed (1)	*some fell alongside the path,*
c	Fate of the seed	*and it was trampled*
		and the birds of the air devoured it.
6a	Location of the seed (2)	*Other seed fell upon the rocky ground,*
b	Fate of the seed	*and when it grew, it withered because it had no moisture.*
7a	Location of the seed (3)	*And other seed fell in the midst of thorns,*
b	Fate of the seed	*and when the thorns grew up with it, they choked it.*
8a	Location of the seed (4)	*And other seed fell into the good earth,*
b	Fate of the seed	*and when it grew it bore fruit, one hundredfold."*
c	Warning	**And as he said these things he cried out,**
		"Let the one who has ears, hear."
9	Question	**His disciples asked him what this parable might mean.**
10a	Explanation	**He said,**
		"It was given to you to know the mysteries of the reign of God;

Continued on next page.

Continued from previous page.

b	Scripture	*but* to the rest [it is] in parables
		so that seeing they do not see
		and hearing they do not understand. (Isa 6:9)

11	Interpretation of the parable	This is [the meaning] of the parable:
		The seed is the word of God.
12a	Comparison to the situation of the hearer (1)	Those that fall alongside the road represent those who hear,
b	Fate of the hearer	then the devil comes and takes the word from their hearts,
		so that they may not believe and be saved.

13a	Comparison to the situation of the hearer (2)	Those that fall upon the rocks are those who, when they hear receive the word with joy,
b	Fate of the hearer	*and* having no root,
		they believe for a season
		and in a season of testing
		they fall away.

14a	Comparison to the situation of the hearer (3)	As for what fell into the thorns, these are those who hear,
b	Fate of the hearer	*and* as they go on,
		they are choked by cares and riches and the pleasures of life
		and they do not bear fruit to maturity.

15a	Comparison to the situation of the hearer (4)	But as for the good soil, these are those who,
b	Fate of the hearer	when they hear the word,
		hold it fast in a good and honest heart and
		bear fruit with endurance.

16a	Proverbial saying	No one after lighting a lamp
b		hides it with a vessel or
		places it under a bed, but
c		places it on a lampstand,
		so that those who enter see the light.

17a	Prophetic aphorism	*For* nothing is hidden that will not become evident,
b	Prophetic aphorism	nor what is covered up that will not become known or brought to light.
18a	Warning	Watch how you hear.
b	Reason	*For* whoever has, it shall be given to him,
c		*and* whoever does not have, even what he thinks he has will be taken from him."

| 19a | Circumstance/ character introduction | **Now his mother and his brothers came to him,** |

Continued on next page.

b		and **they were not able to join him**
		because of the crowd.
20	Announcement	And **it was announced to him,**
		"Your mother and your brothers are standing outside wanting to see you."
21	Response / aphorism	But **he answered and said to them,**
		"My mother and my brothers are these who hear and do the word of God."

Structure and Literary Form

The report of the visit of Jesus' family precedes the parable of the sower in Matthew 13 and Mark 4. Luke places this incident after the parable so that it and the report of the women benefactors bracket the parables about how one listens. It helps explain the women's role and status as Jesus' followers. They have responded authentically and have become part of Jesus' family. Their generous support of his mission reveals the fruit of hearing God's Word well.

How the parable form functions is well illustrated by the parable of the sower. It reflects real life using everyday things, established facts, and familiar happenings to make a connection between the already known and the unknown. It compels the listener to form a judgment that makes that connection. One's stance toward the teller of the parable also affects the listener's understanding. The parable in this case could be dismissed as an agricultural truism that lacks any significance. Or, it can be applied to Jesus' teaching as sowing "the word of God" and taken as a challenge to hear rightly, to make a decision, and to change one's life.

Moule likens parables to the modern political cartoon. The picture itself may please and amuse, but if that is all that happens it has failed its purpose.[4] France avers, "To appreciate it requires some knowledge of the current political scene, and the willingness and perceptiveness to work out the principles the cartoonist wished to illustrate, and to respond in appropriate action. The more you bring to it, the more you get out of it."[5] Parables place the burden of responsibility on the listeners. What will they make of what they hear? For this reason, "parables are not used by speakers who wish to control listeners by telling them exactly what to think and to do and why parables are not well received by persons who wish to be told directly what to think, to believe and to do."[6]

---

4. C. F. D. Moule, "Mark 4:1 – 20 Yet Once More," in *Neo-testementica et Semitica* (ed. E. E. Ellis, and M. Wilcox; Edinburgh: T&T Clark, 1969), 96 – 97.

5. R. T. France, *Divine Government: God's Kingship in the Gospel of Mark* (London: SPCK, 1990), 30.

6. Craddock, *Luke*, 109.

Exegetical Outline

→ **I. Summary: Jesus' itinerant teaching (8:1 – 3)**

    A. Traveling with the twelve disciples through the cities and villages and teaching (8:1)

    B. Traveling with women followers (8:2 – 3)

       1. Delivered from illnesses and demons (8:2)

       2. Supporting Jesus' ministry from their means (8:3)

II. Parable of the sower (8:4 – 8)

    A. Setting: a great crowd (8:4)

    B. Parable (8:5 – 8)

       1. Failure (8:5 – 7)

           a. Sowing along path (8:5)

           b. Sowing upon rocky ground (8:6)

           c. Sowing among thorns (8:7)

       2. Success (8:8)

           a. Sowing into good earth (8:8a)

           b. Hundredfold harvest (8:8b)

III. Interpretation of the parable (8:9 – 15)

    A. Request for explanation (8:9)

    B. Scriptural explanation of the function of parables (8:10)

    C. Interpretation of the parable of the sower (8:11 – 15)

       1. Identification of the seed with the word of God (8:11)

       2. Explanations of the failure (8:12 – 14)

           a. Failure because the devil takes the seed from the listeners' hearts (8:12)

           b. Failure because of a lack of roots in times of testing (8:13)

           c. Failure because of riches and the pleasures and cares of this world (8:14)

       3. Explanation of success: hearing the word, holding it fast, and bearing fruit (8:15)

    D. Three Images (8:16 – 18)

       1. The parable of the lamp (8:16)

       2. Nothing hidden that will not be disclosed (8:17)

       3. Warning to hear rightly (8:18)

IV. Statement about Jesus' expanded family (8:19 – 21)

    A. Arrival of Jesus' blood kin (8:19)

    B. Statement that Jesus' family envelops those who hear and do the word of God (8:20 – 21)

Explanation of the Text

8:1 And it happened that afterward he went about from town to village preaching and proclaiming the good news of the reign of God, and the Twelve were with him (καὶ ἐγένετο ἐν τῷ καθεξῆς καὶ αὐτὸς διώδευεν κατὰ πόλιν καὶ κώμην κηρύσσων καὶ εὐαγγελιζόμενος τὴν βασιλείαν τοῦ θεοῦ καὶ οἱ δώδεκα σὺν αὐτῷ). This summary indicates that the Twelve and the women continued to follow him throughout Jesus' itinerant mission criss-crossing Galilee.[7] The twelve disciples do not serve yet as coworkers in the task but are companions who go *with* him.[8] The journey with Jesus is the basic frame for understanding discipleship. Their growth occurs as they learn from watching and listening to Jesus and from their own missteps.

8:2 – 3 And certain women who had been healed from evil spirits and illnesses, Mary who is called Magdalene, from whom seven demons had gone out, and Joanna the wife of Chuza, a steward of Herod, and Susanna, and many others, helped to support them out of their means (καὶ γυναῖκές τινες αἳ ἦσαν τεθεραπευμέναι ἀπὸ πνευμάτων πονηρῶν καὶ ἀσθενειῶν, Μαρία ἡ καλουμένη Μαγδαληνή, ἀφ᾽ ἧς δαιμόνια ἑπτὰ ἐξεληλύθει, καὶ Ἰωάννα γυνὴ Χουζᾶ ἐπιτρόπου Ἡρῴδου καὶ Σουσάννα καὶ ἕτεραι πολλαί, αἵτινες διηκόνουν αὐτοῖς ἐκ τῶν ὑπαρχόντων αὐταῖς). The description of the women continues the statement about "the Twelve" who were "with him" "and certain women." They also travel with Jesus as disciples would do. Bauckham states, "At this stage of Luke's narrative this is the essence of discipleship

(cf. 6:17; 7:11; cf. Mark 3:14): to accompany Jesus and to witness his ministry."[9]

That Luke assumes these women accompanied Jesus throughout his Galilean tour is confirmed by the angel's reminder of what Jesus told them while he was still in Galilee, "that it is necessary for the Son of Man to be handed over to hands of sinners and to be crucified, and on the third day to rise again" (24:6 – 7). When Luke records these words in 9:18 – 24, they are spoken only to the disciples. Bauckham comments, "Unlike Matthew and Mark, where it comes as something of a surprise to the reader to learn, during the passion narrative, that many women had accompanied Jesus from Galilee and had 'provided' for him (Matt 27:55 – 56; Mark 15:40 – 41), Luke makes clear that these women disciples were constant companions of Jesus from an early stage of the Galilean ministry."[10]

The verb "ministered" (διηκόνουν) in the context means "to provide for" (cf. Matt 25:44; Rom 15:25; Heb 6:10), and the imperfect tense conveys habitual action. Their "means" (τῶν ὑπαρχόντων) is a present participle used to refer to "possessions, property, money, goods" (11:21; 12:15, 33, 44; 14:33; 16:1; 19:8; Acts 4:32). Witherington claims that "some of these women could give only of their time and talents, perhaps in making meals or clothes."[11] They may have done so, but Luke highlights that they supplied financial support for the entire group, probably pooling "their resources in a common fund."[12] Like the woman with the jar

---

7. M. A. Co ("The Major Summaries in Acts: Acts 2,42 – 47; 4,32 – 35; 5,12 – 16: Linguistic and Literary Relationships," *ETL* 68 [1992]: 56 – 57) defines a "summary" as "a relatively independent and concise narrative statement that describes a prolonged situation or portrays an event as happening repeatedly within an indefinite period of time."

8. Bovon, *Luke 1:1 – 9:50*, 300.

9. Bauckham, *Gospel Women*, 112.

10. Ibid., 112 – 13.

11. Ben Witherington III, *Women in the Ministry of Jesus* (SNTSMS 51; Cambridge: Cambridge Univ. Press, 1984), 195 – 96.

12. David C. Sim, "The Women Followers of Jesus: The Implications of Luke 8:1 – 3," *HeyJ* 30 (1989): 53; Bauckham, *Gospel Women*, 113 – 14.

of precious ointment that she unstintingly poured out on Jesus as a token of her love and gratitude, these women responded to Jesus' gracious deliverance with gracious generosity.

Since there were so many women named Mary, Mary Magdalene is distinguished by her home village, which was situated near Tiberias on the west shore of the lake. She is not to be identified as the sinful woman who was forgiven much in the previous episode (7:36–50). Demon possession is not connected to moral failure. Those possessed by demons need deliverance, not forgiveness, and possession by *seven* demons indicates a grievous condition (see 11:24–26).

Nothing else is known about Susanna, but Luke offers tantalizing details about Joanna, who is identified by her husband's name and his connection to Herod. Naming her husband is not necessary to distinguish her from others, as in the case of the many Marys. Chuza could be a manager (ἐπίτροπος) of one of Herod's royal estates (cf. 16:1–8) or a high-ranking official at Herod's court.[13] If the latter, he was a member of the Herodian aristocracy, which explains why Luke identifies her in this way. She has high social status and denotes the gospel's reach into high places.[14]

The gospel is not only for the down-and-out. Joanna is wealthy and uses her wealth in a manner Jesus labels as wise (16:9–13), though it would have been scandalous in her social circle for her to follow Jesus. Bauckham suggests that becoming a disciple was for her "a step across the whole of the social gulf that separated the Tiberian elite from the ordinary people, not to mention the beggars, the prostitutes, the other outcasts with whom Jesus habitually associated." Her high position also may have generated suspicion and resentment from many of Jesus' followers who had experienced Herodian oppression and the burden of taxation that funded the luxurious lifestyle, but Jesus welcomed her as he welcomed tax collectors. Bauckham concludes:

> Among these people, her status brought her no honor, not even her substantial donations to the common fund gave her a place above others. But instead she found a place in what Jesus called his new family of those who were practicing the will of God, his sisters and brothers and mothers, who were therefore also sisters and brothers and mothers to each other.[15]

Did Joanna leave her husband to serve Jesus?[16] If so, as a married woman she "braved public condemnation."[17] She may have been a wealthy widow who had more independence and was free to dispose of her property as she wished.[18]

8:4–5a When a large crowd came together and those from every town journeyed to him, he said in a parable, "The sower went out to sow his seed" (συνιόντος δὲ ὄχλου πολλοῦ καὶ τῶν κατὰ πόλιν ἐπιπορευομένων πρὸς αὐτὸν εἶπεν διὰ παραβολῆς· ἐξῆλθεν ὁ σπείρων τοῦ σπεῖραι τὸν σπόρον αὐτοῦ). The setting of a large gathering of people who come to Jesus from all over testifies to his magnetic attraction. Jesus speaks to them in a parable that has intrinsic allegorical features using transparent metaphors. In Greco-Roman philosophical discussions, for example, the "sower" is a stock analogy for the "teacher," "sowing" for "teaching," "seed" for "words," and "soils" for "students."[19]

13. Bauckham, *Gospel Women*, 134–50.

14. Nolland, *Luke*, 1:366. See also Turid Karlsen Seim, *The Double Message: Patterns of Gender in Luke and Acts* (Nashville: Abingdon, 1994), 35–36.

15. Bauckham, *Gospel Women*, 196.

16. So Bovon, *Luke 1:1–9:50*, 301.

17. Sim, "The Women Followers of Jesus," 55.

18. Bauckham, *Gospel Women*, 135. He makes the intriguing and, to my mind, convincing suggestion that Joanna is the same person identified as Junia, whom Paul greets in Rom 16:7 as prominent among the apostles and one of Paul's relatives (see *Gospel Women*, 165–202).

In a Jewish context, the image is weighted more theologically. Sowing was used as a metaphor for sowing God's Word. God is said to sow the house of Israel in Jer 31:27 – 28 in connection with the new covenant (31:31 – 34; see also Ezek 36:9; Hos 2:21 – 23; 2 Esd. 8:6; 9:30 – 31; *1 En.* 62:8).

Jesus' parable is not about the cultivation of minds through education. It is about God planting a renewed, end-time Israel through Jesus (see 10:2). The planting occurs through Jesus' teaching. How will the crowds who have gathered from everywhere hear and respond? Some are like bad soil, which precludes the seed's success; others are like good soil, in which the seed will flourish and produce an abundant harvest.

8:5b – 8 "While he was sowing, some fell alongside the path, and it was trampled and the birds of the air devoured it. Other seed fell upon the rocky ground, and when it grew, it withered because it had no moisture. And other seed fell in the midst of thorns, and when the thorns grew up with it, they choked it. And other seed fell into the good earth, and when it grew it bore fruit, one hundredfold." And as he said these things he cried out, "Let the one who has ears, hear" (καὶ ἐν τῷ σπείρειν αὐτὸν ὃ μὲν ἔπεσεν παρὰ τὴν ὁδὸν καὶ κατεπατήθη, καὶ τὰ πετεινὰ τοῦ οὐρανοῦ κατέφαγεν αὐτό. καὶ ἕτερον κατέπεσεν ἐπὶ τὴν πέτραν, καὶ φυὲν ἐξηράνθη διὰ τὸ μὴ ἔχειν ἰκμάδα. καὶ ἕτερον ἔπεσεν ἐν μέσῳ τῶν ἀκανθῶν, καὶ συμφυεῖσαι αἱ ἄκανθαι ἀπέπνιξαν αὐτό. καὶ ἕτερον ἔπεσεν εἰς τὴν γῆν τὴν ἀγαθὴν καὶ φυὲν ἐποίησεν καρπὸν ἑκατονταπλασίονα. ταῦτα λέγων ἐφώνει· ὁ ἔχων ὦτα ἀκούειν ἀκουέτω).

Every field in Palestine had its share of rocks and thorns, but the sower is not daunted by the condition of his plot of land and sows liberally using a broadcast method. How the seed fares depends on the condition of the soil. Second Esdras 8:41 offers a helpful parallel: "For just as the farmer sows many seeds in the ground and plants a multitude of seedlings, and yet not all that have been sown will come up in due season, and not all that were planted will take root; so also those who have been sown in the world will not all be saved." The point here that not all the seed sown germinates and not every seedling prospers is used to explain why the mass of humanity will perish in the world to come. Jesus' parable, however, applies the lesson of the various outcomes of sowing seed quite differently to those who are exposed to his message but also adds that most of the seed will produce the desired harvest.

A hardened path leaves the seed exposed to birds so that it is eaten before it can sprout. In rocky soil, the roots from seeds that do germinate cannot penetrate deep enough to sustain growth. Where thorns already abound, the seed is at a disadvantage in competing for nutrients.[20] Good soil by its nature, however, permits the seed to produce an abundant crop. Producing one hundredfold is an extraordinary return (see Gen 26:12).[21]

Luke varies the preposition of what happened to the seed in relation to the soil. Some fell "*alongside* the path" (παρὰ τὴν ὁδόν); some fell "*upon* the rocky ground" (ἐπὶ τὴν πέτραν); some fell "*in the midst of* the thorns" (ἐν μέσῳ τῶν ἀκανθῶν); and some fell "*into* the good earth" (εἰς τὴν γῆν

---

19. Burton L. Mack and Vernon K. Robbins, *Patterns of Persuasions in the Gospels* (Sonoma: Polebridge, 1989), 156. See Plato, *Phaed.* 276E – 277A; Plutarch, *E Delph.* 1 (394 E); Seneca, *Ep.* 38:2; Antiphon, *Frag.* 60; Quintilian, *Inst.* 5.11.24.

20. G. E. M. Suess ("Enemies of the Harvest," *Jerusalem Perspective* 53 [1997]: 18 – 23) identifies 125 species of thorns in Palestine.

21. Matt 13:8 and Mark 4:8 record threefold results, thirty, sixty, and a hundredfold, which refer to the returns on individual plants, producing differing numbers of tillers of wheat and differing numbers of grains on each spike (see John H. Martin, Warren H. Leonard and David L. Stamp, *Principles of Field Crop Production* [New York: Macmillan, 1976], 436).

τὴν ἀγαθήν). For the seed to produce this harvest, it must find "its way into the soil."[22] The first never had a chance to germinate. The second grew but could not survive without any depth of soil. The third grew but was choked out by stronger competition. The fourth took root and grew vigorously. The reference to the four types of soil does not mean that the farmer lost three quarters of the seed. Unless this farmer's field is plagued by flocks of pesky birds, rests on an extensive rocky substratum, or is overrun by thorns, the losses are negligible, as the abundant harvest reveals.

8:9 – 10 His disciples asked him what this parable might mean. He said, "It was given to you to know the mysteries of the reign of God; but to the rest [it is] in parables so that seeing they do not see and hearing they do not understand" (ἐπηρώτων δὲ αὐτὸν οἱ μαθηταὶ αὐτοῦ τίς αὕτη εἴη ἡ παραβολή. ὁ δὲ εἶπεν· ὑμῖν δέδοται γνῶναι τὰ μυστήρια τῆς βασιλείας τοῦ θεοῦ, τοῖς δὲ λοιποῖς ἐν παραβολαῖς, ἵνα βλέποντες μὴ βλέπωσιν καὶ ἀκούοντες μὴ συνιῶσιν). Everyone can understand the farmer's story at an agricultural level, but not everyone can understand how it applies to what God is doing through Jesus. Even the disciples need an explanation, and only Jesus can clarify how his sowing God's Word relates to the mysteries of God's reign. The explanation comes only if one has Jesus to ask.

The "mysteries" (μυστήρια) do not refer to conundrums that the human intellect can puzzle over and eventually figure out, as if they were akin to discovering the double helix structure of DNA. They are heavenly truths concealed from human understanding until they are made known through divine revelation (see Dan 2:28 – 30; 1 Cor 2:6 – 16; 1QH 1.21). The passive voice "it was given" (δέδοται) implies that God is the agent who gives

the secret. Knowing the mysteries has eschatological implications because they have been hidden for ages and are revealed to humans in God's timing in the last age (Rom 16:25; Eph 3:9; Col 1:26).

The quotation from Isa 6:9 is introduced by the conjunction (ἵνα) that can express purpose ("in order that") or result ("with the result that"), and both translations are applicable. It might seem strange to communicate to people through means that are intended to baffle listeners. Hooker comments, "Jewish thought tended to blur the distinction between purpose and result; if God was sovereign, then of course what happened must be his will, however strange this appeared."[23] This quotation from Isaiah is "a classic expression of what happens with prophets" and expresses hyperbolically what has already happened because of the hearers' hardness of heart.[24] The passage from Isa 6:9 – 10 is quoted more fully at the conclusion of Acts (28:26 – 27) with the declaration that the word of this salvation will be sent to the Gentiles who will listen.

8:11 – 14 "This is [the meaning] of the parable: The seed is the word of God. Those that fall alongside the road represent those who hear, then the devil comes and takes the word from their hearts, so that they may not believe and be saved. Those that fall upon the rocks are those who when they hear receive the word with joy, and having no root, they believe for a season and in a season of testing they fall away. As for what fell into the thorns, these are those who hear, and as they go on, they are choked by cares and riches and the pleasures of life and they do not bear fruit to maturity" (ἔστιν δὲ αὕτη ἡ παραβολή· ὁ σπόρος ἐστὶν ὁ λόγος τοῦ θεοῦ. οἱ δὲ παρὰ τὴν ὁδόν εἰσιν οἱ ἀκούσαντες, εἶτα ἔρχεται ὁ διάβολος καὶ αἴρει τὸν λόγον ἀπὸ τῆς καρδίας αὐτῶν, ἵνα

---

22. Green, *The Gospel of Luke*, 325.

23. Morna Hooker, *A Commentary on the Gospel according*

to Mark (Peabody, MA: Hendrickson, 1993), 128.

24. Snodgrass, *Stories with Intent*, 160 – 61.

μὴ πιστεύσαντες σωθῶσιν. οἱ δὲ ἐπὶ τῆς πέτρας οἳ ὅταν ἀκούσωσιν μετὰ χαρᾶς δέχονται τὸν λόγον, καὶ οὗτοι ῥίζαν οὐκ ἔχουσιν, οἳ πρὸς καιρὸν πιστεύουσιν καὶ ἐν καιρῷ πειρασμοῦ ἀφίστανται. τὸ δὲ εἰς τὰς ἀκάνθας πεσόν, οὗτοί εἰσιν οἱ ἀκούσαντες, καὶ ὑπὸ μεριμνῶν καὶ πλούτου καὶ ἡδονῶν τοῦ βίου πορευόμενοι συμπνίγονται καὶ οὐ τελεσφοροῦσιν).

The interpretation matches the pattern of parable, question, and explanation found in the Old Testament.[25] Jesus applies the farming experiences to spiritual realities. "His seed" is explained as "the word of God." The soils represent the various vulnerabilities of the hearers. Seed falling along the path to be eaten by birds recalls the fight for souls that is being waged by Satan against God. Judas's betrayal of Jesus, for example, is directly attributable to Satan's wiles (22:3 – 4; John 13:2, 27).

The thin layer of soil covering a rocky substratum does not allow the Word to plant deep roots. "Receive the word with joy" refers here only to ephemeral emotional excitement (contrast 1 Thess 1:6). Temporary elation does not prepare one for the times when commitment is tested (see 12:1 – 12).

The thorns represent the "cares and riches and the pleasures of [this] life" that constantly threaten to choke the life out of reception of the Word. The "lovers of money" (16:14; see 12:16 – 21; 16:19 – 31; 18:18 – 25) and those consumed by worldly affairs (14:16 – 24) inevitably become stifled in their spiritual growth.

8:15 "But as for the good soil, these are those who, when they hear the word, hold it fast in a good and honest heart and bear fruit with endurance" (τὸ δὲ ἐν τῇ καλῇ γῇ, οὗτοί εἰσιν οἵτινες ἐν καρδίᾳ καλῇ καὶ ἀγαθῇ ἀκούσαντες τὸν λόγον κατέχουσιν καὶ καρποφοροῦσιν ἐν ὑπομονῇ). The farmer meets with varied failures in the field, but the abundant yield offsets any failure, which is why farmers keep farming. The explanation also identifies what makes good soil good. "Hear[ing] the word" requires "hold[ing] it fast," which leads to "bear[ing] fruit with endurance" (21:19). The images of establishing roots (see Col 2:7) and "holding fast the word" imply that more is required than a onetime, joyous reception of the Word. They picture a sustained process that will lay the groundwork for a foundation that will withstand all possible assaults on faith.

8:16 – 17 "No one after lighting a lamp hides it with a vessel or places it under a bed, but places it on a lampstand, so that those who enter see the light. For nothing is hidden that will not become evident, nor what is covered up that will not become known or brought to light" (οὐδεὶς δὲ λύχνον ἅψας καλύπτει αὐτὸν σκεύει ἢ ὑποκάτω κλίνης τίθησιν, ἀλλ᾽ ἐπὶ λυχνίας τίθησιν, ἵνα οἱ εἰσπορευόμενοι βλέπωσιν τὸ φῶς. οὐ γάρ ἐστιν κρυπτὸν ὃ οὐ φανερὸν γενήσεται οὐδὲ ἀπόκρυφον ὃ οὐ μὴ γνωσθῇ καὶ εἰς φανερὸν ἔλθῃ). These two sayings may apply to the hearer or to the one who sows the Word of God.[26] Most interpreters take it as a reference to the disciples who, as lamps that have been lit, must now shine forth to others.[27] This interpretation is more apt for Matt 5:16, "Let your light shine." In the context of explaining why Jesus speaks in parables, the images make more sense when applied to him as the implied agent.[28] The purpose in teaching via a parable is not to obscure the truth and prevent

25. Eugene E. Lemcio, "External Evidence for the Structure and Function of Mark iv.1 – 20; vii.14 – 23; viii.14 – 21," *JTS* 29 (1978): 323 – 38; see Ezek 17:1 – 24; Zech 4:1 – 14.

26. The sayings are repeated in different contexts in 11:33; 12:2; 19:26.

27. See, e.g., Plummer, *Luke*, 222.

28. Ed Ruch, "One More Look at 'Hiding the Light' in Luke 8:16 – 18 and Mark 4:21 – 25," *Notes on Translation* 10 (1996): 11 – 17.

people from understanding (Isa 6:9). Its purpose is to disclose whether hearers will be truly receptive to the teaching.

The original audience, accustomed as they were to oil lamps, would have recognized the obvious foolishness of covering a lamp with a vessel. It would extinguish it. Placing it under a bed, probably made of straw, would not only hide its light but create a fire hazard. Lamps are lit to light up a dark place (2 Pet 1:19), and therefore they are set on lampstands. Similarly, parables are not meant to hide the truth but to display it. The Word of God is intended for "all Israel" (Acts 2:36), not a small circle of initiates. The use of parables is intended to cause light to dawn on a new order of reality.

The second image reinforces the point. Jesus does not couch his teaching in secrecy. His purpose is to reveal the truth about God's reign that has been hidden.

8:18 "Watch how you hear. For whoever has, it shall be given to him, and whoever does not have, even what he thinks he has will be taken from him" (βλέπετε οὖν πῶς ἀκούετε· ὃς ἂν γὰρ ἔχῃ, δοθήσεται αὐτῷ· καὶ ὃς ἂν μὴ ἔχῃ, καὶ ὃ δοκεῖ ἔχειν ἀρθήσεται ἀπ᾽ αὐτοῦ). This third image draws out the consequences of the previous two. If the Word is not hidden, it places the burden on the hearer to hear responsibly. A spiritual axiom reinforces the urgency of understanding Jesus' teaching. If one fails to understand, one will only get mired further in ignorance. Satan can snatch what has been sown, roots cannot penetrate into the ground, and thorns can suffocate any growth. By contrast, understanding begets

further understanding (see Prov 9:9). Understanding means more than intellectual comprehension; it requires submitting to the Word in one's heart.

8:19 – 21 Now his mother and his brothers came to him, and they were not able to join him because of the crowd. And it was announced to him, "Your mother and your brothers are standing outside wanting to see you." But he answered and said to them, "My mother and my brothers are these who hear and do the word of God" (παρεγένετο δὲ πρὸς αὐτὸν ἡ μήτηρ καὶ οἱ ἀδελφοὶ αὐτοῦ καὶ οὐκ ἠδύναντο συντυχεῖν αὐτῷ διὰ τὸν ὄχλον. ἀπηγγέλη δὲ αὐτῷ· ἡ μήτηρ σου καὶ οἱ ἀδελφοί σου ἑστήκασιν ἔξω ἰδεῖν θέλοντές σε. ὁ δὲ ἀποκριθεὶς εἶπεν πρὸς αὐτούς· μήτηρ μου καὶ ἀδελφοί μου οὗτοί εἰσιν οἱ τὸν λόγον τοῦ θεοῦ ἀκούοντες καὶ ποιοῦντες). Luke does not explain why Jesus' family comes to him. In contrast to the note in Mark 3:21, here they do not hear or think that he is out of his mind and they do not come "to take charge of" him. Jesus' mother has been lauded for her humble, faithful obedience to God's Word (1:38, 45), so Luke does not intend for Jesus' comments to portray coolness toward his mother and brothers. No friction exists between them, and "standing outside" is not an indication of their estrangement.[29]

The crowd surrounding Jesus blocks them as it blocked the friends of the paralytic who sought to bring him to Jesus (5:18 – 19). Luke uses this incident to highlight Jesus' declaration that enlarges his family under the reign of God beyond kinship lines.[30] Those who hear and do the Word of God not only are fruitful, they become Jesus' mothers, brothers, and sisters.[31]

---

29. They are identified as followers in Acts 1:14.

30. See Garland, *Mark*, 129 – 34, for Mark's different application of this incident.

31. Luke uses the term "brothers" (οἱ ἀδελφοί) inclusively to include "sisters."

Theology in Application

1. Jesus and Women Disciples

The brief summary about Jesus' followers in 8:1 – 3 reveals four things. First, Luke notes that the Twelve were "with him," which is a key description of what discipleship entails. Giles comments, "In Lukan thought the journey that Jesus takes is one that is essential for the true disciple as well. Luke cannot use the word disciple of anyone who does not actually accompany Jesus."[32] Discipleship is always a journey in the presence of the Lord, and "the faithful disciple only departs from his master's presence at his express command to carry out his will" (see 9:60; 19:29 – 32; 22:8, 13).[33]

Second, the reader can only assume that the women who follow him and minister to the needs of the group from their resources must do so out of gratitude for having been healed of their diseases and exorcised from their demons. Using one's material goods in service of the Lord is the necessary response to Jesus' healing and teaching.[34]

Third, as the category of family is widened to include those "who hear and do the word of God" (8:21), so the category of Jesus' disciples who follow him is widened to include females. The mention of women followers of Jesus is surprising given the attitudes toward women in the first century. To have women disciples "was unheard-of" in this era.[35] One of the charges against Jesus at his trial, according to Marcion's version of Luke 23:2, was associating with women (and children). Women were expected to stay at home as much as possible and to avoid men, even relatives. Men were not to be alone with them or to speak with them on the street (see John 4:9, 27).

One rabbi advised, "Talk not much with womankind. They said this of a man's own wife: how much more of his fellow's wife! Hence the sages have said: He that talks much with womankind brings evil upon himself and neglects the study of the Law and at the last will inherit Gehenna" (*m. ʾAbot* 1:5). Philo describes a crisis in Egypt when the wives of Judeans "who were enclosed [in their houses], and who actually did not come out of their inner chambers, and their young women, who were kept in the strictest privacy, avoiding men's eyes, even of those who were nearest kin, out of modesty, were … being displayed in the public view, not only by persons who were not their kin, but were common soldiers" (*Flaccus* 89). The *T. Reu.* 5:1 – 6 reflects a jaundiced view toward women:

> For women are evil, my children, and by reason of their lacking authority or power over man, they scheme treacherously how they might entice him to themselves by means of their looks. And whenever they cannot enchant by their appearance they

---

32. Giles, "The Church in the Gospel of Luke," 140. See 22:28.
33. Ibid., 141.
34. Hendrickx, *The Third Gospel*, 2B:117.
35. Bovon, *Luke 1:1 – 9:50*, 300.

conquer by a stratagem. Indeed, the angel of the Lord told me and instructed me that women are more easily overcome by the spirit of promiscuity than are men. They contrive in their hearts against men, then by decking themselves out they lead men's minds astray, by a look they implant their poison, and finally in the act itself they take them captive. For a woman is not able to coerce a man overtly, but by a harlot's manner she accomplishes her villainy. Accordingly, my children, flee from sexual promiscuity, and order your wives and your daughters not to adorn their heads and their appearances so as to deceive men's sound minds. For every woman who schemes in these ways is destined for eternal punishment.

This perspective identifies the problem not as a man's lust, which is viewed as uncontrollable, but as women who are the occasion of a man's lust. The solution was therefore to avoid women, to segregate them, to cover them up. Having women followers meant that Jesus expected his disciples to control their desires and to treat women as persons, not objects of lust.

Fourth, there may have been practical reasons for having women followers. They could talk to women freely at wells or market stalls and visit them in homes without touching off a scandal.[36] Bovon notes, however, "The list is form-critically comparable to the lists of male disciples (6:12–16; Acts 1:13; Mark 3:13–19; Matt 10:1–4)."[37] These women disciples "fulfill the conditions Peter specifies in Acts 1:21–22: they have 'accompanied us [the eleven] during all the time that the Lord Jesus went in and out among us, beginning from the baptism of John until the day he was taken from us.'"[38] They are closely connected to the apostles in 23:49; 24:9–10; and Acts 1:13–14, and the three named women correspond to the inner circle of the apostles (9:28) who are singled out from the larger group. Like Peter, Mary Magdalene heads the list.

Since the women traveled with Jesus, they also would have been "sources and guarantors of traditions from the ministry of Jesus."[39] Boman proposes that because women figure prominently in Luke's special material (L), it "derives from a circle of women disciples, including Joanna, who were the eyewitnesses, traditioners, and custodians of a cycle of Gospel traditions."[40] The women are not only ministers to financial needs; they also probably served as the vital ministers of the Word (1:2).

2. Reception of the Word

Fitzmyer captures the essence of the parable of the sower for Luke: "If 'the word of God' is a saving word, one has to react to it with faith."[41] But not everyone does so. Craddock asks, "Why is it that in the same audience some hear and some do not?

36. Bauckham, *Gospel Women*, 197.
37. Bovon, *Luke 1:1–9:50*, 299–300.
38. Bauckham, *Gospel Women*, 188.
39. Ibid., 189.
40. Boman, *Die Jesus-Überlieferung*, 122–37,
41. Fitzmyer, *Luke*, 1:712.

Is it intelligence? Sin? Predestination? God's grace?"[42] He offers no answer because neither does the parable.

God requires only that the seed be broadcast widely. The job is to sow the Word, knowing that not all teaching and preaching will produce a response in everyone. God's Word will meet with adversity and opposition. One cannot preselect what type of soil one prefers to sow the seed. It is to be spread extensively among all kinds of people in all kinds of conditions.

The reign of God that appears in the ministry of Jesus is like seed being sown in a field. It does not come in one fell swoop that promptly upends the old age. Evil does not vanish immediately with the coming of the Christ. The opposing kingdom puts up a fight, causing some to spurn him. But the seed sown by him will produce an abundant harvest because that is the nature of good seed in good soil.

Jesus quotes Isa 6:9 to explain the hardness of heart of those who do not yield to his preaching. Some are going to see but see nothing; some are going to hear but understand nothing. This quotation from Isaiah is "a classic expression of what happens with prophets," and Jesus uses this as a hyperbole to explain what has already happened because of the hearers' hardness of heart.[43] The prophet Ezekiel gets much the same message from the Lord, "But when I speak to you, I will open your mouth and you shall say to them, 'This is what the Sovereign Lord says.' Whoever will listen let them listen, and whoever will refuse let them refuse; for they are a rebellious people" (Ezek 3:27).

Jesus' parable makes it clear that this condition was preexisting in the soil; it was not caused by defective seeds. The unbelief of the listeners is caused not by the obscurity of the parables but by an unreceptive, rebellious heart. The parable and the explanatory quotation have nothing to do with predestination, however. The emphasis is on how one responds to the revelation, which the command to "watch how you hear" stresses.[44] The crowds all heard the same message and offer. Some responded; some did not. Those who failed to respond failed for a variety of reasons. How does one explain the moral and spiritual condition of humans that determines how they will respond to the Word of God? Can it be changed?

Parables cull out those who are unwilling to grasp the mystery of God's reign, but they also reveal the truth to others who will produce the harvest God intends. The veiled revelation separates faith from unfaith. One never knows if any have a receptive heart except by sowing the Word. The light that illumines the truth for some paradoxically highlights the dark shadows in others. Those who do see and hear, however, do not do so on their own because Jesus is talking about "the mysteries of the reign of God." They must come to Jesus and ask him for understanding.

---

42. Craddock, *Luke*, 112.

43. Snodgrass, *Stories with Intent*, 160 – 161. Hooker (*Mark*, 128) explains: "Jewish thought tended to blur the distinction between purpose and result; if God was sovereign, then of course what happened must be his will, however strange this appeared."

44. Snodgrass, *Stories with Intent*, 172.

"The mysteries" are integrally related to Jesus' role as God's Son sowing God's Word and fulfilling God's purpose for Israel. Being dull of hearing, blind, and stiff-necked need not be a permanent condition. Craddock concludes, "Those who lean forward to hear, who invest trust and commitment, who come to the altar of the word seeking, asking, hungering — these are the ones to whom 'more will be given.' "[45] Good listening requires vulnerability to hear what one may not want to hear, acceptance of the truth, expectancy of a future brought by God, and constancy in obeying God's Word.

Those who do not listen will be stripped of their legacy. Peter proclaims to the people in the temple: "For Moses said, 'The Lord your God will raise up for you a prophet like me from among your own people; you must listen to everything he tells you. Anyone who does not listen to him will be completely cut off from their people' " (Acts 3:22 – 23). That warning still applies to the church. God does not require less under God's grace than under the law. To whom more is given, more is expected.

---

45. Craddock, *Luke*, 113.

CHAPTER 24

Luke 8:22 – 39

Literary Context

The mention of the women who were cured of evil spirits and diseases and who followed Jesus (8:2) and the devil's opposition to sowing the Word of God in the interpretation of the parable (8:12) prepare for this next section, which illustrates Jesus' power over the demonic. Jesus demonstrates himself to be Lord over the sea, with the power of the Lord of creation (8:22 – 25), Lord over demons (8:26 – 39), Lord over sickness (8:43 – 48), and Lord over death (8:40 – 42, 49 – 56).

These demonstrations of divine power prepare for Jesus' sending out his disciples to proclaim the reign of God and to heal in 9:1 – 6. They also prepare for the answer to the question "Who then is this?" (8:25), which Jesus will ask his disciples directly in 9:20. The readers have known the answer to this question from the infancy narrative. The disciples gradually learn who Jesus is by observing his mighty power, and the climax will be the declaration from the divine voice in 9:35.

III. Jesus' Ministry in Galilee (4:14 – 9:50)
- C. Are You the One Who Is to Come? (7:1 – 50)
- D. Responding to Jesus and the Word of God (8:1 – 21)
- ➦ **E. Jesus' Power over Creation, Demons, Sickness, and Death (8:22 – 56)**
  - **1. Jesus' Power over the Sea and Legions of Demons (8:22 – 39)**
    - **a. Jesus' Power over the Sea (8:22 – 25)**
    - **b. Jesus' Power over the Gerasene Demoniac (8:26 – 39)**
  - 2. Jesus' Power over Sickness and Death (8:40 – 56)

Main Idea

"In Jesus, the power of God can and does conquer the powers of darkness arrayed against him."[1] Jesus subdues the convulsive power of the wind and the sea that imperil life and expels demons that would destroy human life.

Translation

(See pages 354 – 55.)

Structure and Literary Form

The form of the stilling of the storm is an epiphanic rescue miracle. The exorcism of the legion of demons from the man is also an epiphanic miracle. Both miracles display Jesus' divine power in combat with chaotic powers and reveal his divinity.[2]

The exorcism falls into four sections:

1. The encounter with the man with the command for the demons to be exorcised (vv. 26 – 29)
2. The encounter with the demons with their attempted defense and request (vv. 30 – 32)
3. The conclusion with the expulsion of the demons, the impression on the audience, and the effect on the man, and a request to leave (vv. 33 – 37)
4. The commission to the man to return home and declare what God has done for him (vv. 38 – 39)

The description of the man's previous plight is balanced by the description of his deliverance.

v. 27: the man who had demons	vv. 35, 38: the man from whom demons had gone out
v. 27: he did not wear clothes	v. 35: he is fully clothed
v. 27: he did not live in a house but in the tombs	v. 39: he is commanded to return to his home
v. 28: he prostrated himself before Jesus and shouted	v. 35: he sits calmly at Jesus' feet
v. 29: the demons seized him and drove him into uninhabited places	v. 35: he is in his right mind

---

1. Paul J. Achtemeier, *Jesus and the Miracle Tradition* (Eugene, OR: Cascade, 2008), 10.

2. Ibid., 96 – 97.

Exegetical Outline

➡ **I. Command to go across to the other side of the lake (8:22)**

II. Peril from a sudden gale-force wind (8:23 – 24)
  A. Jesus asleep during the storm (8:23)
  B. Fearful disciples awake Jesus (8:24a)
  C. Jesus rebukes the raging waves and there is calm (8:24b)

III. Reaction to the miracle (8:25)
  A. Jesus' question: "Where is your faith?" (8:25a)
  B. Disciples' question: "Who then is this?" (8:25b)

IV. Encounter with a demoniac in the territory of the Gerasenes (8:26 – 29)
  A. Description of the man's condition (8:26 – 27)
  B. His response to Jesus (8:28)
  C. Jesus command for the unclean spirit to come out of the man (8:29a)
  D. Description of the severity of the man's condition (8:29b)

V. Encounter with the demons (8:30 – 34)
  A. The vast number of the demons (8:30)
  B. Cringing plea to avoid going back into the Abyss (8:31)
  C. Inhabiting a large herd of swine (8:32)
  D. Drowning of the swine and demons (8:33)
  E. The report of the swineherds to the town (8:34)

VI. Encounter with the townspeople (8:35 – 37)
  A. Description of the man's new condition (8:35a-b)
  B. Reaction of fear (8:35c – 36)
  C. Plea for Jesus to leave (8:37)

VII. Encounter with the man (8:38 – 39)
  A. Plea to be with Jesus (8:38)
  B. Commission to return home and declare how much God has done for him (8:39a)
  C. Obedience: declaring how much Jesus had done for him (8:39b)

Luke 8:22–39

8:22a	Circumstance	**It happened** on one of those days that he and his disciples got in a boat,
b	Command	and **he said to them,** *"Let us go to the other side of the lake,"*
c		and **they embarked.**
23a	Crisis	While they were sailing, **he dropped off to sleep.** **A gale-force wind blew down upon the lake,**
c		and **they were taking on water** and **becoming endangered.**
24a	Entreaty	**They came to him and roused him, saying,** *"Master, Master, we perish!"*
b	Miracle	But when he was aroused, **he rebuked the wind and the surging waves of water,** and **they stopped** and **there was calm.**
25a	Rebuking question	**He said to them,** *"Where is your faith?"*
b	Marveling question	**They were afraid and marveled, saying to one another,** *"Who then is this, that he commands even the winds and the water,* *and they obey him?"*
26	Circumstance	**They put in at the region of the Gerasenes,** which is across from Galilee.
27a	Encounter with a demonized man	When he came upon the land, **a certain man of the town who had demons met him.**
b		For a long time he **did not wear clothes and** did not stay in a house but among the tombs.
28a	Submission	When he saw Jesus, **he fell on his face before him,**
b	Encounter with the demons	and **crying out in a loud voice,** **he said,** *"What do you and I have to do with each other,* *Jesus, Son of the Most High God?* *I beg you, do not torment me."*
c	Pleading request	
29a	Command	For **he commanded the unclean spirit to come out from the man.**

Continued on next page.

b	History of the man's condition	For **many times it took hold of him,**
		and **though he was guarded and bound with chains and shackles, he broke** ↵
		the chains,
		and **he was driven by the demon into uninhabited places.**
30a	Question	**Jesus asked him,**
		"*What is your name?*"
b	Response (evasion)	**He said,**
		"*Legion,*"
		because **many demons had entered into him.**
31	Pleading request	And **they were begging him that he not command them to depart into** ↵
		the Abyss.
32a	Granting of the request	Now **there was a large herd of pigs feeding on the hill,**
b		and **they begged him that he permit them to enter into these,**
		and **he permitted them.**
33a		When the demons left the man,
		they entered the pigs,
b		and **the herd hurtled down the steep bank into the lake** and **was drowned.**
34	Report of witnesses	When the herdsmen saw what had happened,
		they fled and **reported it in the town and the countryside.**
35a	Response to the man's restoration	**They went out to see what had happened**
		and **came to Jesus**
b	Circumstance	and **found the man**
		from whom the demons had gone out
		fully clothed,
		restored to sanity, and
		sitting at the feet of Jesus,
c		and **they were afraid.**
36	Report of witnesses	**Those who had seen [what happened] reported how the one who had** ↵
		been possessed by demons was saved.
37a	Request	**Then the whole multitude of people from the Gerasene countryside** ↵
		asked him to depart from them,
		because **they were in the** ↵
		grip of a great fear.
b	Granting of the request	After embarking in the boat,
		he returned.
38a	Request	**The man from whom the demons went out was beseeching him to be with him,**
b	Refusal to grant the request	but **he sent him away, saying,**
39a	Command	"*Return to your house and describe what God did for you.*"
b	Obedience	And **he left, proclaiming to the whole town what Jesus did for him.**

Explanation of the Text

8:22 – 23 It happened on one of those days that he and his disciples got in a boat, and he said to them, "Let us go to the other side of the lake," and they embarked. While they were sailing, he dropped off to sleep. A gale-force wind blew down upon the lake, and they were taking on water and becoming endangered (ἐγένετο δὲ ἐν μιᾷ τῶν ἡμερῶν καὶ αὐτὸς ἐνέβη εἰς πλοῖον καὶ οἱ μαθηταὶ αὐτοῦ καὶ εἶπεν πρὸς αὐτούς· διέλθωμεν εἰς τὸ πέραν τῆς λίμνης, καὶ ἀνήχθησαν. πλεόντων δὲ αὐτῶν ἀφύπνωσεν. καὶ κατέβη λαῖλαψ ἀνέμου εἰς τὴν λίμνην καὶ συνεπληροῦντο καὶ ἐκινδύνευον). Jesus trusts the disciples' skill to navigate these waters and dozes off. Since the lake is 682 feet below sea level with two extensive valleys on the western side that often funneled wind onto the lake and with the heights on the eastern side that could send downdrafts of cool air, it is prone to unexpected squalls.[3]

In the ancient world, however, a raging sea was not simply attributed to atmospheric phenomena but to God (Jonah 1:4) or to the primeval powers of chaos that God subdued in creation (Gen 1:2; Ps 74:12 – 14; Isa 51:9 – 10). The sea had religious significance as the abode of demonic powers that God will ultimately destroy (Rev 21:1).[4] Jesus' sleep also can have religious significance and should not be attributed simply to physical exhaustion, to God granting "sleep to those he loves" (Ps 127:2), or to his trust in God (Pss 3:5; 4:8). Sleep is a symbol of divine rule in ancient Near Eastern literature (see Isa 51:9 – 10). In this context where Jesus demonstrates his power to command the sea, his sleep is a sign of divine sovereignty.[5]

8:24 They came to him and roused him, saying, "Master, Master, we perish!" But when he was aroused, he rebuked the wind and the surging waves of water, and they stopped and there was calm (προσελθόντες δὲ διήγειραν αὐτὸν λέγοντες· ἐπιστάτα ἐπιστάτα, ἀπολλύμεθα. ὁ δὲ διεγερθεὶς ἐπετίμησεν τῷ ἀνέμῳ καὶ τῷ κλύδωνι τοῦ ὕδατος· καὶ ἐπαύσαντο, καὶ ἐγένετο γαλήνη). When the waves threaten to swamp the vessel, the disciples wake Jesus to announce, "We've had it!" Luke's account does not betray any impatience with Jesus on their part for sleeping through their peril (contrast Mark 4:38). This story is not about his absence in times of stress. It is about his divine power to rescue the perishing. Jesus does not pray to God to deliver them from this deadly danger but does what God alone can do: calm the sea by his command (Pss 89:9; 107:28 – 29).

8:25 He said to them, "Where is your faith?" They were afraid and marveled, saying to one another, "Who then is this, that he commands even the winds and the water, and they obey him?" (εἶπεν δὲ αὐτοῖς· ποῦ ἡ πίστις ὑμῶν; φοβηθέντες δὲ ἐθαύμασαν, λέγοντες πρὸς ἀλλήλους· τίς ἄρα οὗτός ἐστιν ὅτι καὶ τοῖς ἀνέμοις ἐπιτάσσει καὶ τῷ ὕδατι, καὶ ὑπακούουσιν αὐτῷ;). Jesus does not chide the disciples for being afraid and having no faith, as he does in Mark 4:40. No verb appears in the clause, and the past tense "Where *was* your faith?" or the present tense "*is*" could be supplied. "Faith" refers to faith in the divine power that is present in his person. When they are in his presence, they should have no fear (Ps 46:1 – 3). The disciples have had the greatest opportunity to see

---

3. A sudden whirlwind (λαῖλαψ ἀνέμου, lit., "a tempest of wind") became an image for sudden disaster and judgment (cf. Jer 25:32).

4. Achtemeier, *Jesus and the Miracle Tradition*, 3 – 10.

5. Bernard F. Batto, "The Sleeping God: An Ancient Near Eastern Motif of Divine Sovereignty," *Bib* 68 (1987): 153 – 77.

and hear Jesus, yet they are filled with doubt and fear in times of danger. When Jesus tells them to go to the other side of the lake, they should know that they will reach their goal. Jesus raises a more critical question in 18:8, "When the Son of Man comes ... will he find faith on the earth?"

The disciples' question, "Who then is this?" makes the point. Only someone with divine power can command the wind. He is Lord over the sea and its diabolical forces. Jesus will require them to give the answer to this question in 9:18–20.

8:26 They put in at the region of the Gerasenes, which is across from Galilee (καὶ κατέπλευσαν εἰς τὴν χώραν τῶν Γερασηνῶν, ἥτις ἐστὶν ἀντιπέρα τῆς Γαλιλαίας). Textual variants offer three options for the name of this region: (1) Gerasenes, modern Jerash, which is around thirty-three miles southeast from the coast; (2) Gadarenes, which is six miles southeast, and (3) Gergesenes, modern El Koursi, which is closer and has nearby the only steep cliff on the eastern shore of the sea. The text allows it to be a reference to a territory controlled by Gerasa and extending to the Sea of Galilee. The variants may have arisen to bring the town into closer proximity to the lake, which is evident in Origen's discussion of the variants.[6] Soutar suggests that it was difficult for uneducated natives to pronounce the second g-sound in Gergesa and it may have contributed to the reading of Gerasa.[7] In spite of all the variants, the key issue is this: Jesus has not only crossed over from Galilee; he has crossed cultural boundaries into Gentile lands where pigs are kept.

8:27–29 When he came upon the land, a certain man of the town who had demons met him. For a long time he did not wear clothes and did not stay in a house but among the tombs. When he saw Jesus, he fell on his face before him, and crying out in a loud voice, he said, "What do you and I have to do with each other, Jesus, Son of the Most High God? I beg you, do not torment me." For he commanded the unclean spirit to come out from the man. For many times it took hold of him, and though he was guarded and bound with chains and shackles, he broke the chains, and he was driven by the demon into uninhabited places (ἐξελθόντι δὲ αὐτῷ ἐπὶ τὴν γῆν ὑπήντησεν ἀνήρ τις ἐκ τῆς πόλεως ἔχων δαιμόνια καὶ χρόνῳ ἱκανῷ οὐκ ἐνεδύσατο ἱμάτιον καὶ ἐν οἰκίᾳ οὐκ ἔμενεν ἀλλ' ἐν τοῖς μνήμασιν. ἰδὼν δὲ τὸν Ἰησοῦν ἀνακράξας προσέπεσεν αὐτῷ καὶ φωνῇ μεγάλῃ εἶπεν· τί ἐμοὶ καὶ σοί, Ἰησοῦ υἱὲ τοῦ θεοῦ τοῦ ὑψίστου; δέομαί σου, μή με βασανίσῃς. παρήγγειλεν γὰρ τῷ πνεύματι τῷ ἀκαθάρτῳ ἐξελθεῖν ἀπὸ τοῦ ἀνθρώπου. πολλοῖς γὰρ χρόνοις συνηρπάκει αὐτόν καὶ ἐδεσμεύετο ἁλύσεσιν καὶ πέδαις φυλασσόμενος καὶ διαρρήσσων τὰ δεσμὰ ἠλαύνετο ὑπὸ τοῦ δαιμονίου εἰς τὰς ἐρήμους).

This is the only exorcism that mentions multiple demons and Jesus' asking for their name, as if to garner power over them. It is also the only one that involves animals and that provokes opposition and a plea for him to leave.

Jesus meets a demonized man who wears no clothes, a sign of his shame and loss of identity (see 10:30), and who is banished to a necropolis, which isolates him from any community. Tombs were known as haunts for demons (see *b. Ber.* 3b; *b. Šabb.* 67a; *b. Giṭ.* 70a; *b. Sanh.* 65b). The demons control this man's speech and actions. His shouts to leave him alone and not to torment him betray that falling at Jesus' feet is only false submission inspired by desperate demons. The demons

6. See Raymond G. Clapp, "A Study of the Place-Names Gergesa and Bethabara," *JBL* 26 (1907): 62–75.

7. J. Soutar, "Gerasenes, Gergesenes," *A Dictionary of Christ and the Gospels* (ed. J. Hastings; New York: Scribners, 1906), 1:643–44. See Vassilios Tzaferis, "A Pilgrimage to the Site of the Swine Miracle," *BAR* 15/2 (1989): 45–51.

recognize who Jesus is, and the title "Son of the Most High God" (1:32, 35, 76) befits this region, since it is found in the LXX as the title that non-Israelites use to refer to the Lord (see Acts 16:17).[8]

In Mark's account, the demons tormenting this man seem to arch their back and hiss at Jesus by invoking a higher power to ward off the exorcism (Mark 5:7). In Luke, the demonic forces controlling the man concede power to Jesus. There is no battle, only a bargaining about the most painless capitulation.[9] The demons torment others but want to avoid being tormented themselves. Luke delays in explaining why the demoniac addresses Jesus in this way and begs him not to torment him. Jesus had commanded the spirit to leave the man.

A flashback presents the details of the man's madness and shattered life, and the futile attempts to subdue him. He has been enslaved by both demons and humans, driven by the one to the haunts of wild animals and clapped by the other in irons and treated like a wild animal. Just as Jesus did not still an average storm but a great gale that would destroy the boat, he will not exorcise demons from one who is marginally possessed but one who is victimized by a legion of demons. Jesus' conquest of the power of the sea where demonic monsters of chaos are believed to reside explains why the demons know that in his presence their defeat is inevitable.

8:30 Jesus asked him, "What is your name?" He said, "Legion," because many demons had entered into him (ἐπηρώτησεν δὲ αὐτὸν ὁ Ἰησοῦς· τί σοι ὄνομά ἐστιν; ὁ δὲ εἶπεν· λεγιών, ὅτι εἰσῆλθεν δαιμόνια πολλὰ εἰς αὐτόν). In *T. Sol.* 18:23, a demon named Mardero says, "I inflict incurable fevers, write my name in some such way in the hours, and I retreat immediately." This

texts reflects the widespread view that knowing the name of powers gave one some power to manipulate them.

But Luke does not present Jesus as engaging in exorcistic sorcery. "Legion" is not a name but an evasive answer that underscores how severely bedeviled this man is. A legion consisted of around 5,600 troops. The man's possession is far worse than that of Mary Magdalene, who was delivered from seven demons (8:2). Like the military "legions of angels" that can come to Jesus' rescue (Matt 26:53), Satan has a legion of demons that fragment humans. Rather than causing Jesus to back down, the huge number of demons highlights the magnitude of his victory.[10]

8:31 And they were begging him that he not command them to depart into the Abyss (καὶ παρεκάλουν αὐτὸν ἵνα μὴ ἐπιτάξῃ αὐτοῖς εἰς τὴν ἄβυσσον ἀπελθεῖν). The Abyss is the place of punishment for evil spirits (see *2 Bar.* 59:5; *1 En.* 10:4; 18:11; 54:5; 88:1; 90:24 – 27; *Jub.* 5:6; Rev 9:1 – 2, 11; 11:7; 17:8; 20:1, 3; see also "Tartarus" in 2 Pet 2:4). The demons do not ask to be allowed to stay in the same region, as in Mark 5:10, but to avoid the eschatological torment (Isa 24:21 – 22).[11] Even demons hate hell. This statement in Luke reveals that the exorcisms have an eschatological dimension.

8:32 – 33 Now there was a large herd of pigs feeding on the hill, and they begged him that he permit them to enter into these, and he permitted them. When the demons left the man, they entered the pigs, and the herd hurtled down the steep bank into the lake and was drowned (ἦν δὲ ἐκεῖ ἀγέλη χοίρων ἱκανῶν βοσκομένη ἐν τῷ ὄρει· καὶ παρεκάλεσαν αὐτὸν ἵνα ἐπιτρέψῃ αὐτοῖς εἰς ἐκείνους εἰσελθεῖν· καὶ ἐπέτρεψεν αὐτοῖς. ἐξελθόντα δὲ τὰ δαιμόνια ἀπὸ τοῦ ἀνθρώπου

8. Green, *The Gospel of Luke*, 339.
9. Bovon, *Luke 1:1 – 9:50*, 327.

10. Klutz, *The Exorcism Stories in Luke-Acts*, 86, n. 11.
11. Twelftree, *Jesus the Exorcist*, 86.

εἰσῆλθον εἰς τοὺς χοίρους, καὶ ὥρμησεν ἡ ἀγέλη κατὰ τοῦ κρημνοῦ εἰς τὴν λίμνην καὶ ἀπεπνίγη). Though large in number, they are beggarly demons. They acknowledge Jesus' superior authority and beg to enter the pigs. The verb "permit" (ἐπιτρέπω) appears twice to underline the fact that Jesus is the one in complete control.

The exorcism has material consequences that are surprisingly destructive to many modern readers. Demons will to inhabit something (see 11:26) and will destroy anything they inhabit. They drove the man into the deserted tombs (8:29), and they drive the pigs into the sea, ironically bringing about their own destruction. Jesus has just demonstrated his power over the sea, and the verb "drowned" (ἀπεπνίγη) placed at the end of the sentence dramatically underscores their end. For Jews, the pigs represent pagan abominations and pagan persecution (see 2 Macc 6:18 – 7:42), and their destruction would prompt no regret.

8:34 – 35 When the herdsmen saw what had happened, they fled and reported it in the town and the countryside. They went out to see what had happened and came to Jesus and found the man from whom the demons had gone out fully clothed, restored to sanity, and sitting at the feet of Jesus, and they were afraid (ἰδόντες δὲ οἱ βόσκοντες τὸ γεγονὸς ἔφυγον καὶ ἀπήγγειλαν εἰς τὴν πόλιν καὶ εἰς τοὺς ἀγρούς. ἐξῆλθον δὲ ἰδεῖν τὸ γεγονὸς καὶ ἦλθον πρὸς τὸν Ἰησοῦν καὶ εὗρον καθήμενον τὸν ἄνθρωπον ἀφ᾽ οὗ τὰ δαιμόνια ἐξῆλθεν ἱματισμένον καὶ σωφρονοῦντα παρὰ τοὺς πόδας τοῦ Ἰησοῦ, καὶ ἐφοβήθησαν).

This report of the reaction to the event is almost as long as the event itself, which reveals its importance. The man is identified three times as the one from whom the demons had gone out (vv. 35, 36, 38). He had broken the fetters with his own power; Jesus did what this man or his community could not do by their own power. He broke the bonds of demons that held him fast. Sitting at Jesus' feet (see 10:39; Acts 22:3) is not only a sign of his new composure but an act of discipleship. Being properly clothed means that he is fit to rejoin his community.

8:36 – 37 Those who had seen [what happened] reported how the one who had been possessed by demons was saved. Then the whole multitude of people from the Gerasene countryside asked him to depart from them, because they were in the grip of a great fear. After embarking in the boat, he returned (ἀπήγγειλαν δὲ αὐτοῖς οἱ ἰδόντες πῶς ἐσώθη ὁ δαιμονισθείς. καὶ ἠρώτησεν αὐτὸν ἅπαν τὸ πλῆθος τῆς περιχώρου τῶν Γερασηνῶν ἀπελθεῖν ἀπ᾽ αὐτῶν, ὅτι φόβῳ μεγάλῳ συνείχοντο· αὐτὸς δὲ ἐμβὰς εἰς πλοῖον ὑπέστρεψεν). The introduction of the verb "saved" (ἐσώθη) applies to the man's physical healing and his spiritual saving. The community obviously does not care that the man is saved. Fear drives their reaction. Perhaps they fear further economic loss, but they are clearly more at home with the presence of the demonic in their midst than the presence of a power that can drive it away. Their rejection of Jesus is similar to what happened to Paul and Silas in Philippi when they exorcised a demon from a female soothsayer (Acts 16:16 – 22).

8:38 – 39 The man from whom the demons went out was beseeching him to be with him, but he sent him away, saying, "Return to your house and describe what God did for you." And he left, proclaiming to the whole town what Jesus did for him (ἐδεῖτο δὲ αὐτοῦ ὁ ἀνὴρ ἀφ᾽ οὗ ἐξεληλύθει τὰ δαιμόνια εἶναι σὺν αὐτῷ· ἀπέλυσεν δὲ αὐτὸν λέγων· ὑπόστρεφε εἰς τὸν οἶκόν σου καὶ διηγοῦ ὅσα σοι ἐποίησεν ὁ θεός. καὶ ἀπῆλθεν καθ᾽ ὅλην τὴν πόλιν κηρύσσων ὅσα ἐποίησεν αὐτῷ ὁ Ἰησοῦς). Verses 38 – 39 record the interaction between Jesus and the man after Luke reports that Jesus has left in v. 37. This technique is similar to the account of Jesus' baptism (3:21 – 22), where what happens at the baptism is described after mentioning that all the people were baptized. It places emphasis on the interaction between the man and Jesus as the stage is cleared of everyone — the demons, swineherds, townspeople, and even the disciples.

Pleading "to be with" Jesus is equivalent to asking to be a disciple. Mary Magdalene and other women who had been healed of evil spirits were allowed to follow him (8:2), but Jesus denies that opportunity to this man.[12] Instead, he commissions him to proclaim what God has done for him in his own land. The townspeople want to keep

Jesus at a safe distance, but the word about Jesus cannot be placed in quarantine. Jesus has restored the man to his community. Yet to be delivered by Jesus brings obligations. For the women, it meant being with him and ministering to his needs sacrificially from their means. For this man, it means announcing far and wide how God had delivered him through Jesus.

The man's proclamation highlights the point. Jesus commands him to return to his home and "describe" (διηγοῦ) what God did for him. He obeys but proclaims (κηρύσσων) "to the whole town" what *Jesus* did for him. He understands that God is working in Jesus.

Theology in Application

1. Faith Rocked by Storms

The storm incident reveals how wrong it is to think that following Jesus will bring an untroubled, soothing life. Storms abound: levees break, tsunamis roar, tornadoes level everything in their path. Metaphoric storms can appear suddenly that shipwreck lives and threaten to scuttle faith. What is required to survive them is not the kind of faith that simply believes that something is true but faith that places complete confidence in God's providential care and protection whatever the dangers. It trusts that even if God does not deliver one from the tidal wave that batters one's life, God will deliver one through it.

Allied troops found the following written on a basement wall when they entered Cologne, Germany, in World War II. It captures the kind of faith that Jesus is talking about: "I believe in the sun even when it is not shining. I believe in love even when feeling it not. I believe in God even when God is silent."

2. Faith in Jesus' Sovereign Power

Stewart declares:

It is a tragedy that the Christian religion is in many minds identified merely with pious ethical behavior and vague theistic beliefs, suffused with aesthetic emotionalism and a mild glow of humanitarian benevolence. This is not the faith which first

---

12. As a presumed Gentile, he does not fit into Jesus' plans for his mission to Israel, just as Jesus, the Jew, does not fit well in Gentile territory. But that situation is temporary, and a witness will remain.

awakened the world like a thousand trumpets and made people feel it bliss in such a dawn to be alive. Men knew what Christianity really was — the entrance into history of a force of immeasurable range.[13]

Achtemeier draws out the theological implications of this miracle: "the miracle of the stilling of the storm indicates in part what the cross, with the resurrection, indicates supremely: in Jesus, the power of God can and does conquer the powers of darkness arrayed against him."[14] The exorcism indicates that in Jesus, God can and does conquer the powers of darkness arrayed against humans. He restores one to equilibrium whom demons drove crazy and no human was able to subdue. This man could not pull himself together on his own or with a therapist but needed a sovereign power to deliver and redeem him. Only Jesus is that sovereign power. The incident with the pigs reveals that evil never goes quietly and is never dismissed to vanish into thin air. It has to be borne away. In a similar manner, Christ on the cross takes the evil in the world into himself and bears it away through his death.

Paul says that all creation groans in anguished anticipation of the day of redemption when all things will be transformed (Rom 8:18–23). For now, we live amid natural calamities and calamities stirred up by human iniquity. The terrestrial storms and spiritual desolation also reveal that the world still languishes in bondage to "the powers of this dark world and ... the spiritual forces of evil in the heavenly realms" (Eph 6:12) that are alien to God and need to be subdued. At the heart of the gospel is an ineradicable assurance that the victory over evil and death has been won, but it is also a victory yet to come.

3. Salvation as Restoration to Wholeness

A man who wore no clothes, lived in the tombs among the dead, and had a long rap sheet hardly seems like a good candidate to be the first to preach the news in this territory awash in paganism. He was a multiple offender whom the authorities had at long last given up trying even to restrain. But like Mary Magdalene, who had been delivered from seven demons (8:2), he was redeemed from his condition by Jesus' powerful word and restored to wholeness.

It has happened to many whose condition is not quite so obvious or public. C. S. Lewis describes his condition before his conversion as "a zoo of lusts, a bedlam of ambitions, a nursery of fears, a harem of fondled hatreds. My name was legion."[15] Using the imagery of the parable of the soils in the previous unit would seem to suggest that persons such as these are hardened, unproductive soil to hear the Word of God and not worth wasting seed by sowing it among them. But the power of God's

13. James S. Stewart, *Thine Is the Kingdom* (New York: Scribner's, 1956), 22.

14. Achtemeier, *Jesus and the Miracle Tradition*, 10.

15. C. S. Lewis, *Surprised by Joy* (New York/London: Harcourt Brace Jovanovich, 1955), 226.

Word can transform even this kind of soil. It can bring salvation, deliverance from the legion of personal demons that assail individuals, and transform the person into a productive proclaimer of the gospel.

The problem is that Christians might tend to avoid the dark haunts where these lost and desperate people may gather. Their scary behavior, as a result of years of maltreatment at the hands of others and their own self-abuse, may make them seem irredeemable, and so they never hear the message of salvation. Jesus is prepared not only to use anyone committed to him to proclaim the gospel, but he is also ready to go anywhere to proclaim it. The whole world, not a small portion of it, needs to be restored to wholeness.

Luke 8:40 – 56

Literary Context

The two miracles recorded here pick up the question that Jesus asked his disciples after calming the raging sea, "Where is your faith?" (8:25), and also recall his answer to John in 7:22: the sick are healed and the dead are raised. He is the one who is to come (7:19 – 20). These two miracles also show how faith saves (7:50; 8:48, 50) by opening oneself up to the power of God to bring healing, peace, and salvation.

Main Idea

When Jesus' divine power meets with human faith, illnesses are healed and death is conquered.

Translation

(See next two pages.)

Luke 8:40–56

8:40	Circumstance	When Jesus returned, **the crowd received him favorably,** for they were all awaiting him.
41a	Character introduction	**And behold, there came a man by the name of Jairus,**
b		who was a ruler of the synagogue,
c	Submission	and when he fell at Jesus' feet,
d	Entreaty	**he pleaded with him to come to his house,**
42a	Reason	because his only daughter, . . .
		who was around twelve years old,
		. . . was dying.
b	Circumstance	While he was going, **the crowds crushed him.**
43a	Character introduction and description of plight	Now **there was a woman who had a discharge of blood for twelve years,**
b		and **[though she had spent her whole living on physicians] she could not ⮠ be healed by anyone.**
44a	Action	**She slipped up from behind and touched the hem of his garment,**
b	Result: healing	and **immediately the bleeding stopped.**
45a	Question	Then **Jesus asked,** *"Who touched me?"*
b	Response	When everyone denied it, **Peter said,** *"Master, the crowds are squeezing you from all sides!"*
46a	Declaration	**Jesus said,** *"Someone touched me,* *for I know that power has gone out from me."*
b	Reason	
47	Response	When the woman saw that she had not escaped notice, **she came trembling and fell before him and announced before all the people ⮠ why she had touched him, and how she was healed immediately.**
48	Declaration	**He said to her,** *"Daughter, your faith has saved you.* *Go in peace."*
49	Report	While he was speaking, **someone came from the [home] of the synagogue ruler, saying,** *"Your daughter has died.* *Do not trouble the teacher any longer."*

Continued on next page.

50	Declaration	When Jesus heard this, **he replied to him,** *"Do not fear,* *only believe,* *and she will be saved."*
51	Circumstance	After he entered into the house, **he did not allow anyone else to come with him,** except Peter, John, and James and the child's father and mother.
52a b	Mourning Declaration	And **they were all weeping** and **beating their breasts over her,** and **he said,** *"Do not weep, for she is not dead but sleeps!"*
53 54	Mocking response Command	**They laughed at him because they knew that she had died.** But **he seized her hand** and **called out,** *"Child, rise!"*
55a b 56a b	Miracle Command Reaction Command	**Her spirit returned** and **she rose immediately,** and **he commanded that something be given to her to eat.** **Her parents were astounded,** and **he ordered them to tell no one what had happened.**

Structure and Literary Form

Luke takes over the bracketing structure of this account from Mark. The story of the dying daughter of a synagogue ruler wraps around the story of a woman with a hemorrhage who intercepts Jesus' rush to the girl's bedside by surreptitiously touching the hem of his garment. The intercalation fills in time in the narrative and serves to heighten the dramatic tension and the miracle's magnitude. During the delay with the woman, the daughter dies. The compositional technique also allows the two intersecting stories to make a similar point. It is wrong, therefore, to treat these two miracles separately. They are tied together.

Exegetical Outline

→ **I. Jesus' return to an expectant Galilee (8:40)**

II. Pleading request from Jairus, a leader of the synagogue, for his dying daughter (8:41 – 42)

III. Touch of a woman in the crowd with an incurable hemorrhage (8:43 – 48)

  A. Description of her suffering (8:43)

  B. Touching Jesus for healing (8:44)

  C. Jesus' recognition that power had gone out from him (8:45 – 46)

  D. Her confession and testimony (8:47)

  E. Jesus' assurance of her healing and commendation of her faith (8:48)

IV. The raising of Jairus's daughter from death (8:49 – 56)

  A. Announcement of the daughter's death (8:49 – 50)

    1. Resignation over her fate: "Do not trouble the teacher" (8:49)

    2. Jesus' exhortation to have faith and insistence that she will be saved (8:50)

  B. Arrival at the house (8:51 – 53)

    1. Limitation of witnesses to Peter, John, and James and the child's parents (8:51)

    2. Jesus' assurance to mourners that the child is not dead but sleeping (8:52)

    3. The mourners' derision and assurance that she is dead (8:53)

  C. Raising the daughter from death (8:54 – 55)

    1. Taking her by the hand and calling her to rise (8:54)

    2. Restoration of her life (8:55)

  D. Astounded reaction of the parents and command to silence (8:56)

Explanation of the Text

8:40 – 42a When Jesus returned, the crowd received him favorably, for they were all awaiting him. And behold, there came a man by the name of Jairus, who was a ruler of the synagogue, and when he fell at Jesus' feet, he pleaded with him to come to his house, because his only daughter, who was around twelve years old, was dying (ἐν δὲ τῷ ὑποστρέφειν τὸν Ἰησοῦν ἀπεδέξατο αὐτὸν ὁ ὄχλος· ἦσαν γὰρ πάντες προσδοκῶντες αὐτόν. καὶ ἰδοὺ ἦλθεν ἀνὴρ ᾧ ὄνομα Ἰάϊρος καὶ οὗτος ἄρχων τῆς συναγωγῆς ὑπῆρχεν, καὶ πεσὼν παρὰ τοὺς πόδας [τοῦ] Ἰησοῦ παρεκάλει αὐτὸν εἰσελθεῖν εἰς τὸν οἶκον αὐτοῦ, ὅτι θυγάτηρ μονογενὴς ἦν αὐτῷ ὡς ἐτῶν δώδεκα καὶ αὐτὴ ἀπέθνησκεν). The people across the lake desperately wanted Jesus to leave; the crowd in Galilee expectantly waits for his return. When he disembarks, a father prostrates himself before Jesus and no less desperately pleads for him to come to his home to deliver his daughter from a mortal illness.

In contrast to the temple, which was run by the high priests, the synagogue was a lay institution run by the local community.[1] Rabbis also did not dominate the synagogue. The synagogue ruler was the presiding officer who attended to the public meetings, maintained order, and bestowed honors

1. Shmuel Safrai, "Synagogue," in *The Jewish People in the First Century: Historical Geography, Political History, Social, Cultural, and Religious Life and Institutions* (CRINT; ed. S. Safrai et al.; Philadelphia: Fortress, 1976), 2:908 – 44.

such as appointing those who would read in the service (*m. Yoma* 7:1; *m. Soṭah* 7:7; Acts 13:15). "Ruler of the synagogue" may also have been an honorific title bestowed on a prominent member of the community. As a ruler of the synagogue, he has high status, but he makes no appeal to it. He does not claim to be worthy for Jesus to do this miracle for him (cf. 7:1 – 10). Instead, he makes himself lowly before Jesus (cf. 1:46 – 55). His abject humility reveals that the synagogue is not uniformly a hotbed of enmity against Jesus (see 12:11; Acts 18:8).

Rabbinic texts classify a girl up to the age of eleven years old as a "child," from eleven years and one day to twelve years and one day as a "minor" (*b. Ketub.* 39a), and from the age of twelve to twelve and a half as a "virgin" (*b. Sanh.* 66b). This daughter is on the cusp of maidenhood and marriageability. That she is also her father's one and only (μονογενής) daughter (see 7:12) adds to the pathos of the moment.

8:42b – 44 While he was going, the crowds crushed him. Now there was a woman who had a discharge of blood for twelve years, and [though she had spent her whole living on physicians] she could not be healed by anyone. She slipped up from behind and touched the hem of his garment, and immediately the bleeding stopped

(ἐν δὲ τῷ ὑπάγειν αὐτὸν οἱ ὄχλοι συνέπνιγον αὐτόν. Καὶ γυνὴ οὖσα ἐν ῥύσει αἵματος ἀπὸ ἐτῶν δώδεκα, ἥτις [ἰατροῖς προσαναλώσασα ὅλον τὸν βίον] οὐκ ἴσχυσεν ἀπ᾽ οὐδενὸς θεραπευθῆναι, προσελθοῦσα ὄπισθεν ἥψατο τοῦ κρασπέδου τοῦ ἱματίου αὐτοῦ καὶ παραχρῆμα ἔστη ἡ ῥύσις τοῦ αἵματος αὐτῆς). Mentioning the crush of the crowds explains why the woman believes she has an opportunity to slip up behind Jesus to touch his garment furtively and slink away unnoticed.

Because the phrase "discharge of blood" (ῥύσει αἵματος) is similar to that used in Lev 15:19 for menstruation, one may assume she suffers from uterine bleeding. Hers is an abnormal discharge, which restricts her interaction with others.

The emphasis in Luke's account is on her hopeless condition (see 13:11; Acts 3:2, 9:33; 14:8), which has caused her impoverishment. Luke does not delve into the Jewish purity laws related to discharges that would cause her to be socially isolated. Those auditors familiar with the law would take it for granted that she was largely banished from normal social intercourse. Greco-Roman auditors unfamiliar with the intricacies of the Mosaic law would also understand her forlorn state since conventional wisdom regarded that the touch of a menstruating woman was harmful (see Pliny, *Nat.* 7.64).

The clause "though she had spent her whole living on physicians" (ἰατροῖς προσαναλώσασα ὅλον τὸν βίον) is absent from early and diversified witnesses.[2] It possibly reflects Luke's rewriting of Mark 5:26 but more likely was omitted by later scribes sensitive to the tradition that Luke was supposedly a physician (Col 4:14).

Both Jairus and the woman believe that Jesus' touch or touching Jesus taps into a power to heal (see 6:19), and her touching Jesus is mentioned four times. The belief that the power of a sacred person is transferred through what one wears or touches was widespread (see Acts 5:15; 19:12). The woman touched the hem (τοῦ κρασπέδου) of Jesus' garment, which probably refers to one of the distinctive blue cords attached to the four corners of the rectangular cloak so that the Israelites would remember their covenant with God to obey the commands (Num 15:38 – 39; Deut 22:12). They would also remind the woman of God's mighty works and perhaps reinforce her belief that God

2. 𝔓[75], B, (D), (it[d]), Syr[s, pal mss], cop[sa], arm, geo.

has raised up "a horn of salvation" for us (Luke 1:68 – 75). Her bleeding was stanched as immediately as the wind and waves stopped at Jesus' command (8:24).

8:45 – 46 Then Jesus asked, "Who touched me?" When everyone denied it, Peter said, "Master, the crowds are squeezing you from all sides!" Jesus said, "Someone touched me, for I know that power has gone out from me" (καὶ εἶπεν ὁ Ἰησοῦς· τίς ὁ ἁψάμενός μου; ἀρνουμένων δὲ πάντων εἶπεν ὁ Πέτρος· ἐπιστάτα, οἱ ὄχλοι συνέχουσίν σε καὶ ἀποθλίβουσιν. ὁ δὲ Ἰησοῦς εἶπεν· ἥψατό μού τις, ἐγὼ γὰρ ἔγνων δύναμιν ἐξεληλυθυῖαν ἀπ᾽ ἐμοῦ). Jesus knows he has been touched in a special way because power has gone out from him, which means that he is also conscious of the power working through him. It is not that he loses power as if he were a battery that discharges energy when used. Rather, God's power is constant (cf. 5:17), and he controls the power going out from Jesus. Jesus knew why he had been touched, and his question is intended to force the woman to come forward publicly, the real test of her faith.

Peter responds incredulously to Jesus' question: "How are we supposed to know, since you are being squeezed from every direction?" His ignorance heightens the sense of Jesus' sovereignty over events.

8:47 When the woman saw that she had not escaped notice, she came trembling and fell before him and announced before all the people why she had touched him, and how she was healed immediately (ἰδοῦσα δὲ ἡ γυνὴ ὅτι οὐκ ἔλαθεν, τρέμουσα ἦλθεν καὶ προσπεσοῦσα αὐτῷ δι᾽ ἣν αἰτίαν ἥψατο αὐτοῦ ἀπήγγειλεν ἐνώπιον παντὸς τοῦ λαοῦ καὶ ὡς ἰάθη παραχρῆμα). Jesus deliberately chooses to touch a leper (5:13), the bier of a widow's son (7:14), and Jairus's dead daughter (8:54). The woman's clandestine touch could have

been interpreted as illegitimately stealing healing from Jesus. But her trembling is not caused by her fear of a reprimand but by awe over this one with such power. Like Jairus, she falls before him, and she declares what he has done for her in front of all the people (see 8:17, 39).

8:48 He said to her, "Daughter, your faith has saved you. Go in peace" (ὁ δὲ εἶπεν αὐτῇ· θυγάτηρ, ἡ πίστις σου σέσωκέν σε· πορεύου εἰς εἰρήνην). Jesus praises this woman for her faith, which must include both her touch *and* her coming forward, identifying herself, and giving a public testimony of her healing. Restoration to health is also viewed as salvation, which comes by faith as well. Faith has nothing to do with confidence in some magical properties attached to Jesus' clothing but is trust in the divine power working through Jesus and God's will to bring healing to brokenness.

Jesus does not simply dismiss the woman when he tells her to go "in peace" but bestows on her the peace of restoration, well-being, and salvation (2:29; 7:50; 10:5 – 6; Acts 10:36). She too is a "daughter."

8:49 While he was speaking, someone came from the [home] of the synagogue ruler, saying, "Your daughter has died. Do not trouble the teacher any longer" (ἔτι αὐτοῦ λαλοῦντος ἔρχεταί τις παρὰ τοῦ ἀρχισυναγώγου λέγων ὅτι τέθνηκεν ἡ θυγάτηρ σου· μηκέτι σκύλλε τὸν διδάσκαλον). The ruler's worst fears come to pass with the news of his daughter's death as "his peace" and hopes are dashed. The bleak message and direction to let Jesus go on his way reflect the messengers' belief that Jesus the healer can do nothing now. Death, in their view, places insurmountable limits on his miraculous powers.

The word that spread throughout Judea and the surrounding country about the raising of the widow's son (7:17) apparently has not reached their ears. The centurion sent word for Jesus not to trouble (σκύλλε) himself by coming any further, but he believed that Jesus need only say the word from where he stood to heal his slave (7:6 – 7). The messengers do not have the faith of the centurion or the woman and would undermine the faith of the father (see 8:12) because they do not know who Jesus is. Jairus must ignore them and trust that Jesus can do all things.

8:50 When Jesus heard this, he replied to him, "Do not fear, only believe, and she will be saved" (ὁ δὲ Ἰησοῦς ἀκούσας ἀπεκρίθη αὐτῷ· μὴ φοβοῦ, μόνον πίστευσον, καὶ σωθήσεται). Jesus is not thrown off guard by this dismal news of the girl's demise. His concern is for the continued faith of the father. Jairus was confident that Jesus could heal his daughter, but he did not bargain for this. Will he have the same confidence that Jesus can save her from death, or will he bow to the pressure from the crowd and believe that all is now lost? The verb "saved" (σωθήσεται) is applied to her restoration, but the phrase expresses the fundamental principle required for spiritual salvation: Do not fear, but believe.

8:51 – 53 After he entered into the house, he did not allow anyone else to come with him, except Peter, John, and James and the child's father and mother. And they were all weeping and beating their breasts over her, and he said, "Do not weep, for she is not dead but sleeps!" They laughed at him because they knew that she had died (ἐλθὼν δὲ εἰς τὴν οἰκίαν οὐκ ἀφῆκεν εἰσελθεῖν τινα σὺν αὐτῷ εἰ μὴ Πέτρον καὶ Ἰωάννην καὶ Ἰάκωβον καὶ τὸν πατέρα τῆς παιδὸς καὶ τὴν μητέρα. ἔκλαιον δὲ πάντες καὶ ἐκόπτοντο αὐτήν. ὁ δὲ εἶπεν· μὴ κλαίετε, οὐ γὰρ ἀπέθανεν ἀλλὰ καθεύδει. καὶ κατεγέλων αὐτοῦ εἰδότες ὅτι ἀπέθανεν). The weeping of the gathered group of friends and relatives turns to the laughter of derision when Jesus blithely announces that the girl is not dead but temporarily asleep. He has not even seen her dead body yet! They know death when they see it, and they know no one who can bring the dead back to life.

The crowd of mourners does not believe that anything more can be done for this girl, just as the physicians assumed that nothing more could be done to stop the woman's hemorrhage. Their skepticism that anyone could be revived from death and their mockery of anyone who said otherwise is perhaps a natural human response. It is the same reaction that Mary Magdalene and the other women get from the apostles when they report that the tomb was empty and that angels had announced to them that Jesus had been raised from the dead. The apostles dismissed it as an idle tale (24:10 – 11). The mourners here create an obstacle to Jairus's faith. He must now ignore them and trust that Jesus can do the impossible by bringing his little girl back to life.

8:54 – 55 But he seized her hand and called out, "Child, rise!" Her spirit returned, and she rose immediately, and he commanded that something be given to her to eat (αὐτὸς δὲ κρατήσας τῆς χειρὸς αὐτῆς ἐφώνησεν λέγων· ἡ παῖς, ἔγειρε. καὶ ἐπέστρεψεν τὸ πνεῦμα αὐτῆς καὶ ἀνέστη παραχρῆμα καὶ διέταξεν αὐτῇ δοθῆναι φαγεῖν). Jesus does not respond to the mockery and does nothing to try to dispel their skepticism. The mention of the girl's "spirit" (τὸ πνεῦμα αὐτῆς) returning is unique to Luke. It may suggest that her spirit had been hovering over her body, but Luke is reflecting on her ability to breathe.[3] Giving her something to eat tangibly confirms that she has

---

3. Fitzmyer, *Luke*, 1:749. Note that πνεῦμα also means "breath."

been restored to life (see 24:41 – 43; Acts 10:41) and needs sustenance.

8:56 Her parents were astounded, and he ordered them to tell no one what had happened (καὶ ἐξέστησαν οἱ γονεῖς αὐτῆς· ὁ δὲ παρήγγειλεν αὐτοῖς μηδενὶ εἰπεῖν τὸ γεγονός). Jesus did not say to the skeptical mourners that he would raise the girl from the dead but that she was not dead, only sleeping. He apparently does not want it broadcast that he raised her from death. The timing for belief in the miracle of resurrection awaits Jesus' own resurrection, which is not simply resuscitation. At this point, Jesus only forestalls death for this girl; his death and resurrection will release death's grasp on believers completely.

Theology in Application

1. Salvation and Healing

In chap. 7 the Jewish elders came to Jesus and only expected him to provide a cure for the centurion's slave (7:3), but when the victim of a disease or a demon responds to Jesus with faith, he offers more than physical well-being. He brings healing through faith, and Luke uses the verb "saved" for both bodily healing (8:35 – 39, 48, 50; 17:19; 18:42; Acts 14:9) and spiritual salvation. This transcendent salvation "originates with God (Lk 1:47), is effected by Christ the Lord (Lk 2:11), and extended not only to the sons of Abraham (Lk 19:9; Acts 13:23, 26), but also to the Gentiles and to the ends of the earth (Acts 13:47)."[4]

The problem is that our culture sees healing primarily through the metaphor of scientific medicine. Kepner says, "The medical model sees disease as a foreign condition against which one's body mobilizes itself to cope; with proper aid, the body will fight disease off with a stepwise fashion, with a resulting end state of health if treatment is successful."[5] This is a linear understanding of healing. The body progresses from a stage of disease to cure. But spiritual healing, which also affects bodily health, is not so simple because it also involves faith. Salvation is more complex than simply experiencing a physical cure. It involves God's initiative and the believer's response in faith. But it also requires a reorientation of the believer's life, conversion, and continuing Christian growth, which often is termed "sanctification." Its culmination awaits the day of the Lord and the final judgment. This process of salvation is complicated by the fact that faith, as the gospel story reveals, can wax and wane and even fail (8:25; 12:28; 18:8; 22:32; see Col 1:22 – 23; 1 Tim 4:1; Heb 10:38 – 39).

Spiritual healing entails a process, but Jesus' healing miracles reveal that it does not occur through one's own or some psychotherapist's inadequate, human resources. It takes place through a divine power unleashed in a person's life. For

---

4. Neal Flanagan, "The What and How of Salvation in Luke-Acts," in *Sin, Salvation, and the Spirit* (ed. D. Durkin; Collegeville, MN: Liturgical, 1979), 206.

5. James I. Kepner, *Healing Tasks: Psychotherapy with Adult Survivors of Childhood Abuse* (Cambridge, MA: Gestalt, 1996), 2.

physical cures, God has granted wonderful advances through medical science. But one may be healthy, wealthy, and even wise, but still alienated from God and beset by a dis-ease created by a spiritual void. No physical cure permanently fends off the various assaults on our mortal bodies, but faith carries one through and allows one to overcome physical maladies. Paul's faith meant that he could glory in his infirmity and see more clearly the grace and power of God working through him (2 Cor 4:7 – 18; 12:1 – 10).

2. Healing for All

The intertwining of these two events conveys a theological point that healing, wholeness, and life are available to all who come to Jesus with faith in his power. The characters are connected coincidentally. The woman has suffered her ailment for twelve years; the synagogue ruler's daughter is twelve years old. The woman has suffered as long as the child has been alive. Other than that, the main characters occupy opposite ends of the economic, social, and religious spectrum. Jairus is a prominent male leader of the community. The woman is nameless, and her wearying disorder isolates her from the community. He has a household and has means. She has been made destitute from seeking treatment for her ailment. He has honor and can approach Jesus directly with his plea for help. She has no honor and no eminent intercessors, as the centurion had (7:1 – 10), and must, she thinks, approach Jesus in a secretive manner from behind.

The two characters share only one thing: their desperate desire for healing and their belief that Jesus has the power to provide it. Both humble themselves before Jesus. Both must publicly recognize Jesus as the source of power. The woman gives her testimony before the crowd that Jesus' power healed her from her seemingly incurable malady. Jairus must ignore the mourners and relatives who deride Jesus' claim to turn his daughter's death into sleep from which she will awake. He must openly commit himself to his belief that Jesus is sufficient to conquer even death. In both cases, their faith is demonstrated by their hoping when all seems hopeless and by their public action. In the woman's case, she wanted to remain anonymous, but she must proclaim publicly what Jesus has done for her. In Jairus's case, he must ignore the emphatic declarations of the mourners that his daughter is beyond hope and trust in Jesus' power. Ironically, he is told to be silent, but this kind of power cannot be kept secret and the story will be told.

26

Luke 9:1 – 17

Literary Context

This larger section (9:1 – 50) sharpens the focus on the relationship of the disciples to Jesus. They are mentioned as the "Twelve," the "apostles," the "disciples," and by individual name twelve times (9:1, 10, 12, 14, 18, 20, 28, 32, 33, 40, 43, 49). They are also shown to have a deficient understanding of Jesus at key points (9:12 – 13, 32 – 33, 40, 45, 49 – 50). The disciples are identified as those who are "with" Jesus, and it becomes clearer why that is necessary. They must be with him to recognize his full identity as God's Son and to listen and learn from him (9:35, 44) before they can go out on mission themselves.

Christology is tied to discipleship and mission. Green comments that "one cannot embody authentic discipleship unless one perceives faithfully the nature of Jesus' person and work; yet, one cannot adequately comprehend Jesus' person and work apart from genuine discipleship."[1] The question of Jesus' identity joins the individual scenes together. When Jesus calmed the sea, the disciples ask, "Who ... is this?" (8:25). When Herod Antipas hears about his miracles, he also asks, "Who is this one about whom I hear such things?" (9:9). Finally, Jesus himself asks his disciples what they think about him. Peter's answer, "the Messiah of God" (9:20), is closely tied to the miracle of the feeding of five thousand. Because the disciples do not completely grasp Jesus' identity and mission, it necessitates that they be with him on the long journey to Jerusalem before they can become fully informed about God's purposes and fully formed to carry out their mission.

Two themes surface that will govern the rest of Luke's narrative. First, Herod's sudden appearance bodes ill for the future, since he has a track record for doing evil (3:19; 9:9). His appearance serves as a solemn reminder that Jesus and his disciples, despite their authority and power, will face murderous opposition. Second, the opinion that Jesus is John returned to life or one of the ancient prophets who has been "raised" affirms God's ability to raise from the dead those who were executed. Earthly powers cannot permanently defeat God's power and purpose.

---

1. Green, *The Gospel of Luke*, 352.

Main Idea

God's power is present in Jesus, and Jesus' power and authority are available to his disciples. He will supply them with all that they need to witness and minister effectively to the world.

Translation

(See next two pages.)

Structure and Literary Form

The structure of the first unit wraps the sending out of the disciples on a mission and their return (9:1 – 6, 10) around Herod's discomfiture over the public speculation about Jesus' identity (9:7 – 9).

Jesus' question to the disciples about what they think about him and Peter's confession that he is God's Messiah (9:18 – 20) follow the feeding of the five thousand. Consequently, the feeding miracle is sandwiched between two episodes that raise the question of Jesus' identity (9:7 – 9, 18 – 20), and it becomes a key event for penetrating the nature of Jesus' identity.

Luke 9:1–17

9:1	Commissioning	When he called the Twelve together,
		he gave them power and authority over all the demons and to heal diseases.
2		**He sent them to proclaim the reign of God and to cure the sick.**
3	Command (1)	**He said to them,**
		"Take nothing for the way,
		neither staff nor bag, nor bread, nor silver, nor two tunics.
4	Command (2)	*And whichever house you enter, remain there and leave from there.*
5	Command (3)	*Whoever does not receive you,*
		when you leave that town,
		shake the dust from your feet as a testimony against them."
6	Obedience	**They went out and were going through the villages preaching the good news and healing everywhere.**
7a	Perplexity	**Then Herod the tetrarch heard all that had happened and was at a loss,**
b	Speculation (1)	**because it was said by some,**
		"John was raised from the dead!"
8a	Speculation (2)	by some,
		"Elijah has appeared!" and
b	Speculation (3)	by others,
		"One of the prophets of old has risen!"
9a	Statement	**Herod said,**
		"I beheaded John.
b	Question	*Who is this one about whom I hear such things?"*
c		**And he kept seeking to see him.**

Ref	Label	Text
10a	Report	When the apostles returned,
b	Circumstance	they reported to him what they did. He took them and withdrew privately to a town called Bethsaida.
11a	Summary	When the crowds knew it,
b		they followed him,
c		and he welcomed them and spoke to them about the reign of God
d		and he healed those who needed to be cured.
12	Dilemma	The day was nearly over, and the Twelve came and said to him, *"Disperse the crowd so that they might go and lodge in the surrounding villages and countryside and find provisions because we are in a deserted place here."*
13a	Command (1)	He said to them, *"You give them [something] to eat."*
b	Objection	They said, *"There are no more than five loaves of bread and two fish for us unless we go and buy food for all this people."*
14a		For there were around five thousand men.
b	Command (2)	He said to his disciples, *"Make them recline in groups of fifty."*
15	Obedience	They did so and made all recline.
16a	Blessing	Then he took the five loaves of bread and two fish and looking up to heaven he blessed them and broke them and
b	Command (3)	gave them to the disciples to set before the crowd.
17a	Miracle	And they ate and all were filled,
b		and they took up what was left over and there were twelve baskets of fragments.

Exegetical Outline

➡ **I. Sending out of the Twelve on a mission to proclaim the reign of God and to heal (9:1 – 6)**

    A. Giving the Twelve authority over demons and diseases (9:1 – 2)

    B. Instructions for the mission (9:3 – 5)

    C. Fulfillment of the mission (9:6)

II. Herod's interest in Jesus (9:7 – 9)

    A. Herod hears about Jesus' works (9:7a)

    B. Herod hears speculation about Jesus' identity (9:7b – 8)

    C. Herod's attempts to see Jesus (9:9)

III. Return and report of the apostles (9:10)

IV. Feeding of the five thousand (9:11 – 17)

    A. The assemblage of a great crowd (9:11)

    B. The disciples' request for Jesus to disperse them (9:12)

    C. Jesus' command for the disciples to feed them (9:13a)

    D. The disciples' appeal to a poverty of resources (9:13b – 14a)

    E. Jesus' command to organize the crowd (9:14b – 15)

    F. The miracle of feeding the crowd with five loaves and two fish (9:16 – 17a)

    G. The gathering of the surplus (9:17b)

Explanation of the Text

9:1 When he called The twelve together, he gave them power and authority over all the demons and to heal diseases (συγκαλεσάμενος δὲ τοὺς δώδεκα ἔδωκεν αὐτοῖς δύναμιν καὶ ἐξουσίαν ἐπὶ πάντα τὰ δαιμόνια καὶ νόσους θεραπεύειν). The centurion recognized Jesus' supernatural authority (7:8), and Jesus has demonstrated his mighty power over demons and disease. He now delegates that same power and authority to the Twelve.[2] Just as he sent the man whom he freed from the legion of demons to proclaim what God had done for him in his own land, he sends the Twelve to proclaim the reign of God to the people of Israel.

9:2 – 4 He sent them to proclaim the reign of God and to cure the sick. He said to them, "Take nothing for the way, neither staff, nor bag, nor bread, nor silver, nor two tunics. And whichever house you enter, remain there and leave from there" (καὶ ἀπέστειλεν αὐτοὺς κηρύσσειν τὴν βασιλείαν τοῦ θεοῦ καὶ ἰᾶσθαι [τοὺς ἀσθενεῖς], καὶ εἶπεν πρὸς αὐτούς· μηδὲν αἴρετε εἰς τὴν ὁδόν, μήτε ῥάβδον μήτε πήραν μήτε ἄρτον μήτε ἀργύριον, μήτε [ἀνὰ] δύο χιτῶνας ἔχειν. καὶ εἰς ἣν ἂν οἰκίαν εἰσέλθητε, ἐκεῖ μένετε καὶ ἐκεῖθεν ἐξέρχεσθε). Jesus gives his disciples a twofold task: to proclaim the reign of God and to heal diseases. Giving them power and authority enables them to heal and cast out demons. The specific commands about provisions and lodging during their mission relate to the first task, proclaiming the reign of God. Taking no food, no money, not even

---

2. Jesus began his ministry with the crowds amazed at his "authority and power" over the unclean spirits (4:36).

an extra tunic, might be perceived as a sign of wretchedness since only the poor lacked a change of clothes.[3] But it is intended to exhibit "their detachment from the cares and concerns of this world and signifies trusting dependence on God."[4]

Jesus cited Deut 8:3, that a person does not live on bread alone (Luke 4:4), to rebuff the devil; he now wants his disciples to be as "radically dependent on God to supply their physical needs" as he has been.[5] He also expects their needs to be met by the hospitality of those who will receive them into their homes and who will receive the word fruitfully. The instruction for them to remain in one house (9:4) cautions them against switching to better-situated patrons. That action would blunt their message by betraying a greater interest in their personal comfort than their mission. They are neither to be beggars, going from house to house, nor peddlers, hawking the gospel for profit.

9:5 "Whoever does not receive you, when you leave that town, shake the dust from your feet as a testimony against them" (καὶ ὅσοι ἂν μὴ δέχωνται ὑμᾶς, ἐξερχόμενοι ἀπὸ τῆς πόλεως ἐκείνης τὸν κονιορτὸν ἀπὸ τῶν ποδῶν ὑμῶν ἀποτινάσσετε εἰς μαρτύριον ἐπ᾽ αὐτούς). Shaking the dust from one's feet (10:11; Acts 13:51; or from the clothes, Acts 18:6) is a symbolic gesture open to a number of interpretations (see also "flinging dust into the air," Acts 22:22 – 23). It has often been suggested that it means that the town is treated as heathen and this gesture is a means of self-purification. It does not mean that they are to sever all relationship with the place, because Jesus sends them back to "Jerusalem, and [to] all Judea and Samaria" (Acts 1:8; see Luke 9:51 – 56). It is far more likely that it is a warning as a "testimony against them" (εἰς μαρτύριον ἐπ᾽ αὐτούς). They

symbolically abandon the place to its impending doom, but even this performative gesture attempts to call them to repentance.

9:6 They went out and were going through the villages preaching the good news and healing everywhere (ἐξερχόμενοι δὲ διήρχοντο κατὰ τὰς κώμας εὐαγγελιζόμενοι καὶ θεραπεύοντες πανταχοῦ). Empowered by Jesus, the disciples are as successful as he has been. Their success is a foretaste of the success they will experience in their mission after the resurrection. The mention of a powerful nemesis, Herod, in the next line reminds the reader that success does not come without significant opposition, suffering, and potential death.

9:7 – 8 Then Herod the tetrarch heard all that had happened and was at a loss because it was said by some, "John was raised from the dead!" by some, "Elijah has appeared!" and by others, "One of the prophets of old has risen!" (ἤκουσεν δὲ Ἡρῴδης ὁ τετραάρχης τὰ γινόμενα πάντα καὶ διηπόρει διὰ τὸ λέγεσθαι ὑπό τινων ὅτι Ἰωάννης ἠγέρθη ἐκ νεκρῶν, ὑπό τινων δὲ ὅτι Ἠλίας ἐφάνη, ἄλλων δὲ ὅτι προφήτης τις τῶν ἀρχαίων ἀνέστη). Luke introduces an interlude while the disciples are off on their mission with the news of Jesus' works reaching and disturbing the powers that be in Galilee. Herod's perplexity ironically sounds the theme of the entire section, "Who is this?"

In Mark 6:17 – 29, the detailed account of Herod's execution of John brackets the disciples' mission, but Luke passes over John's beheading quickly and focuses only on his central concern: the confusion about Jesus identity. Herod is "at a loss" (διηπόρει; see Acts 2:12; 5:24; 10:17), which exposes him as one who hears but does not

3. Gildas Hamel, *Poverty and Charity in Roman Palestine: First Three Centuries CE* (Berkeley: Univ. of California Press, 1990), 76.

4. Resseguie, *Spiritual Landscape*, 97.
5. Heil, *The Meal Scenes in Luke-Acts*, 55.

understand (8:10). More important, his puzzlement prepares for Peter's confession in 9:18–20.

The crowd's ruminations present three options for interpreting who Jesus is. He may be John come back from the grave to haunt his royal nemesis, except that Herod knows that he is dead. Though Jesus' ministry in Galilee has many parallels to that of Elijah, he is more than a forerunner. The crowds do not say that he is *like* one of the ancient prophets but that he *is* one of the ancient prophets who has been raised up. Jesus will declare, however, that the age of the prophets has drawn to a close with John (16:14–17). That Jesus is neither Elijah nor a prophet of old is confirmed by the transfiguration scene, where Elijah and Moses make cameo appearances (9:28–36).[6]

9:9 Herod said, "I beheaded John. Who is this one about whom I hear such things?" And he kept seeking to see him (εἶπεν δὲ Ἡρῴδης· Ἰωάννην ἐγὼ ἀπεκεφάλισα· τίς δέ ἐστιν οὗτος περὶ οὗ ἀκούω τοιαῦτα; καὶ ἐζήτει ἰδεῖν αὐτόν). This brief statement is the only information Luke gives about John's demise. Herod takes full responsibility for his execution and expresses neither regrets nor qualms, which befits one who does evil in the sight of the Lord (3:18–20). His desire to see Jesus is mentioned twice in 23:8, where he wants to see a sign from Jesus, but, as here, he gets no answer and no sign. The reader, then, who also hears such things, must supply an answer to this question and judge whether Peter's confession is right.

9:10–11 When the apostles returned, they reported to him what they did. He took them and withdrew privately to a town called Bethsaida. When the crowds knew it, they followed him, and he welcomed them and spoke to them about the reign of God and he healed those who needed to be cured (καὶ ὑποστρέψαντες οἱ ἀπόστολοι διηγήσαντο αὐτῷ ὅσα ἐποίησαν. καὶ παραλαβὼν αὐτοὺς ὑπεχώρησεν κατ᾽ ἰδίαν εἰς πόλιν καλουμένην Βηθσαϊδά. οἱ δὲ ὄχλοι γνόντες ἠκολούθησαν αὐτῷ· καὶ ἀποδεξάμενος αὐτοὺς ἐλάλει αὐτοῖς περὶ τῆς βασιλείας τοῦ θεοῦ, καὶ τοὺς χρείαν ἔχοντας θεραπείας ἰᾶτο). The disciples return to report to Jesus, and he withdraws with them to Bethsaida, an area beyond Herod Antipas's control. It was elevated to the status of a city in AD 30 by Herod Philip, who commemorated the event by minting coins and renaming it Julia after Augustus's wife Livia Julia.

But Jesus cannot escape the crowds who chase after him. We may assume that they have been fueling the rumors that Elijah, John, or one of the prophets was raised from the dead. Despite needing to retreat with his disciples from the constant tug and pull of the crowds, Jesus welcomes them when they come crashing in on his private refuge. He continues his ministry of teaching and healing. The huge number of these devotees thronging around him is not mentioned until v. 14.

9:12 The day was nearly over, and the Twelve came and said to him, "Disperse the crowd so that they might go and lodge in the surrounding villages and countryside and find provisions because we are in a deserted place here" (ἡ δὲ ἡμέρα ἤρξατο κλίνειν· προσελθόντες δὲ οἱ δώδεκα εἶπαν αὐτῷ· ἀπόλυσον τὸν ὄχλον, ἵνα πορευθέντες εἰς τὰς κύκλῳ κώμας καὶ ἀγροὺς καταλύσωσιν καὶ εὕρωσιν ἐπισιτισμόν, ὅτι ὧδε ἐν ἐρήμῳ τόπῳ ἐσμέν). When it is time to eat, the disciples urge Jesus to send the crowds away. Their frustration with what they see as an impending disaster if something is not done soon may be betrayed by their omission of the polite address "Lord," but it also divulges how quickly they forget Jesus' extraordinary power.

---

6. Darr, *Herod the Fox*, 170.

Compared to the parallel in Mark 6:34, Luke writes that Jesus "welcomed" (ἀποδεξάμενος) the crowd rather than "had compassion on them." He also adds to the disciples' concern that the crowds find a place "to lodge" (καταλύσωσιν) as well as secure food (cf. Mark 6:36). This detail suggests that even in a deserted place the crowds could find provisions and implies that the miracle of the feeding is not done "primarily to satisfy a physical need."[7] It manifests Jesus power *and* hospitality.

The setting has not changed. They are still in Bethsaida or its vicinity and describing it as a "deserted place" (ἐρήμῳ τόπῳ) may seem anomalous, but it has a historical basis tied to its geological history.[8] It may also hark back to God's miraculous feeding of Israel in the wilderness (Exod 16; Ps 78:19 – 20). In such a setting, there can be no chance to wash hands so that they could eat in ritual purity (11:38), no choosing places of honor when they recline (14:8 – 9), and no vetting the guests when they number over five thousand. Since Jesus makes them all "recline" (κατακλίνατε, 9:14b, 15), this miracle is one of *"super-abundant table fellowship,"* which "is symbolic of the *joy* of God's *uncalculating* forgiveness, and a pointer to the eschatological *messianic banquet.*"[9] The disciples, however, automatically assume that the situation is hopeless and do not ask Jesus to do anything more than scatter the crowd.

9:13 – 14a He said to them, "You give them [something] to eat." They said, "There are no more than five loaves of bread and two fish for us unless we go and buy food for all this people." For there were around five thousand men (εἶπεν δὲ πρὸς αὐτούς· δότε αὐτοῖς ὑμεῖς φαγεῖν. οἱ δὲ εἶπαν· οὐκ εἰσὶν ἡμῖν πλεῖον ἢ ἄρτοι πέντε καὶ ἰχθύες δύο, εἰ μήτι πορευθέντες ἡμεῖς ἀγοράσωμεν εἰς πάντα τὸν λαὸν τοῦτον βρώματα. ἦσαν γὰρ ὡσεὶ ἄνδρες πεντακισχίλιοι). The term "people" (τὸν λαόν) recalls the use of this term for "the people of God" — they are not just some "amorphous crowd."[10] The disciples are not to be only recipients of hospitality, as they were on their preaching campaign (9:3 – 5); they are also required to offer hospitality to others (whether any of these were the ones who welcomed them into their homes or not).

The disciples assume that they have no resources to help the crowds and want to send them packing to fend for themselves in the surrounding villages, which would be overrun by such large numbers. Deserted place or not, dearth of supplies or not, they must offer hospitality to others, whether any of these were ones who had welcomed them into their homes or not.[11]

9:14b – 16 He said to his disciples, "Make them recline in groups of fifty." They did so and made all recline. Then he took the five loaves of bread and two fish and looking up to heaven he blessed them and broke them and gave them to the disciples to set before the crowd (εἶπεν δὲ πρὸς τοὺς μαθητὰς αὐτοῦ· κατακλίνατε αὐτοὺς κλισίας [ὡσεὶ] ἀνὰ πεντήκοντα. καὶ ἐποίησαν οὕτως καὶ κατέκλιναν ἅπαντας. λαβὼν δὲ τοὺς πέντε ἄρτους καὶ τοὺς δύο ἰχθύας ἀναβλέψας εἰς τὸν οὐρανὸν εὐλόγησεν αὐτοὺς καὶ κατέκλασεν καὶ ἐδίδου τοῖς μαθηταῖς παραθεῖναι τῷ ὄχλῳ). Arranging the people in groups of fifty again harks

---

7. Wilson C. K. Poon, "Superabundant Table Fellowship in the Kingdom: The Feeding of the Five Thousand and the Meal Motif in Luke," *ExpTim* 114 (2003): 225.

8. See Richard A. Freund, *"Erēmos*: Was Bethsaida a 'Lonely Place' in the First Century CE?" in *Bethsaida: A City by the North Shore of the Sea of Galilee* (ed. R. Arav and R. A. Freund; Kirksville, MO: Truman State Univ. Press, 2004), 183 – 212.

9. Poon, "Superabundant Table Fellowship," 226.

10. Heil, *The Meal Scenes in Luke-Acts*, 59.

11. Luke does not have Mark's more picturesque phrase "by companies" (συμπόσια συμπόσια, Mark 6:39), perhaps because in the Greco-Roman world the word connoted "drinking parties."

back to Israel's wilderness wanderings (Exod 18:21, 25; Deut 1:15) and became a conventional way of numbering the people of Israel.

Elisha fed one hundred men with twenty loaves (2 Kgs 4:42 – 44), but Jesus feeds far more with far less. Before he empowers the disciples to preach and heal everywhere (9:1 – 2, 6) "he now empowers to provide 'all this people' (9:13) the hospitality of a marvelous meal."[12] He assumes the role of host and offers a blessing. The Jewish blessing normally offers a blessing of God ("Blessed are you, O Lord our God … "), but Jesus blesses the bread and fish and that blessing causes them to multiply.[13] Looking up to heaven is the normal attitude in prayer (Job 22:26 – 27), and Jesus looks to heaven as the source of power that brings about the miracle. The multiplication of the loaves and fishes from this meager supply apparently occurs in the process of serving them to the people, not before.

9:17 And they ate and all were filled, and they took up what was left over and there were twelve baskets of fragments (καὶ ἔφαγον καὶ ἐχορτάσθησαν πάντες, καὶ ἤρθη τὸ περισσεῦσαν αὐτοῖς κλασμάτων κόφινοι δώδεκα). Each of the Twelve collected a basket filled with the profusion of leftovers. The crowds cannot complain as the wilderness generation did to Moses (Exod 16:3) or defiantly ask, "Can God really spread a table in the wilderness?" (Ps 78:19). They are all filled.

Theology in Application

1. The Disciples' Authority and Task

The Twelve are empowered and sent out but hardly seem prepared to carry out this momentous task. Their learning occurs in doing what Christ commands them. They also seem completely unprepared to feed more than five thousand, but they are able to do so when they obey him. This sending is the precursor to Jesus' sending them out into the world under the power of the Holy Spirit (Acts 1:8). Those under Jesus' authority will have authority to cast out demons and illnesses and to trample snakes and scorpions (Luke 10:19).

What is curious about the feeding miracle is that Jesus does not deal directly with the crowd. Instead, he commands his disciples to feed the crowd, orders the seating arrangements, and blesses the bread and fish. The disciples' task shifts from exercising Jesus' power over demons and curing illnesses (9:1) to offering Jesus' hospitality to the crowd. Faced with this daunting task and with no resources of their own, the disciples are miraculously able to pull it off, with an abundance of leftovers, by obeying Jesus' commands.

Despite having misgivings that they will not have enough to show hospitality to everyone, they are to receive outsiders and outcasts and bring the broken fragments of humanity together to receive God's beneficence in Christ. They learn that Jesus' power is available to them in all situations and to step out in faith and trust in

12. Heil, *The Meal Scenes in Luke-Acts*, 61.   13. Achtemeier, *Jesus and the Miracle Tradition*, 24.

God's providential care. Their meager resources, five loaves and two fishes, which ultimately feed more than five thousand people, match the meager resources, twelve apostles, whom God will use to spread the gospel to the entire world. It spreads in Acts through their praying, teaching, performing many wonders and signs, and continuing the tradition of fellowship they had with Jesus by breaking bread together and *sharing* with all who had need (Acts 2:42 – 47).

Jesus taught the crowds about the reign of God (9:11), but the reign of God is not just words. Jesus healed those who needed healing. The reign of God also brings action in feeding the hungry — even when they do not ask for help. "All were filled" (9:17) recalls the beatitude in 6:21 ("Blessed are those who hunger now, because they will be filled"), and the abundance of leftovers signifies that God's reign is present in Jesus and points to its promised fulfillment (14:15). Meals with Jesus are always significant, but this feeding has particular "revelatory power" as evidenced by Peter's confession that follows: Jesus is God's Messiah.[14] What disciples learn is that they are Jesus' representatives on earth, that he has empowered them, and that they will be enlightened to know God's will through prayer (9:28). The church can take a cue from Jesus. As Bruner comments on the feeding of the multitude, "He does not give tracts, advise fasting, or counsel patient resignation. He feeds."[15]

2. Deliverance Ministries

The passage about Jesus' granting his followers the authority to do exorcisms leads to the inevitable question: Is it possible for a Christian to be demon-possessed? If Christ is in us (Rom 8:9 – 10; Col 1:27), then the answer is no. Christians are not demon-possessed. But I also believe this to be the wrong question. Instead, we should ask, Is it possible for Christians to be tempted, to be tormented and harassed by the enemy, to open themselves up to addictions and uncontrollable habits, to have a worldly mind-set and be taken advantage of by the enemy, to be subject to divisions and to foster strife within the church, to give way to pride, to be plagued by fear, rejection, spitefulness, enmity, bitterness, anger, shame, guilt, and condemnation? The answer is, obviously, yes. The remedy for these ills, however, is not deliverance from demons but repentance.

It is interesting to note that demon possession and exorcisms are never mentioned in the letters of Paul. The demonized individuals encountered in the New Testament are never Christians, never rebuked, never told to repent, and never told that their sins are forgiven. They are not sinners but victims of a supernatural power that requires a greater divine power to liberate them. It is thus dangerous to ascribe every addiction or destructive behavior to demons, because it may lead one to

14. Culpepper, "The Gospel of Luke," 196.
15. Frederick Dale Bruner, *The Churchbook: A Historical/* *Theological Commentary: Matthew 13 – 28* (Dallas: Word, 1990) 67.

"neglect the more mundane spiritual warfare which each Christian must wage in his or her own heart."[16]

Jesus' commissioning of the disciples to cast out demons (see also the report of the seventy-two, 10:17) raises the question of its application for today. Jesus' ministry is the touchstone for evaluating all deliverance ministries, and striking contrasts exist. Jesus did not engage in dramatic or theatrical exorcisms to wow an audience. I take issue with some of the practices of contemporary deliverance ministries and believe that when they are compared to Jesus' ministry of exorcism, they come up short and lead to error.

Jesus eschewed anything that would seem to be theatrical. He did not parade victims around who had been delivered from demons to validate his authority to others. He did not have them manifest their deliverance in particular ways to prove that he had been successful. He did not tout his credentials as the most experienced or authoritative expert on demons in his day to gain adherents. He did not engage talkative demons in conversation to gather information about their methods, motivations, and goals (contrast the *Testament of Solomon*). He did not make use of any rituals or special prayers. He did not offer special training in deliverance methods, nor did he market formulaic steps to deliverance; he simply gave his followers authority. He did not gain financially from his ministry.

Jesus never flaunted his authority but ministered to hurting and broken people. He was not only the Savior of souls, but also the Good Physician. His miracles of healing were part and parcel of his activity as Savior of the world. In his exorcisms, he demonstrated his authority as the Son of God, and that authority was unique. It is he that bound Satan, not his disciples or us.

One deliverance prayer that I found runs this way and seems to usurp Jesus' role and exalt the exorcist:

> In the Name of the Lord Jesus Christ, I bind and destroy ALL satanic powers, strategies, yokes and bands in Jesus Christ's Name. I bind ALL satanic forces, oppressions, delusions, plans, hindrances and strategies by the power of the Blood of the Lord Jesus Christ. I break these powers off my life, ministry, family, marriage, finances, health, mind and I render them powerless.

The predominance of "I" in this prayer betrays the egotism behind it. It does not simply want God to come and work his power for us; it wants us to work that magic deliverance.

Deliverance ministries assume that demons are behind the inability to stop certain sins and addictions, and they tend to look for the quick fix. But sin is not so easily dispatched. Being rid of these sins requires yielding oneself completely to God, and it can take time. Anne Lamott says of her conversion to belief in God: "I felt changed, and a little crazy. But though I was still like a strained and slightly buckled jigsaw puzzle with some pieces missing, now there were at least a few broken pieces in place."[17] Jigsaw puzzles take time to complete, and this process, when the image is applied to the Christian life, is identified as sanctification.

In composing this commentary on a computer, I have often wanted to change the format and alter the margins, the font, and the page and footnote numbering, and so on. I am not a computer whiz, and when I turned the computer on the next time, it has reverted to the old, default setting. This experience is analogous to fighting sin and temptation in one's life. Often an involuntary reflex setting keeps resurfacing, and it requires a constant effort, grace, and vigilance to bring one's life into sync with the standards of Christ. My computer did not need deliverance but a more skilled operator. The same applies to Christians. What Christians need is not deliverance from demons (from which they have already been delivered) but immersion and submersion in the Holy Spirit. The Spirit is the master programmer who can reset the default mode so that one will not gratify the desires of the flesh (Gal 5:16 – 17).

17. Anne Lamott, *Traveling Mercies: Some Thoughts on Faith* (New York: Pantheon, 1999), 29.

Luke 9:18 – 36

Literary Context

Herod raised the question of Jesus' identity. Peter's confession here that Jesus is the Christ does not solve the issue because Jesus demands silence. He goes on to disclose that the Son of Man must suffer and die and then be raised and that disciples must also take up their cross daily and share his destiny. He then mentions his coming in glory (the parousia). The transfiguration scene, which, according to Luke, occurred around eight days after these words, connects the prediction of suffering with the preview of his eternal glory.

The confession and passion prediction and the transfiguration should not be treated as separate units. Neagoe insists, "Linking Jesus' prediction of his trial with the foregoing question of who he is, or linking it to the subsequent 'journey' to Jerusalem, is not an either-or for Luke, since Jesus' going up to Jerusalem to face trials is for Luke part and parcel of the divine plan for the Messiah."[1] The transfiguration provides heavenly ratification of what Jesus says about his destiny with the glorious appearance of Moses and Elijah speaking with him about his departure. The voice from the cloud that overshadows them provides divine confirmation of Jesus' identity. He is "my Son, the Chosen One" (9:35). This supernatural testimony reveals that Jesus' impending rejection and death do not mean that he is a failed messiah. His passion and resurrection are preordained for "God's Messiah."

The literary connections among these themes form a chiasm:

A Jesus' *identity* as the Messiah stated by Peter (9:20)

    B Jesus' *death and resurrection* stated by Jesus (9:22)

        C Jesus' future coming in *glory* (9:26)

            D Disciples seeing the reign of God in the future (9:27)

        C′ Jesus' *glory* visibly demonstrated in the transfiguration (9:29)

    B′ Jesus' *exodus* (= death, resurrection, and ascension) discussed by Moses and Elijah (9:31)

A′ Jesus' *identity* affirmed by the voice from heaven ("This is my Son," 9:35).[2]

---

1. Neagoe, *The Trial of the Gospel*, 51.   2. Adapted from Crump, *Jesus the Intercessor*, 44 – 45.

As the disciples repeat the speculation of the crowds about Jesus (9:7 – 8, 19) and Peter escalates it by declaring that Jesus is the Messiah, the next level in the chiasm augments the initial statement about Jesus' identity and death. Jesus is not simply the Messiah; he is the Son of God. Jesus' death is not the end of the story; it is an "exodus" that leads to his ascension and heavenly enthronement.

The transfiguration marks a major turning point as Jesus moves from one stage of his ministry to the next. It parallels his baptism at the beginning of his public ministry, when he was also in prayer and a voice from heaven made a similar pronouncement that he is "my Son, the beloved" (3:21 – 22). Nave notes that after Peter's confession "the tone of the gospel becomes severe. Jesus turns his attention to the suffering that awaits him in Jerusalem." During the travel narrative, he will consistently raise the issue of "the costs and conditions of discipleship, emphasizing the importance of self-denial over selfish gain (9:23 – 27)."[3]

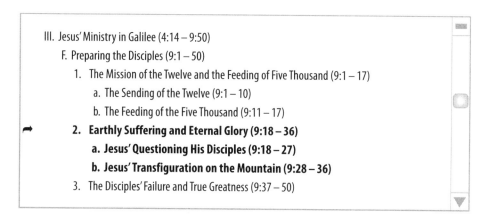

III. Jesus' Ministry in Galilee (4:14 – 9:50)

F. Preparing the Disciples (9:1 – 50)

1. The Mission of the Twelve and the Feeding of Five Thousand (9:1 – 17)
   a. The Sending of the Twelve (9:1 – 10)
   b. The Feeding of the Five Thousand (9:11 – 17)
2. **Earthly Suffering and Eternal Glory (9:18 – 36)**
   a. **Jesus' Questioning His Disciples (9:18 – 27)**
   b. **Jesus' Transfiguration on the Mountain (9:28 – 36)**
3. The Disciples' Failure and True Greatness (9:37 – 50)

Main Idea

Jesus' prediction that he will suffer, die, and be raised and his transfiguration on the mountain reveal how his death intertwines with his eternal glory.

Translation

(See next two pages.)

---

3. Nave, *Repentance in Luke-Acts*, 176.

Luke 9:18–36

9:18a	Prayer	**It happened** *while he was praying alone* that the disciples joined him.
b	Question	**He asked them,** *"Who do the crowds say I am?"*
19a	Speculation (1)	**They answered,** *" 'John the Baptist,' and*
b	Speculation (2)	*others, 'Elijah,' and*
c	Speculation (3)	*others, 'One of the prophets of old has arisen.' "*
20a	Question	**He said to them,** *"Who do you say I am?"*
b	Confession	**Peter answered,** *"The Messiah of God!"*
21	Rebuking command	**He rebuked them and commanded them to tell this to no one, saying,**

22	Passion/resurrection prediction	*"It is necessary for the Son of Man to suffer many things,*
		         to be repudiated by the elders,↲
		           chief priests, and scribes, and
		        to be killed, and
		
		         on the third day
		        to be raised."

23	Command	**He said to all,**
		   "If anyone wants to come after me,
		let him deny himself and
		   take up his cross daily and
		   follow me.

24	Reason (1)	*For whoever desires to save his life will lose it,* *and whoever loses his life because of me will save it.*
25	Reason (2)	*For what does it benefit a person to acquire the whole world and to lose*↲ *or forfeit himself?*

26	Reason (3)	*For whoever is ashamed of me and my words,*
		the Son of Man will be ashamed of this one
		       whenever he comes in his glory and that of↲
		         the Father and of his holy angels.

27	Prophecy	*I say to you truly, there are certain ones standing here who will not taste*↲ *death until they see the reign of God."*

Continued on next page.

28a	Circumstance / Chronological note	It happened about eight days after these words,
b		**he went up a mountain to pray,**
c		taking along Peter and James and John.
29a	Prayer	And while he was praying,
b	Transfiguration	**the appearance of his face became different,**
c		**and his clothing became as white as a flash of lightning.**
30a	Character introduction	**And behold, two men were speaking with him**
b		who were none other than Moses and Elijah,
31a	Description	who appeared in glory,
b	Discussion	**and they were talking of his exodus, which he was about to fulfill in Jerusalem.**
32a	Recognition	**Peter and those who were with him had been heavy-lidded with sleep,**
b		**but staying awake, they saw his glory and the two men standing with him.**
33	Reaction: uninformed declaration	And it happened as they were departing from him, **Peter, not knowing what he was saying, said to Jesus,** *"Master, it is a good thing that we are here,* *so that we may make three tents,* *one for you, one for Moses, and one for Elijah."*
34	Theophany	While he spoke, **a cloud came and overshadowed them;** **and they were afraid as they entered the cloud.**
35a	Divine declaration (informed)	**Then a voice came from the cloud, saying,** *"This is my Son, the Chosen One.*
b	Command	*Listen to him!"*
36	Reaction: silence	After the voice spoke, **they found Jesus alone.** **And they were silent and did not announce to anyone in those days what** **they had seen.**

Structure and Literary Form

The structure links Peter's confession, Jesus' prediction of his passion and resurrection, and sayings on discipleship with an apocalyptic vision of his transfiguration. This section is encircled by statements about Jesus' identity, first from humans and then from God: the erroneous guesses of the crowd (9:19), Peter's declaration that Jesus is "the Messiah of God" (9:20), and the definitive divine declaration that Jesus is "my Son, the Chosen One" (9:35). The structure of the transfiguration scene reveals why Jesus would wish to silence Peter's human confession even though it is correct.

A visible divine manifestation is followed by a frail human response that is wide of the mark.

Jesus' face and clothing are dramatically changed, and Moses and Elijah appear with him in glory to discuss "his exodus" (ἔξοδος, 9:29 – 31). The disciples react by being heavy-eyed, and then Peter makes a wildly flawed proposal (9:32 – 33). This response reveals that humans are not yet ready to comprehend God's plan that will lead to Jesus' glory, and the only appropriate response is silence (9:36) until they can fully understand and know what they are saying about Jesus. The center of the section reveals that a time will come when they do see the connection between suffering and glory and they will clearly see the reign of God (9:27).

Exegetical Outline

→ **I. Jesus' questioning his disciples about his identity and the prediction of his suffering (9:18 – 27)**

    A. Jesus' prayer before asking his disciples about his identity (9:18)

    B. The crowd's speculation (9:19)

    C. Peter's answer: "The Messiah of God" (9:20)

    D. Jesus' rebuke to be silent (9:21 – 26)

        1. Prediction of his passion and resurrection on the third day (9:21 – 22)

        2. Expectation that his followers must deny themselves and take up their cross (9:23 – 26)

            a. Aphorism about losing one's life to save it (9:23 – 24)

            b. Aphorism about gaining the whole world and losing one's soul (9:25)

            c. Warning that those ashamed of the Son of Man will be put to shame at the parousia (9:26)

    E. Prediction that his current followers will see the reign of God (9:27)

II. Jesus' transfiguration on the mountain (9:28 – 36)

    A. Jesus' prayer before the transfiguration (9:28 – 29a)

    B. What the disciples see but do not hear (9:29b – 33)

        1. Jesus' appearance as a divine being during prayer (9:29b-c)

        2. Appearance of Moses and Elijah in glory (9:30 – 31a)

        3. Their discussion of Jesus' departure in Jerusalem (9:31b)

        4. Reaction: Peter's misguided intention to build three shelters (9:32 – 33)

    C. What the disciples hear but do not see (9:34 – 36)

        1. Overshadowing by the cloud of the divine presence (9:34)

        2. Voice from the cloud identifying Jesus as "my Son, the Chosen One" (9:35a)

        3. Command to listen to him (9:35b)

        4. Reaction: Jesus found alone and the disciples' silence (9:36)

Explanation of the Text

9:18 It happened while he was praying alone that the disciples joined him. He asked them, "Who do the crowds say I am?" (καὶ ἐγένετο ἐν τῷ εἶναι αὐτὸν προσευχόμενον κατὰ μόνας συνῆσαν αὐτῷ οἱ μαθηταί, καὶ ἐπηρώτησεν αὐτοὺς λέγων· τίνα με λέγουσιν οἱ ὄχλοι εἶναι;). Praying alone is one of the characteristics of Jesus' prayer life. He already attempted to retire from the crowd (9:10), and now he resumes his quest for privacy. Luke does not tell us what Jesus prays about. Some surmise that he prays about his mission or his newly developing understanding that it will require the passion.[4]

Jesus certainly received insight into his mission through prayer, but Luke is not interested in delineating Jesus' development of his own understanding. Instead, the focus falls on what the disciples learn and witness. This explains the apparent contradiction that Jesus prays alone but his disciples join him. Luke links Jesus' prayer directly to his probe of the disciples' understanding of his identity. Luke also does not locate Peter's momentous confession as the spokesperson for the disciples in the district of Caesarea Philippi (Matt 16:13; Mark 8:27). He ties this confession more closely to the miraculous feeding of the five thousand and Jesus' prayer.[5]

9:19 – 20 They answered, " 'John the Baptist,' and others 'Elijah,' and others, 'One of the prophets of old has arisen.' " He said to them, "Who do you say I am?" Peter answered, "The Messiah of God!" (οἱ δὲ ἀποκριθέντες εἶπαν· Ἰωάννην τὸν βαπτιστήν, ἄλλοι δὲ Ἠλίαν, ἄλλοι δὲ ὅτι προφήτης τις τῶν ἀρχαίων ἀνέστη. εἶπεν δὲ αὐτοῖς· ὑμεῖς δὲ τίνα με λέγετε εἶναι; Πέτρος δὲ ἀποκριθεὶς εἶπεν· τὸν Χριστὸν τοῦ θεοῦ). Jesus is not gauging his poll numbers as a messianic candidate but probing what the disciples have discerned so far. They report the same rumors that aroused Herod's anxiety (9:7 – 8), but Jesus requires them to answer their question voiced in 8:25, "Who then is this?" Peter arrives at the answer that the reader of Luke's gospel already knows from the announcement of the angels (1:32 – 33; 2:11) and the earlier prophecies about his identity (1:32 – 33, 69; 2:26). The miracles they have witnessed, particularly the feeding of the five thousand, confirm for them that he is the divinely appointed Messiah. The crowds also have seen his miracles, but the difference is that in the presence of the praying Jesus, Peter can give the right answer.[6]

Peter's confession in Luke's account differs from Mark's simple "the Messiah" (Mark 8:29) and Matthew's "the Messiah, the Son of the living God" (Matt 16:16). The phrase "the anointed of God" (τὸν χριστὸν τοῦ θεοῦ) appears in 2 Sam 23:1 (2 Kgdms 23:1, LXX), and the genitive "of God" means that he belongs to God, who anointed him (see 1 Sam 24:6; 1 Kgdms 24:7, LXX) and sent him.[7] This answer raises the question about what it means to be *God's* Messiah with a divine commission that may run counter to human yearnings for an earthly, political kingdom that metes out vengeance to enemies and glittering benefits to boosters. God's Messiah must follow the way of suffering.

9:21 – 22 He rebuked them and commanded them to tell this to no one, saying, "It is necessary

---

4. So Charles H. Talbert, "The Way of the Lukan Jesus: Dimensions of Lukan Spirituality," *PRSt* 9 (1982): 243 – 45.

5. Liefield and Pao, "Luke," 174.

6. Crump, *Jesus the Intercessor*, 28.

7. It is not a genitive of source, "derived from" or "dependent on." Wallace (*Greek Grammar*, 109) notes that this is a rare category in Koine Greek: "In cases where there is no verbal head noun, possessive still takes priority over source as an apt label."

for the Son of Man to suffer many things, to be repudiated by the elders, chief priests, and scribes, and to be killed, and on the third day to be raised (ὁ δὲ ἐπιτιμήσας αὐτοῖς παρήγγειλεν μηδενὶ λέγειν τοῦτο, εἰπὼν ὅτι δεῖ τὸν υἱὸν τοῦ ἀνθρώπου πολλὰ παθεῖν καὶ ἀποδοκιμασθῆναι ἀπὸ τῶν πρεσβυτέρων καὶ ἀρχιερέων καὶ γραμματέων καὶ ἀποκτανθῆναι καὶ τῇ τρίτῃ ἡμέρᾳ ἐγερθῆναι). The right answer gets a surprising rebuke from Jesus.[8] Identifying the correct "title" for Jesus does not mean that the answer is correct. The demons got his title right as well (4:41). The disciples know that the crowd's answers are lacking, but they do not know why this answer is deficient or why it should prompt a reproof and the demand to remain silent. The absence of private corrective teaching (Mark 8:31, "he then began to teach them") or blessing (Matt 16:17, "Blessed are you … ") from Luke's account suggests that Jesus treats them as if their answer was on the same level as the crowd's guesswork.[9] Jesus will challenge their traditional framework and categories for understanding what God's Messiah, not simply the Jewish Messiah, must do. God will reveal that he is also the "Son of God."

The first passion prediction in Luke (see also 9:44; 17:25; 18:31 – 33) completes Jesus' follow-up command with a participle, "saying" (εἰπών). This construction makes "a stronger connection between Jesus's Christological identity and his forthcoming passion."[10] "The elders, chief priests, and scribes" will form a uniform front of opposition and conspire to bring about his death. The passive infinitives "to be killed" (ἀποκτανθῆναι) and "to be raised" (ἐγερθῆναι) contrast the agency of

humans and God: humans will kill him but God will raise him from the dead. The absence of any reaction from Peter to this passion announcement (contrast Mark 8:32 – 33) suggests that he does not yet fathom its meaning (9:45; 18:34).

9:23 He said to all, "If anyone wants to come after me, let him deny himself and take up his cross daily and follow me" (ἔλεγεν δὲ πρὸς πάντας· εἴ τις θέλει ὀπίσω μου ἔρχεσθαι, ἀρνησάσθω ἑαυτὸν καὶ ἀράτω τὸν σταυρὸν αὐτοῦ καθ' ἡμέραν καὶ ἀκολουθείτω μοι). The image of taking up a cross and following Jesus derives from the Roman custom of making condemned persons carry their crossbar to the place of execution. It pictures a procession of the condemned and implies that one lives knowing that "life in this world is *already finished.*"[11] The additional phrase "daily" (καθ' ἡμέραν) means that disciples are not in this for a brief period of tribulation, but this self-denial must extend over a natural lifetime.[12] The disciples will follow Jesus literally to Jerusalem, but they will learn what discipleship requires on the way as they hear his teaching and see what he does.

9:24 – 26 "For whoever desires to save his life will lose it, and whoever loses his life because of me will save it. For what does it benefit a person to acquire the whole world and to lose or forfeit himself? For whoever is ashamed of me and my words, the Son of Man will be ashamed of this one whenever he comes in his glory and that of the Father and of his holy angels" (ὃς γὰρ ἂν θέλῃ τὴν ψυχὴν αὐτοῦ σῶσαι, ἀπολέσει αὐτήν· ὃς δ᾽ ἂν ἀπολέσῃ τὴν ψυχὴν αὐτοῦ ἕνεκεν ἐμοῦ οὗτος σώσει αὐτήν. τί γὰρ ὠφελεῖται ἄνθρωπος

---

8. The verb translated "rebuke" (ἐπιτιμήσας) has that nuance everywhere else it occurs in Luke (4:35, 39, 41; 8:24; 9:21, 42, 55; 17:3; 18:15, 39; 19:39; 23:40) and has that meaning here.

9. David P. Moessner, "Luke 9:1 – 50: Luke's Preview of the Journey of the Prophet Like Moses of Deuteronomy," *JBL* 102 (1983): 591.

10. Neagoe, *The Trial of the Gospel*, 51.

11. Marshall, *The Gospel of Luke*, 373.

12. Greg Sterling, "Pray Always — Prayer in Luke/Acts," in *Preaching from Luke/Acts* (ed. David Fleer and David Bland; Abilene, TX: Abilene Christian Univ. Press, 2000), 76.

κερδήσας τὸν κόσμον ὅλον ἑαυτὸν δὲ ἀπολέσας ἢ ζημιωθείς; ὃς γὰρ ἂν ἐπαισχυνθῇ με καὶ τοὺς ἐμοὺς λόγους, τοῦτον ὁ υἱὸς τοῦ ἀνθρώπου ἐπαισχυνθήσεται, ὅταν ἔλθῃ ἐν τῇ δόξῃ αὐτοῦ καὶ τοῦ πατρὸς καὶ τῶν ἁγίων ἀγγέλων). There are three reasons given here why one should submit to Jesus' radical demand. The first, losing one's life to save it, belongs to the paradoxical wisdom found in 6:22 and 18:29. A divine law of unintended consequences kicks in when one tries to save one's life by conforming to the standards, values, and means of this world. One's life will be inevitably and ultimately lost.

The second reason, "What does it benefit a person to acquire the whole world and to lose or forfeit himself?" reinforces the first statement. Multiple examples abound to corroborate this statement. Getting everything one wants gets one nowhere.

The third reason is apocalyptic. Seeking "to acquire the whole world" will inevitably require that one ignore, if not openly despise, Jesus and his teaching. "Being ashamed" reflects a belief that being identified with Jesus brings a loss of status according to the world's calculations (2 Tim 1:8, 12, 16). But the use of the verb in Rom 1:16 suggests additionally that shame is related to the fear that the gospel will somehow disappoint and not accomplish what it promises. Identifying with Jesus recognizes that the gospel is the power of God that will not fail. Those who have failed to give their complete allegiance to Jesus will be put to shame. Consequently, one should evaluate one's present commitment in light of the future age when the righteous will be rewarded and evil people judged. Everything valued in this world will be reversed by God's intervention in the coming age of glory.

The Greek has three genitives that imply that each — the Son of Man, the Father, and the angels — has glory (ἐν τῇ δόξῃ αὐτοῦ καὶ τοῦ πατρὸς καὶ τῶν ἁγίων ἀγγέλων; contrast Mark 8:38 and Matt 16:27, where he comes in the glory of "his Father" and accompanied by angels). Fletcher-Louis declares that this construction envisages "a Christology in which the Son of Man embraces all levels of reality, the human, the angelic and that of God himself."[13]

9:27 "I say to you truly, there are certain ones standing here who will not taste death until they see the reign of God" (λέγω δὲ ὑμῖν ἀληθῶς, εἰσίν τινες τῶν αὐτοῦ ἑστηκότων οἳ οὐ μὴ γεύσωνται θανάτου ἕως ἂν ἴδωσιν τὴν βασιλείαν τοῦ θεοῦ). The final pronouncement leads into the transfiguration scene. The prediction is unfulfilled if it refers to the parousia. Luke's use of the general phrase "the reign of God" rather than the more specific "the reign of God coming with power" (Mark 9:1; Luke 21:27) suggests that he did not intend it to refer to the parousia. If it refers to "certain ones" of the disciples who will witness Jesus' glorious transformation as an anticipatory preview of God's reign, which is recounted in the next episode, it is fulfilled.

But it seems overly dramatic to use the expression "will not taste death" to refer to something that happens a week later. Instead, "see[ing] the reign of God" in Luke means to perceive a spiritual reality "that does not come with observable [signs]" (17:20), that is, "in [their] midst" (17:21), and that can be seen, for example, in Jesus' casting out demons (11:20). Jesus contrasts the disciples with the crowds. The disciples who remain partially blind now but who follow Jesus will see the reign of God in Jesus' death, resurrection, and ascension and in their continuing mission to the world (Acts 1:3).

---

13. Crispin H. T. Fletcher-Louis, *Luke-Acts: Angels, Christology and Soteriology* (WUNT 2/94; Tübingen: Mohr Siebeck, 1997), 226 – 27.

9:28 It happened about eight days after these words, he went up a mountain to pray, taking along Peter and James and John (ἐγένετο δὲ μετὰ τοὺς λόγους τούτους ὡσεὶ ἡμέραι ὀκτὼ [καὶ] παραλαβὼν Πέτρον καὶ Ἰωάννην καὶ Ἰάκωβον ἀνέβη εἰς τὸ ὄρος προσεύξασθαι). Mark and Matthew record this event occurring "after six days," which means that it occurs on the seventh day after his prediction of his death and resurrection. That time span matches the period Moses awaited revelation from God when "the glory of the LORD settled on Mount Sinai. For six days the cloud covered the mountain, and on the seventh day the LORD called to Moses from within the cloud" (Exod 24:16). Luke's "about eight days" (ὡσεὶ ἡμέραι ὀκτώ) is less precise and uses the "normal inclusive rendering of a 'week.'"[14] Perhaps Luke makes this change to distance Jesus from Moses. Jesus is much more than simply a new Moses.

The emphasis falls on "these words" so that the time reference definitely connects this incident to Peter's confession that Jesus is the Messiah and Jesus' announcement of his suffering, death, and resurrection. Peter, James, and John (see 5:10; 8:51) get a preview of Jesus' future glory. The revelation that occurs "is primarily for the benefit of those who accompany Jesus, not for Jesus himself."[15] Jesus already knows and has disclosed his destiny to the disciples. Its purpose is to reveal to them (and the reader) that suffering and death are not incompatible with heavenly glory.

Only Luke mentions that Jesus' purpose for ascending the mountain is to pray, and the radiance occurs *while* he is praying.[16] For Luke, prayer is the way to discover and accept God's plan, and its importance in this incident is emphasized by its repetition in 9:29. Crump comments: "Luke conceives of the prayers of Jesus as a catalyst for the reception of the divinely bestowed insight into the person and character of Christ; once again, through the prayers of Jesus, the disciples see and hear something about who Jesus is."[17]

9:29 And while he was praying, the appearance of his face became different, and his clothing became as white as a flash of lightning (καὶ ἐγένετο ἐν τῷ προσεύχεσθαι αὐτὸν τὸ εἶδος τοῦ προσώπου αὐτοῦ ἕτερον καὶ ὁ ἱματισμὸς αὐτοῦ λευκὸς ἐξαστράπτων). Luke avoids the verb "transfigured" (μεταμορφόω; Matt 17:2; Mark 9:2) and says "the appearance" (τὸ εἶδος) of his face changed ("became different," or "became other," ἕτερον). Luke's understated description thereby avoids any association with what happened to Jesus on the mountain with the pagan myths of gods magically transforming themselves and humans.[18]

Moses' face shone when he came down from the mountain after being in the presence of God (Exod 34:29 – 35). But this alteration of his appearance was a reflected glory and is not comparable to what happens to Jesus. By contrast, Jesus' clothes shine white like lightning, which conveys that he is a divine being (Dan 12:3; Matt 13:43).[19] The

---

14. Hemer, *The Book of Acts in the Setting of the Hellenistic History*, 356. It is unlikely that Luke has "eight days" to tie the event more closely to the Feast of Booths and the command in Lev 23:3 (as Bovon, *Luke 1:1 – 9:50*, 374, contends). That feast does not factor in Luke's interpretation of this event.

15. Green, *The Gospel of Luke*, 380. Simon S. Lee (*Jesus' Transfiguration and the Believers' Transfiguration* [WUNT 2/265: Tübingen: Mohr Siebeck, 2009], 108 – 9) suggests that the accounts of Jesus' appearance in glory to Stephen and Paul in Acts serve to make the Hellenists' experience of Jesus' glory

comparable to that of these three disciples. They too are authoritative witnesses of his glory after his crucifixion for their respective mission.

16. The mountain's identity is irrelevant to Luke (6:12).

17. Crump, *Jesus the Intercessor*, 44.

18. See Ovid's *Metamorphoses*, an epic poem that recounts such Greek and Roman myths.

19. Barbara E. Reid, *The Transfiguration: A Source- and Redaction-Critical Study of Luke 9:28 – 36* (CahRB; Paris: Gabalda, 1993), 115.

language of brightness is reminiscent of Paul's account of his divine encounter with Christ on the Damascus road (Acts 9:3; 22:6, 9, 11; 26:13). Heil interprets it to mean that Jesus is "temporarily transformed by God into a heavenly being while still on earth. It anticipates his future and permanent attainment of glory in heaven as promised to the righteous after their death."[20] This divine reality contrasts dramatically with the contrived reality created by Herod, who dresses Jesus in "shining raiment" after his interrogation of him in the passion narrative (23:11). It further illustrates how humans both misunderstand and always fall short when encountering the divine.

9:30 – 31a And behold, two men were speaking with him who were none other than Moses and Elijah, who appeared in glory (καὶ ἰδοὺ ἄνδρες δύο συνελάλουν αὐτῷ, οἵτινες ἦσαν Μωϋσῆς καὶ Ἠλίας, οἳ ὀφθέντες ἐν δόξῃ). Luke mentions two men speaking with Jesus before identifying them. The "two men" appearing "in glory," which refers to the divine order (9:26; Acts 7:55), loosely connect this scene to the two men in white at the tomb after the resurrection (24:4) and the two men in white at the ascension (Acts 1:10). In the Greek each incident is introduced the same way: "Behold, two men." Then, Luke identifies them in chronological order (as opposed to Mark 9:4) as Moses and Elijah. Their sudden appearance with Jesus refutes the people's mistaken notions that he was Elijah or a recycled prophet (Moses, the prototype).

The significance of their appearance is debated. Since Luke divides Scripture into the Law and the Prophets (2:22; 5:14; 16:16, 29), these two figures

may be symbolic representatives of the Law and the Prophets respectively. This traditional view has fallen into disfavor among modern interpreters, but it best fits their discussion of Jesus' departure ("exodus"), which he is to fulfill, since Luke emphasizes that the Law and the Prophets foretold his destiny (24:27, 44; Acts 3:18; 26:22). In Stephen's sermon in Acts, Moses redeemed Israel from captivity and worked signs and wonders (Acts 7:36). The first time Moses goes to "visit" Israel he is rejected (Acts 7:23 – 29, 35).[21]

Elijah worked miracles, spoke God's authoritative word, issued dire warnings to Israel, and also suffered as a persecuted prophet. He was mysteriously taken up into heaven by a whirlwind. Both men now belong to the realm of glory, where Jesus is ultimately headed (24:26).[22] As two witnesses from heaven who both experienced rejection by Israel, they confirm the truth of Jesus' "words" that he is to undergo rejection, suffering, and death.

9:31b And they were talking of his exodus, which he was about to fulfill in Jerusalem (ἔλεγον τὴν ἔξοδον αὐτοῦ ἣν ἤμελλεν πληροῦν ἐν Ἰερουσαλήμ). In Acts 13:24, Luke terms the beginning of Jesus' ministry as an "entrance" (εἴσοδος). Here, he identifies the termination of his journey as an "exodus" (ἔξοδος). The term appears in Heb 11:22 to designate the departure from Egypt (see Exod 19:1; Num 33:38; 1 Kgs 6:1; Ps 105:8 [104:38]). In 2 Pet 1:15, it is a euphemism for the author's death, an exit from life. Josephus and Philo use the term predominantly in neutral ways rather than as a technical term for the exodus.[23]

Luke's use of this term emphasizes what is

---

20. John Paul Heil, *The Transfiguration of Jesus: Narrative Meaning and Function of Mark 9:2 – 8, Matt 17:1 – 8 and Luke 9:28 – 36* (AnBib 144; Rome: Pontifical Biblical Institute, 2000), 260.

21. Johnson, *The Gospel of Luke*, 19 – 20.

22. Richard J. Dillon, *From Eye-Witnesses to Ministers of the Word: Tradition and Composition in Luke 24* (AnBib 82; Rome:

Pontifical Biblical Institute, 1978), 143.

23. Besides the exodus out of Egypt, Josephus uses it for "roads" or "routes," "setting out," "departure," "marching off," "withdrawal," "excursion," "sallying out for battle," "campaign," "an outcome of a battle," and "exit from life." Philo uses it for the death of Moses (*Moses* 1.268).

fulfilled in Jerusalem, not what happens on the way to Jerusalem. But the exodus does not end in Jerusalem but ends in heaven, when Jesus is taken up into heaven (24:51). The meaning of the word must be related to what is accomplished in Jerusalem, namely, his death, resurrection, and ascension (24:26 – 27, 44 – 47).[24] The reader may assume that Moses and Elijah provide heavenly encouragement for Jesus' next stage in his mission, which will end during Passover in the city that kills the prophets (13:34). Lee contends that this loaded term evoking God's redemptive act for Israel does not convey only Jesus' individual journey but refers to "God's redemptive work revealed through his journey."[25]

9:32 Peter and those who were with him had been heavy-lidded with sleep, but staying awake, they saw his glory and the two men standing with him (ὁ δὲ Πέτρος καὶ οἱ σὺν αὐτῷ ἦσαν βεβαρημένοι ὕπνῳ· διαγρηγορήσαντες δὲ εἶδον τὴν δόξαν αὐτοῦ καὶ τοὺς δύο ἄνδρας τοὺς συνεστῶτας αὐτῷ). In Gethsemane when Jesus prays for deliverance, the disciples are again drowsy (22:45). The disciples are "heavy-lidded with sleep" (ἦσαν βεβαρημένοι ὕπνῳ; lit., "weighed down"), but it need not mean that they are muddleheaded. Bovon notes, "People believed themselves to be near to the divine while sleeping or dreaming."[26] The verb "staying awake" (διαγρηγορήσαντες) can mean that they struggled to stay awake and need not mean that they were fully awakened. Luke implies with the adversative "but" (δέ) that they stayed awake despite their drowsiness. Godet comments:

Perhaps we should regard the choice of this unusual term as indicating a strange state, which many persons have experienced, when the soul, after having sunk to sleep in prayer, in coming to itself, no longer finds itself in the midst of earthly things, but feels raised to a higher sphere, in which it receives impressions full of unspeakable joy.[27]

Luke's language avoids any suggestion that this was a dream vision. It was a real-life experience.[28] The disciples, therefore, see Jesus' divine glory before it will become manifest to all when he comes at the end of the age (9:26).

9:33 – 34 And it happened as they were departing from him, Peter, not knowing what he was saying, said to Jesus, "Master, it is a good thing that we are here, so that we may make three tents, one for you, one for Moses, and one for Elijah." While he spoke, a cloud came and overshadowed them; and they were afraid as they entered the cloud (καὶ ἐγένετο ἐν τῷ διαχωρίζεσθαι αὐτοὺς ἀπ᾽ αὐτοῦ εἶπεν ὁ Πέτρος πρὸς τὸν Ἰησοῦν· ἐπιστάτα, καλόν ἐστιν ἡμᾶς ὧδε εἶναι, καὶ ποιήσωμεν σκηνὰς τρεῖς, μίαν σοὶ καὶ μίαν Μωϋσεῖ καὶ μίαν Ἠλίᾳ, μὴ εἰδὼς ὃ λέγει. ταῦτα δὲ αὐτοῦ λέγοντος ἐγένετο νεφέλη καὶ ἐπεσκίαζεν αὐτούς· ἐφοβήθησαν δὲ ἐν τῷ εἰσελθεῖν αὐτοὺς εἰς τὴν νεφέλην). Peter makes his proposal about the tents as the men were departing (ἐν τῷ διαχωρίζεσθαι αὐτούς). This particular detail, which appears only in Luke's account, suggests that he wanted to prolong their stay by building shelters. If the shelters have any thematic relation to the Feast of Booths, Luke does

---

24. Brevard S. Childs (*The Book of Exodus* [OTL; Philadelphia: Westminster, 1974], 233) argues against any reference to the exodus tradition here and thinks, "The connection is only possible by means of an illegitimate semantic transfer."

25. Lee, *Jesus' Transfiguration and the Believers' Transfiguration*, 118.

26. Bovon, *Luke 1:1 – 9:50*, 376, noting Albrecht Oepke, "καθεύδω," *TDNT*, 3:431 – 33; Horst Balz, "ὕπνος," *TDNT*, 8:545.

27. Godet, *Luke*, 1:491.

28. Fletcher-Louis, *Luke-Acts: Angels, Christology and Soteriology*, 28.

not develop it.[29] Nor does he present Peter wanting to build the tents from fear of being in the presence of the divine.[30]

If Peter sets Moses and Elijah on an equal plane with Jesus in wanting to build a tent shrine for each, it cannot and should not be done. If he wants to tether the glory of God on a leash by causing them to tarry longer and forestall Jesus' predestined "exodus" in Jerusalem, it too cannot and should not be done. Since the tent is related to God's dwelling with Israel (Exod 33:7–14; 40:34; 2 Sam 7:6–7), it is more likely that Luke understands his proposal as inadequate and unnecessary. God's own dwelling comes down and surrounds them and surpasses anything that humans could ever build.

It is unclear who is included in the phrase "they entered the cloud" (ἐν τῷ εἰσελθεῖν αὐτοὺς εἰς τὴν νεφέλην). Does it mean only Jesus, Moses, and Elijah, or does it also include the three disciples? Since the divine voice speaks "from" (ἐκ) the cloud (v. 35), the disciples may be pictured as standing outside it. It is less awkward grammatically if the personal pronouns that are explicit and understood in the verb refer to the disciples: the cloud overshadowed them, they were afraid, and they entered the cloud.

In the Synoptic accounts of the transfiguration, the disciples experience fear at different points. In Mark 9:6, Peter's proposal regarding the tents is attributed to their fright. In Matt 17:6, "they fell facedown to the ground, terrified" on hearing the voice. Luke mentions their fear as they were entering the cloud. One can postulate different reasons why the three evangelists locate the fear where they do in their accounts or simply assume that fear gripped the disciples in waves at successive stages of the event. The cloud is a veil and vehicle of divine glory that signifies God's presence (Exod 24:15–18; 13:21–22; 16:10; 19:9; 40:34; 2 Sam 22:12).[31] It is mentioned three times for emphasis. Fear is the appropriate and natural human response to the divine glory overshadowing them.

9:35 Then a voice came from the cloud, saying, "This is my Son, the Chosen One. Listen to him!" (καὶ φωνὴ ἐγένετο ἐκ τῆς νεφέλης λέγουσα· οὗτός ἐστιν ὁ υἱός μου ὁ ἐκλελεγμένος, αὐτοῦ ἀκούετε). God provides the definitive answer to Herod's question, "Who is this one about whom I hear such things?" but Herod and his ilk will not hear. Will the disciples hear? The revelation comes from the word, not from the supernatural visual effects. The voice from the cloud identifies Jesus as "my Son" *and* "the Chosen One" (ὁ ἐκλελεγμένος; see Isa 41:9; 42:1; 43:10; 44:1), as opposed to "my Son, whom I love" in Matt 17:5 and Mark 9:7.[32] The allusion connects Jesus to the suffering servant (Isa 52:13–53:12) and helps the disciples to interpret Jesus' frightening destiny (and theirs) in terms of God's will and heavenly glory. Chosenness is connected to suffering. The title reappears when the leaders taunt Jesus to save himself on the cross since he is God's "elect one" (23:35).

The command to listen to Jesus means that they should listen to the revelation of God that comes through Jesus rather than the fickle speculations of public opinion (9:18–19) or their yearnings to make Jesus conform to their own expectations of what the Messiah should be and do. Moses prophesied that God would raise up from the people a prophet like him, and they were to listen to him, and everyone who does not listen to him will be rooted out from the people (Acts 3:22–23). Now

29. Contra Bock, *Luke*, 1:870–71.
30. Contra Randall E. Otto, "The Fear Motivation in Peter's Offer to Build τρεῖς σκηνάς," *WTJ* 59 (1997): 106–7, 110–12.
31. A cloud also comes to lift Jesus out of the disciples' sight at the ascension (Acts 1:9).
32. The voice calls him "beloved" in 3:22, but "chosen" and "beloved" are synonymous.

a divine voice confirms that Jesus is that one. He is God's Messiah (9:20), obeys God's will, and declares God's purposes. Those who do not listen and obey will be cut off from the people of God and from salvation.

9:36 After the voice spoke, they found Jesus alone. And they were silent and did not announce to anyone in those days what they had seen (καὶ ἐν τῷ γενέσθαι τὴν φωνὴν εὑρέθη Ἰησοῦς μόνος. καὶ αὐτοὶ ἐσίγησαν καὶ οὐδενὶ ἀπήγγειλαν ἐν ἐκείναις ταῖς ἡμέραις οὐδὲν ὧν ἑώρακαν). Only Luke mentions the disciples' awed silence, which is the only appropriate response to such an event. Their continued silence about what happened means that it cannot be understood until after Jesus' "exodus" — his death, resurrection, and ascension.

Theology in Application

1. Taking Up the Cross of Suffering

The cross was an instrument of death usually reserved for slaves and terrorists. Jesus' demand to his disciples to take up a cross and follow after him should have stunned them, since they had no inkling that he would die by crucifixion. The demand, however, is directed primarily to the readers who know how the story ends, and we must interpret it in light of Jesus' own cross. To bear it means that disciples imitate Jesus and willingly subject themselves to shame and the howling mob to follow God's will. To bear it recognizes that it is not foolishness but the power of God for salvation (1 Cor 1:18), and that as the cross turns out to be the glory of Christ, so it is the glory of Christians. To bear it means that they must put to death self-centered purposes and renounce a wicked world, the realm where people glory in the flesh (Gal 6:13–14). To bear it "daily" means that it has nothing to do with martyrdom but a lifetime of sacrificial living.[33] Wright concludes:

> There was the way of wisdom and the way of folly. Conventional wisdom said, of course, that the way of the Messiah would be the way of fulfilment and self-aggrandizement: those who wanted to gain their lives would have to fight for them, and the devil take the hindmost. Jesus' most subversive teaching, in both form and content, consisted in just this: the way of wisdom meant taking up the cross, dying in order to live.[34]

2. Suffering and Glory

The transfiguration incident transforms the understanding of "glory." Jesus' glory will come from his "self-sacrificing love."[35] It also transforms the understanding of Jesus as "God's Son." Because God "chose him" (9:35; 23:35) and "made this Jesus ... both Lord and Messiah" (Acts 2:36)," "it is appropriate to say of Jesus what otherwise can only be said of God precisely because Jesus is God's perfect instrument."[36]

---

33. Craddock, *Luke*, 130.
34. Wright, *Jesus and the Victory of God*, 315.
35. Ibid.
36. Schweizer, *Luke*, 158.

In contrast to other miracles in Luke, the transfiguration does not show what Jesus can do but who Jesus is and how to interpret his suffering and death. One cannot tell that the cross is glorious by looking at it. It is hidden. Luke "associated it with the glory into which Christ was to enter by the Resurrection and Ascension and in which He would appear at the Parousia."[37]

This is the interpretation of the event in 2 Pet 1:12 – 18. They were "eyewitnesses of his majesty" as "he received honor and glory from God the Father." Since the scene is deliberately connected to Jesus' sayings on his passion and resurrection and parousia, "it foreshadows the time when God will gloriously enthrone Jesus after the degradation on the cross."[38] What is important to see is that the one who descends to the depth of disgrace also ascends to glory. On the cross, his garments are taken from him; in the transfiguration we see him divinely arrayed. On the cross, he dies a humiliating death. In the transfiguration, we see him glorified. Lee comments, "The one who is transfigured on the mountain is the one who is disfigured by anguish, pain and death on the cross. The two cannot be separated."[39] This Jesus is God's Son, who was chosen for this exodus that will lead others out of the darkness into the glorious light through his obedience.

If Peter was trying to extend this sacred moment and prolong the stay of Elijah and Moses, he seeks to "control the holy," which cannot be done.[40] Peter's attempt to sustain this moment of glory is similar to the crowd's trying to prevent him from leaving Capernaum after all his successful miracles and demons shouting out that he is the Son of God (4:40 – 42). His response, "It is necessary for me to proclaim the good news of the reign of God in other cities. I have been sent for this purpose" (4:43), applies here as well. He is under a divine necessity to head toward Jerusalem, and disciples must listen to him, follow his lead, and not try to impose their desires for glory upon his mission.

3. Listening to Jesus

Many commentators point out the various parallels between what happens to Jesus in this scene and the shining face of Moses (Exod 34:29 – 35), but there are marked differences because Jesus is greater than Moses. For example, when Moses said, "The Lord your God will raise up for you a prophet like me from among your own people" (Acts 3:22, citing Deut 18:15), Jesus does not simply appear as a prophet like Moses (or Elijah, for that matter) but as the Son of God who will be "raised" by God from the dead (Acts 3:15). Stettler also draws a vital theological point from the differences between God's appearance to Moses at Mount Sinai and God's appearance on the mount of transfiguration.[41] God revealed himself to Moses in the

37. G. B. Caird, "The Transfiguration," *ExpTim* 67 (1955): 292.
38. Garland, *Mark*, 343 – 44.
39. Dorothy Lee, *Transfiguration* (London/New York: Continuum, 2004), 124 – 25.
40. Johnson, *The Gospel of Luke*, 156.
41. Stettler, "Sanctification in the Jesus Tradition," 165.

formula of self-introduction, "I am Yahweh," and then gave the Decalogue. In the transfiguration, God introduces his Son, "This is my Son, the Chosen One," and then continues, "Listen to him." Jesus' instructions are placed on a level with God's commandments. His words, like God's word, "will not pass away" (21:33).

Peter places Jesus on an equal par with Moses and Elijah in his desire to build three individual shelters for them. Caird explains, "For all their greatness Moses and Elijah belonged to the old order, which was now giving place to a fuller and more adequate revelation of God's character and purpose."[42] Moses, Elijah, and Jesus do *not* represent a new trinity — the Law, the Prophets, and Jesus, who is a bit of both with the added ingredient of grace. Moses and Elijah disappear so that Jesus stands "alone." Moses represents in Luke rigorous legalism (Acts 15:1). In calling down fire from heaven, as a later episode recalls, Elijah, according to Caird, represents a destructive attitude, "typical of the whole Old Testament toward the enemies of God and God's people." Caird expands on this comment:

> For the Old Testament offered life and blessing to the obedient, and atonement to those who sinned in ignorance and error; but to those who wilfully opposed God it offered only God's curse. Now, however, the law of Moses and the spirit of Elijah were both being rendered obsolete by the determination of Jesus to follow the way of the Cross and by His redemptive suffering to reveal God's way of dealing with sin.[43]

4. The Message of Hope

The transfiguration offers a message of hope, but it is shrouded in a paradox. The path of suffering and death leads to glory. It is therefore hard for humans to comprehend since they get only brief glimpses of the glory to come, and these may be as frightening and confusing as they are comforting. The failures of humans after this event reveals that they do not need transfiguration but transformation. Lee observes that the Feast of Transfiguration celebrated in some Christian communions occurs on August 6, when the first atomic bomb detonated to destroy Hiroshima.[44] That fierce fireball of light contrasts with the light of God that promises to transform this world and put an end to its wars that destroy and disfigure humans.

Jesus' transfiguration gives us a preview of the promise of this renewed world and our own transformation. As Paul visualizes it: "And we all, with unveiled face, beholding the glory of the Lord, are being transformed into the same image from one degree of glory to another. For this comes from the Lord who is the Spirit" (2 Cor 3:18 ESV). But Paul also reminds us that the god of this world is still at work to blind the minds of the unbelievers "to keep them from seeing the light of the gospel of the glory of Christ, who is the image of God" (2 Cor 4:4 ESV). This is why the path to glory must still journey through suffering.

42. Caird, "The Transfiguration," 293.
43. Ibid., 293.

44. Lee, *Transfiguration*, 131 – 32.

Luke 9:37 – 50

Literary Context

Luke's account of an exorcism at the behest of a desperate father whose son is bedeviled by a demon follows immediately after the transfiguration, in contrast to Mark and Matthew, which include a discussion between Jesus and the disciples about the timing of the coming of Elijah between the transfiguration and the exorcism story (Matt 17:9 – 13; Mark 9:9 – 13). According to Talbert, this exorcism story does not function as a postlude to the transfiguration but is integral to it: "In Luke all the stress falls on the authority of Jesus, so 9:37 – 43 goes together with the voice from heaven (9:35) to reaffirm Jesus' authority prior to telling his disciples he must be delivered into the hands of men."[1]

Jesus' announcement of his passion (9:44) is also integral to the exorcism. It is uttered *while* the crowd is marveling over all that he is doing (9:43). It continues to highlight a divine paradox. Jesus is God's Son, the Chosen One, who has matchless authority over demonic powers that beleaguer humans in tragic ways. God intends for all to heed him, but he will be rejected, betrayed, and put to death. Luke's omission of any discussion about Elijah as an end-time figure prevents the spotlight on Jesus from drifting away.

Jesus' passion predictions (9:22, 44) that surround the transfiguration reveal the divine necessity of his "exodus" to Jerusalem. In obedience to God's will, he will set his face to go there (9:51). The lengthy travel narrative that follows (9:51 – 19:28) reveals that this journey is also necessary for the disciples' training. This section discloses that they have a steep learning curve before they will be fully prepared to take up their crosses daily and follow him, as he demands (9:23). They fail to exorcise a demon, fail to understand Jesus' second passion prediction, and show themselves to be competitive with one another and contentious with others. Jesus' continuing instruction on the way to Jerusalem will attempt to purge these faults.

1. Talbert, *Reading Luke*, 119.

III. Jesus' Ministry in Galilee (4:14 – 9:50)

   F. Preparing the Disciples (9:1 – 50)

      1. The Mission of the Twelve and the Feeding of Five Thousand (9:1 – 17)

      2. Earthly Suffering and Eternal Glory (9:18 – 36)

    → **3. The Disciples' Failure and True Greatness (9:37 – 50)**

         a. Jesus' Exorcism of a Demon (9:37 – 43a)

         b. Jesus' Prediction of His Betrayal (9:43b – 50)

IV. Jesus' Journey to Jerusalem (9:51 – 19:28)

Main Idea

The magnificence of God's working through Jesus includes deliverance from the oppression of evil powers, the self-giving love of Jesus' sacrificial death, and the initiative of grace to the lowly, with whom Jesus identifies.

Translation

Luke 9:37–50

9:37	Circumstance	It happened on the next day,
		when they had descended from the mountain,
		a large crowd met him.
38a	Character introduction	**And behold, a man from the crowd cried out,**
b	Urgent request	*"Teacher, I beg you to look at my son*
c	Reason	*because he is my one and only.*
39	Description of malady	*And behold, a spirit takes him,*
		and suddenly he yells
		and it shakes him with foaming at the mouth
		and it scarcely leaves him, battering him about.
40	Previous failure	*And I begged your disciples to cast it out, and they were not able."*
41a	Pronouncement	**Jesus answered,**
		"O faithless and crooked generation,
		how long will I be with you and put up with you?
b	Command	*Bring your child here."*
42a	Encounter with the demon	While he was coming,
		the demon threw him down and shook him.

Continued on next page.

b	Exorcism	But **Jesus rebuked the unclean spirit, healed the child, and gave him back to↩ his father.**
43a	Reaction	**All were amazed at the magnificence of God.**
b	Circumstance	While they all were marveling over all that he was doing, **he said to his disciples,**
44a	Attention	*"Fix these words in your ears,*
b	Passion prediction	*for the Son of Man is about to be betrayed into the hands of men."*
45a	Effect (1) incomprehension	But **they remained ignorant about this statement,**
b		and **it was hidden from them so that they did not comprehend,**
c	Fear	and **they were afraid to ask him about this statement.**
46	Effect (2) dispute	**They started an argument among them about which of them was the greatest.**
47	Object lesson	But **Jesus, knowing the thoughts in their hearts, took a little child and placed him by his side and said to them,**
48a	Pronouncement	*"Whoever receives this child in my name, receives me. And whoever receives me, receives the one who sent me.*
b	Pronouncement	*For the least among you all—this one is great."*
49	Boast	**John responded,** *"Master, we saw someone casting out demons in your name and we tried to prevent him, because he does not follow with us."*
50	Pronouncement	**Jesus said to him,** *"Do not prevent him, for whoever is not against you is for you."*

Structure and Literary Form

The disciples' failure to cast out the demon from the son of a desperate father and their attempt to prevent an unfamiliar exorcist who was not following with them but who was successfully casting out demons in Jesus' name brackets Jesus' second prediction of his passion. In both incidents, a child factors into the story, first as a victim and then as an object lesson. The disciples' incomprehension is magnified by their callous dispute over who is the greatest immediately after Jesus announces his impending death. Each of the three incidents concludes with a pronouncement from Jesus (9:44, 48, 50).

Exegetical Outline

→ **I. Jesus' exorcism of a demon (9:37 – 45)**

    A. Jesus' encounter with a desperate father (9:37 – 40)

        1. Plea from a father to help his son (9:37 – 38)

        2. Description of the assaults by an evil spirit (9:39)

        3. The disciples' failure to exorcise it (9:40)

    B. Pronouncement: Jesus' complaint against this generation (9:41a)

    C. Jesus' exorcism of the demon (9:41b – 42)

        1. Jesus' command to bring the boy to him (9:41b)

        2. Final assault by the evil spirit (9:42a)

        3. Rebuke of the evil spirit, healing of the boy, and his restoration to his father (9:42b)

    D. Amazement of the crowd over the magnificence of God (9:43a)

    E. Jesus' pronouncement: The Son of Man will be betrayed (9:43b – 44)

    F. The disciples' incomprehension (9:45)

II. The disciples' dispute over who is the greatest (9:46 – 48)

    A. Dispute over who is the greatest (9:46)

    B. Example of a little child (9:47)

    C. Jesus' pronouncements (9:48)

        1. Those who welcome a child welcome him and the one who sent him (9:48a)

        2. The least among them is the greatest (9:48b)

III. The exorcist stranger (9:49 – 50)

    A. John's report of an attempt to stop a stranger from casting out demons (9:49)

    B. Jesus' pronouncement: Do not interfere with those doing good who are not against you (9:50)

Explanation of the Text

9:37 – 39 It happened on the next day, when they had descended from the mountain, a large crowd met him. And behold, a man from the crowd cried out, "Teacher, I beg you to look at my son because he is my one and only. And behold, a spirit takes him, and suddenly he yells and it shakes him with foaming at the mouth and it scarcely leaves him, battering him about" (ἐγένετο δὲ τῇ ἐξῆς ἡμέρᾳ κατελθόντων αὐτῶν ἀπὸ τοῦ ὄρους συνήντησεν αὐτῷ ὄχλος πολύς. καὶ ἰδοὺ ἀνὴρ ἀπὸ τοῦ ὄχλου ἐβόησεν λέγων· διδάσκαλε, δέομαί σου ἐπιβλέψαι ἐπὶ τὸν υἱόν μου, ὅτι μονογενής μοί ἐστιν, καὶ ἰδοὺ πνεῦμα λαμβάνει αὐτόν καὶ ἐξαίφνης κράζει καὶ σπαράσσει αὐτὸν μετὰ ἀφροῦ καὶ μόγις ἀποχωρεῖ ἀπ᾽ αὐτοῦ συντρῖβον αὐτόν).

Jesus returns from the mountain, where the disciples witnessed his divine glory, to the world of human and demonic mayhem. He immediately encounters another parent desperately concerned for his only child (see 7:12; 8:42), who is being brutalized by an evil spirit. Luke provides vivid details of how it afflicts the boy. The man's desperation is not only caused by helplessly witnessing his son being tormented. This evil threatens to bring an end to his bloodline, and his son's attention-getting affliction brings shame to the family.

9:40 – 41a "And I begged your disciples to cast it out, and they were not able." Jesus answered, "O faithless and crooked generation, how long will I be with you and put up with you?" (καὶ ἐδεήθην τῶν μαθητῶν σου ἵνα ἐκβάλωσιν αὐτό, καὶ οὐκ ἠδυνήθησαν. ἀποκριθεὶς δὲ ὁ Ἰησοῦς εἶπεν· ὦ γενεὰ ἄπιστος καὶ διεστραμμένη, ἕως πότε ἔσομαι πρὸς ὑμᾶς καὶ ἀνέξομαι ὑμῶν;). Even though Jesus had commissioned the disciples and given them authority and power to cast out demons and to heal diseases (9:1 – 6), Luke only records incidents when Jesus casts out demons (8:26 – 56). In the present case, the disciples hit a snag. Luke's version offers no reason why they are unable to expel the demon after they had been so successful earlier.

No mention is made here of anyone's lack of faith or the need for prayer, as in Mark's account (Mark 9:23 – 24, 29). Nevertheless, Jesus responds harshly to the disciples' failure. He lumps them together with the whole mass of the faithless and perverse people of Israel (Deut 32:5, 20; Isa 65:2; Jer 5:21 – 23; Ezek 12:2). The exclamation "How long?" (ἕως πότε) is one of exasperation. What is their fault? In Luke's context, the only explanation for the erosion of the disciples' power over demons is that it is somehow connected to their failure to understand Jesus' prediction of his upcoming passion.

9:41b – 44 "Bring your child here." While he was coming, the demon threw him down and shook him. But Jesus rebuked the unclean spirit, healed the child, and gave him back to his father. All were amazed at the magnificence of God. While they all were marveling over all that he was doing, he said to his disciples, **"Fix these words in your ears, for the Son of Man is about to be betrayed into the hands of men"** (προσάγαγε ὧδε τὸν υἱόν σου. ἔτι δὲ προσερχομένου αὐτοῦ ἔρρηξεν αὐτὸν τὸ δαιμόνιον καὶ συνεσπάραξεν· ἐπετίμησεν δὲ ὁ Ἰησοῦς τῷ πνεύματι τῷ ἀκαθάρτῳ καὶ ἰάσατο τὸν παῖδα καὶ ἀπέδωκεν αὐτὸν τῷ πατρὶ αὐτοῦ. ἐξεπλήσσοντο δὲ πάντες ἐπὶ τῇ μεγαλειότητι τοῦ θεοῦ, πάντων δὲ θαυμαζόντων ἐπὶ πᾶσιν οἷς ἐποίει εἶπεν πρὸς τοὺς μαθητὰς αὐτοῦ· θέσθε ὑμεῖς εἰς τὰ ὦτα ὑμῶν τοὺς λόγους τούτους· ὁ γὰρ υἱὸς τοῦ ἀνθρώπου μέλλει παραδίδοσθαι εἰς χεῖρας ἀνθρώπων).

Jesus takes charge of the situation. He expels the demon despite its last-ditch tactic to throw the boy into a violent paroxysm. He is then restored whole to his father. The account is much briefer than the one in Mark, which has the boy brought forward twice (Mark 9:17, 20), identifies the demon twice (9:17, 25), and mentions two reactions of the demon to Jesus' presence (9:20, 26). Luke also does not include the lengthy interaction with the father or the debriefing with the disciples that appear in Mark and Matthew's accounts (9:28 – 29; cf. Matt 17:19 – 20). The focus in Luke is solely on Jesus and his tremendous power.

The crowd marvels over "the magnificence [τῇ μεγαλειότητι][2] of God," and this is tied to "all that he [Jesus] was doing" (ἐπὶ πᾶσιν οἷς ἐποίει). The crowd's amazement would seem to be the climax to this exorcism, but it is connected to Jesus' restatement of his passion as a genitive absolute, "while they all were marveling" (πάντων δὲ θαυμαζόντων), which introduces it. The climax surprisingly becomes Jesus' restatement of his coming betrayal into the hands of men. Luke omits the transition preceding this statement in Mark 9:30 – 31 that has Jesus leaving and passing

---

2. The term appears in 2 Pet 1:16 to describe Jesus' transfiguration.

through Galilee and teaching his disciples (see Matt 17:22). The result is that this prediction may seem alien to the context, but it serves Luke's theological purpose. Divine majesty will not meet with constant applause from humans but will encounter rejection. Many will fail to see that God works an even mightier deed on the cross with Jesus' death and resurrection.

9:45 But they remained ignorant about this statement, and it was hidden from them so that they did not comprehend, and they were afraid to ask him about this statement (οἱ δὲ ἠγνόουν τὸ ῥῆμα τοῦτο καὶ ἦν παρακεκαλυμμένον ἀπ᾽ αὐτῶν ἵνα μὴ αἴσθωνται αὐτό, καὶ ἐφοβοῦντο ἐρωτῆσαι αὐτὸν περὶ τοῦ ῥήματος τούτου). The disciples hold their peace at this second announcement, but it may be a disapproving silence. The narrator attributes it to their ignorance and fear (Matt 17:23b/Mark 9:32) but adds that they were not yet meant to know. Its significance will remain hidden from them, even as they draw nearer to Jerusalem (18:34). Only after the resurrection, after all has been accomplished, will their minds be opened to understand the Scriptures that God is ultimately behind the handing over of Jesus according to a divine plan (24:45 – 47).

9:46 – 48 They started an argument among them about which of them was the greatest. But Jesus, knowing the thoughts in their hearts, took a little child and placed him by his side and said to them, "Whoever receives this child in my name, receives me. And whoever receives me, receives the one who sent me. For the least among you all — this one is great" (εἰσῆλθεν δὲ διαλογισμὸς ἐν αὐτοῖς, τὸ τίς ἂν εἴη μείζων αὐτῶν. ὁ δὲ Ἰησοῦς εἰδὼς τὸν διαλογισμὸν τῆς καρδίας αὐτῶν, ἐπιλαβόμενος παιδίον ἔστησεν αὐτὸ παρ᾽ ἑαυτῷ, καὶ εἶπεν αὐτοῖς· ὃς ἐὰν δέξηται τοῦτο τὸ παιδίον ἐπὶ τῷ ὀνόματί μου, ἐμὲ δέχεται· καὶ ὃς ἂν ἐμὲ δέξηται, δέχεται τὸν ἀποστείλαντά με· ὁ γὰρ μικρότερος ἐν πᾶσιν ὑμῖν ὑπάρχων οὗτός ἐστιν μέγας).

This argument must have taken place outside of Jesus' hearing, since he must read "the thoughts in their hearts" to know it had taken place. The disciples, however, are not bashful about arguing about who is the greatest in front of Jesus. Another dispute breaks out among them at the most inappropriate time, the Last Supper. Again, it occurs immediately after he has announced his impending betrayal (22:21 – 24).

As an object lesson, Jesus sets a child in their midst. Jesus had no romanticized notions about the qualities of children (see 7:32) and was *not* setting up the child as a model for them to imitate. Children had no power, no status, and no rights, and they were regarded as insignificant and disposable, as witnessed by the exposure of (usually female) children in the Greco-Roman world.[3] Exposure was not done just by the poor but also by the wealthy. Nelson explains, "The harsh reality in antiquity of high infant mortality rates was an important reason for the low view of children: people had to find a way to come to terms with the probability that some if not most of their children would not live to adulthood."[4]

As one who is regarded as small, weak, and dependent, a child is the perfect illustration of those who are the most responsive to God's grace. Those who swagger in their vainglory and wish to be crowned the greatest resist grace. Moessner captures Jesus' meaning well, "There is no point at being at Jesus' side unless one is humble enough to be at a 'child's side.'"[5]

3. Thomas E. J. Wiedemann, *Adults and Children in the Roman Empire* (London: Routledge, 1989), 6 – 7.

4. Peter K. Nelson, *Leadership and Discipleship: A Study of Luke 22:24 – 30* (SBLDS 138; Atlanta: Scholars, 1994), 39.

5. Moessner, "Luke 9:1 – 50," 593.

9:49 – 50 John responded, "Master, we saw someone casting out demons in your name and we tried to prevent him, because he does not follow with us." Jesus said to him, "Do not prevent him, for whoever is not against you is for you" (ἀποκριθεὶς δὲ Ἰωάννης εἶπεν· ἐπιστάτα, εἴδομέν τινα ἐν τῷ ὀνόματί σου ἐκβάλλοντα δαιμόνια καὶ ἐκωλύομεν αὐτόν, ὅτι οὐκ ἀκολουθεῖ μεθ᾽ ἡμῶν. εἶπεν δὲ πρὸς αὐτὸν ὁ Ἰησοῦς· μὴ κωλύετε· ὃς γὰρ οὐκ ἔστιν καθ᾽ ὑμῶν ὑπὲρ ὑμῶν ἐστιν). The same selfish pride that drove the disciples to seek precedence in their in-group rouses them to ensure that outsiders remain outsiders and unempowered.

John's boast is reminiscent of Joshua's plea to Moses when unauthorized prophets arose, "Moses, my lord, stop them!" (Num 11:28). Moses responded, "Are you jealous for my sake? I wish that all the Lord's people were prophets and that the Lord would put his Spirit on them!" (11:29). Jesus responds here with an aphorism, "Whoever is not against you is for you." That word will become clearer when the disciples engage in mission in an increasingly hostile environment (see 21:12, 16 – 17). They will need all of the friends that they can get.

Theology in Application

1. The Suffering Messiah and Understanding Suffering

What is hidden from the disciples is the necessity that the Messiah suffer. Their blindness is rooted in a misunderstanding of God's majesty and a human perception of what constitutes glory. The juxtaposition of a crowd amazed at God's majesty evident in all that Jesus was doing, and the prediction of his rejection and betrayal requires rethinking the nature of that majesty. It is evident in more than just Jesus' mighty deeds of healing and exorcism; it also includes God's magnificent and mysterious plan that will lead him to the cross.

That final battle will not be unlike the exorcism. In this incident, the demon looks like it wins, throwing the lad to the ground in a violent spasm. The Son of Man's betrayal and death on the cross will also look like another triumph for evil. But it will only be temporary. As Paul later recognizes, the cross was "God's wisdom, a mystery that has been hidden and that God destined for our glory before time began." Had "the rulers of this age understood it … they would not have crucified the Lord of glory" (1 Cor 2:7 – 8). The majesty of God is demonstrated in the cross. The resurrection and ascension manifest the defeat of the powers of evil, which want to maul and crush God's creation.

Luke brings out the relationship of child and Father in the midst of suffering in Jesus' prayers to the Father on the Mount of Olives (22:42) and at the moment of his death (23:46). Because Jesus knows suffering, he is able to empathize with and minister to those who experience suffering like that of the distraught father and his stricken son. Throughout the gospel, Jesus actively tackles and defeats the forces that cause suffering in human lives. These take various forms: the evil personified as unclean spirits, various illnesses, and death. He also takes on humans who inflict suffering on others. In Luke's gospel, religious leaders weigh people down with burdens hard to bear (11:46). Today, one may think of the egregious suffering caused by clergy sexual abuse of children and adults.

In his passion, however, Jesus suddenly becomes silent and accepts his destiny to absorb all the worst suffering that humans can inflict on another. The demonic shows its colors by its resort to force. In this case, "the demon threw [the lad] down and shook him" (9:42). Jesus does not triumph through force but by enduring suffering in giving his life.

But often modern disciples are like these first followers of Jesus and fail to exorcise evil. We witness children suffering and dying and parents going through torment. Suffering is a part of life for us, and to cope with it requires accepting the miracles of Jesus as a promise of its end in the purpose of God and learning from Jesus' own suffering to put it in a new, divine perspective. Bowker comments:

> It cannot be doubted that Jesus had the whole fact of pain present to his mind. He lived in the midst of suffering. Yet it did not present itself to him as a problem. Certainly he made no explicit reference to the questions with which Job wrestled. His compassion flowed forth unhindered by any theory of the causes of pain. He never viewed suffering as anything but a great evil. He devoted a large part of his ministry to its alleviation. But he never stood before it confounded or paralysed.... He lived in unbroken communion, and faced all of the problems of life from that position of perfect acquaintance. He knew God. He knew that God's love gathers into its company all the suffering of man and of the whole of sentient creation.[6]

2. Fighting the Battle alongside Others

Because the disciples do not yet understand the greatness of self-sacrificing service, they want to preserve the privileges and honor only for themselves and copyright acting in Jesus' name so that those who do not belong to their group are cut off. Christ's power, however, does not belong to them, nor is it under their control. They do not get to allocate who may use it. The outsider they spy casting out demons in Jesus' name is not pirating the power of Jesus' name, as the sons of Sceva later do (Acts 19:13 – 17), but is acting in good faith. The point, which John misses, is that casting out demons brings glory to God, not to the exorcist. An appropriate sense of lowliness and dependence on God should applaud others who are successful for God, even though they may not be on our team. Disciples must recognize who the real enemy is and not start fruitless fights with presumed competitors. Fighting the battle against Satan will be lonely enough without skirmishing with other saints.

The danger is that Christians may want to define others who are not part of their

6. John Bowker, *Problems of Suffering in Religions of the World* (Cambridge: Cambridge Univ. Press, 1970), 57.

particular group as "the Others." The criterion of accepting their work is that they are doing good in Jesus' name. It does not mean that those who simply are indifferent to Christians and do not openly oppose them are to be counted as belonging to Christ. Jesus refers to those who belong to him but do not necessarily belong to a disciple's particular tribe. As Christianity continues to spread across cultures around the world, Christians are learning to be tolerant of different ways of thinking and doing things. There is to be no rivalry or envy in God's work since all labor for the same King, sharing in his power to accomplish his will.

CHAPTER 29

Luke 9:51 – 62

Literary Context

This unit marks the beginning of Jesus' journey to Jerusalem, where he will fulfill his destiny (9:31). In this gospel, which gives special attention to Samaritans, their first mention does not present them in a positive light. But it fits a literary pattern in Luke. As the baptism (3:21 – 22) introduced the first period of Jesus' ministry, which begins with the rejection at Nazareth, the transfiguration (9:28 – 36) introduces the second period of his ministry, which begins with his rejection in Samaria.

The so-called travel narrative, comprising ten chapters, is a distinctive feature of Luke.[1] In the gospels of Matthew and Mark, Jesus makes the transition from Galilee to Jerusalem in fairly short order. Luke leaves the order found in Mark's narrative and utilizes material that has been traditionally designated as Q (material common to Matthew and Luke and absent from Mark) and L (material unique to Luke). Where the travel narrative ends is debated. Some contend it ends in 18:14, where Luke again picks up the Markan narrative. Others contend that it ends in 19:27 with the conclusion of the parable of the vengeful throne claimant. The most logical ending point, however, is 19:44, because in the next scene Jesus enters Jerusalem and the temple.

Jesus' movement lacks any clear progression that can be traced on a map, and time references are nebulous. Rather than following a specific travel itinerary to Jerusalem, Jesus seems to wander from place to place.[2] The statement in 17:11 that "he was passing through the area between Samaria and Galilee" indicates that he was no closer to Jerusalem than when he began in 9:52, about to enter a village of the Samaritans. His arrival in Jericho (18:35) on the last leg of the journey is sudden and unexpected. Moessner comments, "Either Luke — at his best — has done a mediocre job in fulfilling his desire to give an 'ordered' account, or in 9:51ff. he shifts his aims entirely for grander theological, practical, or aesthetic pursuits."[3] The latter

---

1. The infancy narrative contains two journeys to Jerusalem (2:22 – 38, 41 – 51). Acts also is organized around the journeys of Philip (Acts 8:4 – 40), Peter (9:32 – 11:18), and Paul (12:25 – 28:16).

2. Reinhard von Bendemann (*Zwischen Δόξα und Σταυρός:*

Eine exegetische Untersuchungen der Texte des sogenannten Reiseberichts im Lukasevangelium (BZNW 2/101; Berlin: de Gruyter, 2001), 95 – 98.

3. Moessner, "Luke 9:1 – 50," 581.

alternative is correct. Luke's lack of geographical precision should not be attributed to ignorance or indifference to Palestinian geography but to his theological purposes.

Many interpreters despair of finding an organizing principle and conclude that Luke simply used the travel section to toss in an amorphous selection of traditions from a variety of sources.[4] But this section is more than a haphazard dumping ground for material absent from Mark. Three organizing principles appear to have governed Luke' purpose in this section:

1. The travel narrative shows the movement of salvation from Galilee to Jerusalem; then in Acts, from Jerusalem to the ends of the earth (Acts 1:8, 10:37, 39).

2. The travel narrative has a christological purpose. Luke presents Jesus' journey as "an expression of his readiness to travel his appointed way (to the cross; 12:50; 17:25; 22:22)." As the previous section of Luke "explained his consciousness of himself as Messiah, the second explains his consciousness of his Passion."[5] Jesus is more than some prophetic figure; he is the Son of God (10:22), who embodies the visitation of God (19:44). Scobie comments, "A person's reaction to Jesus determines his or her destiny; those who welcome him and follow his teaching, like Zacchaeus, find salvation (Lk. 19:9); those who do not accept him, like the city of Jerusalem, face God's judgment because they fail to recognize the time of their visitation from God (Lk. 19:44)."[6]

3. The travel narrative has an ecclesiological purpose that invites "readers to see themselves as a community on mission, always on the move, always on the journey, always in the presence of the Lord."[7] Disciples must learn to walk the path of self-denial themselves.[8] This travel setting becomes an opportunity for disciple formation in which Jesus provides instruction on the nature, call, costs, and rewards of discipleship. This instruction becomes a paradigm for the mission of the church.

Various themes emerge: the task of proclaiming the reign of God (9:60; 10:9; 16:16); the nature, cost, mission, and rewards of discipleship (9:57 – 62; 12:4 – 12; 13:24; 14:25 – 34); the necessity of prayer (11:1 – 13; 18:1 – 14); the need for repentance (13:1 – 5; 15:1 – 32; 16:30); the nature of faith (12:28; 17:5 – 6; 18:1 – 8); the proper use of material possessions and the requirement to care for the poor (16:1 – 31); and the necessity of suffering (10:1 – 9). Often throughout his journey

---

4. Von Bendemann (*Zwischen Δόξα und Σταυρός*, 6 – 48) examines the numerous attempts to explain and organize the section and offers another alternative.

5. Schweizer, *Luke*, 165.

6. Scobie, "A Canonical Approach to Interpreting Luke," 334.

7. Giles, "The Church in the Gospel of Luke," 141.

8. Talbert, *Reading Luke*, 119, writes: "The didactic material given in the context of a journey fits Luke's conception of the life of faith as a pilgrimage, always on the move (cf. Acts 9:2; 19:9, 23; 22:4; 24:14, 22 where the Christian faith is designated 'the Way')." John Drury (*Tradition and Design in Luke's Gospel* [London: Darton, Longman, and Todd, 1976], 140) considers this narrative to be "a Christian Deuteronomy — a handbook on the Christian life in the historical setting of a journey to Jerusalem." See also Moessner, "Luke 9:1 – 50," 581 – 82.

someone in the crowd will make a statement or ask a question that allows Jesus to expound on these themes (9:57; 10:25; 11:15, 27, 45; 12:13, 41; 13:1, 23; 14:15; 15:2; 16:14; 17:20, 37; 18:18, 26).

III. Jesus' Ministry in Galilee (4:14 – 9:50)

   F. Preparing the Disciples (9:1 – 50)

      1. The Mission of the Twelve and the Feeding of Five Thousand (9:1 – 17)

      2. Earthly Suffering and Eternal Glory (9:18 – 36)

      3. The Disciples' Failure and True Greatness (9:37 – 50)

➡ **IV. Jesus' Journey to Jerusalem (9:51 – 19:28)**

   A. On Being Disciples (9:51 – 10:42)

      1. The Beginning of Jesus' Journey to Jerusalem (9:51 – 62)

      2. The Mission Campaign of the Seventy-two (10:1 – 24)

Main Idea

Jesus journeys to Jerusalem with a resolute purpose that will culminate in his ascension, and radical self-denial is required of anyone who wishes to follow after him as a disciple.

Translation

Luke 9:51–62

9:51a	Circumstance	It happened
		when the days of leading up to his ascension were being fulfilled,
b	Programmatic note	**he set his face to go to Jerusalem.**
52a	Sending	**And he sent messengers before him.**
b	Obedience	When they left,
		they entered one of the villages of the Samaritans to make preparations for him.
53	Rejection	**And they did not welcome him,**
		because his destination was Jerusalem.
54	Response to rejection	When the disciples James and John saw this,
		they said,
		"Lord, do you want us to command fire to come down from heaven and wipe them out [even as Elijah did]?"

Continued on next page.

55	Response to proposal	But **he turned and rebuked them, [and said,** "You do not know what manner of spirit you are.
56a	Pronouncement	For *the Son of Man is not come to destroy lives, but* *to save them.]"*
b	Departure	And **they went to another village.**
57	Declaration	As they were going on the way, **a certain man said to him,** *"I will follow you wherever you go!"*
58	Pronouncement	**Jesus said to him,** *"Foxes have holes and the birds of heaven have nests,* but *the Son of Man has nowhere to lay his head."*
59a	Command	**He said to another,** *"Follow me!"*
b	Request for exemption	But **he said,** *"Lord, permit me first to go and bury my father."*
60	Refusal/command	**But he said to him,** *"Leave the dead to bury their own dead,* but *you go and proclaim the reign of God."*
61	Declaration and request for exemption	**Another said,** *"I will follow you, Lord,* but *first permit me to bid farewell to the people at home."*
62	Pronouncement	**Jesus said,** *"No one who puts his hand to the plow and keeps looking back is useful* *for the reign of God."*

Structure and Literary Form

Attempts to outline the travel narrative as a "great chiasm, in which parallel stories radiate outward in a careful and deliberate balance from a central point" are to be rejected. Johnson acutely observes, "There are such points of balance to be discovered, obviously, otherwise such theories would be impossible. But the points of resemblance often result as much from the definitions given by scholars as from the stories themselves."[9]

The lack of a readily discernible structure is attributable to the use of dramatic episodic style common to historical writings. Braun argues that Luke adopts a style "characteristic of the style of tragic-pathetic historiography." It features (1) the "absence of a continuous, even flow of narrative"; (2) "the presentation of the story in a series of discrete episodes, which, though linked together with an *egeneto*-formula or other artificial connectors, are independent of each other and so can be understood and appreciated on their own"; (3) "an emphasis on theatrical, virtual scenes";

---

9. Johnson, *The Gospel of Luke*, 163.

(4) "the transposition of abstract ideas into direct speech to heighten the appeal to the reader." This explains the lineup of blocks of episodes connected by "it happened" (*kai egeneto*) in 11:1; 14:1; 17:11. The goal of this style of writing is not simply to present a historical record of the facts but to bring about the "edification and transformation of the audience."[10] The identification of the genre need not be so specific, but the characteristics outlined by Braun are helpful for explaining Luke's style.

Centering the narrative on a journey is not a Lukan literary creation, since journeys are prominent in the Old Testament (and also in Greco-Roman literature, beginning with Homer's *The Odyssey*). Scobie observes, "From the wanderings of the patriarchs, through the epic journey of the exodus, to the homeward trek of the exiles from Babylon, the journey motif has deep roots in the Old Testament."[11] Giles notes how it relates to discipleship: "The disciple, like his Master, is a pilgrim and wanderer in this world, on a path which leads through humiliation into glory." It "finds classical expression in the epistle to the Hebrews."[12] The journey motif reflects continuity with God's working in Israel's salvation history.

This first unit establishes Jesus' destination as Jerusalem and raises the theme of opposition. Here he meets opposition from Samaritans, which allows him to begin teaching on discipleship and the rejection of vengeance. This incident is followed by his responses to three would-be disciples who request to follow Jesus and receive a striking and surprising response from Jesus about the requirements for following him.

Exegetical Outline

→ **I. Jesus' sets his course for Jerusalem (9:51 – 56)**
   A. Rejection by a Samaritan village (9:51 – 53)
   B. Desired retribution by the disciples (9:54)
   C. Rejection of vengeance by Jesus (9:55 – 56)

II. Would-be followers of Jesus (9:57 – 62)
   A. An eager disciple (9:57 – 58)
      1. Aspiration: I will follow you wherever you go (9:57)
      2. Cautionary admonition: The Son of Man has nowhere to lay his head (9:58)
   B. Procrastinating disciples (9:59 – 62)
      1. Request for deferral: Let me bury my father (9:59)
      2. Request denied: Leave the dead to bury the dead (9:60)
      3. Request to return home to bid farewell (9:61)
      4. Request denied: No one can look back (9:62)

10. Willi Braun, "Symposium or Anti-Symposium? Reflections on Luke 14:1 – 24," *TJT* 8 (1992): 71 – 72.

11. Scobie, "A Canonical Approach to Interpreting Luke," 337.

12. Giles, "The Church in the Gospel of Luke," 139. The journey motif continues in Acts. All three of Paul's missionary journeys from Antioch end in a trip to Jerusalem.

Explanation of the Text

9:51 It happened when the days of leading up to his ascension were being fulfilled, he set his face to go to Jerusalem (ἐγένετο δὲ ἐν τῷ συμπληροῦσθαι τὰς ἡμέρας τῆς ἀναλήμψεως αὐτοῦ καὶ αὐτὸς τὸ πρόσωπον ἐστήρισεν τοῦ πορεύεσθαι εἰς Ἰερουσαλήμ). This first verse sounds "the programmatic note for the whole section that is to follow."[13] It introduces the travel narrative to Jerusalem, which is a journey to his passion. "The fulfilment of the days of his ascension" (ἀναλήμψεως) serves as superscription of the travel narrative.[14] The way to the cross leads to glory.

Just as the gospel began in Jerusalem and Jesus' testing by Satan climaxed in Jerusalem (4:9), so Jesus' earthly ministry will end there. The city figures prominently as the destination throughout the travel narrative (9:53, 13:22, 17:11; 18:31; 19:11; 19:28). Jerusalem "is the place of the full manifestation of Jesus as the Christ."[15] Scobie comments, "Not only does he go *to* Jerusalem because that is where he is destined to suffer and die, but also because it is *from* Jerusalem that the gospel is destined to spread outwards to the rest of the known world (Lk. 24:47)."[16] The reference to the "days … being fulfilled" (ἐν τῷ συμπληροῦσθαι τὰς ἡμέρας) recalls the purposes of God being fulfilled (1:1; see Acts 2:1). It complements the statement in 9:31 that Moses and Elijah appeared to him in the transfiguration and "were talking of his

exodus, which he was about to fulfill [πληροῦν] in Jerusalem."

This verse also introduces enigmatically the subject of Jesus' death and ascension. Jesus goes to his death (12:50; 13:33 – 34; 17:25; 18:31), but the final stage of his exodus is described as his being "taken up" (ἀναλήμψεως). This term can refer to his death (*Ps. Sol.* 4:18; Philo, *Moses* 2.291) but more likely to his resurrection and ascension (24:51). The use of the plural "days" suggests that it embraces multiple events. The verb form (ἀναλαμβάνω) appears in Acts 1:2, 11, 22 for Jesus' ascension (see 1 Tim 3:16).[17] The journey to Jerusalem, therefore, is not doom-laden because it will not end there on a cross but in heaven.

"He set his face" (αὐτὸς τὸ πρόσωπον ἐστήρισεν) is a Hebraism that implies a "fixedness of purpose, especially in the prospect of difficulty or danger."[18] Jesus' journey cannot be delayed, and he cannot go home to say good-bye to family. But the expression may echo Ezek 21:2 – 6, which would then hint at the impending judgment of Jerusalem.[19]

"Setting his face toward Jerusalem" also sets up the resistance his company will meet from the Samaritans in the immediate context. It introduces the theme of opposition that Jesus will face along the way.

9:52 And he sent messengers before him. When they left, they entered one of the villages of the

---

13. Hendrickx, *The Third Gospel*, 3A:6.

14. Johannes Schneider, "Zur Analyse des lukanischen Reiseberichtes," in *Synoptische Studien: Alfred Wikenhauser zum siebzigsten Geburtstag* (ed. Josef Schmid and Anton Vögtle; Munich: Zink, 1953), 212.

15. Paul Schubert, "The Structure and Significance of Luke 24," in *Neutestamentliche Studien: Festschrift für Rudolf Bultmann* (BZNW 21; ed. W. Eltester; Berlin: Töpelmann, 1954), 184.

16. Scobie, "A Canonical Approach to Interpreting Luke," 335.

17. It resonates with the "lifted up" sayings in John 3:14; 8:28; 12:32 – 34 (see Acts 2:33). The LXX uses the verb for Elijah's (4 Kgdms 2:9, 11; 1 Macc 2:58; Sir 48:9) and Enoch's (Sir 49:14) departure/ascension.

18. Plummer, *Luke*, 263.

19. Craig A. Evans, " 'He Set His Face': Luke 9,51 Once Again," *Bib* 68 (1987): 80 – 84. See also Ezek 6:2; 13:17; 14:8; 15:7; 20:46; 25:2; 28:21; 29:2; 38:2; Jer 21:10.

Samaritans to make preparations for him (καὶ ἀπέστειλεν ἀγγέλους πρὸ προσώπου αὐτοῦ. καὶ πορευθέντες εἰσῆλθον εἰς κώμην Σαμαριτῶν ὡς ἑτοιμάσαι αὐτῷ). Jesus is heading south to Jerusalem, cutting through Samaria. Most Jews skirted Samaria in traveling to Galilee. Jesus sends "messengers" (ἀγγέλους) as an "advance party" to prepare for the large group of pilgrims "seeking accommodation for the night."[20]

This task may recall Moses sending out messengers "to spy out the land for us and bring back a report about the route we are to take and the towns we will come to" (Deut 1:22).[21] It also recalls the scriptural quotation applied to John in Luke 7:27, who was sent to prepare for another. Tannehill concludes: "The narrator, by the adoption of this language, is suggesting a significant similarity between the role of the disciples in this new phase of Jesus' journeys and the role of John the Baptist."[22]

9:53 And they did not welcome him, because his destination was Jerusalem (καὶ οὐκ ἐδέξαντο αὐτόν, ὅτι τὸ πρόσωπον αὐτοῦ ἦν πορευόμενον εἰς Ἰερουσαλήμ). Jesus' rejection by the village in Samaria at the beginning of the travel section matches the rejection of Jesus at the beginning of his ministry in Galilee. There he stirred up the wrath of the Nazareth synagogue when he referred to Elijah's ministry to the widow of Zarephath in Sidon, which is north of Galilee. The people's long history of mutual hatred and the Samaritans' antipathy toward Jerusalem explain this snub.

9:54 When the disciples James and John saw this, they said, "Lord, do you want us to command fire to come down from heaven and wipe them out [even as Elijah did]? (ἰδόντες δὲ οἱ μαθηταὶ Ἰάκωβος καὶ Ἰωάννης εἶπαν, Κύριε, θέλεις εἴπωμεν πῦρ καταβῆναι ἀπὸ τοῦ οὐρανοῦ καὶ ἀναλῶσαι αὐτούς [ὡς καὶ Ἡλίας ἐποίησεν];). When Jesus sent his disciples out on mission, he commanded them to leave a town that did not welcome them and to shake the dust from their feet as a warning of judgment (9:5; see 10:10 – 11). James and John do not want simply to shake the dust of this town from their feet but to reduce it to dust. In an honor-shame culture, a perceived violation of one's honor is assumed to merit fearsome revenge, which inevitably spirals out of control.[23] One might imagine that this incident explains why James and John earned the nickname "sons of thunder" (Mark 3:17).

If the textual variant "even as Elijah did" is not original to the text, it is an accurate gloss on the text that calls attention to the subtle reintroduction of the Elijah/Elisha motif (see 4:25 – 27). Jesus is in the vicinity where Elijah had incinerated a captain and his fifty men whom King Ahaziah sent to inquire of him (2 Kgs 1:1 – 18). In 9:51 – 62, the two prophets become negative foils. The allusion to what Elijah did highlights the popular misunderstanding about Jesus' identity. The disciples reported that some of the crowds mistook Jesus for Elijah (Luke 9:8). The disciples are also mistaken about Jesus here. They must assume that a "man of God" (2 Kgs 1:10, 12) will wreak divine vengeance on the stubborn and unrepentant. But Jesus is the "Son of God," who teaches a new way that renounces vindictive violence. The incident makes clear that the disciples still have much to learn on the way with Jesus.

20. Marshall, *The Gospel of Luke*, 404.

21. Evans, *St. Luke*, 437.

22. Tannehill, *Unity of Luke-Acts*, 229 – 30.

23. Around AD 51, in the village of Ginea on the border between Galilee and Samaria, one of a large company of pilgrims traveling to celebrate the Passover in Jerusalem was murdered.

Jewish authorities sought justice from the Roman governor Cumanus, who belittled the incident. When word reached the pilgrims in Jerusalem, violent men retaliated by slaughtering everyone and burning the village to the ground (Josephus, *J.W.* 2.12.3 – 7 §§232 – 246; *Ant.* 20.6.1 – 3 §§118 – 136).

9:55 – 56 But he turned and rebuked them, [and said, "You do not know what manner of spirit you are. For the Son of Man is not come to destroy lives, but to save them."] And they went to another village (στραφεὶς δὲ ἐπετίμησεν αὐτοῖς. [καὶ εἶπεν· οὐκ οἴδατε ποίου πνεύματός ἐστε· ὁ γὰρ υἱὸς τοῦ ἀνθρώπου οὐκ ἦλθεν ψυχὰς ἀνθρώπων ἀπολέσαι ἀλλὰ σῶσαι]. καὶ ἐπορεύθησαν εἰς ἑτέραν κώμην). Rather than punish the Samaritans for their enmity, Jesus rebukes his own disciples. The content of this rebuke is also a textual variant. The clauses have weak external support, and the variations among them are typical of later interpolations. They fit well in the context, however, and it would be odd for the story not to culminate in a pronouncement from Jesus. The clauses may have been expurgated from the text because it portrays the apostles in such a bad light.[24] If it is not original, it is a perceptive commentary on the text. Those who resort to vendettas against enemies, whether by swords or by divine fire, reflect the vengeful spirit of Satan, not the merciful spirit of Christ.

9:57 As they were going on the way, a certain man said to him, "I will follow you wherever you go!" (καὶ πορευομένων αὐτῶν ἐν τῇ ὁδῷ εἶπέν τις πρὸς αὐτόν· ἀκολουθήσω σοι ὅπου ἐὰν ἀπέρχῃ). Jesus leads his disciples along the way in fulfillment of Isa 40:3 (Luke 3:4). What they learn cannot be learned in a sterile classroom discussing hypothetical examples. In Acts, Jesus' followers will be identified as those who belong to "the Way" (Acts 9:2; 19:9, 23; 22:4; 24:14; 24:22).[25] Others may want to join him, but he does not take just any volunteer.

9:58 Jesus said to him, "Foxes have holes and the birds of heaven have nests, but the Son of Man has nowhere to lay his head" (καὶ εἶπεν αὐτῷ ὁ Ἰησοῦς· αἱ ἀλώπεκες φωλεοὺς ἔχουσιν καὶ τὰ πετεινὰ τοῦ οὐρανοῦ κατασκηνώσεις, ὁ δὲ υἱὸς τοῦ ἀνθρώπου οὐκ ἔχει ποῦ τὴν κεφαλὴν κλίνῃ). Following Jesus means that one follows an "itinerant teacher, not part of an established community."[26] Jesus has nothing to offer those who seek from him material blessings and security. He does not have what even the beasts of the field and birds of the air possess. But this imagery may have a political edge. Manson points out that "foxes" refer to Israel's political enemies, the Ammonites, in *1 En.* 89, and Jesus identifies Herod as a "fox" (13:32). He concludes that the sense may be:

> ... everybody is at home in Israel's land except the true Israel. The birds of the air — the Roman overlords, the foxes — the Edomite interlopers, have made their position secure. The true Israel is disinherited by them: and if you cast your lot with me and mine you join the ranks of the dispossessed, and you must be prepared to serve God under those conditions.[27]

9:59 – 60 He said to another, "Follow me!" But he said, "Lord, permit me first to go and bury my father." But he said to him, "Leave the dead to bury their own dead, but you go and proclaim the reign of God" (εἶπεν δὲ πρὸς ἕτερον· ἀκολούθει μοι. ὁ δὲ εἶπεν· [κύριε,] ἐπίτρεψόν μοι ἀπελθόντι πρῶτον θάψαι τὸν πατέρα μου. εἶπεν δὲ αὐτῷ· ἄφες τοὺς νεκροὺς θάψαι τοὺς ἑαυτῶν νεκρούς, σὺ δὲ ἀπελθὼν διάγγελλε τὴν βασιλείαν τοῦ θεοῦ). The present imperative "follow" (ἀκολούθει) implies that Jesus is calling the man to begin and to continue to follow him, but, unlike others who receive this command in the narrative, this individual puts Jesus off with an

---

24. J. M. Ross, "The Rejected Words in Luke 9, 54 – 56," *ExpTim* 84 (1972 – 73): 85 – 88.

25. Scobie, "A Canonical Approach to Interpreting Luke," 342.

26. Darrell Bock, *Luke* (NIVAC; Grand Rapids: Zondervan, 1996), 284.

27. T. W. Manson, *The Sayings of Jesus* (London: SCM, 1937), 72 – 73.

excuse. It seems a legitimate one, since burial of the dead touches the heart of Jewish piety as a deed of loving-kindness that gained primacy among all good works (Mark 14:7–8). Burying a parent was the chief responsibility of a son (see Gen 46:4; 49:29; 50:1–5; Tob 4:3; 6:13–15; 14:10–15; Josephus, *J.W.* 5.13.3 §545), and a religious duty that took precedence over all others (*m. Ber.* 3:1). To refuse this duty is tantamount to disobeying God for failing to honor parents.[28]

Jesus' refusal of such a request reveals that he demands of his followers what God demanded of the prophets.[29] He commands with the authority of God. Instone-Brewer concludes, "He was effectively telling a prospective disciple that following him was the most supreme religious commitment imaginable."[30]

"Leave the dead to bury their own dead" sounds extraordinarily harsh to someone in a time of grief. But the "dead" is a metaphorical reference to those who make no response to Jesus' (see Eph 2:1, 5). The premise behind this command is that outside of the sphere of discipleship to Jesus there is only death. The spiritually dead can bury those who are physically dead. If the man postpones discipleship, he belongs to the living dead. The command also conveys a radical sense of urgency. Hengel comments, "There was no more time to be lost and so he had to be followed without procrastination and to the abandonment of all human considerations and ties."[31] It is now or never.

9:61–62 Another said, "I will follow you, Lord, but first permit me to bid farewell to the people at home." Jesus said, "No one who puts his hand to the plow and keeps looking back is useful for the reign of God" (εἶπεν δὲ καὶ ἕτερος· ἀκολουθήσω σοι, κύριε· πρῶτον δὲ ἐπίτρεψόν μοι ἀποτάξασθαι τοῖς εἰς τὸν οἶκόν μου. εἶπεν δὲ ὁ Ἰησοῦς· οὐδεὶς ἐπιβαλὼν τὴν χεῖρα ἐπ᾽ ἄροτρον καὶ βλέπων εἰς τὰ ὀπίσω εὔθετός ἐστιν τῇ βασιλείᾳ τοῦ θεοῦ). The request of this second would-be disciple echoes that of Elisha when Elijah found him plowing a field and threw his mantle over him to follow him and replace him as God's prophet (1 Kgs 19:19–21). Elijah granted Elisha's request to say good-bye; Jesus does not grant this man's request.

Jesus uses the image of plowing, whose balky implements did not allow for wandering attention, to reinforce the point. The use of an aorist participle (ἐπιβαλών) for putting hand to the plow and a present participle (βλέπων) for looking back suggests that "looking back" is more continuous than a momentary glance. The more idiomatic translation "looking back" renders the more literal reading in Greek, "the things behind" (τὰ ὀπίσω). Those "things" that lie behind can include a multiplicity of distractions and longings (see Phil 3:12–14).

The message is that the new reality of God's reign should totally mold every decision in life and that the world as it has been must be left behind without any wistfulness. In the Elisha story, Elisha slaughters the oxen he had been plowing with and roasts them over a fire made from their yoke for his farewell banquet, which signifies his complete break with his past.

---

28. B. R. McCane ("'Let the Dead Bury Their Own Dead': Secondary Burial and Matt 8:21–22," *HTR* 83 [1990]: 31–43) contends that it refers to the custom of secondary burial, and the man asks to postpone following Jesus until the one-year wait before reburial in the ossuary is completed. This interpretation softens the radical nature of Jesus' demand, which uses shock to make the point.

29. God forbade Ezekiel and Jeremiah from lamenting the dead or comforting the mourner to show God's displeasure with the people (Jer 16:5–7; Ezek 24:15–24).

30. David Instone-Brewer, *Traditions of the Rabbis from the Era of the New Testament*; vol. 1: *Prayer and Agriculture* (Grand Rapids: Eerdmans, 2004), 51.

31. Hengel, *The Charismatic Leader*, 15.

Theology in Application

1. Obedience to God

Abraham set out in obedience to God not knowing where he was going (Heb 11:8). Jesus sets out in obedience to God knowing full well where he is going and what will happen to him when he reaches his destination. The controversies with opponents along the way (11:15 – 24, 37 – 53; 13:14 – 17; 14:1 – 6; 15:2; 16:14 – 15) foreshadow the more potent and deadly opposition he will meet in Jerusalem that will bring about his death. Though Jesus "set his face," the references to the days "being fulfilled" and his "ascension" reveal that this is not simply a human decision but a response to the divine necessity laid on him. Going to Jerusalem fulfills God's purposes. "Setting his face" applies to Jesus' single-minded intention to obey God. He knows what awaits him in Jerusalem and goes to meet it with a steely resolve.

2. The Spirit of Elijah and the Spirit of the Lord

Some thought that Jesus was Elijah (9:8, 19), and the textual variant in 9:54 recalls the situation where Elijah called down fire from heaven to incinerate opponents. The disciples do not understand that though Jesus may be Elijah-like (e.g., raising a widow's son as the prophet did), he is not like Elijah. He is not as harsh as Elijah and will not call down fire on the heads of presumed enemies. Caird comments, "This is why Elijah had to disappear from the mountain to give place to Jesus, with his new way of loving enemies and dying for them, and to the new conception of God which that way implied."[32]

Nevertheless, the demands Jesus places on his disciples are harsher. Elijah permitted Elisha to return to say farewell to his family (1 Kgs 19:19 – 21), but Jesus will not permit a would-be disciple to do so (9:61 – 62). The disciples are right in addressing him as "Lord" (9:54), except he is "the Lord," not another prophet like Elijah, and he shows mercy as the Lord does. Rowe's observation is important: The use of "Lord" "subverts the normal associations of rule and power in which a κύριος ['lord'] deals with those who oppose him through means of massive strength and violence and paints a radically different picture, one in which to be Lord is to experience denial and rejection and yet not to respond with violent punishment."[33] It sets the tone for the whole travel narrative leading up to Jesus' crucifixion in Jerusalem.

The disciples expect instant judgment, but the travel narrative reveals that God allows people time to respond before the final judgment (see 13:6 – 9). It is the year of the Lord's favor, not wrath.[34] Jerusalem will not be destroyed immediately for rejecting Jesus but will be given time to respond. Had Jesus yielded to their vindictiveness,

---

32. Caird, *Saint Luke*, 140.
33. Rowe, *Early Narrative Christology*, 126.
34. Stein, *Luke*, 299.

there would have been no point in sending disciples to Samaria (Acts 1:8), and conversions of Samaritans would have been unlikely (17:16; Acts 8:1 – 14; 9:31; 15:3). It would have been another atrocity committed against them by vengeful Jews.

Craddock draws a contemporary application: James and John "bring to mind overzealous evangelists of another generation who extended God's grace to the audience and then tossed balls of hellfire at those who refused the offer."[35] They are intoxicated with their own importance and assume Jesus will use his power to settle their grudges for being rebuffed. As Jesus was not sent into the world to judge it but so that it might be saved through him (John 3:17), so the disciples must become instruments by which this salvation becomes known.

The disciples do not understand Jesus' teaching about his passion (9:45), and they do not understand his teaching about love of enemies (6:27 – 31) either.[36] They must go farther down the road with Jesus and hear the parable of the Samaritan and watch a Samaritan leper return praising God and giving thanks if they are going to have a spirit like his. Jesus is rejected at Nazareth at the beginning of his ministry in Galilee; he is rejected in Samaria at the beginning of his journey to Jerusalem; he is rejected in Jerusalem at the end of his ministry. Rejection is par for the course. Disciples also will have to observe Jesus on the journey and in Jerusalem to understand how to engage in mission in the face of hostility. Only then will they know that the fire Jesus brings to earth (12:49) is not one of destruction, but the fiery tongues of the Spirit (Acts 2:3) that empowers disciples to bear loving witness "in Jerusalem, and in all Judea and Samaria, and to the ends of the earth" (Acts 1:8).

3. The Demands of Discipleship

As opposed to Jesus' own single-minded devotion in setting his face toward Jerusalem, these would-be disciples have their faces twisting in two directions. Disciples learn from these interchanges and from the parable of the dinner guests that there are "no excused absences from the kingdom of God whether they be business commitments, social obligations, or sacred family duties." It underscores the reality that discipleship "is not merely another commitment which we add to the long list of our other commitments, but it is *the* commitment — demanding a reordering of our lives from the bottom up."[37] These "astonishing pronouncements confront each disciple with a choice, one that is focused exclusively on Jesus himself: follow him at high cost or do not follow him at all. No explanations for the demands are given, and there is no attempt at persuasion in the light of the cost."[38] Jesus is not interested in "spring break" or "summer vacation" discipleship. It is all or nothing.

If one is to call Jesus "Lord," then one should be prepared to exercise his lordship

---

35. Craddock, *Luke*, 143.
36. Hendrickx, *The Third Gospel*, 3A:13.
37. Robert C. Tannehill, *The Sword of His Mouth* (Philadel-

phia: Fortress, 1975), 159.
38. Rowe, *Early Narrative Christology*, 132.

and to submit to his commands. These examples address the problem of people who swear allegiance to Christ but do not become true disciples. They profess their belief in Christ but do not act on it.

Ryle has famously written:

> Nothing … has done more harm to Christianity than the practice of filling the ranks of Christ's army with every volunteer who is willing to make a little profession, and to talk fluently of his "experience." It may be painfully forgotten that numbers alone do not make strength and that there may be a great quantity of mere outward religion, while there is very little real grace.… Let us tell them [young people and inquirers] plainly that there is a crown of glory at the end, but let us tell them no less plainly that there is a daily cross on the way.[39]

The cross must be borne before the crown can be worn.

Recent studies have shown that ministers are experiencing increasing burnout and as a result are falling out of the ministry. Some attribute it to the increasing expectation that ministers provide entertainment that makes parishioners feel good about themselves rather than providing moral guidance and admonition and in-depth biblical teaching. The pressure to be successful, which is often measured by numbers, can lead many to water down the gospel and to cater to the whims of the audience. It is unlikely that Jesus would have been successful in this kind of environment with his no-nonsense approach.

Or would he? Many yearn for some kind of direction to their lives and some kind of demanding purpose that cannot be satisfied by theological pabulum and extravaganza worship experiences that never reach the depth of the human soul and its wretched condition. It has been my experience that teachers who make the most demands of students may not be the most popular, but they make the deepest impact. The minister's responsibility is to lay out clearly the radical demands of following Jesus, as Jesus himself did, and not to sugarcoat them with a crowd-pleasing gospel. The minister is also expected to live out these demands, as Paul did for his congregations (e.g., 1 Thess 2:1 – 12), as an example for others.

4. Rejection of Vengeance

Formulaic tales of a hero or heroine taking revenge for some evil done to them or their family members in books, movies, and television shows enjoy popularity because they allow the audience to participate in and cheer on murder and mayhem. Presumably, the audience would never engage in such behavior themselves, but they vicariously enjoy others retaliating against and destroying the evildoers. Such fare

---

39. J. C. Ryle, *Matthew* (Crossway Classic Commentaries; Wheaton: Crossway,1993; repr., New York: R. Carter, 1860), 59.

dangerously whets the appetite for vengeance and makes violence easier to accept when one has been slighted in large or even small ways.

Daily news reports give evidence to this problem. One recent example as I write is particularly egregious. Letters bearing the image of a skull and crossbones were sent to professors at a university with the threat: "Every true Christian should be ready and willing to take up arms to kill the enemies of Christian society." Christ gave his life out of love for us, and if Christians mete out revenge for perceived wrongs, they uproot that love in themselves and replace it with a diabolical energy that destroys themselves and others. They renounce a basic Christian principle, "Do not repay evil for evil or reviling for reviling, but on the contrary, bless, for to this you were called" (1 Pet 3:9 ESV). They also disgrace the name Christian (1 Pet 4:14 – 15) and destroy the opportunity to bear witness and win enemies to Christ. Pedersen contends, "Violence is apparently an expression of strength, but the Israelite considers this strength a delusion, which can only exist for a time, because it does not draw directly from the source of strength, peace and its blessing, which rests in the divine forces."[40]

---

40. Johannes Pedersen, *Israel: Its Life and Culture I – II* (London: Oxford Univ. Press, 1926), 419.

Luke 10:1 – 24

Literary Context

Jesus made clear what discipleship requires, and he continues to train disciples beyond the Twelve. The journey to Jerusalem (9:51) involves a mission that will continue after his work is accomplished there (13:32; 24:46 – 47). As Jesus encounters acceptance and rejection on his way to Jerusalem, so the disciples will in their mission. The emphasis on the requirement of lowliness (9:47 – 48) continues. They are to travel light and accept humbly whatever hospitality is offered them (10:6 – 8). God will provide for their needs (11:3).

In a previous incident, the disciples show their colors by wanting to lord it over each other as the greatest (9:46) and over others who are perceived as rivals (9:49). In this section, Jesus says that God's gracious will is to reveal the truth to "infants," those who are lowly (10:21 – 24). The disciples may want to wreak vengeance on those who reject them (9:52 – 54), but Jesus' followers must learn rejection is par for the course when they proclaim the message. Their assignment is only to preach the gospel and cure those in need, and they must leave any punishment for rejecting the gospel to God alone (10:10 – 16). They must also learn not to bask in the glory of their success but humbly attribute it all to God.

The mission of the seventy-two prepares for the answer to the accusation that Jesus' power comes from Beelzebul (11:15). When demons are cast out by his disciples, Jesus sees Satan's hold on power cracking. This powerful adversary has been dethroned as God's reign advances.

Main Idea

The successful mission of the seventy-two in proclaiming the presence of God's reign and the revelation about Jesus as God's Son reveal that the advance of God's reign is unstoppable and Jesus will ultimately triumph.

Translation

Luke 10:1–24

10:1	Commission			After these things,
		the Lord		**appointed seventy-two others**
		and		**sent them before him two by two to every town and place**
				where he himself↵
				was about to go.
2		**He said to them,**		
				"The harvest is plentiful,
				but the workers are few.
				Pray then to the Lord of the harvest
				that he will dispatch workers into his harvest.
3	Command			*Go! Behold, I send you as lambs into a pack of wolves.*
4	Command			*Do not carry a money bag, nor a backpack, nor sandals, and greet no one↵*
				along the way.
5	Command			*Into whatever house you enter, first say, 'Peace to this house!'*
6	Condition			*If there is a son of peace there, your peace will rest upon him.*
				If not, it will return upon you.
7a	Command			*Remain in this house eating and drinking what they have to offer,*
b	Reason			*for the worker is worthy of his hire.*
c	Command			*Do not move from house to house.*
8	Command (condition)			*Whenever you enter a town and they receive you,*
				eat what is set before you,
9	Command			*and cure the sick in it*
				and tell them,
				'The reign of God has drawn near to you!'
10	Command (condition)			*Whenever you enter a town and they do not receive you,*
				when you go out into the streets,
				say:
11a	Renunciation			*'Even the dust from your town, which has stuck to our feet, we wipe↵*
				off [in protest] against you.
b				*Nevertheless, know that the reign of God has drawn near!'*
12	Prophetic pronouncement			*I tell you, it will be more tolerable for Sodom in that day than for that town.*

Continued on next page.

13a	Condemnation	*Woe to you, Chorazin!*
		Woe to you Bethsaida!
b	Reason	*Because . . .* *if the miracles that happened among you⌒*
		had taken place in Tyre and Sidon,
		. . . they would have repented long ago, sitting in sackcloth⌒
		and ashes.
14		*So, at the judgment it will be more tolerable for Tyre and Sidon than for you.*
15	Condemnation	*And you, Capernaum, you will not be exalted to heaven, will you?*
		You will be brought down into Hades!
16	Pronouncement	*The one who listens to you listens to me,*
		and the one who rejects you rejects the one who sent you."
17	Report	**The seventy-two returned with joy, saying,**
		"Lord, even the demons are subject to us in your name."
18	Prophetic vision	**He said to them,**
		"I observed Satan falling from heaven like a streak of lightning!
19	Reminder	*Behold, I gave you authority* *to trample serpents and scorpions, and*
		over all the power of the enemy,
		and nothing will ever harm you.
20	Admonition	*Nevertheless, do not* *rejoice about this, that the spirits are subject to you,*
		but *rejoice that your names are inscribed in heaven."*
21	Thanksgiving	In that same hour,
		he rejoiced in the Holy Spirit and said,
		"I praise you, Father of heaven and earth,
		that you have *hidden these things from the wise and understanding* *and*
		revealed them to infants.
22a	Pronouncement	*Yes, Father, because that is what was well-pleasing before you.*
		All things have been given to me by my Father,
b		*and no one knows who the Son is except the Father, and*
		who the Father is except the Son and
		whomever *the Son wills to reveal him."*
23	Beatitude	And turning to his disciples,
		he said to them privately,
		"Blessed are your eyes that see what you see!
24	Reason	*For I tell you, many prophets and kings wanted to see what you see and⌒*
		they did not see it, and
		to hear what you hear⌒
		and they did not hear it."

Structure and Literary Form

The form used here is a commissioning of the disciples with a host of commands, pronouncements, and warnings. It concludes with a report of the disciples' success and an important explication of the relationship of Jesus to the Father. It consists of three four-line strophes. Crump outlines it as follows:

I. "I thank you, Father, Lord of heaven and earth,
because you have hidden these things from the wise and the intelligent
and have revealed them to infants;
yes, Father, for such was your gracious will."

II. "All things have been handed over to me by my Father;
and no one knows who the Son is except the Father,
or who the Father is except the Son
and anyone to whom the Son chooses to reveal him."

III. "Blessed are the eyes that see what you see!
For I tell you that many prophets and kings desired
to see what you see, but did not see it,
and to hear what you hear, but did not hear it."[1]

Exegetical Outline

→ **I. Appointment of the seventy-two for mission (10:1 – 16)**
    A. The harvest is plentiful and the laborers few (10:1 – 2)
    B. Special instructions for the mission (10:3 – 11)
        1. Warning of dangers (10:3)
        2. Command to travel light (10:4)
        3. Command to accept any hospitality (10:5 – 8)
        4. Command to cure the sick and announce the reign of God (10:9)
        5. Command to announce the threat of judgment when rejected (10:10 – 11)
    C. Warnings of judgment for rejection of the message (10:12 – 16)
        1. Woes against Chorazin, Bethsaida, and Capernaum (10:12 – 15)
        2. Rejecting the disciples means rejecting Jesus and God (10:16)
II. Return of the seventy-two (10:17 – 24)
    A. Report of success (10:17)
    B. Jesus' vision of Satan's fall (10:18)
    C. Authority over the power of the enemy and divine protection (10:19)
    D. Rejoice in being aligned with God and not success (10:20)

---

1. Crump, *Jesus the Intercessor*, 50 – 51.

E. Jesus' thanksgiving to God (10:21 – 24)

   1. God's gracious will to reveal these things to the lowly (10:21)

   2. God's handing over authority to Jesus (10:22a)

   3. God's handing over the revelation of the Father to Jesus the Son (10:22b)

   4. God's gracious blessing of the disciples to witness this revelation (10:23 – 24)

Explanation of the Text

10:1 After these things, the Lord appointed seventy-two others and sent them before him two by two to every town and place where he himself was about to go (μετὰ δὲ ταῦτα ἀνέδειξεν ὁ κύριος ἑτέρους ἑβδομήκοντα [δύο] καὶ ἀπέστειλεν αὐτοὺς ἀνὰ δύο [δύο] πρὸ προσώπου αὐτοῦ εἰς πᾶσαν πόλιν καὶ τόπον οὗ ἤμελλεν αὐτὸς ἔρχεσθαι). Jesus has been identified as "Lord" by Peter (5:8), the centurion (7:6), James and John (9:54), and would-be disciples (9:59, 61), and the narrator increasingly uses this title to identify him (see 7:13, 19; 10:39, 41; 11:39; 12:42; 13:15; 17:5 – 6; 18:6; 19:8; 22:61). As Lord, he appoints others to go out as a mission advance party during his journey to Jerusalem. The mission task will not be limited to the Twelve.

Sending these people out in pairs is a pattern that continues in Acts (Acts 13:2; 15:27, 39 – 40; 17:14; 19:22; see Luke 7:18 – 19). The pairs provide the double witness prescribed in Deut 17:6; 19:15. In addition, going out in pairs provides companionship, some protection, and accountability. There is no parallel in Jewish history for one to send out others on a mission to proclaim news about the reign of God, and the authority for this action is located in Jesus' own person. This harvest is part of "the long-promised gathering of the people of God (Isa 27:12)."[2]

The manuscripts divide equally in reading either "seventy-two" or "seventy." The two numbers are interchangeable in Jewish traditions. For example, in the list of nations in Gen 10:2 – 31, the MT has "seventy" and the LXX has "seventy-two."[3] What is important is the number's symbolic quality instead of its quantity. As the number twelve is significant for the disciples' mission to the tribes of Israel (9:1 – 6; see 9:17), the number seventy-two is significant (six times twelve) as foreshadowing the mission to all the nations of the world. Nolland asserts, "Luke is fond of anticipations and almost certainly uses the number here to anticipate later mission to all the nations of the earth."[4] It prefigures "the universal mission in Acts" (see Acts 2:5).[5] The total of those sent on mission during Jesus' ministry is seven times twelve.[6]

10:2 He said to them, "The harvest is plentiful, but the workers are few. Pray then to the Lord of the harvest that he will dispatch workers into his harvest" (ἔλεγεν δὲ πρὸς αὐτούς· ὁ μὲν θερισμὸς πολύς, οἱ δὲ ἐργάται ὀλίγοι· δεήθητε οὖν τοῦ κυρίου τοῦ θερισμοῦ ὅπως ἐργάτας ἐκβάλῃ εἰς τὸν θερισμὸν αὐτοῦ). For temporal harvests, there was a surplus of workers ready to go into the fields (see Matt 20:1 – 7), but this spiritual harvest is totally different. The laborers are few because few

2. David L. Tiede, *Luke* (ACNT; Minneapolis: Fortress, 1988), 201.

3. Bruce M. Metzger, "Seventy or Seventy-Two Disciples?" *NTS* 5 (1958 – 59): 299 – 306.

4. Nolland, *Luke*, 2:549.

5. Green, *The Gospel of Luke*, 412.

6. These numbers have symbolic significance as well as a literal meaning. Seven symbolizes completeness, perfection, or wholeness in Scripture (see 8:2), and twelve represents the tribes of Israel.

are willing to work under such stringent demands for so little earthly reward. In Isa 27:12, the Lord God harvests the people, and the assumption is that God "alone can find and authorize harvesters, who will convey announcements of his judgments and signs of his power."[7]

The disciples are charged to go and to pray because it is ultimately the Lord's harvest, not theirs, and everything depends on the Lord's unlimited resources. Identifying Jesus as "the Lord" in 10:1, however, "alerts the reader to a second level of interpretation."[8] Jesus is also "the Lord of the harvest" who sends his disciples out, and when they return, they appropriately address him as "Lord" (v. 17). The high Christology is implicit in this narrative and should not be missed.

10:3 – 4 Go! Behold, I send you as lambs into a pack of wolves. Do not carry a money bag, nor a backpack, nor sandals, and greet no one along the way (ὑπάγετε· ἰδοὺ ἀποστέλλω ὑμᾶς ὡς ἄρνας ἐν μέσῳ λύκων. μὴ βαστάζετε βαλλάντιον, μὴ πήραν, μὴ ὑποδήματα, καὶ μηδένα κατὰ τὴν ὁδὸν ἀσπάσησθε). These mission workers have been following Jesus as he commanded them to do, and now they must go where he commands. An important reason for prayer is that they are being sent among "wolves," primarily an allusion to the officials in the cities (Ezek 22:27; Zeph 3:3). Wolves hunt in packs to prey on and maul defenseless lambs.

Jesus gives them essentially the same instructions about what to take and not to take as he gave the Twelve in 9:3. They are to travel light, but not taking sandals is extreme. It is a token of impoverishment (see 15:22). Minear comments, "Only as beggars without visible resources could they convey invisible resources to other beggars."[9]

Forbidding them to give greetings to those they meet on the road (2 Kgs 4:29) conveys the urgency of their mission. Harvesters cannot dawdle, and they cannot be delayed by the lengthy exchange of niceties that governed etiquette. Jesus may, however, simply be forbidding them from visiting or calling on relatives, which would distract them from their task.[10]

10:5 – 6 Into whatever house you enter, first say, "Peace to this house!" If there is a son of peace there, your peace will rest upon him. If not, it will return upon you (εἰς ἣν δ' ἂν εἰσέλθητε οἰκίαν, πρῶτον λέγετε· εἰρήνη τῷ οἴκῳ τούτῳ. καὶ ἐὰν ἐκεῖ ᾖ υἱὸς εἰρήνης, ἐπαναπαήσεται ἐπ' αὐτὸν ἡ εἰρήνη ὑμῶν· εἰ δὲ μήγε, ἐφ' ὑμᾶς ἀνακάμψει). The message of these workers will detect the "sons of peace." This is a Semitic idiom; those who express in their own way of life that of another or of some quality are called "a son of" that one or thing. "Sons of peace" exude peace, and their character will determine their destiny. Refusing to greet others on the way will cause these followers to stand out; this instruction reveals that the greeting of peace is not simply a conventional greeting but an eschatological wish.[11] Peace takes on a new meaning in light of Acts 10:36: "You know the message God sent to the people of Israel, announcing the good news of peace through Jesus Christ, who is Lord of all."

10:7 – 9 Remain in this house eating and drinking what they have to offer, for the worker is worthy of his hire. Do not move from house to house. Whenever you enter a town and they receive you, eat what is set before you, and cure the sick in it and tell them, "The reign of God has drawn near to you!" (ἐν αὐτῇ δὲ τῇ οἰκίᾳ μένετε, ἐσθίοντες καὶ πίνοντες τὰ παρ' αὐτῶν· ἄξιος γὰρ

7. Minear, *To Heal and to Reveal*, 10.
8. Rowe, *Early Narrative Christology*, 134.
9. Minear, *To Heal and To Reveal*, 72.
10. Bernhard Lang, "Grussverbot oder Besuchsverbot?"

BZ 26 (1982): 75 – 69.
11. Iris Bosold, *Pazifismus und prophetische Provokation: Das Grussverbot Lk 10,4b und sein historischer Kontext* (SBS 90; Stuttgart: Verlag Katholisches Bibelwerk, 1978), 84 – 85.

ὁ ἐργάτης τοῦ μισθοῦ αὐτοῦ. μὴ μεταβαίνετε ἐξ οἰκίας εἰς οἰκίαν. καὶ εἰς ἣν ἂν πόλιν εἰσέρχησθε καὶ δέχωνται ὑμᾶς, ἐσθίετε τὰ παρατιθέμενα ὑμῖν καὶ θεραπεύετε τοὺς ἐν αὐτῇ ἀσθενεῖς καὶ λέγετε αὐτοῖς· ἤγγικεν ἐφ᾽ ὑμᾶς ἡ βασιλεία τοῦ θεοῦ).

When these workers find those who will welcome them, they are entitled to receive their keep, but they are not to become freeloaders, "a parasite at large with no fixed stable" (Horace, *Ep.* 1.15.28; see also Sir 29:23–24). This command makes it clear that their mission is not about them but about what Jesus has sent them to do. Sharing the good news of God's reign with others means they must also share their table fellowship. "Eat what is set before you" would horrify a Pharisee and may anticipate the issue of food that emerges in the mission to Gentiles (see Acts 11:1–18; Gal 2:11–21).

10:10–12 Whenever you enter a town and they do not receive you, when you go out into the streets, say: "Even the dust from your town, which has stuck to our feet, we wipe off [in protest] against you. Nevertheless, know that the reign of God has drawn near!" I tell you, it will be more tolerable for Sodom in that day than for that town (εἰς ἣν δ᾽ ἂν πόλιν εἰσέλθητε καὶ μὴ δέχωνται ὑμᾶς, ἐξελθόντες εἰς τὰς πλατείας αὐτῆς εἴπατε· καὶ τὸν κονιορτὸν τὸν κολληθέντα ἡμῖν ἐκ τῆς πόλεως ὑμῶν εἰς τοὺς πόδας ἀπομασσόμεθα ὑμῖν· πλὴν τοῦτο γινώσκετε ὅτι ἤγγικεν ἡ βασιλεία τοῦ θεοῦ. λέγω ὑμῖν ὅτι Σοδόμοις ἐν τῇ ἡμέρᾳ ἐκείνῃ ἀνεκτότερον ἔσται ἢ τῇ πόλει ἐκείνῃ).

Jesus anticipates that not everyone will openly receive the message of these workers. What will be offensive in their preaching about the presence of God's reign is closely bound to the presence of Jesus and his ministry. Wherever this message is spurned, Jesus orders them to warn the town (collective guilt) that they are inviting God's

judgment; they are to punctuate this warning with a vivid prophetic action of shaking the dust from their feet on a broad avenue so that many will see it. The offer of peace (v. 5) is withdrawn and replaced with a pronouncement of perdition.

The notoriously sinful and Gentile city of Sodom, which went up in smoke (Gen 19:24–29) and is used as a warning example of what will befall the godless (Rom 9:29 [citing Isa 1:9]; 2 Pet 2:6; Jude 7), will fare better in the judgment than these Jewish towns who snub the Messiah and his representatives. The reference to the Sodom saga means that any sons of peace who reside in that town should flee it (17:28–30; 21:21).

10:13–14 Woe to you, Chorazin! Woe to you Bethsaida! Because if the miracles that happened among you had taken place in Tyre and Sidon, they would have repented long ago, sitting in sackcloth and ashes. So, at the judgment it will be more tolerable for Tyre and Sidon than for you (οὐαί σοι, Χοραζίν, οὐαί σοι, Βηθσαϊδά· ὅτι εἰ ἐν Τύρῳ καὶ Σιδῶνι ἐγενήθησαν αἱ δυνάμεις αἱ γενόμεναι ἐν ὑμῖν, πάλαι ἂν ἐν σάκκῳ καὶ σποδῷ καθήμενοι μετενόησαν. πλὴν Τύρῳ καὶ Σιδῶνι ἀνεκτότερον ἔσται ἐν τῇ κρίσει ἢ ὑμῖν).

Jesus launches woes against the cities of Chorazin and Bethsaida, the town of Andrew, Peter, and Philip (John 1:44; 12:21); these towns were near the place where Jesus fed the five thousand (9:10). He compares these towns to the Gentile cities of Tyre and Sidon to the north, which are cursed throughout the Old Testament for their sin and oppression of the people of Israel (Isa 23; Ezek 26–28). Josephus identifies the people from Tyre as their bitter enemies (*Ag. Ap.* 1 §70). They lived in luxury off the food produced in Galilee (see Acts 12:20), while the producers lived at a subsistence level.

To a Jew, to say that these heathen cities, which "heaped up silver like dust, and gold like the dirt of the streets" (Zech 9:3), would have repented and humbled themselves in coarse sackcloth and ashes seems utterly improbable. Claiming that they will have a more tolerable time in the judgment than these Jewish cities also seems incredible and makes clear that rejecting Jesus and his message is far more serious than any other sin.

10:15 And you, Capernaum, you will not be exalted to heaven, will you? You will be brought down into Hades! (καὶ σύ, Καφαρναούμ, μὴ ἕως οὐρανοῦ ὑψωθήσῃ; ἕως τοῦ ᾅδου καταβήσῃ). The three cities are in the same vicinity on the north shore of the Sea of Galilee. Capernaum was mentioned by Jesus in his first sermon in Nazareth when he predicted that they would beseech him to do in their hometown what he did in Capernaum (4:23). Those mighty works (4:31 – 42) ultimately did not do Capernaum much good, since they apparently did not repent. Jesus threatens Capernaum here with a question expecting a negative answer. Its residents will not be exalted to heaven as they might expect but will be cast down into Hades, a place of fiery torment (16:23).

These threats were fulfilled in the Jewish revolt against Rome (AD 60 – 70). Josephus (*J.W.* 3.10.8 – 9 §§516 – 542) describes the beauty and fertility of the area, its feeble defense in a sea battle, and its brutal and total devastation by the Roman general Vespasian, who would soon become emperor. Like Jerusalem, these cities did not know the time of their visitation by God (19:44) or the things that make for peace (19:42). Because they refuse to be gathered, they will be cut off from the people of God.

10:16 The one who listens to you listens to me, and the one who rejects you rejects the one who sent you (ὁ ἀκούων ὑμῶν ἐμοῦ ἀκούει, καὶ ὁ ἀθετῶν ὑμᾶς ἐμὲ ἀθετεῖ· ὁ δὲ ἐμὲ ἀθετῶν ἀθετεῖ τὸν ἀποστείλαντά με). Rejection will not halt the unswerving progress of the campaign. Jesus explains why ignoring his messengers will bring this horrible judgment. To reject them is to reject God who sent them. The parable of vineyard (20:9 – 17) illustrates the inevitable catastrophe that will befall those who reject the servants and the Son.

10:17 The seventy-two returned with joy, saying, "Lord, even the demons are subject to us in your name" (ὑπέστρεψαν δὲ οἱ ἑβδομήκοντα [δύο] μετὰ χαρᾶς λέγοντες· κύριε, καὶ τὰ δαιμόνια ὑποτάσσεται ἡμῖν ἐν τῷ ὀνόματί σου). The seventy-two are just as successful in their mission as the Twelve were (9:10), and they seem joyfully surprised that *even* the demons" were subject to them. The power of Jesus' name is not limited to only a select few (see 9:1 – 6; 9:49). It carries power for all who faithfully use it for God's glory (Acts 3:6, 16; 4:10).

10:18 He said to them, "I observed Satan falling from heaven like a streak of lightning!" (εἶπεν δὲ αὐτοῖς· ἐθεώρουν τὸν Σατανᾶν ὡς ἀστραπὴν ἐκ τοῦ οὐρανοῦ πεσόντα). Jesus' vision of Satan's downfall can be a mental image (see Isa 14:2 – 15) for what has happened or is happening in his own mission and that of the seventy-two.[12] The imperfect tense of the verb, which can be rendered "I was observing" (ἐθεώρουν), lends itself to this interpretation and refers to the course of their successful mission as they were casting out demons. Or, it can be a vision of what will happen in the future.

Gathercole argues that this is a vision of end-time events and the ultimate downfall of Satan.[13] Nolland claims it is a vision of the future akin to those of the Old Testament prophets. The prophets

---

12. Satan either falls "like lightning" from heaven, or he falls the way lightning falls from heaven, suddenly in a flash.

13. Simon J. Gathercole, "Jesus' Eschatological Vision of the Fall of Satan: Luke 10.18 Reconsidered," *ZNW* 94 (2003): 143 – 63.

did not have visions of what had happened or was happening in heaven but what would happen. Jesus "has seen the coming triumph of the kingdom of God over the rule of Satan and has identified this triumph as his own task. He sees this as what God intends to achieve through him."[14]

Jesus, therefore, can put his followers' success in a heavenly perspective that is hidden from them. He projects the limited defeat of demons onto the broader screen of the cosmic conflict between God and the forces of evil. What is happening is not simply the expulsion of random demons that they might come across in their travels but the beginning of the complete overthrow of Satan's rule. The disciples only see the battle picture from the limited perspective of their hand-to-hand combat in the trenches. They have charged into the line of demons and routed them in various skirmishes. Jesus sees the whole war map. Satan has been knocked off his throne in "heaven," representing "the summit of his power,"[15] and is in full retreat. He is still kicking and will unleash woes, but he will assuredly be vanquished. His final defeat will be consummated at the end of time.

The image "like a streak of lightning" (ὡς ἀστραπήν) can imply "suddenly" or refer to lightning's usual downward path. It may picture how lightning often breaks up from one long powerful streak into several weaker strands and does not return to its starting point. It may picture the sudden and instantaneous defeat of evil that will occur at the end.

10:19 Behold, I gave you authority to trample serpents and scorpions, and over all the power of the enemy, and nothing will ever harm you (ἰδοὺ δέδωκα ὑμῖν τὴν ἐξουσίαν τοῦ πατεῖν ἐπάνω ὄφεων καὶ σκορπίων, καὶ ἐπὶ πᾶσαν τὴν δύναμιν τοῦ ἐχθροῦ, καὶ οὐδὲν ὑμᾶς οὐ μὴ ἀδικήσῃ). This

authority to trample serpents and scorpions is all the more impressive for those who travel without sandals. Paul was bitten by a poisonous adder on the island of Malta — the language is vivid, it "fastened itself on his hand" — but he did not die as the natives expected (Acts 28:3 – 5). But Jesus is using these as metaphors for God's divine protection (Deut 8:15) and for crushing evil; "the God of peace will soon crush Satan under your feet" (Rom 16:20). Jesus is not giving clearance to handle snakes (Mark 16:18) to prove one's invulnerability. The point is that "a powerful and resourceful enemy," including the forces of nature, will not be able to stop the success of the Christian mission.[16]

10:20 Nevertheless, do not rejoice about this, that the spirits are subject to you, but rejoice that your names are inscribed in heaven (πλὴν ἐν τούτῳ μὴ χαίρετε ὅτι τὰ πνεύματα ὑμῖν ὑποτάσσεται, χαίρετε δὲ ὅτι τὰ ὀνόματα ὑμῶν ἐγγέγραπται ἐν τοῖς οὐρανοῖς). Jesus switches the focus of their joy from their successes to their own salvation. The source of the disciples' euphoria should not derive from any success they might achieve but from their security in God. In the future, they may meet with utter failure (9:40), but it should not lessen their joy in Christ. Satan has fallen from heaven, but they will be participants in heaven. The image of a heavenly book with the names of the righteous inscribed is traditional (see Mal 3:16 – 17; Phil 4:3; Heb 12:23; Rev 3:5).

This saying serves to check an unbridled delight in power. The returned workers use the present tense, "the demons are subject to us" (ὑποτάσσεται), which is true, but their power derives only from their association with Jesus. The demons submit to Jesus' name, not theirs. Their power is not something that they can treat as their permanent possession to boast about. Their boast

---

14. Nolland, *Luke*, 2:564.
15. Plummer, *Luke*, 279.

16. Dillon, *From Eyewitnesses to Ministers of the Word*, 235.

can only be that God has accepted them and promises them salvation (Rom 5:1 – 2, 11; Gal 6:14).

10:21 In that same hour, he rejoiced in the Holy Spirit and said, "I praise you, Father of heaven and earth, that you have hidden these things from the wise and understanding and revealed them to infants. Yes, Father, because that is what was well-pleasing before you" (ἐν αὐτῇ τῇ ὥρᾳ ἠγαλλιάσατο [ἐν] τῷ πνεύματι τῷ ἁγίῳ καὶ εἶπεν· ἐξομολογοῦμαί σοι, πάτερ, κύριε τοῦ οὐρανοῦ καὶ τῆς γῆς, ὅτι ἀπέκρυψας ταῦτα ἀπὸ σοφῶν καὶ συνετῶν καὶ ἀπεκάλυψας αὐτὰ νηπίοις· ναί ὁ πατήρ, ὅτι οὕτως εὐδοκία ἐγένετο ἔμπροσθέν σου).

Jesus, anointed by the Holy Spirit (3:22; 4:18) and led by the Spirit (4:1), rejoices in God's presence. The phrase "these things" is ambiguous, but since Jesus refers to the revelation of the Son in what follows, it must be that he thanks God for answering his prayers (9:18) and for giving spiritual insight to the disciples into his identity (9:19 – 20).[17] It means, however, that the disciples must accept being categorized as infants. They are no different from the blind man on the margins in Jericho (18:35 – 43) or the hated Zacchaeus (19:1 – 10).

10:22 All things have been given to me by my Father, and no one knows who the Son is except the Father, and who the Father is except the Son and whomever the Son wills to reveal him (πάντα μοι παρεδόθη ὑπὸ τοῦ πατρός μου, καὶ οὐδεὶς γινώσκει τίς ἐστιν ὁ υἱὸς εἰ μὴ ὁ πατήρ, καὶ τίς ἐστιν ὁ πατὴρ εἰ μὴ ὁ υἱὸς καὶ ᾧ ἐὰν βούληται ὁ υἱὸς ἀποκαλύψαι). Luke's narrative on the mission of the seventy-two complements the Great Commission in Matt 28:18 – 20. In Matthew, Jesus announces that all authority in heaven and on earth has been given to him, and then he

commissions his disciples to go make disciples. In Luke, he commissions the disciples to go into the harvest; after they report their success and he reports his vision of Satan's fall, he announces, "All things have been given to me by my Father." Crump lays out the logic:

> A I thank you Father for *revealing* the nature of the Son *to whomever you* choose.
>   B *Only the Father knows the Son*, and
>   C therefore only the Father *can reveal the Son.*
>   B´ Likewise, *only the Son knows the Father.*
> A´ Therefore, only the Son *can reveal* the nature of the Father to *whomever he chooses.*[18]

Crump concludes that Jesus rejoices because God has revealed "Jesus' true person and character to the disciples. Because the disciples have come to know Jesus in this way, he is able, as the only one who knows the Father, to reveal the Father to them as well."[19]

10:23 – 24 And turning to his disciples, he said to them privately, "Blessed are your eyes that see what you see! For I tell you, many prophets and kings wanted to see what you see and they did not see it, and to hear what you hear and they did not hear it" (καὶ στραφεὶς πρὸς τοὺς μαθητὰς κατ᾽ ἰδίαν εἶπεν· μακάριοι οἱ ὀφθαλμοὶ οἱ βλέποντες ἃ βλέπετε. λέγω γὰρ ὑμῖν ὅτι πολλοὶ προφῆται καὶ βασιλεῖς ἠθέλησαν ἰδεῖν ἃ ὑμεῖς βλέπετε καὶ οὐκ εἶδαν, καὶ ἀκοῦσαι ἃ ἀκούετε καὶ οὐκ ἤκουσαν). The woes against the cities are balanced by a beatitude for Jesus' followers. They are to be congratulated because of their privilege to be entrusted with this revelation (see 1 Cor 2:9 – 10). They see and hear because God granted them to see and hear, and they respond properly with faith.

---

17. Crump, *Jesus the Intercessor*, 57.
18. Ibid., 58.
19. Ibid.

Theology in Application

1. Engaging in Mission

The mission of the seventy-two is the gathering of Israel that God promised would take place, but it also foreshadows the disciples' future mission to the whole world. More emphasis is placed on what to do when the mission meets with rejection and expects a divided response from Israel. Those who refuse to be gathered under the kingship of Jesus will be cut off from the people of God. But this discourse also hints that if Gentiles were given this unparalleled opportunity, even infamously sinful cities like Sodom, Tyre, and Sidon would turn to God in repentance. Luke will describe the divided response of Israel as the gospel is carried to the far reaches of the world in Acts, and the surprising positive response of many Gentiles. Those who truly belong to the people of God are only those who submit to Jesus as Lord.

This discourse may have served as a handbook on mission for early Christians. The risen Lord continues to live and act in his church. O'Toole comments:

> He leads us. Our mission is Christ's mission. He gives us our mission and directs us. When we are persecuted, he encourages, supports, and protects us. His power enables us to perform miracles. When we preach, he preaches; when we are heard he is heard. Our salvation, a present experience and reality, comes only from him.[20]

Our mission depends on awakening to the great need for others to hear the gospel and God's desire to gather them. It also depends on prayer, a sense of urgency, accountability to other missionaries, a clear sense of divine commission, a clear sense of the finality of the task in calling others to repent, the blessing of others with peace, joy over success, and a refusal to retaliate over rejection. The missionaries also are warned never to become too impressed with themselves.

Jesus comes to persons through the mediation of his followers. Their behavior must conform to the Lord they represent. Their poor example can cause others not to want to meet Jesus or to use it as an excuse for their refusal to repent. Their moral authority leaks out like the helium from birthday balloons that eventually collapse in a heap when they are guilty of egregious ethical failures. If followers obey Jesus' moral teaching, they will be "blameless and innocent, children of God without blemish in the midst of a crooked and twisted generation, among whom you shine as lights in the world" (Phil 2:15 ESV). They will not engage in mission for what it might profit them. They will not become so enmeshed in whatever society they find themselves and so dependent on their support that they are unable or unwilling to shake the dust from their feet and pronounce God's judgment.

---

20. O'Toole, *The Unity of Luke's Theology*, 61.

2. Cosmic Conflict

Opposition to Jesus is building, and it is more than a clash between wolves and lambs. It is a battle between God and Satan. The reason the disciples are successful in their sorties against Satan's ranks is because "a specific defeat of Satan in heaven preceded the earthly warfare in which the seventy-two are engaged, and enables them to fight."[21] But these are preliminary skirmishes and not the final battle. They portend Satan's inevitable defeat, which is God's fundamental purpose (see John 16:11; 12:31; 1 John 3:8).

The vision of Satan's fall does not make Jesus' death and resurrection superfluous, and the final victory does not even come in Jesus' death and resurrection because Satan continues to work damage in Acts (13:4 – 12; 26:18).[22] But the cross and resurrection do mortal damage to the satanic realm (Heb 2:14). Paul envisions that it is now and not yet. God has highly exalted Jesus and "placed all things under his feet" (Eph 1:21 – 22), but the final nail will be driven in the coffin at the very end (1 Cor 15:24 – 28; see Rev 20:10).

What has already occurred is that Satan is now deposed from his role as the adversary.[23] The term "Satan" is used as the one in heaven who accuses humans (Job 1:6 – 12; 2:1 – 7; Zech 3:1 – 5). Caird comments, "The ejection of Satan means that God's redemptive mercy has delivered men from both the sentence that hung over them and from the guilt and power of sin that held them captive (Rev 12:7 – 12)."[24] Paul understands this when he asks, "Who then is the one who condemns?" and declares that Christ Jesus, who died and was raised and is now at the right hand of God, intercedes for us (Rom 8:34). Satan's fall also means that humans can be delivered from the power of darkness (Acts 26:17 – 18). We no longer have to live under Satan's bondage.

3. The Revelation of the Father and the Son

This passage affirms God's sovereignty in revealing the truth and hiding it. It also reflects Luke's high Christology. Gathercole contends that this passage (along with others, such as the transfiguration) reveals that "Jesus is portrayed as having a heavenly identity — participating in the heavenly realms — already before Easter."[25] Jesus has access to the heavenly council. He sees the fall of Satan. He knows that no harm will come to the disciples. He knows that their names are inscribed in heaven, which is a heavenly secret known only to exalted angels and revealed at the end of the age. He knows whom God has elected. He knows God's heavenly decree. The passage

---

21. Minear, *To Heal and To Reveal*, 12.
22. Green, *The Gospel of Luke*, 419.
23. Fitzmyer, *Luke*, 2:862.
24. Caird, *Saint Luke*, 143.

25. Simon J. Gathercole, *The Preexistent Son: Recovering the Christologies of Matthew, Mark, and Luke* (Grand Rapids: Eerdmans, 2006), 54.

reveals Jesus' intimacy with the Father and his knowledge of heavenly secrets. He is no ordinary prophet but far more as the so-called "thunderbolt from the Johannine heaven" reveals.

To know God, one must know Jesus. If one knows Jesus, then one knows God. Rowe clarifies this insight:

> The Father is not specified as Father apart from the Son, nor the Son as Son apart from the Father. Indeed, this is the point of the use of the article. In no way can the saying be read along generic or parabolic lines: just as a son knows his father and can make him known. The relation, rather, is between "the" Father and "the" Son and … in its very uniqueness it is exclusive (οὐδείς [no one] … εἰ μή [except]). Thus, the only way human beings can know of such a relation is through a revelation in which the awareness of this relation comes to them from outside, as it were. … the knowledge of the relation between the Father and the Son comes only through the will to reveal it.[26]

The revelation about the Father-Son is mediated through the Son in a particular human life and then through the missionaries in the name of the Son. If persons claim to know God and deny that God is revealed in Jesus, they do not fully know God. Jesus' rejoicing in the Holy Spirit opens the door for musing on the economy of the Trinity.

---

26. Rowe, *Early Narrative Christology*, 139 – 40.

CHAPTER 31

Luke 10:25 – 37

Literary Context

Jesus has sent the seventy-two out in pairs to every place he intended to go with instructions for their mission (10:1). He prepared them for success and rejection, but unlike his previous mission instructions (9:1 – 6), he uttered strong threats against Chorazin, Bethsaida, and Capernaum for their failure to respond (10:13 – 15). Many in Israel will be worse off in the judgment than their bitter enemies Tyre and Sidon. When the seventy-two returned with joy that the demons submitted to them, Jesus addressed the incongruity that God unexpectedly had hidden "these things" from the wise and intelligent who failed to respond and revealed them to "infants," the opposite of wise and intelligent, who did respond (10:21). The parable of the Samaritan now amplifies this astonishing result. It is the hated outsider rather than those who serve in the temple in Jerusalem who faithfully obeys the command to love God with every fiber of one's being and to love the neighbor as oneself.

This parable is followed by an incident in the home of Mary and Martha. The close connection between the two units will be discussed in the following section.

Main Idea

Loving God means that one cannot place limits on whom one must love as a neighbor.

Translation

Luke 10:25–37

10:25	Question	**Just then a lawyer rose to put him to the test and said,**
		"Teacher, what must I do to inherit eternal life?"
26	Counterquestion	**He said to him,**
		"What is written in the law?
		How do you read it?"
27	Response	**He answered and said,**
		"You shall love the Lord your God
		with all your heart, and
		with all your soul, and
		with all your strength, and
		with all your mind,
		and [you shall love] your neighbor as yourself." (Deut 6:5; Lev 19:18)
28	Command	**He said to him,**
		"You answered rightly;
		do this and you shall live."
29	Question	**Wanting to justify himself, he said to Jesus,**
		"And who is my neighbor?"
30a	Parable	**Jesus replied,**
		"A certain man was coming down from Jerusalem to Jericho
		and he fell among robbers
b	Violent actions	*who stripped him,*
		beat him, and
		went away leaving him half dead.
31	Character introduction (1)	*By chance a certain priest was coming down that road,*
		and when he spotted him,
		he passed by on the other side.
32	Character introduction (2)	*Likewise, a Levite also came along,*
		and when he came to the place and spotted him,
		he passed by on the other side.
33	Character introduction (3)	*A certain Samaritan who was traveling came upon him,*
		and when he spotted him,
		he was moved with compassion.
34a	Merciful actions	*He went over to him,*
b		*bandaged his wounds after pouring oil and wine on them.*
c		*Then he lifted him up on his own mount and*
		led him to an inn and
		took care of him.

Continued on next page.

Continued from previous page.		
35		On the next day,
	he	took out two denarii,
		gave them to the innkeeper, and
		said,
		'Take care of him, and whatever you need to spend in addition↩
		I will repay you when I come back.'
36	Question	Which of these three, do you think, proved to be a neighbor to the man who↩
		fell among the robbers?"
37a	Response	**He said,**
		"The one who acted with mercy toward him."
b	Command	**Jesus said,**
		"Go and do likewise."

Structure and Literary Form

This account breaks into three segments. In the first segment, a lawyer puts Jesus to the test with the question about how to inherit eternal life. Jesus forces him to provide his own answer to his question with a counterquestion about how to inherit eternal life by prompting him to interpret what the Scripture says. He affirms his answer from Scripture, and Jesus instructs him to do it.

This response precipitates another question from the lawyer about the definition of the neighbor that Scripture commands one to love. In this second segment, Jesus prompts the lawyer to provide the answer to his question from a parable (10:29–35). The magic of parables is that they give us a glimpse of the transcendent through the lens of ordinary existence — a man getting mugged on the Jericho road, the age-old Jewish enmity toward Samaritans. Something incongruous happens in the story that jolts the expectations of the listeners and points to something about God that transcends. It assaults the prejudice that we are always in the right and our enemies are going to hell. The parable has four scenes with the robbers mugging a traveler coming down from Jerusalem on the Jericho road, a priest and then a Levite passing by and leaving him to bleed to death, and a Samaritan who has compassion and offers aid. The Samaritan remedies what the robbers have done by saving the man's life and does what the priest and Levite could have done but did not.

The third segment records the reaction of the lawyer to the parable. Jesus forces him to provide his own answer to his question about the neighbor with a counterquestion. Again, his answer is correct, and again Jesus instructs him to do it (10:36–37). The lawyer is interested in debating the question about who is the neighbor, but Jesus' answer shows he is not interested in debates but in what one *does*. The command "to do" frames the parable (10:28, 37).

Exegetical Outline

→ **I. What must one do to inherit eternal life? (10:25 – 29)**

    A. Question to test Jesus (10:25)

    B. Counterquestion from Jesus about the law (10:26)

    C. Answer: Love God and love your neighbor as yourself (10:27)

    D. Commendation and command to do this (10:28)

    E. Further question: Who is my neighbor? (10:29)

II. Parable of the Samaritan (10:30 – 37)

    A. Setting: a mugging victim (10:30)

    B. Three responses to the wounded man (10:31 – 35)

      1. A priest passes him by (10:31)

      2. A Levite passes him by (10:32)

      3. A Samaritan has compassion on him and renders aid (10:33 – 35)

        a. Dresses his wounds (10:33 – 34b)

        b. Cares for him at an inn (10:34c)

        c. Pays for his care until he returns (10:35)

    C. Question: Who acted as a neighbor? (10:36 – 37)

      1. Answer: the one who showed mercy (10:36 – 37a)

      2. Command to do this (10:37b)

Explanation of the Text

10:25 Just then a lawyer rose to put him to the test and said, "Teacher, what must I do to inherit eternal life?" (καὶ ἰδοὺ νομικός τις ἀνέστη ἐκπειράζων αὐτὸν λέγων· διδάσκαλε, τί ποιήσας ζωὴν αἰώνιον κληρονομήσω;). Teachers sat, and students stood in courtesy, so the lawyer is demonstrating the proper deference to Jesus as the teacher. Luke notifies the reader, however, that the lawyer's intentions are less than sincere. He wishes to put Jesus to the test. The Pharisees, lawyers, and rulers as a class are portrayed as having a proclivity to put Jesus on trial and to justify themselves

(16:15) rather than God (7:29). He is not considering following Jesus as a serious option even if Jesus were to come up with a stirring answer to his question.

The same question is asked by a serious seeker in 18:18. Like modern-day politicians and sports stars who get asked the same questions over and over again, it is likely that Jesus was asked how to inherit eternal life many times (see Matt 22:34 – 40; Mark 12:28 – 34). Jesus spoke his sayings "on numerous occasions, with numerous local variations."[1]

---

1. Wright, *Jesus and the Victory of God*, 288. Manson (*The Sayings of Jesus*, 260) argues regarding the parallel with Mark 12:28 – 31 that Jesus had been teaching on the doctrine of loving God and neighbor before and that it was well-known that this was for him the key for interpreting and understanding the law. He notes that in our world a teacher or preacher need

only put his thoughts in print to reach thousands. In first-century Palestine, however, the only way of communicating great thoughts was to keep repeating them. Manson suggests that the lawyer already knew Jesus' opinion on the matter and had raised the issue to ask the further question, "Who *is* my neighbor?

10:26 He said to him, "What is written in the law? How do you read it?" (ὁ δὲ εἶπεν πρὸς αὐτόν· ἐν τῷ νόμῳ τί γέγραπται; πῶς ἀναγινώσκεις;). Jesus' teaching method avoided giving direct answers, particularly to those only interested in trapping him. This method is captured in the joke: "Why does a Rabbi answer a question with a question?" Answer: "Why shouldn't a Rabbi answer a question with a question?" But Jesus' method is more serious because so much is at stake — inheriting eternal life. One cannot simply follow a guidebook, "Five Steps to Eternal Life." One has to internalize it. So Jesus turns the tables on the lawyer, and the one interrogated becomes the interrogator. As Esler interprets it, "the tone here is quite sharp and rather dismissive: 'You are a lawyer, what do you think?' "[2]

This question could mean, "How do you recite?" presupposing a frequent recitation of a passage, which may explain why the lawyer answers by reciting from the Shema (Deut 6:5) to love God and neighbor.[3] But it is more likely to mean, "How do *you* interpret?"[4] The issue raised by the lawyer is how the law is to be interpreted.

10:27 He answered and said, "You shall love the Lord your God with all your heart, and with all your soul, and with all your strength, and with all your mind, and [you shall love] your neighbor as yourself" (ὁ δὲ ἀποκριθεὶς εἶπεν· ἀγαπήσεις κύριον τὸν θεόν σου ἐξ ὅλης [τῆς] καρδίας σου καὶ ἐν ὅλῃ τῇ ψυχῇ σου καὶ ἐν ὅλῃ τῇ ἰσχύϊ σου καὶ ἐν ὅλῃ τῇ διανοίᾳ σου, καὶ τὸν πλησίον σου ὡς σεαυτόν). The logic behind the conflation of Deut 6:5 and Lev 19:18 is that loving God also requires loving those who have been made in the image of God. But the text reads "neighbor," not your fellow human being. If one believed it was right to hate and destroy those opposed to God, as many devout persons did, reason dictated that these persons could not be classified as neighbors who were to be loved.

One detects, it seems, a desire to limit the scope of this command, who might qualify as neighbor, to validate the human proclivity to dislike of the "other" in such statements as these. The *Letter of Aristeas* 227 reads: "God's very great commandment is that one shall honor one's parents. Next, and close to it, it comes that one shall honor one's friends, for he [God] equals the friend to one's own self." Those who entered in the rule of the community at Qumran were instructed to seek God with all one's heart and all one's soul (1QS 1.1 – 2), but they were required only to love all "the sons of light," fellow members, while they were to detest "the sons of darkness," nonmembers (1QS 1.9 – 11). Jesus' response in this parable challenges the assumption that the pious, observant, full-pedigree Jew gets to determine who falls into the category of enemy or those who oppose God and need not be loved.

10:28 He said to him, "You answered rightly; do this and you shall live" (εἶπεν δὲ αὐτῷ· ὀρθῶς ἀπεκρίθης· τοῦτο ποίει καὶ ζήσῃ). The man is an expert in the law and knows the answer. Jesus says, "Practice what you preach." This response cites Lev 18:5, "Keep my decrees and laws, for the person who obeys them will live by them. I am the LORD" (see Gal 3:12). What is at question for Jesus is not what one *must* do but whether one *does* it.[5] That retort stings, "since it suggests that the

2. Philip F. Esler, "Jesus and the Reduction of Intergroup Conflict: The Parable of the Good Samaritan in the Light of the Social Identity Theory," *BibInt* 8 (2000): 333.

3. Joachim Jeremias, *New Testament Theology: The Proclamation of Jesus* (trans. John Bowden; New York: Scribner's, 1971), 187.

4. J. Duncan M. Derrett, *Law in the New Testament* (London: Darton, Longman & Todd, 1970), 224.

5. Luke emphasizes "doing" (3:10 – 14; 6:47; 8:21).

lawyer may not yet be fulfilling these commandments and may not have life."[6] As far as Jesus is concerned, "having right answers does not mean one knows God."[7]

10:29 Wanting to justify himself, he said to Jesus, "And who is my neighbor?" (ὁ δὲ θέλων δικαιῶσαι ἑαυτὸν εἶπεν πρὸς τὸν Ἰησοῦν· καὶ τίς ἐστίν μου πλησίον;). Is the lawyer a showoff who wants to prove he knows more than the teacher? Perhaps, but the verb "justify himself" has loaded significance. He is not simply trying to recover from some embarrassment. In 16:15, the Pharisees are identified as those who seek to justify themselves (οἱ δικαιοῦντες ἑαυτούς) before people (translated, "You are those who make yourselves look upright in the eyes of others"). Not only would he "justify" himself before God by *doing* something to gain eternal life; he wants to present himself before others as a righteous man.

Bailey surmises that the lawyer's next question, "Who is my neighbor?" expects the answer, "Your relative, your friend, etc.," and he can then proudly announce, "All of these I have fully loved from my youth." Jesus will then be expected to praise him, and the lawyer can bask in the admiration of the people who see his good works praised and his eternal life guaranteed. He can then live with greater confidence based on that praise and the admiration bestowed upon him.[8]

The lawyer wants to know how and where to draw the line. What can be demanded of me? Whom exactly am I required to love? The question implies that there can be a non-neighbor![9]

The lawyer also wants to know from whom can he safely withhold his love. The lawyer wants *halakah* from Jesus. The purpose of *halakah* was

> to determine whether or not a biblical passage does in fact constitute a commandment, if there can be any doubt; to establish the application of a biblical commandment; to define its precise scope and meaning; and to determine precisely what must be done in order to fulfill it.[10]

Linnemann points out that being able to know precisely what is required provides one with a shell inside of which one can live peacefully because everything is familiar. It gives one a sense of certainty and security because everything is cut-and-dried.[11] The story is a means of rescuing this questioner from being destroyed by the spiritual stockade that hems him in and keeps him from loving others.

The definition of neighbor was open to debate. Leviticus 19:17–18 identifies the neighbor whom we are to love as "a fellow Israelite," "anyone among your people." It appears to be limited; the neighbor is one who shares in the election and covenant with you and who knows the duties and rights incumbent on those in that covenant. It does not necessarily embrace all humans.

Leviticus 19:33–34, however, commands: "When an alien resides with you in your land, you shall not oppress the alien. The alien who resides with you shall be to you as the citizen among you; you shall love the alien as yourself, for you were aliens in the land of Egypt: I am the LORD your God" (NRSV). Some extended the definition of

6. Esler, "Jesus and the Reduction of Intergroup Conflict," 333.

7. Craddock, *Luke*, 150.

8. Bailey, *Through Peasant Eyes*, 39. Wright (*Jesus and the Victory of God*, 306) imagines that the man is not trying to deflect criticism and look a fool for having asked such an easy question or that he was seeking Pelagian self-justification. Instead, he was concerned to justify the Jew by "seeking to draw

the boundaries of the covenant at the appropriate place, with (of course) himself inside, and sundry other specifiable categories outside."

9. Derrett, *Law in the New Testament*, 225.

10. E. P. Sanders, *Paul and Palestinian Judaism* (Philadelphia: Fortress, 1977), 76.

11. Eta Linnemann, *Parables of Jesus: Introduction and Exposition* (London: SPCK, 1975), 52.

neighbor to include Gentiles (see *T. Iss.* 5:2; 7:6). Most recognized only full proselytes among the Gentiles as neighbors, while some Pharisees drew the line even more narrowly to exclude nonobserving Israelites.[12] This bias is reflected in *Mekilta Nezikin* 12:11 – 13 on Exod 21:35: "When one man's ox hurts another's — the ox of his neighbor — This excludes the ox of a Samaritan, the ox of a foreigner, and the ox of a resident alien." A similar interpretation emerges in *Sipra Lev.* to 20:10: "If a man commits adultery with the wife of his neighbor ... that excludes the wife of a non-Israelite." A discussion of the phrase "And Hatred of Mankind" in *ʾAbot R. Nat.* 16 leads to this conclusion:

> This teaches that no one should think of saying, " 'Love the Sages but hate the disciples'; or 'Love the disciples but hate the *am ha-aretz*' [the people of the land]. On the contrary, love all these. But hate the sectarians (*minim*), apostates, and informers; and so said David: 'Do I not hate them, O Lord, that hate Thee? And do I not strive with those that rise up against Thee? I hate them with utmost hatred; I count them mine enemies' [Ps 139:21 – 22].
>
> "But does it not say, But thou shalt love thy neighbor as thyself: I am the Lord [Lev 19:18]: and why is that? Because I [the Lord] have created him. Indeed! if he acts as thy people do, thou shalt love him; but if not, thou shalt not love him."

According to *b. Sanh.* 57a, "It has been taught: A Cuthean [the Jewish name for Samaritans] and a [Jewish] shepherd of small cattle need neither be rescued [from a pit] nor may they be thrown [therein]." Both were regarded as robbers.

The lawyer's question really asks, "Who is a Jew?" Jesus' answer is not a story about a good human being but about a Samaritan. The Samaritan,

from the Jewish perspective, is part Jew, part idolater but partly like Israelites in some practices.[13]

10:30 Jesus replied, "A certain man was come down from Jerusalem to Jericho and he fell among robbers who stripped him, beat him, and went away leaving him half dead (ὑπολαβὼν ὁ Ἰησοῦς εἶπεν· ἄνθρωπός τις κατέβαινεν ἀπὸ Ἰερουσαλὴμ εἰς Ἰεριχὼ καὶ λῃσταῖς περιέπεσεν, οἳ καὶ ἐκδύσαντες αὐτὸν καὶ πληγὰς ἐπιθέντες ἀπῆλθον ἀφέντες ἡμιθανῆ). Jesus' story draws on the everyday reality of brutality that plagued the land, an indifferent cleric class, and prejudice toward a hated half-breed, half-heathen neighbor. The Jericho road winds through rocky desert terrain and descends 3,600 feet in the seventeen miles from Jerusalem to Jericho. Jerusalem is 2,300 feet above sea level and Jericho, 1,300 feet below sea level. Robbers were notorious along this route (see Strabo, *Geogr.* 16.2.41, who reports that Pompey had to wipe out strongholds of brigands there; see also Josephus, *J.W.* 2.12.2 §228). They remained a serious threat into the twentieth century.

The robbers could have been the social bandits who lived off the land or even those with connections to the high priest who secured immunity through bribes (see Josephus, *J.W.* 2:274 – 76; *Ant.* 20.9.2 §§206 – 7, 20.9.4 §§213 – 14). They pounce on the lone traveler, strip him of his clothes, beat him, and leave him half dead. Since he is stripped of his clothes and therefore naked, one could tell whether he was circumcised or not. Since he is half dead and presumably mute, however, one could not easily identify his origin.

10:31 By chance a certain priest was coming down that road, and when he spotted him, he passed by on the other side (κατὰ συγκυρίαν δὲ ἱερεύς τις κατέβαινεν ἐν τῇ ὁδῷ ἐκείνῃ καὶ ἰδὼν

12. The covenanters at Qumran also had a limited view of who the neighbor was (see 1QS 1:10, 2:24, 5:25, 9:21; 1QM 1:1).

13. Berel Dov Lerner, "Samaritans, Jews and Philosophers," *ExpTim* 113 (2002): 154.

αὐτὸν ἀντιπαρῆλθεν). The verb "was coming down" (κατέβαινεν) indicates that the priest was coming from Jerusalem. One always went "up" to Jerusalem and went "down" from Jerusalem. Perhaps the priest had finished his tour of duty in the temple (see 1:5 – 8) and was returning to his home in Jericho, which had the largest population of priests outside of Jerusalem.[14] As he came along, he saw the beaten, naked, and half-dead man. The text states briefly that he passed by on the opposite side (ἀντιπαρῆλθεν), implying that he deliberately steered clear of him.

The priesthood in Jerusalem constituted a kind of Jewish nobility and represented the upper stratum of Jewish society. Josephus begins his account of his life with a genealogy and says his family "is no ignoble one"; connection with the priesthood "is that hallmark of an illustrious line" (*Life* 1 §1). The priest, therefore, was likely to have been perceived by the listeners as a notable representative of Jewish piety. As members of a privileged profession, priests were not held in great affection by laity. From an earlier time, Hosea 6:9 complains bitterly: "As marauders lie in ambush for a victim, so do bands of priests; they murder on the road to Shechem, carrying out their wicked schemes." According to a contemporary witness, priests are idolaters, adulterers, money lovers, arrogant, lawless, lascivious, child abusers, and practice bestiality (*T. Levi* 17:11; see also Josephus's account of the brutality of the high priest Ananias [*Ant.* 20 §§205 – 207]).

The priest quickly decides that this beaten man is not a neighbor and is presented with no great moral dilemma over which his conscience struggles. Several considerations may have flashed across his mind in that moment of decision, but Luke does not elaborate. According to *b. Sanh.* 73a, "If a man sees his fellow drowning, mauled by beasts, or attacked by robbers, he is bound to

save him — 'Thou shalt not stand by the blood of thy neighbor!' [Lev 19:16]." If the priest could be sure that this man was a fellow, a neighbor, he was duty bound to save him. But how can he know if he is a neighbor? He is stripped so that there is no distinctive dress to identify him; he is half dead and therefore mute. A warning in Sir 12:1 – 7 cautions about whom one should help:

> If you do good, know to whom you do it,
>   and you will be thanked for your good deeds.
> Do good to the devout, and you will be repaid —
>   if not by them, certainly by the Most High.
> No good comes to one who persists in evil
>   or to one who does not give alms.
> Give to the devout, but do not help the sinner.
>   Do good to the humble, but do not give to the ungodly;
> hold back their bread, and do not give it to them,
>   for by means of it they might subdue you;
> then you will receive twice as much evil
>   for all the good you have done to them.
> For the Most High also hates sinners
>   and will inflict punishment on the ungodly.
> Give to the one who is good,
>   but do not help the sinner. (NRSV)

Not only does the priest have no idea who this man is; he has no idea what kind of man he is. Is he someone worthy of help? If he were a good man, why has this misfortune befallen him? He may offend the Most High by offering aid and thus saving the life of a wretched sinner who will repay him in evil.

If the half-dead man were dead or died in his hands, he would be defiled for seven days for touching a corpse (Num 19:11 – 19; see Hag 2:11 – 13). If he were alive, he could not be sure that he could save the man's life. More significantly, special instructions were enjoined on the priests in Lev 21:1 – 3 about defiling themselves with a

14. Str-B 2:66, 180.

corpse (this issue is further debated in *m. Naz.* 7:1; see *b. Naz.* 47b). These laws were not simply Jewish restrictions; they were widespread throughout the ancient world. Lucian (*Syr. d.* 2.62) writes: "Those priests who bore the corpse of a Galloi priest of Syria were not allowed to enter the temple for seven days; if any priest looked at a corpse he was impure that day and could only enter the temple the following day if he was cleansed." It is best, however, to focus on what the text emphasizes — his callousness in leaving a man (to die) by the wayside rather than showing love and mercy.

10:32 Likewise, a Levite also came along, and when he came to the place and spotted him, he passed by on the other side (ὁμοίως δὲ καὶ Λευίτης [γενόμενος] κατὰ τὸν τόπον ἐλθὼν καὶ ἰδὼν ἀντιπαρῆλθεν). The priest and Levite are mentioned because they represent the ultimate insiders. The Levites were an order of lower clergy who served in the temple as gatekeepers, musicians (chanting, playing lyres, flutes, harps, trumpets, and cymbals), janitors, and haulers. Harrington outlines the contrasts between priests and Levites:[15]

Priests	Levites
offer sacrifices	perform music accompanying sacrifices
disqualified by impurity and blemish	disqualified by impurity but not blemish
serve God directly	serve the priests
guard the Court of the Priests	guard the non-priestly courts
superintend maintenance of temple complex	maintain the temple complex

may not marry a widow or divorcee	may marry a widow or divorcee
may only mourn close relatives	may mourn anyone

What deterred the Levite from assisting the wounded man may be presumed to be the same callousness that deterred the priest. They were temple personnel and represented *Israel's cult*, and they are shown not doing the will of God. What makes this neglect worse is that the audience would probably assume that the beaten man coming down from Jerusalem was likely a pilgrim returning from the temple. Though the priest and Levite lived off of the offerings of pilgrims, they showed no compassion for him. The story presents the failure of religious leaders to be humane and follow the dictates of Scripture, and it cast aspersions on the institution they served.

10:33 A certain Samaritan who was traveling came upon him, and when he spotted him, he was moved with compassion (Σαμαρίτης δέ τις ὁδεύων ἦλθεν κατ᾽ αὐτὸν καὶ ἰδὼν ἐσπλαγχνίσθη). The phrases "priests, Levites, and all the people" define the tripartite division of Israel.[16] The first two characters on the scene "belong to the first two categories of the social hierarchy that dominated post-exilic Judaism," and the audience "would expect the narrative to bring on stage a lay Israelite," the last category of the division. It is a shocker for a Samaritan to appear and act with such compassion.[17] Most Jews agreed that Samaritans belonged to the category of outsider (see 17:18) and non-neighbor. The deviation from the traditional tripartite formula would have jarred Jesus' audience.

---

15. Harrington, *Holiness: Rabbinic Judaism and the Graeco-Roman World*, 71.

16. See 1 Chr 28:21; 2 Chr 34:30; Ezra 2:70; 7:7, 13; 8:15; 9:1; 10:5; Neh 8:13; 11:3, 20; 1QS 2:11, 19 – 21; CD 14:3; 11QTemple 21:4 – 6; 22:8 – 14; 57:12 – 15; 61:8 – 9; Josephus, *Ant.* 4.8.16

§222; 7.14.7 §363; 9.13.1 §260; 11.3.9 §74; 11.4.2 §481, 11.4.7 §107.

17. Michel Gourges, "The Priest, the Levite, and the Samaritan Revisited: A Critical Note on Luke 10:31 – 35," *JBL* 117 (1998): 709 – 13.

In Depth: Jews and Samaritans: An Adversarial History

Samaritans and Jews had a bitter history stemming from their different views of the Samaritans' heritage. According to Jewish accounts, when the native population of Samaria was sent into exile (2 Kgs 17), the king of Assyria brought in colonists from Cutha, Babylon, Hamath, and elsewhere. Others, identified as adversaries of Judah and Benjamin, were brought in to repopulate the area by later Assyrian kings (Ezra 4:2, 10). Their knowledge of Judaism was only a thin veneer over a deep-seated heathen superstition. The early settlers were plagued by lions, so the story goes (2 Kgs 17:25), and they appealed to the authorities to send one of the Jewish priests to instruct them in the local cult so that they might appease the local deity. The result was a syncretistic mixture of paganism and Yahwism.

Consequently, Jewish sources refer to the Samaritans contemptuously as Cutheans or lion converts (*b. Ketub.* 75a – 76a; Josephus, *Ant.* 9.14.3 §§288 – 91). The Samaritans argue that not all of the inhabitants were deported in 722 BC, and some were repatriated after fifty-five years. The Samaritans claimed to be the descendants of these native Israelites. They claimed that the breach with Israel went back to the time of Eli when he set up his apostate sanctuary at Shiloh. The true sanctuary was on Mount Gerizim. This apostasy was continued by the accursed Ezra, who misled the returning exiles to build a temple in Jerusalem. The Samaritans called themselves the Shamerim, the observant, rather than the Shomeronim, the inhabitants of Samaria. They had their own copies of the Pentateuch and rejected the authority of the historical and prophetic books and, of course, any oral tradition. It was Josephus's opinion that when the Jews were prospering, the Cutheans claimed to be kinsmen of the Jews; when they were in trouble, they claimed to be of another race and had nothing to do with them (*Ant.* 9.14.3 §291; 11.8.6 §341).

The vitriolic Jewish hostility toward Samaritans is easily documented (see Sir 50:25 – 26; *T. Levi* 7:2). Samaritans reciprocated the hostility. In 135 – 104 BC, several Samaritan cities were attacked and conquered during the rule of John Hyrcanus. Shechem was destroyed, and the temple on Mount Gerizim was razed (Josephus, *J.W.* 1.2.6 §63; *Ant.* 13.9.1 §256). According to Josephus, this blow was delivered to repay the Samaritans for injuries inflicted on some colonists in Marisa (Josephus, *Ant.* 13.10.1 – 2 §§273 – 281). It was a form of what might be called "ethnic cleansing" today. In the first century, the Samaritans were pro-Roman (Josephus, *J. W.* 1.7.7 §156; 1.8.4 §166) and received both Roman favor and their pagan influence. Herod, the client king of Rome, married a Samaritan (one of ten wives) and built the city of Sebaste in Samaria with a temple dedicated to Caesar. In AD 6 – 9, Josephus reports an incident when the Samaritans infiltrated the crowd of Passover pilgrims in the temple and deposited human bones in the porticoes and throughout the premises of the temple, thus desecrating it (*Ant.* 18.2.2 §§29 – 30). The priests were forced to shut down the temple during Passover to exclude everyone from the temple.

Samaritans were excluded from the temple cult (*m. Šeqal.* 1:5), could not be a witness in a court (except in a divorce, *m. Giṭ.* 1:5) because they were judged to be liars, were lumped together with those of doubtful stock (*m. Qidd.* 4:3, *t. Qidd.* 4:3), and conveyed uncleanness because their daughters were deemed menstruants from the cradle (*m. Nid.* 4:1, *t. Nid.* 5:1). Rabbi Eliezer used to say: "He that eats the bread of the Samaritans is like one who eats the flesh of swine" (*m. Šeb.* 8:10). The public latrines of the Samaritans were off-limits because they are said to bury their miscarriages there. R. Judah, however, contended: "They did not bury them but only threw them away and wild animals dragged them off (*m. Nid.* 7:4). One of the worst names Jesus is called in his ministry is "Samaritan" (John 8:48).

Samaritans were no less hostile toward Jews and probably said mean things too. The point is that the modern reader should interpret the Samaritan's appearance in the parable in light of bitter ethnic conflicts in the modern world to grasp its shock value.

It is important that the person is identified as a Samaritan and not an idolater. The Samaritan understands himself to be under the same Mosaic law as do the lawyer, the priest, and the Levite. A pagan would not, so the parable is not about natural law but about the universal claim of the Mosaic law.

10:34 He went over to him, bandaged his wounds after pouring oil and wine on them. Then he lifted him up on his own mount and led him to an inn and took care of him (καὶ προσελθὼν κατέδησεν τὰ τραύματα αὐτοῦ ἐπιχέων ἔλαιον καὶ οἶνον. ἐπιβιβάσας δὲ αὐτὸν ἐπὶ τὸ ἴδιον κτῆνος ἤγαγεν αὐτὸν εἰς πανδοχεῖον καὶ ἐπεμελήθη αὐτοῦ). Rather than passing by,

the Samaritan goes over to the man and ministers aid. He does not first ask if he might be a fellow Samaritan.[18] He dresses his wounds, puts the man on his mount, probably getting bloody in the process, and leads him on foot to an inn. He takes the form of a servant. It costs him time, effort, and money and is risky. Not only might the robbers still be in the neighborhood ready to pounce again, but the man might die and the family could blame him and demand blood vengeance. The Samaritan, however, is bound by the same law to love one neighbor as the Jew is.

The word for "inn" (πανδοχεῖον) means "welcome for all," and this inn was probably nothing more than a stockade with a gate and porticoes. Oil was used to soften a wound and the wine was

---

18. 2 Chronicles 28:5 – 15 records Samaritans showing such compassion.

poured on to disinfect them (see *m. Šabb.* 19:2, which describes oil and wine mixed for treating circumcision). Derrett finds symbolic significance in all of this:[19] (1) Binding of wounds is imagery that is used of God when he acts to save his people (Isa 1:6; Jer 30:17). (2) Oil and wine were important elements in the temple worship, and the Samaritan who pours oil on the wound pours out the true offering acceptable to God worth more than ten thousands of rivers of oil offered up in the sacrificial cult (Mic 6:6 – 8). The priest and Levite appear dysfunctional outside the temple without their props.

10:35 On the next day, he took out two denarii, gave them to the innkeepe, and said, "Take care of him, and whatever you need to spend in addition I will repay you when I come back" (καὶ ἐπὶ τὴν αὔριον ἐκβαλὼν ἔδωκεν δύο δηνάρια τῷ πανδοχεῖ καὶ εἶπεν· ἐπιμελήθητι αὐτοῦ, καὶ ὅ τι ἂν προσδαπανήσῃς ἐγὼ ἐν τῷ ἐπανέρχεσθαί με ἀποδώσω σοι). Oakman estimates that two denarii represent around three weeks' worth of food for one person or about one percent of an ancient Palestinian family's budget and represents a substantial amount.[20] The Samaritan is willing to pay for all future expenses incurred, no limitations or strings attached. Bornkamm comments that we have no parade of religion and no sentimentality. The Samaritan is careful with his money. He leaves the innkeeper nothing more than what is necessary.[21]

10:36 "Which of these three, do you think, proved to be a neighbor to the man who fell among the robbers?" (τίς τούτων τῶν τριῶν

πλησίον δοκεῖ σοι γεγονέναι τοῦ ἐμπεσόντος εἰς τοὺς λῃστάς;). Many have pointed out that a shift takes place between the first question asked by the lawyer and this question asked by Jesus. The lawyer's question asked, "Who is my neighbor [whom I must love]?" The neighbor is an object. Jesus asks, "Who became neighbor to the man who was victimized by the robbers?" The neighbor is now a subject who acts.

Many have suggested that this was a redactional slip on Luke's part, but they completely miss the significance of this deliberate change. The shift from neighbor as object to neighbor as subject is just the point: "As long as the neighbor remains an object, the issue remains a legal one: What are the limits of my responsibility? Who must I help? How much must I help him?"[22] By changing the question, Jesus requires the lawyer to answer it from the perspective of the waylaid man, from the inferior position of the one who needs help. It reflects the twists that one finds in so many of Jesus' parables. The lawyer's question was asked from the perspective of assumed superiority. My group gets to decide who qualifies as our neighbor and whom we should help.

The way Jesus tells this parable sets up a surprise. The original hearers would not have identified with the clerics and expected the hero to be the third element in the tripartite formula, "priests, Levites, Israelites." They were prepared for the merciful man to be an Israelite. In fact, the Jewish scholar Claude Montefiore contends that the original series indeed was priest, Levite, and Israelite, because he claims that the reference to a Samaritan destroys the logical order![23] The original audience

19. Derrett, *Law in the New Testament*, 220.

20. D. E. Oakman, "The Buying Power of Two Denarii: A Comment on Luke 10:35," *Forum* 3 (1987): 33 – 38.

21. Günther Bornkamm, *Jesus of Nazareth* (trans. I. McCluskey, F. McCluskey, and J. M. Robinson; New York: Harper & Row, 1960), 110.

22. Walter Wink, "The Parable of the Compassionate Samaritan: A Communal Exegesis Approach," *RevExp* 76 (1979): 212 – 13.

23. Claude G. Montefiore, *The Synoptic Gospels* (2nd ed.; New York: Ktav, repr. 1968) 2:467. He claims that it is no less strange than the order, "Priest, Deacon and Frenchman" would be to us.

most certainly would *not* have identified with the Samaritan as we who are so familiar with the parable's punch line do. The only person left in the story with whom they could have identified was the man in the ditch coming down from Jerusalem. The lawyer asked, "What must I do to inherit eternal life?" The parable shifts the question to, "From whom will I accept ministry? Will I accept it from an impure, heretic Samaritan?"[24] The original Jewish audience must enter the ditch and accept a Samaritan as a savior, helper, and healer. They must experience being touched by this unclean enemy who treats a wounded man as a compatriot.[25]

The different vantage point requires that one sees "something positive not in one's own self but in an 'other' who becomes a potential care-giver to oneself."[26] When one needs to be the recipient of mercy, group boundaries become unimportant. If the parable were changed so that a Samaritan was the victim and a Jewish person stopped to assist him, it would simply be a case of *noblesse oblige*: noble rank requires benevolent and honorable conduct. The Jew would be reaching beneath him to an unequal (see such a story in *Qoh. Rab.* 11.1).

10:37 He said, "The one who acted with mercy toward him." Jesus said, "Go and do likewise" (ὁ δὲ εἶπεν· ὁ ποιήσας τὸ ἔλεος μετ᾽ αὐτοῦ. εἶπεν δὲ αὐτῷ ὁ Ἰησοῦς· πορεύου καὶ σὺ ποίει ὁμοίως). The lawyer may not be able to identify who his neighbor is, but he can recognize an act of neighborliness. Because of his deep-seated prejudice, he cannot bring himself to say "the Samaritan" but employs a circumlocution, which drives home the point. The neighbor is someone who acts with compassion and mercy to assist someone in need. It prevents one from defining neighbor as someone whom we must love, which, in effect, reinforces group boundaries. Group divisions and hostilities remain hard and fast if one says, "Even such a one as this requires my help." The shock is that this lawyer must learn a positive lesson from the behavior exhibited by a Samaritan and a negative lesson from that of a priest and a Levite.

The Greek idiom, translated literally, reads "he did mercy with him" (see 1:58, 72). This idiom is reflected in the English wording "compassion, suffering with." English speakers tend to think in terms of doing mercy *to* or *on* another. Showing mercy, however, is something that is to be done *with* people and always makes us vulnerable. For the Samaritan, it meant getting down in the ditch with the victim, getting bloody lifting the man up, walking while another who cannot walk rides, reaching into one's own pocket to pay for another, and risking never being appreciated and perhaps still being hated for all the trouble.

The emphasis in the dialogue framing the parable falls on how to act and the behavior of the Samaritan becomes an example. The verb "to do" (ποιεῖν) is prominent: "What must I *do*?" (10:25); "*do* this and you shall live" (10:28); "the one *doing* [acting with] mercy" (10:37); and the final command, "go and *do* likewise" (10:37). In the parable itself no mention is made of the recovery of the wounded man. Did he lose an eye? Did he change his attitude toward Samaritans? The center of attention is solely on the Samaritan as the one who embodies and therefore teaches the meaning of the law of the love of neighbor, and one must emulate this behavior to have eternal life. It is not simply a matter of reading and reciting but of doing.

24. Robert A. J. Gagnon ("A Second Look at Two Lukan Parables: Reflections on the Unjust Steward and the Good Samaritan," *HBT* 20 [1998]: 1) argues that the parable's shock is lost on modern obtuse readers because of familiarity, and they will situate themselves at the wrong vantage point and identify "with the most sympathetic character in the story." The result is that hearers will be "less likely to be jolted out of complacent notions of how God acts in the world."

25. Wink, "The Parable of the Compassionate Samaritan," 212.
26. Gagnon, "A Second Look," 7.

Theology in Application

1. Eternal Life

If pressed logically, the lawyer's question about how to "inherit" eternal life is pointless. One does not *do* anything to inherit something; one either is or is not an heir.[27] But the question exposes a self-centered concern about ensuring one's own salvation. Jesus' parable focuses on someone who is concerned with saving the life of another. The question also reflects a misconception about eternal life. It views it as something that happens after death as a reward for a life of good deeds. According to Jesus, eternal life is a relationship with God (see esp. John 6:47, 54, 68; 10:27 – 28; 17:3) that begins in this life.

2. Loving God

The command to love the neighbor is linked to the command to love God. The parable would say, if we do not show love to all humanity, we can hardly claim to have loved God (see 1 John 3:14 – 18; 4:8, 10 – 12, 20 – 21). Instead of asking, "Who is my neighbor?" the lawyer should be asking, "Who is God?" Who does God want to benefit with the reign of God?

The lawyer's question, "Who is my neighbor?" reveals that he lives in an ethical/theological system of codified do's and don'ts. That is the way he wants it, because in a system of precise boundaries he can "justify" himself before God and man. He wants an annotated book of regulations and is unconcerned that such a closed system closes him off from his fellow human beings and from real fellowship with God. The account begins with his asking the wrong question, "What must I do to inherit eternal life?"

We may ask a similar question differently, "Why should I want to be like the Samaritan?" The answer might be that we want to do what is required to inherit eternal life so that we can justify ourselves and be commended just like the lawyer. The Samaritan asked no questions. When he saw the wounded man, he could have asked himself, "What's in it for me?" or "Whoever got him may still be in the vicinity. What will happen to me?" If one begins with the wrong questions, one will get the wrong answers. The reign of God is present when one is concerned about the suffering of others and not just one's own advantage.

3. Loving the Neighbor

This parable is often labeled an "example story," but this characterization "can lead interpreters astray, making them think that the parable intends simply to provide a

---

27. Bailey, *Through Peasant Eyes*, 35.

model for humanitarian compassion rather than to answer the question posed by the lawyer who approached Jesus: 'Who is my neighbor?' "[28] The parable's answer is that the neighbor is the one we decided beforehand cannot be my neighbor. The question itself implies that there is such a thing as a non-neighbor; the parable says there is no such person. The kingdom of God leads people to recognize the kin-dom of life. In the parable, all the characters are fellow travelers on a dangerous road.

The parable reveals that "one cannot say in advance who the neighbor is but that the course of life will make this plain enough."[29] Montefiore writes: "Love, it [the parable] tells us, must know no limits of race and ask no enquiry. Who needs me is my neighbour. Whom at the given time and place I can help with my active love, he is my neighbour and I am his."[30] Another Jewish scholar, Leo Baeck, writes about "our fellow man": "All of our yearning and our prayer includes him, for he is our brother, the child of God, united with us in our eternal origin and in the path along which we are commanded to proceed."[31]

The parable could just as well be entitled "The Traveler Beaten to a Pulp and in Need of a Neighbor." When one is lying half dead in a ditch, one views who one's neighbor is quite differently. Trudinger writes: "The lawyer in his superiority had to learn that the neighbor is the one who comes to us in our need. Only when we have known ourselves as ministered unto can we truly minister to others in the spirit of the Good Samaritan."[32]

Gagnon understands this point: "It is the beaten man on the road who must ask '*Who is my neighbor?*' not the Samaritan."[33] When one is at ground zero and if one hopes to survive, one cannot be choosy about one's rescuers. This point has theological ramifications. The Jewish victim does not consent to the Samaritan's ministrations. He submits because he has no other alternative. Scott states: "Grace comes to those who have no other alternative than to accept it. He is so low he cannot help but receive it."[34] Funk avers, "All who are truly victims, truly disinherited, have no choice but to give themselves up to mercy."[35] It becomes a parable of divine mercy expressed through a stranger. Will one accept mercy from one like Jesus who dies on a cross?

4. The So-Called "Good" Samaritan

The Samaritan is not called "good" in the parable but has become the "good" Samaritan in the course of its retelling. The "good" Samaritan has become synonymous with someone who helps another in trouble. But that term is pejorative because it

28. Craig L. Blomberg, *Interpreting the Parables* (Downers Grove, IL: InterVarsity Press, 1990), 75 – 76.

29. Heinrich Greeven, "πλησίον," *TDNT*, 6:317.

30. Montefiore, *The Synoptic Gospels*, 2:468.

31. Leo Baeck, *The Essence of Judaism* (trans. Victor Grubenwieser and Leonard Pearl; New York: Schocken, 1948), 213.

32. L. P. Trudinger, "Once Again, Now, 'Who Is My Neighbour?'" *EvQ* 48 (1976): 161.

33. Gagnon, "A Second Look," 6.

34. Bernard B. Scott, *Hear Then the Parable: A Commentary on the Parables of Jesus* (Minneapolis: Fortress, 1989), 31.

35. Robert W. Funk, "The Good Samaritan as Metaphor," *Semeia* 2 (1974): 79.

implies that he is different from other Samaritans. The adjective "good" stereotypes members of an out group as if they were all the same with this one exception. The question could be raised: Is he good because he stopped or did he stop because he is good? The reality is that he stopped because he obeyed God's command. "Love your neighbor" is not a slogan or a proverb but a divine command.

The parable reveals that love requires self-expenditure for another in need. One cannot say, "I love you, brother," unless one is willing to help in spite of the cost (see John 15:13). The Samaritan risked his life for an unknown person; "to fulfill the command to love God and neighbor, one must often become the Samaritan, the outsider taking a risk in a hostile world."[36]

5. Changing the Face of the Enemy

All cultures have stereotypical images of their enemies. The enemy is the other, the one who is strange. Our enemy is also perceived to be God's enemy. Lamott sagely writes, "You can safely assume you've created God in your own image when it turns out that God hates all the same people you do."[37] This story destroys the Jewish stereotype of the Samaritan as enemy. But it has lost its punch over the centuries. Who in the Western world hates Samaritans today? Substitute a contemporary hated enemy for the Samaritan in the story and it regains it. Bailey confesses that in twenty years of ministry among Middle Eastern Arab Christians he never "had the courage to tell a story to Palestinians about a noble Israeli, nor a story about the noble Turk to the Armenians."[38] When this image becomes reality, it reveals what it means for the reign of God to be in our midst (17:21). When Samaritans help Jews, and Jews abandon their prejudices and embrace their enemies, the kingdom of God is in their midst.[39]

36. John R. Donahue, *The Gospel in Parable: Metaphor, Narrative and Theology in the Synoptic Gospels* (Philadelphia: Fortress, 1988), 134.

37. Anne Lamott, *Bird by Bird: Some Instructions on Writing*

and Life (New York: Anchor, 1995), 22.

38. Bailey, *Through Peasant Eyes*, 48.

39. Wink, "The Parable of the Compassionate Samaritan," 214.

Luke 10:38 – 42

Literary Context

John's gospel has Mary and Martha living in Bethany (John 11:1), two miles outside of Jerusalem (John 11:18). Luke appears to be deliberately ambiguous about the name of their village, "a certain village," because he knows that it is chronologically out of place. Jesus has barely started his long journey to Jerusalem, and it would disrupt the journey motif if Jesus were to arrive so soon at the outskirts of Jerusalem. Luke has apparently moved up an incident associated with Bethany for a purpose, as he did the Nazareth episode. Why he has done so is not easy to discover, but it is important to ask why this account appears where it does. It reinforces the climax of the transfiguration scene in which God booms: "This is my Son, the Chosen One. Listen to him!" (9:35). But what is its relationship to the good Samaritan parable?

Marshall thinks Luke "omitted the name because he does not regard Jesus as being near Jerusalem at this point."[1] Kilgallen counters that this conclusion simply "underlines the problem" about why this incident is placed here. He thinks that Luke has "more likely reduced the known, but inopportune village, to the unknown."[2]

In the context, Jesus rejoiced in the Holy Spirit and thanked God that "these things" have been hidden from the wise and revealed to "infants" (10:21). He then asserted that "all things" have been handed over to him by the Father "and no one knows who the Son is except the Father, and who the Father is except the Son and whomever the Son wills to reveal him" (10:22). He then pronounced the disciples "blessed ... for I tell you, many prophets and kings wanted to see what you see and they did not see it, and to hear what you hear and they did not hear it" (10:23 – 24). The disciples are blessed because what they hear and see far surpasses the blessings granted "the most privileged of history."[3] Mary is, therefore, in an extraordinary position with an extraordinary opportunity (10:42) as Jesus reveals the Father to her through his teaching. Luke places the story in its present location "to emphasize the supreme importance" he attaches "to the teaching of Jesus."[4]

Juxtaposing this story with the parable of the Samaritan clarifies the latter's meaning.[5] The Samaritan's actions were motivated by his feelings of compassion. In the popular mind, he was a good Samaritan, and his actions have been divorced from the teaching of the Lord. Kilgallen points out:

> Possibly the conclusion might be drawn that moral action is motivated by one's feelings. With this troublesome possibility in view, Luke followed the Good Samaritan story with the proper motivation of all moral decision: the word of the Lord. Thus, one can conclude that 10, 25 – 37 and 38 – 42 belong together so that the latter corrects a possible misunderstanding of the former.[6]

The God of Jesus Christ is also the God of Moses, and the commandments of the God of Moses must be obeyed. But these commandments must be interpreted aright, and Jesus is the one who interprets them aright and who must be obeyed. The *teaching of Jesus* is to govern moral action.

IV. Jesus' Journey to Jerusalem (9:51 – 19:28)
   A. On Being Disciples (9:51 – 10:42)
      3. The Parable of the Merciful Samaritan (10:25 – 37)
      4. Mary and Martha (10:38 – 42)
   B. On Prayer (11:1 – 13)
      1. The Model Prayer (11:1 – 4)

Main Idea

Listening to the teaching of Jesus is the most important component of discipleship because it determines how one should serve.

Translation

(See next page.)

---

4. Ibid., 559.   6. Ibid.
5. Ibid., 560.

Luke 10:38–42

10:38a	Travel notice	When they were on their way,
		he entered a certain village,
b	Character introduction	**and a woman by the name of Martha welcomed him into her home.**
39a	Character introduction	**She had a sister named Mary**
b	Posture in relation to Jesus	who sat at the Lord's feet, listening to his word.
40a	Posture in relation to Jesus	**Martha was distracted by all the service.**
b	Complaint	**She came and said,**
		"Lord, do you not care that my sister has left me all alone to serve?
c		*Tell her to help me!"*
41	Rebuke	**The Lord answered her,**
		"Martha, Martha, you are worried and fret about many things.
42	Affirmation	*One thing is essential.*
		For Mary has chosen the best portion, which shall not be taken away from her."

Structure and Literary Form

Martha is the subject of three finite verbs and one participle and is the focus of the account. Mary silently sets the example by sitting at Jesus' feet, listening to his teaching. The structure alternates between the two sisters and highlights the contrast of their different choices. Martha offers hospitality to Jesus (10:38); Mary sits and listens to Jesus (10:39). Martha scurries about with her duties (10:40a) and complains to Jesus about Mary abandoning her and her duties (10:40b). Martha wants Jesus to tell Mary to help her (10:40c). Jesus chides Martha (10:41) and utters a pronouncement that commends Mary's choice (10:42).

Exegetical Outline

➡ I. Martha's attentive hospitality for Jesus (10:38)

II. Mary's attentive listening to Jesus' teaching (10:39)

III. Complaint about Mary's inaction (10:40)

IV. Jesus' response about the one essential thing (10:41 – 42)

    A. Distraction from service (10:41)

    B. The one essential thing: listening to the teaching of Jesus (10:42)

Explanation of the Text

10:38 When they were on their way, he entered a certain village, and a woman by the name of Martha welcomed him into her home (ἐν δὲ τῷ πορεύεσθαι αὐτοὺς αὐτὸς εἰσῆλθεν εἰς κώμην τινά· γυνὴ δέ τις ὀνόματι Μάρθα ὑπεδέξατο αὐτόν). The hospitality offered this itinerant preacher is what Jesus says the disciples sent out on mission must accept (10:5–7). Since Martha welcomed (ὑπεδέξατο) Jesus into her home, it is assumed that this is Martha's home (see 19:6; Acts 17:7). Her cordial reception of Jesus fits the theme of hospitality (10:4–12). She does what was expected for her honored guest (see Jesus' complaints against the Pharisee in 7:36–50). Guests bring obligations in hospitality, and she pulls out all the stops.

10:39 She had a sister named Mary who sat at the Lord's feet, listening to his word (καὶ τῇδε ἦν ἀδελφὴ καλουμένη Μαριάμ, [ἣ] καὶ παρακαθεσθεῖσα πρὸς τοὺς πόδας τοῦ κυρίου ἤκουεν τὸν λόγον αὐτοῦ). Male space and female space were divided in the ancient world, and males and females usually did not intermingle even in the home. Women only crossed into the male world to wait on men and then retreated (unless they were elderly or prostitutes).

The idiom "to sit at someone's feet" meant to study with that person or to become his disciple. Paul, for example, says that he was brought up in Jerusalem at the feet of Gamaliel (Acts 22:3), referring to his education (see Luke 8:35). Listening is necessary for faith to begin (5:1) and leads to discipleship if the Word is held fast (8:11–21; 6:47; 11:28).

10:40 Martha was distracted by all the service. She came and said, "Lord, do you not care that my sister has left me all alone to serve? Tell her to help me!" (ἡ δὲ Μάρθα περιεσπᾶτο περὶ πολλὴν διακονίαν. ἐπιστᾶσα δὲ εἶπεν, κύριε, οὐ μέλει σοι ὅτι ἡ ἀδελφή μου μόνην με κατέλιπεν διακονεῖν; εἰπὲ οὖν αὐτῇ ἵνα μοι συναντιλάβηται). "All the service" (πολλὴν διακονίαν, lit., "much service") in itself is not bad (see 22:24–27). The problem is that the chores associated with waiting on her guest cause her to be "distracted" or "pulled away" (περιεσπᾶτο). Jesus identifies what she is pulled away from in the climax, "the one essential thing." This surprising indictment suggests that the growth of the Word can be choked by well-intentioned overactivity as much as by "cares and riches and the pleasures of life" (8:14).

Martha addresses Jesus as "Lord," but she admonishes him. From her perspective, her sister Mary is out of her proper place and breaching social conventions. She has crossed that social divide and does what her sister deems inappropriate. It prompts her to grumble, "Why are you not bustling about with me where you belong?" Instead of having a private word with Mary or giving her a meaningful look, Martha wipes her dishpan hands on her apron and complains directly to Jesus about her do-nothing sister. Ironically, Martha addresses Jesus as "Lord," but it is Mary "who sits at Jesus' feet and listens to his word, in her position and receptiveness suggesting at least an inchoate awareness of her guest's identity."[7]

10:41 The Lord answered her, "Martha, Martha, you are worried and fret about many things" (ἀποκριθεὶς δὲ εἶπεν αὐτῇ ὁ κύριος· Μάρθα Μάρθα, μεριμνᾷς καὶ θορυβάζῃ περὶ πολλά). Martha expects Jesus to reprove her sister and shoo her back into the kitchen where she belongs.

7. Rowe, *Early Narrative Christology*, 149.

Instead, he reproaches Martha.[8] How is it that one can do everything right and still be wrong? Martha intended to show Jesus love by serving him but fails when she allows her exertion to become a distraction. She also blunders when she criticizes the different service of her sister. Martha wants Mary to be like her, judges her (see 6:41–42), and foreshadows the elder brother's complaint about his sibling, "This is unfair!" (15:25–32). She might respond to Jesus' rebuke, "That evil sister has swayed another person with her charm," but she remains silent.

Alexander charts the contrast between the two sisters:[9]

Mary	Martha
sits at Jesus' feet	welcomes Jesus: serves
listens to Jesus' words	distracted: full of cares and troubled
one thing	many things
the needful thing (commended)	implied: unnecessary things (rebuked)
quietly listens = discipleship role	working in kitchen = women's work and fussing

10:42 "One thing is essential. For Mary has chosen the best portion, which shall not be taken away from her" (ἑνὸς δέ ἐστιν χρεία· Μαριὰμ γὰρ τὴν ἀγαθὴν μερίδα ἐξελέξατο ἥτις οὐκ ἀφαιρεθήσεται αὐτῆς).[10] The word "for" (γάρ) introduces a reason for something that is

unexpressed in Jesus' response to Martha's complaint: "No, I am not concerned about your sister leaving you alone and I will not tell your sister to return to you — for she has chosen a good (better, best) part, which will not be taken from her."[11] "Portion" (μερίς) is used for a portion of food (Gen 43:34; Deut 18:8; 1 Sam 1:4) and also in a metaphorical sense: "You are my portion, LORD; I have promised to obey your words" (Ps 119:57; see also 16:5).

The rendering "the best portion" (τὴν ἀγαθὴν μερίδα) assumes that the positive adjective "good" is used in the place of a superlative adjective, though it could also be in the place of a comparative adjective ("better"). This pronouncement may provide another answer to the lawyer's question, "What must I do to inherit eternal life?" (10:25). The noun "portion" can also be used synonymously for "inheritance": "The Lord is the portion (μερίς) of my inheritance (κληρονομίας) and of my cup" (Ps 15:5 LXX).[12] Alexander comments:

> On the surface, Martha is making a mistake common to hosts: she is in danger of getting so bogged down in the details of hospitality that she forgets the point of the whole exercise, which is to enjoy the company of your guest. This would be a mistake for any host, and with any guest: to that extent, the story, like 14:7–11, works as simply as a piece of advice on etiquette. When the guest is Jesus, however, the mistake assumes cosmic proportions: Martha is in danger of "missing the point" which of all points must not be missed.[13]

---

8. The repetition of her name adds emphasis (see 6:46; 8:24; 13:34; 22:31; 23:21; Acts 9:4; 22:7; 26:14).

9. Slightly adapted from Loveday Alexander, "Sisters in Adversity: Retelling Martha's Story," in *Women in the Biblical Tradition* (Studies in Women and Religion 31; ed. G. J. Brooke; Lewiston, NY: Mellen, 1992), 172.

10. Verses 41–42 contain interesting textual variants, but the key one relates to the phrase "one thing is essential" (ἑνὸς δέ ἐστιν χρεία), which has early and widespread attestation.

The variants reflect confusion over its meaning, which is crucial for understanding the meaning of the incident: (1) "but few things are needful, or [really] only one"; (2) Codex Bezae (D) omits the phrase; and (3) other Western versions omit vv. 41b–42a altogether.

11. John J. Kilgallen, "A Suggestion Regarding *gar* in Luke 10,42," *Bib* 73 (1992): 255–58.

12. Heil, *The Meal Scenes in Luke-Acts*, 76.

13. Alexander, "Sisters in Adversity," 181.

Theology in Application

Thomas Merton claims that in this Mary-Martha episode, "the superiority of contemplation over action is explicitly stated there."[14] The incident, however, does not contrast activity with meditation. Fitzmyer says, "To read this episode as a commendation of contemplative life over against active life is to allegorize it beyond recognition and to introduce a distinction that was born only of later preoccupations."[15] After all, Jesus berates the Pharisee for failing to offer him proper hospitality (7:36 – 50), so he is not censuring Martha for paying attention to this important duty. She is scolded not for hustling and bustling but for fretting and fussing.

Martha functions as the mistress of the house and is distracted by the requirements to manage her household for this important guest. Like the Pharisees, who conscientiously tithe garden herbs while neglecting justice and the love of God (11:42), she is in danger of majoring in minors and passing over what is of chief importance. She needs to learn "to clarify between two important virtues, one being to receive the master and the other being to learn from the teacher."[16] She needs knowledge and insight to help her discern what is best (Phil 1:9 – 10).

Kilgallen argues that this passage confirms the teaching of the "one thing necessary" in the preceding story of the Samaritan. Luke shows that to love God, one must listen to Jesus' words. Hearing is the precondition for doing, and action is the proof of the hearing.[17] "One thing is essential" refers to hearing the Word of God. Mary made the right choice despite the social expectations and pressures. This episode does not teach that sitting down and listening is superior to scurrying about. The previous parable of the Samaritan who shows compassion teaches to "go and do likewise" (10:37). But one is to go and do what Jesus teaches, which requires sitting down and listening to him.

Santayana's "Sonnet III" begins, "O world, Thou choosest not the better part!" This judgment accords with Jesus' assessment of Martha's choice, but the poem uses images of inward vision and a pathway lit one step ahead by a smoky torch of our knowledge to describe how to choose "the better part." By contrast, in Luke, the one who leads us down the better pathway is Jesus, who shines the light ahead, and "divine thought" is taught only by him, not simply by "the soul's invincible surmise."[18] Sadly, the world mostly chooses different guides and different paths, but those paths lead only to despair and destruction.

---

14. Thomas Merton, *Entering the Silence: Becoming a Monk and Writer, The Journals of Thomas Merton, II (1941 – 52)* (ed. J. Montaldo; San Francisco: Harper, 1996), 347. He argues, however, that no opposition exists "between contemplation and activity when they are properly ordered."

15. Fitzmyer, *Luke*, 2:893.

16. Bart J. Koet and Wendy E. S. North, "The Image of Martha in Luke 10,38 – 42 and John 11,1 – 12,8," in *Miracles*

and *Imagery in Luke and John: Festschrift Ulrich Busse* (ed. J. Verheyden, G. Van Belle, and J. G. Van der Watt; BETL 218; Leuven: Peeters, 2008), 65.

17. Ludger Feldkämper, *Der betende Jesus als Heilsmittler nach Lukas* (Veröffentlichungen des Missionspriesterseminars St. Augustin 29; St Augustin: Steyler, 1978), 185.

18. George Santayana, *Poems* (Charleston, SC: BiblioLife, 2009), 5.

Luke 11:1 – 13

Literary Context

Luke has joined together three pericopes and an exhortation to create a unit on prayer. This teaching on prayer is set up by a disciple observing Jesus at prayer and asking him to teach them to pray as John had taught his disciples. It is not directly related to what precedes or follows except for its theme. Jesus' life is undergirded by prayer throughout the narrative, and his devotion to prayer becomes a model for disciples to imitate.

The evidence from Acts reveals that disciples do learn the lesson, and it sustains them when they are sent out on their mission under the power of the Holy Spirit (Acts 1:14, 24; 4:31; 6:6; 7:59; 8:15; 9:11, 40; 11:5; 12:5, 12; 13:3; 16:25; 20:36; 21:5; 27:29; 28:8). The gift of the Holy Spirit that caps the unit as the supreme answer to the disciple's prayer (Luke 11:13) also ties into mission. The Holy Spirit will teach them what they need to say in stressful situations as they stand in the prisoner's dock (12:12).

IV. Jesus' Journey to Jerusalem (9:51 – 19:28)
   A. On Being Disciples (9:51 – 10:42)
→ **B. On Prayer (11:1 – 13)**
   1. The Model Prayer (11:1 – 4)
   2. The Parable of the Reluctant Neighbor (11:5 – 10)
   3. The Parable of the Father Who Gives What His Child Needs (11:11 – 13)
   C. Jesus and Beelzebul; Light and Darkness (11:14 – 36)

Main Idea

Disciples can pray with confidence because God as their Father can be trusted fully to bestow good gifts that they need. God will give them the greatest gift of all, the Holy Spirit.

Translation

Luke 11:1–13

11:1a	Circumstance	**Now it happened that he was in a certain place praying.**
b	Request	When he finished,
		one of his disciples said to him,
		"Lord, teach us to pray, just as John taught his disciples."
2a	Response	**He said to them,**
		"Whenever you pray, say:
b	Address	Father,
c	Petitions related to the Father	let your name be sanctified,
d		your reign come.
3	Petitions related to one's needs	Give us each day our daily bread.
4a		Forgive us our sins
b		as we ourselves forgive everyone in debt to us.
c		Do not bring us into testing."
5a	Hyperbolic illustration	**And he said to them,**
b	Request	"Who of you will have a friend
		and you go to him in the middle of the night and say to him,
c		'Friend, lend me three loaves of bread!
6	Reason	Because my friend has shown up at my house from his⤸ journey,
		and I have nothing to set before him.'
7a	Response	*And* that one will answer from within,
		'Do not trouble me!
b	Reason	The door is already bolted
		and my children are with me in bed!
		I am not able to get up and give you anything!'?
8	Conclusion	I tell you,
		though he will not get up to give anything to him because⤸ he is his friend, indeed,
		because of his shamelessness
		he will get up and give to him whatever he needs."
9a	Exhortation	"*And* I tell you,
b		ask, *and* it will be given to you,
c		seek, *and* you shall find,
d		knock, *and* it shall be opened to you.
10a	Reason	*For* everyone who asks receives,
b		*and* everyone who seeks finds,
c		*and* for everyone who knocks it shall be opened."

Continued on next page.

11a	Hyperbolic illustration	*"What father among you*
b	Request	*whose son* *asks for a fish*
c	Response	*will give him a snake instead of a fish?*
12a	Request	*Or,* *if he asks for an egg,*
b	Response	*will give him a scorpion?*
13a	Conclusion	*Therefore,* *if you who are evil know how☞*
		to give good gifts to your children,
b		*how much more will the Father in heaven give the Holy Spirit to those who☞ ask him?"*

Continued from previous page.

Structure and Literary Form

God as Father is stressed at the beginning (11:2) and at the end (11:13) of the unit on prayer. The request for bread, representing the basic necessities of life, appears in the Lord's Prayer and in both parables. After the address, "Father," the prayer has two third person singular petitions related to God, that God's name be honored by all and that his reign be realized so that he rules over all. It is followed with three second person singular petitions related to the disciples' needs in living their life in faithful service to God.

The model prayer is supplemented by two hyperbolic illustrations (11:5 – 8, 11 – 13) that argue from the lesser to the greater and surround an exhortation to pray (11:9 – 10). Both illustrations begin with a question that assumes a far-fetched situation. No friend would be such a crank as to turn down an urgent, legitimate request to help a neighbor fulfill a sacred duty, no matter how he might be tempted to try to put him off with weak excuses. No father would give his child something harmful or even deadly, a snake or a scorpion, instead of the food that his hungry child needs and requests.

Both parables illustrate why one can expect God to answer prayer. If a grumpy, sleepy neighbor will answer an urgent request at an inopportune hour, how much more will God answer prayer! If a father who belongs to our sinful race will give to his child what is requested and needed, how much more will the Father in heaven give to his children what is most needed! The exhortation to prayer states a principle that further underscores why disciples can approach God in prayer, humbly confident that God will answer.

Exegetical Outline

➤ **I. Jesus' habit of prayer (11:1)**

    A. Observation by disciples (11:1a)

    B. A disciple's request to be taught how to pray (11:1b)

II. The Model Prayer (11:2 – 4)

    A. Address: Father (11:2a-b)

    B. Petitions related to God (11:2c-d)

        1. Let your name be sanctified (11:2c)

        2. Your reign come (11:2d)

    C. Petitions for ourselves (11:3 – 4)

        1. Request for daily sustenance (11:3)

        2. Request for forgiveness (11:4a-b)

        3. Request not to be led into testing (11:4c)

III. Parable of the reluctant neighbor (11:5 – 8)

IV. Exhortation to pray (11:9 – 10)

V. Parable of the father who gives what his child needs (11:11 – 13)

Explanation of the Text

11:1 Now it happened that he was in a certain place praying. When he finished, one of his disciples said to him, "Lord, teach us to pray, just as John taught his disciples" (καὶ ἐγένετο ἐν τῷ εἶναι αὐτὸν ἐν τόπῳ τινὶ προσευχόμενον. ὡς ἐπαύσατο, εἶπέν τις τῶν μαθητῶν αὐτοῦ πρὸς αὐτόν· κύριε, δίδαξον ἡμᾶς προσεύχεσθαι, καθὼς καὶ Ἰωάννης ἐδίδαξεν τοὺς μαθητὰς αὐτοῦ). That Jesus prays (3:21; 5:16; 6:12; 9:18, 28) makes it clear that he is dependent on God's help and direction. Also, it shows that he is not a magician working a sorcerer's tricks in healing others. His power comes from God.

In contrast to Matthew's account of the Lord's Prayer, which appears as part of Jesus' teaching in the Sermon on the Mount, Luke reports that Jesus was praying and that one of his disciples requested that he teach them to pray, just as John had taught his disciples. It is not that the disciples do not know how to pray. Luke wishes to underscore that Jesus' disciples are impressed with the example of Jesus' prayer life.

Luke often mentions that Jesus was alone praying (4:42) or teaching about prayer. Luke alone records that Jesus was praying when the heavens opened at his baptism, the Holy Spirit descended on him, and the voice declared, "You are my Son" (3:21 – 22). Jesus was also praying when he withdrew to the wilderness before his first clash with the Jewish leaders (5:16 – 17), when he was about to choose his disciples (6:12 – 16), and when he asked his disciples, "Who do you say I am?" and he made the first announcement of his passion (9:20).

At the transfiguration, Luke alone records that Jesus took Peter, James, and John up the mountain *to pray*; moreover, the appearance of his face changed and his garment became dazzling white *as he was praying* (9:28 – 29). When the seventy returned from their mission, Jesus rejoiced and offered up a prayer of thanksgiving to God

(10:21 – 22). Furthermore, when Jesus informed Peter at the Last Supper that Satan asked to sift him and that Peter would ultimately deny him three times, Jesus also assured him that he had prayed for him so that his faith would not fail (22:31 – 32). Luke also emphasized that Jesus exhorted his disciples to pray that they might not enter into temptation at Gethsemane, and he prayed this same prayer himself (22:40, 46). Luke alone records Jesus' two prayers on the cross (23:34, 46).

Three parables related to prayer appear only in Luke: the parable of the friend who goes to his sleepy neighbor to request some bread for an unexpected guest (11:5 – 8), the parable of the shameless widow who badgers a wicked judge until she gets a judgment in her favor (18:1 – 8), and the parable of the toll collector and the Pharisee praying in the temple (18:9 – 14).

The unnamed disciple in 11:1 wants Jesus to give them a distinctive prayer that would make them stand out. What will make them distinctive, however, is not the content of their prayer but praying as often and intensely as Jesus does and living out the petitions they make.

11:2a He said to them, "Whenever you pray, say" (εἶπεν δὲ αὐτοῖς· ὅταν προσεύχησθε, λέγετε). The differences between the versions of the prayer preserved in Luke, Matt 6:9 – 13, and *Did.* 8:2, and the addition of a doxology found in a textual variant to Matt 6:13 (apparently modeled on 1 Chr 29:11 – 13), along with the various glosses in the textual tradition have provoked a fruitless attempt to discover the original text of the Lord's Prayer. When it comes to liturgical material, such a task

is impossible, since variations would have existed side by side, as they do even today.[1] Dunn correctly attributes the differences to "liturgical usage" that "both conserves and adapts (slowly)."[2] It is best to trace the variations to oral transmission.[3] The "whenever" (ὅταν) suggests that Jesus understood this prayer to be a prototype for all prayer, not something to be recited verbatim with no variation. Jesus intends the model prayer to function like a tuning fork by which disciples can measure whether their prayers are in the right pitch. It is to be used as an outline that those who pray it may fill out with their own words.[4]

The Lord's Prayer has similarities with the Eighteen Benedictions in Jewish tradition, which also was not a fixed prayer but an outline that could be filled in by the one praying (see *m. Ber.* 4:4; *m. Taʿan.* 2:2). The Lord's Prayer is much briefer than the long Eighteen Benedictions and the shorter *Qaddish* prayer that ended synagogue services. There is no proof that, as they have been preserved in rabbinic literature, either existed or were regularly recited in the time of Jesus.[5] The similarities are attributable to typical Jewish concerns and devotional piety and the yearning for God's reign to be established on earth. The differences are notable, however. The *Qaddish* prayer has a lengthy and ecstatic doxology, proclaiming God's greatness, power, and sovereignty. The Lord's Prayer is bolder with its intimate address, omission of any praise of the attributes of God, and inclusion of specific personal requests.

11:2b Father (πάτερ). Jesus addresses God as Father in his prayer in 10:21 and has said that no

---

1. Joseph Heinemann, *Prayer in the Talmud: Forms and Patterns* (SJ 9; Berlin: de Gruyter, 1977), 43.

2. Dunn, *Jesus Remembered*, 227.

3. Betz, *The Sermon on the Mount*, 370 – 71.

4. Gordon J. Bahr, "Use of the Lord's Prayer in the Primitive Church," *JBL* 84 (1965): 153 – 59. Origen (*Prayer* 18.1) describes

the prayer as one "traced in outline" (τὴν ὑπογραφεῖσαν), "sketched out" (ὑποτετυπωμένην) by the Lord.

5. See Emil Schürer, *The History of the Jewish People in the Age of Jesus Christ* (rev. and ed. G. Vermes, F. Millar, and M. Black; Edinburgh: T&T Clark, 1979), 2:456 – 63.

one knows who the Father is except the Son and whomever he has chosen to reveal him. He teaches his disciples to pray to the Father as a father. This simple address to God in prayer differs markedly from pagan prayers, which were long on invocation to get the attention of the god or gods to which they were praying (see 1 Kgs 18:26 – 29). The gods were believed to have different functions and domains of power under different names, and one had to be sure to utter the right name to get any response. It was like trying to select a winning lottery number just to get an audience with the god, who was assumed to be reluctant to respond.

The gods were also believed to be touchy about being addressed properly, and one had to be careful not to offend them. An example of such a prayer appears in Apuleius's *Metamorphoses* 11.2, where the character Lucius appeals to the "blessed Queen of Heaven, whether Thou be the Dame Ceres … whether Thou be the celestial Venus … or whether Thou be the sister of the god Phoebus … or whether Thou be called terrible Proserpine." After each name, he gives a lengthy recital of the deeds and qualities of the goddess. Jesus teaches that simply calling out to God as Father suffices. The petitioner has no need to add on any extra names or to recite any divine exploits to flatter and cajole God into answering.

The term "father" (πάτερ) was used in the family circle not just by little children and was applied even to beloved and revered teachers by their disciples. It was a term of respect and intimacy. Jesus models prayer as conversation with one with whom we have an intimate relationship. It is to be as simple as a child making known his or her requests to a parent, with no need for eloquence or pretense. In Luke, the image of the Father is one of love, mercy (6:36), benevolence (12:30), forgiveness

(23:34), and jubilation over recovery of a lost child (15:11 – 32).

While the address conveys a deep sense of intimacy with God — Jesus knows God as Father in ways that others do not and cannot — it should not be forgotten that God's fatherhood connotes the need for obedience. Jesus' prayers on the cross reveal that he trusts completely in God as his Father and is completely obedient to his will. To address God as Father, as Jesus does, requires that one also learn from him how to be the Father's faithful child.

11:2c Let your name be sanctified (ἁγιασθήτω τὸ ὄνομά σου). In Hebrew thought, the name is virtually equivalent to the thing itself. The divine name reflects what has been revealed to humans about God.[6] Jesus makes God's name known in John 17:26.

The expression "to sanctify God's name" occurs only in Lev 22:32; Isa 29:23; and Ezek 36:23. Who is to sanctify God's name, humankind or God? Ezekiel records the promise that God will sanctify his own name:

> Therefore say to the house of Israel, Thus says the LORD God: It is not for your sake, O house of Israel, that I am about to act, but for the sake of my holy name, which you have profaned among the nations to which you came. I will sanctify my great name, which has been profaned among the nations, and which you have profaned among them; and the nations shall know that I am the LORD, says the LORD God, when through you I display my holiness before their eyes. (Ezek 36:22 – 23 NRSV).

So I will display my greatness and my holiness and make myself known in the eyes of many nations. Then they shall know that I am the

6. Raymond E. Brown, "The *Pater Noster* as an Eschatological Prayer," *TS* 22 (1961): 186.

LORD. (Ezek 38:23 NRSV; see also Ezek 20:41; *2 Bar.* 21:25).

On the one hand, this first petition may express a plea using the divine passive for God to bring to pass what only God can do, to act to vindicate his holiness.[7] Only God can sanctify his name and bring in his reign. The petition would be similar to Jesus' prayer in John 12:28, which uses the active voice, "Father, glorify your name" (see John 13:31). This request petitions God to intervene directly and cause the world to acknowledge his sovereignty. This petition, then, is not answered by the human response of simply revering God's name.

On the other hand, biblical texts also refer to God's people profaning instead of sanctifying (hallowing) God's name (Lev 22:32; Jer 34:16; Amos 2:7). The *Qaddish* prayer has a parallel petition that refers to humans sanctifying God's name, that is, holding it in highest reverence: "His great name may be magnified and hallowed in the world which he has created according to his will" (see Ps 34:3). Recognition of God's holiness requires that God's people lead a holy life (Lev 11:45; 19:2).[8]

This demand ties in with the promises in Ezek 36 that God will sanctify his name as a result of the eschatological action of his Spirit. It will be accomplished through God's gathering the people from the nations (36:24), cleansing them from all their impurity and idolatry (36:25), giving them a new heart and a new spirit (36:26), creating obedience by putting God's Spirit in them (36:27), and reestablishing them in the land (36:28a). When this happens, the covenant promise, "you will be my people, and I will be your God" (Ezek 36:28; 37:27), will become a reality. God also promises that he will make an everlasting covenant of peace with them; "Then the nations will know that I the LORD make Israel holy, when my sanctuary is among them forever" (Ezek 37:28). Stettler concludes: "It follows that the petition 'hallowed be your name' implies nothing less than the recreation or restitution of Israel as a holy people in fulfilment of this prophecy."[9]

The promise in Ezekiel that God will act to sanctify his name, then, creates the proper human response. With the renewal of God's Spirit, humans will no longer profane God's name but sanctify it through their obedience. This connection explains the surprising conclusion in 11:13. The heavenly Father will give the Holy Spirit to those who ask, and the Holy Spirit will create obedience.

If these are petitions for God to act, Gerhardsson asks why more direct expressions were not used in the prayer. Why did Jesus not phrase these petitions: "sanctify your name," "bring your reign," "do your will"?[10] His answer is that the third person passive imperative is a reverential circumlocution that forestalls the impression that humans can dictate to God. But, more significantly, he concludes that had the requests regarding God's name, reign, and will (in Matthew's version) been expressed with active imperatives, it might have appeared "that God alone is to act." The circumlocutions make it easier to draw a connection between God's action and human reaction: "God's mighty works in sanctifying his name, establishing his reign, and realizing his final redemptive purpose demand a suitable human response."[11]

---

7. Caird, *The Language and Imagery of the Bible*, 29. See also Brown, "The *Pater Noster*," 186; Wright, *Jesus and the Victory of God*, 293.

8. "Sanctifying God's name" also becomes an expression for obedience to God's commands and the vocation of God's people in rabbinic literature (Str-B 1:411 – 18). Jesus and the Pharisees differ over what being a holy people entails and how it will come to pass.

9. Stettler, "Sanctification in the Jesus Tradition," 154.

10. Birger Gerhardsson, "The Matthean Version of the Lord's Prayer (Matt 6:9b – 13): Some Observations," in *The New Testament Age* (ed. W. C. Weinrich; Mercer: Mercer Univ. Press, 1984), 2:213.

11. Ibid.

11:2d Your reign come (ἐλθέτω ἡ βασιλεία σου). This petition echoes Zech 14:9, "And the LORD will become king over all the earth; on that day the LORD will be one and his name one" (NRSV). This petition longs for the reign of the evil one to be overthrown. Jesus' ministry reveals that the reign of God has drawn ever nearer, and his healing ministry (with his disciples) reveals that Satan's power over the world is on its last legs (9:11; 10:9).

11:3 Give us each day our daily bread (τὸν ἄρτον ἡμῶν τὸν ἐπιούσιον δίδου ἡμῖν τὸ καθ' ἡμέραν). The request for bread has been spiritualized as early as Origen and Tertullian as a reference to the Word of God or the bread of the Eucharist, but such an interpretation is to be rejected. We are to ask for provisions for the bare necessities to sustain life, and we offer our prayer to God in humble recognition that without his gracious provision we go without.

The word translated "daily" (ἐπιούσιον) is problematic since it does not appear in extant Greek literature before the New Testament. It consists of a prepositional prefix (ἐπί) plus the participle of the verb "to be" (οὔσιον), which means "essential." The prefix does not alter the meaning, so it means "essential bread," and this meaning can be spiritualized to refer to the Bread of Life.[12] It is unlikely, however, that it refers to the bread of the Eucharist, which would be anachronistic in the context, or to future eschatological bread (14:15; 22:29 – 30), which would be simply a rewording of the petition "your reign come." Luke's addition "each day" (τὸ καθ' ἡμέραν) and the present imperative "give us" (δίδου), implying "keep on giving to us," points to a daily ration of material bread, which many in Jesus' world went without. The parable that follows also includes a request for the bread

of subsistence (11:5). For those in impoverished circumstances like Paul, who said he often went without food and other basic necessities (2 Cor 11:27), the petition has more poignancy. Those who face starvation joyfully welcome the gift of bread for today to make it to tomorrow. Those who live with abundance probably would be dissatisfied if God were to grant this petition literally and provide them only with enough to survive on for today and tomorrow.

The petition recalls the gift of manna delivered to Israel in the wilderness: "in the morning you will be filled with bread" (Exod 16:12). Assurance of having bread for the morrow relieves disciples from worrying about what they will eat and drink (Luke 12:22, 29). This request is only for bare subsistence and is akin to praying to receive the minimum wage in our culture. While Jesus is fully mindful that one does not live by bread alone (4:4), Prov 30:8 – 9 provides a rationale for making this petition:

> Remove far from me falsehood and lying;
>> give me neither poverty nor riches;
>> feed me with the food that I need,
> or I shall be full, and deny you,
>> and say, "Who is the LORD?"
> or I shall be poor, and steal,
>> and profane the name of my God. (NRSV)

A Latin-American prayer reveals how this petition can apply to those who lack bread and those who have abundance: "O God, to those who hunger, give bread; and to those who have bread, give the hunger for justice."[13]

11:4a-b Forgive us our sins as we ourselves forgive everyone in debt to us (καὶ ἄφες ἡμῖν τὰς ἁμαρτίας ἡμῶν, καὶ γὰρ αὐτοὶ ἀφίομεν παντὶ

---

12. See Henri Bourgoin, "ἐπιούσιος expliqué par la notion de préfixe vide," *Bib* 60 (1979): 91 – 96; Werner Förster, "ἐπιούσιος," *TDNT*, 2:592 – 95.

13. Cited by Krister Stendahl, "Your Kingdom Come," *Cross Currents* 32 (1982): 263.

ὀφείλοντι ἡμῖν). In 7:41 – 49 Jesus used the language of canceling debts (Deut 15:2) and connected it to the forgiveness of sins. This petition assumes that those who have been forgiven much not only must show their gratitude to God (7:47) but also must forgive debts owed to them.

The communal emphasis of the prayer is evident in the use of the plural ("our sins," τὰς ἁμαρτίας ἡμῶν; contrast Ps 25:18, "take away all my sins"). It is striking to request that God should forgive us as we forgive others (see Sir 28:2 – 7). The present tense of the verb in the phrase "as we ourselves forgive" (ἀφίομεν) suggests that this must become a habitual discipline (see 17:3 – 4). It does not mean that God's forgiveness of us hinges on our forgiving others first. The Lord's Prayer is to affect the distinctive way that disciples live and not just the distinctive way they pray. It has an ethical thrust; we ought not to expect to receive from God what we are not prepared to bestow on others.[14]

This petition reflects a spiritual axiom that if one is not forgiving, one cannot receive forgiveness. A forgiving spirit is the outstretched hand by which we grasp God's forgiveness. When that hand is closed tightly into a fist, it can receive nothing. Being forgiving is "not the ground on which God bestows forgiveness but the ground on which man can receive it."[15] The petitions for bread and forgiveness open up disciples to the future. They are not to be weighed down by anxiety about bread for tomorrow or by the burden of their past.

11:4c Do not bring us into testing (καὶ μὴ εἰσενέγκῃς ἡμᾶς εἰς πειρασμόν). The "testing" is not specified here. Testing can be by God, but it is not considered in Scriptures to be something negative. Discipline and purification are usually the

object, not punishment and destruction (see 1 Pet 1:6 – 7). Some interpreters interpret the testing eschatologically to refer to the time of trial during the "titanic struggle between God and Satan which introduces the last days" (see Rev 3:10), not to the temptations of everyday life.[16] But why pray for God's reign to break into our world and then pray not to be tested, if the trials are part and parcel of the last days? Moreover, no definite article appears before the noun "testing" (πειρασμόν); therefore, it does not refer to *the* test but to a temptation to sin that could occur at any time in life (see 8:13; 22:40, 46). This petition parallels other Jewish prayers: for example, "bring me not into sin, or into iniquity, or into temptation, or into contempt. And may the good inclination have sway over me and let not the evil inclination have sway over me" (b. Ber. 60b; see 11QPs^a 24.10, "Do not … lead me into difficulties").

The problem with this interpretation, which Porter addresses, is that it may imply that God can lead one into temptation, seemingly contradicting Jas 1:13, which argues that God tempts no one but that we bring on our own troubles and downfall.[17] Temptations were viewed by some in Jesus' day as spiritual muscle builders for the faithful (see b. ʿAbod. Zar. 17ab), and it was not improper to place oneself in temptation in order to overcome it.[18] David's prayer, "Test me, LORD, and try me; examine my heart and my mind" (Ps 26:2; see also 139:23 – 24), was interpreted by the rabbis as a request that God test him so that he could be a proved man of God like Abraham, Isaac, and Jacob. Unfortunately, the rabbis said, God sent him Bathsheba as the test, which he failed rather miserably.[19]

Jesus' model takes exactly the opposite approach:

14. Israel Abrahams, *Studies in Pharisaism and the Gospels* (2nd series; Cambridge: Cambridge Univ. Press, 1924), 96.

15. Manson, *Luke*, 135.

16. Brown, "The *Pater Noster*," 204.

17. Stanley E. Porter, "Mt 6:13 and Lk 11:4: 'Lead Us Not into Temptation,'" *ExpTim* 101 (1989 – 90): 359 – 62.

18. Abrahams, *Studies in Pharisaism and the Gospels*, 2:106.

19. Str-B, 1:140 – 41.

Do not test me; I might not be able to hold up. This prayer becomes a humble admission that we are vulnerable and are likely to succumb to any temptation. Jesus does not teach us to pray for strength to hurdle all difficulties that might arise[20] but to avoid them altogether. It contrasts with the attitude of Peter, when Jesus warns him at the Last Supper that he will be "sifted" by Satan. Peter responds, in effect, "Bring it on!" (22:33). By contrast, Jesus' attitude on the Mount of Olives, when he prays for the cup to be removed (22:42), becomes an illustration of what this petition means. The way to be armed against trial is to pray not to be led into trial. This petition prevents us from the danger of triumphalism (see 1 Cor 10:12).[21]

It is more often than not that humans put God to the test, as Ananias and Sapphira did in tempting the Spirit of the Lord with their fraud (Acts 5:9). It is likely that one of them tempted the other with this scheme that proved so disastrous for them. Temptations come from our fellow human beings, and that is part of living in community. We cannot withdraw from the human condition or human society but must learn to withstand the lures of this world, as Jesus did, by being imbued with the knowledge and truth of Scripture.

11:5 – 6 And he said to them, "Who of you will have a friend and you go to him in the middle of the night and say to him, 'Friend, lend me three loaves of bread! Because my friend has shown up at my house from his journey, and I have nothing to set before him'" (καὶ εἶπεν πρὸς αὐτούς· τίς ἐξ ὑμῶν ἕξει φίλον καὶ πορεύσεται πρὸς αὐτὸν μεσονυκτίου καὶ εἴπῃ αὐτῷ· φίλε, χρῆσόν μοι τρεῖς ἄρτους, ἐπειδὴ φίλος μου παρεγένετο ἐξ ὁδοῦ πρός με καὶ οὐκ ἔχω ὃ παραθήσω αὐτῷ). From the context, the expression, "Who of

you…?" anticipates a negative answer from the listener (cf. 11:11; 12:25; 17:7; John 8:46; Jas 2:15 – 16). The question connotes, "Can any of you imagine…?" and expects the answer, "Certainly not!"

The anticipated response occurs in v. 7 and awkwardly includes the unthinkable response of a selfish neighbor. It should be noted that the parable does *not* begin, "Who of you will be so impudent as to disturb your neighbor in the middle of the night with such a request?" but, "Who of you will have a friend who gives this response?" Jesus' listeners are intended to identify with the petitioner, and the question conveys, "Can you imagine going to a neighbor with this request and getting this kind of response?" The obvious answer is "Certainly not!" since anyone from this culture would sense deeply the responsibility to a guest and would also possess a highly developed sense of shame and honor.

In the example, a friend arrives unexpectedly at midnight. It is sometimes claimed that the guest undertook his journey in the evening to avoid the heat of the day, and arrivals at that time of night were not unusual, though most did their travel during the daylight hours (see Judg 19:6 – 9) from fear of demons at night. The arrival at midnight is assumed to be out of the ordinary and quite unexpected, catching the host off guard.

But regardless of what time a guest might arrive, the host must provide proper hospitality if he is to save face. His cupboard, however, is bare, and there are no twenty-four-hour foodmarts to get the needed supplies. In a small village, one would know who had baked bread that day and might have some left over to spare. The loan of bread could be repaid the next day when his wife baked bread. Given Oriental custom, he must serve, and

20. Contra Jean Carmignac, *Recherches sur le 'Notre Pere'* (Paris: Letouzey & Ane, 1969), 236 – 304; 437 – 45; Marshall, *The Gospel of Luke*, 462.

21. Porter, "'Lead Us Not into Temptation,'" 361.

the guest must eat. He must be able to offer a complete unbroken loaf of bread since a partial, used loaf would be a grave insult. Three loaves probably refer to three rolls, enough for one person.[22] He is not asking his friend to cater a banquet.

The average American would likely be too embarrassed to disturb a neighbor at the witching hour of the night unless the house was on fire. Most would hesitate to barge in on their neighbor past midnight to make such a request for food; and we would never make a demand as this man does, "Lend me three loaves," without so much as a "please." We would be more likely to phrase it: "I hate to trouble you at this late hour, but might I bother you for a second." For an Oriental, however, this would indicate distance between you and the other person. They are supposed to be friends. In a close relationship, a request is not prefaced with "please," but "give me" is quite correct.[23] The host asks with confidence because (1) he is not asking for himself but to honor a friend; (2) he is asking a friend, not just any neighbor; (3) he is asking for the bare minimum required for a simple meal; and (4) his guest is not simply his private guest but, from the perspective of the Oriental, a guest of the entire community. One greeted a visitor: "You have honored our village...." From the host's perspective the sleeping neighbor was duty bound to help him fulfill his duty to this guest of the village.[24]

11:7 "And that one will answer from within, 'Do not trouble me! The door is already bolted and my children are with me in bed! I am not able to get up and give you anything!'?" (κἀκεῖνος

ἔσωθεν ἀποκριθεὶς εἴπῃ, μή μοι κόπους πάρεχε· ἤδη ἡ θύρα κέκλεισται, καὶ τὰ παιδία μου μετ᾽ ἐμοῦ εἰς τὴν κοίτην εἰσίν· οὐ δύναμαι ἀναστὰς δοῦναί σοι). The neighbor is tempted to say no to the petitioner. He lives in a simple, peasant one-room house, and the entire family sleeps together in one room. He wants to put off the host with lame excuses. By saying that the door is bolted and his children are asleep with him in bed, he implies that the commotion of removing the timber locking the door will wake them.[25] From the viewpoint of the listener, who highly esteems the obligation of being a host, these would be incredibly silly excuses—a closed door and sleeping children, who were not as prized in their culture as in ours—what nonsense!

Framed as a question, the parable assumes that no one could expect to get this kind of response from a neighbor in such a crisis. In a Western context, which may not value the need to provide hospitality at all hours of the night for unexpected guests, the situation needs to be changed to convey the urgency and sense of duty. It would be like a friend who calls in the middle of the night to say that his wife is in labor, and he needs to get her to the hospital right away but his car won't start. Could he borrow your car? Who of you would say, "I'm sorry I left the car keys in the kids' bedroom and I'm afraid I might wake them up"? No one but the worst cad would come up with such weak excuses to put him off and leave his friend in the lurch during such an emergency. The neighbor does need to raise a ruckus and keep ringing the doorbell, and they do not even need to be friends

---

22. Jeremias, *The Parables of Jesus*, 157.

23. See J. Duncan M. Derrett, "The Friend at Midnight: Asian Ideas in the Gospel of St. Luke," in *Donum Gentilicum: New Testament Studies in Honour of David Daube* (ed. E. Bammel, C. K. Barrett, and W. D. Davies; Oxford: Clarendon, 1978), 81–84.

24. Bailey, *Poet and Peasant*, 123.

25. The term "bed" (κοίτη) often refers to "the marriage bed," but the wife is not mentioned as being in bed with him out of a sense of decorum. One does not say, "I am lying with my wife in bed" (so David Daube, "Shame Culture in Luke," in *Paul and Paulinism: Essays in Honour of C. K. Barrett* [ed. M. D. Hooker and S. G. Wilson; London: SPCK, 1982], 358).

for one to feel the obligation to respond and offer help.

11:8 "I tell you, though he will not get up to give anything to him because he is his friend, indeed, because of his shamelessness, he will get up and give to him whatever he needs" (λέγω ὑμῖν, εἰ καὶ οὐ δώσει αὐτῷ ἀναστὰς διὰ τὸ εἶναι φίλον αὐτοῦ, διά γε τὴν ἀναίδειαν αὐτοῦ ἐγερθεὶς δώσει αὐτῷ ὅσων χρῄζει). The phrase τὴν ἀναίδεια αὐτοῦ is the major sticking point for interpreting the parable. What does ἀναίδεια mean, and which person is the antecedent of "his"?

The traditional view assumes it belongs to the host and refers to his persistence. It fits the context if one translates the present imperatives in the aphorism that follows, "keep on asking," keep on seeking, keep on knocking" (11:9 – 10). It also seems to parallel the parable that depicts the shameless persistence of a widow who pleads her case every day before an unscrupulous judge, who finally capitulates and grants her wish (18:1 – 8), which also is given as a lesson related to prayer. This interpretation assumes that the host will not be put off by these pitiful excuses and will un-blushingly continue to call out or knock until his friend finally relents.[26]

In this understanding, the word ἀναίδεια is interpreted as something positive. Most modern translations render it "persistence." This rendering leads to the interpretation that if one petitions God again and again, eventually God will be moved to action.[27] Jeremias says that the parable reflects "beggar's wisdom."[28] Marshall attempts to mitigate any view that suggests that God needs to be pestered to get an answer. He contends the point is not: "Go on praying because God will eventually respond to importunity; rather it is: Go on praying because God responds graciously to the needs of his children."[29] If persistence can achieve its purpose with an unwilling neighbor, how much more so will our heavenly Father, who is neither grouchy nor wicked, answer us. If one does not receive an immediate response to prayer, one should continue to pray persistently because God is gracious.

The chief problem with this interpretation is the positive meaning attached to the noun ἀναίδεια. In the LXX, Josephus, and Greek papyri and literature, this word always has a negative connotation. Catchpole states: "It is a quality which always calls forth disapproval."[30] Johnson concludes: "In the first century there is no evidence that the word would have been understood as 'importunity' or 'persistence.'"[31] It is possible for this word to mean relentless when there are other grounds in the context that give clues for this rendering. For example, Oppian (*Halieutica* 2.441 – 50) describes the rainbow wrasse that attack a fisherman in large schools, "stinging relentlessly [ἀναίδεσιν], pursuing stubbornly like flies that vex reapers and do not abate their shamelessness [ἀναίδεια] until they die or have tasted the reaper's dusky blood." Snodgrass, utilizing the TLG database, has found 258 occurrences of this term and determines that its usage is "demonstrably *negative* except those places early Christian writers have assigned a positive use in dependence on Luke 11:8."[32] It is not a neutral term and refers to improper conduct, disgrace, and shameless transgression of

---

26. This interpretation would seem to conflict, however, with Jesus' disparagement of pagan prayer: "they think they will be heard because of their many words" (Matt 6:7).

27. Ernst (*Das Evangelium nach Lukas*, 366) says petitioning God again and again will receive its reward.

28. Jeremias, *The Parables of Jesus*, 159 – 60.

29. Marshall, *The Gospel of Luke*, 462.

30. David R. Catchpole, "Q and the Friend at Midnight (Luke xi.5 – 8/9)," *JTS* 34 (1983): 411.

31. A. F. Johnson, "Assurance for Man: The Fallacy of Translating *Anaideia* by 'Persistence' in Luke 11:5 – 8," *JETS* 22 (1979): 127.

32. Klyne Snodgrass, "ἀναίδεια and the Friend at Midnight," *JBL* 116 (1997): 506 – 8.

the boundaries of propriety (see Sir 25:22). Plutarch refers to a carving in the temple of Athena at Sais that warns: "God hates shamelessness" (*Is. Os.* 363F).[33] The negative connotation of the word was probably turned into a positive quality in the translations because translators could not understand how Christians could act shamelessly or impudently when they go to God in prayer. The problem still perplexes modern translators.[34]

Jesus assumes that the request will be granted for one of two possible reasons. A friend will help out a friend in need. Or, if he is not truly a friend, he will help out to avoid shame. Because of the customs of Oriental hospitality, it would not have been regarded audacious to ask a friend for help to fulfill a sacred duty irrespective of the hour of the night. It would have been the worst effrontery for him not to make the attempt to provide his guest with bread. It is best, then, to interpret the negative behavior that the word ἀναίδεια connotes as belonging to the grumpy neighbor and referring to his sense of shame. The shamelessness has been attributed to the wrong man.

The parable gives no indication that the host refuses to take no for an answer and persists in calling out or continues to pound on the door so that the neighbor must finally yield to his petition to restore his peace and quiet. Unlike the widow, who is described explicitly as coming *every day* to make her loud appeal, the neighbor has asked only once; and, apparently, once was enough. In fact, the sleeper has *already arisen* before any mention of ἀναίδεια. He has already started to respond to the request!

The structure of the parable also supports the reading that shamelessness belongs to the sleeper.

A Request: "lend me three loaves"

  B Reason for the request: "my friend has arrived"

    C Appeal to duty: "I have nothing to set before him"

    C′ Duty refused: "Do not bother me"

  B′ Reason for refusal appealing to duty to children: "The door is shut, my children are asleep"

A′ Request denied: "I am unable to rise and give you anything"

Jesus' interpretation in v. 8 reveals this pattern:

A Though he will not give to him	Sleeper
B having arisen	Sleeper
C not because of being his friend	Sleeper
C′ but because of his shamelessness	(Sleeper?)
B′ having arisen	Sleeper
A′ he will give to him whatever he needs[35]	Sleeper

33. Cited by ibid., 508.

34. Catchpole's ("Q and the Friend at Midnight") proposal to eliminate 11:8 altogether as a confusing addition by the Lukan redactor solves nothing. Hultgren's translation "troublesome persistence" (Arland J. Hultgren, *The Parables of Jesus: A Commentary* [Grand Rapids: Eerdmans, 2000], 227) may fit his construction of the parable's meaning but not the usage of ἀναίδεια.

35. Bailey, *Poet and Peasant*, 128.

Though some argue that the pronoun "his" could refer to the petitioner, the focus is on the sleeper and on what he does and why.

This argument is buttressed further by social considerations about honor and shame in this culture. What will the host do if the sleeper refuses his request? He will go elsewhere to another neighbor in the village, and soon the stinginess of the sleeper will be spread throughout the entire village. This is not a middle-class suburb where people mind their own business behind their privacy fences. The village grapevine will spread the word quickly, "He would not even get up to fulfill this duty because he claimed that his children were asleep; can you imagine?" In a small Palestinian village where the houses abut one another, most would have heard such an interchange already.

The neighbor does not want to lose face by failing to offer hospitality, and his so-called friend would not want to lose face in his community by becoming known for shameless behavior, a chiseler who refuses the request of a friend who wants to fulfill a sacred duty. Scott recognizes that he will act because "he is afraid that he will be disgraced in the village."[36] Both characters in the parable act to avoid disgrace, but the parable focuses on the shame of the one who is asked to give. He does what is expected of him: "Do not say to your neighbor, 'Go, and come again, tomorrow I will give it' — when you have it with you" (Prov 3:28 NRSV). Sirach gives a list of things that one should be ashamed about, including being surly in giving and receiving (Sir 41:19). The sleeper will get up and give the host whatever he wants, not because he is a friend, but to preserve his good name (see Sir 29:14: "A good person will be surety for his neighbor, but one who has lost all sense of shame will fail him"). He grants the request because the neighbor asks and because of the nexus of cultural expectations.

The parable is parallel to the wicked judge and the widow pleading her case but not because both the host and the widow are shamelessly insistent until their request is finally granted but because they both petition scoundrels. The judge cares nothing for justice and nothing for the widow; the sleeper cares nothing for the friend or his duty as a host. But both act to help. The judge acts to avoid a black eye. The sleeper acts to avoid shamelessness that tempted him to offer such feeble excuses to put off his neighbor.

In this parable, everyone's honor is at stake — that of the host, the sleeping friend, and the entire village. The only action in this parable that could be construed as utterly shameless is refusing to grant the request and giving such inane excuses. His hypothetical insolence may be what he wanted to say when he was awakened from sleep, but he does not (γε means "indeed, even, at least"). The assumption is that he will respond because he has to respond given the cultural requirements.

The point of the parable moves from the lesser to the greater. If a friend grants your request in the middle of the night, even though he is asleep and tempted to put you off with the weakest of excuses, he will respond out of a desire to keep his name from shame if not from friendship. How much more readily, then, will a loving God respond to prayer? But the parable also ties into the first petition of the Lord's Prayer for God to sanctify his name. God also has a name and reputation to preserve, who makes a name for himself by redeeming his people and doing great and awesome things for them (2 Sam 7:23). God acts for the sake of his name that it not be profaned in the sight of the nations (Ezek 20:9, 14, 22; see Deut 32:26 – 27). The parable's point is captured in Ezek 36:22 – 23:

---

36. Scott, *Hear Then the Parable*, 91.

Therefore say to the house of Israel, Thus says the Lord GOD: It is not for your sake, O house of Israel, that I am about to act, but for the sake of my holy name, which you have profaned among the nations to which you came. I will sanctify my great name, which has been profaned among the nations, and which you have profaned among them; and the nations shall know that I am the LORD, says the Lord GOD, when through you I display my holiness before their eyes. (NRSV; see also Ezek 36:33 – 36; 39:23 – 28)

Friendship is mentioned four times in the parable: in the introduction, in the request, in the description of the guest, and in the conclusion. Friendship created a tight bond with mutual obligations (see Sir 6:5 – 17). God is Israel's friend (*Mekilta Nezikin* 18 to Exod 22:20 – 23; *Exod. Rab.* 27:1). God also does not sleep. Compare Elijah's mockery of the priests of Baal (1 Kgs 18:27), suggesting that perhaps their gods were musing, had gone on a journey, or were asleep.

11:9 – 10 And I tell you, ask, and it will be given to you, seek, and you shall find, knock, and it shall be opened to you. For everyone who asks receives, and everyone who seeks finds, and for everyone who knocks it shall be opened (κἀγὼ ὑμῖν λέγω, αἰτεῖτε καὶ δοθήσεται ὑμῖν, ζητεῖτε καὶ εὑρήσετε, κρούετε καὶ ἀνοιγήσεται ὑμῖν. πᾶς γὰρ ὁ αἰτῶν λαμβάνει καὶ ὁ ζητῶν εὑρίσκει καὶ τῷ κρούοντι ἀνοιγήσεται). This saying does not commend the virtue of asking, seeking, and knocking so much as highlights God's love and grace that responds to requests (see John 16:24; 14:13 – 14; 15:7). That is why Jesus does not specify what it is that one is to ask for or to seek after, or where one is to knock. The context of these verbs is religious. One asks or seeks God (see Deut 4:29; Isa 55:6; 65:1). One knocks on the gates of mercy.[37] The image of the door appears elsewhere

in Luke to refer to salvation. Jesus warns that it is a narrow door (13:23 – 24) and it can be shut tight (13:25 – 26). God gives obedience to those who ask, the path that leads to life to those who seek it.

11:11 – 12 What father among you whose son asks for a fish will give him a snake instead of a fish? Or, if he asks for an egg, will give him a scorpion? (τίνα δὲ ἐξ ὑμῶν τὸν πατέρα αἰτήσει ὁ υἱὸς ἰχθύν, καὶ ἀντὶ ἰχθύος ὄφιν αὐτῷ ἐπιδώσει; ἢ καὶ αἰτήσει ᾠόν, ἐπιδώσει αὐτῷ σκορπίον;). This illustration begins as does the previous parable with the phrase "Who of you," which appeals to an everyday norm that again prompts the answer, "Certainly none of us." It also deals with a petition for the basic necessity of food and ties into the appeal in the Lord's Prayer for God to provide daily sustenance. It pairs the request for something nourishing with a spiteful and dangerous alternative. The point is not that the alternatives might look alike and trick the child. It is simply that no good parent will give what is deadly to his or her child.

11:13 Therefore, if you who are evil know how to give good gifts to your children, how much more will the Father in heaven give the Holy Spirit to those who ask him? (εἰ οὖν ὑμεῖς πονηροὶ ὑπάρχοντες οἴδατε δόματα ἀγαθὰ διδόναι τοῖς τέκνοις ὑμῶν, πόσῳ μᾶλλον ὁ πατὴρ [ὁ] ἐξ οὐρανοῦ δώσει πνεῦμα ἅγιον τοῖς αἰτοῦσιν αὐτόν). Like the previous parable, this statement also argues from the lesser to the greater to make its point. If parents on earth give good gifts to their children, how much more can God be counted on to give good gifts. It contains two surprising shifts, however. First, the listeners are abruptly dislodged from the role of the good parents who give their children the necessities of life when they are asked

---

37. Str-B, 1:458.

and are now identified as those "who are evil" (see Rom 3:10).

Second, what constitutes a good gift is determined by God, not by the petitioner. It is possible that the petitioner will unwittingly ask for harmful things — something out of the will of God. God, as any good parent and one who is infinitely wiser, will not grant those requests. One may pray for something else, but God's best gift to those who pray is the Holy Spirit.[38]

Theology in Application

1. God as Father

The disciples ask Jesus to teach them to pray. Aside from the model prayer, which serves as an outline for prayer, Jesus gives no instructions on how to pray. Instead, his answer focuses on the graciousness of God, to whom prayer is addressed. Knowing who God is and how God is gracious should shape how one prays.

Dalman declared that any idea that the Jews did not understand God as Father and did not feel an intimate relationship with him until the revelation of the New Testament is incorrect. He wrote: "It was therefore nothing novel when the Fatherly relation of God was also applied within the Jewish community to the individual."[39] Ancient Jewish tradition professed that God had called Israel to be his covenant son (Deut 14:1; Ps 103:13; Hos 11:1), and Isaiah confessed, "You, LORD, are our Father" (Isa 63:16; 64:8). Jeremiah attacked those who hypocritically addressed God as Father but who acted unfaithfully (Jer 3:4, 19). According to the Wisdom of Solomon 2:16 – 20, the righteous man boasts of God as his Father, and the unrighteous put that righteous one to the test with insults, torture, and a shameful death to see if God will indeed protect his child. Sirach prayed to God for discipline to overcome temptations, "O Lord, Father and Master of my life" (23:1, 4); and Tobit exulted: "He is our Lord and he is our God; he is our Father and he is God forever" (Tob 13:4). According to 3 Macc 5:7, Ptolemy ordered Jews to be gathered into the hippodrome to be trampled by five hundred elephants. The victims fervently prayed to "the Almighty Lord and Ruler of all power, their merciful God and Father."

Since Jesus has just said that no one knows who the Father is except the Son and whomever he has chosen to reveal him (10:22), we must assume that his understanding of God as Father reveals something new. It is central to his view of God that he should be addressed as "Father" in prayer. The term "Father" for God appears twenty-one times in the Old Testament, while it appears 255 times in the New Testament. "Our Father" is the one who sends Jesus to the cross to die for our sins and delivers him from death, and he also sends the Holy Spirit, who will enable disciples to proclaim that message to the world.

---

38. Crump, *Jesus the Intercessor*, 133.

39. Gustaf Dalman, *The Words of Jesus* (trans. D. M. Kay; Edinburgh: T&T Clark, 1902), 189.

2. God's Reign

Christ's followers are to pray for God's reign to come, not theirs. God's dominion is divorced from the national or political hopes of any particular group. The petition is not addressed to the Lord God of Israel and asks for no blessings upon the nation.[40] Interpreted eschatologically, this petition is not harmless. God is not only to reign in the heart of individuals but in history and culture. It asks God to bring our world to an end and to bring about a whole new world order and toss the reigning humans off their petty thrones. For those without comfort in this world, this petition is an expression of hope. Those who are impoverished and persecuted yearn for the final fulfillment of God's promises.

3. God's Forgiveness

C. S. Lewis captures the gist of Jesus' teaching:

> We believe that God forgives us our sins; but also that He will not do so unless we forgive other people their sins against us. There is no doubt about the second part of this statement. It is in the Lord's Prayer, it was emphatically stated by our Lord. If you don't forgive you will not be forgiven. No exceptions to it. He doesn't say that we are to forgive other people's sins, provided they are not too frightful, or provided there are extenuating circumstances, or anything of that sort. We are to forgive them all, however spiteful, however mean, however often they are repeated. If we don't, we shall be forgiven none of our own.[41]

Though most people agree that forgiveness is admirable, it is not easy. Alexander Pope's adage, "To err is human; to forgive is divine," may explain why humans so often fail to practice this divine trait. It has been said that some bury the hatchet but leave the handle sticking out of the ground so that it is ready to grasp when they want it. Others ask, "Do I have to forgive if the offender does not repent?" It may never occur to them to ask, "Can the offender repent if I do not forgive?"

Jesus understands that forgiveness is as important for the one who has been hurt as for the one who caused the hurt. Forgiveness keeps one from being clobbered again and again when the memories resurface. Harboring a grudge opens persons up to the danger of defining their lives by how they have been hurt. Forgiveness provides release. Smedes writes, "To forgive is to set a prisoner free and discover that the prisoner was you."[42] After a man took hostages and then killed five young girls and wounded five other children at the Amish West Nickel Mines one-room schoolhouse in Lancaster County, Pennsylvania, on October 2, 2006, the forgiving

40. Plummer, *Luke*, 295.

41. C. S. Lewis, "On Forgiveness," in *The Weight of Glory* (London: SPCK, 1949; repr. San Francisco: HarperCollins, 2001), 178.

42. Lewis B. Smedes, *Forgive and Forget: Healing the Hurts We Don't Deserve* (San Francisco: HarperCollins, 1984).

spirit of the Amish community received as much national attention as the horrific act of violence. Johann Christoph Arnold, the senior elder of the Bruderhof, commented on forgiveness in an interview two days later: "If you hold a grudge, it will live on in your heart until it leads to violence of some kind. If you do not forgive, then you cannot be healed. Forgiveness can heal the forgiver as well as the one who is forgiven. This is what the Amish believe. It will take time, but this is what they now must strive to live out for all the world to see."

Forgiveness leads to greater spiritual and psychological well-being, but it also becomes a witness to the world. This is what God has done in Christ and what God expects from Christ followers.

4. God's Graciousness: Ask, Seek, Knock

While persistence in prayer is commendable (1 Thess 5:17), Jesus does not demand it here. As Crump recognizes, "Luke is not teaching that one may bend God's will by bending God's ear. Prayer offered repeatedly enough is no more guaranteed to effect the desired result than is prayer offered faithfully enough."[43] The pagans mistakenly believed that it was the squeaky wheel that would get the grease. Seneca (*Ep.* 31.5) talks about fatiguing the gods, and Martial (7.60.3) talked about wearing oneself out with petitions. They were more interested in getting answers to their prayers than in praying. Crump remarks, "The distinctive feature of magical thought wherein one seeks to control or compel divine forces to operate in a desired fashion through the careful use of specific techniques, is far removed from the attitudes expressed by Luke."[44]

Jesus encourages boldness in prayer. As the petitioner was forceful, so Christians may be forceful in asking for spiritual gifts no matter how implausible or impossible it might seem. Suppliants can be bold with their demands when they know their rights and the goodness of the Father who knows their needs before they ask and wants to give them good gifts. Jesus teaches that prayer is founded on the goodness of God and lays hold of God's willingness. Prayer is not a spiritual crowbar or a jackhammer that pries open God's willingness to act but a means by which Christians open themselves up to God — to grasp God's will and to be grasped by it. The child does not need to whine constantly to get bread from a loving father. Fathers are supposed to give their children bread. Everything depends on the goodness of God, not the unrelenting ardor of the one asking. The examples Jesus gives reveal that God is keen to answer requests, to be found, to open the door.

There is no reason for us to keep our troubles, worries, and needs bottled up inside of us and bear needless pain because we do not take things to God in prayer. We have a ready audience with God and can air our petitions boldly in prayer (as Jesus

43. Crump, *Jesus the Intercessor*, 131.   44. Ibid., 135 – 36.

himself did on the Mount of Olives). Prayer expresses the yearning to see God's will be done in the world and to orient our lives around it. True prayer seeks to release God's will in our lives. It approaches God with childlike trust: I have nothing and I need help. Luther comments that it shows "that we do not have everything, but that we are in such a condition that there is failure and want everywhere."[45]

Jesus wishes to bestow confidence on his followers in coming to God candidly in prayer, but some have twisted the offer to ask, seek, and knock into asking for selfish ends. The following guidelines can check this inclination. (1) The images that Jesus uses are of a friend asking a friend and a child asking a father for what is necessary. It is no use praying to God in some emergency situation when one has not been in a relationship with the Father. Yet one must be careful not to take that relationship for granted. The parable of the Pharisee and the tax collector praying in the temple (18:9 – 14) reveals that a presumed close relationship to God may be all show and no substance, as it was on the Pharisee's part. And one who may appear to have no relationship to God, the seeming pariah, may cry out in need, as the tax collector does, and be answered.

(2) The spirit of the Lord's Prayer should shape our prayers. James offers a commentary on asking. God gives to all "generously and ungrudgingly" for those who lack wisdom and ask in faith without doubting (Jas 1:5 – 7 NRSV). Those who ask and do not receive must examine themselves to see if they "ask wrongly, to spend it on your passions" (Jas 4:3 ESV). Jesus does not naïvely encourage disciples to ask anything from God. He also does not assure them "that God will give whatever is asked for but that whatever the Father gives will be good."[46] Many saints have thanked God that he did not give what they asked. But Jesus assumes that the petitioner can expect the prayer to be heard and answered by God. The answer may not be what one expected. For example, Paul prayed time and again for his thorn in the flesh to be removed. It was not, but he did receive a more profound answer: "My grace is sufficient for you, for my power is made perfect in weakness" (2 Cor 12:8 – 9).

(3) Seeking is primarily related to seeking the Lord as attested by the Law, the Prophets, and the Psalms and Wisdom books (Deut 4:29; Isa 55:6; Jer 29:14; Ps 27:8 – 9; Prov 8:17). Those who seek the wrong things in life will always come up empty.

5. God's Gift of the Holy Spirit

The Holy Spirit is what the Father promises to give (24:49; Acts 1:4; 2:33), what Jesus brings (3:16; Acts 1:5; 11:16), and what people most need. The reference to the Holy Spirit directly links to the first two petitions in the Lord's Prayer, "Let your name

---

45. Martin Luther, *Commentary on the Sermon on the Mount* (trans. C. A. Hay; Philadelphia: Lutheran Publication Society, 1892), 397.

46. Dunn, *Jesus Remembered*, 555.

be sanctified," and "Your reign come." The boundary between heaven, where God's name and reign are sanctified and acknowledged, and earth, where God's name and reign are profaned and ignored, is bridged by the Holy Spirit, who transforms space and time. The Holy Spirit is the channel of God's grace and blessing (1:15, 35; 4:18; 10:21); he will empower disciples to do as Jesus tells them (6:46).

The discernible presence of the Holy Spirit in disciples' lives betokens that some of the splendor of the world to come has already broken into this present evil age and serves as a guarantee of their final transformation and participation in the future glory God has prepared for them (2 Cor 5:5). The Spirit will also instruct them and help them endure and overcome the trials that will come their way for being Christ's disciples (12:11 – 12). The Spirit delivers the power of God's presence that amply supplies all they could need.

This promise of the gift of the Holy Spirit previews Luke's next volume (24:49; Acts 1:8; 2:1 – 4, 38; 9:31; 11:15; 13:52). In Acts 8:15 – 17, the Spirit is given in answer to prayer. When the Holy Spirit comes upon the disciples after Jesus' ascension in Acts, they experience God's presence as power in a seemingly powerless community, and it leads to an outward thrust in which God's Spirit breaks into the lives of believers and turns human history upside down. It is the Spirit's power that will allow them to be witnesses.

Luke 11:14 – 36

Literary Context

Jesus has been engaged in a ministry that expels demons from people. The reactions have been mixed: from astonishment (4:31 – 37; 9:37 – 43) to excitement (6:17 – 19) to open hostility (8:26 – 39). Luke narrates different reactions to Jesus' exorcism of a demon from a man who is mute. The crowds marvel, but others start a smear campaign and skeptics want more proof that God indeed is working something new in Jesus. This incident also evokes religious praise from a woman. Jesus defends himself against contemptuous accusations. The sacking of Satan's fortifications (11:22) and the defeat of his demonic minions (11:14, 15, 18, 19, 20) are a sign that his domain is crumbling (11:18). Even Jesus' disciples (9:1, 17 – 18) and those who cast out demons in his name (9:49) have success against Satan.

Jesus attributes the opponents' hostile response to a darkness within them that reveals that they have been possessed by the power of darkness that deflects the light so that they cannot see the truth. This leads into the attack on the Pharisees and scholars of the law in the next section. They are guilty of scattering, not gathering, the flock (11:23, 52), and the darkness in them expresses itself in their murderous deeds (11:47 – 51) and in making them Jesus' deadly opponents (11:53 – 54). Jesus' blast against "this evil generation" (11:29, 30, 32, 50), nevertheless, still holds out hope that the invective will cause them to repent because Jesus mixes his polemic (11:29 – 33, 39 – 42a, 43 – 44, 46 – 52) with exhortation (11:33 – 36, 41, 42b).

Main Idea

Jesus' exorcisms are divine invasions into Satan's realm and a sign that God's power works through him. Those who are filled with impenetrable darkness, however, fail to recognize this fact and will be judged for their failure to acknowledge him and to repent.

Translation

(See next two pages.)

Structure and Literary Form

After a brief description of an exorcism with the report of its effect on the crowds (11:14 – 16), the first group of sayings (11:17 – 26) comprise a seven-stage response to counter the defamatory charge that Jesus works through the prince of demons. The sayings adopt a variety of forms — from axioms to parables. An interlude with two beatitudes (11:27 – 28) leads into a denunciation of this generation as evil and three sayings related to the "sign of Jonah" (11:29 – 32). It is followed by three sayings and an exhortation on light and darkness (11:33 – 36). A word association thread runs through the series of sayings. The unclean spirit brings back seven more "evil" than itself (11:26); this generation is "evil" (11:29); and the eye is "evil" (11:34).

The concluding sayings related to light and darkness explain why persons could attribute Jesus' exorcisms to satanic black magic. They are so filled with darkness that they cannot see the light. Consequently, they are destined for judgment.

Luke 11:14–36

11:14a	Circumstance/ exorcism	**And he was casting out a demon (that was) mute,** and it happened that

when the demon went out,
the man who was mute spoke,

| b | Reaction (1) | **and the crowds marveled.** |
| 15 | Reaction (2) | **But some of them said,** |

"*He casts out demons by Beelzebul, the ruler of demons.*"

| 16 | Reaction (3) | **Others, testing him, were seeking a sign from heaven from him.** |
| 17 | Axiom
(Response 1) | **But he knew their thoughts and said to them,** |

"*Every kingdom divided against itself will be laid waste*
and house falls against house.

| 18 | Logical inference
(Response 2) | |

If Satan also is divided against himself,
how will his kingdom stand?
—for you say that I cast out demons by Beelzebul.

| 19a | Comparison
(Response 3) | |

Now   *if I cast out demons by Beelzebul,*
by whom do your sons cast them out?
So, they will be your judges.

| b | | |
| 20 | Challenge
(Response 4) | |

But   *if I cast out demons by the finger of God,*
then the reign of God has come upon you.

| 21 | Parable
(Response 5) | |

When a strong man is fully armed with weaponry,
he guards his house,
and his possessions are secure.

| 22 | | |

As soon as one who is stronger comes upon him and conquers him,
he   *takes away his panoply of armor in which he had put his confidence*
and   *divides the spoils.*

| 23 | Declaration
(Response 6) | |

The one who is not with me is against me,
and the one who does not gather with me scatters.

| 24 | Parable
(Response 7) | |

When the unclean spirit goes out from the man,
it passes through waterless places seeking rest,
and when it does not find it, it says,
'*I will return to my house from which I came.*'

| 25 | | |

When it comes back,
it finds that it has been swept and put in order.

| 26 | | |

Then it goes and brings along seven other spirits more evil than it,
and they enter and dwell there,
and the last [condition] of that man becomes worse than the first."

Continued on next page.

27	Praise	While he was speaking these things,
		a certain woman from the crowd raised her voice and **said to him,**
		"*Blessed is the womb that carried you*
		and the breasts from which you nursed."
28		**But he said,**
		"*Yes, but blessed are those who hear the word of God and keep it.*"
29a	Circumstance	When the crowds were increasing,
b	Declaration	**he began to say,**
		"*This generation is evil.*
		It seeks a sign
		and a sign will not be given to it except the sign of Jonah.
30	Explanation	*For just as Jonah became a sign to the Ninevites,*
		thus will be the Son of Man to this generation.

The queen of the South will be raised in the judgment with the men of ☙
this generation
| 31a | | |
and she will condemn them,
because she came from the ends of the earth to hear the ☙
wisdom of Solomon,

| b | | *and, behold, something greater than Solomon is here.* |

32a		*The men of Nineveh will be raised in the judgment with this generation*
		and they will condemn it,
		because they repented at the preaching of Jonah,

| b | | *and, behold, something greater than Jonah is here.* |

33	Parable	*No one after lighting a lamp puts it in a hidden place but*
		upon a lampstand
		so that those who enter may see the light.

34a	Axiom	*The light of the body is your eye.*
		Whenever your eye is without guile,
		then your whole body is radiant.
b		*But when it is evil,*
		then your whole body is full of darkness.
35	Exhortation	*Therefore,* **pay careful attention to whether the light in you is darkness.**

| 36 | Promise | *If then your whole body is radiant, with no part of it having darkness,* |
| | | *then it will be radiant as when a lamp shines its rays upon you.*" |

Exegetical Outline

→ **I. The source of Jesus' power to cast out demons (11:14–23)**

    A. Setting: casting out the demon of a man that was mute (11:14a)

    B. Reactions to the exorcism (11:14b–16)

      1. Wonder (11:14b)

      2. Slander: Jesus casts out demons by Beelzebul (11:15)

      3. Skepticism: demand for more signs from heaven (11:16)

    C. Jesus' defense (11:17–26)

      1. A divided kingdom falls (11:17)

      2. Satan will not empower the destruction of his own realm (11:18)

      3. By what power do your sons cast out demons? (11:19)

      4. Jesus' exorcisms demonstrate that God's reign has come upon them (11:20)

      5. A stronger man (Jesus) can overwhelm even one who is well-armed (Satan) (11:21–22)

      6. An implied demand to choose sides for or against Jesus (11:23)

      7. The nature of evil spirits is to make things worse not better (11:24–26)

II. Positive Response to Jesus (11:27–28)

    A. Beatitude: Blessed is the mother of such a son (11:27)

    B. Amended beatitude: Blessed are those who hear and keep God's Word (11:28)

III. The sign of Jonah and the warning of judgment (11:29–32)

    A. The sign of Jonah: preaching, judgment, miraculous deliverance (11:29–30)

    B. Comparisons of this generation to the response of non-Israelites in the past (11:31a, 32a)

    C. Jesus is greater than Solomon and Jonah (11:31b, 32b)

IV. Explanation for the rejection of God's light that comes in Jesus and a warning (11:33–36)

    A. God's light is evident for all to see (11:33)

    B. Good eyes receive the light and fill the person with light (11:34a)

    C. Bad eyes shut out the light and fill the person with darkness (11:34b)

    D. Take care that one is filled with light (11:35)

    E. Those who are filled with light will shine (in the judgment) (11:36)

Explanation of the Text

11:14–15 And he was casting out a demon [that was] mute, and it happened that when the demon went out, the man who was mute spoke, and the crowds marveled. But some of them said, "He casts out demons by Beelzebul, the ruler of demons" (καὶ ἦν ἐκβάλλων δαιμόνιον, [καὶ αὐτὸ ἦν] κωφόν. ἐγένετο δὲ τοῦ δαιμονίου ἐξελθόντος ἐλάλησεν ὁ κωφός καὶ ἐθαύμασαν οἱ ὄχλοι. τινὲς δὲ ἐξ αὐτῶν εἶπον· ἐν Βεελζεβοὺλ τῷ ἄρχοντι τῶν δαιμονίων ἐκβάλλει τὰ δαιμόνια). Satan dons a variety of disguises (2 Cor 11:14) and causes all manner of evil, and various names have been given to him. The etymology of the term *Beelzebul*, an alias for Satan, is unclear, but the view that it "derived from the Hebrew words *baʿal* ("lord," Hos 2:18), used mostly of local manifestations of the

Canaanite fertility god who was the chief adversary of the Israelite religion (1 Kgs 18:16–40), and *z*ᵉ*bul* ("exalted dwelling," 1 Kgs 8:13)" is probably right.[1] The origin of the term would not have been understood by Luke's readers, and he simply uses it as another moniker for the ruler of demons. The premise behind the charge and Jesus' response is that the world is "enemy-occupied territory: it belongs by right to God, but through the sin of man it has fallen under the tyranny of Satan, who keeps it in a grip that no power of man can break … the two kingdoms confront one another in war."[2]

Jesus' opponents do not dismiss his exorcisms as some kind of hoax but perversely attribute them to forces of evil, not God. These muckrakers are not identified, but the Pharisees and lawyers who are condemned in the next section are the most likely candidates (see Matt 12:24; Mark 3:22). Jesus' inroads with the crowds threaten them the most, and they have been the most vocal in opposing Jesus. By not identifying these opponents specifically, however, Luke does not limit "this evil generation" to one small party in Judaism.

The church would not have invented this charge, and this accusation reveals that Jesus' contemporaries believed that he performed works of uncommon power. Aune comments, "In Greco-Roman paganism magical procedures were commonly used for acquiring divine revelations and for the securing the aid of an 'assistant daemon' (*paredros daimôn*) who could mediate such revelation and enable the practitioner to perform miraculous feats."[3] Because his mighty deeds are combined with unconventional teaching and activity, they seem suspect. Jesus' enemies refuse to accept that Israel's God was acting in a remarkably new way that requires them to reconsider their religious hopes. Israel's destiny is centered in Jesus.

11:16 Others, testing him, were seeking a sign from heaven from him (ἕτεροι δὲ πειράζοντες σημεῖον ἐξ οὐρανοῦ ἐζήτουν παρ' αὐτοῦ). Some in the crowd demand more proof before committing themselves. The demand for signs to test him recalls Satan's testing of Jesus in the wilderness. In Scripture, signs are public events that confirm a disputed claim (see 2 Kgs 20:1–10; Isa 7:10–11, 18–25; 38:1–20; John 2:13–18; 6:26–31). One also seeks a sign when someone judged to be a pretender does or says strange things. The sign proves the legitimacy of the claimant, but the imperfect tense of the verb "were seeking" (ἐζήτουν) suggests a running quest for proof that will never be satisfied that it has enough evidence to make a commitment.

Signs in general need not comprise anything spectacular or miraculous but must correspond to a prediction of what would occur. Gibson argues that the demand for "a sign from heaven" (σημεῖον ἐξ οὐρανοῦ), however, is different. It refers to "apocalyptic phenomena which embody or signal the onset of aid and comfort for God's elect and/or the wrath that God was expected to let loose against his enemies and those who threaten his people."[4] A sign from heaven is something that "is apocalyptic in tone, triumphalistic in character, and the embodiment of one of the 'mighty deeds of deliverance' that God had worked on Israel's behalf in rescuing it from slavery."[5] These enemies of Jesus may be responding to his preaching about the coming of the reign of God and demanding proof. But it is not yet the time for this kind of sign (Acts 1:6–8). Much more is yet to happen in God's plan for the salvation of the world.

1. Graham H. Twelftree, "Demon, Devil, Satan," *DJG*, 164.

2. Caird, *Saint Luke*, 154–55.

3. David E. Aune, *Prophecy in Early Christianity and the Ancient Mediterranean World* (Grand Rapids: Eerdmans, 1983), 242.

4. Jeffrey B. Gibson, "Jesus' Refusal to Produce a 'Sign' (Mark 8.11–13)," *JSNT* 38 (1990): 45–47.

5. Ibid., 53.

Jesus does not refuse outright to give a sign as he does in Mark 8:11 – 12. The feeding of the five thousand is a sign to the eyes of faith, but since these skeptics raise doubts about his exorcisms, that miracle would have been suspect as well. The upshot is that God does not coerce faith with irresistible proof and does not submit to human demands for verification. Jesus only responds to these challenges with a parable and a direct challenge of his own.

11:17 – 18 But he knew their thoughts and said to them, "Every kingdom divided against itself will be laid waste and house falls against house. If Satan also is divided against himself, how will his kingdom stand? — for you say that I cast out demons by Beelzebul" (αὐτὸς δὲ εἰδὼς αὐτῶν τὰ διανοήματα εἶπεν αὐτοῖς· πᾶσα βασιλεία ἐφ᾽ ἑαυτὴν διαμερισθεῖσα ἐρημοῦται καὶ οἶκος ἐπὶ οἶκον πίπτει. εἰ δὲ καὶ ὁ Σατανᾶς ἐφ᾽ ἑαυτὸν διεμερίσθη, πῶς σταθήσεται ἡ βασιλεία αὐτοῦ; ὅτι λέγετε ἐν Βεελζεβοὺλ ἐκβάλλειν με τὰ δαιμόνια).

The first stage of Jesus' refutation of the charge expresses the premise that a divided kingdom will fall (11:17). The second stage exposes the illogic of Satan trying to undermine his own kingdom and purposes by empowering Jesus to work exorcisms. Why would Satan deputize Jesus to wreak havoc in his own domain? It should be obvious that exorcisms are evidence of God's assault on Satan's powerful grip on human beings. Luke's readers will also know that when the disciples reported their own success in expelling demons, Jesus announced that he saw Satan falling from heaven like a flash of lightning (10:18).

11:19 Now if I cast out demons by Beelzebul, by whom do your sons cast them out? So, they will be your judges (εἰ δὲ ἐγὼ ἐν Βεελζεβοὺλ ἐκβάλλω τὰ δαιμόνια, οἱ υἱοὶ ὑμῶν ἐν τίνι ἐκβάλλουσιν; διὰ τοῦτο αὐτοὶ ὑμῶν κριταὶ ἔσονται). The unexpressed premise behind Jesus' defense is that exorcisms are good for the persons delivered from demons. Those maligning him have not claimed that his exorcisms are somehow unique, so Jesus asks about the source of power behind other exorcists. Do they also expel demons by Satan? The opponents cannot have it both ways. If these others exorcize demons by God's power, then so does Jesus.

"Your sons" (οἱ υἱοὶ ὑμῶν) traditionally has been understood as referring to other Jewish exorcists associated with the Pharisees. In Luke's context, however, it makes more sense for Jesus to refer to his own disciples who successfully performed exorcisms (9:1 – 9; 10:17 – 20) or to those unknown supporters who did them in his name (9:49).[6] If the other exorcists work by the power of God but not in Jesus' name, do they also herald the arrival of God's reign (11:20)? For Luke, God's reign is tied solely to the Spirit-led activity of Jesus. Those exorcists who try to pirate Jesus' name as if it had magical power are struck down (Acts 19:13 – 17; see 13:6 – 12).

Also, why would these exorcists be their judges? The phrase "your sons" can refer to the disciples as the crowd's kinsmen or as Israelites in general (see 1:16; Matt 27:9).[7] This reading connects their exorcisms by Jesus' authority to his own exorcisms as a sign that Satan's kingdom is being decimated and that God's reign has come. It also best explains the judging function assigned to the exorcists: they are the disciples (see 22:30).

---

6. Robert Shirock, "Whose Exorcists Are They?" *JSNT* 46 (1992): 41 – 51.

7. Shirock (ibid., 50) argues the phrase "your sons" may be "a rhetorical device" that says: "These disciples of mine are *your own kinsmen*. Are you willing, in face of their widespread success, to accuse all thirteen (or seventy-three) of us of being possessed by Beelzebul?"

11:20 But if I cast out demons by the finger of God, then the reign of God has come upon you (εἰ δὲ ἐν δακτύλῳ θεοῦ ἐκβάλλω τὰ δαιμόνια, ἄρα ἔφθασεν ἐφ᾽ ὑμᾶς ἡ βασιλεία τοῦ θεοῦ). In the fourth stage of his argument, Jesus dramatically asserts that he is empowered by God, not Beelzebul. The phrase "the finger of God" derives from the Old Testament; there are "no *known* convincing parallels" to this expression in Greek or Roman literature.[8] In Israel's exodus, God revealed his finger by performing miraculous signs that confirmed his salvific intent for Israel. Pharaoh's magicians were flummoxed by gnats and finally conceded that "this is the finger of God" (Exod 8:19). The two stone tablets of the covenant also were written with "the finger of God" (Exod 31:18; Deut 9:10).

Both of these contexts may provide a backdrop for understanding Jesus' phrase. The first allusion points to the self-evident nature of Jesus' exorcisms that anyone should recognize. They are proof of God's creative power working in human affairs. The second allusion underscores the revelatory character of Jesus' exorcisms that is comparable to God's writing the two tablets of the covenant.[9] These two allusions combined suggest that Jesus' exorcisms reveal God's majesty and creative power, which God displays "in order that Israel might 'fear the Lord,' and keep all his commandments."[10]

The phrase "has come upon you" (ἔφθασεν ἐφ᾽ ὑμᾶς) means that God's reign has arrived or overtaken them (see Rom 9:31; Phil 3:16; 1 Thess 2:16), not that it has come near. It expresses a paradox. God's reign is present in Jesus' miraculous activity and the defeat of Satan, and yet it is to be fully consummated in the future.

11:21 – 22 When a strong man is fully armed with weaponry, he guards his house, and his possessions are secure. As soon as one who is stronger comes upon him and conquers him, he takes away his panoply of armor in which he had put his confidence and divides the spoils (ὅταν ὁ ἰσχυρὸς καθωπλισμένος φυλάσσῃ τὴν ἑαυτοῦ αὐλήν, ἐν εἰρήνῃ ἐστὶν τὰ ὑπάρχοντα αὐτοῦ. ἐπὰν δὲ ἰσχυρότερος αὐτοῦ ἐπελθὼν νικήσῃ αὐτόν, τὴν πανοπλίαν αὐτοῦ αἴρει ἐφ᾽ ᾗ ἐπεποίθει, καὶ τὰ σκῦλα αὐτοῦ διαδίδωσιν). The fifth stage of Jesus' argument alludes to Isa 49:24 – 25, where God promises to take prey from the mighty and rescue captives from a tyrant, and Isa 53:12, where the suffering servant will divide the spoil with the strong. The image pictures all-out war in which the strong man is caught unawares by one who is stronger (3:16), and it is impossible to sue for peace (14:31 – 32). The parable is an allegory that refers to Satan, whose defense armaments are inadequate against a stronger Jesus (3:16), who is empowered by God and invades his domain. Garrett writes:

> The dark regions are the realm of Satan, the ruler of the world, who for eons has sat entrenched and well-guarded, his many possessions gathered like trophies around him. The sick and possessed are held captive by his demons; the Gentiles, too, are subject to his dominion, giving him honor and glory that ought to be offered to God. Tragically, even many Jews have acquiesced to Satan's authority. For generations they have resisted the Spirit and rejected the prophets, choosing instead to follow false prophets, who themselves serve the devil as Lord. Hence the Jews are in bondage to the devil as surely as the Israelites were once in bondage to Pharaoh.[11]

---

8. Edward J. Woods, *The 'Finger of God' and Pneumatology in Luke-Acts* (JSNTSup 205; Sheffield: Sheffield Academic, 2001), 243, cf. 61 – 100.

9. Robert W. Wall, " 'The Finger of God' Deuteronomy 9:10 and Luke 11:20," *NTS* 33 (1987): 145.

10. Woods, *The 'Finger of God' and Pneumatology in Luke-Acts*, 245.

11. Garrett, *The Demise of the Devil*, 101.

The final victory is not yet won, but Satan's demise is inevitable as his domain begins to crumble around him.

11:23 The one who is not with me is against me, and the one who does not gather with me scatters (ὁ μὴ ὢν μετ᾽ ἐμοῦ κατ᾽ ἐμοῦ ἐστιν, καὶ ὁ μὴ συνάγων μετ᾽ ἐμοῦ σκορπίζει). The sixth stage of the refutation draws a line in the sand. Those who do not side with Jesus make matters worse by scattering instead of gathering Israel.[12] More seriously, they join forces with Satan, who resists the restoration of Israel.

11:24 – 26 When the unclean spirit goes out from the man, it passes through waterless places seeking rest, and when it does not find it, it says, "I will return to my house from which I came." When it comes back, it finds that it has been swept and put in order. Then it goes and brings along seven other spirits more evil than it, and they enter and dwell there, and the last [condition] of that man becomes worse than the first (ὅταν τὸ ἀκάθαρτον πνεῦμα ἐξέλθῃ ἀπὸ τοῦ ἀνθρώπου, διέρχεται δι᾽ ἀνύδρων τόπων ζητοῦν ἀνάπαυσιν καὶ μὴ εὑρίσκον [τότε] λέγει· ὑποστρέψω εἰς τὸν οἶκόν μου ὅθεν ἐξῆλθον· καὶ ἐλθὸν εὑρίσκει σεσαρωμένον καὶ κεκοσμημένον. τότε πορεύεται καὶ παραλαμβάνει ἕτερα πνεύματα πονηρότερα ἑαυτοῦ ἑπτά, καὶ εἰσελθόντα κατοικεῖ ἐκεῖ· καὶ γίνεται τὰ ἔσχατα τοῦ ἀνθρώπου ἐκείνου χείρονα τῶν πρώτων). This parable is the seventh stage in Jesus' refutation to the charge that he works through Beelzebul. Jesus does not argue that the expulsion of demons does not prevent repossession unless something fills the vacuum that will ward off the next onslaught. Instead, it describes the nature

of demons and the way they work (thirteen verb forms relate the unclean spirit as the subject) to contrast the effect of Jesus' exorcisms. The unclean spirit in the parable does what is natural for unclean spirits to do. They do not find rest in waterless places because of the absence of people. They want to inhabit humans and create disorder, and they regard a human being as simply a convenient place to make their home ("my house").[13]

When the spirit is booted out, it returns to find everything swept and ordered, or ornamented. It probes for weaknesses, and finding "no security system in place" or opposing force, it calls in reinforcements to reclaim its victim and makes things worse seven times over. Kilgallen argues, "The point is that the demons always make things worse — seven times over. Jesus brings about cleanness and order."[14] The demonic powers will not cooperate with Jesus but do everything they can to neutralize and make worse what he does.

11:27 – 28 While he was speaking these things, a certain woman from the crowd raised her voice and said to him, "Blessed is the womb that carried you and the breasts from which you nursed." But he said, "Yes, but blessed are those who hear the word of God and keep it" (ἐγένετο δὲ ἐν τῷ λέγειν αὐτὸν ταῦτα ἐπάρασά τις φωνὴν γυνὴ ἐκ τοῦ ὄχλου εἶπεν αὐτῷ· μακαρία ἡ κοιλία ἡ βαστάσασά σε καὶ μαστοὶ οὓς ἐθήλασας. αὐτὸς δὲ εἶπεν· μενοῦν μακάριοι οἱ ἀκούοντες τὸν λόγον τοῦ θεοῦ καὶ φυλάσσοντες). In contrast to those who accuse Jesus of practicing black magic (11:15) or put him to the test by demanding signs (11:16), an anonymous woman from the crowd unrestrainedly lauds Jesus. She uses synecdoche whereby the womb that gave birth to him and the breasts that nourished him refers to his mother.

---

12. Marshall, *The Gospel of Luke*, 479.

13. John J. Kilgallen, "The Return of the Unclean Spirit (Luke 11,24 – 26)," *Bib* 74 (1993): 58.

14. Ibid.

Praising his mother indirectly praises him: "Your mother must be so proud to have given birth to such a wonderful son." Her beatitude echoes Elizabeth's prophecy about Mary (1:42) and what Mary herself came to believe (1:48).

Jesus' response, with the particle translated "yes, but" (μενοῦν), amends her beatitude because more needs to be said.[15] His mother is not blessed because of the fertility of her womb and the milk in her breasts,[16] but because she listened to God's word, believed it, and acted on it.[17] Jesus' correction reasserts that blessedness is open to all who hear and obey "the word of God" and is not based on kinship (8:21). "The word of God" is that which comes from God and tells of God (see 8:11). In Luke, Jesus is the one who proclaims and embodies it (5:1; 8:11). Ultimately, then, Jesus requires obedience, not praise.

11:29–32 When the crowds were increasing, he began to say, "This generation is evil. It seeks a sign and a sign will not be given to it except the sign of Jonah. For just as Jonah became a sign to the Ninevites, thus will be the Son of Man to this generation. The queen of the South will be raised in the judgment with the men of this generation and she will condemn them, because she came from the ends of the earth to hear the wisdom of Solomon, and, behold, something greater than Solomon is here. The men of Nineveh will be raised in the judgment with this generation and they will condemn it because they repented at the preaching of Jonah, and, behold, something greater than Jonah is here" (τῶν δὲ ὄχλων ἐπαθροιζομένων ἤρξατο λέγειν· ἡ γενεὰ αὕτη γενεὰ πονηρά ἐστιν· σημεῖον ζητεῖ, καὶ σημεῖον οὐ δοθήσεται αὐτῇ εἰ μὴ τὸ σημεῖον Ἰωνᾶ. καθὼς γὰρ ἐγένετο Ἰωνᾶς τοῖς Νινευίταις σημεῖον, οὕτως ἔσται καὶ ὁ υἱὸς τοῦ ἀνθρώπου τῇ γενεᾷ ταύτῃ. βασίλισσα νότου ἐγερθήσεται ἐν τῇ κρίσει μετὰ τῶν ἀνδρῶν τῆς γενεᾶς ταύτης καὶ κατακρινεῖ αὐτούς· ὅτι ἦλθεν ἐκ τῶν περάτων τῆς γῆς ἀκοῦσαι τὴν σοφίαν Σολομῶνος, καὶ ἰδοὺ πλεῖον Σολομῶνος ὧδε. ἄνδρες Νινευῖται ἀναστήσονται ἐν τῇ κρίσει μετὰ τῆς γενεᾶς ταύτης καὶ κατακρινοῦσιν αὐτήν· ὅτι μετενόησαν εἰς τὸ κήρυγμα Ἰωνᾶ, καὶ ἰδοὺ πλεῖον Ἰωνᾶ ὧδε).

The enigmatic sign of Jonah may refer to his divine rescue from certain death (Jonah 1:17–2:10; 3 Macc 6:8), his preaching of repentance (Jonah 3:4–10), or his preaching of judgment (Jonah 3:4). Jesus' reference to "the word of God" in 11:28 suggests that it refers to Jonah's preaching. Jonah did no sign in Nineveh, yet they believed. As he was a "sign" to the Ninevites in his preaching, so Jesus is a "sign" to this generation in his preaching. Danker concludes, "Jesus refuses to offer any other sign but his own person and message."[18]

Fitzmyer notes the irony: since preaching is the only sign this generation will have, it has already been given.[19] Marshall objects to this interpretation because the crowd has asked for some "divine accreditation of Jesus' message." The divine intervention that rescued Jonah from the fish would stand out in the mind of Jesus' contemporaries. The corresponding feature in Jesus' ministry is his resurrection (Acts 1:3; 17:31).[20] Yet even this sign will not lead everyone to repent (16:30). Schmitt links the sign to the description of Jonah in the *Lives of the Prophets* 10.10–11, an image that may have been in the popular consciousness: "And he gave a portent concerning Jerusalem and the whole land, that whenever they should see a stone crying

15. Moule, *Idiom Book of New Testament Greek*, 163–64; Margaret Thrall, *Greek Particles in the New Testament* (Grand Rapids: Eerdmans, 1962), 34–35.

16. Green, *The Gospel of Luke*, 461.

17. Fitzmyer, *Luke*, 2:927.

18. Danker, *Jesus and the New Age*, 236.

19. Fitzmyer, *Luke*, 2:933.

20. Marshall, *The Gospel of Luke*, 485.

out piteously the end was at hand. And whenever they should see all the gentiles in Jerusalem, the entire city would be razed to the ground."[21] Jesus' prophecy in 21:20, 24 is similar.

I conclude that "the sign of Jonah" includes all three elements: the preaching of repentance (5:32; 13:3, 5; 15:7, 10), the preaching of judgment (13:1 – 9, 23 – 30, 34 – 35; 20:9 – 19; 22:20 – 28; 23:28 – 31), and divine rescue (24:5 – 7). But this sign also involves another element that is developed in Acts: openness to outsiders. Grassi observes about the Jonah story that "God has never called upon a prophet to preach to any nation but Israel."[22] The lesson from Jonah is that God is the God of all and that God's steadfast love is accessible to all. The gospel ends with Jesus teaching the written Scriptures to his disciples — that the Christ is to be raised on the third day and that repentance for the forgiveness of sins be preached in his name to all the nations. The sign of Jonah for this generation may also be extended beyond Jesus' earthly ministry to include the mission of his disciples to the ends of the earth and the Gentiles' reception of their message.

In the next saying recalling the experiences of Solomon and the queen of the South and Jonah and the Ninevites, Jesus denounces this generation for failing to heed his preaching. The queen of the South, a non-Israelite, came from the ends of the earth and recognized Solomon's legitimacy and deferred to his wisdom. The Ninevites, also non-Israelites, repented at Jonah's preaching. Jesus is far greater than Solomon or the prophet Jonah because he brings in God's reign, but this generation neither recognizes his authority nor repents. Their continued obduracy will seal their fate in the judgment.

11:33 – 34 No one after lighting a lamp puts it in a hidden place but upon a lampstand so that those who enter may see the light. The light of the body is your eye. Whenever your eye is without guile, then your whole body is radiant. But when it is evil, then your whole body is full of darkness (οὐδεὶς λύχνον ἅψας εἰς κρύπτην τίθησιν ἀλλ' ἐπὶ τὴν λυχνίαν, ἵνα οἱ εἰσπορευόμενοι τὸ φῶς βλέπωσιν. ὁ λύχνος τοῦ σώματός ἐστιν ὁ ὀφθαλμός σου. ὅταν ὁ ὀφθαλμός σου ἁπλοῦς ᾖ, καὶ ὅλον τὸ σῶμά σου φωτεινόν ἐστιν· ἐπὰν δὲ πονηρὸς ᾖ, καὶ τὸ σῶμά σου σκοτεινόν). The axiom about the lamp applies to God's Word (Ps 119:105). God has not hidden the light, but it shines in the world through Jesus. The different reactions to Jesus' deeds of power, however, reveal that people do not all receive it.[23]

The saying about the eye being the light of the body is applied to a person's spiritual condition. As the lamp radiates light into a room, the eye radiates light into "the body," which here refers to the innermost being and personality (Dan 10:6). Garrett argues that this image depicts a person's "state of being" when encountering God or God's salvation, which comes to them as light (1:79; 9:29; Acts 9:3; 22:6, 26:13). The image of darkness depicts the realm of Satan and death (22:53; Acts 13:9 – 11). The imagery is combined in Acts 26:18, where Paul expounds on his commission: "to open their eyes and turn them from darkness to light, and from the power of Satan to God, so that they may receive forgiveness of sins and a place among those who are sanctified by faith in me." Garrett concludes that the "eye imagery functions as a poetic vehicle for characterizing persons' participation in one or another of these realms."[24]

---

21. Götz Schmitt, "Das Zeichen des Jona," *ZNW* 69 (1978): 123 – 29.

22. Joseph Grassi, *Peace on Earth: Roots and Practices from Luke's Gospel* (Collegeville, MN: Liturgical, 2004), 100.

23. There is a textual variant "under a basket" (ὑπὸ τὸν μόδιον), which harmonizes with 8:16, but it is an early interpretation that the saying refers to hiding a light and does not refer to a cellar or crypt where a light would be needed.

24. Susan R. Garrett, "'Lest the Light in You Be Darkness': Luke 11:33 – 36 and the Question of Commitment," *JBL* 110 (1991): 96.

The term "without guile" (ἁπλοῦς) literally means "single." It can have both a medical connotation ("healthy") and an ethical one and can apply to "single-mindedness, sincerity, integrity." In *T. Iss.* 6:1, it is prophesied "that in the end times, persons will abandon single-mindedness [ἁπλότης], guilelessness, and the commands of the Lord, allying themselves with insatiable desire, villainy, and Beliar." Double-mindedness is associated with every work of Beliar (*T. Benj.* 6:7).[25] This explains how an eye can be "evil" (πονηρός), which also has an ethical connotation and not simply a medical one ("unhealthy"). The one with an "evil eye" cannot receive the light and as a result is filled with darkness.

11:35 – 36 "Therefore, pay careful attention to whether the light in you is darkness. If then your whole body is radiant, with no part of it having darkness, then it will be radiant as when a lamp shines its rays upon you" (σκόπει οὖν μὴ τὸ φῶς τὸ ἐν σοὶ σκότος ἐστίν. εἰ οὖν τὸ σῶμά σου ὅλον φωτεινόν, μὴ ἔχον μέρος τι σκοτεινόν, ἔσται φωτεινὸν ὅλον ὡς ὅταν ὁ λύχνος τῇ ἀστραπῇ φωτίζῃ σε). Jesus concludes with an exhortation that is tied to a saying that implicitly refers to the last judgment. If one is filled with darkness, it has eternal consequences; it will lead to damnation with the prince of darkness. If one is filled with light, one will be radiant at the last judgment.

Nebe reads the phrase "will be [ἔσται] radiant" as a volitive imperative, "let it be."[26] But it more naturally refers to the future and alludes to the final judgment when a great light will shine that reveals the secrets in human hearts. A similar saying appears in Matt 13:43: "The righteous will shine like the sun in the kingdom of their Father." The one whose eye is single and who is full of light is counted among the children of light and "will *one day* be made wholly bright."[27]

Theology in Application

1. The Chaos of Evil

Critics of the reliability of the gospels claim that the early church invented sayings and incidents in the life of Jesus, but the church would never have invented the charge that Jesus was in league with Beelzebul. The charge recorded here confirms that Jesus' contemporaries believed that he did works of power. His opponents refused to acknowledge that they were evidence of the presence of God's power working in Jesus and a sign that God's reign had come upon them. They perniciously attributed his power to black magic inspired by satanic forces and refused to accept that Jesus' miracles were the "gracious act of God" producing "beneficent results."[28] Jesus' defense exposes the illogic of such a charge but also illumines the nature of the demonic. It always causes chaos, never healing. Even the secular world understands the irresistible power that evil can exert on people's lives.

Recognizing the power of evil does not mean that people turn to the truth. It also

25. Ibid., 99.
26. Gottfried Nebe, "Das ἔσται in Lk 11,36 — ein neuer Deutungsvorschlag," *ZNW* 83 (1992): 108 – 14.
27. Garrett, "'Lest the Light in You Be Darkness,'" 103.
28. Wright, *Jesus and the Victory of God*, 189.

has the power to lure and to deceive. Good is made to look like evil, and evil is made to look good. Evil abhors a vacuum and seizes every opportunity to take over human lives. Attempts to reform by one's own power are fruitless. While Jesus' image of the returning demons is intended to portray how evil works in contrast to what he does in routing evil, one can infer an additional theological corollary. Emmrich states, "It is not enough to have the power of one ruler routed; one must swear allegiance to the new sovereign, represented by the prophet. One must choose between kingdoms. It is the empty tenement that invites squatters."[29] The trouble is that the secular world does not identify this terror theologically and therefore does not accept the resolution that comes only through Christ.

2. Light versus Darkness

The implication of the sayings about light is that there is no natural, inner light in a human. Light comes from God alone; darkness comes from Satan. People have no power to expel the darkness on their own. They must turn to an external, divine source of power and light to drive out the darkness. But the darkness can become so thick that it can make people blind to the light. A popular expression has it that one "goes over to the dark side." It assumes a measure of volition; a person has rejected the light for the darkness. In doing so, one gives oneself over to a powerful force of darkness that intercepts the light and makes the darkness more impenetrable. The mind blinded by Satan cannot think straight and rebels against the truth (2 Cor 4:4).

Paul uses similar imagery in discussing why his kinsmen have rejected the gospel. He argues that "the god of this age has blinded the minds of unbelievers, so that they cannot see the light of the gospel that displays the glory of Christ, who is the image of God" (2 Cor 4:4). He attributes the positive response to the gospel to God: "For God, who said, 'Let light shine out of darkness,' made his light shine in our hearts to give us the light of the knowledge of God's glory displayed in the face of Christ" (4:6). Strachan comments: "So much of our religion is regarded as a quest in the dark, a venture of faith. God is regarded as waiting to be discovered. The Jewish and Christian conception is that God chooses his people, and reveals Himself to them (John 15:15)."[30]

29. Martin Emmrich, "The Lucan Account of the Beelzebul Controversy," *WTJ* 62 (2000): 184.

30. R. H. Strachan, *The Second Epistle of Paul to the Corinthians* (MNTC; London: Hodder and Stoughton, 1935), 83.

Luke 11:37 – 54

Literary Context

Jesus' metaphorical warning of the unclean spirit that is expelled and returns to find a house swept and put in order and brings in more powerful and deadly demonic reinforcements prepares for the blistering denunciation of the Pharisees and the law scholars in this section. Their reform movement attempted to clean Israel's house and put things in order, but it caused them to focus so much on externals that they failed to do what God requires. It is no wonder that they failed to recognize that the finger of God had come upon them in Jesus' ministry. The consequences, however, are serious. As leaders they will guide the people to their destruction.

Jesus' attack prepares for several themes that follow: the emphasis on giving alms (12:33); the warning against scrambling for honor (14:7 – 11); the accusation that the Pharisees are lovers of money (16:14) and devour widows' houses (20:46 – 47); their continued hostile scrutiny of Jesus (13:1; 14:1; 15:1 – 3); Jesus' continued attack on their empty piety (18:10 – 14) and misinterpretation of Scripture (12:1; 13:10 – 17; 14:1 – 6); the violent deaths of the prophets and of Jesus (13:33 – 34; 18:31 – 33; 19:47); and the warnings about the destruction of Jerusalem and the temple (20:9 – 18; 21:20).

Main Idea

The misinterpretation of what is vital to God leads to an empty religiosity that spills over into violence against those messengers from God who challenge it.

Translation

Luke 11:37–54

11:37	Circumstance	While he was speaking, **a Pharisee asked him to dine with him. He came in and took his place.**
38	Conflict	When the Pharisee saw that he did not first immerse before the meal, **he was amazed.**
39	Rebuke	**The Lord said to him,** *"Now, you Pharisees clean the outside of the cup and platter, but your inside is full of plundering and depravity.*
40	Epithet Question	*Fools, did not the one who made the outside also make the inside?*
41	Command	*But give alms from what is inside and, behold, all things are clean for you.*
42a	Woe	*But woe to you Pharisees,*
b	Reason	*because you tithe the mint, dill, and every herb and neglect justice and the love of God.*
c		*These things it is necessary to do without neglecting those other things.*
43a	Woe	*Woe to you Pharisees,*
b	Reason	*because you love the seats of honor in the synagogues and greetings in the marketplaces.*
44a	Woe	*Woe to you,*
b	Reason	*because you are like unseen graves, and people walk over them without knowing it."*
45	Objection	**A certain law scholar answered and said to him,** *"Teacher, saying things like this insults us too!"*
46a	Woe	**He said,** *"Woe to you law scholars,*
b	Reason	*because you load people down with burdens hard to bear, and you yourselves do not lift a finger to lessen those burdens.*

47a	Woe	Woe to you,
b	Reason	because you build the tombs of the prophets whom your fathers killed.
48	Inference	You are then witnesses and approve the works of your fathers,
		because they killed them, and you build [their tombs].
49	Consequence	Because of this,
		the Wisdom of God also said,
		'I will send them prophets and apostles,
		and some of them they will kill and persecute,'
50		so that the blood of all the prophets . . .
		that has been poured out since the foundation of the world
		. . . might be avenged on this generation,
51a		from the blood of Abel
		to the blood of Zechariah,
		who was killed between the altar and
		the sanctuary.
b	Prophecy	Yes, I tell you, it will be avenged on this generation.
52a	Woe	Woe to you law scholars,
b	Reason	because you took the key of knowledge.
		You yourselves did not enter and you hindered those who were entering."
53a	Circumstance	After he left there,
b	Opposition	**the scribes and Pharisees held an intense grudge against him and quizzed him about many things,**
54		**lying in wait to trap him in something coming from his mouth.**

Structure and Literary Form

Luke uses the meal setting to organize and present traditional material in a coherent account in which Jesus enters (11:37) and leaves (11:53). The context of a Pharisee's home sets the stage for his attack first on pharisaic preoccupations (purity, tithing, and accolades from others; 11:39 – 44) and second on their scholars' interpretation of the law (making it burdensome, concealing the key to knowledge; 11:46 – 52). The first unit contains a silent objection to Jesus' refusal to comply with a pharisaic practice of ritual purity and a response from Jesus about essential purity and the discrepancy between outward and inner purity. He follows this up with three woes against the Pharisees' practices. The second unit is introduced by an objection to this attack by a law scholar, which is followed by three woes for their faulty interpretation of the law.

The woes address a specific indictment of behavior that fails to conform to God's requirements. They express lament. Of all people, these persons who wear their religion on their sleeves should be the ones to set the example of what obedience to God means. The woes also pronounce doom on the listeners if they fail to change their ways (see 11:45 – 47).

Exegetical Outline

→ **I. Setting: failing to wash hands before a meal in a Pharisee's home (11:37 – 38)**

II. Jesus' attack on the Pharisees' practices (11:39 – 44)

    A. Ritual purity versus internal corruption (11:39 – 41)

    B. Tithing minutiae versus ignoring loving God and doing justice (11:42)

    C. Seeking personal honors (11:43)

    D. Causing defilement in others (11:44)

III. Jesus' attack on the law scholars' interpretation of Scripture (11:45 – 52)

    A. Making obedience to the law burdensome (11:45 – 46)

    B. Building memorials to the prophets and sharing in the shedding of righteous blood (11:47 – 51)

    C. Taking away the key of knowledge (11:52)

IV. Conclusion: plotting against Jesus (11:53 – 54)

Explanation of the Text

11:37 – 38 While he was speaking, a Pharisee asked him to dine with him. He came in and took his place. When the Pharisee saw that he did not first immerse before the meal, he was amazed (ἐν δὲ τῷ λαλῆσαι ἐρωτᾷ αὐτὸν Φαρισαῖος ὅπως ἀριστήσῃ παρ' αὐτῷ· εἰσελθὼν δὲ ἀνέπεσεν. ὁ δὲ Φαρισαῖος ἰδὼν ἐθαύμασεν ὅτι οὐ πρῶτον ἐβαπτίσθη πρὸ τοῦ ἀρίστου). Another Pharisee invites Jesus to dine (see 7:36), and the phrase "while he was speaking" (ἐν δὲ τῷ λαλῆσαι) suggests that he was in the audience and not offended by what Jesus was saying. But Jesus does startle him when he does not immerse before the meal.

Immersing (ἐβαπτίσθη) presumably refers to immersing the hands before a meal, which was connected to purity issues and not hygiene.[1] This pharisaic practice was based on a view of how one contracted defilement in daily activities and how one might remove it. Furstenburg explains: "Impurity can flow from one object to another, from food to body and then again to other food, and it can pass through many stages before dying out."[2] Hands easily transmitted impurity to food and liquids: "If his hands were dirty all becomes unclean" (m. Yoma 2:2). Consuming unclean food would defile their inner parts. That would have a detrimental effect on their program of prayer and study of the law.[3] Hauck comments, "Uncleanness is not just a lack of cleanness. It is a power which positively defiles."[4]

The righteous could not be filled with Torah and prayer if they were defiled. Therefore they sought to avoid it. According to m. Yad. 1:1, "[To render the hands clean] a quarter-*log* or more [of water] must be poured over the hands [to suffice] for one person." This quantity (equal to an egg and a half) acted as a spiritual detergent. The Pharisee must have assumed that Jesus followed this practice if he was "amazed" at his failure to do so. A later rabbinic tradition likens eating bread without previously washing the hands to having intercourse with a harlot (b. Soṭah 4b). According to b. Ber. 60b, "When he washes his hands he should say, 'Blessed is He who has sanctified us with his commandments and commanded us concerning the washing of hands.'" Only priests, however, are commanded to wash hands (Exod 30:19 – 21; see 40:12). The Pharisees' oral tradition extended this custom to all persons, not just priests, and as a preparation for eating all food, not just holy offerings. Jesus must believe that unclean hands that touch food and liquid do not defile persons if they consume them.

11:39 – 41 The Lord said to him, "Now you Pharisees clean the outside of the cup and platter, but your inside is full of plundering and depravity. Fools, did not the one who made the outside also make the inside? But give alms from what is inside and, behold, all things are clean for you" (εἶπεν δὲ ὁ κύριος πρὸς αὐτόν· νῦν ὑμεῖς οἱ Φαρισαῖοι τὸ ἔξωθεν τοῦ ποτηρίου καὶ τοῦ πίνακος καθαρίζετε, τὸ δὲ ἔσωθεν ὑμῶν γέμει ἁρπαγῆς καὶ πονηρίας. ἄφρονες, οὐχ ὁ ποιήσας τὸ ἔξωθεν καὶ τὸ ἔσωθεν ἐποίησεν; πλὴν τὰ ἐνόντα δότε ἐλεημοσύνην, καὶ ἰδοὺ πάντα καθαρὰ ὑμῖν ἐστιν). Jesus' response to his Pharisee host's unspoken criticism is more fiery and caustic than his response to his Pharisee host's unspoken

---

1. See Garland, *Mark*, 271 – 73.
2. Yair Furstenberg, "Defilement Penetrating the Body: A New Understanding of Contamination in Mark 7.15," *NTS* 54 (2008): 188.
3. J. C. Poirier, "Why Did the Pharisees Wash Their Hands?" *JJS* 46 (1996): 217 – 33.
4. Friedrich Hauck, "καθαρός," *TDNT*, 3:416.

criticism in 7:36 – 50, and once again is a breach of dinner etiquette. He first chastises Pharisees for their attention to the external ritual purity of cups and platters while ignoring their own inner defilement. Instead of being filled with light (11:34), they are filled with the darkness of plundering, driven by their greed and wickedness. Calling the host and his gathering of fellow Pharisees "fools" lumps them in with the godless (12:20; cf. Ps 14:1).

In matters of ritual purity, the inside of the cup is primary. A clean outside does not affect the ritual status of the inside. If the inside is unclean, the whole vessel is unclean.[5] Jesus accuses the Pharisees of cleansing only the outside of the cup when it comes to moral and spiritual matters, contrary to what is required in ritual matters concerning cups.[6] Maccoby concludes: "Outward observance is useless without inner moral purity, but that when such purity exists, outward virtuous behaviour will follow inevitably."[7] A saying from the Talmud (b. ʿErub. 65b) claims a person is known by "his cup," "his purse," and "his anger." To no surprise, those who neglect justice and love for God will have cups and plates full of plunder from extortion and robbery. If they want to cleanse something, they should start with what is most important, their hearts.

To "give alms" is the detergent that cleanses rapacity. "From what is inside" (τὰ ἐνόντα) is difficult and can be understood as an accusative of respect, "in connection with what is inside."[8] It would refer to the rapacious greed inside the Pharisees. It also makes sense as the second direct object of the verb "give" and refers to the contents of the utensils. The cup and plate are full because of their avarice (see Isa 3:14), and if they were to give away the plunder as alms, it would cleanse

them of their greed in the process.[9] Rendering the phrase "what is in one's power" may also capture the sense. One gives alms from what one has.

The story of Cornelius in Acts 10 illustrates this point. Though he disregarded Jewish purity laws as a Gentile, he was a devout man who feared God, prayed constantly, and gave alms (Acts 10:2). God declared him to be "clean" (Acts 10:15; 11:9).

11:42 But woe to you Pharisees, because you tithe mint, dill, and every herb and neglect justice and the love of God. These things it is necessary to do without neglecting those other things (ἀλλὰ οὐαὶ ὑμῖν τοῖς Φαρισαίοις, ὅτι ἀποδεκατοῦτε τὸ ἡδύοσμον καὶ τὸ πήγανον καὶ πᾶν λάχανον, καὶ παρέρχεσθε τὴν κρίσιν καὶ τὴν ἀγάπην τοῦ θεοῦ· ταῦτα δὲ ἔδει ποιῆσαι κἀκεῖνα μὴ παρεῖναι). Jesus launches a fusillade of woes that recalls the prophets' powerful denunciations of the people. The woe is akin to a curse that warns against catastrophe, which looms should the current behavior be continued. Doom can only be averted by swift repentance. The woe is a combination of righteous indignation and pain and often expresses pathos through irony.[10]

The first woe ironically attacks the Pharisees for being scrupulous about tithing trifles while being unscrupulous and neglecting something of major importance, justice. Jesus may be using hyperbole to exaggerate how they pay elaborate attention to inconsequential things since "rue" is specifically exempt from being tithed according to m. Šeb. 9:1 and "mint" is never mentioned in rabbinic literature. Tithing "mint, dill, and every herb" expands the natural interpretation of Deut 14:22 – 23 ("your grain, new wine and olive oil" and "the firstborn of your herds and flocks"). It

5. Hyam Maccoby, "The Washing of Cups," JSNT 14 (1982): 7.
6. Ibid., 4.
7. Ibid., 7.
8. Nolland, Luke, 2:664.
9. So Hays, Luke's Wealth Ethics, 121.
10. James G. Williams, "Irony and Lament: Clues to Prophetic Consciousness," Semeia 8 (1977): 51 – 71.

need not reflect sham piety to be hyperexacting in tithing but may result from a serious interpretation of the phrase "the yield of your seed" (Deut 14:22 NRSV).[11] Like the Pharisee who fasts twice a week and tithes all that he acquires (18:12), these people take things to the extreme.

Jesus does not dismiss the significance of conscientious tithing. They do need to do "these things," but they are meaningless if the one who tithes fails to love God (Deut 6:5) and do justice (Mic 6:8). Jesus therefore changes the paradigm of what really counts for holiness.[12] Those who are holy devote themselves to the love of God and its corollary, the love of neighbor, which entails devotion to justice.

The problem is that the Pharisees concentrate on more easily accomplished, but insignificant, pieties, to the neglect of broad, difficult to measure principles that are much harder to fulfill. Neither loving God nor doing justice can be limited to 10 percent but requires all one's heart, soul, strength, and mind (10:27). Jesus has shown that loving God requires loving the neighbor, and that is open-ended and far more costly (10:25–37). With the emphasis on giving alms in the preceding verse, it is implied that God "requires generosity beyond mere tithing."[13]

11:43 Woe to you Pharisees, because you love the seats of honor in the synagogues and greetings in the marketplaces (οὐαὶ ὑμῖν τοῖς Φαρισαίοις, ὅτι ἀγαπᾶτε τὴν πρωτοκαθεδρίαν ἐν ταῖς συναγωγαῖς καὶ τοὺς ἀσπασμοὺς ἐν ταῖς ἀγοραῖς). The seats of honor in the synagogue may to refer to elevated seats, separate from the congregation and restricted to those with the highest status. The synagogue was intended to be a place for prayer and the study of God's Word, but these leaders use

it to accrue prestige for themselves rather than to honor God. In the marketplace, they bask in the veneration shown them by others as the paragons of devotion to God. The human hunger for prominence, however, exposes their show of devotion to God to be just that—all show, no substance.

11:44 Woe to you, because you are like unseen graves, and people walk over them without knowing it (οὐαὶ ὑμῖν, ὅτι ἐστὲ ὡς τὰ μνημεῖα τὰ ἄδηλα, καὶ οἱ ἄνθρωποι [οἱ] περιπατοῦντες ἐπάνω οὐκ οἴδασιν). The third woe attacks the Pharisees for not being what they seem. Jesus exposes them as frauds.

Contact with a grave rendered a person unclean for seven days (Num 19:16), and consequently gravesites were carefully marked. Ironically, Jesus accuses those who so assiduously avoid defilement of being the worst source of defilement, corpse defilement. Because of the wickedness interred within them, these enforcers of purity are like doctors who, while serving their patients, unknowingly spread a plague. Like an invisible grave, no one realizes that they have been defiled from contact with the Pharisees until it is too late. Since one walks over an unmarked grave unwittingly, one may never recognize it. Since they reject the purposes of God (7:30), those who follow their lead are headed for destruction.

11:45–46 A certain law scholar answered and said to him, "Teacher, saying things like this insults us too!" He said, "Woe to you law scholars, because you load people down with burdens hard to bear, and you yourselves do not lift a finger to lessen those burdens" (ἀποκριθεὶς δέ τις τῶν νομικῶν λέγει αὐτῷ· διδάσκαλε, ταῦτα λέγων καὶ ἡμᾶς ὑβρίζεις. ὁ δὲ εἶπεν· καὶ ὑμῖν τοῖς νομικοῖς

11. Matthew's "dill and cumin" are subject to tithing according to *m. Maʿaś.* 4:5 and *m. Demai* 2:1 (Matt 23:23).

12. Marcus J. Borg, *Conflict, Holiness and Politics in the Teaching of Jesus* (Harrisburg, PA; Trinity Press International, 1984), 116.

13. Hays, *Luke's Wealth Ethics*, 166.

οὐαί, ὅτι φορτίζετε τοὺς ἀνθρώπους φορτία δυσβάστακτα, καὶ αὐτοὶ ἑνὶ τῶν δακτύλων ὑμῶν οὐ προσψαύετε τοῖς φορτίοις). Pharisees were laymen who were concerned to do what the law enjoined, avoid doing what it forbade, and thereby tried to fulfill the basic requirement that Israel be holy to the Lord. Not all Pharisees were expert interpreters of the law. One of their law scholars objects that they too are included in this attack and complains that Jesus is being offensive. As law scholars, they interpret the will of God for others, and Jesus unloads on them for substituting burdensome minutiae for God's will.

Interpreters of Scripture have two options: "to define in ever more detail, to impose ever more precision, to formulate ever more rules, and thus to lay ever more burdens upon those who would conform to the will of God (cf. Acts 15:10), or to ease the burdens, to limit the rules, and to highlight broad principles."[14] The law scholars have chosen the former; Jesus, the latter. Tithing "mint, dill and every herb" is a good example of their characteristic practice of adding greater specificity to the law (Lev 27:30; Deut 14:22), of making a fence around the law, and of making obedience to it more exacting. They offer no leniency, no relief, and no forgiveness to the sinner and the nonobservant who collapse under the load or who simply give up trying to bear it (see Acts 15:10).

11:47–48 Woe to you, because you build the tombs of the prophets whom your fathers killed. You are then witnesses and approve the works of your fathers, because they killed them, and you build [their tombs] (οὐαὶ ὑμῖν, ὅτι οἰκοδομεῖτε τὰ μνημεῖα τῶν προφητῶν, οἱ δὲ πατέρες ὑμῶν ἀπέκτειναν αὐτούς. ἄρα μάρτυρές ἐστε καὶ συνευδοκεῖτε τοῖς ἔργοις τῶν πατέρων ὑμῶν, ὅτι αὐτοὶ μὲν ἀπέκτειναν αὐτούς, ὑμεῖς δὲ οἰκοδομεῖτε). The number of martyred prophets grew in popular legend, and building tombs to memorialize them was an attempt to disown any guilt. How does this seemingly pious action implicate them in the murder of the prophets? If this is a reference to literal memorials, they do not celebrate the prophets' murders but declare: "'Had we lived in the days of the prophets, unlike our fathers we would have heeded them.' The irony is that they live in the days of the Messiah, and their guilt far surpasses that of their fathers ... [see 11:29–32; Acts 7:52–60]."[15]

They are the spiritual heirs of these past murderers because they also resist the will of God and will do the same thing to God's messengers who are sent to them. Jesus implies, "You like only dead prophets, not living ones."[16] Dead prophets cannot trouble or threaten them. Like their forefathers, they resist all who call them to account: prophets (7:30), the Messiah, and his apostles. Immediately after Jesus' jeremiad against them, they plot against him.

It is possible that Jesus does not refer to building actual tombs but makes a play on words. The scholars were known as "builders" or "edifiers" (see *m. Miqw.* 9:6; *b. Šabb.* 114a) in interpreting the law, and Jesus may turn this phrase against them.[17] Their barren and false interpretations of the law stifle the prophets. The prophets' cries for justice, among other things, are entombed and silenced by the scholars' hairsplitting over such things as the tithing of spices. They are foolish builders (6:47–49). Other "builders" will reject the

14. David R. Catchpole, "Temple Traditions in Q," *Templum Amicitiae* (ed. W. Horbury; JSNTSup 48; Sheffield: JSOT, 1991), 311.

15. David E. Garland, *The Intention of Matthew 23* (NovTSup 52; Leiden: Brill, 1979), 81.

16. Hendrickx, *The Third Gospel*, 3A:170.

17. Garland, *The Intention of Matthew 23*, 164–65. See J. Duncan M. Derrett, "'You Build the Tombs of the Prophets' (Lk. 11,47–51, Mt. 23,29–31)," *SE* IV (TU 102; Berlin: Akademie, 1968), 187–93.

cornerstone (20:17, citing Ps 118:22 – 23) and will become a stone of stumbling to others.

11:49 – 51 Because of this, the Wisdom of God also said, "I will send them prophets and apostles, and some of them they will kill and persecute," so that the blood of all the prophets that has been poured out since the foundation of the world might be avenged on this generation, from the blood of Abel to the blood of Zechariah, who was killed between the altar and the sanctuary. Yes, I tell you, it will be avenged on this generation (διὰ τοῦτο καὶ ἡ σοφία τοῦ θεοῦ εἶπεν· ἀποστελῶ εἰς αὐτοὺς προφήτας καὶ ἀποστόλους, καὶ ἐξ αὐτῶν ἀποκτενοῦσιν καὶ διώξουσιν, ἵνα ἐκζητηθῇ τὸ αἷμα πάντων τῶν προφητῶν τὸ ἐκκεχυμένον ἀπὸ καταβολῆς κόσμου ἀπὸ τῆς γενεᾶς ταύτης, ἀπὸ αἵματος Ἅβελ ἕως αἵματος Ζαχαρίου τοῦ ἀπολομένου μεταξὺ τοῦ θυσιαστηρίου καὶ τοῦ οἴκου· ναί, λέγω ὑμῖν, ἐκζητηθήσεται ἀπὸ τῆς γενεᾶς ταύτης).

Abel is the first righteous man murdered in Scripture (Gen 4:1 – 16), and Zechariah is the son of Jehoiada the priest, who denounced the people for transgressing God's commandments (2 Chr 24:20 – 22). He announced that because they had forsaken God, God had forsaken them. King Joash ordered him stoned and Zechariah's dying words were, "May the LORD see this and call you to account." The reference to Zechariah suggests that 2 Chronicles may have been placed last in a current canonical order. Zechariah, then, would be the last man murdered in the Scriptures. In English, the image is more easily conveyed as all the righteous blood shed from A to Z.

The problem for "this generation" is that

righteous blood pollutes the land and cries out until it is avenged (Gen 4:10 – 11; Job 16:18; Isa 26:21; Ezek 24:7 – 8; Joel 3:19; Lam 4:13; *1 En.* 47:1 – 4; *As. Mos.* 9:6 – 7). God is the avenger of blood (Deut 32:43; 1 Kgs 2:32, 37; 2 Kgs 9:7, 26; 24:4; Jer 26:15; Acts 5:28).

11:52 "Woe to you law scholars, because you took the key of knowledge. You yourselves did not enter and you hindered those who were entering" (οὐαὶ ὑμῖν τοῖς νομικοῖς, ὅτι ἤρατε τὴν κλεῖδα τῆς γνώσεως· αὐτοὶ οὐκ εἰσήλθατε καὶ τοὺς εἰσερχομένους ἐκωλύσατε). The key opens the door to knowledge; and since Jesus is speaking to law scholars, the key refers to the interpretation of Scripture. In their hands, the law that was intended to lead one to God has become an obstacle course.

11:53 – 54 After he left there, the scribes and Pharisees held an intense grudge against him and quizzed him about many things, lying in wait to trap him in something coming from his mouth (κἀκεῖθεν ἐξελθόντος αὐτοῦ ἤρξαντο οἱ γραμματεῖς καὶ οἱ Φαρισαῖοι δεινῶς ἐνέχειν καὶ ἀποστοματίζειν αὐτὸν περὶ πλειόνων, ἐνεδρεύοντες αὐτὸν θηρεῦσαί τι ἐκ τοῦ στόματος αὐτοῦ). Not surprisingly, the scribes and Pharisees do not appreciate this tirade directed against them. If they are anything like Paul (see Phil 3:5 – 6), they knocked themselves out trying to be righteous. Jesus challenges nearly everything that they have built their religious lives around, and it sparks the knee-jerk reaction of bearing a grudge against their detractor that will not be satisfied until he bears a cross.

Theology in Application

H. G. Wells was right in this description of Jesus:

He was like some terrible moral huntsman digging mankind out of the snug burrows in which they had lived hitherto. In the white blaze of this kingdom of his there was no property, no privilege, no pride and precedence; no motive indeed and no reward but love. Is it any wonder that men were dazzled and blinded and cried out against him?[18]

Jesus flushes the Pharisees and law scholars out from the safe lair of their supposed sanctity and exposes them to the light of day. He condemns them for allowing their religious practices and interpretations to get in the way of their obedience to God. He accuses them of exalting meaningless religious trivialities that cloak their inner depravity. He claims that their fastidiousness impedes others from obeying God. They cry out in protest, for their practices are not meaningless to them. But Harrington contends, "The purity laws were emphasized because they plainly distinguished Israel from non-Israel and defined Israel as physical and dependent on history and genealogy not on a universal, spiritual idea."[19] Jesus emphasizes the universal, spiritual idea that identifies Israel, and, as a consequence, this emphasis opens the door for those who do not observe the law as the Pharisees interpret it to be included in Israel. This indiscriminating openness sparks their ire.

Jesus' hermeneutic "resolutely places the gift before the demand, divine grace before human obedience."[20] He does not conceive of the law as a series of "innumerable obstacles" so that those who surmount them can boast of their achievement. According to Jesus, it is instead "a series of generous warnings addressed to pilgrims who are ill-suited for life."[21] When they fail, they encounter God's grace. Those who claim to succeed, spurn God's grace. But their success is only an illusion that comes from making out the test, grading it themselves, and awarding themselves an "A." They are in for a rude awakening.

Johnson identifies the intention of this conflict discourse as protreptic. It is aimed at the Christian audience and provides a negative counterimage to a positive ideal. He argues, "The purpose of polemic is not so much the rebuttal of the opponent as the edification of one's own school. Polemic was primarily for internal consumption."[22] It is not intended as a history lesson about the evils of Jesus' first-century foes but as a warning to Christian leaders not to commit the same sins or they will face

---

18. H. G. Wells, *The Outline of History, Being a Plain History of Life and Mankind* (Garden City, NY: Garden City, 1956), 362.

19. Harrington, *Holiness: Rabbinic Judaism and the Graeco-Roman World*, 164.

20. François Bovon, "The Law in Luke-Acts," in *Studies in Early Christianity* (Grand Rapids: Baker, 2003), 69.

21. Ibid.

22. Luke Timothy Johnson, "The New Testament's Anti-Jewish Slander and the Conventions of Ancient Rhetoric," *JBL* 108 (1989): 433.

the same condemnation. These tendencies plague humankind, and Christian leaders are no less susceptible to them.

Religious people of all stripes can easily fool themselves into believing that their exhaustive religiosity covers their sins. Jesus' attack on these representative religious leaders for their moral turpitude that strips all of their religiosity of any meaning is an attack on all who seek honor for themselves, wear public masks of piety, and expect adoration. They are no less guilty of intellectual duplicity and moral corruption. They hide behind the power of their religious authority that permits them to continue their abuse with impunity.

The Pharisees are guilty of majoring in minors and minoring in majors. They spin their wheels calculating the tithe for tiny amounts of herbs and vegetables, while ignoring the most important commands: to love God and one's neighbor (10:27). Tithing is fine, but focusing on the percentage of what one gives permits one to neglect how much one keeps for oneself. Justice may require unloading large proportions of one's wealth for the benefit of the poor. It may be the only way to cleanse greed. After the parable of the rich fool, Jesus commands his disciples to sell their possessions and give alms (12:33). Hays calls almsgiving "a spiritual wonder drug." It cleanses sin and rapacity (11:41). It imitates the generosity of God (6:35–36), and it brings an eternal reward (16:9).[23] It shares God's concern for the welfare of the poor. As the encounter with the rich ruler reveals (18:18–23), alms cannot be limited to loose change or even to one's surplus.

23. Hays, *Luke's Wealth Ethics*, 172.

Luke 12:1 – 12

Literary Context

The opening phrase of this section, translated "in these circumstances" (12:1), literally reads "at which things" (ἐν οἷς). It could be rendered as a time phrase, "meanwhile," but Luke intends to link the following sayings to the Pharisees' stalking Jesus and firing antagonistic questions at him to trap him. Their overt opposition to Jesus sets the stage for his instructions to his disciples, who will face similar adversity. They will join the long line of God's messengers who will be persecuted and killed (11:49; see 6:22 – 23), and they need to be prepared for that future. Faced with increasing hostility, Jesus encourages them to meet terror with fearless confession, assured of God's providential protection.

The gathered crowd, numbering in the thousands, does not factor in the beginning of this discourse, which extends through 13:9, since Jesus does not address them but his disciples. In the discourse, Jesus alternates back and forth between addressing the crowds (12:13 – 21, 49 – 59; 13:1 – 9) and the disciples (12:1 – 12, 22 – 48). He begins by indirectly continuing his assault on the Pharisees with admonitions, warnings, and promises that apply specifically to the disciples. In the context, the question is: Who should be the leaders of the people: the Pharisees, who are filled with greed, load down the people with impossible burdens, and take away the key to knowledge, or Jesus and his disciples, who proclaim the forgiveness of sins (24:47)? The Pharisees and law scholars will lead this generation to inevitable destruction (11:39 – 52), and the disciples must avoid those mistakes. But more, they cannot restrict the truth to hushed discussions in back rooms but must be ready to proclaim it fearlessly far and wide and be ready to face the consequences when it meets resistance and persecution.

The images of the final judgment in the discourse prepare for the warnings of judgment that follow (12:15 – 48; 13:1 – 9). Jesus' followers will not get a bye in the judgment. Consequently, they are to live their lives in full recognition that they will be held accountable to God for all that they say and do.

IV. Jesus' Journey to Jerusalem (9:51 – 19:28)

    D. Woes against the Pharisees and Lawyers (11:37 – 54)

➡   **E. On the Current Eschatological Crisis and Preparing for the Last Judgment (12:1 – 13:9)**

       1. Call to Fearless Confession (12:1 – 12)

       2. The Parable of the Rich Fool and Storing Up Treasure with God (12:13 – 34)

Main Idea

In the face of opposition, Jesus calls his disciples to fearless confession, assured of God's providential care for them.

Translation

(See next page.)

Structure and Literary Form

The discourse consists of promises, warning sayings, a Son of Man saying, and exhortations; these are brought together to exhort fearless confession in times of terror. It divides into four sections. Jesus (1) warns the disciples to steer clear of the hypocrisy of the Pharisees (12:1 – 3); (2) exhorts them to fear God and not any human adversary (12:4 – 7); (3) discusses the fate of those who confess the Son of Man and those who deny and blaspheme against the Holy Spirit (12:8 – 10); and (4) gives assurance that the Holy Spirit will teach them what to say in moments of trial (12:11 – 12).[1]

---

1. Martin W. Mittelstadt, *The Spirit and Suffering in Luke-Acts* (JPTSup 26; London/New York: T&T Clark, 2004), 66.

Luke 12:1–12

12:1a	Circumstance	In these circumstances, when a crowd of many thousands gathered,
		so that they trampled on one another,
b	Warning	**he began to say first to his disciples,**
		"Beware of the leaven of the Pharisees, which is their hypocrisy.
2	Promise	Nothing is covered up that will not be uncovered and
		hidden that will not become known.
3	Promise	*Therefore,* whatever you said in the dark will be heard in the light,
		and what you whispered in the ear in inner rooms will be proclaimed on the rooftops.
4	Admonition	I say to you, my friends, do not fear those who kill the body and
		after these things
		have nothing more that they can do.
5	Admonition	*But I will warn you whom to fear:* Fear him who, after the killing, has power to cast [you] into Gehenna.
		Yes, I say to you, fear this one.
6a	Rhetorical question	Do not five little sparrows sell for two small coins?
b	Assertion	*Yet* not one of them is neglected before God.
7	Admonition/encouragement	Indeed, even the hairs of your head are all counted.
		Do not fear!
		You are worth more than little sparrows.
8	Promise/assurance	I say to you, everyone who bears testimony about me before men,
		the Son of Man also will bear testimony before God's angels,
9	Promise/warning	*but* whoever denies me before men
		will be denied before God's angels.
10	Promise/warning	*And* everyone who will say a word against the Son of Man, it will be forgiven him,
		but whoever blasphemes against the Holy Spirit will not be forgiven.
11	Admonition	Whenever they bring you to the synagogues, rulers, and authorities,
		do not be anxious how you will defend yourselves or what you will say,
12	Assurance	*for the Holy Spirit will teach you in that hour what it is necessary to say."*

Exegetical Outline

→ **I. Setting and warning about the hypocrisy of the Pharisees (12:1 – 3)**

    A. Beware of hypocrisy (12:1)

    B. Promise: What is hidden will be revealed (12:2 – 3)

II. Exhortation to fear only God, not human powers (12:4 – 7)

    A. Humans can only kill; God can cast one into Gehenna (12:4 – 5)

    B. God knows the disciples intimately and cares for them (12:6 – 7)

III. Confessing the Son of Man; blaspheming against the Holy Spirit (12:8 – 10)

    A. Confessing the Son of Man brings eternal rewards (12:8)

    B. Denying the Son of Man brings eternal condemnation (12:9)

    C. Antagonists who oppose the Holy Spirit will not be forgiven (12:10)

IV. Promise of the Holy Spirit's aid at the moment of confession before worldly authorities (12:11 – 12)

Explanation of the Text

12:1 In these circumstances, when a crowd of many thousands gathered, so that they trampled on one another, he began to say first to his disciples, "Beware of the leaven of the Pharisees, which is their hypocrisy" (ἐν οἷς ἐπισυναχθεισῶν τῶν μυριάδων τοῦ ὄχλου, ὥστε καταπατεῖν ἀλλήλους, ἤρξατο λέγειν πρὸς τοὺς μαθητὰς αὐτοῦ πρῶτον· προσέχετε ἑαυτοῖς ἀπὸ τῆς ζύμης, ἥτις ἐστὶν ὑπόκρισις, τῶν Φαρισαίων). The Pharisees' attempts to blacken Jesus' reputation have failed as thousands trip over one another to gather around him. Jesus intends to drive a wedge between the disciples and these dominant interpreters of Judaism.

"Leaven" (ζύμη) is sourdough that could easily become tainted and spread poison to the rest of the dough in baking.[2] That is why in Scripture it is a symbol of corruption and the infectious power of evil (Exod 12:17 – 20; 23:18; 34:18; Lev 2:11, 6:17; Hos 7:4; 1 Cor 5:6 – 8; Gal 5:9). Jesus accuses the Pharisees of having a hidden, corrupting influence on the people. The Aramaic for "leaven" and "word" were homonyms,[3] and Matt 16:12 retains that connection: the "leaven" is their "teaching."[4] In Luke's context (11:37 – 52), the "leaven," which is their "hypocrisy," may also apply to their teaching.

The Pharisees appear to be faithful interpreters of God's will, but their inner corruption and false piety contaminate all they do and spread a contagion to all who follow them. Their interpretations are false. Disciples must dissociate themselves completely from their unhealthy teaching. Failing to heed this warning will be injurious to their spiritual health.

"Many thousands" (τῶν μυριάδων) gather around Jesus. In Acts 21:20, "many thousands" among the Jews are zealous for the law and also believe in Jesus. If they allow themselves to be deceived by false teaching (see Acts 15:1 – 2), they will fall away and lead others to destruction.

---

2. "Virus" might be a better modern image for the hidden danger that can infect and destroy.

3. Athanase Negoiṭă and Constantin Daniel, "L' énigme du levain and Mc, viii15; Mt xvi 6; et Lc xii 1," *NovT* 9 (1967): 310 – 14.

4. See Garland, *The Intention of Matthew 23*, 104 – 17.

12:2 – 3 Nothing is covered up that will not be uncovered and hidden that will not become known. Therefore, whatever you said in the dark will be heard in the light, and what you whispered in the ear in inner rooms will be proclaimed on the rooftops (οὐδὲν δὲ συγκεκαλυμμένον ἐστὶν ὃ οὐκ ἀποκαλυφθήσεται, καὶ κρυπτὸν ὃ οὐ γνωσθήσεται. ἀνθ᾽ ὧν ὅσα ἐν τῇ σκοτίᾳ εἴπατε ἐν τῷ φωτὶ ἀκουσθήσεται, καὶ ὃ πρὸς τὸ οὖς ἐλαλήσατε ἐν τοῖς ταμείοις κηρυχθήσεται ἐπὶ τῶν δωμάτων). What is covered up and hidden is the significance of Jesus' deeds and the nature of his relationship to the Father, not the secrets in people's hearts that they try to conceal. The Pharisees sought to defame Jesus and to prevent the truth from coming out (11:14 – 16). What must be exposed are not an individual's hypocrisies but the truth of the gospel that centers on Jesus' mission from God. This statement is a promise, not a caution.

Despite the dangers, the truth will not be whispered in the safety and secrecy of alcoves but proclaimed publicly and boldly (see 8:17). As "no one after lighting a lamp puts it in a hidden place but upon a lampstand so that those who enter may see the light" (11:33), so no one who believes the gospel will limit it to private discussions. It has an inner power that compels persons to proclaim it (see Acts 4:18 – 20). Bovon writes: "The transparency of the gospel is their best weapon."[5]

12:4 – 5 I say to you, my friends, do not fear those who kill the body and after these things have nothing more that they can do. But I will warn you whom to fear: Fear him who, after the killing, has power to cast [you] into Gehenna. Yes, I say to you, fear this one (λέγω δὲ ὑμῖν τοῖς φίλοις μου, μὴ φοβηθῆτε ἀπὸ τῶν ἀποκτεινόντων τὸ σῶμα καὶ μετὰ ταῦτα μὴ ἐχόντων περισσότερόν τι ποιῆσαι. ὑποδείξω δὲ ὑμῖν τίνα φοβηθῆτε· φοβήθητε τὸν μετὰ τὸ ἀποκτεῖναι ἔχοντα ἐξουσίαν ἐμβαλεῖν εἰς τὴν γέενναν. ναί, λέγω ὑμῖν, τοῦτον φοβήθητε). The call to be fearless anticipates the violence that will come from the Pharisees (11:48 – 49), among others. Jesus gave his disciples authority to cast out demons and to heal every disease but not to fend off persecution. They will face deadly opposition that will put their allegiance to the test.

For the first time, Jesus addresses his disciples as "friends." Many in Luke's Greco-Roman audience would understand the significance of "friend" from its Roman political context (see John 19:12). It referred to those loyalists in the emperor's favored circle. A "friend of Caesar" was under his protection. Those who mess with Caesar's friends will hear from Caesar. In the same way, Jesus' "friends" (φίλοι) are his protégés and will receive his support in their desperate circumstances.[6]

Jesus poses two questions to help his disciples assess accurately the real danger they will face in proclaiming the truth about him. First, he asks what kind of fear should hold sway over disciples: a timid, self-protective fear of their persecutors, or awe of God's sovereign power? What is to be feared more, bodily death or eternal death (see 4 Macc 13:14 – 15)? Luke must assume that his readers would understand from the context that Gehenna (γέεννα, the Greek transliteration of the Hebrew "Valley of Hinnom") refers to a place of punishment after death.

12:6 – 7 Do not five little sparrows sell for two small coins? Yet not one of them is neglected before God. Indeed, even the hairs of your head are all counted. Do not fear! You are worth more than little sparrows (οὐχὶ πέντε στρουθία πωλοῦνται ἀσσαρίων δύο; καὶ ἓν ἐξ αὐτῶν οὐκ

---

5. Bovon, *Das Evangelium nach Lukas (Lk 9,51 – 14,35)*, 251 (author's translation).

6. Hendrickx, *The Third Gospel*, 3A:179.

ἔστιν ἐπιλελησμένον ἐνώπιον τοῦ θεοῦ. ἀλλὰ καὶ αἱ τρίχες τῆς κεφαλῆς ὑμῶν πᾶσαι ἠρίθμηνται. μὴ φοβεῖσθε· πολλῶν στρουθίων διαφέρετε). The second question reminds disciples of their value to God. Jesus is not commenting on what a bargain little sparrows are but is arguing from the lesser to the greater.[7] He portrays God as knowing things that humans do not know, the number of hairs on their heads, and caring about things they do not care about, what happens to little sparrows. If God does not dismiss from the mind the little sparrows sold in the market, it follows that God will not ignore what happens to disciples who remain loyal to Jesus. They will not be "given over to oblivion" or "neglected."

The background for this perspective is Ps 84:3 and Jesus' statement in Luke 10:20, that their "names are inscribed in heaven." The saying about God's knowing the number of their hairs on their heads may be coupled with 21:18, where Jesus promises his disciples that not a hair of their head will be harmed when they are under fire and betrayed and hated by all (see Acts 27:34; cf. 1 Sam 14:45; 2 Sam 14:11; 1 Kgs 1:52). The point here, however, is not that God will rescue them from danger (see the death of Stephen in Acts 7:54 – 60), but that they should fear only the one who is able to know the number of their hairs and who has the power to cast them into Gehenna after death.

12:8 – 9 I say to you, everyone who bears testimony about me before men, the Son of Man also will bear testimony before God's angels, but whoever denies me before men will be denied before God's angels (Λέγω δὲ ὑμῖν, πᾶς ὃς ἂν ὁμολογήσῃ ἐν ἐμοὶ ἔμπροσθεν τῶν ἀνθρώπων, καὶ ὁ υἱὸς τοῦ ἀνθρώπου ὁμολογήσει ἐν αὐτῷ ἔμπροσθεν τῶν ἀγγέλων τοῦ θεοῦ· ὁ δὲ ἀρνησάμενός με ἐνώπιον τῶν ἀνθρώπων ἀπαρνηθήσεται ἐνώπιον τῶν

ἀγγέλων τοῦ θεοῦ). This prophecy anticipates the context of hostility awaiting Jesus' followers after his death, which is more fully described in 21:12 – 19. Disciples will be subject to harsh oppression and will be tempted to fall into a panic and renounce their faith. Jesus envisions "a future scene when the Lord Jesus, having achieved victory and honor, acknowledges those who supported him and disowns (v. 9) those who repudiated him during the present age."[8]

In contrast to the Pharisees, who are lauded by others on earth, the disciples can expect to be only objects of scorn. But the Son of Man, a circumlocution for Jesus that has an eschatological connotation, will be the advocate of these faithful ones and laud them in the heavenly court. If they have denied him, however, he will become their prosecutor. They lose their status as "friends" and will be condemned.

12:10 And everyone who will say a word against the Son of Man, it will be forgiven him, but whoever blasphemes against the Holy Spirit will not be forgiven (καὶ πᾶς ὃς ἐρεῖ λόγον εἰς τὸν υἱὸν τοῦ ἀνθρώπου, ἀφεθήσεται αὐτῷ· τῷ δὲ εἰς τὸ ἅγιον πνεῦμα βλασφημήσαντι οὐκ ἀφεθήσεται). This saying anticipates what Luke will narrate in the passion narrative and Acts. A word against the Son of Man refers to a denunciation or rejection of Jesus. Peter, for example, will deny Jesus three times (22:34, 57, 61). The people will reject him and demand his death (23:13 – 25). These sins can be forgiven if they repent because they have acted in ignorance (Acts 3:12 – 15, 19 – 21). But when Jesus is exalted at the right hand of God and God's promise of the Holy Spirit has been poured out on the disciples (22:69; Acts 2:33), those who deliberately reject and suppress the signs worked through

---

7. "Little sparrows" (στρουθία) is the diminutive form of "sparrow" (στρουθός).

8. Liefeld and Pao, "Luke," 220.

the Spirit saddle themselves with an insurmountable load of guilt.

The account in Acts 4:16 – 18 shows how this warning connects to the disciples' testimony about Jesus that is inspired by the Spirit. The priestly hierarchy recognizes that the apostles have performed a notable sign in healing a lame man at the gates of the temple (Acts 3:1 – 26), but they seek to muzzle the word about Jesus' power from spreading further among the people and forbid them from speaking or teaching in the name of Jesus.[9] Their intractable opposition to the apostles' testimony and to the Holy Spirit's work (Acts 5:32 – 33; 7:51 – 52) solidifies their rejection of the message and seals their fate and that of those who follow their lead.

12:11 – 12 Whenever they bring you to the synagogues, rulers, and authorities, do not be anxious how you will defend yourselves or what you will say, for the Holy Spirit will teach you in that hour what it is necessary to say (ὅταν δὲ εἰσφέρωσιν ὑμᾶς ἐπὶ τὰς συναγωγὰς καὶ τὰς ἀρχὰς καὶ τὰς ἐξουσίας, μὴ μεριμνήσητε πῶς ἢ τί ἀπολογήσησθε ἢ τί εἴπητε· τὸ γὰρ ἅγιον πνεῦμα διδάξει ὑμᾶς ἐν αὐτῇ τῇ ὥρᾳ ἃ δεῖ εἰπεῖν). This saying foreshadows and parallels the ominous warnings about the future that Jesus delivers in 21:12 – 19. The verb "defend" (ἀπολογήσησθε) is used in the context of the law court to defend oneself against charges (see Acts 26:1 – 2, 24; and the noun form in Acts 22:1; 2 Tim 4:16). When they are standing in the dock, it will not be a battle of wits with earthly authorities. The Holy Spirit will take control of what needs to be said in the hour of trial during their interrogation. The ultimate goal of the Spirit's intervention is not to get the accused off the hook but to convict the hearers of the truth of the gospel (see 2 Tim 4:17). That is why the defenses of Peter and John (Acts 4:5 – 23), Stephen (6:15 – 7:60), and Paul (Acts 22:1 – 21; 26:1 – 23) before the authorities under the inspiration of the Spirit are sermons, not speeches for the defense.

Theology in Application

1. Fearless Confession

Jesus' sayings in this section anticipate what is narrated in Acts. The promise is that the truth will be proclaimed. What begins behind the closed doors of an upstairs room (Acts 1:13) will soon spill out onto the streets of Jerusalem and will continue to be proclaimed unhindered to the ends of the earth (Acts 28:31). The disciples who proclaim the gospel will face pressure from those who would deny, denigrate, and suppress the work of the Holy Spirit. Their lives may be threatened for their proclamation. In that moment of crisis, they will face the decision to acknowledge and proclaim the Son of Man or to deny him. They will be tempted to equivocate or be silent. They also will be tempted not to trust the power of the Holy Spirit or God's providential care.

To fear the powers of the world and to acquiesce to them is to doubt Jesus' power as the resurrected Lord who reigns over all. These powers are false powers. They can

---

9. The parallels are noted by Odette Mainville, "Le péché contre l'Esprit annoncé en Lc 12,10, commis en Acts 4:16 – 18: une illustration de l'unité de Luc et Actes," *NTS* 45 (1999): 38 – 50.

take life, but they cannot create or give life. When they have killed, they are through, but God is not. God has power over life and death and a person's ultimate destiny after death. If God is attentive to what happens to even the slightest of creatures, certainly God will show care for Jesus' followers. If God cares enough to number their hairs, they are certainly prized. If they perish, they will not perish eternally. The persecution and even the death of Jesus' followers do not mean that God's redemptive purpose somehow has been derailed. Green comments, "Jesus' instruction is permeated by his vision of God, who has ultimate oversight in the unfolding of earthly events."[10]

These sayings reveal that while salvation is present, it is also future and yet to be fully revealed. One's behavior in this life affects one's salvation in the future. The warning comes that if one falls away in a time of testing (8:13), one risks the certainty of being denounced by Jesus in the judgment. But the passage is filled with assurances for disciples. The truth cannot be suppressed (Acts 5:34 – 39); the Holy Spirit will powerfully intercede in times of trial so that the truth will be proclaimed. Should disciples suffer for their testimony, those sufferings are not eternal. In the context, however, the blasphemy against the Holy Spirit is not something that Jesus warns disciples against. He is giving assurance that when they proclaim the truth, God is in complete control and those who resist their proclamation with violence will pay the penalty.

2. Blasphemy against the Spirit

Jesus does not direct this threat connected to blaspheming against the Spirit to his disciples, who are assumed to be faithfully proclaiming the Word. It is directed against "opponents who rise up to combat God's word wherever it is proclaimed."[11] It is not intended to be an open-and-shut theological proposition but is uttered in a polemical context that is designed to give assurance and confidence to Christian disciples who are proclaiming God's Word in a hostile environment. Like Jesus, they will have to endure defamation of their character and preaching by opponents who attempt to discredit a message that threatens their worldview, status, and sacred cows. What makes this sin so serious is that it reveals a deliberate rejection of the work of the Holy Spirit, which makes repentance improbable and, therefore, forgiveness impossible.

To say this sin is unforgivable, however, makes the point of the seriousness of this sin through hyperbole. Sadly, many Christians (like the great hymn writer William Cowper) have suffered from agonizing delusions that they had committed the unforgivable sin sometime in their past. Frank McCourt humorously recounts his confusion as a youth over the unforgivable sin that has bedeviled many Christians.

---

10. Green, *The Gospel of Luke*, 479.   11. Mittelstadt, *The Spirit and Suffering in Luke-Acts*, 84.

He knows that some sins are worse than others, which is why his church has various categories of sin, "the sacrilege," "the mortal sin," "the venial sin." Then there is the "unforgivable sin," which is a great mystery to him because you do not know if you have committed it if you do not know what it is. He fears being kicked out of the confession box and doomed to be tormented forever by devils in hell.[12]

Paul, however, is an example of one who opposed the Holy Spirit and violently persecuted the church (Acts 8:3; 9:1 – 2; Gal 1:23; 1 Cor 15:9; 1 Tim 1:14 – 16), but he responded to God's call. Had he continued to reject the forgiveness of sins offered in Jesus, to disparage it, and to squelch its proclamation by force or intimidation, he would have shut himself off from forgiveness and from salvation. But he became a recipient of God's forgiving grace (cf. 1 Tim 1:13 – 14).

---

12. Frank McCourt, *Angela's Ashes: A Memoir* (New York: Simon and Schuster, 2000), 124.

Luke 12:13 – 34

Literary Context

The parable of the good Samaritan addressed one aspect of what one must do to inherit eternal life: love one's neighbor. This parable of a rich fool and the sayings that follow it are the first in a series of parables and instruction that address another component of how one inherits eternal life: love God with all one's substance.

Throughout the travel narrative, Jesus addresses the issue of how disciples should use material possessions. The parable of the rich fool and instructions about how to store treasure in heaven vividly sound this leitmotif. Jesus has just condemned the Pharisees as "fools" because of their greed, being "full of plundering and depravity" (11:39 – 40). The rich fool is an example of those who are "lovers of money" (16:14) and who do not use their possessions wisely by giving alms and being hospitable to the poor but by serving their own selfish ends. His implied postmortem judgment fits the eschatological tenor of the discourse (12:1 – 59) with its warnings to fear the one who can cast your soul into Gehenna (12:5) and to be prepared for the unexpected coming of the Son of Man (12:40, 46). Death, when one will be called to account, also comes unexpectedly.

Main Idea

Fools do not take into account the inevitability of death in planning how to use wisely and properly their possessions, which are gifts from God, so as to please God rather than themselves.

Translation

Luke 12:13–34

12:13	Demand	**Then someone from the crowd said to him,**
		"Teacher, tell my brother to give me a share of the family inheritance."
14	Question	**But he said to him,**
		"Man, who appointed me a judge or arbitrator over your claims?"
15a	Warning	**Then he said to them,**
		"Watch and be on guard against all greed!
b	Reason	*For one's life is not defined by the abundance of possessions."*
16	Parable	**And he told them a parable, saying,**
		"The land of a certain rich man produced a good crop.
17a	Interior monologue	*And he debated with himself, saying,*
b	Dilemma	*'What shall I do, because I do not have enough space to store my crops?'*
18	Solution	*And he said,*
		'I will do this!
		I will tear down my granaries and build bigger ones,
		and I will store there all my wheat and good things.
19	Expected Result	*And I will say to my soul,*
		"Soul, you have laid up many good things for many years.
		Take it easy, eat, drink, and live it up?"'
20	Actual result	*But God said to him,*
		'Fool! This very night your soul will be demanded of you.
		And the things you have hoarded, whose will they be?'
21	Axiom	*It will be like this for everyone who stores up treasures for himself and is ⤴*
		not rich toward God."
22	Admonition	**He said to his disciples,**
		"Because of this I say to you,
		do not be anxious about your life, what you will eat;
		nor about your body, what you will wear.
23	Reason	*For life is more than food and the body is more than clothing.*
24a	Illustration (1)	*Consider the ravens because they neither sow nor harvest;*
		they have no storerooms or granaries, yet God feeds them.
b	Declaration	*You are far more valuable than birds!*
25	Rhetorical question	*Who of you will add a single minute to your life span by worrying?*
26	Inference	*Therefore,*
		if you cannot do such a little thing as that,
		why are you anxious about the rest?

Continued on next page.

27a	Illustration (2)	*Consider the lilies how they grow,*
		and they do not labor nor spin.
b		*I say to you, not even Solomon was arrayed as gloriously as one of these.*
28a	Inference	*If God clothes the grass of the field like this,*
		which is here today⏦
b		*and tomorrow becomes fuel for the oven,*
c		*how much more [will God clothe] you, O little-faithed ones!*
29	Admonition	*As for you, do not become obsessed about what you will eat and what you⏦*
		will drink
		and do not be anxious.
30	Reason	*For the pagan world seeks after all these things,*
		and your Father knows that you need them.
31a	Command	*Indeed, seek his reign,*
b	Promise	*and all these things will be given to you.*
32a	Command	*Do not fear, little flock,*
b	Promise	*because it is the Father's good pleasure to give to you his reign.*
33a	Command	*Sell your possessions and give alms.*
b	Command	*Make purses for yourselves that will not wear out,*
c	Command	*get a treasure in heaven that will not run out, where a robber cannot come⏦*
		near nor a moth ruin.
34	Axiom	*For where your treasure is, there also your heart will be."*

Structure and Literary Form

A bystander's selfish demand that Jesus compel his brother to divide a family inheritance sets up a discussion of greed. Jesus responds with a parable that is addressed to the crowd. It gives a negative example of one who stores up treasures for himself and not with God (12:16 – 21). It falls into four movements: the land producing a bountiful harvest (12:16), the problem of how to store this abundance (12:17), the solution to build new barns (12:18 – 19), and God's direct intrusion in judgment (12:20).

The next unit (12:22 – 34) addresses the disciples and develops how to store treasure with God. The unit contains two commands not to be anxious, followed by two enthymemes (a syllogism in which one of the premises is not expressed but implied) about birds being fed and flowers being clothed, which illustrate the point that God will take care of them. It concludes with the command to give alms as a way to store treasure with God.

Exegetical Outline

→ **I. Setting: a request to divide a family inheritance (12:13 – 14)**

II. Jesus' response to the crowd (12:15 – 21)

    A. Warning about greed (12:15)

    B. Illustration of the futility of greed: the parable of a rich fool (12:16 – 21)

III. Jesus' response to the disciples (12:22 – 34)

    A. Command not to be anxious (12:22 – 30)

        1. First rationale: life is more than food and clothing (12:22 – 23)

        2. Enthymeme from the world of birds related to food (12:24)

            a. Birds are fed by God (12:24a)

            b. You are worth more than birds (12:24b)

        3. Second rationale: no one can increase one's life span through worry (12:25 – 26)

        4. Enthymeme from the world of flowers related to clothing (12:27 – 30)

            a. The flowers of the field are arrayed beautifully (12:27)

            b. Flowers become the grass of the field and become fuel for ovens (12:28a)

            c. Unexpressed middle term: you are worth more than the flowers/grass of the field (12:28b)

            d. Conclusion: God will clothe you (12:28c)

        5. Reiteration of the command not to be anxious (12:29)

        6. Third rationale: anxiety is pagan and God knows one's needs (12:30)

    B. Command and promise: Seek God's reign and God will give what one needs (12:31 – 32)

    C. Command: Give alms (12:33 – 34)

Explanation of the Text

12:13 Then someone from the crowd said to him, "Teacher, tell my brother to give me a share of the family inheritance" (εἶπεν δέ τις ἐκ τοῦ ὄχλου αὐτῷ· διδάσκαλε, εἰπὲ τῷ ἀδελφῷ μου μερίσασθαι μετ' ἐμοῦ τὴν κληρονομίαν). A man interrupts Jesus' teaching (12:1 – 12) to try to persuade him to settle a dispute with his brother over the division of their father's inheritance. Inheritance disputes were common, and it would not have been unusual for one with a complaint to bring his case to a religious leader, since the Mosaic law embraced the civil and criminal as well as ritual and moral law.[1] Hock notes that inheritance disputes would have been more frequent and vital "because wealth was far more likely to be inherited than earned."[2]

Presumably, the man wants Jesus to exercise moral suasion on his brother. He is certainly the younger brother who has not received his due from his elder brother now in control of their father's estate. Marshall surmises that the elder brother wants to keep the family property intact while the

---

1. See Num 27:10 – 11; 36:2 – 10; Deut 21:15 – 17, which outline specific laws concerning inheritance. See *m. B. Bat.* 8 – 9 for rabbinic legal discussions on inheritance.

2. Ronald F. Hock, "The Parable of the Foolish Rich Man (Luke 12:16 – 20) and Graeco-Roman Conventions of Thought and Behavior," in *Early Christianity and Classical Culture: Comparative Studies in Honor of Abraham J. Malherbe* (NovTSup 110; ed. J. T. Fitzgerald et al.; Leiden: Brill, 2003), 183.

younger brother wants to take his share and separate it from family ownership. If this is accurate, a division of the property would mean a reduction in the overall wealth of the family.

It is one thing to say, "Rabbi, my brother and I are at odds over our inheritance, would it be possible for you to mediate?" To command Jesus to mediate the dispute is a different sort of request. This younger brother, by contrast, commands Jesus to assert his authority to do what he has already decided needs to be done, to force his brother to make some kind of settlement, which would finalize the already broken relationship. This interruption in Jesus' teaching is a rude reminder of how oblivious the average listener can be to his message about God's reign invading all of life and turning the world and its values upside down. The man represents the attitude of many who are so wrapped up in their own petty concerns they are deaf to Jesus' warnings about coming tribulations (12:11 – 12). He is only concerned about how he can get his hands on some cash that he thinks is due him.

12:14 But he said to him, "Man, who appointed me a judge or arbitrator over your claims?" (ὁ δὲ εἶπεν αὐτῷ· ἄνθρωπε, τίς με κατέστησεν κριτὴν ἢ μεριστὴν ἐφ' ὑμᾶς;). Jesus' response may reflect culturally expected humility that does not seek to do something that belongs to another's province,[3] but it is more likely that Jesus responds curtly because he does not brook fools easily. More important, Jesus is not a divider but a reconciler. In Greek, the difference between these two words is slight: "arbitrator" (μεριστής), and "reconciler" or "mediator" (μεσίτης). Moses addressed inheritance laws, but Jesus is greater than Moses and has a task far greater than to settle legal squabbles.

12:15 Then he said to them, "Watch and be on guard against all greed! For one's life is not defined by the abundance of possessions" (εἶπεν δὲ πρὸς αὐτούς· ὁρᾶτε καὶ φυλάσσεσθε ἀπὸ πάσης πλεονεξίας, ὅτι οὐκ ἐν τῷ περισσεύειν τινὶ ἡ ζωὴ αὐτοῦ ἐστιν ἐκ τῶν ὑπαρχόντων αὐτῷ). Jesus directs his next response not to the man but to his disciples whom he has been teaching (12:1). The man stands as a prime example of avarice that disciples must avoid.

12:16 And he told them a parable, saying, "The land of a certain rich man produced a good crop" (εἶπεν δὲ παραβολὴν πρὸς αὐτοὺς λέγων· ἀνθρώπου τινὸς πλουσίου εὐφόρησεν ἡ χώρα). As Jesus responds to this intrusion to his disciples, the crowds are able to listen in (12:1). The parable tweaks classical wisdom that is found, for example, in Sir 11:18 – 19: "One becomes rich through diligence and self-denial, and the reward allotted to him is this: when he says, 'I have found rest, and now I shall feast on my goods!' he does not know how long it will be until he leaves them to others and dies." Jesus classifies such a one as a fool. Seneca philosophized:

> How stupid to plan out the years that lie ahead when you are not even master of tomorrow. What madness to start out with long-term hopes, thinking, "I'll buy and sell and build, I'll lend money and take back more, and I'll gain positions of honor. And when I'm too old and tired, I'll retire." Believe me when I tell you everything is unsure, even for the most fortunate. (*Ep.* 101.4)

Seneca did not apply this wisdom to his own life, nor did he consider that there would be a judgment before God, but his statement reveals that Jesus' parable would have resonated across cultures.

That "the land ... produced a good crop" is

3. Bruce J. Malina, *The New Testament World: Insights from Cultural Anthropology* (Atlanta: John Knox, 1981), 78.

another way of saying that God produced it (cf. Ps 104:14). The Hebrews assumed that everything belonged to God (see Pss 24:1; 50:10 – 12). Note Paul's discussion of apostolic labor: God gives the growth through the miracle of divine power after humans have planted and watered (1 Cor 3:6 – 7). Jesus' parable in Mark 4:26 – 29 of the seed scattered on the ground states that it grows "all by itself" (αὐτομάτη) and the farmer does not know how it grows. This means God is behind the growth of seeds and the production of harvests. Philo says this explicitly: the earth bears of itself "independently of all skill in the husbandman" (*Creation* 167).

The rich man in this parable gives no acknowledgment of God for his bounty. His soliloquy contradicts Ps 24:1, "The earth is the LORD's, and everything in it" (see Ps 50:12), by containing five my's: "my crops," "my granaries," "my wheat," "my good things," and "my soul." For him, it is all about "me," not God or anyone else. His soliloquy also contains six "I's." He is totally self-absorbed.

12:17 And he debated with himself, saying, "What shall I do, because I do not have enough space to store my crops?" (καὶ διελογίζετο ἐν ἑαυτῷ λέγων· τί ποιήσω, ὅτι οὐκ ἔχω ποῦ συνάξω τοὺς καρπούς μου;). Luke's parables frequently include an inner dialogue (12:45; 15:17; 16:3; 18:4; 20:13). By being made privy to the internal musings of a character, the auditor gets a "realistic sympathy for the dilemmas of ordinary human existence."[4]

Selew notes that this type of speech reveals a character's "true values and motivations." Jesus "paints realistic portraits of ordinary people caught being themselves, quick sketches of authentic, though troubled individuals, grasping for help or advantage in life's crucial moments." The device also allows us to "see ourselves reflected in his little people caught in awkward places. The frantic thoughts and calculations, the desperate attempts to claw out of trouble, these defining moments of the Farmer, the Lost Son, the Judge or the Steward, could just as well be our own."[5] Observing them react to life situations allows disciples to gauge how they should react in light of God's inbreaking reign.

The farmer faces the dilemma of a bumper crop and bulging barns. He sees his quandary "as a practical rather than a moral dilemma."[6] He has a surplus, and the only question that enters his mind is the practical one: "Where can I store it to preserve it all for myself?" It never occurs to him that he is already rich and does not need any more.

12:18 And he said, "I will do this! I will tear down my granaries and build bigger ones, and I will store there all my wheat and good things" (καὶ εἶπεν· τοῦτο ποιήσω, καθελῶ μου τὰς ἀποθήκας καὶ μείζονας οἰκοδομήσω καὶ συνάξω ἐκεῖ πάντα τὸν σῖτον καὶ τὰ ἀγαθά μου). The rich man's solution to tear down the old barns and build new and bigger ones reveals that he is either totally unaware of or totally rejects the kind of thinking that speaks of storing treasures in heavenly barns and

---

4. Donahue, *The Gospel in Parable*, 126.

5. Philip Selew, "Interior Monologue as a Narrative Device in the Parables of Luke," *JBL* 111 (1992): 252. See also Bernhard Meininger, *Metaphorik, Erzählstruktur und szenischdramatische Gestaltung in den Sondergutgleichnissen bei Lukas* (NTAbh 24; Münster: Aschendorff, 1991). Hock ("The Parable of the Foolish Rich Man," 186 – 89) argues that it is more accurate to term it *ēthopoiia*, which appears in the *Progymnasmata* as an exercise for constructing how a speech might have

been spoken on a certain occasion. He assumes, however, that the parable derives from Luke reflecting Greco-Roman conventions. There is no reason not to assume that Jesus could construct parables with characters voicing interior monologues that revealed their situation and character without having been instructed in the Greco-Roman schoolroom. Ideas do not flow in pipelines.

6. Selew, "Interior Monologue as a Narrative Device," 245.

being rich toward God (12:21, 33 – 34). According to Wisdom, a fool's godlessness reveals itself in the lust for more and more.[7]

This solution to the problem runs counter to the strictest Jewish piety, which Jesus espouses. What was superfluous for one day should be given for the relief of others. It is expressed in Tob 4:16: "Give some of your food to the hungry, and some of your clothing to the naked. Give all your surplus as alms, and do not let your eye begrudge your giving of alms." Jesus taught his disciples to pray, "Give us each day our daily bread" (11:3), not a year's or even a week's supply. This man had plenty for this day, next month, and for many years to come, while there were beggars like Lazarus (16:19 – 31) and widows with barely two lepta to rub together (21:1 – 4) haunting the land. The inner dialogue reveals that the real problem for this man is not his surplus. It is his greed, the ruthless appetite to have more and more of what one already has regardless of the consequences to others.

12:19 "And I will say to my soul, 'Soul, you have laid up many good things for many years. Take it easy, eat, drink, and live it up'" (καὶ ἐρῶ τῇ ψυχῇ μου, ψυχή, ἔχεις πολλὰ ἀγαθὰ κείμενα εἰς ἔτη πολλά· ἀναπαύου, φάγε, πίε, εὐφραίνου). The farmer assumes that hoarding his grain will give him security. One might assume that if prices go up, he will be able to sell at the highest price and profit from the needs of others. This practice is condemned in Prov 11:26: "People curse the one who hoards grain, but they pray God's blessing on the one who is willing to sell." The words of Jeremiah are also apropos: "Like the partridge hatching what it did not lay, so are all who amass wealth unjustly; in mid-life it will leave them, and at their end they will prove to be fools" (Jer 17:11 NRSV).

The rich man echoes the philosophy expressed in Eccl 8:15: "So I commend enjoyment, for there is nothing better for people under the sun than to eat, and drink, and enjoy themselves, for this will go with them in their toil through the days of life that God gives them under the sun" (NRSV; see Eccl 2:24; 3:13; 5:18; Isa 22:13; 1 Cor 15:32). His self-satisfied contemplation of an exciting old age reveals that he mistakenly assumes that the abundant life is connected to an abundance of material things. He is an example of the covetous person consumed by his cravings (12:15). Not only will he not feast again on earth; he will not feast at the heavenly banquet.

12:20 But God said to him, "Fool! This very night your soul will be demanded of you. And the things you have hoarded, whose will they be?" (εἶπεν δὲ αὐτῷ ὁ θεός· ἄφρων, ταύτῃ τῇ νυκτὶ τὴν ψυχήν σου ἀπαιτοῦσιν ἀπὸ σοῦ· ἃ δὲ ἡτοίμασας, τίνι ἔσται;). The fear of the Lord is the beginning of wisdom (Prov 1:7; 9:10), and Jesus warns the crowd that one should fear the one who has the power to cast your soul into hell and not those who can kill only the body (12:4 – 5). It is the fool who says in his heart, "There is no God" (Pss 14:1; 53:1 – 4; Rom 1:21 – 22), and by his words and deeds this rich man reveals that he is a practical atheist. He has completely forgotten about God. But God steps into this story, as God is wont to do, right in the midst of his moneymaking and merrymaking and calls him a fool. The man intended for his hoard of good things to contribute to living it up. There is a play on words for the Greek reader. The nominal form based on the verb "live it up" (εὐφραίνου; i.e., εὔφρων) is similar to the epithet "fool" (ἄφρων).[8]

This man has a bigger problem than bulging

---

7. Fitzmyer, *Luke*, 2:972.

8. The man would be judged a fool from a worldly perspective because he prepares to enjoy his good things and never does (see Seneca, *Ep.* 13.16 – 17). From a theological perspective, he is a fool for being rapacious and full of greed.

barns that he fails to face. He is mortal. Securing his economic future does not mean that his future is secure (Ps 10:4 – 13; Prov 1:32; cf. Job 21:16). The one who began the story behind the scenes by producing the growth of the field now makes a direct appearance and exposes the farmer's foolishness. Since death is inevitable (Eccl 3:19 – 22; 5:12 – 16) and its timing is unknown, that should inform what one should do with disposable wealth.[9]

The conclusion has an indefinite third person plural verb and reads literally, "they are demanding [or requiring] your soul of you" (τὴν ψυχήν σου ἀπαιτοῦσιν ἀπὸ σοῦ). The "they" may refer back to the "many good things" in v. 19 and mean that his possessions have taken possession of his life. It could also be a circumlocution for God (see 6:38, 16:9; 23:31) and simply mean that God requires his soul tonight.

According to 1 Chr 29:14 (see Hag 2:8), God is the sole owner of all that we possess, including our very selves. This axiom of Israel's faith is expressed in *m. ʾAbot* 3:8: God owns us. Wisdom 15:8 contains a statement that reflects the major premise of this parable: "With misspent toil, these workers form a futile god from the same clay — these mortals who were made of earth a short time before and after a little while go to the earth from which all mortals are taken, when the time comes to return the souls that were borrowed." Because the man is a fool, he forgot that our lives are on temporary loan from God. All of the "I's" and "my's" in his interior monologue are shortsighted. He is going to die, as all humans eventually do, rich and poor.

Again, this point accords with the Wisdom tradition. In Eccl 8:8, the preacher says, "As no one has power over the wind to contain it, so no one

has power over the time of their death" (see also Jas 4:13 – 16). But when this man is making his plans, he is not dead yet. He has until tonight to make things right, but he does not know how little time he has.

God next asks the fool about all of the things he has prepared: "Whose will they be?" This question parallels the psalmist's condemnation of his persecutors, identified as "those who trust in their wealth and boast of their great riches" (Ps 49:6). In Ps 49:7 – 9, he reflects that no one can ransom his life from God so that he can live forever and never see the pit. He continues, "the foolish and the senseless also perish, *leaving their wealth to others*" (Ps 49:10, see vv. 16 – 20; see also Ps 39:6; Eccl 2:21; Sir 11:18 – 19; 14:15). The rhetorical question connects to the request of the bystander who is locked in a dispute with his brother over the family inheritance (12:13). One can imagine the family of the rich man in the parable gathering to mourn his sudden death and then arguing about who is going to get all the good things stashed away in the big barns. Some will never speak to one another again.

The basic warning about the misuse of wealth, which Jesus expresses here in parable form, is captured in a woe pronouncement in *1 En.* 97:8 – 10:

> Woe to you who acquire silver and gold, but not in righteousness, and say, "We have become very rich and have possessions and have acquired everything that we desired. Now let us do what we have planned, for we have gathered silver and filled our storehouses, and as many as water are the husbandmen of our houses." Like water your life will flow away, for riches will not stay with you; they will quickly go up from you, for you acquired everything in wickedness, and you will be given over to a great curse.

---

9. See *T. Ab.* 1:4 – 5, where the archangel Michael is sent by God to the "very rich" Abraham to "tell him about his death so that he may arrange for the disposition of his possessions" (see also 4:10 – 11; 8:9 – 11; 15:1, 7). Even before this angelic "commander in chief" Abraham proved recalcitrant.

12:21 It will be like this for everyone who stores up treasures for himself and is not rich toward God (οὕτως ὁ θησαυρίζων ἑαυτῷ καὶ μὴ εἰς θεὸν πλουτῶν). This conclusion assumes that the man in the parable, whom others might admire as shrewd and successful, made a disastrously bad investment. He stored the wrong kind of treasure in the wrong place and is spiritually bankrupt (see 18:18 – 30). He should have been storing treasure with God. The next unit describes how to be rich with God.

12:22 He said to his disciples, "Because of this I say to you, do not be anxious about your life, what you will eat, nor about your body, what you will wear" (εἶπεν δὲ πρὸς τοὺς μαθητάς· διὰ τοῦτο λέγω ὑμῖν, μὴ μεριμνᾶτε τῇ ψυχῇ τί φάγητε, μηδὲ τῷ σώματι τί ἐνδύσησθε). The conclusion of this unit advises us to store up riches in heaven by disposing of riches on earth by giving alms. What prevents this kind of generosity? Anxiety that one may not have enough for oneself. Jesus shows his disciples that anxiety is useless and unfounded.

In developing the lesson from the rich fool, Jesus does not bid disciples to be indifferent toward life. He is concerned that people have the material necessities for life, which is why one prays for daily bread. But he is aware of the tyranny of things. From his perspective, earthly treasure is a snare because it causes one to invest one's heart in the material world and to rest on its false security. Since material things are so easily lost (Prov 23:4 – 5), they are also a cause of anxiety. Anxiety prevents one from being focused entirely on God. Danger arises when persons become so engrossed in ensuring their material well-being that they go to pieces when it is threatened or is taken from them.

12:23 For life is more than food and the body is more than clothing (ἡ γὰρ ψυχὴ πλεῖόν ἐστιν τῆς τροφῆς καὶ τὸ σῶμα τοῦ ἐνδύματος). Anxiety over food and clothing is rooted in a fatal illusion that human needs are only physical. Worry about such things is like a flashing warning light that a basic conflict exists between one's trust in God and one's selfish concern for material security.

12:24 Consider the ravens because they neither sow nor harvest; they have no storerooms or granaries, yet God feeds them. You are far more valuable than birds! (κατανοήσατε τοὺς κόρακας ὅτι οὐ σπείρουσιν οὐδὲ θερίζουσιν, οἷς οὐκ ἔστιν ταμεῖον οὐδὲ ἀποθήκη, καὶ ὁ θεὸς τρέφει αὐτούς· πόσῳ μᾶλλον ὑμεῖς διαφέρετε τῶν πετεινῶν). Tannehill notes that the illustration from the world of flowers and birds to support Jesus' admonition not to worry is not forceful if it is viewed as ordinary observations about birds and flowers. The portrait only works if the repetition of the pattern breaks through the hearers' entrenched view of the world and engages their imagination so that they "begin to wonder which is the real world, the world of our anxiety, or this other world of which the birds and flowers are images."[10]

In the first stage of the argument, Jesus leads his audience to reflect on the ravens, which, according to Lev 11:15 and Deut 14:14, are classified as unclean and an abomination. Yet God feeds these birds without their having to sow or reap (see Job 38:41). The reference to ravens may be intended to recall when God commanded the ravens to feed Elijah by the Kerith Ravine (1 Kgs 17:4, 6). The picture is intended to trigger a contrast between an ideal world of the birds being fed by God with our own hustle and bustle and elaborate structures to amass food in barns. R. Simeon b. Eleazar is purported to have said: "Hast thou ever seen a wild

---

10. Tannehill, *The Sword of His Mouth*, 66.

animal or a bird practising a craft? — they have their sustenance without care and were they not created for naught else but to serve me? But I was created to serve my Maker. How much more then ought not I have my sustenance without care?" (*m. Qidd.* 4:14; *t. Qidd.* 5:15). Jesus' illustration emphasizes that God feeds birds in the same way that God brings forth a harvest.

Dio Chrysostom argued:

> Consider the beasts yonder, and the birds, how much freer from trouble they live than man, and how much more happy, and how much healthier and stronger they are, and how each of them lives the longest life possible, although they have neither hands nor human intelligence. And yet, to counterbalance these and their other limitations they have one very great blessing — they own no property. (*Serv.* 10:16)

The assumption is that owning property creates anxiety. Jesus, who owned nothing, might agree; but for him the problem is not owning property but having too much while others have nothing.

The conclusion "You are far more valuable than birds!" could be punctuated as a question or a statement, and I have chosen to read it as an emphatic statement. The unexpressed conclusion to this syllogism is that since God feeds birds and since humans are more valuable to God than birds, God will feed you. Therefore, worry reveals a lack of trust in God.

12:25 – 26 Who of you will add a single minute to your life span by worrying? Therefore, if you cannot do such a little thing as that, why are you anxious about the rest? (τίς δὲ ἐξ ὑμῶν μεριμνῶν δύναται ἐπὶ τὴν ἡλικίαν αὐτοῦ προσθεῖναι πῆχυν; εἰ οὖν οὐδὲ ἐλάχιστον δύνασθε, τί περὶ τῶν λοιπῶν μεριμνᾶτε;). The second stage of the argument draws on the impossibility of adding any time to one's life span. The introductory phrase, "Who of you?" anticipates an emphatic answer:

"No one!" The mortality rate remains steady at 100 percent, and even those who eat healthily and exercise regularly have no control over when they will die. The image is deliberately absurd: Who grows by worrying about their height? (ἡλικία can refer to stature.) Who can add a foot to his life? Worry not only can cut life short; it makes it miserable while it lasts.

12:27 Consider the lilies how they grow, and they do not labor nor spin. I say to you, not even Solomon was arrayed as gloriously as one of these (κατανοήσατε τὰ κρίνα πῶς αὐξάνει· οὐ κοπιᾷ οὐδὲ νήθει· λέγω δὲ ὑμῖν, οὐδὲ Σολομὼν ἐν πάσῃ τῇ δόξῃ αὐτοῦ περιεβάλετο ὡς ἓν τούτων). The third stage of the argument pictures the lilies of the field that neither toil nor spin and yet they increase. Jesus continues that these wildflowers are not merely clothed but are clad with such grandeur that not even the proverbially magnificent King Solomon could match it (1 Kgs 9:26 – 10:29; 2 Chr 9:13 – 28; Eccl 2:1 – 11).

12:28 If God clothes the grass of the field like this, which is here today and tomorrow becomes fuel for the oven, how much more [will God clothe] you, O little-faithed ones! (εἰ δὲ ἐν ἀγρῷ τὸν χόρτον ὄντα σήμερον καὶ αὔριον εἰς κλίβανον βαλλόμενον ὁ θεὸς οὕτως ἀμφιέζει, πόσῳ μᾶλλον ὑμᾶς, ὀλιγόπιστοι). Jesus dramatically switches the direction of his argument by now calling the flowers "the grass of the field." He is not being sentimental about flowers. The "grass of the field" was a standard image for something inconsequential (see *b. Sanh.* 102a), and its withering is used as an image for human finitude.

The tension between the glorious raiment of the flowers and their final insignificance leads to the question: How much more gracious will God be with humans? The argument accords with the psalmist's wonder, "What is mankind that you are mindful of them, human beings that you care for them?" (Ps 8:4), but it argues it in another way: What are birds that you are mindful of them; flowers that you care for them? The unexpressed middle term, "You are worth more than the flowers/grass of the field," leads to the conclusion that God will provide the necessities of life and clothe his disciples.

12:29 – 30 As for you, do not become obsessed about what you will eat and what you will drink and do not be anxious. For the pagan world seeks after all these things, and your Father knows that you need them (καὶ ὑμεῖς μὴ ζητεῖτε τί φάγητε καὶ τί πίητε, καὶ μὴ μετεωρίζεσθε· ταῦτα γὰρ πάντα τὰ ἔθνη τοῦ κόσμου ἐπιζητοῦσιν, ὑμῶν δὲ ὁ πατὴρ οἶδεν ὅτι χρῄζετε τούτων). To be seeking "all these things" (anxiously) is identified as a pagan activity. Pagans seek after all these things because they do not know God and are deceived about what is crucial in life. The awareness of God's love for us and our love for God casts out all anxiety. If God provides daily bread in answer to our prayer, why should one frantically seek after it and seek after more than one needs?

12:31 – 32 Indeed, seek his reign, and all these things will be given to you. Do not fear, little flock, because it is the Father's good pleasure to give to you his reign (πλὴν ζητεῖτε τὴν βασιλείαν αὐτοῦ, καὶ ταῦτα προστεθήσεται ὑμῖν. Μὴ φοβοῦ, τὸ μικρὸν ποίμνιον, ὅτι εὐδόκησεν ὁ πατὴρ ὑμῶν δοῦναι ὑμῖν τὴν βασιλείαν). Logic and reason do not necessarily rid one of anxiety. Only those who are confident in the coming of God's reign and who live out that confidence will be set free from anxiety's stranglehold. This saying

does not mean that if one seeks first God's reign, it will pay off in all kinds of material bounty. If one truly submits to God's rule, one will be unconcerned about material abundance (see Phil 4:12 – 13). One will receive much more that has ultimate significance (see 22:28 – 30).

12:33 Sell your possessions and give alms. Make purses for yourselves that will not wear out, get a treasure in heaven that will not run out, where a robber cannot come near nor a moth ruin (πωλήσατε τὰ ὑπάρχοντα ὑμῶν καὶ δότε ἐλεημοσύνην· ποιήσατε ἑαυτοῖς βαλλάντια μὴ παλαιούμενα, θησαυρὸν ἀνέκλειπτον ἐν τοῖς οὐρανοῖς, ὅπου κλέπτης οὐκ ἐγγίζει οὐδὲ σὴς διαφθείρει). The locale where treasure is kept ultimately determines its value. The earth is temporal; heaven is eternal. The way to store wealth in heaven is to give it away on earth. Storing one's treasure on earth refers to accumulating and hoarding possessions as the rich fool did.[11] Jesus gives an example of how one can store treasure in heaven. Giving money away to the needy, a deed of loving-kindness, is equivalent to storing wealth in heavenly treasuries (see Sir 29:10 – 11; Tob 4:8 – 9; see *m. Peʾah* 1:1; *b. B. Bat.* 11a).

12:34 For where your treasure is, there also your heart will be (ὅπου γάρ ἐστιν ὁ θησαυρὸς ὑμῶν, ἐκεῖ καὶ ἡ καρδία ὑμῶν ἔσται). The heart is the center for making decisions. What one treasures reveals everything about a person's heart. The implication is that if one's heart is tied to the ephemeral things of this world, one's heavenly treasure will be bankrupt, and it will prove to be a ruinous investment when God requires one's soul.

---

11. *1 Enoch* 97:9 berates the rich for having gathered silver and having "filled their storehouses (treasuries)" with money (like water).

Theology in Application

1. The Foolhardy Pursuit of Wealth

The average listener was probably not unlike James and John, who said to Jesus, "We want you to do for us whatever we ask" (Mark 10:35). The man who tried to wring from Jesus a legal decision in his favor is, like them, only concerned about himself. He is a classic example of soil that is ruined by an infestation of thorns. The cares of this age and the delight in riches choke out a proper response to the Word (8:14).

Many Westerners live in a materialistic, consumerist culture that bombards them with the message that success is having more things that will let them live a better life. Advertisers goad people to want more and promise that fulfillment, bliss, and well-being are just a purchase away. Such activity only breeds discontent, and many never learn that an abundance of things creates an abundance of worries.

Being rich and the pursuit of greater riches pose an even greater danger, however. Moses warns the people of Israel about to enter the land flowing with milk and honey that God said to him, when "they have eaten and are full and grown fat, they will turn to other gods and serve them, and despise me and break my covenant (Deut 31:20 ESV). They will say, "My power and the might of my hand have gotten me this wealth" (Deut 8:17 ESV). A life oriented toward riches rather than God is a life oriented toward death.

The rich man in the parable suffers from the peril of plenty. Mark Twain, in his "The Revised Catechism," lampooned the rapacity of his age: "What is the chief end of man? — to get rich. In what way? — dishonestly if he can; honestly if he must." Jesus' parable excoriates a consumerist culture, in which one wag has said, "We can't make enough money to buy all the stuff that we want but don't need."

In affluent cultures, most do not worry about getting fed but worry that they may not have as much as the next person. Consequently, if one were to read about this man in something other than a parable of Jesus entitled "The Rich Fool," one would more likely envy his good fortune than pity his avarice. The one who is so diligent in his quest to preserve his wealth is no fool according to human wisdom. He is more likely to be regarded as farsighted and shrewd, able to see the big picture and make daring business decisions. But such a person deludes himself into thinking that he is the master of his fate and that he can make himself invulnerable to the vicissitudes of this mortal life. He puts his trust in what he possesses rather than in God. As a result, he has plenty to live on, but nothing to live for.

The parable casts a spotlight on the values of our everyday life from the vantage point of eternity. From there, covetousness looks foolish. Those who invest only in themselves, their security, and their comfort and pleasure have made a bad investment in the end. They are spiritually and morally bankrupt. The paraphrase in *The*

Message captures the idea beautifully, "That's what happens when you fill your barn with Self and not with God" (12:21). The parable assumes that everyone must give a final accounting before God for how they have made use of God's bounty.

The man in the parable is a "fool" because he failed to use his possessions wisely and was oblivious to the certainty of death and its uncertain timing. He spent his last day alive selfishly planning for a long future. He was going to settle back and take it easy and enjoy the fruits of what he regarded as *his* bounty, not God's. He was careful and astute when it came to preparing for his comfort and security in this life but careless and stupid when it came to preparing for his ultimate destiny with God. Hock comments, "By foolishly thinking that the goods for his body were the goods for his soul, the rich man thereby neglected his soul which thus became impoverished, impoverished in the sense of lacking in virtue — self-control certainly, given his hedonistic lifestyle, but also perhaps in justice, wisdom and courage."[12]

By inference, Jesus' questioner is also a fool in his pursuit of material benefits at the expense of brotherly love. Hock cites a father's response in Longus's ancient novel *Daphnis and Chloe*. He tells his son not to be distressed when he learns that he will now receive only a portion of the inheritance instead of it all when his long-lost brother returns: "for there is no better possession than a brother.... Rather, love one another."[13]

2. Anxiety versus Generosity

The warning against anxiety and the command to store up treasure in heaven through almsgiving draws the lesson to be learned from the negative example of the rich fool. Lowery comments: "The imperative to relinquish and redistribute wealth grows out of the assurance that God provides sustenance and beauty sufficient for good life. Generosity flows from confidence in God's willingness and ability to provide."[14]

A harvest is a miraculous gift from God, but the farmer did not treat his bumper crop as an opportunity for sharing with others from God's bounty but as an occasion to keep more for himself and to hedge against future bad harvests. Such actions are rooted in fear that one may not have enough. "Fear," as Lowery notes, "breeds obsession with survival. It is a small step then to idolatry, the vain attempt to substitute certitude for faith, to find security in that which can be controlled rather than which simply must be trusted." By contrast, "faith sees the abundance as surplus to be shared, because God can be trusted to provide enough next year, as well."[15] When the world is divided up between the have-mores and the have-nothings, the love of neighbor should determine the answer to the question, "What shall I do with my surplus?"

---

12. Hock, "The Parable of the Foolish Rich Man," 195.
13. Ibid., 184, citing *Daphn.* 4.24.4.
14. Lowery, "Sabbath and Survival," 162.
15. Ibid.

Jesus allows that material things are necessary for life (12:16, 22 – 32), but a greater abundance of these things does not lead to a greater abundance of life.[16] Nor does it lead to greater peace and security. Instead, as Bultmann notes, "the person who supposedly has the world at his disposal is [often] its victim."[17] That person is often confused about what is really important in life. That is why Paul advises in 1 Cor 7:31 that one should "use the things of the world, as if not engrossed in them." The man in the parable learns too late that the only possessions worth having and storing up are those that death cannot snatch away. He also never gets to enjoy his "good things." The truth is that greater happiness derives from the experience of sharing things with others than from miserly attempts to accumulate and to stash them away.

3. Worry Devastates Discipleship

The quest for economic security prevents one from becoming a disciple who will follow Jesus all the way to the cross. Therefore, Jesus commands his disciples not to become so worried by concerns for daily sustenance or material prosperity that it causes them to be too distracted to function as disciples. Anxiety leads to nervousness, a want of courage, loss of confidence, misgivings, despondency, hankering for security at all costs, and even panic. None of these emotions characterizes a faithful disciple.

Jesus is not discouraging forethought but nervous anxiety. Sowing, reaping, and gathering (traditional male functions) and toiling and spinning (traditional female functions) can be done with anxiety or with faith. Manson writes that Jesus is not simply contrasting the beauty of nature with human artistry but making this point:

> the flower has a glory of its own not by any effort of its own, but simply by being what God meant it to be, no more no less. The ambitions and pride of a Solomon may and do run counter to God's will, so that the more he becomes what he desires to be, the less he resembles what God meant him to be. He is clothed indeed with a glory of sorts, but it is a glory that comes short of the divine glory revealed in wild flowers. In the natural world God's will is done because there is no other will competing with his. In the world of self conscious beings the case is different. Pitting their wills against God's they can fall below the level of the beasts of the field or inanimate things. That is the risk of freedom. On the other hand, they have the capacity of bringing their wills into subjection to God's will: and so of rising to a higher glory.... If the glory of Solomon falls below that of the lilies of the field, the light of the knowledge of the glory of God in the face of Jesus is something immeasurably far above anything in the natural world.[18]

16. Manson, *The Sayings of Jesus*, 271.

17. Rudolf Bultmann, *Theology of the New Testament* (trans. K. Grobel; New York: Scribner, 1951), 1:351.

18. T. W. Manson, *The Teaching of Jesus: Studies in Its Form and Content* (2nd ed.; Cambridge: Cambridge University Press, 1967), 164.

Luke 12:35 – 59

Literary Context

This section continues the theme of eschatological crisis and making the right decisions in light of it so as to be prepared. Death may come at an unexpected hour (12:20); the Son of Man will come at an unexpected hour (12:40). The assurances of security and the promise of reward (12:32) are now sandwiched by the warning to fear God, who has the power to cast them into Gehenna (12:5) and who will punish them severely if they are careless in their responsibilities or abuse their station (12:46 – 48).

Disciples should fear being unprepared when they are called to account. In the context, they are to be prepared to withstand persecution, to use their possessions wisely, and to be faithful in carrying out their responsibilities as servants in God's household. The setting for most of the images in this unit comes from the world of the household, which requires keeping lamps lit and doorkeepers on watch, masters returning unannounced, potential burglars breaking in, managers doling out food rations, rewards for faithful servants with greater responsibility, and harsh punishment for lax and iniquitous servants.

The last warnings about being blind to the urgency of the present time (12:54 – 56) and making a settlement with a plaintiff before being hauled into court and remanded to prison until the last penny is paid (12:57 – 59) are addressed to the crowds. These warnings prepare for the next unit (13:1 – 9), in which Jesus exhorts Israel to repent lest they all perish. Reconciliation with God is still possible. The warnings, however, apply beyond the impending crisis that will overtake Israel to the crisis of the coming of the Son of Man and the last judgment. The warnings are therefore universal in scope; everyone must be obedient. A reckoning with God will occur, and the present is always a time of critical decision.

Main Idea

To be prepared for the coming of the Son of Man, which can happen at any hour, disciples must faithfully discharge their duties.

Translation

(See next two pages.)

Structure and Literary Form

The sayings and parables recorded here, which are in the manner of an apocalyptic discourse, divide into three units. The first (12:35 – 40) contains warnings for disciples always to be prepared because they do not know the hour when they will be called to account. It includes the illustrations of the servants waiting for the master to return from the wedding banquet and the householder not knowing when a thief will break in. It concludes with the statement that the Son Man will come at an unexpected time. The second unit (12:41 – 48) contains illustrations of faithful and unfaithful servants that serve as warnings to all but are especially applicable for Christian leaders. The third unit (12:49 – 59) contains sayings related to the crisis created by Jesus' coming.

Exegetical Outline

➡ **I. Be prepared for the return of the Son of Man (12:35 – 40)**

    A. Be dressed for action (12:35a)

    B. Have lamps lit (12:35b)

    C. Be alert like a slave for the master's return (12:36 – 39)

    D. The Son of Man comes, like a thief does, at an unexpected hour (12:40)

II. Sayings are applicable to all (12:41)

Luke 12:35–59

12:35a	Command	"Be dressed for action
b		*and* keep your lamps lit.
36a	Command	Be like those waiting for their master to return from the wedding banquet
b	Purpose	*so that* when he arrives and knocks they⤴
		immediately open the door for him.

37a	Beatitude	Blessed are those slaves whom the master finds keeping watch.
b		Amen, I say to you,
		he will dress himself for service,
		have them sit, *and*
		come to serve them.

38	Beatitude	If he comes in the middle of the night or near the end and⤴
		finds them [doing] so,
		those are blessed.
39		But know this,

if the house master had known what hour the thief⤴
comes,
he would not have allowed [him] to break into his house.

40a	Command	Be ready,
b	Reason	*because* the Son of Man comes at an hour when you do not think⤴
		[he will come]."

41	Question	**Peter said,**
		"Lord, are you telling this parable for us or also for everyone?"
42	Parable	**The Lord said,**
		"Who then is the faithful and
		prudent manager

whom the master will put in charge of his serving staff
to give them their portion of food at the⤴
proper time?

| 43 | Beatitude | Blessed is that slave whom his Lord finds doing this when he comes. |
| 44 | | Truly, I tell you, he will put him in charge over all he owns. |

45	Interior monologue	But if that slave says in his heart,
		'My Lord is delayed in coming,' and
		if he begins to beat the men and women⤴
		servants and to eat and drink and get drunk,
46a		the Lord of that slave will come on a day he does not expect and an hour⤴
		he does not know,
b	Punishment	*and* he will cut him in two and put him with the unfaithful.

Continued on next page.

Continued from previous page.

47a		*That slave . . .*
		who knew the will of his Lord, but
		did not prepare for or do his will,
b	Punishment	*. . . will be whipped with many lashes.*
48a		*But the one . . .*
		who did not know and did deserve blows
b	Punishment	*. . . will be whipped lightly.*
c		*But to everyone to whom much is given, much will be required,*
		and to whom much is given, even more will be demanded.
49a	Statement of	*I came to cast fire on the earth;*
	purpose	
b	Question	*what do I wish if it is already kindled?*
50	Answer	*Now I have an immersion to undergo, and how I am pressed⮌*
		until it is completed!
51a	Question	*Do you think that I have come to give peace to the earth?*
b	Answer	*No, I tell you, but rather division.*
52a	Prophecy	*From now on, there will be five in one house and they will be divided,*
		three against two and two against three.
b	Conflict	
53a		*They will be divided,*
b		*father against son and*
		son against father,
c		*mother against daughter and*
		daughter against mother,
d		*mother-in-law against daughter-in-law and*
		daughter-in-law against mother-in-law."

54	Illustration	**He also told the crowds,**
		"When you see a cloud rising in the west, you immediately say,
		'A thunderstorm is coming';
		and so it happens.
55		*And whenever you see wind blowing from the south, you say,*
		'It will be scorching hot';
		and it happens.
56	Reproach	*Hypocrites!*
		You know how to evaluate the appearance of the earth and the sky,
		but do you not know how to evaluate this time?
57		*Why do you not judge for yourselves what is right?*
58	Reason/parable	*For as you go with your accuser before the ruler,*
		on the way endeavor to come to a settlement with him
		so that he will not drag you before the judge, and
		the judge hand you over to the bailiff, and
		the bailiff throw you in prison.
59	Conclusion	*I tell you, you will never get out from there until you have paid back⮌*
		the last cent."

III. **Faithful and unfaithful servants (12:42 – 48)**

    A. A faithful manager will feed the household and be rewarded with greater responsibility (12:42 – 44)

    B. Unfaithful servants will abuse responsibility and will be severely punished (12:45 – 48)

IV. **Jesus' purpose (12:49 – 53)**

    A. To kindle fire on the earth (12:49)

    B. To undergo a baptism (12:50)

    C. To bring division (12:51 – 53)

V. **Recognition of the coming crisis (12:54 – 59)**

    A. Ability to recognize weather signs but not the signs concerning the present time (12:54 – 57)

    B. Seizing the opportunity to make reconciliation (12:58 – 59)

Explanation of the Text

12:35 Be dressed for action and keep your lamps lit (ἔστωσαν ὑμῶν αἱ ὀσφύες περιεζωσμέναι καὶ οἱ λύχνοι καιόμενοι). "Be dressed for action" interprets the image of girding the loins that derives from the loose-flowing robes worn in Jesus' day. They were tied up with a sash whenever one prepared for action (17:8) or for travel (Acts 12:8). The perfect tense of the participle "having been girded" (περιεζωσμέναι) plus the imperative "be" (ἔστωσαν) implies that one is always dressed for action. Moses instructed Israel to eat the Passover with their loins girded so that they could depart at any moment (Exod 12:11), and this image may tie into the warning to beware of the leaven of the Pharisees (Luke 12:1), since leavened bread was also forbidden so that they could be ready for their sudden departure (Exod 12:15).

Lighting lamps is mentioned in 11:33 – 36. If the light goes out, they are in darkness and the darkness creeps in them. Here the image is connected to readiness (see Matt 25:1 – 13).

12:36 – 39 Be like those waiting for their master to return from the wedding banquet so that when he arrives and knocks they immediately open the door for him. Blessed are those slaves whom the master finds keeping watch. Amen, I say to you, he will dress himself for service, have them sit, and come to serve them. If he comes in the middle of the night or near the end and finds them [doing] so, those are blessed. But know this, if the house master had known what hour the thief comes, he would not have allowed [him] to break into his house (καὶ ὑμεῖς ὅμοιοι ἀνθρώποις προσδεχομένοις τὸν κύριον ἑαυτῶν πότε ἀναλύσῃ ἐκ τῶν γάμων, ἵνα ἐλθόντος καὶ κρούσαντος εὐθέως ἀνοίξωσιν αὐτῷ. μακάριοι οἱ δοῦλοι ἐκεῖνοι, οὓς ἐλθὼν ὁ κύριος εὑρήσει γρηγοροῦντας· ἀμὴν λέγω ὑμῖν ὅτι περιζώσεται καὶ ἀνακλινεῖ αὐτοὺς καὶ παρελθὼν διακονήσει αὐτοῖς. κἂν ἐν τῇ δευτέρᾳ κἂν ἐν τῇ τρίτῃ φυλακῇ ἔλθῃ καὶ εὕρῃ οὕτως, μακάριοί εἰσιν ἐκεῖνοι. τοῦτο δὲ γινώσκετε ὅτι εἰ ᾔδει ὁ οἰκοδεσπότης ποίᾳ ὥρᾳ ὁ κλέπτης ἔρχεται, οὐκ ἂν ἀφῆκεν διορυχθῆναι τὸν οἶκον αὐτοῦ). The images that follow draw on the unpredictability of two events, one expected, the return of the master, and the other unexpected, a burglary, to support why one should always be ready for action.

It is a notable household that has doorkeepers, and the first image pictures them faithfully performing their duties in the master's absence while waiting for his return from a wedding banquet. Romans divided the time from 6:00 p.m. to 6:00 a.m. when guards were posted into four three-hour watches (see Mark 13:35, evening, midnight, cock-crow, and dawn). Midnight divides the second and third watches. The Hebrew and Greek pattern was to divide the night into three watches. The second and third watch would last from midnight to dawn. This latter time frame is more likely here and suggests a longer wait and the greater likelihood that the servants will doze off and not hear the master's knock.

The parable does not require that Jesus be the returning master to make its point, just as the next one, the thief coming at night (12:39), need not refer to Jesus. The image is of a thief-like surprise (1 Thess 5:1 – 2; 2 Pet 3:10; Rev 3:3; 16:15). Householders should take precautions. Doorkeepers need always to be at their post and to be alert, and those caught unawares will face severe punishment. The image of a master serving his faithful slaves when he returns, however, differs significantly from what normally would be done (see 17:7 – 10). It reflects a world turned upside down. Since Jesus tells his disciples at the Last Supper that he is among them as one who serves (22:24 – 27), readers may connect the arriving "master" (τὸν κύριον, "Lord," v. 36) with Jesus. They may also see an allusion to the heavenly banquet.[1]

One anticipates the arrival of the master who eventually will come home, but one normally does not anticipate the arrival of a thief since robbers do not book appointments to burglarize nor do they send warning notices. The only protection against them is constant vigilance. The responsible party moves up the scale of servants and is identified as the "house master" (ὁ οἰκοδεσπότης).

12:40 Be ready, because the Son of Man comes at an hour when you do not think [he will come] (καὶ ὑμεῖς γίνεσθε ἕτοιμοι, ὅτι ᾗ ὥρᾳ οὐ δοκεῖτε ὁ υἱὸς τοῦ ἀνθρώπου ἔρχεται). In Jesus' context,

the Son of Man is in their midst, and yet many are blind to it and will be caught off guard in the moment of crisis. They do not know the time of God's visitation (19:44). In the readers' context, the images mean that they must always be ready because the timing of the end is unknown (Mark 13:32; Acts 1:7). It is likely to occur when they least expect it. Trying to pin down precise dates on some apocalyptic timetable chart is a useless exercise and distracts one from more urgent duties that prepare for the return of the Son of Man (see Acts 1:11). Readiness means "faithfulness in service and constancy in witness."[2]

12:41 – 42 Peter said, "Lord, are you telling this parable for us or also for everyone?" The Lord said, "Who then is the faithful and prudent manager whom the master will put in charge of his serving staff to give them their portion of food at the proper time?" (εἶπεν δὲ ὁ Πέτρος· κύριε, πρὸς ἡμᾶς τὴν παραβολὴν ταύτην λέγεις ἢ καὶ πρὸς πάντας; καὶ εἶπεν ὁ κύριος· τίς ἄρα ἐστὶν ὁ πιστὸς οἰκονόμος ὁ φρόνιμος, ὃν καταστήσει ὁ κύριος ἐπὶ τῆς θεραπείας αὐτοῦ τοῦ διδόναι ἐν καιρῷ [τὸ] σιτομέτριον;). Jesus has been addressing the disciples (12:1, 4, 22), though the crowds are also present (12:1, 13, 54). Peter, as the disciples' spokesman, asks, "Are these instructions applicable to us? Are we like those slaves who serve in the household?" Jesus does not answer directly. Peter (and the readers) must figure out for themselves how it applies. What follows only emphasizes, "The steward is answerable (in fidelity) to the master who appointed him, as well as answerable (in fidelity) to the other slaves."[3]

12:43 – 44 Blessed is that slave whom his Lord finds doing this when he comes. Truly, I tell you, he will put him in charge over all he owns

1. Green, *The Gospel of Luke*, 501.
2. Tiede, *Luke*, 241.

3. Johnson, *The Gospel of Luke*, 206.

(μακάριος ὁ δοῦλος ἐκεῖνος, ὃν ἐλθὼν ὁ κύριος αὐτοῦ εὑρήσει ποιοῦντα οὕτως. ἀληθῶς λέγω ὑμῖν ὅτι ἐπὶ πᾶσιν τοῖς ὑπάρχουσιν αὐτοῦ καταστήσει αὐτόν). The translation should not be "master" but "Lord" to make it clear that the one whom Peter addresses as "Lord" is also the one who will return. The reference to "his Lord" "ties the parable to the larger Lukan story."[4] When the slave is scrutinized by his Lord and found faithful, the reward is to move up in responsibility (see 19:17).

12:45 – 48 But if that slave says in his heart, "My Lord is delayed in coming," and if he begins to beat the men and women servants and to eat and drink and get drunk, the Lord of that slave will come on a day he does not expect and an hour he does not know, and he will cut him in two and put him with the unfaithful. That slave who knew the will of his Lord, but did not prepare for or do his will, will be whipped with many lashes. But the one who did not know and did deserve blows will be whipped lightly. But to everyone to whom much is given, much will be required, and to whom much is given, even more will be demanded (ἐὰν δὲ εἴπῃ ὁ δοῦλος ἐκεῖνος ἐν τῇ καρδίᾳ αὐτοῦ· χρονίζει ὁ κύριός μου ἔρχεσθαι, καὶ ἄρξηται τύπτειν τοὺς παῖδας καὶ τὰς παιδίσκας, ἐσθίειν τε καὶ πίνειν καὶ μεθύσκεσθαι, ἥξει ὁ κύριος τοῦ δούλου ἐκείνου ἐν ἡμέρᾳ ᾗ οὐ προσδοκᾷ καὶ ἐν ὥρᾳ ᾗ οὐ γινώσκει, καὶ διχοτομήσει αὐτὸν καὶ τὸ μέρος αὐτοῦ μετὰ τῶν ἀπίστων θήσει. Ἐκεῖνος δὲ ὁ δοῦλος ὁ γνοὺς τὸ θέλημα τοῦ κυρίου αὐτοῦ καὶ μὴ ἑτοιμάσας ἢ ποιήσας πρὸς τὸ θέλημα αὐτοῦ δαρήσεται πολλάς· ὁ δὲ μὴ γνούς, ποιήσας δὲ ἄξια πληγῶν, δαρήσεται ὀλίγας. παντὶ δὲ ᾧ ἐδόθη πολύ, πολὺ ζητηθήσεται παρ᾽ αὐτοῦ, καὶ ᾧ παρέθεντο πολύ, περισσότερον αἰτήσουσιν αὐτόν).

The image shifts from a slave who is inattentive and shirks his duty to one who is villainous and abuses his authority. The slave believes that the master's absence and delay permit him to fall into evil ways with impunity. The horrible punishment of dismemberment for shirking one's duty reinforces why they should fear God (12:4 – 5). Being cut in two reflects an extreme penalty and need not be literal but may be symbolically appropriate for one with divided loyalties. The reveling may be done with the food and drink intended for the other servants who must go without.

Different levels of punishment will be meted out to those who know the master's will and do not do it (see Acts 22:14; Rom 2:18; Jas 4:17; 2 Pet 2:21) and to those who do not know the master's will and do not do it. The latter "should have been anxious to find it [the master's will] out."[5] The bottom line is that all those who fail to perform their duty for whatever reason will be punished.

Gifts bring responsibilities. The Father gives good gifts to those who ask (11:13), and the disciples have been given to know the secrets of the reign of God (8:10), the power and authority over demons, and the ability to heal (9:1), and it is the Father's pleasure to give them the reign of God (12:32). Consequently, the disciples who have been entrusted with so much have the greatest responsibility. Those who prove treacherous will not only have these gifts taken away (8:18; 19:26), they will suffer the greatest punishment, for they have no excuse.

12:49 – 50 I came to cast fire on the earth; what do I wish if it is already kindled? Now I have an immersion to undergo, and how I am pressed until it is completed! (πῦρ ἦλθον βαλεῖν ἐπὶ τὴν γῆν, καὶ τί θέλω εἰ ἤδη ἀνήφθη; βάπτισμα δὲ ἔχω βαπτισθῆναι, καὶ πῶς συνέχομαι ἕως ὅτου

---

4. Rowe, *Early Narrative Christology*, 153 – 54.

5. Plummer, *Luke*, 333.

τελεσθῇ). "Fire" is a negative image in Luke (3:9, 17; 9:54; 17:29; see Rev 8:5 – 7), and the immediate context is one of judgment (12:45 – 48, 58 – 59) and division (12:51 – 53). Casting fire on the earth, then, is not related to the Holy Spirit that comes on the disciples after the resurrection (Acts 2:3 – 4) but refers to destructive judgment that also brings purification by separating out the evil from the good.[6] The people who are not God's true people will reject God's way of salvation and will be cut off. It is the winnowing that John prophesied would occur, and the chaff will be consumed in an unquenchable fire (Luke 3:16 – 17).

The wish may be unfulfilled, which is the way it is often translated, "and how I wish that it was already kindled!" (καὶ τί θέλω εἰ ἤδη ἀνήφθη).[7] I interpret it instead as a fulfilled wish that is progressing and punctuate it as a question: "What do I wish if it is already kindled?" This reading matches the structure of the next saying in v. 51 that contains a question and its answer. The fire has already been kindled in Jesus' public ministry, and the answer to his question "What do I wish?" comes in v. 50. He has set his face to go to Jerusalem (9:51), and he wishes that his task were already completed when the fire would engulf him and bring redemption to sinful humanity.[8]

The image of immersion derives from the Old Testament as a metaphor for "being overwhelmed by catastrophe."[9] Jesus refers to his impending death (9:22, 44). In 13:32 – 33, a verb closely related to the one translated here as "completed" (τελεσθῇ) is used in connection to his death. The way to Jerusalem that will accomplish God's purpose (18:31) results in rejection, suffering, and death (17:25). "I am pressed" (συνέχομαι) does not entail distress. It reflects Jesus' intense focus that occupies him to accomplish the urgent task set before him (see Acts 18:5; 2 Cor 5:14). He is compelled by the divine "must" and is "totally governed by this."[10]

12:51 – 53 Do you think that I have come to give peace to the earth? No, I tell you, but rather division. From now on, there will be five in one house and they will be divided, three against two and two against three. They will be divided, father against son and son against father, mother against daughter and daughter against mother, mother-in-law against daughter-in-law and daughter-in-law against mother-in-law (δοκεῖτε ὅτι εἰρήνην παρεγενόμην δοῦναι ἐν τῇ γῇ; οὐχί, λέγω ὑμῖν, ἀλλ᾽ ἢ διαμερισμόν. ἔσονται γὰρ ἀπὸ τοῦ νῦν πέντε ἐν ἑνὶ οἴκῳ διαμεμερισμένοι, τρεῖς ἐπὶ δυσὶν καὶ δύο ἐπὶ τρισίν, διαμερισθήσονται πατὴρ ἐπὶ υἱῷ καὶ υἱὸς ἐπὶ πατρί, μήτηρ ἐπὶ τὴν θυγατέρα καὶ θυγάτηρ ἐπὶ τὴν μητέρα, πενθερὰ ἐπὶ τὴν νύμφην αὐτῆς καὶ νύμφη ἐπὶ τὴν πενθεράν).

People might think that Jesus came to bring peace from such passages as Isa 9:5 – 7 and Zech 9:9 – 10 that speak of a Davidic heir. Readers might also think that from the angel's announcement in Luke 2:14. The announcement of Solomon's birth in 1 Chr 22:9 identifies him as "a man of peace and rest" and specifies that God "will grant Israel peace and quiet during his reign." But something greater than Solomon is here and something worse is in store for Israel. It is ominous that in Luke 19:38, the crowd mentions only peace in heaven, not on earth, and then Jesus weeps over a city that does not know the things that make for peace and consequently will know no peace (19:42).[11]

---

6. Marshall, *The Gospel of Luke*, 547.

7. Plummer, *Luke*, 334, notes it "does rather serious violence to the Greek," and many trace it to an Aramaism (Isa 9:5; Sir 23:14).

8. The "now" (δέ) serves as a linking marker and can mean "that is" (see BDAG).

9. Plummer, *Luke*, 334. See 2 Sam 22:5; Pss 42:7; 69:1 – 2; Isa 43:2.

10. Helmut Köster, "συνέχω, συνοχή," *TDNT*, 7:882.

11. Hendrickx, *The Third Gospel*, 3A:260.

The Roman peace was false and only preserved the existing order. The strife Jesus describes is the inevitable result created by preaching the gospel. It brings perturbation, conviction, disarray, mental confusion, and family divisions. Responding to God's offer may indeed create strife since not all will accept it. The time of decision will create a divided response, not only in Israel, but in the most basic unit of society, the family, which will be pulled apart (see Mic 7:6). Michaelis writes, "The one who decides for Jesus must be prepared for the enmity even of those most closely related to him."[12]

12:54 – 57 He also told the crowds, "When you see a cloud rising in the west, you immediately say, 'A thunderstorm is coming'; and so it happens. And whenever you see wind blowing from the south, you say, 'It will be scorching hot'; and it happens. Hypocrites! You know how to evaluate the appearance of the earth and the sky, but do you not know how to evaluate this time? Why do you not judge for yourselves what is right?" (ἔλεγεν δὲ καὶ τοῖς ὄχλοις· ὅταν ἴδητε [τὴν] νεφέλην ἀνατέλλουσαν ἐπὶ δυσμῶν, εὐθέως λέγετε ὅτι ὄμβρος ἔρχεται, καὶ γίνεται οὕτως· καὶ ὅταν νότον πνέοντα, λέγετε ὅτι καύσων ἔσται, καὶ γίνεται. ὑποκριταί, τὸ πρόσωπον τῆς γῆς καὶ τοῦ οὐρανοῦ οἴδατε δοκιμάζειν, τὸν καιρὸν δὲ τοῦτον πῶς οὐκ οἴδατε δοκιμάζειν; τί δὲ καὶ ἀφ' ἑαυτῶν οὐ κρίνετε τὸ δίκαιον;).

The crowds are still gathered around Jesus and his band of disciples, and he warns them to recognize the signs of the coming crisis. Weather in Palestine is determined by the west and east winds. In Palestine, west winds bring in cool air from the sea and can carry rain. East winds, originating in the desert, bring a heat wave (Gen 41:6; Ezek 17:10; Hos 13:15). Bovon notes that in the Mediterranean areas, it is the south wind from the Sahara that brings the scorching heat. He concludes that Luke adapted "the meteorological situation to his own country, namely, Greece."[13]

Jesus calls them "hypocrites." A "hypocrite" in this instance is not someone who pretends to be something he or she is not. The term applies to the incongruity that they can interpret accurately the weather signs in the heavens but cannot interpret accurately the signs of God's heavenly intervention. It may imply that they are deliberately oblivious. "This time" (τὸν καιρὸν ... τοῦτον) refers to the presence of God's Messiah, which kindles the time of decision and hastens the time of judgment. They do not recognize how cloudy their future looks if they do not recognize the time of their visitation (19:44) or that a scorching fire of judgment looms on the horizon.

12:58 – 59 For as you go with your accuser before the ruler, on the way endeavor to come to a settlement with him so that he will not drag you before the judge, and the judge hand you over to the bailiff, and the bailiff throw you in prison. I tell you, you will never get out from there until you have paid back the last cent (ὡς γὰρ ὑπάγεις μετὰ τοῦ ἀντιδίκου σου ἐπ' ἄρχοντα, ἐν τῇ ὁδῷ δὸς ἐργασίαν ἀπηλλάχθαι ἀπ' αὐτοῦ, μήποτε κατασύρῃ σε πρὸς τὸν κριτήν, καὶ ὁ κριτής σε παραδώσει τῷ πράκτορι, καὶ ὁ πράκτωρ σε βαλεῖ εἰς φυλακήν. λέγω σοι, οὐ μὴ ἐξέλθῃς ἐκεῖθεν, ἕως καὶ τὸ ἔσχατον λεπτὸν ἀποδῷς).

Jesus is not giving mundane advice about how to avoid going to court and jail. With the coming judgment, the audience is in dire straits and does not know it. In this parabolic warning, what the secular judge will do in a lawsuit is what God will do in the judgment.[14] The warning is not

---

12. W. Michaelis, "μάχαιρα," *TDNT*, 4:526.

13. François Bovon, "Meteorology in the Synoptics (Luke 12:54 – 56 par.)," in *Studies in Early Christianity* (Grand Rapids:

Baker Academic, 2003), 40 – 41, 43.

14. The "bailiff" (ὁ πράκτωρ) was in charge of the debtor's prison and carried out the punishment.

addressed to individuals but to Israel. In the context, Jesus refers to God's coming judgment on Israel, which is temporal, rather than to the last judgment.[15] Reconciliation is still possible, but Jesus underscores the gravity of the situation by insisting that even such a small amount, the last cent, must be repaid. After the verdict is rendered, it is too late to settle.

Theology in Application

1. Being Prepared for the End

We are duly warned that the end comes without warning. Inevitably, it will catch people as unprepared as in the days of Noah, when his generation was swept away by the flood. They were so involved in everyday pursuits that they were oblivious to the disaster soon to overtake them (17:26 – 27). Jesus calls every generation to interpret the present time rightly. Bovon comments:

> As a prudent farmer or skilled sailor can foresee the weather, so we must learn not only to consider the present, that is, our time, but also to discover the future that is latent in the present. We need to do both; to read human history in our own reality and, more importantly, to decipher God's plan present in it.[16]

Today, many are closely attuned to the slightest shifts in the stock market so that they can make shrewd investments at the right time. These same people take no notice of the working of God in the world. Like the rich fool, they will be surprised when God intervenes in the midst of their worldly pursuits.

The image of masters and slaves is foreign to most contemporary readers, but the idea of being given responsibility and being called on the carpet for neglecting one's duties or being saluted for performing well is not foreign. Some may have experience in getting ready and waiting for an inspection review that will occur on a definite date, but it is different when one knows an event is coming but does *not* know when. Ceaseless vigilance can be tiring.

Yet that is what Jesus expects. Christians know they are on the edge of time. They are not to be on edge and filled with anxiety, but they are to be about their business for God. Yet it is easy to be lulled to sleep during the interim. Faith can wane, effort can decline, and commitment can vanish. Study, prayer, and self-discipline can be edged out by worldly pursuits. The true motive for being ever vigilant is not because the end is just around the corner, but because when it comes suddenly and unexpectedly, like death, it will be impossible then to prepare. It will be too late.

15. Brent Kinman, "Debtor's Prison and the Future of Israel (Luke 12:57 – 59)," *JETS* 42 (1999): 411 – 25.

16. Bovon, "Meteorology in the Synoptics," 43.

2. Serving Faithfully

It is more difficult to serve faithfully, to hope steadfastly, and to wait patiently when the timetable is uncertain. But as Summers claims, "The ultimate test of genuine faith is the demonstration of faith through a life of fidelity."[17] Jesus' instructions particularly apply to how church leaders should carry out their duties. Vigilance is required, but also responsible service. As good servants, they should perform their duties not only when they are under the watchful eye of their master but also when he is absent. Church leaders are required to be watchful (Acts 20:26 – 31a) but also faithful and reliable (Eph 6:21; Col 1:7).

Readiness concerns how leaders treat and relate to other people. Church leaders are involved in distributing food (9:13 – 17; Acts 6:1 – 3; 1 Cor 11:17 – 22), and food is also a metaphor for giving spiritual nourishment through teaching (1 Cor 3:2; Heb 5:12 – 14). The one who feeds others spiritual bread need not worry about the timing of the parousia. They are not to be domineering (2 Cor 1:24; 1 Pet 5:3) or exploit others selfishly. They are not to be drunkards (1 Tim 3:3, 8; Titus 1:7) or abuse their power. Paul sums it up: Those who serve in positions of leadership/stewardship in the church are to be found trustworthy (1 Cor 4:2).

Sadly, headlines continue to publicize the egregious failures of religious leaders. As one example, the scourge of clergy sexual abuse is an extreme abuse of power that has devastated the lives of victims, destroyed others' faith in God, and dragged the reputation of the church in the dirt. The horrible punishments pictured in this discourse cause many to blanch, but they seem apt for those who molest children and adults behind the cloak of sanctity.

3. Family Disruption

Jesus does not intend to drive a wedge into family loyalties, but a rupture may result from the choices that individuals make for or against God. Priorities need to be reordered. This disruption even in families cannot be avoided as long as there are some who prefer darkness to light (John 3:17 – 21). Justin Martyr (*2 Apol.* 2.2) describes the family disruption that occurred. A Christian woman divorced her husband because of her disapproval of his dissolute life, and he denounced her as a Christian and her teacher was sentenced to death. It is much like the fire that John prophesied would happen that separated the wheat from the chaff. Godet comments, "Without the cross, the conflagration lighted on the earth by the presence of Jesus would very soon be extinguished, and the world would speedily fall back to its undisturbed level."[18]

---

17. Summers, *Commentary on Luke*, 162.   18. Godet, *Commentary on Luke*, 2:136.

Luke 13:1 – 9

Literary Context

This unit concludes the discourse beginning in 12:1 that deals with preparation for the last judgment. It is peppered with exhortations to be ready for the judgment that may come at any moment. This final warning immediately follows Jesus' parabolic saying about the weather signs (12:54 – 56) and his concern that Israel recognize that they live in a time of crisis. They cannot be blasé in presuming that God's judgment is remote or that it will not touch them. Since they can interpret the heavens to know whether it will rain or whip up a hot south wind, why are they unable to interpret the significance of the present time from the signs of the kingdom of heaven?

In this scene, when Jesus is informed of an atrocity committed by Pilate against Galileans offering sacrifice, he brings up another catastrophe that occurred in Jerusalem. He warns his audience that they had better not detach themselves from these events but take heed. With an apocalyptic, doomsday perspective, he warns that these things point to their own destruction looming on the horizon. They may not be crushed by one of the great fortress towers at Jerusalem or become the sacrificial victims at one of the great religious feasts, but they are careening toward utter disaster unless they repent. The absence of any concrete sign of judgment may only be an indication that God is giving them one last chance. The warning is implicit: there may be a wideness to God's mercy, but there is a limit to God's patience.

Main Idea

Now is the time to repent. The disasters mentioned in this passage did not befall sinners guilty of particularly heinous crimes but serve as weathercocks pointing to what will happen to all sinners if they do not repent.

Translation

(See next page.)

Structure and Literary Form

The structure consists of an atrocity story reported to Jesus. Jesus responds unexpectedly by turning the story against his audience by warning them to repent. Roman atrocities are not to become a rallying cry for revenge. This first warning is followed by a description of a second catastrophe and a second, similar warning to repent. A warning parable then caps the argument.

Exegetical Outline

➡ **I. Complaint about Pilate's atrocity against Galileans (13:1)**

  II. Jesus' response: Repent! (13:2 – 3)

  III. Jesus' example from the tower of Siloam catastrophe (13:4)

  IV. Jesus' response: Repent! (13:5)

  V. Development of the point with the parable of the fig tree (13:6 – 9)

Luke 13:1–9

13:1	Atrocity story	At the same time **some who were present made known to him** the story of the Galileans whose blood Pilate had mixed with the blood of their sacrifices.
2a	Response	**He answered and said to them,**
b	Question	*"Do you suppose that these Galileans were worse sinners than all other Galileans* *because they suffered in this way?*
3a	Answer	*No, I tell you!*
b	Warning	*But if you do not repent,* *you will all perish in the same way!*
4a	Catastrophe story	*Or those eighteen people who were killed when the tower in Siloam fell on them,*
b	Question	*do you suppose that these were greater offenders than all the people dwelling in Jerusalem?*
5a	Answer	*No, I tell you!*
b	Warning	*But if you do not repent,* *you will all perish in the same way!"*
6a	Parable	**And he told this parable.** *"A certain man had a fig tree, which had been planted in his vineyard,*
b		*and he came looking for fruit on it but did not find any.*
c		*He said to his vinedresser,*
7a		*'Look, for three years I came looking for fruit on this fig tree and have found none.* *Chop it down!*
b		*Why should it waste the soil?'*
8a		*He replied to him,*
b		*'Sir, leave it for another year,* *and I will dig around it and* *throw some manure on it.*
9		*And if it bears fruit next year [well and good],* *but if not, you will chop it down.'"*

Explanation of the Text

13:1 At the same time some who were present made known to him the story of the Galileans whose blood Pilate had mixed with the blood of their sacrifices (παρῆσαν δέ τινες ἐν αὐτῷ τῷ καιρῷ ἀπαγγέλλοντες αὐτῷ περὶ τῶν Γαλιλαίων ὧν τὸ αἷμα Πιλᾶτος ἔμιξεν μετὰ τῶν θυσιῶν αὐτῶν). Some anonymous persons in the crowd inform Jesus about certain Galileans who were slaughtered by Pilate, the Roman prefect of Judea (3:1; see Acts 3:13; 4:27; 13:28).[1] Their blood was said to have been mixed with their sacrifices, which warrants the assumption that they were either in the temple offering sacrifices or going to the temple to offer sacrifices when they were killed.

Josephus records several atrocities in his works: the butchering of six thousand Pharisees in Jerusalem by Alexander Janneus when they objected to his offering sacrifice (*J.W.* 13.13.1 §§372 – 73), the slaughter of three thousand protesters in Jerusalem by Herod Archelaus during Passover (*J.W.* 2.1.2 §§8 – 13; *Ant.* 17.9.3 §§213 – 18), and the massacre ordered by Pilate of armed Samaritans who gathered to view the sacred vessels that Moses was purported to have buried on Mount Gerizim (*Ant.* 18.4.1 §§85 – 87). The bloodletting of unruly dissidents perceived to be threats to the status quo was not unusual in Judea as the authorities used violence to stifle unrest, maintain the peace, and secure their hold on power.

Josephus makes no mention of this outrage against the Galileans, however, but it may not have merited his attention because it was not large-scale carnage or because it did not fit his purposes. Josephus writes disparagingly of "Galileans," describing many inhabitants as "ever craving for revolution, by temperament addicted to change and delighting in sedition" (*Life* 17 §87). As a client of the Roman emperor's family, he disapproved of rebellious actions by Jews that ultimately led to the current decimation of Israel. We may guess that these victims were not innocents caught up in some random sweep by Pilate but that this strong-arm tactic was an overreaction against those perceived to be agitators of some stripe.

13:2 He answered and said to them, "Do you suppose that these Galileans were worse sinners than all other Galileans because they suffered in this way?" (καὶ ἀποκριθεὶς εἶπεν αὐτοῖς· δοκεῖτε ὅτι οἱ Γαλιλαῖοι οὗτοι ἁμαρτωλοὶ παρὰ πάντας τοὺς Γαλιλαίους ἐγένοντο, ὅτι ταῦτα πεπόνθασιν;). Luke does not tell us why these persons brought this incident to Jesus' attention. Did they wish to evoke an outburst against Pilate's sacrilegious cruelty or a dispassionate comment about the guilt of the Galileans? In his response, Jesus does not denounce Pilate as that "fox" (cf. 13:32), or rail against the Roman occupation of God's land, or attempt to stir up the crowd to join a Galilean rights movement that should fight to the death to drive the infidel from the land.

Jesus already has warned that the blood of Abel to Zechariah, who was murdered between the altar and the sanctuary, will be charged against this generation (11:51), so the hands of Jews are no less bloodstained by similar outrages. If anyone thought that these wretches were guilty of some horrible sin to suffer such a gruesome fate, Jesus does not condemn these Galileans as particularly sinful. The announcement of their deaths leads him to a different conclusion: Take this as a warning for all Israel.

---

1. Interruptions like this are common in Luke (7:37; 8:19; 10:25; 11:27, 37; 12:13).

Jesus identifies the victims as "sinners," which may be startling to those who broached the topic. My guess is that the reporters of this news and Jesus' audience regarded them as poor unfortunates, passive resisters in a just cause, and they expected Jesus indignantly to utter some malediction against Pilate as a representative of the evil Roman Empire. When he labels these hapless victims as "sinners" and lumps all other Galileans in the same category, he turns the case into an unwelcome reality check intended to force them to come to grips with the real issue facing them. It is not what Pilate has done; it is what God will do to all sinners. No one stands guiltless before God, and all Galileans alike will perish unless they repent.[2]

13:3 No, I tell you! But if you do not repent, you will all perish in the same way! (οὐχί, λέγω ὑμῖν, ἀλλ᾿ ἐὰν μὴ μετανοῆτε πάντες ὁμοίως ἀπολεῖσθε). Jesus challenges the crowd's assumptions, as he did in 12:51, with the statement, "No, I tell you." His response counters any mistaken theological notion that catastrophes like this only happen to sinners who deserve it (see Job 4:7; 8:4, 20; 22:5), while those who imagine themselves to be righteous have nothing to fear. The absence of any concrete signs of judgment in one's life is not a sign of one's righteousness or that a reckoning is not right around the corner (see 12:57 – 59). One may not distance oneself from the victims with such remarks as, "We are all sinners, of course, but not as bad as some."[3]

All are sinners, and all are deserving of punishment. Since these sinners met with a catastrophe, every other sinner in Galilee had better take heed from what befell their contemporaries. A bell is tolling, Jesus warns. Unless they dramatically change their ways of thinking and acting and start living according to his teaching, they are doomed. They need to know how to interpret the present time. It is the last hour "before the catastrophe of God's judgment breaks forth."[4]

13:4 – 5 Or those eighteen people who were killed when the tower in Siloam fell on them, do you suppose that these were greater offenders than all the people dwelling in Jerusalem? No, I tell you! But if you do not repent, you will all perish in the same way! (ἢ ἐκεῖνοι οἱ δεκαοκτὼ ἐφ᾿ οὓς ἔπεσεν ὁ πύργος ἐν τῷ Σιλωὰμ καὶ ἀπέκτεινεν αὐτούς, δοκεῖτε ὅτι αὐτοὶ ὀφειλέται ἐγένοντο παρὰ πάντας τοὺς ἀνθρώπους τοὺς κατοικοῦντας Ἰερουσαλήμ; οὐχί, λέγω ὑμῖν, ἀλλ᾿ ἐὰν μὴ μετανοῆτε πάντες ὡσαύτως ἀπολεῖσθε). Sinners are not confined to Galilee, and Jesus brings up the tragic demise of eighteen Jerusalemites who were killed in the collapse of the tower of Siloam. Josephus also never mentions this particular calamity, and we can only guess that it occurred during the construction or repair of a city wall or of the aqueduct leading to the pool of Siloam.

Pilate appropriated money from the temple's sacred treasury to build the aqueduct into Jerusalem, precipitating riots by outraged Jews (Josephus, *J.W.* 2.9.4. §175; *Ant.* 18.3.2 §60), and the accident could be indirectly connected to Pilate. Pilate could be the common denominator in both incidents cited. If this accident were to be perceived as some kind of divine punishment, God struck what would seem to be the wrong people — the supposedly innocent laborers rather than a perpetrator of evil against Israel.[5] Again, Jesus repeats the warning: these poor souls were no worse sinners than any

---

2. Josephus recounts going to pacify a brigand chief named Jesus in Galilee who plotted against his life. He informs him that he was not ignorant of the plot but would forgive "if he would show repentance and prove his loyalty to me" (*Life* §110).

3. Schweizer, *Luke*, 219.

4. Bornkamm, *Jesus of Nazareth*, 87.

5. Referring to this catastrophe with the tower of Siloam killing eighteen as a wake-up call for all Israel to repent would

other Judeans. All sinners in Israel will likewise perish unless they repent.

Jesus views Israel as headed on a collision course with Rome. Judgment looms on the horizon. Why focus on isolated incidents when all who inhabit Galilee and Jerusalem are in danger of perishing? The repetition of the dire warning heightens the sense of urgency. One might even draw the implication that Rome could be an instrument of divine justice against sinners of Israel, as Babylon was in the days of the exile.[6] Wright argues that for Jesus, repentance also carries the connotation that Israel must "abandon revolutionary zeal." It means to repent of nationalist violence and to "give up their way of being Israel."[7]

13:6 And he told this parable. "A certain man had a fig tree, which had been planted in his vineyard, and he came looking for fruit on it but did not find any" (ἔλεγεν δὲ ταύτην τὴν παραβολήν· συκῆν εἶχέν τις πεφυτευμένην ἐν τῷ ἀμπελῶνι αὐτοῦ, καὶ ἦλθεν ζητῶν καρπὸν ἐν αὐτῇ καὶ οὐχ εὗρεν). This parable continues Jesus' response and reinforces the urgency of the hour. It reflects the everyday practice of planting fig trees in vineyards (see Mic 4:4). Since it is planted in a vineyard, this tree has not been ignored but has received special treatment. Fig trees yield two crops annually, one around May-June, and the most important one in August-October. The budding of fig trees belongs to the early signs of spring, which is the background for another parable about signs of the times (see Matt. 24:32 – 35; Mark 13:28 – 30; Luke 21:29 – 33).

The fig tree is a potent image in Scripture. It is the only tree specifically mentioned in the garden of Eden, since it provided a covering for Adam and Eve. It appears as a figure related to the blessings of the Promised Land (Deut 8:7 – 8). The image of everyone sitting under his vine and fig tree during Solomon's era is one of blessing, peace, prosperity, and safety (1 Kgs 4:25; Mic 4:4). The fig tree, therefore, evokes images of Israel's golden past and hopes for a blessed future.[8] Conversely, the destruction of the fig tree represents a curse on the land (Joel 1:6 – 7; Amos 4:9).

As the vineyard is used in the Old Testament as a metaphor for Israel (Ps 80:8; Isa 5:1 – 7; Jer 2:21), the fig tree is used as a metaphor for Judah or Jerusalem (Jer 8:13; 24:1 – 10; Mic 7:1; Hos 9:10; see *2 Bar.* 39:1 – 8; *m. ʾAbot* 3:18; *Pesiq. Rab.* 60b for the tree as a metaphor for the leaders). The fig tree then becomes a transparent metaphor for Jerusalem or the temple (Hag 2:18 – 19; see the cursing of the fig tree in Mark 11:12 – 14, 20 – 25).[9] The deaths cited in Luke 13:1 – 5 occur in Jerusalem, and Jesus takes this as an ominous omen of what lies ahead.

A question arises whether the fig tree is newly planted or is an older tree. Jeremias argues that the parable has in mind a newly planted fig tree. If so, according to Lev 19:23 – 25, the fruit from that tree is forbidden for the first three years. The fourth year's fruit is to be dedicated to the Lord. The fifth year's fruit may be eaten. According to Jeremias's reconstruction of the parable, the owner has come for six years seeking fruit and concludes that since the tree has never borne fruit in that time, it must be hopelessly barren.[10]

The parable contains no indication that this

---

probably have been as welcomed in the first century as using the attack on the World Trade towers in New York, killing thousands, as a call for the United States to repent. The question naturally arises: "Why should we repent? It is the evil perpetrators who must repent or perish."

6. Manson, *The Sayings of Jesus*, 163.

7. Wright, *Jesus and the Victory of God*, 250, 254.

8. Scott, *Hear the Parable*, 338.

9. See Garland, *Mark*, 439 – 42.

10. Jeremias, *The Parables of Jesus*, 170. Bailey (*Through Peasant Eyes*, 82) contends that nine years would have passed: three years for the tree to grow; three years when they fruit was forbidden (Lev 19:23), and three years of seeking fruit.

fig tree was a new tree that has never borne fruit. The use of the imperfect of "had" (εἶχεν) and the perfect participle "planted" (πεφυτευμένην) functions as a pluperfect periphrastic. It places the emphasis on the results that existed in past time.[11] To render it, "A man had a fig tree planted in his vineyard" (NRSV) may wrongly imply that the fig tree has been newly planted. The perfect tense is better rendered: "A man had a fig tree growing in his vineyard" (REB). This translation suggests that Jesus pictures an older tree once fruitful, but for the last three years it has not borne fruit.

Some have seen in the reference to three years an allusion to the ministry of Jesus. This interpretation is imposed on the text, however, since there is no indication in Luke how long Jesus' ministry lasted. The three years may not refer to a specific period of three years but may be an idiomatic way of referring to "a long time" that has tried the patience of the owner (see 2 Cor 12:8).[12] For a long time, the owner has patiently come looking for fruit from this tree.[13]

13:7 He said to his vinedresser, "Look, for three years I came looking for fruit on this fig tree and have found none. Chop it down! Why should it waste the soil?" (εἶπεν δὲ πρὸς τὸν ἀμπελουργόν· ἰδοὺ τρία ἔτη ἀφ᾽ οὗ ἔρχομαι ζητῶν καρπὸν ἐν τῇ συκῇ ταύτῃ καὶ οὐχ εὑρίσκω. ἔκκοψον [οὖν] αὐτήν· ἱνατί καὶ τὴν γῆν καταργεῖ;). Since fig trees absorb large amounts of nutrients from the soil, an unproductive tree was doubly useless since it sapped nourishment from the vines. The owner sensibly commands the tree be cut down. Why should it use up the ground?

The owner's frustration over the tree's lack of productivity matches Jesus' own frustration at the

end of Luke 13. He compares himself to a mother hen desperately trying to gather her brood under her wings to protect them, but they will not be gathered and instead scoot away in different directions (13:34). The frustrated expectations aptly apply to the relationship between God and Israel. God desires that Israel (Galilee and Jerusalem) repent and accept the offer of salvation, but they stubbornly resist. The door for repentance is still open but not for much longer. Their refusal will lead to certain destruction — destruction as inevitable as that destined for a fruitless tree or for a defenseless chick left to the mercy of foxes and vultures.

13:8 – 9 He replied to him, "Sir, leave it for another year, and I will dig around it and throw some manure on it. And if it bears fruit next year [well and good], but if not, you will chop it down" (ὁ δὲ ἀποκριθεὶς λέγει αὐτῷ· κύριε, ἄφες αὐτὴν καὶ τοῦτο τὸ ἔτος, ἕως ὅτου σκάψω περὶ αὐτὴν καὶ βάλω κόπρια. κἂν μὲν ποιήσῃ καρπὸν εἰς τὸ μέλλον· εἰ δὲ μή γε, ἐκκόψεις αὐτήν). The parable takes a surprise turn when the gardener boldly intercedes for the tree. He requests that the inevitable be put off for another year to give the tree one more chance.

Jesus' original audience may or may not have been familiar with an ancient tradition in *Ahiqar* 8:35 (seventh to sixth century BC) and preserved in three versions, Syriac, Arabic, and Armenian. An unfruitful tree pleads not to be cut down and promises to produce in the next year. The owner refuses because its past record promises little change in productivity. In Jesus' parable, the vinedresser does what is unexpected by appealing on behalf of the tree. He pledges to dig around the tree and put manure on it in an attempt to save

11. See Wallace, *Greek Grammar*, 584, 647.

12. Erich Klostermann, *Das Lukasevangelium* (3rd ed.; HNT; Tübingen: Mohr [Siebeck] 1975), 143.

13. Charles W. Hedrick ("Prolegomena to Reading Parables: Luke 13:6 – 9 as a Test Case," *RevExp* 94 [1997]: 179 – 97) describes the lack of consensus among scholars on the meaning of this parable and claims a wide range of interpretations might be plausible and valid.

it. Jeremias claims that this would be unusual because the fig tree normally does not require such care. Bailey reads this as an example of "insult humor." He identifies the fig tree as a metaphor for the religious hierarchy in the vineyard of Israel and notes that the tree is not pruned and watered but manured.[14] What they need is a load of dung spread around them.

The "if" clause ("if it bears fruit next year") is left hanging in the Greek text and is not followed by an apodosis (a "then" clause). Modern translations fill in a response, "well and good," or "fine" (NIV). The performance record of the tree, however, does not hold much promise that it will meet the deadline. Will this special handling have any effect? Can fruitfulness come from barrenness without something more than an extra heaping of manure — some miraculous intervention? How much production counts as a success — a quart, a peck, a bushel of figs?

In light of John's threat that "every tree that does not bear good fruit is cut down and thrown into the fire" (3:9) and Jesus' stern warnings about

trees that bear bad fruit (6:43 – 45), the auditors might expect the same thing to happen to the fig tree as happened to the tree in the story of *Ahiqar*. The request will be denied, and the tree will get axed. But in Jesus' parable, the master gives no response; final judgment will be postponed to grant the tree one more year to bear fruit. The threat of judgment then becomes a call for repentance. But the time is short; its judgment will come at "an hour when you do not think" (see 12:35 – 40). It has until next season! A barren fig tree will not be allowed to encumber the ground forever. God cannot afford profitless trees. The tree must respond to this extra special care or it will be cut down.

Fitzmyer draws a contrast between the context and the parable.[15] The Galileans died from human malice; the Jerusalemites, from chance. He claims that they were not personally responsible for the evil that befell them. By contrast, the hearers of the parable will be destroyed by their own lack of productivity. They *will be* responsible for the catastrophe that will befall them if they fail to produce the fruits of repentance.[16]

Theology in Application

How does the parable apply to Jesus' context and ministry? Kilgallen contends: "the presence of Jesus is the presence of the vinedresser; his appeals to repent, i.e., produce good fruit for God, are those efforts of the vinedresser during the time of the owner's patience, a patience, which the parable suggests, does have an end."[17] Plutarch's discussion in *On the Delays of the Divine Vengeance* reveals that the problem Jesus has in awakening his Jewish audience to their danger is a pervasive human one. Plutarch cites Thucydides on the effects that an overdue debt of merited punishment has on people: It "strengthens the wrongdoer in confidence and boldness" (*Mor.* 549E). Since the blow has not fallen, wrongdoers may fool themselves into thinking

---

14. Bailey, *Through Peasant Eyes*, 84.

15. Fitzmyer, *Luke*, 2:1005.

16. This story becomes an acted parable in Matt 21:18 – 20/ Mark 11:12 – 25; see William R. Telford, *The Barren Temple and*

the Withered Tree (JSNTSup 1; Sheffield: JSOT, 1980).

17. John J. Kilgallen, "The Obligation to Heal (Luke 13, 10 – 17)," *Bib* 82 (2001): 409.

that they have escaped the divine punishment due them or that others are the ones who are due punishment.

For this reason, Jesus struggles to pierce Israel's false sense of security and to get the people to produce the fruit of repentance. Paul's argument in Rom 2:1 – 11 provides an apt commentary on Jesus' parable and call to repent. He cautions any Jew who dares to judge others who are no less guilty and who may be tempted to assure themselves, "Well, judgment has not fallen yet; we got away with it," by declaring:

> Do you despise the riches of his kindness and forbearance and patience? Do you not realize that God's kindness is meant to lead you to repentance? But by your hard and impenitent heart you are storing up wrath for yourself on the day of wrath, when God's righteous judgment will be revealed. For he will repay according to each one's deeds. (Rom 2:4 – 6 NRSV)

Jesus seeks to correct theological misconceptions about what God will do with an impenitent Israel. An interpretation of Habakkuk in the Dead Sea Scrolls declares: "God will not destroy His people by the hand of the nations; God will execute judgment of the nations by the hand of his elect" (1QpHab 5.3 – 4). By contrast, Jesus asserts the opposite. Repentance was the only way to escape the looming judgment that would come at the hands of a pagan nation.

In this context, Wright argues that Jesus' call to repentance was not simply the cry of a moralistic reformer urging people to turn from private sin but had eschatological and political ramifications. In Jesus' context, repentance "would have carried the connotations of 'what Israel must do if YHWH is to restore her fortunes at last.'"[18] This repentance required more than some inward religious transformation. He claims, "it was a *political* call, summoning Israel as a nation to abandon one set of agendas and embrace another."[19]

Jesus' original audience may have been shocked and baffled by his threat that Israel, not Rome or its governor, will be held accountable for their sins and is destined for judgment lest they repent. Today, "sin and judgment" are less familiar concepts but no less unpopular. The idea of a "judgment day" sounds so "judgmental." Consequently, people today will be equally shocked and baffled by being characterized as sinners destined for judgment. They do not feel a need to confront their own sinfulness and therefore have no compunction that will lead them to change their orientation and behavior. They may also feel it is unfair when God lets bad things happen to "good" people and may contend that God one day will have to answer for this injustice. But they themselves do not feel that they need to answer for their own selfish rebellion against God or for their nonchalance toward God's reign. Sometimes disasters can become wake-up calls to take stock and to repent.

---

18. Wright, *Jesus and the Victory of God*, 249.   19. Ibid., 251.

Luke 13:10 – 21

Literary Context

The story is connected to its context as an illustration of the failure of many to interpret the present time (12:56). God's reign brings liberation through merciful and miraculous healing of a woman bent double for eighteen years, but the "hypocrites" (12:56; 13:15) are unable or refuse to discern its presence in their midst. Consequently, they will fail to repent (13:3, 5). For them, it is business as usual as they confine God's power to calendrical and legal restrictions.

This story is linked to the following parables about the mustard seed and the leaven by "therefore" (οὖν, rarely used in Luke at the beginning of a unit). These parables are part of Jesus' teaching in the synagogue (13:10) and illustrate how some might fail to recognize the presence of the reign of God. It may seem to burst forth in mysterious and unorthodox ways, but its effects are undeniable. The miracle serves as proof that God's reign has commenced, however invisible it might be even to accredited religious leaders. The story in which a bent-over woman is made to stand up straight while Jesus' opponents are doubled over in shame prepares for the theme of reversal that emerges in the following chapters.

Main Idea

The Sabbath is a time that celebrates God's mercy and God's liberation from bondage. Jesus' divine mission to bring release to captives and to restore Israel does not go on a hiatus on the Sabbath.

Translation

(See next page.)

Structure and Literary Form

The first story combines a healing/exorcism, a subdued conflict story, and a pronouncement. The Sabbath healing controversy is a recurring type-scene in Luke, and the reader has come to expect certain reactions and responses. O'Toole identifies its structure as two panels hinged together.[1] In the first panel, Jesus' action triggers two results: the woman is healed instantly and praises God for it, and the synagogue ruler instantly takes offense and criticizes it as a violation of the Sabbath. In the second panel, Jesus' word incites two responses: the opponents are put to shame while the crowd rejoices over all the glorious things done by him. The story's contrasts help divulge its aim:

ox and donkey	daughter of Abraham
being bound in a stall	being bound by Satan
being loosed (physically)	being loosed (spiritually with physical consequences)
necessity to work six days	necessity for divine healing/liberation on any day including the Sabbath

The question Jesus answers in this episode is not, "What is permitted on the Sabbath?" but, "Why does healing take place on this day?"[2] As Willimon aptly summarizes it, "The clash with authority is not over the rules but over *who* rules."[3] God does not relinquish power to Satan simply because it is the Sabbath but acts through Jesus to undo Satan's evil works. After Jesus makes this point, the incident concludes with two parables about the mystery of God's reign.

1. Robert F. O'Toole, "Some Exegetical Reflections on Luke 13,10–17," *Bib* 73 (1992): 86–87.

2. Jewish Sabbath legislation was no longer an issue for Luke's audience, and he uses this episode for other purposes (M. Dennis Hamm, "The Freeing of the Bent Woman and the Restoration of Israel: Luke 13.10–17 as Narrative Theology," *JSNT* 31 [1987]: 23).

3. William H. Willimon, "Lord of the Sabbath," *Christian Century* 108/16 (1991): 515.

Luke 13:10–21

13:10 Circumstance — Now **he was teaching in one of the synagogues on the Sabbath,**

11 Character introduction — **and** behold **there was a woman** who   she was   had a spirit of infirmity for eighteen years and stooped over and unable to straighten up completely.

12a Summons —   When Jesus saw her, **he summoned her and said,**

b Pronouncement — *"Woman, you have been set free from your infirmity."*

13a Healing — **He laid hands on her, and instantly she was straightened up**

b Response: praise — **and she began to praise God.**

14a Response — **The ruler of the synagogue became indignant**   because Jesus healed on the Sabbath

b Pronouncement — **and   kept saying to the crowd in response:** *"There are six days on which it is necessary to work. Come on one of them to be healed and not on the Sabbath day!"*

15a Response — **But the Lord responded to him and said,** *"Hypocrites!*

b Question — *Does not each one of you set free his ox or donkey from its stall on the Sabbath and lead it to drink?*

16 Pronouncement — *This woman is a daughter of Abraham, whom Satan bound for eighteen years. Is it not necessary to set her free from this bondage on the Sabbath day?"*

17a Circumstance / Response: shame —   When he said these things, **all of his opponents were put to shame,**

b Response: rejoicing — **and all the crowd began to rejoice over all the marvelous things that were being done by him.**

18 Introductory question — **He therefore said,** *"What is the reign of God like? And to what shall I compare it?*

19 Parable — *It is like a mustard seed that a man took and threw into his own garden, and it grew and became a tree, and all the birds of heaven settled in its branches."*

20 Introductory question — **And again he said,** *"To what shall I compare the reign of God?*

21 Parable — *It is like leaven that a woman hides in three measures of flour until it leavens the whole batch."*

Exegetical Outline

→ **I. Healing in a synagogue on the Sabbath (13:10 – 14)**

    A. Setting (13:10)

    B. The description of a woman's infirmity and its duration (13:11)

    C. Jesus' healing intervention (13:12 – 13a)

        1. Pronouncement: She is set free (13:12)

        2. Laying on hands and healing (13:13a)

    D. The woman's response: praise of God (13:13b)

    E. A religious leader's response (13:14)

        1. Indignation (13:14a)

        2. Pronouncement: No healing on the Sabbath (13:14b)

II. Jesus' defense (13:15 – 17)

    A. Questions (13:15 – 16)

        1. Watering an ox or donkey on the Sabbath (13:15)

        2. Healing a daughter of Abraham (13:16)

    B. Response (13:17)

        1. Shame on the part of the opponents (13:17a)

        2. Rejoicing on the part of the crowd (13:17b)

III. Parables about God's Reign (13:18 – 21)

    A. The mustard tree that shelters all the birds of heaven (13:18 – 19)

    B. Leaven that leavens the dough (13:20 – 21)

Explanation of the Text

13:10 Now he was teaching in one of the synagogues on the Sabbath (ἦν δὲ διδάσκων ἐν μιᾷ τῶν συναγωγῶν ἐν τοῖς σάββασιν). Jesus makes his last appearance in a synagogue in Luke. Teaching is appropriate to a synagogue setting, and Luke presents Jesus teaching through a miracle that sparks a controversy. The synagogue setting takes the reader back to Jesus' first appearance in Nazareth, where he announced on a Sabbath his anointing by God's Spirit to proclaim release to the captives (4:16 – 21).[4] That is precisely what he does here by announcing to a woman bound by Satan, "You have been set free."

13:11 And behold, there was a woman who had a spirit of infirmity for eighteen years and she was stooped over and unable to straighten up completely (καὶ ἰδοὺ γυνὴ πνεῦμα ἔχουσα ἀσθενείας ἔτη δέκαοκτὼ καὶ ἦν συγκύπτουσα καὶ μὴ δυναμένη ἀνακύψαι εἰς τὸ παντελές). Luke does not provide a medical diagnosis of the woman's condition but describes it as "a spirit of infirmity" (πνεῦμα ... ἀσθενείας, or "spirit of weakness"). This is an Aramaism that means "a spirit that causes infirmity" (cf. Acts 16:16, "a spirit of divination" NRSV). Luke's description of her malady, using positive wording ("she was stooped over")

---

4. Plummer, *Luke*, 343.

and negative wording ("unable to straighten up completely"), stresses the severity of her ailment.[5] Specifying twice how long she has been disabled ("eighteen years" [ἔτη δέκαοκτώ], and in 13:16 "ten and eight years" [δέκα καὶ ὀκτὼ ἔτη]) is puzzling, but it hooks this story to the previous pericope (13:4, the eighteen who died at the tower of Siloam, which perhaps suggests her infirmity is not her fault) and can simply represent a long time.[6] Her disability was severe, plagued her much of her life, and was undoubtedly well-known.[7]

13:12 When Jesus saw her, he summoned her and said, "Woman, you have been set free from your infirmity" (ἰδὼν δὲ αὐτὴν ὁ Ἰησοῦς προσεφώνησεν καὶ εἶπεν αὐτῇ· γύναι, ἀπολέλυσαι τῆς ἀσθενείας σου). The woman does not come to the synagogue seeking a cure for her condition. Jesus takes the initiative in seeing and calling the woman over to him, and she joins him as the center of attention. He addresses her, not the demon, in announcing the word of liberation. She "has been set free" (ἀπολέλυσαι, perfect tense) from her ailment, and, as Jesus will clarify later, she has also been released from the bondage of Satan. The passive voice represents a theological passive, which is crucial for Jesus' defense when the synagogue ruler objects to the healing. He has not worked a cure; God has.

13:13 He laid hands on her, and instantly she was straightened up and she began to praise God (καὶ ἐπέθηκεν αὐτῇ τὰς χεῖρας· καὶ παραχρῆμα ἀνωρθώθη καὶ ἐδόξαζεν τὸν θεόν). The woman had been freed from Satan's thralldom before Jesus lays hands on her, and this action is more likely a compassionate act of assurance than the final touch "to complete the physical cure" (see 4:40).[8] She is "instantly" restored, and the healing has two effects. First, "she was straightened" (ἀνωρθώθη). This translation preserves the passive voice that points to divine intervention: "she was straightened up." Hamm points to the use of this verb in the LXX to refer "to the (usually future) restorative action of God."[9] Sirach 11:12 is a relevant example: "There are others who are slow and need help, who lack strength and abound in poverty; but the eyes of the Lord look kindly upon them; he lifts them out of [ἀνώρθωσεν] their lowly condition."

Second, the woman begins to praise God (ἐδόξαζεν, an ingressive imperfect), which is the appropriate response to this divine deliverance.[10] "Her eighteen years of affliction have not destroyed her spirituality."[11] She comes to the synagogue demanding nothing special from God but praises him when she is healed. Her praise discloses that she recognizes God's work and power at work in Jesus.

5. W. Radl, "Ein 'doppeltes Leiden' in Lk 13,11? Zu einer Notiz von Günther Schwarz," *BN* 31 (1986): 35 – 36. Attempted medical diagnoses of the woman's disorder miss the point.

6. Nolland, *Luke*, 2:724.

7. Summers, *Commentary on Luke*, 167. Others emphasize its symbolic significance. The number eighteen can evoke memories of the period of Israel's bondage to enemies (Moab [Judg 3:13 – 14]; the Philistines and Ammonites [Judg 10:8]; see Danker, *Jesus and the New Age*, 261). It may have christological value as the sum of the two letters (which also serve as numbers in Greek) that are used to abbreviate Jesus' name (the *nomen sacrum* IH with an overstroke) (Mikeal Parsons, *Body and Character in Luke and Acts: The Subversion of Physiognomy in Early Christianity* [Grand Rapids: Baker, 2006], 89 – 95). Her ailment is not to be regarded as a "punishment" for some sin (Heidi Torgerson, "The Healing of the Bent Woman: A Narrative Interpretation of Luke 13:10 – 17," *CurTM* 32.3 (2005): 179 – 80).

8. Plummer, *Luke*, 342.

9. Hamm, "The Freeing of the Bent Woman," 28. He also notes that in 21:28 "standing up straight" describes the posture one is to take when the signs of the coming Son of Man begin to happen (p. 33), but a connection to this passage seems stretched.

10. See 2:20; 4:15; 5:25; 5:26; 7:16; 13:13; 17:15; 18:43; 23:47.

11. O'Toole, "Some Exegetical Reflections on Luke 13,10 – 17," 87.

13:14 The ruler of the synagogue became indignant because Jesus healed on the Sabbath and kept saying to the crowd in response: "There are six days on which it is necessary to work. Come on one of them to be healed and not on the Sabbath day!" (ἀποκριθεὶς δὲ ὁ ἀρχισυνάγωγος, ἀγανακτῶν ὅτι τῷ σαββάτῳ ἐθεράπευσεν ὁ Ἰησοῦς, ἔλεγεν τῷ ὄχλῳ ὅτι ἓξ ἡμέραι εἰσὶν ἐν αἷς δεῖ ἐργάζεσθαι· ἐν αὐταῖς οὖν ἐρχόμενοι θεραπεύεσθε καὶ μὴ τῇ ἡμέρᾳ τοῦ σαββάτου). A synagogue ruler's assignment was to govern what happened in the synagogue, and presumably he had invited or permitted Jesus to teach.[12] He does not directly challenge Jesus. His attack is oblique as an aside to the audience. His objection "it is necessary to work" (δεῖ ἐργάζεσθαι) implies that Jesus has "worked" a cure and therefore violated the Sabbath.[13] His message to the crowd is, "This is not the day for healing. Let those afflicted by Satan go away and come again some other day during the week if they wish to be cured."

The synagogue official sees the world only through the prism of law, and it distorts his reasoning. He does not see the woman as an individual afflicted by Satan and desperate for release but rather as a nuisance who gets in the way of his ultimate concern, namely, maintaining Sabbath restrictions. She is not in a life-or-death situation, and it will not hurt for her to be bent over one more day. The ruler also cannot see that this healing is a divine work but equates what has happened with

"human work." Jesus' response, however, makes clear that it is a divine liberation, like Israel's liberation from the bondage in Egypt.[14]

13:15 But the Lord responded to him and said, "Hypocrites! Does not each one of you set free his ox or donkey from its stall on the Sabbath and lead it to drink?" (ἀπεκρίθη δὲ αὐτῷ ὁ κύριος καὶ εἶπεν· ὑποκριταί, ἕκαστος ὑμῶν τῷ σαββάτῳ οὐ λύει τὸν βοῦν αὐτοῦ ἢ τὸν ὄνον ἀπὸ τῆς φάτνης καὶ ἀπαγαγὼν ποτίζει;). The plural "hypocrites" (ὑποκριταί) indicates that Jesus addresses a wider audience than simply the ruler. Hypocrisy normally is related to a conflict between saying one thing and doing another, conscious or unconscious pretense. In 12:56, however, Jesus labels those who can forecast the weather from the signs in the earth and the sky but who cannot discern the signs of God's presence when it is staring them in the face as "hypocrites" (see 11:16). In this instance, "hypocrisy" does not refer to playacting but is tied to "end-time blindness."[15] Here, they cannot see God working through Jesus in this Sabbath miracle. The hypocrisy of the opponents may apply to their false exposition of the law that concocts contrivances to protect property (farm animals) while showing no concern for the needs of human beings.[16]

Jesus takes for granted that his audience recognizes the practical necessity of loosing their oxen or donkeys and leading them to water even on the Sabbath.[17] He compares the woman's binding to

12. Synagogue rulers generally appear in a favorable light in Luke-Acts. Jairus is a leader of the synagogue who falls at Jesus' feet in supplication (8:41). Other synagogue officials invite Paul and Barnabas to speak in their synagogue (Acts 13:13–43). Crispus, another ruler of the synagogue, became a believer in the Lord in Corinth (Acts 18:8). Sosthenes, on the other hand, was also a ruler in a synagogue in Corinth and apparently was an instigator in bringing Paul up on charges before Gallio (18:17). Paul refers to "our brother Sosthenes" in 1 Cor 1:1. If this refers to the same person, it is possible that he too became a believer in Jesus.

13. On the significance of the Sabbath for Jews, see comments on 6:1–11.

14. Bovon, *Das Evangelium nach Lukas (Lk 9,51–14,35)*, 403.

15. Hamm, "The Freeing of the Bent Woman," 34.

16. See discussion of the term "hypocrisy" in Garland, *The Intention of Matthew 23*, 96–117.

17. This act may require undoing knots. The later rabbis apparently debated the issue, and R. Judah laid down the general rule: "None is accounted culpable for [tying or untying] any knot that is not lasting" (*m. Šabb.* 15:1–2). See also the tortu-

the binding of farm animals who are not free to get a drink unless let loose by their masters. The difference is that the woman has been tethered for eighteen years and has not been set free even for one day during that time.[18] He impales them on the horns of their own legal logic that ferrets out loopholes in applying the law. They understand that oxen and donkeys require and deserve proper care, and they interpret the law to permit it. Is a person not as important as a beast of burden (see 12:7; see 1 Cor 9:8 – 10)? Animals are unbound on the Sabbath; this woman was unbound on the Sabbath. The difference is that she was unbound by God, and she was not set free from a stall but from the captivity of Satan.

13:16 "This woman is a daughter of Abraham, whom Satan bound for eighteen years. Is it not necessary to set her free from this bondage on the Sabbath day?" (ταύτην δὲ θυγατέρα Ἀβραὰμ οὖσαν, ἣν ἔδησεν ὁ σατανᾶς ἰδοὺ δέκα καὶ ὀκτὼ ἔτη, οὐκ ἔδει λυθῆναι ἀπὸ τοῦ δεσμοῦ τούτου τῇ ἡμέρᾳ τοῦ σαββάτου;). Nothing is said of this woman's piety (1:6), her prayers (1:13; Acts 10:4, 31), or her faith (7:9, 50; 8:48; 17:19; 18:42) that make her deserving of this deliverance. The only qualification mentioned is that she is a daughter of Abraham (see 19:9; Acts 13:26) and therefore destined to be a recipient of the covenant blessing promised to the seed of Abraham: "He has come to the aid of his servant Israel, [to prove] he has not forgotten mercy to Abraham and his seed forever, just as he spoke to our fathers" (1:54 – 55; see Acts 3:25).[19] She is another example of the lowly being lifted up.

By identifying the woman's healing as a deliverance from Satan, Jesus lifts this miracle above the cross fire of legal debates and places it in the realm of messianic expectations. He clarifies that her restoration by God's power means that God is working through Jesus to restore Israel and to throw off the shackles of Satan. Luke looks at Jesus' ministry as a battle with Satan (10:18; 11:14 – 23; 22:3, 31) and at disease as evidence of Satan's tyrannous influence (Acts 10:38).

Jesus' declaration "is it not necessary" (οὐκ ἔδει) counters the leader of the synagogue's declaration "it is necessary" (δεῖ) in 13:14. Jesus does not revoke the law of Moses but interprets it differently according to his messianic mission to set free the oppressed. He is under a "must" from God, and this Sabbath day belongs to the "today" of divine liberation that Jesus announced in 4:18 – 21. The Sabbath "celebrated release from captivity, from bondage, as well as from work."[20] Deuteronomy 5:15 makes this clear: "Remember that you were a slave in the land of Egypt, and the LORD your God brought you out from there with a mighty hand and an outstretched arm; therefore the LORD your God commanded you to keep the sabbath day" (NRSV). That is why this deliverance is *most* appropriate on the Sabbath.

13:17 When he said these things, all of his opponents were put to shame, and all the crowd began to rejoice over all the marvelous things that were being done by him (καὶ ταῦτα λέγοντος αὐτοῦ κατησχύνοντο πάντες οἱ ἀντικείμενοι αὐτῷ, καὶ πᾶς ὁ ὄχλος ἔχαιρεν ἐπὶ πᾶσιν τοῖς ἐνδόξοις τοῖς γινομένοις ὑπ᾽ αὐτοῦ). The response to Jesus'

---

ous casuistry in the legal decisions outlined in *m. ʿErub.* 2:1 – 4 that permits a public well to have the semblance and status of a private domain so that persons can bring their stock to it on the Sabbath to drink without violating the law regarding Sabbath limits.

18. Nolland, *Luke*, 2:724.

19. The term "daughter of Abraham" is used to designate the whole community in *b. Sukkah* 49b and *b. Sanh.* 94b. Paul makes clear that a daughter or son of Abraham is not limited to the ethnic descendants of Abraham but applies also to Gentile believers (Gal 3:7).

20. Wright, *Jesus and the Victory of God*, 394.

miracle and argument splits the community. At first glance, the crowd's presence may seem insignificant, but its role in this scene is crucial. Matters of honor and shame must be witnessed publicly to have an effect. Jesus exposes the leaders' hypocrisy, and the crowd rejoices. In so doing, the crowd publicly affirms Jesus' place of honor while the synagogue leader, and others with him, are put to shame (Isa 45:16; see Luke 21:15).

The crowd adds to the woman's praise of God with rejoicing, the proper response to what God is doing through Jesus (see 5:26; 7:16; 17:15; 18:43). The term "marvelous things" (ἔνδοξοι) is associated in the LXX with the mighty deeds of the Lord during the exodus (Exod 34:10; Deut 10:21).[21] This echo is another reminder that the Sabbath is a day of celebration of God's deliverance.

13:18–19 He therefore said, "What is the reign of God like? And to what shall I compare it? It is like a mustard seed that a man took and threw into his own garden, and it grew and became a tree, and all the birds of heaven settled in its branches" (ἔλεγεν οὖν· τίνι ὁμοία ἐστὶν ἡ βασιλεία τοῦ θεοῦ καὶ τίνι ὁμοιώσω αὐτήν; ὁμοία ἐστὶν κόκκῳ σινάπεως, ὃν λαβὼν ἄνθρωπος ἔβαλεν εἰς κῆπον ἑαυτοῦ, καὶ ηὔξησεν καὶ ἐγένετο εἰς δένδρον, καὶ τὰ πετεινὰ τοῦ οὐρανοῦ κατεσκήνωσεν ἐν τοῖς κλάδοις αὐτοῦ). The two parables are connected to the previous incident by "then" or "therefore" (οὖν). Jesus compares God's reign surprisingly to a mustard seed that grows into a tree that shelters all the birds of heaven in its branches. It is surprising because the mustard plant is a bush that is mostly hollow and will hardly provide a suitable nesting place for birds. It

also seems undesirable to have birds nesting in a garden (see 8:5). Pliny (*Nat.* 19:170–71) describes mustard as growing "entirely wild, though it is improved by being transplanted: but on the other hand when it has once been sown it is scarcely possible to get the place free of it, as the seed when it falls germinates at once."

Nothing is said about the proverbial smallness of the mustard seed (Matt 13:31; 17:20), so the point is not related to the contrast between small beginnings and great results. Instead, the point falls on the end result, "all the birds of heaven" nesting in the branches.[22] "All the birds of heaven" is as much an exaggeration as the mustard shrub becoming a tree. The image contrasts dramatically with the lofty cedar of Lebanon, which, in Ezekiel, was a symbol of the haughty greatness of mortal kingdoms that will be brought low (Ezek 17:22–24; 31:1–17; see also Ps 37:35; Isa 2:13).[23] The mustard "tree," by contrast, symbolizes God's reign as improbably inglorious and humble and yet enormously successful.

13:20–21 And again he said, "To what shall I compare the reign of God? It is like leaven that a woman hides in three measures of flour until it leavens the whole batch" (καὶ πάλιν εἶπεν· τίνι ὁμοιώσω τὴν βασιλείαν τοῦ θεοῦ; ὁμοία ἐστὶν ζύμῃ, ἣν λαβοῦσα γυνὴ [ἐν]έκρυψεν εἰς ἀλεύρου σάτα τρία ἕως οὗ ἐζυμώθη ὅλον). The second parable is also surprising in comparing God's reign to "leaven" (ζύμη). Leaven is sourdough, which had an inherent danger of becoming tainted and then poisoning batch after batch; it was an apt symbol of the infectious power of evil (Exod 12:15–20; 23:18; 34:18; Lev 2:11; 6:17; Hos 7:4; Luke 12:1;

---

21. It complements the response of the crowd to the healing of the paralyzed man in 5:26. They glorified God and were filled with awe and said that they had seen "strange things" (παράδοξα).

22. Jeremias (*The Parables of Jesus*, 147) contends that

"settled" or "nesting" (κατεσκήνωσεν) is an eschatological term used to symbolize the incorporation of the Gentiles in the people of God (see *Jos. Asen.* 15:6).

23. See Robert Funk, "The Looking-Glass Tree Is for the Birds," *Int* 27 (1973): 3–9.

1 Cor 5:6 – 8; Gal 5:9). Plutarch (*Quaest. rom.* 289F) comments, "Yeast [leaven] is itself also the product of corruption, and produces corruption in the dough with which it is mixed … and altogether the process of leavening seems to be one of putrefaction; at any rate if it goes too far, it completely sours and spoils the dough" (see also see Pliny, *Nat.* 18:26).

Comparing the reign of God to leaven inverts the common images of the sacred and profane. From the perspective of his pharisaic opponents, Jesus' view of God's reign, which ignored ceremonial purity concerns (11:38), violated their interpretation of Sabbath rules (6:1 – 11; 14:1 – 6), and accepted sinners and tax collectors (5:30; 15:1 – 2) was indeed a corrupting force.

The metaphor of leaven, while disorienting, focuses on the end result (like the first parable). Bread cannot rise without leaven. Jesus' teaching and healing ministry set in motion an invisible process that would change Judaism and the world. Like leaven, it has an inward vitality that gives it the power to affect with its own quality whatever it touches.[24] The leaven disappears when mixed with the dough, but it permeates it and inexorably does its work. As leaven has the power to transform the dough into something new while at the same time maintaining continuity with the old, God's reign is transforming Judaism.

It would also have been jarring to many in Jesus' audience that he connects the reign of God to a woman baking. The amount of meal, "three measures of flour" (σάτα τρία), is also large. It is about thirty-six quarts, close to fifty pounds. This is not a typical amount for a peasant household's daily bread-making but suitable only for a large, festive party. The dissonant images, when taken together, prepare for the equally whimsical images of banquets with the guests of honor coming from surprising quarters, the four winds (13:24 – 30), the highways and alleys (14:16 – 24), and a far country (15:11 – 32). Those whom one would expect to be in attendance, however, are shut out. God's reign will rescue the lost and the marginalized and restore those oppressed by Satan and be a cause for celebration. But it will exclude the clubby, self-righteous people who resist including these others, murmur against this iconoclastic vision of what God is doing, and want to enter God's kingdom on their own terms.

Theology in Application

1. Determining God's Will

How does one determine what is God's will? If, as the synagogue ruler's contends, healing is prohibited on the Sabbath, then God wills that this woman be excluded from divine help on this day. This incident, however, reveals the patent absurdity that God would refrain from delivering people on the Sabbath and permit "the Sabbath to be a time when Satan's dominance and causing of evil is not opposed."[25] God is interested in not only release from work but also release from Satan and any form of

---

24. C. L. Mitton, "Leaven," *ExpTim* 84 (1972 – 73): 340.

25. O'Toole, "Some Exegetical Reflections on Luke 13,10 – 17," 88.

bondage or enslavement. The Sabbath, in fact, celebrates God's redemption. Kilgallen concludes:

> From the words Jesus uses, one is encouraged to think of that meaning of the Sabbath that celebrates the freedom of Abraham's children from Egypt, symbolically the land of slavery, darkness, false gods, and so of Satan. It seems certain from his vocabulary that Jesus wants the synagogue leader to think in terms of this sense of the Sabbath when he sees Jesus cure (set free) on the Sabbath.[26]

The Sabbath is not to be an end in itself that enslaves humans with its restrictions but a time when people can celebrate who God is as a liberating God. Dorothy Bass reminds us that keeping the Sabbath helps us "to remember one's freedom and to recall the One from whom that freedom came, the One from whom it still comes."[27]

The Christology in this episode is implicit and subtle. Jesus' act has "redemptive-historical import" and is in line with why the Sabbath is celebrated.[28] Since Jesus is engaged in a fight against cosmic powers, he must exercise his power for the good of others and destroy Satan's works. The miracle is a sign of God's favor to his people through the coming of his Son, who is anointed with power. "Jesus' ministry of healing exemplifies the mercy inherent to God's coming reign."[29] The miracle points to God's reign being established on earth and is a foretaste of the final release from all bondage that awaits God's people in the age to come.

The introductory statement to the parables, "the reign of God ... is like," assumes that Jesus has divine authority to explain what God's rule is like. The parables convey that God's reign is already present in Jesus' work. The startling images in the parables (mustard and leaven) have been dulled by their retelling over the years, but they appropriately convey that Jesus' ministry will shatter expected norms. He does not come as a mighty, military Messiah who gives Israel dominion over the world as the top cedar (Ezek 17:22 – 24), but as a lowly mustard tree. Despite appearances and expectations, this tree will shelter all the birds of heaven, which will include even Gentiles.

Like leaven, what Jesus unleashes in Israel will totally transform it into something new. It works silently and powerfully. The cure of the bent-over woman on the Sabbath shows how it affects the law. Jesus does not abrogate the law but reinterprets and transforms it. For Jesus, the law is valid only when understood through the lens of merciful action that serves the needs of the poor, the sick, and the infirm.

---

26. Kilgallen, "The Obligation to Heal (Luke 13, 10 – 17)," 406.

27. Dorothy Bass, *Receiving the Day: Christian Practices for Opening the Gift of Time* (San Francisco: Jossey-Bass, 2000), 48.

28. Joel B. Green, "Jesus and a Daughter of Abraham (Luke 13:10 – 17): Test Case for a Lucan Perspective on Jesus' Miracles," *CBQ* 51 (1989): 651.

29. Torgerson, "The Healing of the Bent Woman," 176.

2. Caring for Those with Physical Impairment

The story of the bent-over woman who lived with her debilitating impairment for so many years offers an opportunity to deal with the issue of physical disabilities. Often, people with disabilities are notably absent or excluded from church life. Derrett notes, "The Qumran sect hoped to exclude all disqualified persons, to which the temple-taboos were transferred."[30] The basis for their attitude was the legal strictures in Lev 21:16 – 24 (see 2 Sam 5:8). For Christians, physical deformity does not manifest some hidden depravity or sin, nor does it cut one off from God or his people. This woman has remained an active worshiper in her synagogue despite her disability. Only with difficulty, however, could she lift up her eyes to the hills and look for her help (Ps 121:1). She was bent over, face to the ground like a bound draft animal. Jesus brings her center stage and cures her.

Many with disabilities, however, will not be cured as this woman was, but they may be healed. We might generalize Crossan's observations about a cure for AIDS. While those with illnesses might hope to be cured, if they are not, "we can still heal the illness by refusing to ostracize those who have it, by empathizing with their anguish, and by enveloping their sufferings with both respect and love."[31] They can be made to feel whole even when they suffer from physical brokenness. Paul endured his unnamed physical malady, which he described as "a thorn in [the] flesh, a messenger of Satan, to torment me" (2 Cor 12:7), and something that was off-putting to others, but he proclaimed the gospel energetically throughout the Mediterranean despite it. Moreover, he learned from it that God's grace alone sustained him (2 Cor 12:9 – 10).

In this case, the woman is affirmed as someone with unique dignity as "a daughter of Abraham," which is used as a term of honor in 4 Macc 15:28; 18:20 for the brave mother of the seven sons who were martyred for their faith. Like Israel redeemed by God from Egypt, she is a slave to her illness no more and may walk erect (Lev 26:13). Walking erect, however, can be a spiritual metaphor even for those who are physically bent over or confined in some way. What is important is that one who was bound by Satan is transformed into one who is bound for heaven.

---

30. J. Duncan M. Derrett, *Studies in the New Testament*, vol. 5: *The Sea-Change of the Old Testament in the New* (Leiden: Brill, 1989), 130.

31. John Dominic Crossan, *Jesus: A Revolutionary Biography* (San Francisco: HarperCollins, 1994), 81.

Luke 13:22 – 35

Literary Context

With his first travel notice since 9:51, Luke reminds the reader that Jesus is still on his way to Jerusalem. The concluding verses of this section (13:33 – 35) recall Jesus' first prediction of his passion (9:22). He goes to Jerusalem, not to escape from the likes of Herod, but to die according to God's plan that controls his destiny. This discourse continues the themes of judgment and separation and the consequences of rejecting Jesus. The time left for an unfruitful fig tree to encumber the ground (13:6 – 9) is growing dangerously short. Will an unfruitful, unrepentant Israel retain its place? The decision to repent (13:3, 5) must be made now before it's too late, and repentance now entails following Jesus. The images of closed doors and exclusion and a surprising guest list at a banquet (13:25 – 29) are developed further in the parable of the great banquet (14:16 – 24). Stubborn Israel is in peril of being excluded from salvation.

Jesus compares salvation to straining to enter a narrow door, and the next chapter provides examples of how difficult that is. It requires strength, commitment, and effort to "hate" father and mother, wife and children, brothers and sisters, and even life itself (14:26), to carry a cross (14:27), and to say goodbye to all one possesses (14:33). Those who decline to make these sacrifices cannot be Jesus' disciples, and they too will forfeit salvation.

Main Idea

God's reign will not be derailed by hostility from human rulers or by Israel's unbelief as Jesus marches on to accomplish God's purpose in Jerusalem.

Translation

Luke 13:22–35

13:22	Travel notice	**Jesus went through town after village,** teaching and making his way to Jerusalem.
23a	Question	**Someone asked him,**
		"Lord, are those who are saved few in number?"
b	Answer	**He said to them,**
24	Command/warning	*"Strain to enter the narrow door,*
		because many, I tell you, will seek to enter and
		will not have the strength to do so.
25a	Parable	*After the master of the house rises and shuts the door, and*
		you stand outside and begin to knock on the door, saying,
b	Entreaty	*'Lord, open up for us!'*
c	Rejection	*then he will answer in reply,*
		'I do not know who you are.'
26	Entreaty	*Then you will begin to say,*
		'We ate and drank before you and you taught in our streets.'
27	Rejection	*And he will say to you,*
		'I do not know where you come from.
		Get away from me, all you workers of iniquity!'
28	Reversal	*There will be weeping and gnashing of teeth,*
		whenever you see Abraham and Isaac and Jacob and
		all the prophets in the kingdom of God, and
		you being cast outside.
29		*And they will have come from east and west and from north and south*
		and will recline in the kingdom of God.
30	Pronouncement	*Behold, the last will be first and the first will be last."*
31	Warning	At that same hour,
		some Pharisees came and said to him,
		"Get away from here, because Herod wants to kill you."
32	Response	**He said to them,**
		"Go tell this fox,
		'Behold, I am casting out demons and curing people today and tomorrow,
		and on the third day I will reach my goal.'

Continued on next page.

33	Pronouncement	*Nevertheless, it is necessary for me to go today, tomorrow, and the next day, because it is impossible for a prophet to be killed⟲ outside of Jerusalem.*
34	Lament	*Jerusalem, Jerusalem, who kills the⟲ prophets and stones those sent to her, how many times I wanted to gather your children in the way a hen gathers⟲ her brood under her wings,* *and you would not [be gathered]!*
35	Prophecy	*Behold, your house is abandoned to you.* *And I tell you, you will not see me until you say,* *'Blessed is the one who comes in the name of the Lord.'"* (Ps 118:26)

Structure and Literary Form

The passage is framed by the report of Jesus' journey as he goes through one town and village after another and teaches the people on his way to Jerusalem (13:22), and his prophecy about how he will be received in Jerusalem as a prophet (13:33 – 35). The passage contains an assortment of Jesus' prophetic sayings in a variety of forms: parable, pronouncement, lament, and prophecy of doom. It divides into two units. The first (13:22 – 30) warns about the danger of being excluded from the saved. The second (13:31 – 35) warns about the danger to Jerusalem for rejecting Jesus and affirms that Jesus will accomplish God's purpose for him despite rejection.[1] The ending provides an enigmatic answer to the opening question, "Are those who are saved few in number?" (13:23). The saved will be those who welcome Jesus and proclaim, "Blessed is the one who comes in the name of the Lord" (13:35).

Exegetical Outline

➡ **I. Question about the number who will be saved (13:22 – 30)**

    A. Setting (13:22)

    B. Question about the number of the saved (13:23)

    C. Command to enter the narrow door (13:24)

    D. Parable of the shut door excluding those who seek to enter too late (13:25 – 27)

    E. Exclusion from the banquet in the kingdom of God and inclusion of outsiders (13:28 – 30)

---

1. Robert J. Shirock ("The Growth of the Kingdom in Light of Israel's Rejection of Jesus: Structure and Theology in Luke 13:1 – 35," *NovT* 35 [1993]: 15 – 29) divides all of 13:1 – 35 into a chiasm:

  A 13:1 – 9 Fig tree
    B 13:10 – 17 Healing of bent woman
      C 13:18 – 19 Parable of the mustard seed
      C' 13:20 – 21 Parable of the leaven
    B' 13:22 – 30 Narrow door
  A' 13:31 – 35 Warning about Herod

II. The necessity of Jesus' death in Jerusalem (13:31 – 35)

A. Refusal to run from Herod to complete his work in Jerusalem (13:31 – 32)

B. The divine necessity of dying in Jerusalem (13:33)

C. Lament over Jerusalem's recalcitrance (13:34 – 35)

Explanation of the Text

13:22 – 24 Jesus went through town after village, teaching and making his way to Jerusalem. Someone asked him, "Lord, are those who are saved few in number?" He said to them, "Strain to enter the narrow door, because many, I tell you, will seek to enter and will not have the strength to do so" (καὶ διεπορεύετο κατὰ πόλεις καὶ κώμας διδάσκων καὶ πορείαν ποιούμενος εἰς Ἱεροσόλυμα. εἶπεν δέ τις αὐτῷ· κύριε, εἰ ὀλίγοι οἱ σῳζόμενοι; ὁ δὲ εἶπεν πρὸς αὐτούς· ἀγωνίζεσθε εἰσελθεῖν διὰ τῆς στενῆς θύρας, ὅτι πολλοί, λέγω ὑμῖν, ζητήσουσιν εἰσελθεῖν καὶ οὐκ ἰσχύσουσιν).

Luke reminds us that Jesus is continuing to wind his way toward Jerusalem (cf. 13:33), and along the way someone asks him about the number of those who will be saved (see 2 Esd 9:13 – 16). This query may have been prompted by the previous parables. A mustard plant can only provide shelter for small birds, and three measures of dough can only feed a couple hundred. Jesus responds enigmatically with two more parables. His answer does not get bogged down in a theoretical discussion about the number of the saved but turns to a baleful warning about how many will squander the opportunity and be left out in the cold.[2]

Jesus first compares salvation to entering a narrow door, which requires exertion. Its narrowness suggests that it is not a grand ornamented portal that one can saunter through. It is less frequented because it is less inviting and requires strength of will and a struggle to follow Jesus on an arduous journey of discipleship.[3] The rich can hardly squeeze through (18:24 – 25), and one has to make a decision to enter it now before it is too late. That decision will determine salvation or exclusion from salvation. Wanting to enter it, however, is not enough; it requires earnest effort.

13:25 – 27 After the master of the house rises and shuts the door, and you stand outside and begin to knock on the door, saying, "Lord, open up for us!" then he will answer in reply, "I do not know who you are." Then you will begin to say, "We ate and drank before you and you taught in our streets." And he will say to you, "I do not know where you come from. Get away from me, all you workers of iniquity!" (ἀφ᾽ οὗ ἂν ἐγερθῇ ὁ οἰκοδεσπότης καὶ ἀποκλείσῃ τὴν θύραν, καὶ ἄρξησθε ἔξω ἑστάναι καὶ κρούειν τὴν θύραν λέγοντες· κύριε, ἄνοιξον ἡμῖν, καὶ ἀποκριθεὶς ἐρεῖ ὑμῖν· οὐκ οἶδα ὑμᾶς πόθεν ἐστέ. τότε ἄρξεσθε λέγειν· ἐφάγομεν ἐνώπιόν σου καὶ ἐπίομεν, καὶ ἐν ταῖς πλατείαις ἡμῶν ἐδίδαξας· καὶ ἐρεῖ λέγων ὑμῖν· οὐκ οἶδα [ὑμᾶς] πόθεν ἐστέ· ἀπόστητε ἀπ᾽ ἐμοῦ πάντες ἐργάται ἀδικίας).

The second metaphor picks up on the image of the door and envisions one knocking to enter after the door has been shut. It had been open as "an invitation for any who wish to enter,"[4] but

---

2. Godet, *Luke*, 2:124; Green, *The Gospel of Luke*, 528.

3. The verb "strain" (ἀγωνίζομαι) appears in Paul's letters (1 Cor 9:25; Col 1:29; 4:12; 1 Tim 4:10; 6:12; 2 Tim 4:7) for fighting the good fight. The present tense implies "keep on straining."

4. Summers, *Commentary on Luke*, 170.

now it is closed. The householder is addressed as "Lord," and the picture envisions people desperately seeking "to enter, *after the time of salvation is past*."[5] Knocking now is of no avail (see 11:10). The Lord's rebuff, "I do not know where you come from" (13:27), does not refer to their geographical origin but to their spiritual roots. They are bitterly identified as "workers of iniquity" (see Phil 3:2; 2 Cor 11:13). Jesus taught in their streets and ate with them, but because they rejected him, they betray they have nothing else in common. Obviously, being physically near to Jesus provides no great advantage over those who will come to the banquet in the kingdom of God from far and wide.

13:28 – 30 There will be weeping and gnashing of teeth, whenever you see Abraham and Isaac and Jacob and all the prophets in the kingdom of God,[6] and you being cast outside. And they will have come from east and west and from north and south and will recline in the kingdom of God. Behold, the last will be first and the first will be last (ἐκεῖ ἔσται ὁ κλαυθμὸς καὶ ὁ βρυγμὸς τῶν ὀδόντων, ὅταν ὄψεσθε Ἀβραὰμ καὶ Ἰσαὰκ καὶ Ἰακὼβ καὶ πάντας τοὺς προφήτας ἐν τῇ βασιλείᾳ τοῦ θεοῦ, ὑμᾶς δὲ ἐκβαλλομένους ἔξω. καὶ ἥξουσιν ἀπὸ ἀνατολῶν καὶ δυσμῶν καὶ ἀπὸ βορρᾶ καὶ νότου καὶ ἀνακλιθήσονται ἐν τῇ βασιλείᾳ τοῦ θεοῦ. καὶ ἰδοὺ εἰσὶν ἔσχατοι οἳ ἔσονται πρῶτοι καὶ εἰσὶν πρῶτοι οἳ ἔσονται ἔσχατοι).

The third picture envisions the eschatological banquet (see Isa 25:6) with the patriarchs (Abraham, Isaac, and Jacob) and the prophets reclining to eat and joined by a crowd from all points of the compass. Others are left outside, weeping and gnashing their teeth. The messianic banquet that was to bring joy and satisfaction will bring for many, even in Israel, only despair.

This image broaches the topic of the reversal of the end-time judgment and recalls John's ominous word that God is able to raise up children to Abraham from these stones (3:8) and Jesus' woes against the rich (6:24 – 26), the cities of Chorazin, Bethsaida, and Capernaum (10:13 – 15), and the Pharisees and law scholars (11:42 – 52). Those who belong to Israel do not have racial priority that automatically secures them a place at the table, despite the fact that many took it for granted that "all Israel will have a share in the world to come" (see *m. Sanh.* 10:1, citing Isa 60:21; *b. Sanh.* 90a).[7] The earlier reference to Elijah's and Elisha's ministry to Gentiles reveals that "God's salvific initiative can pass over Israel's own distress" (4:25 – 27), and Acts 28:28 shows that God's plan includes Gentiles in salvation "on an equal basis with the Jews."[8]

The people coming from all over should not automatically be equated with Gentiles. In Jesus' context and in Luke's, it more likely includes the gathering of the lost tribes of Israel (Isa 43:5 – 6). Bergren summarizes what may have been believed about their anticipated return in Jesus' day. In contrast to the sinfulness of the present authorities and inhabitants of the land, "their [the lost tribes'] moral status and way of life in exile were highly idealized."[9] These people are not included on a

---

5. Plummer, *Luke*, 529.

6. The "kingdom of God" (ἡ βασιλεία τοῦ θεοῦ) is more apt as the translation here since it obviously pictures a location rather than God's dynamic rule.

7. According to a discussion in *b. Sanh.* 98b, "R. Giddal said in Rab's name: The Jews are destined to eat [their fill] in the days of the Messiah. R. Joseph demurred: Is this not obvious; who else then should eat — Hilek and Bilek?" The latter are fictitious names, like Tom, Dick and Harry, and this response means that the days of the Messiah will not be enjoyed by just anyone other than Jews.

8. Michael Wolter, "Israel's Future and the Delay of the Parousia, according to Luke," in *Jesus and the Heritage of Israel: Luke's Narrative Claim upon Israel's Legacy* (ed. David P. Moessner; Harrisburg, PA: Trinity Press International, 1999), 310 – 11.

9. Theodore A. Bergren, "The 'People Coming from the East' in 5 Ezra 1:38," *JBL* 108 (1989): 675 – 83.

whim but are those who would have responded to the gospel, like those who are gathered from every nation at Pentecost (Acts 2:5 – 43).

13:31 At that same hour, some Pharisees came and said to him, "Get away from here, because Herod wants to kill you" (ἐν αὐτῇ τῇ ὥρᾳ προσῆλθάν τινες Φαρισαῖοι λέγοντες αὐτῷ· ἔξελθε καὶ πορεύου ἐντεῦθεν, ὅτι Ἡρῴδης θέλει σε ἀποκτεῖναι). The reference to Herod's malevolence balances the reference to Pilate's atrocities in 13:1. The two will figure in the plot to put Jesus to death and become fast friends (23:12; Acts 4:26). Jesus' constant travel probably kept him from being apprehended sooner for his inflammatory message.

Some claim that malevolent motives lie behind this warning. They are trying to drive him into a trap in Jerusalem where he will come under the power of the Sanhedrin, and his followers will panic.[10] Or, they use this ruse simply because they want him out of their hair and sphere of influence.[11] Or, perhaps they are trying to expose him as a false prophet for rejecting God's plan (7:30) by seeking to save himself.[12] Such speculation is unwarranted. Luke is neither concerned with their motives for warning Jesus nor with Herod's motives for wanting to do away with him. The scene simply sets up Jesus' response, his acceptance of his divine mission with its attendant fate, and his lament over Jerusalem. Neither the Pharisees nor Herod direct his destiny; only God does.

13:32 He said to them, "Go tell this fox, 'Behold, I am casting out demons and curing people today

and tomorrow, and on the third day I will reach my goal'" (καὶ εἶπεν αὐτοῖς· πορευθέντες εἴπατε τῇ ἀλώπεκι ταύτῃ· ἰδοὺ ἐκβάλλω δαιμόνια καὶ ἰάσεις ἀποτελῶ σήμερον καὶ αὔριον καὶ τῇ τρίτῃ τελειοῦμαι). For many, the "fox" metaphor suggests someone who is crafty, sly, or cunning. Green notes, however, that there is no hint in the narrative that Herod is "particularly cunning or crafty."[13] It is more likely that Jesus refers to him as an insignificant person (Neh 4:3; 2 Esd 13:35 LXX).[14]

Buth claims that the metaphor fits the rabbinic use of fox that challenges Herod's inability to carry out his threat and attacks his pedigree and morality. He offers the following possible translations to convey the intent of the original: "Weakling, small fry, usurper, poser, clown, insignificant person, cream puff, nobody, weasel, jackass, tin soldier, peon, hick, pompous pretender, jerk, upstart."[15] In an article titled "Kings Are Lions, but Herod Is a Fox," Hermanson argues that Jesus is saying that Herod is no lion but a jackass.[16]

As he did in his reply to John (7:22), Jesus sums up his ministry with the signs of the Messiah's works (see Acts 2:22; 10:38).[17] The miracles are things that originally attracted Herod's interest in Jesus (9:7; 23:8). Jesus' answer affirms that "the course of the Messiah is determined, and will not be abbreviated or changed because of threats from Herod."[18] He has a goal to reach (τελειοῦμαι, "complete, accomplish, carry through completely"). The verb could be taken as a passive to mean "I am perfected" (ASV) or when "I am

10. So Plummer, *Luke*, 348, who likens it to the plot of Amaziah in Amos 7:10 – 17.

11. Marshall, *The Gospel of Luke*, 571.

12. Johnson, *The Gospel of Luke*, 221.

13. Green, *The Gospel of Luke*, 536.

14. Petronius (*Sat.* 44) has a character say, "Today, when people are at home they tend to think of themselves as lions, but in public they're just foxes" (cited by Danker, *Jesus and the New Age*, 265).

15. Randall Buth, "That Small-Fry Herod Antipas, or When a Fox Is Not a Fox," *Jerusalem Perspectives* 40 (1993): 7 – 9, 14. He cites *m. ʾAbot* 4:15; *j. Šabb.* 10.5 38c; *j. Šeb.* 9.5 39a; *b. B. Qam.* 117a; *b. B. Meṣ.* 84b; *b. Ḥag.* 14a.

16. E. A. Hermanson, "Kings Are Lions, but Herod Is a Fox: Translating the Metaphor in Luke 13:32," *BT* 50 (1999): 235 – 40.

17. Plummer, *Luke*, 349.

18. Ibid., 350.

brought to an end (by God)."[19] Luke uses it, however, in 2:43 to mean "complete" and in Acts 20:24 to mean "to finish" the course. Its meaning here is strikingly similar to Johannine usage (John 4:34; 5:36; 17:4; 19:28). Jesus uses a similar verb in his last announcement of his coming death: "Behold we are going up to Jerusalem. And the things written by the prophets about the Son of Man will be accomplished" (Luke 18:31).

The "third day" is not literal but refers to a short period of time, which in this context is determined only by God. It also has symbolic significance as the time of God's rescue (Hos 6:2; Jonah 1:17). Jesus has already told his disciples that after undergoing rejection by the elders, chief priests, and scribes, and experiencing suffering and death, he will be raised "on the third day" (9:22).

13:33 Nevertheless, it is necessary for me to go today, tomorrow, and the next day, because it is impossible for a prophet to be killed outside of Jerusalem (πλὴν δεῖ με σήμερον καὶ αὔριον καὶ τῇ ἐχομένῃ πορεύεσθαι, ὅτι οὐκ ἐνδέχεται προφήτην ἀπολέσθαι ἔξω Ἰερουσαλήμ). Jesus will not escape death by escaping from Herod's grasp. He follows God's plan expressed in a divine "must." His response reflects his intimate knowledge of God's will.

Luke mentions Jerusalem ninety-nine times compared with forty-nine times in the rest of the New Testament, and here it looms ominously, like Mount Doom in *The Lord of the Rings*, as the place most dangerous for prophets. It embodies the traditions, attitudes, leadership, and institutions of Israel, and any who challenge these things, as prophets are wont to do, are likely to meet with a violent end (see Acts 7:52). In Jesus' context, Jerusalem is the headquarters of a religious hierarchy that is more interested in preserving their power than in hearing what God has to say. They are the ones who will destroy Jesus in.

13:34 Jerusalem, Jerusalem, who kills the prophets and stones those sent to her, how many times I wanted to gather your children in the way a hen gathers her brood under her wings, and you would not [be gathered]! (Ἰερουσαλὴμ Ἰερουσαλήμ, ἡ ἀποκτείνουσα τοὺς προφήτας καὶ λιθοβολοῦσα τοὺς ἀπεσταλμένους πρὸς αὐτήν, ποσάκις ἠθέλησα ἐπισυνάξαι τὰ τέκνα σου ὃν τρόπον ὄρνις τὴν ἑαυτῆς νοσσιὰν ὑπὸ τὰς πτέρυγας, καὶ οὐκ ἠθελήσατε). Jesus may have uttered this lament more than once (see Matt 23:37 – 38), and Luke records it here well before he enters Jerusalem. As God is a frustrated fig tree owner disappointed over a fruitless nation (13:6 – 9), so Jesus is a frustrated mother hen.[20] Judgment is certain for rejecting Jesus, but it is meted out reluctantly. The shelter of God's wings is a vivid metaphor for God's protection (Ruth 2:12; Pss 17:8; 36:7; 57:1; 61:4; 63:7; 91:4; Isa 31:5; 2 Esd 1:30; *2 Bar.* 41:3 – 4). This brood, however, refuses God's protection (see Isa 65:1 – 2), and Jerusalem lies exposed and primed for destruction as a result.

13:35 Behold, your house is abandoned to you. And I tell you, you will not see me until you say, "Blessed is the one who comes in the name of the Lord" (ἰδοὺ ἀφίεται ὑμῖν ὁ οἶκος ὑμῶν. λέγω [δὲ] ὑμῖν, οὐ μὴ ἴδητέ με ἕως [ἥξει ὅτε] εἴπητε· εὐλογημένος ὁ ἐρχόμενος ἐν ὀνόματι κυρίου). Jesus expresses guarded hope combined with a prophecy of doom.[21] "Your house" may not refer to the temple, since it is known as God's house, but to Israel itself. Jeremiah, however, refers to the temple as "this house" that will become desolate (Jer 22:5 – 6 NRSV). If Jesus does refer to the temple, then he no longer regards it as God's house, but already as a den of robbers (cf. 19:46).

---

19. Fitzmyer, *Luke*, 2:1031.
20. Shirock, "The Growth of the Kingdom in Light of Israel's Rejection of Jesus," 19 – 20.
21. Ibid., 28.

Theology in Application

1. The Narrow Door of Salvation

Jesus' challenge for his followers to "strain to enter the narrow door" reveals that God's offer of free grace does not rule out human effort (see 1 Cor 9:25–27; Phil 2:12–13). Manson comments that God opens the door of salvation for us to enter, but it is narrow. One has to struggle through rather than stroll in. If people fail to enter it, it is not because God's refuses to admit them. It means they want to enter on their own terms and "not on the only terms on which entrance is possible."[22] It will be particularly difficult for the high and mighty and the rich.

The disciples will later ask, "Who then can be saved?" (18:26). Jesus' answer reveals a paradox. Salvation is impossible for mortals but only possible for God (18:27). The strength to enter comes only from God (Phil 4:13). The lament reveals God's passion to save, but salvation requires accepting God's offer of grace through Jesus and heeding his teaching by reorienting one's life accordingly. It is not that God decides who will be allowed to enter and who will be shut out but that God acknowledges who has entered and who has refused to enter. It means that Israel will be redefined as those who heed God's call and submit to God's righteousness that is revealed in Jesus as the Messiah (Rom 9–11).

2. Resistance to Jesus

The christological element of this passage is subtle and emerges in Jesus' statement that he would gather Jerusalem under his wings. "To gather" (ἐπισυνάξαι) is "the regular word for the hope of God's restoration" (Pss 106:47; 147:2; Isa 52:12 [LXX]; Jer 31:8–10; Zech 2:10 [LXX]; 2 Macc 1:27; 2:18).[23] Jesus claims to take God's role as the one who would gather Israel. The image of gathering Jerusalem under his wings is also striking. Stettler comments that it "can be understood if we think of the wings of the cherubs above the Ark of the Covenant as the place of God's indwelling and of atonement in the priestly code. Jesus thus identifies with the divine *Shekinah* dwelling in the Temple at Jerusalem."[24]

The gathering of Israel requires ransoming and redeeming them (Jer 31:11). God will accomplish this through Jesus' death in Jerusalem. Jesus presents his death as that of a prophet. Dillon notes:

> Prophecy, as a principal form of communication between God and man, is inevitably also a volatile ground of contention between the two realms. Precisely the one whom God *accredits*, man *repudiates*; thus it is that divine forgiveness and human

---

22. Manson, *The Sayings of Jesus*, 125.
23. Evans, *St. Luke*, 564.
24. Stettler, "Sanctification in the Jesus Tradition," 156.

conversion become the prerequisites of God's rule, and thus the bitter course charted for all who stand in the prophets' tradition.[25]

It is no surprise that this iconoclastic prophet, who has challenged hallowed traditions, the temple, and the religious hierarchy, will meet with death. But it is not simply the tragic death of another rejected prophet. It is one that is brought about by divine necessity. Jesus connects his exorcisms and healing to finishing his work on the third day, which means they are only a foretaste of the liberation that his death brings.

The citation from Psalm 118:26 most obviously refers to Jesus' entrance into Jerusalem when the crowds shout, "Blessed is the king who comes in the name of the Lord" (19:37 – 38). This psalm had developed messianic connotations in Jesus' day, which explains why the Pharisees try to get Jesus to squelch the crowd's jubilation (19:39). The implication is that there is still time for Israel to repent and turn to God.

The prophetic pronouncement echoes another part of the psalm: "Open for me the gates of the righteous; I will enter and give thanks to the Lord. This is the gate of the Lord through which the righteous may enter" (Ps 118:19 – 20). The prayer has been answered. The gate has been opened, but one cannot simply stroll through it, and it will not remain open forever.

Jesus quotes the psalm again in 20:17, "The stone that the builders rejected, this one has become the cornerstone" (Ps 118:22; see Acts 4:11). The implication is that Jesus is the stone that has been rejected. In the psalm, they offer their blessing from "the house of the Lord" (Ps 118:26), but Jesus' pronouncement that "my house" has been abandoned is ominous (see Jer 12:7). When it has become "their house," it has become only a shell. Schweizer draws a contemporary application to the church:

> But when the living God forsakes the house, the walls of the magnificent temples and churches may remain standing (cf. 21:5), but all the religious activity and all the theological expertise cannot conceal the fact that they are empty, "deserted by all good spirits," and that it is only a question of time until the fall to ruin (vs. 35). They will be visited only by tourists with an interest in art history, whose guides repeat the terrifying echo, "This is the temple of Yahweh" (Jer. 7:4).[26]

25. Dillon, *From Eye-Witnesses to Ministers of the Word*, 126.   26. Schweizer, *Luke*, 232.

Luke 14:1 – 6

Literary Context

This dinner episode is the third and last in the home of a Pharisee (see 7:36 – 50; 11:37 – 54). Given Jesus' recriminations against the Pharisees and legal experts at the last meal (11:37 – 54), the reader may be surprised to find him invited back to a leading Pharisee's home, assuming that word of the previous fracas was sure to get around.

It is not surprising, however, to find Jesus again going into attack mode and lambasting his host and his guests. He challenges them for their self-centered manipulation of Sabbath rules, their hankering after seats of honor and public recognition, their neglect of the poor and outcasts, and their rude rejection of the invitation extended by Jesus to join in the festivities of the banquet that exalts the poor and outcasts and rejoices with sinners who repent. The section begins with dinner guests, consisting of respected peers of one of the top leaders of the Pharisees, enjoying a banquet, and it ends with Jesus' parable in which the dinner guests enjoying a banquet populated by a motley crew of outcasts and poor people from the fringes of respectable society (14:7 – 24).

The previous chapter prepares for what follows in this section. The controversy over healing on the Sabbath comes up for the third and last time (see 6:1 – 11; 13:10 – 17). This passage seems to be repetitive with its similarities to the incident in 13:10 – 17: the presence of the ruler of the synagogue/a ruler from the Pharisees (13:14; 14:1), the challenging issue whether it is appropriate to heal on the Sabbath (13:14; 14:3), a Sabbath healing (13:12; 14:4), the use of the verb "release" (ἀπέλυσεν) to emphasize the healing (13:12; 14:4), and the analogy of treatment of animals on the Sabbath — unbinding them and leading them to drink and rescuing them (and a child) from a pit (13:15; 14:5). The healing fulfills what Jesus has just announced he will continue to do in response to Herod's intimidation: "Go tell this fox, 'Behold, I am casting out demons and curing people today and tomorrow, and on the third day I will reach my goal'" (13:32). Neither Herod's threats nor the Pharisees' hostile surveillance will stop him from his mission of healing and liberation.

But how else might the point of the incident differ from the previous Sabbath healing? Tannehill suggests that the man with dropsy (today more commonly called edema) "represents those persons to whom Jesus offers wholeness in spite of religious regulations that would restrict his ministry." He is an example of the poor, disabled, blind, and lame who are mentioned later in Jesus' discourse (14:13, 21).[1] But the use of the disease of dropsy as a metaphor for consuming passions, gluttony, and greed (see the discussion below) adds a new twist that makes this healing an apt introduction to the issues related to wealth and generosity that will occupy Jesus' attention in the following units.

IV. Jesus' Journey to Jerusalem (9:51 – 19:28)
    F. On Recognizing the Reign of God (13:10 – 15:32)
        1. The Release of a Bent Woman on the Sabbath and the Parables of the Mustard Tree and Leaven (13:10 – 21)
        2. The Accomplishment of God's Purpose despite Rejection (13:22 – 35)
            a. Question about the Number Who Will Be Saved (13:22 – 30)
            b. The Necessity of Jesus' Death in Jerusalem (13:31 – 35)
➡   **3. Healing the Man with Dropsy (14:1 – 6)**
        4. Banquet Invitations (14:7 – 14)

Main Idea

Jesus cures unhealthy cravings that plague humans and stifle life.

Translation

(See next page.)

Structure and Literary Form

This incident is a mixture of a healing and conflict story. Jesus initiates the conflict with two rhetorical questions that challenge the opponents' application of the law. He heals the victim and reduces the opponents to silence.

---

1. Robert C. Tannehill, "The Lukan Discourse on Invitations (Luke 14,7 – 24)," 1605.

Luke 14:1–6

14:1	Circumstance	On one occasion **he went to the house of one of the leaders of the Pharisees** ⤴
		to eat a meal on the Sabbath,
		and they were keeping a close eye on him.
2	Circumstance	**And behold, a certain man who had dropsy was before him.**
3	Challenging	**And answering, Jesus said to the legal experts and other Pharisees,**
	rhetorical question	*"Is it lawful to heal on the Sabbath or not?"*
4a	Audience's response	**And they were silent.**
b	Healing	**So he took hold of him, healed him, and released him.**
5	Challenging	**And he said to them,**
	rhetorical question	*"Which of you whose son or ox falls into a well will not immediately pull* ⤴
		him out on the day of the Sabbath?"
6	Audience's response	**And they were not able to answer to these things.**

Exegetical Outline

→ **I. Setting: Jesus is invited to the home of a Pharisee with a hostile audience (14:1)**

II. Encounter with a man with dropsy (14:2 – 6)

   A. Confrontation with the legal experts and Pharisees with a challenging question about healing on the Sabbath (14:2 – 3)

   B. Silence of the legal experts and Pharisees (14:4a)

   C. Healing and release of the man with dropsy (14:4b)

   D. Confrontation with the legal experts and Pharisees with a challenging question from their own practice about healing on the Sabbath (14:5)

   E. Silence of the legal experts and Pharisees (14:6)

Explanation of the Text

14:1 On one occasion he went to the house of one of the leaders of the Pharisees to eat a meal on the Sabbath, and they were keeping a close eye on him (καὶ ἐγένετο ἐν τῷ ἐλθεῖν αὐτὸν εἰς οἶκόν τινος τῶν ἀρχόντων [τῶν] Φαρισαίων σαββάτῳ φαγεῖν ἄρτον καὶ αὐτοὶ ἦσαν παρατηρούμενοι αὐτόν). The Sabbath was a joyous time (Neh 8:9 – 12) when families feasted on the food prepared on the previous day (Exod 16:23). Luke does not tell us why this Pharisee (presumably) invited Jesus into his home for the Sabbath dinner. Were his intentions malicious, so that he wanted to trap him in some indiscretion, or were they benign and he offered hospitality because Jesus was making a pilgrimage to Jerusalem? That Jesus attended this dinner shows that he was just as intent on winning self-righteous Pharisees as he was the so-called flagrant sinners. The note that they were keeping a close eye on him suggests that the meal fellowship was convivial only on the surface.

His host could be another ruler of the synagogue, as in 13:14. It is more likely that he is one of the eminent leaders of the Pharisees who exerted moral authority in the movement as a ruler (i.e., a magistrate, 12:58), or as a member of the Sanhedrin who adhered to pharisaic practices. The point for Luke in the context is that he would be numbered among the elite in his circle and was surrounding himself at his dinner party with a charmed coterie of local worthies.

The company includes "legal experts" (νομικοί), who are also Pharisees (14:3). Not all Pharisees were legal scholars (see 5:30, 6:35); they simply followed the rules governing purity, tithing, and Sabbath observance that were dictated by the recognized legal experts among them who puzzled over such things and issued decisions. It is no surprise that the Pharisees are watching Jesus closely and with hostile intent (see the other uses of the verb "to keep an eye on," "to watch closely" [παρατηρεῖν] in 6:7 and 20:20). The verb can imply that they were lying in wait and ready to pounce. They had been doing so for some time as Jesus continued to flaunt their interpretations of the law and to call attention to the flaws in their legal technicalities and the mendacity of their hypocrisies.

Their response is a far cry from what one would expect after Jesus has just announced that he is the one coming in the name of the Lord (13:35). Instead of strewing his way with cries, "Blessed is the one who comes," they look at him gravely with furrowed brows, trying to spot some incriminating slip in regard to the law with which they could slander him (see 11:53 – 54). Their enmity reminds the reader that, despite this Sabbath respite, Jesus is on a journey to his death. It recalls Ps 37:32: "The wicked lie in wait for the righteous, intent on putting them to death." Because of this, this Pharisee's house will also be "abandoned of salvation" (13:35a).[2]

14:2 And behold, a certain man who had dropsy was before him (καὶ ἰδοὺ ἄνθρωπός τις ἦν ὑδρωπικὸς ἔμπροσθεν αὐτοῦ). Braun asserts that this man's "brief cameo role is to be a physical, visual representation of an ethos craving desire."[3] There is no reason to believe that his presence is an unexpected disturbance, like the woman in 7:36 – 50.[4] He has no speaking part in the scene, and the opponents are silent as well. In contrast to the earlier account of the "bent woman" whom Jesus' healed on the Sabbath (13:13, 14, 17), no one rejoices over the healing, nor does anyone express indignation over its occurring on the Sabbath. The absence of such responses may suggest that Luke intends for this parallel story to take the Sabbath healing to a new level of meaning and that Braun is right. The metaphorical significance attached to the healing of this particular disease is of key importance.

Dropsy refers to an abnormal accumulation of liquid in cells or tissue causing swelling and poor circulation, and the swollen limbs and belly would make this man's condition obvious to all. A primary symptom of dropsy was an unquenchable thirst in a body already bloated, but drinking only made the victim thirstier and worsened the disease. In the Greco-Roman world, dropsy was seen as the consequence of gluttony, and thus it was often used as a metaphor for greed and lust.[5]

---

2. David P. Moessner, _Lord of the Banquet: The Literary and Theological Significance of the Lukan Travel Narrative_ (Minneapolis: Fortress, 1989; repr., Harrisburg, PA: Trinity Press International, 1998), 157.

3. Willi Braun, _Feasting and Social Rhetoric in Luke 14_ (SNTSMS 85; New York: Cambridge Univ. Press, 1995), 41.

4. Tannehill, "The Lukan Discourse on Invitations (Luke 14,7 – 24)," 1605. My assumption is that he is one of the invited guests. His disease does not make him impure. In _b. Šabb._ 33a,

three kinds of dropsy are identified: that caused by sin (see also _Lev. Rab._ 15.2; _b. Yebam._ 60b), that caused by fasting, and that caused by "delayed calls of nature." Three rabbis (Samuel the Little, Abaye, and Raba) are identified as having suffered from it with the clarification that their condition was _not_ a punishment for some sin. This man's condition does not make him an outcast. There is nothing in the text to suggest that he came seeking healing from Jesus.

5. Braun, _Feasting and Social Rhetoric in Luke 14_, 30 – 37.

Polybius (13.2.2) said, "in the case of a dropsy the thirst of the sufferer never ceases and is never allayed by the administration of liquids from without, unless we cure the morbid condition of the body itself, so it is impossible to satiate the greed for gain, unless we correct by reasoning the vice inherent in the soul."[6]

Dropsy was a label for money lovers. According to Stobaeus (*Flor.* 3.10.45), "Diogenes compared money-lovers to dropsies: as dropsies, though filled with fluid crave drink, so money-lovers, though loaded with money, crave more of it, yet both to their demise. For, their desires increase the more they acquire the objects of their cravings."[7] Ovid (*Fast.* 1.215–16) wrote similarly of dropsy: "So he whose belly swells with dropsy, the more he drinks, the thirstier he grows. Nowadays nothing but money counts: fortune brings honors, friendships; the poor man everywhere lies low."[8] Lucian (*Gall.* 21–23) said that the rich are subject to a host of ills, including dropsy, as a consequence "of their extravagant dinners." This man's body reflects his spirit.

The Pharisees, labeled as money lovers (16:14), need to be healed of their moral dropsy, their greedy desire for personal wealth and honor. There is one in their midst who can heal them of their unquenchable selfish social and material ambition.

14:3 And answering, Jesus said to the legal experts and other Pharisees, "Is it lawful to heal on the Sabbath or not?" (καὶ ἀποκριθεὶς ὁ Ἰησοῦς εἶπεν πρὸς τοὺς νομικοὺς καὶ Φαρισαίους λέγων· ἔξεστιν τῷ σαββάτῳ θεραπεῦσαι ἢ οὔ;). They look on Jesus as someone with a shady reputation when it came to strict Sabbath observance, and he answers their unspoken thoughts with a rhetorical question. Jesus has posed the question before (6:9), and he has already healed three times on the Sabbath (4:31–37; 6:6–11; 13:10–17) and proclaimed himself to have divine authority to do so as Lord of the Sabbath (6:5). The issue whether or not it is permissible to heal on the Sabbath is not the main one in this passage.[9] As noted in the In-Depth note below, the Pharisee's oral tradition made concessions in the case of emergencies, but this man's condition, though it could lead to sudden death (see *b. ʿErub.* 41b), would not have been considered an emergency that warranted healing. The challenge exposes the Pharisees' inadequacies as interpreters of the law, and the examples Jesus will give of their violations of the Sabbath reveal that they are motivated more by self-interest than by obedience to God.

14:4 And they were silent. So he took hold of him, healed him, and released him (οἱ δὲ ἡσύχασαν. καὶ ἐπιλαβόμενος ἰάσατο αὐτὸν καὶ ἀπέλυσεν). Before Jesus receives an answer, he heals the man by taking hold of him. It is unclear how this action relates to the cure. The verb "take hold" (ἐπιλαμβάνομαι) can also imply that Jesus helps or assists him (see Heb 2:16) or that he lays hold of the disease.[10] If the verb "released" (ἀπέλυσεν) is translated "dispersed" (cf. 9:12), it may suggest that the man was not one of the guests at the dinner party. His hasty departure might forestall being harried by the disapproving guests.

---

6. As cited in ibid., 36.

7. As cited in ibid., 37. He cites other examples (e.g., Plutarch, *Mor.* 524A–D; p. 35).

8. As cited in ibid., 37.

9. Halvor Moxnes (*The Economy of the Kingdom: Social Conflict and Economic Relations in Luke's Gospel* [Philadelphia: Fortress, 1988], 136) contends that seeking honor from other people characterized social interaction. By "protecting the purity of Israel through a strict observance of Sabbath rules," the Pharisees maintain their prominent position but also "keep outside this system of exchange" — the sick, poor, and unclean. These persons are the focus of 14:1–25. This perspective adds a new wrinkle for understanding the Pharisaic interest in Sabbath observance. It solidifies their superior status in social relations.

10. LSJ, 642.

The incident, however, is parallel to the healing of the bent woman in 13:12, and the same verb is used when she is cured: "When Jesus saw her, he summoned her and said, 'Woman, you have been set free (ἀπολέλυσαι) from your infirmity.'" It may mean, then, that Jesus released this man from the ailment and the spiritual condition of gluttony and greed associated with it.

On another Sabbath, Jesus declared that his mission was to proclaim "release to the captives" (4:18). As God's Son, he has been able to vanquish easily Satan, demons, and sickness, but he is also able to overcome a no less deadly spiritual disease — human greed. He is able to remove everything that blocks life.[11] This healing sets the stage for his teaching on money and care for the poor that will follow.

14:5 And he said to them, "Which of you whose son or ox falls into a well will not immediately pull him out on the day of the Sabbath?" (καὶ πρὸς αὐτοὺς εἶπεν· τίνος ὑμῶν υἱὸς ἢ βοῦς εἰς φρέαρ πεσεῖται, καὶ οὐκ εὐθέως ἀνασπάσει αὐτὸν ἐν ἡμέρᾳ τοῦ σαββάτου;). The question "Which of you?" (τίνος ὑμῶν) seeks to elicit agreement from the audience because the answer seems obvious. All of us would do this. A textual variant reads "donkey" (ὄνος) instead of "son" (υἱός). A later scribe probably made the change to make it agree with 13:15 ("Does not each one of you set free his ox or donkey from its stall on the Sabbath and lead it to drink?"; see Exod 21:33 – 34; Deut 22:4).

It also may have seemed incongruous to link a child to a beast of burden. But the text yields a paronomasia when translated back into Aramaic: *bᵉra* ("son") and *bᵉ⁽ira* ("ox") and *bera* ("well").[12] The wording also matches the fourth commandment in Deut 5:14: "but the seventh day is a sabbath to the LORD your God. On it you shall not do any work, neither you, nor your son or daughter, nor your male or female servant, nor your ox, your donkey or any of your animals, nor any foreigner residing in your towns, so that your male and female servants may rest, as you do." "Son" stands first in the list among family members, and "ox" stands first among farm animals.

The dilemma of a child or beast falling into a well or pit brings two commands into conflict: the command to keep the Sabbath holy and the demand that one should help lift up a neighbor's donkey or ox who has fallen in the road (Deut 22:4), even if it belongs to one who hates him (Exod 23:5). Jesus' argument runs like this: If his opponents are willing to violate the Sabbath to save an animal, why do they object to his healing a person on the Sabbath? His question, however, interjects the note of self-interest. If it were a child, and particularly their child, they will not wait until the Sabbath is over but will "immediately" (εὐθέως) rush to save him. If it is their animal, they will hasten to set it free. This rhetorical question implies that this man seized with dropsy is a child of God whose life is endangered, but they are indifferent to his plight.

11. Bovon, *Das Evangelium nach Lukas (Lk 9,51 – 14,35)*, 476.

12. Marshall, *The Gospel of Luke*, 580.

The Rabbis and the Sabbath

According to *m. Yoma* 8:6, breaking the Sabbath in a life-or-death situation was permitted. All of the rabbis agreed that saving a life takes precedence over keeping the Sabbath. They disagreed over what is the scriptural basis for this conclusion. In *Mekilta Shabbata* 1 (on Exod 31:12), for example, the section begins by discussing the command, "Thou shalt not do any manner of work," and concludes that even such activities that "only detract from the restfulness of the day" are prohibited. It continues:

> Once R. Ishmael, R. Eleazar b. Azariah and R. Akiba were walking along the road followed by Levi the netmaker and Ishmael the son of R. Eleazar b. Azariah. And the following question was discussed by them: Whence do we know that the duty of saving life supersedes the sabbath laws? [Giving medicine falls into the category of grinding because medicines were prepared on the spot by picking (reaping) and grinding herbs into powders.] R. Ishmael, answering the question, said: "Behold if a thief be found breaking in," [he can be killed in self-defense even on the Sabbath, although it is not explicitly mentioned in the text, without acquiring blood guilt] (Exod 22:1). Now of what case does the law speak? Of a case when there is doubt whether the burglar came merely to steal or to kill. Now by using the method of *qal wahomer* [the light and the heavy] it is to be reasoned: Even shedding of blood, which defiles the land and causes the Shekinah to be removed, is to supersede the laws of the sabbath if it is to be done in protection of one's life. How much more should the duty of saving life supersede the sabbath laws!

Other rabbis ruled that if an animal falls into a stream of water on the Sabbath, it is not pulled out, but provisions are made for it where it lies so that it should not perish (*b. Šabb.* 128b; *b. B. Meṣ.* 32b). A ruling from the Dead Sea Scrolls is far more strict: No beast was to be helped to give birth on the Sabbath and none that had fallen into a cistern or into a pit was to be lifted out on the Sabbath (CD 11:13 – 14; see also 4Q265 7:6 – 7).

Jesus is not dealing with rabbinic casuistry but actual practice. The amendment of Sabbath restrictions had been accepted in practice, and Jesus appeals to this reality.

14:6 And they were not able to answer to these things (καὶ οὐκ ἴσχυσαν ἀνταποκριθῆναι πρὸς ταῦτα). At first, his fellow diners were "silent" (v. 4); now, they are powerless to answer. This phrase may be translated, "they had no power to reply."[13] Johnson notes that according to Cicero (*Inv.* 1.32.54) silence means consent, and it is surprising since these people could make a case against it.[14] In this case, their silence is evidence of their smarting pride and the power of Jesus' word to confute them. If they objected to his logic, they would be forced to say that they did not regard this man as worth saving on the Sabbath.

Theology in Application

The Pharisees' silence before Jesus' questioning is damning. He does not provide a theological rationale for healing on the Sabbath; he simply does it. He also removes this issue from the cross fire of legal debate and places it in the arena of what is humane. Why must this man, who is a son of Abraham, wait one more day to be set free from his affliction? If they answer, "Because it's the Sabbath," they expose their self-centeredness. This man's problem is not their problem; he is not their child or ox. People can be quite legalistic in strictly applying rules to others, but when they are hit with similar problems, they are quick to bend them. When it is my problem, it becomes a crisis for which loopholes can be found. This hypocrisy among religionists leads to the cynical definition of "Christian" in Ambrose Bierce's "The Devil's Dictionary": "one who believes that the New Testament is a divinely inspired book admirably suited to the spiritual needs of his neighbor."[15]

The silence of the Pharisees is also damning when compared to other healing accounts in Luke. Elsewhere, healing evokes joy and praise of God. This healing meets only with resistance.

What is most important are the metaphorical implications of healing this disease. As noted above, dropsy is linked to the unquenchable desire of the rich for more of what they already have — money and elite status. The silent disapproval of the witnesses suggests that they will not be cured of their love of money (16:14) or their quest for honor (14:7 – 11). What characterizes all of the wealthy with their bloated bank accounts is their lack of contentment and satisfaction with what they have.

This passage has direct application to a consumerist culture that hungers and thirsts after all the wrong things that ultimately contribute to physical diseases and to spiritual dis-ease. Since nothing really fills the cavernous emptiness inside people, they always want more. Greed drives the sabbathless pursuit of riches in modern societies, and it scorns the gift of rest that the Sabbath brings to humanity and to the

---

13. Plummer, *Luke*, 356.
14. Johnson, *The Gospel of Luke*, 223.

15. Ambrose Bierce, *The Collected Writings of Ambrose Bierce* (New York: Carol, 1989), 211.

world. What Jesus offers is the restoration of personal worth to each individual and release from the deadly cravings that destroy life.

In a sermon, Augustine not only captures the essence of what I believe is the point of this passage, using the metaphor of dropsy, but his interpretation of "ask, and it shall be given to you" (11:9) captures the theme of the following passages that are related to the use of money. The antiquated language of the translation is apt because its message is so foreign to the ears of a consumerist culture whose motto is: "Get all you can, can all you get, and sit on your can."

> There is gold, there is silver; they are good, not such as can make thee good, but whereby thou mayest do good. Thou hast gold and silver, and thou desirest more gold and silver. Thou both hast and desirest to have; thou are at once full and thirsty. This is a disease not opulence. When men are in the dropsy, they are full of water, yet always thirsty.[16]

Augustine goes on to say, "Thou hast money, deal it out freely.... Thy money is diminished, thy righteousness is increased. That is diminished which thou must soon have lost, that diminished which thou must soon have left behind thee; that increased which thou shalt possess for ever."[17]

16. Augustine, *Sermons on Selected Lessons of the New Testament*; vol. 1: *Matthew, Mark, Luke* (trans. R. G. MacMullen; London: John Henry Parker; J. G. F. and J. Rivington, 1844), 114.
17. Ibid., 115.

Luke 14:7 – 14

Literary Context

Two questions from chapter 13, "What is the reign of God like?" (13:18, 20), and "Are those who are saved few in number?" (13:23), receive further answers in chapter 14. The first question prompted Jesus' comparison of the reign of God to a mustard tree, where the birds of the air nest in its branches, and to leaven, whose small amount is hidden in the lump of dough but produces irrefutable effects (13:18 – 21).

These are subversive images that challenge expectations, and they prepare us for the radical picture of the eschatological banquet that Jesus gives later in chapter 14. When one of the dinner guests trumpets, "Blessed is the one who eats at the banquet in the reign of God" (14:15), it provokes Jesus' parable about a banquet (14:16 – 24; see comments on next section). The host plans a feast for the prim and proper elite, who suddenly all come up with last-minute excuses that prevent them from attending. The feast is then transformed when a mob of misfits are escorted into the banquet. God's kingdom banquet will include those whom the upper crust would never consider inviting: the poor, the crippled, the blind, and the lame.

Will the saved be few? The answer is less than comforting. The emphasis in 14:7 – 11, 12 – 14, 16 – 24 is on invitations. The perfect passive participle "invited" (κεκλημένοι; 14:7, 24) brackets the teaching on invitations and banquets, and the verb to invite (καλέω, "call") appears eleven times. Though many will be included from all over (13:29), those who complacently assume that they will be in that number instead will be locked out (13:24 – 27; 14:24).

Main Idea

Seeking worldly honor and status is a futile endeavor, and doing so to the neglect of the poor and outcasts will earn God's condemnation. Honoring the dishonored will reap its reward in the resurrection of the just.

Translation

Luke 14:7–14

14:7	Circumstance	**Then he told those who were invited a parable** as he noticed how they were choosing the seats of honor,
		and he said to them,
8a	Circumstance	*"Whenever you are invited by someone to wedding feasts,*
b	Prohibition	*do not sit in the seat of honor*
9a	Reason	*lest someone more distinguished than you has been invited by him.*
b		*And* *when he arrives,* *the one who invited you will say to you,* *'Give up your seat to this one.'*
c		*And then, covered with shame, you will have to go down to the last seat.*
10a	Circumstance	*But* *whenever you are invited,*
b	Positive command	*go and take the last seat*
c	Reason	*so that whenever the one who invited you comes, he may say to you,* *'Friend, move up to a more worthy seat.'* *Then you will be honored before all the company.*
11	General principle (proverb) supporting the command	*Because* *everyone who exalts himself will be humbled,* *and* *everyone who humbles himself will be exalted."*
12a	Address to host	**Then he turned to the one who invited him and said,**
b	Indefinite temporal clause	*"Whenever you give a meal or banquet,*
c	Prohibition	*do not summon your friends, your family, your other relatives, or your rich neighbors,*
d	Reason	*lest they invite you in return and that shall become your repayment.*
13a	Circumstance	*But* *whenever you give a reception,*
b	Positive command	*invite the poor, crippled, lame, blind.*
14	General principle (beatitude) supporting the command	*You will be blessed, because they cannot repay you, for you will be repaid in the resurrection of the just."*

Structure and Literary Form

Luke identifies Jesus' saying here as "a parable" (14:7), but it is quite unparabolic compared to other parables in the gospel. It is more a warning couched as sage advice with a wisdom saying (14:11) and a beatitude (14:14). The two warnings in 14:8 – 10 follow a similar pattern with an indefinite temporal clause, prohibition, reason, indefinite temporal clause and positive command, reason, and general principle supporting the reasons, and they are bound together by the verb "to invite" (καλέω).

Jesus' counsel to his fellow guests and his host would seem to be advice on gracious living related to table etiquette and compiling guest rosters were it not for the climaxes in 14:11 and 14, which introduce what God will do in the final judgment. Theological passives are used here: those who exalt themselves "will be humbled" (by God), and those who humble themselves "will be exalted" (by God); and those who include the poor and the outcasts to share in their feasts "will be repaid" (by God) in the day of resurrection. These pronouncements make clear that Jesus' advice concerning worldly issues involving human preoccupations with honor and shame will have eternal ramifications. Rather than seeking kudos from humans, one should concentrate on honoring those whom God honors. Johnson observes, "His advice therefore is 'parabolic' because it parodies the 'good advice' of worldly wisdom only to subvert it by the more radical demand of the kingdom."[1]

Exegetical Outline

➡ I. Reproaching fellow guests for scrambling for the seats of honor (14:7 – 10)

   II. Exaltation (14:11)

   III. Reproaching the host for inviting only those who can repay the honor (14:12 – 13)

   IV. Beatitude (14:14)

---

1. Johnson, *The Gospel of Luke*, 227.

Explanation of the Text

14:7 Then he told those who were invited a parable as he noticed how they were choosing the seats of honor, and he said to them (ἔλεγεν δὲ πρὸς τοὺς κεκλημένους παραβολήν, ἐπέχων πῶς τὰς πρωτοκλισίας ἐξελέγοντο, λέγων πρὸς αὐτούς). The setting is still the dinner at the Pharisee's house (14:1), and Jesus observes the guests jockeying to grab the seats closest to the host that will bestow on them the badge of highest ranking in the social pecking order. The couches in the dining area were assigned traditional rankings.[2] Where one sat indicated one's rank relative to that of the other guests.[3] In his *Table Talk* (1.2), Plutarch's remarks show how much importance was placed on following accepted social protocol in Greco-Roman society:

> My brother Timon, upon an occasion when he was host to a considerable number of guests, bade them each as they entered take whatever place they wished and there recline, for among those who had been invited were foreigners as well as citizens, friends as well as kinsmen, and in a word, all sorts of people. Now when many guests were already assembled, a foreigner came up to the door of the banquet room, like a grandee out of a comedy, rather absurd with his extravagant clothes and train of servants; and when he had run his eyes round the guests who had settled in their places, he refused to enter, but withdrew and was on his way out when a number of the guests ran to fetch him back, but he said that he saw no place left worthy of him.

Plutarch's father said, "If he had arranged the placing of his guests at the beginning as I told him to do, we would not be under suspicion of disorderliness" (*Mor.* 615 C-D).

The guests had been eyeing Jesus (14:1), but Jesus turns the tables by inspecting them. He has already pronounced a woe on a group of Pharisees for their love of the seats of honor in the synagogues and being greeted with respect in the marketplaces (11:43). He will characterize them as those who seek righteousness in the sight of others (16:15), which is a means of acquiring honor before others. Much later, he will warn his disciples not to be like the scribes who parade about in long robes, crave to be saluted with stately greetings in public, and seek the places of honor at banquets (20:46). This scene depicts this itch for honor in action as the guests make a mad dash for the seats of honor as if it were a game of musical chairs.

14:8–9 Whenever you are invited by someone to wedding feasts, do not sit in the seat of honor lest someone more distinguished than you has been invited by him. And when he arrives, the one who invited you will say to you, "Give up your seat to this one." And then, covered with shame, you will have to go down to the last seat (ὅταν κληθῇς ὑπό τινος εἰς γάμους, μὴ κατακλιθῇς εἰς τὴν πρωτοκλισίαν, μήποτε ἐντιμότερός σου ᾖ κεκλημένος ὑπ' αὐτοῦ, καὶ ἐλθὼν ὁ σὲ καὶ αὐτὸν καλέσας ἐρεῖ σοι· δὸς τούτῳ τόπον, καὶ τότε ἄρξῃ μετὰ αἰσχύνης τὸν ἔσχατον τόπον

---

2. One finds directions on how to arrange guests according to their importance in *t. Ber.* 5:5; *b. Ber.* 46b; Josephus, *Ant.* 15.2.4 §21. In the community assembly of the Qumran, they sat "each one according to his dignity" (1QSa 2.16–17, 21). According to 1QS 2.19–23:

> The priests shall enter in order foremost, one behind the other, according to their spirits. And the Levites shall enter

after them. In third place all the people shall enter in order, one after another, in thousands, hundreds, fifties and tens, so that each Israelite may know his standing in God's Community in conformity with an eternal plan. And no-one shall move down from his rank nor move up from the place of his lot.

3. Dennis Smith, "Table Fellowship as a Literary Motif in the Gospel of Luke," *JBL* 106 (1987): 617.

κατέχειν). The host determines the seating order at a banquet. The lesson turns on the shame incurred when someone with greater status arrives, and the host publicly requires one to give way for this more distinguished guest. The self-promoter must then get up and move to a lower station. The last seat will be the only one available.

Dinners were regarded as barometers of one's prestige in the gathering and the community. For such an occasion to bring public shame would be almost unbearable to a social climber. Jesus assumes that the diners naturally seek public approval from the host and fear any public reproach. After a taste of glory, the person called down will be ashamed of his fallen estate and, valiantly trying to look otherwise, will be betrayed by his ashen face (Isa 29:22).

Honor and shame were matters of life and death, and saving face was more important than garnering wealth. Jesus wishes to wake up his audience to life and death issues that are truly life-and-death issues with eternal ramifications. If self-admiration and exaltation can lead to disastrous consequences in human social settings, it will lead to even more disastrous results in the final judgment.

14:10 But whenever you are invited, go and take the last seat so that whenever the one who invited you comes, he may say to you, "Friend, move up to a more worthy seat." Then you will be honored before all the company (ἀλλ᾽ ὅταν κληθῇς, πορευθεὶς ἀνάπεσε εἰς τὸν ἔσχατον τόπον, ἵνα ὅταν ἔλθῃ ὁ κεκληκώς σε ἐρεῖ σοι· φίλε, προσανάβηθι ἀνώτερον· τότε ἔσται σοι δόξα ἐνώπιον πάντων τῶν συνανακειμένων σοι). The advice not to seek a higher status may seem, at first glance, to be similar to what is found in Prov 25:6 – 7 ("Do not exalt yourself in the king's presence, and do not claim a place among his great men; it is better for him to say to you, 'Come up

here,' than for him to humiliate you before his nobles"). Or, it may be viewed as comparable to a saying attributed to R. Hillel ("My humiliation is my exaltation, and my exaltation is my humiliation" [*Lev. Rab.* 1:5]), or the advice given by Plutarch ("Dinner of the Seven Wise Men"):

> "When we have taken our places," continued Thales, "we ought not to try to discover who has been placed above us, but rather how we may be thoroughly agreeable to those placed with us.... For, in every case, a man that objects to his place at the table is objecting to his neighbor rather than to his host, and he makes himself hateful to both." (*Mor.* 149A-B).

The point is: There is always someone more admirable, more important than oneself.

But Jesus is not dispensing mundane wisdom on how to avoid embarrassment at banquets or how cunningly to finagle special recognition when one is singled out to move to a higher place. He rejects entirely any desire to bask in the ephemeral admiration of others and uses this meal setting to warn about God's judgment. Such people assiduously seek honor from others while forgetting the judgment of God. What is worse, the Lord of the Banquet is in their midst, and they do not recognize him, defer to him, or endorse his divine mission.

14:11 Because everyone who exalts himself will be humbled, and everyone who humbles himself will be exalted (ὅτι πᾶς ὁ ὑψῶν ἑαυτὸν ταπεινωθήσεται, καὶ ὁ ταπεινῶν ἑαυτὸν ὑψωθήσεται). The passive voice implicitly has God as the one meting out the recompense, not humans (see Ezek 17:24). Self-seeking is ultimately self-defeating, but it is an immutable divine principle that "God opposes the proud, but shows favor to the humble" (Jas 4:6; 1 Pet 5:5; see Ezek 31). This declaration makes it clear that Jesus is talking about far more than table manners. The banquet serves as both a metaphor for relationships in God's reign and a warning of God's judgment. Those who arrogate to themselves places of honor in religious circles ultimately will find themselves put in their place by God and possibly excluded from the banquet altogether.

14:12 Then he turned to the one who invited him and said, "Whenever you give a meal or banquet, do not summon your friends, your family, your other relatives, or your rich neighbors, lest they invite you in return and that shall become your repayment" (ἔλεγεν δὲ καὶ τῷ κεκληκότι αὐτόν· ὅταν ποιῇς ἄριστον ἢ δεῖπνον, μὴ φώνει τοὺς φίλους σου μηδὲ τοὺς ἀδελφούς σου μηδὲ τοὺς συγγενεῖς σου μηδὲ γείτονας πλουσίους, μήποτε καὶ αὐτοὶ ἀντικαλέσωσίν σε καὶ γένηται ἀνταπόδομά σοι). "Do not summon"[4] is a present prohibition, which suggests a customary habit, "do not *habitually* call."[5] Jesus is not forbidding inviting one's family, friends, and neighbors to meals (see 15:3–7, 8–10; Acts 10:24) but forbids inviting them exclusively. It is similar to his comments in Matt 5:47 about greeting only brothers and sisters.

The host is no less self-centered than the guests clambering over one another for the seats of honor. He invites only the honorable in his social circle who can reciprocate and bestow future benefits and honor on him. By inviting persons to his banquet, he honors a patron, repays clients, reinforces their loyalty by putting them further in his debt, or seeks out new alliances. The aim is to schmooze with the "influential, powerful, and well-connected" to one's own advantage.[6]

Plutarch referred to "the friend-making power of the table" (*Quaest. conv.* 612D). Hospitality was regarded as a utilitarian investment "designed to return a net gain in status, honour, and influence."[7] The system ran on "balanced reciprocity." Receiving invitations from the elite confirms and maintains one's status as a member of the elite. When the elite accept an invitation to dine, it confirms and maintains their status as a member of the elite. Consequently, guest lists were scrutinized so that the guests would have the proper social rank. If one could not repay the honor in some way, one was unlikely to be invited. The key word is "repayment." All of these categories of persons listed — friends, family, relatives, rich neighbors — can repay the favor. The next four categories of persons listed — "the poor, crippled, lame, blind" — cannot.

14:13 But whenever you give a reception, invite the poor, crippled, lame, blind (ἀλλ᾽ ὅταν δοχὴν ποιῇς, κάλει πτωχούς, ἀναπείρους, χωλούς, τυφλούς). Luke uses five different words for meals in the illustrations from banquets: "to eat bread" (lit. trans. of φαγεῖν ἄρτον, 14:1, 15); "wedding banquet" (γάμος, 14:8; see 12:36), which can also have eschatological connotations (Isa 25:6; Matt 25:10; Rev 19:7, 9; 2 Esd 2:38); "meal" (ἄριστον, 14:12; textual variant in 14:15), which can refer to any kind of meal from breakfast to dinner (11:38; Matt 22:4; Tob 2:1); "banquet" (δεῖπνον, 14:12, 16, 17, 24), which usually refers to the main meal toward evening or a formal banquet; and "reception" (δοχή, 14:13; see 5:29).

The verb "invite" (κάλει) is a present imperative with an ingressive-progressive force: "begin

---

4. The verb now is "summon" (φώνει) instead of "invite" (κάλει).

5. Plummer, *Luke*, 358; Wallace, *Greek Grammar*, 724.

6. K. C. Hanson and D. E. Oakman, *Palestine in the Time of Jesus: Social Structures and Social Conflicts* (Minneapolis: Fortress, 1998), 75.

7. Braun, "Symposium or Anti-Symposium? Reflections on Luke 14:1–24," 75. See Gabriel Herman, *Ritualized Friendship and the Greek City* (Cambridge: Cambridge Univ. Press, 1987), 121–23.

and continue."[8] This command echoes the Deuteronomic commands to invite the Levites, the resident aliens, the orphans, and the widows, so that they "may come and eat and be satisfied, and so that the LORD your God may bless you in all the work of your hands" (Deut 14:29; cf. 16:11, 14; 26:11).[9] Luke's list reverberates throughout the gospel beginning with Jesus' first sermon announcing that the Spirit of the Lord has anointed him to bring good news to the poor, to proclaim release to the captives, recovery of sight to the blind, and to let the oppressed go free (4:18); to the Beatitudes announcing blessing on the poor, hungry, mourners, and reviled (6:20 – 22); and to the announcement to the envoys of John the Baptist about the results of Jesus' ministry (the blind receive their sight, the lame walk, the lepers are cleansed, the deaf hear, the dead are raised, the poor have good news brought to them, 7:22). The poor appear in every list and always in an important position, either first or last.

This advice about whom to invite for dinner would present different dynamics as such people entered the banquet. The crippled, lame, and blind could not scramble for the seats of honor but each would have to be helped to the table. It also would disregard the purity or impurity of those invited. It would make the Pharisees' obsessions over such things irrelevant. While the movement of the Pharisees overrode class distinctions — being a part of this movement depended entirely on education and religious practices — it created new kinds of distinctions based on purity charts. A group concerned with bodily integrity and ritual taboos was also concerned to keep its membership, the social body, free from contamination.[10]

It therefore erected different kinds of social barriers corresponding to categories of clean/unclean.

Mary Douglas concludes "that holiness is exemplified by completeness. Holiness requires that individuals should conform to the class to which they belong. And holiness requires that different classes of things shall not be confused."[11] Fastidious Pharisees would not welcome such at their table, yet Jesus recommends inviting the incomplete and impure. Though they cannot participate in Israel's earthly worship because of their impurity, he implies in the next parable (14:15 – 24) that they will be guests of honor at the heavenly banquet. They will be like Lazarus, who, though denied the discarded scraps from rich man's table, was escorted by angels to the place of honor next to Abraham in the heavenly realm (16:22 – 23).

In the cultural circles of the elite and would-be elite in the Hellenistic world, to invite the poor and outcasts would be perceived as a reckless waste of social capital. The elite did not hobnob with people they did not know, and they were above associating with those regarded as the lower breeds. Plutarch, for example, affirms that Chilon, one of the seven sages in "The Dinner of the Seven Wise Men,"

> showed most excellent judgment when he received his invitation yesterday in not agreeing to come until he had learned the name of every person invited. For he said that men must put up with an inconsiderate companion on shipboard or under the same tent, if necessity compels them to travel or to serve in the army, but that to trust to luck regarding the people one is to be associated with at table is not the mark of a man of sense. (*Mor.* 148A; see also *Mor.* 708 D)

---

8. Wallace, *Greek Grammar*, 721.

9. These Old Testament commands provide the backdrop for Abraham's response to the rich man in Hades that if his brothers will not repent listening to Moses and the prophets, they will not repent if someone were to come back to them

from the dead (16:30 – 31).

10. Donahue, *The Gospel in Parable*, 144.

11. Mary Douglas, "The Abominations of Leviticus," in *Anthropological Approaches to the Old Testament* (ed. B. Lang; Philadelphia: Fortress, 1985), 112.

Social outcasts have nothing to offer, and to welcome people like this would be to thumb one's nose at this well-guarded system and to invite social ostracism as payback.[12] As Tannehill notes, "it could cost them their positions in their families and social class."[13]

Jesus' seemingly innocent advice is unexpectedly revolutionary. It ignores the Pharisees' purity stratification as irrelevant and rejects social stratification altogether. It is a concrete application of his demand in 6:32 – 36 to be merciful to all and expect nothing in return. In light of the dire prophecy about the rich in 1:46 – 55, the rich are invited to step up and exalt those of low degree and fill the hungry with good things. If they do not, the assurance that the rich will be sent away empty applies to them, and they will become the forlorn.

14:14 You will be blessed, because they cannot repay you, for you will be repaid in the resurrection of the just (καὶ μακάριος ἔσῃ, ὅτι οὐκ ἔχουσιν ἀνταποδοῦναί σοι, ἀνταποδοθήσεται γάρ σοι ἐν τῇ ἀναστάσει τῶν δικαίων). Jesus rejects the system based on balanced reciprocity (see 6:35, if one lends expecting nothing in return, one should also give expecting nothing in return, not even gratitude). Moxnes terms it "*redistribution*, a one-way flow from those who have to the have-nots."[14] The cultural conventions governing giving and receiving meant that when one person outgave another, that person gained status as the superior in the relationship while the other moved down a rung in the status ladder.

Receiving a gift, consequently, put one under considerable social and financial pressure to reciprocate in kind. If one could not, one must not only accept inferior status but also return the favor by bestowing honor and praise, offering verbal thanks, and professing a sense of debt to the benefactor. Jesus eliminates the issues of power and status that the giving of gifts generated by introducing God into the equation. The assumption is that the bond between people — in this case, the haves and have-nots — is triangular. Repayment would come from God at the resurrection, not from the recipients of any benevolence. This teaching eviscerates the traditional patron-client relationship that governed society throughout the ancient world.[15] Since the Pharisees believed in the resurrection and held that God would dish out rewards and punishments in the judgment, it should ring true for them.

Jesus omits the resurrection of the unjust (see Acts 24:15, where Paul declares to the governor Felix, "I have the same hope in God as these men themselves have, that there will be a resurrection of both the righteous and the wicked") because he is not teaching about the resurrection. He is simply qualifying the basis on which one can expect to receive rewards in the resurrection. This beatitude serves as the positive antithesis to the stark warning in the story of the rich man and Lazarus (16:19 – 30).[16] The rich man fared sumptuously while disregarding Lazarus who starved at his gate, and he ended up tormented in Hades. To avoid such a fate, one should invite the poor.[17]

---

12. Richard L. Rohrbaugh, "The Pre-Industrial City in Luke-Acts: Urban Social Relations," in *The Social World of Luke-Acts: Models for Interpretation* (ed. Jerome H. Neyrey; Peabody, MA: Hendrickson, 1991), 145.

13. Robert C. Tannehill, "The Lukan Discourse on Invitations (Luke 14,7 – 24)," 1608.

14. Moxnes, *The Economy of the Kingdom*, 133.

15. Ibid.

16. Tannehill, *Unity of Luke-Acts*, 183.

17. The sentiment is also echoed in *1 En.* 108:8 – 13.

Theology in Application

1. The Desire for Recognition

It is a widespread human tendency to want to be observed and admired by others and to want a higher rank. Jesus' disciples are not immune to arguing over preferred positions and their imagined rankings (9:46 – 48; 22:24 – 27). This human problem permeated Paul's churches. Paul tells the Philippians, "Do nothing out of selfish ambition or vain conceit. Rather, in humility value others above yourselves" (Phil 2:3), and he follows this admonition with the example of Christ (2:5 – 11). He exhorts the Romans, "Live in harmony with one another. Do not be proud, but be willing to associate with people of low position" (Rom 12:16). He writes this admonishment from Corinth, where these problems particularly plagued the Corinthian church and disrupted their celebration of the Lord's Supper (see 1 Cor 11:17 – 34; cf. 1 Tim 6:17).[18] They were imbued in a concern for honor, which permeated Corinthian culture long before they became Christians.

This absorption with honor spans cultures and centuries. We may confess in prayer that we are worms of the dust and sing about amazing grace that saves wretches like us, but we love our little distinctions — and from God's perspective they are indeed little. When God's evaluation of our niche in his reign does not match our own assessment of our worth, the consequences will bring far more than shame.

This unit, which seems innocuous, overthrows the domination system created by social, moral, and religious establishments. Green maintains that Luke's ideal is that relationships in the believing community are to be "defined by egalitarianism and mutuality, not by webs of exchange that turn gifts into a never-ending cycle of repayment and debt."[19] Jesus overtly attacks social climbing and social stratification, which pervaded the ancient world.

But the elite were not the only ones preoccupied with the honor race: "The plebeian was as preoccupied with honor as the patrician, the client as the patron, the woman as the man, the child as the adult."[20] Cicero observes, "Nature has made us . . . enthusiastic seekers after honour, and once we have caught, as it were, some glimpse of its radiance, there is nothing we are not prepared to bear and go through in order to secure it" (*Tusc.* 1.2.4; 2.24.58). By contrast, "meekness and humility are basic to the proper attitude believers should display in their relationship toward God, and service to the needy is characteristic of the proper attitude one should have toward others."[21]

---

18. See David E. Garland, *1 Corinthians* (BECNT; Grand Rapids: Baker, 2003), 533 – 57.

19. Joel B. Green and Michael Pasquarello III, *Narrative Reading, Narrative Preaching: Reuniting New Testament Interpretation and Proclamation* (Grand Rapids: Baker, 2003),

60 – 61. See Peter Garnsey and Richard Saller, *The Roman Empire: Economy, Society and Culture* (Berkeley: Univ. of California Press, 1987), 148 – 59.

20. Barton, *Roman Honor*, 11.

21. Stein, *Luke*, 388.

2. God's A-List

The Pharisees' approach to the reign of God and the people of God sought to solidify categories that clearly identify who was excluded and who was included. Jesus hints "at a life-world in which honor is measured and granted along unforeseen lines."[22] "A-List" is a term that was first used in Hollywood for the most bankable movie stars, but its usage has been expanded to apply to anyone who is admired and has desirable social status. These are the celebrities one could only wish to have at one's dinner party. God, however, welcomes those who seem not even to make anyone's Z-list. The list of those to be invited shows that God values the humbled and the poor. The scale of who is in and out has been turned upside down.

Jesus invites persons to come to his table who can never repay the gift he bestows on them by giving his life for them. In the context of the churches in Luke's time, "persons previously treated as outsiders, strangers, would be embraced as members of one's extended kin group."[23] Jesus' followers are to cultivate "a *disposition* deriving from their numbering themselves among the lowly."[24] One's status and prestige is determined in the world by evaluating others who are not disinterested parties, and also by climbing the social ladder or fighting others off to hang on to their rung.

In God's reign, God ascribes a person's station, not others. This invasion of divine reality frees people from engaging "in the mad scramble for the little badges of recognition afforded by human society."[25] As Schweizer observes, it frees them from "the need always to advance their own cause and come out on top or to count the profit," "to have to impress others," and to "compare ourselves with others and define our own value on that basis." It allows us "to be unconditionally generous"; "then we could take our places without worrying whether we were second or tenth, where [whether] we were lame or [whether] we were blind."[26] This truth also frees people from shame. Shame comes when one's own evaluation of one's honor is not shared by others. Jesus' disciples need not join in the scrimmage for honor because they know who they are in God's eyes.

---

22. Green, *The Gospel of Luke*, 552.
23. Ibid., 553.
24. Doble, *The Paradox of Salvation*, 121.
25. Malcolm Tolbert, "Luke," in *The Broadman Bible Commentary*; vol. 9: *Luke to John* (ed. Clifton J. Allen; Nashville: Broadman, 1970), 119.
26. Schweizer, *Luke*, 236.

Luke 14:15 – 24

Literary Context

The parable of the banquet is the last scene in the context of the dinner at the home of a ruler of the Pharisees (14:1). The parable symbolizes another dimension of the eschatological banquet, which Jesus mentioned in 13:28 – 29. There he visualized another surprising twist to what may have been conventional expectations by affirming that Abraham, Isaac, and Jacob and all the prophets will sit at table in the reign of God, joined by all those from east and west, north and south, while the workers of iniquity — apparently, those who may have expected to be included — are cast out, weeping and gnashing their teeth. In this parable, the surprising twist is that the participants in the banquet are not the first invited, the elite, but the poor and outcasts. In the immediate context, the parable contains social criticism of the dominant class that used banquets to further their hankering for social status while ignoring the poor. It is also a warning to Christian readers "who may have to choose between their social advantages and the call to follow Jesus."[1]

---

1. Robert C. Tannehill, "The Lukan Discourse on Invitations (Luke 14,7 – 24)," 1607.

Main Idea

Not everyone who might expect to participate in the celebration of the reign of God at the end of the age will be included. Some will exclude themselves by their obsession with their worldly affairs, showing contempt for the one who has invited them. They also will exclude themselves by showing contempt for the poor and the outcasts.

Translation

Luke 14:15–24

14:15	Beatitude/ circumstance	When one of those eating with him heard these things, **he said,** *"Blessed is the one who eats at the banquet in the reign of God."*
16a b	Response: Parable of the Banquet	And **he said to him,** *"A certain man gave a great banquet and invited many.*
17	Sending/ announcement	*He sent his servant at the hour the banquet was ready to tell those who had been invited, 'Come because it is already prepared!'*
18a	Excuses	*And they began unanimously to excuse themselves.*
b	Sample excuse (1)	*The first said to him, 'I have purchased a field and I am compelled to go see it. I ask you, have me excused.'*
19	Sample excuse (2)	*And another said, 'I have purchased five yoke of oxen and I am on my way to test them. I ask you, have me excused.'*
20	Sample excuse (3)	*And another said, 'I have married a wife and because of this I am not able to attend.'*
21a	Report of the servant (1)	*The servant reported to his master these things.*
b	Reaction of the host (1)	*Then the master of the house became angry and said to his servant, 'Go quickly into the boulevards and alleyways of the city and bring in the poor, crippled, lame, and blind here.'*
22	Report of servant (2)	*The servant said, 'Lord, I have done what you ordered and there is still room.'*
23	Reaction of the host (2)	*The master said to the servant, 'Go out into the country roads and along the hedges and compel them to come in so that my house might be filled.'*
24	Pronouncement	*For I say to you, none of those persons who were invited will taste of my banquet."*

Structure and Literary Form

The parable is framed by references to eating in a banquet (14:15, 24). It is prompted by a fellow guest glibly braying on about the joys of eating at the banquet of the reign of God, and the last verse declares that not everyone will participate in the banquet.

The parable is similar to the parable of the wedding feast in Matt 22:1 – 14 but with striking differences. Matthew's parable is about a king giving a wedding party for his son (Matt 22:2); Luke's is about a "certain man" giving a great dinner (Luke 14:16). In both Matthew and Luke, the invitation is issued three times: in Matthew, twice to the invited and once to the uninvited; in Luke, once to the invited and twice to the uninvited. In Matthew, the king sends out servants to summon those invited and he gets the report that they do not want to come (Matt 22:3). In the second sending of the servants, the guests make light of it, go off to attend to business, and treat them shamefully and kill them (Matt 22:5 – 6). In Luke, a single servant summons those invited to come to the feast, and he meets with a sudden onslaught of excuses, three samples of which are given (Luke 14:18 – 20).

Both hosts are angry at being treated so disrespectfully (Matt 22:7; Luke 14:21). In Matthew, the king musters an army for a military campaign and destroys the murderers and burns their city, even though it is part of his own domain (Matt 22:7). He then has his servants go into the highways and byways to invite whomever they find to join in the feast (Matt 22:8 – 9). In Luke, the angry householder sends his servant into the city and then outside the city to bring in guests who are identified as the poor, maimed, blind, and lame (Luke 14:21). His goal is to fill his house (Luke 14:23). The punishment for those who refused to come is that they will not get to eat of the feast (Luke 14:24). In Matthew's parable, Jesus notes that the hall is filled with both good and evil (Matt 22:10), and the denouement has the king coming to observe the feast and spotting a man without appropriate wedding clothes. He has him summarily thrown out where there is weeping and gnashing of teeth (Matt 22:11 – 14).

The comparison reveals that the Lukan version places an emphasis on the nature of the excuses of those invited and the social status of the replacement guests. While that parable is more realistic in its details and Matthew's more allegorical, both symbolize issues related to the banquet at the end of the age and the judgment of God.

Exegetical Outline

→ **I. Introduction about the banquet of the reign of God (14:15)**

II. The parable of the banquet (14:16 – 23)

    A. Invitation to many (14:16 – 17)

    B. Last minute excuses by all of those invited (14:18 – 20)

        1. The excuse of having purchased a field (14:18)

        2. The excuse of needing to test a team of oxen (14:19)

        3. The excuse of marrying a wife (14:20)

    C. Invitation to the outcasts of the city (14:21 – 22)

    D. Second invitation to outcasts outside of the city (14:23)

III. Pronouncement about the exclusion of those first invited to the banquet (14:24)

Explanation of the Text

14:15 When one of those eating with him heard these things, he said, "Blessed is the one who eats at the banquet in the reign of God" (ἀκούσας δέ τις τῶν συνανακειμένων ταῦτα εἶπεν αὐτῷ· μακάριος ὅστις φάγεται ἄρτον ἐν τῇ βασιλείᾳ τοῦ θεοῦ) A guest picks up on the word "blessed" and the mention of the resurrection in 14:14 to make a pious declaration that anticipates the joys of the messianic banquet (lit., "eating bread in the reign of God"; see Rev 19:9). He may have wanted to change the subject out of some discomfort over the discussion of the poor and lame (14:13 – 14) or to avert any further embarrassing confrontations.

This guest's statement, however, serves two purposes. First, it makes a theological link between the invitations to a banquet (14:7 – 14) and the banquet celebrating God's reign (see Isa 25:6; 1 En. 62:14). Banquet invitations become a symbol of God's reign. Second, it exposes the confidence and complacency of guests who take for granted that they will be included in that number who will dine joyously in the reign of God. Jesus punctures that sanguine expectation with this parable.

The Pharisees gathered around the table can get nothing right. Jesus even turns a pious bromide against them. He seizes on this declaration as a teachable moment, but are the Pharisees teachable? The reign of God is not pious talk about a future hope but requires action in the face of its present invasion into the world in the person of Jesus (16:16; 17:20 – 21), particularly as it relates to caring for the poor. The parable explores the issue of the identity of those who would be resurrected and participate in the banquet. It pointedly raises the question for the listeners gathered at this dinner. Will they honor Jesus as their benefactor, accept his invitation, and be present at his table in the reign of God (22:30), or will they lose out on this blessedness because of their business quests, their preoccupation with family, and their disdain for the host and the other guests who show up?

14:16 And he said to him, "A certain man gave a great banquet and invited many" (ὁ δὲ εἶπεν αὐτῷ· ἄνθρωπός τις ἐποίει δεῖπνον μέγα καὶ ἐκάλεσεν πολλούς). The great feast and the large number invited suggest that the host is a man of some means. The nature of the excuses offered by those who give him the brush-off suggests that they too were persons of means.

14:17 He sent his servant at the hour the banquet was ready to tell those who had been invited, "Come because it is already prepared!" (καὶ ἀπέστειλεν τὸν δοῦλον αὐτοῦ τῇ ὥρᾳ τοῦ δείπνου εἰπεῖν τοῖς κεκλημένοις· ἔρχεσθε, ὅτι ἤδη ἕτοιμά ἐστιν). Double invitations were customary among the upper class when they were entertaining (Est 5:8; 6:14; Philo, *Creation* 78: "Just as givers of a banquet, then, do not send out the summonses to supper till they have put everything in readiness for the feast … [so God prepared the world]"; see also Apuleius, *Metam.* 3.12; *Lam. Rab.* 4:2). Depending on who and how many people accepted the invitation, the host must decide on what or how many animals to slaughter and cook. When the food was prepared, it had to be eaten that night. They could not put leftover fatted calf, for example, in the freezer. Therefore, the guests who accepted an invitation are honor-bound to attend when they are informed by the servant that the meal is ready.

The emphasis is on the banquet being ready. The preparations have been completed. Guests cannot simply drop by when it suits them. Now is the time of decision.

14:18a And they began unanimously to excuse themselves (καὶ ἤρξαντο ἀπὸ μιᾶς πάντες παραιτεῖσθαι). All of a sudden, the servant of the host is hit with a barrage of excuses that decline the invitation. Many have been invited, and Jesus gives only a sampling of three of their excuses (compare the sampling of the report of three results from a total of ten servants in the parable of the minas [19:16–21]). The phrase translated "unanimously" literally is "from one" (ἀπὸ μιᾶς [feminine]) and could be completed by the feminine nouns "voice" (φωνῆς, "with one voice") or "mind" (γνώμης, "with one mind"). It is a suspicious coincidence

that every last one of those invited comes up with last-minute reasons why they cannot come and do so "with one accord" or "in concert." It recalls Jesus' lament in 13:34 about wanting to gather Israel as a mother hen gathers her chicks under her wings, "and you would not."

The chorus of sudden pretexts to beg off attending the banquet raises several questions. Are they legitimate excuses that the host should fully understand, or are they transparently weak and a slap in the face?

Linnemann maintains that these are not weak excuses and that they should not be taken as a deliberate slight of the host. Rather, they are legitimate excuses that will simply delay their arrival. These people plan to show up at the banquet later. Favorable business opportunities suddenly arose, and the people wish to use the remaining hours of daylight to finish business matters that might otherwise fall through before they come to the banquet; after all, "the banquet will not run away."[2] This explanation is possible since references in Jewish literature describe the length of time during which invited guests could arrive late and be welcomed, and this grace period was indicated by a cloth hung over the door. After the three introductory courses had been served, the cloth was removed and any latecomer would be turned away.[3]

Linnemann's reconstruction assumes that these invitees are "in the act of" buying and that they are rushing to get things done before the Sabbath starts, which would then preclude any further investigation of fields or testing of animals after the setting of the sun. Since the third excuse breaks the pattern and does not say, "I am about to marry a wife," she argues that it is a secondary addition to the parable and fits the tendency to multiply

---

2. Linnemann, *Parables of Jesus*, 89.
3. Joachim Jeremias, *Jerusalem in the Time of Jesus* (trans. F. H. and C. H. Cave; London: SCM, 1969), 93, citing *t. Ber.* 4:10; *Lam. Rab.* 4:4; *b. B. Bat.* 93b.

excuses that is exemplified by the parallel parable in *Gos. Thom.* 64.

It seems an unlikely coincidence that the entire guest list suddenly has some pressing eleventh-hour business that needs attention. It smacks of some kind of conspiracy among the guests that was designed to embarrass the host. No one shows up late to find there is no room (contrast Matt 25:1 – 14). The guests do not ask if they can come later but ask to be *excused* from attending the banquet. A host may be irked by their tardiness, but it is their refusal to come that sparks his fury. If the host simply wanted to exclude these people who thought that they could slip in a little late, he simply could have removed the cloth over the door (if this were the practice in this time). He did not hastily have to invite a crowd in from off the streets so that there would be no room for the latecomers. He did so to fill his house, which otherwise would have been empty. The story about the tax collector Bar Mayaan in the Jerusalem Talmud (*j. Ḥag.* 2:2, 77d; *j. Sanh.* 6:6, 23c) may lend support to a conspiracy theory against the host.

Sanders offers another explanation for the excuses by drawing a parallel with the four acceptable excuses for exemption from the service in the army of the faithful (Deut 20:5 – 8; 24:5). The grounds for exemption are both social and economic.[4] The problem with this interpretation is that the host is not setting off on a holy war; he is holding a banquet. These Old Testament excuses apply to exemption from a year of military duty, not banquets. Sanders counters that the parable describes (allegorically) the great eschatological banquet. He points out that holy war legislation was viewed as eschatological at Qumran (1QM 10:5 – 6; 1Qsa).[5] Therefore, he concludes, "battle and banquet should be seen in the same light."[6]

Aside from the fact that the excuse about marriage is the only real parallel to the excuses found in Deuteronomy, these same excuses are commented on in *m. Soṭah* 8:1 – 7, and it is concluded that they only apply in a battle waged of free choice. In a battle waged in a religious cause, everyone, including the bridegroom, must go forth. Therefore, the Mishnaic commentary may parallel Jesus' parable in depicting an occasion when the excuses of Deuteronomy *do not* apply.[7]

Rorhbaugh argues quite differently from a sociological perspective that the excuses are diversionary and "conceal the real reason for the social disapproval." None of those invited risks breaking ranks and coming to the banquet shunned by others in their elite circle.[8] Given the social conventions of double invitations, it seems that the sudden and absurd refusals show "a coordinated act of ostracism ... inform[ing] the host that he is no longer socially acceptable."[9] Braun offers that such a boycott by the urban elite would have shamed the host, both directly and indirectly through the resulting chain reaction of humiliating rumors, forcing a conversion of social and class identity and commitments.[10] What remains unclear is what is wrong with the host or the supper that causes these people to shun the invitation.

Since Luke's gospel is peppered with warnings against allowing worldly concerns from impeding answering the invitation that Jesus extends for

4. James A. Sanders, "The Ethic of Election in Luke's Great Banquet Parable," in *Essays in Old Testament Ethics* (ed. James L. Crenshaw and John T. Willis; New York: Ktav, 1974), 245 – 71.

5. Ibid., 257.

6. Ibid., 260.

7. Donahue, *The Gospel in Parable*, 141 – 42.

8. Richard L. Rohrbaugh, "The Pre-Industrial City in Luke-Acts: Urban Social Relations," in *The Social World of Luke-Acts: Models for Interpretation* (ed. Jerome H. Neyrey; Peabody, MA: Hendrickson, 1991), 142 – 43.

9. Tannehill, "The Lukan Discourse on Invitations (Luke 14,7 – 24)," 1614.

10. Braun, *Feasting and Social Rhetoric in Luke 14*, 106 – 31.

all to come under the reign of God, the excuses may serve a multiple function. They show how "the cares and riches and pleasures of life" (8:14) can choke the Word. But nothing in life should be allowed to preempt responding to the invitation. They also show a callous contempt for the one who issues the invitation.

14:18b The first said to him, "I have purchased a field and I am compelled to go see it. I ask you, have me excused" (ὁ πρῶτος εἶπεν αὐτῷ· ἀγρὸν ἠγόρασα καὶ ἔχω ἀνάγκην ἐξελθὼν ἰδεῖν αὐτόν· ἐρωτῶ σε, ἔχε με παρῃτημένον). Fitzmyer claims, "The reader should not ask why he did not inspect it before he bought it, that would be to miss the point of the story."[11] But would not the original audience have asked themselves that question? "I have a necessity to go see it" is the literal rendering of the phrase and seems to stretch the truth. If the banquet is held in the evening, the man would have little daylight left even for a superficial examination. Who buys a field without having first seen what he is buying? Inspection normally occurs long before the purchase of the land. Bailey likens this excuse to saying that "I have just bought a house over the phone, and I must go now to take a look at it and see the neighborhood."[12] But it may be that this excuse is intended as an example of one who is totally fixated on his business affairs. He is like those in the days of Lot who were "buying and selling, planting and building" and were oblivious to the danger of the hour (17:28 – 30).[13]

14:19 And another said, "I have purchased five yoke of oxen and I am on my way to test them. I ask you, have me excused" (καὶ ἕτερος εἶπεν· ζεύγη βοῶν ἠγόρασα πέντε καὶ πορεύομαι δοκιμάσαι αὐτά· ἐρωτῶ σε, ἔχε με παρῃτημένον). "I go" (πορεύομαι) is in the present tense and implies, "I am on my way." This invitee pleads no special necessity to do so. He is already on his way to test the oxen to see if they will perform well when they are yoked together.[14] Apparently, he had not done so prior to buying them. If he has already bought the animals, what is the urgency? Examining them could wait until the next day.

Bailey likens this excuse to calling your wife and canceling dinner because you have just bought a used car over the phone and you are now going to the used car lot to find out what kind it is, how old it is, and whether or not it will start.[15] Again, the absurdity of the excuse matches the ridiculous amount of time and energy that people spend on meaningless ventures to the neglect of answering to God.

14:20 And another said, "I have married a wife and because of this I am not able to attend" (καὶ ἕτερος εἶπεν· γυναῖκα ἔγημα καὶ διὰ τοῦτο οὐ δύναμαι ἐλθεῖν). This excuse means that he said last week that he would attend the banquet, but today he says that he will be busy with his new bride this evening (the banquet would be for men only). He implies that he is going to stay home in an effort to fulfill the command to be fruitful and multiply.[16] Bailey points out that in an Oriental

11. Fitzmyer, *Luke*, 2:1056.

12. Bailey, *Through Peasant Eyes*, 96. Bock, *Luke*, 2:1274, however, cites Str-B, 2:208 and *b. ʿAbod. Zar.* 15a for examples of post-purchase inspections.

13. Two mentions of fields in Acts reveal two contrasting attitudes. Judas used the proceeds of his betrayal of Jesus to buy a field (Acts 1:18 – 19); Barnabas sold a field and gave the proceeds to the apostles to be distributed to the needy (4:36 – 37).

14. Green, *The Gospel of Luke*, 560, notes: "Five yoke of oxen would work a farm over one hundred acres and indicates a man of substantial wealth."

15. Bailey, *Through Peasant Eyes*, 98.

16. Sjef Van Tilborg ("The Meaning of the word γαμέω in Lk 14:20; 17:27; Mk 12:25 and in a number of Early Jewish and Christian Authors," *HvTSt* 58 [2002]: 802 – 10) contends that there are enough classical Greek, early Jewish, and Christian texts that use the verb (γαμέω) in the sense of "to have sexual contact" rather than "to marry" and it has that meaning here (see Luke 17:27; Mark 12:25).

society it would be considered extremely crude to hint of honeymoon activities.[17] What makes this excuse worse is that he does not even ask to be excused as the others did, which only serves to compound the insult to the host.

The excuses escalate in bad manners, though the value of the grounds for the excuses also increases: field, animals, and wife. The first says, "I am compelled to go to see the field. I ask you (pray), have me excused" The second says simply, "I am on my way" and mentions no necessity. The third is not going anywhere; he is going to stay home and does not ask to be excused. "Because of this I am not able to attend" is tantamount to saying "I will not attend" (see 11:7). Again, this excuse may illustrate those who are "marrying [and] being given in marriage" as in the days of Noah (17:27). Their preoccupations with mundane matters will cause them to miss the banquet, and they will be swept away by the flood of destruction. Note Jesus' subsequent proclamation about discipleship in 14:26 (the next section).

14:21 The servant reported to his master these things. Then the master of the house became angry and said to his servant, "Go quickly into the boulevards and alleyways of the city and bring in the poor, crippled, lame, and blind here" (καὶ παραγενόμενος ὁ δοῦλος ἀπήγγειλεν τῷ κυρίῳ αὐτοῦ ταῦτα. τότε ὀργισθεὶς ὁ οἰκοδεσπότης εἶπεν τῷ δούλῳ αὐτοῦ· ἔξελθε ταχέως εἰς τὰς πλατείας καὶ ῥύμας τῆς πόλεως, καὶ τοὺς πτωχοὺς καὶ ἀναπείρους καὶ τυφλοὺς καὶ χωλοὺς εἰσάγαγε ὧδε). The host was first described as "a certain man" (ἄνθρωπός τις), then as a "master" (κύριος), and now as the "master of the house"

(οἰκοδεσπότης). Irritation is a common response to refused dinner invitations, and the excuses enrage the host, which is even more understandable if they were transparently feeble excuses. Derrett contends, "Contempt for equals is so scorching as to make life impossible and survival doubtful. Honour and respect, and the visible and recognisable signs of it, are necessary to daily life."[18]

Those invited have publicly snubbed the host, and his community esteem among his peers has plummeted. It is unlikely that he seeks some kind of revenge against those originally invited by filling up his house with those whom they would dismiss as a bunch of rabble. They are not going to weep and gnash their teeth for being excluded from joining this crowd. The replacement guests are precisely those listed by Jesus in 14:12 – 14 who could never repay the favor. In his desire to fill his house, has the master undergone a social conversion and now rejects "the system of social reciprocity" that influenced his first invitations?[19]

The boycott, if that is what it was, fails to abort the banquet. The party goes on as scheduled even if the headliners fail to show. The host will not allow his food to go to waste, and the house is filled so that every place will be taken by those invited in off the streets. These are people who would never make it on anyone's party list. This second invitation extends to those from the wider public roads inside the city, where the nonelite might gather, and the narrower alleyways, where the poorest live. These are persons "whom the walls and gates of the central precincts of pre-industrial cities were designed to shield from view. They are the very ones the walls were meant to keep in their proper place."[20] The verb translated as "bring in"

17. Bailey, *Through Peasant Eyes*, 98 – 99.

18. J. Duncan M. Derrett, *Jesus's Audience: The Social and Psychological Environment in Which He Worked* (New York: Seabury, 1973), 42.

19. So Heil, *The Meal Scenes in Luke-Acts*, 109. Green, *The*

Gospel of Luke, 562, concurs that "this householder has raised the stakes considerably further by completely rejecting the very social order that gave power and significance to those who had heaped shame on him."

20. Rohrbaugh, "The Pre-industrial City in Luke-Acts," 144.

(εἰσάγαγε) implies that they are "led in" (see 22:54; Acts 9:8; 21:37; 22:24), not simply invited.

The guests who eventually share in the meal are strikingly different from those first invited. When the parable is read as symbolic of the eschatological feast, the revised guest list includes the very ones whom the covenanters at Qumran believed would be excluded. In the Rule of the Congregation (1Q28a [1QSa] 2.5 – 22), the subject concerns those who may be admitted to the community council and sit at the table when the Messiah comes and those who may not. A list in the War Scroll (1QM 7.4 – 6) of those who are forbidden to approach the field of battle in the great holy war of the last days is similar. These lists parallel Lev 21:17 – 23, which enumerates those who may not approach the altar to offer the bread of God:

Lev 21:17 – 23	1QSa 2.5 – 22	1QM 7.4 – 6
any blemish	defiled in the flesh	lame
blind	paralysis in feet or hands	blind
lame	lame	paralysis
mutilated face	blind	any indelible blemish
limb too long	deaf	impurity of the flesh
broken foot or hand	mute	
hunchback	defiled by visible blemish	
dwarf	tottering old man	
blemish in eyes	senility	
itching disease		
scabs		
crushed testicles		

If this kind of discriminatory thinking forms the backdrop for the parable, Jesus challenges the assumptions about the identity and ritual purity of the elect and turns upside down the way that many thought things would be when the Messiah came. In the reign of God, the outcast will no longer be cast out. According to Isa 35:5 – 6, the blind, deaf, lame, and mute are those who will benefit from the coming salvation of God. The blind will see, the deaf will hear, the lame will leap, and the mute will shout for joy (Luke 7:22). In Jesus' parable, these become the guests of honor while those who thought themselves to be most worthy to sit in the places of honor will not simply be dispatched to the lowest seats (14:7 – 14), they will be excluded from the feast. Others who truly value the invitation will take their places.

Inviting the poor to a meal is also mentioned in Tob 2:2, but they are supposed to be the poor "of our people among the exiles in Nineveh, who is wholeheartedly mindful of God." In the parable the guests brought in off the streets may or may not be "wholeheartedly mindful of God," and they are not first quizzed before they are admitted. They come and are not offended in the least that they were not the first ones invited but were brought in as second-string emergency replacements.

14:22 – 23 The servant said, "Lord, I have done what you ordered and there is still room." The master said to the servant, "Go into the country roads and along the hedges and compel them to come in so that my house might be filled" (καὶ εἶπεν ὁ δοῦλος· κύριε, γέγονεν ὃ ἐπέταξας, καὶ ἔτι τόπος ἐστίν. καὶ εἶπεν ὁ κύριος πρὸς τὸν δοῦλον· ἔξελθε εἰς τὰς ὁδοὺς καὶ φραγμοὺς καὶ ἀνάγκασον εἰσελθεῖν, ἵνα γεμισθῇ μου ὁ οἶκος). The large number of invitations (v. 16) means that a large number of substitute guests are necessary. The first sending does not fill the house, and the householder bids the servant to canvass "the roads outside the city" for guests.[21] The areas outside the

---

21. Plummer, *Luke*, 363.

city would have been inhabited by outcast groups (ethnic groups, tanners, traders, beggars, prostitutes), who required access to the city but were not permitted to live within it.[22] Green asserts that "this householder will include *anyone* among his table guests — that is, no one is too sullied, too wretched, to be counted as a friend at table." Thus, "'the roads and lanes' of the city would be where those of very low status lived, whether because of their despised occupation, their family heritage, their religious impurity, their poverty or some other cause."[23]

To ensure a full house, the householder now tells his servant to "compel" (ἀνάγκασον) them to come in. "Compel" does not entail using force. Given the conventions regarding invitations, the persons would have possibly resisted because they could not repay. Barton notes:

> In Plautus's *Asinaria* the poor man is not only embarrassed but deeply suspicious of the kindly and equal treatment afforded him by his rich neighbor. We might describe the poor man's anxiety as fear of being patronized. The respect shown him by his rich neighbor threatens to make him even more hopelessly in debt to, and so more vulnerable to, an already powerful man.[24]

Consequently, these persons must be compelled in the sense of being resolutely urged to come. They must be convinced it is a genuine invitation and not a cruel prank or an attempt to subjugate them further. Paul's advice in 2 Tim 4:2 is an apt description of what is intended in the context of inviting persons to accept God's offer of grace: "Preach the word; be prepared in season and out of season; correct, rebuke and encourage — with great patience and careful instruction."

14:24 For I say to you, none of those persons who were invited will taste of my banquet (λέγω γὰρ ὑμῖν ὅτι οὐδεὶς τῶν ἀνδρῶν ἐκείνων τῶν κεκλημένων γεύσεταί μου τοῦ δείπνου). The "you" (ὑμῖν) is plural, which raises the question, who is speaking and who is being addressed? If this is the host of the parable speaking, he had sent out only one servant, and he must be addressing someone other than the lone servant; otherwise it would require the singular "you" (σοί). The only group of people present are the poor who have been invited off the streets, and the master could be thundering against those first invited who refused to attend. Or, the master "steps as it were on to the apron of the stage and addresses the audience."[25]

If it is Jesus speaking, this dinner at a Pharisee's house ends as badly as the previous one in 11:42 – 52 with its barrage of woes. The pronouncement formula ("for I say to you"; λέγω γὰρ ὑμῖν) matches what Jesus uses elsewhere in the gospel to draw a point. No character in a parable speaks like this.[26] Thus, I interpret it as Jesus' address to the diners in the Pharisee's house as he applies the parable directly to them. The pronouncement knocks the air out of the smug sense of security implicit in the opening beatitude by one of the guests. The banquet no longer is a local affair that a crowd of malcontents sought to sabotage or were too preoccupied to attend. It is the banquet of the reign of God (14:15). Jesus asserts that God's banquet is *his* banquet, which fits the beatitude in Rev 19:9, "Then the angel said to me, 'Write this: Blessed are those who are invited to the wedding supper of the Lamb!' And he added, 'These are the true words of God.'"

---

22. Rohrbaugh, "The Pre-Industrial City," 144 – 45.
23. Green, *The Gospel of Luke*, 561.
24. Barton, *Roman Honor*, 225.
25. Linnemann, *Parables of Jesus*, 90.
26. Of the thirty-three times the phrase "I tell you" is ut-

tered by Jesus in Luke, four occur at the conclusion of parables (13:35; 18:8, 14; 19:26; see 4:24, 25; 7:9, 26, 28; 10:12, 24; 11:8, 51; 12:5, 22, 37, 44, 51; 13:3, 5, 24; 15:7, 10; 17:34; 18:17, 29; 19:40; 21:3, 32; 22:16, 18, 37). Once, it is spoken by John the Baptist (3:8).

Theology in Application

1. The Exclusion from the Reign of God of the Privileged Who Are Complacent

When Jesus first alluded to the eschatological banquet and to himself as the Lord of that banquet, he urged his audience to be prepared as faithful servants for his sudden arrival (12:35 – 48). In a surprising reversal of roles, the Lord will serve those servants who were watching and faithful (12:37, 42 – 43), and the unfaithful and corrupt servants will be beaten (12:47 – 48). Now, the audience takes the role of potential guests. Those first invited will be excluded and those who normally would be blacklisted will be included in the roster of special guests.

As this parable applies to the context of Jesus' ministry in Luke's gospel, his inclusive invitation to one and all to enter the kingdom of God, coupled with the offer of grace, becomes a stumbling block to those who insist on limiting the invited to the religious upper crust. The Pharisees who think they are shoo-ins to attend the eschatological banquet as honored guests will be shut out (see Isa 65:13 – 14). "None of those persons who were invited will taste of my banquet" is a statement in the world of the parable that expresses the seriousness of turning down the invitation from Jesus. It should not be pressed to mean that no Pharisee or Jew could be saved. Paul, the Pharisee, is an example of one who initially rejected the invitation as a persecutor of the church but who was not written off by God. The parable dramatizes the paradox that the first can indeed become last — and not only last, but totally shut out. It is a warning to all who regard themselves as privileged with God that they can cause themselves to be cut off from all of God's privileges.

The parable has multiple quills that can stick in the auditors and do their work to reshape their current vision of life and the reign of God. First, the parable lends itself to an allegorical reading. As Tannehill observes:

> Telling a story enables the traditional material to enter new configurations. A religious teacher of Jesus' time and place who told a story about a master who gives a banquet could probably expect the audience to interpret it in terms of the banquet in God's reign. The teacher could use this expectation, however, to undermine other expectations (e.g., concerning the participants in that banquet) through a surprising twist in the story. This observation relates to the debate about so-called "allegorical" elements in the parables of Jesus. Certain stereotypical identifications are probably presupposed, but these enable the parable to work as a parable. They provide the horizon of expectation which in the parable can rework to produce unexpected results.[27]

---

27. Tannehill, "The Lukan Discourse on Invitations (Luke 14,7 – 24)," 1609.

The references to the resurrection of the just (14:14) and to eating bread in the reign of God (14:15), which precipitate Jesus' response with a parable, quite naturally encourage the auditor to think of the great banquet at the end of the age. Jesus also has just employed this imagery in 13:22 – 30. The parable would then be saying something about the participants in the messianic banquet — the great party that God will throw at the end of the age. The threat that those who refuse to come will not taste of this meal has eternal implications. If the parable is interpreted in light of 2:34 – 35 ("the falling and rising of many in Israel") and 13:24 (the "many … [who] will seek to enter and will not have the strength to do so"), it is pointing to the exclusion of many who viewed themselves as the elect or called of God.

The parable takes up the story at the second invitation when everything has been prepared and the meal is ready, and it is possible to apply it to Jesus' ministry. In Jesus' call we have the decisive summons to salvation.[28] God's first invitation had long since been issued by the prophets, and the chosen ones have accepted it. Jesus issues the final summons. At the decisive hour, however, they balk when Jesus announces that the feast is ready. Tax collectors and sinners are responding (5:29 – 30; 15:1; 19:7 – 10), but the so-called righteous ones who think they need no repentance (15:7) refuse to come. It is not uncommon to interpret this passage in terms of Rom 11:11: "Because of their transgression, salvation has come to the Gentiles." The poor, crippled, lame, and blind from the streets of the city could represent the outcasts within Israel and the guests from the highways and hedges as those beyond the pale of Judaism, namely, the Gentiles.[29] The parable could be construed to convey that Israel's rejection means salvation to the Gentiles. As Stein states it:

> The second sending is unique to Luke and speaks of the entrance of the Gentiles into God's kingdom. The rejection of Jesus and the kingdom by official Judaism (14:24) precipitated the inclusion of Israel's outcasts (4:18, 7:22) and the Gentiles (Acts 13:47 – 48; 18:6; 28:25 – 28). The great reversal had taken place. Alas, Israel, however, was rejected (13:34 – 35). They ignored the day of visitation, the "now" of Jesus' ministry (4:21; cf. 2 Cor 6:2).[30]

God will have a people even if, as John the Baptist warned, God has to raise up children to Abraham from stones (3:8) or has to invite the riffraff off the street. Some also note that the commission to fill the house remains unfulfilled when the

---

28. Walter Grundmann, *Das Evangelium nach Lukas* (THKNT; 4th ed.; Berlin: Evangelische Verlaganstalt, 1966), 299.

29. The term translated "hedges" (φραγμοί) appears in Eph 2:14 to refer to the dividing wall of hostility that Christ has abolished in his flesh. See *Let. Aris.* 139: "In his wisdom the legislator, in a comprehensive survey of each individual part, and being endowed by God for the knowledge of universal truths, surrounded us with unbreakable (or unbroken)

palisades (φραγμοί) and iron walls to prevent our mixing with any of the other peoples in any matter, being thus kept pure in body and soul, preserved from false beliefs, and worshiping the only omnipotent over all creation."

30. Stein, *Luke*, 394. See also John Martin Creed, *The Gospel according to Luke* (London: Macmillan, 1930), 192; Marshall, *The Gospel of Luke*, 585 – 86; Fitzmyer, *Luke*, 2:1053; Bock, *Luke* (NIVAC), 395.

parable closes, so that it symbolizes the church's continuing mission to the Gentiles (see Rom 11:25). If those who are gathered from east, west, north, and south come to sit at table in the reign of God with Abraham, Isaac, and Jacob (13:23 – 30) refer to Gentiles, then those who ate and drank in Jesus' presence and in whose streets Jesus taught but who are now cast out could refer to the Jews.

Interpreting the first group as "the Jews" or "the Jewish elite," however, is overly simplistic and misleading. While some Jews do reject the gospel in Luke-Acts, many, including priests, respond positively (Acts 5:14 – 16; 6:7; 13:47; 18:6, 8; 21:20; 28:23 – 28). The response is mixed, but it is wrong to interpret this parable as implying that the Gentiles are included because of the rejection by some Jews. As Green recognizes, "According to this reading, the inclusion of 'the poor' would be for God a kind of afterthought, an alternative course of action forced upon him by his need to have a full house (v 23) and by having surprisingly been spurned by those first invited."[31] To say, "There will be no second chance for the pious in Israel," as Evans does,[32] contradicts Paul's argument in Rom 11. And why identify the Gentiles with the poor, or, as Evans identifies them, "vagrants"?[33] If those who reject the summons refer only to the Jewish leaders, why were they the only ones originally invited? Had they accepted the invitation, the possibility of further invitations for the poor and outcast would never have arisen.[34]

One cannot ignore the metaphorical reference to the eschatological banquet, but the three different groups could be explained simply by the law of three. The second and third invitations underscore the host's strong desire and desperate attempt to fill up his banquet. If the focus of the parable is on the identity of the guests who will dine at table in the reign of God, it makes the point that they will include those who do not make it on anyone's A-list except God's. The guests are at the opposite end of the spectrum — religiously and socially — of those first invited. The clubby members of the social register who move in the best of circles and believe themselves to be the insiders will miss out. Jesus implies that this surprising shift is already happening in his ministry. God's reign has arrived, and those who will enjoy the banquet are the derelicts who are neither physically whole nor healthy. The parable serves as a vindication of his fellowship with sinners and/or as a part of his theme of the great reversal and the Lukan context with the parables in chapter 15.

2. Concern and Help for the Poor

The parable has an ethical thrust. It shows that to invite the poor is to do what God is doing, to invite those who are not ordinarily on anyone's guest list, and, according to the Pharisees' standards, should be rejected.

31. Green, *The Gospel of Luke*, 556.
32. Evans, *St. Luke*, 575.
33. Ibid., 574.
34. Green, *The Gospel of Luke*, 557, n. 146.

Banquets were closely related to one's status in a community and governed by shame and honor. When one wanted to signal one's prestige or to tap the barometer of one's prestige in the community, one entertained. Accepting an invitation recognized the status of the host and brought with it the responsibility to reciprocate to remain on an equal footing.[35] What Jesus recommends is that the rich invite the poor to join in the time of rejoicing and expect nothing in return, not even praise, which turns the system upside down. It is a call to charity. They are to be like Tobit, who, when he arrived home and found an abundance of food prepared for him, told his son, "Go … and bring whatever poor person you may find of our people … who is wholeheartedly mindful of God, and … I will wait for you, until you come back" (Tob 2:2). The difference is that Jesus does not insist that those invited should be "mindful of the Lord;" they should be just willing to come.

In a Hellenistic setting, this parable would be regarded as "something akin to a social revolution."[36] The reason is that the fundamental rationale for gift-giving in a Hellenistic society was to "establish reciprocal relations which could be cashed in at a later date." Therefore, one was "generous" to those who were in a position to return you a favor. The sort of people whom the host invites — beggars, lame cripples, and the blind — could never repay. Any repayment one might receive for inviting such folks would take place only at the resurrection.[37]

For the rich in Luke's audience, the parable serves as a call to associate with people of low status, which would scandalize their friends for violating the system that barred people of low status. It would bring ostracism, which would bring financial consequences. It meant to "renounce the privileges of his social class and identify with the poor."[38] Rohrbaugh suggests that the parable reflects the shaky social position of the Christian elite who would be ostracized by their peers for their association with the poor who were attracted to Christianity and that Luke uses the parable "to confront the rich of his own community who are avoiding association with poor Christians."[39] It would be apt as "a warning to members of the Christian community who may have to choose between their social advantages and the call to follow Jesus."[40]

The host opened himself up to social ridicule by opening his doors to a ragtag group of outcasts, but so does God, who has chosen what the world regards as foolish — the low and despised to shame the wise and the high and mighty (1 Cor 1:26 – 28). The folks who declined to attend can taunt the host, saying that he cannot give a banquet without having to invite the common people off the street. But, as

35. Derrett, *Jesus's Audience*, 43.

36. Philip F. Esler, *Community and Gospel in Luke-Acts: The Social and Political Motivations of Lukan Theology* (SNTSMS 57; Cambridge: Cambridge Univ. Press, 1987), 194.

37. See A. R. Hands, *Charities and Social Aid in Greece and Rome* (London: Thames and Hudson, 1968).

38. Tannehill, "The Lukan Discourse on Invitations (Luke 14,7 – 24)," 1614.

39. Rohrbaugh, "The Pre-Industrial City,"142.

40. Tannehill, "The Lukan Discourse on Invitations (Luke 14,7 – 24)," 1607.

Minear puts it, "God chooses the company of sinners, who cannot repay his generosity."[41] This parable reinforces the principle enunciated in 13:30 that the first will be last and the last first. It also recalls the promise that God will exalt the humble and fill the hungry with good things while sending the rich away empty (1:52 – 53).

The difference is that these persons exclude themselves. The excuses that kept the no-shows away reveal that they are persons whose lives are wrapped up entirely in earthly enterprises. Their last-minute excuses reveal their true priorities. Heil comments, "All of those invited to the great dinner began to excuse themselves because of their selfish preoccupation and craving, 'dropsical' desire to acquire property and increase their wealth and social status" (see the interpretation of the healing of the man with dropsy, 14:1 – 6).[42] They were all winners, and they had to spend a lot of time to keep being successful and to stay on top. There are so many deals to be made; who has time for this inconsequential party that only interferes with our pressing affairs? They are self-absorbed and spend their lives consumed by their consumption of material things.

The banquet will not be called off because of their absence, and they will not be able to attend on their own terms and arrive whenever they like. The first two excuses require persons of means, but the last excuse can apply to anyone on the social spectrum. Paul's comments in 1 Cor 7:29 – 31 are an apt commentary of what Jesus expects to be learned from this parable.

The parable describes a situation that offers grace to the outcast and excludes the privileged. It therefore serves as a warning. Manson's comments deserve repeating: "No one can enter the kingdom without the invitation of God, and no man can remain outside of it but by his own deliberate choice. Man cannot save himself; but he can damn himself."[43]

3. The Mission to Fill God's Banquet Hall

Humans take radical steps to fill their banquet hall; how much more will God! Heil recognizes that this story of the householder "provides the audience with a model for not being discouraged by the rejections of their announcement that the kingdom of God has arrived (10:1 – 12) but to turn to those who are better disposed to accept and appreciate it."[44] The conclusion that there is still room reveals that when applied to God, "the mission of God seems never to be complete."[45]

41. Paul S. Minear, "Some Glimpses of Luke's Sacramental Theology," *Worship* 44 (1970): 325.

42. Heil, *The Meal Scenes in Luke-Acts*, 107.

43. Manson, *The Sayings of Jesus*, 130.

44. Heil, *The Meal Scenes in Luke-Acts*, 110.

45. Hultgren, *The Parables of Jesus*, 339.

CHAPTER 45

Luke 14:25 – 35

Literary Context

The surprising largess of the host in the previous parable, extending an invitation to a banquet to those normally excluded, comes as undeserved grace. This illustration of the grace of the kingdom is followed appropriately by warnings, as the audience shifts from the diners in the Pharisee's home to the crowds. Jesus' warnings about the challenges of discipleship are not new; they have appeared earlier in the gospel (see 8:4 – 21; 9:23 – 27, 57 – 62; 12:13 – 59). The parable of the banquet invites a wide sweep of people to fill the house (14:23). All are invited to accept God's grace, but with grace comes demand.

The thrust of the sayings and parables in this section parallel the conclusion to the similar parable of the banquet in Matt 22:11 – 14. In Matthew, the banquet hall is filled with "the bad as well as the good" (22:10). When the king comes to observe his guests and spies a man without a wedding garment, he has him unceremoniously expelled into "the darkness, where there will be weeping and gnashing of teeth" (22:13). The parable has allegorical features, and the meaning of the wedding garment is elusive. It most likely refers to the man's character and lack of righteousness (5:20).[1] Luke lays out the requirements placed on those who accept the gracious invitation to the banquet more transparently. The demands following the parable forestall any presumption that all discipleship involves is just showing up. Discipleship is not an invitation to ease and comfort but demands sacrifice and suffering.

1. Garland, *Reading Matthew*, 223 – 27.

Main Idea

Discipleship requires the uncompromising sacrifice of a cruciform life, the ready acceptance of possible martyrdom, single-minded devotion, and dogged tenacity.

Translation

(See next page.)

Structure and Literary Form

This unit has four warning sayings about the cost of discipleship that wrap around two cautionary parables. Two warnings about the cost of discipleship and the necessity of bearing a cross (14:26, 27) precede the two parables about the tower builder and the warring king (14:28 – 30, 31 – 32); the parables are followed by two warnings about leaving one's possessions and the uselessness of unsalty salt (14:33, 34 – 35).

Exegetical Outline

→ **I. Setting (14:25)**
  II. Two warnings about the commitment required for discipleship (14:26 – 27)
     A. The requirement of hating one's family and one's own life (14:26)
     B. The requirement of bearing one's cross (14:27)
  III. Two parables about the commitment required for discipleship (14:28 – 32)
     A. Parable of the tower builder (14:28 – 30)
     B. Parable of the warring king (14:31 – 32)
  IV. Two warnings about the commitment required for discipleship (14:33 – 35a)
     A. The requirement of giving up one's possessions (14:33)
     B. The uselessness of saltless salt (14:34 – 35a)
  V. Conclusion (14:35b)

Luke 14:25–35

14:25	Circumstance	**Now large crowds were traveling with him, and he turned and said to them,**
26	Negative warning about discipleship	"Whoever comes to me and does not hate his own father, mother, wife, children, brothers, and sisters and even his very own life is not able to be my disciple.
27	Negative warning	Whoever does not bear his own cross and come after me is not able to be my disciple.
28a	Parable about discipleship (1)	For who . . . among you who wanting to build a tower
b	Deliberation	. . . does not first sit down and calculate the cost to see if he has the means to bring it to completion?
29	Consequence	Otherwise, when he has laid the foundation and does not have the means to finish it, everyone who sees it will begin to mock him, saying,
30		'This man began to build and did not have the means to finish.'
31	Parable about discipleship (2)	Or what king . . . pondering whether to go to war with another king
	Deliberation	. . . does not first sit down and deliberate whether he is able with an army of ten thousand to oppose an army of twenty thousand set against him?
32	Consequence	Indeed, if he decides he cannot win, while the other king is still far away, he will send an emissary to sue for peace.
33	Negative warning about discipleship	Consequently, every one of you who does not say good-bye to all that you possess is not able to be my disciple.
34	Negative warning about discipleship	Salt is good, but if salt should lose its savor, how will it be re-salted?
35a		It is good for nothing, not even for the earth or the dung heap, and must be thrown out.
b	Concluding warning	Let those who have ears, listen."

Explanation of the Text

14:25 Now large crowds were traveling with him, and he turned and said to them (συνεπορεύοντο δὲ αὐτῷ ὄχλοι πολλοί, καὶ στραφεὶς εἶπεν πρὸς αὐτούς). The mention of large crowds (see 12:1) traveling with Jesus marks his departure from the Pharisee's home and the resumption of his journey to Jerusalem. Most of the specific teaching on discipleship occurs on the road in a public setting. The large crowds represent a pool of potential disciples,[2] and they follow because they recognize something rare and special about Jesus (9:18 – 19) and suspect that something rare and special is about to happen. They trail along to satisfy their curiosity and perhaps to get a ringside seat.

The majority will not fully grasp the implications of what it means to be with Jesus. A big difference exists between simply going along with (συμπορεύομαι) Jesus and following him (ἀκολουθέω) as a disciple (5:11, 27 – 28; 9:23; 18:22, 28, 43; see 9:57 – 62; 22:54). Craddock asks, "Is this march to Jerusalem a parade? The crowds must think so; everyone loves a parade."[3] But this parade will not end in a twenty-one-gun salute and bands playing "Hail to the Chief" in the temple. It is more a funeral cortège — for both Jerusalem, which will be judged for failing to respond to the Messiah, and for Jesus, who will be condemned by the authorities.

The crowds need to know that it will not be enough to say that they were there, heard his teaching, saw his miracles, and ate with him. He already has warned that some will say at the last judgment, "We ate and drank before you and you taught in our streets"; and he will respond, "I do not know who you are" or "where you come from" (13:25 – 27). Jesus' disciples are those who change

every priority in their lives and conform to his way of the cross, and so he lets them know what it will cost.

14:26 Whoever comes to me and does not hate his own father, mother, wife, children, brothers, and sisters and even his very own life is not able to be my disciple (εἴ τις ἔρχεται πρός με καὶ οὐ μισεῖ τὸν πατέρα ἑαυτοῦ καὶ τὴν μητέρα καὶ τὴν γυναῖκα καὶ τὰ τέκνα καὶ τοὺς ἀδελφοὺς καὶ τὰς ἀδελφάς ἔτι τε καὶ τὴν ψυχὴν ἑαυτοῦ, οὐ δύναται εἶναί μου μαθητής). It may seem odd to instruct disciples to love their enemies (6:35) but to hate their family. But Jesus is using hyperbole to capture the seriousness of his demand. "To hate" does not refer to enmity but is a Semitic expression that conveys indifference to one and preference for another: "I love A and hate B," which means "I prefer A to B" (see Gen 29:30 – 33; Deut 21:15 – 17; Mal 1:2 – 3; Luke 16:13; Rom 9:13).[4]

Nolland argues that the meaning of this expression entails more than simply "to love less than," citing Deut 33:8 – 9 as an example. He thinks it fits "the Greek philosophical tradition reaching back to Socrates that, in the name of single-minded devotion to truth, devalued family loyalties and concern for one's own bodily life and its needs (see Epictetus, *Diatr.* 3.3.3 – 5; Xenophon, *Mem.* 1.2.49 – 55)."[5] But the parallel text in Matt 10:37 – 38 argues for the interpretation that "to hate" means "to love less": "Anyone who loves their father or mother more than me is not worthy of me." The command to honor mother and father is still valid (18:20; see John 19:26 – 27), but Jesus will warn that those who attempt to serve two masters will hate the one and love the other (16:13). Family

2. Green, *The Gospel of Luke*, 564.
3. Craddock, *Luke*, 181.
4. Evans, *St. Luke*, 577.
5. Nolland, *Luke*, 2:762.

is not to become one's master; only Jesus is to have that role. Love for him is to take precedence over all other loves.

Natural affections can undermine faithfulness to God and provide us with excuses to back down in our commitment: "My family must come first; I must care for them." The "hatred" of family is of a piece with denying oneself (9:23). What it means is best illustrated by the disciples who left everything to follow him (5:11), and by Jesus' refusal to allow a would-be disciple to put off discipleship to return to bury his father (9:59 – 60) and to allow another to return to say farewell to his family (9:61 – 62). Jesus himself has demonstrated the single-minded devotion to the kingdom that required slighting his family and rejecting their claims on him (2:43 – 50; 8:19 – 21).

The phrase "is not able to be my disciple" occurs three times (14:26, 27, 33) at the conclusion of each saying about discipleship. Luke's language, "is not able" (οὐ δύναται), differs from the parallel sayings in Matthew, "is not worthy of me" (οὐκ ἔστιν μου ἄξιος, Matt 10:37 – 38; see 22:8) and places the emphasis on moral strength instead of moral worth.

14:27 Whoever does not bear his own cross and come after me is not able to be my disciple (ὅστις οὐ βαστάζει τὸν σταυρὸν ἑαυτοῦ καὶ ἔρχεται ὀπίσω μου οὐ δύναται εἶναί μου μαθητής). This word repeats Jesus' challenge in 9:23 (see comments) and makes concrete the idea of hating one's life. It is impossible to overemphasize the shame associated with crucifixion in the ancient world (Heb 12:2). The demand to carry or bear the cross is in the present tense (βαστάζει), probably stressing the ongoing quality of living in this manner. Although the qualification "daily" that is included

in 9:23 is absent here, the daily nature of the cross-bearing is implicit in the context. If carrying one's cross is parallel to repudiating one's family, social ties, and even life itself, then it is not a onetime experience.

Jesus expects nothing that he has not already accepted for himself. He was not a passive victim but incited the world against himself by his message and the life he lived. His crucifixion in Jerusalem did not happen to him "as the act of an evil destiny.... According to the gospels, Jesus himself set out for Jerusalem and actively took the expected suffering upon himself."[6]

Jesus' ultimatum to disciples is similar to Joshua's defiant bugle call to the Israelites (Josh 24:19 – 28). Joshua remonstrated with them, "You cannot serve the Lord, for he is a holy God. He is a jealous God; he will not forgive your transgressions or your sins. If you forsake the Lord and serve foreign gods, then he will turn and do you harm, and consume you, after having done you good" (Josh 24:19 – 20 NRSV). The people accepted the challenge and said they would serve the Lord. Joshua then laid down the conditions for serving the Lord and set up a stone in the sanctuary as a witness to their words and a warning if they disobeyed. Luke does not tell us how the throng of people tagging along after Jesus responded to his challenge.

14:28 For who among you who wanting to build a tower does not first sit down and calculate the cost to see if he has the means to bring it to completion? (τίς γὰρ ἐξ ὑμῶν θέλων πύργον οἰκοδομῆσαι οὐχὶ πρῶτον καθίσας ψηφίζει τὴν δαπάνην, εἰ ἔχει εἰς ἀπαρτισμόν;). The question "Who among you?" (cf. 14:5) is intended to elicit agreement from the audience because the answer is obvious: no one among us would do anything

---

6. Jürgen Moltmann, *The Crucified God* (trans. R. A. Wilson and J. Bowden; Minneapolis: Fortress, 1993), 51.

this imprudent (see also 11:5, 11; 12:25; 15:4; 17:7). It also draws in the whole audience. They are all potential disciples if they are willing to make the radical commitment that Jesus requires.

Manson contends that the tower should not be pictured as some grandiose fortification. That would be the work of a ruler, and rulers, for the most part, have the wherewithal to complete their undertakings. Since the parable is addressed to a largely rural audience, the tower may refer to a farm building, like the one mentioned in the parable of the wicked tenants (Matt 21:33; Mark 12:1, a detail absent from Luke's version).[7] The mention of laying a foundation suggests to some, however, that it is a more substantial building and that it might serve a military and defensive function like the tower of Siloam (13:4).[8] A military purpose would make a better connection to the next comparison of a king going to war.[9] This first comparison with the tower reflects a defensive posture; the second comparison, an attack mode.

Connected to discipleship, the enemy onslaught comes from Satan. Satan will enter Judas (22:3) and sift Peter (22:31). Disciples require a defensive fortification to withstand satanic assault or they will be overrun and utterly fail.

The first point of comparison between tower building and discipleship is calculating the cost. Jesus assumes that people are usually careful not to embark on some project without making reasonably sure of their ability to carry it through to a successful end. No one would ever start on such a project as constructing a tower without first sitting down and calculating the cost. The phrase "first sit down" (πρῶτον καθίσας) reappears in 14:31 and is key to both comparisons. "To sit down"

characterizes someone deliberating and tallying the cost (ψηφίζει τὴν δαπάνην; see the use of the verb in Rev 13:18, which assumes discernment in being able to calculate the number of the beast). One has to sit down and take stock before one can rise up to meet the challenge.

14:29 – 30 Otherwise, when he has laid the foundation and does not have the means to finish it, everyone who sees it will begin to mock him, saying, "This man began to build and did not have the means to finish" (ἵνα μήποτε θέντος αὐτοῦ θεμέλιον καὶ μὴ ἰσχύοντος ἐκτελέσαι πάντες οἱ θεωροῦντες ἄρξωνται αὐτῷ ἐμπαίζειν λέγοντες ὅτι οὗτος ὁ ἄνθρωπος ἤρξατο οἰκοδομεῖν καὶ οὐκ ἴσχυσεν ἐκτελέσαι). The point turns on the desire to avoid shame. Fear of public ridicule will prevent anyone from starting to build something that cannot be completed. No one wants to wind up with an encumbrance that one can neither finish nor abandon and that will stand as a monument to one's imprudence and lack of resources. It announces to the world that one started to build and was not strong enough to finish it. If the tower was built to guard against marauders, it will only serve to advertise weakness and may even become an invitation to attack. If, however, the person calculates the cost carefully before starting to build, he will spend all that is necessary to finish his building.

When the image is connected to discipleship, Judas is infamous as the betrayer of Jesus. He is joined by Ananias and Sapphira (Acts 5:1 – 11), Demas (2 Tim 4:10), and Hymenaeus and Alexander (1 Tim 1:20) in the failed disciple hall of shame in the New Testament.

7. Manson, *The Sayings of Jesus*, 281.
8. Michael P. Knowles, "'Everyone Who Hears These Words of Mine': Parables on Discipleship (Matt 7:24 – 27//Luke 6:47 – 49; Luke 14:28 – 33; Luke 17:7 – 10; Matt 20:1 – 16)," in

The Challenge of Jesus' Parables (ed. R. N. Longenecker; Grand Rapids: Eerdmans, 2000), 292 – 93.
9. Josephus (*J.W.* 3.2.3 §25) refers to "a strong tower" in a village.

14:31 Or what king pondering pondering whether to go to war with another king does not first sit down and deliberate whether he is able with an army of ten thousand to oppose an army of twenty thousand set against him? (ἢ τίς βασιλεὺς πορευόμενος ἑτέρῳ βασιλεῖ συμβαλεῖν εἰς πόλεμον οὐχὶ καθίσας πρῶτον βουλεύσεται εἰ δυνατός ἐστιν ἐν δέκα χιλιάσιν ὑπαντῆσαι τῷ μετὰ εἴκοσι χιλιάδων ἐρχομένῳ ἐπ᾽ αὐτόν;). Regardless of whether the second comparison pictures a king threatened by an army looming in the distance and spoiling for a fight, something that was not uncommon in Israel's experience, or a king intent on a war of aggression, he is outnumbered two to one. He must first sit down and calculate whether he has the wherewithal to engage in battle to conquer or to drive off the enemy (see Prov 24:3 – 6).

14:32 Indeed, if he decides he cannot win, while the other king is still far away, he will send an emissary to sue for peace (εἰ δὲ μή γε, ἔτι αὐτοῦ πόρρω ὄντος πρεσβείαν ἀποστείλας ἐρωτᾷ τὰ πρὸς εἰρήνην). Fear of an overwhelming defeat by the enemy will lead the king to negotiate surrender (see 2 Sam 8:8 – 11; 1 Chr 18:9 – 11). He wants to avoid courting defeat in battle, which promises to bring far worse consequences than the humiliation of submission. Failure in this case does not simply open one to scorn from neighbors but will result in being conquered, put on exhibit, and either executed or sold into slavery. But if the king believes he can win, he will fling every last soldier into the battle. Just as war requires total dedication to win, so discipleship requires total dedication. There can be no token discipleship.

14:33 Consequently, every one of you who does not say good-bye to all that you possess is not able to be my disciple (οὕτως οὖν πᾶς ἐξ ὑμῶν ὃς οὐκ ἀποτάσσεται πᾶσιν τοῖς ἑαυτοῦ ὑπάρχουσιν οὐ δύναται εἶναί μου μαθητής). The conclusion draws the consequences of what precedes, beginning in 14:26. The verb translated "say good-bye" (ἀποτάσσεται) is used five other times in the New Testament to mean "to bid farewell" (Mark 6:46; Luke 9:61; Acts 18:18, 21; 2 Cor 2:13). Here it has a figurative meaning: "to renounce, to get rid of, to break free from" (*Herm. Mand.* 6.2.9, "to break from the angel of wickedness").[10]

The term used here for one's possessions (τὰ ὑπάρχοντα) always refers to earthly possessions in the New Testament. The "everything" refers to each and every thing (πᾶσιν) just as Jesus addresses each and every person (πᾶς) who wants to be his disciple. Simon, James, and John (5:11) and Levi (5:28) are reported to have left everything to follow him. Twice, Jesus advises people to sell their possessions and distribute proceeds to the poor — once to his disciples (12:33) and once to a rich man (18:22). Peter also informs him that they have left their own things (τὰ ἴδια) and followed him (18:28), and the pattern of sacrificial giving continues in the Christian community after the resurrection (Acts 2:45; 4:34).

14:34 Salt is good, but if salt should lose its savor, how will it be re-salted? (καλὸν οὖν τὸ ἅλας· ἐὰν δὲ καὶ τὸ ἅλας μωρανθῇ, ἐν τίνι ἀρτυθήσεται;). The Greek reads literally, "if salt becomes foolish" (i.e., tasteless, unsalty). It is impossible for pure sodium chloride (NaCl) to lose its saltiness, but salt in Palestine was obtained from the evaporation of Dead Sea water and contained a mixture of salt,

---

10. Philo uses this verb to refer to Moses' fasting for forty days and nights, which he connects to renouncing "the whole belly," the things that create pleasure (*Alleg. Interp.* 3.142). Josephus uses it to refer to Esther refusing all food and drink and comforts (*Ant.* 11.6.8 §232). In *2 Clem.*, it is used to mean "bidding farewell" to things of this world (adultery, corruption, love of money, and deceit; 6:4 – 5) and "enjoyments" (16:2).

gypsum, and carnallite. The salt crystals could dissolve, leaving a residue that looked like salt but without any salty tang.

The salt metaphor appears twice elsewhere in the gospels with different referents. "You are the salt of the earth" (Matt 5:13) is coupled with two brief parables: a city set on a hill cannot be hidden; no one lights a lamp only to extinguish it at once by putting it under a basket. It clarifies the disciples' vocation in the world. They carry on the covenant calling of Israel in the world.[11]

Mark 9:49 – 50 contains two salt sayings: "Everyone will be salted with fire"; and "Salt is good, but if it loses its saltiness, how can you make it salty again? Have salt among yourselves, and be at peace with each other." The first means that the disciples will be purified by persecution. The second is closer to Luke's meaning, "If they do not manifest the distinctive characteristics Jesus requires, they are not real disciples and are worthless to him."[12] In Luke's context, the image of salt relates to discipleship and applies to the characteristics Jesus has just enumerated: the readiness "to renounce kin, comfortable living, and life itself for the sake of being Jesus' disciple"[13] A false form of discipleship may look like salt, but the gradual process of leaching leaves only a zestless pile of waste.

14:35 "It is good for nothing, not even for the earth or the dung heap, and must be thrown out. Let those who have ears, listen" (οὔτε εἰς γῆν οὔτε εἰς κοπρίαν εὔθετόν ἐστιν, ἔξω βάλλουσιν αὐτό. ὁ ἔχων ὦτα ἀκούειν ἀκουέτω). The adjective "fit" (εὔθετόν) appears in 9:62 in relation to

discipleship where Jesus declares unfit anyone who puts a hand to the plow and looks back. The text does not say that it is unfit to be used on food, but unfit for the earth or the dung heap. Malina claims that Jesus develops

> the point from the concrete picture of the outdoor Palestinian earth-oven or kiln, called earth (see Ps 12:6; Job 28:5). Fire in such an earth-oven was produced by burning dung. To make the dried dung burn, the bottom of the kiln was faced with plates of salt, and the dung itself was sprinkled with salt. The salt served as a chemical agent that helped the dung to burn. However, over time, the heat of the oven would cause the salt plates to undergo a chemical reaction which made the salt plates impede and stifle the burning of the dung. It is when the salt crystals chemically change that they must be thrown out — the salt has lost its saltiness.[14]

The image might then imply that disciples are to be a kind of fire catalyst, like salt, but it is left undeveloped. The picture is only of the failure of the salt to be salt.

The question about how the saltiness will be restored assumes that it is impossible to do so (see Heb 6:1 – 8). It is fit for nothing. The disciple who becomes saltless is worse than one who never started out as a disciple. This warning to disciples employs hyperbole. It should not be taken to mean that one might be better off never attempting to become a disciple. When it comes to discipleship, it is all or nothing. Those who fail to give their all to Jesus are in the same boat as those who never take the first step. Both are destined for damnation in the judgment.

---

11. Garland, *Reading Matthew*, 61.
12. Garland, *Mark*, 370.

13. Summers, *Commentary on Luke*, 181; see Plummer, *Luke*, 366.
14. Malina, *The New Testament World*, 119.

Theology in Application

1. The Total Demand of Discipleship

Many who come to Christ have no idea in advance what this decision will eventually cost them. The church makes the problem of those falling by the wayside worse when things get tough (see the interpretation of the parable of the sower, 8:13 – 14) by soft-selling the requirements of discipleship. Church leaders can become too interested in keeping up attendance and keeping down conflict and, as a result, dilute Jesus' radical demands. Some may be anxious about turning off people. This unit makes clear that discipleship is costly. If it is to be compared to a king preparing to go to war, disciples must be prepared to throw everything into a life-and-death battle. It will not be a gentle stroll through a rose garden.

In other words, discipleship is only "for those who have considered the worth of the enterprise with Jesus and are prepared to pay the price for sharing it."[15] Jesus does not hide his extreme requirements in the fine print but proclaims them boldly in headlines. The object is not to scare potential disciples away, which it may well do, but to enlist those who are ready to stake all with fervor on a decision that they have first considered in cold blood. Faithful discipleship that will stick it out to the end does not rest on a momentary burst of feeling. Enthusiasm may wane as quickly as it blazes up.

Jesus makes a total demand that would crush the autonomous spirit of those who want to do their own thing or who are in it for what they can get out of it. He does not want disciples who simply want to go along for the ride, soaking up his teaching while leaving fundamental values, loyalties, and manner of life unchanged. For Jesus, discipleship is an either/or proposition and is to be entered into with fear and trembling because it requires transformation.

2. The Renunciation of All Things for Christ

To follow Jesus requires being able to renounce all material goods and possessions. It entails giving up the quest for earthly security that material wealth promises. It is the trap that Judas fell into when he betrayed his Lord for money (22:3 – 5). It requires the abandonment of all projects, plans, and personal goals that one cooks up in the course of one's life, usually for the purpose of redounding to one's personal honor. Schweizer makes the challenging observation that "there is no such thing as a totally middle-class discipleship."[16]

The tendency in an affluent culture is to dilute Jesus' radical demands. To follow Jesus is not a "low-risk" or "low-cost" venture, however, as his personal example

---

15. Manson, *The Sayings of Jesus*, 281.   16. Schweizer, *Luke*, 242.

makes clear.[17] Disciples cannot play it safe. To become a disciple of Jesus is to embark on a stony path leading to an uncertain future in this life and the possibility that a cross will stand at the end of the road (9:62; 14:27). It requires being able to give up the intrinsic love for one's own life. Peter, who will follow Jesus from afar after his arrest and will deny him under gentle pressure (22:54 – 62), shows how hard it is to bear the cross with him all the way to the end.

To follow Jesus means to loosen sacred family ties (8:19 – 21; 11:27 – 28; 9:59 – 60; 14:26; 18:28 – 30). Disciples must be willing to sacrifice what they love most in the world — to give up something that goes against the promptings of human nature — the love of wife, child, and family. This word cannot be easily softened, perhaps only ignored. What it means is that discipleship to Christ must take precedence over all other relationships in life and the securities they offer. It requires redefining those relationships with some measure of detachment.

The demands to forsake family and material security are introduced in 9:57 – 62 when Jesus responds to three potential followers. In 12:49 – 53, he emphasizes the divisiveness of his message, explaining that even families will be divided and relatives will oppose disciples. In 18:18 – 30, Jesus addresses "a certain ruler" who becomes sad at Jesus' demand that he sell everything he owns. These incidents reveal that the choice is not between Jesus and the devil. It is far more subtle. It is between Jesus and our strongest allegiances: Jesus and family, Jesus and business, or Jesus and profit. These stipulations become a stumbling block that God uses to reveal our heart's desire, which may be unknown even to us. They become a means of revelation that will either draw us closer to God or alienate us further.

This call for self-denial may seem extreme and unreasonable, but "the point of discipleship is to be like one's master."[18] This is what Jesus did. Subordinating security, home, and family to Christian commitment does not mean that one discards these things entirely. Renouncing them is not for the sake of renunciation, but for the purpose of service. Bernadicou comments, "True love and concern for family, friends, and one's own self (see 14:26, 27, 33) depend upon a genuine discernment of values in the Christ." He continues, "One renounces selfish concern out of trust in God's love which must inevitably express itself in love for one's fellowman."[19]

3. Counting the Cost of Not Following Christ

The emphasis in the two parables of the tower builder and the king going to war is on counting the cost. Becoming a disciple of Jesus is a serious matter, as costly as building a tower, as dangerous as going to war when you are outnumbered by two

17. Knowles, " 'Everyone Who Hears These Words of Mine,' " 295.

18. Paul J. Bernadicou, "The Spirituality of Luke's Travel Narrative," *Review for Religious* 36 (1977): 458.

19. Ibid.

to one. But discipleship is not a matter of prudent risk management. From a worldly point of view, becoming a disciple is clearly imprudent since the enemy's power seems so overwhelming. But one should also count the cost of *not* following Jesus.

What the text does not spell out is that one will lose everything anyway whatever one's choice. Knowles points out, "The only question is whether one will lose all as a follower of Jesus and for the sake of God's reign, or as one who refuses to follow and obey. Which, in other words, is the more promising course of action?"[20] Counting the cost and concluding that the risk is too great and not worth the effort is not a viable option. Unconditional surrender to an invading king, if it is Satan, for example, will lead to ultimate ruin.[21] One therefore should count the cost of *not* following Jesus. If the option is unconditional surrender to Jesus or to Satan, the former is the only one that will prove to be the wise choice.

If the characters of the tower builder and the king in the two parables are assumed to possess the resources to carry out the contemplated tasks before them, the connection to the potential disciple breaks down. The New Testament makes clear that those who depend on their own meager resources and feeble powers are doomed to fail. The fight will be lost and the enterprise abandoned. Disciples can only depend on the power and resources of God that make them sufficient despite their weakness (2 Cor 3:4; 4:7 – 12; 12:9 – 10).

Josephus has King Agrippa speak against the war with Rome by bidding the rebels to compare their lack of resources with Rome's might, and the speech can provide a new perspective on this parable:

> What are the troops, what is the armor, on which you rely? Where is your fleet to sweep the Roman seas? Where is your treasury to meet the cost of your campaigns? Do you really suppose that you are going to war with Egyptians and Arabs? Will you shut your eyes to the might of the Roman empire and refuse to take the measure of your weakness? (*J.W.* 2.16.4 §§361 – 62)

Jesus' parable suggests that even when one counts the costs and thinks one's resources are adequate to face the enemy, they are not. Disciples can only put their confidence in God. Conversely, when one counts the costs and thinks one's resources are *inadequate* to face the enemy, they are adequate because one can only rely on God.

---

20. Knowles, " 'Everyone Who Hears These Words of Mine,' " 294.

21. P. G. Jarvis ("Expounding the Parables V: The Tower-Builder and the King Going to War [Luke 14:25 – 33]," *ExpTim* 77 [1966]: 196 – 98) identifies the opposing king as Satan.

Literary Context

Jesus has invited those with ears to hear to listen to what he is saying (14:35), and those who draw near to hear him are the tax collectors and "sinners" (see 7:29 – 30).[1] The disreputable assemblage shifts from the physically impure (14:13, the crippled, lame, and blind) to the spiritually impure. The Pharisees and the scribes continue to monitor Jesus' behavior and object to the unsavory cast of characters he gathers around him at table (5:30). They also continue to object to the celebratory note in Jesus' ministry (7:34).

The grumbling of Jesus' enemies resonates with that of the wilderness generation who complained when they failed to recognize God's presence with them.[2] Their churlishness discloses a failure to interpret the significance of the present time (12:54 – 56) or to see God's reign at work in Jesus' ministry (13:18 – 21). Jesus does not excoriate them as "hypocrites" who shut the door of the kingdom of heaven against others, refusing to enter themselves and refusing entry to others (Matt 23:13). Instead, these parables are essentially an invitation not to repeat the mistakes of the former "grumblers" of Israel who met with disastrous consequences. They justify his association with "sinners" and invite them to share in God's delight over reclaiming the lost.

The banquet theme continues from chapter 14. Each parable in chap. 15 — the shepherd, the woman, and the father — has a feast. The celebrations recall the party baking implied in the parable of the leaven, which Jesus says characterizes God's reign (see comments on 13:20 – 21). This unit discusses the first two of these parables.

---

1. If Jesus insists that renunciation is a basic requirement of discipleship, that is what the tax collector Levi did in leaving everything to follow him (5:27 – 28). He then threw a great banquet, filling his house with a large crowd of tax collectors and others (5:29), again, what Jesus bids people to do.

2. Exod 15:24; 16:2, 7 – 8; 17:3; Num 11:1; 14:2, 27, 29, 36; 16:11, 41; 17:5; Deut 1:27; 1 Cor 10:10; Heb 3:7 – 19.

Main Idea

The repentance of others must be met with joy and celebration.

Translation

(See next page.)

Structure and Literary Form

The basic structure of these twin parables is similar:

- Introduction
- Lost object
- Exhaustive searching
- Finding
- Rejoicing
- Application

In the conflict setting, the parables offer a seemingly innocuous response and allow Jesus to challenge his critics indirectly by drawing them into a story. The singular "parable" in 15:3 indicates that Luke understands the three parables to form one unit. In the initial hearing of the parables, the shepherd is a shepherd, the woman a woman, and the father a father. As the listeners allow themselves to be transported away in their imaginations from the story's literal arena, they encounter the surprise and shock of another reality. The actions of the shepherd, woman, and father become metaphors for what God is doing through Jesus.

Luke 15:1–10

15:1	Circumstance	**All the tax collectors and sinners were drawing near to him to hear him.**
2	Conflict	**And the Pharisees and scribes were grumbling, saying,** "This one receives 'sinners' and eats with them."
3	Response: parable (1)	**And he told them this parable, saying:**
4a	Character introduction	"What man among you . . . who has one hundred sheep and
b	Loss	having lost one of them
c	Search	. . . will not leave the ninety-nine in the desert to go for the lost one until he finds it?
5	Recovery and joy	And when he finds it, he carries it back on his shoulders rejoicing.
6	Celebration	And when he arrives home, he will invite his friends and neighbors, announcing to them, 'Rejoice with me because I have found my lost sheep.'
7	Conclusion	I say to you, like this scene, there will be joy in heaven, only more so, over one sinner who repents than over ninety-nine righteous ones who do not have need to repent."
8a	Response: parable (2) Character introduction	Or what woman . . . who has ten coins,
b	Loss	if she should lose one of them,
c	Search	. . . will not light a lamp and sweep her house seeking for it diligently until she finds it?
9a	Recovery	And when she finds it,
b	Celebration	she will announce it to her friends and neighbors, 'Rejoice with me because I have found my lost coin.'
10	Conclusion	I say to you, like this scene, there will be joy before God's angels over one sinner who repents."

Exegetical Outline

→ **I. Setting (15:1 – 2)**

    A. Jesus hosts sinners (15:1)

    B. The Pharisees and scribes murmur against him (15:2)

II. Jesus' response to the murmuring (15:3 – 10)

    A. The parable of the shepherd (15:3 – 6)

    B. Application to seeking the lost and rejoicing (15:7)

    C. The parable of the woman (15:8 – 9)

    D. Application to seeking the lost and rejoicing (15:10)

Explanation of the Text

15:1 All the tax collectors and sinners were drawing near to him to hear him (ἦσαν δὲ αὐτῷ ἐγγίζοντες πάντες οἱ τελῶναι καὶ οἱ ἁμαρτωλοὶ ἀκούειν αὐτοῦ). The section begins with the narrator telling us that all the tax collectors and sinners were drawing near to hear Jesus, and the reader is left to infer that his preaching good news is what attracts them. The imperfect periphrastic "were drawing near" (ἦσαν ... ἐγγίζοντες) may signal something that was happening right then or, more likely, refers to a recurring activity — "as was their custom." To draw near to Jesus in order to hear him is to draw near to the reign of God (10:24; 17:21).

The tax collectors (οἱ τελῶναι) were not the tax barons but those who collected tolls, tariffs, imposts, and customs. They were drawn from the ranks of those who were so desperate that they were willing to engage in a dishonorable profession to survive. Most took more than official fees to make a living and developed a reputation for dishonesty as a class. John tells them to take no more than what was properly due (3:12 – 13), and the Pharisee in his prayer in the temple lumps them together with robbers, evildoers, and adulterers (18:11). Tax collectors were outside the law,

and the scribes and Pharisees object that Jesus appears to do nothing to bring them under the law.

The sinners (οἱ ἁμαρτωλοί) could be apostate Jews (1 Macc 1:34; 2:44, 48) who were not simply the wrong sort of people but notorious and persistent lawbreakers who brought dishonor to their fellow Jews. They could comprise the godless who are presumed to be without hope. More likely, the Pharisees labeled them sinners because they were not meticulous or did not care to obey their rulings on purity standards of the Mosaic law (see John 7:49). "Sinners," then, can simply be those who do not practice religion the way others think they should.

According to *1 En.* 82:4 – 7, sinners are those Jews who wrongly reckoned the months and the feasts and the years; according to *Pss. Sol.* 1:8; 2:3; 7:2; 8:12 – 13; 17:5 – 8; 23, they are Jewish opponents of the "devout"; according to *As. Mos.* 7:3, 9 – 10, they are Jews with different interpretations of ritual purity requirements. In the Dead Sea Scrolls, sinners are Jews who did not hold to the sectarian interpretation of the Qumran community (CD 4:8; 1QS 5:7 – 11; 1QH 7:12). Luke, however, says nothing about the nature of their sin. From Jesus' perspective, the sinners are those who, like the prodigal son, are lost and alienated from the Father and need to be restored.

15:2 And the Pharisees and scribes were grumbling, saying, "This one receives 'sinners' and eats with them" (καὶ διεγόγγυζον οἵ τε Φαρισαῖοι καὶ οἱ γραμματεῖς λέγοντες ὅτι οὗτος ἁμαρτωλοὺς προσδέχεται καὶ συνεσθίει αὐτοῖς). The scribes and Pharisees have grumbled before about Jesus eating with tax collectors and sinners (5:29 – 30), but now they refer to him contemptuously as "this one" (οὗτος; see 7:39) and do not ask for an explanation for his conduct. From their perspective, it invalidates any claim that he is of God. Sharing a meal with another was regarded as a token of "mutual acceptance and solidarity."[3]

The use of the present tense ("receives" [προσδέχεται] and "eats with" [συνεσθίει]) suggests an ongoing pattern, which the Pharisees construe as a violation of the instructions laid down throughout Scripture not to associate with evildoers. This prohibition is particularly prominent in Proverbs, but the psalmist says: "Blessed is the one who does not walk in step with the wicked or stand in the way that sinners take or sit in the company of mockers" (Ps 1:1; cf. Isa 52:11). According to *Mek. Amalek* 3 on Exod 18:1, "The wise say, 'Let not a man associate with sinners even to bring them near to the Torah.'"

What is worse, Jesus "receives 'sinners'"; that is, he hosts them. It is one thing to call them to repentance, as John the Baptist did; it is quite another to treat them as if they were in some way respectable and acceptable. Juel captures what irks the Pharisees: "Jesus' willingness to welcome to his table those whose lives demonstrate contempt for God's law conjures up the real possibility of undermining moral seriousness and determination. The possibility of bringing all of life under the sacred canopy of God's law is threatened by actions that suggest that God is not serious about the law."[4]

Jesus snubbed the whole system of ranking and classifying people, to the disadvantage of the Pharisees who worked so hard to attain their status with the authority to circumscribe boundaries and to serve as the gatekeepers. The Pharisees did not care that Jesus associated with these people in order to bring them to repentance (5:32) and to restore them to Israel.[5] They had their own vision of how God's reign would take shape and who should qualify for membership. Meals became a means of establishing clear boundaries that showed who was in and who was out.

Luke uses the intensive form of the verb for grumbling (διεγόγγυζον; contrast ἐγόγγυζον in 5:30), and the imperfect tense suggests customary behavior.[6] The same noisome attitude that characterized the wilderness generation and led to their destruction had taken hold of the Pharisees and scribes as they misinterpreted the ministry of Jesus.[7]

---

3. Nelson, *Leadership and Discipleship*, 63.

4. Donald Juel, "The Lord's Prayer in the Gospels of Matthew and Luke," in *The Lord's Prayer* (ed. Daniel L. Migliore; PSBSup 2; Princeton: Princeton Theological Seminary, 1992), 68. Linnemann (*Parables of Jesus*, 86) comments similarly that Jesus does "not observe the boundary between sinners and righteous; it is as if the dam which is to protect society against the overflowing of sin has been breached."

5. See Maccoby, *Early Rabbinic Writings*, 132.

6. The sound resemblance between the verbs ἐγγίζοντες in v. 1 ("drawing near") and διεγόγγυζον ("grumbling") highlights the dissimilarity in the actions between the two groups.

7. The issue of whom one could legitimately eat with was not confined to the ministry of Jesus. Table fellowship with sinners set the stage for table fellowship with Gentiles. It arose early on in the Christian mission when the question became, How should one relate to Gentiles? Peter required a special vision of what no longer should be considered clean or unclean prior to the arrival of messengers from the Gentile centurion, Cornelius; even then he balked at entering a Gentile's house (Acts 10:1 – 33). And he was called to task by the circumcision in Jerusalem for actually going to those who were uncircumcised and eating with them (Acts 11:2 – 3). Paul testified that the matter had not yet been settled when at Antioch, Peter,

15:3 And he told them this parable, saying (εἶπεν δὲ πρὸς αὐτοὺς τὴν παραβολὴν ταύτην λέγων). Jesus' enemies see no relationship between the purpose of God and the ministry style of Jesus, and the parables that follow are Jesus' answer to their objections. The singular "parable" in 15:3 is used so that all three parables are to be understood as a unified response to the Pharisees' challenge. The antecedent of "them" (αὐτούς) includes both the soured scribes and Pharisees and the tax collectors and sinners who have drawn near "to hear him." Both groups, presumably, would have different reactions to "the parable."

15:4 What man among you who has one hundred sheep and having lost one of them will not leave the ninety-nine in the desert to go for the lost one until he finds it? (τίς ἄνθρωπος ἐξ ὑμῶν ἔχων ἑκατὸν πρόβατα καὶ ἀπολέσας ἐξ αὐτῶν ἓν οὐ καταλείπει τὰ ἐνενήκοντα ἐννέα ἐν τῇ ἐρήμῳ καὶ πορεύεται ἐπὶ τὸ ἀπολωλὸς ἕως εὕρῃ αὐτό;). The image of the shepherd and his flock is used in the Old Testament to represent God's care for his flock Israel.[8] A late rabbinic legend associates a story of a lost sheep with Moses' worthiness to lead Israel. While Moses was feeding the sheep of his father-in-law in the wilderness, a young lamb ran away. Moses went looking for it and found it at a well where it had stopped for a drink. Moses said to the sheep, "I did not know that you ran away because of thirst; you must be weary." So Moses took the kid on his shoulders and carried it back. Then God said: "Because thou hast mercy in leading the flock of a mortal, thou wilt assuredly tend to my flock, Israel" (*Exod. Rab.* 2:2).

Some might expect the opening question to be met with a resounding, "None of us would abandon ninety-nine sheep to search for only one!" No responsible person would ever think of leaving ninety-nine sheep in the wilderness to go in search of one.[9] It could result in the loss of a hundred sheep.[10] This conclusion is misplaced in a Palestinian setting. The phrasing of the question recurs in Luke (11:5, 11; 12:25; 14:5, 28; 17:7) and anticipates a definite answer: "None of us who had a hundred sheep and lost one *would not* leave the ninety-nine and go in search of the one!"[11] The phrase "what man among you" reveals that Jesus does not describe some exceptional case but "typical behavior."[12] This is exactly what a shepherd is expected to do. He would not nonchalantly say, "You win some; you lose some."

One hundred sheep is a large flock, and we can assume that other shepherds would be present to watch over the sheep. In 1 Sam 17:28, David's eldest brother, Eliab, asked him: "Why have you come down here? And with whom did you leave those few sheep in the wilderness?" The question assumes that one leaves sheep with others, and David indeed left the sheep with a keeper (1 Sam 17:20). The original Palestinian audience would not need to be told that the shepherd had others in the wilderness to watch over the sheep, and he could leave the ninety-nine with them as he went to look for the lost one. Adding extra characters in the story would take the spotlight off the shepherd

Barnabas, and others were persuaded by men from James not to eat with Gentiles (Gal 2:11–14).

8. Gen 48:15; 49:24; 2 Sam 5:2; Pss 23; 78:71; 80:1; Isa 40:10–11; 49:9; Jer 23:3; 31:10–14; 50:19; Ezek 34:11–22; Mic 4:6–8.

9. Mary Ann Tolbert, *Perspectives on the Parables: An Approach to Multiple Interpretations* (Philadelphia: Fortress, 1979), 55–56.

10. In the parallel version in *Gos. Thom.* 107, the missing

sheep is described as the largest, and it is said that the shepherd loved this sheep more than all the others, which explains why the shepherd leaves the others.

11. The parallel in Matt 18:12 is phrased differently but requires the answer "yes" to the question, "Will he not [οὐχὶ] leave the ninety-nine on the hills and go to look for the one that wandered off?"

12. Linnemann, *Parables of Jesus*, 65.

who will stop at nothing to recover the lost sheep. At the end of the day, he intends to have a hundred sheep and not be left with only one.[13]

The sheep would have been counted as they entered into the fold and passed under the shepherd's staff (Jer 33:13; Ezek 20:37). Apparently, the shepherds counted the flock in the wilderness, found one to be missing, and one of them went to find it while the others either stayed or probably led the sheep home, since the shepherd, after finding the lost sheep, returns home. Leaving out these extraneous details and stating that the shepherd leaves the ninety-nine in the wilderness serves to underscore what is at issue. The implication that "one" is more important than "ninety-nine" highlights the "the emotion that is felt over a loss."[14] The value of something becomes heightened when it becomes lost.

Without the shepherd's help, the lost sheep could not find its way back to the flock.[15] Luke places the emphasis on the shepherd's determination to recover what was lost; he will search *"until he finds it"* (ἕως εὕρῃ αὐτό). Matthew's parallel version (Matt 18:10–14) is less certain about the outcome: "if he should happen to find it" (lit. trans. of καὶ ἐὰν γένηται εὑρεῖν αὐτό).

15:5 And when he finds it, he carries it back on his shoulders rejoicing (καὶ εὑρὼν ἐπιτίθησιν ἐπὶ τοὺς ὤμους αὐτοῦ χαίρων). Nothing is said about the time and effort spent on searching for the sheep, nor does the story end when the shepherd finds it. When he finds the sheep, his job has just begun; the sheep must now be restored to the flock. Since sheep will often lie down helplessly and refuse to budge, the shepherd must carry it back on his shoulders (Isa 40:11; see 49:22). Irrespective of the burden—a sheep may weigh as much as seventy pounds—he rejoices.

15:6 And when he arrives home, he will invite his friends and neighbors, announcing to them, "Rejoice with me because I have found my lost sheep" (καὶ ἐλθὼν εἰς τὸν οἶκον συγκαλεῖ τοὺς φίλους καὶ τοὺς γείτονας λέγων αὐτοῖς· συγχάρητέ μοι, ὅτι εὗρον τὸ πρόβατόν μου τὸ ἀπολωλός). Wendland observes, "In a communal society, personal joy must be shared to be genuine."[16] The recovered sheep therefore becomes an occasion for communal joy. Sinners who have been lost from the community should also inspire communal joy, not grumbling, when they are recovered. The imperative "rejoice with me" (συγχάρητέ μοι) is repeated as the climax in the next parable (15:9). A synonym, "celebrate" (εὐφραίνω, 15:23, 32), appears in the two climaxes of the last parable and an explanation is added as to why it is imperative to do so (15:24, 33). This appeal to rejoice declares the main point of all three parables.

15:7 I say to you, like this scene, there will be joy in heaven, only more so, over one sinner who repents than over ninety-nine righteous ones who do not have need to repent (λέγω ὑμῖν ὅτι οὕτως χαρὰ ἐν τῷ οὐρανῷ ἔσται ἐπὶ ἑνὶ ἁμαρτωλῷ μετανοοῦντι ἢ ἐπὶ ἐνενήκοντα ἐννέα δικαίοις

13. Another possible interpretation: Israel is described as a lost sheep in the Old Testament (Ps 119:176; Isa 13:14; 53:6; Jer 23:1; Zech 10:2) and in the teaching of Jesus (Matt 10:6; 15:24). If the lost sheep represents Israel, who are the ninety-nine left in the wilderness? The conclusion to the parable refers to ninety-nine righteous ones who need no repentance, which would seem to be an allusion to the Pharisees. Were they not also lost sheep of Israel? The parable vividly illustrates God's concern to restore the remnant of Israel: "I will surely gather all of you, O Jacob, I will gather the survivors of Israel; I will set them together like sheep in a fold, like a flock in its pasture; it will resound with people" (Mic 2:12 NRSV).

14. Linnemann, *Parables of Jesus*, 66.

15. Jeremias, *The Parables of Jesus*, 134.

16. Ernst R. Wendland, "Finding Some Lost Aspects of Meaning in Christ's Parables of the Lost—And Found (Luke 15)," *TrinJ* 17ns (1996): 39.

οἵτινες οὐ χρείαν ἔχουσιν μετανοίας). Jesus scores the point of the parable with the solemn pronouncement, "I say to you" (λέγω ὑμῖν). The translation "like this scene" attempts to render the adverb (οὕτως; lit., "thusly, so") to show that Jesus connects and compares the earthly celebration to a heavenly one.

The shepherd does not compliment the ninety-nine for not wandering off, nor does he rejoice over them. Is the statement that they "do not have need to repent" to be taken at face value or is it ironical? The focus may be on only those who are "obviously lost," and Jesus accepts that those who do not need to repent are truly righteous.[17] He said that he had come to call sinners to repentance, not the righteous (5:32), and the scribes and Pharisees would naturally assume that they indeed were the righteous who did not need repentance.

This attitude manifests itself in Simon the Pharisee, who did not consider himself to be a debtor (7:36–50), and in the Pharisee in the temple, who thanked God he was not like other sinners (18:9–14). Their assumptions are obviously in error, and since this parable is aimed at those who are murmuring, it is fair to assume that Jesus uses gentle irony. Both John and Jesus demand repentance of everyone, and no one should presume to be exempt from this demand. In the context, the scribes and Pharisees need to repent of their grumbling and refusal to accept God's acceptance of sinners lest they go the way of the grumbling wilderness generation.

15:8–9 Or what woman who has ten coins, if she should lose one of them, will not light a lamp and sweep her house seeking for it diligently until she finds it? And when she finds it, she will announce it to her friends and neighbors, "Rejoice with me because I have found my lost coin" (ἢ τίς γυνὴ δραχμὰς ἔχουσα δέκα, ἐὰν ἀπολέσῃ δραχμὴν μίαν, οὐχὶ ἅπτει λύχνον καὶ σαροῖ τὴν οἰκίαν καὶ ζητεῖ ἐπιμελῶς ἕως οὗ εὕρῃ; καὶ εὑροῦσα συγκαλεῖ τὰς φίλας καὶ γείτονας λέγουσα· συγχάρητέ μοι, ὅτι εὗρον τὴν δραχμὴν ἣν ἀπώλεσα). The coins are drachmas, a Greek silver coin equated with the Roman denarius. It was the price of a sheep and one-fifth the price of an ox.[18]

The lost coin may have been part of a set that made it more valuable, perhaps as part of a headdress that was a component of a woman's dowry handed down to her from her family.[19] This popular interpretation, however, is unlikely because these headdresses had forty to fifty coins and were owned by wealthier women who might loan them out to poorer families to be worn during wedding celebrations.[20] The coins may simply represent the sum total of her savings because she is clearly not a woman of means. She lives in a one-room peasant hut with small slits for windows since the light of her oil lamp lights her entire house.

15:10 I say to you, like this scene, there will be joy before God's angels over one sinner who repents (οὕτως, λέγω ὑμῖν, γίνεται χαρὰ ἐνώπιον τῶν ἀγγέλων τοῦ θεοῦ ἐπὶ ἑνὶ ἁμαρτωλῷ μετανοοῦντι). In both vv. 7 and 10 the point is scored: all heaven rings with joyous laughter. The phrases "in heaven" (v. 7) and "before God's angels" (see 12:9) are a pious way of avoiding talking about God's emotions. It communicates that God jumps for joy. Angels began the story announcing good news to all persons and singing for joy (2:13–15); here, Jesus implies that God rejoices when sinners respond to the good news.

17. W. O. E. Oesterley (*The Gospel Parables in the Light of Their Jewish Background* [London: SPCK, 1936], 180) argues that Jesus did not use irony.

18. BDAG, 261.

19. Jeremias, *The Parables of Jesus*, 133.

20. Shelagh Weir, "Bridal Headdress from Southern Palestine," *PEQ* 105 (1973): 101–9.

Theology in Application

1. Concern for What is Lost

Many have pointed out that both parables underscore the endless trouble that humans will take to recover lost property — they search *until* they find it — and their deep satisfaction when they succeed. As Jesus' response to the grumbling of the scribes and Pharisees, the parables imply that the tax collectors and sinners, despite appearances, also belong to God. God not only wants them back; God will take endless trouble to find them and bring them back. This point does not mean that the shepherd's hunting for his lost sheep or the woman's searching for her lost coin represents God. It is rather the case that Jesus uses the argument from the lesser to the greater. If a shepherd will go to this much effort to recover a sheep and if a woman will go to this much effort to recover a coin, how much more effort will God exert to recover a lost person!

Ninety-nine percent or 90 percent are great percentages, but it is not good enough for God. We cannot say, "Since God has us, God has enough. What more could God want?" If a family of ten were to sit down to Sunday dinner and discovered that little Sarah is not present, the head of the family does not gruffly respond, "She knows what time we eat, and if she's not here, that's her problem." Nor does that one say, "Nine of us are here. That is 90 percent and good enough." Nor does that one grumble when the rest of the family starts looking for little Sarah, "Why bother looking for her? Let's eat." Then three months later, someone asks, "Do you remember little Sarah who used to be a member of our family; I wonder whatever became of her?" In the context, Jesus would be saying to the Pharisees, "I seek the lost for God; so should you."

2. Jesus' Transforming Power

The problem is that the Pharisees looked down on sinners while Jesus looked for them. The Pharisees believed that forgiveness was available only to those sinners who made restitution and returned to the faithful observance of the law, and they shunned contact with people whom they labeled "the people of the land" because of a fear of defilement and uncertainty over whether their foodstuffs had been properly tithed or prepared. They engaged in defensive religion, fending off what was judged to be contaminating, the way one might attack a weed. Betz and Riesner make the case that Jesus would argue with the Pharisees that it was not Ezek 44 with its emphasis on all of the ordinances of the temple, those who may be included and excluded from the sanctuary, and the fine differences between the holy and the common, "that was the Magna Carta for priestly service." Rather, it was Ezek 34, "the chapter about the good shepherd, that defined Jesus' attitude to Israel." [21] The quality of a royal shepherd is revealed by concern for the sick and strays among the flock (Ezek 34:4, 12, 16).

Jesus had no fear of contamination, physical or spiritual, because his power was able to overcome both physical and spiritual disease. Wink concludes: "Holiness … was not something to be protected; rather it was God's numinous transforming power. God's holiness cannot be sullied; it can only prevail."[22] Jesus welcomes sinners and dines with them because he does not fear being corrupted by them but seeks to transmit blessing on them. He does more than preach repentance to sinners; he finds them, dines with them, and effects their forgiveness. To use the imagery from 5:31 (Jesus' first response to the Pharisees' complaint), he did not set up office hours to consult with the sick only after they had been cured. He sought out the sick.

3. The Divine Initiative

Jesus does more than imply that he models the behavior of the shepherd and the woman (harmless stories in and of themselves). He defends his actions by pointing out their relation to what goes on in the heavenly realm: "Parallel to the earthly realm there is a heavenly realm, in which the inner reality of the earthly situation is revealed."[23] Implicit in this parallel is the premise that "Jesus' action is God's action."[24] Jesus' rejoicing before tax collectors and sinners, where purity issues seem of no concern, is likened to God's rejoicing before the angels. The heavenly parallel makes these two parables most provocative. This is what God is like, Jesus says, and this is why I act as I do, since I act "under his orders and in his stead."[25] To murmur against me is to murmur against God.

In contrast to the parallel in Matthew where the sheep wanders away from the flock (Matt 18:12, πλανηθῇ), the shepherd is said to have lost one of the sheep (ἀπολέσας ἐξ αὐτῶν ἕν). Does this assume negligence on the part of the shepherd, like the criminal negligence of the shepherds of Israel in the Old Testament (see Ezek 34:1 – 6; Jer 23:1 – 4)? If so, Ezekiel announces that God will take over the role of shepherd, who will seek the lost sheep and bring back the strayed (Ezek 34:11 – 16). If these parables vindicate Jesus' own activity in seeking out the lost and conferring God's grace on them, they contain an enormous christological claim. They imply that what Jesus does is nothing less than the action of God, who takes the initiative in recovering the lost.

Manson's astute comment is widely quoted, "But the characteristic feature of

21. Otto Betz and Rainer Riesner, *Jesus, Qumran and the Vatican: Clarifications* (New York: Crossroad, 1994), 133 – 34.

22. Walter Wink, *Engaging the Powers: Discernment and the Resistance in a World of Domination* (Minneapolis: Fortress, 1992), 117.

23. Fletcher-Louis, *Luke-Acts: Angels, Christology and Soteriology*, 74.

24. Ibid.

25. Jeremias, *The Parables of Jesus*, 139.

these two parables is not so much joy over the repentant sinner as the Divine love that goes out to seek the sinner before he repents."[26] Sheep and coins do not repent for getting lost. Bornkamm concludes similarly that "salvation and repentance have ... now changed places." For Jesus' audience of Pharisees "repentance is the first thing, the condition which affords the sinner the hope of grace, it is now the case that repentance comes by means of grace."[27] For Jesus, grace is the first thing, and repentance comes as a response to grace.

All of the parables in this chapter have a celebration: the characters experienced so much joy, they had to invite folks to help them enjoy their joy. Affluent Western-ers may smile at having a lost-and-found party over a sheep or a recovered coin.[28] This is precisely the point. Jesus has us reflect on the way people behave when they recover what is ultimately some trivial possession. A lost object, however, can take on an exaggerated value to the one who has lost it. If people celebrate extravagantly when they retrieve what has been lost, how much more will God celebrate when God recovers a lost person! The scowling religiosity of people represented here by the scribes and Pharisees who expect God to be less concerned and joyful about lost sinners than they themselves are about some animal or trinket has no place in the kingdom of God.

4. Breaking Down Prejudices

The parables also deconstruct the pharisaic prejudices through the main char-acters Jesus introduces. For some rabbis, shepherds were added to a list of unworthy trades (ineligible to be witnesses in judicial cases) because they were suspected of intentionally leading their sheep to graze on other people's land and of being thieves (*m. Qidd.* 4:14; *m. B. Qam.* 10:9; *b. Sanh.* 25b). Josephus, for example, attempts to parry objections that Moses kept sheep (Exod 3:1) by adding the explanation that in those days the wealth of barbarian races consisted in sheep (*Ant.* 2.11.2 §263). The *Midrash to Psalm* 23 contains the comment of R. Jose b. Hanina, which expresses the ambivalence about the shepherd metaphor: "In the whole world you find no occupa-tions more despised than that of the shepherd, who all of his days walks about with this staff and his pouch." He tries to justify why David presumes to call "the Holy One, blessed be He, a shepherd" of all things. The answer: "The ancients know more about these things than we do. So out of loyalty to the tradition, God is my shepherd and we must accept it."[29]

When Jesus addresses the Pharisees, "What man among you who has one hun-dred sheep and having lost one of them...?" he would offend their sensitivities. It would be like asking a pastors' conference, "Which of you owning a tavern, having

26. Manson, *The Sayings of Jesus*, 284.
27. Bornkamm, *Jesus of Nazareth*, 83.
28. Danker, *Jesus and the New Age*, 169.
29. Cited by Scott, *Hear Then the Parable*, 414.

a hundred bottles of beer on the wall, and losing one will not turn on the lights and search high and low until you find it, and then let everyone have one on the house to celebrate?"

Since women were considered to be inferior in matters religious, some point out that Jesus uses a woman to illustrate what God is doing. A parallel parable in rabbinic literature has a man:

> R. Phineas b. Jair expounded: "If you seek wisdom as silver, that is, if you seek the things of the law as hidden treasures — A parable: If a man loses a *sela* or an *obol* in his house, he lights lamp after lamp, wick after wick, till he finds it. Now does it stand to reason: if for these things which are only ephemeral and of this world a man will light so many lamps and lights till he finds where they are hidden, for the words of Torah which after the life of both this world and the next world, ought you not to search as for hidden treasures." (*Cant. Rab.* 1.1.9)

The use of a woman and a shepherd as examples implicitly rejects the attitude that they are religiously inferior in some way.[30]

---

30. Ibid, 158.

Luke 15:11 – 32

Literary Context

This parable continues Jesus' response to the complaints about his welcoming and eating with sinners. In the previous two parables, the community of friends and neighbors celebrates the recovery of the lost object. No one stands off and sulks. This parable, however, dramatizes contrasting responses to repentance and the recovery of the lost.[1] The older brother is like these Pharisees who reckon themselves as faithful servants and who look down on others and begrudge any unmerited grace shown to them (see 7:29 – 30). The parable expands on the theme of God as Father (the term occurs twelve times; cf. also 11:1 – 13; 12:22 – 34) in showing mercy to sinners.

Main Idea

God allows sin's punishment to work itself out in the lives of those who willfully desert him and try to go it alone. But God's grace can draw them back home and God's love welcomes even those who seem irretrievably lost but who repent. God's joy over their repentance and return must be shared by all who claim to be God's children.

---

1. Nave, *Repentance in Luke-Acts*, 183.

Translation

(See next two pages.)

Structure and Literary Form

The third parable is much longer than the previous two, and the percentage of loss increases from one out of a hundred and one out of ten to one out of two. The loss is even more devastating because it is a son, not an animal or a coin. The parable divides into two parts: the father's interaction with the youngest son (rebellion, repentance, acceptance, and celebration) and the father's interaction with the older son (resistance and insistence).

Exegetical Outline

→ **I. Setting: A father had two sons (15:11)**

II. The younger son (15:12 – 24)

    A. Demand for his inheritance and his departure (15:12 – 13a)

    B. Wasting his living in living it up (15:13b – 14a)

    C. Famine and poverty (15:14b – 16)

    D. Awakening (15:17 – 19)

    E. Forgiveness, restoration, and celebration (15:20 – 24)

III. The older son (15:25 – 32)

    A. Anger over his father's reception of his brother (15:25 – 28a)

    B. His father's plea to join the celebration (15:28b)

    C. His litany of complaints (15:29 – 30)

    D. His father's pronouncement (15:31 – 32)

        1. Love for his older son (15:31)

        2. Necessity to celebrate the younger son's return (15:32)

Luke 15:11–32

		And **he said,**
15:11	Response: parable (3) Character introduction	"A certain man had two sons.
12a	Request	And the younger of them said to his father, 'Father, give to me the portion of [your] property that falls to me.'
b	Response	And he distributed his estate among them.
13a	Action	And not long after this, the younger gathered together all his things and journeyed to a distant land
b		and there he squandered his estate living wastefully.
14	Consequences of action	And when he had spent all that he had, a severe famine hit that land, and he began to suffer from want.
15		And he went and joined himself to one of the citizens of that land, and he sent him into his fields to feed pigs.
16		And he longed to fill his belly with the carob pods the pigs were eating, and no one gave him anything to eat.
17	Interior monologue: reaction to the consequences	And when he came to himself, he said, 'How many of my father's hired hands have more than enough to eat, and I am being destroyed here with starvation?
18		I will arise and go to my father, and I will say to him, 'Father, I have sinned against heaven and before you.
19		I am no longer worthy to be called your son. Employ me as one of your hired hands.''
20a	Action	Then he arose and went to his father.
b	Reaction (1)	While he was still some distance away, his father spotted him, had compassion on him, and ran to him and fell upon his neck and kissed him.
21	Confession	His son said to him, 'Father, I have sinned against heaven and before you, I am no longer worthy to be called your son.'
22	Response	Then his father called to the servants, 'Quickly, bring the best robe and put it on him and give him a ring for his hand and shoes for his feet.

23	Celebration	*And bring the fattened calf, slaughter it, and let us celebrate and eat,*
24a	Explanation	*because this my son was given up for dead and came to life again;*
b		*he was lost and has been found.'*
		And they began to celebrate.
25	Character introduction	*Meanwhile, his older son was in the field, and as he drew near to the house, he heard the music and dancing.*
26	Description of celebration	*He called one of the servants and asked what all this commotion might be about.*
27		*He told him,*
		'Your brother is here, and your father slaughtered the fattened calf because he has received him safe and sound.'
28a	Reaction (2)	*He became angry and did not want to come in,*
b	Response	*so his father went out to him and pleaded with him.*
29	Complaint	*But he answered his father and said,*
		'Look! So many years I have served you and never disobeyed your command, and you never gave me so much as a kid goat to celebrate with my friends!
30		*When this son of yours who devoured your estate with whores arrives, you slaughter for him the fattened calf?'*
31	Response	*He said to him,*
		'Child, you were always with me, and everything that is mine is yours.
32a	Explanation	*But it is necessary to celebrate and to rejoice*
b		*because this your brother was given up for dead and came to life again, was lost and is found.'"*

Explanation of the Text

15:11 And he said, "A certain man had two sons" (εἶπεν δέ· ἄνθρωπός τις εἶχεν δύο υἱούς). The parable's focus falls on the father and his reaction to his two sons. He appears in both sections of the parable: the return of the younger son from the far country, and the return of the older son from the field. Consequently, any title given to this parable should make clear that the father, not the sons, is the central figure.

15:12 And the younger of them said to his father, "Father, give to me the portion of [your] property that falls to me." And he distributed his estate among them (καὶ εἶπεν ὁ νεώτερος αὐτῶν τῷ πατρί· πάτερ, δός μοι τὸ ἐπιβάλλον μέρος τῆς οὐσίας. ὁ δὲ διεῖλεν αὐτοῖς τὸν βίον). Sons did not normally demand their inheritance before the death of their father, but the warning against dividing an inheritance during a father's lifetime in Sir 33:20 – 24 suggests that such a thing was occasionally done, and many a rash father lived to regret it.[2] To ask for the inheritance is a way of saying to a father, "I wish you were already dead, but since you aren't, I can't wait any longer."

Donahue maintains that the son's request "should not be considered as rebellion or a desire for unwarranted freedom."[3] Jesus' listeners, however, would have thought that the younger son's place was to stay home, to labor, and to obey his father as the older son did. Such a request harms the family's reputation and damages its wealth, perhaps irretrievably. They would have asked, "How could he treat his father like that and expose him and his family to such scorn and shame?"

The readers of Luke are reminded of the man who made the inappropriate request that Jesus intercede and coerce his brother to give him his share of an inheritance (12:13 – 21). The request exposed his greed and selfishness and is met with a parable about a "fool." By demanding his inheritance, the younger son here sows discord in the family (one of six things the Lord hates, see Prov 6:16 – 19). A Roman audience, which considered *pietas*, dutiful respect toward parents (as well as the gods and fatherland), as the cornerstone of morality, also would have looked askance at such a brazen request that exposed the lack of loyalty toward the father.

The father meets the son's "impatience with patience" and submits to his request.[4] According to the law, the older son would receive a double portion (Deut 21:15 – 17). This provision protected the firstborn son in case the father might favor another of his wives and give preference to her son. The younger son is often the father's favorite in the Old Testament (Isaac over Ishmael, Joseph and Benjamin over Reuben and his brothers).

15:13 And not long after this, the younger gathered together all his things and journeyed to a distant land and there he squandered his estate living wastefully (καὶ μετ᾽ οὐ πολλὰς ἡμέρας συναγαγὼν παντα ὁ νεώτερος υἱὸς ἀπεδήμησεν εἰς χώραν μακρὰν καὶ ἐκεῖ διεσκόρπισεν τὴν οὐσίαν αὐτοῦ ζῶν ἀσώτως). Fitzmyer notes the possibility that the word "to gather together" (συναγεῖν) connotes "to convert into money."[5] When he asked for his inheritance, the younger son does not suggest that he will use it to bankroll his abandonment of the family. His motives to sunder these relationships are not mentioned in the text and therefore are not vital to its interpretation.

2. Tobit 8:21and the legal discussion in *t. Ketub.* 8:5 about fathers signing their property over to their sons also indicates that it was done.

3. Donahue, *The Gospel in Parable*, 153.
4. Derrett, *Law in the New Testament*, 106.
5. Fitzmyer, *Luke*, 2:1087. See Plutarch, *Cat. Min.* 6.7.672c.

Jewish emigration from Palestine was common, since it was often visited by famine and foreign troops. The trading centers of the Diaspora offered the hope of more favorable economic opportunities. In this culture, however, preserving family relationships was of utmost value, and this son spurns his duties to his father and ruptures family ties to pursue his selfish interests in what he imagines to be fairer climes.

Jesus reports ever so briefly that his living is wasted (διεσκόρπισεν; see 16:1) in carefree, spendthrift, or debauched living. The noun form "prodigality" (ἀσωτία) appears in Eph 5:18; Titus 1:6; and 1 Pet 4:4 and is related to getting drunk with wine, debauchery, and dissipation. It is left to the older brother to fill in the suspected details of his profligacy — he "devoured your estate with whores" (15:30) — but the adverb "wastefully" (ἀσώτως) does not require sexual immorality. It may simply mean that he engaged in a reckless orgy of spending.[6] His folly is a story replayed many times in the lives of the young before and since. One father laments, "Our son Castor along with others by riotous living has squandered all his own property."[7] His situation was not unusual if the papyrus letter found in Egypt of one Antonius Longus is any indication:

> Greetings: I hope you are in good health; it is my constant prayer to Lord Serapis. I did not expect you to come to Metropolis, therefore I did not go there myself. At the same time I was ashamed to go to Kanaris because I am so shabby. I am writing to tell you I am naked. I plead with you forgive me. I know well enough what I have done myself. I have learned my lesson. I know my mistake. I have heard from Dostumos who met you in the area of Arsinoe. Unfortunately, he told you everything. Don't you know I would rather be

a cripple than owe so much as a cent to any man? I plead with you....

> Antonius Longus, your son.[8]

In the context of Jewish Wisdom literature, however, the son's actions take on religious significance. Wisdom contains extensive warnings about this kind of foolish behavior and its inevitable results: "Do not give yourself to prostitutes, or you may you lose your inheritance" (Sir 9:6; see Prov 5:1 – 14; 23:26 – 35; 29:3); "whoever loves pleasure will become poor; whoever loves wine and olive oil will never be rich" (Prov 21:17). The consequences of such behavior in the moral universe envisioned in Proverbs are unavoidable:

> For human ways are under the eyes of the LORD,
>   and he examines all their paths.
> The iniquities of the wicked ensnare them,
>   and they are caught in the toils of their sin.
> They die for lack of discipline,
>   and because of their great folly they are lost.
>   (Prov 5:21 – 23 NRSV)

15:14 – 15 And when he had spent all that he had, a severe famine hit that land, and he began to suffer from want. And he went and joined himself to one of the citizens of that land, and he sent him into his fields to feed pigs (δαπανήσαντος δὲ αὐτοῦ πάντα ἐγένετο λιμὸς ἰσχυρὰ κατὰ τὴν χώραν ἐκείνην, καὶ αὐτὸς ἤρξατο ὑστερεῖσθαι. καὶ πορευθεὶς ἐκολλήθη ἑνὶ τῶν πολιτῶν τῆς χώρας ἐκείνης, καὶ ἔπεμψεν αὐτὸν εἰς τοὺς ἀγροὺς αὐτοῦ βόσκειν χοίρους). A severe famine drives the destitute young man to slop pigs for a Gentile. Wallowing in sin, he now wallows with hogs. The Jews had a well-organized system of almsgiving in the Diaspora, but instead of casting himself on the mercy of whatever Jewish community might be there, this younger son joins himself

---

6. Werner Foerster, "ἄσωτος, ἀσωτία," *TDNT*, 1:506 – 7.
7. P.Flor 99.6 – 7, cited in Milligan, *Greek Papyri*, 71 – 72.
8. BGU 846.

to a Gentile. The upshot is that "he has lost his familial, ethnic, and religious identity."[9]

Pigs and Gentiles were considered equivalent by the Jews. Pigs were unclean animals (Lev 11:7, Deut 14:8). To eat swine's flesh was a means to get Jews to renounce their faith. Antiochus Epiphanes forced Jews to eat swine's flesh as part of his program of Hellenization and of undermining Jewish allegiance to their law (see 1 Macc 1:47 – 49; 2 Macc 6:18 – 31; 7:1 – 42). This explains the curse in the Talmud: "Cursed be the man who keeps swine and cursed be the man who teaches his son Greek wisdom" (*b. B. Qam.* 82b). The younger son seemingly has passed the point of no return, like the tax collectors and sinners who also seem irretrievably lost to Israel.

15:16 And he longed to fill his belly with the carob pods the pigs were eating, and no one gave him anything to eat (καὶ ἐπεθύμει χορτασθῆναι ἐκ τῶν κερατίων ὧν ἤσθιον οἱ χοῖροι, καὶ οὐδεὶς ἐδίδου αὐτῷ). Despite his job, he was in desperate straits. The use of the imperfect verbs "he longed" (ἐπεθύμει), "were eating" (ἤσθιον), and "gave" (ἐδίδου) indicates a continual state of deprivation. Wiedemann points out that looking after cattle, goats, and pigs were

> "marginal" occupations in antiquity — not only because the hours and responsibility made them unpleasant, and attacks by robbers or wild beasts made the job dangerous, but also because pastures were "marginal" places, uncultivated woods and mountains far from the city, and herdsmen were cut off from social life for months at a time. Thus these jobs were suited to slaves, not freemen.[10]

The owner apparently valued keeping his pigs fed more than keeping his swineherder fed. The young man would gladly have filled his belly with what he fed the pigs, the leguminous fruit (sweet pulp) of the carob tree (κεράτια, lit., "little horns"). Almsgiving was not considered in the pagan world to be a virtue that the gods would reward, and that son has become so valueless that no one thought he was worth bestowing any benefaction on him. Again, his plight comes as no surprise to those schooled in Wisdom: "Whoever disregards discipline comes to poverty and shame" (Prov 13:18); "the righteous eat to their hearts' content, but the stomach of the wicked goes hungry" (Prov 13:25; see 10:3).

15:17 And when he came to himself, he said, "How many of my father's hired hands have more than enough to eat, and I am being destroyed here with starvation?" (εἰς ἑαυτὸν δὲ ἐλθὼν ἔφη· πόσοι μίσθιοι τοῦ πατρός μου περισσεύονται ἄρτων, ἐγὼ δὲ λιμῷ ὧδε ἀπόλλυμαι). Is the statement "he came to himself" or "he came to his senses" an indication of repentance? Some argue no.[11] It may only mean that he woke up (see Acts 12:11) and recognized his situation was irredeemable, and his empty stomach drove him to return home. To avoid starving to death, he then takes action, hoping to receive some sympathy from his father. He would be little different from the unjust steward (16:1 – 8) trying to escape his wretchedness and salvage his future with a desperate ploy.

Clues from the prodigal's interior monologue in which he acknowledges his sin and resolves to return home suggest, however, that his forlorn state prepares him to remember heaven and his father and to repent. In the later rabbinic homiletic

---

9. Donahue, *The Gospel in Parable*, 153.

10. Thomas E. J. Wiedemann, "Slavery," in *Civilization of the Ancient Mediterranean: Greece and Rome* (ed. M. Grand and R. Kitzinger; New York: Charles Scribner's Sons, 1988), 1:586.

11. Selew, "Interior Monologue as a Narrative Device," 246; Scott, *Hear Then the Parable*, 116; Kenneth E. Bailey, *Jacob and the Prodigal: How Jesus Retold Israel's Story* (Downers Grove, IL: InterVarsity Press, 2003), 103 – 7.

tradition, an interpretation of Isa 1:19 – 20 construed the phrase being "devoured by the sword" as a consequence of rebelling against God, and it was taken to mean that Israel would be forced by their destitution to "eat carobs." R. Aha commented, "Israel needs carobs to lead them to repentance" (*Lev. Rab.* 35.6; see parallel versions in *Lev. Rab.* 13.4; *Cant. Rab.* 1.4 §4). The Palestinian rabbis are remembered to have said regarding the verse, "In the days of her affliction and wandering Jerusalem remembers" (Lam 1:7): "when the son goes barefoot he recalls the comfort of his father's house" (*Lam. Rab.* 1.7 §34).

The image of returning is also tied to repentance throughout Scripture (e.g., Isa 55:7; Jer 3:12; Hos 14:1 – 2). The immediate context assumes that the tax collectors and sinners gathered around Jesus because they had repented, and their meals together were celebrations of God's grace and forgiveness (see 5:27 – 32). Luke's gospel highlights that the tax collectors in particular were responsive to the preaching and baptism of John that called for repentance (3:12 – 13; 7:29). "He came to himself" must mean that the younger son snapped out of it, and it marks the beginning of his repentance.[12] How deep his repentance runs will only become clear from what he does *after* being received so generously by his father, but the parable concludes with the homecoming party.

The parable's abrupt ending reveals that it is *not* about a son's repentance but about a father's love. It is the father who drives the plot by indirectly drawing the son to return home because he remembers his father's goodness even to hired hands.

15:18 – 19 **"I will arise and go to my father, and I will say to him, 'Father, I have sinned against**

heaven and before you. I am no longer worthy to be called your son. Employ me as one of your hired hands'" (ἀναστὰς πορεύσομαι πρὸς τὸν πατέρα μου καὶ ἐρῶ αὐτῷ· πάτερ, ἥμαρτον εἰς τὸν οὐρανὸν καὶ ἐνώπιόν σου, οὐκέτι εἰμὶ ἄξιος κληθῆναι υἱός σου· ποίησόν με ὡς ἕνα τῶν μισθίων σου). Until the son rises and returns home, his reconciliation with his father will be impossible. Therefore, remorse must be combined with action. The younger son's rising is the beginning of his transformation from death to life.

The confession that he has sinned against heaven, which is a circumlocution for God, echoes Exod 10:16: "Pharaoh quickly summoned Moses and Aaron and said, 'I have sinned against the Lord your God and against you'" (see also Num 21:7). Bailey contends that the audience of Pharisees would know their Scriptures, recognize the echo, and know that Pharaoh had no intention of repenting. Like Pharaoh, he thinks the lad is only mouthing these words of repentance to soften his father's heart.[13]

Such a reading is too cynical and misunderstands how repentance is presented in Luke-Acts. The difference is that the young man adds that he has proven himself unworthy to be a son and will offer to become his father's temporary help, dissociated from the family. Nave defines repentance in Luke-Acts as abandoning one's former ways of thinking and living "and adopting new ways of thinking and living consistent with the lifestyle prescribed in the teachings of Jesus."[14] The son's confession demonstrates how he now recognizes the errors of his ways and must now change. His actions show the appropriate changes in behavior and thinking (more important than any emotional feelings of remorse), and his joyous reception by

---

12. The prayer of Solomon in 1 Kgs 8:46 – 48 is a parallel. He asks God to forgive the people after they sin and are given over to an enemy and are carried away captive to a far or near land, and then they repent and plead, "We have sinned, we have

done wrong, we have acted wickedly."
13. Bailey, *Jacob and the Prodigal*, 106.
14. Nave, *Repentance in Luke-Acts*, 168 – 69.

his father shows how repentant sinners should be received (as in 5:27 – 39).[15]

The boy's misery is real, and his recognition that he is to blame for it is also real. It is a promising sign that he does not blame his big brother for his plight or get angry with life for being dealt a bad hand.[16] He accepts full responsibility for his predicament. He admits he has destroyed the relationship with his father. He has proved himself unworthy to be a son. Like the woman desperate to have her daughter made well and willing to accept the role of a dog to get just a scrap of healing from Jesus (Mark 7:24 – 30), the son comes crawling home to throw himself on the mercy of his father. He does not know what his father's attitude might be toward him, but he does know his father's track record for treating hired hands kindly. They have more than enough to eat. The son concludes it is far better to return home in shame and work as a day laborer than to be treated as he is now by his current pagan master.

The younger son recognizes that he has fractured the relationship with his father and is not even acceptable as a slave in his father's house. A day laborer is different from a slave in that he is not part of the household. In some respects the slave could be better off. For example, Job laments that human beings have a hard lot on earth and their days are like that of a hireling who ekes out a day-to-day existence (Job 7:1). By contrast, according to Prov 17:2, "A prudent servant will rule over a disgraceful son and will share the inheritance as one of the family."

15:20 Then he arose and went to his father. While he was still some distance away, his father spotted him, had compassion on him, and ran to

him and fell upon his neck and kissed him (καὶ ἀναστὰς ἦλθεν πρὸς τὸν πατέρα ἑαυτοῦ. ἔτι δὲ αὐτοῦ μακρὰν ἀπέχοντος εἶδεν αὐτὸν ὁ πατὴρ αὐτοῦ καὶ ἐσπλαγχνίσθη καὶ δραμὼν ἐπέπεσεν ἐπὶ τὸν τράχηλον αὐτοῦ καὶ κατεφίλησεν αὐτόν). The father has compassion on his son *before* he can utter his confession, and his reception of him exceeds the boy's wildest dreams and shows that he has been forgiven. It also exceeds what anyone in the audience would have thought prudent and violates what Wisdom would lead one to expect.

It would not have been unrealistic for the father to kill the son rather than the fattened calf. The son fit the category of a rebellious son, a glutton, and a drunkard, who could be stoned (Deut 21:18). Or, the father could have put the son on probation. But the father is as compassionate as God, who longs for the return of his erring son Ephraim (Jer 31:18 – 20). The story begins with the statement, "A certain man had two sons," and nothing the boy has done makes him an un-son. The father does not require that his son first demonstrate that he has truly repented and proven that his motives are pure before he showers his love upon him.

The father sees his son coming at a distance, has compassion on him, and runs to him in his exuberance. Some claim that running is beneath the dignity of an Oriental elder because it suggests that he is not in control of his time or resources, and he would have humiliated himself pulling up his long robes and bearing his legs as he dashes out to greet his son.[17] According to Sir 19:30, the nobleman is known by his gait, that is, by the slow, dignified pace that betokens his stature in the community. But in Gen 33:4, Esau did the same thing when his brother Jacob appeared. He "ran to meet Jacob

---

15. Ibid., 182, n. 167. Nave goes on to say, "To question the motivation for and the authenticity of the younger son's repentance is to miss the point of the parable."

16. Dan Otto Via Jr., *The Parables: Their Literary and Exis-*

tential Dimension (Philadelphia: Fortress, 1967), 168.

17. Jeremias, *The Parables of Jesus*, 130; Kenneth E. Bailey, *Finding the Lost: Cultural Keys to Luke 15* (St. Louis: Concordia, 1992), 143 – 46.

and embraced him; he threw his arms around his neck and kissed him." Can we expect anything less from a father who loves his son, longs for his return, and sees him coming down the road? He will naturally run to greet him. The celebrations for recovered sheep and coins in the previous parables prepare us for the father's excitement over the return of his son.

Before the prodigal gets out one word of the confession he has been practicing all the way home, his father throws his arms around his neck and kisses him. The father's love is not conditioned by confession. The father has endured the trials of having a foolish son (see Prov 10:1; 17:21, 25; 19:18, 26; 20:20; 22:15; 23:22 – 25; 28:24), but he refrains from giving him a sermon when he comes home: "Didn't I tell you how it would go for you? Now will you listen to your father?" He does not give speeches but shows forgiveness through actions. In the same way, by receiving sinners and eating with them, Jesus' actions speak louder and more convincingly than a sermon or a lecture on God's loving mercy or the need to repent.

15:21 – 22 His son said to him, "Father, I have sinned against heaven and before you, I am no longer worthy to be called your son." Then his father called to the servants, "Quickly, bring the best robe and put it on him and give him a ring for his hand and shoes for his feet" (εἶπεν δὲ ὁ υἱὸς αὐτῷ· πάτερ, ἥμαρτον εἰς τὸν οὐρανὸν καὶ ἐνώπιόν σου, οὐκέτι εἰμὶ ἄξιος κληθῆναι υἱός σου. εἶπεν δὲ ὁ πατὴρ πρὸς τοὺς δούλους αὐτοῦ· ταχὺ ἐξενέγκατε στολὴν τὴν πρώτην καὶ ἐνδύσατε αὐτόν, καὶ δότε δακτύλιον εἰς τὴν χεῖρα αὐτοῦ καὶ ὑποδήματα εἰς τοὺς πόδας). When the boy finally gets a chance to give his speech of contrition, the father interrupts him before he gets to the part

about becoming a hireling by giving him gifts that betoken his complete acceptance as a son.

Bailey questions whether the father actually interrupts the son. He argues that after this show of forgiveness "the prodigal changes his mind and in a moment of genuine repentance surrenders his plan to save himself and lets his father find him."[18] This interpretation is driven by a theological agenda that presumes that humans cannot return to God without God's assistance and that the father, therefore, must "find" the son. He defines repentance as "acceptance of being found."[19] This definition is only partly true. Perhaps the son decides to drop his proposal after being showered with his father's love, but the reader only knows that his planned speech has been cut short. What is important is that the father has no intention of letting him work his way back into his favor. The son confesses his sin and his unworthiness, and the father takes over from there with surprising and exorbitant grace akin to what Isaiah promises, "Before they call I will answer; while they are still speaking I will hear" (Isa 65:24).

No one had given the prodigal anything when he was in dire straits among the Gentiles, and now he is given everything by one whom he has severely wounded. In the words of one scholar, "The embrace, the kiss, the robe, the ring, and the sandals together symbolize the love, forgiveness, reconciliation and honor bestowed upon the younger son by the father."[20] These gifts make clear that he still has the status of son. The robe was a ceremonial sign of authority, and the ring confirms his full sonship and the right of inheritance (see Gen 41:41 – 42; 1 Macc 6:15).[21]

15:23 "And bring the fattened calf, slaughter it, and let us celebrate and eat" (καὶ φέρετε

18. Bailey, *Jacob and the Prodigal*, 109.
19. Ibid.
20. Nave, *Repentance in Luke-Acts*, 182.

21. Clean clothing is used as a metaphor for repentance in the interpretation of Eccl 9:8 in *b. Šabb.* 153a.

τὸν μόσχον τὸν σιτευτόν, θύσατε, καὶ φαγόντες εὐφρανθῶμεν). The father has the fattened (τὸν σιτευτόν, "grain-fed") calf killed, which would have been an animal used for a special feast (see 1 Sam 28:24–25) and presumably belongs to the older brother after the division of the inheritance. Killing such a large animal means that the father intends to invite a large crowd, perhaps the entire community, to participate in the celebration. The younger son who had been deprived of food as a pig keeper will now feast and be feted as the returned son.

15:24 "Because this my son was given up for dead and came to life again; he was lost and has been found." And they began to celebrate (ὅτι οὗτος ὁ υἱός μου νεκρὸς ἦν καὶ ἀνέζησεν, ἦν ἀπολωλὼς καὶ εὑρέθη. καὶ ἤρξαντο εὐφραίνεσθαι). The image of death and life resonates throughout the New Testament (Rom 8:13; Eph 2:1). The aorist tense of ἀνέζησεν is often translated "is alive," but here it has an ingressive function that stresses the beginning of his entrance into the state of life ("came to life again").

15:25 Meanwhile, his older son was in the field, and as he drew near to the house, he heard the music and dancing (ἦν δὲ ὁ υἱὸς αὐτοῦ ὁ πρεσβύτερος ἐν ἀγρῷ· καὶ ὡς ἐρχόμενος ἤγγισεν τῇ οἰκίᾳ, ἤκουσεν συμφωνίας καὶ χορῶν). The older son returns from the fields where he presumably has been working all day to find that his younger brother has been given the red-carpet treatment. He "draws near" (ἤγγισεν) like the tax collectors and sinners (15:1), but his reaction is like the Pharisees and scribes. He grumbles, irritated by the joyous celebration, which he regards as unseemly.

15:26–28a He called one of the servants and asked what all this commotion might be about.

He told him, "Your brother is here, and your father slaughtered the fattened calf because he has received him safe and sound." He became angry and did not want to come in (καὶ προσκαλεσάμενος ἕνα τῶν παίδων ἐπυνθάνετο τί ἂν εἴη ταῦτα. ὁ δὲ εἶπεν αὐτῷ ὅτι ὁ ἀδελφός σου ἥκει, καὶ ἔθυσεν ὁ πατήρ σου τὸν μόσχον τὸν σιτευτόν, ὅτι ὑγιαίνοντα αὐτὸν ἀπέλαβεν. ὠργίσθη δὲ καὶ οὐκ ἤθελεν εἰσελθεῖν). The older brother will not join in the heavenly rejoicing over one sinner who repents (cf. 15:10). He perhaps assumes (correctly) that his brother came home only because he ran out of money. He also assumes that he had blown it and needed to be taught a lesson. The older brother probably would have thought the hired hand option should have been given more serious consideration. His anger seems justified. He has been the responsible son who fulfilled his duty to his father and worked in the fields.[22] He has upheld the interests of the family's honor and welfare and should be the one who is honored.

15:28b So his father went out to him and pleaded with him (ὁ δὲ πατὴρ αὐτοῦ ἐξελθὼν παρεκάλει αὐτόν). The older son's refusal to join this public celebration gravely dishonors his father, but, as Jesus gently tries to coax the resentful Pharisees and scribes with these parables to receive repentant sinners with joy, so the father tries to coax his faithful son to rejoice over the recovery of his lost brother. He leaves the festivities, which he hosts, to go out into the chill of the evening air to his older son cooling his heels. He does not need to do this. He could have sent the slaves out to fetch him and give the order, "Get in here right now!" and the "good" son would have been in the house in two minutes. But the father loves this son and goes out to him to implore him to come in. He

---

22. Wolfgang Pöhlmann, *Der Verlorene Sohn und das Haus* (WUNT 68; Tübingen: J. C. B. Mohr [Paul Siebeck], 1993), 70.

only entreats or "pleads" (παρεκάλει; the verb can also mean "comfort"); he does not command. It turns out that the father is as powerless with the older son as he was with the youngest.

15:29 But he answered his father and said, "Look! So many years I have served you and never disobeyed your command, and you never gave me so much as a kid goat to celebrate with my friends!" (ὁ δὲ ἀποκριθεὶς εἶπεν τῷ πατρὶ αὐτοῦ· ἰδοὺ τοσαῦτα ἔτη δουλεύω σοι καὶ οὐδέποτε ἐντολήν σου παρῆλθον, καὶ ἐμοὶ οὐδέποτε ἔδωκας ἔριφον ἵνα μετὰ τῶν φίλων μου εὐφρανθῶ). The father runs into a buzz saw of complaints from his older son. He disdainfully compares his faithfulness with the irresponsibility of his sibling (see 18:11 – 12), and that spirit may explain why the younger son wanted to leave in the first place.

More important, the older son's complaints reveal the truth about his relationship with his father. Neither child apparently had a deep father-son relationship. The younger wanted to split; the older stayed home but served his father with the heart of a time-server eyeing a reward. One was prodigal in heart and body; the other, prodigal only in heart. For one, the culpability is obvious; for the other, it is less obvious.

The older son believes his father has taken him for granted despite his years of conscientious obedience. He fails to address his father with respect and launches into a litany of complaints: "Look! So many years I have served you." The verb "served" (δουλεύω) does not imply that he chafed under some sense of bondage to his father as if it were slavery. The verb is used in Acts 20:19 to refer to Paul's humble service to the gospel (see Gal 5:13; cf. Phil 1:1; 2:22), and it is the most common term for service of God in the LXX, "not in the sense of

an isolated act, but in that of total commitment to the Godhead."[23]

He has served his father faithfully and never disobeyed a command (see Deut 26:12 – 13 and the confession of those who faithfully tithed "according to all you commanded. I have not turned aside from your commands nor have I forgotten any of them"). His attitude reveals four problems:

1. He belongs to the category of those who think that they need no repentance (15:7) and therefore do not repent.
2. He appeals to his faithful service to compare himself favorably to his brother; he deserves his father's love, while his brother deserves rejection.
3. In doing his duty (see 17:9 – 10), he expects to receive a special reward from his father. Clearly, he derives little joy from his steadfast service (contrast Paul's statements in Phil 2:17 – 18).
4. His ambition "to celebrate with my friends" is no different from his younger brother's desires, who presumably lived it up with his friends (15:13).

What this older son would do, slaughtering a kid goat, is markedly different from what the father has done, slaughtering a calf. In both cases, the entire animal would need to be consumed or it would go to waste, so slaughtering a calf means that the father intended to invite most of the village's inhabitants to the homecoming party that evening. The older son's goat, however, would entail "only a small celebration — for just me and my friends!"[24] He would exclude both his father and his brother from his little reception! He represents what the Pharisees do. They gather in their small cliques and eat in purity. By contrast, Jesus' celebration will invite the whole village and include all the outcasts who would never be invited to a Pharisee's home.

23. Karl Rengstorf, "δοῦλος," *TDNT*, 2:267.

24. Bailey, *Poet and Peasant*, 186 – 87.

15:30 **"When this son of yours who devoured your estate with whores arrives, you slaughter for him the fattened calf!"** (ὅτε δὲ ὁ υἱός σου οὗτος ὁ καταφαγών σου τὸν βίον μετὰ πορνῶν ἦλθεν, ἔθυσας αὐτῷ τὸν σιτευτὸν μόσχον). It is unclear how the older son would know that this lurid accusation against his brother was true. Is this charge a projection of his imagination — that is what he would have done had he been out in the far country? Does it reveal that his heart was in the far country all along, while his body stayed home and was dutifully obedient? Or does he repeat the rumors that have been flying around the village?

It is clear that the older brother is more concerned about lost property wasted on high living than he is about a lost son and brother. He is convinced that his brother has reaped what he sowed. According to Prov 13:18, "Whoever disregards discipline comes to poverty and shame, but whoever heeds correction is honored." Just the reverse appears to be taking place in this story, and the older brother cannot understand how his father could be made glad by this wastrel's return. What galls him is that he gets no say in whether his father should welcome this playboy back.

That he is not a true son who loved his father or a true brother is further revealed by his begrudging his father's joy over the return of the younger son, his brother. He refers to the returning prodigal as "this son of yours" (ὁ υἱός σου οὗτος). He cannot bring himself to say, "this my brother." When the father rejoices that the bond of fellowship with his younger son is restored, the older son reveals that he never wanted the split to be mended. He thereby shares the same guilt of the younger son for breaching family relationships. He cherishes the broken relationship between the father and his younger son by which he can come off as the better son, obeying every command and slaving away in the fields.

15:31 **He said to him, "Child, you were always with me, and everything that is mine is yours"** (ὁ δὲ εἶπεν αὐτῷ· τέκνον, σὺ πάντοτε μετ᾽ ἐμοῦ εἶ, καὶ πάντα τὰ ἐμὰ σά ἐστιν). The father does not respond to allegations about his younger son's behavior. Whatever sins he may have committed is not the point. He has been restored. He now gently tries to restore his older son to the family, calling him "child." He does not dismiss his son's obedience and reassures him that showing grace toward his brother does not diminish his status with the father or his love for him. Is it not the reward and joy of a son to be with the father? Apparently, that was not enough. He did not need to ask to have his little celebration — limited as it was to his friends. The father had already generously given him his inheritance. It was his goat after all, and he could do what he wanted.

15:32 **"But it is necessary to celebrate and to rejoice because this your brother was given up for dead and came to life again, was lost and is found"** (εὐφρανθῆναι δὲ καὶ χαρῆναι ἔδει, ὅτι ὁ ἀδελφός σου οὗτος νεκρὸς ἦν καὶ ἔζησεν, καὶ ἀπολωλὼς καὶ εὑρέθη). The older brother's bitter complaint serves as an occasion for the father to explain the acceptance of his wayward son and his joy in receiving him, just as the Pharisees' complaint served as an occasion for Jesus to explain God's acceptance of sinners. This conclusion drives home the point for those who have complained that God's grace is too indiscriminate, "that love bestowed on the sinner is not an injustice to them ... rather, it is something which they themselves must share if they are to understand the merciful ways of divine favor."[25] The father

---

25. Charles Homer Giblin, "Structural and Theological Considerations on Luke 15," *CBQ* 24 (1962): 24.

reminds his older son that the returning prodigal is "your brother." Giblin offers that "the personal triad of father-son-brother" is "the heart" of the structure of the parable and "perhaps the core of its theology."[26] It underscores that they are a family, and families do not run on the intricate calculus of a merit system.

The repetition of the conclusion of the first act (15:24) — that he was dead and has come to life again, was lost and is now found — underscores its importance. When the dead are revived and the lost found, "it is necessary … to rejoice" (χαρῆναι ἔδει). The translation "it was fitting" (RSV, see KJV, "it was meet") is misleading. The verb "it is necessary" has a connection with salvation in Luke (see 2:49; 4:43; 9:22; 13:16, 33; 17:25; 19:5; 22:37;

24:7, 26, 44). Joy is the only option. Grumbling cuts one off from the salvation that comes in Jesus. The older son represents those who resent heaven's joy and resist it on earth. He must do more than keep commands but must join the party and learn that forgiveness is greater than justice.

The parable ends with the older brother standing outside, and we do not know whether he comes in or not. The invitation is open. He may come into the celebration but only on the father's terms — grace. While sinners need to leave behind their filth, the righteous need to leave behind their righteousness. The chapter closes with the Pharisees still standing outside, and we do not know whether they will join in the rejoicing over the recovery of the lost members of the family.

Theology in Application

Many have said that this parable expresses the gospel in a nutshell. It highlights three theological issues: repentance, God's unconditional love, and the joyful welcome of sinners.

1. The Nature of Repentance

The parable makes clear that sinners, like the younger son in this parable, can extricate themselves from their miserable predicament — "I am perishing" — through repentance. Desperation and repentance are often concomitant. Persons often find God at the end of their rope. Moule observes, "Real repentance feels like death."[27] Ann Lamott describes the beginning of her conversion after she was doing well as an author but had become an alcoholic and bulimic. One night, feeling weak and drunk and miserable, she said:

> I became aware of someone with me, hunkered down in the corner and I just assumed it was my father, whose presence I had felt over the years when I was frightened and alone. The feeling was so strong that I actually turned on the light for a moment to make sure no one was there — of course, there wasn't. But after a while, in the dark again, I knew beyond any doubt that it was Jesus. I felt him as surely as I feel my dog lying nearby as I write this.

26. Ibid., 25.

27. C. F. D. Moule, *Essays in New Testament Interpretation* (Cambridge: Cambridge Univ. Press, 1982), 254.

And I was appalled. I thought about my life and my brilliant hilarious progressive friends, I thought about what everyone would think of me if I became a Christian, and it seemed an utterly impossible thing that simply could not be allowed to happen. I turned to the wall and said out loud, "I would rather die."[28]

Of course, that is exactly what repentance requires, to die to this world. The good news is that one dies with Christ (Rom 6:8, 2 Cor 7:3, Col 2:20; 2 Tim 2:11) so that one will live with him.

Repentance, therefore, requires stooping low, which is infinitely costly to self-esteem. It requires a change of thinking and acting and a renunciation of previous intentions and deeds (Isa 55:7). Anyone who calculates, "I will sin and repent; I will sin and repent," will not receive forgiveness (see Sir 5:4–7; *m. Yoma* 8:9; *'Abot R. Nat.* 39; 2 Pet 2:22). It requires painful confession that does not presume on the Father's forgiveness and heaven's remission of his sins. Also, it requires the recognition that forgiveness cannot be earned.

The three parables in this chapter confirm that Luke understands repentance to involve "both divine and human action."[29] Questions challenging the genuine repentance of the prodigal miss the theological point that repentance is also God's gift (see Acts 5:31; 11:18). Tannehill asserts, "The assumption that repentance is the human contribution to salvation and forgiveness is the divine contribution is not only theologically shallow but also ignores indications in Luke-Acts that God's saving purpose and action are manifest in the act of repentance itself."[30]

The paradoxical mystery that repentance involves both human and divine action is portrayed in the three parables in this chapter. In the first two parables, the lost objects (sheep and coin) are passive figures that are diligently sought. These parables "suggest that the experience of repentance may be more like being found by someone who searches with great determination than like achieving something through our own determination."[31] The parable depicting the two sons is different and reflects "the human decision to return," so that "the same act of repentance can be viewed as God's saving action in a person's life and as a human decision." Though repentance is obligatory, it can never be understood as a human achievement that puts God in one's debt.[32] Donahue comments, "Awareness of sin and accepting personal responsibility for it are the beginning of his [the son's] return."[33]

Repentance may be most difficult for the righteous, who seemingly need no repentance. Prodigal sinners leave the filth of the pigsty behind. Righteous sinners,

---

28. Lamott, *Traveling Mercies*, 49.
29. Tannehill, *The Shape of Luke's Story*, 91.
30. Ibid.
31. Ibid.
32. Peter Pokorný, "Lukas 15, 11–32 und die lukanische

Soteriologie," in *Christus bezeugen: Festschrift für Wolfgang Trilling zum 65. Geburtstag* (ETS 59; ed. Karl Kertelge, Traugott Holtz, and Claus-Peter März; Leipzig: St. Benno, 1989), 188.
33. Donahue, *The Gospel in Parable*, 154.

however, must leave their imagined righteousness behind. It requires abandoning self-assured boasts about obedience and a preoccupation with rewards. It requires giving up their disdain for others who seem less obedient and their expectations that these deserve to be rejected by God.

2. The Father's Unconditional Love

The younger son does everything that is expected of a roguish, irresponsible youngest son. The father, however, does what is unexpected. Bailey cites the Egyptian Protestant scholar Ibrahim Sa'id, who commented:

> The shepherd in his search for the sheep, and the woman in her search for the coin, do not do anything out of the ordinary beyond what anyone in their place would do. But the actions the father takes in the third story are unique, marvelous, divine actions which have not been done by any father in the past.[34]

The parable presents us with a recklessly extravagant father who is "lavish and wasteful in the love expended to both sons."[35] Both sons acted as if their father's love was conditional. They needed to do something to restore or to maintain the relationship with the father. The younger son wanted to humble himself as a hired servant and perhaps earn his way back into his father's good grace. The older son was slavishly obedient and expected his younger brother to wallow in his shame and to crawl around the farm in sackcloth and ashes. Instead, he now parades about in a fine robe. The older son thought that his faithful obedience should earn him special favor with his father and that his brother's waywardness excluded him from any favor. Juel comments: "The elder brother's protest gathers up all the resentment of responsible people, who have committed themselves to holding off the chaos that threatens to sweep away civilized life and expect nothing more than justice."[36]

The parable conveys that both sons were cherished by the father because they were sons, not because of what they did or did not do. The same applies to God's love for us. We are not loved on the basis of conditions that are dictated in advance as in a contract — I will love you, if you do or be such and such. It may seem to the righteous, however, that such love is profligate. They may fear that there is not enough of God's love to go around to include everyone. They may fear that they have been abandoned or taken for granted in the search for the lost and the joyful welcome when they are recovered. The parable conveys that God's generosity and joyful reception of the lost does not disinherit the righteous or impoverish them.

34. Bailey, *Jesus through Middle Eastern Eyes*, 100.
35. Ibid., 157.
36. Juel, "The Lord's Prayer in the Gospels of Matthew and Luke," 68.

3. Acceptance of Others Saved by Grace

The father's excited joy in receiving his son mirrors Jesus' festive meals with sinners. The older son's refusal to rejoice over his brother's return highlights the difficulty many have of accepting repentant sinners, particularly if they have been notorious sinners. This parable captures God's intention to gather a community based on grace and not on the strict calculus of merits and demerits that can engender a mercenary spirit in dealing with God and others. If persons do not seek the lost themselves, they must at least rejoice at their recovery and favorable reception by God. Those who accept Christ must accept others accepted by Christ.

Yet those who identify themselves as righteous and obedient may balk at the idea of mercy and forgiveness for sinners because they fear that it only seems to give comfort to the enemies.[37] They need to recognize that while we were *all* enemies, we were justified by faith, received peace with God, obtained access to divine grace, received the hope of sharing the glory of God, and were reconciled to God through the death of his Son (Rom 5:1 – 2, 10).

---

37. Garrison Keillor, *Life among the Lutherans* (ed. H. Harden; Minneapolis: Augsburg, 2009), 173.

Luke 16:1 – 13

Literary Context

This story about a dishonest agent perplexes most readers. When accused of wasting his master's goods, he tries to salvage his future by squandering more of his master's goods. While he still has the books, he has his master's debtors significantly reduce the amounts they owe in hopes that they will remember his kindness to them and take him in when he is jobless. How can the Lord commend the dishonesty of a clever rogue? What do malfeasance and fraud have to do with the reign of God?

The answers do not come easily. Over a century ago, Plummer pronounced: "The literature on this subject is voluminous and unrepaying."[1] More recently, Topel avers: "The literature dealing with the parable is staggering, and after all the effort expended, its meaning still eludes us."[2] Creed simply declares it to be "an unedifying story."[3] These opinions, however, fail to take account of how the parable works in its literary context.

The parable follows the parable about a prodigal son who acted decisively and wisely to extricate himself from his predicament by returning to his father. In the present parable another character who has gotten himself into a mess acts decisively, if not honestly, to try to save his future. This parable, however, is applied to the issue of the right use of wealth that dominates Luke 16. In view of the crisis of the hour created by the arrival of the reign of God (13:1 – 9), what is the most prudent way to handle one's possessions? Each of the three units begins similarly:

- 16:1 There was a certain rich man …
- 16:14 The Pharisees, who are lovers of money …
- 16:19 There was a certain rich man …

The aphorisms that follow the parable of the unrighteous agent help to interpret it. They urge a faithful use of wealth, "what is not yours," to ensure receiving "true riches" from God. These sayings draw out what it means to sit down and count the

1. Plummer, *Luke*, 381.
2. L. John Topel, "On the Injustice of the Unjust Steward: Lk 16:1 – 13," *CBQ* 37 (1975): 216.
3. Creed, *Luke*, 203.

cost (14:28, 31) and "to say goodbye to all that you possess" to be Jesus' disciple (14:33). The parable of the rich man and Lazarus (16:19 – 31) reinforces the point that wealth must be shared with the poor (12:13 – 21, 32 – 34; 13:13 – 14) if one is to have any hope of participating in the world to come.

IV. Jesus' Journey to Jerusalem (9:51 – 19:28)

    F. On Recognizing the Reign of God (13:10 – 15:32)

➡   **G. On the Faithful Use of Wealth (16:1 – 31)**

       1. The Unrighteous Agent (16:1 – 13)

       2. Jesus' Teaching on Money and the Reign of God and the Law and the Prophets (16:14 – 18)

       3. The Parable of the Rich Man and Lazarus (16:19 – 31)

Main Idea

Disciples should learn from the children of this world, who act boldly and decisively as they try to ensure their earthly future, also to act boldly and decisively — but to ensure their eternal future. As this agent recognizes his crisis and moves shrewdly to hedge his security in this world, so disciples should shrewdly use their worldly possessions, which are only on temporary loan from God, in deeds of mercy to store up treasures for themselves in heaven.

Translation

(See pages 640 – 41.)

Structure and Literary Form

This unit contains a parable followed by four spiritual axioms and a concluding command. Each explains and applies the parable's point. Many contend that vv. 1 – 7 contain the parable, and vv. 8 – 9, 10 – 13 are a secondary interpretation of the parable that was appended later. Still others contend that vv. 1 – 8 contain the parable ending with the master's reaction to the agent, and this view is refined by those who think the parable is limited to vv. 1 – 8a and vv. 8b – 9, 10 – 13 add a later interpretation. I argue that vv. 1 – 7 contain the parable, and vv. 8 – 9 are the application of the parable by Jesus, and vv. 10 – 13 reinforce the point.

The question of where the parable ends is tied to another question: Who praises the agent in v. 8 and why? If it is the agent's master who praises him, why would he do so? If it is the Lord who praises him, what has the agent done that is spiritually praiseworthy?[4] I will argue that Jesus is "the Lord" who praises the agent, and he applies this example of sharp practice to the issue of the redistribution of wealth, which runs throughout the travel narrative. The aphorisms are parallel in form with each statement taking the argument a step forward.

Exegetical Outline

→ **I. Parable of the agent bound up in the world of unrighteousness (16:1 – 7)**

   A. An agent's crisis (16:1 – 2)

   B. The agent's decisive action to win friends for himself (16:3 – 7)

II. Affirmation of the agent's shrewdness (16:8 – 9)

   A. The Lord's praise of the agent's shrewdness (16:8a-b)

   B. Comparison to the lack of shrewdness on the part of the children of light (16:8c)

   C. Command to distribute Mammon to win friends for oneself in heaven (16:9)

III. Trustworthiness in the use of money (16:10 – 12)

   A. Trustworthiness in small things is a condition for promotion to greater things (16:10)

   B. Trustworthiness in a specious thing like Mammon is a condition for being entrusted with what is genuine (16:11)

   C. Trustworthiness in what belongs to another is a condition for being given what is your own (16:12)

IV. Divided allegiance (16:13)

   A. Servants cannot serve two masters (16:13a)

   B. Disciples cannot serve God and Mammon (16:13b)

Explanation of the Text

16:1 And he said to his disciples, "There was a certain rich man who had an agent and charges were brought to him that this one was squandering his goods" (ἔλεγεν δὲ καὶ πρὸς τοὺς μαθητάς· ἄνθρωπός τις ἦν πλούσιος ὃς εἶχεν οἰκονόμον, καὶ οὗτος διεβλήθη αὐτῷ ὡς διασκορπίζων τὰ ὑπάρχοντα αὐτοῦ). Since parables "are short and have no time for elusive character development," they draw on a repertory of stock figures and "rely on the cultural associations brought by the hearers to the evocation of stock figures."[5] Sensitivity to the historical and cultural associations "that were automatic to the original hearers" is crucial for understanding the parable.[6] In an affluent society such as the Western world today, a "certain rich man" may be a sympathetic character, since wealth is something admired and envied. In Jesus' peasant society, however, "a certain rich man" would automatically evoke antipathy. He is like the rich men in the parables in 12:16 – 21 and 16:19 – 31,

---

4. For a history of interpretation, see Dennis J. Ireland, "A History of Recent Interpretation of the Parable of the Unjust Steward (Luke 16:1 – 13)," *WTJ* 51 (1989): 293 – 318; and his *Stewardship and the Kingdom of God: An Historical, Exegetical and Contextual Study of the Parable of the Unjust Steward in Luke 16:1 – 13* (NovTSup 70; Leiden: Brill, 1992); and Richard

Dormandy, "Unjust Steward or Converted Master?" *RB* 109 (2002): 512 – 27.

5. Philip L. Culbertson, *A Word Fitly Spoken: Context, Transmission, and Adoption of the Parables of Jesus* (Albany: SUNY Press, 1995), 17.

6. Ibid., 19.

Luke 16:1–13

16:1a	Character introduction	**And he said to his disciples,**
b		"There was a certain rich man who had an agent
c		and charges were brought to him that this one was squandering his goods.
2	Dismissal	When he called him in, he said to him,
		'What is this I hear about you?
		Hand over the account of your management, *for* you are no longer able to continue as agent.'
3a	Interior monologue	The agent said to himself,
		'What shall I do *because* my master is taking the position of agent away from me?
b		I am not strong enough to dig.
c		I am ashamed to beg.
4a	Decision	I know what I will do
b	Purpose	*so that* people will receive me *into* their households *after* I am no longer the agent!'
5	Action (1)	When he called his master's debtors one by one, he said to the first,
		'How much do you owe my master?'
		And he said,
		'One hundred measures of olive oil.'
		And he said to him,
6		'Take your contract, sit down, and quickly write fifty.'

7	Action (2)	Then he said to another,
		'How much do you owe?'
		And he said,
		'A hundred measures of wheat.'
		He said to him,
		'Take your contract and write eighty.'"
8a	Praise	**And the Lord praised the agent [bound up, as he was, in the world] of unrighteousness**
b	Reason	because he acted shrewdly,
c		because **worldlings are more shrewd in taking advantage of their opportunities than are the children of light.**
9a	Command	"And I say to you,
		Make friends with unrighteous Mammon,
b	Rationale	*so that* when it fails they will receive you in eternal habitations.
10	Aphorism (1)	The one who is trustworthy with what is insignificant will be faithful with what is much more significant;
		and the one who is untrustworthy with what is insignificant
		will be untrustworthy with what is much more significant.
11	Aphorism (2)	If therefore you are not trustworthy with unrighteous Mammon, who will entrust you with true riches?
12	Aphorism (3)	*And if* you are not trustworthy with what belongs to another, who will give you what is yours?
13a	Aphorism (4)	No servant is able to serve two masters, *for* he will hate the one and love the other, *or*
		he will help the one and disregard the other.
b	Command	You are not able to serve God and Mammon!"

someone guilty of reprehensible avarice and readily identifiable as a villain or dishonorable person.[7]

Malina shows that in Jesus' world, those classified as "the rich" were the dishonest, greedy rich
who deprived others of what was rightfully theirs
by accumulating for themselves more than their
fair share. Being a creditor was how the rich got
richer, and being a debtor was how the poor got
poorer. Jesus pronounced woes on those who were
rich and full (6:24 – 25; see 1:53) and compared
those who delight in riches and pleasures to the
seed sown among thorns, which chokes the Word
and makes it unfruitful (8:14). He tells his disciples that it is impossible for a rich man to enter the
kingdom of God (18:24 – 27), presumably because
the rich got their wealth at the expense of others.
In a limited goods economy, the assumption was
that everyone could have the necessities of life if
others did not have too much.[8]

Since all goods were assumed to exist in limited amounts, which could neither be increased
nor expanded, it follows that someone who was
rich when so many were poor had acquired that
wealth at the expense of others who were deprived
and denied what is theirs.[9] This attitude was deep-
seated. Jerome reflects it when he affirmed "the
truth in a saying of a philosopher, 'Every rich man
is either wicked or the heir of wickedness.'"[10]

The rich man here has entrusted the business
management of his estate to an agent (or steward)
who was empowered to make all legal transactions with third parties in the name of his master
(see 19:12 – 27). He was authorized to negotiate

such contracts at his discretion. Consequently,
one had to be careful in selecting an agent. Columella (*Rust.* 11.1.7) advises how a steward should
be trained and what qualities one should look
for: competence, fidelity, and goodwill toward
the owner. He warns against the sleepyheaded
idler who spends his time gambling and in bawdy
houses (*Rust.* 1.8.1) and urges choosing someone
who is abstemious in wine, sleep, and sexual indulgence (*Rust.* 11.1.13 – 14). He also recommends
selecting someone who has a good mind but is illit-
erate "because not knowing his letters he is either
less able to falsify accounts or is afraid to do so
through a second party because that would make
another aware of the deception" (*Rust.* 1.8.4). He
advises that the landowner should exercise personal supervision because it will help avoid losses
caused by a careless or greedy steward.

If the agent turns out to be careless or greedy,
Columella blames it on the "the fault of the master,
inasmuch as he has the authority to prevent such a
person from being placed in charge of his affairs,
or to see to it that he is removed if so placed" (*Rust.*
1.7.5). On distant estates, he recommends that it is
better for them to be farmed by free farmers than
to be managed by slave overseers who are careless
and dishonest, who charge the sowing of far more
seed than is actually sown, and who lessen the
amount of threshing by trickery or carelessness
(*Rust.* 1.7.6 – 7). The agent in this story lacks the
qualities expected of a reliable agent.

Columella's advice on hiring stewards also exposes the master's negligence. He is out of touch

---

7. See Sir 13:3 – 4: "A rich person does wrong, and even adds insults; a poor person suffers wrong, and must add apologies. A rich person will exploit you if you can be of use to him, but if you are in need he will abandon you." See also the condemna-tions of the rich in Jas 2:6 – 7; 5:1 – 6; *1 En.* 62:1 – 5.

8. Bruce J. Malina, "Wealth and Poverty in the New Testa-ment," *Int* 41 (1987): 361.

9. Malina, *The New Testament World*, 75 – 76. Leasing land

was a main source of wealth for the rich. It was also a source of great anguish for the poor tenant, who frequently was barely able to eke out an existence off the land that used to belong to his fathers. The land was probably lost when the small-time farmer was drowned in a sea of indebtedness.

10. Jerome, "Homily on Psalm 83," cited by Arthur A. Just Jr., *Luke* (ACCS; Downers Grove, IL: InterVarsity Press, 2003), 290.

and needs to be informed about what is going on with his business if he does not want his goods to be wasted.

Charges are raised against the agent that he is squandering his master's property. The verb "squandered" (διασκορπίζω) is the same verb that describes the prodigal son's profligacy (15:13). How the agent has wasted his master's goods — through mismanagement, swindling, or extravagant self-indulgence (see 12:45) — is not specified. Apparently, this mismanagement is widely known: "What is this I hear about you?" (16:2; see similar expressions in Gen 12:18; 20:9; 42:28). Such gossip would make the master look like a fool, and he must take action to save his reputation and protect his investment.

The verb rendered "to bring charges" (διαβάλλω) can mean "to slander" or "to accuse unjustly" (see 2 Macc 3:11; 4 Macc 4:1; Josephus, *Ant.* 7.11.3 §267) or simply "to denounce" (Dan 3:8; Josephus, *Ant.* 12.4.4 §176). If the first meaning applies, then the charges are untrue and are brought by those who want the agent fired. Since the agent makes no attempt to deny the accusations or to beg for mercy, as the servant does in Matt 18:26, we can presume that his silence represents his guilt (see Matt 22:12). He accepts that he has been caught with his hand in the till and is about to lose his job.

16:2 When he called him in, he said to him, "What is this I hear about you? Hand over the account of your management, for you are no longer able to continue as agent" (καὶ φωνήσας αὐτὸν εἶπεν αὐτῷ· τί τοῦτο ἀκούω περὶ σοῦ; ἀπόδος τὸν λόγον τῆς οἰκονομίας σου, οὐ γὰρ δύνῃ ἔτι οἰκονομεῖν). Derrett outlines the Jewish law of agency that provides an important backdrop for understanding the freedom of the agent to act on his master's behalf and the constraints on

the master to get restitution for any malfeasance. (1) A man's agent is like himself. Anything done by the agent within the scope of his agency binds his master (*b. B. Meṣ.* 96a; *b. B. Qam.* 113b; *b. Qidd.* 41b–42a). (2) As long as his agency lasts (i.e., he is not repudiated publicly), he can bind his master in relation to third parties and is not himself liable for any loss because of his incompetence or negligence.[11]

When the master tells the agent to give him the account of his stewardship, he is requesting the books, the financial statement of all that was in the agent's charge. The master must have the books before he can transfer the stewardship to someone else. While the agent still has the books, however, he quickly takes action to ensure some measure of acceptance in the community when he no longer has the leverage of his position.

16:3 The agent said to himself, "What shall I do because my master is taking the position of agent away from me? I am not strong enough to dig. I am ashamed to beg" (εἶπεν δὲ ἐν ἑαυτῷ ὁ οἰκονόμος· τί ποιήσω, ὅτι ὁ κύριός μου ἀφαιρεῖται τὴν οἰκονομίαν ἀπ᾽ ἐμοῦ; σκάπτειν οὐκ ἰσχύω, ἐπαιτεῖν αἰσχύνομαι). We overhear the agent's soliloquy, just as we do the rich fool's (12:17–19), the prodigal son's (15:17–19), and the unjust judge's (18:4–5), all of whom evaluate their respective situations. He focuses all his mental energy on safeguarding his future without a job. How will he survive? The present tense of the verb "is taking away" (ἀφαιρεῖται) suggests a process is involved in ousting the agent, which gives him time to act.

"I am not strong enough to dig" (see Aristophanes, *Birds* 1432) means he is either too physically weak or too lazy to do manual labor. Or, he may regard himself to be above the vulgar herd

---

11. Derrett, *Law in the New Testament*, 52–55. This idea of stewardship is reflected in Paul's understanding of his apostle-ship (1 Cor 4:1–2, 9:17; Eph 3:2; Col 1:25; see Titus 1:7; 1 Pet 4:10).

who must sweat and toil for a living. Since almost everyone in Jesus' peasant audience had to dig — i.e., engage in manual labor — his soliloquy makes him an unsympathetic character.[12] The rascal remains oblivious that this crisis is of his own making. His first loyalty is to his own comfort and status, and he desperately engages in damage control to avoid ever having to do real work or having to panhandle. Becoming someone who sponges off the hospitality of others is more acceptable to him. Unlike the prodigal son, who, when faced with the crisis of his poverty (15:19), was willing to make himself as his father's hired hand, presumably to dig in the fields, this man is unwilling to demean himself with honest labor.

16:4 "I know what I will do so that people will receive me into their households after I am no longer the agent!" (ἔγνων τί ποιήσω, ἵνα ὅταν μετασταθῶ ἐκ τῆς οἰκονομίας δέξωνταί με εἰς τοὺς οἴκους αυτῶν). The aorist verb pictures this agent lighting upon an idea: "I've got it!" (ἔγνων). He has a narrow window of opportunity to act before he must physically hand over the accounts to the master. The agent knows that when word gets out about his dismissal, he will be scorned by his social equals, other agents, and debtors. Reemployment as an agent will be impossible. He has no future unless he does something, and he recognizes that he must strike fast to secure goodwill for himself.

His soliloquy reveals his inner motivations and thoughts to the listener while concealing his true, less-than-honorable motivations from the debtors.[13] This interior monologue also reveals that he remains unchanged after being caught in misconduct. He does not think, "Maybe I should repent"; rather, he remains the clever rogue who continues his underhanded, scheming ways: "How can I get out of this smelling like a rose?" In wanting to be "received into their households," his aim is to become a freeloader, a professional house guest who lives off other people. His hope is that at least one of the debtors will be grateful enough to bestow on him this favor.

16:5–7 When he called his master's debtors one by one, he said to the first, "How much do you owe my master?" And he said, "One hundred measures of olive oil." And he said to him, "Take your contract, sit down, and quickly write fifty." Then he said to another, "How much do you owe?" And he said, "A hundred measures of wheat." He said to him, "Take your contract and write eighty" (καὶ προσκαλεσάμενος ἕνα ἕκαστον τῶν χρεοφειλετῶν τοῦ κυρίου ἑαυτοῦ ἔλεγεν τῷ πρώτῳ· πόσον ὀφείλεις τῷ κυρίῳ μου; ὁ δὲ εἶπεν· ἑκατὸν βάτους ἐλαίου. ὁ δὲ εἶπεν αὐτῷ· δέξαι σου τὰ γράμματα καὶ καθίσας ταχέως γράψον πεντήκοντα. ἔπειτα ἑτέρῳ εἶπεν· σὺ δὲ πόσον ὀφείλεις; ὁ δὲ εἶπεν· ἑκατὸν κόρους σίτου. λέγει αὐτῷ· δέξαι σου τὰ γράμματα καὶ γράψον ὀγδοήκοντα).

The agent concocts a plan to trim the amount owed by his master's debtors. The phrase "one by one" (ἕνα ἕκαστον, "each one") implies that a number of debtors are called in and that we are given only two examples of typical debtors who have their bonds reduced. When he asks them, "How much do you owe?" (vv. 5, 7), he is establishing an agreement that the amount recorded on the contract is correct. He does not cancel the whole

---

12. Xenophon records a conversation of Socrates with a certain Eutherus who had lost his fortune due to war and was reduced to earning his living as a manual laborer. Socrates warns him that as he gets older, he will find it harder to survive and encourages him to seek work as a works or estate agent. He responds, "I absolutely refuse to be liable to be called to account by anyone" (*Mem.* 2.8.1–5). He prefers manual labor to accepting a position that involves personal service to a master.

13. From Resseguie (*Spiritual Landscape*, 59), who applies it to the parable of the unjust judge.

debt because that would immediately call attention to the fraud. He lets the debtors alter their promissory notes or make out new ones in their own hand so it would arouse no suspicions.

Are these people in debt tenants or merchants? If they are tenant farmers, rent normally consisted of a share of the crop (*t. Demai* 4:30; 6:2, 5–6; *m. Ḥal.* 4:7). The debts are rather substantial, equivalent to the amount King Artaxerxes decreed could be provided to Ezra to support the temple worship in Jerusalem (Ezra 7:22).[14] Kloppenborg estimates that this debt represents "a half-share rent for almost 200 acres, which is twenty times the size of an average family plot."[15] The debtors certainly are not peasants eking out a subsistence living from the land but persons of means.

The steward is now forced by his dire straits to take into consideration the welfare of those whom he had been able to disregard because of his position of authority over them. The agent takes action on the basis of the principle of reciprocity (quid pro quo), which governed relationships in society (6:31–35). By having these people doctor the balance due, he makes them accomplices in the fraud and "contrives adroitly to put his master's debtors under a lasting obligation to himself."[16] He hopes that he will be able to cash in on these obligations when he is thrown out.[17]

16:8 And the Lord praised the agent [bound up, as he was, in the world] of unrighteousness because he acted shrewdly, because worldlings are more shrewd in taking advantage of their opportunities than are the children of light (καὶ ἐπῄνεσεν ὁ κύριος τὸν οἰκονόμον τῆς ἀδικίας ὅτι φρονίμως ἐποίησεν· ὅτι οἱ υἱοὶ τοῦ αἰῶνος τούτου φρονιμώτεροι ὑπὲρ τοὺς υἱοὺς τοῦ φωτὸς εἰς τὴν γενεὰν τὴν ἑαυτῶν εἰσιν). The phrase translated literally "agent of unrighteousness" (ὁ οἰκονόμος τῆς ἀδικίας) is similar to "unrighteous Mammon" (τοῦ μαμωνᾶ τῆς ἀδικίας) in 16:9 and is an attributive or Hebraic genitive, which places the emphasis on unrighteousness (see 18:6). In the context, however, the phrase is used in contrast to the "children of light." It is not "a description of his particular character or of his particular deed, but an expression that assigns him to a certain group or category of people: He belongs to this world as opposed to the children of light."[18] The expression describes "a man who is completely bound up in this world in which ἀδικία [unrighteousness] is the ruling principle."[19]

The shocker comes when the unrighteous agent is praised for his actions, for acting "shrewdly" (φρονίμως). Most translations identify the one who praises the agent as "the master" (ὁ κύριος) in the parable, the same person mentioned in v. 3

14. The first "measure" (βάτος), a transliteration of the Hebrew, is a liquid measure equivalent to nine gallons. One hundred "baths" equals around 900 gallons. The second measure (κόρος) is also a transliteration of the Hebrew; it is a dry measure that has been variously described (e.g., Josephus, *Ant.* 3.15.3 §321 and 15.9.2 §314) as equivalent to ten to fifteen bushels.

15. John S. Kloppenborg, "The Dishonoured Master (Luke 16,1–8a)," *Bib* 70 (1989): 482.

16. Manson, *The Sayings of Jesus*, 182.

17. For this reason, attempts to interpret the agent as some kind of allegorical representation of Christ who forgives debts is untenable. Contra William Loader, "Jesus and the Rogue in Luke 16,1–8a: The Parable of the Unjust Steward," *RB* 96

(1989): 518–32; Colin Brown, "The Unjust Steward: A New Twist?" in *Worship, Theology and Ministry: Essays in Honor of Ralph P. Martin* (JSNTSup 87; ed. by M. Wilkins and T. Paige; Sheffield: JSOT, 1992), 121–45. To speculate that this fraud would, ironically, become a benefaction for the poor as the wholesalers pass on the cost reductions to the wider populace takes us wide afield of the parable (contra Ronald A. Piper, "Social Background and Thematic Structure in Luke 16," in *The Four Gospels, 1992: Festschrift Frans Neirynck* [BETL 100; ed. F. Van Segbroeck et al.; Leuven: Leuven Univ. Press, 1992], 2:1649–52).

18. Hans Kosmala, "The Parable of the Unjust Steward in the Light of Qumran," *ASTI* 3 (1964): 114–15.

19. Ibid., 115.

("my master"; ὁ κύριός μου) and v. 5 ("his master's"; τοῦ κυρίου ἑαυτοῦ). Scott contends that the master's praise of the servant is part of the unexpected in the art of storytelling.[20] Nevertheless, it seems highly improbable that this rich financier, who was upset about his assets being wasted by his agent, would suddenly find an even greater loss of his assets commendable. Several proposals have attempted to explain why the master would praise the agent for cheating him. I list three views that I disagree with and then give my own interpretation.

(1) Bailey conjectures that the agent reflects on the fact that he is fired and not jailed. He contends that the agent would have been held accountable for malfeasance and would have been jailed. The master, according to this view, treated him with unusual mercy — even generosity. The agent seizes on the grace of the master and summons the debtors, who assume that he is still in charge. Bailey imagines that the debtors would ask why he was doing this, and the steward would respond: "I talked the old gentleman into it."[21] The master discovers that the villagers are toasting him "as the most generous man who ever rented land in this district."[22] He chooses not to void the contracts and instead basks in the praise won him by the actions of the agent.[23] The agent guesses instinctively that the master was generous and merciful. He risks everything on this aspect of his master's nature, hoping that he would act generously again. The hero of the story, then, becomes the master who appears to enjoy being outwitted. Barth claims that he responds this way "because he is

a good and gracious lord who in a critical situation, instead of appealing to law, order, morality, fair business practice proves to be generous in an unprecedented manner. This master is pleased to see the agent set everything on one card: the master's goodness."[24]

Other parables of Jesus portray the whimsical behavior of a king (Matt 18:23 – 35) or a vineyard owner (Matt 20:1 – 16), but this interpretation collapses because the agent could not be jailed for incompetence and the contracts could not be declared invalid. He could only be dismissed and publicly reproached.[25] The parable gives no hint that the landowner was interested in garnering a reputation as a generous man, and evidence exists in Luke that landowners had no interest in earning good reputations (see 19:21). In Luke, "rich man" and "generous" are mutually exclusive terms.[26] In addition, this interpretation ignores that the text explicitly says that the agent acts in hope of gaining hospitality from those people after he has turned in his books (16:4), not in hope of retaining his job. This reading of the parable erroneously turns it into an allegory where the master corresponds to God.

(2) Another view argues that the agent deducts hidden interest that was being charged the debtors. Despite the biblical ban on usury (Exod 22:25; Lev 25:36 – 37; Deut 15:7 – 8; 23:19 – 20), devious means were contrived to circumvent the appearance of charging interest while at the same time garnering it, often at exorbitant rates.[27] Some argue that the agent has the debtors change their notes by removing the interest. In the case of the oil, the interest

---

20. Scott, *Hear Then the Parable*, 175, n. 8.

21. Bailey, *Poet and Peasant*, 100.

22. Ibid., 101.

23. Ibid.

24. Markus Barth, "The Dishonest Steward and His Lord: Reflections on Luke 16:1 – 13," in *From Faith to Faith* (ed. D. Y. Hadidian; Pittsburgh: Pickwick, 1979), 72.

25. See Derrett, *Law in the New Testament*, 54.

26. Luke does not identify Joseph of Arimathea as a "rich man," as he is in Matt 27:57, but as a "good and righteous man" (Luke 23:50).

27. Charging interest is assumed in the parables of the minas in 19:23.

would have been 100 percent (800 measures cut down to 400); in the case of the wheat, the interest was 20 percent (1000 measures cut down to 800). By removing the interest charges, the master was not cheated out of anything to which he was legally entitled, which mitigates the supposed dishonesty of the agent. The interest charged has been interpreted in two ways.

According to Derrett, the interest premium accrued to the master. When he discovers what has happened, he relishes the undeserved reputation among the debtors for righteous dealing.[28] According to Fitzmyer, the interest charges went to the agent as part of his service commission. The agent foregoes his profits from usury to please the debtors and to gain a favorable reception from them when he is removed from his position.[29] This prudent and sacrificial action is what elicits the praise of the master.

This interpretation assumes that Luke's audience would understand the intricacies of covertly usurious loans and ignores that the debt is owed the master, not the agent, and that only he is harmed by the decreased amounts. It also assumes that the master either did not authorize but knew of the usurious nature of the contracts, or that if he did authorize them, he was not concerned about making a profit. This assumption is undermined by the fact that the agent urges the debtors to write the new bonds "quickly" (v. 6) in their own hand. That urgency suggests a deliberate attempt to defraud the master. He does not simply have the bills marked paid because that would be a dead giveaway that foul play was afoot. The master did not know what was originally recorded on the bills, and they could be safely altered.[30] This view also

requires that the master somehow learns about the doctoring of the accounts despite the fact that he does not have them. Who tells him? His anonymous informers? The agent? The debtors? His own inspection of the books?

If Fitzmyer is correct, the agent was only removing his commission from the bonds. But why is the agent not interested in his profits to tide him over during his unemployment? The answer might be that he knew he would be unable to collect since he would no longer be the agent. But the parable makes no hint that this was what he was thinking. All attempts to remove the element of dishonesty on the part of the agent are misguided. His plan for his future security involves dissociating himself from the owner in the nick of time in hopes that the debtors will reciprocate and receive him in their households.

(3) Some argue that the story reflects the trickster motif found in the farces of Roman slave comedy.[31] The master's admiration of his agent is the customary response of owners who are outsmarted by their wily slaves. The story picks up a common theme that satirizes the rich with the flatterer/swindler who always needs a host. The problem with this view is that Luke is not writing Roman farce. The chagrin of one who has been bamboozled in one of Plautus's comedies, for example, does not lead to good-natured praise of the culprit, but anger:

> The more I consider the matter inside myself
> The more I get angrier, pained and beside myself.
> The manner in which I was flimflammed, the way
> I couldn't perceive when they led me astray!

---

28. Derrett, *Law in the New Testament*, 72.

29. Joseph A. Fitzmyer, "The Story of the Dishonest Manager (Lk 16:1 – 13)," *TS* 25 (1964): 23 – 42; Fitzmyer, *Luke*, 2:1098.

30. As a landlord, Cicero (*De or.* 1.48.250) refers to matters related to account books as "complicated and often troublesome."

31. See Bernard Heininger, *Metaphorik, Erzählstruktur und szenisch-dramatische Gestaltung in den Sondergutgleichnisse bei Lukas* (NTAbh 24; Münster: Aschendorff, 1991), 168.

O when this is known I'll be mocked through
    the city,
When I reach the forum the whole world will
    say:
"That clever old chap was bamboozled today!"
    (*Capt.* 781 – 87)[32]

(4) I argue that the one who praises the agent's
shrewdness is Jesus, identified as "the Lord" (ὁ
κύριος) in v. 8. The story breaks off abruptly in
v. 7 before reaching the denouement. We do not
know if the fraud was successful or not. We are not
told what happens to the agent or the rich man and
can only assume that the agent was fired, as he expected, and the rich man was none the wiser about
how badly he had been fleeced.[33] The parable is
not a human interest story, and Jesus focuses only
on the agent's quick thinking and decisive action
in a crisis as an example for his disciples.

The use of "lord" (κύριος) unambiguously refers to the master in vv. 3 and 5 when it is modified
by "my" and "his." Unfortunately, many modern
translations wrongly translate v. 8 as if "his" were
in the Greek text ("his Lord"; see ASV, NASB,
NRSV).[34] The text has "the Lord" (ὁ κύριος), and
in Luke the absolute use of "Lord" with the definite

article without any modifier usually refers to Jesus
(7:13, 19; 10:1; 11:39; 12:42; 13:15; 17:5, 6; 18:6; 19:8;
23:61; 24:34).[35] If Jesus is "the Lord" who praises
the agent, this construction ("the Lord praised the
unrighteous agent" [τὸν οἰκονόμον τῆς ἀδικίας])
parallels the conclusion to the parable about the
wicked judge in 18:6: "The Lord said, 'Listen to
what the unrighteous judge [ὁ κριτὴς τῆς ἀδικίας]
says!'" This direction is followed, as in 16:9 – 10, by
an application of the parable in 18:7 and a declaration, "I say to you," in 18:8.[36] Jesus does not bring
the parable that immediately precedes to a narrative close (15:11 – 32), and he does not do so in this
parable either. What is important is not the conclusion to the agent's story but Jesus' application of
his behavior to issues of discipleship.[37]

Further clues make it clear that Luke understands that Jesus is "the Lord" who praises the
agent. (1) The owner is identified in 16:1 as "a certain rich man" who deals in large loans. In Luke,
since those who are rich in material things are
portrayed as devoted to Mammon (16:13) and not
rich toward God (12:21), it would be incongruous
for him to serve as a positive character or the one
who scores the point of the parable (see 1:53; 6:24;

---

32. Erich Segal, *Roman Laughter: The Comedy of Plautus* (2nd ed.; New York/Oxford: Oxford Univ. Press, 1987),
120 – 21.

33. Even if the master is the one who praises the agent, we
do not know what happens next. Does the master now allow
the agent to continue in his position? Why would an owner decide at one moment to dismiss someone who had been wasting
his goods, either through mismanagement or dishonesty, and
then at another moment dramatically change his mind when
he learns that his losses are now even greater? Why would he
run the risk of having more of his property squandered by an
agent who has demonstrated himself to be both dishonest and
clever?

34. Many more translations render it "the master," and
egregiously the NLT paraphrases it "the rich man," completely
abandoning the Greek text.

35. See 12:36 ("their master"); 12:43 ("his master"); 12:45
("my master"); 12:46 ("master of that servant"); 12:47 ("his
master"); 14:21, 22 ("his master"); 16:3 "my master"); 16:5 ("his

master"); 19:16, 18, 20, 25 ("Master" direct address); 19:33 ("its
masters"); 20:13, 15 ("the master of the vineyard"). The three
exceptions are in 12:37, 42 and 14:23, where it unambiguously
refers to the character in the parable, but the character may
also be interpreted as an allegorical figure representing God.

36. The sudden shift from indirect speech in v.8b ("the Lord
praised ... because") to direct speech in v. 9, ("I say to you ...")
appears in 5:14 and Acts 23:22; 25:4 – 5 (see BDF §470, noting
that a New Testament author finds it "quite impossible ... to
maintain indirect discourse in an extended passage. Instead he
reverts without fail to the direct."

37. Jesus also interjects his comments on the action in
14:24. Ryan S. Schellenberg ("Which Master? Whose Steward?
Metalepsis and Lordship in the Parable of the Prudent Steward
[Lk. 16.1 – 13]," *JSNT* 30 [2008]: 263 – 88) appeals to Gérard
Genette's identification of a trope dubbed *metalepsis*, in which
the boundaries of narrative levels are blurred so that "the Lord"
can refer to both the master in the parable and the Lord who
tells it.

14:12; 18:23; 21:1).[38] Modern affluent readers may want the rich owner to be gracious and whimsical, as we imagine ourselves to be, but Jesus would not have shared this view (see above on v. 1).

This rich man is another lover of money (16:14). In fact, all the characters in this parable are "worldlings" (οἱ υἱοὶ τοῦ αἰῶνος τούτου, "the sons of this age"), members of "this corrupt generation," from which Christians must break loose (Acts 2:38 – 40). The original hearers will have heard this story as a confederacy of rogues: a dishonest rich man who serves Mammon, a tricky business agent who defrauds his master to save himself, and well-to-do merchants who profit from the deception.[39] The poor and the needy, who always seem to be exploited by the wealthy and the middlemen,[40] appear only when the agent dreads the prospect of joining their ranks. The rich man, by virtue of being identified as a rich man, would have been viewed by the auditors as a protagonist of evil like the wicked judge (18:1 – 6). Jesus' audience would not be appalled by the agent's flagrant dishonesty, since they would delight in the rich man being duped.[41]

A modern analogy from the world of movies may help us better understand the original audience's perspective. Plots in which crooks plan a clever heist of a gambling casino do not evoke sympathy for the victimized casino owner. The audience does not care about the dishonesty of the safecrackers, who are the heroes of the story, but admires their streetwise cunning, enjoys the suspense, and hopes they get away with it. The casino, perceived as a den of robbers, gets no sympathy, because it is assumed that it gets what

it deserves and will quickly make up its losses. A plot in which an accountant for a Mafia boss defrauds him by donating millions of his ill-gotten gains to charity and then makes his escape evokes the same response. No one feels that a grave injustice has been done to the victimized mafioso. In the same way, "a certain rich man" would evoke no sympathy from Jesus' audience — except from those who are lovers of money (16:14).

(2) If the changing of the bonds was done behind the master's back, as the story suggests, the master would not have known about it to react. There is no reason to believe that he uncovers the fraud. He does not have the books and did not keep up with day-to-day transactions because he had to be told that the agent was squandering his property.

(3) The word "shrewdly" (φρονίμως) is used in an eschatological context by Jesus in 12:42 in its adjectival form. It is unlikely that it would reappear on the lips of someone like a rich creditor.

(4) It is even more unlikely for the rich man to use the phrase "the children of this age" ("worldlings"), since the rich man would be a classic example of "a child of this age" who thinks only in terms of this age and its possibilities and who orders his life with little thought given to God. This language reflects the apocalyptic concept of two ages and only makes sense on the lips of Jesus. The children of light belong to the age to come (see Eph 5:8; 1 Thess 5:5).

The statement "because worldlings are more shrewd in taking advantage of their opportunities than are the children of light" offers the rationale why Jesus would laud flagrant dishonesty in the

---

38. A rich man appears as the antihero in two other parables: 12:16; 16:19. Zacchaeus is described as a chief tax agent and rich (19:2), but he repents and unloads his wealth.

39. Oesterley, *The Gospel Parables in Light of Their Jewish Background*, 197 – 98.

40. See *1 En.* 48:8: "In those days, the kings of the earth and

the mighty landowners shall be humiliated on account of the deeds of their hands"; 62:3: "On the day of judgment, all the kings, the governors, the high officials, and the landlords shall see and recognize him" who will judge them.

41. Even members of the ruling class felt contempt for what Seneca calls "stupid rich men" (*Ep.* 27).

midst of making the parable's point. Jesus passes no moral judgment on the agent's actions; he simply uses those actions as a foil to challenge his disciples. Given the end-time crisis facing everyone (13:5), disciples should prepare for the future reckoning by employing their material possessions shrewdly.

What Jesus regards as "shrewd," however, differs from how the world defines it. Jesus has warned that those who do not renounce all that they possess are not able to be his disciples (14:33). He has told them to store up treasures with God by selling their possessions and giving alms (12:21, 33). Franklin comments, "Wealth is a mark of God's disfavor, a guarantee of impending doom, so the only thing is to use it in order to gain an escape from this almost inevitable fate."[42]

The story, though addressed to the disciples, applies to everyone. Let them follow the example of the agent, a typical son of this age. His sights are set only on this world, but he recognized the critical nature of his situation and took bold steps to make entry into his new life as easy as possible. Here is a man of the world who took charge of a situation in such a way as to overcome the threat.

The audience is in the same situation as the agent threatened with imminent disaster (12:54 – 59; 13:1 – 5). The difference is that their very souls are at risk. They are to imitate the agent's concern for the future by not allowing things simply to take their course. When everything was at stake, the agent staked everything on this daring course of action. If worldlings such as this fellow act so astutely to protect their ephemeral self-interests in this world, should not disciples seize the moment and act astutely to ensure their interests in the world to come, which is eternal? The point of the parable is akin to Jesus' saying in Matt 10:16: "Be wise (φρόνιμοι) as serpents" (NRSV). The serpent is no more an attractive example for wisdom than the dishonest agent. But both represent an essential characteristic that disciples should have — prudence, which the challenge of the hour demands.

Jesus also laments that the children of this world show more concern for the security of their earthly existence and act more decisively to guarantee it than the children of light do in securing their eternal existence. The disciples are therefore told to imitate the agent by dissociating themselves from wealth. Here was a man governed by unrighteousness (ἀδικία) who acted while there was still a chance for him to act.[43] "Like the friend who obliged his neighbor by giving him whatever he wanted for his midnight guest but not out of friendship, and like the judge who heard the widow's case but not out of any sense of responsibility, the steward showed charity to the debtors but it was not from charity."[44] The disciples, as children of light, however, are not governed by unrighteousness and have expectations only for the world to come. Should they not demonstrate the same kind of prudent wisdom that looks ahead to the future when it comes to how they use wealth? Disciples are to exploit wisely the money at their disposal by disposing of it to benefit others.

16:9 "And I say to you, Make friends with unrighteous Mammon, so that when it fails they will receive you in eternal habitations" (καὶ ἐγὼ ὑμῖν λέγω, ἑαυτοῖς ποιήσατε φίλους ἐκ τοῦ μαμωνᾶ τῆς ἀδικίας, ἵνα ὅταν ἐκλίπῃ δέξωνται ὑμᾶς εἰς

---

42. Eric Franklin, *Christ the Lord: A Study in the Purpose and Theology of Luke-Acts*, (London: SPCK, 1975), 156.

43. The point would be similar to the admonition in Luke 12:57 – 59 from the perspective of the debtor (see Matt 5:25 – 26). Settle with the accuser while you are on the way to the judge lest you eventually wind up in prison. This warning appears in Luke in the context of being able to discern the times (Luke 12:54 – 56).

44. David Daube, "Neglected Nuances of Exposition in Luke-Acts," *ANRW* 2/25/3 (1984): 2329.

τὰς αἰωνίους σκηνάς). If "the Lord" in v. 8 refers to Jesus, then the change from the third person to the first person, "and I say to you," suggests that a tradition has been joined to help interpret the parable and explain how Jesus could have praised a crook.[45] Many assume that vv. 9 – 13 contain independent sayings that have been added by Luke by loose catchword associations.

"Mammon" (μαμωνᾶ), the key word in the sayings that follow (16:9, 11, 13; see Matt 6:24; 2 Clem. 6:1), is a transliteration into Greek of an Aramaic term that does not appear in the Old Testament. It may derive from the root ʾmn ("trust") and refer to that in which one trusts because it appears to provide security.[46] It refers to property or anything of value and was used as a neutral term for "money," "wealth," or "goods." It is synonymous with "goods" (τα ὑπάρχοντα) in v.1, which the agent has squandered.[47] Few would have regarded wealth as something "inherently evil," which is demonstrated by the commentary on Deut 6:5 in m. Ber. 9.5: " '[thou shalt love the LORD thy God …] with all thy strength' " [that is], 'with all thy wealth (mammon).' "[48] When money was obtained from bribes, fraud, oppression, or usury, it is identified as tainted (see Tg. Onq. on Gen 37:26; Sam. Tg. 12:3). By contrast, Jesus always uses the term "Mammon" in a derogatory sense; it is something inherently evil and dangerous.

"Unrighteous Mammon" (τοῦ μαμωνᾶ τῆς ἀδικίας, an attributive or Hebraic genitive) can refer to ill-gotten gains, but, for Jesus, there is no such thing as "righteous Mammon." If "unrighteousness" (ἀδικία) connotes what is false and untrustworthy (John 7:18; Rom 2:8; 2 Thess 2:12),[49] the phrase implies that all wealth is untrustworthy and deceives with false promises. It provides no real security. Caird contends that for Jesus, "All money, however acquired, is tainted unless it is used in God's service."[50] The transliteration "Mammon" is kept in the translation rather than rendering it as "money" because it retains a negative connotation as something (like an idol) that competes with God for human devotion.

Make friends for yourselves "with [ἐκ] unrighteous Mammon" is a prepositional phrase meaning "by means of." The prodigal son threw away his money (διασκόρπισεν) in high living, but it won him no friends and his habitation became a pigsty (15:13 – 15). The agent wasted his master's money (διασκορπίζων, 16:1), but then used it in hopes of gaining friends on earth among his master's debtors to be received into their houses. He recognized that money could be a means for securing his next life. The money was not his; it belonged to his master. In the same way, Jesus believes that our money is not ours but belongs to God.[51] The "friends" are likely to be "the poor."

The phrase "when it fails" hints that Mammon is destined to give out. It is not a question of if it should come to pass but when it will. It will be of no use in the world to come, as Zephaniah makes clear: "Neither their silver nor their gold will be able to save them on the day of the LORD's wrath" (Zeph 1:18a; see also 1 En. 63:10: "Our souls are satisfied with the mammon of unrighteousness, yet for all that we descend into the flame of Sheol's pain"). It has no clout in heaven because its shine will be eclipsed by the glory of God. Therefore, it becomes useless to its owner, as illustrated in the

---

45. See Jeremias, The Parables of Jesus, 45 – 46.

46. Friedrich Hauck, "μαμωνᾶς," TDNT, 4:388 – 89; H. P. Rüger, "μαμωνᾶς," ZNW 63 (1973): 127 – 31.

47. See m. Sanh. 1:1, "cases concerning property [mammon]."

48. Max Wilcox, "Mammon," ABD, 4:490. See Prov 3:9, "Honor the LORD with your wealth."

49. Evans, St. Luke, 598.

50. Caird, Saint Luke, 189.

51. This pious conviction is expressed in m. ʾAbot 3:7: "Give unto him what is his for thou and what thou hast are his; and it is written in David, "For all things come of thee, and of thine own have we given thee [1 Chr 29:14]."

parables of the rich fool ("and the things you have hoarded, whose will they be?" 12:20) and of the rich man who enjoyed good things in his life but suffered torment in death (16:25). Jesus' advice to sell your possessions and give alms to store up treasure in heaven that "will not run out" (12:33) becomes more urgent.

The agent only hoped that he would be taken into the houses of others after being discharged from his position. His security will last only as long as their houses last, and, since they are debtors, that security looks shaky. The disciples, by contrast, hope to be taken into eternal tabernacles beyond this world when they die. Their security is ensured by God and lasts forever. Jesus speaks of being received into "eternal habitations" (εἰς τὰς αἰωνίους σκηνάς) because it reflects the image of God's tabernacling or sheltering his people in heaven (Rev 7:15; 21:3). It refers to the home of those who have found favor with God (16:22; 23:43).

The "they" who will "receive you" again may be "the poor," who form a welcoming committee for their benefactors. Or, "they" might refer to (1) one's "good works," which are personified and judged by the rabbis to be advocates (Tob 4:7 – 11; 12:8 – 9; m. ʾAbot 4:11; t. Peʾah 4:21; b. B. Bat. 10a; b. Šabb. 32a); (2) "the angels," who whisk Lazarus to the bosom of Abraham (16:22); or (3) a circumlocution for God (see 12:20; m. Yoma 8:9).

16:10 – 12 The one who is trustworthy with what is insignificant will be faithful with what is much more significant; and the one who is untrustworthy with what is insignificant will be untrustworthy with what is much more significant. If therefore you are not trustworthy with unrighteous Mammon, who will entrust you with true riches? And if you are not trustworthy with what belongs to another, who will give you what is yours? (ὁ πιστὸς ἐν ἐλαχίστῳ καὶ ἐν πολλῷ πιστός ἐστιν, καὶ ὁ ἐν ἐλαχίστῳ ἄδικος καὶ ἐν πολλῷ ἄδικός ἐστιν. εἰ οὖν ἐν τῷ ἀδίκῳ μαμωνᾷ πιστοὶ οὐκ ἐγένεσθε, τὸ ἀληθινὸν τίς ὑμῖν πιστεύσει; καὶ εἰ ἐν τῷ ἀλλοτρίῳ πιστοὶ οὐκ ἐγένεσθε, τὸ ὑμέτερον τίς ὑμῖν δώσει;).

The three aphorisms express how masters normally deal with their slaves. They reward trustworthiness with more trust; they penalize untrustworthiness with denial of trust. The aphorisms, however, are not examples of worldly wisdom; they have eschatological implications and apply to the way God will deal with his servants. They assert that how one uses money in this world (a testing ground) will determine what one will receive in the next world. The reference to "trustworthiness" may help us see that Jesus does not advocate dishonesty or brazen opportunism, as this parable might imply when mistakenly interpreted. Disciples are to be trustworthy. They are only to imitate the steward's quick-witted action in the face of peril. Trustworthiness in what is "insignificant" (ἐν ἐλαχίστῳ) is a condition for promotion to be trusted with something greater. "What is insignificant" refers to material possessions. In Jesus' estimation they are trivial. Righteously disposing of Mammon by helping the poor, for example, will lead to being entrusted by God with true wealth.

In the same way, trustworthiness with a specious thing like Mammon that belongs to this world is a condition for being entrusted with what is genuine (τὸ ἀληθινόν). Trustworthiness in what belongs to another (ἐν τῷ ἀλλοτρίῳ) is a condition for being given what is "your own" (τὸ ὑμέτερον). This statement implicitly expresses that wealth does not belong to its presumed owner on earth. It reaffirms the basic premise that everything belongs to God and is on temporary loan to humans, who are fools if they think it is theirs. Wealth has been given to us by God in trust to use in the service of others. What is "your own" relates to the

Father's good pleasure to give Jesus' little flock the kingdom (12:32; see 18:29 – 30). If ἀλλότριος refers to "what is foreign to you" or "contrary to your own concerns," it implies that wealth is an alien possession. It is something foreign to the children of light who have broken free from its power.

16:13 **"No servant is able to serve two masters, for he will hate the one and love the other, or he will help the one and disregard the other. You are not able to serve God and Mammon!"** (οὐδεὶς οἰκέτης δύναται δυσὶ κυρίοις δουλεύειν· ἢ γὰρ τὸν ἕνα μισήσει καὶ τὸν ἕτερον ἀγαπήσει, ἢ ἑνὸς ἀνθέξεται καὶ τοῦ ἑτέρου καταφρονήσει.

οὐ δύνασθε θεῷ δουλεύειν καὶ μαμωνᾷ). A slave could be the property of two masters, but the slave could not give equal devotion to both. One or the other master will rule. This conclusion to the discussion of the use of money means that one's ultimate allegiance cannot be divided. One cannot be devoted to making money and to serving God. The two are mutually exclusive. One is either the slave of Christ or the slave of Mammon (see Rom 6:19 – 22). Money is akin to a demonic power that can mesmerize us with its attractions and claim our service. The double-minded person will inevitably fall sway to money and devote energy to its service.[52]

Theology in Application

1. The Inevitability of Having to Give an Account to God

The children of this age are smarter than the children of light when it comes to acting in their best interests. They are motivated by self-interest and self-preservation and concern themselves only with this world. The sons of light should be concerned about the world to come, but they act more like the rich man in the parable that follows. If the children of light understood what their true self-interest is, they would be motivated by it to act no less decisively and boldly than the children of this age, and they would then concentrate their energies on serving others. They would use whatever worldly opportunities they have to attain otherworldly ends by helping the needy in this world.

The agent in this parable only thinks in terms of how to make his life in the here and now comfortable after he has to give an account of his earthly stewardship. Christians know that all will have to give an account to God (Matt 12:36; 1 Cor 3:12 – 15; 1 Pet 4:5). We should focus our energies on doing what is pleasing to God.

2. The Dangers of Wealth

Accepting and applying the point of this parable and the statements that interpret it are far more difficult than figuring out the point of the parable. The parable asks,

52. Barth, "The Dishonest Steward and His Lord," 66.

"How can I as one of the children of light make the best use of money now so that when I am unemployed in this world (i.e., dead), I will have a new employer (God) in the age to come who will give me an eternal home?"[53] Wealth means "weal" or "well-being," but this is deceptive. How does one define well-being? The accumulation of riches will do one no good when one is dead. It can do one good when death comes if one has used material wealth wisely in life.

This view is illustrated in rabbinic literature when a pagan asks R. Akiba, " 'Why does your God, being the lover of the needy, not Himself provide for their support?' R. Akiba replied: 'By charity wealth is to be made a means of salvation; God the Father of both the rich and the poor, wants the one to help the other, and thus to make the world a household of love' " (*b. B. Bat.* 10a).[54] The parable and its interpretation imply that sharing wealth is not just something good that should be done for the poor but is a means of saving one's soul from danger. As a spiritual discipline, giving to others loosens the grip of Mammon on one's heart. It explains why Jesus commands disciples to give to those who beg of you (6:30). It is not simply because they are in such great need but because we are.[55] In doing something for others we do something for ourselves.

Bovon claims that since Mammon "is the negative counterpart of God, it is logical that the renunciation of possessions becomes the corollary of faith in Christ the Lord."[56] Is one a slave to Mammon or slave to God? But it is more than that. As Barth observes, wherever money is at issue there is danger to life. It is not a neutral or harmless commodity; it possesses high voltage and explosive energy.[57] It strikes reverence in the heart. The danger of Mammon is that it creates a love of acquisition and an appetite for self-gratification, while deadening the instinct for self-sacrifice. It deceives one into believing that it offers security (see Luke 12:15). Gagnon captures the dilemma for Christians:

> Yet the people of God too often succumb to the allure of money and material possessions, treating them as ends in themselves and as objects that bring security by the very possession of them. More precisely, they find themselves caught between two different systems and two different ends: claiming attachment to the world above and the age to come, but in their "Mammon" working to secure their life in this world below and this present age. If their end is consonant with their status as "children of light," then money and resources must be viewed as objects to serve that end and contribute to its attainment.[58]

53. Gagnon, "A Second Look," 4.

54. See also *Lev. Rab.* 34:4: "If the poor man stands in the company of the medium man and says to him: 'Give me charity, and he gives to him, then 'the Lord giveth light to the eyes of them both'; the one obtains temporal life and the other the life of the world to come."

55. I am indebted to Emily McGowan for this insight.

56. François Bovon, "Studies in Luke-Acts: Retrospect and Prospect," in *Studies in Early Christianity* (Grand Rapids: Baker, 2003), 34.

57. Barth, "The Dishonest Steward and His Lord," 69.

58. Gagnon, "A Second Look," 4 – 5.

Derrett notes: "When we give to God we give him what is his; and when we give to the poor we merely redistribute God's wealth."[59] According to Jesus, the wise use of money is to get rid of it through almsgiving (11:40 – 41; 12:33 – 34; 19:1 – 10), canceling debts, and loaning without expecting to get anything back (6:34 – 35). This generosity with one's possessions is what Luke tells us characterized the early Christian community (Acts 2:44 – 45; 4:32, 34; 6:1 – 6; 11:27 – 30). The foolish use of money is exemplified by the parables of the rich fool (12:13 – 21) and the rich man and Lazarus (16:19 – 31), and, in Acts, the stories of Judas (Acts 1:16 – 20) and Ananias and Sapphira (5:1 – 11).

---

59. Derrett, _Law in the New Testament_, 74.

49

Luke 16:14 – 18

Literary Context

The series of statements in this unit are sandwiched between two parables that both begin, "There was a rich man" (16:1, 19). It exposes the true nature of those who might reject Jesus' teaching about wealth expressed in the parables and offers a caveat that Jesus' teaching accords with the law. The Pharisees, declared here to be "lovers of money," become foils who represent those who appear to be righteous but scoff at Jesus' teaching about Mammon. Their piety is a sham. Being a lover of money cancels out any claim to righteousness and puts one in the class of an idolater. The statement about the permanence of the law (16:17) prepares for the conclusion of the next parable about the adequacy of the law and the prophets on this subject (16:29) and the ironic prediction, "If they do not listen to Moses and the prophets, they will not be persuaded if someone rose from the dead" (16:31).

Main Idea

The teaching of Jesus on money accords with God's will expressed in the law and the prophets. Those who reject it cannot regard themselves as righteous.

Translation

Luke 16:14–18

16:14a	Narrative aside	**The Pharisees, . . .** **who are lovers of money,**
b	Response of bystanders	**. . . were listening to all these things** and **were mocking him.**
15	Rebuke	And **he said to them,** *"You are those who make yourselves look upright in the eyes of others,* *but God knows your hearts, because what is exalted among humans is an*↵ *abomination before God.*
16a	Explanation	*Up until John, [there were only] the law and the prophets.*
b		*Since then, the good news of the reign of God is proclaimed, and everyone*↵ *is being pressed to enter it.*
17	Clarification of the law's permanence	*It would be easier for heaven and earth to pass away than for one comma*↵ *to drop out of the law.*
18	Substantiation of the clarification	*Everyone who divorces his wife and marries another commits adultery,* *and the one who marries a woman divorced from her husband commits*↵ *adultery."*

Structure and Literary Form

The structure consists of a response to the previous sayings by dubious Pharisees, who serve as a foil. Jesus' rebuke of their false righteousness follows, coupled with a statement about the spiritual crisis created by the preaching of the reign of God since John. The new situation is altogether different from the time of the law and the prophets and demands a decision. This statement is followed by a caveat that the law and the prophets are not passé. This caution is confirmed by an axiom from Jesus' teaching that is applied figuratively. As marriage is designed to be a permanent relationship, so the law and the prophets are a permanent expression of God's will.

Exegetical Outline

→ **I. The Pharisees' reaction to the previous teaching on money (16:14)**

  II. Jesus' condemning response (16:15)

  III. The newness and urgency associated with the proclamation of the reign of God (16:16)

  IV. The reaffirmation of the validity of the law (16:17 – 18)

Explanation of the Text

16:14 The Pharisees, who are lovers of money, were listening to all these things and were mocking him (ἤκουον δὲ ταῦτα πάντα οἱ Φαρισαῖοι φιλάργυροι ὑπάρχοντες, καὶ ἐξεμυκτήριζον αὐτόν). The Pharisees shift from grumbling about Jesus' association with sinners (15:2) to open disdain over his teaching on money. Luke explains their scoffing with an aside that lifts the veil on their hidden motives. They are "lovers of money." Jesus' teaching about money emphasizes giving alms, inviting the down-and-outs to banquets, and not leaving beggars to starve to death at one's doorstep. Danker is therefore right that a "lover of money" is someone who is stingy when it comes to the poor (see 4 Macc 2:8 – 9).[1]

Not all Pharisees were lovers of money, but they serve as the scapegoats in this section, representatives of those who pass themselves off as devoutly obedient to God but whose greater obeisance to the things of this world proves the contrary. This sin is not simply one among many but is "the ultimate sin of idolatry."[2] In *T. Jud* 18:2, 6 and 19:1, the idolater is associated with the money lover.[3] The Pharisees are singled out as a cautionary example because others esteemed them as paragons of religious virtue and respected their decrees. God, however, knows what truly lurks in their hearts, as does Jesus, who has already reproached them for being full of greed and wickedness (11:39). The truth comes out when they not only do not heed Jesus' warning about the dangers of Mammon but mock it. Luke's narrative aside reveals this divine point of view to the audience and further undercuts any claims by the Pharisees to be upright religious leaders. They may believe that money is

a sign of God's favor, a rightful reward for their right conduct. It is not.

16:15 And he said to them, "You are those who make yourselves look upright in the eyes of others, but God knows your hearts, because what is exalted among humans is an abomination before God" (καὶ εἶπεν αὐτοῖς· ὑμεῖς ἐστε οἱ δικαιοῦντες ἑαυτοὺς ἐνώπιον τῶν ἀνθρώπων, ὁ δὲ θεὸς γινώσκει τὰς καρδίας ὑμῶν· ὅτι τὸ ἐν ἀνθρώποις ὑψηλὸν βδέλυγμα ἐνώπιον τοῦ θεοῦ). The Greek reads literally: "You are those who justify yourselves before human beings" (ὑμεῖς ἐστε οἱ δικαιοῦντες ἑαυτοὺς ἐνώπιον τῶν ἀνθρώπων). It implies that the Pharisees are primarily interested in creating the outward appearance of righteousness (see 18:9) to win honor from humans. Approval from those who gaze with admiration at their faux piety has more immediate rewards than approval from God, who is less easily impressed and whose rewards await the age to come.

Outward displays of piety can be deceiving, and Jesus has made it clear that the Pharisees and lawyers are specialists in deluding both others and themselves with their religiosity (11:39 – 54; 12:1). Their positive self-evaluation flies in the face of God's evaluation of them. To "make [*themselves*] look upright" also sets them apart from those who "justif[y] *God*" (7:29). The problem here is that the Pharisees consider themselves "just" despite holding a view about money that is antithetical to God's.

What humans exalt is left undefined, but from the immediate context it can include the desire for honor (14:7 – 14), for exclusivity (15:1 – 2), for Mammon (16:13), and for luxurious comfort

---

1. Danker, *Jesus and the New Age*, 282.
2. Moxnes, *The Economy of the Kingdom*, 151.

3. T. E. Schmidt, "Burden, Barrier, Blasphemy: Wealth in Matt 6:33, Luke 14:33, and Luke 16:15," *TJ* 9 (1988): 181.

(16:19). These things are an "abomination before God" because humans exalt and prefer them over God. The term "abomination" (βδέλυγμα) appears in the LXX in the polemic against idolatry (Deut 7:25 – 26; 1 Kgs 14:24; Isa 1:13; 44:19; 66:3). The implication is that the Pharisees serve Mammon, and those who serve Mammon are idolaters. Since there is no call for them to change their attitudes and behavior, as in 11:39 – 41, one may assume that they are regarded as so hardened in their ways that repentance is now nearly impossible.

16:16 Up until John, [there were only] the law and the prophets. Since then, the good news of the reign of God is proclaimed, and everyone is being pressed to enter it (ὁ νόμος καὶ οἱ προφῆται μέχρι Ἰωάννου· ἀπὸ τότε ἡ βασιλεία τοῦ θεοῦ εὐαγγελίζεται καὶ πᾶς εἰς αὐτὴν βιάζεται). The phrase "until John" (μέχρι Ἰωάννου) may be inclusive of John as belonging to the period of the law and the prophets or exclusive of him as belonging to the new era of salvation. Jesus qualifies his earlier affirmation that John is the greatest of the prophets by stating that the least in the reign of God is greater than he is (7:26 – 28). This surprising diminution of John's status implies that he belongs to the era of the law and the prophets (compare Paul and Moses in 2 Cor 3:4 – 18).

This ranking is confirmed in Acts, which characterizes Luke's gospel narrative as an account of all that *Jesus* began to do (Acts 1:1), asserts that the message of salvation spread throughout Galilee

after John's immersion ministry (10:36 – 37), and makes clear that John's water immersion was superseded by immersion in the Holy Spirit (1:5; 19:1 – 7). John urgently summoned the people to an immersion of repentance in preparation for the coming reign of God and inaugurated something new, the good news of the reign of God. This good news is embodied in Jesus' ministry and surpasses the epoch of the law and the prophets. John serves as a transitional figure for Luke because he can use the verb "to proclaim good news" (εὐαγγελίζω) with John as the subject (3:18).[4] He thinks of him as standing in both eras.[5]

How is this reference to John relevant to the context of a controversy over Mammon? Luke has informed his audience that the people submitted to John's immersion and justified God; that is, they acknowledged God's plan that was coming to light and making a claim on them. The Pharisees, by contrast, are singled out for rejecting God's purpose for themselves by refusing to repent and be immersed (7:29 – 30). Luke does not simply record that John preached repentance and immersed the crowd but provides an excerpt of his message condemning injustice and insisting that repentance requires sharing with the poor (3:10 – 14). The Pharisees' "love of money," then, would be a primary reason why they turned a deaf ear to John's call to repent and why they brush off the new period in salvation history that his preaching began.

The Greek contains no verb in the phrase "the

---

4. The verb appears ten times in Luke, fifteen times in Acts, and only once in the other gospels (Matt 11:5).

5. We need not rehash the debate with Conzelmann that Luke divided God's dealings with his people in three successive epochs: the period of Israel recorded in the Old Testament, the period of Jesus' ministry in the center of time, and the period of the church (*The Theology of St. Luke*, 16, 22 – 27). This theory, applied to this verse, led him to argue that John was excluded from the kingdom. Most recent scholars would affirm the uniqueness of Jesus' ministry while seeing John as a transitional figure who is involved in both eras. K. N. Giles

correctly recognizes that Luke thinks in terms of "one unfolding plan in which important events are carefully prepared for and integrated with one another" ("The Church in the Gospel of Luke," 122). For a helpful survey, see Michael Bachmann, "Johannes des Täufer bei Lukas: Nachzügler oder Vorläufer," in *Wort in der Zeit: Neutestamentliche Studien: Festgabe für Karl Heinrich Rengstorf* (ed. W. Haubeck and M. Bachmann; Leiden: Brill, 1964), 123 – 55. For a more general discussion of the reception of Conzelmann's periodization of salvation history, see François Bovon, *Luke the Theologian* (2nd rev. ed; Waco, TX: Baylor Univ. Press, 2006), 11 – 77.

law and the prophets until John," and interpreters supply a variety of options: the law and the prophets "were in effect" (NRSV); "were" (REB); "lasted" (NAB); "were in force" (GWT); "were proclaimed" (NIV); "were your guides" (NLT). The context makes clear that Jesus does not wish to imply that the law and the prophets have now been superseded and can be scrapped. Nolland's translation and interpretation best grasps the intention that the law and the prophets have been supplemented by the good news of God that Jesus proclaims: "[There was only] the law and the prophets until John."[6]

Moses and the prophets govern how one relates to one's neighbor (10:25 – 28) and how the rich man and his brothers should live to avoid torment in Hades (16:29, 31). The law of Moses, the prophets, and the Psalms also map out and clarify the meaning of the ministry, death, and resurrection of Jesus (24:44; Acts 3:11 – 26; 28:23). The law and the prophets are the foundation of Christian preaching of the gospel (Acts 13:15).

The advent of God's reign delivers something new, and it leaves the Pharisees aghast because it contravenes their interpretation of the law. It offers the possibility for all sorts of sinners and disreputable people to submit to God to escape the fiery wrath to come (3:10 – 14; 4:36; 5:26; 7:16 – 17; 9:43; 18:43). It also breaks Satan's oppressive stranglehold (13:10 – 17).

The proclamation of the good news of God's reign marks a dramatic shift so that the law and the prophets must now be understood "in light of the manifestation of God's purpose within the ministry of Jesus."[7] The law and the prophets, however, are not to be relegated to the dustbin of history. They must be interpreted differently in terms of God's grace for sinners. This was the stumbling block for the Pharisees and for some in the early church as God's grace was extended to include even Gentile sinners.

How to translate the verb I render "being pressed" (βιάζεται) presents a notorious problem. Is it to be read as a passive or middle voice? As a passive voice, it can mean "to be violated, to be forced, to be oppressed." As a middle voice, which is the most common usage, it can mean "to force a way through, to use force upon, to violate, to urge." Does it have a positive or negative connotation in this context? Are people physically assaulting the reign of God, or are they metaphorically taking the reign of God by storm, that is, zealously pushing their way into the kingdom? Who is meant by "everyone" (πᾶς)?

If the verb is rendered positively, as the majority of versions do, it is demonstrably untrue that "everyone tries to enter it by force" (NRSV, a conative sense), or "everyone forces a way in" (REB), or "forces his way into it" (ESV). The Pharisees, for example, do not rush to enter the reign of God but scurry in the opposite direction. The parables of the children in the marketplace (7:32 – 34) and of the sower (8:5 – 15) also contradict this interpretation. Even would-be followers of Jesus do not push their way into God's reign but try to put off their commitment to attend to family responsibilities (9:59 – 62), and the reign of God creates violent division within families because not all (12:51 – 53) strive ardently to enter it but some resist it.

The same kind of problem rises from the negative hostile rendering, "everyone uses force against it."[8] This is manifestly untrue. The Pharisees have not physically assaulted Jesus or plotted his death. Only Herod might qualify as one who has done violence to the kingdom by beheading John (9:9) and seeking to kill Jesus (13:31).

---

6. Nolland, *Luke*, 2:813.

7. Green, *The Gospel of Luke*, 603.

8. This interpretation best fits the parallel saying in Matt 11:12.

Rendering this verb as a passive "everyone is pressed to enter it" (see NET; NRSV marginal note) best fits the context and the universal reference to "everyone." It would parallel the passive "is proclaimed" (εὐαγγελίζεται) in the first clause and match the images in previous parables of compelling persons to enter the banquet (14:23), resolutely searching for what has been lost (15:1 – 10), and pleading with an elder son to join the party to celebrate his younger brother's return (15:25 – 32). It would also fit the use of the verb in the LXX to mean "to urge or to invite insistently" (Gen 33:11; Judg 13:15 – 16; 19:7; 2 Sam 13:25, 27; 2 Kgs 5:23 [textual variant]; see also 4 Macc 2:8; 8:24; 11:25). Luke uses the more intensive form of the verb (παραβιάζομαι) in 24:29 and Acts 16:15 to mean "to urge strongly, to prevail upon" (see LXX, 1 Sam 28:23; 2 Kgs 2:17; 5:16). It does not connote forcing people against their will.

A papyrus document (*P.Oxy.* II:294:16 – 18, dated around AD 22) uses the verb with a similar meaning: "I (Sarapion) am being pressed by friends to become a member of the household of Apollonius, the chief usher."[9] The urgency of "being pressed" does not imply that persons are compelled to enter against their will, as if at gunpoint, but recognizes that it is a "narrow door" (13:24) and it requires pressure for people to choose to enter it. Cortés and Gatti conclude that the verb refers here to moral force or insistence and translate the clause, "and every person is *insistently urged* to enter into it (the kingdom)."[10] This interpretation also makes the best sense of "everyone" (πᾶς) and the universality of God's reign.

Rendering the phrase as "being pressed" or

"insistently urged" adds another distinction to the time of the announcement of the reign of God compared with the time of the law and the prophets. Repentance has always been obligatory, but now it is all the more urgent because what God is doing in Jesus' ministry is climactic and final.[11] It is not just the fate of the nation Israel that is at stake; it is the fate of their very souls.

16:17 It would be easier for heaven and earth to pass away than for one comma to drop out of the law (εὐκοπώτερον δέ ἐστιν τὸν οὐρανὸν καὶ τὴν γῆν παρελθεῖν ἢ τοῦ νόμου μίαν κεραίαν πεσεῖν). This statement affirms what all faithful Jews believed about the perpetuity of the law.[12] The "comma" (κεραία) refers to something projecting like a horn and may refer to a serif of a Hebrew letter that distinguishes it from a similar letter. It is not some insignificant squiggle, since it is a crucial mark that denotes what letter is intended. In the same way, commas, when they are misplaced or altered, can change the whole meaning of a sentence.

The statement does not say that the law will not pass away, but that heaven and earth will sooner pass into extinction than that the law will fail. The law and the prophets, therefore, cannot be dismissed or ignored. Those who insist on obedience to the law, as the Pharisees do, had better listen carefully to what the law says about care for the poor (let alone what it foretells about the reign of God and the Messiah). In asserting the compatibility of the Mosaic law with reason, the author of 4 Macc maintains:

As soon as one adopts a way of life in accordance

9. Cited by Juan B. Cortés and Florence M. Gatti, "On the Meaning of Luke 16:16," *JBL* 106 (1987): 253.

10. Ibid., 248; see also P.-H. Menoud, "The Meaning of the Verb βιάζεται in Luke 16.16," in *Jesus Christ and the Faith: A Collection of Studies* (trans. E. M. Paul; Pittsburgh: Pickwick, 1978), 193 – 201.

11. John J. Kilgallen, "The Purpose of Luke's Divorce Text (16,18)," *Bib* 76 (1995): 234.

12. See Deut 4:2; Bar. 4:1; 4 Ezra 9:37; *Jub.* 2:33; 6:14; *2 Bar.* 77:15; Philo, *Moses* 2.3; Josephus, *Ag. Ap.* 1.8 §§42 – 43.

with the law, even though a lover of money, one is forced to act contrary to natural ways and to lend without interest to the needy and to cancel the debt when the seventh year arrives. If one is greedy, one is ruled by the law through reason so that one neither gleans the harvest nor gathers the last grapes from the vineyard. (4 Macc 2:8 – 9)

From this perspective, if one simply obeys the letter of the law, even when disinclined to obey it, it will prevent one from giving way to natural inclinations toward gluttony and selfishness.

16:18 Everyone who divorces his wife and marries another commits adultery, and the one who marries a woman divorced from her husband commits adultery (πᾶς ὁ ἀπολύων τὴν γυναῖκα αὐτοῦ καὶ γαμῶν ἑτέραν μοιχεύει, καὶ ὁ ἀπολελυμένην ἀπὸ ἀνδρὸς γαμῶν μοιχεύει). Nothing prepares the reader for a saying about divorce in this context, and it does not seem an apt conclusion to the preceding statements or a lead-in to the following parable. Some contend that Luke inserted it here to mean that the law and the prophets remain valid but must be refracted through the lens of Jesus' interpretation of the law. As Nolland argues, "The present verse is meant to be illustrative of the way in which the demands of the kingdom of God take up and confirm the imperatives of the law and the prophets (Exod 20:14; Lev 18:20; Deut 5:18; Mal 2:14 – 16), but go on to be yet more demanding in very specific ways."[13] This view is more suited to the Matthean context of the antitheses, where the divorce teaching appears and Jesus says, "It has been said ... but I tell you ..." (Matt 5:17 – 20; 31 – 32). That backdrop appears to be read into Luke.

Another option is that Jesus uses the divorce issue to condemn the Pharisees' misinterpretation of God's intention for marriage.[14] Again, this view assumes Mark's context for the divorce saying (Mark 10:2 – 12; see also Matt 19:3 – 9). Luke does not inform the reader what the Pharisees might believe about divorce, so Jesus does not challenge their interpretation. It is also unlikely that "divorce" is added to provide an additional example of what is an abomination to God, because Luke offers no other specific examples of "abominations."[15]

Kilgallen argues that this assertion is not included to present Jesus' teaching on divorce and marriage. When compared to the parallels in Matt 5:32; 19:9; Mark 10:11 – 12; and 1 Cor 7:10 – 11, Luke's formulation of the statement suggests that it "had reached the point in tradition where it could be abstracted from its normal context and used as a self-contained *quasi* proverb."[16] Paul appeals to Jesus' teaching in 1 Cor 7:10 – 11 as something the Corinthians would already know. In Luke's context, the saying about the permanence of marriage functions to substantiate the statement about the law and the prophets.[17]

The argument runs like this: the presence of the reign of God creates something new and "the present *is* different from the past." That newness, however, does not mean that the law and the prophets are no longer in effect. Jesus squelches such a notion with the assertion that they endure, which is then supported by Jesus' well-known view about the indissolubility of marriage.[18] The divorce saying has a figurative function that reinforces the point that Jesus' teaching and the law and the prophets cohere. They can be severed from each other, as a marriage can be sundered, but such a disjoining is outside of God's intention and will have disastrous results.

---

13. Nolland, *Luke*, 2:822.
14. Grundmann, *Das Evangelium nach Lukas*, 324.
15. Contra Johnson, *The Gospel of Luke*, 255.

16. Kilgallen, "The Purpose of Luke's Divorce Text," 233.
17. Ibid., 230.
18. Ibid., 238.

Theology in Application

1. The Continuing Validity of the Law

This connecting unit reiterates that John's prophetic ministry was preparatory (1 – 2; 3:1 – 22; 7:18 – 35) but adds that it marked a bridge that crossed over from the old economy of salvation to the new. With Jesus, a new epoch in salvation history has begun. Luke's Christian readers know that the law does not bring salvation. It is not good news. One thing that is new with the coming of Christ is the justification of sinners on the basis of faith. Luke records Paul asserting this truth in Acts: "I want you to know that through Jesus the forgiveness of sins is proclaimed to you. Through him everyone who believes is set free from every sin, a justification you were not able to obtain under the law of Moses" (Acts 13:38 – 39). This declaration accords with Paul's statements in his letters (Rom 3:20, 24, 26, 28, 30; 5:1; Gal 2:16; 3:11; 5:4).

But Paul's statement that Christ is the end of the law (Rom 10:4) can be misunderstood. George asks, "If the law cannot save but only condemn, if it cannot remove transgressions but actually increases them, if we are no longer under its harsh discipline, if Christ is the end (*telos*) of the law for all who believe, then does the law have any continuing normative significance for the Christian?"[19] The answer is, "Yes, it does" (Rom 7:12), and the problem that this teaching also addresses in this unit is that God's grace can be just as distorted by antinomianism as by legalism (Rom 3:8).

Freedom from the law does not mean freedom from moral restraints. Freedom from sin does not mean freedom to sin. Christ's followers cannot be aloof to moral law. The passage clarifies that the newness Christ brings does not mean that the law and the prophets are now obsolete. The law is not the polar opposite of the gospel but is also the Word of God. It contains God's purposes that point to Christ and are unveiled by him (24:27, 44 – 45). In the context, the ethical thrust of the law and the prophets remains in force. This truth is confirmed by the next parable: Listen to Moses and the prophets (16:29), particularly what they say about care for the poor. One who is subject to the law of Christ (1 Cor 9:21) is subject to the law that commands the love of neighbor.

Luke applies this lesson here in the context to the use of money and care for the poor. Craddock comments, "The realism of these sayings is simply that life consists of a series of seemingly small opportunities."[20] Tests come with the presentation of a poor man, the person in need of a cup of cold water, a visit in prison, or a gift of clothing. Most would not openly identify themselves as money lovers, particularly those with religious commitments (see the warnings in 1 Tim 6:10; 2 Tim 3:1 – 5). Anyone who neglects the poor, however, is a money lover, flouts God's law and his prophets, and is in danger of damnation.

19. Timothy George, *Galatians* (NAC; Nashville: Broadman and Holman, 1994), 268.

20. Craddock, *Luke*, 192.

2. The Permanence of Marriage and the Problem of Divorce

I have argued that the inclusion of Jesus' comment on divorce is not intended to give instructions about divorce and remarriage. Instead, it is used to illustrate something about the permanent validity of the law and the prophets. As marriage binds husband and wife in a permanent union, so the law and the prophets are permanently bound and cannot be jettisoned or disjoined. The humor in a cartoon behind a question asked of a newly married couple, "Are you planning a long marriage following the ceremony?" is rooted in a basic assumption that marriage is a lifetime commitment. Those who pledge in the marriage ceremony that they will to stay together "for better, for worse, for richer, for poorer, in sickness and in health, till death do us part" believe that the permanence of marriage is the premise, not just an ideal.

This assumption may be reflected behind the attitude of those today who live together as husband and wife, yet do not marry. They may fear that marriage is too binding a commitment and they may prove unable to keep their promises. Even Seneca's cynical remark that women in his day no longer blush to be divorced, count the years not by the consuls but by their different marriages, and divorce in order to be married and marry in order to be divorced (*Ben.* 3.16.2) reflects an underlying sense that something is amiss when people engage in serial marital unions. Marriage should not be treated so cavalierly.

In our era, marriages can be legally dissolved in the law court, but it is a fantasy to think that it is possible for the divorced to go back to being single. Whitworth and Keith write, "Divorce is leaving part of the self behind, like the rabbit who escapes the trap by gnawing one leg off."[21] To shift to a less violent metaphor, "married partners are like two plants that have grown together in the same pot for years so that their roots become intertwined. It is well nigh impossible to uproot one without affecting the other."[22] The continuing effects of the marriage union after a divorce are poignantly captured by Elizabeth W. Garber's poem, "The Best Ex-Husband You Could Ever Ask For."[23] It is therefore the church's task to help partners strengthen and maintain the sanctity of their marriages by confronting openly all the forces that can cause them to fall apart.

Marriage provides a wonderful opportunity to expose and then exterminate any forms of selfishness that lurk in our lives. Many, however, ultimately fail in this task. While divorce is a deplorable but inescapable fact of life because of the sinful nature of the human condition, it is not to be treated lightly, but neither is it to be treated as

---

21. Carl A. Whitaker and David V. Keith, "Counseling the Dissolving Marriage," in *Klemer's Counseling in Marital and Sexual Problems: A Clinician's Handbook* (ed. R. F. Strathmann and W. J. Hiebert; 2nd ed.; Baltimore: Williams & Wilkens, 1977), 71.

22. Diana S. Richmond Garland and David E. Garland,

Beyond Companionship: Christians in Marriage (Philadelphia: Westminster, 1986; repr. Eugene, OR: Wipf and Stock, 2003), 169.

23. Elizabeth W. Garber, *Listening Inside the Dance: A Life in Maine Infused with Tango* (Belfast, ME: Illuminated Sea Press, 2005), 20–21.

the unpardonable sin. Any broken marriage falls short of God's will, but this applies to any sin. Then what? Where does one go from there? The principle of the salvage and redemption of broken sinners runs through the gospel of Luke. If someone were to fracture a leg, he or she would go to a specialist to see what can be done to re-build it as best as possible. One cannot turn back the clock and undo the injury, but one must ask what the options are for the future and how God's grace can heal the brokenness.

3. The Evil Toll of Adultery

Jesus' words about adultery may seem harsh, but he does not soft-pedal the evil effects that infidelity has on a marriage. The traditional marriage vow includes the line, "forsaking all others," and infidelity adulterates the marriage bond, not simply the marriage vow. Our culture tends to downplay its effects by using euphemisms such as playing around, having a fling, engaging in hanky-panky, getting a bit on the side. Even the word "affair" diminishes the gravity of the effects of this sin. But it is the worst form of treachery that ravages the lives of the innocent spouse, any children in the marriage, and other family members and friends. It leaves emotional scars that sometimes never heal.

While adultery is done in secret, when it is exposed, as sins inevitably are, it is like a spiritual earthquake that demolishes trust, faith, and self-esteem. It is like pollut-ing a drinking well with poison or releasing a toxic gas into the air ducts of a home. Adultery leaves the innocent spouse subject to humiliation, depression, and suicidal thoughts and causes them to wonder if they could ever be loved again or if they could ever risk loving another again.

It is possible to make up rather than break up after adultery, but the healing pro-cess may take a long time. God is sufficient to bring redemption, restoration, and reconciliation to shattered lives and shipwrecked marriages.

50

Luke 16:19 – 31

Literary Context

This parable illustrates two themes that emerge from the preceding sayings. The kingdom is open to everyone, especially to paupers like Lazarus, and the laws concerning such things as the treatment of the poor are still in force. If one ignores Moses and the prophets, one will be in danger of being excluded.[1] It also illustrates that what is esteemed among humans is an abomination to God. The rich man is clean, well off, and, according to the conventional wisdom of his set, favored by God. By contrast, Lazarus is unclean, penniless, and, one might assume, disfavored by God. Neither prosperity nor impoverishment is a reliable gauge of a person's standing with God. The rich man demonstrates total ignorance of Jesus' advice in 14:13 – 14: "Whenever you give a reception, invite the poor, crippled, lame, blind. You will be blessed, because they cannot repay you, for you will be repaid in the resurrection of the just." As a result, the rich man is damned.

---

1. Talbert, *Reading Luke*, 159.

Main Idea

Wealth is not a barometer of one's standing before God. It is both a source of peril and obligation. Using it wrongly and ignoring the welfare of the unfortunate will bring divine judgment.

Translation

(See next page.)

Structure and Literary Form

This parable highlights a stark contrast between the lifestyles of the rich man and poor Lazarus. Their fates intersect because Lazarus has been placed at the gate of the rich man and because they both die at the same time. In death, their circumstances are reversed. The parable's structure divides into three parts: a narration of what occurs on earth before death (16:19 – 22); a dialogue between the rich man and Abraham in the life after death (16:22 – 26); and a continuation of the dialogue applied to the living (16:27 – 31).

Exegetical Outline

➡ **I. Before death: enjoying luxury in the face of starvation (16:19 – 21)**
  II. Death: burial by men and delivery by angels (16:22)
  III. After death: the great reversal (16:23 – 31)
    A. Rich man's first request: Have Lazarus relieve my torment (16:23 – 24)
    B. Abraham's response: The chasm is unbridgeable (16:25 – 26)
    C. Rich man's second request: Send Lazarus to warn my brothers (16:27 – 28)
    D. Abraham's response: Let them read the Scriptures (16:29 – 31)

Luke 16:19–31

16:19a	Character introduction	*"There was a certain rich man*
b		*and he dressed himself in purple and the finest linen*
c		*and dined sumptuously every day.*
20a	Character introduction	*And there was a certain poor man*
b		*by the name of Lazarus*
c		*who was laid, covered with sores, at the rich⤴ man's gate.*
21a		*And he longed to be filled from the scraps that were falling from the rich⤴ man's table,*
b		*but, it gets worse, dogs came and licked his sores.*
22a	Death	*It so happened that the poor man died,*
b		*and the angels carried him back home to the bosom of Abraham.*
c	Death	*And the rich man died*
d		*and was buried.*
23	Circumstance	*And in Hades he was in torment, and raising his eyes he saw Abraham far⤴ off and Lazarus in his bosom.*
24a	Request (1)	*Crying out, he said,*
		'Father Abraham!
		Have mercy on me
		and send Lazarus to dip the tip of his finger in water and cool off⤴ my tongue,
b	Reason	*because I am suffering pain amidst these flames.'*
25	Rejection/explanation	*Abraham said,*
		'Child!
		Do you remember that you received your good things in your life,
		and Lazarus in turn received only bad?
		But now he is comforted here, and you are suffering pain.
26	Explanation	*And besides this, there is fixed a great chasm between us and you*
		so that those who might want to cross from⤴ here over to you are not able,
		nor are they able to cross over from⤴ there to us.'
27	Request (2)	*He said,*
		'I ask you, then, Father, that you send him to my father's house,
28	Reason	*for I have five brothers,*
		that he might warn them so that⤴ they will not come to this place of torment.'
29	Rejection/explanation	*Abraham said to him,*
		'They have Moses and the prophets, let them read them.'
30	Rebuttal	*But he said,*
		'No, Father Abraham!
		If someone would rise from the dead and go to them, they would repent.'
31	Rejection/explanation	*He said to him,*
		'If they do not listen to Moses and the prophets,
		they will not be persuaded if someone rose from the dead.'"

Explanation of the Text

16:19 There was a certain rich man and he dressed himself in purple and the finest linen and dined sumptuously every day (ἄνθρωπος δέ τις ἦν πλούσιος, καὶ ἐνεδιδύσκετο πορφύραν καὶ βύσσον εὐφραινόμενος καθ᾽ ἡμέραν λαμπρῶς). The introduction of the parable, "There was a certain rich man," is identical to the introduction of the parable in 16:1, and the rich man's character brings with it the same negative associations discussed in the comments on 16:1 – 13. It is unusual for Jesus to describe the clothing of a character, and it serves to characterize the rich man further (see 7:25) and to set him in direct contrast with Lazarus with his sores and rags. The rich man is clothed in garments worthy of a king (Judg 8:26).[2] He also wears the most expensive imported Egyptian underwear. "Finest linen" (βύσσος) was the most delicate and most expensive fabric known to the ancient world.

The diet of the average person was soup, bread, and fruit. Feasting would normally only occur at weddings. The rich man fares sumptuously every day, probably as a connoisseur of the finest cuisine. The verb translated "dine" (εὐφραινόμενος) appears in the parable of the prodigal son (15:23, 24, 29, 32) and can be translated "to make merry" or "to celebrate." It refers here to the enjoyment of food. In the parable of the rich fool, his last wish is "to eat, drink, and live it up" (εὐφραίνου; 12:19).

Lucian portrays a rich man as one who "gorges himself on all these good things, belching, receiving his guest's congratulations and feasting without a break" (*Sat.* 21). He also claims that the poor imagine that the rich were "gorging alone behind closed doors" (*Sat.* 32). In this rich man's case, it is true. Feasting "every day" makes him like the generation of the flood, eating and drinking and completely unaware of the looming calamity that would destroy them (17:27). He lives the good life fencing himself off from the cries of despair outside his gate. The echo from Lam 4:5, "Those who once ate delicacies are destitute in the streets. Those brought up in royal purple now lie on ash heaps," bodes ill for this man (see Rev 17:4).

16:20 And there was a certain poor man by the name of Lazarus who was laid, covered with sores, at the rich man's gate (πτωχὸς δέ τις ὀνόματι Λάζαρος ἐβέβλητο πρὸς τὸν πυλῶνα αὐτοῦ εἱλκωμένος). Lazarus is the only named character in Jesus' parables. The name facilitates the dialogue when the rich man calls out from his torment. That the rich man recognized him and knew his name makes him all the more culpable for ignoring Lazarus's plight. The name also gives Lazarus a measure of personhood. The rich man has no identity except as a rich man.[3]

The etymology of the name "Lazarus" (the Greek form of Eleazar, which, in Hebrew, means "God has helped" or "God is my help") is suggestive but probably eluded Luke's first readers since the evangelist does not explain it (see Matt 1:23; Acts 4:36; 13:8). Nevertheless, Jesus may have chosen this name to hint at the contrast between the self-sufficient rich man, who helps himself (and helps himself to too much), and the utterly dependent Lazarus, whom no one helps except God and whose angels whisk him away to a blessed afterlife.[4]

2. "Purple" (πορφύραν) represents dyes for blue, rose, scarlet, amethyst, and violet that were imported from Tyre. In 1 Macc 8:14, the Romans are praised for not having a king (during the time of the Republic) or wearing purple as a mark of pride.

3. The name for the rich man that is sometimes used, "Dives," derives from the Vulgate translation and means "rich man" in Latin. 𝔓75, the oldest text of Luke, has "rich man whose name was Neves" (ὀνόματι Νευης).

4. See Abrahams, *Studies in Pharisaism and the Gospels*, 203.

Lazarus is described as "laid" or "thrown" (ἐβέβλητο) in front of the rich man's gate. "Laid" may be intransitive and imply that he was ill or crippled. It is used in Matt 8:6 to describe the centurion's servant, who lay paralyzed at home. If it is intransitive, he is as helpless as the victim mugged on the Jericho road and similarly ignored. If it means that he was "laid" by others at this rich man's gate, it raises another issue. He would have been brought to the gate of rich man's home with the expectation that he would receive alms.

The word for gate (πυλών) is used especially for the large gates of entrances to temples or dwellings (Acts 12:10; 14:13). It implies that the man has an impressive gateway or gatehouse guarding the entry to his home. It advertises his wealth and keeps out undesirable riffraff. The gate may be closed, but it does not mark an unbridgeable divide like the chasm between heaven and Hades. The rich man can open the gate and pass through it to offer aid to the poor on the other side. Instead, Lazarus is left to suffer from starvation and physical torment within a stone's throw of epicurean excess.

16:21 And he longed to be filled from the scraps that were falling from the rich man's table, but, it gets worse, dogs came and licked his sores (καὶ ἐπιθυμῶν χορτασθῆναι ἀπὸ τῶν πιπτόντων ἀπὸ τῆς τραπέζης τοῦ πλουσίου· ἀλλὰ καὶ οἱ κύνες ἐρχόμενοι ἐπέλειχον τὰ ἕλκη αὐτοῦ). The rich man indulges his every desire, but Lazarus is described further as longing to be filled with what is falling (τῶν πιπτόντων, present tense) from the rich man's table. Lazarus yearns only to be a scavenger eating out of the rich man's garbage can after the feast is over. He does not dream of being invited to the feast or even having a table for himself. It is not that he envies the delicacies

the rich man enjoys; he wants only to be filled (χορτασθῆναι) as the famished prodigal did (see 15:16; Jas 2:16) with whatever bits might fall off the table for pet dogs to devour (Mark 7:27–28).[5] The rich man with his full belly does not even bother throwing his leftover scraps to Lazarus.

"But even" (ἀλλὰ καί; "not only so but") implies "it gets worse." Lazarus is so weak from hunger that he is too feeble to fend off the dogs nosing him. The original audience would have imagined the ravenous street curs, not cuddly puppies, that ran loose in packs coming to nose around him and lick his sores. Dogs are regarded as unclean animals and are often mentioned as eating the bodies of the dead (1 Kgs 14:11; 16:4; 21:19, 23, 24; 22:38). While the rich man probably ate in ceremonial purity, Lazarus wastes away in the midst of filth. The details contrast someone who has it all with someone who has absolutely nothing.

16:22 It so happened that the poor man died, and the angels carried him back home to the bosom of Abraham. And the rich man died and was buried (ἐγένετο δὲ ἀποθανεῖν τὸν πτωχὸν καὶ ἀπενεχθῆναι αὐτὸν ὑπὸ τῶν ἀγγέλων εἰς τὸν κόλπον Ἀβραάμ· ἀπέθανεν δὲ καὶ ὁ πλούσιος καὶ ἐτάφη). Death strikes both men. In Ps.-Phoc. 110–113 we read:

> Not to the grave can we take aught of our wealth
> 　or possessions.
> Dead men are equal in death — though God
> 　rules over their spirits.
> Common to all is their fate, common to all is
> 　their homeland,
> All men are equal in Hades, pauper and
> 　monarch together.

Jesus' parable challenges this truism from Hellenistic Jewish wisdom. Lazarus and the rich man

---

5. These may not be crumbs that fell accidentally (see Matt 15:27) but big pieces of bread used to clean or dry the hands after the diners had dipped them into the dishes of gravy (see Jeremias, *The Parables of Jesus*, 184).

are *not* equals in Hades. Only one is in Hades, and Hades is not pictured here as the repose for the spirits of the dead, but as a place of extreme torment.

The rich man died and was buried, and we can assume he had a lavish funeral appropriate for a man of his social class. As a rich man, he may have been buried in an elaborate tomb. What could be expected for Lazarus? There is no mention of a burial. He was destined for a pauper's grave at best, but, contrary to all expectations, Jesus says that he was carried away to the bosom of Abraham by angels. God is never explicitly mentioned in the story, but the readers of Luke know that these angels are God's angels (see 1:11; 2:9; 12:8; Acts 5:19; 8:26; 12:7, 23) and are sent by God (Luke 1:26; Acts 12:11).

The translation of the verb "to be carried back home" (ἀπενεχθῆναι) is based on van der Horst's argument that the compound verb with the preposition "from" (ἀπο-) often connotes the notion of "back to where it belongs" or "deservedness" or "of what is due." He argues that Luke uses the verb here to mean more than that poor Lazarus was "carried away" but to convey that he was taken to Abraham's bosom, where he belonged and where he was entitled to be. Lazarus's conveyance to Abraham's bosom becomes confirmation of the beatitude, "Blessed are the poor, because yours is the reign of God" (6:20).[6]

According to a legend in *T. Ab.* 20:10 – 15, the archangel Michael stood with multitudes of angels beside Abraham when he died, and "they bore his precious soul in their hands in divinely woven linen" and "escorted his precious soul and ascended into heaven, singing the hymn of the thrice holy to God, the master of all, and they set

it (down) for the worship of the God and Father." God then orders:

> Take, then, my friend Abraham into Paradise, where are the tents of the righteous ones and where the mansions of my holy ones, Isaac and Jacob, are in his bosom, where there is no toil, no grief, no moaning, but peace and exultation and endless life and the abodes of my holy ones, Isaac and Jacob, in his bosom, where is not toil, neither grief nor mourning; but peace, and exultation, and life everlasting [cf. *T. Ash.* 6:4 – 5].

Lazarus gets the same royal treatment when he dies that Abraham was imagined to have received.

16:23 – 24 And in Hades he was in torment and raising his eyes he saw Abraham far off and Lazarus in his bosom. Crying out, he said, "Father Abraham! Have mercy on me and send Lazarus to dip the tip of his finger in water and cool off my tongue, because I am suffering pain amidst these flames" (καὶ ἐν τῷ ᾅδῃ ἐπάρας τοὺς ὀφθαλμοὺς αὐτοῦ, ὑπάρχων ἐν βασάνοις, ὁρᾷ Ἀβραὰμ ἀπὸ μακρόθεν καὶ Λάζαρον ἐν τοῖς κόλποις αὐτοῦ. καὶ αὐτὸς φωνήσας εἶπεν· πάτερ Ἀβραάμ, ἐλέησόν με καὶ πέμψον Λάζαρον ἵνα βάψῃ τὸ ἄκρον τοῦ δακτύλου αὐτοῦ ὕδατος καὶ καταψύξῃ τὴν γλῶσσάν μου, ὅτι ὀδυνῶμαι ἐν τῇ φλογὶ ταύτῃ).

The parable's imagery of Hades is found in Jewish literature that describes the afterlife for the wicked: (a) torment (16:23; see 4 Macc 13:15; (b) the dead of one locale being able to see the others (see 4 Ezra 7:31 – 44; 80 – 87, 93; *2 Bar.* 51:5 – 6; *1 En.* 22; *As. Mos.* 10:10); (c) thirst (see 4 Ezra 8:59); (d) flames (see Sir 21:9 – 10; *1 En.* 10:13, 18:11 – 12; 63:10; Isa 66:24). The idea of a yawning chasm is also found in Virgil (*Aen.* 6.540 – 543). These details are not intended to describe the nature of

---

6. P. W. van der Horst, "Abraham's Bosom, the Place Where He Belonged: A Short Note on ἀπενεχθῆναι in Luke 16:22," *NTS* 52 (2006): 142 – 44.

Hades but to underscore the great reversal that has taken place for the two men in the afterlife. The rich man now experiences the hellish existence that Lazarus endured on earth, but the torment is exponentially greater and irreversible.

Being in the bosom of Abraham is an image for a blessed state in death.[7] If it refers to a child lying in his parent's lap (John 1:18; *b. Yebam.* 77a), this feature draws a sharp contrast between the rich man who cries out to Father Abraham, while Lazarus is embraced by Abraham on his lap.[8] A feast is in mind (see 13:28–30), and Lazarus, of all people, has the place of honor and is able to lean close toward Abraham in his bosom as the beloved disciple did with Jesus (see John 13:23; *2 Clem* 4:5). Unlike the guests who scrambled for the seat of honor next to the host (Luke 14:7–14), Lazarus, who never was invited to an earthly banquet, is escorted to the seat of honor by angels.

The point is clear: a beggar, once sick and hungry with no earthly pretensions, becomes rich in eternity. Lazarus is indeed helped and comforted. The rich man, once healthy and wealthy and enjoying nothing but the finest in life, now suffers the worst torment in death, his last two requests denied. The parable luridly illustrates the theme found throughout Luke of the exaltation of the poor and the humbling of the rich (1:52–53; 4:18; 6:21, 24, 25; 16:15). It also encapsulates Old Testament themes that God will not ignore the affliction of the afflicted (Ps 22:24–26), and those who close their ears to the cry of the poor will themselves cry out and not be heard (Prov 21:13; see *1 En.* 101–3).

Lazarus, lying sick on the ground, used to have to look up while the rich man passed by him going through his gate. Now the rich man must look up to see Abraham and Lazarus at a heavenly feast. He

was so used to power in his old life and the clout his money gave him that he acts as if things are unchanged even in Hades. He does not repent and thinks that he can order Abraham to send Lazarus to be his lackey. This detail reveals that he recognized Lazarus and knew his name! He could not have been unaware that Lazarus was lying at his gate. Though he never spared a thought for Lazarus's needs during his lifetime, the rich man, self-centered even in death, thinks he should minister to his suffering now. How many times did Lazarus cry out to him as he went through his gate, "Have mercy on me!" (see 17:13; 18:38–39)? The rich man could have eased the agony of Lazarus on earth, but Lazarus cannot help the rich man in Hades.

The rich man's appeal to Abraham as "father" is precisely what John warned against (Luke 3:8). One's fate is determined by one's mercy toward the poor, not by one's relationship to Abraham or through the merits of the fathers.

16:25–26 Abraham said, "Child! Do you remember that you received your good things in your life, and Lazarus in turn received only bad? But now he is comforted here, and you are suffering pain. And besides this, there is fixed a great chasm between us and you so that those who might want to cross from here over to you are not able, nor are they able to cross over from there to us" (εἶπεν δὲ Ἀβραάμ· τέκνον, μνήσθητι ὅτι ἀπέλαβες τὰ ἀγαθά σου ἐν τῇ ζωῇ σου, καὶ Λάζαρος ὁμοίως τὰ κακά· νῦν δὲ ὧδε παρακαλεῖται, σὺ δὲ ὀδυνᾶσαι. καὶ ἐν πᾶσι τούτοις μεταξὺ ἡμῶν καὶ ὑμῶν χάσμα μέγα ἐστήρικται, ὅπως οἱ θέλοντες διαβῆναι ἔνθεν πρὸς ὑμᾶς μὴ δύνωνται, μηδὲ ἐκεῖθεν πρὸς ἡμᾶς διαπερῶσιν).

Addressing the rich man as "child" (τέκνον, a

---

7. See 4 Macc 13:17: "For if we so die, Abraham and Isaac and Jacob will welcome us, and all the fathers will praise us";

and *b. Qidd.* 72b: "Today he sits in Abraham's lap."
8. So Creed, *Luke*, 212; Manson, *The Sayings of Jesus*, 299.

term of affection, see 2:48; 15:31), Abraham explains the reasons for the reversal by reminding him that he had received all his good things in his life while Lazarus received only bad things.[9] This explanation gives no theological or moral rationale for his plight and seems hardly to suffice. To the rich man's credit, he does not respond with a "Yes, but…." He accepts this answer. Readers may recall Mary's declaration, "He filled the hungry with good things and sent the rich away empty" (1:53), but the parable leaves them to figure out on their own the reasons for this turn of events.

Abraham stresses the impossibility of granting the request because of the "great chasm" (χάσμα μέγα). That gulf marks the finality of death and emphasizes that it is now too late. It warns that the adage "Let us eat and drink, for tomorrow we die" does not tell the whole story. After death, comes judgment. The rich man goes to his fiery torment because he ate and drank too much when one at his doorstep had nothing. His circumstances illustrate the woe on the rich found in *1 En.* 96:5 – 6:

> Woe unto you who eat the best bread! And drink wine in large bowls, trampling upon the weak people with your might. Woe unto you who have water available to you all the time, for soon you shall be consumed and wither away, for you have forsaken the fountain of life.

The great gap between the rich and the poor in earthly life is bridgeable. In the life beyond, the chasm widens and becomes unbridgeable.[10]

16:27 – 28 He said, "I ask you, then, Father, that you send him to my father's house, for I have five brothers, that he might warn them so that they will not come to this place of torment" (εἶπεν δέ· ἐρωτῶ σε οὖν, πάτερ, ἵνα πέμψῃς αὐτὸν εἰς τὸν οἶκον τοῦ πατρός μου, ἔχω γὰρ πέντε ἀδελφούς, ὅπως διαμαρτύρηται αὐτοῖς, ἵνα μὴ καὶ αὐτοὶ ἔλθωσιν εἰς τὸν τόπον τοῦτον τῆς βασάνου). The rich man still does not fathom the status granted to Lazarus and wants Abraham to send him to bear testimony to his five brothers so that they will not come to this horrible place. "Warn" (διαμαρτύρηται) means "to testify," but in the context it means "to protest solemnly, admonish." What Lazarus would warn them about must be inferred. Would he warn them that living in the lap of luxury while ignoring abject poverty at their doorstep is dangerous to their spiritual health?

This second plea may seem to reflect a concern on the part of the rich man for others, but his family was regarded as an extension of himself. In looking out for his brothers, the rich man is still looking out for his own interests. A defense, "Yes, but he cared for his family," does not wash. The Old Testament identifies the poor as one's brother as well (see Lev 25:25, 35, 39; Deut 15:7, 9, 11; Neh 5:7), but the rich man never gave a thought for these brothers. His plea may also be an attempt at self-justification. Had someone only warned him, he may imply, he would not have come to this wretched state.

His plea scores the point. Unless his brothers repent — that is, change their ways of behaving and thinking, particularly as it relates to their relationships to the poor and their use of their

9. A later rabbinic tradition expands on Abraham's hospitality to the angels at the Oaks of Mamre (Gen 18:1 – 15) and contends that he would seek out travelers to offer food and drink in his house and leave them provisions in stately mansions on highways (*ʾAbot R. Nat.* 7).

10. The lesson is similar to Deborah's deathbed admonition, according to *L.A.B.* 33:2 – 3: "Only direct your heart to the Lord your God during the time of your life, because after your death you cannot repent of those things in which you live … obey my voice; while you have the time of love and the light of the Law, make straight your ways." (see Eckart Reinmuth, "Ps.-Philo, *Liber Antiquitatum Biblicarum* 33,1 – 5 und die Auslegung der Parabel Lk 16:19 – 31," *NovT* 31 [1989]: 16 – 38).

wealth — they are headed for perdition. John uttered this warning in 3:11.

16:29 Abraham said to him, "They have Moses and the prophets, let them read them." (λέγει δὲ Ἀβραάμ· ἔχουσι Μωϋσέα καὶ τοὺς προφήτας· ἀκουσάτωσαν αὐτῶν). Abraham's terse response is less than solicitous. The Scriptures already give plenty of warnings. Deuteronomy 30:11 – 14 is apropos: The commandment "is not too difficult for you or beyond your reach." One need not ask, "Who will ascend into heaven to get it and proclaim it to us so we may obey it?" "The word is very near you; it is in your mouth and in your heart so you may obey it." The problem is that the word is not in their hearts, particularly the word commanding care for the poor.

The reference to Moses and the prophets picks up on the affirmation of their continuing validity as a guide for ethical conduct (16:16 – 18). The prophets sound three themes related to wealth and charity:

- God desires that persons comfort the poor even more than offering sacrifices (Isa 58:6 – 10).
- The rich who abuse the poor are denounced (Isa 1:23; 3:13 – 15; 10:1 – 3; Ezek 22:29; Amos 6:4; 8:4 – 6; Mic 2:1 – 2).
- The rights of the poor will be respected in the eschatological future (Isa 11:1 – 4; 26:1 – 6; 61:1).[11]

Had the rich man read the prophets, he would have known that his failure to meet the needs of the poor would provoke God's wrath and bring retribution (Jer 5:26 – 29; 22:13 – 19; Amos 2:6 – 7; 4:1 – 3; 5:11 – 15). Reading Moses and the prophets

also points to the coming of the Messiah and helps explain Jesus' suffering and death (see 24:27, 44).

16:30 – 31 But he said, "No, Father Abraham! If someone would rise from the dead and go to them, they would repent." He said to him, "If they do not listen to Moses and the prophets, they will not be persuaded if someone rose from the dead" (ὁ δὲ εἶπεν· οὐχί, πάτερ Ἀβραάμ, ἀλλ᾽ ἐάν τις ἀπὸ νεκρῶν πορευθῇ πρὸς αὐτοὺς μετανοήσουσιν. εἶπεν δὲ αὐτῷ· εἰ Μωϋσέως καὶ τῶν προφητῶν οὐκ ἀκούουσιν, οὐδ᾽ ἐάν τις ἐκ νεκρῶν ἀναστῇ πεισθήσονται). The rich man's final plea also falls flat, "but if someone were to come back from the dead, they would repent."[12] Abraham says, "No!" Hunter paraphrases: "If a man cannot be humane with the Old Testament and Lazarus on his doorstep, nothing will teach him otherwise."[13] Someone coming back from the dead, like Marley's ghost in Dickens' *A Christmas Carol*, is not going to convince those who, as lovers of money, are not persuadable.

Herod heard rumors that John or one of the prophets was raised from the dead. It piqued his curiosity but did not lead him to repentance (9:7 – 9; 13:31). In John's gospel, when Jesus raised a man from the dead, coincidentally named Lazarus, it did not produce repentance but precipitated a plot to kill Jesus (John 11:45 – 53). In Matthew, the story by the guards at the tomb about Jesus' resurrection only provoked the leaders to invent a lie and bribe the guards to squelch the truth (Matt 28:11 – 15). Something more than a dramatic return from the dead must soften hardened hearts.

11. Roman Garrison, *Redemptive Almsgiving in Early Christianity* (JSNTSup 77; Sheffield: JSOT, 1993), 48.

12. It may be implied that the rich man's brothers were influenced by Sadducean theology and do not believe in the

resurrection. But, according to Jesus, Moses also proclaimed the resurrection (20:37).

13. Archibald M. Hunter, *Interpreting the Parables* (Philadelphia: Westminster, 1960), 81.

Theology in Application

1. The False Gospel of Health and Wealth

In Lucian's *Demon.* 43, the question, "What are things like in Hades?" receives the sarcastic answer: "Wait, and I will see that you get information directly from the place." The details of the tormented thirst and the great chasm rivet the attention of many, but Jesus does not tell this parable to describe the horrors of Hades. Bauckham contends that the story is not a literal, eyewitness description of the fate and situation of the dead but a parable that directs attention "away from the apocalyptic revelation of the afterlife back to the inexcusable injustice of the coexistence of rich and poor."[14]

The reversal that the parable describes turns a popular theology on its ear. Many in Jesus' day and today believe that riches are a stamp of God's approval for a righteous life. It is something ordained by God.

> The rich man in his castle,
> the poor man at his gate,
> God made them high and lowly
> and ordered their estate.

If Lazarus is at the bottom of the heap, according to this perspective, it is because it is his destiny or because he is lazy. If the rich man is at the top of the food chain, it is because it is his destiny or because he was industrious. Jesus' parable challenges any such view and also invalidates the false gospel of health and wealth.

Alcorn writes: "Seeking fulfillment in money, land, houses, cars, clothes, boats, campers, hot tubs, world travel, and cruises has left us bound and gagged by materialism — and like drug addicts, we pathetically think that our only hope lies in getting more of the same."[15] Some preachers feed this habit by offering a gospel based on "ifs." You can have all these things *if* you do, believe, or think such and such. It is reminiscent of Satan's line: it will all be yours, *if* you worship me (4:7). But when it is all yours, you find that it has been a bad bargain. It not only does not bring happiness and fulfillment; it brings discontent and divine condemnation.

2. The Authority of the Scriptures

The lead-up to the parable (16:16–18) and the parable's climax argue that Moses and the prophets are abiding guides for governing our conduct in this world and have not been superceded by the ministry of Jesus. The law, for example, in Deut 15:7–11

---

14. Richard Bauckham, "The Rich Man and Lazarus: The Parable and the Parallels," *NTS* 37 (1991): 233, 245–46. Contrast Marshall, *The Gospel of Luke*, 633; Fitzmyer, *Luke*, 2:1129; and Nolland, *Luke*, 2:827.

15. Randy C. Alcorn, *Money, Possessions and Eternity* (rev. ed.; Wheaton: Tyndale, 2003), 39.

directly applies to the rich man. It demands that believers are not to "be hardhearted or tightfisted toward [their needy neighbor]," but they must be openhanded to the poor and needy and give to them liberally and ungrudgingly. Then, the Lord will bless them. If the law is obeyed, there will be no one in need in the land (Deut 15:4).

Isaiah's words are even more applicable to a rich man feasting away in his home: "Is not this the kind of fasting I have chosen … to share your food with the hungry and to provide the poor wanderer with shelter — when you see the naked, to clothe them, and not to turn away from your own flesh and blood?" (Isa 58:6–7). Ezekiel 16:49 is no less damning in identifying the guilt of Sodom as her pride, excess of food, and prosperous ease while refusing to aid the poor and needy.

This parable is not about world hunger but about the hunger of one man whose name the rich man knows and who is right on his doorstep. The rich man's sin is eating a full meal in the face of a starving person. His home has become a sepulcher in which he shuts himself up with his servants and gourmet food and shuts out the world of poverty and hunger. As Nave correctly sees, the rich man is not condemned to perish in Hades because he was rich but because "he failed to repent of his greed and selfishness by sharing his resources with Lazarus."[16]

Abraham's final answer to the rich man, "They have Moses and the prophets, let them read them," assumes that the reading and proclamation of the Scriptures are more effective than some spectacular show (see Acts 8:26–39). Some today, however, seem to believe that the Bible needs some assistance to get through to people, something more spectacular, entertaining, and in tune with modern society. This parable would argue that if the Bible is not sufficient, then nothing is sufficient. "True faith arises out of an encounter with the Word."[17]

When Christians read this passage, they would naturally think of the resurrection of Jesus (see 9:35, the transfiguration and the statement, "Listen to him!"). If Christians do not respond to someone like Lazarus with Moses, the prophets, Jesus, the New Testament, and the Holy Spirit, what will become of them?

16. Nave, *Repentance in Luke-Acts*, 187.
17. Thorwald Lorenzen, "A Biblical Meditation on Luke 16:19–31: From the Text toward a Sermon," *ExpTim* 87 (1975): 40.

Luke 17:1 – 10

Literary Context

Jesus continues to address the disciples (16:1; 17:1), but in the presence of the Pharisees who can still overhear what he says. The focus is on the spiritual formation of the disciples so that they will not become like the Pharisees who are presented as disregarding "the little ones" and being unmoved by the plight of sinners and unforgiving. Luke organizes 17:1 – 19 around the issue of faith: faith forgives (17:1 – 4); it can do all things (17:5 – 6); it is humbly obedient (17:7 – 10); and it is grateful (17:11 – 19).[1]

Main Idea

Faith overcomes stumbling blocks and forgives those who sin. A small amount works wonders and serves in humble obedience.

---

1. Paul J. Achtemeier, "The Lucan Perspective on the Miracles of Jesus: A Preliminary Sketch," *JBL* 94 (1975): 554.

Translation

Luke 17:1–10

17:1a Warning woe **And he said to his disciples,**

"It is inevitable that stumbling blocks that cause people to sin will come,

b but woe to that one who causes them to happen.

2 It would be   better for that one   to be cast into the sea with a millstone fastened around his neck

than   to be responsible for causing one of these little ones to stumble and sin.

3a Command Watch yourselves!

b Command If your brother sins, reprove him.

And if he repents, forgive him.

4 Command And   even if he sins against you seven times in a day and turns to you and says,

'I repent,'

you will forgive him."

5 Request **The apostles said to the Lord,**

"Increase our faith."

6 Response **And the Lord said,**

"If you have faith the size of a mustard seed,

you could say to this sycamine tree,

'Be uprooted and be planted in the sea,'

and it would obey you.

7 Parable Who among you will say to a slave who comes in from the field after plowing or tending sheep,

'Come at once and sit down at table'?

8 Will you not rather say,

'Fix me something to eat and gird yourself to wait on me until I have eaten and drunk.

And afterward, then you may eat and drink'?

9 You do not show special favor to the slave because he did what you commanded, do you?

So it is also with you.

10 Command When you have done everything that has been commanded, you must learn to say,

'We are unworthy slaves;

we only did what we were supposed to do.'"

Structure and Literary Form

The structure mixes three different forms. It begins with a severe warning with a woe, followed by an inquiry and an aphorism about faith, and then a parable. The organizing principle of these fragments of Jesus' teaching is related to how faith is to play itself out in the disciples' service. The warning not to be a cause of stumbling to others and the command to forgive a person who persistently offends but asks for forgiveness (17:1–4) is met with the disciples' request to increase their faith to be able to pull off these directives (17:5–6). The parable (17:7–10) then addresses the motivation behind obeying and serving Jesus.

Exegetical Outline

→ **I. Warnings about stumbling blocks leading to sin (17:1–4)**

    A. They are inevitable (17:1a)

    B. Those who cause them will be judged (17:1b–2)

    C. Those who sin need to be reproved and forgiven (17:3–4)

II. Teaching on faith (17:5–6)

    A. Disciples' request for faith (17:5)

    B. A little faith works wonders (17:6)

III. Parable on faithfulness (17:7–10)

    A. Faithfulness earns no special reward (17:7–9)

    B. Faithfulness is the basic requirement (17:10)

Explanation of the Text

17:1 And he said to his disciples, "It is inevitable that stumbling blocks that cause people to sin will come, but woe to that one who causes them to happen" (εἶπεν δὲ πρὸς τοὺς μαθητὰς αὐτοῦ· ἀνένδεκτόν ἐστιν τοῦ τὰ σκάνδαλα μὴ ἐλθεῖν, πλὴν οὐαὶ δι' οὗ ἔρχεται). Disciples are not removed to a utopia where they are sealed off from temptations. The world is full of those who would resist God's purposes, and some will even identify themselves as disciples. In his farewell speech to the elders of Ephesus, Paul warns of fierce wolves who will enter the flock and draw disciples away (Acts 20:29–30).

17:2 It would be better for that one to be cast into the sea with a millstone fastened around the neck than to be responsible for causing one of these little ones to stumble and sin (λυσιτελεῖ αὐτῷ εἰ λίθος μυλικὸς περίκειται περὶ τὸν τράχηλον αὐτοῦ καὶ ἔρριπται εἰς τὴν θάλασσαν ἢ ἵνα σκανδαλίσῃ τῶν μικρῶν τούτων ἕνα). The image of the rich man's torment in the previous parable provides a backdrop for understanding how it would be better to drown than to be guilty of causing a little one to sin. A disciple is fully responsible for his or her influence on others (see Rom 14:13; 1 Cor 8:9–10; 1 John 2:10; Rev 2:14).

"These little ones" (τῶν μικρῶν τούτων) are not identified, but the context would suggest that it would include people like Lazarus (16:20 – 21), the prodigal son (15:11 – 32), tax collectors and sinners (15:1), the poor, crippled, lame, and blind (14:13, 21), the man with dropsy (14:1 – 6), and the crippled woman (13:11 – 16). "Little one" or "small" has the connotation of immature pupil or young, immature scholar in rabbinic literature.[2] They seem insignificant on the world's scale of values or irredeemable in some imagined divine scale of values. Jesus' statement about the infants (18:15 – 17) reveals that all should be acutely conscious of their insignificance before God, but also that the so-called little ones are not insignificant to God. Consequently, one should receive them in Jesus' name and never be the cause of their falling away.

17:3 – 4 Watch yourselves! If your brother sins, reprove him. And if he repents, forgive him. And even if he sins against you seven times in a day and turns to you and says, "I repent," you will forgive him (προσέχετε ἑαυτοῖς. ἐὰν ἁμάρτῃ ὁ ἀδελφός σου ἐπιτίμησον αὐτῷ, καὶ ἐὰν μετανοήσῃ ἄφες αὐτῷ· καὶ ἐὰν ἑπτάκις τῆς ἡμέρας ἁμαρτήσῃ εἰς σὲ καὶ ἑπτάκις ἐπιστρέψῃ πρὸς σὲ λέγων· μετανοῶ, ἀφήσεις αὐτῷ). From the welcome given the prodigal son, one might get the impression that sin is something to be ignored, but this is not the case. The admonition in *T. Gad* 6:3 ("So love one another from the heart; if anyone sins against you, speak to him peaceably, banishing the poison of hatred, and keeping not guile in your soul. If he confesses and repents, forgive him") shows how this command is at home in Jewish piety.

"Brother" (ὁ ἀδελφός) is the New Testament term for a fellow disciple and underscores the kinship created in Christ among his followers. When the brother misses the mark, he or she is to be confronted and corrected. It is far easier for those

provoked with sinners to talk about them behind their backs than to confront them face to face. The elder son's attitude toward his brother who had come home chastened and submissive provides an example that disciples must avoid. The community of disciples is not to be a community of snipers. Stauffer spells out the implications: "Reproof should be accompanied by the awareness of common guilt before God and therefore by a spirit of unconditional forgiveness."[3]

17:5 The apostles said to the Lord, "Increase our faith" (καὶ εἶπαν οἱ ἀπόστολοι τῷ κυρίῳ· πρόσθες ἡμῖν πίστιν). The disciples' request to increase their faith may seem to come out of the blue. But they recognize that these requirements not to cause others to stumble and always to be forgiving are formidable tasks that require greater faith.

17:6 And the Lord said, "If you have faith the size of a mustard seed, you could say to this sycamine tree, 'Be uprooted and be planted in the sea,' and it would obey you" (εἶπεν δὲ ὁ κύριος· εἰ ἔχετε πίστιν ὡς κόκκον σινάπεως, ἐλέγετε ἂν τῇ συκαμίνῳ [ταύτῃ]· ἐκριζώθητι καὶ φυτεύθητι ἐν τῇ θαλάσσῃ· καὶ ὑπήκουσεν ἂν ὑμῖν). Jesus responds to this request with a typically vivid and extreme image to assure disciples that they can do this now without a divine infusion of supplemental faith.

This sentence is in the form of a mixed condition. The apodosis with the untranslatable particle (ἄν) plus the imperfect indicative (ἐλέγετε) is that of a second class (unreal) condition that is presumed to be contrary to fact. The protasis of a second class condition normally has "if" (εἰ) plus a secondary tense (imperfect or aorist) in the indicative mood and assumes that the condition is not in fact realized; but here, the verb "you have" (ἔχετε) is in the present tense, which would be used in a

---

2. Otto Michel, "μικρός," *TDNT*, 4:649 – 50.

3. Ethelbert Stauffer, "ἐπιτιμάω, ἐπιτιμία," *TDNT*, 2:625.

first class (real) condition that assumes, for the sake of argument, the reality of the condition.

If one translates this verse as a contrary to fact condition, "if you had faith," it implies that the disciples do not have even this tiny amount of faith. The statement then becomes a mild rebuke: If they just had a little faith, they could do wonders. If one translates it, however, as a first class condition, it assumes the truth of the statement, at least for the sake of argument: "If you have faith." Their own request to increase their faith takes for granted that they already have it, and Jesus' answer does not correct or rebuke them. It assumes that they have faith enough and do not need to ask for more.

This response fits a pattern throughout Luke. In 8:25, Jesus mildly chides the disciples for showing fear during the storm on the lake, "Where is your faith?" which assumes that they have faith. By contrast, the parallel in Mark 4:40 reads, "Do you still have no faith?" and in Matt 8:26 he berates them as "you of little faith." In Luke 22:42, Jesus informs Peter that he has prayed that when he passes through his bitter failure, his faith will not fail. Again, he assumes that Peter has faith, and it will be faith enough to overcome his collapse under fire and to turn and strengthen his brothers. Luke's tendency toward a more positive portrayal of the disciples justifies a positive rendering of this sentence.

Removing a sycamine is a localized image. It is a black mulberry (*morus nigra*) with a proverbially extensive and deep root system (*m. B. Bat.* 2:11; *y. Ber.* 9:2, 14a; *Gen Rab.* 13:17). Uprooting it completely was deemed to be a hopeless task, comparable to uprooting a mountain as the parallel saying in Matt 17:20 states (see also Matt 21:21; Mark 11:23; 1 Cor 13:2). Planting it in the sea seems a rather bizarre thing to do and even more

impossible. The implication of the saying is that a little faith can work wonders.

17:7 Who among you will say to a slave who comes in from the field after plowing or tending sheep, "Come at once and sit down at table"? (τίς δὲ ἐξ ὑμῶν δοῦλον ἔχων ἀροτριῶντα ἢ ποιμαίνοντα, ὃς εἰσελθόντι ἐκ τοῦ ἀγροῦ ἐρεῖ αὐτῷ· εὐθέως παρελθὼν ἀνάπεσε;). The phrase "Who among you" (τίς δὲ ἐξ ὑμῶν) anticipates an emphatic "No one of us" and has been utilized in previous parables. It presents an exaggerated situation, given the ways of the world, to make the point. In spite of his exhausting work in the field, everyone would assume that the slave must fulfill his other duties in the house.

The attitude toward slaves expressed in Sir 33:25–30 provides a backdrop for understanding the assumptions behind the parable's reality. It reflects the Mediterranean worldview that a master should maintain boundaries to maintain respect and that slaves should not be treated as friends:

Fodder and a stick and burdens for a donkey;
   bread and discipline and work for a slave.
Set your slave to work, and you will find rest;
   leave his hands idle, and he will seek liberty.
Yoke and thong will bow the neck,
   and for a wicked slave there are racks and tortures.
Put him to work, in order that he may not be idle,
   for idleness teaches much evil.
Set him to work, as is fitting for him,
   and if he does not obey, make his fetters heavy.
Do not be overbearing toward anyone,
   and do nothing unjust.

The parable turns on the assumption "that the slave alone, not the master, remains under obligation."[4] Jesus makes no comment about the injustice

4. Michael P. Knowles, "Reciprocity and 'Favour' in the Parable of the Undeserving Servant (Luke 17:7–10)," *NTS* 49 (2003): 256.

of the institution of slavery. He simply draws from this everyday reality to make a point about the disciple's responsibilities as God's servant.

17:8 Will you not rather say, "Fix me something to eat and gird yourself to wait on me until I have eaten and drunk. And afterward, then you may eat and drink"? (ἀλλ᾽ οὐχὶ ἐρεῖ αὐτῷ· ἑτοίμασον τί δειπνήσω καὶ περιζωσάμενος διακόνει μοι ἕως φάγω καὶ πίω, καὶ μετὰ ταῦτα φάγεσαι καὶ πίεσαι σύ;). "Will you not rather say" (with the use of οὐχί) expects the answer "yes" — this is exactly what a master would say to the slave, no matter how hard he has worked in the field. This master is presumed to be a man of modest income; his plowman is also the herdsman and the cook. The parable's point balances the exhortation in 12:35 – 38. In that parable, the situation is reversed. The master shows up at midnight and finds the slaves alert, and he has them sit down and girds himself to serve them. That illustration pictures the coming of Christ at the end time and the judgment when the slaves' earthly duties have come to an end.

17:9 You do not show special favor to the slave because he did what you commanded, do you? (μὴ ἔχει χάριν τῷ δούλῳ ὅτι ἐποίησεν τὰ διαταχθέντα;). The Greek "not" (μή) expects the answer "no." The question reads (lit.), "Does he have favor (ἔχει χάριν) for the slave?" This phrase may refer to the master's gratitude toward the slave for his service. The construction "to have favor" (ἔχειν χάριν) plus the dative case means "to thank" in 1 Tim 1:12 and 2 Tim 1:3. But this phrase may also mean to "show favor" or to give some special benefit (see 3 Macc 5:20). The parable is driven by an assumption about the service of slaves that is summarized by Seneca (*Ben.* 3.18), who asks,

"Can a slave confer a benefit? Is his service, however lavish, not merely a duty to his lord, which as it springs from constraint, is undeserving of gratitude?" In other words, by fulfilling his ordinary duties the slave does not become the master's patron.[5]

The master and slave in the parable are ciphers for God and those who serve God. Since the parable is not about master-slave relationships but about service to God, it torpedoes the utilitarian expectations in the ancient world about service rendered to the gods. Those imbued with Greco-Roman religious assumptions thought that offering public worship to the gods and following prescribed rules should elicit some favor or benefit in return; otherwise, one would move on to serve a more accommodating god. The gods are expected to reciprocate with special favor for being honored or served by the worshiper.

Jesus argues that fulfilling one's duties to God "elicits no reciprocal obligation on the part of the master/God."[6] Resseguie captures the point: "*Obedience is based on divine initiative and human obligation, rather than on human initiative and divine obligation.*"[7] The parable makes clear that the relationship between God and those serving God is not akin to a patron-client relationship in which the client receives benefactions from the patron in return for service and support. To make this point clearer, the phrase is rendered "You do not *show special favor* to the slave" rather than "You do not *show gratitude.*"

17:10 So it is also with you. When you have done everything that has been commanded, you must to learn say, "We are unworthy slaves; we only did what we were supposed to do" (οὕτως καὶ ὑμεῖς, ὅταν ποιήσητε πάντα τὰ διαταχθέντα ὑμῖν, λέγετε ὅτι δοῦλοι ἀχρεῖοί ἐσμεν, ὃ

---

5. Green, *The Gospel of Luke*, 614.
6. Knowles, "Reciprocity and 'Favour,'" 260.

7. Resseguie, *Spiritual Landscape*, 51.

ὠφείλομεν ποιῆσαι πεποιήκαμεν). Verses 7 – 9 have the listeners look at things from the point of view of the master only to flip them into the position of slave in this last line.[8] It does not continue as the reader might have expected, "So command your servants...." Rather, it concludes, we must confess that we are unworthy servants after doing all that has been commanded. We should not say as the older brother did, "Look! So many years I have served you" (15:29; cf. 18:12, 21). The present parable responds, "So what?" Our service to God, who now becomes the Master, has not put God in our debt. Having done all that we were bidden to do, the best we can hope for is that God retains us as servants.

The adjective "unworthy" (ἀχρεῖοι) is applied to the servant who had done nothing with the talent that was given to him except to bury it (Matt 25:30), and he is chucked into the outer darkness. In Luke's context, however, this slave has not shirked his duties but has fulfilled them, so it is better to understand the unworthiness to mean that we are not worthy of any special praise.

The Pharisees have taken it on the chin throughout this part of the travel narrative, but their spiritual heirs record similar views about rewards as this parable: there are no rewards from God because of our merit. For example, Antigonus of Soko said: "Be not slaves that minister to the master for the sake of receiving a bounty, but be like slaves that minister to the master not for the sake of receiving a bounty; and let the fear of Heaven be upon you" (*m. ʾAbot* 1:3). Rabbi Joḥanan b. Zakkai said: "If thou practiced much Torah claim not much merit for thyself, for to this end wast thou created" (*m. ʾAbot* 2:8). Paul, a former Pharisee, says the same thing about his apostolic calling: "For when I preach the gospel, I cannot boast, since I am compelled to preach. Woe to me if I do not preach the gospel!" (1 Cor 9:16). One cannot expect reward for works of supererogation, because there are no such things. Nor can one ever boast before God (Rom 3:27; 1 Cor 1:29; Eph 2:9) or expect to be offered seats of honor on the left and right of Christ in his glory (Mark 10:37).

Theology in Application

1. Growing Faith

The disciples have at least some faith, and Jesus assures them that it is sufficient to do the impossible. They do not need *more* faith; the little faith they have is enough already to do what Jesus requests. But one should not interpret this assertion to suggest that spectacular wonders are in view. Sensational feats are done to inspire awe, which is not Jesus' intention.

The marvel that Jesus has in mind may seem more mundane, but it is no less a marvel. It is not causing little ones to stumble, graciously reproving other disciples for their sin, and forgiving them again and again when they repent. Faith is not a form of magic that enables us to control nature or to get God to do our bidding.

---

8. A similar flip-flop occurs in 11:11 – 13, where the listener starts out as a beneficent parent meeting a child's requests and then becomes one who is evil supplicating a heavenly Father.

Faith is a response to God's initiative that trusts that we are empowered to do what God requires. If we wait until we can say we have enough faith to do what Jesus asks, we will probably never do anything. The request to give us more faith is rooted in unfaith. As Green perceptively observes, "'faith' is not so much a possession as a disposition."[9] Doing what is required results in growing faith.

2. Faithfully Discharging One's Duty to God

The parable moves from the lesser to the greater in making its theological point. Manson captures its gist: "If a mere man is entitled to make such far-reaching demands on the services of his servant, and that merely for his own profit and comfort, how much more is God entitled to require the utmost from His servants in the manifestation and extension of His kingdom among humans."[10] One should expect no pats on the back or give oneself pats on the back for doing what is required by God.[11]

The parable presents us with the uncomfortable reminder that we are but slaves of Christ and nothing more, and that Christ is an unrelenting master who exacts complete obedience and nothing less. If such service and submission are expected in earthly slave-master relationships, how much more so in human relationships with God. Faithful service does not exalt the slaves and change their roles. After faithfully discharging their duties, slaves are not promoted to the master level but are required to continue discharging their duties faithfully.

The parable requires total self-denial of the slave. Similarly, slaves of Christ cannot expect to tend to their own needs first; instead, their lot is to do everything the master requires. The duties expected in the context are not to cause others to stumble (17:1 – 3a), to forgive the brother (17:3b – 4), and to have faith even the size of a mustard seed (17:5). But these are not the sum total of the duties required; there is always something more to do. As in the saying, "A mother's work is never done," so it is with the servant of Christ — the work is never done. One can never ask, "What must I do to inherit eternal life?" and then say, "I have done it." One can never claim to have settled accounts with God.

3. Service with No Eye for Reward

The parable may have been directed against "Pharisaic self-righteousness,"[12] but it would have been just as applicable to the disciples (9:46 – 48; 22:24 – 27). Luke also may have considered it applicable to apostolic evangelists vested with special authority in mission. They may have "a penchant for claiming that their work is finished when they come from the field into the house; they also have a tendency to assign

9. Green, *The Gospel of Luke*, 613.
10. Manson, *The Sayings of Jesus*, 302.

11. Schweizer, *Luke*, 264.
12. Jeremias, *The Parables of Jesus*, 193.

priority and superiority to their 'field work.'"[13] It is universally applicable to any who think they have done a full day's work and deserve special recognition and perks. Meritorious service does not put the Master in one's debt: "He has not done anything or given any service the master was not entitled to demand in the first place."[14] This theology drives Paul's understanding of his apostolic calling as expressed in 1 Cor 9.[15]

The parable also challenges a view of religion that believes that one can earn merit before God or that God's purpose is to serve us. The parable corrects a religious mind-set that is obsessed with self by bringing up duties. Followers of Christ are to be servants, no more and no less. The eschatological warnings that follow in 17:20 – 37 remind us of God's coming invasion into the world when everyone will be called to account.

13. Paul S. Minear, "A Note on Luke 17:7 – 10," *JBL* 93 (1974): 85.

14. Manson, *The Sayings of Jesus*, 302.

15. See Garland, *1 Corinthians*, 421 – 37.

CHAPTER 52

Luke 17:11 – 19

Literary Context

This incident complements the previous parable (17:7 – 10) that the master never owes gratitude to his slave. Gratitude instead is owed the master — in this case, God as benefactor. Luke's placement of the incident provides a real-life example of the exceptional faith required by Jesus' teaching, and it affirms that faith saves. This historical encounter also presents an example of faith and spiritual perception among the down-and-outs, which is reinforced by the parables and stories in chapters 18 – 19. The use of reversal that transcends social boundaries — a Samaritan returning to offer homage to Jesus — prepares for the question in 18:8: "When the Son of Man comes ... will he then find faith on the earth?" It may not be found among those one would expect.

Main Idea

Faith recognizes Jesus as the source of healing and expresses itself in gratitude and praise to him.

Translation

Luke 17:11–19

17:11	Circumstance	When he was on his way to Jerusalem, **he was passing through the area between Samaria and Galilee.**
12	Character introduction	As he entered into a certain village, **ten men with a skin disease met him, standing at a distance.**
13	Request	**They raised their voices, saying,** *"Jesus, Master, have mercy on us!"*
14a	Response	When he saw them, **he said,** *"Go show yourselves to the priests."*
b	Miracle	**And it happened that as they were going, they were cleansed.**
15	Reaction	**One of them, when he saw that he was healed, turned back, glorifying God ⤸ with a loud voice.**
16a	Worshipful thanksgiving	**He fell on his face before Jesus' feet, giving him thanks,**
b	Character description	**and he was a Samaritan.**
17	Response	**Jesus responded by saying,** *"Were there not ten cleansed? Where are the other nine?*
18	Criticism	*Can it be that this foreigner was the only one to be found who turned back ⤸ to give praise to God?"*
19	Pronouncement	**He said to him,** *"Rise! Go! Your faith has saved you!"*

Structure and Literary Form

The structure of the passage falls into two parts. The first part records the healing of ten lepers in a border area between Samaria and Galilee (17:11 – 14). The lepers who are healed are not distinguished from one another. The second part records the return of a Samaritan to Jesus to offer praise to God and obeisance to Jesus (17:15 – 19). Jesus scores the point with a surprised question and a pronouncement. He asks why only "this foreigner" of the ten lepers returned to him to give praise to God and declares that he is saved by his faith. The structure can be diagramed as follows.[1]

Part 1	Part 2
A Ten come to Jesus	A´ One comes to Jesus
B Ten keep distance	B´ One at Jesus' feet
C Ten cry for mercy	C´ One praises God for receiving mercy
D Jesus sends the ten	D´ Jesus sends the one
E Ten are cleansed	E´ One is saved

Exegetical Outline

→ I. **Plea for mercy (17:11 – 13)**

  II. **Obedience and healing (17:14)**

  III. **Gratitude, return, and obeisance (17:15 – 16)**

  IV. **Ingratitude and indifference (17:17 – 18)**

  V. **Gratitude a mark of saving faith (17:19)**

Explanation of the Text

17:11 When he was on his way to Jerusalem, he was passing through the area between Samaria and Galilee (καὶ ἐγένετο ἐν τῷ πορεύεσθαι εἰς Ἰερουσαλὴμ καὶ αὐτὸς διήρχετο διὰ μέσον Σαμαρείας καὶ Γαλιλαίας). Luke reminds the reader that Jesus is still winding his way slowly toward Jerusalem (9:51; 13:22; 17:11; 18:35; 19:11, 28, 41). The identification of a locale "along the border of" or "between Samaria and Galilee" may suggest that he "is walking through a liminal zone, a place of transition, a place 'between,' where neither Galilean nor Samaritan is at 'home.'"[2] Luke holds little interest in geographical clarity, which may be attributable to drawing on disparate oral

---

1. Adapted from Frederick J. Gaiser, "Your Faith Has Made You Well: Healing and Salvation in Luke 17:12 – 19," *WW* 16 (1996): 294.

2. John T. Carroll, "Luke 17:11 – 19," *Int* 53 (1999): 405.

traditions about Jesus and weaving them into a narrative in a travel setting. Readers are not to track Jesus' journey on a map (and we should remember that Luke writes to a mapless culture).

17:12 – 13 As he entered into a certain village, ten men with a skin disease met him, standing at a distance. They raised their voices, saying, "Jesus, Master, have mercy on us!" (καὶ εἰσερχομένου αὐτοῦ εἴς τινα κώμην ἀπήντησαν [αὐτῷ] δέκα λεπροὶ ἄνδρες, οἳ ἔστησαν πόρρωθεν. καὶ αὐτοὶ ἦραν φωνὴν λέγοντες· Ἰησοῦ ἐπιστάτα, ἐλέησον ἡμᾶς). On the nature of the skin disease (leprosy), see the discussion on 5:12 – 14. The men with this disease were required by the law to separate themselves from others, to live outside the camp, and to warn of their presence so that they would not convey their uncleanness to others (Lev 13:45 – 46; Num 5:2). The common affliction of these men has erased their ethnic differences, and, like the homeless today, they probably lived together to help support one another.

The phrase "he is unclean" is a constant refrain in any text dealing with leprosy. The leper, like a corpse, was the first of the "fathers of uncleanness," that is, a prime source of ritual impurity, not of disease. Proof of this is the statement in *m. Neg.* 3:1, that the rules concerning leprosy signs apply only to Israelites: "All can contract uncleanness from leprosy-signs excepting gentiles and resident aliens." According to the law, only when a person is declared unclean by a priest is that person considered unclean. Therefore, in *Sipra* to Lev 14:36, it is *not* recommended that a person be examined for the presence of the disease before a festival or a marriage celebration; otherwise, he or she could be forced to miss it.

A wife of a leper was allowed to share exile with her husband, and they could and did cohabit (see Uzziah's son, Jotham, born while he was leprous, according to *b. Mo'ed Qaṭ.* 7b, *b. Ker.* 8b). Ideally,

lepers were also permitted to come to the house of study as long as they entered first and left last and were separated from the rest by a wall ten handbreadths in height and four cubits in width (*m. Neg.* 13:12; *t. Neg.* 7:11). These measures were not designed to prevent spreading the disease but to prevent spreading the impurity.

The major problem for lepers was the social ostracism the law prescribed. A leper was banished from the city and society. Josephus attempted to counter the slanderous accusation that the Jews had originally been driven out of Egypt because they were lepers by pointing out that Moses himself had banished lepers outright from the camp so that they could have no contact with others. The leper in no way differed from a corpse (Josephus, *Ant.* 3.11.3 §264), so that the cure of a leper was akin to raising the dead.

The cleansing of a leper restores the victim to life and to the community, and these lepers cry out desperately and audaciously to Jesus as the "Master" to have mercy on them. In this case, to show mercy means that they will be cleansed of their leprosy. In this incident, the ten may be restored to their respective communities, but only one seeks to join a community created by Jesus where ethnic distinctions between Jew and Samaritan are obliterated.

17:14 When he saw them, he said, "Go show yourselves to the priests." And it happened that as they were going, they were cleansed (καὶ ἰδὼν εἶπεν αὐτοῖς· πορευθέντες ἐπιδείξατε ἑαυτοὺς τοῖς ἱερεῦσιν. καὶ ἐγένετο ἐν τῷ ὑπάγειν αὐτοὺς ἐκαθαρίσθησαν). Jesus' command assumes that their healing will occur on the way to the priests, and all ten exhibit trust in that word. Jesus sends them to the priests because only a priest is authorized to examine persons and pronounce that they have the skin disease or that they have been cleansed from it. The priest cannot heal, only diagnose. That is why Lev 13 – 14 goes into such detail describing various conditions to help the priest look for the presence or absence of particular physical signs — such as skin color change, hair color, infiltration, extension, or ulceration of the skin. After the priest inspects the skin and notarizes that someone has been cleansed of the disease, the victim was required to go to the temple to offer the prescribed sin offerings specified in Lev 14. Only then could that person be reintegrated into society.

The healing occurred in the process of obeying Jesus' command. The lepers have done nothing to deserve this cure except to beg for mercy from Jesus and trust his instructions to go, as if they were already healed. Jesus appears to have done nothing as well. There is no healing touch, no prayer of intercession, and no special directions to induce the cure. But Jesus does "see" the lepers, and this look is filled with both mercy and power. As God looked favorably on Elizabeth to take away the disgrace of her barrenness (1:25), Jesus may be seen as looking favorably on the lepers to take away the humiliation of their leprosy.

17:15 One of them, when he saw that he was healed, turned back, glorifying God with a loud voice (εἰς δὲ ἐξ αὐτῶν, ἰδὼν ὅτι ἰάθη, ὑπέστρεψεν μετὰ φωνῆς μεγάλης δοξάζων τὸν θεόν). The language of "seeing" (ἰδών), "returning" (ὑπέστρεψεν) and "glorifying God" (δοξάζων τὸν θεόν) recalls the response of the shepherds after the angelic announcement of Christ's birth and their visit to the manger. They "returned, glorifying and praising God for all that they had heard and seen" (2:20).[3]

When this particular leper sees he is cured, he also sees who has effected that cure.[4] The eyes of faith are opened for him to see (see 18:42 – 43). He forgets about the priests and his longing to get back to some semblance of normal life as soon as possible and turns back to offer homage to his benefactor. In effect, by seeing for himself that he has been healed, he takes over the priestly function for himself.[5] Seeing and returning to Jesus "amounts to his conversion" and is the most pivotal thing that happens.[6] Hamm argues that in recalling historical encounters concerning vision, Luke does so in a way "that symbolizes the deeper seeing which is the faith that perceives Jesus' true identity and acts upon it."[7] The need to thank the one instrumental in his healing also overrides the need to get notarized by a priest according to Mosaic regulations. The other lepers who were healed apparently see no reason to return to give thanks to Jesus.

This Samaritan's piety matches another Samaritan's charity (10:30 – 35). The one showed mercy; the other pled for mercy. Luke does not tell us why a Samaritan is the only one to return any more than we are told why only a Samaritan renders aid to a mugging victim. Somehow, they are able to see things differently from others. A priest and Levite see a mugging victim on the side of the road (10:31 – 32) and pass him by. A Samaritan sees him and is filled with pity and is moved to help him (10:33 – 35). Jewish lepers go to the priests who can inspect them and observe that the signs of leprosy have disappeared, but only a Samaritan leper sees that he has been healed by God. Their special way of seeing leads to their appropriate responses. God expects compassion for a neighbor and praise for healing.

---

3. Dennis Hamm, "What the Samaritan Leper Sees: The Narrative Christology of Luke 17:11 – 19," *CBQ* 56 (1994): 283.

4. Note that the Samaritan is "healed" (17:15); the others, who are presumably Jews, are "cleansed" (17:14, 17).

5. Annette Weissenrieder, *Images of Illness in the Gospel of*

Luke (WUNT 2/164; Tübingen: Mohr Siebeck, 2003), 186.

6. Hans Dieter Betz, "The Cleansing of the Ten Lepers (Luke 17:11 – 19)," *JBL* 90 (1971): 318.

7. Dennis Hamm, "Sight to the Blind: Vision as Metaphor in Luke," *Bib* 67 (1986): 458.

17:16 He fell on his face before Jesus' feet, giving him thanks, and he was a Samaritan (καὶ ἔπεσεν ἐπὶ πρόσωπον παρὰ τοὺς πόδας αὐτοῦ εὐχαριστῶν αὐτῷ· καὶ αὐτὸς ἦν Σαμαρίτης). The man glorifies God and subjugates himself before Jesus, falling on his face at his feet. Luke uses this formula to spotlight characters who exemplify the essence of faith.[8] Only the Samaritan has demonstrated the proper response when God works miracles.

17:17 – 18 Jesus responded by saying, "Were there not ten cleansed? Where are the other nine? Can it be that this foreigner was the only one to be found who turned back to give praise to God?" (ἀποκριθεὶς δὲ ὁ Ἰησοῦς εἶπεν· οὐχὶ οἱ δέκα ἐκαθαρίσθησαν; οἱ δὲ ἐννέα ποῦ; οὐχ εὑρέθησαν ὑποστρέψαντες δοῦναι δόξαν τῷ θεῷ εἰ μὴ ὁ ἀλλογενὴς οὗτος;). Three questions from Jesus in these two verses make the point. The questions emphasize that all ten were healed, but only one, a Samaritan of all people, found it in his heart to return to Jesus to thank him and glorify God. This incident recalls 4:27, when Jesus' sparked a furor in the synagogue at Nazareth by pointing out that in the time of Elisha *only* Naaman, a Syrian, was healed of his leprosy despite the presence of many lepers in Israel. The difference is that the majority of those cured of their leprosy are full-fledged Jews. This incident fits the theme expressed in 7:9, "Not even in Israel have I found such faith." The least likely somehow sees what others cannot see and responds.

The questions also stress that gratitude is due Jesus. Josephus wrote regarding leprosy: "But if any by supplication to God obtains release from this disease and recovers a healthy skin, such a one returns thanks to God by divers sacrifices" (*Ant.* 3.11.3 §264). The ten lepers with one voice boldly appealed to Jesus for mercy. Only one returned to show gratitude. Jesus' astonishment reveals that the other nine also should have returned. Receiving divine mercy should evoke concrete expressions of gratitude and praise (7:36 – 50; see also Ps 30:10 – 12).

The text radically subverts the significance of the temple's rituals and sacrifices when offering praise to God and thanks to Jesus not only suffice for making the required offerings (Lev 14:1 – 32) but surpass it. It is also significant that Jesus' term for the Samaritan as a "foreigner" (ἀλλογενής) is the same term that appears on the inscriptions found on the balustrades surrounding the temple warning that "no alien" (μηθένα ἀλλογενής) may go beyond this point and will suffer the penalty of death if they are caught doing so.[9] One alienated from the temple is not alienated from God but is considered a part of Israel and "saved" apart from the temple.

17:19 He said to him, "Rise! Go! Your faith has saved you!" (καὶ εἶπεν αὐτῷ· ἀναστὰς πορεύου· ἡ πίστις σου σέσωκέν σε). The command emphasizes that faith saves. All the lepers acted on faith that they would be cleansed in making their way to a priest to be examined. Only to this one who returned does Jesus say, "Your faith has saved you" (see 7:50; 8:48, 50; 18:42). The use of the verb "saved" (σέσωκεν) shows that physical cleansing (καθαρίζω) from ritual impurity and healing (ἰάομαι) have nothing to do with salvation. Jesus' purpose is not to provide miracles but to offer a saving relationship to God through him.

---

8. Terrance McCaughey, "Paradigms of Faith in the Gospel of St. Luke," *ITQ* 45 (1978): 177 – 84.

9. Noted by Weissenrieder (*Images of Illness in the Gospel of Luke*, 98 – 99), though she interprets its significance differently.

Theology in Application

1. Faith in Jesus

The disciples had asked Jesus to increase their faith. It becomes clear that a vital faith is faith in Jesus and that it produces gratitude to Jesus. The Samaritan appealed to Jesus, as did the other nine, but he returned to Jesus instead of going off to a priest to get clearance to return to society. As Danker puts it, the Samaritan "came to the right place."[10] The other nine lepers missed salvation because they had not seen it. Did they intend to postpone thanks until their cure was certified by a priest? If so, it would be too late. If they should see Jesus again, they would certainly give him a nod of appreciation. Jesus had accomplished what they wanted and was now forgotten. Schweizer comments that healing can lead away from salvation when we only want something from God and not God in this something.[11] These ungrateful former lepers may represent the ingratitude of Israel, who forgot the works of God (see Ps 106:7).

Salvation comes unexpectedly to those who have been written off by the self-assured who regard themselves as shoo-ins for salvation. It comes to the outcasts, pariahs, and so-called heretics. The Samaritan looked like a double loser as a Samaritan (the pagan half-breed from the Jewish perspective) and as a leper, but salvation came when he publicly demonstrated faith and gratitude to Jesus. Their acceptance by God may be galling to those who want others to be left out and to be beyond the pale. Jesus erected no walls that said, "Keep out," but instead he broke down walls and moved across geographical, national, ritual, and racial barriers to embrace all humans. The incasts are no different from the outcasts when it comes to God's healing grace and salvation, which know no caste system. In Luke's stories that contrast Jews and Samaritans, the priest and Levite and the nine lepers do not measure up to the behavior or faith of the Samaritans (see Rom 2:13 – 29).

2. Encountering God in Healing

The incident also shows that while many receive healing in their lives, only a few (see 13:23) "encounter God in their healing."[12] Why is it that the Samaritan "sees" and the other nine do not? The text does not explain, and the response of faith remains a mystery. Perhaps the others took God for granted, or they were too distracted by the religious rituals they would need to perform to pay any attention to God, or they were simply ungrateful by nature. Faith and thanksgiving are inseparable. True Christians therefore experience God's grace intensely and allow their gratitude for what God has done for them in Christ to shape their whole lives.

---

10. Danker, *Jesus and the New Age*, 291.
11. Schweizer, *Luke*, 269.

12. Gaiser, "Your Faith Has Made You Well," 295.

Luke 17:20 – 37

Literary Context

Hartman recognizes that this section does not have "an informative function, foretelling future events." It tells us nothing about how near or how distant or delayed the day of the Son of Man is. Instead of giving a calendar of future events, "it has an admonitory function" that exhorts "the reader to lead a life worthy of the Son of Man, having such a future in mind."[1] This view is supported by the connection of this discourse to what follows in 18:1 – 30, which contain only ethical admonitions.

The teaching in this section imposes "demands on those who look forward to the coming of the Son of Man, *or* to inheriting eternal life, *or* to being saved, *or* to being taken away — all of them seem to have meant more or less the same thing to the reader!"[2] Despite the chapter division, 18:1 – 8 does not begin a new episode "since there is no new action, no new place, no new constellation of characters, no new time."[3] What follows in 18:1 – 8 illustrates what is required to be saved when the Son of Man comes: diligent prayer and faith. The conclusion to the parable (18:8) caps off the section by offering the assurance that God will bring vindication and deliver the elect. It adds an implicit admonition to maintain faith during the adversity of the interim.

---

1. Lars Hartman, "Reading Luke 17,20 – 37," in *The Four Gospels, 1992: Festschrift Frans Neirynck* (BETL 100; ed. F. van Segbroeck et al.; Leuven: Leuven Univ. Press, 1992), 1672.

2. Ibid., 1675.

3. Ibid., 1671.

Main Idea

The end will not come according to human calculation or observation, but when it comes it will be visible to all. It will bring conflagration and destruction, but the elect will be safely delivered from it if they do not become imbedded in the things of this world.

Translation

(See next page.)

Structure and Literary Form

The opening question from the Pharisees allows Jesus to launch his admonitions related to the coming of the reign of God. After quickly dismissing an eschatological perspective that assumes that the coming of his reign can be charted by observable signs, implicitly associated with the wrongheaded Pharisees (17:20 – 21), Jesus directs a fuller response to his disciples.

In 17:22, Luke introduces a change in the audience from the Pharisees to the disciples and a corresponding shift in perspective from the present to the future.[4] The subject matter also shifts to the coming days of the Son of Man (17:22 – 37). The reign of God is currently in their midst, so there is no need to say, "Look, here it is!" or "There it is!" (17:21); but the days of the Son of Man are different. It marks the shift from the present evil age to the age to come.

Jesus' departure from this earthly life will mark a new era that will bring intense longing among believers, spawning the danger that false prophets claiming that the Son of Man has returned will deceive the faithful. Verse 24 explains why the disciples should discredit any such feverish speculation. Jesus compares the coming of the days of the Son of Man to lightning flashing across the whole sky. Its course cannot be mapped out in advance, and it is not hidden but overwhelmingly obvious as it lights up the horizon. Verse 25 reiterates the necessity of the Son of Man's suffering and death that brings about his departure. Verses 26 – 30 compare the days of the Son of Man to the catastrophes overtaking the generations of Noah and of Lot. The comparison consists of three elements: (1) distraction with the mundane business of life; (2) rescue of those who are warned of the coming destruction; and (3) destruction. This comparison is followed by further assurances, warnings, and admonitions

---

4. I follow Steven L. Bridge (*Where the Eagles Are Gathered: The Deliverance of the Elect in Lukan Eschatology* [JSNTSup 240; London: Sheffield Academic, 2003], 25 – 27) in the analysis of the structure.

Luke 17:20–37

17:20a	Question	When he was asked once by the Pharisees when the reign of God comes,
b	Response	**he answered,**
		"*The reign of God does not come with observable [signs].*
21a		*Nor will they say,*
		'Look, here it is!'
		or 'There it is!'
b	Explanatory clause	*for behold, God's reign is in your midst."*
22	Prophecy	**He said to the disciples,**
		"*Days will come when you will desire to see one of the days of the Son of Man*
		and you will not see them.
23a		*They will say to you,*
		'Look there!'
		'Look here!'
b	Admonition	*Do not go out;*
		do not go in search of it.
24a	Explanatory clause	*For as lightning flashes and lights up the heavens from one side to the other,*
b		*so will the Son of Man be [in his day].*
25	Prophecy	*But first it is necessary for him to suffer many things and*
		to be rejected by this generation.
26	Illustration (1)	*Just as it was in the days of Noah, so it will be in the days of the Son of Man.*
27a	Distraction	*They were eating, drinking, marrying, being given in marriage*
b	Rescue	*until the very day that Noah entered into the ark,*
c	Destruction	*and the flood came and destroyed them all.*
28a	Illustration (2)	*Likewise, just as it was in the days of Lot,*
b	Distraction	*they were eating and drinking, buying and selling, planting and building,*
29a	Rescue	*but*
		on the day that Lot left Sodom,
b	Destruction	*it rained fire and sulfur from heaven and destroyed all of them—*
30	Comparison	*it will be like that on the day that the Son of Man is revealed.*
31a	Admonition	*On that day, anyone on the housetop who has belongings in the house*
		must not come down to take them away;
b	Admonition	*and likewise anyone in the field must not turn back.*
32	Admonition	*Remember Lot's wife.*
33	Axiom	*Whoever tries to make his or her life secure will lose it,*
		but whoever loses his or her life will keep it.
34	Prophecy/separation	*I tell you, on that night there will be two in one bed;*
		one will be taken and the other left.
35	Prophecy/separation	*There will be two women grinding meal together;*
		one will be taken and the other left."
36	Textual variant	
37a	Question	**Then they asked him,**
		"*Where, Lord?"*
b	Response	**He said to them,**
		"*Where the body is,*
		there also the eagles will be gathered up together."

concerning "that day" and "that night" (17:31 – 35). Some will be rescued, while others will be left.

The Pharisees raise the question of "when," but the disciples raise the question of "where." The issue of "where" brackets the discourse. The second part of Jesus' answer to the question "when" identifies *where* it is: "[It] is in your midst" (17:21). Jesus' answer to the disciples' question identifies whither they are rescued.

Exegetical Outline

→ **I. Pharisees' question about calculating the coming of God's reign (17:20a)**

II. The answer to the question "When?" (17:20b – 21)

    A. God's reign does not come with observable signs (17:20b)

    B. Only deceivers will say that God's reign is "here" or "there" (17:21a)

    C. God's reign is already in their midst (17:21b)

III. The absence of the Son of Man (17:22 – 23)

    A. Jesus' absence will create intense longing in his disciples (17:22)

    B. Warning against deceivers who say that the Son of Man is "here" or "there" (17:23)

IV. The appearance of the Son of Man (17:24 – 30)

    A. The appearance of the Son of Man likened to lightning (17:24)

    B. The necessary suffering and rejection of the Son of Man causing his absence (17:25)

    C. The appearance of the Son of Man likened to the days of Noah (17:26 – 27)

    D. The appearance of the Son of Man likened to the days of Lot (17:28 – 30)

V. Assurances/warnings concerning what will happen "on that day" (17:31 – 35)

    A. Assurances/warnings concerning the evacuation of the righteous (17:31 – 33)

    B. Assurances/warnings concerning the separation of humanity (17:34 – 35)

VI. The answer to the question "Where?" (17:37)

Explanation of the Text

17:20 When he was asked once by the Pharisees when the reign of God comes, he answered, "The reign of God does not come with observable [signs]" (ἐπερωτηθεὶς δὲ ὑπὸ τῶν Φαρισαίων πότε ἔρχεται ἡ βασιλεία τοῦ θεοῦ ἀπεκρίθη αὐτοῖς καὶ εἶπεν· οὐκ ἔρχεται ἡ βασιλεία τοῦ θεοῦ μετὰ παρατηρήσεως). The Pharisees' question about when the reign of God will come reflects their blindness. God's reign has already broken into the world through Jesus' ministry.

Jesus dismisses their question as misguided. God's reign has not announced itself with pyrotechnic, triumphalistic, apocalyptic phenomena that make its presence indisputable, but it has come in a disarming way, like a mustard seed or like leaven (13:18 – 21). As Wright reconstructs their point of view, they were looking for "tangible, this-worldly points of reference."

If Pilate was still governing Judea, then the kingdom had not come. If the Temple was not rebuilt, then the kingdom had not come. If the Messiah had not arrived, then the kingdom had not come. If the pagans were not defeated and/or flocking to Zion for instruction, then the kingdom had not come.[5]

Jesus rejects the idea that the coming of God's reign can be predicted through something "observable" (παρατήρησις), which most recent commentators connect to "the observation of the movement of heavenly bodies, woes, wars, family strife, social collapse, natural disasters, and the breakup of the cosmic order." I relate the noun instead to the hostile demand that Jesus produce a "sign from heaven" to validate his ministry (11:16), and to Jesus' declaration that no sign will be given a sign-seeking, evil generation (11:29 – 32; see 23:8). I therefore add "signs" in brackets to convey this idea.

The translation of the NRSV ("things that can be observed") is misleading because there *are* observable components to the advent of God's reign (9:27). For example, it is visible in the ingathering of sinners and the resulting celebration. The Pharisees, however, are blind to such evidence. Jesus makes the point that the coming of God's reign differs from the advent of the end. Those who fix their eyes myopically on obedience to the minutiae in the law or who squint into the distance to calculate the timing of the end from observable events will miss seeing what is staring them in the face.

17:21 Nor will they say, "Look, here it is!" or "There it is!" for behold, God's reign is in your midst (οὐδὲ ἐροῦσιν· ἰδοὺ ὧδε ἤ· ἐκεῖ, ἰδοὺ γὰρ ἡ βασιλεία τοῦ θεοῦ ἐντὸς ὑμῶν ἐστιν). The emphatic placement of the present tense verb "is" (ἐστιν) at the end of the phrase underscores that God's reign is a present reality and not a glimmer of hope.[6] A rare word is taken to mean "within" or "among" (ἐντός). Three options have dominated interpretation.[7]

(1) Jesus may imply that God's reign is an internal reality. The word ἐντός occurs elsewhere in the New Testament only in Matt 23:26 to refer to the inside of a cup (see also LXX Pss 38:4; 102:1; 108:22; Isa 16:11). According to Holmén's research, the early church fathers who cite this verse not only understood it to mean "within," they appear to know no other alternative meaning.[8] Several versions therefore render it, "the kingdom of God is within you" (KJV, ASV, NIV 1984). This translation is questionable, however. If Jesus refers to God's reigning activity, it seems highly inappropriate to say that God's reign is within the Pharisees, given their attitudes.[9] They are like those who are full of darkness, not light (11:33 – 36). Also, God's reign is not portrayed in Luke as some kind of inner psychological reality, nor is it akin to the presence of the Spirit. Marshall comments, "Jesus speaks of men entering the kingdom, not of the kingdom entering men."[10] The reign of God is not something Luke portrays as indistinguishable from the Spirit of God that dwells within individuals (Rom 8:11).

---

5. Wright, *Jesus and the Victory of God*, 223.

6. Contra A. J. Mattill, *Luke and the Last Things: A Perspective for the Understanding of Lukan Thought* (Dillsboro, NC: Western North Carolina Press, 1979), 198 – 201. The use of the present "comes" (ἔρχεται) in 17:20 is a futuristic present.

7. See Bent Noack, *Das Gottesreich bei Lukas: Eine Studie zu Lk 17,20 – 24* (SymBU 10; Uppsala: C. W. K. Gleerup, 1948), for a brief history of interpretation.

8. Tom Holmén, "The Alternatives of the Kingdom: Encountering the Semantic Restrictions of Luke 17,20 – 21 (ἐντὸς ὑμῶν)," *ZNW* 87 (1996): 223.

9. C. C. Carargounis ("Kingdom of God/Kingdom of Heaven," *DJG*, 423 – 24) counters that the phrase "is Luke's way of expressing the inward nature and dynamic of the kingdom of God, rather than refer to any actual presence within or among the Pharisees." This reading makes the narrative context irrelevant for interpretation.

10. Marshall, *The Gospel of Luke*, 655.

(2) Another possibility is that it means "within your reach, grasp, or possession."[11] It is related to the ability to repent and have the word of faith in the heart (see Deut 30:14; Rom 10:17). It might then correspond to the demand to strive to enter through the narrow door (13:24). The problem with this interpretation is that it places too much emphasis on human control over God's reign and does not answer the question the Pharisees have asked.[12] They asked *when* God's reign is coming, but this answers *how* one enters it. It would also seem that this answer requires an additional explanation or exhortation: "Repent and believe the good news!" (Mark 1:15). Beasley-Murray calls it "an unexpressed corollary,"[13] but its absence in the context makes this interpretation unlikely.

(3) Matill presents over forty usages of the word (ἐντός) over the span of one thousand years and finds seven well-attested meanings.[14] The meaning "among" or "in the midst of" has legitimate support, and the narrative context can be the determining guide for understanding what it means here. The meaning that seems to make the best sense in this context with a plural pronoun is "in your midst" (NASB, ESV, TNIV, NIV 2011) or "among you" (NJB, NAB, NRSV). It refers to the present reality embodied in the preaching and healing of Jesus (7:22 – 23; 9:27; 11:20).[15] It explains why God's reign does not come with apocalyptic warning signs (17:20). They are pointless because Jesus is the sign of the presence of God's reign, which expresses the paradoxical already/not yet reality of God's reign (see 10:9, 11; 21:31;

22:16, 18).[16] Jesus tries to direct the Pharisees' gaze away from the future to the present. Their problem is that they cannot read the signs of the times (12:54 – 56).

17:22 He said to the disciples, "Days will come when you will desire to see one of the days of the Son of Man and you will not see them" (εἶπεν δὲ πρὸς τοὺς μαθητάς· ἐλεύσονται ἡμέραι ὅτε ἐπιθυμήσετε μίαν τῶν ἡμερῶν τοῦ υἱοῦ τοῦ ἀνθρώπου ἰδεῖν καὶ οὐκ ὄψεσθε). The Pharisees drop out of the picture, and Jesus addresses the disciples on the topic of the coming day(s) of the Son of Man. The Old Testament can refer to the "day(s) coming" as a time of "anticipated judgment and distress" (see Isa 39:6; Jer 7:32; 9:25; 19:6; 48:12; 49:2; 51:52; Hos 9:7; Amos 4:2; 8:11).[17] If the references to "the day[s] of the Son of Man" in vv. 24, 26 govern its meaning in this verse,[18] those days are not only characterized by the oblivion of sinners; they also bring deliverance, as in the case of Noah and Lot.

Earthly distress and Jesus' absence underlie the yearning. God's reign is no longer incarnate "in [their] midst." As Peter declares to the people of Jerusalem, Jesus must remain "until the time comes for God to restore everything" (Acts 3:21). The disciples "will *not* see" those days during their lives on earth, and their suffering will produce intense yearning and crying out. The days will come, however, in God's timing.

17:23 – 24 They will say to you, "Look there!" "Look here!" Do not go out; do not go in search

11. C. H. Roberts, "The Kingdom of Heaven (Lk. xvii.21)," *HTR* 41 (1948): 1 – 8; A. A. Rüstow, "Zur Deutung von Lukas 17:20 – 21," *ZNW* 51 (1960): 197 – 224; George R. Beasley-Murray, *Jesus and the Kingdom of God* (Grand Rapids: Eerdmans, 1986), 102 – 3; Fitzmyer, *Luke*, 2:1161 – 62.

12. Bridge, *Where the Eagles Are Gathered*, 159.

13. Beasley-Murray, *Jesus and the Kingdom of God*, 103.

14. Mattill, *Luke and the Last Things*, 204 – 7.

15. Daniel 4:2 – 3 connects God's reign to present signs and wonders. See Hartman, "Reading Luke 17,20 – 37," 1666.

16. See Bock, *Luke* (NIVAC), 193 – 97.

17. Beasley-Murray, *Jesus and the Kingdom of God*, 314. Jesus fluctuates between using the plural "days" (vv. 22, 26) and the singular "day" (vv. 24, 27, 29, 30, 31; see v. 34 and then "night").

18. Ibid.

of it. **For as lightning flashes and lights up the heavens from one side to the other, so will the Son of Man be [in his day]** (καὶ ἐροῦσιν ὑμῖν· ἰδοὺ ἐκεῖ· ἰδοὺ ὧδε· μὴ ἀπέλθητε μηδὲ διώξητε. ὥσπερ γὰρ ἡ ἀστραπὴ ἀστράπτουσα ἐκ τῆς ὑπὸ τὸν οὐρανὸν εἰς τὴν ὑπ᾽ οὐρανὸν λάμπει, οὕτως ἔσται ὁ υἱὸς τοῦ ἀνθρώπου [ἐν τῇ ἡμέρᾳ αὐτοῦ]). Because the desire for earthly deliverance will be so intense, disciples will be vulnerable to being hoodwinked by false sightings.

The lightning image offers an explanation why they are not to go out in search of the Son of Man when people excitedly exclaim, "Here!" or "There!" (v. 23). Luke does not refer to lightning that falls vertically from the sky (like Satan's fall, 10:18) but lightning that flashes across the sky in an overwhelming fashion that is unmistakably visible (lit., "from the [region] under heaven to the [region] under heaven"). The Son of Man will not make secret appearances to only a few; his coming will be obvious to all.

While the parallel saying in Matt 24:27 compares the lightning to "the coming of the Son of Man," Luke compares it to the Son of Man himself. Lightning accompanies God's appearances on earth in Exod 19:16 – 24; 2 Sam 22:15; Pss 18:14; 77:18 (see also *2 Bar.* 53:8 – 10), and Luke emphasizes the glorification of the Son of Man (see 9:29, where in the transfiguration his garments became "as a flash of lightning"). Like lightning, the Son of Man's arrival will be sudden, eye-catching, glorious, frightening, and celestial.

17:25 But first it is necessary for him to suffer many things and to be rejected by this generation (πρῶτον δὲ δεῖ αὐτὸν πολλὰ παθεῖν καὶ ἀποδοκιμασθῆναι ἀπὸ τῆς γενεᾶς ταύτης). This is the fifth of six passion predictions in Luke (see also 9:22, 44; 18:32 – 33; implicit 12:50; 13:32 – 33)

and is introduced almost as an aside. It is the only passion prediction in the synoptic tradition to be found in an eschatological discourse. In the context referring to the glorious coming of the Son of Man, it may correct any expectation of glory without suffering. The path of suffering leads to glory, and this saying reminds readers that the affliction and rejection Jesus suffered at the hands of his generation does not end with his death.

"This generation" applies to those who will put Jesus to death, but his disciples will continue to be afflicted and rejected by their generations (see 18:1 – 8). The oppression will not be rectified until the parousia, which brings universal judgment. Plummer interprets it to mean, "Just as the thought of impending suffering needs to be cheered by that of future glory, so the thought of future glory needs to be chastened by that of impending suffering."[19]

17:26 – 27 Just as it was in the days of Noah, so it will be in the days of the Son of Man. They were eating, drinking, marrying, being given in marriage until the very day that Noah entered into the ark, and the flood came and destroyed them all (καὶ καθὼς ἐγένετο ἐν ταῖς ἡμέραις Νῶε, οὕτως ἔσται καὶ ἐν ταῖς ἡμέραις τοῦ υἱοῦ τοῦ ἀνθρώπου· ἤσθιον, ἔπινον, ἐγάμουν, ἐγαμίζοντο, ἄχρι ἧς ἡμέρας εἰσῆλθεν Νῶε εἰς τὴν κιβωτόν καὶ ἦλθεν ὁ κατακλυσμὸς καὶ ἀπώλεσεν πάντας). Bridge argues that the image from "the days of Noah" suggests that "the days of the Son of Man" cannot mean that it "will come as an unexpected catastrophe."[20] Noah had time to warn everyone, build an ark, and gather animals. Lot was warned the night before and lingered before leaving (Gen 19:12 – 22). He contends that the references to these figures may instead place an emphasis on

---

the righteous survivors being rescued. He cites Glasson's earlier observation:

> The time of crisis is described, not as the day when the flood came, but "the day that Noah entered into the ark," not the day when it rained fire from heaven, but "the day that Lot went out from Sodom." Had it been the purpose of Jesus merely to illustrate sudden judgment, there would have been no need to mention Lot at all.[21]

The point is well taken. In Wis 10:6 – 9, for example, Lot is referred to as a righteous man who was rescued when the wicked, ungodly were perishing to make the point, "Wisdom rescued from troubles those who served her" (Wis 10:9). This idea reappears in 2 Pet 2:7, which speaks of God's rescuing Lot, "a righteous man, who was distressed by the depraved conduct of the lawless." In 1 Pet 3:20, the days of Noah are connected to his rescue, "a few people, eight in all, were saved," and not to the suddenness of the flood. Bridge concludes that the point of comparison is that Noah and Lot were saved from divine judgment, and "Luke's point is not the suddenness of the judgment but the removal of the righteous."[22]

17:28 – 30 Likewise, just as it was in the days of Lot, they were eating and drinking, buying and selling, planting and building, but on the day that Lot left Sodom, it rained fire and sulfur from heaven and destroyed all of them — it will be like that on the day that the Son of Man is revealed (ὁμοίως καθὼς ἐγένετο ἐν ταῖς ἡμέραις Λώτ· ἤσθιον, ἔπινον, ἠγόραζον, ἐπώλουν, ἐφύτευον, ᾠκοδόμουν· ᾗ δὲ ἡμέρᾳ ἐξῆλθεν Λὼτ ἀπὸ Σοδόμων, ἔβρεξεν πῦρ καὶ θεῖον ἀπ᾽ οὐρανοῦ καὶ ἀπώλεσεν πάντας. κατὰ τὰ αὐτὰ ἔσται ᾗ

ἡμέρᾳ ὁ υἱὸς τοῦ ἀνθρώπου ἀποκαλύπτεται). The reference to Lot is absent from the parallels in Mark and Matthew. Luke adds "buying and selling, planting and building" to what Noah's generation was doing, "eating, drinking, marrying." All of these are normal activities.

What is noteworthy is that Jesus does not mention the sins of Noah's or Lot's generation that brought judgment. Instead, what he notes is their "living in complete disregard to what was coming, immersed in their daily occupations and pleasures, planning and arranging their lives with no thought beyond their immediate interests, self-sufficient and self-satisfied, until catastrophe overwhelmed them (Gen 6:11ff. 7:21ff)."[23] These activities can interfere with heeding God's call (14:18 – 20) and being wholeheartedly committed to God (12:18 – 19; 14:26; 18:28; see 1 Cor 7:29 – 31). But in the context of Jesus' concern for the poor throughout the travel narrative, Ezekiel's comments about Sodom's guilt are pertinent: "This was the guilt of your sister Sodom: she and her daughters had pride, excess of food, and prosperous ease, but did not aid the poor and needy" (Ezek 16:49 ESV).

Lot is mentioned because, like Noah, he was saved from destruction that overtook his generation. When Noah and Lot "have been taken out of the firing line," then total devastation, from flood or from fire and sulfur, befell the others.[24] In the context, according to Bridge, it reinforces "the idea that the evacuation of the righteous will precede the eschatological destruction."[25] The scenario presented is that when the Son of Man "is revealed" (1 Cor 1:7; 2 Thess 1:7; 1 Pet 1:7, 13),

---

21. T. F. Glasson, *The Second Advent: The Origin of New Testament Doctrine* (3rd ed.; London: Epworth, 1963), 82 – 83.

22. Bridge, *Where the Eagles Are Gathered*, 41. The parallel to Luke 17:27 in Matt 24:39 has "and they knew nothing." Luke may have omitted this phrase so as not to lessen their

culpability since ignorance in Luke-Acts is forgivable (23:34; Acts 17:30).

23. Manson, *The Sayings of Jesus*, 144.

24. Nolland, *Luke*, 2:861.

25. Bridge, *Where the Eagles Are Gathered*, 43.

the elect will be rescued and then disaster and destruction will consume those left.

17:31 – 32 On that day, anyone on the housetop who has belongings in the house must not come down to take them away, and likewise anyone in the field not must turn back. Remember Lot's wife (ἐν ἐκείνῃ τῇ ἡμέρᾳ ὃς ἔσται ἐπὶ τοῦ δώματος καὶ τὰ σκεύη αὐτοῦ ἐν τῇ οἰκίᾳ, μὴ καταβάτω ἆραι αὐτά, καὶ ὁ ἐν ἀγρῷ ὁμοίως μὴ ἐπιστρεψάτω εἰς τὰ ὀπίσω. μνημονεύετε τῆς γυναικὸς Λώτ). Disciples are to remember that Lot's wife disobeyed the command and looked back (Gen 19:17, 26). The context suggests that the emphasis is on not turning back as Lot's wife did (see 9:62).

Neither the Old Testament nor Luke indicates why she looked back. Was she concerned about family and friends? Did she want to fetch her belongings, or did she look longingly after them? Did she begrudge giving up the comfort of her old life in Sodom? If so, she was not quite prepared to leave everything even when she knew that everything she so cherished in Sodom was soon to be destroyed. Whatever the reason, Jesus admonishes disciples to be obedient and resolute. As Bridge observes, it "introduces the point that deliverance demands nothing less than a wholehearted commitment on the part of the elect. In other words, even on 'that day' one can still jeopardize salvation by simply turning back."[26]

17:33 Whoever tries to make his or her life secure will lose it, but whoever loses his or her life will keep it (ὃς ἐὰν ζητήσῃ τὴν ψυχὴν αὐτοῦ περιποιήσασθαι ἀπολέσει αὐτήν, ὃς δ᾽ ἂν ἀπολέσῃ ζῳογονήσει αὐτήν). In its context, this saying applies to securing one's life by breaking off

all attachments to earthly goods (see Matt 16:25; Mark 8:35; Luke 9:24). In the conflagration, all earthly things will be destroyed.

17:34 – 35 I tell you, on that night there will be two in one bed; one will be taken and the other left. There will be two women grinding meal together; one will be taken and the other left (λέγω ὑμῖν, ταύτῃ τῇ νυκτὶ ἔσονται δύο ἐπὶ κλίνης μιᾶς, ὁ εἷς παραλημφθήσεται καὶ ὁ ἕτερος ἀφεθήσεται· ἔσονται δύο ἀλήθουσαι ἐπὶ τὸ αὐτό, ἡ μία παραλημφθήσεται ἡ δὲ ἑτέρα ἀφεθήσεται). It is possible that the term for "bed" can refer to a "dining couch" (κλίνης; see the textual variant in Mark 7:4). But the time frame at night points to them being in bed. The image has no sexual overtones and reflects less affluent times when people did not enjoy the luxury of private bedrooms. The emphasis in these illustrations is placed on the separation of persons who are side by side and closely related. It reinforces that as in the days of Noah and Lot when some were rescued and others were not, so it will be on that day when the Son of Man appears. The passive verbs represent divine passives: the Son of Man will rescue them. Those who are not taken will be left to face the inferno.

17:37 Then they asked him, "Where, Lord?" He said to them, "Where the body is, there also the eagles will be gathered up together" (καὶ ἀποκριθέντες λέγουσιν αὐτῷ· ποῦ, κύριε; ὁ δὲ εἶπεν αὐτοῖς· ὅπου τὸ σῶμα, ἐκεῖ καὶ οἱ ἀετοὶ ἐπισυναχθήσονται). The multitude of suggested meanings reveals that this text is "notoriously elusive."[27] Bridge identifies twenty interpretations.[28] In Matthew's gospel, the saying is linked to the lightning simile and refers to the universal visibility of Jesus' coming (Matt 24:27 – 28). In Luke, the

---

26. Ibid.

27. Ronald A. Piper, *Wisdom in the Q Tradition: The Aphoristic Teaching of Jesus* (SNTSMS; Cambridge: Cambridge Univ.

Press, 1989), 139.

28. Bridge, *Where the Eagles Are Gathered*, 3.

saying is separated from the lightning simile and placed in the climactic position of the discourse at the end. This placement indicates that the saying's meaning in Luke differs from that in Matthew.

It is wrong to interpret the disciples' question as a futile one that stems from their ignorance and that Jesus' answer is deliberately evasive. If that were the case, it would mean that he is ruder to his own disciples than to the Pharisees.[29] The answer, however, is enigmatic, which lends itself to a variety of interpretations.

The correct interpretation will not ignore the basic thrust of the disciples' question, "Where?" For example, interpreting the saying as comparing the speed of the eagle or the vulture (translations vary between the two, Job 9:25–26; Hab 1:8) to the swiftness of the coming of the Son of Man fails to answer their question. Taking it as a reference to a lack of preparation — when vultures gather, the prey is already dead — also does not provide an answer to this question. The same is true for interpretations that link the answer to the nature of the final judgment — its inevitability, mercilessness, or thoroughness. Interpreting the saying as referring to the visible presence of the Son of Man when he comes, like vultures hovering over carrion (Job 39:26–30), fits Matthew's context, not Luke's.

Interpreting the saying as a macabre image of the nature of the judgment that pictures vultures tearing into the kill also ignores the question, "Where?" Luke does not use the noun "corpse" or "carcass" (πτῶμα), which appears in Matt 24:28, but "body"(σῶμα). This difference in wording is not simply attributable to a stylistic desire to change a coarse word "corpse" to something more delicate. Bridge's interpretation of this saying is the most convincing because it offers an answer to the disciples' question. He takes it as a metaphor that pertains to those who are taken (17:34–35). The "eagles" (ἀετοί) represent the righteous who are being borne away. He argues lexically for the translation of the noun as "eagles," since another word (γύψ) is the usual Greek word for "vulture."[30] The question "Where?" (ποῦ) means whither are they taken (see John 14:5; 16:5), and the answer is to "the body" (σῶμα), which represents the Lord. The "body" is not a reference to a lifeless corpse but "signifies the crucified Lord as a living entity, namely, the resurrected Christ."[31] The image of eagles being "gathered" (ἐπισυναχθήσονται) pictures the eschatological ingathering of the elect (Ps 106:47; 2 Macc 1:27; 2:7–8, 18).

The disciples' question does not reflect spiritual dullness but "proceeds logically from the rather cryptic disappearances described in vv. 34–35."[32] They want to know where the elect will be taken when they are saved from destruction. The answer is obscure, and the disciples will not be able to understand it until after the resurrection when they can recognize Jesus as the risen Lord, remember his words, and interpret the events in light of God's purposes in Scripture. Only after the passion and resurrection can they recognize the "body" as the one given for them by Jesus (22:19), who was raised from the dead and transported to glory (24:3, 23, 26).

---

29. Ibid, 5. Bridge provides an in-depth critique of the various proposals.

30. Luke appears to have interpreted the image in light of the tradition of the eagle as a deliverer of the elect (Exod 19:3–6; Deut 32:10–12; *1 En.* 96:1–2; 4Q 504 [frag 6] 6–8),

carrying them into the realm of the divine (Bridge, *Where the Eagles Are Gathered*, 66).

31. Ibid., 52.

32. Ibid., 51.

Theology in Application

1. The Timing of the End

In this brief discourse, Jesus stymies any attempt to calculate with precision when the return of the Son of Man will occur so that it can be entered into a calendar or end-time chart. Like the reign of God, it does not come with observable signs. A time line, however, can be derived from this difficult passage:[33]

Jesus' ministry | Ascension | Interim Period | Son of Man's Revelation | New Age

This schema prevents the danger of an overrealized eschatology that Paul challenges in 2 Tim 2:17 – 18.[34] It also places the persecutions of Jesus' disciples in divine perspective during the interim when they may be afflicted with discouragement about the delay and doubt about whether God will ultimately vindicate his people. Dillon states that the declaration in 17:25 "is meant to place the travails of a missionary church, longing for the sight of her hidden Lord (v. 22; cp. Acts 3,21) ... under the challenge and consolation of the Lord's own destiny."[35] The missionary church will take the same journey that Jesus did through the successive stages of suffering (see Acts 5:41; 9:15 – 16) to resurrection.

This conviction runs throughout Luke-Acts. Paul instructs the churches to "strengthen" their "souls," and he encourages them to continue in the faith by asserting, "We must go through many hardships to enter the kingdom of God" (Acts 14:22). He proclaims this message after he and Barnabas were stoned and left for dead in Lystra. Disciples should be confident in God's final vindication not only when they experience the beneficial manifestations of God's reign in this life but also when they experience tribulation on behalf of God's reign.

The coming of the Son of Man will be universal and cosmic in scope (17:24, 30). There will be no mistaking the fact that it has arrived. It will come suddenly, however, when people are distracted by the pursuits of everyday life (eating, drinking, marrying, giving in marriage, buying, selling, planting, and building). There will be no warning shots fired across the bow to alert people to the imminent judgment.

Again, attempts to set dates for Christ's return must be rejected. The period of time until that event is indeterminate. When it does come, it will be unexpected and a surprise. Christians do not prepare themselves by graphing out time charts and different scenarios. They do prepare themselves by their faithful witness and ethical conduct befitting their repentance. In the meantime, God will continue to visit

---

33. Ibid., 40. The phrase the "days will come" (17:22) refers to the interim period; "one of the days of the Son of Man" (17:22) refers to Jesus' ministry or eschatological reign during this interim; "the Son of Man ... [in his day]" (17:24) refers to the Son of Man's revelation; "the days of the Son of Man" (17:26) refers to the interim period just prior to the day of revelation; and "on the day," "on that day" (17:30, 31) refer to the day of revelation.

34. Talbert, *Reading Luke*, 168.

35. Dillon, *From Eye-Witness to Ministers of the Word*, 209.

his people with judgment and redemption; and as in the days of the Old Testament, God's people will continue to endure humiliation and tribulation until "the times of the Gentiles," the time of oppression, "are fulfilled" (21:24).

2. The Deliverance of the Elect and Judgment of the Unrighteous

The closing lines liken "the eschatological 'day' to a sequence of events in which the evacuation of the righteous precedes total annihilation (17:26 – 30)."[36] The righteous followers of Christ will be rescued and gathered to the Son of Man to avoid punishment (17:34 – 37; see Heb 9:28). But they must give evidence of wholehearted allegiance to their true hope for survival. Consequently, they should be careful not to become overly attached to worldly possessions or caught up too much in worldly pursuits. They should be prepared for the deliverance to occur at any time. Danker comments: "Precisely because everything goes on as usual, the disciple cannot carry on business as usual."[37] One cannot be seeking to gain one's life in the here and now without endangering one's life in the coming age. Losing one's life now ensures preserving it at the parousia. It requires single-minded devotion and a willingness to leave all behind. When it comes, there can be no looking back. Bridge states: "As was the case with Noah and Lot, the eschatological deliverance of the elect will depend on their ability to relinquish their former lives completely."[38]

The rejection of Christ and the persecution of his followers (17:25) will precipitate a devastating judgment on the unrighteous. They will be left behind as they were in the days of Noah and Lot "to suffer their inevitable destruction."[39] Sadly, being intimately linked with someone in this life does not mean that they cannot be separated from each other to face completely different fates in the judgment (17:34 – 35). Those who are left will not only face devastation; they will be excluded from God's reign. No specific criteria are given as to why one will be taken and the other left, and readers are left to figure that out for themselves.

---

36. Bridge, *Where the Eagles Are Gathered*, 55.
37. Danker, *Jesus and the New Age*, 293.
38. Bridge, *Where the Eagles Are Gathered*, 47.
39. Ibid., 55.

54

Literary Context

This parable should not be separated from the eschatological discourse that precedes it (17:20 – 37) as the beginning of a new chapter because it forms its conclusion. It differs from the sayings discourse only in its form as a parable. The teaching directed to the disciples began with a statement about longing to see the days of the Son of Man (17:22), and it comes to a fitting conclusion with the application of the parable, "when the Son of Man comes …" (18:8).

The vocabulary in the parable has eschatological implications. The verb "to give justice, avenge" (ἐκδικεῖν) appears only here in Luke (18:3, 5),[1] but the noun form "justice" (ἐκδίκησις, 18:7, 8) appears in 21:22 to refer to "the days of vengeance." The noun has an eschatological connotation in 2 Thess 1:7 – 8, where Paul alludes to the suffering of Christians and looks forward to the day "when the Lord Jesus is revealed from heaven with his mighty angels in flaming fire, inflicting vengeance [ἐκδίκησιν] on those who do not know God and on those who do not obey the gospel of our Lord Jesus" (NRSV). In Rev 6:10, the martyrs cry out from underneath the altar supplicating the Lord to judge and avenge their blood (see Rev 19:2); it is a supplication for the final vindication. The verb "to be patient" (μακροθυμεῖν) appears in 2 Pet 3:8 – 9 in an eschatological context to explain that the Lord's timetable seems frustratingly slow only when clocked by impatient humans. The Lord is patient in bringing the end and its judgment because he does not want anyone to perish but all to come to repentance. The adverbial phrase "quickly" (ἐν τάχει) also appears in eschatological contexts in the New Testament (Rev 1:1; 22:6).

The literary context reveals that this parable is not simply about how one should pray but relates directly to prayer for the Lord to come and set things right — a prayer that is all the more urgent on the lips of those suffering affliction. It assures listeners that the Lord takes note of their affliction and will act swiftly to vindicate them, but it also warns that they need to endure so that they can stand before the Son of Man when he comes to deliver them (21:36).

---

1. This verb and its related noun also appear in Acts 7:24, where it reports how Moses avenged his wronged countryman (see Rom 12:19; 2 Cor 7:11, 10:6; Heb 10:30; 1 Pet 2:14).

Main Idea

Disciples must pray with persistence while waiting for their vindication lest they fall away during the period of delay when injustice abounds.

Translation

Luke 18:1–8

18:1	Parable expressing the point	**And he told this parable to them** about how it is necessary for them always to pray and not become ✎ disheartened,
2a	Character introduction (1)	saying, "A certain judge was in a certain city,
b		who neither feared God nor showed regard for people.
3a	Character introduction (2)	*And* there was a widow in that city
b		*and* she used to come to him, saying, 'Give me justice against my adversary!'
4a	Time reference	*For a time,* he was unwilling [to act], *but* after a while he said to himself,
b	Interior monologue	'Though I do not fear God or show any regard for people,
5a		*yet* *because* this widow pesters me,
b		I will have to give her justice
c		*so that* she will not wear me out in the end with her continual appeals.'"
6	Admonition	**The Lord said,** "Listen to what the unrighteous judge says!
7	Interpretive question	Will not God bring justice for his elect who cry to him night and day, though he waits patiently [to act] for them?
8a	Pronouncement	I say to you that he will bring justice for them quickly.
b	Motivational question	When the Son of Man comes, however, will he then find faith on the earth?"

Structure and Literary Form

The structure follows the pattern of an introduction that expresses the point followed by a parable that illustrates the point. It is followed by an application of the point with two questions. The first question (18:7) is answered with a pronouncement (18:8a). The next question (18:8b) goes unanswered and therefore contains an implicit admonition.

Exegetical Outline

→ I. **Axiom: Always pray and do not lose heart (18:1)**

II. **Example of the unjust judge and persistent widow (18:2 – 5)**
   A. A pitiless, hard-boiled judge (18:2)
   B. A relentless, aggrieved widow (18:3)
   C. The judge succumbs to the widow's dogged tenacity (18:4 – 5)

III. **Application to God's delay in bringing vindication (18:6 – 8)**
   A. From the lesser to the greater: If an unjust judge acts, how much more will a gracious God? (18:6 – 7)
   B. Pronouncement: God will act to vindicate the elect (18:8a)
   C. Motivational question: Will the Son of Man find faith when he comes? (18:8b)

Explanation of the Text

18:1 And he told this parable to them about how it is necessary for them always to pray and not become disheartened (ἔλεγεν δὲ παραβολὴν αὐτοῖς πρὸς τὸ δεῖν πάντοτε προσεύχεσθαι αὐτοὺς καὶ μὴ ἐγκακεῖν). The context for this exhortation is the danger that Christians might become disheartened in the midst of affliction before the return of the Son of Man to deliver them (17:22 – 37). It applies to the generation of Jesus' disciples who will endure tribulations because of their faith (21:12 – 19) and to all Christians who must enter the reign of God through many persecutions (Acts 14:22). Christians pray, "Your reign come" (11:2), and "Come, Lord Jesus" (Rev 22:20; cf. 1 Cor 16:22); yet nothing seems to happen, at least according to their limited time perspective.

Impatient humans dislike delay and expect God to be more punctual in meeting their immediate needs. When disciples face persecution and martyrdom for their faith and most of them are fainting from fear (21:12), they will particularly long to see the days of the Son of Man (17:22) and may fall into despair when deliverance from their affliction seems remote and their hopes seem illusory.

The verb "to become disheartened" (ἐγκακεῖν) can also mean "to grow weary" (see Gal 6:9; 2 Thess 3:13). Paul uses the verb when he says he does not lose heart (2 Cor 4:1, 16) though he is afflicted in every way, crushed, perplexed, persecuted, struck down, and always given up to death for Jesus' sake (2 Cor 4:8 – 10). He admonishes those addressed in the letter to the Ephesians not to become discouraged over his sufferings (Eph 3:13). Jesus' admonition implicitly assumes that troubles are in store for disciples in the days to come (21:12 – 19, 35 – 36). Growing weary makes one unready for the day of the Son of Man (17:26, 30).

18:2 Saying, "A certain judge was in a certain city, who neither feared God nor showed regard for people" (λέγων· κριτής τις ἦν ἐν τινι πόλει τὸν θεὸν μὴ φοβούμενος καὶ ἄνθρωπον μὴ ἐντρεπόμενος). The community courts were staffed by local notables who had social and political eminence. As a city judge, this man would be a member of the urban elite and would hold a position of honor.[2] His high status accords him, he thinks, the luxury of neither fearing God nor showing any regard for others.

He is first introduced as someone brazenly impious (18:2), and then he characterizes himself in this way (18:4). The characters in Jesus' parables are rarely described in abstract terms, and the reader usually learns of their life stance from their behavior or from an interior monologue. This characterization is thus an important factor for understanding this parable. This judge is the antithesis of what a judge in Israel was ideally supposed to be (see Sus 5).

When Jehoshaphat appointed judges, he exhorted them:

> Consider what you are doing, for you judge not on behalf of human beings but on the LORD's behalf; he is with you in giving judgment. Now, let the fear of the LORD be upon you; take care what you do, for there is no perversion of justice with the LORD our God, or partiality, or taking of bribes. (2 Chr 19:6 – 7 NRSV)

He also charged them: "He gave them these orders: You must serve faithfully and wholeheartedly in the fear of the LORD" (2 Chr 19:9). The judge of Israel is to be like God in his impartial judging and therefore must have the fear of God in his heart.

The verb "showed regard" in the active voice means "to make ashamed" (ἐντρέπειν; 1 Cor 4:14); in the passive voice it means "to be put to shame" (2 Thess 3:14; Titus 2:8); and in the middle voice it means "to have regard for, respect" (Mark 12:6). The verb could mean that the judge is incapable of being put to shame before others.[3] He does not flinch when someone cries out to him, "For shame!" While this sense of shamelessness may be true, it is more likely that Luke uses the verb to mean "to show regard for, respect." In the parable of the wicked tenants (20:9 – 17), after the tenants abused the owner's slaves who were dispatched to collect the rent, the vineyard owner decides to send his "beloved son," thinking, "They will respect [ἐντραπήσονται] this one" (20:13). Instead, the tenants demonstrated they neither feared God nor showed regard for anyone by killing the son. The description of the judge as not fearing God or showing regard for people presents him as a callous impenitent and sets up the expectation that receiving justice from him will be impossible for a powerless widow.

The discourse of the ungodly in Wis 2:10 – 11 captures the attitude of this judge: "Let us oppress the righteous poor man; let us not spare the widow or regard the gray hairs of the aged. But let our might be our law of right, for what is weak proves itself to be useless." A beatitude in *2 En.* 42:9 reads: "Blessed is the one who judges righteous judgment for the orphan and the widow, and who helps anyone who has been treated unjustly!" But this judge doesn't care about God's blessing and will not give orphans and widows the time of day.

The judge also flouts the biblical ideal that one find favor "with the LORD and with people" (see

---

2. Scott, *Hear Then the Parable*, 178.

3. Ceslas Spicq ("La parabole de le veuve obstinée et du judge inerté aux decisions impromptues [Lc xviii, 1 – 8]," *RB* 68 [1961]: 68 – 90) translates the verb as "failing in a sense of honor." See also Plummer, *Luke*, 412; Bailey, *Through Peasant Eyes*, 131 – 32.

1 Sam 2:26; Prov 3:4; Luke 2:40, 52). It is an ideal also found in the Roman world. Dionysius of Halicarnassus condemns the Roman conspirators as "neither fearing the wrath of the gods nor regarding the indignation of men" (*Ant. rom.* 10.10.7).[4] Therefore, this judge is presented as someone beyond the limits of normal social pressures that govern relationships with others.[5] As a judge, he is a scofflaw who shrugs off God and gives others the cold shoulder. He loves neither God nor neighbor (10:25 – 28). A widow making an appeal for justice before this kind of judge has zero chance.

18:3 And there was a widow in that city and she used to come to him, saying, "Give me justice against my adversary!" (χήρα δὲ ἦν ἐν τῇ πόλει ἐκείνῃ καὶ ἤρχετο πρὸς αὐτὸν λέγουσα· ἐκδίκησόν με ἀπὸ τοῦ ἀντιδίκου μου). The widow was one of the special categories of persons (including orphans and foreigners) under the protection of God.[6] Philo writes that God

> provides for the orphans and widows because they have lost their protectors, in the first case parents, in the second husbands, and in this desolation no refuge remains that men can give; and therefore they are not denied the hope that is greatest of all, the hope in God, Who in the graciousness of His nature does not refuse the task of caring for and watching over them in their desolate condition. (*Spec. Laws* 1.310)

Losing a husband usually meant that a widow had no financial support but also that she had no protector. Widows were particularly vulnerable to those who would "devour" their living (20:47). A widow who must make her own appeal has no man to defend her.[7] The judge's portrayal would hardly inspire hope in anyone bringing litigation before him. He is likely to put his judicial decisions up for sale to the highest bidder, and she has no resources. If she wants this judge "to set things right" (ἐκδικεῖν), she is barking up the wrong tree. He will not become her advocate if there is nothing in it for him except doing justice.

Jesus does not tell us what injustice she has suffered.[8] One can surmise that it was related to a financial settlement related to the death of her husband. Women could not inherit directly from their husbands (*m. B. Bat.* 8:1), but they were entitled to be maintained from their husband's estate (*m. Ketub.* 11:1; 12:3) or to receive their *ketuba*, an amount of money in a prenuptial agreement that would be given to the wife in the event of divorce (*m. Ketub.* 4:2; 5:1). According to *m. Ketub.* 4:12, a widow can remain in the house of her husband and be supported from his estate until the heirs are willing to give her the *ketuba*, her marriage settlement. When they do that, they can then send her away. She has no more rights.

Whatever the injustice, this widow must

---

4. See also Livy, who describes a commander as one who lacked respect for "the laws," "the senate's majesty," and "even for the gods" (*Hist.* 13.12.3.4 – 5). Josephus uses the verb to describe the attitude of the rabble who massacred Jewish innocents in Caesarea, "without even the slightest regard [ἐντραπέντες] for the Romans, who regarded as enemies only us who had revolted" (*J.W.* 7.8.7 §362).

5. A similar description can be found in Josephus (*Ant.* 10.5.2 §83) of Joakeimos (Jehoiakim): "He proved to be unjust [ἄδικος] and wicked [κακοῦγος] by nature and was neither reverent toward God nor kind [ἐπιεικής] toward men."

6. See Exod 22:22 – 24; Deut 10:17 – 18; 24:17; 27:19; Job 22:9; Pss 68:5; 146:9; Prov 15:25; Isa 1:17; 10:2 – 3; 54:4; Jer

7:6; 22:3; Zech 7:10; Mal 3:5; Jas 1:27. They figure prominently in Luke-Acts: Anna (2:36 – 38), the widow of Zarephath (4:25 – 26), the widow of Nain (7:11 – 17), the widow with two mites (21:2 – 3), the Hellenist widows (Acts 6:1), and Dorcas and the widows (9:36 – 41).

7. See Naomi's lament when she becomes widowed (Ruth 1:20 – 21).

8. Wendy Cotter ("The Parable of the Feisty Widow and the Threatened Judge [Luke 18.1 – 8]," *NTS* 51 [2005]: 336 – 37) contends that "she has prepared a petition for the offending person to be prosecuted in court, but the judge denies that she has sufficient grounds and refuses to proceed."

venture alone into the forbidding male realm of the public courts if she is to get redress. Persistence is her only weapon. The imperfect of "to come" ("she used to come," ἤρχετο) implies that she came repeatedly. The typical court scene in the Middle East was not marked by somber decorum but a great din of shouting and pushing. This woman would be heard only because she was the shrillest.[9] She skips any honorific title in her appeal to the judge and pleads her case persistently and loudly.

18:4 For a time, he was unwilling [to act], but after a while he said to himself, "Though I do not fear God or show any regard for people" (καὶ οὐκ ἤθελεν ἐπὶ χρόνον. μετὰ δὲ ταῦτα εἶπεν ἐν ἑαυτῷ· εἰ καὶ τὸν θεὸν οὐ φοβοῦμαι οὐδὲ ἄνθρωπον ἐντρέπομαι). True to character, the judge initially ignores the widow's pleas for justice. He prefaces his decision by agreeing with the appraisal that he has a heart of marble and feels no awe of God. Giving into this widow will ruin his reputation as hard-bitten and impassive to others' plight.

18:5 "Yet because this widow pesters me, I will have to give her justice so that she will not wear me out in the end with her continual appeals" (διά γε τὸ παρέχειν μοι κόπον τὴν χήραν ταύτην ἐκδικήσω αὐτήν, ἵνα μὴ εἰς τέλος ἐρχομένη ὑπωπιάζῃ με). The widow has found a crack in the judge's steely facade. To put a stop to her constant badgering, he decides to act in her behalf despite his bluster about his lack of humanity. The verb translated "wear out" (ὑπωπιάζειν) was used as a boxing term for a blow that results in the bruising

below the eye. Paul uses it when he refers to pummeling his body that he might subdue it (1 Cor 9:27). If this is meant literally, the judge decides to vindicate her lest finally she comes and gives him a pounding that will result in a black eye.[10] He may be afraid of a slap in the face, which is the archetypal insult (Matt 5:39; Isa. 50:6; *m. B. Qam.* 6:8).

But is he really afraid that the widow will finally lose it and haul off and hit him? Her coming every day and shrilly crying for justice may be tolerated, but she would not be allowed to resort to blows. Schottroff dismisses it as "sexist sarcasm." This woman has not behaved submissively as she ought, and the judge assumes that she might be capable of anything, including violence against him.[11] Derrett argues that the verb does not refer to blackening the eye but to blackening one's face, meaning "to be slandered." He suggests that the judge is afraid that people are going to wink and say that her pleading her case with him every day is just a smokescreen for a sexual liaison. This heartless judge, then, does care what people say or think about him and will act to save his reputation. Derrett takes the point to mean that God has a reputation to lose as well. For his name's sake, God will do justice for his people.[12]

The verb can also mean to "wear down, wear out." This is most likely its meaning here. In a test of wills, the widow's pestering gets the judge to give up. He will do whatever she requires just to get rid of her. Manson describes it as a war of attrition.[13] The judge turns out to be more afraid of this widow, who will not take "no" for an answer, than he is of God.

9. Bailey, *Poet and Peasant*, 134–35.

10. Cotter ("The Parable of the Feisty Widow and the Threatened Judge [Luke 18.1–8]," 338–42) argues for a literal translation. She contends the woman is not meekly submissive and helpless but spunky and capable of a violent assault. The judge's vanity determines his decision; he fears losing face from walking around town with a black eye delivered by a woman.

11. Luise Schottroff, *Lydia's Impatient Sisters: A Feminist Social History of Early Christianity* (trans. B. and M. Rumscheidt; Louisville: Westminster John Knox, 1995), 104.

12. J. Duncan M. Derrett, "Law in the New Testament: The Unjust Judge," *NTS* 18 (1971–72): 190–91.

13. Manson, *The Sayings of Jesus*, 306.

18:6 The Lord said, "Listen to what the unrighteous judge says!" (εἶπεν δὲ ὁ κύριος· ἀκούσατε τί ὁ κριτὴς τῆς ἀδικίας λέγει). "The Lord" refers to Jesus, who draws the conclusion to the parable (see 16:8) but does not give its point. "Listen" means that the audience must draw the inference about how this story about a wicked judge applies to God. Though the judge is godless, corrupt, and unjust, he responds to this widow's constant clamor just to bid her good riddance. Reasoning from the lesser to the greater, Jesus leads us to infer, if this widow, against all odds, gets her case settled in her favor because of her persistence, how much more will those receive who supplicate God, who is both loving and just.

The magistrate is characterized as a "judge of unrighteousness" (ὁ κριτὴς τῆς ἀδικίας, an attributive genitive), which means that he belongs to this present evil age (see 16:9, 11). By contrast, God is impartial, takes no bribe, and "defends the cause of the fatherless and the widow, and loves the foreigner residing among you, giving them food and clothing" (Deut 10:17 – 18). Sirach 35:14 – 19 provides an instructive parallel to this parable:

> Do not offer him a bribe, for he will not
>   accept it …
> for the Lord is the judge,
>   and with him there is no partiality.
> He will not show partiality to the poor;
>   but he will listen to the prayer of one who
>   is wronged.
> He will not ignore the supplication of the orphan,
>   or the widow when she pours out her
>   complaint.
> Do not the tears of the widow run down her
>   cheek
>   as she cries out against him who has caused
>   them to fall?

18:7 Will not God bring justice for his elect who cry to him night and day, though he waits patiently [to act] for them? (ὁ δὲ θεὸς οὐ μὴ ποιήσῃ τὴν ἐκδίκησιν τῶν ἐκλεκτῶν αὐτοῦ τῶν βοώντων αὐτῷ ἡμέρας καὶ νυκτός καὶ μακροθυμεῖ ἐπ' αὐτοῖς;). This question about justice for those who suffer injustice and must cry out day and night limits the application of what this parable says about prayer. It clearly does not mean that those who are persistent in prayer will get whatever they ask. It puts their insistent cries in an eschatological context (compare Bar 4:21 – 25). Their cry for God to set things right is another way of praying, "Your reign come" (Luke 11:2). The model for this prayer is another widow in Luke's story, Anna, who never left the temple but fasted and prayed night and day, pleading to God to bring the redemption of Jerusalem (2:37 – 38).

The "elect" (τῶν ἐκλεκτῶν) appears elsewhere in Luke only in 23:35 and refers to the mocking of Christ as "the elect one." The taunt, "He saved others; let him save himself," implies that the elect of God will certainly not be allowed to suffer so ignominiously if he were truly elect (cf. Mark 13:20, 22, 27). Jesus' deliverance, however, does not come immediately. He must pass through death.

"Though he waits patiently [to act] for them" (μακροθυμεῖν; "though he bear long with them," KJV) translates this verb, which can mean "to wait patiently, be slow or delay, be patient or forbearing."[14] That God gives a patient hearing to the constant appeals of the elect who cry out for his reign to come may seem odd. Consequently, some take it to refer to the timing of the vindication of the elect. God will respond quickly (see Hab 2:3; Sir 21:5). The REB renders it in relation to the appearance of delay, "He will give them justice soon enough." But this translation and that of the NRSV, "And will

---

14. Marshall, *The Gospel of Luke*, 674 – 75, lists nine different interpretations.

not God grant justice to his chosen ones who cry to him day and night? Will he delay long in helping them?" (see also ESV, NASB), seem no less odd. Why must the faithful cry to God day and night if God does not delay in helping them?

I render it concessively as addressing the problem that vindication has been long delayed.[15] In the immediate context, the Pharisees ask Jesus when the reign of God is coming (17:20), which may betray the anxiety of Luke's readers who expect it should come soon (see 19:11). When Jesus turns to his disciples and warns that the time is coming when they will long to see the "days of the Son of Man" and will not see them (17:22), it implies delay. The parable concludes this section with an encouragement to keep praying despite the sense of disappointment under the stress.

Linnemann says that a church that is persecuted and oppressed cries fervently for vindication, but as one day follows another, doubt can gnaw away at faith and the question will be raised whether the day of the Lord will ever come.[16] This despondency need not apply only to the church after the resurrection. During the ministry of Jesus, Israel continued to be oppressed (see the image of the bereft widow applied to Israel in Isa 49:21; Lam 1:1) and longed for deliverance. The answer Jesus gives is essentially the same one given to the martyrs crying out beneath the altar in Rev 6:11: wait a little longer. God will move, but in God's own timing. God is also "longsuffering toward their persecutors."[17] He gives them time to repent.

18:8 I say to you that he will bring justice for them quickly. When the Son of Man comes, however, will he then find faith on the earth? (λέγω ὑμῖν ὅτι ποιήσει τὴν ἐκδίκησιν αὐτῶν ἐν τάχει. πλὴν ὁ υἱὸς τοῦ ἀνθρώπου ἐλθὼν ἆρα εὑρήσει τὴν πίστιν ἐπὶ τῆς γῆς;). Jesus assumes that the supplication is for God's final vindication of the elect. The parable assures that those who pray to God for this final vindication will be answered. But Jesus turns the tables on those who might express exasperation with God's delay (see the same switch in 17:7–10). He affirms that God will not fail to act, but how does it stand with those who pray? When the Son of Man comes, will he find faith on earth, including in those so desperately praying for God to do something? The consoling message shifts to a warning of judgment.[18]

---

15. See the KJV, "though he bear long with them?" and the NJB, "even though he still delays to help them." See LSJ, 1074.

16. Linnemann, *Parables of Jesus*," 122.

17. C. E. B. Cranfield, "The Parable of the Unjust Judge and the Eschatology of Luke-Acts," *SJT* 16 (1963): 300.

18. Klaus Haacker, "Das Gleichnis von der bittenden Witwe (Lk 18,1–8)," *TBei* 25 (1994): 277–84.

Theology in Application

1. Prayer to a Loving and Just God

The parable confirms the Pauline injunctions to pray without ceasing (1 Thess 5:17), to persevere in prayer (Rom 12:12; Eph 6:18), and to devote yourselves to prayer (Col 4:2). But it may be easily misinterpreted to mean that God eventually wears down and responds to persistence. The message is *not* that it pays to pester God because God eventually will respond, or that the squeaky wheel gets the grease. Instead, the point is that God, who demands justice and is sympathetic to the plight of his people, will bring final vindication. Believers may boldly plead with God in prayer, "Your reign come," and know that they are not dealing with an apathetic, wicked crook who metes out favorable decisions to the highest bidder. They pray to a loving, caring God who has promised deliverance and has the power to accomplish it. The difference is that Christians are not like the widow and God is not like the judge. Believers do not approach God as if they were poor bag ladies. They are identified as "the elect" and already have a relationship with God. Will God not vindicate his elect?

The widow in the parable has no other connections, no other options. The judge is her only hope. As the widow determinedly casts her future hopes in the hands of this judge, so Christians must place all of their hope in God as the only hope they have.

2. Prayer for Final Vindication

The parable must be interpreted in light of its eschatological context and Jesus' warnings about the days of the Son of Man (17:20 – 37). It is not about prayer in general but prayer for final vindication (see 2 Thess 1:3 – 10). The widow who has the gumption to entreat a judge forcefully becomes a figure for God's people crying out for rescue. The connection assumes that they are suffering injustice and are seemingly defenseless in this world while being led to slaughter. This pictures them as the exact opposite of the queenly harlot in Rev 18:7, who sits on her throne bedecked with jewels and the blood of the martyrs dripping from her lips (Rev 17:6). She represents the haughty world power of Rome that will soon come to grief and go up in smoke (Rev 18). Her vaporous terrestrial power explains why God's people cry out to him to rescue them because they live in a worn and weary world where oppression abounds. But the path to glory passes through the dark veil of suffering (17:25; 24:26).

Is God slow to help? It depends on how one defines slow and from whose perspective (see 2 Pet 3:8). In the midst of affliction and crying out, "How long, Sovereign Lord?" (Rev 6:10), it is easy to become impatient and lose heart when nothing happens according to one's own timetable. Once again in Luke, prayer is the antidote to a potential spiritual toxin. It is not that it makes God hasten the day. As Crump notes, "the timing of God's will does not ignore the disciples' prayers, but it is established independently of such prayers."[19] The question is whether or not we will live with faith and prayer in the face of persecution and oppression.

If Christians expect God to work according to their own time charts of the end and hope to escape hardship, they are more vulnerable to despair and will give up on prayer when they are beset by affliction and when God's chronology does not match theirs. For Luke, the end is near, not in the sense that it will occur within months, but in the sense that

> since *the* decisive event of history has already taken place in the ministry, death, resurrection, and ascension of Christ, all subsequent history is a kind of epilogue, an interval inserted by God's mercy in order to allow men time for repentance, and, as such an epilogue, necessarily in a real sense short, even though it may take a very long time.[20]

The ending of the parable shifts the focus. The question is not whether God will respond to our prayers but whether we will respond to God and trust his faithfulness to fulfill all the promises (see 1:20; 45; 24:45). Christians must endure to the end and can only endure through prayer. Prayer feeds faith, lifts up drooping hands, and strengthens weak knees (Heb 12:12).

19. Crump, *Jesus the Intercessor*, 132.   20. Cranfield, "The Parable of the Unjust Judge and the Eschatology of Luke-Acts," 300–301.

Luke 18:9 – 14

Literary Context

The readers should be accustomed to surprise twists in the parables that are unique to Luke. The Samaritan is the one who offers mercy while the temple functionaries pass by a beaten man. The prodigal brother is received joyously by the father while the older brother, who had faithfully served his father, cuts himself off from the celebration. Poor Lazarus is whisked away to the bosom of Abraham while the rich man suffers in the torment of Hades. A tax collector who cries out for mercy is declared more upright than a Pharisee who knocks himself out going above and beyond what the law requires as he tries to please God.

In the context, the preceding parable (18:1 – 8) affirms that God answers the prayers of the saints. This parable affirms that God also answers the prayers of sinners. It reinforces the principle that those who exalt themselves above others will be humbled; those who humble themselves will be exalted (18:14; see 14:11).[1] The surprise element, however, helps to focus the topic of how one will be taken and another left (17:34 – 35).

This subject is developed further in the story of a rich ruler who had obeyed all of the commandments from his youth but who ruefully walks away from Jesus, rejecting his demand to abandon his attachment to his wealth by giving it to the poor (18:18 – 30). Jesus' reaction, "How hard it is for those who have possessions to enter into the reign of God," jolts the listeners (18:24). No less surprising is his outreach to Zacchaeus, a despised, rich, chief tax collector. When Zacchaeus pledges to divest his wealth and ill-gotten gains by giving it to the poor and to make amends with those he has cheated, Jesus proclaims him to be a "son of Abraham" and declares that salvation has come to his house (19:1 – 10).

Luke identifies the audience of this parable as those who trusted in themselves that they were righteous (δίκαιοι), that is, properly observant in their duty before God and thus in a right relationship with God. Nothing could have been more shocking than for Jesus to declare that a tax collector, the sinner par excellence, was more upright than a Pharisee, the epitome of piety. In his complete dependence on God, the sinner who cries out is like those who receive the reign of God as a child.

---

1. Bridge, *Where the Eagles Are Gathered*, 30.

Main Idea

Being upright requires acknowledging that one is a sinner before God and asking for pardon, not reciting all of one's pious accomplishments.[2]

Translation

Luke 18:9–14

18:9	Introduction	**He spoke this parable to certain ones** who had convinced themselves that they were upright and disdained everyone else.
10a	Introduction of characters	*"Two men went up to the temple to pray,*
b		*one was a Pharisee*
c		*and the other a tax collector.*
11a	Posture	*The Pharisee stood and began to pray these things to himself,*
b	Prayer	*'God, I thank you that I am not like the rest of humanity, the swindlers, the unjust, the adulterers, or even like this tax collector here.*
12		*I fast twice a week;*
		I give one tenth of all that I acquire.'
13a	Posture	*The tax collector stood afar off and would not lift up his eyes to heaven but instead beat his breast, saying,*
b	Prayer	*'God, make atonement for me, the sinner!'*
14a	Pronouncement	*I say to you,*
		this [tax collector] went down to his house more upright than that [Pharisee],
b	Rationale	*because everyone who exalts himself will be humbled,*
		and the one who humbles himself will be exalted."

2. Robert Doran, "The Pharisee and the Tax Collector: An Agonistic Story," *CBQ* 69 (2007): 265.

Structure and Literary Form

The form of this story is a parable that compares two people on an issue — in this case, who is more upright in honoring God. The least likely candidate is dubbed superior. There is a striking contrast between the number of words describing the two individual's stances and prayers. Five words describe the Pharisee's stance and twenty-nine narrate his prayer. Nineteen words describe the tax collector's stance and six words narrate his prayer.

Exegetical Outline

→ I. The disdain of those who suppose themselves to be righteous toward others (18:9)

II. Setting: temple worship (18:10)

III. The prayer of a self-righteous Pharisee (18:11 – 12)

IV. The prayer of an unrighteous tax collector (18:13)

V. Jesus' surprise declaration that the tax collector was more upright (18:14)

Explanation of the Text

18:9 He spoke this parable to certain ones who had convinced themselves that they were upright and disdained everyone else (εἶπεν δὲ καὶ πρός τινας τοὺς πεποιθότας ἐφ᾽ ἑαυτοῖς ὅτι εἰσὶν δίκαιοι καὶ ἐξουθενοῦντας τοὺς λοιποὺς τὴν παραβολὴν ταύτην). The Pharisees may not have departed since their question in 17:20. The verb "convinced" ("to trust, have confidence" [τοὺς πεποιθότας]) appears in 11:22 in the parable of the strong man, who guarded his own palace and possessions in peace until someone stronger took away the armor in which he trusted and divided the spoil. In this parable, Jesus will assail and take away what the hearers have put their trust in, namely, their self-assurance that they are upright before God.

18:10 "Two men went up to the temple to pray, one was a Pharisee and the other a tax collector" (ἄνθρωποι δύο ἀνέβησαν εἰς τὸ ἱερὸν προσεύξασθαι, ὁ εἷς Φαρισαῖος καὶ ὁ ἕτερος τελώνης). We may be conditioned by the word "pray" (προσεύξασθαι) to visualize these two men going to the temple for private devotions. Nothing could be further from the truth. There were two periods for public prayer, the third hour (9:00 a.m.) and the ninth hour (3:00 p.m.; see Acts 3:1) during the twice-daily whole offering, or Tamid, service (see Exod 29:38 – 42; Num 28:2 – 8). A Jewish audience would assume that these men were joining in the corporate worship of the people when they prayed during the burning of the incense and waited to receive the priestly benediction (see 1:10, 21; Jdt 9:1; Sir 50:19; *m. Tamid* 5:1).[3]

18:11 The Pharisee stood and began to pray these things to himself, "God, I thank you that I am not like the rest of humanity, the swindlers, the unjust, the adulterers, or even like this tax collector

---

3. Bailey, *Through Peasant Eyes*, 145 – 46; Hamm, "Tamid Service," 215, 224; contra Nolland, *Luke*, 2:875.

here" (ὁ Φαρισαῖος σταθεὶς πρὸς ἑαυτὸν ταῦτα προσηύχετο· ὁ θεός, εὐχαριστῶ σοι ὅτι οὐκ εἰμὶ ὥσπερ οἱ λοιποὶ τῶν ἀνθρώπων, ἅρπαγες, ἄδικοι, μοιχοί, ἢ καὶ ὡς οὗτος ὁ τελώνης). A Pharisee is chosen as a foil because they were well-known for excelling others in their religious observances and for their exact interpretation of the law (Josephus, *J.W.* 1.5.2 §110; see Phil 3:4 – 6). They were caricatured even in rabbinic literature for being over the top in practicing their piety (see *b. Soṭah* 22b). The Pharisee serves as a picture postcard of those who imagine themselves to be righteous, but whose self-image is at odds with God's judgment. Both men are characterized by their stances and their prayers. The Pharisee stands (see 19:8; Acts 2:14; 17:22; 27:21) and testifies about himself.[4]

Prayers were usually uttered aloud (see *L.A.B.* 50:5). The Pharisee's prayer may seem to mirror sincere prayers found elsewhere (Pss 17:1 – 7, 26; 26:1 – 12; 1QH[a] 15:34 – 35; *b. Ber.* 28b), and he gives thanks to God, who has given him his lot. He asks nothing from God because he thinks he needs nothing. Seeking God's mercy and forgiveness seems unnecessary. From what follows, he has already made out the exam, graded it himself, and given himself an A+.

His prayer functions to reveal what he assumes it means to honor God and to be "upright." He has developed a righteousness scale by which he can gauge his and other's rectitude and reports to God what he has done and what others have not done (see Deut 26:1 – 15). He testifies that he is on the Lord's side and is not like those who dishonor God by violating the Ten Commandments (robbers, evildoers, and adulterers). His reference to "this tax collector" (οὗτος ὁ τελώνης) drips with contempt.

18:12 "I fast twice a week; I give one tenth of all that I acquire" (νηστεύω δὶς τοῦ σαββάτου, ἀποδεκατῶ πάντα ὅσα κτῶμαι). Fasting was obligatory only on the Day of Atonement (Lev 16:29, 31; 23:27, 29, 32; Num 29:7), but this Pharisee goes beyond what is enjoined in Scripture by fasting twice a week. His motive may have been to atone for his own sins (*Ps. Sol.* 3:7 – 8) and the sins of others, to prevent further catastrophe befalling Israel,[5] or to supplicate God for Israel's deliverance (Jdt 4:8 – 12). Jewish asceticism apparently had become proverbial in the Greco-Roman world since Suetonius has the phrase "not even a Jew fasts so scrupulously" (*Aug.* 76). By contrast, Jesus and his disciples were known for not fasting but for eating (5:33 – 34) and having fellowship with those who were disreputable (15:1 – 2).

Jesus accused Pharisees of being full of greed and wickedness (11:39) and lovers of money, of neglecting justice while tithing mint, rue, and herbs (11:42). This Pharisee takes tithing a step further. He gives to God an additional one tenth of whatever he buys. He goes to this extreme as a precaution in case the producer had not paid the proper tithes enjoined in Deut 14:22. The Mishnah tractate *Demai* (lit., "dubious, suspicious") covers the topic of produce not certainly tithed and assumes that any produce bought from "the people of the land" (the unobservant) is to be treated as untithed, unless one knows otherwise: "He that undertakes to be trustworthy [scrupulous] must give tithe from what he eats and from what he sells and from what he buys [to sell again]; and he may not be the guest of an Am ha-aretz" (*m. Demai* 2:2; see *j. Demai* 1:3; 22a).

---

4. Bailey (*Through Peasant Eyes*, 147 – 48) argues that the Pharisee stood "by himself" (which would be supported by the reading in codex Bezae [D], which has καθ' ἑαυτόν). Luke normally introduces a character's soliloquy with the phrase ἐν ἑαυτῷ, not πρὸς ἑαυτόν (7:39, 12:17, 16:3, 18:4), but the use

of the preposition πρός here matches 24:12 (Peter marveling "to himself").

5. According to *b. Giṭ.* 56a, R. Zadok observed fasts for forty years in order that Jerusalem might not be destroyed.

18:13 The tax collector stood afar off and would not lift up his eyes to heaven but instead beat his breast, saying, "God, make atonement for me, the sinner!" (ὁ δὲ τελώνης μακρόθεν ἑστὼς οὐκ ἤθελεν οὐδὲ τοὺς ὀφθαλμοὺς ἐπᾶραι εἰς τὸν οὐρανόν, ἀλλ᾽ ἔτυπτεν τὸ στῆθος αὐτοῦ λέγων· ὁ θεός, ἱλάσθητί μοι τῷ ἁμαρτωλῷ). The tax collector is chosen because he belongs to a class associated with notorious sinners (see 5:30, 7:34, 15:1, 19:2 – 7; see *m. Šeb.* 39:9). Instead of taking the Lord's side, he has chosen to take the Romans' side by serving their system of tax collection. He stands at a distance from the sanctuary and the gathered crowd because he considers himself to be unworthy to stand with God's people before the altar. Perhaps he is conscious of Ps 24:3 – 6. He has neither clean hands nor a pure heart and does not belong here on God's holy hill. He is spiritually "far away" and painfully aware of his sins.

Lifting up one's eyes to heaven was the normal attitude in prayer (see Ps 123:1; Mark 6:41; 7:34; John 11:41, 17:1). The tax collector does not lift up his eyes because of his sense of shame.[6]

Gestures of despair were not normally part of Jewish prayer. "Beat his breast" is a sign of extreme sorrow, which women normally did at funerals (see 23:27; cf. 23:48). It was rare for men to do so (Josephus [*Ant.* 7.10.5 §252] records David as beating his breast over the death of his son Absalom). This detail shows that the tax collector is so overwhelmed by the chasm he feels exists between himself and God that he is oblivious to his surroundings.

The tax collector does not bore God with a recital of his unworthiness. The definite article before the noun (τῷ ἁμαρτωλῷ) may mean he contrasts himself with the Pharisee and accepts his verdict that he is a sinner. The Pharisee is the righteous one; he is *the* sinner. The definite article may point to him as being "in a class by himself." He identifies himself as "the worst of all sinners."[7]

His prayer matches pleas in the Old Testament (see Pss 25:11; 79:9; the verb ἱλάσκομαι is used in the LXX Pss 24:11; 78:9; see also in the Apocrypha, Pr Man 1:9 – 14). Bailey contends that his outburst is precipitated by the fact that he prays during the corporate worship of the morning or evening atonement sacrifice.[8] The prayer should not be translated "be merciful to me" because the verb ἐλεέω (see 18:38) is not used. Rather, the verb ἱλάσκομαι is used, which occurs in Heb 2:17 to mean "make an expiation." Related noun forms occur in Rom 3:25; Heb 9:5; 1 John 2:2, 4:10 to refer to an atonement sacrifice; and this seems best to fit the setting if it occurs during the daily sacrifice for the people.[9] The tax collector's attitude before God matches that commended in a later rabbinic tradition:

> R. Bibi b. Abaye said: How should a person confess on the eve of Yom Kippur? He should say: "I confess all the evil I have done before You; I stood in the way of all evil; and as for the evil I have done, I shall no more do the like; may it be Your will, O Lord my God, that You pardon me for all my iniquities, and forgive me all my transgressions, and grant me atonement for all my sins." (*Lev. Rab.* 3:3)[10]

The tax collector experiences the anguish of the temple's promise of atonement from the daily sacrifice and the reality of his own sinful life. The forgiveness offered in the temple sacrifice confirmed by the priestly benediction does not apply to the likes of him. In his brokenness, he cries

---

6. See *1 En.* 13:5: "They could no longer speak or raise their eyes to heaven out of shame for their sins."

7. Wallace, *Greek Grammar*, 222 – 23.

8. Bailey, *Through Peasant Eyes*, 154.

9. Hamm, "Tamid Service," 224.

10. Cited by Doran, "The Pharisee and the Tax Collector," 268.

out, "God, make atonement for me!" Atonement for tax collectors was notoriously difficult. To receive forgiveness one must repent, and to repent one must make recompense (see 19:1 – 10). From Luke's perspective, God is preparing an atonement sacrifice that will expiate this man's sin apart from the temple sacrifices.

18:14 I say to you, this [tax collector] went down to his house more upright than that [Pharisee], because everyone who exalts himself will be humbled, and the one who humbles himself will be exalted (λέγω ὑμῖν, κατέβη οὗτος δεδικαιωμένος εἰς τὸν οἶκον αὐτοῦ παρ᾽ ἐκεῖνον· ὅτι πᾶς ὁ ὑψῶν ἑαυτὸν ταπεινωθήσεται, ὁ δὲ ταπεινῶν ἑαυτὸν ὑψωθήσεται). Jesus picks up on the contemptuous use of the demonstrative pronoun "this one" by the Pharisee and provides a different verdict of the tax collector: "This one" (οὗτος) is more upright than "that one" (ἐκεῖνον). The structure reveals the intent to contrast the two men ("two men … the one … the other")[11] and supports translating the phrase as a comparative ("more upright than that one" [δεδικαιωμένος … παρ᾽ ἐκεῖνον].[12] It should not be translated as "justified," as if it were a forensic term. The issue addressed by the parable is who serves God best, "who is truly observant of God's honor?"[13] The surprising answer is that the tax collector does, but the Pharisee with all of his works of supererogation falls short.

The theological principle that those who exalt themselves will be humbled and those who humble themselves will be exalted is repeated from 14:11 and captures the point. The Pharisee exalted himself above another before God. The tax collector humbled himself as *the* sinner. Jesus' response to the humble thief on the cross who confesses his crimes and begs for Jesus to remember him when he enters his reign further illustrates this principle (23:40 – 42).

Theology in Application

1. The Scandal of God's Grace

Jesus' original audience is identified as those who are "convinced" that they are upright. For Luke's readers, the Pharisee serves as an example (like the older brother) of those who hinder others — whomever they may be, God-fearers, Gentiles, the marginalized — from receiving God's grace. Accepting those of bad reputation is always a problem for those who deem themselves of good reputation. Those who deem themselves righteous according to their own standards are like Paul, who testifies that at one time no one could have more "confidence" in the flesh than he. He was a zealous Pharisee, and when it came to righteousness that derives from obedience to the law, he judged himself to be "faultless" (Phil 3:4 – 6).

The parable teaches in a nutshell what Paul argues at length, namely, that all have sinned and fallen short of the glory of God (Rom 3:23); that "Scripture has locked up

---

11. See other comparisons in 13:2, 4 with the preposition παρά.

12. Doran, "The Pharisee and the Tax Collector," 265. See

BDF §185.3. In codex Bezae (D) the word "more" (μᾶλλον) is added to the text to make it specific.

13. Doran, "The Pharisee and the Tax Collector," 259 – 70.

everything under the control of sin, so that what was promised, being given through faith in Jesus Christ, might be given to those who believe" (Gal 3:22); and that there can be no boasting in the presence of God (1 Cor 1:29). The punch line to Jesus' parable would have stunned the religious sensibilities of all who heard it. It is not that a righteous Pharisee is placed on the same level before God as an outcast sinner, but that an outcast sinner who pleads for mercy is more upright.

God's grace is always scandalous. But what is implicit in the parable and can be seen only when it is read after Jesus' death and resurrection is that the temple sacrifices are made irrelevant. They do not bring atonement to either man. When the tax collector pleads during the temple sacrifice that an atonement be made for him, the believer knows that God has provided it through the death of the teller of this parable. Feuillet contends that the tax collector's justification and receiving atonement anticipates the justification and atonement offered in Jesus' death. He argues that the verbs "being justified" and "humbling oneself" and "being exalted" in the conclusion are hidden allusions to the Servant Songs (Isa 52–53), particularly Isa 52:13; 53:8, 11, where these verbs occur.[14] Jesus' body broken, his blood poured out for others (22:19–20), and his resurrection and exaltation open the way to the forgiveness of sins (24:47; Acts 5:31; 10:43; 13:38; 26:18).

2. The Unrighteous Prayer of the Righteous One Who Is Proud

Where does the Pharisee go wrong? (1) He is self-absorbed. He lives in smug complacency, assuming that everything is in order between himself and God. He has a zeal for God, but it is a deluded zeal (see Rom 10:2–3). He imagines that he can cash in his religious accomplishments like chips. He comes boldly to God and can name all the good things he has done and every sin he has not done that others do.[15] In the judgment, he expects to go through the "express lane": ten sins or less. Ezekiel 33:13 serves as an appropriate warning: "If I tell a righteous person that they will surely live, but then they trust in their righteousness and do evil, none of the righteous things that person has done will be remembered; they will die for the evil they have done."

(2) He wants to stand out. Performing deeds above the requirements of the law leads to showing off (see Matt 6:1; 23:5).

(3) He finds security in comparing himself to others. He pumps up his own performance by highlighting the defects of others. It prevents him from understanding how God could show mercy to sinners. If God has mercy on sinners, he thinks it jeopardizes his special status. Consequently, he would not want this tax collector

14. Andre Feuillet, "La signification christologique de Luc 18,14 et les références des Evangiles au Serviteur souffrant," *NV* 55 (1980): 188–229.

15. Compare the statement in *b. Sukkah* 45b: "If the saved numbered only one hundred, I and my son are among them; and if only two, they are I and my son."

to repent because then he would have no one with whom to compare himself so favorably before God. If everybody repents, he will no longer stand out and be special to God. No one can expect justification before God without also accepting God's justification of others and showing love, not contempt, for neighbors.

(4) He is devout with a bad attitude. One cannot be truly righteous and disdain others.[16]

(5) He implicitly pronounces judgment on others who are less dutiful and is ready to profess their sins without confessing his own. Schweizer notes: "He tries in his prayer to commit God to condemning the tax collector." He forgets that God loves those who come with empty hands as well as those who labor mightily.[17] He wants to box God in by preempting divine grace. The problem is that he also puts himself in a box, because he cannot be forgiven either. By excluding another from grace he excludes himself. He represents "an exclusive attitude that Luke later seems to connect with the temple and its representatives"[18]

(6) He forgets that God alone is holy. Contrast his prayer with Hannah's, "There is none holy like the LORD; there is none besides you" (1 Sam 2:2 ESV). God's holiness should cause all to recognize their own unworthiness. Paul expresses this point in Rom 3:23: "All have sinned and fall short of the glory of God." But Paul also explains that justification comes through faith as a gift, not by earning it through obedience to the law. It comes through faith in the sacrifice of atonement of Jesus' blood (Rom 3:21 – 25).

3. The Righteous Prayer of the Unrighteous One Who Is Desperate

If the parable gives a snapshot of what God requires, what does the tax collector do right? (1) He pays no attention to anyone else and focuses only on his own sinful condition in the eyes of God. (2) He offers up no defense but comes with a broken and contrite heart and a sense of unworthiness (see Pss 34:6, 18; 51:17). He recognizes that he is as good as dead and is ready to receive the reign of God like a child (18:17) by acknowledging his lowliness. God welcomes the hopeless, despairing sinner. James 4:8 – 10 provides an apt commentary:

> Come near to God and he will come near to you. Wash your hands, you sinners, and purify your hearts, you double-minded. Grieve, mourn and wail. Change your laughter to mourning and your joy to gloom. Humble yourselves before the Lord, and he will lift you up.

---

16. Jerome Kodell, "Luke and the Children: The Beginning and End of the Great Interpolation (Luke 9:46 – 56; 18:9 – 23)," *CBQ* 49 (1987): 424.

17. Schweizer, *Luke*, 283.

18. Geir Otto Holmås, " 'My House Shall Be a House of Prayer': Regarding the Temple as a Place of Prayer in Acts with the Context of Luke's Apologetical Objective," *JSNT* 27 (2005): 407.

4. Recognizing Oneself in the Parable

Two dangers lurk in the theological application of this story. First, one can become as preoccupied with one's sin as the Pharisee was preoccupied with his righteousness. Humility can be just as self-absorbed. Jesus does not admonish us to adopt a humble posture rather than a proud one but to give up all posturing. Niebuhr explains that the power of prayer is not found in the "poverty of our asking, but according to the richness of God's grace."[19]

Second, the Pharisee and the tax collector have changed places in modern times. Everyone knows the end of the story and everyone hates self-righteous snobs and usually sympathizes with the underdog. Achtemeier recognizes, "We identify with the tax collector and feel silent gratitude that we are decent and humble rather than being self-righteous like that shameful Pharisee."[20] We can be like the Sunday school teacher who goes through the lesson and says at the end, "Now, children, let us bow our heads and thank God we are not like that Pharisee."

Manson says that the two men have changed places today, and the tax collector comes to pray and thank God he is not like those "canting humbugs, hypocrites and killjoys whose chief offense is that they take their religions seriously." [21] In every sermon, the publican walks out the door justified and presumably continues his same old life, only to come back again and again in other sermons to confess all over again and receive another halo. The poor Pharisee busting his buttons to please God gets the thumbs-down every time. The introduction to the parable cries out for readers to see their inner Pharisee and that they are no better than anyone else despite their religious accomplishments. Jesus' encounter with Zacchaeus, which follows (19:1 – 10), reveals that receiving God's grace requires the reformation of one's life and balances the simple cry for mercy.

19. Reinhold Niebuhr, *Justice and Mercy* (San Francisco: Harper & Row, 1974), 12.

20. Paul J. Achtemeier, "The Ministry of Jesus in the Synoptic Gospels," *Int* 35 (1981): 162.

21. Manson, *Sayings of Jesus*, 312.

Luke 18:15 – 34

Literary Context

This section joins four seemingly disparate units together to make a statement about what is required to be a disciple of Jesus and to inherit eternal life. O'Toole comments:

> Children, unlike adults, realize that they are receivers, and this is probably why Luke chose to put this story about them right after the parable of the Pharisee and the tax collector. The tax collector resembles the children in that he humbles himself, unlike the Pharisee who represents those who trusted in themselves that they are righteous (cf. Lk 18:9).[1]

This section rehearses themes that have surfaced in chapters 14 – 18 relating to wealth and discipleship and prepares for Jesus' entrance into Jerusalem to suffer and die. Since no transitions or change in the audience occurs, Jesus' pronouncement about the infants and the reign of God, the question the rich ruler asks about inheriting eternal life, the thunderbolt dictum that those attached to their possessions will hardly enter into the reign of God, the appalled reaction of bystanders, and the disciples' request for reassurance because of the sacrifices they have made to follow Jesus are all part of the same scene. Only the passion and resurrection prediction is spoken privately to the disciples.

Receiving the reign of God as a little child (v. 17) and following Jesus (vv. 18, 22) relate to the issue of discipleship. Inheriting eternal life (v. 18), having treasure in heaven (v. 22), entering into the reign of God (vv. 24 – 25), being saved (v. 26), and receiving eternal life in the age to come (v. 30) convey identical ideas. The two themes are capped off by Jesus' announcement of his suffering and his resurrection. The juxtaposition of these units conveys that to receive eternal life one has to become a disciple of Jesus. To be a disciple of Jesus one must receive the reign of God as a little child, be willing to renounce one's possessions and even family, and be prepared to follow him even to a shameful death. Those still shackled to the wealth of this world are unlikely to make the right choices.

---

1. O'Toole, *The Unity of Luke's Theology*, 145.

Main Idea

The way to eternal life is through discipleship to Jesus, which entails becoming as dependent as an infant, breaking ties to material goods, and taking up one's cross and following Jesus.

Translation

(See next two pages.)

Structure and Literary Form

Mark concludes Jesus' response to Peter with the statement that the first shall be last and the last first (Mark 10:31), and then Jesus goes up to Jerusalem and actually walks ahead of the disciples while he explains where they are going and what will happen to him (Mark 10:32). Luke does not have these details, and the result is that Jesus' prediction of his passion and resurrection (18:31 – 33) is tied closely to what precedes:

- infants as exemplars of the requirements for discipleship
- renunciation of the attachment to possessions as a requirement for discipleship
- renunciation even of attachment to family as a requirement for discipleship
- Jesus' suffering as an exemplar of what is required of disciples

The different characters in these scenes come to Jesus wanting something from him. The parents want blessing for their children; the rich man, assurance of eternal security; and the disciples, assurance of a reward for their sacrifice. Each scene is capped by a pronouncement by Jesus. Jesus' last passion prediction in the gospel sums up everything. Discipleship will have its earthly and eternal reward, but it requires following one who will die a shameful death. Eternal life comes as an impossible gift from God, but it comes to those who are able to receive it as helpless infants and who commit themselves wholeheartedly to God's reign.

Luke 18:15–34

18:15a	Action	**People were trying to bring even infants to him** so that he might touch them.
b	Rebuke	When the disciples saw it, **they began to rebuke them.**
16a	Response/rebuke	**Jesus called to them and said,** *"Let the little children come to me and stop hindering them,*
b	Explanation	*for the reign of God belongs to such as these.*
17	Pronouncement	*Amen, I say to you, whoever does not receive the reign of God as a little child will never enter it."*
18	Question seeking reassurance	**And a certain ruler asked him,** *"Good teacher, what shall I do to inherit eternal life?"*
19	Deflection	**Jesus said to him,** *"Why do you call me 'good'?* *No one is good except one—God.*
20	Simple answer	*You know the commandments,* *'You shall not commit adultery;* *you shall not murder;* *you shall not give false witness;* *honor your father and mother.'"* (Exod 20:12-16; Deut 5:16-20)
21	Response	**He said,** *"All these things I have kept from my youth."*
22a	Substantial answer	When Jesus heard this, **he said to him,** *"One thing is still missing for you.*
b	(command)	*Sell all that you have and distribute it to the poor*
c	(promise)	*and you will have treasure in heaven,*
d	(command)	*and come follow me."*

23a	Response (dismay)	**But when he heard these things he became very sad**
b	(reason)	because he was exceedingly rich.
24a	Response (dismay)	**Jesus looked at him [became very sad] and said,**
b	Pronouncement	*"How hard it is for those who have possessions to enter into the reign of God!*
25	Reason (hyperbole)	*For it is easier for a camel to pass through the eye of a needle than for a rich person to enter the reign of God."*
26	Exclamation	**Those who heard this said,** *"Who then can be saved?"*
27	Explanation	**He said,** *"What is impossible for humans is possible for God."*
28	Request for assurance	**Peter said,** *"Look, we have left our possessions and followed you."*
29	Promise	**He said to them,** *"Amen, I say to you that there is no one who has left house or wife or brothers or parents or children because of the reign of God*
30		*who will not receive back many times more in this age and eternal life in the age to come."*
31a	Passion/resurrection	**Then taking the Twelve aside, he said to them,** *"Behold, we are going up to Jerusalem.*
b	Prediction	*And the things written by the prophets about the Son of Man will be accomplished.*
32		*For he will be handed over to the Gentiles and be mocked, humiliated, and spat upon;*
33a		*and after scourging him, they will kill him.*
b		*Then on the third day he will rise again."*
34	Incomprehension	**And they understood nothing of these things; indeed this word had been hidden from them, and they had no idea what he was talking about.**

The passage contains Jesus' dialogues with the disciples about receiving the reign of God as a child (18:15 – 17), with the rich man about eternal life (18:18 – 25), with the audience about his saying on riches (18:26 – 27), and with Peter about the reward for leaving everything to follow him (18:28 – 30). This theme of self-surrender is followed up by Jesus' private announcement to his disciples about his own passion and resurrection (18:31 – 34).

Exegetical Outline

➡ **I. Parents' desire for their infants to be blessed (18:15 – 17)**

    A. Parents seek out Jesus to touch their infants to bless them (18:15a)

    B. Disciples hinder them from coming to Jesus (18:15b)

    C. Jesus' pronouncement: one must receive the reign of God as a little child (18:16 – 17)

II. A rich ruler's query about eternal life (18:18 – 27)

    A. How does one attain eternal life? (18:18)

    B. Answer: obey the commandments (18:19 – 20)

    C. Assumption that he has successfully completed the requirements (18:21)

    D. Rejection of the requirement to sell everything and follow Jesus (18:22 – 23)

    E. Pronouncement that the rich will hardly enter the reign of God (18:24 – 25)

    F. Reaction: "Who then can be saved?" (18:26)

    G. Answer: salvation comes from God's grace alone (18:27)

III. Peter's query about the reward of discipleship (18:28 – 30)

    A. Disciples have left home and possessions (18:28)

    B. Pronouncement that disciples will receive much in this life and eternal life (18:29 – 30)

IV. Jesus' announcement of his passion (18:31 – 34)

Explanation of the Text

18:15 People were trying to bring even infants to him so that he might touch them. When the disciples saw it, they began to rebuke them (προσέφερον δὲ αὐτῷ καὶ τὰ βρέφη ἵνα αὐτῶν ἅπτηται· ἰδόντες δὲ οἱ μαθηταὶ ἐπετίμων αὐτοῖς). The saying in v. 16, "Let the little children come to me," is so familiar that it is easy to ignore that Luke identifies those who are brought to Jesus as "infants" (τὰ βρέφη). Since infant mortality was so high, "the picture is one of peasant women, many of whose babies would be dead within their first year, fearfully holding them out for Jesus to touch."[2] Jesus' touch has healed others, even raised them from the dead (5:13; 7:14; 22:51), so many others have tried to touch him for healing and blessing (6:19; 8:44). The parents hope that his touch will protect their infants from evil and preserve their lives, and they assume that he would be glad to bless them.[3]

Like churlish gatekeepers, the disciples begin to

---

2. Malina and Rohrbaugh, *Social-Science Commentary on the Synoptic Gospels*, 243.

3. The imperfect verb is rendered as a conative imperfect, "were trying to bring" (προσέφερον) since the disciples hin-

rebuke those bringing their infants to Jesus. They may want to determine who does and who does not have access to Jesus, but, more importantly, their resistance betrays a belief that infants were inconsequential. They have no "merit or achievement," something very much on the mind of the rich ruler and the disciples in the later scenes and the Pharisee in the previous parable.[4] Their actions allow Jesus to make a crucial point: infants are models of how the reign of God is to be received (see 10:21 – 22).

18:16 Jesus called to them and said, "Let the little children come to me and stop hindering them, for the reign of God belongs to such as these" (ὁ δὲ Ἰησοῦς προσεκαλέσατο αὐτὰ λέγων· ἄφετε τὰ παιδία ἔρχεσθαι πρός με καὶ μὴ κωλύετε αὐτά, τῶν γὰρ τοιούτων ἐστὶν ἡ βασιλεία τοῦ θεοῦ). Disciples are to enable rather than to hinder persons from coming to Jesus and receiving the blessings of the gospel (see Acts 8:36; 10:47, where the verb "stand in the way of" [κωλύετε] occurs). Jesus must intercede on behalf of the parents and the children, who represent those most vulnerable. Jesus consistently sides with those on the fringe and considered expendable — the least, those who have no rights, those held cheap by others. The new community he founds embraces the little ones rather than banishing them: "To receive a little child is to accept and esteem even the lowliest of human society."[5]

But how is it that the reign of God belongs to such as these? In the context, the persons who respond to the challenge of God's reign are like these — the tax collector crying for mercy in the temple, the blind man sitting in the dust on the side of the road in Jericho, Zacchaeus scampering up the branches of a tree. All three were spurned by others. The rich ruler, however, seemingly fixed in life with his wealth and his show of piety, spurns Jesus' requirements.

18:17 Amen, I say to you, whoever does not receive the reign of God as a little child will never enter it (ἀμὴν λέγω ὑμῖν, ὃς ἂν μὴ δέξηται τὴν βασιλείαν τοῦ θεοῦ ὡς παιδίον, οὐ μὴ εἰσέλθῃ εἰς αὐτήν). This saying may mean that one must receive the reign of God (1) as one receives a little child; (2) as a little child receives it; or (3) as though one were a little child. The last option is most likely. Jesus does not say that we are to become like little children, and he does not refer to some inherent quality in children, such as their imagined receptivity, humility, trustfulness, lack of self-consciousness, transparency, hopefulness, openness to the future, simplicity, freshness, excitement, or any other idealized quality that commentators often attribute to children. None of these virtues were associated with children in first-century culture, and they reflect a contemporary, sentimental view of children.[6]

In light of the preceding parable of the tax collector who pled for mercy from God out of his helplessness, Luke must have had in mind the child's total helplessness and dependence on others, which explains the mention of "infants." Infants do not display the qualities mentioned above; they are utterly helpless and dependent on others

---

dered them. The next imperfect verb is rendered as an ingressive imperfect, "they began to rebuke them" (ἐπετίμων), since this would not be continuous or customary action after Jesus corrected them.

    4. Craddock, *Luke*, 212.

    5. Fitzmyer, *Luke*, 2:817.

    6. Wiedemann (*Adults and Children in the Roman Empire*, 186) writes: "Classical society relegated children, together with

women, old men, and slaves, to the margins of community life." See also Beryl Rawson, "Children in the Roman Familia," in *The Family in Ancient Rome* (ed. B. Rawson; Ithaca, NY: Cornell Univ. Press, 1986), 170 – 200; and James Francis, "Children and Childhood in the New Testament," in *The Family in Theological Perspective* (ed. S. Barton; Edinburgh: T&T Clark, 1996), 65 – 85.

for survival. Consequently, infants are open to being helped; in fact, they cry out for help, even when others object to their cries. They are not self-sufficient but receive everything as a gift. Likewise, disciples are to receive the reign of God as those who are totally helpless and recognize their total dependence on God for their salvation.[7]

This model sets up how the next scenes are to be interpreted. The rich ruler (18:18–30), the disciples (18:24–30), the blind man (18:35–43), and Zacchaeus (19:1–10) become examples of either failure or success in receiving the kingdom as a little child.

18:18 And a certain ruler asked him, "Good teacher, what shall I do to inherit eternal life?" (καὶ ἐπηρώτησέν τις αὐτὸν ἄρχων λέγων· διδάσκαλε ἀγαθέ, τί ποιήσας ζωὴν αἰώνιον κληρονομήσω;). Only Luke identifies this man as a ruler (ἄρχων), which places him in the negative company of other "rulers" mentioned in Luke: Herod, Philip, and Lysanius (3:1, 19; 9:7). In both Matt 19:16 and Mark 10:17, the rich man approaches Jesus expecting to glean an interpretation of Moses to assist in his strategic plan to inherit eternal life. In Luke, the man does not "come to Jesus." He has just heard Jesus say, "Whoever does not receive the reign of God as a little child will never enter it" (18:17). The ruler's question should be understood as a response, "Good teacher, what will it take for someone like me to inherit eternal life?"

18:19 Jesus said to him, "Why do you call me 'good'? No one is good except one — God" (εἶπεν δὲ αὐτῷ ὁ Ἰησοῦς· τί με λέγεις ἀγαθόν; οὐδεὶς ἀγαθὸς εἰ μὴ εἷς ὁ θεός). Jesus deflects the idle flattery with the statement, "No one is good except one." The ruler may have expected Jesus to reciprocate by also calling him "good" (ἀγαθός), but Jesus makes clear that one may not use the word "good" casually. His first remark alludes to the first commandment to have no other gods before the one God, which directs the rich ruler to the source of what he seeks. By pointing beyond any form of moral goodness to God himself, Jesus reprises the point of the parable of the Pharisee and tax collector: entrance into the reign of God only comes via the miracle of God's grace. It cannot be earned; it can only be accepted with humility and faith.

18:20 You know the commandments, "You shall not commit adultery; you shall not murder; you shall not give false witness; honor your father and mother" (τὰς ἐντολὰς οἶδας· μὴ μοιχεύσῃς, μὴ φονεύσῃς, μὴ κλέψῃς, μὴ ψευδομαρτυρήσῃς, τίμα τὸν πατέρα σου καὶ τὴν μητέρα). Jesus' first answer is less than earthshaking. To the question, "What must I do?" Jesus breezily responds, "Keep the commandments!" It is an obvious answer that mirrors Abraham's answer to the rich man's last-ditch request from Hades: "They have Moses and the prophets, let them read them" (16:29; see 16:31).

Jesus lists five commandments: murder, adultery, stealing, bearing false witness, and honoring mother and father.[8] This answer is different in form from the one the lawyer gives to his own similar question in 10:25–27 ("You shall love the Lord your God with all your heart, and with all your soul, and with all your strength, and with all your mind, and [you shall love] your neighbor as yourself"), but it basically has the same thrust.

---

7. Stephen Fowl ("Receiving the Kingdom of God as a Child: Children and Riches in Luke 18.15ff.," *NTS* 39 [1993]: 153–58) offers another possible dimension to this image. Children will "drop what they are doing and attach themselves to an object of desire." This "single-minded vigour" characterizes "the disciples, the blind man in Jericho and Zacchaeus" (158).

8. The fifth commandment occurs last perhaps because it is formulated as a positive command. In the context of Roman society, it is clear that Jesus' teaching upholds what was regarded as the basic unit of society, the family.

The commands listed affect the neighbor and can be subsumed under the command to love your neighbor. They all have to do with kinship and community, and the implication is that Jesus is primarily concerned with the ruler's attitude toward his neighbor. The ruler comes with a selfish question about his own future security. Jesus redirects his attention to others, which requires selflessness.

18:21 He said, "All these things I have kept from my youth" (ὁ δὲ εἶπεν· ταῦτα πάντα ἐφύλαξα ἐκ νεότητος). If the ruler has indeed kept all these commandments from his youth, he is like the ninety-nine who need no repentance (15:7), the older brother who served his father so many years and never transgressed one of his commands (15:29), and the Pharisee who professes he has never committed adultery or other sins (18:11 – 12), and he joins the list of those who have convinced themselves that they are upright (18:9). He does not ask if he lacks anything (as in Matt 19:20). In Luke, his triumphant assertion assumes that he can know where he stands with God according to his measurable achievements on the obedience scale, and he should pass with flying colors.

18:22 When Jesus heard this, he said to him, "One thing is still missing for you. Sell all that you have and distribute it to the poor and you will have treasure in heaven, and come follow me" (ἀκούσας δὲ ὁ Ἰησοῦς εἶπεν αὐτῷ· ἔτι ἕν σοι λείπει· πάντα ὅσα ἔχεις πώλησον καὶ διάδος πτωχοῖς, καὶ ἕξεις θησαυρὸν ἐν [τοῖς] οὐρανοῖς, καὶ δεῦρο ἀκολούθει μοι). Jesus uncorks a surprise, however, and apprises him that he lacks one thing. Matt 19:21 and Mark 10:21 have Jesus respond, "Sell what you possess" (ESV), but Luke has, "Sell *all* that you have," in keeping with the

radical demands associated with discipleship (14:33). Parceling out his wealth to the poor, who, in Luke, comprise the destitute like Lazarus, repeats Jesus' counsel in 16:9 – 13 (see 19:8). This command is not unique to the rich man and his situation. Renouncing your possessions is a requirement for discipleship (14:33), and others have left everything to follow Jesus (5:11, 27 – 28; 18:28 – 30).

18:23 But when he heard these things he became very sad because he was exceedingly rich (ὁ δὲ ἀκούσας ταῦτα περίλυπος ἐγενήθη· ἦν γὰρ πλούσιος σφόδρα). Bailey comments that if Jesus had given the ruler a checklist of expensive good works to fund or carry out, he may have begun them with great enthusiasm.[9] Jesus asks too much of him. This rich man does not think it is worth the sacrifice because he believes he has so much to give up. As Cain's countenance fell when his offering was not accepted (Gen 4:5), so this ruler's face is frozen in a rictus of surprise and horror when he is told that his record of obedience does not measure up to all that God requires. "Very sad" (περίλυπος) is the same word used to describe Jesus' overwhelming grief in Gethsemane in Matt 26:38 and Mark 14:34. It is also used of Herod's reaction when he heard the request for the head of John (Mark 6:26). Sadness does not always lead to repentance.

Jesus lays open this ruler's soul and exposes the truth that he does not love God with all his heart, soul, and strength. He ignores the poor, except perhaps with token handouts. His exceeding wealth, not God, is really his lord. Consequently, "he has not kept the first and greatest commandment, requiring complete trust in God and self-giving love for the neighbor, encountered in the poor (cf. 10:27)."[10] He wants to serve both God

---

9. Bailey, *Through Peasant Eyes*, 167.

10. John Gillman, *Possessions and the Life of Faith: A Reading of Luke-Acts* (Collegeville, MN: Liturgical, 1991), 88.

and Mammon (16:13), but he must sever all ties to Mammon if he has any hope of eternal life. As Craddock eloquently captures his problem:

> … he has lain too long in silken ease, fared too well at banquet tables, rested too comfortably on the security of his surplus, moved too far from the cries of the hungry, enjoyed too obviously the envy of those less prosperous, assumed too much that he could buy everything he needed. He depends on his money. In short, he is an idolater.[11]

Resseguie comments, "To receive the treasure he wants, the ruler must give up the treasure he has."[12] He needs to shake the gold dust from his feet, but he is grieved because he cannot envision life without his abundant possessions. Usually, those who possess riches are possessed by them. He is devoted to his wealth with its comet's tail of zeroes and the envy that it evokes in others.

Hellerman states a principle that we have stressed above in the discussion of the rich man in the parable of the unjust agent regarding Jesus' teaching about wealth in a first-century context: "The extensive Pentateuchal legislation and concern about land apportionment assumes an important truth: in a *limited goods* society, when one person (or group) has *more,* then someone else inevitably ends up with *less.*"[13] If the rich ruler had truly kept all those commandments, he would not be "exceedingly rich" (πλούσιος σφόδρα). With this in mind, Jesus' command to sell all his possessions and distribute them to the poor is his interpretive summary of the commandments he listed.

18:24 Jesus looked at him [became very sad] and said, "How hard it is for those who have possessions to enter into the reign of God!" (ἰδὼν δὲ αὐτὸν ὁ Ἰησοῦς [περίλυπον γενόμενον] εἶπεν· πῶς δυσκόλως οἱ τὰ χρήματα ἔχοντες εἰς τὴν βασιλείαν τοῦ θεοῦ εἰσπορεύονται). Rather than walking away, as he does in Matt 19:22 and Mark 10:22, the rich man does not move. Jesus therefore addresses his testimony about how hard it is for those with possessions to enter the reign of God (= inherit eternal life, v. 18; to be saved, v. 26) directly to the rich ruler: "Jesus looked at him and said."[14] Luke has shown that Jesus has a unique prophetic vision that can spiritually diagnose people with a look. The ruler knows he falls short and will miss out on his hope for eternal life. That Jesus "became very sad" (περίλυπον γενόμενον) is a textual variant, but it fits Luke's tendency to include poignant details (7:13; 19:41; 22:62). It also fits his tendency to use a word ("sad," v. 23) "and then use it again soon afterward."[15]

"Possessions" (τὰ χρήματα, "property, money"; see Acts 4:37) is a better translation than "wealth," because many might assume that this ruler was a special exception because he was "exceedingly rich." The term basically refers to a thing that one needs or uses. The principle enunciated here applies to all (14:33), not just to those who are wealthier than others.

18:25 For it is easier for a camel to pass through the eye of a needle than for a rich person to enter the reign of God (εὐκοπώτερον γάρ ἐστιν κάμηλον διὰ τρήματος βελόνης εἰσελθεῖν ἢ πλούσιον εἰς τὴν βασιλείαν τοῦ θεοῦ εἰσελθεῖν). Jesus uses hyperbole to announce that either the rich will enter into the reign of God with difficulty,

---

11. Craddock, *Luke,* 214.

12. Resseguie, *Spiritual Landscape,* 110.

13. Joseph H. Hellerman, "Wealth and Sacrifice in Early Christianity: Revisiting Mark's Presentation of Jesus' Encounter with the Rich Young Ruler," *TJ* 21/2 (2000): 151.

14. Luke has the present tense of the verb "they enter"

(εἰσπορεύονται) rather than the future, which appears in Matt 19:23 and Mark 10:23.

15. Henry J. Cadbury, "Four Features of Lucan Style," in *Studies in Luke-Acts* (ed. L. E. Keck and J. L. Martyn; Nashville: Abingdon, 1966), 100.

or the wealthy will hardly enter into the reign of God. The imagery suggests the latter. The "eye of a needle" is the smallest opening imaginable, and the camel was the largest animal in Palestine (cf. Matt 23:24, where camels are contrasted with gnats). The image of an elephant passing through the eye of the needle is found in the Babylonian Talmud, which was compiled in Mesopotamia where elephants were the largest animals (*b. Ber.* 55b; *b. B. Meṣ.* 38b).

The widely held belief that there was a gate in Jerusalem named "The Needle's Eye" and that a camel could get through if it threw off its burden, got down low, and sucked in its insides is a myth. Theophylact (eleventh century) apparently is the first to make this suggestion that it was the name of a gate, but since Luke uses a different word for "needle" (βελόνη) than appears in Mark 10:25 (ῥαφίς), it is unlikely, let alone that it ruins the hyperbole. If a gate had been called "The Needle's Eye," one term would have been used.[16] The dumbfounded reaction of the bystanders that follows this saying also rules out any attempt to soften its shock effect. They are startled because the image conveys that it is all but impossible for the rich to be saved.

18:26 – 27 Those who heard this said, "Who then can be saved?" He said, "What is impossible for humans is possible for God" (εἶπαν δὲ οἱ ἀκούσαντες· καὶ τίς δύναται σωθῆναι; ὁ δὲ εἶπεν· τὰ ἀδύνατα παρὰ ἀνθρώποις δυνατὰ παρὰ τῷ θεῷ ἐστιν). The ruler has asked, "What shall *I* do?" (v. 18) and has asserted, "All these things *I* have kept" (v. 21). He assumes that entering into the kingdom of heaven is something that he can do on his own and is therefore very much unbabylike. He is self-sufficient. Salvation for humans is only possible with God (see 1:37). The bystanders

assume that someone so rich and so outwardly pious must be favored by God, and if the highly favored are excluded from the reign of God, the question, "Who then can be saved?" is inevitable (see 13:23).

Jesus' answer is a generalized statement about "things"; "what is impossible" (τὰ ἀδύνατα) and "possible" (δυνατά) are neuter plurals. The problem applies not just to the super-rich. None can be saved through his or her own efforts.

18:28 – 30 Peter said, "Look, we have left our possessions and followed you." He said to them, "Amen, I say to you that there is no one who has left house or wife or brothers or parents or children because of the reign of God who will not receive back many times more in this age and eternal life in the age to come" (εἶπεν δὲ ὁ Πέτρος· ἰδοὺ ἡμεῖς ἀφέντες τὰ ἴδια ἠκολουθήσαμέν σοι. ὁ δὲ εἶπεν αὐτοῖς· ἀμὴν λέγω ὑμῖν ὅτι οὐδείς ἐστιν ὃς ἀφῆκεν οἰκίαν ἢ γυναῖκα ἢ ἀδελφοὺς ἢ γονεῖς ἢ τέκνα ἕνεκεν τῆς βασιλείας τοῦ θεοῦ, ὃς οὐχὶ μὴ [ἀπο]λάβῃ πολλαπλασίονα ἐν τῷ καιρῷ τούτῳ καὶ ἐν τῷ αἰῶνι τῷ ἐρχομένῳ ζωὴν αἰώνιον). Peter does not seem to show well in this question. If he wants to know what the return will be on the disciples' considerable investment of following Jesus (5:11), then he is as self-absorbed as the rich ruler. Luke does not understand Peter's question to imply that since they have left everything to follow Jesus, they ought to receive something in return, as if he has already forgotten the point of the parable about the servant in 17:7 – 10. His question serves two purposes in Luke's context.

(1) The question presents an opportunity before Jesus arrives in Jerusalem to reinforce explicitly the requirements for discipleship and eternal life. Jesus has told disciples, "Every one of you who

---

16. Paul S. Minear, "The Needle's Eye: A Study in Form Criticism," *JBL* 61 (1942): 157 – 69.

does not say goodbye to all that you possess is not able to be my disciple" (14:33). The encounter with the rich ruler underscores this requirement. He also insisted, "Whoever comes to me and does not hate his own father, mother, wife, children, brothers, and sisters and even his very own life is not able to be my disciple" (14:26). Commitment to Jesus must supersede allegiance to family and clan. Peter's affirmation reveals that the disciples have shown that commitment. Jesus also says, "Whoever does not bear his own cross and come after me is not able to be my disciple" (14:27; see 9:23). By pulling the disciples aside in the next scene to give the last passion prediction (18:31 – 33), Jesus strengthens this aspect of the requirements for discipleship. The disciples, however, will not grasp this necessity until after the resurrection.

(2) The question sets the stage for Jesus to present his vision for an alternative social reality. Jesus intensifies it by specifying that they might have left "house or wife or brothers or parents or children because of the reign of God." The ruler asks about future salvation. Jesus' answer speaks about the future promise rooted in present commitments and practices. Receiving back "many times more" (πολλαπλασίονα) is not to be taken literally in the case of wives but reflects the reality of a new community created by commitment to Jesus that transcends bloodlines and disciples' ethnic and economic backgrounds.

Jesus knows that the bonds of affection within the group will be intensified and invested with deeper meaning precisely because disciples may become isolated from their family and will be separated from the world. But this new family of believers creates "a surrogate kinship group in which material resources are to be freely shared according to need and availability in such a way as to eliminate the socio-economic inequities."[17]

18:31 Then taking the Twelve aside, he said to them, "Behold, we are going up to Jerusalem. And the things written by the prophets about the Son of Man will be accomplished" (παραλαβὼν δὲ τοὺς δώδεκα εἶπεν πρὸς αὐτούς· ἰδοὺ ἀναβαίνομεν εἰς Ἰερουσαλήμ, καὶ τελεσθήσεται πάντα τὰ γεγραμμένα διὰ τῶν προφητῶν τῷ υἱῷ τοῦ ἀνθρώπου). Jesus addresses the disciples alone for the last time about the mystery of what is about to take place. This passion/resurrection prediction provides the most explicit details (see 9:22, 44; 17:25; see also the allusions to his passion without reference to the Son of Man, 12:50; 13:32 – 33). As noted above, Luke does not conclude Jesus' response to Peter with an aphorism (cf. Mark 10:31), and he does not speak to them about his passion/ resurrection on the way (Mark 10:32 – 33), so that this prediction is tied closely to what precedes. How does it all tie together?

Marshall offers that it is "a commentary on the preceding saying": "although eternal life is promised, the path to it is by way of the suffering of Jesus."[18] This reading is on target, but Marshall fails to see the connection with the previous incidents. Neagoe argues that this prediction of his passion/resurrection clarifies further how life is obtained by the seeker.[19] Jesus does not simply demand that the rich ruler disencumber himself of all of his possessions; he also tells him to "follow me." To follow someone who says that he is headed to Jerusalem to suffer and die implies that to inherit eternal life may require suffering and dying as well.

This final prediction, then, increases the stakes for what it means to follow Jesus and to inherit eternal life. It is not enough to keep the

17. Hellerman, "Wealth and Sacrifice in Early Christianity," 156.

18. Marshall, *The Gospel of Luke*, 689.
19. Neagoe, *The Trial of the Gospel*, 57.

commandments from your youth or to relinquish one's attachment to possessions and family ties for the sake of the reign of God. One has to follow Jesus to the cross and carry one's own cross. Peter says more than he knows at the Last Supper: "Lord, I am ready even to go to prison with you and to face death" (22:33).

18:32 – 33 For he will be handed over to the Gentiles and be mocked, humiliated, and spat upon; and after scourging him, they will kill him. Then on the third day he will rise again (παραδοθήσεται γὰρ τοῖς ἔθνεσιν καὶ ἐμπαιχθήσεται καὶ ὑβρισθήσεται καὶ ἐμπτυσθήσεται καὶ μαστιγώσαντες ἀποκτενοῦσιν αὐτόν, καὶ τῇ ἡμέρᾳ τῇ τρίτῃ ἀναστήσεται). This prediction covers three aspects of Jesus' passion/resurrection: his trial (being handed over to the Gentiles [see Acts 4:25 – 26] with its mockery), his execution (scourging and death), and his resurrection on the third day. The third day is emphasized in Luke (see 9:22; 13:32; 24:7, 21, 46; Acts 10:40).

18:34 And they understood nothing of these things; indeed this word had been hidden from them, and they had no idea what he was talking about (καὶ αὐτοὶ οὐδὲν τούτων συνῆκαν καὶ ἦν τὸ ῥῆμα τοῦτο κεκρυμμένον ἀπ᾽ αὐτῶν καὶ οὐκ ἐγίνωσκον τὰ λεγόμενα). When the twelve-year-old Jesus stayed in the temple to be about the things of his Father (2:49), his parents did not understand (2:50). Disciples also do not understand what Jesus is talking about even though he has told them explicitly three times and several times hinted at the events to take place in Jerusalem. Their incomprehension is stated rather than illustrated by their next actions, as it is in Mark 10:35 – 45.

Jesus is the only one to understand his destiny. He knows specifically what is in store for him in Jerusalem and that it is all part of God's plan laid out in Scripture. Things remain hidden from the disciples until after the crucifixion and resurrection. Only then are the disciples' eyes opened so that they can make sense of what has happened through the Scriptures. The additional explanatory statement in 18:31b, "And the things written by the prophets about the Son of Man will be accomplished," is a crucial line that stresses the correspondence between the Old Testament and Jesus' passion (see 24:44 – 48). The disciples may not see now, but what is hidden will be revealed (8:16 – 17). They can understand after the resurrection and after Jesus elucidates the Scriptures for them.

Theology in Application

1. Receiving God's Reign and Inheriting Eternal Life

The interaction with this rich man who claims to have obeyed God's commandments faithfully is followed by an interaction with the rich Zacchaeus, who is despised by one and all as a disreputable chief tax collector. Why does Jesus reject an upright, upstanding citizen like this man with a downbeat message of total sacrifice and then turn around and welcome a disreputable lowlife like Zacchaeus with an upbeat message of grace? Welcoming Zacchaeus into the fold of his supporters invites only scorn. This paradox underscores how one is to receive God's reign and inherit eternal life.

The real contrast is between powerless infants and the ruler, not Zacchaeus and the ruler. Gillman comments, "The rich ruler acts as the antithesis of the children. He teaches us about receiving the kingdom like a child by acting as a counterexample. The children, who know nothing of attachment to power and wealth, will receive the kingdom."[20] No one who is self-sufficient can enter the reign of God, but riches tend to foster a sense of self-sufficiency. Receiving eternal life does not come from keeping the commandments or through achieving extraordinary merit. For Jesus, these are not even the port of entry into discipleship, as evidenced by his response to Zacchaeus and the dying thief on the cross. The rich man is not told to try harder but to surrender everything. Bailey comments: "No one unaided *enters* the kingdom. No one achieves great things and *inherits* eternal life. An inheritance is a gift, not an earned right."[21] One can only approach God like a child who is helpless and dependent.

2. The Challenge of Riches

Jesus' response to the rich ruler makes it clear that he does not associate God's favor with prosperity. James goes so far as to say that God chose the poor who are rich in faith to be heirs of the promised kingdom (Jas 2:5). Hays remarks:

> [This] will require of us not only imaginative reflection but also costly change. No matter how much hermeneutical squirming we may do, it is impossible to escape the implications of the New Testament's address to us: imaginative obedience to God will require of us a sharing of possessions far more radical than the church has ordinarily supposed.... For the church to heed the New Testament's challenge on the question of possessions would require nothing less than a new Reformation.[22]

Entering the kingdom of God is the result of wise spiritual investments, and Jesus asks persons to exchange their present possessions, securities, and status for something better. He sets the example by giving up his own life, what most would consider their most precious possession, to obey God's will. The incident illustrates that one has to lose one's life to gain it (9:24 – 25). It also illustrates that one cannot serve two masters (16:16 – 17). Kelley observes, "The list of commandments the rich man claimed to have followed is from the second table of the law, those dealing with interpersonal ethics." His problem, however, is his disobedience of the first commandment forbidding idolatry. "Wealth became this man's idol." To inherit eternal life, then, "he must completely give up his idolatrous relationship with wealth." He concludes, "This saying does not require the universal and physical dispossession by all disciples but it does require renouncing the ownership of all possessions by all

---

20. Gillman, *Possessions and the Life of Faith*, 86.
21. Bailey, *Through Peasant's Eyes*, 167.
22. Richard B. Hays, *The Moral Vision of the New Testa-*

ment: A Contemporary Introduction to New Testament Ethics (San Francisco: HarperCollins, 1996), 468.

disciples."[23] The dilemma for rich people is this: "lepers (Luke 5:12; 17:13) and blind people (Luke 18:41) want to be set free from that which inhibits them, rich people usually do not."[24]

This tendency explains the various attempts to veil the meaning of the text by reducing the size of the camel to a rope, supposing that "camel" mistranslates an original Aramaic word for "rope," or to enlarge the size of the needle's eye by making it the name for a low gate in Jerusalem. The resulting interpretations produce only spiritual bromides — for example, that one need only throw off one's burdens and get down low to squeeze through. The rich need not worry and may keep their riches as long as they are humble. They also need not worry about obeying all the commandments. Jesus might as well have said, "Rich camels cannot go to heaven," for all the impact these interpretations make on people's lives. One takes the edge off the sting of Jesus' teaching at one's peril. This is such a striking assault on the rich who may feel at ease in Zion that it should only provoke the shocked reaction, "Who then can be saved?"

Throughout Luke, Jesus has addressed the issue of the right and wise use of wealth. He does not exclude the rich from discipleship or from the reign of God, but they must come to terms with Jesus' warnings by seriously evaluating their attachment to their worldly goods. My assumption is that Theophilus was a rich patron who helped publish Luke-Acts, a costly project, and Luke would have been addressing others like him about how they should use their wealth. They could and should use it to help the poor and to advance the cause of the gospel.

We find examples of such people in their various cameo appearances in the New Testament. Barnabas sold a field to allow the proceeds to be used for the needy in the fellowship (Acts 4:36 – 37). Lydia was well-to-do as a dealer in purple who offered hospitality to Paul and his comrades (16:14 – 15). Gaius hosted the whole church in Corinth (Rom 16:23). Phoebe was a benefactor to Paul and many others (16:1 – 2). The church cannot do without the help of those who have means and who know that in Christ they can also do without (Phil 4:11b – 13). As a result, they lay their wealth at the feet of Christ for his service.

23. Timothy W. Kelley, "Tale of Two Searchers," in *Preaching from Luke/Acts* (ed. D. Fleer and D. Bland: Abilene, TX: ACU, 2000), 54 – 55.

24. Mark Allan Powell, "Salvation in Luke-Acts," *WW* 12 (1992): 9.

Luke 18:35 – 43

Literary Context

Jesus meets a blind beggar as he approaches Jericho, and then he encounters a rich tax collector, Zacchaeus, as he passes through the city.[1] Like the blind beggar, Zacchaeus is unable to see Jesus (19:3). The crowd serves as an obstacle to both men: they rebuke the blind beggar when he cries out to Jesus for help; they block Zacchaeus's view of Jesus and openly complain when Jesus invites himself to his home (19:7).

But both men remain resolute in their quest to get help from Jesus or to see him. The beggar will not stop crying out; Zacchaeus runs ahead of the crowd and climbs a tree. Jesus announces that both men are saved (18:42; 19:9): the blind man by his faith; Zacchaeus by his repentance demonstrated by unloading his wealth from ill-gotten gains. The blind man suffers from physical blindness but sees spiritually. Zacchaeus encounters a physical obstacle that prevents him from seeing Jesus but is cured of his spiritual blindness.

The blind man is the only person in Luke to identify Jesus as "the Son of David" (see 3:31), and the messianic hopes specifically associated with David have not been sounded since the infancy narrative (1:27, 32, 69; 2:4, 11). The title reminds readers that Jesus is the Messiah in the line of David as he prepares for his royal entry into Jerusalem. The use of this title by a blind man begging for mercy makes it clear that Jesus does not enter Jerusalem as a firebrand. The title applies to one who hears the cries of the oppressed, shows mercy, brings healing, and evokes praise to God. The blind man does not cry out for deliverance from foreign domination but deliverance from his blindness. Calling him also "Lord" (18:41) prepares for 20:41 – 44. Jesus is David's Lord, not simply heir to his throne.

---

1. In Mark, Jesus encounters the blind beggar as he leaves Jericho (Mark 10:46). For explanations of the differences, see Bock, *Luke*, 2:1502 – 4.

Main Idea

Jesus is the Messiah who brings recovery of sight to the blind and sets free the oppressed (4:18), but their hearts must be prepared to see who Jesus is if they are to be healed by his power.

Translation

(See next page.)

Structure and Literary Form

This miracle account divides into three parts. The first (18:35 – 39) consists of a blind man's appeal to Jesus for mercy, a rebuke from the crowd, and a second, more urgent, appeal. The second part (18:40 – 42) consists of Jesus' questioning of the man, his third appeal (this time for specific healing), and Jesus' commendation of his faith that restores his sight. The third part (18:43) describes the outcome of the healing with the blind man following Jesus and glorifying God and the crowd now joining in with praise of God.

Luke 18:35–43

18:35a	Circumstance	As he drew near to Jericho,
b	Character introduction	**a certain blind man was sitting beside the road begging.**
36	Question	When he heard a crowd passing by, **he inquired what this might be.**
37	Answer	**They announced to him,** *"Jesus the Nazarene is passing through."*
38	Cry for help	**Then he started shouting,** *"Jesus, Son of David, have mercy on me!"*
39a	Rebuke	**Those who were in the lead rebuked him to be silent,**
b	Cry for help	**but he cried out all the more,** *"Son of David, have mercy on me!"*
40a	Command	**Jesus stopped and commanded that he be brought to him.**
b		As he was drawing near, **he asked him,** *"What do you want me to do for you?"*
41a	Question	
b	Cry for help	**He said,** *"Lord, that I might see again!"*
42a	Command	**Jesus said to him,** *"Let your sight be restored.* *Your faith has saved you."*
b	Explanation	
43a	Healing	**Then, immediately, he could see again,**
b	Response (1) following	**and he followed him, glorifying God.**
c	Response (2) praise	**Then all the people who saw this gave praise to God.**

Exegetical Outline

→ **I. Jesus' approach to Jericho (18:35 – 39)**

    A. Cry for mercy from a blind beggar (18:35 – 38)

    B. The crowd's attempt to silence the blind man (18:39a)

    C. The blind man's persistence in crying out for mercy (18:39b)

II. Mercy from Jesus (18:40 – 42)

    A. Jesus' question: What do you want? (18:40 – 41a)

    B. The blind man's specific plea: to see again (18:41b)

    C. Healing and commendation of his faith (18:42)

III. Response to the healing (18:43)

    A. Following Jesus and praising God (18:43a-b)

    B. The crowd's praise of God (18:43c)

Explanation of the Text

18:35 As he drew near to Jericho, a certain blind man was sitting beside the road begging (ἐγένετο δὲ ἐν τῷ ἐγγίζειν αὐτὸν εἰς Ἰεριχὼ τυφλός τις ἐκάθητο παρὰ τὴν ὁδὸν ἐπαιτῶν). The mention of Jericho reveals that Jesus is nearing the last leg of the journey before traversing the steep road up to Jerusalem. It was located fifteen miles northeast of Jerusalem and a few miles west of the Jordan River and north of the Dead Sea. A blind man sits in the dust by the roadside anticipating the generosity of pilgrims headed toward Jerusalem. Eye afflictions were common in Palestine, and poverty was ubiquitous. His condition has forced him to beg to sustain life. The commotion accompanying Jesus as he is about to pass by excites the blind beggar's curiosity. This must be someone important, and those in the lead inform him that Jesus the Nazarene is passing through.

Hartsock notes the differences from Mark's account of the story (Mark 10:46 – 52). In Mark he has a name, Bartimaeus, and he immediately knows who Jesus is. In Luke, the blind man needs to be told who is passing by. He sits by the side of the road begging, which underscores his helplessness. In Mark, he throws off his cloak and springs up to come to Jesus, but in Luke he must be assisted and is brought to Jesus.[2]

18:36 – 38 When he heard a crowd passing by, he inquired what this might be. They announced to him, "Jesus the Nazarene is passing through." Then he started shouting, "Jesus, Son of David, have mercy on me!" (ἀκούσας δὲ ὄχλου διαπορευομένου ἐπυνθάνετο τί εἴη τοῦτο. ἀπήγγειλαν δὲ αὐτῷ ὅτι Ἰησοῦς ὁ Ναζωραῖος παρέρχεται. καὶ ἐβόησεν λέγων· Ἰησοῦ, υἱὲ Δαυίδ, ἐλέησόν με). It is likely that Jesus is part of a convoy of pilgrims preparing to go up the dangerous Jericho road to Jerusalem to celebrate the Passover, but everywhere he goes he attracts special attention and crowds.

Somehow the blind man connects the dots from "Jesus the Nazarene" to "Son of David." Luke's readers might attribute his insight to a general conviction that blindness increased mental perception.[3] It sets up a contrast with those who have physical sight but are spiritually blind, like the rich ruler, who was blinded by his riches. But what follows suggests that Jesus' identity as the Son of David is not so much the key in this passage as the man's persistence. It parallels the persistence of the widow in the parable in seeking justice (18:1 – 5) and Zacchaeus's persistence in seeking to see Jesus (19:1 – 10).

18:39 Those who were in the lead rebuked him to be silent, but he cried out all the more, "Son of David, have mercy on me!" (καὶ οἱ προάγοντες ἐπετίμων αὐτῷ ἵνα σιγήσῃ, αὐτὸς δὲ πολλῷ μᾶλλον ἔκραζεν· υἱὲ Δαυίδ, ἐλέησόν με). Like the infants whom the disciples dismissed, this blind man is judged by the crowd to be inconsequential and a nuisance. Those in the front of the pack mercilessly scold him to shut up. They reflect a widespread view that he is one of the expendables; society has no place or need for such people. The crowd's attempt to silence his cries says to him, "You do not matter to anyone, and least of all to someone important like Jesus." They mistakenly assume that Jesus, on his way to Jerusalem, shares their prejudice and would not delay his trip for

2. Chad Hartsock, *Sight and Blindness in Luke-Acts: The Use of Physical Features in Characterization* (BibInt 94; Leiden: Brill, 2008), 183 – 84.

3. Wolfgang Schrage, "τυφλός, τυφλόω" *TDNT*, 8:271.

someone who was excluded from participation in the temple worship (Lev 21:18; 2 Sam 5:8).

The community may also want to silence this man's embarrassing cries because they call attention to their lack of care for him. But their attempt to stifle his messianic cries to Jesus as the "Son of David" is parallel to the Pharisees' attempt to curb the enthusiastic cheers of Jesus' followers as they soon shout messianic slogans when he enters Jerusalem (19:37 – 40).

The blind man will not be silent, and he cries out all the more shrilly. His persistence is like that of the widow who will not be put off in Jesus' parable (18:1 – 5). The beggar's faith will not be throttled by the crowd that apparently cannot see who Jesus is. Like Zacchaeus, he will overcome obstacles and persist in shouting all the more to Jesus, Son of David, for help.

18:40 – 41 Jesus stopped and commanded that he be brought to him. As he was drawing near, he asked him, "What do you want me to do for you?" He said, "Lord, that I might see again!" (σταθεὶς δὲ ὁ Ἰησοῦς ἐκέλευσεν αὐτὸν ἀχθῆναι πρὸς αὐτόν. ἐγγίσαντος δὲ αὐτοῦ ἐπηρώτησεν αὐτόν· τί σοι θέλεις ποιήσω; ὁ δὲ εἶπεν· κύριε, ἵνα ἀναβλέψω). Though Jesus is nearing the last stage of his journey with the cross looming on the horizon (18:31 – 34), he can still hear the cries of the desperate. He stops (σταθείς , lit., "stood"). The question "What do you want me to do for you?" probes to see if he only wants a handout (see Acts 3:1 – 5). The answer "Lord, that I might see again!" reveals the same faith that the lepers showed when they cried out to Jesus. But they were not so presumptuous as to ask for anything more than mercy; they did not ask to be cleansed (17:11 – 19). Only God could cleanse leprosy; and it was also

widely believed that blindness was impossible to heal.[4] The answer to the question presumes that Jesus as Son of David has the power to restore his sight.

18:42 Jesus said to him, "Let your sight be restored. Your faith has saved you" (καὶ ὁ Ἰησοῦς εἶπεν αὐτῷ· ἀνάβλεψον· ἡ πίστις σου σέσωκέν σε). This is Jesus' last miracle before he enters Jerusalem. It takes us back to the beginning when Jesus announced in his hometown synagogue in Nazareth that he had been anointed to preach good news to the poor and to give to the blind "recovery of sight" (4:18). Being identified as "Jesus the Nazarene" reinforces that connection. The miracle of restoring sight also reconfirms that he is the one who is to come (7:18 – 23).

No emphasis is placed on the course of the miracle itself. Jesus only speaks; he does not touch. Special importance falls on the blind man's "faith," and it provides another answer to the question "Who ... can be saved?" (18:26) — those who have faith.

18:43 Then, immediately, he could see again, and he followed him, glorifying God. Then all the people who saw this gave praise to God (καὶ παραχρῆμα ἀνέβλεψεν καὶ ἠκολούθει αὐτῷ δοξάζων τὸν θεόν. καὶ πᾶς ὁ λαὸς ἰδὼν ἔδωκεν αἶνον τῷ θεῷ). The blind man is transformed from being a beggar sitting along the way to a person who can see and follow Jesus on the way to Jerusalem. He now has both sight and insight. Jesus does not ask him to follow him, as he does the rich ruler (18:22), but his voluntarily following Jesus illustrates how those with nothing readily do so. He has no worldly attachments to encumber him and hold him back.

---

4. Ibid.

Theology in Application

The last two miracles worked by Jesus in the gospel restore sight to a blind person and a severed ear to one of his enemies (22:50 – 51). Seeing and hearing are crucial for receiving the good news of God's reign. With his sight restored, the blind man is a paradigm of what conversion entails: following Jesus and glorifying God.

The blind man also represents those who are most receptive to God's reign. Those who are humbled by others and pushed to the margins of society and those who humble themselves will be exalted (18:14). A blind person in this age was totally dependent on others. The crowd treats him as someone who is insignificant and contemptible. They will give him information — it is Jesus who is passing by — but they will do nothing to help him receive aid from Jesus (see Lev 19:14).

The blind man's plea recalls God's mercy on Israel in the past and the anticipation of the outpouring of that mercy with the coming of the Messiah in the infancy narrative (1:50, 54, 58, 72, 78). It recognizes Jesus as that Messiah, the Son of David (see 1:27, 69; 3:31), who will show mercy to the needy and helpless. Here is one who can only humbly rely on God's mercy; he represents those who cry out more ardently for it and receive it with greater enthusiasm. The man receives his physical sight through his internal sight that recognizes Jesus as the merciful Son of David and trusts his power to heal him. Faith leads to insight, which in turn leads to following Jesus, to salvation, and to God's praise (Eph 1:3 – 14).

There are reports of medical breakthroughs that restore sight to the blind — for example, using stems cells from one's own eye to bring new sight to those blinded by burns. But spiritual blindness does not lend itself to such medical breakthroughs. It explains why Jesus asks the seemingly odd question of the blind man, "What do you want?" Philo refers to "the blind race of common men" who see but are blind because they choose evil rather than the good (*Heir* 76 – 77). They will always give the wrong answer to this question.

The blind man's response, however, reveals that he understood his need to see again. He was so desperate for healing that he would not be put off by the crowd's insistence that he hush. It also required him to state publicly his faith that Jesus was able to restore his sight. Jesus' response that his faith saved him reveals that he had an even greater need. The blind man saw who Jesus really was, and Jesus saw what the blind man really needed and provided both physical healing and salvation. The following story about Zacchaeus (19:1 – 10) reveals "that not being able to see Jesus was far more serious than not being able to see!"[5] The blind man's following Jesus on the way to Jerusalem, where a cross awaits him, also reveals that insight into Jesus means nothing if does not lead to obedience and following Jesus.

---

5. Eugene LaVerdiere, *Dining in the Kingdom* (Chicago: Liturgical Training, 1994), 110.

Luke 19:1 – 10

Literary Context

Zacchaeus's encounter with Jesus functions as a foil to that of the rich ruler (18:18 – 30). Both men are described as rich and both hold high office ("ruler" [ἄρχων], 18:18; "chief tax collector" [ἀρχιτελώνης], 19:2). But Jesus instructs only the rich ruler to distribute his goods to the poor (18:22). He makes no direct demands of Zacchaeus. Instead, he invites himself to his home. Zacchaeus responds to Jesus' surprising insistence with rejoicing (19:6), and he pledges to give half of his goods to the poor and to make restitution for any dishonest dealings (presumably with the other half; 19:8). The rich man, by contrast, refused to distribute his wealth to the poor and turned away from Jesus deeply saddened (18:23).

In the earlier story, Jesus then observed that it is easier for a camel to pass through the eye of a needle than for a rich man to enter into the reign of God. This bombshell prompts his listeners to ask, "Who … can be saved?" (18:25 – 26). The incident with Zacchaeus offers an answer when Jesus pronounces that today salvation has come to his house (19:9). While the rich ruler fancied himself to be righteous ("all these things I have kept from my youth," 18:21) and probably persuaded others to share that same good opinion of himself, he declined to share his goods with the poor. The townsfolk deem Zacchaeus to be unrighteous as one who sold out his people by collaborating with Rome to become a profiteering chief tax collector. Jesus overrules that verdict because Zacchaeus has the correct attitude toward wealth.

This incident complements the parable of the Pharisee and the tax collector (18:9 – 14). The tax collector walked out the door "more upright" by virtue of his humble confession of unworthiness, but the story of Zacchaeus checks an interpretation that salvation comes without any demand. The tax collector cannot continue his same old life and think that is all he needs to do to receive another halo; he cannot simply confess the same sins without any reformation of his life (see Rom 6:1 – 11).

Jesus' encounter with Zacchaeus in the midst of Jericho also parallels the preceding incident with the blind man, which occurred as he drew near to Jericho (18:35). The crowd presents an obstacle for both men who want to see Jesus (18:36; 19:3). They rebuke the blind man for crying out to Jesus, but Jesus intervenes by commanding that he be brought to him (18:39 – 40). Zacchaeus must break away from the crowd to see Jesus, and Jesus commands him to come down from a tree to host him, evoking the crowd's indignation (19:5 – 7). The blind man glorifies God when he is healed, and the crowd joins in praising God in response to the healing. Zacchaeus's promise to give to the poor and rectify past wrongs may count as praise of God, but Luke does not narrate how the crowd reacts to Jesus' announcement about salvation coming to his house. Do they continue to grumble?

IV. Jesus' Journey to Jerusalem (9:51 – 19:28)

   J. On Entering the Reign of God (18:9 – 19:28)

      1. The Parable of the Pharisee and the Tax Collector (18:9 – 14)

      2. Entering the Reign of God (18:15 – 34)

      3. The Healing of a Blind Man (18:35 – 43)

      4. Jesus Meets Zacchaeus (19:1 – 10)

      5. The Parable of the Vengeful Throne Claimant (19:11 – 28)

Main Idea

The renunciation of wealth, charity toward the poor, and the reformation of one's life in response to grace open the way to salvation.

Translation

(See next page.)

Structure and Literary Form

The incident consists of two panels.[1]

First panel (19:2 – 5)	Second panel (19:6 – 10)
Zacchaeus seeks to see Jesus (19:3a)	Zacchaeus meets Jesus (19:6)
Crowd interferes (19:3b)	Crowd objects (19:7)
Zacchaeus overcomes obstacle (19:4)	Zacchaeus overcomes obstacle (19:8)
Climax: Jesus speaks — "Today" (19:5)	Climax: Jesus speaks — "Today" (19:9 – 10)
Connecting hinge: "Hurry and come down" (19:5 – 6)	

The form of this story is mixed. It combines a quest story with a pronouncement.

1. Robert F. O'Toole, "The Literary Form of Luke 19:1 – 10," *JBL* 110 (1991): 112 – 13.

Luke 19:1–10

19:1	Circumstance	**He entered Jericho and was passing through it.**
2a	Character introduction	**And behold, a man named Zacchaeus [was there].**
b		**He was a chief tax collector and he was rich.**
3a	Obstacle	**He was seeking to see who Jesus is,**
b		**and he was not able [to see]**
		from the crowd
		because he was small.
4a	Surmounting the obstacle	**So he ran ahead and climbed a sycamore tree to see him,**
b		because he was about to pass through that way.
5a	Encounter	When Jesus came to the spot,
		he looked up and said to him,
b	Command	*"Zacchaeus, hurry and come down!*
c	Justification	*For today it is necessary for me to lodge in your house."*
6	Response to the command	**So he hurried and climbed down and received him with rejoicing.**
7	Obstacle	**All who saw this began to grumble, saying,**
		"He goes to find lodging with a man who is a sinner!"
8a	Surmounting the obstacle	**Zacchaeus stood there and said to the Lord,**
		"Behold, one half of my possessions, Lord, *I will give to the poor;*
b		*and if I have extorted anything from anyone,* *I will repay fourfold."*
9a	Pronouncement	**Then Jesus said to him,**
		"Today, salvation has come to this house!
b		*Because he too is a son of Abraham!*
10	Conclusion/justification	*For the Son of Man came to seek and to save the lost."*

Exegetical Outline

→ **I. Zacchaeus's desire and endeavor to see Jesus (19:1 – 4)**

  II. Jesus' desire to stay with Zacchaeus (19:5)

  III. Zacchaeus's joyful response (19:6)

  IV. The crowd's hostile response (19:7)

  V. Zacchaeus's public repentance (19:8)

  VI. Jesus' public vindication of Zacchaeus (19:9 – 10)

Explanation of the Text

19:1 – 2 He entered Jericho and was passing through it. And behold, a man named Zacchaeus [was there]. He was a chief tax collector and he was rich (καὶ εἰσελθὼν διήρχετο τὴν Ἰεριχώ. καὶ ἰδοὺ ἀνὴρ ὀνόματι καλούμενος Ζακχαῖος, καὶ αὐτὸς ἦν ἀρχιτελώνης καὶ αὐτὸς πλούσιος). The interjection "behold" (ἰδού) focuses attention on Zacchaeus. He is no tax underling, like Levi (5:27). The Romans auctioned off the collection of indirect taxes (tolls, tariffs, and customs) to the highest bidders, which may have been an individual or a group of individuals. By farming out the collection of these taxes, the Roman governor could count on receiving a fixed sum from the beginning of the year and reduce overhead expenses.

Because the tariffs were unfixed, this arrangement opened the door to fraud and extortion.[2] The lessee could charge whatever he wanted to cover expenses and make a profit, but he would also have to bear any losses. The term "chief tax collector" (ἀρχιτελώνης) appears only here in Greek literature and may denote that Zacchaeus is either the head of a group of partners who joined together to obtain the contract, the sole owner of the contract, or someone hired by the partners to supervise the operation.

He is rich, presumably because he has raked in big payoffs since Jericho was a significant import and export post. As a chief tax collector and a rich man he represents "the sinner supreme."[3] Despite his riches, he remains on the margins of society — disdained, if not hated, as a despicable, greedy, and laughable character.

19:3 He was seeking to see who Jesus is, and he was not able [to see] from the crowd because he was small (καὶ ἐζήτει ἰδεῖν τὸν Ἰησοῦν τίς ἐστιν καὶ οὐκ ἠδύνατο ἀπὸ τοῦ ὄχλου, ὅτι τῇ ἡλικίᾳ μικρὸς ἦν). Zacchaeus's elfin stature is made memorable in lines from the children's song, "Zacchaeus was a wee little man." Physical descriptions of characters in the gospels are rare, and this description may be included to explain why he could not see Jesus from the crowd (ἀπὸ τοῦ ὄχλου, not "because of the crowd") and had to climb a tree.[4] His short stature and the large crowd presented an obstacle that had to be overcome for him to satisfy his quest.

Luke does not tell us why he wants to see who Jesus is. The text implies that he simply wants a vantage point to get a glimpse of Jesus, nothing more. Beyond the text, we might imagine that he had experienced social ostracism, isolation, and contempt and had heard (4:14, 37) that Jesus received sinners and tax collectors (5:27 – 32; 15:1 – 2). Consciously or unconsciously, he may have been looking for the salvation Jesus offered.[5]

19:4 So he ran ahead and climbed a sycamore tree to see him, because he was about to pass through that way (καὶ προδραμὼν εἰς τὸ ἔμπροσθεν ἀνέβη ἐπὶ συκομορέαν ἵνα ἴδῃ αὐτόν, ὅτι ἐκείνης ἤμελλεν διέρχεσθαι). The crowd might make way for someone who was respected in the community, but it would not do so for someone like Zacchaeus. Running ahead, he shamelessly scurries up a tree and perches on a limb. Zacchaeus's resolve means that he does not mind

2. Otto Michel, "τελώνης," *TDNT*, 8:98, n. 105; See Schürer, *The History of the Jewish People*, 1:374 – 76.

3. John O'Hanlon, "The Story of Zacchaeus and the Lukan Ethic," *JSNT* 12 (1981): 9.

4. This explanation is more likely than Mikeal C. Parsons' (" 'Short in Stature': Luke's Physical Description of Zacchaeus,"

NTS 47 [2001]: 51 – 53) suggestion that it was "commonplace to associate outer physical characteristics with inner qualities" and that short people were prejudged to be small-minded. These features are not developed in the incident.

5. Robert C. Tannehill, "The Story of Zacchaeus as Rhetoric," in *The Shape of Luke's Story*, 79.

looking ridiculous in his quest.[6] Bailey suggests that since sycamore fig trees have large leaves as well as low branches Zacchaeus may have hoped to remain unseen.[7]

19:5 When Jesus came to the spot, he looked up and said to him, "Zacchaeus, hurry and come down! For today it is necessary for me to lodge in your house" (καὶ ὡς ἦλθεν ἐπὶ τὸν τόπον, ἀναβλέψας ὁ Ἰησοῦς εἶπεν πρὸς αὐτόν· Ζακχαῖε, σπεύσας κατάβηθι, σήμερον γὰρ ἐν τῷ οἴκῳ σου δεῖ με μεῖναι). Zacchaeus was seeking to learn who Jesus is and discovers that Jesus already knows who he is. Jesus does not ask if it is convenient but informs him that he "must" stay at his home (see 9:4). This strange necessity is explained by the conclusion in v. 10. It is part of Jesus' divine mission to seek and save the lost.

19:6 So he hurried and climbed down and received him with rejoicing (καὶ σπεύσας κατέβη καὶ ὑπεδέξατο αὐτὸν χαίρων). The parables in Luke 15 portrayed rejoicing from the vantage point of those who recover what they have lost (15:5 – 7, 9 – 10). Zacchaeus's rejoicing (χαίρων) lets the reader see joy from the perspective of the one who is lost and is found. The joy is also expressed in a meal, which becomes a celebration (15:22 – 24, 32).[8]

19:7 All who saw this began to grumble, saying, "He goes to find lodging with a man who is a sinner!" (καὶ ἰδόντες πάντες διεγόγγυζον λέγοντες ὅτι παρὰ ἁμαρτωλῷ ἀνδρὶ εἰσῆλθεν καταλῦσαι).

The verb used here (καταλῦσαι) means "to rest, lodge" (see 9:12). The Pharisees and scribes earlier grumbled over Jesus' hosting tax collectors and sinners (5:30; 15:2). That mean-spirited outlook now extends to the whole crowd. They grouse about Jesus going to be a guest of this pariah. They expect Jesus to be on their side in snubbing Zacchaeus. It costs Jesus to go home with Zacchaeus because he now joins him as an object of ostracism.

19:8 Zacchaeus stood there and said to the Lord, "Behold, one half of my possessions, Lord, I will give to the poor; and if I have extorted anything from anyone, I will repay fourfold" (σταθεὶς δὲ Ζακχαῖος εἶπεν πρὸς τὸν κύριον· ἰδοὺ τὰ ἡμίσειά μου τῶν ὑπαρχόντων, κύριε, τοῖς πτωχοῖς δίδωμι, καὶ εἴ τινός τι ἐσυκοφάντησα ἀποδίδωμι τετραπλοῦν). Zacchaeus responds appropriately by calling Jesus "Lord," offering hospitality, and displaying the right attitude toward his wealth. Since the verbs "I give" (δίδωμι) and "I restore" (ἀποδίδωμι) are in the present tense, Zacchaeus may be announcing his repentance and a pledge to change (a futuristic sense), or he may be protesting his innocence by expressing what was his customary action (an iterative sense). Fitzmyer contends that Zacchaeus is defending himself against the crowd's perception of him as a sinner and is not repenting.[9] He neither begs for mercy (17:13; 18:38) nor expresses sorrow for his past misdeeds (15:21; 18:13). The "if" (εἴ), according to Fitzmyer, refers to any incident where Zacchaeus might have

---

6. The healing of the paralytic (5:17 – 26) shares commonalities with the story of Zacchaeus. The desire to see Jesus is blocked by the crowd, which necessitates that the friends "climb up" (ἀναβαίνω) the roof. Jesus takes notice and gives a surprising, positive response that meets with objections from others.

7. Bailey, *Jesus through Middle Eastern Eyes*, 177 – 79.

8. The meal is not mentioned explicitly but is implied by the term "lodge."

9. Fitzmyer, *Luke*, 2:1220 – 21. See also Richard C. White, "A Good Word for Zacchaeus? Exegetical Comment on Luke 19:1 – 10," *LTQ* 14 (1979): 89 – 96; and "Vindication for Zacchaeus," *ExpTim* 91 (1979 – 80): 21 – 25; Alan C. Mitchell, "Zacchaeus Revisited: Luke 19,8 as a Defense," *Bib* 71 (1990): 153 – 76; and "The Use of συκοφανεῖν in Luke 19,8: Further Evidence for Zacchaeus's Defense," *Bib* 72 (1991): 546 – 47. This view is successfully refuted by Dennis Hamm, "Luke 19:8 Once Again: Does Zacchaeus Defend or Resolve?" *JBL* 107 (1988):

discovered that his men were involved in extortion or kickbacks and strongly affirms that he immediately took action to rectify it.

This reading of the text almost makes him sound as if he were saying, "I haven't done anything wrong, and I won't do it again." Such an interpretation is ruled out by other clues in the narrative. First, tax collectors are lumped together with sinners throughout the gospel (5:30; 7:34; 15:1; see Matt 5:46; 18:17; 21:31 – 32) and are assumed to need repentance (3:12 – 13) and mercy (18:13). Rabbinic texts further illustrate how tax collectors were regarded by others and why they were hated. It was not only their collaboration with the Romans but their notorious dishonesty that made them so despised. Had Zacchaeus been so generous, as Fitzmyer contends, why does the crowd harbor such antagonism toward him? He would be acclaimed rather than scorned.

His affirmation is more likely a promise to bear the "fruits ... of repentance" that John demanded of tax collectors and soldiers (3:8, 12 – 14), but it is far more. He will not merely desist from dishonest appraisals and extortion; he will repay all that he had defrauded to his victims, plus a self-levied penalty. Marshall contends: "The conditional clause is to be translated 'From whomsoever I have wrongfully exacted anything,' and thus does not put the fact of extortion in doubt, but rather its extent."[10]

Zacchaeus accepts for himself the law imposed on rustlers who were compelled to make double restitution (if an animal was alive) or fourfold or fivefold restitution (if an animal died; Exod 22:1,

3 – 4; 2 Sam 12:6).[11] Horsley contends from inscriptional evidence that the fourfold recompense matches a Roman milieu. Zacchaeus was "offering to provide restitution in the same proportion as he would have been liable to under Roman law if he had been brought to court."[12]

Second (in response to Fitzmyer), how could Zacchaeus regularly be giving half of his possessions to the poor and restoring fourfold any discovered extortion and still be rich?[13] It is more likely that Zacchaeus is enthusiastically announcing a change in his life's direction. He will now attend to the needs of the poor. Johnson acidly observes that Zacchaeus "clearly has not impoverished himself (half a bundle can still be a bundle)."[14] But he is not trying to keep half of his goods for himself and get off with less than that demanded of the rich man in 18:22.

Zacchaeus identifies two separate groups who will receive his wealth: the poor and the victims of extortion. The poor would have been less likely to carry goods through his customs house to be fleeced by his tax enterprise. Zacchaeus needs to retain the other half of his wealth if he is to make good on his commitment to restore fourfold to those he swindled.[15] The result is that when Jesus opens up his heart to him, Zacchaeus opens up his heart to the poor.

Third, if this speech were a protest of his innocence, Zacchaeus would be no less sanguine about his righteousness than the Pharisee in Jesus' parable (18:11 – 12) or the rich man who claims to have kept all the commandments from his youth

436 – 37; and "Zacchaeus Revisited Once More: A Story of Vindication or Conversion?" *Bib* 72 (1991): 249 – 52; and by Fernando Méndez-Moratalla, *The Paradigm of Conversion in Luke* (JSNTSup 252; London: T&T Clark, 2004), 153 – 80.
    10. Marshall, *The Gospel of Luke*, 698.
    11. The laws of restitution require paying the full amount back plus 20 percent (Lev 6:1 – 7; Num 5:7), but Zacchaeus goes

far beyond the law's requirements.
    12. G. H. R. Horsley, *New Documents Illustrating Early Christianity* (North Ryde, NSW: The Ancient History Documentary Centre, Macquarie University, 1981), 2:72 – 73.
    13. O'Toole, "The Literary Form of Luke 19:1 – 10," 109, n. 9.
    14. Johnson, *The Gospel of Luke*, 286.
    15. Tannehill, "The Story of Zacchaeus as Rhetoric," 75 – 76.

(18:21). He would be the only person in Luke, and a rich person at that, whose claims to be upright are endorsed by Jesus. It is far more likely that Zacchaeus stands in contrast to those "who had convinced themselves that they were upright and disdained everyone else" (18:9). He is disdained by everyone else because of his notorious unrighteousness. The point seems to be that even sinners whom everyone judges to be beyond the pale of hope can find salvation through Jesus.[16]

Fourth, Jesus would not announce that salvation has come to "this house," that is, that Zacchaeus is saved, unless he were in need of saving. The announcement of salvation is tied to repentance and the forgiveness of sins (1:77; Acts 2:21; 38, 40; 5:31). The assertion that it happens "today" (σήμερον, v. 9) indicates that a dramatic change has taken place. The conclusion in v. 10 that the Son of Man came to seek and save the lost implies that Zacchaeus was a sinner who was lost. When he was found, he repented in response.

19:9 Then Jesus said to him, "Today, salvation has come to this house! Because he too is a son of Abraham!" (εἶπεν δὲ πρὸς αὐτὸν ὁ Ἰησοῦς ὅτι σήμερον σωτηρία τῷ οἴκῳ τούτῳ ἐγένετο, καθότι καὶ αὐτὸς υἱὸς Ἀβραάμ ἐστιν). "Today" introduces crucial statements related to the immediate availability of the promise of salvation (2:11; 4:21; 5:26; 13:32 – 33; Acts 13:33). Jesus' pronouncement foreshadows the unexpected announcement to the thief on the cross, "Today, you will be with me in paradise!" (23:43). Jesus gives the reason that salvation has come to Zacchaeus's house: *because* (καθότι) he *too* (καὶ αὐτός, for emphasis) is a "son of Abraham."

In the judgment of the crowd, Zacchaeus's collaboration with the oppressor of God's people and his swindling would have excluded him from the promises to Abraham and his descendents (1:55).

But the preaching of John made it clear that not all children of Abraham by birth are children of Abraham spiritually (3:8). Zacchaeus qualifies as a "son of Abraham" because he bears fruit befitting his repentance. He gives back his fraudulent gains, gives to the poor, and, if he stays in his job, will "collect no more taxes than has been authorized" for him to collect (3:12 – 13).

Zacchaeus's entire household would have been assumed to be implicated in his guilt (see Josh 7) and is also included in his salvation (see Acts 10:2; 11:14; 16:15, 31). Jesus speaks to Zacchaeus in the third person because it is not simply a private conversation between the two of them but a direct confrontation of the crowd. The crowd who obstructed Zacchaeus's access to Jesus by rejecting him as a sinner and collaborator and who objected to Jesus' abiding with him needs to hear this announcement. Jesus overturns their assessment that Zacchaeus is a sinner who is forever excluded from God's people. When Jesus goes to his house *today* (19:5), salvation arrives *today* (see 1:69, 71, 77). It comes to "this house," but it will pass over the grumbling crowd. The declaration provides another answer to Peter's implied question, "What shall we have for following you?" (18:28). The answer is "salvation."

19:10 For the Son of Man came to seek and to save the lost (ἦλθεν γὰρ ὁ υἱὸς τοῦ ἀνθρώπου ζητῆσαι καὶ σῶσαι τὸ ἀπολωλός). Zacchaeus only wanted "to see" Jesus, but he finds one who was on a quest for him. Jesus seeks to gather him in as a shepherd gathers lost sheep (Ezek 34:11 – 16, which uses the image to refer to God). The reason why it is "necessary" for him to stay with Zacchaeus (19:5) is because his divine mission to seek the lost requires it. When finally he sees Jesus, he learns who he truly is — the rescuer of the lost, the

---

16. If Zacchaeus belonged to the group of "tax collectors" who repented, "justified God," and was immersed with John's

immersion (7:29), it seems that it would have been worthy of mention.

restorer of dignity, his Savior. A variation of this statement also appears in 5:32, and it brackets and interprets Jesus' ministry prior to his entry into Jerusalem and the passion narrative.[17]

The basic outline of the Zacchaeus story matches the conversion of Levi (5:27 – 32). Jesus calls to him out of the blue (5:27). He leaves everything in response (5:28). He hosts him in his home (5:29). Others object to Jesus' association with "tax collectors and sinners" (5:30). Jesus then pronounces that he has come to call sinners to repentance, not the righteous (5:32).

Theology in Application

1. Salvation from God's Initiative

Barclay claims that determination to achieve a goal is the point of the story: "Zacchaeus was short of stature but large of heart and overcame his disadvantage by determination."[18] This reading veers dangerously close to false doctrine: "salvation by determination." The sequence of the story may also unintentionally mislead the reader to infer that salvation comes as a reward for works — in this case, the promise of good works. Zacchaeus announces that he will give half of his goods to the poor and make fourfold restitution to those who were defrauded. Jesus then announces that salvation has come to this house.

What precedes Zacchaeus's announcement is most important, however. Jesus invites himself to Zacchaeus's home, and he responds to this act of grace. Jesus' invitation to dine with him is all that is needed to compel his repentance. He responds to this offer of grace by ridding himself of "the damning weight" of wealth acquired at the expense of others.[19] Instead of being a story about determination or works, it reinforces the theological truth that God comes to us when "we are without merit, without ability to please God, and without reason to think that we can be saved or helped."[20]

Luke's entire gospel is driven by God's initiative in offering forgiveness and reconciliation, and Jesus' initiative with this tax collector exemplifies that divine initiative. Jesus stops and spots Zacchaeus hidden in the branches, tells him to hurry and come down, and announces that it is necessary for him to lodge in his house (19:5). According to Maly, "that gesture alone was more than enough to change the heart of a sinner and to make him proclaim his new way of life publicly."[21] Augustine writes that grace "is bestowed on us, not because we have done good works, but that we may be able to do them" (*Spir. et litt.* 16).

---

17. Nave, *Repentance in Luke-Acts*, 184, n. 174.

18. William Barclay, *The Gospel of Luke* (Philadelphia: Westminster, 1955), 244.

19. Kelley, "Tale of Two Searchers," 61.

20. Jason Byassee, "Be Happy: The Health and Wealth Gos-

pel," *Christian Century* 112/14 (July 12, 2005): 22.

21. Eugene H. Maly, "Sin and Forgiveness in the Scriptures," in *Sin, Salvation, and the Spirit* (ed. D. Durkin; Collegeville, MN: Liturgical, 1979), 47.

The conclusion that the Son of Man has come to seek and save the lost (19:10) means that Zacchaeus did not determinedly chase down grace. He wanted to see Jesus, but the text does not say why. Was it simply curiosity, like Herod's desire to see him (23:8)? Or did it reflect some deeper, subconscious longing that he could not put in words? Whatever the motive, the result is clear. Divine forgiveness came to him as a surprise when he deserved nothing and did not even dare to hope to receive it.

2. Repentance: The Name of the Game

In Luke, the release of sins is tied to repentance. Rabbinic literature discusses the repentance of those involved in usury (both the lender and the borrower) and the question is posed, "When are they judged to have repented?" The answer: "When they tear up their bills and undergo a complete reformation, that they will not lend [on interest] even to a Gentile." Another rabbi, R. Nehemia, interprets what this means: "They [the Rabbis] did not mean a mere verbal repentance, but a reformation that involves monetary reparation. How so? He must declare: 'I, so and so, have amassed two hundred *zuz* by trading in Sabbatical produce, and behold, here they are made over to the poor as a gift'" (*b. Sanh.* 25b).[22]

This rabbinic discussion and the story about Zacchaeus illustrate that Jesus and the rabbis would agree on what constitutes genuine repentance. First, it entails sincere regret. Second, it requires a verbal confession (see 18:13). For Zacchaeus, the confession was public but directed "to the Lord" (19:8). Third, repentance demands that one stop the guilty behavior. Finally, when money is involved, it requires restitution and/or charity. This last step means that repentance is more than a fleeting gust of emotional melodrama but has implications for one's long-range future and should show up in the bank balance.

This account overtly introduces the theological conviction that salvation comes from one's response to Jesus and is conferred by Jesus. Wright asserts: "Jesus declared on his own authority that Zacchaeus was a true son of Abraham, and that salvation had 'today' come to his house. In other words, what Zacchaeus would normally have obtained through visiting Jerusalem and participating in the sacrificial cult, Jesus gave to him on the spot."[23]

The grumbling and rejoicing in this account hark back to the setting of the parables of the lost in chap. 15, which climax in the father's declaration, "But it is necessary to celebrate and to rejoice because this your brother was given up for dead and came to life again, was lost and is found" (15:32). It makes clear that the reprobates with dubious reputations can be a part of the community of faith when they repent.

---

22. The assumption was that one who profited from sabbatical trading could not be rehabilitated until the next sabbatical year comes around, and R. Nehemia modifies this interpretation to allow for repentance (and forgiveness) to occur before then.

23. Wright, *Jesus and the Victory of God*, 257.

The response of caring for the poor reinforces the points made in chap. 16. Psychologically, removing a sense of guilt requires more than just saying to a sinner, "All is forgiven." It requires action and restitution on the part of the one who needs forgiveness.

God takes the initiative in offering forgiveness, but there can be no salvation without repentance. It demands: "Change your heart and mind about what is important in life, and then change your life accordingly."[24]

---

24. John P. Meier, *Matthew* (New Testament Message; Wilmington: Michael Glazier, 1980), 23.

CHAPTER 59

Luke 19:11 – 28

Literary Context

In Matt 25:14 – 30, the similar parable of the talents occurs in the context of four other parables delivered on the Mount of Olives as part of Jesus' eschatological discourse (Matt 24 – 25). Its allegorical features relate to the final judgment. The master returns only after a "long time" (Matt 25:19), and the "wicked, lazy" servant (25:26) not only has his talent confiscated but is cast "outside, into the darkness, where there will be weeping and gnashing of teeth" (Matt 25:30; see 8:12; 13:42, 50; 22:13; 24:51). In Luke, the parable stands alone and is set prior to Jesus' entry into Jerusalem. It is introduced to correct those who supposed that "the reign of God was about to appear immediately" (19:11). "Jesus' spatial proximity to Jerusalem" does not signal "the temporal proximity of the revelation of divine rule."[1]

Luke's parable also differs significantly from Matthew's with the additional details of a nobleman going to a far country to receive a kingdom (19:12), the resistance of his citizens who hate him and send an embassy to protest against him (19:14), and the final destruction of the enemies who are slaughtered before him (19:27). If one interprets Luke's parable using Matthew's more familiar parable of the "talents" as the template, these elements seem extraneous to its point. In Luke's context, however, they are key details. The interpretation associated with the more familiar Matthean allegory of the talents and related to stewardship should not be allowed to override Luke's text. In the same way that Luke's parable of the banquet is similar to Matthew's parable of the wedding banquet but makes a quite different point, so this parable has a different meaning. Since the fearful and idle servant is not thrown into the outer darkness, as in Matt 25:30, and is not punished except to be publicly reprimanded and to have his one mina taken from him (Luke 19:22 – 24), Luke does not present this as an allegory of accountability at the final judgment.

The literary context is vital for discerning how this parable functions. The surrounding narrative is peppered with notices about Jesus drawing near to Jerusalem (18:35; 19:11, 28, 37, 41). Jesus has been recognized by the blind man in Jericho

---

1. Wolter, "Israel's Future and the Delay of the Parousia, according to Luke," 313.

as the "Son of David" (18:38 – 39), which heightens the political expectations (see 1:32 – 33). The parable is meant to be read as the prelude to Jesus' humble entrance into Jerusalem on a donkey to receive his kingship ("Blessed is the king who comes in the name of the Lord" 19:38). The contrasts between Jesus, a benevolent Savior who weeps over Jerusalem (19:41), and an evil tyrant king (19:12, 27) who is hated by his people and wants to see his opponents slaughtered in his presence are dramatic. The parable's purpose is to correct any notion that the reign of God is "to 'appear' as a political institution, the kingdom of God cannot be 'observed' (17:20 – 21) like the Roman Empire."[2]

God's reign is already present, in their midst (11:20; 17:20 – 21), but it does not make its appearance in ways that people are accustomed to expect. Its king is unlike earthly tyrants who have armies that bring vengeance, trampling, and desolation (21:20 – 24). As in 22:24 – 27, Jesus contrasts himself with the kings of the Gentiles. They lord it over others and crown themselves with titles such as "benefactor." Jesus comes as one who serves and gives himself for others. This parable should be read as a subtle subversion of Roman imperial ideology that highlights how Jesus' sovereignty differs: he is humble, gives his life for others, and dies forgiving his enemies. This king comes to seek and save the lost.[3]

It must be pointed out, however, that others read the literary context differently. The introduction to the parable (19:11) clearly asserts that it was intended to dampen political expectations that his approach to Jerusalem aroused.[4] Strauss interprets the parable to mean in the context that though Jesus is rightly proclaimed as king, the Son of David by a prescient blind man, he "will receive his kingdom in a 'distant country' (= heaven) from whence he will return to judge those who have rejected his kingly authority." He is the messianic King (1:32 – 33; 1:68 – 75), but "his reign will not be initiated at this entrance into Jerusalem but rather at his exaltation-enthronement at God's right hand."[5] In his death and resurrection he departs to receive kingly authority and will return in judgment. The Zacchaeus story corrects any view that Jesus comes as "the conquering Son of David of contemporary Judaism (see *Ps. Sol.* 17; 4 Ezra 13; 4QpIsa[a]; 1QS b 5,24 – 26) dealing retribution to Israel's enemies but rather as the compassionate Son of Man seeking and saving the lost (i.e. the role of the messiah as set out in Lk. 4.18 – 19, 7.20 – 23)."[6]

Strauss provides solid arguments for his interpretation, but I would not interpret the parable so allegorically that many of its details are pressed to point to something

---

2. Bridge, *Where the Eagles Are Gathered*, 143, n. 85.

3. Most interpret this parable as an allegory of the Son of Man returning for judgment (see Acts 17:31) to remind disciples in a time after Jesus' death that the Lord's absence is not permanent and they must faithfully discharge their commission. In my view, this interpretation does not fit Luke's narrative context.

4. The widespread interpretation that the parable was intended to justify and explain the delay of the parousia for the later church (so, e.g., Conzelmann, *The Theology of St. Luke*, 113, 121; Marshall, *The Gospel of Luke*, 702) has no merit, particularly in the literary context.

5. Strauss, *The Davidic Messiah in Luke-Acts*, 309 – 10.

6. Ibid., 311.

else. The Zacchaeus story could be read as the way to undo the hated and oppressive Roman imperial tax system through the conversion of individual agents rather than through a violent rebellion, much as the submission of the Roman centurion to Jesus' authority subverts the authority of the Roman military power (7:1 – 10). Jesus embodies the things that make for peace (19:42) by giving his life for others rather than taking life, which is intended to lead to the conversion and salvation of people, not their destruction.

IV. Jesus' Journey to Jerusalem (9:51 – 19:28)

    J. On Entering the Reign of God (18:9 – 19:28)

        1. The Parable of the Pharisee and the Tax Collector (18:9 – 14)

        2. Entering the Reign of God (18:15 – 34)

        3. The Healing of a Blind Man (18:35 – 43)

        4. Jesus Meets Zacchaeus (19:1 – 10)

➡   **5. The Parable of the Vengeful Throne Claimant (19:11 – 28)**

    V. Jesus in Jerusalem (19:29 – 21:38)

Main Idea

The vengeful king contrasts with the rule of King Jesus, the Messiah, who comes into the world to bring peace and goes to Jerusalem to give his life for others, not to destroy them.

Translation

Luke 19:11–28

19:11	Circumstance	As they were listening to these things,
		he proceeded to tell a parable
		because he was near to Jerusalem and
		they thought that the reign of God was about to appear↻
		immediately.
12	Parable/ introduction of main character	**He therefore said,**
		"A certain nobleman went to a faraway land to acquire a kingdom for↻ himself and to return.
13	Command	*When he summoned ten servants, he gave them each ten minas and told them, 'Do business until I come back!'*

Continued on next page.

14	Opposition	*His citizens hated him, and they sent an embassy after him, saying,*
		'We do not want this one to reign over us.'
15	Accounting	*When he↵*
		returned after acquiring the kingdom,
		he had these servants who had been given the money summoned
		so that he↵
		might learn how they fared in their business.
16	Report (1)	*The first came and reported,*
		'Master, your mina has produced ten minas.'
17	Reward	*He said to him,*
		'Well done, good servant,
		because you have been faithful in little,
		here, have authority over ten cities.'
18	Report (2)	*The second came and said,*
		'Your mina, master, made five minas.'
19	Reward	*He said also to this one,*
		'And you be over five cities.'
20	Report (3)	*And the other came and said,*
		'Master, behold, [here is] your mina,
		which I had and kept in a handkerchief.
21	Rationale	*For I feared you because you are a harsh man.*
		You collect what you did not deposit,
		and you reap what you did not sow.'
22	Condemnation	*He said to him,*
		'I will condemn you from your own words, evil servant.
		You knew that I am a hard man, who collects what I did not deposit↵
		and reaps what I did not sow.
23		*Then why did you not give my money to the bank,*
		and when I came, I might have earned some interest from it?'
24	Punishment	*He said to those present,*
		'Take the mina from him
		and give it to the one who has ten minas.'
25	Objection	*They said to him,*
		'Master, he [already] has ten minas!'
26	Rationale	*'I tell you that to everyone who has it shall be given,*
		and from the one who does not have it shall be taken.
27	Retribution for opposition	*As for these enemies of mine who did not want me to reign over them,*
		lead them here and slaughter them in my presence.'"
28	Circumstance/ travel notice	After he spoke these things,
		he continued on ahead going up to Jerusalem.

Structure and Literary Form

The parable is an expanded form of Mark 13:34: a man goes on a journey and when he leaves home, he puts his servants in charge, each with his own work, and commands the doorkeeper to be on the watch. The present parable includes the commission, reports, and the reward and punishment of the man's servants but also an extra detail that combines historical and allegorical features. The man is a nobleman who leaves to seek a kingdom and is opposed by his citizens. When he returns as the king, he gruesomely destroys his opponents. The parable is sandwiched between two notices about Jesus' nearing Jerusalem (19:11) and his going on ahead to the city (19:28). Since he will enter Jerusalem as a king, his deportment as a humble king contrasts dramatically with the ruthlessness of the nobleman in the parable, who represents the kings of the world as they lord it over others (22:25).

Exegetical Outline

➡ **I. Jesus nearing Jerusalem heightens expectations about the reign of God (19:11)**

II. Parable of the nobleman (19:12 – 27)

    A. Departure to receive a kingdom (19:12)

    B. Commission of servants to earn profits (19:13)

    C. Embassy of opponents to oppose his rule (19:14)

    D. Delayed return after receiving a kingdom (19:15 – 27)

        1. Settling accounts with servants (19:15 – 26)

            a. First servant is rewarded for faithfulness (19:15 – 17)

            b. Second servant is rewarded for faithfulness (19:18 – 19)

            c. Third servant is punished for negligence (19:20 – 26)

        2. Slaughtering citizens who opposed him (19:27)

III. Jesus continues on to Jerusalem (19:28)

Explanation of the Text

19:11 As they were listening to these things, he proceeded to tell a parable because he was near to Jerusalem and they thought that the reign of God was about to appear immediately (ἀκουόντων δὲ αὐτῶν ταῦτα προσθεὶς εἶπεν παραβολὴν διὰ τὸ ἐγγὺς εἶναι Ἰερουσαλὴμ αὐτὸν καὶ δοκεῖν αὐτοὺς ὅτι παραχρῆμα μέλλει ἡ βασιλεία τοῦ θεοῦ ἀναφαίνεσθαι). If my interpretation of the context is correct, this parable is not "an apocalyptic warning about the conduct of the faithful during the delay of the parousia,"[7] which is then followed by an illustration of the swift judgment facing those who reject Jesus' sovereignty. Since Luke's parable does not include the statement, found in Matt 25:19, that the nobleman returns "after a long time," no emphasis falls on a delayed return. To argue so ignores that Luke specifically ascribes the audience's anticipation that the reign of God is about to appear to the fact that Jesus *is drawing near to Jerusalem* (see 24:21). The mention of present salvation ("today") and "son of Abraham" in the previous episode (19:9 – 10) could have awakened traditional expectations about Jerusalem's redemption (2:38).[8] The audience may assume that God's reign will take on an earthly manifestation after the manner of earthly kings and kingdoms.

19:12 He therefore said, "A certain nobleman went to a faraway land to acquire a kingdom for himself and to return" (εἶπεν οὖν· ἄνθρωπός τις εὐγενὴς ἐπορεύθη εἰς χώραν μακρὰν λαβεῖν ἑαυτῷ βασιλείαν καὶ ὑποστρέψαι). This detail is not an allusion to any specific historical event, but it does fit what Jews had experienced in their history. Josephus's account of Hyrcanus and Aristobulus scrapping for royal power with all of the intrigue, hostilities, embassies, murders, and promise to bestow cities on allies is similar (*Ant.* 14.1.1 – 6 §§1 – 97). Josephus blames the internecine fighting between these two for the Jews' loss of freedom and subjection to the Romans and to a despised aristocracy (*Ant.* 14.4.5 §77; 5.4 §91).

Later, when King Herod died, he left his kingdom to three surviving sons, Archelaus, Antipas, and Philip. The bequest had to be confirmed by the Romans, and Archelaus traveled to Rome to gain the support of the emperor Augustus. The Judeans revolted and also sent an embassy of fifty to oppose his appointment because of his brutality (Josephus, *Ant.* 17:8.1 §188; 17.8.2 §§228 – 342; 17.9.3 §222; 17.11.1 – 4 §§299 – 320; *J.W.* 2.2.1 – 7 §§14 – 38; 2.6.1 – 2 §§80 – 92). Before setting out on his journey, Archelaus entrusted his castle and treasuries to his officers (*J.W.* 2.2.2 §18). When he returned to Jerusalem as a tetrarch rather than king, he deposed the high priest Joazar and replaced him with Eliezer.[9]

The nobleman cannot represent Jesus, as so many commentators mistakenly assume. The term "noble" (εὐγενής) is an earthly evaluation that derives from the perverted standards of this world and is particularly applicable to Roman citizens

7. Contra Lane C. McGaughy, "The Fear of Yahweh and the Mission of Judaism: A Postexilic Maxim and Its Early Christian Expansion in the Parable of the Talents," *JBL* 94 (1975): 237. This view is represented by many other commentators. Few have treated the parable in any depth; see the bibliographical note in Francis D. Weinert, "The Parable of the Throne Claimant (Luke 19:12, 14 – 15a, 27) Reconsidered," *CBQ* 39 (1977): 505, n. 1.

8. Vittorio Fusco, "'Point of View' and 'Implicit Reader' in Two Eschatological Texts (Lk 19,11 – 28; Acts 1,6 – 8)," in *The Four Gospels, 1992: Festschrift Frans Neirynck* (BETL 100; ed. F. Van Segbroeck; Leuven: Leuven Univ. Press, 1992), 2:1678.

9. See also the embassy to Rome sent by Judas Maccabeus to form an alliance to oppose Demetrius I Soter from seizing the Seleucid throne (1 Macc 8:17 – 19; Josephus, *Ant.* 12.10.1 §§389 – 92).

(see 1 Cor 1:26), not to Jesus, born in humble circumstances in Bethlehem. It is a stretch to equate the "faraway land" with heaven. The nobleman goes to "acquire" or "take" (λαβεῖν) royal power, but Jesus is born Messiah (2:11, 26), a role equated with king in 23:2 and Acts 17:7. The nobleman is hated by his citizens, who dispatch an embassy to thwart his attempt to assume royal power. Jesus' entry into Jerusalem is met with rejoicing by a crowd of disciples (19:37 – 38), and "the people" do not oppose him during the passion narrative. The newly anointed king distributes cities to his lackeys, and this detail is not to be allegorized as a spiritual symbol of greater responsibilities or treasure in heaven. The cities represent cities.

The last servant characterizes the nobleman as an austere man who reaps where he does not sow, and he expects to earn interest from the bankers, a great impiety to Jews except when dealing with foreigners (Exod 22:25; Lev 25:35 – 38; Deut 23:19 – 20). The servant's picture of the king as a hard man is not some mistaken exaggeration of an embittered slave but is borne out when the king has his enemies executed in front of him. This bloodlust characterizes the world's tyrants, not Jesus. He is the one who is slaughtered in giving his life for others but asks the Father to forgive the perpetrators (23:34). Weinert rightly concludes that the narrative features of supposedly sending an embassy to oppose Jesus' divine enthronement and the vengeful treatment of enemies "are allegorically unintelligible from a Christian point of view."[10] Who can send an embassy to heaven?

19:13 When he summoned ten servants, he gave them ten minas and told them, "Do business until I come back!" (καλέσας δὲ δέκα δούλους ἑαυτοῦ ἔδωκεν αὐτοῖς δέκα μνᾶς καὶ εἶπεν πρὸς αὐτούς· πραγματεύσασθε ἐν ᾧ ἔρχομαι). Luke has

ten servants, but only three appear in the reckoning (19:16 – 27). In Matthew's parable of the talents, the master discriminates and gives to each servant according to his own ability (Matt 25:15). Matthew's parable also has them entrusted with larger currency, the talent. In Luke, each servant receives the same amount. The mina in Luke is worth about one-sixtieth of a talent (= one hundred denarii), which is a paltry sum for someone who can dole out cities as a reward. The servants must trade in hostile circumstances, since the citizens hate the nobleman (19:14), and one of the servants attempts to conserve what he has.

19:14 His citizens hated him, and they sent an embassy after him, saying, "We do not want this one to reign over us" (οἱ δὲ πολῖται αὐτοῦ ἐμίσουν αὐτόν καὶ ἀπέστειλαν πρεσβείαν ὀπίσω αὐτοῦ λέγοντες· οὐ θέλομεν τοῦτον βασιλεῦσαι ἐφ᾽ ἡμᾶς). Sending embassies to Rome to protest egregious abuses by the governors or client kings was not uncommon in this era (see Philo's treatise *On the Embassy to Gaius*), and this detail is a bit of realia. While opposition to Jesus as Lord and King may be rife among the priestly aristocracy, this detail in the parable hardly represents citizens sending an embassy to God to protest Jesus' reign.

19:15 – 19 When he returned after acquiring the kingdom, he had these servants who had been given the money summoned so that he might learn how they fared in their business. The first came and reported, "Master, your mina has produced ten minas." He said to him, "Well done, good servant, because you have been faithful in little, here have authority over ten cities." The second came and said, "Your mina, master, made five minas." He said also to this one, "And you be over five cities" (καὶ ἐγένετο ἐν τῷ ἐπανελθεῖν αὐτὸν λαβόντα τὴν βασιλείαν

10. Weinert, "The Throne Claimant Reconsidered," 507.

καὶ εἶπεν φωνηθῆναι αὐτῷ τοὺς δούλους τούτους οἷς δεδώκει τὸ ἀργύριον, ἵνα γνοῖ τί διεπραγματεύσαντο. παρεγένετο δὲ ὁ πρῶτος λέγων· κύριε, ἡ μνᾶ σου δέκα προσηργάσατο μνᾶς. καὶ εἶπεν αὐτῷ· εὖγε, ἀγαθὲ δοῦλε, ὅτι ἐν ἐλαχίστῳ πιστὸς ἐγένου, ἴσθι ἐξουσίαν ἔχων ἐπάνω δέκα πόλεων. καὶ ἦλθεν ὁ δεύτερος λέγων· ἡ μνᾶ σου, κύριε, ἐποίησεν πέντε μνᾶς. εἶπεν δὲ καὶ τούτῳ· καὶ σὺ ἐπάνω γίνου πέντε πόλεων).

Compared to Matthew's version, the account of the trading experiences of the servants is absent and their reports briefer as the story moves more quickly to its denouement. Only the first servant is praised as "good" whereas in Matthew both the first and second servants are equally praised with the double adjectives "good and faithful." The emphasis in Luke is not on the performance of the servants, since no mention is made that they were "faithful in a few things" as in Matt 25:21, 23. The reward given to the good servants in Matthew's version is vague and spiritualized. They are set "over many things," and they are invited to enter their "master's happiness" (Matt 25:21, 23). In Luke, the reward is specific: a gift of ten cities to the first, five cities to the second (Luke 19:17, 19).

19:20 And the other came and said, "Master, behold, [here is] your mina, which I had and kept in a handkerchief" (καὶ ὁ ἕτερος ἦλθεν λέγων· κύριε, ἰδοὺ ἡ μνᾶ σου ἦν εἶχον ἀποκειμένην ἐν σουδαρίῳ). The "evil" servant in Matthew buried his talent (25:18, 25). In Luke, he wrapped his mina in a cloth napkin (σουδαρίῳ). According to the Mishnaic law of damages, burying money was considered to be the best security against theft and freed one from liability. If anyone tied up entrusted money in a cloth, however, he was responsible to make good any loss incurred because he exercised inadequate care of the entrusted deposit

(*m. B. Meṣ.* 3:10). From this perspective, not only did the servant disobey the command to do business with the mina, he was careless in keeping what was entrusted to him even though he did not lose it.

19:21 "For I feared you because you are a harsh man. You collect what you did not deposit, and you reap what you did not sow" (ἐφοβούμην γάρ σε, ὅτι ἄνθρωπος αὐστηρὸς εἶ, αἴρεις ὃ οὐκ ἔθηκας καὶ θερίζεις ὃ οὐκ ἔσπειρας). The servant defends his behavior by describing his master as a hard-boiled, grasping predator. The imagery of a harsh man (αὐστηρός, from the verb, αὔω, "to dry up, wither") is that of a "tough, uncompromising, punctilious financier,"[11] which is never applied to God in the Bible and certainly does not apply to Jesus. The phrase "you collect what you did not deposit" (αἴρεις ὃ οὐκ ἔθηκας) literally reads, "you take what you did not put down," and these are commercial terms. Plato cites "take not up what you laid not down" as a venerable law and says that those who flout it will be punished by the gods (*Laws* 11.913C-D). Josephus cites "taking what one did not deposit" in a list of crimes that the Jewish law punished more severely than the laws of other nations (*Ag. Ap.* 2.30 §216).[12] Afraid of losing the sum given to him by such an exacting bloodsucker, the servant does nothing.

19:22 – 24 He said to him, "I will condemn you from your own words, evil servant. You knew that I am a hard man, who collects what I did not deposit and reaps what I did not sow. Then why did you not give my money to the bank, and when I came, I might have earned some interest from it?" He said to those present, "Take the mina from him and give it to the one who has ten minas" (λέγει αὐτῷ· ἐκ τοῦ στόματός σου κρίνω σε, πονηρὲ δοῦλε. ᾔδεις ὅτι ἐγὼ ἄνθρωπος

11. BDAG, 152. 12. See BDAG, 1004.

αὐστηρός εἰμι, αἴρων ὃ οὐκ ἔθηκα καὶ θερίζων ὃ οὐκ ἔσπειρα; καὶ διὰ τί οὐκ ἔδωκάς μου τὸ ἀργύριον ἐπὶ τράπεζαν; κἀγὼ ἐλθὼν σὺν τόκῳ ἂν αὐτὸ ἔπραξα. καὶ τοῖς παρεστῶσιν εἶπεν· ἄρατε ἀπ᾽ αὐτοῦ τὴν μνᾶν καὶ δότε τῷ τὰς δέκα μνᾶς ἔχοντι). The king makes no attempt to refute this servant's characterization of himself but affirms it and uses it to justify this third servant's condemnation. He had claimed that he was afraid, but if that were true, he would have put the money in a bank (or with a money dealer) and at least collected some interest. Instead, he wrapped the money in a napkin and did not even bury it for safekeeping. Since the servant was careless with his trust, he has the mina taken from him.

Reiterating the master's characteristics as a harsh man underscores that he is a tyrant. His actions reveal that the servant was *not* operating under an illusion and "did not recognize his master's true character."[13] His pitilessness is evidenced by his taking away what the third servant has and giving it to the more productive servant and by the slaughter in his presence of those who opposed his rule.

19:25 – 26 They said to him, "Master, he [already] has ten minas!" "I tell you that to everyone who has it shall be given, and from the one who does not have it shall be taken"** (καὶ εἶπαν αὐτῷ· κύριε, ἔχει δέκα μνᾶς. λέγω ὑμῖν ὅτι παντὶ τῷ ἔχοντι δοθήσεται, ἀπὸ δὲ τοῦ μὴ ἔχοντος καὶ ὃ ἔχει ἀρθήσεται). The new king's command to take the one mina from the unproductive servant and give it to servant with ten minas is not an eschatological judgment. He does not have the power to punish him by casting him into the outer darkness where there will be weeping and gnashing of teeth

(Matt 25:30). He does not represent God or Jesus, as he does in the Matthean parable. The fearful servant did not produce with what he had; he now has nothing.

Others in the king's circle object to this redistribution of funds to the productive servant: "He already has ten minas."[14] The king's justification for this action is a piece of conventional wisdom that simply means "the rich get richer." It is not the conclusion to the parable; it simply reflects the cynical callousness of a king who is a man of the world. Here, it does not convey a spiritual lesson as it does in Matt 25:28 – 29 (cf. Matt 13:12), and it is not comparable to the saying in Luke 12:48 because it is uttered by this vengeful throne claimant, not by Jesus. Superimposing the interpretation of the Matthean parable and this saying on Luke's parable prevents one from understanding its meaning in Luke's context.[15]

19:27 "As for these enemies of mine who did not want me to reign over them, lead them here and slaughter them in my presence" (πλὴν τοὺς ἐχθρούς μου τούτους τοὺς μὴ θελήσαντάς με βασιλεῦσαι ἐπ᾽ αὐτοὺς ἀγάγετε ὧδε καὶ κατασφάξατε αὐτοὺς ἔμπροσθέν μου). The butchery of enemies is what foreign kings do (2 Kgs 25:6 – 7, 18 – 21; Jer 39:5 – 7; 52:9 – 11, 24 – 27). It is also what Joshua did to the five kings (Josh 10:16 – 27) and Samuel did to Agag (1 Sam 15:33). It is what the disciples thought was warranted for the inhospitable Samaritan town. When the town rebuffed Jesus, James and John urged him to call down fire from heaven as a reprisal. Jesus rebukes them and moves on to another village (9:51 – 56).

Slaughter is not what Jesus does. It is what the Romans do and will do to Jerusalem when the city

---

13. Contra Danker, *Jesus and the New Age*, 309, and many others.

14. This exclamation is absent from codex Bezae (D) and some Old Latin, Syriac, and Coptic versions. The single mina

seems superfluous to one who now has authority over ten cities.

15. The same may be said of attempts to reconstruct some hypothetical, "original" parable from the two different parables.

is surrounded by armies and its inhabitants will be dashed to the ground, fall by the sword, and be taken into captivity (19:43 – 44; 21:20 – 24). In a Roman triumph, the victors brandished their war trophies, paraded their prisoners of war through the streets, and executed these captives when the cavalcade reached its destination. In my view, Luke does not attribute this kind of threatening action to God or Jesus. For example, Luke's version of the parable of the great banquet (14:15 – 24), in contrast to Matthew's (Matt 22:1 – 14), does not have the enraged host sending troops to destroy those who rebuffed him and murdered his servants and to burn their city (Matt 22:7).

19:28 After he spoke these things, he continued on ahead going up to Jerusalem (καὶ εἰπὼν ταῦτα ἐπορεύετο ἔμπροσθεν ἀναβαίνων εἰς Ἱεροσόλυμα). Jesus' destination is Jerusalem, where he will become a victim of brutal violence at the hands of the priestly leaders and the Romans. He goes as an anointed King who will not dish out punishment to those who would resist him and do away with him but will instead appeal to God that they be forgiven (23:34).

Theology in Application

1. The Human Lust to Rule

This parable is *not* a salvation-history allegory in which the nobleman going to a far land represents Jesus' ascension to heaven to receive his kingdom, and his return and slaughter of the enemies represent the parousia and final judgment, no matter how often this interpretation is repeated. Jesus has already received his kingdom. At the Last Supper, Jesus tells his disciples that he confers on them a kingdom just as the Father has conferred on him a kingdom (22:29; see 12:32). Nor does this parable teach the moral lesson "that during the absence of the ascended Christ each of his disciples is expected to carry on with his or her duties of Christian mission, seeking to do the most that can be done."[16] The focus of the parable is not on the third servant but on the king in each scene as he deals with three servants and his adversaries. The parable prepares for a contrast between the rulers of this world and Jesus, who is poised to enter Jerusalem as a king.[17]

God's reign does not mirror the way worldly kingdoms operate. They depend on political infighting, military power, and the annihilation of enemies. The rulers of this world lust to rule and wreak vengeance on those who resist their will to power. It is the way of the kings of this world to go to war against other kings (14:31 – 32) and to seek more status, more power, more land, and more taxes. Those who resist the domination of the kings of this world will bear the brunt of their cruel oppression. The kings of the world may have their lackeys, who perform well and get their share

---

16. Hultgren, *The Parables of Jesus*, 289.

17. Craig A. Evans (*The Bible Knowledge Background Commentary: Matthew-Luke* [Colorado Springs, CO: Cook, 2003], 467) comments that the parable was applied to principles of stewardship in the life of the church when it "became separated from its original social and economic context" and when memory of Archelaus had faded.

of cities over which to rule, but their power is limited. Their trophies are only temporal and temporary. The real power belongs to the King, who brings peace, metes out justice, and shows compassion and mercy.

The Jewish leaders bring Jesus to the Roman governor, Pilate, with the charge that he claims to be a king (23:2 – 3). But Pilate is stymied (particularly in John's account, John 18:33 – 38). As a Roman official, he was conditioned to think of kingship and kingdoms in terms of power politics and military strategic weapons. He found the charge that Jesus was a king to be ludicrous, as did Herod Antipas. Jesus had no army, put up no resistance, and did not put on royal airs. What Pilate could not fathom was that Jesus' kingdom is in the world and over the world, but it does not derive from the world's possibilities. His kingship is built on the sovereignty of the truth. His destiny is to give his life for others rather than to annihilate them.

2. God's Reign of Peace

As Jesus neared Jerusalem, his followers may have taken for granted that the same old human story of how one takes power and establishes a kingdom was in play. They may have anticipated that Jesus would restore the glory days of the kingdom of David (see Acts 1:6). They would gain supremacy through brute force to secure dominance over their enemies, and their supremacy would be obvious to all.

But the reign of God is conducted on a totally different strategy. Smith writes, "Earthly kings subdue enemies; God subdues enmity. His victories must be interior before they can be exterior. He does not subjugate but he conquers."[18] That is why "God's kingdom has no geographical borders, no capital city, no parliament building, no royal trappings that you can see. Its followers live right among their enemies, not separated from them by a border fence or a wall. It lives, and grows, on the inside of humans."[19] That is also why praying "Your reign come" requires that hearts be transformed.

The future of God's people hinges on their accepting God's ways and not aligning themselves with the overlords who govern human empires. Church history reveals, however, that Christians have had a hard time understanding that God does not win over the opposition through violence and domination. Christ's followers still get it wrong in thinking that such means are justified by their supposed good end. The problem is that they do not fully realize that the real enemy to be vanquished is Satan, not human opponents. The passion narrative and the resurrection show God's way for defeating this enemy.

---

18. Hannah Whitall Smith, *The Christian's Secret of a Happy Life* (rev. ed.; Boston: Willard Tract Repository, 1885), 263.

19. Philip Yancey, *The Jesus I Never Knew* (Grand Rapids: Zondervan, 1995), 248.

Luke 19:29 – 46

Literary Context

After the long journey to Jerusalem, the climactic point has arrived. The opening travel notice in 19:28 connects Jesus' entry into Jerusalem to the previous parable about the vengeful throne claimant ("after he spoke these things"), and it serves as a bridge between the two units (see 19:11). Jesus enters the city as a royal figure, but unlike the throne claimant, he comes humbly riding on a colt and heading ultimately to his death on a cross.

This is not a triumphal entry as the Romans practiced it. There are no military trappings, no trophies of war, no captives, and no white horse — none of the things associated with triumphal processions. It is to be compared to the celebratory welcomes of a royal or other dignitary.[1] Jesus comes as a king, not a king of war but a king of peace. Luke links Jesus' pronouncement of judgment on the city with the events surrounding his entry. It quickly moves from the disciples' shouts of joy to Jesus' wail of lament as he knows he must pull against the gravitational power of the temple, which has fallen into enemy hands.

Main Idea

Jesus enters Jerusalem as the messianic King, and his coming as the Lord brings joy or calamity, depending on how he is received.

---

1. Brent Rogers Kinman, "Parousia, Jesus' 'A-Triumphal' Entry, and the Fate of Jerusalem (Luke 19:28 – 44)," *JBL* 118 (1999): 280 – 84.

Translation

Luke 19:29–46

19:29a	Circumstance	Now it happened

         as he drew near to Bethphage and Bethany at the mountain called Olives,

| b | Commission | **he sent two of his disciples, saying,** |
| 30a | Prophecy | *"Go to the village ahead* |

     and as you enter, you will find a tethered colt that no one has ever sat upon.

| b | Command | *Loose it and lead it [here].* |
| 31 | | *If anyone asks you,* |

       'Why are you loosing it?'

    you will say this,
     'The Lord needs it.'"

| 32 | Obedience | **So those who were sent left and found [it] just as he told them.** |

| 33 | Reaction | As they were loosing the colt, |

its lords said to them,
  "Why are you loosing the colt?"

| 34 | Response | **They said,** |

  "The Lord needs it."

| 35a | | **They led it to Jesus** |
| b | | **and threw their garments on the colt and** |

    mounted Jesus on it.

| 36 | Circumstance | While he went on, |

they were spreading their garments on the way.

| 37a | | As he now drew near to the ↵ |

descent from the Mount of Olives,

| b | Homage | **the multitude of disciples all together began to praise God,** rejoicing with a ↵ |

               loud voice
           for all the mighty works they ↵
           had seen,

| 38a | Acclamation | saying, |

     "Blessed is the king who ↵
    comes in the name of the Lord.

| b | Scripture | *In heaven peace and ↵* |

    glory in the highest." (Ps 118:26)

39a	Character introduction	**And certain ones of the Pharisees from the crowd said to him,**
b	Objection	*"Teacher, rebuke your disciples!"*
40	Prophecy	**He answered them,**

   "I say to you, if these will become silent, the stones will cry out."

| 41a | Circumstance | And as he drew near and saw the city, |
| b | | **he burst into tears over it, saying,** |

Continued on next page.

42	Lament	*"If you, even you, only knew on this day the things that make for peace,* *but now it is hidden from your eyes.*
43	Prophecy	*Because the days will come upon you* *and your enemies will set up siege works against you, and encircle you,* *and hem you in on every side.*
44a		*And they will dash you to the ground and your children within [your walls],* *and they will not leave one stone upon another within [your walls]*
b		*because you did not know the time of your visitation."*
45a	Circumstance	**Then he entered the temple**
b	Prophetic protest	**and began to cast out the sellers, telling them,**

46	Explanation from
	Scripture
		"It stands written,
		    'My house shall be a house of prayer,' (Isa 56:7)
		    but you have made it a hideout for bandits!" (Jer 7:11)

Structure and Literary Form

Jesus' climactic entry into Jerusalem divides into four scenes. The first three scenes describe preparations for Jesus and begin with the verb "to draw near" (ἐγγίζω; 19:29, 37, 41); the last scene presents him entering (εἰσελθών) the temple (19:45). Each scene alludes to or directly quotes Scripture (19:35 – 36, 38, 44, 46). From their Old Testament context, the first two allusions would lead one to expect triumph for Jerusalem; the last two, only judgment.

1. Preparations to enter the city from the Mount of Olives (19:28 – 36)
2. Acclamations nearing the descent from the Mount of Olives (19:37 – 40)
3. Lament over the impending destruction of the city (19:41 – 44)
4. Entrance into the temple and pronouncement of judgment (19:45 – 46)

The scenes compare to the familiar "celebratory welcomes" of royal or other dignitaries who expected certain protocol to be followed when they arrived (*parousia*) in cities. Kinman highlights the normal features of such a reception:

1. Welcome was commonly bestowed on kings and other ruling figures.
2. The welcome was normally extended when the dignitary approached the city.
3. The religious and political elite and other welcomers would meet the dignitary and escort him back to the city.
4. The large body of citizens would mark the occasion by wearing ornamental clothing.
5. The dignitary would be lauded by speeches presented to him on behalf of the city expressing their privilege at receiving his visitation.[2]

---

2. Ibid., 284. One would expect that Pilate, as governor, would have received such a reception when he transferred from his headquarters in Caesarea to Jerusalem during the volatile Passover season.

Given these conventions, Kinman concludes:

> Jerusalem's hardened spiritual condition is epitomized by its failure to recognize its king. He is not met by city officials, nor fêted by the leading citizens nor escorted back to the city. The encounter with the Pharisees is a rejection, and the nonappearance of the high priests, other officials, and the citizens of Jerusalem is an affront. The rejection is made clearer by the fact that Luke has gone to some lengths to stress that Jesus is king. Although he is the king, he is not received as one by Jerusalem.[3]

Jesus receives the same rebuff from Jerusalem that he received from the Samaritan town (9:51 – 55). Ancient readers would know that the city's indifference to Jesus the King courted certain reprisal, since kings did not brook insults with forbearance. A king's *parousia* "was frequently brought to an end by the visit of the guest to the local temple."[4] Jesus' entrance into the temple in this case turns into a symbolic act and oblique announcement of its destruction. Jesus will not be the king who will decimate the city in revenge; the Roman rulers will. Jerusalem did not receive the King of Peace and did not recognize the things that make for peace, and they will be ravaged in a war against Roman hegemony.

Exegetical Outline

➡ **I. Jesus draws near to Jerusalem (19:29 – 44)**

    A. Preparations (19:29 – 36)

    B. Response to entrance (19:37 – 40)

        1. Acclamation from the disciples (19:37 – 38)

        2. Objections from the Pharisees (19:39 – 40)

    C. Jesus' lament over Jerusalem's recalcitrance (19:41 – 44)

        1. Weeping over Jerusalem's hardened spiritual condition (19:41 – 42)

        2. Prophecy of its destruction (19:43 – 44)

II. Entrance to the temple (19:45 – 46)

    A. Prophetic sign of judgment (19:45)

    B. Scriptural explanation (19:46)

---

3. Ibid., 293 – 94.   4. Ibid., 283.

Explanation of the Text

19:29 Now it happened as he drew near to Bethphage and Bethany at the mountain called Olives, he sent two of his disciples (καὶ ἐγένετο ὡς ἤγγισεν εἰς Βηθφαγὴ καὶ Βηθανιὰ[ν] πρὸς τὸ ὄρος τὸ καλούμενον Ἐλαιῶν, ἀπέστειλεν δύο τῶν μαθητῶν). Jesus approaches the city via the main Jerusalem-to-Jericho road to Bethphage. Both Bethphage and Bethany are assumed by Luke to be on or near the summit of the Mount of Olives. According to *m. Menaḥ.* 11:2, Bethphage marked the limit of the boundary of Jerusalem.

Zechariah 14 forms an important but discordant backdrop, because everything one might expect from this prophecy is inverted. According to Zechariah, the Lord comes to the Mount of Olives (cf. Zech 14:4) to rescue the city from its terrible oppression at the hands of the nations. But here in Luke Jesus does not come to fight against the nations and rescue Israel from her enemies. Jesus does come as the king (cf. Zech 14:9) and he will be worshiped as king (14:16), but this king utters a mournful lament over the city because he knows that it is doomed. Jerusalem will not "be secure" (contrast Zech 14:11). The city's inexorable ruin lies in the near future, not in the past (see Luke 19:43 – 44). The writing is on the wall, but they cannot see it.

To punctuate the city's judgment, this section ends with Jesus' entering the temple and carrying out an audacious prophetic protest that forebodes its destruction (19:45 – 46). He drives out the traders, which resonates with Zech 14:21b ("And on that day there will no longer be a [merchant] in the house of the Lord Almighty").

The echoes from Zechariah reveal that King Jesus, who comes to the city from the Mount of Olives, will be a different kind of king. He is not a warlike Messiah who will put Israel on equal military footing with her oppressors and wage victorious battle against them. He comes to deliver all humanity, not just Israel, from an even more deadly enemy. A war-fevered nation will not welcome this kind of king of peace, will not be guided in the way of peace (Luke 1:79), and will be destroyed by its obstinacy.

19:30 Saying, "Go to the village ahead and as you enter, you will find a tethered colt that no one has ever sat upon. Loose it and lead it [here]" (λέγων· ὑπάγετε εἰς τὴν κατέναντι κώμην, ἐν ᾗ εἰσπορευόμενοι εὑρήσετε πῶλον δεδεμένον ἐφ᾽ ὃν οὐδεὶς πώποτε ἀνθρώπων ἐκάθισεν, καὶ λύσαντες αὐτὸν ἀγάγετε). Since Jesus has walked everywhere else in his ministry and did not mount the colt until he reaches the eastern boundary of the city, this departure from his custom is a calculated symbolic act. Actions speak louder than words but not always as clearly. The disciples recognize the subtle messianic connotations.[5] Zechariah 9:9 (see also 1 Kgs 1:32 – 35) lies behind Jesus' pointed choice of riding in on a colt:

> Rejoice greatly, Daughter Zion!
> Shout, Daughter Jerusalem!
> See, your king comes to you,
> righteous and victorious,
> lowly and riding on a donkey,
> on a colt, the foal of a donkey.

Horses were associated with war, and, according

---

5. In 2 Sam 18:9, it is noted that when Absalom's hair got caught in the branches of a large terebinth he was riding an ass, which was symbolic of his claim to kingship. In 2 Sam 19:26, Mephibosheth rode an ass as a symbol of his royal claim that he would make for the old house of Saul had the insurrection of Absalom succeeded. In 1 Kgs 1:38, David instructs Zadok the priest, Nathan the prophet, and Benaiah son of Jehoida to mount Solomon on King David's ass as he rides to his anointing as king in order to secure his claim over that of Adonijah.

to the psalmist, the war horse's image of great might is connected to the vain hope of military victory (Ps 33:17; see Prov 21:31; Isa 43:17; Zech 9:10; see Rev 6:2–8). The colt in Zechariah's context is connected to peace and humility. That this particular colt had not been ridden before makes it suitable for a sacred purpose and worthy of a king.[6]

Jesus has declared his ministry to be one of "release" or setting loose (cf. 4:18), and my translation of the verb λύω, which appears five times in a short span, attempts to retain that image by rendering the verb "loose" (λύσαντες) rather than "untie." The ultimate "release" will come from his death and resurrection. The references to the colt being tethered and loosed may also echo Jacob's blessing of Judah, which prophesied that "the scepter will not depart from Judah" and mentions "tether[ing] his donkey to a vine, his colt to the choicest branch" (Gen 49:10–11). Later rabbis associated this text with Zech 9:9 and gave it messianic associations (*b. Ber.* 56b–57a; *Gen. Rab.* 99:8).

If this connection is valid, it serves to contrast Jesus as the royal Messiah. The royal figure in Gen 49:11–12 "tethers his own beast to the vine in order to satiate himself on the richness of wine and milk," a testament to "royal excess and self-indulgence."[7] Jesus' disciples loose the colt, and he will ride into Jerusalem on this borrowed animal, a symbol of his reduced circumstances and renunciation of wealth (and very unlike the throne claimant in the previous parable). He does not arrive as his royal highness but his royal lowness.

19:31 If anyone asks you, "Why are you loosing it?" you will say this, "The Lord needs it" (καὶ ἐάν τις ὑμᾶς ἐρωτᾷ· διὰ τί λύετε; οὕτως ἐρεῖτε· ὅτι ὁ κύριος αὐτοῦ χρείαν ἔχει). Jesus manifests

prophetic foreknowledge in dispatching the anonymous disciples. He knows that the colt will be in the village and prepares them with what to say to those who object to their taking charge of it: "The Lord needs it." It is grammatically possible to translate the phrase "its lord [master] needs it." But Luke frequently uses the absolute "the Lord" (ὁ κύριος) throughout his gospel. The statement has the ring of a royal requisition formula.[8]

Speculation on whether Jesus made prior arrangements with the owners, who will release it at the secret password, weakens Luke's purpose. He presents Jesus as a king claiming the divine right to conscript animals from his subjects (see 1 Sam 8:16–17). Luke does not have "some people standing there" objecting to the disciples' untying the colt, as in Mark 11:5, but "its lords" (οἱ κύριοι αὐτοῦ; "its masters," v. 33), which draws a contrast between them and Jesus to make clear who "the Lord" truly is.

19:32–36 So those who were sent left and found [it] just as he told them. As they were loosing the colt, its lords said to them, "Why are you loosing the colt?" They said, "The Lord needs it." They led it to Jesus and threw their garments on the colt and mounted Jesus on it. While he went on, they were spreading their garments on the way (ἀπελθόντες δὲ οἱ ἀπεσταλμένοι εὗρον καθὼς εἶπεν αὐτοῖς. λυόντων δὲ αὐτῶν τὸν πῶλον εἶπαν οἱ κύριοι αὐτοῦ πρὸς αὐτούς· τί λύετε τὸν πῶλον; οἱ δὲ εἶπαν· ὅτι ὁ κύριος αὐτοῦ χρείαν ἔχει. καὶ ἤγαγον αὐτὸν πρὸς τὸν Ἰησοῦν καὶ ἐπιρίψαντες αὐτῶν τὰ ἱμάτια ἐπὶ τὸν πῶλον ἐπεβίβασαν τὸν Ἰησοῦν. πορευομένου δὲ αὐτοῦ ὑπεστρώννυον τὰ ἱμάτια αὐτῶν ἐν τῇ ὁδῷ).

Viewing this event through the lens of modern Palm Sunday services may cause us to misperceive

---

6. According to *m. Sanh.* 2:5, no one else may ride a king's horse. The theme is continued when Jesus is buried in a rock-hewn tomb in which no one had been buried (23:53).

7. Nolland, *Luke*, 3:924.

8. Ethelbert Stauffer, "Messias oder Menschensohn?" *NovT* 1 (1956): 85.

what is happening. There is no indication in the text that it is Sunday. There are no palms but only cloaks (19:36; it is only John 12:13 that mentions the palms), and no children appear. It is not a fickle crowd that praises God joyfully but the whole multitude of disciples. The disciples use their garments as a saddle and then spread their garments along the way in much the same way Jehu was welcomed as king (2 Kgs 9:13; see also the late legend in *Yalquṭ Exodus* 168, which claims that when Moses was proclaimed king of Kush, the people took off their garments and spread them on the ground). Again, the details signal Jesus' royalty.

19:37 As he now drew near to the descent from the Mount of Olives, the multitude of disciples all together began to praise God, rejoicing with a loud voice for all the mighty works they had seen (ἐγγίζοντος δὲ αὐτοῦ ἤδη πρὸς τῇ καταβάσει τοῦ ὄρους τῶν Ἐλαιῶν ἤρξαντο ἅπαν τὸ πλῆθος τῶν μαθητῶν χαίροντες αἰνεῖν τὸν θεὸν φωνῇ μεγάλῃ περὶ πασῶν ὧν εἶδον δυνάμεων). The disciples can see the city before them as they begin their descent. They all begin to raise their voices in praise of God for the mighty works they have seen Jesus do. The emphasis is on seeing. Only disciples could make this acclamation because they have recognized God's power working in Jesus and that Jesus had been chosen by God. They may not see that the days of the miracles are over. Jesus enters the city to die and will be enthroned as king on a cross, which will bring even greater benefactions to the people. The greatest mighty work, the resurrection, which is to be worked by God, awaits.

19:38 Saying, "Blessed is the king who comes in the name of Lord. In heaven peace and glory in the highest" (λέγοντες· εὐλογημένος ὁ ἐρχόμενος, ὁ βασιλεὺς ἐν ὀνόματι κυρίου· ἐν οὐρανῷ εἰρήνη καὶ δόξα ἐν ὑψίστοις). To emphasize Jesus' royalty,

Luke has the disciples praise him as "the king" (see John 12:13) instead of crying, "Blessed is the coming kingdom of our father David!" (Mark 11:10). The coming kingdom of David has nationalistic implications that would be politically inflammatory and misleading to Luke's readers. Instead, the disciples speak of "peace," and Jesus weeps because Jerusalem does not know what makes for peace. Jesus enters as the one who brings peace.[9]

The acclamation that Jesus is king is no less defiant to the Roman establishment — Jesus is executed as king of the Jews (23:38) — but it does not limit Jesus' kingship to a political entity, and a minor one at that. The scope of his kingship embraces heaven. Also, in contrast to the hue and cry raised in Mark 11:10, this acclamation shifts the emphasis from the expectation of the messianic kingdom coming with him to the person of Jesus as the eschatological king who brings divine peace and glory from heaven.

The disciples' exultation echoes Ps 118:26, "Blessed is he who comes in the name of the LORD" (see Luke 13:34 – 35). But the shouts do not come from the people, and they do not emerge from "the house of the LORD," as in the psalm. From the temple comes only stony silence. It is spiritually desolate and will soon lie physically desolated. Since Jesus comes in the name of the Lord, to reject him is to reject God. Jerusalem will not have peace or favor but war and wrath. Jesus' lament (13:34) that Jerusalem kills those sent to her and is unwilling "to be gathered" will be fulfilled. His prophecy (13:35) that they will not see him until they say, "Blessed is the one who comes in the name of the Lord," awaits fulfillment.

Luke customarily omits the occasional Semitic transliterated words found in the tradition. Instead of "Hosanna in the highest heaven," which frames the cries in Matt 21:9 (cf. Mark 11:9; John

---

9. Strauss, *The Davidic Messiah in Luke-Acts*, 314.

12:13), Luke has "in heaven peace and glory in the highest," which dramatically contrasts with the king in the previous parable, who brings reckoning and death.[10] The cries echo the words of the angel Gabriel, who announces Jesus' conception to Mary (1:32 – 33), and the angelic choristers who announce his birth to the shepherds (2:14).

19:39 And certain ones of the Pharisees from the crowd said to him, "Teacher, rebuke your disciples!" (καί τινες τῶν Φαρισαίων ἀπὸ τοῦ ὄχλου εἶπαν πρὸς αὐτόν· διδάσκαλε, ἐπιτίμησον τοῖς μαθηταῖς σου). The Pharisees make their last appearance in Luke in their regular role as irascible wet blankets. They have seen nothing of God in what Jesus has done and regard the messianic clamor of his disciples as shocking and perhaps dangerous if it should goad the Romans. Consequently, they insist that he suppress this blasphemous acclaim by rebuking his disciples.

Sanders contends that the mixture of the Zechariah passage and Ps 118 would have been "explosive."[11] Psalm 118 was a royal psalm recited on the annual enthronement of the king. He states: "It would have been all right to recite it as one among many psalms in celebration of a festival, but it would have been blasphemous to reenact it with its original royal meanings to those not otherwise convinced of the claim."[12] The psalm was not to be read and enacted that way until the Messiah came. And when he did come, it would surely be the authorities and leading citizens of the city who would welcome him, not a boisterous rabble.

Jesus indeed had rebuked his disciples earlier when he commanded them to keep quiet about his identity after Peter identified him as "the Messiah of God" (9:20 – 21). Now, with his death looming on the horizon, he allows this word to be proclaimed all the way down the mountain to the temple, and he accepts their messianic applause.

19:40 He answered them, "I say to you, if these will become silent, the stones will cry out" (καὶ ἀποκριθεὶς εἶπεν· λέγω ὑμῖν, ἐὰν οὗτοι σιωπήσουσιν, οἱ λίθοι κράξουσιν). Jesus' response that the stones would cry out if his disciples remained silent reaffirms his promise in 12:3 that nothing can stop the good news from being shouted from the housetops. It also recalls John's rebuke of the crowds who came for baptism: God can raise up children to Abraham from these stones. God can also make stones cry out in recognition of his Son.

This image fits the biblical witness that nature becomes involved in recognizing God's work (Ps 96:12 – 13; Isa 44:23; 55:12). The verbal parallel in Hab 2:11 suggests, however, that if geology has to take up the task of theology, then it is an implicit judgment on Jerusalem. In Hab 2:6 – 20, judgment comes upon the city because it has fostered bloodshed, injustice, and the oppression of the poor, and the stones cry out in accusation. The reference to the stones in the present verse, however, may have nothing to do with judgment but pictures Jesus' arrival in the city as so momentous that it requires a response — "if not a human one, then another."[13] Possibly, it is an allusion to Gentiles, who were regarded as insentient stones when it came to understanding anything related to God.[14] When Jesus dies on the cross, a Gentile declares

---

10. Nolland, *Luke*, 3:927, comments, "Jesus is now on his way to royal rule, but only in the terms that 19:11 – 28 has defined." In my opinion, he is on his way to royal rule in a way that is exactly *the opposite* of how it is defined in 19:11 – 28.

11. James A. Sanders, "A Hermeneutic Fabric: Psalm 118 in Luke's Entrance Narrative," in *Luke and Scripture: The Function of Sacred Tradition in Luke-Acts* (ed. James A. Sanders and

Craig A. Evans; Eugene, OR: Wipf and Stock, 2001), 143.

12. Ibid., 143 – 44.

13. Craddock, *Luke*, 227 – 28; see also Brent Rogers Kinman, "'The Stones Will Cry Out' [Luke 19,40] — Joy or Judgment?" *Bib* 75 [1994]: 232 – 35.

14. Arthur A. Just Jr., *Luke* (Concordia Commentary; St. Louis: Concordia, 1996), 152, 748.

that he is righteous (23:47). The primary point of the saying is that silencing the disciples and even silencing Jesus will not negate that Jesus is King, nor will it derail God's purposes.

19:41 And as he drew near and saw the city, he burst into tears over it (καὶ ὡς ἤγγισεν ἰδὼν τὴν πόλιν ἔκλαυσεν ἐπ᾽ αὐτήν). Jesus' tears stem from his foreknowledge of the city's impending destruction because of her refusal to accept him and because they will choose the way of the sword (see Jer 9:1; 13:17; 14:17). Paul felt no less grief over Israel's recalcitrance (Rom 9:1 – 5). Tears will flow from the daughters of Jerusalem for Jesus when he leaves the city on his way to the cross, but he says they are misdirected (23:28). It is they who are most to be pitied.

19:42 Saying, "If you, even you, only knew on this day the things that make for peace, but now it is hidden from your eyes" (λέγων ὅτι εἰ ἔγνως ἐν τῇ ἡμέρᾳ ταύτῃ καὶ σὺ τὰ πρὸς εἰρήνην· νῦν δὲ ἐκρύβη ἀπὸ ὀφθαλμῶν σου). "On this day" (ἐν τῇ ἡμέρᾳ ταύτῃ) refers to "the time of your visitation" (19:44), which is nearing its end. "Peace" recalls the priest Zechariah's prophecy in 1:78 – 79: "By the compassionate mercy of our God, upon whom the dawn from on high will visit [ἐπισκέψεσται] us, to shine light for those who sit in darkness and in the shadow of death, to direct our feet into the path of peace." "Peace" relates to peace with God (Rom 5:1), but in this context it also refers to external concord (see 14:32), particularly with Rome, which will ultimately destroy the city after a futile rebellion. According to Josephus, Titus was appalled by the story of a mother's cannibalism of her infant during the siege of Jerusalem and declared himself innocent

of this abomination because he had offered the Jews "peace" and "amnesty," but they were past reason and preferred sedition and war (*J.W.* 6.3.5 §§214 – 19).

The "but now" (νῦν δέ) breaks off the statement without a conclusion (aposiopesis) and makes the unfulfilled wish more poignant. What "is hidden" (ἐκρύβη) are "the things that make for peace."[15] Their ignorance is emphasized in Acts 13:27: "The people of Jerusalem and their rulers did not recognize Jesus, yet in condemning him they fulfilled the words of the prophets that are read every Sabbath." They are responsible for ignoring the light, which will result in the fall of Jerusalem; yet the use of the passive voice "is hidden" suggests that this spiritual blindness is part of the divine will. Evans comments on this paradox: "Luke shows that he regarded that fall, even though brought about by human agency, as occupying a decisive place in the divine plan of history as that was being put into effect in the mission and death of Jesus."[16] The question is, will their eyes be opened (see 24:16, 31; 2 Cor 3:14 – 16)?

19:43 – 44 Because the days will come upon you and your enemies will set up siege works against you, and encircle you, and hem you in on every side. And they will dash you to the ground and your children within [your walls], and they will not leave one stone upon another within [your walls] because you did not know the time of your visitation (ὅτι ἥξουσιν ἡμέραι ἐπὶ σὲ καὶ παρεμβαλοῦσιν οἱ ἐχθροί σου χάρακά σοι καὶ περικυκλώσουσίν σε καὶ συνέξουσίν σε πάντοθεν, καὶ ἐδαφιοῦσίν σε καὶ τὰ τέκνα σου ἐν σοί, καὶ οὐκ ἀφήσουσιν λίθον ἐπὶ λίθον ἐν σοί, ἀνθ᾽ ὧν οὐκ ἔγνως τὸν καιρὸν τῆς ἐπισκοπῆς σου). Zechariah's prophecy that Israel will be

---

15. It is possible to render the clause with the next verse: "But now it is hidden from your eyes that the days will come upon you and your enemies."

16. Evans, *St. Luke*, 685.

saved from her enemies and from the hand of all who hate her (1:71, 74) will come to naught if it refers to political enemies. Jesus now forewarns in vividly gruesome detail how Jerusalem will be destroyed (see 21:5 – 6, 20 – 24; 23:28 – 31). The city rejected the King of Peace and instead would foolishly revolt against Roman power because they did not want the Romans to rule over them, and the upshot would be a city and temple lying in smoking ruins.

While the details of this prophecy accord with Josephus's description of the city's destruction in his account of the Jewish war (see *J.W.* 5.11.4 §466; 5.12.2 §508), it is not a prophecy shaped by later events and placed on the lips of Jesus. The language fits ancient military operations and what so often happens in war, and it parallels, for example, Ezekiel's prophecy and the description of the sacking of Solomon's temple in 587 BC.[17] Jesus could see where Israel was heading and knew that their infidelity to God and obstinacy would bring God's judgment.

The "time [or season] of your visitation" refers in the Old Testament to the coming of God, whether for rescue (see Gen 21:1; 50:24 – 25; Exod 3:16; 4:31; 13:19; Jer 15:15; Ps 106:4) or for judgment (Isa 10:3; Jer 6:15; 10:15). The statement reflects a high Christology, since it is Jesus who visits Jerusalem. Rowe claims that Luke is deliberately ambiguous "because it is inclusive of both God and Jesus. The visitation of Jesus is the presence of God coming to Jerusalem as κύριος [Lord]."[18] Jesus has come for their good, proclaiming salvation (the verb form is used in 1:68, 78; 7:16); but if they turn away and reject him, his coming becomes the basis

for judgment. Rejection of Jesus is "tantamount" to the rejection of God.[19]

19:45 Then he entered the temple and began to cast out the sellers (καὶ εἰσελθὼν εἰς τὸ ἱερὸν ἤρξατο ἐκβάλλειν τοὺς πωλοῦντας). Since Luke does not specifically report that Jesus enters Jerusalem but enters the temple, he must equate the two. Jerusalem's fate is therefore the temple's fate, and vice versa. Compared to the lengthier accounts of Jesus' actions in the temple in Matt 21:10 – 22 and Mark 11:11 – 25, Luke pares down the details to a bare minimum.

Luke omits any reference to the cursing of the fig tree that brackets Mark's telling of the cleansing of the temple. One possible explanation for this omission is that Luke will record that Jesus' disciples continually gather in the temple to bless God after his resurrection (24:53; Acts 2:46; 3:1; 5:20 – 21, 42; 21:26; 22:17). He reports that Jesus' actions are directed only against the merchants to prevent this action from being interpreted by Greco-Roman readers as defiling a temple, regarded as a serious crime (Rom 2:22). In Luke, Jesus is not charged with threatening the temple or mocked as one who would destroy the temple (contrast Matt 26:60 – 61; 27:29; Mark 14:57 – 58; 15:29). On the contrary, he takes control of the temple through his teaching (19:47 – 48).[20]

Luke's bare-bones account, then, may reflect his sensitivity to the reality that in the Greco-Roman world temple desecration was a serious offense. In Acts 24:5 – 6, Tertullus accuses Paul before the governor Felix of being a pestilent fellow, an agitator, a ringleader of the Nazarene sect, and a temple

---

17. C. H. Dodd, "The Fall of Jerusalem and the 'Abomination of Desolation,'" in *More New Testament Studies* (Manchester: Manchester Univ. Press, 1968), 74 – 77. See Isa 29:3; 37:33; Jer 6:6, 15; 10:15; 52:4 – 5; Ezek 4:1 – 3; 21:22. Jeremiah 6:15 (LXX) refers to them being destroyed in the "time of their visitation."

18. Rowe, *Early Narrative Christology*, 166.
19. McComiskey, *Lukan Theology in the Light of the Gospel's Literary Structure*, 305.
20. If any cleansing of the temple occurs, it takes place through Jesus' teaching (see J. M. Dawsey, "Confrontation in the Temple: Luke 19:45 – 20:47," *PRSt* 11 [1984]: 153 – 65).

desecrator, which means that he is an enemy of the peace that Rome has brought to Israel (Acts 24:2) and is worthy of death (see Paul's defense in 25:8).

Since the temple probably lies in ruins when Luke writes, the issue of its relevance is moot for him. It is more likely that Luke abbreviates his account of Jesus' action in the temple because he wishes to center everything on Jesus' statement in 19:46. Holmås contends, "The trade in the temple precinct is given no emphasis, but is simply epitomized as that which the temple has become, as it is expressed in Jesus' prophetic statement in v. 46: the temple is no longer living up to its call 'as a house of prayer', but has become a cave for bandits."[21] Jesus' teaching in the temple demonstrates his supremacy over the temple.

19:46 Telling them, "It stands written, 'My house shall be a house of prayer,' but you have made it a hideout for bandits!" (λέγων αὐτοῖς· γέγραπται· καὶ ἔσται ὁ οἶκός μου οἶκος προσευχῆς, ὑμεῖς δὲ αὐτὸν ἐποιήσατε σπήλαιον λῃστῶν). Luke does not have the qualification that the temple is to be a house of prayer "for all nations" (Mark 11:17), which derives from Isa 56:7. It serves to make the contrast between "house of prayer" and "bandits' den" more stark. The explicit citation from Jeremiah derives from a long section that roundly condemns the temple's corruption that has made it a place of false security where bandits retreat to their hideout to seek asylum from justice. They reassure themselves that they are safe and secure from all alarms by reciting the mantra, "This is the temple of the LORD, the temple of the LORD, the temple of the LORD" (Jer 7:4). They have turned the temple into a different kind of sanctuary, a devil's lair that gives asylum to murdering thieves.

The Jeremiah passage also contains a specific threat that the temple would be destroyed (remember "Shiloh," Jer 7:12, 14). The people lived in a fantasy, imagining that they were invincible because God could never allow his temple to be destroyed. By interpreting his actions with this verse from the middle of this jeremiad, Jesus makes clear that he is not attempting to reform the temple and remold it into a house of prayer. But the wickedness and opposition to Jesus remains and will soon mobilize against him. What Jesus has done was a daring prophetic sign that warns of God's judgment.[22]

Theology in Application

1. The Bringer of True Peace

Though Jesus engages in provocative street theater by entering Jerusalem on a mount that betokens his royal dignity as an earthly king, Luke understands this to be a divine visitation. If the people do not respond with welcome, they will face judgment. Jesus' action in the temple is not simply that of an irate prophet symbolically warning of judgment but one of God pronouncing judgment. The problem is that the inhabitants of Jerusalem and the temple's tenants do not recognize Jesus for who he is and do not know what makes for peace. Thus, they will not sue for peace (14:32) but instead will attempt to resist this divine visitation with violence. Their indifference,

---

21. Holmås, "'My House Shall Be a House of Prayer,'" 407.

22. Peter W. L. Walker, *Jesus and the Holy City: New Testament Perspectives in Jerusalem* (Grand Rapids: Eerdmans, 1996), 63; Holmås, "'My House Shall Be a House of Prayer,'" 408.

hostility, and resistance to Jesus are symptomatic of human indifference, hostility, and resistance to God's intervention in the world and their lives.

It is empirically obvious that the world does not know what makes for earthly peace. It is attributable to their ignorance of God and God's ways. True peace does not come through the violent exercise of superior power, as the Romans would have it. Peace refers to salvation (Rom 5:1) and comes only through Jesus as the Lord of all (Acts 10:36). Because humans do not know what makes for peace, it is now a heavenly quality.[23] It is "peace in heaven." Nolland astutely observes that at Jesus' birth the angels from heaven celebrate what is happening on earth. As he approaches death, which will lead to his exaltation, the disciples celebrate what is happening in heaven. He cites Col 1:20 and Rev 12:10 as theological parallels.[24] The "peace in heaven," then, "is that of the reconciliation which the Messiah comes to effect between God and the earth."[25] Doble writes, "in the Lukan scheme of things [peace] lay on the other side of Jesus' [being taken up]."[26] Peace comes from his passion, resurrection, and ascension and from worshiping him as the Lord (Acts 2:33).

2. The Bringer of Reformation

What do Jesus' arrival and actions in the temple mean for the status of the temple whose sacrifices are supposed to offer atonement? God told Solomon that he had chosen the temple as a house of sacrifice where he would be attentive to the prayers made in this place (2 Chr 7:12 – 18). But God warned in the same breath:

> But if you turn away and forsake the decrees and commands I have given you and go off to serve other gods and worship them, then I will uproot Israel from my land, which I have given them, and will reject this temple I have consecrated for my Name. I will make it a byword and an object of ridicule among all peoples. This temple will become a heap of rubble. All who pass by will be appalled and say, "Why has the LORD done such a thing to this land and to this temple?" People will answer, "Because they have forsaken the LORD, the God of their ancestors, who brought them out of Egypt, and have embraced other gods, worshiping and serving them — that is why he brought all this disaster on them." (2 Chr 7:19 – 22)

According to the messianic hopes expressed in *Ps. Sol.* 17:30, the son of David will "purge Jerusalem (and make it) holy as it was even in the beginning." But that hope is not to be. Luke begins his gospel with the temple appropriately functioning as a place of worship and prayer (1:8 – 22), and he begins the continuing saga in Acts with the disciples going to the temple to pray. They also proclaim the power of the "name of Jesus" there (Acts 3:1 – 4:22). As the story progresses in both the gospel and Acts, however, the temple's sanctity diminishes. Its degradation is directly tied

23. Fitzmyer, *Luke*, 2:1251.
24. Nolland, *Luke*, 3:927.
25. Godet, *Luke*, 2:230.
26. Doble, *The Paradox of Salvation*, 30.

to the failure to understand who Jesus is and what this divine visitation means. In the gospel of Luke, the temple now becomes the focus of opposition to Jesus. In Acts, its caretakers try to stifle Jesus' disciples and destroy their message.

Luke does not include the phrase that derives from Isa 56:7 and appears in Mark 11:17 that the temple is to be a house of prayer "for all nations." Omitting that phrase "indicates that he sees no future role for the temple."[27] Gentiles will not be flocking to Jerusalem to worship Israel's God in the temple, as many Jews believed would happen in the end time. Stephen's speech stresses the temple's irrelevance as a house "made by human hands" (Acts 7:47 – 50). Luke's account of Paul's arrest in the temple subtly ties it to the issue of the acceptance of Gentiles by noting that the doors of the temple were shut when Paul was seized (21:30). The temple doors are shut to Gentiles and their advocates while the doors of the kingdom are swung wide open.[28] According to Green, "in the Lukan vision, Gentiles would not come to the temple to find Yahweh; rather, the Lord goes out, through his witnesses, to the Gentiles (cf. Acts 1:8)."[29]

The prophecy of Jerusalem's destruction means that the year of grace (4:19) will come to an end and be replaced by the "days of vengeance" (21:22). This destruction has theological consequences. As Green recognizes,

> If Jerusalem is utterly destroyed (with no stone left on another, v 44), then its socio-religious role is also decimated. If Jerusalem is no longer the center of the world, then the status distinctions it embodied and propagated are no longer definitive.[30]

The "segregating zones" with the architectural barriers forbade entry to various categories of outsiders and reinforced the superiority of priest over layperson, male over female, Jew over Samaritan, and Jew over Gentile. Talbert trenchantly summarizes further theological implications. First, the Jesus movement is completed Judaism, the true Israel. Second, the nation-race is no longer synonymous with the people of God. There is no soteriological function for the nation as such. Third, one becomes a part of God's people by making an individual decision for Jesus.[31] Not one stone of the temple edifice will be left on top of another. What remains, however, is the rock of Jesus' teaching in the temple. Luke records that teaching in what follows.

3. The Ones Who Resist Reformation

The corruption of the temple with its encrustation of ritual traditions that excluded so many and its monopoly of power afforded to so few represents a danger that can infect Christian churches and institutions. History, ancient and modern, shows similar problems resurfacing again and again in the church. Religious leaders, like secular leaders, can acquire the trappings of power and privilege, the titles and

---

27. Holmås, "'My House Shall Be a House of Prayer,'" 407.

28. Frank Stagg, *The Book of Acts: The Early Struggle for an Unhindered Gospel* (Nashville: Broadman, 1955), 224.

29. Green, *The Gospel of Luke*, 694.

30. Ibid., 682.

31. Talbert, *Reading Luke*, 214.

the wealth, through impenetrable, closed structures or through family connections, or they can seize them through political machinations. Once in power, they seek to disempower and exclude others, assuming that the more power others might have, the less power they can have. Consequently, they are always on the defensive to preserve their institutional power and to resist any prophet who proclaims divine truth that would dethrone them and transform the institution. To serve selfish ends, they transmute falsehoods into accepted truths. They enforce conformity of practice and belief to reinforce their domination. They ignore the biblical mandate to show mercy and resort to injustice and call it justice. They tout a theology of glory that glorifies them. They desire to control divine power and channel it to abet their own evil purposes.

This brand of leadership earns God's judgment. What makes it so reprehensible is that it brings contempt for Christ's church, obscures the truth of the gospel, and leaves the sheep shepherdless and vulnerable to the wolves.

Luke 19:47 – 20:8

Literary Context

In Matt 21:18 – 22 and Mark 11:12 – 14, 20 – 25, Jesus' cursing of the barren fig tree is interposed between Jesus' temple action and the Jewish leaders' challenge of his authority. Its absence from Luke's narrative results in tying together more closely the account of his entrance into Jerusalem and the temple and the account of the leaders' intentions to destroy Jesus and to challenge his authority. Conflict over authority dominates this larger unit (19:47 – 20:40) and leads to the question who the Son of David truly is — he is David's Lord (20:41 – 44). Then, Jesus condemns those who profit from the temple cultic system and who in turn oppress the weak and try to whitewash their venality with shows of false piety (20:45 – 21:4). The rejection of Jesus' authority and the corruption surrounding the temple cult sets up Jesus' prophecy of the temple's total destruction (21:5 – 38).

Main Idea

Jesus' source of authority is the same as John's. If people do not believe him and submit to his authority, they invite the judgment John warned about in his preaching.

Translation

Luke 19:47–20:8

19:47a	Introduction of time, place, and characters	**Then he was teaching every day in the temple.**
		The chief priests and scribes . . . along with the first ones of the people
b	Conflict	**. . . were seeking to destroy him.**
48a	Frustration	**And they did not find anything that they could do,**
b	Reason	for the whole people were hanging on him
c		as they listened to him.
20:1a	Circumstance	**It happened one day**
b		as he was teaching the 🕊 people in the temple and preaching good news,
c	Conflict	**the chief priests and the scribes with the elders came [to him],**
2a	Opponents' question/challenge	**and they said to him,**
b		*"Tell us: by what authority do you do these things,*
c		*or who is the one who gave you this authority?"*
3	Jesus' counterquestion	**He answered and told them,**
		"I will also ask you something, and you tell me.
4		*The immersion of John, was it from heaven or was it from men?"*
5a	Deliberation	**They discussed it among themselves, saying,**
b	(positive evaluation)	*"If we say 'from heaven,' he will say,* *'Why did you not believe him?'*
6	(negative evaluation)	*But if we say 'from men,'* *the whole people will stone us,* for *they are convinced that John was a* 🕊 *prophet."*
7	Opponents' answer	**So they answered that they did not know from where it came.**
8	Jesus' answer	**Then Jesus said to them,** *"Neither will I tell you by what authority I do these things."*

Structure and Literary Form

The large section 19:47 – 21:38 reports Jesus' teaching in the temple and the conflict it arouses.[1] The summary statements that Jesus is teaching in the temple, the people hang on him and listen to his teaching in 19:47 – 48, and all the people come early to the temple to listen to him teach in 21:37 – 38 frame this section.[2] It divides into three sections (20:1 – 44; 20:45 – 21:4; 21:5 – 36), each introduced by an identification of the characters addressed (20:1; 20:45; 21:5).

Introduction		
	19:47 – 48	Jesus' teaching arousing conflict
Subscene A		Direct conflict with the temple establishment (20:1 – 44)
	20:1 – 8	By what authority?
	20:9 – 19	The parable of the vineyard tenants
	20:20 – 26	Rendering to God and to Caesar
	20:27 – 40	On the resurrection
	20:41 – 44	The Messiah as David's Son is David's Lord
Subscene B		Indirect Conflict (20:45 – 21:4)
	20:45 – 47	Beware of the scribes
	21:1 – 4	The widow's example that shames the rich
Subscene C		Future Conflict (21:5 – 36)
	21:5 – 9	Introduction: the fate of the temple
	21:10 – 28	Eschatological discourse
	21:29 – 33	The sign of the fig tree
	21:34 – 36	Final warnings
Conclusion		
	21:37 – 38	Temporary cessation of conflict

The present incident is the first of three conflict stories prompted by a question raised by his opponents intended to discredit or entrap him. The scene forms a chiastic pattern:

A The high priests, scribes, and the first ones of the people seek to kill Jesus but are unable to do anything against him. (19:47 – 48a)

   B All the people hang on to what they hear from Jesus (19:48b)

   B′ Jesus teaches and preaches good news to the people (20:1a)

A′ The priests and the scribes with the elders challenge Jesus' authority (20:1b – 2)[3]

---

1. The following outline is adapted from the careful analysis of Blake R. Grangaard, *Conflict and Authority in Luke 19:47 to 21:4* (Studies in Biblical Literature 8; New York: Lang, 1999), 43 – 44.

2. Ibid., 44 – 45.

3. Jon A. Weatherly, *Jewish Responsibility for the Death of Jesus in Luke-Acts* (JSNTSup 106; Sheffield: Sheffield Academic, 1994), 72.

Exegetical Outline

→ I. The high priests, scribes, and the first ones of the people seek to kill Jesus but are unable to do anything against him (19:47 – 48a)

II. All the people hang on to what they hear from Jesus (19:48b-c)

III. Jesus teaches and preaches good news to the people (20:1a-b)

IV. The priests and the scribes with the elders ask Jesus by what authority he does these things (20:1c – 2)

V. Jesus' counterquestion about the immersion of John (20:3 – 4)

VI. The leaders' deliberation and decision to plead ignorance (20:5 – 7)

VII. Jesus' refusal to answer their question (20:8)

Explanation of the Text

19:47 Then he was teaching every day in the temple. The chief priests and scribes along with the first ones of the people were seeking to destroy him (καὶ ἦν διδάσκων τὸ καθ᾽ ἡμέραν ἐν τῷ ἱερῷ. οἱ δὲ ἀρχιερεῖς καὶ οἱ γραμματεῖς ἐζήτουν αὐτὸν ἀπολέσαι καὶ οἱ πρῶτοι τοῦ λαοῦ). The temple precincts are the venue for the conflict over Jesus' teaching that follows. The key players are the people, who form an eager audience, and the chief priests and scribes, who will engage in guerrilla-style tactics, making futile attempts to discredit Jesus' authority.

Jesus' return to the temple takes us back to his Father's house (2:49), which he has reclaimed (19:45 – 46) for his teaching. Instead of listening to and questioning the teachers (2:46), he is now *the* teacher. No mention is made that Jesus "worships" (2:37), "prays" (1:10; 18:10), or "offers sacrifice" in the temple. For Luke, his teaching is the most important thing happening in the temple during this week. Jesus has taught throughout his ministry (4:14 – 15; 5:17; 13:10), and the imperfect periphrastic "was teaching" (ἦν διδάσκων, presenting the action as customary) and the adverbial phrase

"every day" (τὸ καθ᾽ ἡμέραν), which appears in this verse and in the note at the end of the section (21:37), underscore this activity. Even his mortal enemies acknowledge him as "Teacher" (20:21, 28, 39; 21:7), though hypocritically.

The temple has become the place for Jesus' teaching and preaching, but it has not been cleansed of its evil caretakers. The chief priests, the scribes, and the first ones of the people take over the role of chief antagonists from the Pharisees and the conflict escalates into something far more deadly.[4] They are determined to do away with Jesus and have the wherewithal to do so. Failing to snare him in the traps they set to discredit him, they will set in motion the events that lead to Jesus' crucifixion by conspiring with Judas to betray him, committing the temple police to arrest him in a secluded spot, and concocting charges to hand him over to Pilate. The Romans would have ignored him unless he had precipitated some political unrest (see Gallio's response in Acts 18:14 – 16).

"Two fundamentally different visions of God's purpose, the character of leadership, and the

---

4. "The first ones of the people" occurs only here in the NT and appears to correspond to "the elders" mentioned first in

9:22 and "the elders" in 20:1. It reflects Josephus's term "principle citizens" (*J. W.* 2.17.3 §411).

nature of Israel's redemption" clash head-on in their encounters with Jesus.[5] The priests have oversight of the temple business by virtue of their birth. The legal specialists (scribes) and the ruling elites are involved by virtue of their knowledge or their wealth because the temple is the nerve center of religion and politics for Israel. It is not as if any of these actors had an ancestral foot firmly planted on Sinai that gave them some divine right of oversight of the temple. Their power derives from the goodwill of the Romans, since the Roman governor appointed the high priest and even kept his vestments in custody in the Antonio fortress.[6] Consequently, Realpolitik directs their agenda, not God. They busy themselves with attempts to gain some tactical advantage to destroy this upstart lest he undermine their governance and the privileges that come with it.

19:48 And they did not find anything that they could do, for the whole people were hanging on him as they listened to him (καὶ οὐχ εὕρισκον τὸ τί ποιήσωσιν, ὁ λαὸς γὰρ ἅπας ἐξεκρέματο αὐτοῦ ἀκούων). The "people" are distinguished from the leaders who seek his death. They not only hang on every word of his teaching; they hang so close to him (ἐξεκρέματο αὐτοῦ) that they prevent the leaders from getting to him.[7] It is reminiscent of the scene where the men could not get their paralyzed friend to Jesus because a huge crowd blocked the way, and they had to cut through the roof (5:19). The large crowd once again is in the way but now forms a temporary barrier of protection. That the leaders will accomplish their malevolent purpose is not in doubt; how they will carry it off is.

20:1 – 2 It happened one day as he was teaching the people in the temple and preaching good news, the chief priests and the scribes with the elders came [to him], and they said to him, "Tell us: by what authority do you do these things, or who is the one who gave you this authority?" (καὶ ἐγένετο ἐν μιᾷ τῶν ἡμερῶν διδάσκοντος αὐτοῦ τὸν λαὸν ἐν τῷ ἱερῷ καὶ εὐαγγελιζομένου ἐπέστησαν οἱ ἀρχιερεῖς καὶ οἱ γραμματεῖς σὺν τοῖς πρεσβυτέροις, καὶ εἶπαν λέγοντες πρὸς αὐτόν· εἰπὸν ἡμῖν ἐν ποίᾳ ἐξουσίᾳ ταῦτα ποιεῖς, ἢ τίς ἐστιν ὁ δούς σοι τὴν ἐξουσίαν ταύτην;). "Preaching good news" (εὐαγγελιζομένου) is distinct from "teaching" (διδάσκοντος), but it is not defined. The verb is specifically connected to good news for the poor in 4:18 and 7:22, but in 4:43; 8:1; 9:6; and 16:16 it describes the general content of his preaching. It must be connected to the announcement of the forgiveness of sins (see 5:20; 7:47 – 48; 24:47), which is inflammatory in the setting of the temple cult as a direct challenge to it. After Jesus' death and resurrection, the temple will no longer be the locus for such forgiveness.

The deputation from the priestly hierarchy questions Jesus' authority to do these things (ταῦτα), which in the context refers to his temple action and his teaching and preaching. The crowds were amazed by the authority of his teaching and miracles from day one (4:32, 36). He has demonstrated his authority on earth to forgive sins (5:24), and a centurion recognized that he has a special authority that outstrips his and that of his superiors.

But the temple leaders see themselves as authorized by heaven to regulate the temple, and with it came the responsibility to query whether a self-proclaimed prophet was acting under the authority of God (7:16, 26, 39) or under that of Beelzebul (11:15). Their question here, however, is insincere

---

5. Green, *The Gospel of Luke*, 700.

6. Vitellius granted the high priest the right to keep them again in the temple after Pilate was recalled (Josephus, *Ant.*

15.11.4 §§403 – 8; 18.4.3 §§90 – 95; 20.1.1 §§6 – 9).

7. The verb "hang" (ἐξεκρέματο) takes a genitive as its object (αὐτοῦ), as can the verb "listen" (ἀκούων).

and is no different from the two others posed to Jesus in this section (20:22, 33). His enemies are setting a trap. If he says he does these things by divine authority, they can attack him as a false prophet. If he does what he does by human authority, it would imply that he is simply a troublemaker bent on usurping Roman law and order.

Most consider the two parts of the question to be synonymous, but Godet argued long ago that they are not. The first question concerns "the *nature* of Jesus' commission: Is it divine or human?" The second question concerns "the *immediate agent* through whom He has received it."[8] They want him to claim divine authority publicly so that they can condemn him publicly for blasphemy. If he denies that he acts with divine authority, they can also condemn him for blasphemy for usurping divine authority.

20:3 – 4 He answered and told them, "I will also ask you something, and you tell me. The immersion of John, was it from heaven or was it from men?" (ἀποκριθεὶς δὲ εἶπεν πρὸς αὐτούς· ἐρωτήσω ὑμᾶς κἀγὼ λόγον, καὶ εἴπατέ μοι· τὸ βάπτισμα Ἰωάννου ἐξ οὐρανοῦ ἦν ἢ ἐξ ἀνθρώπων;). Hardened as they are, these Jewish leaders will not accept his divine authority to forgive sins, judge the temple, or teach in it, no matter how he answers. Jesus feels no need to explain or give an account of himself to these opponents but instead parries their demand by turning the tables on them. He takes control of the threatening situation with a counterquestion. Those who approach Jesus with hostility never receive direct answers or incontrovertible proofs.

Jesus deflects the challenge of his enemies by asking about John, who began his public ministry during the priesthood of Annas and Caiaphas

(3:2). Green notes, "How one has responded to John serves as a barometer of one's orientation to the divine purpose (7:29 – 30)."[9] "Heaven" is a circumlocution for God. The narrative makes clear from the words of the Spirit-filled Zechariah that John is a prophet commissioned by God (1:76). He is also presented as Jesus' forerunner (1:16 – 17, 76; 3:16). If his authority were not from heaven, he was a false prophet well-deserving of the death that he suffered under Herod (see Deut 18:20). But if his authority was from heaven, then he testified that Jesus was greater than he (3:16).

This counterquestion about John's immersion is also pertinent because John came preaching an immersion of repentance for the forgiveness of sins that bypassed the temple cult.[10] John's ministry rejected the ways that one traditionally became right with God by means of sacrifices. If his ministry was from heaven, the temple has become passé, and God is prepared to strike down unrepentant, unfruitful trees with an ax, throw them into the fire, and then raise up children to Abraham from the stones.

20:5 They discussed it among themselves, saying, "If we say 'from heaven,' he will say, 'Why did you not believe him?'" (οἱ δὲ συνελογίσαντο πρὸς ἑαυτοὺς λέγοντες ὅτι ἐὰν εἴπωμεν· ἐξ οὐρανοῦ, ἐρεῖ· διὰ τί οὐκ ἐπιστεύσατε αὐτῷ;). The reader is let in on the interchange among the authorities and their quandary as they mull over the different possible answers. The verb translated "discussed" (συλλογίζομαι) means "to calculate" (from which we get the noun syllogism) and is a minor variation from the verb (διαλογίζομαι) used in 20:14 to describe the murderous deliberations of the tenants.

The delegation is not worried that they might

---

8. Godet, *Commentary on Luke*, 2:236 – 37.

9. Green, *The Gospel of Luke*, 701.

10. The "immersion of John" (τὸ βάπτισμα Ἰωάννου) is a

subjective genitive, "the immersion that John performed." Accepting John's immersion, from Luke's perspective, leads inescapably to accepting Jesus (see Acts 18:24 – 26).

give the wrong answer but that the correct answer would subvert their own domination. They cannot say that John's authority came from heaven because that would incriminate them for having ignored it. They cannot say that his authority was not from heaven and that he was a fraud, because the people had decided he was a prophet. In the hour of decision for Israel, they refuse to commit one way or the other; and their answer is controlled by their fear of the people.

Because the leaders rejected John, they reveal that they also reject the purposes of God (7:30); but, ironically, they will unintentionally carry them out by orchestrating Jesus' death. It is out of the question for them even to consider for a moment that Jesus could be acting with divine authority. Prophets are unwelcome in Jerusalem (13:34). Pleading "agnostic neutrality,"[11] "We do not know" exposes their incompetence for understanding the way God works in the world and God's will for Israel. They do not know the time of the divine visitation (19:44). Consequently, they forfeit any right to be the temple's divinely authorized custodians.

20:6 – 7 "If we say 'from men,' the whole people will stone us, for they are convinced that John was a prophet." So they answered that they did not know from where it came (ἐὰν δὲ εἴπωμεν· ἐξ ἀνθρώπων, ὁ λαὸς ἅπας καταλιθάσει ἡμᾶς, πεπεισμένος γάρ ἐστιν Ἰωάννην προφήτην εἶναι. καὶ ἀπεκρίθησαν μὴ εἰδέναι πόθεν). As Danker comments, "Fear of the people takes precedence over their fear of God."[12] They are governed only by self-interest and worry more that a wrong answer might stoke the ire of the people against them than that it will kindle God's righteous wrath. They fear being stoned (see also Acts 5:26), the penalty for blasphemy, but have no qualms about

stoning others (13:34; Acts 7:57 – 60). Stoning was also the penalty for those who tried to turn the people away from the Lord their God (Deut 13:10).

From their perspective, as Jesus' enemies they stood for order over anarchy, as long as they were the ones giving the orders. They shut themselves off from the possibility of divine intervention, if it destroys their "continued favor and elevated status within Israel."[13] Their evasive answer is hypocritical, like defendants in modern times who claim they "do not remember" so as not to incriminate themselves.

20:8 Then Jesus said to them, "Neither will I tell you by what authority I do these things" (καὶ ὁ Ἰησοῦς εἶπεν αὐτοῖς· οὐδὲ ἐγὼ λέγω ὑμῖν ἐν ποίᾳ ἐξουσίᾳ ταῦτα ποιῶ). Jesus will not answer them directly, even when he is interrogated at his trial (22:67 – 68). All they get from him is the parable that follows (20:9 – 19). It is spoken to the people and not to the leaders, whom he now snubs. They are left to stew on the sidelines as they overhear Jesus validate his authority enigmatically in the parable — he is the Son. He also transparently warns them of their tenuous position with God as managers of a vineyard that is in default for nonpayment and on the verge of intensifying their guilt for murdering the Son.

While Jesus' enemies correctly surmise that the parable contains an implicit threat to their tenancy of the temple, it serves only to inflame their hostility. They do not understand its true significance related to God's requirement to bear fruit and the identity of "the beloved Son" as God's Son. But silencing opponents, as Jesus does throughout this section, does not stifle their animosity towards him. It only fuels their resolve to do away with him once and for all.

---

11. Paul S. Minear, *Saint Mark* (Layman's Bible Commentary; London: SCM, 1962), 111.

12. Danker, *Jesus and the New Age*, 317.
13. Green, *The Gospel of Luke*, 702.

Theology in Application

1. Institutional versus Divine Authority

This incident raises the issue of who can claim divine authority. The source of Jesus' authority has already been answered in the narrative (3:21 – 22; 4:18): it comes from God. The authority of the priestly hierarchy is founded on tradition and family ties; it is tied to an institution. Jesus' authority is based on his direct prophetic calling by God and is tied to his unique relationship to God. Deluded by the grandeur of the temple surrounding the priests and by their years of special privilege, they think they have the last word on who gets to say what God is or is not doing. Their word, however, comes from a god who speaks exactly as they do. The resurrection makes clear that the true God has the last word and has not yet spoken.

Nolland notes the contrast between the Jewish leaders, whose power derives from an institution (the temple), and the Christian movement, whose power derives from the Spirit of God. The contingent of Jewish leaders is governed by self-protective behavior; Christian discipleship "by contrast, bases itself on commitments for which one is prepared to die."[14] The Jewish leaders fear losing their headlock on political power; Christian discipleship has no fear going head-to-head with power to proclaim the truth of the gospel (Acts 4:5 – 22; 5:12 – 42). This encounter teaches that the power associated with a temporal office and an institution is no match for one who comes with a divine commission.

Authority is the primary concern of the chief priests, and Jesus has challenged that authority. For them, authority is a matter of status; it distinguishes them from the people they fear, and as a result, they seek to keep the people subjugated economically and religiously. True authority, such as Jesus possessed (4:32, 36; 5:24; 7:6 – 8), comes from the Spirit and does not always work through official, human channels. It does not come from inherited status, for Jesus has no priestly pedigree. Jesus can confer this authority to others (9:1; 10:19), and disciples in Acts will do things by the authority of Jesus Christ, whom they proclaim as Lord.

Consequently, when the leaders do succeed in doing away with him, they will not do away with this authority, because it belongs to God (Acts 1:7). In Acts, the chief priests' attempts to stifle the movement through violence and threats of violence (5:29; 9:14; 25:5, 26:10, 12) fail every time because the Word of God will not be shackled.

---

14. Nolland, *Luke*, 3:944.

2. The Impotence of the Temple Institution

To have the kind of faith Jesus seeks, one has to arrive at the conclusion by whose authority Jesus is working and teaching. The thief on the cross and the centurion will come to realize that God is working through Jesus. But faith like this is hard to come by — especially in those bent on gaining or preserving status and power for themselves. Satan promised Jesus that he would give him authority of all the kingdoms of the world if he would only bow down and worship him (4:5 – 7). Had Jesus done so, the priestly hierarchy may have been more enthusiastic and acquiescent. They are not interested in the inconvenient truth that challenges their supremacy. Any institution that cares more about preserving its influence and authority than serving God guarantees its irrelevance and sows the seeds of its own destruction.

What stirs the leaders to action is Jesus' teaching and preaching good news in the temple. In light of the parable of the Pharisee and the tax collector (18:9 – 14), the people need to hear good news preached in this sacred place. The tax collector cries out, overwhelmed by his guilt and alienation from God, for mercy — for an atoning sacrifice that would lift his burden of sin and remove his shame. The temple cult offers nothing for the likes of him. The good news is that even those in his state can have sins forgiven.

Luke 20:9 – 19

Literary Context

Jesus directs this parable to the people gathered in the temple, but it is also addressed to the Jewish leaders still standing on the sidelines. The parable provides an oblique answer to their question about his authority. To paraphrase the poet Diane Wikosky, "Poetry is the art of saying what you mean but disguising it." Jesus' parables also say what he means but disguise it.

Jesus comes as the beloved Son of the Lord of the vineyard. He has already warned his disciples that the Son of Man will be rejected by the elders, chief priests, and scribes and that he will undergo suffering and be killed (9:22). With this allegorical parable, he insinuates to the people within earshot of the elders, chief priests, and scribes that the tenants of the vineyard will kill the Son. The leaders perceive the parable is about them, but they do not hear the warning of God's judgment. Consequently, the parable only increases their resolve to kill him, fulfilling the plot of the parable. By destroying the Son they unwittingly destroy themselves.

In Luke's context, the parable is a barbed allegory that transparently attacks the authority of the temple hierarchy. They are knocked off their high horses and equated with tenant farmers, landless peasants, who default on the rent due the owner and defiantly intimidate and murder his agents. They are deluded fools who think that they can take over the vineyard for themselves by doing away with the Son.

Main Idea

The rejection of Jesus as the heir by the leaders is done with malice aforethought, but it is done without knowing that they also are rejecting God, forfeiting their tenancy of God's vineyard, and leading the nation to destruction.

Translation

(See next page.)

Structure and Literary Form

The structure of this parable with allegorical elements consists of the planting of a vineyard by the owner, three sendings of servants to collect rent from the tenants, and three progressively worse abuses of the servants. It then contains an interior monologue of the owner of the vineyard about what to do next. It culminates with the sending of his son and the murder of that son by the tenants. At the conclusion of the parable, Jesus asks a rhetorical question that he answers himself. What will the Lord of the vineyard do? He will destroy the tenants and give the vineyard to others.

The parable provokes two reactions. First, the people to whom the parable is addressed (20:9) respond that this could not happen (20:16b). Jesus corrects this response with a scriptural proof text (20:17 – 18). The second response comes from the scribes and chief priests, who correctly surmise that the parable and its conclusion have been aimed at them, and they secretly plot Jesus' death.

Exegetical Outline

→ I. **The planting of God's vineyard (20:9 – 16a)**

    A. Leasing to tenants (20:9)

    B. The sending of the servants to collect the fruit owed and their mistreatment (20:10 – 12)

    C. The sending of the Son and his murder (20:13 – 15a)

    D. The punishment of the tenants (20:15b – 16a)

  II. **The people's shocked response (20:16b)**

  III. **Christological citation from Scripture (20:17 – 18)**

  IV. **The leaders' plot to destroy Jesus (20:19)**

Luke 20:9–19

20:9a	Introduction of parable characters and circumstance	**Then he began to tell this parable to the people.**
b		*"A certain man planted a vineyard*
c		*and leased it to tenant farmers*
d		*and went away for a long time.*
10a	Time note	*And in due season,*
b	Sending (1)	*he sent a servant to the tenant farmers*
		so that they might give him the fruit from the vineyard.
c	Response (1)	*But after beating him, the tenant farmers sent him away empty-handed.*
11a	Sending (2)	*Again, he sent another slave.*
b	Response (2)	*That one they beat, dishonored, and sent away empty-handed.*
12a	Sending (3)	*Again, he sent a third.*
b	Response (3)	*They badly wounded this one and cast him out.*
13a	Interior monologue	*The Lord of the vineyard said,*
		'What shall I do [now]?
b	Decision/sending (4)	*I will send my beloved son!*
		It may be that they will respect this one.'
14a	Deliberation	*When the farmers saw him, they reasoned among themselves,*
b	Decision	*'This is the heir!*
		Let's kill him so that the inheritance might become ours.'
15a	Response (4)	*Then they cast him outside the vineyard and killed him.*
b	Question to listeners	*Now what will the Lord of the vineyard do?*
16a	Answer	*He will come and destroy these farmers*
		and he will give the vineyard to others."
b	Response	**Upon hearing this, they said,**
		"Never!"
17	Scriptural proof text	**But he looked them straight in the eye and said:**
		"What then is this that stands written:
		'The stone that the builders rejected, this one has become the ⤶
		cornerstone'? (Ps 118:22)
18	Interpretation	*Everyone who falls upon that stone will be smashed to pieces,*
		and it will crush to pieces whomever it falls upon."
19a	Deliberation/ decision	**Then the scribes and chief priests sought to lay hands on him at that very** ⤶
		moment,
b		**but they were afraid of the people,**
c		for **they knew that he spoke this parable against them.**

Explanation of the Text

20:9 Then he began to tell this parable to the people. "A certain man planted a vineyard and leased it to tenant farmers and went away for a long time" (ἤρξατο δὲ πρὸς τὸν λαὸν λέγειν τὴν παραβολὴν ταύτην· ἄνθρωπός [τις] ἐφύτευσεν ἀμπελῶνα καὶ ἐξέδετο αὐτὸν γεωργοῖς καὶ ἀπεδήμησεν χρόνους ἱκανούς). The vineyard is a transparent image from the Old Testament for God's relations to his chosen people, Israel.[1] Brooke argues that contemporary Jewish exegesis understood the image of "the vineyard" and its component elements to represent Jerusalem and contends that the parable is obviously about "Israel in miniature, that is Jerusalem, its temple and its cult."[2]

Luke's readers may not know that a huge, golden grapevine with grape clusters signifying Israel as God's fruit-bearing vine surrounded the entrance into the temple sanctuary (Josephus, *Ant.* 15.11.3 §395; see Tacitus, *Hist.* 5.5). But the original hearers gathered in the temple would be more likely to make the connection. Jesus has come to the temple and found it wanting (19:45–46), and the conclusion has the leaders admit that the parable is about them (20:19). Who the tenants in the parable represent is not obvious, however.[3] It only becomes clear as the story progresses that Jesus refers to the leaders.

The reference to a "long time" (χρόνους ἱκανούς), according to Tiede, highlights the owner's forbearance: "God did not rush the vineyard or look for produce before the time came (v. 10)."[4] The allegory echoes the reference to God's planting a vineyard in Isa 5:1–7 (though it is more explicit in Mark and Matthew). The differences from Isaiah are illuminating.[5] In Isaiah, the owner did not receive a harvest because the vineyard did not produce an adequate one. In Jesus' allegory, the vineyard produces fruit, but the tenants rebelliously withhold it from the owner. In Isaiah, the judgment falls on the vineyard. In Jesus' allegory, it falls on the tenants, and the vineyard is given to others. From this comparison, it becomes clear that Jesus condemns the leaders. They serve themselves instead of God. They rejected John the Baptist and his demands for the fruits of repentance (3:8), and they will do violence to Jesus, who came to warn them and to set things right.

20:10–12 And in due season, he sent a servant to the tenant farmers so that they might give him the fruit from the vineyard. But after beating him, the tenant farmers sent him away empty-handed. Again, he sent another slave. That one they beat, dishonored, and sent away empty-handed. Again, he sent a third. They badly wounded this one and cast him out (καὶ καιρῷ ἀπέστειλεν πρὸς τοὺς γεωργοὺς δοῦλον, ἵνα ἀπὸ τοῦ καρποῦ τοῦ ἀμπελῶνος δώσουσιν αὐτῷ· οἱ δὲ

1. Klyne Snodgrass, *The Parable of the Wicked Tenants: An Inquiry into Parable Interpretation* (WUNT 2/27; Tübingen: Mohr Siebeck, 1983), 76. See Ps 80:8–13; Isa 5:1–7; 27:2–5; Jer 2:21; 12:10; Ezek 19:10–14; Hos 10:1.

2. George J. Brooke, "4Q500 1 and the Use of Scripture in the Parable of the Vineyard," *DSD* 2 (1995): 284.

3. Harrington (*Holiness: Rabbinic Judaism and the Graeco-Roman World*, 102) observes: "The agricultural restrictions and requirements on Israel maintain the fundamental principle that God owns the land, causes its fertility and therefore deserves its produce. The people of Israel are his tenants and as such have

the right to work and benefit from the land. Recognizing God's ownership and their dependence on him for their continuing bounty, they present him, through his priestly representatives, with prescribed portions of the produce and livestock. This activity releases the rest of the crops and animals for normal, Israelite use. The tenants have acknowledged the sovereignty of the Landowner, who promises to guarantee fertility."

4. Tiede, *Luke*, 340.

5. Timothy J. Geddert, *Watchwords: Mark 13 in Markan Eschatology* (JSNTSup 26; Sheffield: JSOT, 1989), 120–21.

γεωργοὶ ἐξαπέστειλαν αὐτὸν δείραντες κενόν. καὶ προσέθετο ἕτερον πέμψαι δοῦλον· οἱ δὲ κἀκεῖνον δείραντες καὶ ἀτιμάσαντες ἐξαπέστειλαν κενόν. καὶ προσέθετο τρίτον πέμψαι· οἱ δὲ καὶ τοῦτον τραυματίσαντες ἐξέβαλον).

Luke records three sendings of servants and their mistreatment. The first servant has the stuffing knocked out of him and is sent away empty-handed (20:10). This detail could imply something far worse; he was "stripped of any valuables he had."[6] The second is beaten but is also treated shamefully and sent away empty-handed (20:11). The third is wounded and cast out (20:12). The mistreatment recalls the abuse of the prophets whom God repeatedly sent to Israel. The word "servant" (δοῦλος) is used in the Old Testament to refer to the prophets (see 1 Kgs 14:18; 15:29; 18:36; 2 Kgs 9:36; 10:10; 14:25; and the phrase "his servants the prophets" in Amos 3:7; Jer 7:25; Dan 9:6). The following Old Testament passage is pertinent as a backdrop for understanding the allegory's description of the servants' abuse:

> Furthermore, all the leaders of the priests and the people became more and more unfaithful, following all the detestable practices of the nations and defiling the temple of the LORD, which he had consecrated in Jerusalem.
>
> The LORD, the God of their ancestors, sent word to them through his messengers again and again, because he had pity on his people and on his dwelling place. But they mocked God's messengers, despised his words and scoffed at his prophets until the wrath of the LORD was aroused against his people and there was no remedy. (2 Chr 36:14 – 16)

Conventional wisdom had it that the prophets inevitably suffered a martyr's fate (see *Jub* 1:12 – 13).

Their persecution is a prominent theme in the New Testament (Matt 5:12, 23:31 – 39; Luke 13:33 – 34; Acts 7:52; 1 Thess 2:15; Heb 11:36 – 38).

"In due season" (καιρῷ) recalls Jesus' warning in 19:44, "And they will dash you to the ground and your children within [your walls], and they will not leave one stone upon another within [your walls] because you did not know the time [καιρόν] of your visitation." "Due season" in this context represents more than harvest time but "a critical time."[7]

20:13 The Lord of the vineyard said, "What shall I do [now]? I will send my beloved son! It may be that they will respect this one" (εἶπεν δὲ ὁ κύριος τοῦ ἀμπελῶνος· τί ποιήσω; πέμψω τὸν υἱόν μου τὸν ἀγαπητόν· ἴσως τοῦτον ἐντραπήσονται). The owner of the vineyard, now identified as "the Lord of the vineyard" (ὁ κύριος τοῦ ἀμπελῶνος), deliberates on what to do next. "It may be" (ἴσως; "perhaps, probably") suggests the extravagant risks God takes to accomplish his purposes and highlights Jesus' precarious situation.[8] He has entered the hangout of a gang of murderers who do not want their sanctuary threatened and will do anything to defend their turf, which they believe belongs to them.

"My beloved son" (τὸν υἱόν μου τὸν ἀγαπητόν) recalls the announcement of the voice from heaven at Jesus' immersion (3:22; see Isa 5:1) and transfiguration (9:35). The Septuagint normally translated "beloved" (ἀγαπητός) for the Hebrew word *yâḥîd*, which means "only." Young suggests that the word not only retains the connotation of "beloved" but also implies "his *only* son."[9] Evidence from the Dead Sea Scrolls (4Q Flor 1:11 on 2 Sam. 7:11; 1QSa 2:11 – 12 on Ps 2:7) referring to the "Son of God"

---

6. Evans, *St. Luke*, 699.

7. It is significant that a rabbinic legend has it, "When Solomon built the Sanctuary, he planted therein all sorts of precious golden trees, which brought forth fruit in their season" (*b. Yoma* 39b; 21b). In the legend, idolaters entering the sacred space caused the trees to dry up.

8. Grangaard, *Conflict and Authority*, 86.

9. Brad H. Young, *Jesus and His Jewish Parables: Rediscovering the Roots of Jesus' Teaching* (New York: Paulist, 1989), 285, 309, n.15.

and "Son of the Most High" make it possible that the audience could have interpreted the reference to "the son" messianically as they deciphered the allegory in their minds. The "beloved son" is certainly on a different level than "the servants" of the Lord of the vineyard.

20:14 When the tenant farmers saw him, they reasoned among themselves, "This is the heir! Let's kill him so that the inheritance might become ours" (ἰδόντες δὲ αὐτὸν οἱ γεωργοὶ διελογίζοντο πρὸς ἀλλήλους λέγοντες· οὗτός ἐστιν ὁ κληρονόμος· ἀποκτείνωμεν αὐτόν, ἵνα ἡμῶν γένηται ἡ κληρονομία). The tenants' recognition of the son does three things. First, it deepens their guilt. They will kill one whom they *know* to be the son.[10] Second, recognizing him as "the heir" (ὁ κληρονόμος) reinforces the idea that this is the "only" son. Killing him, they think, will clear the path for them to take possession of the vineyard. Third, identifying him as "the heir" reinforces the truth that they are only temporary tenants, capable of being replaced. It is not their inheritance and never will be.

20:15a Then they cast him outside the vineyard and killed him (καὶ ἐκβαλόντες αὐτὸν ἔξω τοῦ ἀμπελῶνος ἀπέκτειναν). In Luke's version of the parable, only the son is murdered, not any of the servants (cf. Matt 21:35; Mark 12:5). If the vineyard represents the temple and Jerusalem, the detail of casting him outside is to be expected. Executions took place outside the city to avoid ritual defilement (Acts 7:58). But the farmers will also cast the body outside the vineyard to avoid defiling it. Later Christian readers of Luke, however, could easily interpret this detail as an allusion to Jesus' crucifixion "outside the city gate" (Heb 13:12).

20:15b – 16 "Now what will the Lord of the vineyard do? He will come and destroy these farmers and he will give the vineyard to others." Upon hearing this, they said, "Never!" (τί οὖν ποιήσει αὐτοῖς ὁ κύριος τοῦ ἀμπελῶνος; ἐλεύσεται καὶ ἀπολέσει τοὺς γεωργοὺς τούτους καὶ δώσει τὸν ἀμπελῶνα ἄλλοις. ἀκούσαντες δὲ εἶπαν· μὴ γένοιτο). As Jesus does in other parables in Luke, he does not leave it for his listeners to connect the dots but concludes the parable with his own interjection to score the point. He spells out the consequences of the tenants' actions with a prophetic warning (the three verbs are in the future tense). The vineyard owner morphs from one who is seemingly impotent into one who is able to wreak terrible vengeance. The tenants will be wiped out and the vineyard given to others.

Do the scribes and chief priests or the people blurt out the reaction, "Never!" (μὴ γένοιτο, lit., "may it not be")? Since Jesus addresses the people with the parable (20:9), it is most likely that they are the ones who exclaim in shock.[11] Perhaps they shudder at the prospects of destruction because they recognize "that their own interests are in jeopardy."[12] If Jerusalem and the temple go, so do their hopes for material and spiritual security. Jerusalem was the center of the Judean economy, and Josephus says it dominated "all the neighborhood as the head towers above the body" (*J.W.* 3.3.5 §54). If this is correct, they do not ask the question that the crowds posed to John the Baptist, "What then should we do?" (3:10 – 13). They prefer to live in a state of denial.

Kloppenborg makes the case, however, that the people are reacting to everything they heard in the parable and not simply to the conclusion about the destruction of the tenants and the reletting

---

10. The phrase "let's kill him" (ἀποκτείνωμεν αὐτόν) is the same one Joseph's brothers use (Gen 37:20a LXX).

11. Paul's use of the phrase shows it is packed with emotion

(Rom 3:4, 6, 31; 6:2, 15; 7:7; 9:14; 11:1, 11; 1 Cor 6:15; Gal 2:17; 3:21; 6:14).

12. Grangaard, *Conflict and Authority*, 91.

of the vineyard to others.[13] The people must be distinguished from the priestly hierarchy, who do react in a self-serving way. The people may not have discerned that the tenants in the parable are to be linked to the leaders, and therefore they express horror over such criminal behavior by the tenants. When the participle "hearing" (ἀκούσαντες) in the plural appears elsewhere in Luke, it refers to hearing an entire story, not simply a single preceding statement.[14]

In my view, with the passage from Scripture and its interpretation, Jesus corrects and challenges the people's response by connecting the story and his conclusion about the tenants' punishment to present circumstances. The scriptural citation becomes a prophecy. These horrible things have been played out in the leaders' treatment of prophets in the past, and most recently John, and they will be played out in their murder of the Son. The criminal behavior of the tenants in the parable is not as mind-boggling as it might seem, and it will meet with a harsh reckoning.

20:17 But he looked them straight in the eye and said: "What then is this that stands written: 'The stone that the builders rejected, this one has become the cornerstone'?" (ὁ δὲ ἐμβλέψας αὐτοῖς εἶπεν· τί οὖν ἐστιν τὸ γεγραμμένον τοῦτο· λίθον ὃν ἀπεδοκίμασαν οἱ οἰκοδομοῦντες, οὗτος ἐγενήθη εἰς κεφαλὴν γωνίας;). The verb translated "looked them straight in the eye" (ἐμβλέψας) implies an intensity (see 22:61) that underscores the serious nature of what Jesus is about to say. Presumably, he stares at those to whom he spoke the parable (20:9), but it would have been fitting for

him to be looking at the Jewish leaders as he says these things. They are the targets of the allegory and have a greater vested interest in the survival of the temple because of the privileges and wealth it accords them. They also have the power to try to make sure that the "never" (μὴ γένοιτο) applies to Jesus as well. He will never be able to get away with saying things like this in their temple again. But the warning also applies to the people. They too are in danger for joining their leaders in rejecting him.

Jesus cites Ps 118:22 (LXX Ps 117:22) as a proof text that the very thing they dread will happen. In Matt 21:42 and Mark 12:11, the citation continues with Ps 118:23, "The LORD has done this, and it is marvelous in our eyes." The absence of this additional verse in Luke results in an emphasis on the rejection of the stone. This rejection is not "marvelous" but tragic. Though it contributes to the fulfillment of God's purposes and is tied to divine necessity, since it is it prophesied in the Scripture (Luke 24:44–46), rejecting the cornerstone will have horrific consequences for Jerusalem.

Jesus' response contains a play on words in Hebrew between the word "son" (bēn) and "stone" (ʾeben) that is lost in translation (in both Greek and English).[15] The rejected stone is "the Son," and the verb "rejected" (ἀπεδοκίμασαν) appears in Jesus' first passion prediction: "It is necessary for the Son of Man to suffer many things, to be repudiated by the elders, chief priests, and scribes, and to be killed" (9:22). The "builders" is a transparent reference to the leaders of Israel, who identified themselves as "the builders of Israel."[16]

---

13. John S. Kloppenborg, *The Tenants in the Vineyard: Ideology, Economics, and Agrarian Conflict in Jewish Palestine* (WUNT 2/195; Tübingen: Mohr Siebeck, 2006), 211–14.

14. See 1:66; 2:18; 4:28; 19:11. The singular participle appears in 7:9; 8:50; 18:22, 23, 23:6 and refers to the preceding statement.

15. Matthew Black, "The Christological Use of the Old

Testament in the New Testament," *NTS* 18 (1971): 11–14. The wordplay is found in Exod 28:9–10; Josh 4:6–7; and possibly Lam 4:1–2; see also Josephus, *J.W.* 5.6.3 §272.

16. Fitzmyer, *Luke*, 2:1282. CD 8:12; 4:19 refers to the builders of the feeble wall, which is probably an epithet alluding to the temple leadership.

The citation from the psalm (cited again in Acts 4:11) implies that a new structure is to be built, but Luke's second volume will make clear that it is not to be a literal building made of stone (see Acts 7:44 – 53). Jesus' rejection by the leaders of Israel, who will coerce the Roman governor to execute him, will ensure the temple's destruction and their demise. They do not take into account the possibility of a resurrection that allows him to become "the cornerstone for a renewed 'temple,' a renewed centre and focus for the people of God as they will be in the future."[17]

20:18 Everyone who falls upon that stone will be smashed to pieces, and it will crush to pieces whomever it falls upon (πᾶς ὁ πεσὼν ἐπ᾽ ἐκεῖνον τὸν λίθον συνθλασθήσεται· ἐφ᾽ ὃν δ᾽ ἂν πέσῃ, λικμήσει αὐτόν). When Simeon greeted the child Jesus in the temple at the beginning of the story, he announced that he was destined to contribute to the rise and fall of many in Israel (2:34). The

proverb, perhaps an expansion and application of Isa 8:14 – 15 and Dan 2:44, asserts that those who oppose the Son/stone will be destroyed. The keystone falling from its heights will crush them. The cornerstone, lying on the ground, will destroy whoever trips over it.

20:19 Then the scribes and chief priests sought to lay hands on him at that very moment, but they were afraid of the people, for they knew that he spoke this parable against them (καὶ ἐζήτησαν οἱ γραμματεῖς καὶ οἱ ἀρχιερεῖς ἐπιβαλεῖν ἐπ᾽ αὐτὸν τὰς χεῖρας ἐν αὐτῇ τῇ ὥρᾳ, καὶ ἐφοβήθησαν τὸν λαόν, ἔγνωσαν γὰρ ὅτι πρὸς αὐτοὺς εἶπεν τὴν παραβολὴν ταύτην). The scribes and chief priests are naturally incensed that Jesus teaches against them (see a similar reaction in Acts 7:54) and wins the hearts and minds of the people in the process. They fear a great tidal swell of popular support for him, which only stiffens their resolve to kill him.

Theology in Application

1. Rebellion against God

There is no need to try to peel away the layers of allegory in this parable in an attempt to get back to the original parable uttered by Jesus, as many interpreters have tried to do.[18] This parable is a transparent indictment of the leaders in Jerusalem for their malfeasance and perversion of their office.[19] They belonged to the ruling class, who became wealthy from their large land holdings. They lived well off the peasants, who leased the land from them.[20] Consequently, they would have naturally sympathized with the dilemma of a landowner who must cope with deadbeat, rebellious tenants. The parable, however, places them in the role of murderous tenants who re-

17. Geddert, *Watchwords*, 123. The term translated "cornerstone" (κεφαλὴν γωνίας, lit., "head of the corner") could refer to the wedge-shaped stone at the center and summit of an arch that locks the other stones together, the keystone or capstone. But it is more likely to refer to a cornerstone that lays the foundation to shore up the junction of two walls of a building. It is chosen with care and laid with peculiar solemnity.

18. See Brooke, "4Q500 1 and the Use of Scripture in the

Parable of the Vineyard," 268 – 94.

19. Charles H. Giblin, *The Destruction of Jerusalem according to Luke's Gospel: A Historical-Typological Moral* (AnBib 107; Rome: Pontifical Biblical Institute, 1985), 66.

20. Martin Goodman, *The Ruling Class of Judea: The Origins of the Jewish Revolt against Rome AD 66 – 70* (Cambridge: Cambridge Univ. Press, 1987), 55 – 75.

neged on their debts and abused the ones sent to collect payment. Brooke highlights an important point:

> The allegorical character of the parable should not be downplayed as secondary and insignificant. The vineyard should not be understood solely in terms of real situations in first-century Palestine, but in light of the scriptural allusion which rests behind its use as that was understood in contemporary Jewish texts, such as 4Q500; the vineyard is Israel in miniature, Jerusalem and its temple and all that takes place on the altar. The motif of election is significant, not in terms of Christian displacement of Israel, but in terms of who may participate in the cult, in the right worship of God. It is the authorities in the temple who are undermined, challenged and displaced, not Israel as a whole. The prooftext from Psalm 118 is remarkably coherent with the opening parts of the parable, so much so that it can be deemed an integral part of the pericope (as the use of בנה in 4Q500 helps us see). The literary context of the parable is thoroughly suitable to its use of scripture; Jesus is portrayed as in the temple, challenging those in charge. Indeed the historical context portrayed suggests that the use of scripture in the pericope as a whole is not the result of the creative work of the early church, but goes back to Jesus himself. To a Jesus who even taught in the temple.[21]

The logic behind the tenants' thinking — if they kill the heir, the vineyard would become theirs — should not be interpreted as a realistic hope.[22] Theologically, the parable paints a vivid picture of human willful rebellion against God. The tenants have rejected the reality that they are creatures of God who simply live in God's vineyard. They want to be the lords of the vineyard. God stands in the way of their plans, and so they brutalize or kill any of God's messengers who remind them of the reality. They recognize the heir "but rejected him because they were unwilling to relinquish control over the vineyard to its rightful owner."[23]

The parable also shows how stupid and miscalculating rebellion against God is. The tenants do not know that this Son is appointed "heir of all things" (Heb 1:2; see Rom 8:17). They do not want to know how to inherit eternal life. Their focus is only on this world and how to ensure security in this life. The problem is that their delusional ambitions sow the seeds of their own destruction. Humans often believe that killing off their opponents will get them power, but they are sadly mistaken. In this parable, they brutalize others and kill to get control of a little vineyard. Humans who try to control their own future without God always suffer from the law of unintended consequences and always are destined to lose.

Sometimes the rebellion against God takes a more passive form; God is simply ignored. A writer discusses the contrast between the study of the New Testament in

---

21. Brooke, "4Q500 1 and the Use of Scripture in the Parable of the Vineyard," 294.

22. For example, Hultgren (*The Parables of Jesus*, 362 – 63)

conjectures that the owner had died and the son had come to claim the vineyard, or the owner signed it over to his son.

23. Talbert, *Reading Luke*, 189.

societies that have "undergone the scientific, historical and industrial revolutions" and study that is done in a "young-church environment," such as Africa or Asia. He makes this devastating observation:

> … the long standing Christian heritage which began as a revolution, has paradoxically enough led to the Westerner taking God for granted. He is someone whose ways are known, whose reactions can be gauged, who will do the decent thing and see that justice and goodness will triumph. He can therefore be safely ignored. Yet the New Testament is solely concerned with trying to convey something explosive about a living God.[24]

This explosive God will blow up the complacency of those who think they can safely ignore him and will demolish supposedly sacrosanct religious institutions that try to substitute empty rituals and token service for radical submission and earnest obedience.

2. God's Forbearance and Patience

The prolonged refusal of the owner to come in judgment becomes a symbol of God's patience and the blessedness of God's grace (see Rom 2:4; 2 Pet. 3:9). But God has every intention of collecting the rent. Authority in God's vineyard brings accountability. Leaders who fail to feed the sheep because they are wrapped up in their own little world of political machinations to preserve their privilege will be destroyed and replaced. God will not be trifled with (Rom 2:1 – 11) and will reckon with human faithlessness. Paul develops this idea in 1 Cor 3:5 – 17.

3. Jesus as the Son

The parable reveals that Jesus was fully conscious of his sonship in relation to the Lord of the vineyard and fully conscious of his impending death at the hands of the authorities. Those who question the authenticity of the parable also question both of these possibilities. The rejected stone has become a stone of stumbling (the crucified Christ). Rejecting the cornerstone or falling on that stone are metaphors for rejecting Jesus, which is tantamount to rejecting God. In parable form, this story reaffirms the necessity of the suffering of the Messiah.[25] The world of the parable, when it is applied to Jesus, is not intended to imply that God did not know the outcome of the sending of his Son. It is necessary for him to suffer.

24. N. Q. King, "Reflections on New Testament Study from a Young-Church Environment," *SE III* (TU 88; Berlin: Akademie-Verlag, 1964), 81.

25. R. Alan Culpepper, "Parable as Commentary: The Twice-Given Vineyard [Luke 20:9 – 16]," *PRSt* 26 (1999): 161 – 62.

Luke 20:20 – 26

Literary Context

The Jewish leaders begin their attempts to trap Jesus and gather incriminating evidence that they can use to destroy him. In this incident, they send stand-ins who pose as sympathizers to bait him with a politically and religiously loaded question.

V. Jesus in Jerusalem (19:29 – 21:38)

    B. Jesus' Teaching in the Temple (19:47 – 21:38)

        1. Jesus' Teaching in the Temple and the Challenge to His Authority (19:47 – 20:8)

        2. The Parable of the Vineyard Tenants (20:9 – 19)

➡   **3. The Question about Tribute to Caesar (20:20 – 26)**

        4. The Question about the Resurrection (20:27 – 40)

Main Idea

One is to give to God what belongs to God, oneself. If one does business with the state, one owes it the tax it demands, but no more.

Translation

Luke 20:20–26

20:20a	Deception	**They watched closely and sent spies who played the role of being righteous** in order to trap him by his word
b	Purpose	so that they might betray him to the authoritative jurisdiction of the ✍ governor.
21	False flattery	**Then they asked him,** "*Teacher, we know that you speak and teach correctly* *and do not show anyone partiality* *but truly teach the way of God.*
22	Question	*Is it lawful for us to pay tribute tax to Caesar or not?*"
23	Assessment	**Perceiving their craftiness, he said to them,**
24a	Command and question	"*Show me a denarius.* *Whose image and inscription are on it?*"
b	Answer	**They said,** "*Caesar's.*"
25a	Pronouncement	**He said to them,**
b		"*Well then, give back to Caesar the things that belong to Caesar and*
c		*to God the things that belong to God.*"
26a	Response	**They were unable to trap him** in his word in the presence of the people,
b		and marveling at his answer, **they fell silent.**

Structure and Literary Form

This account is a pronouncement story. It is structured around a challenging question that sets up a trap, which is followed by a clever response that silences the opponents.

Exegetical Outline

→ I. Setting a political and religious trap (20:20 – 22)

  II. Evading the trap (20:23 – 24)

  III. Pronouncement: give back to God what belongs to God (20:25 – 26)

Explanation of the Text

20:20 They watched closely and sent spies who played the role of being righteous in order to trap him by his word so that they might betray him to the authoritative jurisdiction of the governor (καὶ παρατηρήσαντες ἀπέστειλαν ἐγκαθέτους ὑποκρινομένους ἑαυτοὺς δικαίους εἶναι, ἵνα ἐπιλάβωνται αὐτοῦ λόγου, ὥστε παραδοῦναι αὐτὸν τῇ ἀρχῇ καὶ τῇ ἐξουσίᾳ τοῦ ἡγεμόνος). Since the temple leaders are afraid to take action against Jesus openly, they put him under surveillance (cf. 6:7; 14:1; Acts 9:24) and send spies (ἐγκαθέτους) who pass themselves off as sympathetic to his teaching in order to gather evidence against him. These double agents play the role (ὑποκρινομένους) of being righteous by asking a question whether it is theologically admissible to pay tribute to a pagan ruler. Their purpose ("so that" [ὥστε]) is to catch him saying something subversive that they can use to spur the Roman governor to take action against him.[1]

20:21 Then they asked him, "Teacher, we know that you speak and teach correctly and do not show anyone partiality but truly teach the way of God" (καὶ ἐπηρώτησαν αὐτὸν λέγοντες· διδάσκαλε, οἴδαμεν ὅτι ὀρθῶς λέγεις καὶ διδάσκεις καὶ οὐ λαμβάνεις πρόσωπον, ἀλλ᾽ ἐπ᾽ ἀληθείας τὴν ὁδὸν τοῦ θεοῦ διδάσκεις). Outsiders or strangers use "teacher" as a respectful address twelve times in Luke, and in this sequence of conflict the term occurs twice (20:28, 39). The spies fawn over Jesus with flattering words, as Satan did in his temptations, but Jesus consistently deflects all forms of flattery. Their charade serves to emphasize his role in the temple as a teacher who teaches the way of God (see Ps 51:13; Isa 2:3).

20:22 "Is it lawful for us to pay tribute tax to Caesar or not?" (ἔξεστιν ἡμᾶς Καίσαρι φόρον δοῦναι ἢ οὔ;). The question "Is it lawful?" (ἔξεστιν) can be a legitimate one: Can one pay tribute to Caesar without dishonoring the one and only God in some way? It is a real dilemma, given the political reality of Roman rule. But these spies hope to use Jesus' response against him. One who shows no partiality does not equivocate, and they expect a straightforward and uncompromising answer about what God demands. Does Jesus agree to full cooperation with the Romans as modeled by the priestly hierarchy? Or does he openly reject Roman rule? Were he to deny the legitimacy of Roman domination over Israel and advocate nonviolent resistance, it would be no less offensive to the Romans than violent rejection of their rule.[2]

The word "tribute" (φόρος) is used to refer to "'tribute' paid to a foreign ruler, whether as a 'land-tax' or 'poll-tax.'"[3] Weiss notes that the word "carried with it the odium of bondage."[4] Gibson summarizes what the tax meant to the Jews. Economically, it represented an additional, bitter financial burden, since it was added to other civic and religious taxes. The result was that taxes totaled nearly 30 to 40 percent of a person's income. Politically, the tribute went to support the hated imperial court in Rome and the pagan cult of the Roman state. It kept the subject nation ever mindful of its domination by a superior Roman power and represented tacit assent to the legitimacy of

---

1. The translation "the authoritative jurisdiction" (τῇ ἀρχῇ καὶ τῇ ἐξουσίᾳ) renders the phrase as a hendiadys in which the two nouns "rule" and "authority" are coordinated and subordinated to one another to express a more complex idea.

2. Compare the examples of Eleazar and the mother with seven sons passively resisting Antiochus Epiphanes recounted in 2 Macc 6–7.

3. Konrad Weiss, "φέρω …," *TDNT*, 9:81.

4. Ibid.

these institutions. Theologically, it was an infringement of the first commandment with the blasphemous imagery and a denial of God's ownership of the land.[5]

Given the inflammatory nature of the issue, the spies may anticipate that Jesus will give a bellicose response. The Galilean firebrand Judas fiercely opposed the imposition of the tax, which led to an uprising in AD 6 – 7. His battle cry was, "No tribute that puts God's land and people under the hegemony of foreigners."[6] Should Jesus openly oppose the tax, it would be tantamount to inciting rebellion against Rome, which warranted execution (23:2). Should Jesus, however, answer "Yes" to the question, it would negate any messianic claim he might make, since everyone expected the Messiah to deliver Israel from such subjection. Luke's birth narrative, however, makes clear that Jesus' family obediently complied with the decree of Emperor Augustus to register for taxation purposes (2:1 – 7). Jesus is a Galilean but not an agitator fomenting revolt.

20:23 – 24 Perceiving their craftiness, he said to them, "Show me a denarius. Whose image and inscription are on it?" They said, "Caesar's' (κατανοήσας δὲ αὐτῶν τὴν πανουργίαν εἶπεν πρὸς αὐτούς· δείξατέ μοι δηνάριον· τίνος ἔχει εἰκόνα καὶ ἐπιγραφήν; οἱ δὲ εἶπαν· Καίσαρος). Jesus is not caught off guard by their guile and outmaneuvers them by setting his own trap in asking them to produce a denarius. Coins were

used for propaganda in the ancient world, and this coin proclaimed Roman imperialistic ideology.

This coin had the effigy of the emperor and the superscription on one side: *TI[berius] CAESAR DIVI AVG[usti] F AVGVSTVS* (Emperor Tiberias Son of the Divine Augustus). On the reverse side, some coins had a female figure facing right, seated on a throne, wearing a crown and holding a scepter in the right hand and a palm or olive branch in the left. The superscription reads: *PONTIF[ex] MAXIM[us]* (Chief Priest). In other words, the coin advertises Tiberius as a divine or semidivine being as the son of the divine Augustus. The woman is a priestess or the wife of Augustus, Livia, the mother of Tiberias, and proclaims the Pax Romana that has put all other nations in subjection.[7]

The denarius oozes idolatry, and Jesus highlights this fact by asking them about the images and inscription on it. By possessing such a coin the would-be informers incriminate themselves as those who are impious by bringing such an unsanctioned, portable graven image into God's temple.[8]

20:25 He said to them, "Well then, give back to Caesar the things that belong to Caesar and to God the things that belong to God" (ὁ δὲ εἶπεν πρὸς αὐτούς· τοίνυν ἀπόδοτε τὰ Καίσαρος Καίσαρι καὶ τὰ τοῦ θεοῦ τῷ θεῷ). Jesus' famous answer begins, in Luke, with an inferential particle, "well then" (τοίνυν). The verb is best translated "give back" (ἀπόδοτε) rather than simply "render" or "give." Jesus simply points out that they already

5. Gibson, *The Temptations of Jesus*, 306 – 9.

6. According to Josephus, Judas incited a revolt when the tribute was imposed after Archelaus was deposed and a Roman governor was installed to govern Judea. He upbraided his countrymen "as cowards for consenting to pay tribute to Romans and tolerating mortal masters" (*J.W.* 2.8.1 §118; see Acts 5:37).

7. See H. St. J. Hart, "The Coin of 'Render unto Caesar …' (A Note on Some Aspects of Mark 12:13 – 17; Matt. 22:15 – 22;

Luke 20:20 – 26," in *Jesus and the Politics of His Day* (ed. E. Bammel and C. F. D. Moule; Cambridge: Cambridge Univ. Press, 1984), 242 – 48.

8. The parallel in *Gosp. Thom.* 100 has them showing him a gold coin, which misses the whole point. Suetonius (*Tib.* 58) highlights the coin's religious associations by noting that one could be punished for taking it into the toilet or a bordello (noted by Ulrich Luz, *Matthew 21 – 28* [trans. J. E. Crouch; Hermeneia; Minneapolis, Fortress, 2005], 65, n. 39).

acknowledge Caesar's authority by having in their possession a coin bearing his image. If they play with Caesar — they are ready to hand Jesus over to the governor — and use Caesar's money, they will have to play by Caesar's rules and pay Caesar's taxes.

These spies did not ask about God, but Jesus' addition, "and to God the things that belong to God," is the key to the whole passage. It is not an afterthought but comes at the climax, which means that this passage is not about what is owed the state but what is owed God. What is left in doubt is whether these opponents play by God's rules and pay back to God what belongs to him, or are like the tenants in the previous parable, who refused to give to the owner of the vineyard

the fruit owed to him. Readers must fill in what it means to give back to God what belongs to God "from the biblical and Jewish tradition."[9]

20:26 They were unable to trap him in his word in the presence of the people, and marveling at his answer, they fell silent (καὶ οὐκ ἴσχυσαν ἐπιλαβέσθαι αὐτοῦ ῥήματος ἐναντίον τοῦ λαοῦ, καὶ θαυμάσαντες ἐπὶ τῇ ἀποκρίσει αὐτοῦ ἐσίγησαν). In trying to catch Jesus in some fatal slip, they are trapped by their own cleverness and expose both their ineptitude and culpability. As Doble points out, however, "silenced opponents are not vanquished opponents."[10] Being foiled by Jesus in this argument will not stop the leaders from fabricating the charge that Jesus forbade paying taxes to Caesar (23:2).

Theology in Application

One must be cautious in developing general applications from Jesus' pronouncement about taxes because it is context specific. Jesus is responding here to the trickery of spies trying to entrap him. His pronouncement does not spell out precisely what belongs to Caesar and what to God, but it can be inferred.

1. The Limitation of What is Rightfully Caesar's

"Give back to Caesar" does not acknowledge Caesar's authority so much as confine it to those things that have his image stamped on them, namely, money, which Jesus dismisses as Mammon, an idol. Things like denarii are trivial compared to God's reign; so why not give Caesar these things?[11] Jesus dismisses the money gifts of the rich to God as mere tokens compared to the widow who gives her whole "life" (βίος, that is, all she has to support her life, 21:1 – 4). What God requires is one's whole life.

9. Luz, *Matthew 21 – 28*, 67.
10. Doble, *The Paradox of Salvation*, 207.
11. Daniel Patte, *The Gospel According to Matthew: A Struc-*
tural Commentary on Matthew's Faith (Philadelphia: Fortress, 1987), 309 – 10.

2. God's Unlimited Rights

The unstated premise behind all that Jesus teaches is our primary responsibility to God. The "things that belong to God" cannot be limited to coins. The whole earth and all that is in it is his (see Ps 24). God's demands are infinitely greater and so are God's rewards and punishments. Since we are created in the image of God (see Gen 1:26; Isa 44:5; see Ezek 18:4), we owe God our very selves.[12]

3. The Provisional Authority of Legitimate Governments

Early Christians adopted a positive view of the role of the government and assumed that it owed its authority to God (Rom 13:1 – 7; 1 Tim 2:1 – 2; Titus 3:1 – 2; 1 Pet 2:13 – 17; *1 Clem.* 61; Justin, *1 Apol.* 17.3; Tertullian, *Apol.* 30). These various statements related to human government apply to cases where it exercises its authority legitimately. Dalman concludes that Jesus

> did not consider the political dominance of the Romans to be any infringement on the sovereignty of God. It is not the rule of foreigners over the nation, but the rule of all ungodly powers in the inner life, that the sovereignty of God aims at removing; and it is no human agency, not even the Messiah, that by earthly means establishes this sovereignty, but God Himself.[13]

The book of Revelation makes it clear, however, how easily earthly powers submit to and become the willing tool of satanic powers. Jesus' pronouncement, therefore, must be tempered by his assertion, "No servant is able to serve two masters, for he will hate the one and love the other, or he will help the one and disregard the other" (16:13).

When the New Testament affirms that Jesus is Lord, it contains a subtext: Caesar is not. Again, an unstated premise in Jesus' teaching assumes that the government's authority is provisional, because the reign of God makes all earthly rulers irrelevant and excessive subservience to them irreverent. Isaiah affirms that God "hands nations over to [one from the east] and subdues kings before him. He turns them to dust with his sword, to windblown chaff with his bow" (Isa 41:2). Paul affirms that the rulers of this world are passing off the stage (see 1 Cor 7:29 – 31), and at the end Christ will hand over "the kingdom to God the Father after he has destroyed all dominion, authority and power. For he must reign until he has put all his enemies under his feet" (1 Cor 15:24 – 25).

---

12. This interpretation goes back to Tertullian, who interpreted this passage to mean: "Render unto Caesar, the image of Caesar, which is on the money, and *unto God*, the image of God, which is in man; so that thou givest unto Caesar money, unto God thine own self" (*Idol.* 15; *Marc.* 4.38.3). See Charles

H. Giblin, " 'The Things of God' in the Question concerning Tribute to Caesar [Lk 20:25; Mk 12:17; Mt 22:21]," *CBQ* 33 (1971): 522 – 23.

13. Dalman, *The Words of Jesus*, 138.

Jesus' critique of the Roman superpower is "broadly in line with the entire biblical and prophetic tradition," and its basis is "the prophetic claim, 'the Lord is our judge, the Lord is our ruler, the Lord is our king, he will save us' (Isa.33.22)."[14] But Jesus does not call his followers to revolt to dismantle human power structures and replace them with other human power structures that his followers control. They are not called to be antigovernment. The biblical witness is that governments are permitted by God to rule in their sphere under "the sphere of God's overarching providence and power." Bryan comments, "Caesar, like all who rule from Pharaoh onward, would ignore or oppose that providence and power at his peril."[15]

The purpose of earthly rulers is to promote God's peace and justice. When they fail to do that, when they fail to submit to God's sovereignty, when they fail to admit and repent from past wrongs, they must be confronted and warned that God's judgment is inevitable. Bryan shares his memory of Archbishop Desmond Tutu's release from prison during the era of apartheid in South Africa. A journalist asked, "'How long do you intend to go on defying the South African government?' With a gentle smile, the Archbishop replied, "But we are not *defying* anyone. We are simply trying to obey God.'"[16]

14. Christopher Bryan, *Render to Caesar: Jesus, the Early Church, and the Roman Superpower* (Oxford: Oxford Univ. Press, 2005), 9.

15. Ibid., 51.

16. Ibid., 130.

Luke 20:27 – 40

64

Literary Context

The Sadducees' question about the resurrection is a setup intended to ridicule the belief rather than to entrap Jesus. But the issue of resurrection is crucial in the context of Luke. Jesus has prophesied that he will suffer and die at the hands of the authorities in Jerusalem, and his fate is sealed as the opposition closes in on him. He has also prophesied that he will be vindicated when God raises him from the dead on the third day. If there is no resurrection, this prophecy is delusional, wishful thinking. In this third challenge in the temple, Jesus continues to best his opponents, revealing their godlessness and the truth about God.

V. Jesus in Jerusalem (19:29 – 21:38)

    B. Jesus' Teaching in the Temple (19:47 – 21:38)

        3. The Question about Tribute to Caesar (20:20 – 26)

        4. The Question about the Resurrection (20:27 – 40)

        5. The Question about David's Son, Warnings about Self-Absorbed Scribes, and the Example of a Poverty-Stricken Widow (20:41 – 21:4)

Main Idea

In his confrontation with the Sadducees, Jesus teaches that the dead will be raised to a new existence that cannot be compared to earthly experiences.

Translation

Luke 20:27–40

20:27	Character introduction	**Certain ones of the Sadducees, who deny that there is a resurrection, came up and asked him,**
28	Scriptural premise	*"Teacher, Moses wrote for us,*
		'If a man's brother should die, and
		he had a wife but was childless,
		he should take his brother's widow to raise up descendants for his brother.' (Deut 25:5)
29	Hypothetical case	*Now, there were seven brothers.*
		The first one took a wife and died childless.
30		*Then the second*
31		*and the third took her,*
		and likewise the seven died childless.
32		*Finally, the woman also died.*
33a		*Now in the resurrection, whose wife will the woman be?*
b		*For the seven had her as a wife."*
34	Jesus' response	**Jesus said to them,**
		"The sons of this age marry and are given in marriage.
35	Assertion	*But those counted worthy to attain that age, . . .*
		that is, the resurrection from the dead,
		. . . neither marry nor are given in marriage.
36	Explanation	*For they cannot die anymore*
		because they are equal to the angels and
		are sons of God,
		being sons of the resurrection.
37	Scriptural refutation	*That the dead are raised Moses also revealed in the 'bush passage' where he says,*
		'The Lord is the God of Abraham, the God of Isaac, and the God of Jacob.'
		(Exod 3:15-16)
38	Pronouncement	*Now, God is not the God of the dead but of the living,*
		for they all live to him."
39	Reaction	**Some of the scribes responded,**
		"Teacher, you said it well."
40	Capitulation	**For they dared not ask him another question.**

Structure and Literary Form

This account is a pronouncement story. It is structured around a challenging question that attempts to confound Jesus with a hypothetical question relating to what happens in the resurrection. Luke does not have the statements in Mark that peremptorily refute the Sadducees: "You are badly mistaken" (Mark 12:27), and "You do not know the Scriptures or the power of God" (Mark 12:24). The emphasis is on Jesus' teaching, not the confrontation. His response first highlights the incompatibility between earthly life and the resurrection life and then provides scriptural proof for the resurrection. The conclusion notes that some of the scribes praise his answer, and the opponents have been silenced once again.

Exegetical Outline

  ➡ **I. Conundrum designed to debunk belief in the resurrection (20:27 – 33)**

     II. Jesus' response (20:34 – 38)

        A. Resurrection existence transcends earthly existence and is not comparable (20:34 – 36)

        B. Scripture proves that God will not abandon the elect to death (20:37 – 38)

     III. External confirmation of Jesus' superior wisdom (20:39 – 40)

Explanation of the Text

20:27 Certain ones of the Sadducees, who deny that there is a resurrection, came up and asked him (προσελθόντες δέ τινες τῶν Σαδδουκαίων, οἱ ἀντιλέγοντες ἀνάστασιν μὴ εἶναι, ἐπηρώτησαν αὐτόν). The Sadducees make the first and only appearance in this gospel (see Acts 4:1; 5:17; 23:6 – 8). Most of what is known about them derives from the writings of those who were hostile to them, but the sources concur that they did not believe in a resurrection or that the soul survives death (see Acts 23:8; Josephus, *J.W.* 2.8.14 §165; *Ant.* 18.1.4 §16; *b. Nid.* 70b). This may be attributable to their rejection of traditions found outside the Pentateuch. The riddle they put to Jesus is aimed at making belief in the resurrection look ridiculous.[1]

Luke has no interest in informing his readers about the Sadducees — who they were or what they believed and why, except for this one crucial issue. They simply serve as a foil that allows Jesus to assert the assurance of the resurrection.

20:28 "Teacher, Moses wrote for us, 'If a man's brother should die, and he had a wife but was childless, he should take his brother's widow to raise up descendants for his brother'" (λέγοντες· διδάσκαλε, Μωϋσῆς ἔγραψεν ἡμῖν, ἐάν τινος ἀδελφὸς ἀποθάνῃ ἔχων γυναῖκα, καὶ οὗτος ἄτεκνος ᾖ, ἵνα λάβῃ ὁ ἀδελφὸς αὐτοῦ τὴν γυναῖκα καὶ ἐξαναστήσῃ σπέρμα τῷ ἀδελφῷ αὐτοῦ). The assumption behind this practice was

---

1. According to a rabbinic tradition in *b. Nid.* 70b, the Sadducees tease their opponents: "Do the resurrected have to go through ritual cleansing because they had contact with a corpse?"

that death cuts off a man's life and threatens to blot out his name forever from Israel if he has no male heirs. The Mosaic law sought to lessen this calamity through the custom of levirate marriage (*levir* is Latin for "husband's brother"). His name may be carried on by the male progeny sired by his brother and the man's surviving wife (Gen 38:8; Deut 25:5–10). The law also lessened the privation for a widowed and childless woman who otherwise would be defenseless with no secure place in her family or society. Josephus points out that this practice made sure that the deceased man's property remained with the relatives (Josephus, *Ant.* 4.8.3 §§254–55).

20:29–33 Now, there were seven brothers. The first one took a wife and died childless. Then the second and the third took her, and likewise the seven died childless. Finally the woman also died. Now in the resurrection, whose wife will the woman be? For the seven had her as a wife (ἑπτὰ οὖν ἀδελφοὶ ἦσαν· καὶ ὁ πρῶτος λαβὼν γυναῖκα ἀπέθανεν ἄτεκνος· καὶ ὁ δεύτερος καὶ ὁ τρίτος ἔλαβεν αὐτήν, ὡσαύτως δὲ καὶ οἱ ἑπτὰ οὐ κατέλιπον τέκνα καὶ ἀπέθανον. ὕστερον καὶ ἡ γυνὴ ἀπέθανεν. ἡ γυνὴ οὖν ἐν τῇ ἀναστάσει τίνος αὐτῶν γίνεται γυνή; οἱ γὰρ ἑπτὰ ἔσχον αὐτὴν γυναῖκα). The conundrum based on the Mosaic custom would seem to make belief in the resurrection seem outlandish. In their crude example, the first of seven brothers died with no children to carry on his name.[2] Each of the other brothers married the widow in turn, and each of them died childless. Finally the widow died. Barely concealing their sniggers, they ask Jesus, "When they are raised from the dead, whose wife will she be, since they all had her?"

20:34–36 Jesus said to them, "The sons of this age marry and are given in marriage. But those counted worthy to attain that age, that is, the resurrection from the dead, neither marry nor are given in marriage. For they cannot die anymore because they are equal to the angels and are sons of God, being sons of the resurrection" (καὶ εἶπεν αὐτοῖς ὁ Ἰησοῦς· οἱ υἱοὶ τοῦ αἰῶνος τούτου γαμοῦσιν καὶ γαμίσκονται, οἱ δὲ καταξιωθέντες τοῦ αἰῶνος ἐκείνου τυχεῖν καὶ τῆς ἀναστάσεως τῆς ἐκ νεκρῶν οὔτε γαμοῦσιν οὔτε γαμίζονται· οὐδὲ γὰρ ἀποθανεῖν ἔτι δύνανται, ἰσάγγελοι γάρ εἰσιν καὶ υἱοί εἰσιν θεοῦ τῆς ἀναστάσεως υἱοὶ ὄντες).

The first stage of the answer argues two things. First, it asserts that their premise is mistaken. They picture the resurrected life as simply an extension of the life they know on earth, only longer. The two spheres of existence, however, are not comparable. The resurrected are equal to angels (ἰσάγγελοι). Those who are resurrected, like angels, have no need to propagate. They have transcended the "mortal limits of this age."[3] Being "a son of God" is more significant than being the son of some mortal father. Union with God, not producing a quiver full of heirs, ultimately thwarts death.

Second, Jesus raises the more vital question whether all will attain the resurrection. Luke introduces a moral tone to Jesus' words not found in Mark 12:25. Kilgallen notes, "This addition means that, rather than concentrating on the question that the Sadducees pose to him, Jesus thinks it vastly more important to concentrate on requirements for entry into the life to come."[4] The implication is that not all (such as his questioners) are worthy. It recalls questions raised earlier by

---

2. These seven brothers contrast with the seven brothers, martyred for their faith, who die trusting in God and the resurrection (2 Macc 7:1–42; see 4 Macc 7:19; 16:24–25; see the story of Sarah whose seven husbands died before she married

Tobias, Tob 3:7–17; 6:10–8:18).

3. Grangaard, *Conflict and Authority*, 118.

4. John J. Kilgallen, "The Sadducees and Resurrection from the Dead: Luke 20,27–40," *Bib* 67 (1986): 482.

the disciples: "Lord, are those who are saved few in number?" (13:23); "Who then can be saved?" (18:26).

20:37 – 38 That the dead are raised Moses also revealed in the "bush passage" where he says, "The Lord is the God of Abraham, the God of Isaac, and the God of Jacob." Now God is not the God of the dead but of the living, for they all live to him (ὅτι δὲ ἐγείρονται οἱ νεκροί, καὶ Μωϋσῆς ἐμήνυσεν ἐπὶ τῆς βάτου, ὡς λέγει κύριον τὸν θεὸν Ἀβραὰμ καὶ θεὸν Ἰσαὰκ καὶ θεὸν Ἰακώβ. θεὸς δὲ οὐκ ἔστιν νεκρῶν ἀλλὰ ζώντων, πάντες γὰρ αὐτῷ ζῶσιν). The second stage of the answer argues from Scripture (Exod 3:15 – 16). Before Scripture was divided up into chapters and verses, one could only refer to the general section in which a specific verse occurs, such as the "bush passage." Moses spoke about more than levirate marriage.

The later rabbis wrestled with the scriptural proof of the resurrection, asking, "How is resurrection derived from the Torah?" (b. Sanh. 90b – 91a). They appeal to various passages (Exod 6:4; 15:1; Num 18:28; 15:31; Deut 11:9, 21; 31:16). Jesus does not start with human possibilities but the nature of God. Those who no longer exist can have no God, so for God to be the God of these patriarchs, God must be the God of the living. Kilgallen concludes from the context of the citation from Exodus, "When Yahweh identifies Himself as God, he refers to the power on which His love can call; to be Yahweh is to produce only life."[5]

20:39 – 40 Some of the scribes responded, "Teacher, you said it well." For they dared not ask him another question (ἀποκριθέντες δέ τινες τῶν γραμματέων εἶπαν· διδάσκαλε, καλῶς εἶπας. οὐκέτι γὰρ ἐτόλμων ἐπερωτᾶν αὐτὸν οὐδέν). Who these scribes are makes no difference to Luke. They serve as another witness to confirm Jesus' mastery of the Scriptures. Jesus silences his opponents who deny that there is a resurrection, and they now slink away defeated. The point has been made.

Theology in Application

1. Belief in the Resurrection

Jesus challenges the Sadducees' assumption that resurrection life in the world to come will be like life on earth, only longer. Such carnal views of the afterlife offering the promise of uninterrupted earthly delights remain widely shared today. Jesus' cursory remarks offer few clues about the resurrection life, except that it will be totally dissimilar from this worldly one. It is beyond the capability of our human, corporeal minds to imagine. Paul's citation in 1 Cor 2:9 is apt, "What no eye has seen, what no ear has heard, and what no human mind has conceived — the things God has prepared for those who love him." Jesus' response to the Sadducees turns attention away from speculation about the nature of the life to come to preparation for it in this life.

Jesus does not offer objective, mathematical proof to refute those who deny the resurrection. His answer is grounded in the testimony of Scripture and faith in God. Looking for indubitable proof kills faith. The most important facts of life cannot be

---

5. Ibid., 491.

proven. Take, for example, the fact that your spouse loves you and is faithful. If you wanted to prove it, you could hire a private investigator to tail the spouse to make sure; but it would prove nothing and kill the love. Proof comes from living with someone and being able to look back and see the evidence of love and commitment from past events.

The proof text that Jesus cites from the law assumes a long story behind the names of Abraham, Isaac, and Jacob. As Schweizer observes, these names reveal that God is not God in general but the God of Abraham, Isaac, and Jacob, the God who binds himself to individuals. One learns from the story of God's relationship with these men that "it is not only true as long as this individual will be strong and good; it will also be true when he or she will be weak or low." God "does not elect anybody in order to throw him in the trash can. As God's presence with me does not cease when I am sleeping or dreaming or irresponsible in a fever or unconscious, it will not cease when death overcomes me. If God did not forsake Israel, even when it turned away from him, how should he leave the individual in death?"[6]

One also learns from the "bush passage" that God will not abandon his people forever to be slaves in Israel but will deliver them out of their bondage. In the same way, God does not abandon the elect to the power of Sheol but will deliver them from death in the resurrection. As Talbert states it: "when God has a relationship with someone, that relationship is not terminated by death: God will not allow an enemy of his, death, to destroy that which means so much to him (cf. Rom. 8:35 – 39)."[7]

The last phrase in v. 38, "they all live to him," finds parallels in 4 Macc 7:19 and 16:25 (see also 4 Macc 13:17). It implies that any perspective that limits itself to this finite, physical world will see the death of a physical body as the end. Those who view death from God's perspective, however, know the full story. The "all" does not imply some universalism but refers in the context to "those counted worthy to attain that age, that is, the resurrection from the dead" (20:35). They may vanish from the face of the earth, but they do not vanish into nothingness. They live to God because God gives them life.

Christianity has had a positive effect on society. Women are no longer repeatedly expected to marry their brothers-in-law simply to perpetuate the name of her husband with a male heir. The story of Tamar and Judah (Gen 38) bears out how that situation does not make for a promising marital relationship. Because of Christian moral influence over the centuries, parents adopt children out of compassion for them and give them love and hope for a better future, not simply to continue their own name into the future.

But most adoptive parents want healthy babies or children, which contrasts with God's adoption of us as children of God. Lamott cites the story of parents in her

---

6. Eduard Schweizer, "Resurrection — Fact or Illusion?"
HBT 1 (1979): 144.

7. Talbert, *Reading Luke*, 227.

church who adopted a special-needs child. The adoption agency's questionnaire asked, "'Could you adopt an addicted baby? A child with a terminal illness? With mild retardation? With moderate retardation? With tendencies toward violence against others?" Her pastor interjected, "God is an adoptive parent, too, who chose us all." God says, "Sure, I'll take the kids who are addicted or terminal. I pick all the retarded kids, and of course the sadists. The selfish ones, the liars...."[8]

2. Till Death Do Us Part

Jesus' response to the riddle assumes that since death is no more, marriage is no longer needed to propagate the human species. In this world, family relationships are time limited. How long is one a husband or a wife? The answer from the marriage ceremony is, "Till death do us part." Earthly families live on only in memories and photographs that eventually fade away. Family relationships in the life to come will be transcended. For Jesus, the life here and now is to be governed by the values of life to come. Therefore, life cannot be totally centered around the biological family (see 1 Cor 7:29 – 31).

Paul affirms that Christians are "children of God" (Rom 8:14 – 15; Gal 3:26; 4:5 – 6), and this passage helps clarify why. Adam as the son of God (3:38) sinned and died. Jesus the Son of God obeyed and was resurrected. Evans explains that those "who believe in Jesus will follow in his steps, no longer subject to death."[9]

8. Lamott, *Traveling Mercies*, 254 – 55.
9. Craig A. Evans, "Jesus and the Spirit: On the Origin and Ministry of the Second Son of God," in *Luke and Scripture: The* *Function of the Sacred Tradition in Luke-Acts* (ed. J. A. Sanders and C. A. Evans; Minneapolis: Fortress, 1993), 45.

Luke 20:41 – 21:4

Literary Context

One by one, Jesus has overmastered all the religious authorities determined to do him in with trick questions. He now takes the offensive and asks his own question about David's Son, which recalls the acclamation of the blind man on the outskirts of Jericho (18:38 – 39) and the shouts of those celebrating his royal entry into Jerusalem (19:38). He poses his own exegetical riddle that asks: What is the relationship of the Messiah to David? He hints that "the better category for making sense of the Messiah is 'Lord' (cf. 2:11)."[1] That Jesus is Lord will be made manifest by his resurrection by God (24:34; Acts 2:36). Therefore only a few could answer the question correctly before the resurrection.

The mention of scribes devouring the houses of widows leads into a story that contrasts the gift of an impoverished widow to the temple coffers with the gifts of the rich. The false piety of the scribes who make a show of long prayers while fleecing widows matches the false piety of the rich who make large, public donations to the temple in the presence of a widow with only two mites to her name. Presumably, this widow is one whose house has been devoured (20:47). Marshall comments, "If the leaders of Jewish religion treated such pious people in the way criticised by Jesus in 20:47, it followed that the system was ripe for judgment. It is no accident that the prophecy of the destruction of the temple follows."[2] Those who deprive aliens, orphans, and widows of justice are cursed (Deut 27:19), and any abuse of widows will bring God's judgment (Exod 22:22 – 24; Isa 10:1 – 4; Ps 94:1 – 7).

The touching vignette of a widow who gives all she has to God with no thought for the morrow complements Jesus' entry into the temple when he drove out the stall keepers and pronounced the place a "hideout for bandits" (19:46). It recalls the warning in Mal 3:5:

> Then I will draw near to you for judgment; I will be swift to bear witness against the sorcerers, against the adulterers, against those who swear falsely, against those who oppress the hired workers in their wages, the widow and the orphan, against those who thrust aside the alien, and do not fear me, says the LORD of hosts. (NRSV)

---

1. Green, *The Gospel of Luke*, 724.

2. Marshall, *The Gospel of Luke*, 752.

This scene sets up the discourse on the eschatological judgment. The widow's selflessness, giving all her living for God, also prepares for the even greater sacrifice that Jesus himself will make, giving his life for others.

V. Jesus in Jerusalem (19:29 – 21:38)

    B. Jesus' Teaching in the Temple (19:47 – 21:38)

        4. The Question about the Resurrection (20:27 – 40)

        5. The Question about David's Son, Warnings about Self-Absorbed Scribes, and the Example of a Poverty-Stricken Widow (20:41 – 21:4)

          a. Question about the Messiah as David's Son (20:41 – 44)

          b. Warnings against the Scribes (20:45 – 47)

          c. Example of a Widow (21:1 – 4)

        6. The Destruction of the Temple and the Coming of the Son of Man (21:5 – 38)

Main Idea

The Messiah is not "a purely nationalistic figure" but will transcend King David in a way not anticipated by popular interpretation.[3] Self-absorbed impiety and perfunctory piety will be judged by God. The reign of God belongs to those who give their lives wholeheartedly to God's service.

Translation

(See next page.)

Structure and Literary Form

The question about the Messiah as David's Son appears to be a pronouncement story, but those who are addressed do not respond. They have already been silenced (20:40). The question shows up the theological failure of the scribes who have influenced the popular understanding of the Messiah. They fail to recognize from Scripture that he is David's Lord. The next scene castigates them for their moral failures. The third scene contrasts a widow's unpretentious, costly piety with the scribes' impiety and the showy, blasé piety of the rich. The three scenes expose the theological and moral bankruptcy of the leaders associated with the temple.

---

3. Danker, *Jesus and the New Age*, 324 – 25.

Luke 20:41–21:4

20:41	Question	**He said to them,**
		"How is it that people say that the Christ is David's Son?
42	Scriptural proof	*For David himself says in the book of the Psalms:*
		'The Lord said to my Lord,
		sit at my right hand,
43		*until I make your enemies a footstool for your feet.'* (Ps 110:1)
44	Question (repetition)	*If David therefore calls him Lord, then how is he his Son?"*
45a	Circumstance	As the whole people continued listening,
b		**he said to his disciples,**
46a	Warning	*"Beware of the scribes*
b	Explanation	who *desire to walk around in [special] stoles and*
c		love *greetings in the marketplaces and*
d		*the first seats in the synagogues and*
e		*places of honor at dinners.*
47a		*They devour widows' houses and pray long prayers for show.*
b	Judgment	*They shall receive a greater judgment."*
21:1	Circumstance	**Then he looked up and saw the rich** who were tossing their gifts into the 🕊
		collection chest.
2	Character introduction	**He also saw a certain needy widow** tossing in two cents.
3a	Announcement	**He said,**
		"I say to you truly,
b		*this poor widow has tossed in more than all.*
4a	Explanation	*For these tossed into the gift collection chest [a portion] of their abundance,*
b		*but she from her want threw in her entire living."*

Exegetical Outline

→ **I. Question about the Messiah as David's Son (20:41 – 44)**

    A. Jesus' challenging question about the Messiah as David's Son (20:41)

    B. Complication: David addresses him as Lord in Ps 110 (20:42 – 43)

    C. Implication: the Messiah is more than the Son of David (20:44)

II. Warnings against the scribes (20:45 – 47)

    A. Warning to beware of scribes (20:45 – 47a)

        1. They parade their status (20:45 – 46b)

        2. They crave special recognition (20:46c)

        3. They seek places of honor (20:46d-e)

        4. They oppress the poor (20:47a)

        5. They cover up their rapacity with showy displays of piety (20:47a)

    B. Warning that they will receive condemnation (20:47b)

III. Example of a widow (21:1 – 4)

    A. The rich put (large) gifts in the treasury (21:1)

    B. A widow gives two pennies (21:2)

    C. Comparison between the two (21:3 – 4)

        1. The rich gave from their overabundance (21:3 – 4a)

        2. The widow gave from her utter poverty (21:4b)

Explanation of the Text

20:41 He said to them, "How is it that people say that the Christ is David's Son?" (εἶπεν δὲ πρὸς αὐτούς· πῶς λέγουσιν τὸν Χριστὸν εἶναι Δαυὶδ υἱόν;). The identity of "them" (αὐτούς) is unspecified, but it is probably aimed at the scribes just mentioned, who took an interest in biblical conundrums. The audience shifts to the disciples in the hearing of the crowds in v. 45 as Jesus openly condemns the scribes, the so-called religious experts. The ones who say that the Christ is David's Son are also left general, which portrays it as conventional wisdom, but most likely this too refers to the scribes. The Sadducees had no interest in speculation about a Davidic Messiah since their power was centered in a priestly aristocracy.

Luke takes for granted that the Messiah is the Son of David (1:32, 69) and identifies Joseph's lineage as belonging to the house of David (1:27; 2:4). This assumption has biblical roots (2 Sam 7:12 – 16; Isa 9:2 – 7; 11:1 – 9; Jer 23:5 – 6; 30:9; 33:14 – 18; Ezek 34:23 – 24; 37:24) and can be found in contemporary Jewish literature (*Pss. Sol.* 17:21; 4QFlor 1.11 – 13; 1QS 9.11; 4; 2 Esd 12:32).

20:42 – 44 For David himself says in the book of the Psalms: "The Lord said to my Lord, sit at my right hand, until I make your enemies a footstool for your feet." If David therefore calls him Lord, then how is he his Son? (αὐτὸς γὰρ Δαυὶδ λέγει ἐν βίβλῳ ψαλμῶν· εἶπεν κύριος τῷ κυρίῳ μου· κάθου ἐκ δεξιῶν μου ἕως ἂν θῶ τοὺς ἐχθρούς σου ὑποπόδιον τῶν ποδῶν σου. Δαυὶδ οὖν κύριον αὐτὸν καλεῖ, καὶ πῶς αὐτοῦ υἱός ἐστιν;). Jesus cites the book of Psalms along with the Law of Moses and the Prophets as pointing prophetically to his resurrection and ascension (24:44). The psalms — in this case Ps 110:1 — also help clarify his identity. The question, "If David therefore calls him Lord, then how is he his Son?" (20:44), suggests that Davidic descent is not the most important thing about the Messiah.

This idea was foreshadowed in Jesus' genealogy. It affirms Jesus' Davidic lineage but identifies him as the son of Joseph with some ambivalence, "as was thought" (3:23). This statement alludes to his virginal conception by the Holy Spirit, which points to a far greater, divine status.

Jesus' question does not deny the Davidic descent of the Messiah, which was well established (*Pss. Sol.* 17:21; Rom.1:3). His answer, however, suggests that "Son of David" is not adequate as a category for understanding "God's Messiah" (23:35). He is not David junior and he is more than a mere human deliverer and king. The argument rests on three premises: The speaker in Ps 110 is David (the Masoretic text and LXX designate it as "a psalm of David"); the one addressed in v. 1 is the Messiah; and the use of "my Lord" implies his superiority over the speaker.[4] Jesus does not explicitly claim to be this Messiah, but his answer is loaded with latent meaning.

First, Jesus' appeal to the psalm redefines the role of the Davidic Messiah. France maintains, "The messianic dominion was not to be won by his own power, but would be conferred on him by God, and would be exercised in a realm higher than that of a national kingship, at the right hand of God."[5] Jesus as Messiah will win no victories on the battlefield but will die a shameful death by crucifixion. Yet he will win an even greater victory over cosmic powers through God's deliverance of him in the resurrection. He is not simply the Messiah of Israel but the Savior of the world. He is heir to David's throne (1:32), yet he will not reign from Jerusalem but from heaven as the "Son of the Most High" (1:32, 35).

Second, Jesus' interpretation connects the Messiah's identity to his "lordship," and the psalm implies "the pre-existence of the Messiah as Lord. The angelic announcement in the infancy narrative declared that a Savior, who is the Messiah, *the Lord* is born in the city of David (2:11)." Elizabeth identifies him as "my Lord" in 1:43. Lee concludes:

> The early Christian belief in Jesus as Lord — if not preexistent Lord — ultimately goes back to something that Jesus himself suggested during his earthly ministry in such a way that the question would probably arise for his audience, especially his disciples as they pondered on what he had said. It is then entirely not out of the question that Jesus could have alluded to himself not only as the long-awaited messiah but as pre-existent Lord, although at the time they would not have picked that up.[6]

Third, Jesus interprets Ps 110:1 as a prophecy awaiting fulfillment. The psalm is taken to affirm the Messiah's ultimate vindication (see 22:69). Jesus has notified his disciples that as the Messiah he will die. Sitting at right hand of God prophesies his exaltation to the place of honor (Acts 2:33 – 35; 5:31; 7:55). At God's right hand, he rules at God's side, has full authority to act on God's behalf, and will vanquish all his enemies.

This passage becomes an important reminder as a prelude to Jesus' passion. The enemies are those who oppose Jesus (not the Gentiles). Danker comments: "Zechariah never dreamed that the 'enemies' (Luke 1:71) might have their headquarters in Jerusalem."[7] They may put Jesus to death but they will not triumph. The enemies to be

4. R. T. France, *Jesus and the Old Testament* (Downers Grove, IL: InterVarsity Press, 1971), 102.

5. Ibid., 103.

6. Aquila H. I. Lee, *From Messiah to Preexistent Son* (WUNT 2/192; Tübingen: Mohr Siebeck, 2005), 231.

7. Danker, *Jesus and the New Age*, 325 – 26.

defeated will extend to all of the cosmic enemies and include even the most feared enemy of all, death (1 Cor 15:24 – 28).

20:45 – 47 As the whole people continued listening, he said to his disciples, "Beware of the scribes who desire to walk around in [special] stoles and love greetings in the marketplaces and the first seats in the synagogues and places of honor at dinners. They devour widows' houses and pray long prayers for show. They shall receive a greater judgment" (ἀκούοντος δὲ παντὸς τοῦ λαοῦ εἶπεν τοῖς μαθηταῖς αὐτοῦ· προσέχετε ἀπὸ τῶν γραμματέων τῶν θελόντων περιπατεῖν ἐν στολαῖς καὶ φιλούντων ἀσπασμοὺς ἐν ταῖς ἀγοραῖς καὶ πρωτοκαθεδρίας ἐν ταῖς συναγωγαῖς καὶ πρωτοκλισίας ἐν τοῖς δείπνοις, οἳ κατεσθίουσιν τὰς οἰκίας τῶν χηρῶν καὶ προφάσει μακρὰ προσεύχονται· οὗτοι λήμψονται περισσότερον κρίμα).

The scribes have been party to the attempts to destroy Jesus (19:47; 20:19, 20, 26), but they are now suddenly singled out, even though they have not been identified as overhearing Jesus' teaching or involved in the attempts to trap him with the question about taxes or the challenge about the resurrection. This diatribe is not a call for the scribes to repent since the warning is issued specifically to the disciples. They are not simply to be on guard against them; they are to avoid becoming like them.

Jesus lists five fatal flaws in the scribes' conduct that are rooted "in a consuming zeal for attention."[8] They are classic examples of those who exalt themselves (14:11; 18:14). (1) They parade about in elaborate stoles that advertise their special status and wealth. (2) They relish receiving accolades in public places. (3) They are the ones who push

and shove to get top billing at banquets and places of honor in religious settings (14:7 – 11). (4) Their long prayers are for show and do not truly address God because they substitute length for substance and urgency in prayer (see 18:9 – 14). Their show of piety covers up their greed. (5) What is worse, their wealth and status derive from oppressing impoverished widows, who are particularly vulnerable (18:2 – 5) and who should receive special care (Acts 6:1). In his "den of robbers" speech, Jeremiah warns that God will dwell in the temple only if they do not oppress the alien, the orphan, and the widow (Jer 7:6).

21:1 Then he looked up and saw the rich who were tossing their gifts into the collection chest (ἀναβλέψας δὲ εἶδεν τοὺς βάλλοντας εἰς τὸ γαζοφυλάκιον τὰ δῶρα αὐτῶν πλουσίους). Jesus looks up from his teaching to watch those who are giving offerings of money for the temple treasury. Whether the gifts are for alms,[9] the temple building,[10] or the sustenance of the temple worship[11] makes no difference. The scene allows Jesus to take one last swipe at the rich who increase their wealth by preying on vulnerable widows or who simply ignore them, which makes them no less culpable.

The "collection chest" is an interpretation of a word that literally means "treasury" or "treasure room" (γαζοφυλάκιον).[12] Johnson goes so far as to contend that it refers to the "chamber of secrets" in the temple where one could give in secret and the poor could receive alms in secret (*m. Šeqal.* 5:6; *Sipre Deut.* 15:10).[13] But one does not throw money into (τοὺς βάλλοντας εἰς) a room, so it is more likely that Luke refers to a receptacle into which the money is dropped. The phrase parallels the one in v. 4, which also is best interpreted as referring to the receptacles. The term "treasury"

8. Resseguie, *Spiritual Landscape*, 94.
9. Johnson, *The Gospel of Luke*, 315.
10. Tiede, *Luke*, 354.

11. Nolland, *Luke*, 3:980.
12. BDAG, 149.
13. Johnson, *The Gospel of Luke*, 315.

applies to the area where the collection chests were found, and by metonymy refers to the thirteen horn-shaped receptacles, wide at the bottom and narrow at the top to prevent theft, set up to collect money for various funds.[14]

The warning in Matt 6:2, "So when you give to the needy, do not announce it with trumpets, as the hypocrites do," may shed light on how Jesus' attention was diverted from his teaching and how he would know how much they gave. This saying does not refer to some trumpet fanfare that people used to call attention to their gifts but to making the trumpet-like receptacles (called šôpᵉrôt) resound noisily as they tossed in their large gifts.[15] One can imagine the loud clang as the rich pitch in their hefty offerings; that would contrast with the faint tinkle made by the widow's two tiny coins.

21:2 He also saw a certain needy widow tossing in two cents (εἶδεν δέ τινα χήραν πενιχρὰν βάλλουσαν ἐκεῖ λεπτὰ δύο). Widows can be identified by their dress, and they are assumed to be impoverished as a matter of course. Luke describes this widow poetically as "needy" (πενιχράν). The "cent" (λεπτόν) was the smallest coin in circulation in Palestine, approximately 1/132 of a denarius, the daily wage of a day laborer (Matt 20:2). If this is all that she had, she is more than simply poor; she has nothing left and now has "beggar's status."[16]

21:3 – 4 He said, "I say to you truly, this poor widow has tossed in more than all. For these tossed into the gift collection chest [a portion] of their abundance, but she from her want threw in her entire living" (καὶ εἶπεν· ἀληθῶς λέγω ὑμῖν ὅτι ἡ χήρα αὕτη ἡ πτωχὴ πλεῖον πάντων ἔβαλεν. πάντες γὰρ οὗτοι ἐκ τοῦ περισσεύοντος αὐτοῖς ἔβαλον εἰς τὰ δῶρα, αὕτη δὲ ἐκ τοῦ ὑστερήματος αὐτῆς πάντα τὸν βίον ὃν εἶχεν ἔβαλεν). The phrase "I say to you truly" (ἀληθῶς λέγω ὑμῖν) introduces examples of discipleship in 9:27 and 12:44. The Greek idiom "they tossed into the gifts" (ἔβαλον εἰς τὰ δῶρα) is strange but parallels the expression in 21:1 so that "the gifts" would be another way to refer, by metonymy, to the "offering-chest." Her "entire living" (πάντα τὸν βίον) refers to all that she has to subsist on (8:43; 15:12, 30).

Her gift is so meager that it is hardly worth noticing, but Jesus extols it over the more substantial amounts dropped in by the rich because this woman gives what common sense and the instinct for self-preservation would say she should not give. She had next to nothing and now has nothing. The contrast is between one who gives from her "want" or "lack" (ἐκ τοῦ ὑστερήματος αὐτῆς) and those who give from their surplus, between one who gives everything and those who give a portion. The translation "[a portion] of their abundance" (ἐκ τοῦ περισσεύοντος) highlights the partitive genitive. After their donations, they are still rich.

The rich might be as extravagant as the widow and lay all their wealth on the line for some risky investment that promises to repay with even greater riches, but they are unlikely to do as this widow does, to expose themselves to financial insecurity (or in her case, to worsen it) by means of charity. Her sacrificial giving demonstrates selfless devotion to God (like Anna's, 2:36 – 38) and models what it means to give back to God what is God's (20:25). She gives her whole self. Luke uses the incident to demonstrate "the distinction between the righteous and the wicked, between those who serve God and those who do not" (Mal 3:18).

---

14. M. Šeqal. 6:5 (see 2:1, 6:1) refers to receptacles set up to collect for the temple's various sacrifices ("new shekel dues," "old shekel dues," "bird offerings," "young birds for the holocaust"), for the temple's accouterments ("wood," "frankincense,"

"gold for the mercy-seat"), and six for "freewill offerings."

15. Neil J. McEleney, "Does the Trumpet Sound or Resound? An Interpretation of Matthew 6:2," *ZNW* 76 (1985): 43 – 46.

16. Grangaard, *Conflict and Authority*, 168.

Theology in Application

1. Jesus: Son of David, David's Lord

Jesus discredits the popular notion that the Messiah would be a nationalistic figure who would restore Israel to its former glory in the gilded age of David. Jesus is the Messiah, the Son of David, but he is far more. The question Jesus asks, "If David therefore calls him Lord, then how is he his Son?" goes unanswered in the scene, but Luke provides the answer in his sequel work. In Acts 2:29 – 36, Peter provides the answer in citing Pss 16:10 and 110:1 and applying these passages to God's raising Jesus from the dead. David speaks of a "holy one" who "was not abandoned to the realm of the dead, nor did his body see decay" (Acts 2:27, 31, citing Ps 16:10). He could not be speaking about himself; he died and was buried, and his tomb was standing in their midst as a monument (Acts 2:29). God swore to David that one of his descendants would ascend his throne. He is identified as a prophet (2:30a), and David predicted the resurrection of the Messiah (Acts 2:31, repeating Ps 16:10).

Peter concludes that David was pointing to Jesus, whom God raised up, and he and the other apostles are witnesses to that fact. Jesus is now exalted at the right hand of God. (Acts 2:32 – 33). The psalms do not refer to David himself because he "did not ascend in heaven" (Acts 2:34) to the right hand of God. Psalm 110:1 is then cited as proof of the ascension of Jesus. The conclusion is that David refers to Jesus who was crucified and whom God has made both Lord and Messiah (Acts 2:36).

Peter's sermon at Pentecost helps explain the juxtaposition of the question about the resurrection and the question about David's Son. The resurrection of Jesus is crucial to his identification as the Lord whom the psalmist addresses. Were there no possibility of resurrection, none of this could be true. With Jesus' resurrection by God and his ascension to heaven, whatever paradigms might be swirling around in people's minds about the Messiah, how he will appear and what he will do, must be reassessed according to what happened to Jesus.

If there were no expectations of a suffering Messiah in the time of Jesus, previous assumptions must be abandoned. Believing that a man who dies on the cross is the Messiah and the Son of God requires a radical shift in worldview.

2. Jesus at the Right Hand of God

While Jesus as the Son of David may seem to have little resonance with contemporary audiences who are not steeped in Jewish messianic expectations, the image of Jesus enthroned at the right hand of God is significant. It does not simply identify Jesus' location or serve as a mark of honor but denotes that he has been given the reins of power. He has dominion over the entire universe (Eph 1:20 – 23). He is not an absentee Lord who looks down from some heavenly perch but is ever present and active in creation through the Spirit: "All the self-imposed limitations of humanity ceased when he sat down on high."[17]

The image of God's right hand is used for God's involvement in creating the world (Isa 48:13), bringing deliverance to Israel and shattering the enemy (Exod 15:6, 12), bringing them to the Promised Land (Ps 44:1 – 3), and showing steadfast love and saving and rescuing those who take refuge in God (Pss 17:7; 60:5). Jesus adopts this role in re-creation and in a new deliverance from sin and death. The imagery is powerfully applied to Jesus in the rest of the New Testament. Paul affirms that after Jesus was raised and is at the right hand of God, he intercedes so effectively for us that no power, no circumstance can separate us from his love (Rom 8:34 – 39). The image is also used to exhort Christians to live their lives under this perspective (Col 3:1).

3. Frauds and the Truehearted

Jesus does not challenge the scribes for their misreading of Scripture but for their behavior. Behavior, not bad exegesis, disqualifies them as legitimate interpreters. Danker cites Epictetus (*Diatr.* 3.23.35) to show that the scribes did not have a corner on vanity or venality. They put on "a fancy cloak, or dainty mantle, and mount the speaker's stand."[18] Jesus does not warn the disciples against coming under the influence of the scribes but against becoming like them.

A story in rabbinic literature has a priest turn away a woman bringing a handful of meal as an offering. God says, however, to accept it because she has brought her life (*Lev. Rab.* 107a). Jesus' interpretation of the widow's gift makes the same point. What others might think unwise or too paltry to count, God accepts. She has given her "life." This radical self-abandonment in devotion to God prepares for Jesus, who will give even more, his very life for others. The implication is that God welcomes giving that comes out of deep sacrifice, not gifts that are simply the leftovers of abundance. This explains why tithing is not a New Testament concept, because it allows one to ignore how much one keeps.[19]

The Macedonians were models of the kind of giving Jesus praises. They gave generously beyond their ability to give "in the midst of a very severe trial" and out of "their extreme poverty." But most importantly, "they gave themselves first of all to the Lord, and then by the will of God also to us" (2 Cor 8:2 – 5). They did not plead poverty to escape from giving but pled with Paul for the opportunity to give. The

---

17. Herbert Lockyer, *All the Doctrines of the Bible* (Grand Rapids: Zondervan, 1964), 57.

18. Danker, *Jesus and the New Age*, 327.

19. A. G. Wright ("The Widow's Mites: Praise or Lament? — A Matter of Context," *CBQ* 44 [1982]: 256 – 65) contends that Jesus laments that the widow's gift leaves her penniless: "She has been taught and encouraged by religious leaders to donate as she does, and Jesus condemns the value system that motivates her action" (262). Fitzmyer, *Luke*, 2:1321, and Green, *The Gospel of Luke*, 728 – 29, endorse this interpretation, and I agree that it applies to the parallel in Mark (see Garland, *Mark*, 482 – 83). But this reading does not fit the context for Luke, where the emphasis falls on what is the true measure of one's gift.

New Testament does not demand that one give to the point of destitution. When Paul gives the Corinthians instructions about the grace-gift for the saints, he knows that many in the church lived at subsistence levels and tells them that their gift is to come out of their surplus. Paul instructs them, "On the first day of every week, each one of you should set aside a sum of money in keeping with your income" (1 Cor 16:2). The phrase "in keeping with your income" is literally a passive voice ("what [each one] has been prospered"), which reminds them that it is God who has given them their abundance, and they only give back to God what is God's in the first place.

The widow represents "the poor" whom Jesus pronounced "blessed" (6:20) and to whom he preached good news in the temple. But she will not receive good news from the temple cult or from the temple management. The story about the early church's care for widows (Acts 6:1 – 6) reveals that injustice to widows can occur among Christians and is not limited to the temple. The Hellenist widows were neglected in the early church until something was done to correct the problem. Those who are full of the Spirit and wisdom must care for the needy widows in their midst. Otherwise, they expose themselves as frauds.

Luke 21:5 – 38

Literary Context

Jesus moves from discussing true and false types of religious behavior to a discussion of the destruction of the temple, which has proven false under the priestly leadership. Jesus' final teaching in the temple announces its imminent demise, but he isolates that calamity from the coming of the Son of Man. It is not the final eschatological event.

This discourse comprises the third eschatological oration in Luke. Each one is longer with more specific details than the previous one. The first (12:35 – 40) places an emphasis on watchfulness because the Son of Man will come at an unexpected hour. The second (17:20 – 37) places an emphasis on the suddenness and celestial manifestation of the Son of Man's coming and the rescue of the righteous from the destruction that awaits the unrighteous, who will be left. The present discourse places an emphasis on the destruction of the temple, which will occur during the interim and it is not a harbinger of the eschaton.

The second half of the discourse (21:25 – 38) reiterates the assurance of the second discourse: the coming of the Son of Man will be visible to all and the righteous will be redeemed from the trouble coming upon the world. The conclusion (21:34 – 36) reiterates the warning of the first discourse that disciples are to be ready (12:40). The parable of the fig tree (21:29 – 33) is sandwiched in between to underscore the certainty of Jesus' prophecies concerning the destruction of the temple and the coming of the Son of Man.

Main Idea

Tumultuous times are coming before the end, and disciples will be persecuted for their faith. During the time of waiting, they must remain calm, wise, faithful, and prepared through prayer, resting in the assurance that they will be delivered in the end.

Translation

Luke 21:5–38

21:5	Introduction	As some were remarking about the temple,
		how it was adorned with beautiful stones and gifts⳥
		consecrated to God,
		he said,
6a	Pronouncement	*"As for these things that you see,*
b		*the days will come*
c		*in which no stone will be left upon another and*
		will not be destroyed."
7a	Questions	**They asked him,**
b	(Part 1)	*"Teacher, when then will these things happen*
c	(Part 2)	*and what will be the sign that they are about to take place?"*
8a	Warning admonition	**He said,**
		"See that you are not led astray!
b	Explanatory clause	*For many will come in my name announcing,*
		'I am he!' and
		'The time has drawn near!'
c	Warning admonition	*Do not go after them!"*
9a	Circumstance	*Whenever you hear about wars and uprisings,*
b	Admonition	*do not be terrified,*
c	Explanatory clause	*for it is necessary for these things to take place first,*
d	Pronouncement	*but the end does not [follow] immediately."*
10	Prophecy about the interim	**Then he began to tell them,**
		"A nation will rise against a nation and
		a kingdom against a kingdom.
11		*There will be great earthquakes and famines,*
		outbreaks of disease in various places,
		horrors, and
		great signs from heaven.
12	Warnings	*Before these things [take place],*
		they will lay their hands on you and persecute you,
		handing you over to synagogues and jails and
		hauling you before kings and governors
		because of my name.

Continued on next page.

Continued from previous page.

13	Result	It will turn out for you to be [an opportunity] to bear witness.
14	Admonition	*Therefore,* determine in your minds not to prepare your court defense in↵
		advance,
15	Explanatory clause	*for* I will give you a voice and wisdom,
		which all who oppose you will not be able to↵
		counteract or contradict.

16	Warning	You will be betrayed even by parents, brothers, relatives, and friends,
		and they will kill some of you.
17		*And* you will be hated by all
		because of my name,

| 18 | Assurance | *and* not a hair from your head will perish. |
| 19 | Admonition | By your endurance, gain your souls! |

20a	Circumstance	When you see Jerusalem encircled by armies,
b		know then that her desolation has drawn near.
21a	Admonitions	Then let those who are in Judea flee to the hills, and
b		those in her midst get out, and
c		those in the countryside not enter.

| 22 | Explanatory clause | Because these are [the] days of vengeance |
| | | so that all that has been written may be fulfilled. |

23a	Lament	Woe to those who are pregnant and those who are nursing infants in those↵
		days,
b	Prophetic explanatory clause	*for* great calamity will fall upon the land and wrath against this people.
24a	Prophecy	Some will fall by the edge of the sword
b		*and* others will be led into captivity to all the nations
c		*and* Jerusalem will be trampled by the Gentiles,
d		until the times of the Gentiles are fulfilled.

25a		There shall be signs in the sun, moon, and stars and
b		on earth distress among the nations,
		anxiety over the uproar *from* the sea and↵
		surging waves.

26		People will pass out *from* fearful foreboding over what is coming upon the↵
		world,
		for the powers of heaven will be shaken.
27	Culmination	Then they shall see the Son of Man coming *on* a cloud *with* power and↵
		great glory.

| 28 | Assuring admonition | As these things begin to take place, |
| | | stand up straight and raise your heads because your redemption draws near." |

Continued on next page.

29	Illustration	**And he told a parable to them,** *"Look at the fig tree and all the trees.*
30		*Whenever they put out leaves,* *you can see for yourselves and* *know that the summer is already near.*
31	Admonition	*So also you, . . .* *when you see these things taking place,* *. . . know that the reign of God is near.*
32	Affirmation	*Amen, I tell you, this generation will not pass away until all things take place.*
33		*Heaven and earth will pass away,* *but my words will not pass away.*
34	Admonition	*Be alert so that your hearts are not burdened by dissipation and⮠* *drunkenness and worries of life and* *that day catch you*
35a		*like an unexpected trap.*
b	Explanatory clause	*For it will come upon all who dwell on the face of the whole earth.*
36	Admonition	*Keep alert in every time,* *praying that you may be strong enough to flee all these things that are⮠* *about to take place and* *to stand before the Son of Man."*
37	Concluding scene	**He was in the temple teaching every day** **and he would go out every night and stay on the mountain that is called "Olives."**
38		**And all the people would get up early in the morning to hear him in the temple.**

Structure and Literary Form

Questions about the temple's destruction and signs related to the end of the world wrap around the warning of the disciples' persecution during the necessary interim — after Jesus' death and prior to Jerusalem's destruction, and then after that event to the end of history. The frequency of the admonitions in this section reveals that Jesus is not interested in imparting information about the timing of Jerusalem's coming destruction or the coming of the end. The discourse's purpose is primarily "exhortative in function," not "informative."[1] Jesus wishes to prescribe wise conduct during the tempestuous interim. The key verbs are "see," "do not …," "determine," "gain by endurance," "flee," "stand up straight," "keep alert," and "pray."

Giblin structures the passage around the three times that the narrator notes Jesus'

---

1. Anders E. Nielsen, *Until It is Fulfilled: Lukan Eschatology according to Luke 22 and Acts 20* (WUNT 2/126; Tübingen: Mohr Siebeck, 2000), 215.

own words: "he said" (ὁ δὲ εἶπεν, 21:8); "he began to tell them" (ἔλεγεν αὐτοῖς, 21:10); "he told a parable to them" (εἶπεν παραβολὴν αὐτοῖς, 21:29). Jesus' answer is divided into three stages: (1) a negatively phrased warning about the false signs of the end time (21:8 – 9); (2) three movements that give a positively phrased answer about the true end-time scenario (21:10 – 11), prior necessities for the disciples (21:12 – 19), and a development of the answers in 21:10 – 11 (21:20 – 28); and (3) two movements on the proximity of the kingdom (21:29 – 33) and a concluding exhortation on how to avoid these things and to stand before the Son of Man (29:34 – 36).[2]

The structure may also follow a chiastic pattern:

A   Questions concerning the temple's demise and the end (21:5 – 7)
    B   The signs preceding the temple's demise (21:8 – 11)
       C   The persecution of the disciples (21:12 – 19)
    B′   The destruction of Jerusalem (21:20 – 24)
A′   The end of the world and the coming of the Son of Man (21:25 – 33)

The problem with this structure is that it leaves out concluding admonitions about being prepared (21:34 – 36) and the concluding reference to Jesus' teaching the crowds in the temple (21:37 – 38), which marks the end of the inclusio that began in 19:47 – 48. It is best to see this section as two panels, the first treating preparation for the destruction of Jerusalem (21:5 – 24) and the second, preparation for the coming of the end (21:25 – 36), with a summary wrapping up Jesus' teaching in the temple (21:37 – 38).

Exegetical Outline

➡ **I. Questions concerning the temple's demise (21:5 – 7)**

   II. The signs preceding the temple's demise (21:8 – 11)

   III. The persecution of the disciples (21:12 – 19)

   IV. The destruction of Jerusalem (21:20 – 24)

   V. The end of the world and the coming of the Son of Man (21:25 – 28)

      A. Signs of crisis in the heavens (21:25a)

      B. Signs of crisis on earth (21:25b)

      C. Panic among people (21:26)

      D. Coming of the Son of Man (21:27)

      E. Assurance that followers will be rescued (21:28)

   VI. The parable of the fig tree and the certainty of the fulfillment of Jesus' words (21:29 – 33)

   VII. Concluding admonitions: watch and pray (21:34 – 36)

   VIII. Jesus' teaching in the temple to popular acclaim (21:37 – 38)

---

2. Giblin, *The Destruction of Jerusalem according to Luke's Gospel*, 78 – 87.

Explanation of the Text

21:5 As some were remarking about the temple, how it was adorned with beautiful stones and gifts consecrated to God, he said (καί τινων λεγόντων περὶ τοῦ ἱεροῦ ὅτι λίθοις καλοῖς καὶ ἀναθήμασιν κεκόσμηται εἶπεν). In Luke, Jesus does not leave the temple for the Mount of Olives to teach about the end of the temple and the end of time (as in Mark 13:2–3) but delivers his discourse in the temple complex. His admonitory instruction is precipitated by "some" (τινων) bystanders, not the disciples, admiring the temple's stones and adornment. The mention of "the gifts consecrated to God" (ἀναθήμασιν) along with the beautiful stones ties this scene back to the widow and the rich making offerings to the temple (21:1–4; contrast Mark 13:1–2, which mentions the "buildings").

These onlookers respond like excited tourists dazzled by the temple's ornamental splendor, and Jesus appears to overhear them. The sanctuary's measurements were rather modest; and since they were dictated by the law, they could not be expanded. To match his aspirations of grandeur, King Herod determined to enhance the temple's significance by increasing the size of its setting (see Josephus, *J.W.* 1.21.1 §401). Construction began in 20/19 BC (see John 2:20) and finished in AD 62. It was widely acclaimed as a glorious complex of buildings (Pliny, *Nat.* 5.15.70; Tacitus, *Hist.* 5.8; *b. Sukkah* 51b). Some of the stones that went into this expansion were prodigious in size (the "massive stones" evoke awe in Mark 13:1).

The temple was a showcase for the quality of Herodian masonry and stone-carving as evidenced by the extant passageways leading up to the temple forecourt. They had elaborate geometric and floral motifs with vines and acanthus leaves.

Josephus also mentions columns of the "purest white marble" in the porticoes (*J.W.* 5.5.2 §190). A golden vine was wreathed around the entrance into the sanctuary (Josephus, *J.W.* 5.5.4 §§210–12). *M. Middot* 3:8 records: "Whosoever gave a leaf, or a berry, or a cluster as a freewill-offering, he brought it and [the priests] hung it thereon." Josephus describes the golden vine as a "marvel of size and artistry to all who saw with what costliness of material it had been constructed" (*Ant.* 15.11.3 §395).

21:6 "As for these things that you see, the days will come in which no stone will be left upon another and will not be destroyed" (ταῦτα ἃ θεωρεῖτε ἐλεύσονται ἡμέραι ἐν αἷς οὐκ ἀφεθήσεται λίθος ἐπὶ λίθῳ ὃς οὐ καταλυθήσεται). Jesus' response begins with a pendant nominative, and he speaks to the disciples in the hearing of the starry-eyed onlookers. His prophecy that no stone will be left upon another repeats his prediction in 19:44. The temple, despite its beauty and its sanctity as the presumed locale of God's presence, will be destroyed once again (see Jer 22:5; Mic 3:12). "The days will come" (ἐλεύσονται ἡμέραι) does not refer to some distant eschatological future but to the near future (see 5:35; 17:22; 19:43; 23:29).[3] The temple's massive grandeur can foster a false sense of invulnerability and safety. Those mesmerized by the temple's magnificence will be blind to its looming destruction.

21:7 They asked him, "Teacher, when then will these things happen and what will be the sign that they are about to take place?" (ἐπηρώτησαν δὲ αὐτὸν λέγοντες· διδάσκαλε, πότε οὖν ταῦτα ἔσται καὶ τί τὸ σημεῖον ὅταν μέλλῃ ταῦτα γίνεσθαι;). Those asking the question are probably

---

3. Bridge, *Where the Eagles Are Gathered*, 117–18.

not the circle of disciples, since only those who are on the outside address him as "teacher" in Luke (7:40; 9:38; 10:25; 11:45; 12:13; 18:18; 19:39; 20:21, 28, 39). Jesus is teaching in the hearing of the people (20:45), and Luke tells us that they gather every day in the temple to hear him (21:37 – 38).

The question in Luke's text differs from the parallel in Mark 13:4 in three ways. Luke does not have "all" before the second ταῦτα (lit., "these things"), uses the verb "to take place" (γίνεσθαι) rather than "to be finished" (συντελεῖσθαι, "to be fulfilled"), and introduces the question with "then" (οὖν). The result is that the question about "these things" would seem to be tied to the series of events preceding the temple's destruction and not the eschatological drama associated with the end of the world.[4] Others argue that there is no distinction between the temple catastrophe and the universal eschatological perspective in other parts of the discourse (see 21:9, 19, 24, 27 – 28, 31, 33).[5]

Jesus places the destruction of the temple in the context of eschatological events leading up to the end of the world, but that event does not mark the immediate end of the world. It is one example of the political upheavals, though a preeminent one for Israel, that are to come before the end. They are living in the last days (Acts 2:17), but the timing of the end cannot be too narrowly restricted to events surrounding the temple's destruction.

The questioners want to know the "sign" that can give them ample warning before these things happen. Josephus, after the fact, points to portents that had signaled the destruction of the city: a star that looked like a sword standing over the city, a cow giving birth to a lamb, strange lights seen in the sanctuary, a comet that lasted a year. He also mentions false prophets who told the people to go

to the temple to receive the signs of their salvation (see *J.W.* 6.5.1 – 3 §§274 – 85). These signs tend to be more appropriate for "Ripley's Believe It or Not." By contrast, Jesus will identify as "signs" realities that humans have grown accustomed to as part of the normal course of life (war, earthquakes, famines, plagues, terrifying events, 21:10 – 11). These events are difficult to discern as "signs" — particularly when people judge participating in a war to be evidence of one's devotion to God, as in the case of the Jewish revolt against Rome.

21:8 He said, "See that you are not led astray! For many will come in my name announcing, 'I am he!' and 'The time has drawn near!' Do not go after them!" (ὁ δὲ εἶπεν· βλέπετε μὴ πλανηθῆτε· πολλοὶ γὰρ ἐλεύσονται ἐπὶ τῷ ὀνόματί μου λέγοντες· ἐγώ εἰμι, καί· ὁ καιρὸς ἤγγικεν. μὴ πορευθῆτε ὀπίσω αὐτῶν). Jesus' response is directed to the disciples, who can understand and heed what he is saying. His answer ignores the question of "when?" and gives little specific information about any sign because there is no one "sign." He simply warns them not to be deceived by those claiming to come in his name and announcing, "I am he." These may claim to be messianic deliverers or to have authority to speak and act for God (see Acts 5:36 – 37; 21:38). This warning assumes that Jesus will be physically absent from his disciples, and that the period of his absence will be long enough that wishful fantasies of quick deliverance will make them susceptible to imposters.

The cry "The time has drawn near!" parallels Lam 4:18 in the context of Jerusalem's imminent destruction and basically means "our days are numbered." It may be a call to battle stations

4. So Fitzmyer, *Luke*, 2:1331; Schweizer, *Luke*, 314; and Bridge, *Where the Eagles Are Gathered*, 118 – 19.

5. So Marshall, *The Gospel of Luke*, 762, 764; Bock, *Luke*, 2:1663, 1666; Nielsen, *Until It Is Fulfilled*, 213; and Vittorio

Fusco, "Problems of Structure in Luke's Eschatological Discourse," in *Luke and Acts* (ed. G. O'Collins and G. Marconi; New York/Mahwah: Paulist, 1991), 73 – 74.

or to get ready to receive deliverance from God. Josephus records that during the war with Rome, a large crowd met their deaths when a false prophet proclaimed "that God commanded them to go up to the temple court, to receive the tokens of their deliverance." He continues:

> Numerous prophets, indeed, were at this period suborned by the tyrants to delude the people by bidding them to await help from God, in order that desertions might be checked and that those who were above fear and precaution might be encouraged by hope. In adversity man is quickly persuaded; but when the deceiver actually pictures release from prevailing horrors, the sufferer wholly abandons himself to expectation. (*J.W.* 6.5.2 §§286 – 87)

Jesus gives fair warning that even when unimaginable and frightening catastrophes occur, like the temple's destruction, the end of the world is not yet.

21:9 Whenever you hear about wars and uprisings, do not be terrified, for it is necessary for these things to take place first, but the end does not [follow] immediately (ὅταν δὲ ἀκούσητε πολέμους καὶ ἀκαταστασίας, μὴ πτοηθῆτε· δεῖ γὰρ ταῦτα γενέσθαι πρῶτον, ἀλλ᾽ οὐκ εὐθέως τὸ τέλος). Chaos is not a sign of the end, but a sign of human fallenness throughout the ages. Jeremiah warned about it (Jer 51:46), as did Daniel (Dan 11:44). Wars and uprisings, which comprise human history, are "the unfolding of miscalculations"[6] when nations seek to get hold of what they want or think they deserve. As a result,

international unrest, famine, and pestilence will be inevitable, but no precise timetable can be charted from these things.

"The end" (τὸ τέλος) refers to the end of the temple.[7] Josephus uses the term in this way (*J.W.* 5.11.2 §459).[8] It is the crack of doom for the temple's world but not for the whole world. The holy city and the temple have been destroyed before in the course of Israel's history, and it did not signify the end of times. The temple's demolition that will occur in the near future is simply a historical event — disastrous to be sure, but not an eschatological turning point. It is the inevitable consequence of the malfeasance of leaders who rejected God's Messiah and his ways and of hotheaded revolutionists who trusted in their own might and engaged in a reckless and futile war.

Jesus therefore admonishes his followers to let these conflagrations take their course, knowing in advance that they must occur and have no part in their ultimate deliverance.[9] These events should spark terror only among those who do not trust that God controls the ultimate outcome of history. Christians are not to panic and are not to join in the fight.

Tacitus's description of the chaotic times of the late 60s fits what Jesus prophesied would happen:

> The history on which I am entering is that of a period rich in disasters, terrible with battles, torn by civil struggles, horrible even in peace. Four emperors fell by the sword; there were three civil wars, more foreign wars, and often both at the same time.... Italy was distressed by disasters

---

6. The phrase comes from Barbara W. Tuchman, *Stillwell and the American Experience in China, 1911 – 45* (New York: Macmillan, 1970), 132.

7. So Fitzmyer, *Luke*, 2:1336; Nolland, *Luke*, 3:992.

8. Bridge, *Where the Eagles Are Gathered*, 120. He notes (121) that Josephus uses similar language to describe the temple's demise: "do not be led astray" *(J.W.* 6.5.4 §313); "many will come" *(J.W.* 6.5.2 §286); "in my name" *(J.W.* 6.5.3 §§300 – 309);

"the time is near" *(J.W.* 6.5.4 §312); "do not go out after them" *(J.W.* 6.5.2 §286); "wars" (61 times); "insurrections" (24 times); "do not be alarmed" *(J.W.* 6.4.6 §255); "earthquake" *(J.W.* 6.6.3 §§299 – 300); "famines" (38 times); "pestilences" *(J.W.* 6.9.3 §421); "terrors" *(J.W.* 6.5.2 §§290 – 309); "great signs from heaven" *(J.W.* 6.5.3 §§281, 296 – 300).

9. Nolland, *Luke*, 3:991.

unknown before or returning after the lapse of the ages.... Beside the manifold misfortunes that befell mankind there were prodigies in the sky and on the earth, warnings given by thunderbolts, and prophecies of the future, both joyful and gloomy, uncertain and clear. (*Hist.* 1.2.3)

21:10 – 11 Then he began to tell them, "A nation will rise against a nation and a kingdom against a kingdom. There will be great earthquakes and famines, outbreaks of disease in various places, horrors, and great signs from heaven" (τότε ἔλεγεν αὐτοῖς· ἐγερθήσεται ἔθνος ἐπ᾽ ἔθνος καὶ βασιλεία ἐπὶ βασιλείαν. σεισμοί τε μεγάλοι καὶ κατὰ τόπους λιμοὶ καὶ λοιμοὶ ἔσονται, φόβητρά τε καὶ ἀπ᾽ οὐρανοῦ σημεῖα μεγάλα ἔσται). This translation assumes that the singular anarthrous nouns for nation (ἔθνος) and kingdom (βασιλεία) are a specific reference to the Jewish nation (7:5; 23:2) revolting against Rome, which will ultimately precipitate Jerusalem's destruction.[10] This saying does not predict isolated skirmishes in far-off places or a general conflagration. Jesus is concerned here only with the destiny of Israel. Here is the sign: when Israel rises up against Rome, the demolition of the temple is at hand.

Natural disasters will occur. These will trigger famine, which will trigger epidemics and add to the miseries of the victims. Jesus does not clarify what will be the nature of the "horrors" or "dreadful portents" (φόβητρα) and the great signs from heaven.

21:12 Before these things [take place], they will lay their hands on you and persecute you, handing you over to synagogues and jails and hauling you before kings and governors because of

my name (πρὸ δὲ τούτων πάντων ἐπιβαλοῦσιν ἐφ᾽ ὑμᾶς τὰς χεῖρας αὐτῶν καὶ διώξουσιν, παραδιδόντες εἰς τὰς συναγωγὰς καὶ φυλακάς, ἀπαγομένους ἐπὶ βασιλεῖς καὶ ἡγεμόνας ἕνεκεν τοῦ ὀνόματός μου). "Before these things," that is, the revolt against Rome and the accompanying disaster that will befall the city (vv. 9 – 11), disciples will be persecuted. Luke inserts the warnings about this persecution (vv. 12 – 19) in between the preceding signs leading up to the temple's destruction (vv. 8 – 11) and the description of Jerusalem's desolation (vv. 20 – 24).

This section foretells the story of the disciples' mission in the face of bitter opposition before the outbreak of the fateful war against Rome in AD 66 – 70. Acts narrates various persecutions of Christ's followers using the same language.[11] Paul and Barnabas consider persecution to be the normal state of affairs: "We must go through many hardships to enter the kingdom of God" (Acts 14:22). The disciples' crime will be their allegiance to Jesus ("because of my name," see 6:22)[12] and proclaiming repentance and forgiveness of sins in his name to all the nations (24:47). The cause of the persecution (see also v. 17) is also the basis of the positive outcome.[13] They will be rescued by him.

Knowing that Jesus predicted that this persecution would occur relieves his followers from worrying that things have gone badly wrong when it takes place. Everything is moving according to God's seemingly inscrutable plan (see 11:49 – 51).

21:13 It will turn out for you to be [an opportunity] to bear witness (ἀποβήσεται ὑμῖν εἰς μαρτύριον). The narrative in Acts helps unpack the

10. Johnson, *The Gospel of Luke*, 321.

11. "Lay hands on you" (Acts 4:3, 5:18; 12:1; 21:27); "persecute" (Acts 9:4 – 5; 22:7 – 8; 26:14 – 15); "hand over" (Acts 8:3; 12:4; 21:11; 22:4; 27:1; 28:17); "to synagogues" (Acts 6:9; 9:2; 19:8 – 9; 22:19; 26:11); "jails" (Acts 5:19 – 25; 8:3;

12:4 – 17; 16:23 – 40; 22:4, 19; 26:10); "kings" (Acts 9:15; 12:1; 25:23 – 28:28); "governors" (Acts 23:24, 26, 33; 24:1, 10; 26:30; see also 13:7; 18:12).

12. Acts 4:17 – 18; 5:28, 40 – 41; 9:14 – 16; 21:13; 26:9.

13. Nielsen, *Until It Is Fulfilled*, 226.

meaning of this statement (Acts 4:33; 22:18; 23:11). When the disciples are hauled before authorities, they are not simply defendants on trial but bold witnesses to the gospel.[14] Throughout Acts, the disciples turn the prisoner's dock into a pulpit, ignoring the consequences (Acts 4:5 – 12; 7:1 – 60).

21:14 – 15 Therefore, determine in your minds not to prepare your court defense in advance, for I will give you a voice and wisdom, which all who oppose you will not be able to counteract or contradict (θέτε οὖν ἐν ταῖς καρδίαις ὑμῶν μὴ προμελετᾶν ἀπολογηθῆναι ἐγὼ γὰρ δώσω ὑμῖν στόμα καὶ σοφίαν ᾗ οὐ δυνήσονται ἀντιστῆναι ἢ ἀντειπεῖν ἅπαντες οἱ ἀντικείμενοι ὑμῖν). The disciples will not need to memorize or rehearse some eloquent spiel to help them wriggle out of tight situations in the courtroom. The concern is not to secure an acquittal but to confront their accusers with the gospel and acquit themselves faithfully (see 1 Pet 3:14 – 16). All the speeches in Acts are delivered extemporaneously, but the disciples' wisdom derives from God, not from their clever rhetoric (see 1 Cor 1:17 – 2:5).

What is guaranteed to the disciples is their successful witness to Jesus, not their safety or release, which is illustrated in Acts 4:14 ("But since they could see the man who had been healed standing there with them, there was nothing they could say") and 6:10 ("But they could not stand up against the wisdom the Spirit gave him as he spoke"; see also 4:29; 18:9 – 10).

21:16 You will be betrayed even by parents, brothers, relatives, and friends, and they will kill some of you (παραδοθήσεσθε δὲ καὶ ὑπὸ γονέων καὶ ἀδελφῶν καὶ συγγενῶν καὶ φίλων, καὶ θανατώσουσιν ἐξ ὑμῶν). The trials will be all the more tortuous because sometimes they will be caused through a betrayal by family and friends.

"Brothers" may include "fellow Jews" (Acts 7:2; 22:1), which is no less scandalous or heartbreaking.[15] The betrayal is the result of placing allegiance to Jesus above father and mother, wife and children, brothers and sisters, and even life itself (14:26 – 27), who then feel that they have been betrayed by the disciple.

21:17 And you will be hated by all because of my name (καὶ ἔσεσθε μισούμενοι ὑπὸ πάντων διὰ τὸ ὄνομά μου). Hatred will come from all directions (see Acts 24:5; 28:22; 1 Pet 2:12; 4:14). "Because of my name" restates the cause of all the distress that awaits them (see v.12). The enmity that disciples will face is why Jesus warned against anyone following him in a rush of enthusiasm. Disciples must first sit down and count up the cost (14:25 – 35).

21:18 And not a hair from your head will perish (καὶ θρὶξ ἐκ τῆς κεφαλῆς ὑμῶν οὐ μὴ ἀπόληται). This statement seems to contradict Jesus' warning that some of them will die (v. 16). The phrase "not a hair from your head will perish" appears in the Old Testament to refer to physical protection (cf. 1 Sam 14:45; 2 Sam 14:11; 1 Kgs 1:52), and Paul uses it to assure his fellow sea voyagers that none of them will perish (Acts 27:34).

Attributing the apparent contradiction to different sources that Luke sloppily cobbled together does not explain what it meant for him. In Jesus' words of comfort to disciples in times of trial in 12:4 – 7, having one's hairs numbered by God does not mean that one is immune from being put to death. The sparrows are watched by God, but they still fall to the earth. The story in Acts reveals that some disciples will be protected; others will die at the hands of their oppressors. Stephen is stoned (Acts 7:57 – 60); Peter and John are set free (4:1 – 31). James, the brother of John, is slain by Herod; Peter escapes Herod's hands when he is liberated from

---

14. Neagoe, *The Trial of the Gospel*, 134.   15. Ibid., 135.

jail by an angel (12:1 – 11). Paul experiences narrow escape after narrow escape, surviving stoning (14:19 – 20), beatings, mob action (21:27 – 32), shipwreck (27:4 – 44), and snakebite (28:3 – 6).

For Luke, this assurance must refer to their deliverance to accomplish God's purposes (see Phil 1:21 – 26). Whether the outcome is death or life, the disciples' will have spiritual protection and the promise of ultimate deliverance (Luke 12:4 – 5). Whatever may happen to them in their mission, they need not fear those who have power only to destroy physical life.

21:19 By your endurance, gain your souls! (ἐν τῇ ὑπομονῇ ὑμῶν κτήσασθε τὰς ψυχὰς ὑμῶν). Mark 13:13 has "the one who stands firm to the end [τέλος] will be saved." Luke uses the noun "the end" to refer to the destruction of the temple (v.9), so it would be inappropriate to insert it here. It would be "nonsensical" to imply "that whoever survives the destruction of Jerusalem will be eternally saved."[16] The disciples must endure persecution beyond that catastrophe.

Luke also has "gain your souls" (κτήσασθε τὰς ψυχὰς ὑμῶν) rather than "shall be saved" (σωθήσεται). This translation accepts the aorist middle imperative rather than the future middle indicative (κτήσεσθε, "you will gain") as the best attested and more difficult reading and fits the context of exhortation (see vv. 34, 36).

"Souls" here refers to true life or "essential being."[17] This command restates Jesus' radical demands of disciples for an eschatological context, losing one's life to save it (9:24; 17:33).[18] The meaning is, "Endurance, not violence, is the Christian's protection, and it shall save the soul, and the *true* life, even if it loses all else."[19]

21:20 When you see Jerusalem encircled by armies, know then that her desolation has drawn near (ὅταν δὲ ἴδητε κυκλουμένην ὑπὸ στρατοπέδων Ἰερουσαλήμ, τότε γνῶτε ὅτι ἤγγικεν ἡ ἐρήμωσις αὐτῆς). Jesus returns to the subject of the destruction of Jerusalem and the temple destruction and "elaborates on the catastrophe itself."[20] He reiterates his earlier warning that Jerusalem will be surrounded by armies, and then the defeated inhabitants will be subject to carnage and captivity as the walls crumble under the force of the Roman war machine (see 19:43). He warns that whenever they see Jerusalem encircled by armies (see the description in Josephus, *J.W.* 5.2.1 – 5 §§47 – 97; 6.2.1 §93; 6.2.7 §§149 – 56), they can be sure that its desolation is near. There will be no divine intervention, and it is not the end of the world.

Consequently, Luke refers to the "desolation" (ἐρήμωσις) of Jerusalem, not an enigmatic, apocalyptic "'abomination that causes desolation' standing where it does not belong" (Mark 13:14) that only applies to the temple's desecration. It is a time of great wrath against the entire city for rejecting Jesus, and it will engulf guilty and innocent alike in its destruction (see Jer 4:7; 7:34; 22:5; 25:18; 44:6, 22).

21:21 Then let those who are in Judea flee to the hills, and those in her midst get out, and those in the countryside not enter (τότε οἱ ἐν τῇ Ἰουδαίᾳ φευγέτωσαν εἰς τὰ ὄρη καὶ οἱ ἐν μέσῳ αὐτῆς ἐκχωρείτωσαν καὶ οἱ ἐν ταῖς χώραις μὴ εἰσερχέσθωσαν εἰς αὐτήν). During the war with Rome, many from the countryside entered the city hoping to find refuge from the invading army in this walled citadel. Jesus warns that it is no longer

16. Bridge, *Where the Eagles Are Gathered*, 126.
17. Talbert, *Reading Luke*, 231.
18. Just, *Luke* (Concordia), 795.
19. F. W. Farrar, *St. Luke* (Cambridge Bible for Schools and Colleges; Cambridge: Cambridge Univ. Press, 1895), 317. Endurance will also contribute to their bearing fruit (8:15).
20. Bridge, *Where the Eagles Are Gathered*, 127.

a place of refuge (Jer 4:6). Its doom is sealed. Walls, fortifications, and weapons are useless if God is not on their side (Jer 21:8 – 10; 38:2).

Running for the hills is not a cowardly retreat but a deliberate break with Jerusalem and the false theology of security that views it as sacrosanct and inviolable (see Jer 51:6; Rev 18:4). "Leaving the city and its temple to their fate is recognition that Jerusalem no longer has a role to play in salvation history."[21] The nation, its temple, and the holy city are no longer tied to redemption. Consequently, disciples are to avoid becoming entangled in the nation's fate.

21:22 Because these are [the] days of vengeance so that all that has been written may be fulfilled (ὅτι ἡμέραι ἐκδικήσεως αὗταί εἰσιν τοῦ πλησθῆναι πάντα τὰ γεγραμμένα). This statement gives the reason why they should flee the city. These are the days of vengeance (see Deut 32:35; Jer 51:6; Hos 9:7), when God judges disobedience. Luke's phraseology (τοῦ plus the infinitive) here expresses result rather than purpose, "so that all that has been written be fulfilled." The many prophecies warning of Jerusalem's destruction at the hands of the Babylonians in 587 BC are understood to apply still in this new situation when even more is at stake. It is not God's purpose to destroy but the inevitable result of disobedience and rebellion.

21:23 Woe to those who are pregnant and those who are nursing infants in those days, for great calamity will fall upon the land and wrath against this people (οὐαὶ ταῖς ἐν γαστρὶ ἐχούσαις καὶ ταῖς θηλαζούσαις ἐν ἐκείναις ταῖς ἡμέραις· ἔσται γὰρ ἀνάγκη μεγάλη ἐπὶ τῆς γῆς καὶ ὀργὴ τῷ λαῷ τούτῳ). Jesus does not lament the temple's destruction but the suffering of those

caught in the cataclysm. Modern readers who have witnessed the grim-visaged pictures of victims of genocide can better understand the torment suffered by those trapped in the midst of hostilities. Jesus bewails the traumatic suffering of mothers who will vainly try to protect their unborn children and infants but will not be spared from the carnage that will fall on the land.

21:24 Some will fall by the edge of the sword and others will be led into captivity to all the nations and Jerusalem will be trampled by the Gentiles, until the times of the Gentiles are fulfilled (καὶ πεσοῦνται στόματι μαχαίρης καὶ αἰχμαλωτισθήσονται εἰς τὰ ἔθνη πάντα, καὶ Ἰερουσαλὴμ ἔσται πατουμένη ὑπὸ ἐθνῶν, ἄχρι οὗ πληρωθῶσιν καιροὶ ἐθνῶν). Falling by the sword recalls the bitter prophecy of Ezek 21:6 – 12. The image of trampling implies desecration and disrespect, and once again the people of Israel will be led into captivity.

Josephus, known for exaggerating numbers, puts the tally of the Jews killed by the Romans at 1,100,000 (*J.W.* 6.5.1 §§271 – 73; 6.9. 3 §420). He claims that the captives led away to be displayed in Rome and sent off as slaves to various provinces and Egyptian mines numbered 97,000 (*J.W.* 7.5.3 §138; 7.5.4 §154; 6.9.3 §420). He gives a gruesome account of the starvation of those under siege in Jerusalem. He claims that one mother took her baby from her breast, killed it, and roasted it for food (*J.W.* 6.3.4 §§201 – 11). He composed his history as a client of the ruling Flavian family in Rome and paints a sympathetic picture of the Roman general Titus Flavius regretting Jerusalem's great desolation. He places blame on the Jews themselves, who forced Titus's hand (*J.W.* 7.5.2 §§112 – 15). Jesus' foreknowledge of the terrible suffering prompted

---

21. Schweizer, *Luke*, 317. Craig Koester ("The Origin and Significance of the Flight to Pella Tradition," *Luther Northwestern Theological Seminary* 51 [1989]: 90) discusses the tradition of the Christians fleeing from Jerusalem to Pella that is said to have contributed greatly to the growth and spread of Christianity.

his tears as he approached Jerusalem (19:41 – 44) and will result in his lament over the daughters of Jerusalem when he leaves the city to be crucified (23:27 – 31).

Luke does not include the statement found in Mark 13:10 that the gospel must first be proclaimed to the nations (Gentiles). Instead, he refers more enigmatically to "times of the Gentiles" (καιροὶ ἐθνῶν). This phrase may apply to the period of mission to the Gentiles (Rom 11:25 – 27; Tob 14:6), the period of foreign domination (see Dan 2:21; 7:1 – 8:27; 9:24 – 27), or a synthesis of both ideas. Nolland takes it as a reference to the judgment on the Gentile nations "that corresponds to the judgment upon Jerusalem."[22] The instruments of Israel's judgment will themselves be judged.

The charge to proclaim repentance and forgiveness of sins in Jesus' name to all nations, however, appears at the climactic end of the gospel (24:46 – 47) and at the beginning and the conclusion of Acts (Acts 1:8; 28:28). Luke understands this venture to be the uppermost task in the next chapter of salvation history. It is most likely that the phrase the "times of the Gentiles" here refers to this mission to the nations.

21:25 – 26 There shall be signs in the sun, moon, and stars and on earth distress among the nations, anxiety over the uproar from the sea and surging waves. People will pass out from fearful foreboding over what is coming upon the world, for the powers of heaven will be shaken (καὶ ἔσονται σημεῖα ἐν ἡλίῳ καὶ σελήνῃ καὶ ἄστροις, καὶ ἐπὶ τῆς γῆς συνοχὴ ἐθνῶν ἐν ἀπορίᾳ ἤχους θαλάσσης καὶ σάλου. ἀποψυχόντων ἀνθρώπων ἀπὸ φόβου καὶ προσδοκίας τῶν ἐπερχομένων τῇ οἰκουμένῃ, αἱ γὰρ δυνάμεις τῶν οὐρανῶν σαλευθήσονται). After the destruction of Jerusalem and the "times of the Gentiles," the focal point shifts to the end of the world and the coming of the Son of Man. Luke does not have any phrase that connects this passage to what precedes, as do Mark 13:24 ("in those days") and Matt 24:29 ("after the distress of those days"). Luke must not see these events as connected.[23] The result is that the timing of events in relation to one another remains vague. Jerusalem's destruction only portends the judgment that awaits the entire world at the end of history.

The structure of vv. 25 – 26 is chiastic:

A Signs in sun, moon, and stars
   B On earth distress among the nations
   B′ Fearful foreboding over what is coming upon the world
A′ Powers of heaven shaken

With the sun, moon, stars, earth, and sea in an uproar, it will seem like "all hell has broken loose," as the *Message* paraphrases this verse. The prophets use sensational, figurative language of cosmic upheaval to describe the destruction of cities and other political disasters (Isa 13:10; 34:4; Ezek 32:7; Joel 2:10; 3:15 [4:15]; see also Isa 13:7; 17:12).[24] Matthew and Mark use this imagery in association with the destruction of the Jerusalem (Mark 13:19 – 20), but Luke links it with the approach of the final consummation and coming of the Son of Man (see Acts 2:19 – 21, citing Joel 2:30 – 32).

The imagery conveys "the climactic judgement upon the nations."[25] All human beings who are

---

22. Nolland, *Luke*, 3:1002 – 4.

23. Stein, *Luke*, 512.

24. Caird, *Saint Luke*, 232, notes that the sea was regarded as "the reservoir of evil things (Rev 13:1)" and the heavenly bodies were "identified with the gods of oriental and Greco-Roman religion, and regarded by Jews as angelic beings created by God and allowed by him to preside over the destinies of pagan nations (Deut 32:8; Isa. 24:21; 34:1 – 4)." When these powers are shaken, it represents "the overthrow of pagan imperial supremacy."

25. Nolland, *Luke*, 3:1006.

left (see comments on 17:22 – 37) will experience a great terror (see 17:27, 29). Modern disaster movies capture this fearful foreboding,[26] but they lack any notion of God's involvement or how one might be saved except through violence or the valiant resolve of a courageous few. In Jesus' scenario, nothing will avail humans in this crisis.

21:27 Then they shall see the Son of Man coming on a cloud with power and great glory (καὶ τότε ὄψονται τὸν υἱὸν τοῦ ἀνθρώπου ἐρχόμενον ἐν νεφέλῃ μετὰ δυνάμεως καὶ δόξης πολλῆς). The parallel in Mark 13:26 has the plural "clouds" (see Dan 7:13 – 14), but Luke has the singular "cloud" (νεφέλῃ) because it represents the divine presence (Exod 19:16; 24:16; 34:5; Num 11:25; Luke 9:34 – 35; Acts 1:9) rather than a mode of divine transport (Ps 104:3). Luke also has "great glory" (δόξης πολλῆς) rather than "great power" (Mark 13:26), which contrasts with the humble associations of his first coming swaddled in a manger and attended by shepherds. The one coming with "power" will dethrone "all dominion, authority and power" and "put his enemies under his feet" (1 Cor 15:24 – 26).

21:28 As these things begin to take place, stand up straight and raise your heads because your redemption draws near (ἀρχομένων δὲ τούτων γίνεσθαι ἀνακύψατε καὶ ἐπάρατε τὰς κεφαλὰς ὑμῶν, διότι ἐγγίζει ἡ ἀπολύτρωσις ὑμῶν). "These things" refers to the eschatological portents described in vv. 25 – 26, not the events beginning with v. 8. Lifting up one's head fits the celestial return of Jesus promised in Acts 1:9 – 11.

"Redemption" (ἀπολύτρωσις) is used only here in Luke and refers to deliverance not from sin but from tribulation, brought about by the defeat of all forces hostile to God (Rom 8:23; Eph 4:30). It is akin to being "exalted to heaven" and the opposite of being brought down to Hades (Luke 10:15).

Are believers to stand up straight and lift up their downcast heads and expect their redemption after all that is described in vv. 25 – 27 occurs?[27] They will then be redeemed "shortly *after* the revelation of the Son of Man — as it does in Mk 13:26 – 27."[28] According to Mark 13:26 – 27, after the Son of Man comes, he will send out the angels and gather his elect from the ends of the earth. Bridge argues that Luke omits this reference to sending out angels because he "considered Lk 17:37 to be a sufficient substitute for Mk 13:27" and tended "to avoid doublets." He may also have considered the eschatological role that Mark assigns to the angels to be problematic.[29]

If the phrase "as these things begin to take place" (ἀρχομένων δὲ τούτων γίνεσθαι) denotes the onset of the end-times sequence, the redemption of God's people could occur prior to the anguish experienced by the inhabitants of the earth (21:25 – 26). According to Bridge, this option is best because the third person is used in v. 27 and the second person in v. 28. He argues, "This shift implies that Jesus' followers (the plural 'you') are not included among those who witness the cosmic upheavals with trepidation ('they')." Believers have been evacuated and removed from the distress overtaking unbelievers during this conflagration.[30]

---

26. "Fearful foreboding" reads φόβου καὶ προσδοκίας as a hendiadys.

27. "Stand up straight" (ἀνακύψατε) is the same command given to the woman who was bent over in bondage to Satan for eighteen years (13:11).

28. Bridge, *Where the Eagles Are Gathered*, 138.

29. Ibid., 135 – 37.

30. Bridge (ibid., 138, n. 65) also notes: "The gathering of the righteous to their Lord prior to the final judgment could also presuppose their involvement in it. This idea is conveyed in Lk 22:30, where Jesus promises his disciples that they 'will sit on thrones judging the twelve tribes of Israel' (cf. Mt 19:28)."

21:29–30 And he told a parable to them. "Look at the fig tree and all the trees. Whenever they put out leaves, you can see for yourselves and know that the summer is already near" (καὶ εἶπεν παραβολὴν αὐτοῖς· ἴδετε τὴν συκῆν καὶ πάντα τὰ δένδρα· ὅταν προβάλωσιν ἤδη, βλέποντες ἀφ᾽ ἑαυτῶν γινώσκετε ὅτι ἤδη ἐγγὺς τὸ θέρος ἐστίν). The fig tree loses it leaves in the winter, but it is one of the first trees to bud in the spring. When it does so, it is a sign that summer is near. In Luke, the warning does not come just from the budding of a fig tree (Mark 13:28) but from "all the trees" because he writes to an audience that may be unfamiliar with Palestinian fig trees. If they can interpret the signs of the coming summer, they should be able to interpret the signs of the coming consummation. Anyone can see it for themselves and need not be informed by others who claim to have special knowledge.

21:31 So also you, when you see these things taking place, know that the reign of God is near (οὕτως καὶ ὑμεῖς, ὅταν ἴδητε ταῦτα γινόμενα, γινώσκετε ὅτι ἐγγύς ἐστιν ἡ βασιλεία τοῦ θεοῦ). The "reign of God" (ἡ βασιλεία τοῦ θεοῦ) should not be confused with human activity. Here it is used as a synonym for the eschaton (9:26–27; 11:2; 14:15; 17:20–21; 19:11; 22:30).

21:32 Amen, I tell you, this generation will not pass away until all things take place (ἀμὴν λέγω ὑμῖν ὅτι οὐ μὴ παρέλθῃ ἡ γενεὰ αὕτη ἕως ἂν πάντα γένηται). "This generation" has been explained in many ways. The more plausible interpretations have it refer to (1) the Jewish contemporaries of Jesus (11:29–32, which means Jesus was mistaken, if he refers to the end of time); (2) the Jews as a race; (3) wicked humanity (see 9:41); (4) humanity in general (see 16:8); (5) Luke's own generation; and (6) the generation of the end time, that is, the last generation that sees "these things" preceding the coming of the Son of Man.

The last option seems best. With reference to the pouring out of God's Spirit and "wonders in the heavens above and signs on the earth below," Acts 2:17–21 makes it clear that the last days have already begun ("In the last days, God says …"). Schweizer draws on the eschatological speculation in the Habbakuk pesher that "the final generation" comprises "several generations (1QpHab 2:7; 7:2) because 'the time of the end is extended' (7:7)."[31] If this accords with Jesus' thinking, then it refers to all the generations after his resurrection to the last one. There is no reason to resort to Farrar's picturesque image to explain how Jesus may have gotten it wrong about the timing of the eschaton: "Prophecy is like a landscape in which time and space are subordinated to eternal relations, and in which events look like hills seen chain behind chain which to the distant spectator appear as one."[32]

The word about "this generation" is then a word of comfort. Jesus intends "to inspire rather than inform."[33] The words of Jesus will endure forever. Heaven and earth are transient and will pass away. When they do, Christ's followers who adhere to Jesus' words will not pass away with them; they will have been rescued (as the faithful were in the days of Noah and of Lot, 17:26–30).

21:33 Heaven and earth will pass away, but my words will not pass away (ὁ οὐρανὸς καὶ ἡ γῆ παρελεύσονται, οἱ δὲ λόγοι μου οὐ μὴ παρελεύσονται). This statement expresses the major concern. Jesus' words are ultimate and must be obeyed.

---

31. Schweizer, *Luke*, 322.
32. Farrar, *St. Luke*, 315. See also Nolland, *Luke*, 3:1010–11.
33. Nielsen, *Until It Is Fulfilled*, 229.

21:34–35 Be alert so that your hearts are not burdened by dissipation and drunkenness and worries of life and that day catch you like an unexpected trap. For it will come upon all who dwell on the face of the whole earth (προσέχετε δὲ ἑαυτοῖς μήποτε βαρηθῶσιν ὑμῶν αἱ καρδίαι ἐν κραιπάλῃ καὶ μέθῃ καὶ μερίμναις βιωτικαῖς καὶ ἐπιστῇ ἐφ᾽ ὑμᾶς αἰφνίδιος ἡ ἡμέρα ἐκείνη ὡς παγίς· ἐπελεύσεται γὰρ ἐπὶ πάντας τοὺς καθημένους ἐπὶ πρόσωπον πάσης τῆς γῆς). This warning echoes Eccl 9:12: "No one knows when their hour will come: As fish are caught in a cruel net, or birds are taken in a snare, so people are trapped by evil times that fall unexpectedly upon them."

Vigilant prayer is the only way to prepare (18:1; see Eph 6:18). "Drunkenness" can refer to more than inebriation but also being drunk on one's own illusions. The opposite is being soberly aware that "the day of the Lord will come like a thief in the night" (1 Thess 5:2–7).

21:36 Keep alert in every time, praying that you may be strong enough to flee all these things that are about to take place and to stand before the Son of Man (ἀγρυπνεῖτε δὲ ἐν παντὶ καιρῷ δεόμενοι ἵνα κατισχύσητε ἐκφυγεῖν ταῦτα πάντα τὰ μέλλοντα γίνεσθαι καὶ σταθῆναι ἔμπροσθεν τοῦ υἱοῦ τοῦ ἀνθρώπου). The exhortation to pray so that they do not quiver in fear and lose heart during the interim recalls the parable of the widow and the judge in 18:1–8, which appears at the end of the previous eschatological discourse (17:20–37). Jesus becomes the model of praying in the face of death on the Mount of Olives (22:39–46).

Summers claims that the call to "be strong enough to flee all these things" (κατισχύσητε ἐκφυγεῖν) does not mean "to avoid but to come

through them victoriously."[34] This reading seems to stretch the meaning of the verb "to flee." It refers to the demand that followers take flight from Jerusalem before it is too late (21:21) and appears in 3:7, when John scoffs at the crowds who come to him in hopes of escaping the coming wrath. Bridge contends that by escaping, Jesus has in mind "the evacuation of the righteous.... Survival ... depends on *not* being on the 'face of the earth.'"[35] This view fits the interpretation of 17:26–37.

"Standing before the Son of Man" recalls Mal 3:2: "But who can endure the day of his coming? Who can stand when he appears?" (see Rev 6:17; cf. Jude 24). Luke would interpret the one who comes as the Son of Man, who comes in glory and judgment. Fletcher-Louis notes that the image is found in the Similitudes of *1 En.* (48:10; 50:4; 62:8–9) and in 4Q185 1.8–9, in which the righteous are able to stand and the unrighteous fall down on their faces before the divine judge. He concludes that the righteous can stand because they are not condemned but also because they have a transformed, exalted, and perhaps heavenly identity.[36]

21:37–38 He was in the temple teaching every day and he would go out every night and stay on the mountain that is called "Olives." And all the people would get up early in the morning to hear him in the temple (ἦν δὲ τὰς ἡμέρας ἐν τῷ ἱερῷ διδάσκων, τὰς δὲ νύκτας ἐξερχόμενος ηὐλίζετο εἰς τὸ ὄρος τὸ καλούμενον Ἐλαιῶν. καὶ πᾶς ὁ λαὸς ὤρθριζεν πρὸς αὐτὸν ἐν τῷ ἱερῷ ἀκούειν αὐτοῦ). Despite his dire predictions of destruction, the crowds continue enthusiastically to swarm around Jesus as he teaches in the temple from morning until evening. The mention of his nightly sojourns on the Mount of Olives prepares for his arrest and explains how Judas would know where to lead the posse to arrest him (see John 18:2).

34. Summers, *Commentary on Luke*, 266.
35. Bridge, *Where the Eagles Are Gathered*, 145.
36. Fletcher-Louis, *Luke-Acts: Angels, Christology and Soteriology*, 233–34.

Theology in Application

1. The Temple's Demise

The temple is no longer a status symbol of God's abiding favor and will be destroyed along with Jerusalem. The structure of the discourse describing this disaster interrupts the chronological flow of events. The signs preceding the assault on Jerusalem (vv. 8 – 11) and the details describing its downfall (vv. 20 – 24) are interrupted by a description of the persecution of the disciples (vv. 12 – 19). Bridge suggests that vv. 8 – 11 and vv. 20 – 24 form a literary inclusio around the persecution of the disciples. The treatment of Jesus and his followers provides an explanation why the temple and Jerusalem will be destroyed.[37] He contends that since many of these events "have already come to pass" when Luke writes, he "uses Jesus' prophecies as proof to his readers that the recent events, however terrible, were in accordance with God's will and affirm God's sovereignty (vv. 29 – 33)."[38] This crushing blow was an act of God and teaches, once again, that God brings judgment in historical events. It warns about the inevitable consequences when a nation ignores God and does what is evil (see Jer 18:7 – 10).

These events do not have an immediate chronological tie to the end of time, so they do not help in mapping out the sequence of the end-time drama. But they can be charted:[39]

Jesus' death (c. AD 30)	End of Acts (c. AD 60)	Destruction of the Temple (AD 70)	Eschaton
Persecution of the disciples (21:12 – 19)	Signs (21:8 – 11)	Fall of Jerusalem (21:20 – 24a)	Eschaton (21:25 – 28)
		Times of the Gentiles (21:24b)	

Jesus makes no mention of the temple's restoration because it will have become irrelevant. Forgiveness of sins will come in Jesus' name (24:47), and the focus of redemption is the coming of the Son of Man in power and glory (v. 27), not the rebuilding of a desolate city.

2. The Reality of Evil

The description of suffering and destruction underscores the reality of evil in the world. The horrors of history reveal that this is not the best of all possible worlds. Humankind has a propensity toward malice. People may hate war but cannot seem to

---

37. Bridge, *Where the Eagles Are Gathered*, 127, n. 38   39. Ibid., 132.
38. Ibid., 147.

live in peace. Even those who claim to be God's own special people rebel and wreak atrocities. As Paul says, we live in a time when all creation groans in aching longing for the redemption of this world from the bondage to terrestrial and spiritual powers (Rom 8:18 – 25).

But Jesus' eschatological teaching reveals that wars, suffering, and death have no ultimate meaning or hold on Christians. The narrative of Jesus' passion and resurrection that follows illustrates the pattern of suffering and vindication that will apply to all followers of Christ. Allison writes, "But if Jesus had known the depths of tribulation and despair, he had also passed through them to the other side; he had attained the eschatological glory. . . . His vindication after his passion is the pledge to Christians that, ultimately, those who trust in God will overcome the ambiguities of this life and enter into a better world."[40]

3. Trinitarian Doctrine

Jesus makes the extraordinary promise that *he* will be with his disciples, not to comfort them in their trials but to give them convicting speech (v. 15). This promise is extraordinary because it is what we find God assuring various prominent Old Testament figures (Exod 3:12; 4:10 – 12; Judg 6:14, 16; Jer 1:7 – 9; Ezek 1:28 – 2:9). In Luke 12:11 – 12, Jesus assures his disciples that they need not worry about what to say when they are arraigned before synagogues, rulers, and authorities, "For the Holy Spirit will teach you in that hour what it is necessary to say" (12:11 – 12; see Mark 13:11). Buckwalter declares:

> Jesus' prophetic self-claim . . . stands as perhaps the most revealing statement of Luke's personal christological estimation of Jesus in the two volumes. It represents, in fact, the only instance in the synoptic tradition where Jesus, before his death, directly identifies himself with a post-resurrection work among his disciples as their exalted Lord. The way Luke illustrates its fulfillment in Acts implies that this was *how — he believed, at least — the earthly Jesus had envisioned it.*[41]

Luke understands the Holy Spirit to inspire the preaching in Acts (Acts 4:8, 31; 6:10; 7:55; 13:9). His gospel tells us what Jesus began to do and to teach; the Acts of the Apostles tells us what he continued to do and teach through the Spirit. The risen Lord is present through the Spirit.[42]

In a similar vein, Jesus makes the extraordinary promise to his disciples after his resurrection, "I am sending the promise of my Father upon you" (24:49). The promise is the sending of the Holy Spirit. What makes this promise extraordinary is that earlier he says that the heavenly Father will give the Spirit to those who ask

40. Dale C. Allison Jr., *The End of the Ages Has Come* (Philadelphia: Fortress, 1985), 173 – 74.

41. H. Douglas Buckwalter, *The Character and Purpose of Luke's Christology* (SNTSMS 89; Cambridge: Cambridge Univ. Press, 1996), 211.

42. O'Toole, *The Unity of Luke's Theology*, 48.

(11:13); and in Acts 2:33 Peter declares that the events and word at Pentecost comes from the disciples "hav[ing] received from the Father the promised Holy Spirit." In this sending of the Spirit, Luke understands the exalted Jesus to be on the same level as the heavenly Father.

4. Mission and Persecution

Verses 12–19 foretell the story of the disciples' mission that will be narrated in Acts before the outbreak of the fateful war against Rome in AD 66. Luke is writing after the city lies smoldering in ruins and the church is now situated in the period where 21:25 begins. He assumes that these are the last days (Acts 2:17–18). During the uncertainty of the day and hour awaiting the coming of the Son of Man, believers are to make good use of their lives, praying for strength in the trials they may face and using the times of persecution and imprisonment as opportunities to bear witness to the gospel.

This accords with Paul's view that being on trial presents an opportunity for the defense and confirmation of the gospel (Phil 1:7). One who endured persecution in a South American torture cellar said all Christian doctrines disappeared then. The only thing that sustained him was knowing that Jesus had also been on the wrong side of a whip and that Jesus was with him. That confidence allowed him to proclaim his faith all the more boldly (see Phil 1:12–14).

Fosdick observes:

> The New Testament begins with a massacre of innocent children; it is centered in the crucifixion; it ends with a vision in which the souls of the martyred saints under the altar cry, "How long, O Master?" The Book was written by men whose familiar experiences were excommunications, persecutions, and martyrdoms. Their faith was not like a candle flame, easily blown out by a high wind, but like a great fire fanned into a more powerful conflagration.[43]

The fearless witness of Christians in the face of persecution paradoxically fuels the flames of evangelism. The movement of the Holy Spirit in the lives of the believers recorded in Acts reveals that the harder opponents tried to combat it, the stronger, more resilient, more unpredictable, and more unstoppable it became. Like a nuclear explosion that unleashes radioactivity, the Holy Spirit emits the spontaneous release of "Christoactivity," an unseen force that cannot be contained and penetrates everything. Persecution is often the trigger that detonates the explosion of mission activity.

43. Harry Emerson Fosdick, *A Guide to Understanding the Bible* (New York: Harper, 1938), 193.

5. The End

Two units of this discourse deal with events of the end time (vv. 25 – 28, 34 – 36). Both units have thematic parallels with 17:20 – 37. First, they allude to the rescue of believers from the cataclysm that arrives with the coming of the Son of Man. They are to stand up, raise their heads because their redemption is near (v. 28), and pray that they have the strength to escape when these things take place and to stand before the Son of Man (v. 36).[44]

Second, persons should expect the unexpected. Redemption for some and destruction for others can come at any time. Be prepared because that day is sprung like a trap ready to snap shut at any moment. It will not be localized but will envelop all people throughout the earth.

Third, Bridge notes that the change from the Son of Man to the reign of God "suggests that [Luke] seeks to distinguish between the return of the Lord and the kingdom of God." He contends:

> It appears, therefore, that Luke subscribes not to a realized eschatology but to what perhaps may be called a realized "kingdomology." Jesus' parable allows Luke to look backwards from his own position in history and to demonstrate to his readers, on the basis of "these things" (i.e. the persecution of the disciples, the omens preceding the destruction of the temple, the fall of Jerusalem, and the dispersion of the Jews), that the kingdom of God has indeed been inaugurated. For Luke, this kingdom is now a present rather than post-historical reality.[45]

This explains the statement that follows in 21:31 and his statement in 9:27 ("I say to you truly, there are certain ones standing here who will not taste death until they see the reign of God." From Luke's perspective, these things have come to pass.

Sadly, the whole subject of the end of time and Christ's return has been the playground of cranks and fanatics. Over the centuries, various people have massaged various biblical texts with little regard to context to prove that Christ would return in this or that year and on this or that day. All have been proven wrong, but this failure has not dissuaded others from attempting to chart out timetables for the end. These errors, often proclaimed with clamorous zeal, have caused many others either to shy away from dealing with the question altogether or to dismiss the blessed hope of the future as fantasy. Jesus' statements about the end should make it clear that no calculation or watching for signs will avail anything. Scouring current news headlines for clues to decipher some apocalypse code in the Bible is futile. As someone has said, "Trying to determine what is going on in the world by reading newspapers is like trying to tell the time by watching the second hand of a clock."

---

44. Bridge, *Where the Eagles Are Gathered*, 147.   45. Ibid.

Too often attention to the return of Christ is selfishly oriented. The question asked, as Cullmann points out, is: "What will my fate be? Rather, it is necessary to consider the plan of salvation which God is pursuing *vis-à-vis* the world as a whole. How ironical that the Christian Church is constantly reproached with concentrating all its interest on the selfish happiness of the individual in the world beyond!"[46] Christ's return completes his work that encompasses God's plan for the whole creation, not just for individuals. The martyrs who had been slaughtered for their testimony for the word of God cry out from beneath the altar, "How long, Sovereign Lord?" The answer they get is to wait, to take their rest a little while longer (Rev 6:9 – 11). There is more yet to be accomplished and more suffering for other Christians yet to endure as God's purposes are worked out. The self-centered view of the end is always too myopic ever to see what God is really doing in the world.

The public's fascination with end-of-the-world disaster movies may suggest that a vague sense of apocalyptic doom looms on the horizon. Something out there is determined to destroy us, and everything is falling apart. Resolution is brought through human struggle and courage and maybe the wave of a magical wand. In an article entitled "It's the End of the World, and We Love It," Mark Moring comments on the film adaptation of Cormac McCarthy's *The Road* and reveals how theologically vapid and ultimately hopeless Hollywood's version of deliverance is. At the end of the movie, a father and son have finally reached the coast after traversing by foot a devastated landscape and staving off all kinds of dangers. They huddle together on "a beach littered with whale and human skeletons":

> The boy, about age 10, has never seen the sea. "What's on the other side?" he asks. "Nothing," replies his father, suffering from malnutrition and weakness after fending off all sorts of evils. All along he has encouraged his son to maintain hope — to "carry the fire" — but has slowly lost his own. The boy, who believes there's still goodness somewhere in their dark and dying world, looks out to the sea and says, "There must be something."[47]

Moring concludes his article, "Hollywood may not know that the answer has already been revealed, that a Father and his Son wait on the other shore." Christian eschatology should bring sanity and a sense of peace to counter the false prophets of every age who stir up fear and hysteria. No matter how bleak things appear, God's future assures the end of evil and the rescue of the righteous.

46. Oscar Cullmann, "The Return of Christ," in *The Early Church* (Philadelphia: Westminster, 1956), 148.

47. Mark Moring, "It's the End of the World, and We Love It," *Christianity Today* 54/3 (March 2010): 44 – 45.

67

Luke 22:1 – 6

Literary Context

The approach (22:1) and the arrival (22:7) of the Passover forms "a literary inclusion" that envelopes the plot to kill Jesus (22:2 – 6).[1] Judas prepares to betray the Passover Lamb while Peter and John prepare the Passover Feast. Luke possibly omits the anointing scene in Mark 14:3 – 9 because he tends to avoid doublets and has a similar account in 7:36 – 50. Satan's entering Judas throws into relief the onslaught of evil that seeks to destroy Jesus and commandeer his disciples (see 22:31, 53).

Main Idea

Satan can take control of those who let down their guard and open themselves up to temptation, even those who are closest to Jesus, to lead them to commit unthinkable acts of betrayal.

---

1. Heil, *The Meal Scenes in Luke-Acts*, 168, n. 5.

Translation

Luke 22:1–6

22:1	Chronological circumstance	**Now** the Festival of Unleavened Bread, which is called Passover, was drawing ⌁ **near.**
2	Character reintroduction	**The chief priests and the scribes were seeking how to do away with him,** for **they were afraid of the people.**
3a	Character introduction	**Then Satan entered Judas,**
b		who is called Iscariot and was among the number of the Twelve.
4	Response	**He went away and** **discussed** **with the high priests and the captains [of the temple guard]** **how he might hand him over to them.**
5	Agreement	**They rejoiced and agreed to give him money.**
6	Agreement	**So, he promised and began to seek a good occasion to hand him over to them** . without the crowd ⌁ [interfering].

Structure and Literary Form

The account of the plan to overcome Jesus' popularity and do away with him contains two scenes. The leaders determine that Jesus must die but fear a public outcry. A disciple of Jesus provides the means to capture him away from the crowd and makes it possible for the secret plans to be carried out.

Exegetical Outline

➡ I. Leaders plot to kill Jesus (21:1 – 2)

II. Satan enters Judas, one of the Twelve (21:3)

III. Judas joins the plot (21:4 – 6)

Explanation of the Text

22:1 Now the Festival of Unleavened Bread, which is called Passover, was drawing near (ἤγγιζεν δὲ ἡ ἑορτὴ τῶν ἀζύμων ἡ λεγομένη πάσχα). Luke dates the beginning of the ministry of John the Baptist (3:1 – 2) but does not date Jesus' death except during a Passover season. "The Festival of Unleavened Bread" (ἡ ἑορτὴ τῶν ἀζύμων) was originally a separate seven-day festival celebrated after Passover from Nisan 15 to 21. The two festivals had essentially become one since they were celebrated together and Passover required unleavened bread (2 Chr 35:17; 1 Esd 1:19; Josephus, *Ant.* 3.10.5 §249; 14.2.1 §21; 17.9.3 §213). Luke clearly links the two (see Acts 12:3; 20:6).

Passover memorializes the time when God spared the firstborn of Israel and delivered them from their bondage. It would now be remembered by Christians as the time when God's firstborn would die, and all humankind would be delivered from bondage to Satan and sin.

22:2 The chief priests and the scribes were seeking how to do away with him, for they were afraid of the people (καὶ ἐζήτουν οἱ ἀρχιερεῖς καὶ οἱ γραμματεῖς τὸ πῶς ἀνέλωσιν αὐτόν, ἐφοβοῦντο γὰρ τὸν λαόν). Luke has emphasized that the chief priests feared that the people's veneration of Jesus might lead to some trouble, and they were nervous about taking direct action against him (19:47 – 48; 20:19; 21:37 – 38; see 20:6).

22:3 Then Satan entered Judas, who is called Iscariot and was among the number of the Twelve (εἰσῆλθεν δὲ Σατανᾶς εἰς Ἰούδαν τὸν καλούμενον Ἰσκαριώτην, ὄντα ἐκ τοῦ ἀριθμοῦ τῶν δώδεκα). According to 4:13, when the devil failed in his testing of Jesus, he departed until another opportune time arose. It does not mean that

he now returns to the fray after quitting the field of battle for a long time. Satan has always been lurking in the shadows and now makes a move to exploit the weakness of one of the Twelve. He conducts a sneak attack against Jesus through his disciples, Judas and Simon (22:31), and he will have his hour (22:53). Satan seizes a beachhead in Judas, who turns to his own way, turns on Jesus, and prepares to turn him over to the authorities. Satan had faced one defeat after another but now has a temporary success with a receptive Judas.

As Crump frames it, "Satan does not tempt Judas, *he enters Judas.*"[2] Satan enters to control his actions. Luke does not explain how Judas allowed Satan to enter. Plummer contends, "there is no hint that Judas is now like a demoniac, unable to control his own actions. Judas opened the door to Satan. He did not resist him, and Satan did not flee from him."[3] Luke is only interested in the results of Judas's coming under Satan's bidding.

At the outset of the passion narrative, the lineup of opposition to Jesus takes shape: the high priests and scribes, representing human agency, and Satan, representing supernatural agency. Satan operates behind the scenes but engages in an all-out onslaught against Jesus' followers. Satan enlists a faltering disciple to sell out Jesus and sifts the others with the intention of causing them to fall away forever from the faith (22:31 – 32). The high priests will soon engage the Roman governor, Pilate, and he will enlist Herod; together they will comprise a troika of evil set against Jesus.

22:4 He went away and discussed with the high priests and the captains [of the temple guard] how he might hand him over to them (καὶ ἀπελθὼν συνελάλησεν τοῖς ἀρχιερεῦσιν

---

2. Crump, *Jesus the Intercessor*, 164.

3. Plummer, *Luke*, 490.

καὶ στρατηγοῖς τὸ πῶς αὐτοῖς παραδῷ αὐτόν). Under Satan's control, Judas has already decided to betray Jesus and goes to the leaders in the temple hierarchy to make a deal on how it might best be arranged. He already knows that they want to get their hands on Jesus to get rid of him.

"The captains [of the temple guard]" (στρατηγοῖς) translates a term that was used popularly for "the highest official" in a Hellenistic city ("chief magistrate," praetor; Acts 16:20, 22, 35 – 36, 38). Luke uses this term, familiar to his Greco-Roman readers, to refer to "the commanders" responsible for the temple (Acts 4:1; 5:24).[4]

22:5 They rejoiced and agreed to give him money (καὶ ἐχάρησαν καὶ συνέθεντο αὐτῷ ἀργύριον δοῦναι). The verb "agreed" (συνέθεντο) can be used to mean "to work out a mutually agreeable contract."[5] It implies that Judas bargained with them on the price for betrayal. The leaders respond out of their joy, and Satan used money to becharm Judas and to control his heart, as he will also "fill" Ananias's heart (Acts 5:1 – 6).

22:6 So, he promised and began to seek a good occasion to hand him over to them without the crowd [interfering] (καὶ ἐξωμολόγησεν, καὶ ἐζήτει εὐκαιρίαν τοῦ παραδοῦναι αὐτὸν ἄτερ ὄχλου αὐτοῖς). According to 4:13, Satan left Jesus "for a while" (ἄχρι καιροῦ). The root word for "time" (καιρός) can mean "opportune time," and it reappears here as "a good occasion" or "opportune time" (εὐκαιρίαν). This promise reveals most clearly what Judas betrayed about Jesus. He made known to the Jewish leaders the time and place where they could capture Jesus quietly and take him into custody away from the crowds to avoid rousing a commotion.

Theology in Application

1. The So-called Gospel of Judas

The so-called *Gospel of Judas* was part of a Coptic language papyrus codex discovered in 1978 and is likely the same work that Irenaeus (AD 180) summarized and attacked in his *Against Heresies* as the product of a Gnostic sect called the Cainites. It purports to record conversations between Jesus and Judas during the week of the Passion. It begins: "The secret account of the revelation that Jesus spoke in conversation with Judas Iscariot during a week three days before he celebrated Passover." The document reflects a later Gnosticism that was hostile to the creator God of the Old Testament, who was viewed as malevolent, and toward the physical creation, which was regarded as the realm of corruption and erroneous beliefs. Truth and salvation could only be found by escaping the physical flesh via saving knowledge.

According to this apocryphal gospel, Judas is the elect one who alone possesses this special knowledge and is superior to the disciples, who are painted as lesser lights. They are caught up with the physical world while Judas pays heed to the spiritual. Jesus secretly approves and authorizes the betrayal and affirms Judas for

---

4. BDAG, 947 – 48. See further, Schürer, *The History of the Jewish People*, 2:277 – 78.

5. BDAG, 975.

"sacrificing the man that clothes me" — in other words, for assisting him in shedding the outward flesh that anchors his divine spark to this world.

The *Gospel of Judas*, probably written to subvert the orthodox leadership of the church, contradicts the canonical gospels. Mark gives no reason for Judas's actions. Matthew and John attribute it to greed. Luke and John attribute it to Satan. But these answers have not satisfied modern readers, who want to plumb the depths of Judas's soul to discover why he *really* did something so shocking. Other explanations abound. The *Gospel of Judas* simply seizes the opportunity to fill in the gap in the text to provide another conjecture that fits the author's theological and sociological agenda. But we should listen to what God's Word says about the truth, not some apocryphal writing.

2. Judas's Reasons for Betraying Jesus?

Asking why Judas did what he did is a fruitless quest that is probably more interested in getting him and ourselves off the hook. I conclude that "attempts to find *the* reason or reasons to explain why Judas did what he did are frequently diversions that prevent us from looking at our own potential betrayal. If we convince ourselves that Judas acted for this or that reason, we can also convince ourselves that we would not succumb to such perfidy."[6] The tradition that Satan entered him (John 13:2, 27; see 6:70) and that he was enticed by money are sufficient explanations. If one of the Twelve could be guilty of such treachery, for whatever reason, then any follower of Jesus could do the same or worse. All must be on their guard because Satan still prowls like a roaring lion hunting someone to devour (1 Pet 5:8).

The mission activity of Jesus and of the early missionaries is interpreted as a deliverance from the power of Satan (10:18; 11:18; 13:16; Acts 26:18). But Luke's account makes it clear that Satan has not been completely defanged and continues to plague disciples, even after the pouring out of the Holy Spirit (see Acts 5:3). The image of "entering" resembles demonic possession (8:30; 11:24–26), but Judas deliberately chose to be directed by Satan and to collude with those who wanted to destroy Jesus. Brown notes, "Unlike the demons who talk and act through their human captives (e.g. Lk 8,30; 9,39) Satan appears in 22,3 as a transcendent force, a heavenly counterpart to the earthly reality to which Judas has fallen captive."[7]

Since the discussion with the high priests involved bargaining with them about the price, he became captive to money, "unrighteous Mammon" (16:9, 11; see Acts 1:18), and Satan is the heavenly counterpart to money. In this case, the money "takes on the character of something demonic and opposed to God."[8] What is important

---

6. Garland, *Mark*, 522.

7. Schuyler Brown, *Apostasy and Perseverance in the Theology of Luke* (AnBib 36; Rome: Pontifical Biblical Institute, 1969), 85.

8. Ibid.

to Luke is that this warning and those that immediately follow set up the contrast between Satan as Adversary and Jesus as Advocate.[9]

3. Betrayal and Redemptive History

Is the betrayal required for the course of redemptive history? The testimony elsewhere in the New Testament is that God handed Jesus over (Rom 4:25; 8:32) or that Jesus handed himself over (Gal 2:20; Eph 5:25; see John 18:1 – 9). What is decreed by the divine necessity (δεῖ) is only that the Son of Man must "go" (22:22a). There had to be a giving of life, but there did not have to be a betrayal. Given the reality of human and superhuman evil, however, betrayal is not something surprising.

In his speech about replacing Judas (Acts 1:15 – 26), Peter cites the Psalms (Acts 1:20) not to show that this treachery was somehow foreordained but to show that the ultimate ruin of the one guilty of such an act was foretold and that another can take his place. It was foreknown, but Judas made the free choice to forfeit his place among the apostles "to go where he belongs" (Acts 1:25). He does not do the will of God that was made known to him by Christ through secret revelations, as the *Gospel of Judas* would have it. He catastrophically succumbs to temptation so that human sin is interlaced with God's saving action.

---

9. Crump, *Jesus the Intercessor*, 164.

Luke 22:7 – 20

Literary Context

Many important events and discussions in Jesus' ministry take place around a table in Luke, and this last meal is a culmination of his ministry with his disciples. Here Jesus discusses his coming betrayal and arrest, the meaning of his death, and the disciples' tasks as future leaders of the church.[1] Minear captures the essence of the meal: "The table becomes a place where human need meets divine grace, where the presence of Jesus transforms the sad remembrance of things past into the glorious promise of things to come."[2]

The directions for preparing for the meal set up the prophecies that follow relating to his destiny and that of the disciples. Jesus exhibits the same prophetic foreknowledge as he did when he dispatched his disciples to get the colt for his entry into the city (19:29 – 34). His precise knowledge of what they will find reinforces the theme that runs through the Last Supper: what has been foreordained by God is also foreknown by Jesus. Because his predictions regarding securing the room for their meal are fulfilled to the letter (22:8 – 13), the reader can trust that his other prophecies will also be fulfilled. Jesus is not being swept away by events but is in command and is accomplishing his divine mission.

- VI. Jesus' Suffering and Death (22:1 – 23:49)
  - A. Judas's Selling Out to Satan and the High Priests (22:1 – 6)
  - **B. Jesus' Last Supper (22:7 – 20)**
  - C. Jesus' Parting Words to His Disciples (22:21 – 38)

---

1. du Plessis, "The Saving Significance of Jesus and His Death on the Cross," 527.

2. Minear, "Some Glimpses of Luke's Sacramental Theology," 325.

Main Idea

At the Last Supper, Jesus conveys through the symbols of bread broken and wine poured out that his death will inaugurate a new covenant with God that brings the expiation of sins.

Translation

Luke 22:7–20

22:7	Temporal episode marker	**Then came the day of Unleavened Bread** on which it was necessary to sacrifice the Passover lamb.
8	Commission	**He then sent Peter and John, saying,** *"Go make ready for us that we may eat the Passover."*
9	Question	**They said to him,** *"Where might you want us to make it ready?"*
10a	Prediction	**He said to them,** *"Behold, when you enter the city, a man carrying an earthenware vessel of water will meet you.*
b	Command	*Follow him into the house he enters.*
11a	Command	*Say to the master of the household,*
b	Inquiry	*'The teacher says to you,* *Where is the guest room where I may eat Passover with my disciples?'*
12a	Prediction	*That one will show you a large room upstairs [already] arranged.*
b	Command	*Make ready there."*
13a	Obedience	So when they went,
b	Fulfillment	**they found everything to be just as he had told them,**
c	Obedience	and **they made ready for the Passover.**
14	Temporal episode marker	When the hour arrived, **he reclined [at table] and the apostles with him.**
15		**Then he said to them,** *"I greatly desired to eat this Passover with you before I suffer.*
16	Vow	*For I say to you, I will not eat it until the time when it is fulfilled in the reign of God."*
17a	Action	Then after taking the cup and blessing it,
b	Command	**he said,** *"Take this and distribute it among yourselves.*
18	Vow	*For I say to you, from now on I will not drink from the fruit of the vine until the reign of God comes."*
19a	Action	Then after taking the loaf and blessing it, **he broke and gave it to them, saying,**

Continued on next page.

b	Explanation	*"This is my body, which is being given for you.*
c	Command	*Do this in remembrance of me."*
20a	Action	**And he did the same thing with the cup after supper, saying,**
b	Explanation	*"This cup is the new covenant in my blood, which is being poured out for you."*

Structure and Literary Form

The structure of the Last Supper consists of Jesus' command to prepare for the Passover, followed by the disciples' question of where they are to do so. The question meets with a prediction that is fulfilled to the letter. The Last Supper then contains three sets of double sayings. The first concerns Jesus' passion (22:15 – 16); the second, the cup (22:17 – 18); and the third, the bread and the cup (22:19 – 20).[3]

Exegetical Outline

→ **I. Preparation for the Passover (22:7 – 13)**

    A. Announcement of the coming sacrifice for the Passover (22:7)

    B. Commission of Peter and John to prepare for the Passover (22:8 – 13)

        1. Commission of the disciples (22:8)

        2. Question about where (22:9)

        3. Prediction of a sign and command to follow the person (22:10 – 12a)

        4. Command to prepare the Passover there (22:12b)

        5. Obedience to the command and fulfillment of the prediction (22:13)

II. The Last Supper (22:14 – 20)

    A. Solemn introduction of Jesus arriving with the apostles at the appointed hour (22:14)

    B. Double saying about Jesus' passion (22:15 – 16)

        1. Desire to eat with his disciples before his passion (22:15)

        2. Confident assurance that his passion will lead to eschatological fulfillment in the reign of God (22:16)

    C. Double saying about the cup (22:17 – 18)

        1. Blessing of the cup and its distribution (22:17)

        2. Confident assurance that it will lead to eschatological fulfillment in the reign of God (22:18)

    D. Double saying about bread and cup (22:19 – 20)

        1. Blessing of the bread, its distribution, and interpretation — my body given for you (22:19)

        2. Blessing of the cup and interpretation — my blood poured out for you (22:20)

---

3. Evans, *St. Luke*, 781.

Explanation of the Text

22:7 Then came the day of Unleavened Bread on which it was necessary to sacrifice the Passover lamb (ἦλθεν δὲ ἡ ἡμέρα τῶν ἀζύμων, [ἐν] ᾗ ἔδει θύεσθαι τὸ πάσχα). Luke introduces Jesus' last meal with the statement that it "was *necessary* to sacrifice the Passover lamb" (ἔδει θύεσθαι τὸ πάσχα), while Mark 14:12b identifies it simply as the time "when it was customary to sacrifice the Passover lamb." Luke portrays Jesus' death as a matter of divine necessity (9:22; 13:33; 22:37; 17:25; 24:7, 26, 44; Acts 1:16; 17:2 – 3), and this reference to the necessity of the Passover sacrifice anticipates and parallels the necessity of Jesus' sacrificial death. This phrase and Jesus' statement that "the Son of Man goes as it has been ordained" (v. 22) have God's predetermined purposes enfolding the account of the Last Supper.

This opening statement "reminds the audience that the death of the Passover lamb was the sacrificial death that saved Israel from death in the original Passover event before their exodus from Egypt."[4] The emphasis on the Passover (22:1, 7, 8, 11, 13) "seems to imply that some form of deliverance is to be accomplished through Jesus' death."[5] The blood of Jesus that will be "poured out," however, is more efficacious than that of the Passover lamb sprinkled on the doorposts because it establishes a new covenant that brings the forgiveness of sins.

"The day of Unleavened Bread" is perhaps Luke's term. He uses it to apply to the general time period when the Passover lambs were sacrificed, the Passover day that occurred after sunset according to Jewish time reckoning, and the following day that began the weeklong Feast of Unleavened

Bread. The reference reminds the audience that Jesus consistently observed Jewish religious practices (cf. Acts 20:16), but what occurs during this feast will change its meaning for Christ's followers forever.

22:8 He then sent Peter and John, saying, "Go make ready for us that we may eat the Passover" (καὶ ἀπέστειλεν Πέτρον καὶ Ἰωάννην εἰπών· πορευθέντες ἑτοιμάσατε ἡμῖν τὸ πάσχα ἵνα φάγωμεν). In Mark 14:12, the disciples first prod Jesus with a question about where they should prepare to eat the Passover. In Luke, Jesus is the one who brings up the issue of eating the meal and sends Peter and John to make preparations. Jesus' initiative in directing the preparation for the meal is reminiscent of the procurement of the colt for his entry into Jerusalem (19:29 – 34) and makes clear that after the Jewish leaders and Judas have plotted his destruction (22:1 – 6), Jesus is not simply a pawn in the hands of fate but an agent in control of all these events.

Luke names the disciples who are sent (in Mark 14:13, they are unnamed). Peter and John (along with James) witnessed the transfiguration (9:28) and will become prominent figures in the emerging church (Acts 3:1, 3, 11; 4:13, 19; 8:14). Preparing for the meal would involve taking their lamb in the afternoon to the temple and joining one of three lines to have the animal slaughtered. Priests would catch the blood in gold or silver vessels, pass the carcass along the line until it reached the priest next to the altar, where it was offered as a sacrifice. When the entrails were removed, the animal was returned to the owners for roasting (see *m.*

4. Heil, *The Meal Scenes in Luke-Acts*, 167 – 68. The verb "to sacrifice" appears in Exod 12:21 (LXX) and the noun in Exod 12:27 (LXX).

5. Nelson, *Leadership and Discipleship*, 58.

Pesaḥ. 5). The disciples would also have to prepare the room and provide the unleavened bread, wine, and dishes of herbs. These leading disciples are therefore portrayed as servants who ready the table for the others, a theme that surfaces in one of Jesus' sayings at the supper (22:24 – 27).[6]

Their preparations give a new twist on what it means to go before the Lord "to prepare his ways" (1:76; see 3:4). These two disciples are not simply preparing for a religious rite but for Jesus' sacrificial death. In the account of the meal that follows, nothing is mentioned about eating the Passover lamb. What they eat is the bread, which Jesus gives to them and interprets as a symbol of his own sacrifice for them. His bloody death is represented by the cup. This night will be seared on the disciples' memories, and this event transforms the meaning of Passover for his followers as Jesus himself becomes the Passover Lamb (1 Cor 5:7)!

22:9 – 10 They said to him, "Where might you want us to make it ready?" He said to them, "Behold, when you enter the city, a man carrying an earthenware vessel of water will meet you. Follow him into the house he enters" (οἱ δὲ εἶπαν αὐτῷ· ποῦ θέλεις ἑτοιμάσωμεν; ὁ δὲ εἶπεν αὐτοῖς· ἰδοὺ εἰσελθόντων ὑμῶν εἰς τὴν πόλιν συναντήσει ὑμῖν ἄνθρωπος κεράμιον ὕδατος βαστάζων· ἀκολουθήσατε αὐτῷ εἰς τὴν οἰκίαν εἰς ἣν εἰσπορεύεται). None of the disciples apparently know where they will eat the Passover, which requires them to ask "Where?" The uncertainty ensures secrecy so that Jesus can impart his final instructions to his disciples without fear of interference from the malevolent authorities. Jesus directs Peter and John to an unusual spectacle that would be easy to spot, since women normally fetched water. The man would lead them to the place.

22:11 – 13 "Say to the master of the household, 'The teacher says to you, Where is the guest room where I may eat Passover with my disciples?' That one will show you a large room upstairs [already] arranged. Make ready there." So when they went, they found everything to be just as he had told them, and they made ready for the Passover (καὶ ἐρεῖτε τῷ οἰκοδεσπότῃ τῆς οἰκίας· λέγει σοι ὁ διδάσκαλος· ποῦ ἐστιν τὸ κατάλυμα ὅπου τὸ πάσχα μετὰ τῶν μαθητῶν μου φάγω; κἀκεῖνος ὑμῖν δείξει ἀνάγαιον μέγα ἐστρωμένον· ἐκεῖ ἑτοιμάσατε. ἀπελθόντες δὲ εὗρον καθὼς εἰρήκει αὐτοῖς καὶ ἡτοίμασαν τὸ πάσχα).

The meal will take place in a private household as Scripture prescribes (Exod 12:3 – 4). No "guest room" (τὸ κατάλυμα) had been available to Jesus and his family at his birth (2:7), but now he has the authority as "the teacher" to request and expect hospitality in the guest room of this house. No disciple of Jesus addresses him as "teacher" in Luke, and the owner of the house is probably someone who knows him from his public teaching in the temple.

22:14 When the hour arrived, he reclined [at table] and the apostles with him (καὶ ὅτε ἐγένετο ἡ ὥρα, ἀνέπεσεν καὶ οἱ ἀπόστολοι σὺν αὐτῷ). The reference to "the hour" (ἡ ὥρα) almost has the ring of John's "hour" (John 13:1). It is not simply a chronological reference but a solemn chiming of the hour heralding the doom-laden events to come.

22:15 Then he said to them, "I greatly desired to eat this Passover with you before I suffer" (καὶ εἶπεν πρὸς αὐτούς· ἐπιθυμίᾳ ἐπεθύμησα τοῦτο τὸ πάσχα φαγεῖν μεθ᾽ ὑμῶν πρὸ τοῦ με παθεῖν). The Greek contains a Hebraism with a verb and cognate noun that literally reads, "with desire I desired" (ἐπιθυμίᾳ ἐπεθύμησα). The construction

---

6. Green, *The Gospel of Luke*, 313.

lends force to the verb and underscores the gathering's importance to Jesus. Jesus sent Peter and John to prepare the Passover so that "we may eat" it (vv. 8, 11), but Jesus now announces that he will not eat. Since in 15:16 and 17:22, the verb "to desire" plus an infinitive expresses an unfulfilled wish, Jesus means, "I would dearly have liked to eat this Passover with you," but he takes a vow of abstinence (vv. 16, 18).[7]

22:16 "For I say to you, I will not eat it until the time when it is fulfilled in the reign of God" (λέγω γὰρ ὑμῖν ὅτι οὐ μὴ φάγω αὐτὸ ἕως ὅτου πληρωθῇ ἐν τῇ βασιλείᾳ τοῦ θεοῦ). "For I say to you" (λέγω γὰρ ὑμῖν) conveys solemnity and is repeated in v. 18. The reference to the reign of God recalls the excited outburst of the dinner guest who gushed, "Blessed is the one who eats at the banquet in the reign of God" (14:15), and Jesus' prophecy that people will come from east and west, from north and south, and will eat in the reign of God (13:29). Jesus now looks forward to the consummation at the end of the age (22:29 – 30). Heil comments, "This accords with the future, prophetic orientation of the Passover meal, which looked forward to the fulfillment in God's kingdom of the great salvific deeds of the past celebrated and made present during the Passover meal."[8] Jesus' death and resurrection will be God's culminating salvific deed and will fulfill the hope of Israel.

22:17 Then after taking the cup and blessing it, he said, "Take this and distribute it among yourselves" (καὶ δεξάμενος ποτήριον εὐχαριστήσας εἶπεν· λάβετε τοῦτο καὶ διαμερίσατε εἰς ἑαυτούς). Jesus serves as the host. He does not drink from his own cup but instead gives it to each of his disciples to drink. Danker insists that this gesture after Jesus' surprising oath and the fact that the disciples all would have had their own cups would have made a profound impression on them.[9] Drinking the cup of someone was understood to be a means of entering into a communion relationship with that person to the point that one shares that person's destiny for good or ill (see Ps 16:4 – 5). After the resurrection, the disciples could recognize in retrospect that sharing Jesus' cup "unites them all to Jesus on his way to death."[10]

22:18 "For I say to you, from now on I will not drink from the fruit of the vine until the reign of God comes" (λέγω γὰρ ὑμῖν [ὅτι] οὐ μὴ πίω ἀπὸ τοῦ νῦν ἀπὸ τοῦ γενήματος τῆς ἀμπέλου ἕως οὗ ἡ βασιλεία τοῦ θεοῦ ἔλθῃ). The disciples do not yet realize that Jesus is destined to drink another cup, the cup of suffering (22:42). Jeremias offers three possible motivations for his vow of abstinence. (1) "Jesus may have intended to make clear to his disciples the irrevocable nature of his decision to prepare the way for the kingdom of God by his vicarious suffering. He burns his bridges."[11] This vow, then, reflects Jesus' longing to fulfill his mission (see 12:50).

(2) The vow conveys his desire to make clear to his disciples that he belongs to the age of the consummation, not the present age, and he provides an example of self-giving that collides with the prevailing norms of the world.

(3) The vow imparts to his disciples his certainty that the reign of God will come despite the

---

7. This statement may be tied to the chronological issues surrounding the passion narrative. It is possible that Jesus' fervent wish may be unfulfilled because he refers to the approaching Passover that will occur on the next day. He knew he would be in the hands of the authorities and unable to celebrate the meal (see John 13:1; 18:28, 39; 19:14). For a summary of the chronological issues, see Raymond E. Brown, *The Death of the Messiah* (2 vols.; New York: Doubleday, 1994), 2:1350 – 78.

8. Heil, *The Meal Scenes in Luke-Acts*, 173.

9. Danker, *Jesus and the New Age*, 345.

10. Heil, *The Meal Scenes in Luke-Acts*, 173.

11. Jeremias, *The Eucharistic Words of Jesus*, 216.

dark hours that lie ahead. These three options are not mutually exclusive and together give a fuller picture of Jesus' intention.

22:19 Then after taking a loaf and blessing it, he broke and gave it to them, saying, "This is my body, which is being given for you. Do this in remembrance of me" (καὶ λαβὼν ἄρτον εὐχαριστήσας ἔκλασεν καὶ ἔδωκεν αὐτοῖς λέγων· τοῦτό ἐστιν τὸ σῶμά μου τὸ ὑπὲρ ὑμῶν διδόμενον· τοῦτο ποιεῖτε εἰς τὴν ἐμὴν ἀνάμνησιν). A notorious textual variant appears in 22:19b – 20. The external evidence of manuscripts supporting the longer reading that describes Jesus' words and distribution of the bread and the cup is overwhelming.[12] Two guiding principles of textual criticism that give deference to the (1) shorter and (2) more difficult reading lead some to conclude these verses were absent from the original manuscript and were inserted at a later time in the course of copying the text. Jeremias rightly counters, "It is difficult to assume that an interpolation could have been introduced in *all* Greek manuscripts except D."[13] The longer reading allows for two parallel sayings about eating and drinking:

22:15 – 16	eat this Passover	"I will not eat"
22:17 – 18	takes cup	"I will not drink"
22:19	takes bread	Interpretation: "this is my body"
22:20	takes cup	Interpretation: "new covenant in my blood"[14]

The argument that the omission of the longer text may have originated from a scribe's attempt to get rid of the two cups at the Lord's Supper (vv.17 and 20) does not hold. Why would the scribe omit vv.19b – 20 instead of vv.17 – 18 and thereby avoid the problem of having the drinking of the cup precede eating the bread, since this order does not conform to church practice?[15]

Jeremias contends that the longer text was probably omitted out of a desire to protect the secret words of a Christian sacrament, intended only for believers, from being profaned by the misinterpretation of heathens.[16] Billings offers a more likely explanation for its omission in the Western text. In the second century, after the break with the synagogue and with their aggressive missionary proselytism, "Christians received more negative attention as a 'third race' (*tertium genus*) distinct from that of Greco-Roman paganism and Judaism."[17] Christians were accused of Oedipodean intercourse and Thyestean banquets, which had cannibalistic connotations that might be reinforced by references to drinking human blood.[18] These accusations fed persecution, and Christian apologists, like Justin, were not able to overcome it.[19] Billings concludes:

> The concentration of apologetic literature of this time is "entirely unique." The nature of the accusations, as evidenced by the responses to them, focuses attention most acutely on the Christian meal observance and the final practices associated

12. The longer text is found as early as AD 150 in Justin Martyr's *1 Apol.* 66. It is represented in ancient text types from both East and West. Only one Greek manuscript, D, supports the shorter text, and this manuscript is notoriously erratic. It is followed by a small number of versions (it[b,e], syr[c], syr[s], syr[p]).

13. Jeremias, *The Eucharistic Words of Jesus*, 144 – 45.

14. Talbert, *Reading Luke*, 207.

15. It is found in *Did.* 9:1 – 3.

16. So Jeremias, *The Eucharistic Words of Jesus*, 156 – 69.

17. Bradly S. Billings, "The Disputed Words in the Lukan Institution Narrative (Luke 22:19b – 20): A Sociological Answer to a Textual Problem," *JBL* 125 (2006): 513. See his full-length work, *Do This in Remembrance of Me: The Disputed Words of the Lukan Institution Narrative: A Historico-Exegetical, Theological, and Sociological Analysis* (LNT 314; London: T&T Clark, 2006).

18. Billings, "The Disputed Words in the Lukan Institution Narrative (Luke 22:19b – 20)," 517.

19. Ibid., 521 – 22.

with it. The allegations of Thyestean cannibalism, which have already led to outrages in Lyons, mean that the words of institution attributed to Jesus are, in this climate of suspicion, rumor, hysteria, highly likely to be misunderstood and/or misappropriated (as already familial language among the believers and other rituals such as the kiss of peace are with less serious consequences).... The Christian communities of the first two centuries, almost everywhere in the extant literature, understand and interpret the Eucharist in essentially realistic language, increasing dramatically the possibility of "outsiders" misunderstanding or misappropriating eucharistic language.[20]

Billings' conclusion that the later sociohistorical situation prompted the alteration of the text is persuasive. A scribe considered it prudent to omit the words of institution to forestall any further misunderstanding and subsequent allegations and persecution.

Jesus gives the traditional blessing of the bread at a meal a new twist by saying that the bread is his body. The subject and predicate connected by the verb "is" (ἐστιν) are not to be taken as identical, and the copula is better translated "represents" or "symbolizes." When Jesus breaks the bread and distributes it to the disciples, it means that what has happened to this bread will happen to me. The broken bread given to the disciples also symbolizes that his passion will benefit them. The implication is that his body is being offered as a sacrifice for them, like the Passover lamb.

This "remembrance" (ἀνάμνησιν) of Jesus is not a reminder or commemoration of him, as one might find on tomb inscriptions, but, like the Passover meal, a re-presentation that proclaims the saving significance of his sacrificial death until he comes (1 Cor 11:26). The past is never merely the past but is relived in the present. As the Passover

remembers God's deliverance of Israel from the bondage of Egypt (Exod 12:14; 13:3, 8; Deut 16:3), so the re-presentation of this meal remembers God's deliverance of all believers through the cross of Jesus, giving them salvation.

The remembrance entails being mindful of God's deliverance in Christ, which should have direct consequences for behavior. It requires reflection on his sacrifice, worship of him, and obedience to his commands. It obligates disciples to be servants who bestow true benefits on others (22:24 – 30), to resist Satan so as to stand firm in faith and to strengthen others (22:31 – 34), and to face violent hostility with courage and grace (22:35 – 38).

22:20 And he did the same thing with the cup after supper, saying, "This cup is the new covenant in my blood, which is being poured out for you" (καὶ τὸ ποτήριον ὡσαύτως μετὰ τὸ δειπνῆσαι, λέγων· τοῦτο τὸ ποτήριον ἡ καινὴ διαθήκη ἐν τῷ αἵματί μου τὸ ὑπὲρ ὑμῶν ἐκχυννόμενον). The cup after the meal is also given a new symbolic interpretation. Jesus associates the blood with the cup, not the wine. It reflects sensitivity to the Jewish aversion to "drinking blood" (Lev 3:17; 7:26; Deut 12:16, 23 – 25; 15:23; 1 Sam 14:32; 1 Chr 11:15 – 19) and "prevents the misunderstanding of a magical transformation of substances."[21]

Jesus accepts the necessity of his death laid out in God's plan of salvation (9:22; 17:25). The verb "poured out" (ἐκχυννόμενον) is passive. Heil connects the use of this verb to sacrifices in the Old Testament:

"To pour out the blood" of someone means to murder him (Gen 9:6; Isa 59:7; Ezek 18:10). And since the plot to murder Jesus is underway (22:2), his blood is already in the process of being poured out. But Jesus' blood is also being poured out as the sacrificial blood that establishes the new

---

covenant. That the covenantal blood of Jesus is being "poured out" (ἐκχυννόμενον) reminds the audience of how Moses poured (ἐνέχεεν) half of the sacrificial blood of the covenant into bowls, and the other half he poured forth (προσέχεεν) before the altar of God (LXX Exod 24:6). As the priest "pours out" (ἐχεεῖ) the blood of the sacrificial animals on the altar as a sin offering to atone for the sins of the people (LXX Lev 4:7, 18, 25, 30, 34), so the sacrificial blood of Jesus is being "poured out" in death to establish the new covenant that definitively unites God to his people though his forgiveness of their sins.[22]

Jesus' blood surpasses the blood of the Passover lamb placed on doorposts before the Exodus because it establishes a new covenant, recalling the promise of Jer 31:31 – 34. The new covenant was necessary because the people continued to sin, and it promises to be different because God declares, "I will put my law in their minds and will write it on their hearts," and "I will forgive their wickedness and remember their sins no more." Heil concludes: "Thus, the sacrificial blood of the death of Jesus now fulfills this hope by establishing 'the new covenant' by which God promises his new, definitive, eschatological forgiveness of sins."[23] In this new covenant, "Jesus' blood becomes a means of expiation provided by God."[24]

Theology in Application

1. The Continuation of Jesus' Table Fellowship

In the Passover meal, Israel "not only relived and made present their past salvific exodus from Egypt, in which God liberated them from slavery and death by 'passing over' their houses sprinkled with the blood of the Passover lamb (Exod 12:1 – 30; Deut 16:1 – 8), but also anticipated their share in God's future and final salvation."[25] The Lord's Supper retains "the threefold orientation" to the past, present, and future as did the Passover, but it replaces the Passover for Christians. It reenacts the covenant established through Jesus' death, reinforces the unity of believers with Christ and one another, and reminds believers of Jesus' pledge that all will be fulfilled in the age to come. It is understandable how it became central for the early church. Schweizer comments:

> In contrast to all other religious communities of their time, the early Christians had no temple, no statues, no priests, no special cult; the only thing visible was a table with a meal around which they came together every week. It was the continuation of the table fellowship of Jesus, and especially of that meal on the last evening together. It was a definitive gift from God and a central manifestation of the truth the church brought to the world.[26]

---

22. Ibid., 179.
23. Ibid.
24. Francis Giordano Carpinelli, "Do This as *My* Memorial (Luke 22:19): Lucan Soteriology of Atonement," *CBQ* 61 (1999): 88.

25. Heil, *The Meal Scenes in Luke-Acts*, 167.
26. Schweizer, *Jesus, the Parable of God*, 47.

2. Jesus' Atoning Death

Many argue that Luke avoided or muted ransom theology in his gospel. If 22:19b – 20 is considered to be a later scribal addition, the only passage in Luke that specifically mentions the blood of Christ that inaugurates a new covenant is eliminated. The absence of this passage, it is said, accords with the general tenor of Luke, which otherwise does not have a specific statement that Jesus died on behalf of anyone.[27] In what seems to be a circular argument, Caird contends that Luke would not have recorded 22:20 (= Mark 14:24) because it appears to concentrate the whole of God's redemption in the cross.[28] If these verses were original to Luke (as is argued above), du Plessis maintains that the pouring out of Jesus' blood is only "the symbol and seal of the new covenant He made with them" and "the *guarantee* of this loyalty and care."[29] Jesus' death is not interpreted as a sacrifice to expiate sin, but "the highest price a human being can pay to show that He cares for his followers, and that they may know and be reminded how much he cares."[30] Luke, it is argued, passed over his death quickly as "a necessary prelude before his glorification" (see 24:25 – 27).[31]

In my view, this interpretation is misleading. Luke does not mute the idea of atonement connected to Jesus' death in Acts 20:28: "The Holy Spirit has made you overseers. Be shepherds of the church of God, which he bought with his own blood." His death brings the remission of sins (Acts 3:17 – 19; 5:30 – 31; 10:43; 13:38 – 39).[32] Moessner challenges the redactional analyses that have attempted to discern Luke's supposed view of the atonement. He argues that in Hellenistic poetics meaning is conferred by the movement of the plot, and he makes an important point overlooked by redaction critics:

> … there is no "point" for direct speech when the plot itself makes the significance of an event clear (Aristotle, *Poetics* 19.7 – 8). Direct-speech commentary is at best a secondary means of emplotment, configured for rhetorical emphasis and entertainment. Thus in asking whether Luke signifies the death of Jesus as atoning for sin, we will have to read/hear the plot of Luke-Acts within its plotted "continuity"; speeches of main characters as well as narratorial comments will be an important place to look, but they will not be the primary media of significance.[33]

---

27. Luke 22:27 parallels Mark 10:45 (Matt 20:24 – 28) about Jesus coming as one who serves, but it omits the reference to Jesus' death as a ransom for many that is found in Mark's text. In 22:37, Luke cites Isa 53:12: "He was reckoned with the lawless," but stops short of quoting the rest of the verse, "he bore the sin of many, and made intercession for the transgressors."

28. Caird, *Saint Luke*, 238.

29. du Plessis, "The Saving Significance of Jesus and His Death on the Cross," 526.

30. Ibid., 534.

31. Caird, *Saint Luke*, 238.

32. Reginald H. Fuller, "Luke and the Theologia Crucis," in *Sin, Salvation, and the Spirit* (ed. D. Durkin; Collegeville, MN: Liturgical, 1979), 216 – 18. He points out that it is unfair to "contrast Luke unfavorably with Mark as regards his soteriology," and notes that Luke "has exactly the same number of explicit references to the cross as salvific event as does Mark" (219).

33. Moessner, "Reading Luke's Gospel as Ancient Hellenistic Narrative," 134.

Luke emphasizes that the central thrust of all the Scriptures is that the Christ must suffer. Though only a small portion of Isa 53 is actually quoted in the Last Supper narrative (22:37), the entire context in Isaiah governs Luke's interpretation of Jesus' death. The atoning effect of Jesus' death is revealed by the story rather than by declarations. Jesus is substituted for the sinner Barabbas as the one who will die (23:18 – 19). Through his death, he saves others and promises that the self-confessed guilty evildoer will be with him in paradise (23:39 – 43). In his narrative arrangement, "Jesus is presented to the Lord with a sacrifice of redemption as the firstborn of Israel [2:22 – 23]; in the 'end,' Jesus presents himself to the Lord as a sacrifice for the redemption of Israel and all the nations."[34]

The Last Supper also conveys Jesus' acceptance of sinners for whom he dies. The long series of meals and references to celebrations in Luke (5:27 – 32; 7:36 – 50; 9:11 – 17; 14:15 – 24; 15:2; 19:5 – 7) were tangible signs of forgiveness, acceptance, and mercy to sinners, and this last meal is the culmination. It affirms that God has acted to break down every barrier to save humanity in Jesus.

3. Do This

The emphasis in this account falls on the self-giving of Jesus that the disciples are to imitate. "Do this" does not refer simply to repeating the ritual or recalling the memory of Jesus, "but making the same self-gift that Jesus made."[35] Jesus' selfless act stands in stark contrast to the disciples' contest for honor and it is what needs to repeated (see 1 Cor 11). The Christian Lord's Supper is based on Jesus' sacrificial death for others. The attitude that led him to give his life in obedience to God should characterize the attitude of those who join with him in this Supper.[36]

When Paul appeals to the original Lord's Supper tradition to correct the abuses of the Lord's Supper in Corinth (1 Cor 11:23 – 26), he is trying to counter the values of the dominant culture that had seeped into that church that were antithetical to the message of the cross. The Corinthians failed to work out the theological implications of the Supper. They were accustomed in their culture to use banquets as theater to showcase one's wealth and social preeminence and as a means to augment one's social-climbing ambitions. The Lord's Supper was part of a full meal (1 Cor 11:33) that brought together a broad slice of Corinthian society. Many of these believers had only their Christian faith in common. Rubbing elbows with the poorer members rubbed against the human tendency to want to socialize with persons of one's own rank or to demonstrate that one was somehow superior. The host probably invited into his triclinium his closest friends or the most distinguished among the believers. The rest took their places in the atrium, where conditions were inferior. The meal

---

34. Ibid., 151.

35. Jerome Kodell, *The Eucharist in the New Testament*

(Collegeville, MN: Liturgical, 1991), 115 – 16.

36. Garland, *1 Corinthians*, 550.

was a potluck affair, except that there was no expectation that one needed to share what one brought with anyone else. It opened the door to indulgence and indifference, and one group gorged themselves while another group went hungry (1 Cor 11:21).

The question for Paul is simply this: Does the practice of the Lord's Supper proclaim the Lord's death (1 Cor 11:26)? Proclaiming the Lord's death means more than simply announcing that this Supper represents that Jesus died for us (Rom 5:8). It means living out the implications of Jesus' dying for us. Inconsiderateness, indifference, and lovelessness (1 Cor 11:22) toward brothers and sisters for whom Christ died (1 Cor 8:11) amount to nothing short of an inexcusable disregard for Christ's saving expiatory death for all.

Devouring their own portion while ignoring the have-nots who had to go without contrasts with what Jesus did at the Last Supper. The wealthier members took bread, broke it, and gobbled it down; Jesus took bread, broke it, and shared it with others. The wealthier members took on their own behalf; Jesus, on others' behalf. The former acted selfishly; Jesus selflessly gave to others. Paul confirms that Jesus' command to "do this" means more than reenacting a religious rite. It means pointing to Jesus' sacrifice of his life for others and following suit. If one proclaims the Lord's death in the Lord's Supper, one cannot despise others, shame them, allow them to go hungry, or overindulge oneself.

The Lord's Supper should accentuate the communion that Christians have with Christ and also with one another as brothers and sisters in Christ (1 Cor 10:16 – 17). The Lord's Supper should be a time when it is clear that "if one part suffers, every part suffers with it; if one part is honored, every part rejoices with it" (1 Cor 12:26).

Luke 22:21 – 38

Literary Context

Liturgical interests have often led to such a preoccupation with the words of the institution of the Lord's Supper that few realize that the center of gravity in Luke's narrative shifts from the sayings during the supper to the sayings *after* the supper. Luke recasts and deliberately places sayings related to disciples in this solemn context, and they form the climax to the supper.[1] Luke turns the spotlight off Jesus for a moment as Jesus reflects his care for the plight of the disciples and their future mission. He is more absorbed by the predicament of his disciples after his death than he is by his own death that looms on the immediate horizon. The reference to his own fate in 22:37 is intended solely as a warning to his disciples that they can expect no better treatment than their Master receives.

What links these groups of sayings together? (1) They all concern the relationship between Jesus and his disciples and reveal both the impending treachery of the disciples and their ultimate hope. The disciples' response to what Jesus says, however, reveals the vast gulf that exists between them. It is as if Jesus' teaching has made no impact on them whatsoever, but this teaching will be remembered in the life of the church. "Do this in remembrance of me" (22:19) does not apply only to liturgical actions repeated in the Last Supper but to the manner of life enjoined by and modeled by Jesus.

(2) A limit is placed on the damage that will be done by the disciples' failures. Judas will betray him to death, but his death accomplishes God's will. The internecine dispute reveals the petty jealousies the disciples have been harboring and their incomprehension about the way of the cross. It will lead to failure at a crucial moment but will not lead to ultimate disaster. They are assured that they will sit at the messianic banquet and on thrones. Peter (along with the others) will be sifted with

---

1. The sayings occur in quite different contexts in Mark and Matthew:
    22:24 – 27 = Mark 10:41 – 45/Matt 20:24 – 28
    22:28 – 30 = Matt 19:28
    22:35 recalls Luke 9:3; 10:4.

what Satan hopes is the sieve of destruction so that his faith falls through the mesh, but Jesus has prayed for him so that he is assured that he will recover and become a pillar of strength for his brother apostles. Disciples, spoiling for a fight, will want to mix it up with those who come to arrest Jesus. One will draw his sword and impetuously strike the high priest's servant. Jesus, by contrast, has no sword and puts up no resistance. He undoes the damage of their violence by healing the injured ear, saying, "That's enough!" (lit.), "Leave it until this" or "Up to this and no further!" (22:49 – 51).

VI. Jesus' Suffering and Death (22:1 – 23:49)

    A. Judas's Selling Out to Satan and the High Priests (22:1 – 6)

    B. Jesus' Last Supper (22:7 – 20)

➡   **C. Jesus' Parting Words to His Disciples (22:21 – 38)**

    D. Jesus' Prayer and Arrest on the Mount of Olives (22:39 – 53)

Main Idea

The path of discipleship and true greatness passes through service and trials and follows the example set by Jesus.[2]

Translation

Luke 22:21–38

22:21	Circumstance/ exclamation	*"But look!* *The one who betrays me is with me!* *His hand is on the table!*
22a	Explanation	*Because the Son of Man goes as it has been ordained,*
b	Woe	*but woe to that man through whom he is betrayed."*
23	Response	**Then they began to argue among them** over which of them it might be who ↯ was about to do this.
24	Dispute	**A quarrel broke out among them** over which of them was to be considered the ↯ greatest.
25	Response/negative example	**He said to them,** *"The kings of the Gentiles lord it over them* *and those who wield authority over them are called benefactors.*

Continued on next page.

---

2. Nelson, *Leadership and Discipleship*, 246 – 47.

26a	Contrast	It is not to be this way with you.
b	Admonition	Let the one who is greatest among you become as the youngest and
c		the leader become as the one who serves.
27a	Justification with rhetorical questions	*For* who is greater, the one who reclines at table or the one who serves?
b		Is it not the one who reclines?
c	Positive example	*But* I am among you as one who serves.
28	Affirmation	You have remained with me throughout my trials.
29	Bequeathal formula	And I bestow on you, just as my Father bestowed on me, a kingdom,
30a	Eschatological assurance	so that you may eat and drink at my table in my reign,
b		*and* you will sit on thrones judging the twelve tribes of Israel."
31	Warning	"Simon, Simon!
		Look! Satan has demanded to sift you like wheat.
32a	Assurance	*But* I have pled for you so that your faith will not fail.
b	Command	When you turn, strengthen your brothers."

33	Protest of loyalty	**He said to him,**
		"Lord, I am ready even to go to prison with you and to face death!"
34	Prophecy	**He said,**
		"I say to you, Peter, the rooster will not crow today, *until* you deny three times that you [even] know me."

35a	Retrospective question	**He then said to them,**
		"When I sent you without a purse, bag, or sandals, you did not lack anything, did you?"
b	Response	**They said,**
		"Nothing."

36	Warning commands	**He said to them,**
		"*But now,* let the one who has a purse take it, and likewise a bag. *And* let the one who does not have a sword sell his cloak and buy one.
37a	Explanation	*For* I tell you, it is necessary that this that has been written about me⳨ be completed, namely, 'He was reckoned with the⳨ lawless.' (Isa 53:12)
b	Assertion	*For* in fact, this [prophecy] about me is coming to its culmination."

38a	Response	**They said,**
		"Lord! Look, here are two swords!"
b	Rebuke	**He said to them,**
		"Enough!"

Structure and Literary Form

The sayings of Jesus recorded at the table are like the "table talk" scenes elsewhere in the gospel, but these come at the end of his life. The scene has parallels with the testamentary genre, in which a man about to die gathers his people around him to bid them farewell, and these final words include exhortations, recollections, and predictions.[3] The first and last sayings make clear that Jesus is surrounded by sinners.

Exegetical Outline

→ I. **The hand of the betrayer (22:21 – 23)**
    A. Announcement of the betrayer (22:21)
    B. Fulfillment of Scripture (22:22a)
    C. Pronouncement of a woe (22:22b)
    D. The disciples' speculation about who among them would do such a thing (22:23)
  II. **The dispute over greatness (22:24 – 27)**
  III. **The rewards of perseverance (22:28 – 30)**
  IV. **The sifting of the disciples (22:31 – 34)**
  V. **The warning about future danger (22:35 – 38)**

Explanation of the Text

22:21 "But look! The one who betrays me is with me! His hand is on the table!" (πλὴν ἰδοὺ ἡ χεὶρ τοῦ παραδιδόντος με μετ' ἐμοῦ ἐπὶ τῆς τραπέζης). Jesus' words of interpretation over the bread and wine end abruptly with his announcement that the hand of the betrayer is at the table. Jesus has known what the reader knows (22:1 – 6). He has prophesied that he would be betrayed into the hands of men (9:44), and when Judas was first introduced as one of the disciples, he was identified as the one who would become a traitor (6:16). Jesus will be betrayed into the hands of men by the hand of Judas, who has just received the bread from Jesus. What none of the players in these treacherous events knows is that they play into the hand of God. It is not Satan, the priestly hierarchy,

or Judas who is in control. It is the hand of God that is really behind Jesus' death and is accomplishing God's inscrutable purpose. Jesus gives over his own life (διδόμενον, 22:19) for others, and he is being given over by God.

22:22 Because the Son of Man goes as it has been ordained, but woe to that man through whom he is betrayed (ὅτι ὁ υἱὸς μὲν τοῦ ἀνθρώπου κατὰ τὸ ὡρισμένον πορεύεται, πλὴν οὐαὶ τῷ ἀνθρώπῳ ἐκείνῳ δι' οὗ παραδίδοται). The verb "ordained" (ὁρίζω) conveys the idea that God has determined what will take place (see Acts 10:42; 17:26, 31). The interjection "but woe!" (πλὴν οὐαί) parallels the interjection "but look!" (πλὴν ἰδού) in 22:21 and introduces *"the proper evaluation of Jesus'*

---

3. On the testamentary genre, see ibid., 97 – 119.

betrayal."[4] What happens to Jesus fulfills God's plan of salvation, but it does not mean that the one who betrays him bears no guilt. What happens to Jesus is ordained, but it is not ordained that Judas would betray him.

As Brown interprets Acts 1:16 – 20: "The Scripture reveals the necessity of the *divine retribution* [for the treason], but not of the treason itself."[5] The woe implies that Judas will be cut off from salvation, and he will not eat and drink at Jesus' table in his reign (v. 30). Judas does not die by his own hand but from an accident: "he fell headlong [and] his body burst open" (Acts 1:18), which can be viewed as an act of God (see Acts 12:23 and the death of Herod).

22:23 Then they began to argue among themselves about which of them it might be who is about to do this (καὶ αὐτοὶ ἤρξαντο συζητεῖν πρὸς ἑαυτοὺς τὸ τίς ἄρα εἴη ἐξ αὐτῶν ὁ τοῦτο μέλλων πράσσειν). In Mark and Matthew, the disciples are sorrowful at this announcement and seek assurance from Jesus that they are not the one, "Surely you don't mean me?" (Matt 26:22; Mark 14:19). In Luke's account, they become defensive and contentious. Presumably, they try to ferret out the culprit. Clivaz claims, however, that the hand that betrays him has twelve names.[6] One

will hand him over, but the others will betray him in other ways.

22:24 A quarrel broke out among them over which of them was to be considered the greatest (ἐγένετο δὲ καὶ φιλονεικία ἐν αὐτοῖς, τὸ τίς αὐτῶν δοκεῖ εἶναι μείζων). Their argument over the betrayer devolves into an even more unseemly squabble over who among them is the greatest.[7] The unbridled ambition of James and John that leads them to request to sit on Jesus' right and left when he comes into his reign (Mark 10:35 – 45, absent from Luke) seems to have infected all of the disciples. One cannot think of a more inappropriate time for the disciples to bicker over who is the greatest. The deadly sin of the heathen — the lust for fame and glory — rears its ugly head at the Last Supper. Had they also scrambled for the seats of honor before the meal (cf. 14:7)? This dispute sullies this holy moment and causes us to blush for the disciples.[8]

The disciples are asking who is to be "considered" (δοκεῖ) greater than the others — who seems to be the greatest "in the eyes of the world."[9] Preoccupation with being recognized, receiving acclaim, and having influence inevitably leads to contentiousness, betrayal, and denial.[10] Jesus' response makes clear that true greatness has nothing to do with appearances or the opinions of others.

4. Heil, *The Meal Scenes in Luke-Acts*, 182; Crump, *Jesus the Intercessor*, 164. See 17:1, scandals will come, "but woe to that one who causes them."

5. Brown, *Apostasy and Perseverance in the Theology of Luke*, 94. He points out that Luke does not have Jesus declare at his arrest, "But the Scriptures must be fulfilled," as in Mark 14:49, but "this is your hour and the dominion of darkness" (22:53).

6. Claire Clivaz, "Douze noms pour une main: nouveaux regards sur Judas à partir de Lc 22.21 – 2," *NTS* 48 (2002): 416.

7. Luke normally presents the disciples in a positive light, but here we see a negative picture. The noun "quarrel" (φιλονεικία) implies "contentiousness" rather than friendly rivalry. Fourth Maccabees 1:26 provides an apt context for its

negative usage in a discussion of malevolent tendencies: "In the soul it is boastfulness, covetousness, thirst for honor, rivalry, and malice" (cf. also 1 Cor 11:16; Prov 10:12; Ezek 3:7; 2 Macc 4:4; 4 Macc 8:26).

8. The Lord's Supper was also an occasion for sundering community around similar issues in Corinth (1 Cor 11:17 – 34; see Garland, *1 Corinthians*, 533 – 57).

9. Heil, *The Meal Scenes in Luke-Acts*, 183. It recalls Paul's ambivalent reference to James, Peter, and John as "those esteemed [δοκοῦντες] as pillars" (Gal 2:9; see vv. 2, 6).

10. Ian Sloan, "The Greatest and the Youngest: Greco-Roman Reciprocity in the Farewell Address, Luke 22:24 – 30," *SR* 22 (1993): 67.

22:25 He said to them, "The kings of the Gentiles lord it over them and those who wield authority over them are called benefactors" (ὁ δὲ εἶπεν αὐτοῖς· οἱ βασιλεῖς τῶν ἐθνῶν κυριεύουσιν αὐτῶν καὶ οἱ ἐξουσιάζοντες αὐτῶν εὐεργέται καλοῦνται). Rather than confronting and condemning the disciples with a frontal attack, Jesus gently chides them through a comparison with the values of pagan grandees.[11] The will to power is a basic human drive; and in the heathen world, the great ones are those who best bend the wills of others to conform to their own. The word "lord it over them" (κυριεύουσιν αὐτῶν) here means to "exercise power over them" (Rom 6:9, 14; 2 Cor 1:24) and likely "implies the tendency towards compulsion or oppression which is immanent in all earthly power, and not merely in political."[12] In the Oriental experience, the monarch speaks, and the rest can only obey.

"Benefactor" is an honorific title typically bestowed as "a gesture of praise in compensation for a good deed."[13] When Vespasian returned to Rome as the new emperor after the defeat of the Jewish rebels, the crowds hailed him "their Benefactor and Savior" (Josephus, *J.W.* 7.4.1 §71). According to Dio Chrysostom (*De lege* 75.7 – 8; *1 Glor.* 66.2), public recognition was "more precious than life itself" for the benefactor. Danker claims that Jesus' comparison does not reject the role of benefactor

but "the interest in domination that is evidenced by many rulers who try to mask their tyranny with a flourish of public works."[14]

Gifts required reciprocity. Monuments are erected for patricians to proclaim themselves as do-gooders. Those who "are called" (καλοῦνται) "benefactors" (εὐεργέται; or who "claim" that title, if the verb is read as the middle voice) bestow patronage on others so that they might have influence over them and domineer over them.[15] Green highlights how insidious this system was. Private giving was necessitated because public treasuries were inadequate to the advantage of the rich:

> Private benefaction was the primary means by which the wealthy were legitimated as those most deserving of public office and prestige in the community. In order to provide leadership, wealth was required, so only the wealthy could provide leadership and thus enjoy the honor and self-advancement reserved for those who gave so "generously."[16]

22:26 – 27 It is not to be this way with you. Let the one who is greatest among you become as the youngest and the leader become as the one who serves. For who is greater, the one who reclines at table or the one who serves? Is it not the one who reclines? But I am among you as one who serves (ὑμεῖς δὲ οὐχ οὕτως, ἀλλ᾽ ὁ μείζων

11. David J. Lull ("The Servant-Benefactor as a Model of Greatness [Luke 22:24 – 30]," *NovT* [1986]: 289 – 305) fails to make the case that "benefactor" should be interpreted as a positive example — doing the greatest good for the greatest number. Nelson counters,

> To say that kings, rulers and authorities are called benefactors is not *in and of itself* a negative portrayal. It is only in light of the progression of thought in content (i.e. vv 23 – 24, 26 – 27) that the picture of kings and rulers takes on a negative hue. It is probable, then, that Luke wishes to pinpoint something negative about *ordinary* patterns of ruling (not just oppressive rule) and *usual* concerns for public honor (not just the improper acquisition of titles). (*Leadership and Discipleship*, 154)

See also Peter K. Nelson "The Flow of Thought in Luke 22:24 – 27," *JSNT* 43 (1991): 113 – 23.

12. Werner Foerster, "ἔξεστιν …," *TDNT*, 2:575.

13. Bruce W. Winter, "The Public Honouring of Christian Benefactors: Romans 13.3 – 4 and 1 Peter 2.14 – 15," *JSNT* 34 (1988): 90 – 91.

14. Frederick W. Danker, *Benefactor: Epigraphic Study of a Graeco-Roman and New Testament Semantic Field* (St. Louis: Clayton, 1982), 324.

15. See the reference to Ptolemy III of Egypt as Euergetes (Benefactor) in the prologue to Sirach.

16. Green, *The Gospel of Luke*, 768; citing Garnsey and Saller, *The Roman Empire*, 33.

ἐν ὑμῖν γινέσθω ὡς ὁ νεώτερος καὶ ὁ ἡγούμενος ὡς ὁ διακονῶν. τίς γὰρ μείζων, ὁ ἀνακείμενος ἢ ὁ διακονῶν; οὐχὶ ὁ ἀνακείμενος; ἐγὼ δὲ ἐν μέσῳ ὑμῶν εἰμι ὡς ὁ διακονῶν). Disciples are to be like God, "to give without expectation of return, even to the wicked and ungrateful (6:35 – 36)."[17] Honor is due God alone, so disciples must give up their fantasies of grandeur. They must also reappraise their ideas about power and greatness according to the pattern set by Jesus.[18] Jesus' model upends the norm.

Jesus sets up a series of contrasts and inverts the normal rankings:

greatest	youngest (26b)
leader	servant (26c)
diner	table servant (27a)
diner	Jesus the table servant (27 b-c)

The youngest normally serve others who have seniority; the great ones are the ones served by others. The disciples, however, have been served by Jesus, but they would be seriously mistaken to regard themselves as belonging to the class of the great. Jesus flips the ladder of success. The one who serves is greatest (see the emphasis on service in 12:35 – 37, 42 – 46; 17:7 – 10; Acts 6:1 – 6). The disciples are interested in titles; Jesus offers them towels instead. Greatness is not determined by how many serve you, but how you serve others.

Luke says nothing about what Jesus does to serve the disciples at table. His service must refer to his pouring out his life's blood for others (vv. 19 – 20).[19] Jesus therefore demonstrates what

it means to be a true benefactor. By giving his life, he bestows benefits (salvation) on all humankind.

22:28 You have remained with me throughout my trials (ὑμεῖς δέ ἐστε οἱ διαμεμενηκότες μετ᾽ ἐμοῦ ἐν τοῖς πειρασμοῖς μου). Jesus affirms what can be affirmed about his disciples. After his gentle rebuke for their hunger for fame, he recalls their commitment to stick it out with him (οἱ διαμεμενηκότες μετ᾽ ἐμοῦ, perfect tense) throughout his trials (τοῖς πειρασμοῖς). The "you" (ὑμεῖς) is emphatic. Because they have stood by him, Jesus prays for them (22:32), instructs them (22:25, 27, 40), and corrects them (22:38, 51). He also sets an example for them to witness and emulate. The subsequent boldness of Peter and John (Acts 4:13) can be partially attributed to having "remained" with Jesus. But this statement is more hortatory than declarative. It defines disciples as those who remain with Jesus in times of trial.

The "trials" are not defined but must refer to things they could recognize — the times when he experienced hostility, rejection, and slander, when Jesus was accused of working black magic through Satan. They could also include the times when they were challenged about their Lord's embarrassing association with sinners. One disciple, however, has already abandoned ship, and the others will experience a loss of nerve when Jesus is arrested. But Luke paints his account of Jesus' passion with the hues of relief and confidence, reflecting the joy that is experienced after the birth of a child that melts away all the pain of the labor. From Luke's perspective, the victory has been won. He does not magnify the painful past and the disciples' failures but exudes

---

17. Green, *The Gospel of Luke*, 768.

18. Nielsen (*Until It Is Fulfilled*, 126) notes that Jesus' statement differs from the parallel statements in Mark 9:33 – 37/10:42 – 45 and Matt 18:1 – 4/20:25 – 28 because "his argument does take as its point of origin something that is potential, that is, the question of how the disciples will attain exaltation, for in Luke the greatness of the disciples is pre-

sumed, though only in reinterpreted form, meaning on the conditions of a servant. Their eschatological position is already determined."

19. John 13:1 – 20 connects Jesus' washing the feet of his disciples at the Last Supper to the redemptive power of his death (Senior, *The Passion of Jesus in the Gospel of Luke*, 69, n. 13).

optimism, looking at the past from the perspective of the disciples' later recovery and success.[20]

22:29 And I bestow on you, just as my Father bestowed on me, a kingdom (κἀγὼ διατίθεμαι ὑμῖν καθὼς διέθετό μοι ὁ πατήρ μου βασιλείαν). Jesus assures his disciples that their faithfulness will be rewarded in the age to come. It is a "dramatic elevation to seats of privilege and power" after Jesus reproached them for their passion for worldly acclaim and enjoined them to assume the lowly status of domestic slaves who serve others.[21] The verb "bestow" (διατίθεμαι) can mean "assign, confer" and need not have a testamentary meaning.[22]

This statement harks back to other sayings in Luke. The angel Gabriel announced that God would give Jesus the throne of David (1:32; see Dan 7:13 – 14), and Mary exulted that God brings down the powerful from their thrones and lifts up the lowly (1:52). Jesus told his disciples to seek the kingdom (12:31), but then notes that it comes as a gift (12:32). Here it is a reward for abiding with Jesus. This promise prepares for the assurance Jesus gives the repentant criminal on the cross, who pleas to be remembered by Jesus when he comes into his reign (23:42).

22:30 So that you may eat and drink at my table in my reign, and you will sit on thrones, judging the twelve tribes of Israel (ἵνα ἔσθητε καὶ πίνητε ἐπὶ τῆς τραπέζης μου ἐν τῇ βασιλείᾳ μου, καὶ καθήσεσθε ἐπὶ θρόνων τὰς δώδεκα φυλὰς κρίνοντες τοῦ Ἰσραήλ). To eat with the king is to be elevated to high status (2 Sam 9:7; 1 Kgs 2:7; Jer 52:32 – 33). This promise is not intended to conjure up the image of "Jesus and his apostles dining alone in royal splendor."[23] The repentant criminal will be there along with the disenfranchised

(14:21 – 23) and those from east and west and north and south (13:29). Senior notes that in Luke, "dining in the kingdom is a metaphor of inclusion, not of privilege."[24]

Matthew 19:28 has "you ... will also sit on twelve thrones, judging the twelve tribes of Israel." Luke omits "twelve thrones" because Judas has already shifted his allegiance to those who looked like the winners. Judas reclines at table with Jesus, but he will forfeit his place and his throne by choosing the wrong kingdom. He will go to his own place (Acts 1:25).

The "twelve tribes" represent "the people of Israel reunited as the people of God into their traditional twelve tribes in the eschatological kingdom of God."[25] The saying stresses the disciples' continuity with Israel and is a fulfillment of the scriptural promises to Israel (see 2:25, 38; 24:21).[26] They are going to be like the judges of ancient Israel who rallied the people and rescued them from their enemies — only the enemies are not political but spiritual foes.

22:31 Simon, Simon! Look! Satan has demanded to sift you like wheat (Σίμων Σίμων, ἰδοὺ ὁ σατανᾶς ἐξῃτήσατο ὑμᾶς τοῦ σινιάσαι ὡς τὸν σῖτον). Luke tends to reflect positively on the past and to record past failures in the light of subsequent success. He does not emphasize the disciples' precarious hold on faith with the prediction that they will all forsake Jesus and flee (cf. Matt 26:31; Mark 14:26 – 27). In Luke's arrest scene, the disciples do not run for their lives in a panic.

No mention is made here of what the disciples will do when Jesus is arrested. Consequently, Luke does not place Jesus' prediction of Peter's denial in a context of competitive braggadocio, as it is in Matthew and Mark where Peter crows, "Even if all

---

20. See Nielsen, *Until It Is Fulfilled*, 126.

21. Nelson, *Leadership and Discipleship*, 221.

22. So ibid., 198 – 205.

23. Senior, *The Passion of Jesus in the Gospel of Luke*, 73 – 74.

24. Ibid., 74.

25. Heil, *The Meal Scenes in Luke-Acts*, 189.

26. Nelson, *Leadership and Discipleship*, 222.

fall away, I will not" (Mark 14:29). Luke couches the prediction of Peter's ignominious denial in the context of a satanic onslaught coming full tilt at all of the disciples, and he uses it as an opportunity to assert Peter's ultimate victory. In fact, Jesus' confident intercession on his behalf and the word of victory when he turns is mentioned *before* any mention of Peter's denial. Luke's account of Peter's denial does not have him denying his faith in his Master but denying knowing him (22:57), that he is "one of them" (22:58), and knowing what they are saying when they accuse him of being with him (22:60).

Using a vivid metaphor, Jesus informs Peter that Satan has demanded "to sift you" (ὑμᾶς τοῦ σινιάσαι). Jesus uses his given name "Simon," which recalls when Jesus first encountered and called him and when Simon confessed that he was a sinful man and begged Jesus to leave him (5:1 – 10). The "you" is plural. It makes no sense "to sift only one corn stalk,"[27] and Peter is not the only one who will be sifted. It implies violent shaking, in this case, to separate them from Jesus and to eliminate them from salvation. Satan in his arrogance sets out to bring the faithful crashing down (see Job 1:8 – 12; 2:3 – 7; Luke 8:12 – 15). Peter's denial becomes a centerpiece in the narrative because he will be the one who will strengthen the others after they have fallen through the sieve and scattered like chaff.

22:32 But I have pled for you so that your faith will not fail. When you turn, strengthen your brothers (ἐγὼ δὲ ἐδεήθην περὶ σοῦ ἵνα μὴ ἐκλίπῃ ἡ πίστις σου· καὶ σύ ποτε ἐπιστρέψας στήρισον τοὺς ἀδελφούς σου). Satan's demand is countered by the prayer of Jesus, and he can give Peter

the ultimate assurance that his faith will not be eclipsed. He will lead the disciples in falling before he will turn around and lead them in their rising.[28] Peter is up against something more than the weakness of the flesh (Mark 14:38). It will not be his strength of resolve but Jesus' intercession that prevents the process of sifting from reaching its intended end — the destruction of his faith.

Luke describes Jesus' intercession with a verb that suggests intensity ("I have pled," [ἐδεήθην]).[29] It is used in Luke to describe various people pleading urgently with Jesus (5:12; 8:28, 38; 9:38). In Heb 5:7, the noun form "petitions" (δεήσεις) describes Jesus' supplications, expressed with loud cries and tears, to the one who could save him from death. From Luke's perspective, Jesus' prayer is infallible. According to Foerster, Jesus plays the role assumed by the archangel Michael as a heavenly intercessor in Jewish apocalyptic and rabbinic literature.[30]

Jesus confidently commands Peter, "When you turn [ἐπιστρέψας, implying his repentance, see 17:4; Acts 3:19], strengthen your brothers." It implies that the satanic sifting will shake their faith and resolve as well. The verb "to turn" is intransitive. It is not his task to get the others to turn, but only to strengthen them. Findlay says, "Peter only 'turned' because the Lord 'turned' first" (22:61).[31] Strengthening others defines the apostolic task elsewhere in the New Testament (see Acts 14:22; 15:32, 41; 18:23; Rom 1:11; 1 Thess 3:2, 13; 1 Pet 5:10). In Acts, Peter strengthens the other apostles in a variety of ways. Not only does he take leadership in reconstituting the Twelve (Acts 1:15 – 26), preaching at Pentecost (2:14 – 41), and facing down the same priests and Sanhedrin that had Jesus executed (4:1 – 31; 5:17 – 32, 40 – 42), he also inaugurates and defends the mission to Gentiles (10:1 – 11:18).

27. F. J. Botha, "*Humas* in Luke xxii.31," *ExpTim* 64 (1952 – 53): 125.

28. Moessner, "Reading Luke's Gospel as Ancient Hellenistic Narrative," 143.

29. David M. Stanley, *Jesus in Gethsemane* (New York: Paulist, 1980), 195.

30. Werner Foerster, "Lk 22.31f," *ZNW* 46 (1955): 131 – 33.

31. Findlay, *The Gospel according to St. Luke*, 225.

22:33 He said to him, "Lord, I am ready even to go to prison with you and to face death!" (ὁ δὲ εἶπεν αὐτῷ· κύριε, μετὰ σοῦ ἕτοιμός εἰμι καὶ εἰς φυλακὴν καὶ εἰς θάνατον πορεύεσθαι). Peter rashly promises to follow Jesus to prison and in death. He perceives himself to be ready, but his participation in the disciples' wrangling over rank suggests he is not. Ironically, going to prison (absent from Matt 26:35 and Mark 14:31) and facing death is exactly what will be required of true disciples (21:12; see Acts 5:18; 12:1 – 5; 16:23; 22:4; 26:10). Before they are truly ready to endure trials, they need to witness the example of Jesus and receive the power of the Holy Spirit.

22:34 He said, "I say to you, Peter, the rooster will not crow today, until you deny three times that you [even] know me" (ὁ δὲ εἶπεν· λέγω σοι, Πέτρε, οὐ φωνήσει σήμερον ἀλέκτωρ ἕως τρίς με ἀπαρνήσῃ εἰδέναι). The rooster's crow matches Peter's cocky boastfulness. As the strutting, crowing king of the chicken coop, the rooster is a proverbial example of foolish pride. Its sound will snap Peter awake to recognize the scope of his failure but also will remind him of Jesus' assurance.

22:35 He then said to them, "When I sent you without a purse, bag, or sandals, you did not lack anything, did you?" They said, "Nothing" (καὶ εἶπεν αὐτοῖς· ὅτε ἀπέστειλα ὑμᾶς ἄτερ βαλλαντίου καὶ πήρας καὶ ὑποδημάτων, μή τινος ὑστερήσατε; οἱ δὲ εἶπαν· οὐθενός). Jesus muses over the good old days when he was able to send the disciples out and they received hospitality (9:3; 10:4). They relied entirely on the goodwill of their hosts in their preaching tours. This dependence on the charity of others is not dissimilar to what Josephus says about the Essenes:

> On the arrival of any of the sect from elsewhere, all the resources of the community are put at their disposal, just as if they were their own; and they enter the houses of men whom they have never seen before as though they were their most intimate friends. Consequently, they carry nothing whatever with them on their journeys, except arms as a protection against brigands. In every city there is one of the order expressly appointed to attend to strangers, who provides them with raiment and other necessities. (*J.W.* 2.8.4 §124)

What is remarkable is that Jesus characterized the disciples' mission as sending them out "as lambs into a pack of wolves" (10:3). Things will get far worse.

22:36 He said to them, "But now, let the one who has a purse take it, and likewise a bag. And let the one who does not have a sword sell his cloak and buy one" (εἶπεν δὲ αὐτοῖς· ἀλλὰ νῦν ὁ ἔχων βαλλάντιον ἀράτω, ὁμοίως καὶ πήραν, καὶ ὁ μὴ ἔχων πωλησάτω τὸ ἱμάτιον αὐτοῦ καὶ ἀγορασάτω μάχαιραν). "But now" (ἀλλὰ νῦν) signals two radical changes that Jesus' execution on a cross will precipitate. First, the tide of popularity will shift against them. When they go out on mission again, they can expect only trouble. Because their Lord will face the worst, done in by some who zealously believe they are doing God a service by killing him (see 22:52), the disciples must also expect the worst. Before, Jesus enjoined his disciples to sell their possessions and give alms (12:33). Now, they must take a purse and a bag, and they must be prepared to sell all and buy a sword. This word therefore cancels Jesus' directive in 10:4 and prepares the reader for another sending of the disciples (10:8).

This sending will mark a second change. They will no longer be traversing in a familiar, safe orbit but will be moving into new, foreign territories (24:47; Acts 1:8).[32] This mission will meet with

32. Schweizer, *Luke*, 391.

hardship and violent opposition (see Paul's list of hardships in 2 Cor 11:23 – 27).

The command to take a purse and bag and to sell their cloak to buy a sword lends itself to many interpretations, but I agree with Moo that the command "is a metaphorical indication of the new situation of hostility which the disciples will confront because of Jesus' being reckoned as a transgressor."[33] The citation from Isa 53:12 that follows gives the reason for this command ("for I tell you," λέγω γὰρ ὑμῖν). A sword is a weapon designed to wound or kill. Are disciples now to live by the sword, like Esau (Gen 27:40), or become experts in war, making preparations for an imminent, final messianic struggle?[34] It is possible that Jesus recommends securing swords as a means to protect themselves on their travels (see Neh 4:8), but we see no evidence of the disciples resorting to self-defense in Acts or Paul's letters.[35]

The sword has appeared in Luke as a metaphor for the opposition Mary will face (2:35), and if Luke changed the term "sword" found in the saying in Matt 10:34 to "division" (see 12:49 – 53), he understood the term "sword" metaphorically. A metaphorical interpretation here best fits Jesus' teaching on nonviolence elsewhere in the gospels (6:27 – 36) and his rebuke of the disciples for lashing out with swords in self-defense at his arrest (22:51). He seeks to convey that the times ahead are going to get rough. The sword represents the opposite of peace (Lev 26:6, 25, 33). They will be targets, but Jesus does not authorize them to

retaliate. The command to buy swords is akin to saying: "Keep your powder dry." It is not intended to be taken literally. It means they will need every resource they have.

22:37 For I tell you, it is necessary that this that has been written about me be completed, namely, "He was reckoned with the lawless." For in fact, this [prophecy] about me is coming to its culmination (λέγω γὰρ ὑμῖν ὅτι τοῦτο τὸ γεγραμμένον δεῖ τελεσθῆναι ἐν ἐμοί· τό· καὶ μετὰ ἀνόμων ἐλογίσθη· καὶ γὰρ τὸ περὶ ἐμοῦ τέλος ἔχει). The statement "this that has been written about me" (τοῦτο τὸ γεγραμμένον … ἐν ἐμοί) affirms that "what originally concerned the servant of God in Isa 53:12 now concerns Jesus and is reaching its final goal, its eschatological completion (τέλος) in his death."[36] For Jesus, the Scriptures disclose "his marching orders" and interpret what happens to him in his passion (see 24:26, 44).[37] Now, everything is on the verge of being accomplished (see the use of verb "to finish, accomplish" [τελέω] related to Jesus' passion in 12:50; 18:31; Acts 13:29).

This prophecy is not fulfilled when Jesus is crucified between two "criminals" (κακοῦργοι, 23:33), since they are not identified as "lawless" (ἄνομοι). Moo contends: "The fulfillment of Jesus' prophecy should be seen as the events of the passion as a whole, which picture the sinless Messiah rejected, mocked and crucified by his own people — in a phrase 'treated as a transgressor.'"[38] Jesus' treatment at the hands of the authorities should tip off

33. Douglas J. Moo, *The Old Testament in the Gospel Passion Narratives* (Sheffield: Almond, 1983), 134 – 35.

34. Hans-Werner Bartsch, "Jesu Schwertwort, Lukas xxii.35 – 38," *NTS* 20 (1973 – 74): 190 – 203. Jesus does not refer to knives instead of swords to allude to the disciples' need to return to fishing (so W. Western, "The Enigma of the Swords," *ExpTim* 50 (1938 – 39): 377; "The Enigma of the Swords, St. Luke xxii, 38," *ExpTim* 52 (1940 – 41): 357). Jesus also does not betray his sympathy with the violence of the Zealot cause, a view discredited by Martin Hengel (*Victory over Violence*

[trans. David E. Green; Philadelphia: Fortress, 1973]).

35. Howard Clark Kee, *Christian Origins in Sociological Perspective* (Philadelphia: Westminster, 1980), 122.

36. Heil, *Meals Scenes in Luke-Acts*, 194. The text reads literally "comes to an end" (τέλος ἔχει; see the same phrase in Mark 3:26).

37. Cosgrove, "The Divine ΔΕΙ in Luke-Acts," 174.

38. Moo, *The Old Testament in the Gospel Passion Narratives*, 137.

the disciples as to what lies in store for them. Hays points out, however, that the command here to buy a sword is linked to the prophecy from Isaiah: Buy a sword, *for* I tell you (λέγω γὰρ ὑμῖν) the prophecy about me needs to be fulfilled.[39] The prophecy could be fulfilled by the disciples who brandish their swords as if they were lawless brigands.

22:38 They said, "Lord! Look, here are two swords!" He said to them, "Enough!" (οἱ δὲ εἶπαν· κύριε, ἰδοὺ μάχαιραι ὧδε δύο. ὁ δὲ εἶπεν αὐτοῖς· ἱκανόν ἐστιν). The point of the saying is lost on the disciples. When Jesus uses metaphors, he is taken literally; when he gives direct commands, he is taken metaphorically. There is talk of swords, and they can understand that. Peter has just asserted that he is ready to die for the cause (22:33). The disciples remain blind to the necessity of his death (9:44 – 45; 18:31 – 34). They know about taking life (see 9:51 – 55) but have yet to comprehend giving one's life freely for others. The appearance of the swords at the supper provides narrative preparation for the disciples' sword assault when Jesus is arrested on the Mount of Olives (22:49 – 51), but that is not the only reason Luke records this exclamation.[40]

One of the characteristics in the meal scenes in Luke is that Jesus exposes the secrets lurking in the hearts of his table companions (7:36 – 50; 10:38 – 42; 11:37 – 54; 14:7 – 24), and during this Last Supper he uncovers the one who is about to betray him, the one who will deny him, and those who will use swords. They cannot hide their sinful hearts from him (see 2:35).[41] Jesus' command does not cause them to go buy swords. They cheerily announce that they possess two swords, revealing what they "have already done out of fear."[42] The Last Supper of Jesus tragically reveals the huge gulf that separates himself and his disciples.

"Enough" (ἱκανόν ἐστιν) can mean "it is sufficient" or "adequate." If so, it is an ironic response and makes clear that Jesus does not envisage any real preparation for an armed uprising led by twelve men wielding two swords. It is laughable to think that Jesus pronounces them combat ready. "Enough" (ἱκανόν) is in the singular, however, and it would not apply to the swords but must refer to something else.

It is possible that Jesus cuts off the conversation, as if to say, "Drop it" (see the usage of this word group in Deut 3:26 and Ezek 45:9 in the LXX).[43] The disciples have totally misunderstood, and Jesus' response may have a double meaning. It calls a halt to the conversation, and it implies that their announcement is enough to confirm that they are lawless and he is reckoned among them. Others simply take it to mean that it is enough to fulfill the prophecy.[44]

39. Hays, *Luke's Wealth Ethics*, 97.

40. These could have been the butcher knives used in the slaughtering the Passover lamb since the identical term is used in the LXX for Abraham's knife in Gen 22:6, 10, when he is about to sacrifice Isaac.

41. Nelson, *Leadership and Discipleship*, 67.

42. Tannehill, *Unity of Luke-Acts*, 267; see also Paul S.

Minear, "A Note on Luke xxii 35 – 38," *NovT* 7 (1964 – 65): 128 – 34.

43. See Thayer, *Greek-English Lexicon of the New Testament*, 300. See also 1 Kgs 19:4; 1 Chr 21:15.

44. Minear, "A Note on Luke xxii 35 – 38," 131; Hays, *Luke's Wealth Ethics*, 97.

Theology in Application

1. The Danger of Betrayal

The statement that the hand of the betrayer is at the table warns that everyone is capable of betraying the Lord. Merely being present at the Lord's table, therefore, is "not assurance of perseverance. Indeed, only Jesus' intimates can betray him!"[45] Eating and drinking with Jesus also do not ensure that he will vouch for one in the judgment (13:22 – 30).

Jesus' announcement that what is about to happen to him has been ordained makes it clear that God does not require human wickedness to accomplish his purposes. God is able to accomplish them *despite* human wickedness and satanic assault. Why did Jesus not pray for Judas as he said he did for Simon? Crump surmises: "Either Jesus had included Judas in his prayers, but God denied this aspect of his request; or Jesus has not included Judas in his intercession, and so without Jesus' protective advocacy Judas was left to experience the full measure of Satan's will."[46] In my view, Judas was already lost to Satan. He was not "fated" to do what he did but became a consenting "conspirator."[47] By contrast, Peter does not *will* to deny knowing his master. He is ambushed by indwelling sin and the weakness of the flesh. He does not do what he wants but what he hates (Rom 7:14 – 20).

One might infer from v. 31 that Satan asked permission from God to sift the disciples, but this inference would be incorrect. If God had granted permission, what is the point of Jesus' prayer for them? The middle force of the verb means "to demand," which makes it "most probable that Satan demands of the disciples themselves that they surrender to his temptations, for the followers, like the master, are his enemies."[48] Jesus knows full well the power of Satan's temptations; only those who resist temptation to the end know the full force of temptation (4:1 – 13). The disciples, however, each in their own way, will wilt under the pressure.

2. The Danger of the Misuse of Power

There is a danger for some to misconstrue Jesus' words and think that he wants us to abdicate leadership roles and abandon the use of power to become humble servants of all. We are not to grasp for power, but refusing to exercise power that is given to us creates a perilous vacuum. What Jesus is concerned about is how power that is lawfully granted is to be used.

---

45. Frank J. Matera, *Passion Narratives and Gospel Theologies: Interpreting the Synoptics through Their Passion Stories* (New York: Paulist, 1986), 163.

46. Crump, *Jesus the Intercessor*, 165.

47. Tiede, *Luke*, 383, 388.

48. Michael Patella, *The Death of Jesus: The Diabolical Force and the Ministering Angel: Luke 23,44 – 49* (CahRB 43; Paris: Gabalda, 1999), 63.

Jesus' teaching particularly applies to those who aspire to authority in the church. His words about service do not mean that he is averse to the exercise of power and authority. Service does not imply servitude. He is only opposed to domineering others and oppressing them. He does not reject authoritative leadership but authoritarian leadership, the modus operandi of the world's despots. Tiede describes Jesus' alternative vision of authority:

> Far from the "divine right of kings" based on might or lineage, the legitimacy of this power is based on service. This authority is clearly revealed in the Messiah who reigned in self-sacrifice.... This vision of authority is part of the saving gospel of what God has done. God's way of ruling sets a new standard and yields evangelical wisdom concerning the legitimate exercise of power.[49]

Leadership in the church is not to be top-down but should come from the posture of humble status and humble service.[50] Nelson avers, "In the Christian community there will be leadership, but it is to involve the subjection of the leader to even the 'lowliest' members."[51] Paul's view of what it means to be an apostle fully accords with this perspective, which is so contrary to values of the dominant culture (see 1 Cor 3:5 – 9; 4:8 – 13; 9:19 – 23; 2 Cor 1:24). He knows himself to have special authority as God's apostle, but he is also God's servant with other apostles, working together with his people, not lording over them.

Jesus also cynically implies that those who receive the title "benefactor" bestow benefits on others to keep them subservient and to foster the myth that the elite are generous and therefore praiseworthy. They give out their largesse to maintain their power and to receive public acclaim. Satan tried to entice Jesus by showing him all the kingdoms of the world and promising to give him all this authority and the accompanying glory, "because it has been handed over to me and I can give it to whomever I want" (4:6). For Luke, all worldly kingdoms are satanic. Note that it is "their" kings, not "ours." The church stands over against them, and their rulers are a foil to Jesus. He sets the example of what it means to be a benefactor by using his power, "doing good and healing all who were under the power of the devil" (Acts 10:38).

The supreme example of greatness and benefaction is Jesus' giving his life for others. He is the host of the gathering, but he says he is there paradoxically as a servant. Yet he performs no servant act. How does he serve? For Luke, it is clear. He must refer to his impending sacrificial death, which is clear from his interpretation of his distribution of the bread and cup. The continued celebration of the meal as a memorial to Jesus should result in sacrificial leadership like his.

---

49. David L. Tiede, "The Kings of the Gentiles and the Leader Who Serves: Luke 22:24 – 30," WW 12 (1992): 24.

50. Nelson, Leadership and Discipleship, 260.
51. Ibid., 172.

3. The Danger of Being Sifted

Unlike Job's situation (see Job 9:33, "If only there were someone to mediate between us, someone to bring us together"), Peter has an advocate with the Father who intercedes on his behalf.[52] But Peter does not know that he is tottering on a precipice and is about to plunge to the earth. After his nosedive, his estimation of his own prowess to hold fast must come down several pegs, and he must learn, as Paul did (2 Cor 12:9 – 10) and as all followers must, to rely on the grace and strength of God. Disciples cannot stockpile this grace and strength beforehand but must learn from Jesus' own example of prayer on the Mount of Olives that they are dependent on God from hour to hour. When they become aware of that, they will be more likely to pray than to talk big and be less likely to swoon in a crisis.

The sifting will not stop after Jesus' passion. It continues as disciples take up their cross on a daily basis (9:23 – 24). The persecution will intensify as they are hauled before kings and governors, punished in synagogues and prisons, and led to the gallows (21:12). The supreme irony is that as the sieve isolates the chaff, the sifting also purifies. Through Jesus' powerful intercession they will not be defeated by their failure. After his death and resurrection and the coming of the Holy Spirit, they will be able to resist the devil, who prowls around like a roaring lion, and to remain steadfast in their faith in the midst of suffering. They will come to know that the "the God of all grace, who called you to his eternal glory in Christ, after you have suffered a little while, will himself restore you and make you strong, firm and steadfast" (1 Pet 5:10).

4. The Danger of Violence

Jesus does not intend to send out his disciples on mission armed to the teeth. It would be considered ludicrous for a contemporary mission-sending agency to present new missionaries with swords (or guns) for their journey at their commissioning. The crozier, the shepherd's crook, replaces swords. The two swords are not an allegorical reference to the power of the state and the church, but expose the disciples' fears as they seek to hedge their bets — securing swords to protect themselves in case God lets them down. The swords show how hopelessly inadequate human resources and preparations are. They cannot put their trust in bows or think that swords can save them (Ps 44:6). Satan's clients wield swords (Luke 22:52), but Satan is not defeated by an arms race and counterviolence. Nor does God's reign advance via strong-arm tactics (John 18:36 – 37; Rev 13:14). It advances by the power of God's truth.

If the disciples think they can combine preaching the gospel with brass knuckles, Jesus must correct them. The reign of God does not advance by taking life but by giving one's life. The disciples address Jesus as "Lord," and Rowe comments, "The nature

---

52. Crump, *Jesus the Intercessor*, 155.

of Jesus' Lordship is radically misunderstood if interpreted as the power to destroy opponents by means of the sword. In this way, the disciples, with their incomprehension and rash action (22:38, 39), threaten to twist or, at best, obfuscate the meaning of Jesus' identity as κύριος [Lord]."[53]

This scene can be linked to James and John's wanting Jesus to call down fire and destroy the Samaritans (9:52 – 56). The disciples have not learned much since then. Political power may grow out of the barrel of a gun, but Jesus eschews all violence. The early Christian community was established on the experience of the power of the Crucified and Risen One, who renounced all external means of exerting power and announced his readiness to serve and give his life. Christ's power derives from what appears to be total powerlessness.

This kind of power is invisible and never can be measured by worldly criteria, but it is the power that ultimately triumphs. Holy head-breakers and militia monks who have obediently carried out the expectations of church leaders to outmuscle any opposition have littered history with corpses, and, in the process, lost half the world.[54] They won skirmishes but lost the battle that can only be won with "the sword of the Spirit, which is the word of God" (Eph 6:17).

5. Salvation from One Reckoned with Sinners

The prophecy from Isa 53:12 that Jesus says is about to reach its fulfillment is the theological key that makes sense of all of the sayings in this section. "He was reckoned with the lawless" is meant to recall the continuation of Isa 53:12 ("for he bore the sin of many, and made intercession for the transgressors") and the context of this chapter in Isaiah. That one of the disciples would betray Jesus, that they all argue at this point over who is the greatest, that one would deny him, and that some possessed two dagger swords reveal that the disciples belonged as much to the transgressors as did the two malefactors crucified with Jesus.

Simon Peter confesses that he is a sinful man on his first meeting with Jesus (5:8). This fact is driven home after he denies Jesus for the third time, after the rooster crows, and after Jesus looks at him. He leaves the stage weeping bitterly (22:60 – 62). As those who also are "lawless," the disciples will fail miserably, but the verse from Isaiah continues: "he bore the sins of many and because of their sins he was given over" (LXX). Every meal recorded in Luke finds Jesus ringed by sinners (5:29 – 32; 7:36 – 50; 11:37 – 52; 14:1 – 24; 15:2). His death, however, takes away their iniquity and opens the way to their hope. That Jesus is reckoned with transgressors explains why he must give over his body and pour out his blood (22:19 – 20).

53. Rowe, *Early Narrative Christology*, 181.
54. See Philip Jenkins, *Jesus Wars: How Four Patriarchs, Three Queens, and Two Emperors Decided What Christians Would Believe for the Next 1,500 Years* (New York: HarperOne, 2010).

The Servant Songs of Isaiah provide the theological backdrop for Luke's understanding of Jesus' passion as he makes constant allusions to it throughout the narrative. In addition to this direct quotation from Isa 53:12, Jesus is in their midst as one who serves (22:27), who, like the lamb, goes silently to slaughter (23:9; Isa 53:7); who is taken away by a perversion of justice (Isa 53:8); and who is declared to be the righteous one (23:47; Isa 53:11). Larkin argues convincingly that the citation of Isa 53:12 indicates Luke understood Jesus' death as vicarious atonement.[55] Heil avers that being reckoned with sinners is part of being given over by God

> to a sacrificial death that atones for sins and that effects a new covenant by which God will forgive sins (22:19 – 20). So, also the reckoning of Jesus with the lawless is ultimately God's reckoning (ἐλογίσθη as divine passive) of him with the lawless so that by his being given over to death he can take away their sins, their lawlessness.[56]

Being with the lawless means that Jesus' "sacrificial death which fulfills God's scriptural plan atones for the sins of the lawless, especially his 'lawless' disciples."[57]

---

55. W. J. Larkin Jr., "Luke's Use of the Old Testament as Key to His Soteriology," *JETS* 20 (1977): 325 – 35.

56. Heil, *The Meal Scenes in Luke-Acts*, 194.

57. Ibid., 195.

70

Luke 22:39 – 53

Literary Context

Luke does not report that Jesus prays in the temple, the house of prayer; he only teaches there. Instead, he prays on the Mount of Olives. This scene puts the finishing touches on his instructions to the disciples. They are to learn from him how to pray in the face of severe testing, which he has warned they soon will encounter (22:31, 35 – 36).

The scene also prepares for and underscores the necessity of Jesus' suffering that follows. It sets the coming conflict beyond the stage of human plots and tactics to the level of God's eternal will.

VI. Jesus' Suffering and Death (22:1 – 23:49)
    B. Jesus' Last Supper (22:7 – 20)
    C. Jesus' Parting Words to His Disciples (22:21 – 38)
→   **D. Jesus' Prayer and Arrest on the Mount of Olives (22:39 – 53)**
    E. Peter's Denial and the Mockery of Jesus (22:54 – 65)

Main Idea

Through his prayer, Jesus seeks to know God's will and align himself with it and provides an example to disciples. Intense prayer guards against the danger of apostasy and creates vigilance.

Translation

(See next page.)

Luke 22:39–53

22:39	Circumstance	**He came out and went,** according to his custom, to the Mount of Olives; and **the disciples followed him.**

40a   When he arrived at the place,

b   Command   **he said to them,**
           "Pray that you not enter into temptation."

41a   Prayer   Then **he withdrew from them** about a stone's throw away

b   and kneeling down **he began to pray,**

42a   Request   *saying, "Father,*
          if you will it, take this cup away from me.

b   Submission   *Nevertheless, let your will, not mine, be done."*

43   Angelic intervention   **Then an angel from heaven appeared to him, strengthening him.**

44a   Prayer   And   becoming [steeled] for combat,
          he prayed all the more fervently,

b   **and his sweat became like drops of blood falling upon the ground.**

45   And   when he rose from prayer,
          he went to the disciples and found them sleeping from grief.

46a   Question   **He said to them,**
          "Why are you sleeping?

b   Command   *Rise, pray that you not enter into temptation."*

47a   Character introduction   While he was speaking,
          behold, a crowd [arrived],

b   Betrayal   **and the one called Judas, one of the Twelve, came up to them**
          and he drew near to Jesus to kiss him.

48   Rebuking question   **Jesus spoke to him,**
          "Judas, with a kiss do you betray the Son of Man?"

49   Question   When those around him saw what was about to happen,
          they said,
          "Lord, should we smite with the sword?"

50   Violent action   **And one of them smote the high priest's servant and cut off his right ear.**

51a   Rebuke   **But Jesus said,**
          "That's enough!"

b   Healing   And   when he touched the ear,
          he healed it.

52   Rebuking question   Then **Jesus said to the chief priests and the captains [of the temple guard]**
                           and elders,
          "Have you come out with swords and clubs as [you would] against a bandit?

53a   *Every day I was with you in the temple*
          and you did not lay hands on me,

b   Pronouncement   *but this is your hour and the dominion of darkness!"*

Structure and Literary Form

The exhortation to "pray that you not enter into temptation" (22:40, 46) brackets this scene, which falls into a chiastic pattern.[1]

> A Pray not to enter into temptation (22:40)
>   B Jesus withdraws from the disciples, kneels and prays (22:41)
>   C Prayer: "Father, if you will it ..." (22:42)
>   D Father's answer: angel from heaven appears (22:43)
>   C′ Prayer "in agony" with sweat like blood (22:44)
>   B′ Rising from prayer he came to his disciples (22:45)
> A′ Pray not to enter into temptation (22:46)

Exegetical Outline

➡ **I. Jesus in prayer (22:39 – 46)**

  A. Jesus' exhortation for his followers to pray (22:39 – 40)

  B. Jesus' example of prayer: opening himself up to God's will (22:41 – 42)

  C. Divine strengthening for battle (22:43 – 44)

  D. Disciples demoralized by not praying (22:45)

  E. Jesus' exhortation for his disciples to pray (22:46)

II. Jesus' arrest (22:47 – 53)

  A. Judas's betrayal of Jesus with a kiss (22:47 – 48)

  B. A follower's betrayal of Jesus with a sword (22:49 – 51)

  C. The temple officialdom's betrayal of God in their confederacy with Satan (22:52 – 53)

Explanation of the Text

22:39 He came out and went, according to his custom, to the Mount of Olives; and the disciples followed him (καὶ ἐξελθὼν ἐπορεύθη κατὰ τὸ ἔθος εἰς τὸ ὄρος τῶν ἐλαιῶν, ἠκολούθησαν δὲ αὐτῷ καὶ οἱ μαθηταί). Jesus goes to the usual place on the Mount of Olives, knowing that the traitor will lead his enemies to find him there.[2] Mentioning that the disciples follow him draws attention to the issue of discipleship. They must also learn to follow him in prayer.

22:40 When he arrived at the place, he said to them, "Pray that you not enter into temptation" (γενόμενος δὲ ἐπὶ τοῦ τόπου εἶπεν αὐτοῖς· προσεύχεσθε μὴ εἰσελθεῖν εἰς πειρασμόν). Luke does not identify what the place is. The focus is on the command to pray, which forms an inclusio with 22:46. There is no additional charge "to watch" (as in Matt 26:38; Mark 14:34) because Luke's emphasis in this section is on prayer. That command to pray not to enter into temptation

---

1. Brown, *The Death of the Messiah*, 1:182.

2. Luke omits Hebrew and Aramaic terms and does not identify the place as "Gethsemane" (Matt 26:36; Mark 14:32).

recalls the last petition in the Lord's Prayer (11:4) and Jesus' warning in 21:36, "Keep alert in every time, praying that you may be strong enough to flee all these things that are about to take place." Temptation (πειρασμόν) refers to a time of testing that is dangerous, because those who have no root will fall away (8:13). Prayer establishes roots in divine soil that not only absorbs its nutrients but also holds one securely when the winds of testing batter one's faith.

22:41 Then he withdrew from them about a stone's throw away and kneeling down he began to pray (καὶ αὐτὸς ἀπεσπάσθη ἀπ᾽ αὐτῶν ὡσεὶ λίθου βολήν, καὶ θεὶς τὰ γόνατα προσηύχετο). Luke does not report that Jesus separates Peter, James, and John from the rest of the disciples to share the experience with him, as in Matt 26:37 and Mark 14:33. The result is that Jesus provides a lesson on prayer to every disciple, not just an inner circle. Luke also makes no mention of Jesus' emotions, his "distress," being "troubled," and "sorrow to the point of death" (Mark 14:33 – 34). Instead, it is the disciples who are overcome by grief, which causes their sleep (22:45). Luke does not report that Jesus falls on the ground (Mark 14:35) or on his face (Matt 26:39). Instead, he assumes a normal posture for prayer by kneeling (Acts 7:60; 9:40; 20:36; 21:5).

22:42 Saying, "Father, if you will it, take this cup away from me. Nevertheless, let your will, not mine, be done" (λέγων· πάτερ, εἰ βούλει παρένεγκε τοῦτο τὸ ποτήριον ἀπ᾽ ἐμοῦ· πλὴν μὴ τὸ θέλημά μου ἀλλὰ τὸ σὸν γινέσθω). In Matt 26:39 and Mark 14:35, Jesus prefaces his request with "Father, if it is possible." Luke's version, "Father, if you will it," underscores that the events

about to take place are part of God's will and plan. Jesus follows his own advice to the disciples to pray to avoid trial. He is not like Peter, who prematurely boasts of his readiness (22:33).

A textual variant occurs in the request to remove this cup from me. "Take" (παρένεγκε), a second aorist imperative, is found in the majority of the better witnesses and conforms to Mark's account. Other texts have a second aorist infinitive (παρενέγκαι), "if you wish *to take* this cup from me," followed by an aposiopesis, a breaking off (see 19:42), which implies that this is a preference, but it is not a direct request. The thought is suspended with "nevertheless" (πλήν), which breaks off the discussion and emphasizes what is important. It should be translated "nevertheless, "however," "in any case," or "only."[3] Jesus is not itching to go through the harrowing suffering that looms ahead. He does affirm that his own will does not enter into consideration. It is God's will alone that is to be done (Acts 21:14). This presentation accords with Jesus' attitude toward his death throughout Luke: he has an immersion to undergo and is pressed until it is completed (12:49 – 50). He has recognized all along that he "must" follow this course (13:31 – 33; 18:31).

22:43 – 44 Then an angel from heaven appeared to him, strengthening him. And becoming [steeled] for combat, he prayed all the more fervently, and his sweat became like drops of blood falling upon the ground (ὤφθη δὲ αὐτῷ ἄγγελος ἀπ᾽ οὐρανοῦ ἐνισχύων αὐτόν. καὶ γενόμενος ἐν ἀγωνίᾳ ἐκτενέστερον προσηύχετο· καὶ ἐγένετο ὁ ἱδρὼς αὐτοῦ ὡσεὶ θρόμβοι αἵματος καταβαίνοντες ἐπὶ τὴν γῆν). Many copies of Luke omit the appearance of the angel to Jesus,[4] and, consequently, many English translations place it

3. BDAG, 826.
4. 𝔓[69vid], 𝔓[75], ℵ[a], A, B, T, W, 579, 1071*, syr[s], bo, arm[mss], geo, numerous lectionaries, Marcion, Clement, Origen, Athanasius, Ambrose, Cyril, John Damascus. It is marked by obeli and asterisks in Δ[c] Π[c] 892[c] 1079 1195 1216 and shifted to Matthew in f[13] and several lectionaries.

in brackets or consign it to a footnote. The text-critical principle of the shortest reading persuades many that it was not a part of Luke's original text. Some consider the vocabulary to be un-Lukan and argue that Luke never refers to an angel as an "angel from heaven" (ἄγγελος ἀπ' οὐρανοῦ) but regularly employs the phrase "angel of the Lord" (Luke 1:11; 2:9; Acts 5:19; 8:26; 12:7, 23), "God's angel" (Luke 12:8, 9; 15:10; Acts 10:3), or "holy angel" (Acts 10:22). The latter term appears only once, so Luke could also have used the phrase "angel from heaven" only once. The angels who appear in the story are also never silent in Luke but come with a message.

Brown refutes the argument offered by some that these verses destroy a suggested chiastic pattern to vv. 40 – 46:

A 22:40 Pray not to enter into temptation
  B 22:41 Jesus withdrew from the disciples, knelt, and prayed
    C 22:42 The prayer
  B′ 22:45 Rising from prayer he came to his disciples
A′ 22:46 Pray not to enter into temptation

He dismisses it as a case of exaggerated chiasm-detection that plagues modern scholarship. One could detect such a meaningless chiasm in modern pulp fiction:

A character Z comes in
  B Z sits down
    C Z says something
  B′ Z gets up
A′ Z goes out

Having Jesus' prayer answered by the angel, in fact, does not detract from the flow of thought but

adds to the chiastic pattern (as noted in the "Structure and Literary Form" section above).

An equal number of significant copies of Luke include this passage.[5] It is easier to see why this text might have been deliberately expunged rather than added. It could be interpreted to imply Jesus' subordination to an angel (see Col 1:18; 2:15, 18; Heb 1:4 – 7, 13 – 14). Sweating so profusely, like drops of blood pouring out, may make Jesus seem too human. Celsus used it in his attack on the claims that Jesus was divine (Origen, *Cels.* 2.24). The earliest orthodox fathers cite the passage against Docetists, who denied that Jesus was fully human (Justin, *Dial.* 103.8; Irenaeus, *Haer.* 3.16.1).

That it was appealed to in doctrinal disputes does not mean that it was created and inserted for polemical purposes. Brown notes that Docetists, for example, could have easily responded that it was not the divine Savior who prayed.[6] The following arguments from internal evidence tip the scales toward its inclusion in the original text.

(1) The unique vocabulary may be attributable to the unique nature of the story, but the account so matches Lukan style that Brown argues, if Luke himself did not compose this passage, then the author consciously or unconsciously imitated Lukan style.[7]

(2) Some heavenly manifestation often follows prayer in Luke-Acts (1:13; 3:21 – 22; 9:28 – 31; Acts 10:2 – 3, 9; 12:5 – 11). Brown contends that Luke "may have found it difficult to follow Mark in not having Jesus receive a discernible answer to his prayer about the hour/cup. Consequently Luke may have turned to another tradition … involving an answer through an angel."[8] Its inclusion means that a heavenly manifestation occurs after Jesus'

5. ℵ[b], D, K, L, X, Δ*, Γ, Θ, Π*, Ψ, f[1,] 565, 700, 1071[c], many lectionaries, aur, b, c, d, e, ff[2], i, l, q r[1], vg, syr, arm, eth, Diatessaron, Justin, Ireneaeus, Hippolytus, Dionysius, Arius (according to Epiphanius), Eusebius, Hilary, Caserius-Nazianzus, Gregory-Nazianzus, Didymus, Ps-Dionysius, Epiphanius, Chrysosotom, Jerome, Augustine, Theodoret, Leontius, Cosmos, Facundus.

6. Brown, *The Death of the Messiah*, 1:184.
7. Ibid., 1:182.
8. Ibid., 1:183.

prayer at three crucial junctures in the story: at his baptism (3:21 – 22), his transfiguration (9:28 – 36), and his prayer on the Mount of Olives.

(3) Angels make frequent appearances in Luke-Acts and usually bring a message (1:11 – 20, 26 – 38; 2:9 – 14; 24:23; Acts 5:19 – 20; 8:26; 10:3, 7, 22; 11:13; 12:7, 23; 23:9; 27:23), but nonspeaking angels appear in Luke 12:9 and 15:10. At this point in the story, having an angel speak, as one does to spur on Paul in Acts 27:23 – 24 in an hour of crisis, might make the angel seem superior to Jesus in some way. Jesus' words and actions trump any cheering encouragement from an angel.

(4) In every pericope of the passion, Luke adds his own material to put his unique stamp on the story. Brun argues that Luke never shortens Mark without adding special material of his own.[9]

(5) The angel's appearance recalls Jesus' temptation in the wilderness. The devil cited Ps 91:11 to Jesus to conjure up the image of God's protection of the righteous in times of need (4:9 – 12). An angel comes here but not to protect Jesus from harm (see Matt 26:53). Luke presents Jesus' preparation for death as akin to getting ready for a rigorous battle. The phrase translated "for combat" (ἐν ἀγωνίᾳ) does not need to connote mental anguish, a product of fear, as it does in English, but refers to "a state of readiness and alertness to take part" in a decisive battle.[10] It pictures "the concentration of powers" in the face of mortal conflict.[11]

The context is that of "a victorious struggle," not agonizing distress.[12]

These details, therefore, do not "militate against the thrust of Lucan authorship in that they add emotional details to what is otherwise a sober abridgement of Mark," as Fitzmyer claims.[13] Note that the phrase occurs *after* the angel appears to strengthen him! The angel places Jesus in the state of being *en agônia*, and it is God's answer to Jesus' prayer (see John 12:28 – 29).[14] The cup will not be removed, but an angel comes to steel him for the battle. The angels did not come to minister to him in the wilderness after Satan tempted him, as they do in Matt 4:11 and Mark 1:13. An angel appears now, however, before an even greater battle against Satan and the hour of the power of darkness. Satan has been biding his time, waiting for the opportune moment to return for the final onslaught (4:13). The angel's coming signifies that God will not take away "the cup" from Jesus, but he will drink it with divine assistance.[15] The "cup" is an *agôn*, a battle, that Jesus' Ant*agon*ist intends to use to destroy him.

It is best not to interpret the phrase "his sweat became like drops of blood" (ἐγένετο ὁ ἱδρὼς αὐτοῦ ὡσεὶ θρόμβοι αἵματος) as bloody sweat, although this phenomenon was not unknown in the ancient world. Luke uses a simile to convey likeness short of identity (compare "tongues of fire that separated," Acts 2:3).[16] Jesus' sweat is so

9. Lyder Brun, "Engel und Blutschweiss Lc 22:34 – 35," *ZNW* 32 (1933): 273 – 74.

10. Christopher M. Tuckett, "Luke 22,43 – 44: The 'Agony' in the Garden and Luke's Gospel," in *New Testament Textual Criticism and Exegesis: Festschrift for J. Delobel* (ed. A. Denaux; BETL 161; Leuven: Leuven Univ. Press, 2002), 138 – 39.

11. Ethelbert Stauffer, "ἀγών ...," *TDNT*, 1:140. The word ἀγωνία occurs only here in the New Testament. The verb form is used to mean "to fight" or "to strive" (ἀγονίζεσθαι; see 13:24; John 18:36; 1 Cor 9:25; Col 1:29; 4:12; 1 Tim 4:10; 6:12; 2 Tim 4:7). Paul uses it for struggling in prayer (Col 4:12).

12. Neyrey, *The Passion According to Luke*, 58 – 62.

13. Fitzmyer, *Luke*, 2:1444.

14. Crump, *Jesus the Intercessor*, 121.

15. Assisting angels appear in martyriological writings (1 Kgs 19:5 – 8; Dan 10:13, 18 – 19 [3:49, 92 LXX]; 3 Macc 5:51; 6:18 – 21), but these are not valid parallels because these angels vanquish the adversaries. Were they true parallels, Jesus would not have needed to suffer his passion. Robert J. Karris ("Luke 23:47 and the Lucan View of the Death of Jesus," *JBL* 105 [1986]: 68 – 70) argues strongly that Luke does not present Jesus' death as that of an innocent martyr.

16. See also the phrases "like a dove" (3:22); "like a streak of lightning" (10:18); "like unseen graves" (11:44).

profuse that it poured out as if he were cut and bleeding. We use the metaphor "sweating bullets," but it has negative connotations. For Jesus, being bathed in sweat signifies his readiness for the ensuing encounter. Brown affirms, "It describes the supreme tension and readiness of the combatant covered with sweat at the start of the contest. In that spirit, Jesus rises from his prayer ready to enter trial, even as he mercifully tells his disciples to pray that they be spared from that trial (22:46)."[17] Through prayer and the strengthening of the angel, Jesus is ready for the showdown during the hour of the dominion of darkness.

22:45 And when he rose from prayer, he went to the disciples and found them sleeping from grief (καὶ ἀναστὰς ἀπὸ τῆς προσευχῆς ἐλθὼν πρὸς τοὺς μαθητὰς εὗρεν κοιμωμένους αὐτοὺς ἀπὸ τῆς λύπης). Luke does not present Jesus returning to the disciples three times, finding them sleeping each time, and urging them to watch and pray as in Mark 14:37–42. That sequence may be taken to imply that he is struggling to come to grips with his destiny and seeking their support. Instead, Luke reports that Jesus "rose from prayer" (ἀναστὰς ἀπὸ τῆς προσευχῆς), which means more than he stopped praying and stood up. It implies that he was buoyed *from* prayer in contrast to the disciples who were sleeping "*from* grief" (ἀπὸ τῆς λύπης; see Isa 50:11 LXX). He becomes a model of how to pray to resist temptation and now is able to give himself over to his enemies. Prayer allows him to foresee what is coming, understand it as God's will, and submit to the violence.

Luke omits any reference to Jesus' grief (contrast Mark 14:34) because of his sensitivity to its negative connotations for a Greco-Roman

audience. Neyrey's survey of "grief" in Stoic philosophers and Hellenistic Jewish circles reveals that it was viewed as: (1) one of the four cardinal evil passions; (2) the typical punishment for sin; and (3) an indication of guilt.[18] Grief torments and corrodes the soul, causes one to shrink back, and results in a loss of power. The disciples' collapse is attributable to their allowing themselves to become victims of grief. By contrast, Jesus remains composed, fearless, and positive, able to perceive the divine will and obey it. He therefore can meet death nobly.

22:46 He said to them, "Why are you sleeping? Rise, pray that you not enter into temptation" (καὶ εἶπεν αὐτοῖς· τί καθεύδετε; ἀναστάντες προσεύχεσθε, ἵνα μὴ εἰσέλθητε εἰς πειρασμόν). The disciples sleep (see 9:32) and can only free themselves from grief's paralysis through prayer. But Jesus' example of prayer shows it is easier said than done. Beck comments:

> If Luke represents the disciples as trying, within their limits, to be obedient to Jesus, and carrying out the command to pray, he may have considered that, if the demands of prayer were such that even Jesus sustained them only with difficulty and with angelic help, the disciples would have been totally exhausted by them.[19]

Battles are won or lost on the field of prayer, but even prayer can be a battle.

22:47–48 While he was speaking, behold, a crowd [arrived], and the one called Judas, one of the Twelve, came up to them and he drew near to Jesus to kiss him. Jesus spoke to him, "Judas, with a kiss do you betray the Son of Man?" (ἔτι αὐτοῦ λαλοῦντος ἰδοὺ ὄχλος, καὶ ὁ λεγόμενος

17. Raymond E. Brown, *A Crucified Christ in Holy Week: Essays on the Four Passion Narratives* (Collegeville, MN: Liturgical, 1986), 50.

18. Neyrey, *The Passion According to Luke*, 50–54.

19. Brian E. Beck, "*Imitatio Christi* and the Lucan Passion Narrative," in *Suffering and Martyrdom in the New Testament: Studies Presented to G. M. Styler* (ed. William Horbury and Brian McNeill; Cambridge: Cambridge Univ. Press, 1981), 40.

Ἰούδας εἷς τῶν δώδεκα προήρχετο αὐτοὺς καὶ
ἤγγισεν τῷ Ἰησοῦ φιλῆσαι αὐτόν. Ἰησοῦς δὲ εἶπεν
αὐτῷ· Ἰούδα, φιλήματι τὸν υἱὸν τοῦ ἀνθρώπου
παραδίδως;). It may seem that Jesus does not get a
direct answer to his prayer, unless one judges Judas's showing up to be the answer. One normally
greeted a teacher or rabbi with a kiss on the hand
or on the cheek if one considered oneself to be an
equal (see 7:45, "You gave me no kiss"). See the
parting kiss given to Paul by the Ephesian elders
(Acts 20:37). In Mark 14:45 Judas addresses Jesus as
rabbi and kisses him. He could have kissed him af-
fectionately (the same word appears in Luke 15:20)
or kissed him on the hand. The customary greeting of respect is turned into a sign of infamy and
death, which Jesus brings out with his question.

**22:49 – 50 When those around him saw what
was about to happen, they said, "Lord, should we
smite with the sword?" And one of them smote
the high priest's servant and cut off his right ear**
(ἰδόντες δὲ οἱ περὶ αὐτὸν τὸ ἐσόμενον εἶπαν·
κύριε, εἰ πατάξομεν ἐν μαχαίρῃ; καὶ ἐπάταξεν
εἷς τις ἐξ αὐτῶν τοῦ ἀρχιερέως τὸν δοῦλον καὶ
ἀφεῖλεν τὸ οὖς αὐτοῦ τὸ δεξιόν). The answer to
the question, "Should we smite with the sword?"
is, "Never." If disciples are to take up the sword, it
is to be a different kind of sword than the one that
the world takes up. Unfortunately, "those around
[Jesus]," whom Luke tactfully does not identify as
"the disciples," already have their swords drawn.
Bock notes that the form of the question in Greek
beginning with εἰ "usually indicates the expectation of an affirmative reply," and goes on to state,
"They have no inkling that their interpretation
might be mistaken."[20] Consequently, one of them
does not wait for an answer before striking.

The blow with a sword may have been a wild
strike that found the high priest's servant's ear by
chance, or it may have been deliberately and provocatively aimed at him. It was taken as a grave
insult against one's own person if one's servant
were attacked or mistreated (see 2 Sam 10:4 – 5
[1 Chr 19:4 – 5]; Luke 20:9 – 11).[21] Josephus records
Antigonus lacerating his rival Hyrcanus's ear with
his own teeth to disqualify him forever from re-
suming the high priesthood (Josephus, *J.W.* 1.13.9
§270; see also *t. Parah* 3:8).

**22:51 But Jesus said, "That's enough!" And when
he touched the ear, he healed it** (ἀποκριθεὶς δὲ ὁ
Ἰησοῦς εἶπεν· ἐᾶτε ἕως τούτου· καὶ ἁψάμενος τοῦ
ὠτίου ἰάσατο αὐτόν). In Mark 14:48 – 49, Jesus rebukes only those who came out against him with
swords and clubs. In Matt 26:52 – 54, Jesus rebukes
the swordsman with an aphorism, "All who draw
the sword will die by the sword," announces that
his arrest fulfills Scripture, and then rebukes the
arresting party and reiterates that what is taking
place is in fulfillment of the Scriptures. In Luke,
Jesus rebukes the swordsman and any others who
might be tempted to join the melee with the command to stop (lit., "leave it until this" [ἐᾶτε ἕως
τούτου]).

Jesus then heals the man's ear, which is a sign
of forgiveness to those who have come to take
him prisoner. Jesus' last miracle recorded in Luke
reveals a total rejection of violence in his name.
More important, Jesus intervenes to prevent the
divine necessity of the cross from being hindered.
As Cosgrove states it, "vengeance must await its
own time and cannot be allowed to impede the
way of the passion."[22]

20. Bock, *Luke*, 2:1770.
21. Benedict T. Viviano ("The High Priest's Servant's Ear:
Mark 14:47," *RB* 96 [1989]: 88) argues that the term "servant"
could refer to the prefect of the priests.

22. Cosgrove, "The Divine ΔEI in Luke-Acts," 180 – 81.

22:52–53 Then Jesus said to the chief priests and the captains [of the temple guard] and elders, "Have you come out with swords and clubs as [you would] against a bandit? Every day I was with you in the temple and you did not lay hands on me, but this is your hour and the dominion of darkness!" (εἶπεν δὲ Ἰησοῦς πρὸς τοὺς παραγενομένους ἐπ᾽ αὐτὸν ἀρχιερεῖς καὶ στρατηγοὺς τοῦ ἱεροῦ καὶ πρεσβυτέρους· ὡς ἐπὶ λῃστὴν ἐξήλθατε μετὰ μαχαιρῶν καὶ ξύλων; καθ᾽ ἡμέραν ὄντος μου μεθ᾽ ὑμῶν ἐν τῷ ἱερῷ οὐκ ἐξετείνατε τὰς χεῖρας ἐπ᾽ ἐμέ· ἀλλ᾽ αὕτη ἐστὶν ὑμῶν ἡ ὥρα καὶ ἡ ἐξουσία τοῦ σκότους). In Mark, the crowd *comes from* the chief priests,

scribes, and elders, but in Luke it *consists of* the chief priests, temple officers, and elders. They work their treachery under the cover of darkness.

Jesus' rebuke specifically links the temple officialdom with Satan's dominion and its moral darkness. They will have their hour, but it is an hour that will only last until the resurrection. Darkness may cover the whole land on Good Friday (23:44), but first light on Sunday reveals the truth. The puppets of the power of darkness cannot know that God will take their presumed triumph in snuffing out Jesus' life on the cross and will turn it into salvation.

Theology in Application

Jesus does not pray for the hour to pass if it is possible (Mark 14:35, see 14:41). He does not say "all things are possible for you" but expresses things in terms of the divine will, "if you will." It means that he does not concern himself with "theoretical possibilities" but with "the actualities of God's determination."[23] If it were God's will, then God would do so.[24] Jesus knows that the Father looks after those whom he does not want to suffer; however, it is the will of the Father, expressed in the Scripture, that Jesus must suffer. What can be inferred from Jesus' prayer on the Mount of Olives for the theology of prayer is that prayer is designed to make God's will known to the one who prays, not to make the pray-er's will known to God. Prayer opens the window "through which man may 'see' God's activity and, perhaps, become a part of it."[25] The very act of praying, then, can express the idea "not my will but thine be done" as those who pray open themselves up to God and God's will.

Jesus' condemnation of the violence that is done in his name has not been taken sufficiently seriously in the history of the church. Violence breeds violence. The sword's blade can kill the victim at a literal level, but the handle kills the holder at another level. Jesus is against war, and one must answer to him if one seeks to justify it in his name. The disciples may mean well and may make excuses for their actions, but they completely misread the situation. The attempt to defend Jesus with violence goes against what he has tried to teach them (6:27–28). They may call him "Lord," but their actions belie their obedience to all that he has commanded. Using Satan's

---

23. Crump, *Jesus the Intercessor*, 122.
24. Ibid., 126.

25. Ibid.

means to fight Satan's minions only betrays the cause of Christ.[26] The disciples are ready to kill someone whom Jesus is ready to die for. The enemies are not devils, and the disciples are not avenging angels.[27]

This is the last time in Luke that Jesus uses his divine power to heal. Healing the ear of the high priest's servant is not an oddment of medical curiosity. It reveals Jesus' healing power, his power over evil, and his rejection of violence. In Luke's passion, he also forgives the brutish soldiers who execute him and blesses the felon who is crucified with him. These acts reveal that his suffering and death are intended to bring healing to a lost world as well as light to a dark world. Jesus would not want to leave even his murderous enemy unhealed. He also intervenes miraculously to undo the violent resistance that might waylay the divine plan that is leading him to the cross.

---

26. Culpepper, "The Gospel of Luke," 9:437.   27. From a conversation with my colleague Terry York.

71

Luke 22:54 – 65

Literary Context

Peter denies knowing Jesus *before* Jesus is questioned by the Jewish court (contrast Matt 26:57 – 58, 69 – 75; Mark 14:53 – 54, 66 – 72; John 18:12 – 18, 25 – 27). This narrative sequence underscores that before Peter can become a confessing disciple, he needs a demonstration of how to do this from his Lord. After he witnesses Jesus' bold testimony before the Jewish leaders, after learning how to pray from Jesus' example, and after being filled with the Holy Spirit, he too can witness with boldness before Jewish councils and the Herods and Pilates of the world. Peter's threefold denial of Jesus fulfills to the letter Jesus' prophecy that this would happen (22:34). The irony is that it occurs in the context of Jesus' being mocked and taunted to prophesy (22:63 – 64).

In this scene, everything occurs in the high priest's courtyard. Since Jesus is able to look at Peter and the mockery of Jesus occurs in the same courtyard before his hearing, Luke presents Peter as denying any knowledge of his Lord while in his presence. Witnessing his chief apostle collapse in a heap of denials adds acute pain to Jesus' mockery by his enemies.

VI. Jesus' Suffering and Death (22:1 – 23:49)
    C. Jesus' Parting Words to His Disciples (22:21 – 38)
    D. Jesus' Prayer and Arrest on the Mount of Olives (22:39 – 53)
➡   **E. Peter's Denial and the Mockery of Jesus (22:54 – 65)**
    F. Jesus on Trial (22:66 – 23:25)

Main Idea

Jesus' identity as "the Lord" is not threatened by the fallibility of his followers or the perceptions of an ignorant rabble. He meets failure with forgiveness, encouragement, and hope, and torturous mockery with dignified silence.[1]

---

1. Rowe, *Early Narrative Christology*, 179.

Translation

Luke 22:54–65

22:54	Circumstance	When they arrested him, **they led him away and entered into the high priest's house.** **Peter was following from afar.**
55		When they lit a fire in the middle of the courtyard and sat down together, **Peter sat in their midst.**
56	Accusation	When a certain slave girl saw him sitting in the light, **she stared intently at him and said:** *"This one was also with him!"*
57	Denial	**He denied it, saying,** *"I do not know him, woman!"*
58a	Accusation	After a short while, **another spotted him and said,** *"You are one of them also!"*
b	Denial	**Peter said,** *"Man, I am not!"*
59	Accusation	After about an hour had passed, **another was firmly insisting, saying,** *"Upon the truth, this one was indeed with him,* *for he is also a Galilean!"*
60a	Denial	**Peter said,** *"Man, I do not know what you are saying!"*
b	Fulfillment of prophecy	Immediately, while he was speaking, **the rooster crowed.**
61a		**The Lord turned and looked at Peter.**
b	Response: remembrance	**Peter then remembered the word of the Lord, how he said,** *"Before the cock crows tonight* *you will deny me three times."*
62	Response: retreat/ regret	And **he went out and wept bitterly.**
63	Mockery	Now **the men who were holding him began to mock him and beat him.**
64	Taunt	**They also blindfolded him and kept asking him,** *"Prophesy! Who is it that struck you?"*
65	Taunt	And **blaspheming, they spoke many other things against him.**

Structure and Literary Form

Jesus is led to the high priest's house and is then mocked by his captors, who taunt him to prophesy; these two scenes wrap around a scene describing Peter's threefold denial that he is a disciple. Jesus had prophesied Peter would deny him three times that evening (22:34). The structure underscores the fulfillment of Jesus' prophecy to the letter as Peter denies any association with Jesus three times when others accuse him of being with him.

Exegetical Outline

→ **I. Transition to the high priest's courtyard (22:54–55)**

II. Peter's three denials (22:56–60)

    A. Denial that he knows Jesus (22:56–57)

    B. Denial that he was one of them (22:58)

    C. Denial that he knows what they are talking about (22:59–60a)

    D. Crowing of the rooster (22:60b)

III. Jesus' presence and look at Peter (22:61a)

IV. Peter's revelation (22:61b–62)

    A. Peter's recollection of Jesus' prophecy (22:61b)

    B. Peter's retreat with bitter weeping (22:62)

V. Mockery of Jesus as a prophet (22:63–65)

Explanation of the Text

22:54 When they arrested him, they led him away and entered into the high priest's house. Peter was following from afar (συλλαβόντες δὲ αὐτὸν ἤγαγον καὶ εἰσήγαγον εἰς τὴν οἰκίαν τοῦ ἀρχιερέως· ὁ δὲ Πέτρος ἠκολούθει μακρόθεν). The "high priesthood of Annas and Caiaphas" is cited in 3:2, but "the high priest" who orchestrated the arrest and is preparing to arraign Jesus before the Roman governor is unnamed here. Luke has no interest in him as an individual. He simply represents the religious power structure aligned against Jesus (9:22; 19:47; 20:19; 22:2).

The disciples had followed Jesus to the Mount of Olives, but they disappear from the narrative as he is led away by his captors. Peter partially keeps his promise to go with Jesus (22:33) but follows at a safe distance and plucks up enough courage to enter into the headquarters of the enemy's camp. What he has in mind is unclear; but, all alone and not having prayed, he exposes himself to intense satanic sifting that reveals his boast of undying loyalty to be nothing but hot air.

22:55 When they lit a fire in the middle of the courtyard and sat down together, Peter sat in their midst (περιαψάντων δὲ πῦρ ἐν μέσῳ τῆς αὐλῆς καὶ συγκαθισάντων ἐκάθητο ὁ Πέτρος μέσος αὐτῶν). Peter joins Jesus' captors by their fire, but he is not as complicit in the crime as Judas was. Where Judas has gone is unknown. There is no indication he was present to identify his fellow follower.

22:56–57 When a certain slave girl saw him sitting in the light, she stared intently at him and said: "This one was also with him!" He denied it, saying, "I do not know him, woman!" (ἰδοῦσα δὲ αὐτὸν παιδίσκη τις καθήμενον πρὸς τὸ φῶς καὶ ἀτενίσασα αὐτῷ εἶπεν· καὶ οὗτος σὺν αὐτῷ ἦν. ὁ δὲ ἠρνήσατο λέγων· οὐκ οἶδα αὐτόν, γύναι). Senior notes that in Mark the fire "warms" Peter (Mark 14:54), but in Luke it "throws light on" him and exposes him in the darkness of the hour (Luke 22:53) in more ways than one.[2] The dim firelight apparently is enough to make out Peter's features, or perhaps he gave himself away in some way when he entered the courtyard.

A "slave girl" (παιδίσκη; see Acts 12:13; 16:16) "stares intently at him" (ἀτενίσασα) and announces her suspicions to the gathered company that he was with Jesus. According to John 18:16, she was the doorkeeper. What gives him away, she does not say, but Peter, the rock, begins to crack; and Jesus' prophecy that he would deny knowing him (22:34) is fulfilled. The irony is that Jesus had asked Peter earlier, "Who do you say I am?" Peter responded, "The Messiah of God!" (9:20). Jesus also warned that whoever denies him before others will be denied before the angels of God (12:9). Peter's denial may not be driven purely by fear but also because his hopes and expectations for Jesus as the Messiah are being dashed before his eyes (see 24:21). Tolbert explains it: "To die when there is hope for victory is one thing; to die for a lost cause, quite another."[3]

Luke does not gloss over the shame of Peter's denial, but he does not present it as bleakly as do Mark and Matthew. Peter does not deny his Lord with oaths and curses (Matt 26:72, 74; Mark 14:71),

and the word "deny" (ἠρνήσατο) appears only in this verse and in the aorist tense. After this first denial, Luke narrates that Peter simply "said" (Luke 22:58, 60).

22:58 After a short while, another spotted him and said, "You are one of them also!" Peter said, "Man, I am not!" (καὶ μετὰ βραχὺ ἕτερος ἰδὼν αὐτὸν ἔφη· καὶ σὺ ἐξ αὐτῶν εἶ. ὁ δὲ Πέτρος ἔφη· ἄνθρωπε, οὐκ εἰμί). Apparently, the slave girl's alarm was ignored, but Peter draws attention from others. "One of them" (ἐξ αὐτῶν) implies that Jesus and his followers have become infamous in these circles.

22:59–60 After about an hour had passed, another was firmly insisting, saying, "Upon the truth, this one was indeed with him, for he is also a Galilean!" Peter said, "Man, I do not know what you are saying!" Immediately, while he was speaking, the rooster crowed (καὶ διαστάσης ὡσεὶ ὥρας μιᾶς ἄλλος τις διϊσχυρίζετο λέγων· ἐπ' ἀληθείας καὶ οὗτος μετ' αὐτοῦ ἦν, καὶ γὰρ Γαλιλαῖός ἐστιν. εἶπεν δὲ ὁ Πέτρος· ἄνθρωπε, οὐκ οἶδα ὃ λέγεις. καὶ παραχρῆμα ἔτι λαλοῦντος αὐτοῦ ἐφώνησεν ἀλέκτωρ). A third person repeats the same accusation as the slave woman and swears that Peter is one of them. The proof is that he is "a Galilean." Galileans with their different accent (see Acts 2:7) would probably stand out like a sore thumb in the high priest's courtyard, but the term may connote more than that someone hails from that area. It may reflect a Judean prejudice that Galileans were country bumpkins who could be easily deluded into following a charlatan (Acts 5:37).

Peter's third denial is punctuated by the crowing of a rooster, just as Jesus predicted. The lack of a definite article before "rooster" (ἀλέκτωρ) suggests that Luke refers to a bird crowing (see 3 Macc

---

2. Senior, *The Passion of Jesus in the Gospel of Luke*, 96.

3. Tolbert, "Luke," 173.

5:23) and not the end of the Roman watch by that name (between 12:00 midnight and 3:00 a.m.). Its raucous cry is an ironic rebuke that makes a sad joke of Peter's cocksure assertion that he would follow Jesus to prison and death.

22:61 The Lord turned and looked at Peter. Peter then remembered the word of the Lord, how he said, "Before the cock crows tonight you will deny me three times" (καὶ στραφεὶς ὁ κύριος ἐνέβλεψεν τῷ Πέτρῳ, καὶ ὑπεμνήσθη ὁ Πέτρος τοῦ ῥήματος τοῦ κυρίου ὡς εἶπεν αὐτῷ ὅτι πρὶν ἀλέκτορα φωνῆσαι σήμερον ἀπαρνήσῃ με τρίς). Only Luke notes that after Peter had denied knowing Jesus the third time, the Lord turned and looked at him. It means that Peter denied knowing Jesus *in his presence*. It is after Jesus looked at him, not after the cock crow, that Peter remembers the prophecy, characterized as "the word of the Lord," about his impending collapse. Despite Peter's denial of him, Jesus remains "the Lord." The phrase also reinforces Jesus' role as a prophet (Isa 1:10; 28:14; Jer 1:14; 2:31; Hos 1:1; 4:1; Joel 1:1; Amos 5:1; 7:16; Jonah 1:1; Mic 1:1; 4:2; Zeph 1:1; Hag 1:1; Zech 1:1).

The silent look from Jesus eclipses the menacing stares of the others gathered around the fire and jolts Peter back to reality. He remembered the Lord's word that prophesied his denial, but did he also remember his word, "whoever denies me before men will be denied before God's angels" (12:9)? Jesus' look, however, would not have been an "I told you so" kind of look or a withering glare of disappointment and reproach. Instead, one can imagine that it would have been a look of forgiveness and encouragement. It carried hope for the future. Peter later must also remember the Lord's prophecy of his recovery and everything the Lord said and did at the Last Supper to interpret his death.

22:62 And he went out and wept bitterly (καὶ ἐξελθὼν ἔξω ἔκλαυσεν πικρῶς). Many note that

the bitter weeping is a sign that Peter begins "to turn" as Jesus prophesied. It takes him full circle back to the time when he first recognized that in Jesus' presence he was an unworthy sinner (5:8). At that time he begged Jesus to leave him; now, he leaves Jesus to his tormentors. Apparently, no one bothers to follow him as he leaves the scene (and neither does the narrator). Luke will only record Peter's running to the tomb to find it empty (24:12), but he takes center stage in the beginning of Acts. As Jesus promised, he and the other disciples ultimately will persevere. The bond will not be broken.

22:63 Now the men who were holding him began to mock him and beat him (καὶ οἱ ἄνδρες οἱ συνέχοντες αὐτὸν ἐνέπαιζον αὐτῷ δέροντες). The mockery precedes the interrogation of Jesus. "The men who were holding" Jesus (οἱ ἄνδρες οἱ συνέχοντες) implicate "the chief priests and the captains [of the temple guard] and elders," who composed the arresting party (22:52). The verb "mock" (ἐμπαίζω) in this context means to make a fool out of somebody by torture (see also 23:11, 36; Matt 27:29, 31, 41; Mark 15:20, 31; 2 Macc 7:10). It also fulfills what Jesus predicted would happen to him (Luke 18:32). Luke is circumspect in describing what was done to Jesus. He does not mention that they spat on Jesus or placed the crown of thorns on his head (Mark 15:16 – 20).

22:64 – 65 They also blindfolded him and kept asking him, "Prophesy! Who is it that struck you?" And blaspheming, they spoke many other things against him (καὶ περικαλύψαντες αὐτὸν ἐπηρώτων λέγοντες· προφήτευσον, τίς ἐστιν ὁ παίσας σε; καὶ ἕτερα πολλὰ βλασφημοῦντες ἔλεγον εἰς αὐτόν). These ruffians must have heard the word on the street that Jesus was some kind of prophet (7:16, 39; 24:19). In their ignorance they ridicule him as a pathetic deceiver who is now exposed.

Luke has no interest in reporting that Jesus was subjected to some kind of cruel game of blind-man's bluff but wishes to highlight the irony. As his enemies ask him to "prophesy," Jesus' most recent prophecies at the Last Supper have been fulfilled to the letter. He has been betrayed by one of the Twelve; Peter has denied him three times before the rooster crowed; and he has been reckoned with transgressors when he was treated as a robber (22:52). The fulfillment of the prophecy that Peter would turn and strengthen his brothers will occur after the resurrection. The fulfillment of the prophecy that his disciples will sit on thrones judging the twelve tribes of Israel awaits the end of the age.

Taunting him to prophesy also highlights what Jesus, the prophet, said happens to prophets in Jerusalem: they are killed (13:33 – 35; see 6:22 – 23), and their blood will be on the heads of their killers (11:47 – 51). The continuation of the "other things" they spoke against him is characterized by Luke as blasphemy (βλασφημοῦντες).

Theology in Application

1. The Example of Peter

What made Peter follow the arresting party into the high priest's courtyard? Was it wounded pride that still stung from Jesus' prophecy at the supper that he would cave in and deny him three times? Did he want to prove Jesus wrong? Was he still overly self-confident? Or did he simply want to be close by to see what would happen so that he could boast to his comrades, "I was there"?

We do not know Peter's motivation for following from afar, but this rash decision brings him into the lions' den of the enemy's camp. His embarrassing, cowardly lies are fully and vividly narrated, but he was not the only one who failed that night. Jesus told him that when he "turned," he was to strengthen his brothers. They too failed, but their failures are not narrated. Peter's failure highlights how pathetic empty boasts can be, and he is not alone. We are often guilty of the same thing when we sing lines from hymns like "All to Jesus I surrender," "Wherever He leads, I'll go," or "Take my silver and my gold, not a mite would I withhold."

Peter failed because he tried to blend in. He apparently could not take the cold stares of disapproval from those he did not even know. The reality is that Christians can never blend in completely and always invite the harsh judgment of outsiders, unless they choose to be utterly silent. Many choose this option because they do not want to associated with a religion sneeringly dismissed as naïve, archaic, and behind the times and only for the gullible and lowbrow. So they withdraw into a shell in shamed silence. Unlike Peter, we should never underestimate our capacity for disloyalty.

Peter could not say after this incident, "I have learned my lesson. This will never happen to me again." If he learned anything, it is that the flesh is weak and Satan's sieve is very fine. He can fail at any time — and when he least expects it. His strength comes only from the Lord's strength. He will always be a penitent who can offer no excuse. The example of Peter's failure puts in a word for a little less spiritual self-esteem and a little more spiritual dissatisfaction on our part. From his broken heart, he is humbled and gains wisdom. The story is not covered up but is told, presumably because Peter tells it. When Peter turned to strengthen his brothers, he had learned that "all have sinned and fall short of the glory of God" (Rom 3:23).

2. The Example of Jesus

First Peter 2:21 affirms that Christ's suffering leaves an example for his followers to follow in his steps. Without the example of Jesus' boldly giving his witness before the Jewish council, king, and governor, and without the power of the Spirit, disciples will fail as Peter does in this scene.

In Acts, Stephen is a model of one who imitates Jesus' example. (1) He was charged with basically the same crimes as Jesus, faced the same leaders of the council and a crowd stirred up by them, and gave his bold testimony without wavering. (2) He saw the Son of Man standing at the right hand of God (Acts 7:54 – 55), which is what Jesus at his trial said would happen (Luke 22:69). That passage contains the only occurrence of the title "Son of Man" outside the Gospels and the only occurrence of it on the lips of anyone other than Jesus (not including the phrase "one like a son of man" in Rev 1:13 and 14:14). (3) At his death, Stephen prayed as Jesus did, "Lord Jesus, receive my spirit" (Acts 7:59; see Luke 23:46 [from Ps 31:5]). (4) Like Jesus he forgave his executioners, "Lord, do not hold this sin against them" (Acts 7:60; see Luke 23:34).

Though Peter fails miserably here, Jesus' prayer, look, and omniscient assurance preserve him. His failure combined with the continuation of the story in Acts reminds us that disciples are in it "for the long haul and need all the hope and encouragement they can get."[4]

---

4. Dean Smith, "We Will Pray: Preaching about Prayer in Luke/Acts," in *Preaching from Luke/Acts* (ed. D. Fleer and D. Bland; Abilene, TX: ACU Press, 2000), 101 – 2.

Luke 22:66 – 23:25

Literary Context

Since Jesus' entry into Jerusalem, Luke has documented the Jewish leaders' intent to do away with Jesus (19:47 – 48; 20:19 – 20; 22:2). Now their plotting reaches its denouement. After arresting Jesus by stealth, they build a case against him with trumped-up charges and prosecute him before the Roman governor, who ultimately capitulates to their will.

In contrast to Jesus' trial before the council in Mark, Luke does not mention any charge that Jesus spoke out against the temple. False witnesses do not give testimony; the high priest plays no part in the proceedings; and the council does not accuse Jesus of blasphemy (see Mark 14:55 – 64). The result is that Luke's account highlights the christological claims about Jesus. He is "the Son of Man [who] will be seated at the right hand of the power of God," and he is "the Son of God." Luke's presentation of Jesus' trial confirms that he "is the Christ promised in Scripture — through his life, death, resurrection and exaltation he has fulfilled the promises made to the fathers."[1]

The trial serves as a fulfillment of Jesus' prophecy of what would happen to him (see 9:22; 13:33; 18:32). It also establishes for the reader, if not for the actors in the scene, his innocence. Luke's purpose is not to uphold Jesus as merely innocent but to show him to be "the righteous sufferer."[2] It also prepares for the experience of the disciples in Acts before other Herods (Acts 12:1 – 23; 25:13 – 26:32) and other Roman governors (13:4 – 12; 18:12 – 17; 23:23 – 26:32).

VI. Jesus' Suffering and Death (22:1 – 23:49)

    D. Jesus' Prayer and Arrest on the Mount of Olives (22:39 – 53)

    E. Peter's Denial and the Mockery of Jesus (22:54 – 65)

➡   **F. Jesus on Trial (22:66 – 23:25)**

    G. The Crucifixion of Jesus (23:26 – 49)

---

1. Strauss, *The Davidic Messiah in Luke-Acts*, 343.   2. Neagoe, *The Trial of the Gospel*, 86 – 89.

Main Idea

As the righteous sufferer, Jesus is sentenced to be crucified by a tidal wave of irrational malevolence that is blind to the truth.

Translation

Luke 22:66–23:25

22:66	Circumstance	As soon as ⮌ day came,
		the body of elders of the people, the chief priests, and scribes gathered,
		and they led him away to their council.
67a	Question	**They said,**
		"Are you the Christ? Tell us!"
b	Response (1)	**He said to them,**
		"If I tell you,
		you will not believe.
68	Response (2)	*If I ask you a question,*
		you will not answer.
69	Prophetic declaration	*From now on, the Son of Man will be seated at the right hand of the power ⮌ of God."*
70a	Question	**They all said,**
		"Are you the Son of God?!"
b	Response	**He said to them,**
		"You say that I am."
71	Resolution	**They said,**
		"Why do we need any more testimony?
		For we ourselves have heard [it] from his own lips."
23:1	Circumstance	**Then the whole bunch of them rose up and led him to Pilate.**
2a	Accusations	**They began to accuse him, saying,**
b		*"We found this man corrupting our nation and*
c		*forbidding the payment of taxes to Caesar and*
d		*calling himself the Messiah, a king."*
3a	Question	**Pilate asked him, saying,**
		"Are you king of the Jews?"
b	Response	**He answered him,**
		"So you say."
4	Attempted resolution	**Pilate said to the chief priests and the crowds,**
		"I find no grounds for charging this man."

Continued on next page.

5	Accusation	**They kept insisting, saying,**
		"He stirs up the people with his teaching
		throughout the whole of Judea, from Galilee, where he began, all⳨
		the way to here."

| 6 | Circumstance | When Pilate heard this, |
| | | **he asked if the man were a Galilean.** |

7a		When he heard that he was from Herod's [jurisdiction of] power,
b		**he sent him off to Herod,**
		who was himself in Jerusalem during these days.
8a	Reintroduction of	When Herod saw Jesus
	character	**he was very glad,**
b		for he had wanted to see him for a long time
c		because he had heard about him and
		was hoping to see some sign performed by him.
9a	Questions	**He asked him many questions,**
b		but **he did not answer him.**

10	Accusations	**The chief priests and scribes had stood by and accused him vigorously.**
11a	Mockery	**Herod himself joined his soldiers in treating him with contempt and mocking⳨**
		him,
b	Circumstance	and **they put shining raiment on him**
		and **sent him back to Pilate.**
12a	Historical side note	**Herod and Pilate became friends with one another from that same day,**
b		for previously **enmity had existed between them**.

13	Circumstance	**Pilate then called together the chief priests, the rulers, and the people.**
14	Pronouncement	**He said to them,**
	of innocence	*"You brought me this man as one who was misleading the people,*
		and behold, after examining him before you, I do not find your charges⳨
		against this man to be valid.
15		*Neither has Herod,*
		for he sent him back to us.
		Behold, he has done nothing worthy of death.
16	Attempted resolution	*Therefore, I will have him chastised with blows and release him."*
17	Textual variant	
18	Cry for death	**Then they all cried out together, saying,**
		"Take this one,
		release Barabbas to us!"
19	Introduction of	**(This was someone who had been thrown into prison for starting a certain⳨**
	character	**uprising in the city and for murder).**
20	Attempted resolution	**Again, Pilate spoke to them**
		because he wanted to release Jesus.

| 21 | Cry for death | But **they kept shouting out,** |
| | | *"Crucify him, crucify him!"* |

Continued on next page.

Continued from previous page.

22a	Attempted resolution/ pronouncement of innocence	**He said to them a third time,** *"Why? What evil has this one done?*
b		*I found no grounds for death in him.*
c		*After chastising him with blows, I will release him."*
23a	Cry for death	**But they kept demanding with loud shouts for him to be crucified,**
b		**and their shouts were overpowering.**
24	Capitulation	**So Pilate decreed that what they asked be granted.**
25a		**He released the one whom they asked for,**
b		the one who had been thrown into prison because of the uprising and murder,
c		**and he handed Jesus over to their will.**

Structure and Literary Form

The structure contains three interrogations of Jesus: before the Jewish leaders (22:66 – 71); before Pilate, the Roman governor (23:1 – 5); and before Herod the tetrarch (23:6 – 12). It concludes with the gathering of the Jewish leaders with Pilate and the verdict that condemns Jesus to death (23:13 – 25). The final scene alternates between Pilate's declarations of Jesus' innocence and attempts to let him go (23:13 – 16, 20, 22), and the crowd's pressure demanding his death (23:18 – 19, 21, 23). It ends with Pilate's capitulation to their wishes (23:24 – 25). The narrative shows that though the governor convicts Jesus and has him executed, the Jewish leaders through the crowds have prevailed upon him to do so.

Exegetical Outline

→ **I. The Sanhedrin hearing (22:66 – 71)**

   A. Question: Are you the Christ? (22:66 – 67a)

   B. Response (22:67b – 69)

       1. Refusal to answer because of their unbelief (22:67b – 68)

       2. Prophetic declaration: The Son of Man is being vindicated even now (22:69)

   C. Question: Are you the Son of God? (22:70a)

   D. Response: ambivalent answer (22:70b)

   E. Decision that he has condemned himself by his testimony (22:71)

II. Trial before Pilate (23:1 – 5)

   A. The charges against Jesus (23:1 – 2)

1. Jesus perverts the nation (23:1 – 2b)

2. Jesus forbade paying tribute to Rome (23:2c)

3. Jesus claimed to be a king (23:2d)

   B. Jesus' ambivalent answer (23:3)

   C. Pilate's first declaration of Jesus' innocence (23:4)

   D. Further charge that Jesus' teaching from Galilee to Jerusalem incites the people (23:5)

III. The Appearance before Herod (23:6 – 12)

   A. Pilate sends Jesus to Herod (23:6 – 7)

   B. Jesus' silence before Herod (23:8 – 9)

   C. The high priests' accusations against Jesus (23:10)

   D. Herod's mockery of Jesus (23:11)

   E. The new alliance between Herod and Pilate (23:12)

IV. Jesus Sentenced to Die (23:13 – 25)

   A. Pilate's second declaration of innocence (23:13 – 16)

   B. The cry for the release of Barabbas, an insurrectionist (23:17 – 19)

   C. Pilate's proposal to release Jesus (23:20)

   D. Shouts to crucify him (23:21)

   E. Pilate's third declaration of innocence and proposal to release Jesus (23:22)

   F. Shouts to crucify him (23:23)

   G. Pilate's capitulation: Barabbas released; Jesus handed over to their will (23:24 – 25)

Explanation of the Text

22:66 As soon as day came, the body of the elders of the people, the chief priests, and scribes gathered, and they led him away to their council (καὶ ὡς ἐγένετο ἡμέρα, συνήχθη τὸ πρεσβυτέριον τοῦ λαοῦ, ἀρχιερεῖς τε καὶ γραμματεῖς, καὶ ἀπήγαγον αὐτὸν εἰς τὸ συνέδριον αὐτῶν). Daylight breaks through, but the "power of darkness" still casts a pall over the scene. Luke records a short informal hearing before the Jewish leaders in the morning. The makeup of the gathering (elders, chief priests, and scribes) represents "the broadest possible official representation of Israel" and matches the passion predictions.[3]

They lead Jesus away either to their "council" or to a place, "their council chamber" (εἰς τὸ συνέδριον αὐτῶν), perhaps "the hall of hewn stone" (*m. Mid.* 5:4). The use of the term in Acts, however, suggests that it refers to a council (see Acts 4:15; 5:27, 34; 6:12, 15; 23:6, 20, 28; 24:20). There would have been a central council in Jerusalem, but Saldarini is correct that "its membership, structure, and powers are not clear in the sources and probably varied with political circumstances."[4] It is unlikely that this body was an assembly of scholars (the Sanhedrin) debating and enacting points of law for the community as envisioned at a much later time in the Mishnah and Talmud. Under the Romans, this body would have consisted of the power brokers: the guild of leading priests and wealthy aristocracy, such as Joseph of Arimathea (Matt 27:57).

Since there was no bureaucracy of Roman

3. Neyrey, *The Passion according to Luke*, 71.

4. Anthony Saldarini, "Sanhedrin," *ABD*, 5:979.

officials to handle all of the administrative matters, the amount of jurisdiction that a Roman governor could manage was limited. Consequently, a large part of the everyday chores of government and administration was carried out by the local council. They had the power to arrest, take evidence, and make a preliminary examination for the purpose of presenting a prosecution case before a governor for a formal trial.

22:67a They said, "Are you the Christ? Tell us!" (λέγοντες· εἰ σὺ εἶ ὁ Χριστός, εἰπὸν ἡμῖν). The leaders have already determined to destroy Jesus and do not meet now to gather and to judge the evidence but only to establish a charge that they can present to the governor. They ask two questions of Jesus, "Are you the Christ?" and "Are you the Son of God?" Then they lead him off to Pilate.

The absence of the false witnesses and the charge that Jesus threatened to destroy the temple (Matt 26:59 – 63; Mark 14:55 – 61a; see Acts 6:13 – 14) allow the focus to fall solely on Jesus' identity rather than on side issues or misrepresentations.[5] Jesus is not silent but speaks out boldly (a model for the disciples in Acts, who will speak out boldly before the Jewish leaders, governors, and kings).

22:67b – 69 He said to them, "If I tell you, you will not believe. If I ask you a question, you will not answer. From now on, the Son of Man will be seated at the right hand of the power of God" (εἶπεν δὲ αὐτοῖς· ἐὰν ὑμῖν εἴπω, οὐ μὴ πιστεύσητε· ἐὰν δὲ ἐρωτήσω, οὐ μὴ ἀποκριθῆτε. ἀπὸ τοῦ νῦν δὲ ἔσται ὁ υἱὸς τοῦ ἀνθρώπου καθήμενος ἐκ δεξιῶν τῆς δυνάμεως τοῦ θεοῦ).

The first part of Jesus' response recalls his refusal to answer the leaders when they asked him about the source of his authority for his actions in the temple (20:1 – 8). Israel had a tragic track record for turning a deaf ear to God's emissaries, and Jesus' assertion that they would not accept his testimony recalls Jeremiah's warning to Zedekiah that prefaces an oracle of doom (Jer 38:15 [45:15, LXX]). It implies that "their problem is not lack of evidence for his Messiahship but lack of openness to the possibility of belief."[6]

Whatever answer Jesus gives, they will not believe him (see John 10:24 – 26). Their refusal to believe means that they are guilty of more than speaking a word against the Son of Man but the unforgivable sin of resisting the Holy Spirit (12:10 – 12).[7] Their hardness of heart presents an insurmountable barrier to repentance and reconciliation. Whatever question he asks them, they will not answer (20:1 – 8, 17, 44).

The second part of his answer asserts "his sovereign authority" over his interrogators[8] and his "victory and the expectation of posthumous honor."[9] "From now on" (ἀπὸ τοῦ νῦν) asserts that he is *already* vindicated and enthroned despite appearances to the contrary.[10] The ascension, which forms the climax of the gospel (24:51) and sounds the opening bars in Acts (Acts 1:9), confirms this confession. Stephen's vision further clarifies Jesus' identity as the Son of God. When he was being stoned to death, filled with the Holy Spirit, he looked into heaven and "saw the glory of God, and Jesus standing at the right hand of God" (see Acts 7:55 – 56; cf. 2:33 – 34; 5:31).[11]

5. Neagoe, *The Trial of the Gospel*, 64.

6. Ibid., 65.

7. Buckwalter, *The Character and Purpose of Luke's Christology*, 218 – 19.

8. Fletcher-Louis, *Luke-Acts: Angels, Christology and Soteriology*, 227 – 28.

9. Peter J. Scaer (*The Lukan Passion and the Praiseworthy Death* [New Testament Monographs 10; Sheffield: Sheffield Phoenix, 2005], 95) notes that this theme is common in the presentation of noble deaths.

10. Luke's account does not have "you will see" (Mark 14:62) because they are incapable of seeing anything.

11. Joseph Plevnik, "Son of Man Seated at the Right Hand of God: Luke 22,69 in Lucan Christology," *Bib* 72 (1991): 331 – 47.

Jesus' presence at the right hand of God confirms for Luke his identity as the Son of God and explains the omission here of any reference to "coming on the clouds of heaven" (an allusion to Dan 7:13 found in Jesus' response in Mark 14:62). Luke does not want the reader to confuse the eschatological judgment of the Jewish leaders with Jesus' exaltation.[12] Luke's text makes clear that Jesus as the earthly Messiah is inseparable from the resurrected heavenly Lord. A coin minted in AD 55 depicts the recently deified emperor Claudius, who died in AD 54, sitting at the right hand of the deified emperor Augustus atop a chariot drawn by four elephants.[13] The audience should understand that it is not a deified Caesar who sits next to God but the crucified Jesus.

22:70 They all said, "Are you the Son of God?!" He said to them, "You say that I am" (εἶπαν δὲ πάντες· σὺ οὖν εἶ ὁ υἱὸς τοῦ θεοῦ; ὁ δὲ πρὸς αὐτοὺς ἔφη· ὑμεῖς λέγετε ὅτι ἐγώ εἰμι). Luke divides Mark's single question, "Are you the Messiah, the Son of the Blessed One?" (Mark 14:61) into two questions that prompt two different responses. The result is that the title "Christ" is distinguished from the title "the Son of God." This second question, "Are you the Son of God?" makes it crystal clear that the council knew the distinction between the political term "Christ" and the religious term "Son of God." They do not mention the religious term when they bring their accusations to Pilate but solely emphasize the political term.

The only legitimate charges against Jesus might be religious, but Pilate would have no interest in any religious squabbles among the Jews that did not constitute a threat to Roman rule. Any issue concerning religious beliefs would have been quickly dismissed by the governor, as happened when the Corinthian Jews brought charges against Paul. Gallio, the proconsul of Achaia, said to them: "If you Jews were making a complaint about some misdemeanor or serious crime, it would be reasonable for me to listen to you. But since it involves questions about words and names and your own law — settle the matter yourselves. I will not be a judge of such things" (Acts 18:14 – 15).

Luke creates the impression that the council deliberately trumps up only a false political charge against Jesus. Jesus' aloof response, "*You say* that I am," may mean, "If you want to present that charge in a Roman court, you can say whatever you want." Jesus knows that they do not believe it, but the emphatic phrasing of "you say" (ὑμεῖς λέγετε) brings out an irony. What they "say" to condemn Jesus is also all they need to say "to believe in him."[14] They resist saying it as a confession of faith.

The religious question, "Are you the Son of God?" marks the climax of the hearing and harks back to the annunciation (1:32 – 35), the voice of God at the baptism (3:22), the temptation by Satan (4:3, 9), and the voice from the cloud at the transfiguration (9:35). It stresses that Jesus as Messiah must be seen through the lens of the reality of Jesus' sonship from God.[15] He will not reign over the house of Jacob simply as a political ruler, and his never-ending reign will not be a political one (1:33). The angel's annunciation to Mary reveals that Jesus is Son of God in a unique and mysterious way.[16] His crucifixion makes his being the Son of God even more mysterious.

---

12. Buckwalter, *The Character and Purpose of Luke's Christology*, 218 – 19.

13. Harold Mattingly, *Coins of the Roman Empire in the British Museum*; vol. 1: *Augustus to Vitellius* (London: Trustees of the British Museum, 1923), 1:201 (plate 38).

14. John Paul Heil, "Reader-Response and the Irony of Jesus before the Sanhedrin in Luke 22:66 – 71," *CBQ* 51 (1989): 282.

15. John J. Kilgallen, "Jesus' First Trial: Messiah and Son of God (Luke 22,66 – 71)," *Bib* 80 (1999): 401 – 14.

16. Ibid.

22:71 They said, "Why do we need any more testimony? For we ourselves have heard [it] from his own lips" (οἱ δὲ εἶπαν· τί ἔτι ἔχομεν μαρτυρίας χρείαν; αὐτοὶ γὰρ ἠκούσαμεν ἀπὸ τοῦ στόματος αὐτοῦ). They have heard the testimony of Jesus that will become the foundation of the apostles' testimony. Because their hearts are hardened, they think only in terms of what charge they can use against him to destroy him. They believe they have nailed him with this confession and will have him literally nailed to a cross.

23:1 Then the whole bunch of them rose up and led him to Pilate (καὶ ἀναστὰν ἅπαν τὸ πλῆθος αὐτῶν ἤγαγον αὐτὸν ἐπὶ τὸν Πιλᾶτον). The council's next step fulfills what Jesus prophesied that he would be rejected by "the elders, chief priests, and scribes" and "handed over to the Gentiles" (9:22; 18:32). They hand Jesus over to a foreign power in hopes of persuading it to implement a death penalty that they could not carry out themselves.

Pilate has been introduced in 3:1 and 13:1 and his name also appears in Acts. Pilate was officially called "prefect" (*praefectus Ioudaeae*), and the governor was called a "procurator" only after AD 44. He was responsible for maintaining order and commanded army auxiliary units in the province, which was a minor one.[17] Pilate, as governor, had the power of life and death over all the inhabitants of his province (see Josephus, *J.W.* 2.8.1 §117). The trial and the statements in Acts 3:13 and 13:28 reveal, however, the Jewish leaders are the primary forces behind Jesus' death. They demand that he be killed, and Pilate unwillingly consents. But Luke's

account does not let Pilate off the hook. Luke presents a wicked religious institution joining hands with an immoral government (Acts 4:27).

23:2 They began to accuse him, saying, "We found this man corrupting our nation and forbidding the payment of taxes to Caesar and calling himself the Messiah, a king" (ἤρξαντο δὲ κατηγορεῖν αὐτοῦ λέγοντες· τοῦτον εὕραμεν διαστρέφοντα τὸ ἔθνος ἡμῶν καὶ κωλύοντα φόρους Καίσαρι διδόναι καὶ λέγοντα ἑαυτὸν Χριστὸν βασιλέα εἶναι). No criminal code existed for the malefactor who was a non-Roman citizen tried in the provinces. It was technically known as a "trial outside the system," and the governor was quite free to make his own rules and judgments as he saw fit, to accept or reject charges, and to fashion whatever penalties he chose within reason. Since there were no public prosecutors, the prosecution's case was brought by private parties (*delatores*; see also Acts 24:1 – 9, with Tertullus presenting the case against Paul before Felix, the governor; 25:6 – 7, 15 – 19).[18]

The Jewish leaders bring three precise and formal accusations that are political in nature and paint Jesus as a revolutionary firebrand. The reader knows that all three charges are patently false. The first charge is general and accuses Jesus of inciting the people with his teaching (see *b. Sanh.* 43a, which claims that Jesus "practiced sorcery and enticed Israel to apostasy"). To a Roman, this accusation would imply fomenting anti-Roman feelings. The province of Judea existed on the edge of the Roman Empire and was given to turmoil. Consequently, the Romans were not

---

17. Provinces that had legionary forces permanently stationed in them were under a senatorial legate.

18. Peter Garnsey (*Social Status and Legal Privilege* [Oxford: Clarendon, 1970], 91) explains: "Jury-court procedure was accusatorial. The praetor simply presided over the contest between accuser and accused and pronounced the verdict of the jury. The *cognitio* procedure, on the other hand, was inquisitorial, and gave immense power to the judge. He sought and questioned witnesses, and interrogated the accused. Before passing sentence he regularly consulted his advisers, but was not bound by their counsel. The judge was able to vary the penalty according to his own social prejudices."

indifferent to any threats of unrest in such a vital area.

But Jesus has not perverted the nation; it was already perverse (9:41). He taught the way of God (20:21), but they have judged it to be subversive because in leading the nation to God, he led them away from the elite, Jewish leaders.[19] Jesus had no intention of stirring up a revolt but instead lamented that Jerusalem did not know what makes for peace (19:41 – 44) and was headed on a collision course with Rome that would result in its annihilation. To readers familiar with the Greek Scriptures, the charge of "corrupting our nation" (διαστρέφοντα τὸ ἔθνος ἡμῶν) puts him in the same company with Moses and Elijah. Pharaoh accused Moses of "turning my people [διαστρέφετε τὸν λαόν μου] away from their work" (Exod 5:4 LXX). King Ahab identified Elijah as the "troubler of Israel" (ὁ διαστρέφων; 1 Kgs 18:17).[20]

The second charge contends that Jesus forbade the people to pay Roman taxes. Readers know that his parents enrolled for the census, which was the basis for levying Roman taxes. They also know that the accusers are blatantly lying. When the scribes and chief priests tried to entrap Jesus on the question of tribute to Rome, he did not reject paying to Caesar what he was owed (20:20 – 26).

The third charge is that he claimed to be "the Christ," which is defined for Pilate as equivalent to "a king."[21] Many people assumed that Jesus was some kind of political Christ (see 19:38, "Blessed is the king who comes in the name of the Lord!"). Luke does present him as the royal Davidic Messiah, the legitimate heir to the throne (2:11, 26; 4:41; 9:20; 20:41 – 44), but Jesus never identifies

himself as the Christ nor accepts the political overtones associated with the title.[22] He would be King and Christ in a quite different sense from what most of his supporters may have hoped for or expected. Consequently, Rome has nothing to fear from him, at least on the surface. On the theological level, the charges are true (see below).

23:3 Pilate asked him, saying, "Are you king of the Jews?" He answered him, "So you say" (ὁ δὲ Πιλᾶτος ἠρώτησεν αὐτὸν λέγων· σὺ εἶ ὁ βασιλεὺς τῶν Ἰουδαίων; ὁ δὲ ἀποκριθεὶς αὐτῷ ἔφη· σὺ λέγεις).

Josephus recounts the "temerity" of the rebel Athronges for aspiring to be the king of the Jews in the time leading up to the revolt against Rome and laments that "Judea was filled with brigandage. Anyone might make himself king as the head of a band of rebels" (Ant. 17.10.7 – 8 §285). It is not surprising that Pilate seizes on this particular charge. The Romans took seriously the charge of maiestas, a crime that directly or indirectly diminished the sovereign power or grandeur of the state, emperor, or people.

Jesus' answer, "So you say" (σὺ λέγεις) may be equivalent to a sarcastic, "Whatever," or "What does it look like to you?" Ancient readers in the Greco-Roman world would likely view Jesus' refusal to answer as a sign of his brave resistance. Jesus refuses to confess as if he were guilty of some crime, because he is not under Pilate's power. Barton states: "Confession was the speech of those who had succumbed to the power of another." It was the speech of those under compulsion. "Confession was the act of someone whose spirit had been broken … someone who, as we say in English, had 'cracked.' "[23] The philosophers believed

---

19. Heil, "Reader-Response," 176.

20. Daryl Schmidt, "Luke's 'Innocent' Jesus: A Scriptural Apologetic," in Political Issues in Luke-Acts (ed. Richard J. Cassidy and Philip J. Scharper; Maryknoll, NY: Orbis, 1983), 119.

21. The Thessalonian Jews brought similar charges against Paul and Silas in Acts 17:6 – 7: (1) they were turning the world

upside down; (2) they acted against the decrees of Caesar; (3) they said that there was another king, Jesus.

22. See Strauss, The Davidic Messiah in Luke-Acts.

23. Barton, Roman Honor, 147. Most confessed (whether guilty or innocent) under the blows of the lash (see Seneca, Ep. 82.7).

that those whose spirit was not fortified by philosophy would collapse under pressure. Jesus does not "crack," but it is because he is fortified by the Spirit and prayer.

23:4 Pilate said to the chief priests and the crowds, "I find no grounds for charging this man" (ὁ δὲ Πιλᾶτος εἶπεν πρὸς τοὺς ἀρχιερεῖς καὶ τοὺς ὄχλους· οὐδὲν εὑρίσκω αἴτιον ἐν τῷ ἀνθρώπῳ τούτῳ). One can guess that Pilate may have become suspicious about Jesus' guilt of this crime because Jesus did not appear militant either in his manner or words. He may also have been aware that his followers made no serious armed resistance before or after his arrest. Pilate's quick declaration, therefore, reveals that Jesus' innocence was obvious to anyone whose judgment was not clouded by poisonous malevolence. He asks essentially the same questions of Jesus as the Jewish leaders and receives the same answers. But Pilate, who the readers know is an evil character (13:1), is able to discern Jesus' innocence.

Luke underscores Jesus' innocence throughout his passion narrative:

1. Pilate declares Jesus innocent of all charges three times (23:4, 14, 22).
2. Herod confirms this judgment (23:15).
3. Jesus is contrasted with Barabbas, a seditionist and murderer (23:18 – 19, 25).
4. Jesus is crucified with two persons identified as "criminals" (23:32, 39), and one declares that they are receiving the due reward for their evil deeds but Jesus has done nothing to deserve this punishment (23:41).
5. The centurion in charge of the execution declares that Jesus was "righteous" (23:47).
6. Joseph of Arimathea is described as "a good and righteous man," someone open to the reign of God, and a member of the council who had *not* consented to their purpose and deed (23:50 – 51).
7. The righteousness (innocence) of Jesus is affirmed throughout Acts (Acts 3:14; 7:52: 13:28).

23:5 They kept insisting, saying, "He stirs up the people with his teaching throughout the whole of Judea, from Galilee, where he began, all the way to here" (οἱ δὲ ἐπίσχυον λέγοντες ὅτι ἀνασείει τὸν λαὸν διδάσκων καθ᾽ ὅλης τῆς Ἰουδαίας, καὶ ἀρξάμενος ἀπὸ τῆς Γαλιλαίας ἕως ὧδε). The leaders continue to hammer at Pilate and reiterate the charge that Jesus "stirs up the people" (ἀνασείει τὸν λαόν), which implies that they do not count themselves among these masses. The people indeed have been stirred, but the Jewish leaders hide the real reason behind their concern. They are upset because his so-called incendiary teaching threatens their privileged status and control as he confronts them with the reign of God.

Mentioning that his teaching began in Galilee and spread to Judea is not intended to bring up the image of Judas the Galilean, who rejected paying tribute to Rome and incited a revolt (Acts 5:37; Josephus, *J.W.* 2.8.1 §118).[24] It recalls the story's beginning (4:14; see Acts 10:37) and sets up the referral to Herod. More important, it expresses Luke's theological conviction that God's purpose is accomplished "in its totality as a walk or a way" (see 9:51; 13:22, 32 – 33; 17:11; 18:31; 19:11, 28; 24:47).[25] The teaching, namely, the gospel, has come all the way to Jerusalem and will go on to the ends of the earth (24:47; Acts 1:8). The story of what Jesus began to do in Galilee and what the Holy Spirit continues to do through his disciples cannot be stopped by the Jewish leaders or by the power of the Roman Empire and its puppets.

---

24. Sean Freyne (*Galilee: From Alexander the Great to Hadrian 323 BCE to 135 CE* [Edinburgh: T&T Clark, 1980], 208 – 55) has shown that the popular image of Galilee as a hotbed of revolutionary activity is exaggerated.

25. Bovon, *Luke the Theologian*, 42.

23:6 – 7 When Pilate heard this, he asked if the man were a Galilean. When he heard that he was from Herod's [jurisdiction of] power, he sent him off to Herod, who was himself in Jerusalem during these days (Πιλᾶτος δὲ ἀκούσας ἐπηρώτησεν εἰ ὁ ἄνθρωπος Γαλιλαῖός ἐστιν·καὶ ἐπιγνοὺς ὅτι ἐκ τῆς ἐξουσίας Ἡρῴδου ἐστὶν ἀνέπεμψεν αὐτὸν πρὸς Ἡρῴδην, ὄντα καὶ αὐτὸν ἐν Ἱεροσολύμοις ἐν ταύταις ταῖς ἡμέραις). The hearing before Herod Antipas appears only in Luke. The tradition may have derived from Joanna, the wife of Chuza, Herod's steward (8:3), or from Manaen, a member of Herod's court (Acts 13:1).

As prefect, Pilate was of the equestrian rank (knight). In this rank he would have had no assistants of a similar status and no bureaucracy of Roman officials to handle all of the administrative matters. The governor could and normally did seek advice from others. Festus, for example, consulted with Herod Agrippa about what to do about Paul (Acts 25:13 – 27). When Pilate learns that Jesus is a Galilean, it is reasonable for him to seek Herod's advice on the matter. As a Roman ally, Herod could be relied upon to judge whether or not Jesus was dangerous to Roman rule. As one familiar with Jewish ways, Herod would know what "Christ" ("anointed one") meant, and he would also know more about Jesus' activities in Galilee.

Pilate does not intend to dump the affair in Herod's lap but to get his opinion and advice on the matter. Herod has been introduced (along with Pilate) as the tetrarch of Galilee in 3:1. He imprisoned John for publicly rebuking him for marrying his brother's wife along with other "evil things" (3:19 – 20). When he was baffled by the news being spread abroad about Jesus and the rumors that John the Baptist had been raised from the dead, he sought "to see" Jesus (9:7 – 9). Pharisees later warned Jesus that Herod wanted to kill him (13:31). Given his hostility and track record, the reader would not expect this transfer to Herod to bode well for Jesus.

The translation "Herod's [jurisdiction of] power" (ἐκ τῆς ἐξουσίας Ἡρῴδου) seeks to preserve the image that what is happening is all part of the "hour and the dominion [ἐξουσία] of darkness" (22:53).[26] Herod belongs to the dark side. But his sphere of power is only a minor, backwater outpost, and his hold on power only fleeting. Readers familiar with the history might see the irony. His father, Herod the Great, had the title "King of the Jews" (Josephus, *Ant.* 16.10.2 §311), but the emperor Augustus specifically refused to bestow that title on Herod Antipas when his father died. He sliced up and parceled out the former "kingdom" to his brothers (Josephus, *Ant.* 17.18.1 §188; 17.9.4 §§224 – 27l; 17.11.4 §318; *J.W.* 2.2.3 §§20 – 22; 2.6.3 §§93 – 95).

Josephus also alleges that later on in AD 37, Herod's wife, Herodias, was so jealous when his nephew, Herod Agrippa, received the title "king" from the emperor Gaius Caligula that she encouraged him to request the title for himself. This request led to his downfall. Opponents used it as an opportunity to bring charges that he harbored plans for rebellion with a stash of weapons, and he was dismissed and sent into exile (Josephus, *Ant.* 18.7.1 – 2 §§240 – 56; *J.W.* 2.9.6 §§181 – 83). But right now, Herod is face-to-face with the true King of Israel, who is also falsely accused of trying to spark an insurrection.

23:8 When Herod saw Jesus he was very glad, for he had wanted to see him for a long time because he had heard about him and was hoping to see some sign performed by him (ὁ δὲ Ἡρῴδης ἰδὼν τὸν Ἰησοῦν ἐχάρη λίαν, ἦν γὰρ ἐξ ἱκανῶν χρόνων

---

26. Brown, *The Death of the Messiah*, 1:765.

θέλων ἰδεῖν αὐτὸν διὰ τὸ ἀκούειν περὶ αὐτοῦ καὶ ἤλπιζέν τι σημεῖον ἰδεῖν ὑπ᾽ αὐτοῦ γινόμενον). The seeing/hearing theme is emphasized: Herod was glad to *see* Jesus; he had wanted to *see* him; he had been *hearing* about him; he was hoping to *see* some sign. By identifying him as one who hoped to see Jesus, he may seem to be like Zacchaeus (19:3 – 4). Noting, however, that he only hoped to see a sign from him reveals that he belongs to the evil generation that seeks a sign (see 11:16, 29).

Since Herod had not repented at the preaching of John the Baptist, he was unprepared to see or hear anything. He does not belong to "[Wisdom's] children" (7:35). Darr comments: "Correct response to Jesus is dependent on true recognition, and recognition requires right perception, and, in turn, true perception is not possible without repentance, faith and the abnegation of all self-righteousness and abuse of power or privilege."[27] Signs come only to those who have surrendered already to God.[28]

23:9 He asked him many questions, but he did not answer him (ἐπηρώτα δὲ αὐτὸν ἐν λόγοις ἱκανοῖς, αὐτὸς δὲ οὐδὲν ἀπεκρίνατο αὐτῷ). Jesus' silence creates dramatic tension. Herod has no power over someone who remains silent. The result is that Herod not only does not "*see* a sign, but also does not *hear* a sound from Jesus. Thus, Jesus' refusal to perform or speak has a symbolic effect: the visual and acoustic vacuum created mirrors the spiritual blindness and deafness of Herod and the accusers."[29]

For readers familiar with the Greek Old Testament, Jesus' silence likely would be interpreted in light of Isa 53:7: "He was oppressed and afflicted, yet he did not open his mouth." For Greco-Roman readers, "Jesus' behavior could be interpreted as an

expression of admirable self-control, perhaps even nobility."[30] In his account of Herod the Great's killing his wife Mariamne, Josephus lauds her "greatness of spirit" as she remained silent before false accusations. She went to her death "with a wholly calm demeanor and without change of colour" (*Ant.* 15.7.5 §236).

23:10 The chief priests and scribes had stood by and accused him vigorously (εἱστήκεισαν δὲ οἱ ἀρχιερεῖς καὶ οἱ γραμματεῖς εὐτόνως κατηγοροῦντες αὐτοῦ). The Jewish leaders function as prosecutors in trying to get Jesus convicted of a crime, and they continue to press their case with Herod. The pluperfect "had stood by" (εἱστήκεισαν) means that they were present throughout the interrogation to prevail upon Herod to take their side against Jesus.

23:11 Herod himself joined his soldiers in treating him with contempt and mocking him, and they put shining raiment on him and sent him back to Pilate (ἐξουθενήσας δὲ αὐτὸν [καὶ] ὁ Ἡρῴδης σὺν τοῖς στρατεύμασιν αὐτοῦ καὶ ἐμπαίξας περιβαλὼν ἐσθῆτα λαμπρὰν ἀνέπεμψεν αὐτὸν τῷ Πιλάτῳ). Herod joins in the soldiers' mockery of Jesus, perhaps out of frustration when he refused to respond to any of his questions. Dressing Jesus in "shining raiment" (ἐσθῆτα λαμπράν) when he sends him back to Pilate is not part of the mockery by the soldiers (contrast Mark 15:20) but is intended to communicate something to Pilate.[31] It relates to Pilate's statement in v. 15 that Herod also found the charges to be groundless since Luke does not record that Herod relayed any other message to Pilate about this so-called king. The shining garments may mock Jesus' claim to be royalty and indicate that he did not take the

27. Darr, *Herod the Fox*, 193.
28. Schweizer, *Luke*, 352.
29. Darr, *Herod the Fox*, 197.
30. Green, *The Gospel of Luke*, 805.
31. Darr, *Herod the Fox*, 200.

charges seriously. It communicates that Jesus was a deluded peasant worthy only of derision.

The word "raiment" (ἐσθῆτα) is used for the robes of Herod Agrippa I (Acts 12:21), but there it is modified by the adjective "royal," not "shining" (λαμπράν) (see Josephus, *Ant.* 19.8.2 §344). The phrase "fine clothes" is used of the splendid clothing of the rich in Jas 2:3, but in Acts 10:30 the phrase describes the "shining clothes" of an angel. The adjective is used for white garments (BDAG) and may allude to the allegation that Jesus is a divine figure (see 9:29; 24:4). The reader may recognize the irony that the shining apparel conveys the truth about Jesus.

23:12 Herod and Pilate became friends with one another from that same day, for previously enmity had existed between them (ἐγένοντο δὲ φίλοι ὅ τε Ἡρῴδης καὶ ὁ Πιλᾶτος ἐν αὐτῇ τῇ ἡμέρᾳ μετ᾽ ἀλλήλων· προϋπῆρχον γὰρ ἐν ἔχθρᾳ ὄντες πρὸς αὐτούς). Luke does not explain what caused the enmity between Herod and Pilate or why this event produces a rapprochement. Herod was probably susceptible to flattery and pleased by what he took to be a friendly gesture by Pilate to consult him. The two could also have a good laugh over this pathetic peasant and the Jewish leaders' nervousness about him. Both will go down in history for executing someone sent by God. Herod executed John; and Pilate, Jesus. These former enemies may have reconciled with one another, but neither was reconciled with God.[32]

Luke interprets their collaboration as a fulfillment of Ps 2:1 – 2: the kings of the earth and rulers gathered together against the Lord and his Christ (Acts 4:24 – 28). The trial before Herod is therefore part of Luke's christological apologetic based on prophetic fulfillment and further establishes that

Jesus is God's Christ. Neagoe concludes: "Luke's dominant concern is to further his case that Jesus' sufferings and subsequent death show him to be the suffering righteous one whose coming the Old Testament prophecies [including Isa 52:13 – 53:12; see Acts 8:32 – 33] had long announced."[33]

23:13 Pilate then called together the chief priests, the rulers, and the people (Πιλᾶτος δὲ συγκαλεσάμενος τοὺς ἀρχιερεῖς καὶ τοὺς ἄρχοντας καὶ τὸν λαόν). Pilate seems to take control by calling together the high priests and rulers of the people. Ironically, the people (τὸν λαόν) whom Jesus is accused of leading astray (23:5) appear on the side of the chief priests and rulers. They join their leaders in demanding the release of Barabbas, a felon, and Jesus' death by crucifixion. It raises the question, who is really corrupting the people? It also raises the question about who is in control. Pilate loses control and capitulates to their outcries. His feeble protests and attempts to release Jesus fail.

23:14 – 15 He said to them, "You brought me this man as one who was misleading the people, and behold, after examining him before you, I do not find your charges against this man to be valid. Neither has Herod, for he sent him back to us. Behold, he has done nothing worthy of death" (εἶπεν πρὸς αὐτούς· προσηνέγκατέ μοι τὸν ἄνθρωπον τοῦτον ὡς ἀποστρέφοντα τὸν λαόν, καὶ ἰδοὺ ἐγὼ ἐνώπιον ὑμῶν ἀνακρίνας οὐθὲν εὗρον ἐν τῷ ἀνθρώπῳ τούτῳ αἴτιον ὧν κατηγορεῖτε κατ᾽ αὐτοῦ· ἀλλ᾽ οὐδὲ Ἡρῴδης, ἀνέπεμψεν γὰρ αὐτὸν πρὸς ἡμᾶς, καὶ ἰδοὺ οὐδὲν ἄξιον θανάτου ἐστὶν πεπραγμένον αὐτῷ). Pilate gives a lengthy declaration of his and Herod's findings: the charges have not been substantiated, and Jesus is innocent. As the governor, Pilate had

32. Jay M. Harrington, *The Lukan Passion Narrative: The Markan Material in Luke 22,54 – 23,25: A Historical Survey,* 1891 – 1997 (NTTS 30; Leiden: Brill, 2000), 797.

33. Neagoe, *The Trial of the Gospel,* 81.

free rein to manage the Judean affairs as he liked. He could reject the charges brought against Jesus, as the governor Gallio did in the case of Paul in Acts 18:12 – 17. But Pilate's verdict is to be overruled by the crowd.

23:16 Therefore, I will have him chastised with blows and release him (παιδεύσας οὖν αὐτὸν ἀπολύσω). The offer to have Jesus "chastised with blows" (παιδεύσας) refers to flogging, precisely what was done to a certain prophet named Jesus bar Ananias just before the war against Rome. He had denounced the city, the sanctuary, and the people and warned of its coming destruction. The incensed leaders arrested and beat him. When he continued with his cries against them, they brought him before the Roman governor, Albinus. Despite being "whipped till his bones were laid bare," he made no supplication and continued to pronounce woes against Jerusalem. Albinus took him to be a lunatic and let him go, much to the aggravation of the Jewish leaders (Josephus, *J.W.* 6.5.1 §§300 – 309).

23:17 - 19 Then they all cried out together, saying, "Take this one; release Barabbas to us!" (This was someone who had been thrown into prison for starting a certain uprising in the city and for murder) (ἀνέκραγον δὲ παμπληθεὶ λέγοντες· αἶρε τοῦτον, ἀπόλυσον δὲ ἡμῖν τὸν Βαραββᾶν· ὅστις ἦν διὰ στάσιν τινὰ γενομένην ἐν τῇ πόλει καὶ φόνον βληθεὶς ἐν τῇ φυλακῇ). Verse 17, which contains an explanation that the governor was *obligated* to offer paschal amnesty to a prisoner, is omitted by significant and widespread early witnesses. Those that include the text insert it at different places, before v. 18 or after v. 19, and with slightly different wording. It is therefore unlikely that it appeared in Luke's original text. It was probably modeled on Matt 27:15 and Mark 15:6 and added to the text to explain why the crowd would insist on releasing Barabbas.[34] Otherwise, this demand seems to come out of the blue. But that is precisely Luke's purpose. The clamor for Barabbas accentuates the intense malevolence toward Jesus. The noisy chants for Jesus' death will prevail (vv. 18, 21, 23).

The rehearsal of Barabbas's crimes reinforces the miscarriage of justice against Jesus. By choosing an insurrectionist over Jesus, the hypocrisy behind the leaders' charges against him is exposed. They, not Jesus, are the real enemies of peace and of Rome. Barabbas is truly guilty of the very crimes they have charged Jesus with committing — inciting the people. He has actually sparked an insurrection, and worse, he has committed murder. Jesus has rejected violence and poses no overt threat to Roman order. The crowds are implicated in the guilt of the Jewish leaders, who have orchestrated this audacious injustice by joining in (cf. "all," [παμπληθεί]) the chorus of shouts to "take" him and "crucify him."[35] The result is that Pilate will sentence to death a man he declares to be innocent and will release a man declared to be a rebel and murderer for no apparent reason other than to appease a rabid crowd.[36]

23:20 - 21 Again, Pilate spoke to them because he wanted to release Jesus. But they kept shouting out, "Crucify him, crucify him!" (πάλιν δὲ ὁ Πιλᾶτος προσεφώνησεν αὐτοῖς θέλων ἀπολῦσαι τὸν Ἰησοῦν. οἱ δὲ ἐπεφώνουν λέγοντες· σταύρου σταύρου αὐτόν). The situation escalates so that now they demand that Jesus be put to death. The cries reveal the deadly power of a group where

---

34. Barabbas is a patronym, like Bartimaeus (Mark 10:46) and Barjonah (Matt 16:17), and means "son of Abba" or "Abbas."

35. "Take him" (αἶρε τοῦτον) is essentially the same cry

they will shout out against Paul (Acts 21:36; 22:22).

36. Helen K. Bond, *Pontius Pilate in History and Interpretation* (SNTSMS 100; Cambridge: Cambridge Univ. Press, 1998), 159.

people may act much differently and more violently than they would if they were alone. Pilate, who is alone, demonstrates himself to be pitifully weak and is all the more culpable for executing one whom he knows to be innocent. He is overpowered by their persistence and refusal to budge from their demands.

23:22 – 24 He said to them a third time, "Why? What evil has this one done? I found no grounds for death in him. After chastising him with blows, I will release him." But they kept demanding with loud shouts for him to be crucified, and their shouts were overpowering. So Pilate decreed that what they asked be granted (ὁ δὲ τρίτον εἶπεν πρὸς αὐτούς· τί γὰρ κακὸν ἐποίησεν οὗτος; οὐδὲν αἴτιον θανάτου εὗρον ἐν αὐτῷ· παιδεύσας οὖν αὐτὸν ἀπολύσω. οἱ δὲ ἐπέκειντο φωναῖς μεγάλαις αἰτούμενοι αὐτὸν σταυρωθῆναι, καὶ κατίσχυον αἱ φωναὶ αὐτῶν. καὶ Πιλᾶτος ἐπέκρινεν γενέσθαι τὸ αἴτημα αὐτῶν).

Pilate's feeble ploys to release Jesus fail. Scourging could serve as a warning to a potential troublemaker (Acts 16:22; 2 Cor 11:25) as well as the prelude to crucifixion. But crowds will not settle for letting Jesus off with only a warning, no matter how severe. Pilate cannot stand up to the extreme pressure of the crowd and capitulates. He is shown to be a pawn in the hands of those he is supposed to rule, and he allows justice to break down.

23:25 He released the one whom they asked for, the one who had been thrown into prison because of the uprising and murder, and he handed Jesus over to their will (ἀπέλυσεν δὲ τὸν διὰ στάσιν καὶ φόνον βεβλημένον εἰς φυλακὴν ὃν ᾐτοῦντο, τὸν δὲ Ἰησοῦν παρέδωκεν τῷ θελήματι αὐτῶν). The statement that Pilate handed Jesus over "to their will" (τῷ θελήματι αὐτῶν) is ironic. In a collision of wills with the Jewish leaders, the Roman governor loses, but unbeknownst to all of the actors in this scene, it is really God's will that triumphs (22:42). Jesus will enter God's glory through suffering (24:26), and the cross will forever be the sign of God's love and forgiveness for rebellious humanity.

By saying that "he handed Jesus over to their will," Luke does not mean to imply that the Jewish leaders crucified Jesus. Readers familiar with crucifixion as a Roman punishment would know that Pilate then turns Jesus over to a contingent of his own soldiers.[37] Weatherly notes that "Luke does not always carefully specify the subjects of third person verbs or the antecedents of third person pronouns."[38] In the crucifixion scene, the soldiers and Jewish leaders are presented as separate groups. Only Roman soldiers would be responsible for creating the *titulus* "King of the Jews." Also, Joseph of Arimathea must go to Pilate to request Jesus' body (23:52). That request assumes that Jesus was crucified under his authority.

Theology in Application

1. God's Plan for Salvation

Luke's account makes clear that Jesus and his followers are not intent on overthrowing the social order or the state. But if Luke's purpose was to defend Christians before Roman officials, none of them would have been impressed with Pilate's performance. After one question and an enigmatic response, Pilate remarkably pronounces Jesus innocent (23:4). He should have been more suspicious of the charge of

37. Brown, *The Death of the Messiah*, 1:857 – 59.

38. Weatherly, *Jewish Responsibility*, 65 – 66.

political sedition. The Roman governor is shown to be impotent, submitting to the bidding of the Jewish leaders he is supposed to govern.

But Luke was not motivated simply to show that Jesus' death was a travesty of justice caused by the malevolent Jewish leaders or to make the case that Christianity was "no threat to Rome, nor to the order and stability so prized by the Romans."[39] He presents it as part of God's plan for salvation. Even though Pilate has protested Jesus' innocence three times and his judgment was correct, the plan of God will not be diverted either by Jewish injustice or Roman justice. Jesus is turned over by the gracious will of God to the deadly will of humans to show how the power of God counters the power of darkness. Bovon writes, "For a moment the will of God will be that the will of the devil triumphs."[40]

This paradox is expressed in Acts 2:23: "This man was handed over to you by God's deliberate plan and foreknowledge; and you, with the help of wicked men, put him to death by nailing him to the cross" (cf. Acts 5:30; 10:38). Peter proclaims the upshot of God's plan: "Jesus Christ of Nazareth, whom you crucified but whom God raised from the dead ... Jesus is 'the stone you builders rejected, which has become the cornerstone.' Salvation is found in no one else, for there is no other name under heaven given to mankind by which we must be saved" (Acts 4:10b – 12).

2. The Guilt of the Religious Leaders

The temple hierarchy is interested in theology only insofar as it can be used to serve their interests and preserve their status and privileges. They perceive Jesus as a threat to that status and callously use the sanctity of the temple as grounds for their sanctimonious scheme to destroy him. They are no different from all of the cynical, politically savvy, self-serving, and pretentious religious leaders of the church who have followed in their train.

Jenkins describes the crisis stirred up by the doctrinal issue of the nature of Christ faced by the fifth-century church. It unleashed centuries of bitter feuding and violence between Christians. He shows that the zeal with which church leaders quarreled over seemingly trifling word choices describing the nature of Christ was not a sign that they were keenly attentive to theological nuances. They were primarily driven by their social associations for which the words were banners and pennants around which to rally. It wasn't that they lost sleep over the truth of the claim that Jesus and the Father were *homoousion* ("of same substance") or the claim that the two were *homoiousion* ("of similar substance"). They were ultimately vying for supremacy and power. They fretted about whether the Homoousions or the Homoiousions were going to run the church.[41]

39. Esler, *Community and Gospel in Luke-Acts*, 218.

40. François Bovon, "The Lucan Story of the Passion," in *Studies in Early Christianity* (WUNT 161; Tübingen: Mohr Siebeck, 2003), 79.

41. Jenkins, *Jesus Wars*, 199 – 226.

This same attitude is captured in a dialogue between an abbot and Brother William of Baskerville in Eco's *The Name of the Rose* about how one spots heretics. The abbot opines:

> You see? You yourself can no longer distinguish between one heretic and another. I at least have a rule. I know that heretics are those who endanger the order that sustains the people of God. And I defend the empire because it guarantees this order for me. I combat the Pope because he is handing the spiritual power over to the bishops of the cities, who are allied with the merchants and the corporations and will not be able to maintain this order. We have maintained it for centuries. And as for the heretics, I also have a rule, and it is summed up in the reply that Arnold Amalaricus, Bishop of Cîteaux, gave to those who asked him what to do with the citizens of Beziers: "Kill them all, God will recognize His own."[42]

Christian leaders can align themselves with the powers solely to preserve the order that safeguards their power to rule over others, but they will find themselves opposing the will and the power of God.

3. The Guilt of All

The trial also brings out the irony that Jesus is the true leader of Israel, not the Jewish leaders. They are the ones who mislead Israel. Danker's salient observations are worth citing in full:

> History records that preservation of religious tyranny through appeal to public order and social stability is not a rare phenomenon. The more discerning have pointed out that many people become confused when they are told that they are being confused. Forming one's own judgment is the capital offense. Religious institutions that claim for themselves the right to protect faithfully their teachings by immunizing themselves against dissident instruction and activity are scarcely in a position to deny the same right to Caiaphas and his associates. They were certainly correct in their conclusions respecting the threat that Jesus posed to the maintenance of some of their traditions. Measured by the yardstick of time-honored institutional prudence, Caiaphas was justified by his procedures.[43]

Are "the people" to be implicated in the guilt of the Jewish leaders? One could argue that the guilt of the Jewish leaders for the death of Jesus is distinguished from the innocence of the multitude of the people.[44] The people have not been Jesus' enemies. They have stymied the leaders' attempts to destroy him and have hung on his every word in the temple (19:47 – 48; 21:38). It is the rulers of the people,

42. Umberto Eco, *The Name of the Rose* (trans. W. Weaver; San Diego: Harcourt Brace Jovanovich, 1983), 153.

43. Danker, *Jesus and the New Age*, 365.

44. See G. Rau, "Das Volk in der lukanischen Passionsgeschichte, eine Konjektur zu Lk 23:13," *ZNW* 56 (1965): 45 – 51; Weatherly, *Jewish Responsibility*, 63 – 64.

not the people, who seek Jesus' death. "The crowds" appear with the Jewish leaders before Pilate (23:4), and they may assume that they join in the cry for the release of Barabbas (23:18). Exegetically, this view falls short and shortchanges an important theological point in the text.

Ascough interprets the people's shift of allegiance against Jesus as parallel to Peter's denial of Jesus.[45] Luke does not present their rejection of Jesus as final. In Acts 3:13 – 14, Peter reminds the people of their guilt — that they denied Jesus in the presence of Pilate when he decided to release him — in his summons to them to repent.[46] He does not mention that he also denied him in the high priest's courtyard, but the reader can pick up on the connection. Peter wept bitterly over what he did, and the crowds will show similar contrition after Jesus' crucifixion (Luke 23:48). Repentance is possible for them as it was for Peter, and indeed they respond to the apostles' preaching in large numbers in Acts 2:12 – 41; 3:9 – 4:4. Had they not been guilty, "they would have nothing of which to repent."[47]

Luke's trial scene presents the theological truth that all are guilty and have fallen short of the glory of God (Rom 3:23). The people along with the Jewish leaders and Pilate represent a microcosm of humanity who are all guilty of Jesus' death. The text invites the reader to examine Jesus' unjust death and to examine his or her own guilt. When this is done, the conclusion can only be the same as that of the criminal crucified with Jesus: "Indeed, we [have been judged] justly, for we are getting paid back for what we have done, but this one has done nothing harmful" (23:41).

---

45. Richard S. Ascough, "Rejection and Repentance: Peter and the People in Luke's Passion Narrative," *Bib* 74 (1993): 356 – 61.

46. Frank Matera, "Responsibility for the Death of Jesus according to the Acts of the Apostles," *JSNT* 39 (1990): 79.

47. Ascough, "Rejection and Repentance," 358.

Luke 23:26 – 49

Literary Context

Betrayed by one disciple and denied by another, Jesus is now derided by his enemies while he dies on a cross. The story of Jesus' earthly ministry reaches its denouement with his execution. Jesus remains calm in the face of death, just as he was in the face of his malevolent accusers. In the crucifixion, his trust in God's providential care that delivers him through his suffering and death and vindicates him is most evident. It prepares for the resurrection narrative that follows. The meaning of Jesus' death is epitomized in his prayer for forgiveness of the perpetrators of his death and his specific offer of grace to a wrongdoer who repents and declares his faith in Jesus. The one who is condemned to death is the one who pardons others from their sins and opens the way to paradise.

Main Idea

The scoffers ironically state the truth: Jesus is God's Messiah, the King of the Jews who saves others. The commander of the execution squad declares him to be "righteous," someone obedient to God's will. Jesus' words reveal the love of a Father to forgive sins and offer reconciliation and the power of his death to open the way to paradise.

Translation

Luke 23:26–49

23:26a	Circumstance	**And** as they led him away,
b	Conscription	**they . . .** took hold of a certain Simon,
		a Cyrenian,
		who was coming from the countryside, and
		. . . laid the cross on him to bear it behind Jesus.
27a		**A large number of the people were following,**
b	Lament	**and women were beating their breasts and wailing for him.**
28a	Jesus' response	**Jesus turned to them and said,**
b	Lament/warning	*"Daughters of Jerusalem, do not weep for me,*
		but weep for yourselves and for your children.
29a	Reason for the lament	*Because behold, the days are coming when they will say,*
b	Ironic beatitude	*'Blessed are the barren and*
c		*the wombs that did not give birth and*
d		*the breasts that did not nurse.'*
30	Cry of despair	*Then they will begin to say to the mountains,*
		'Fall on us!' and
		to the hills,
		'Cover us!'
31	Proverb	*For if these things are done when the tree is green,*
		what will happen when the tree is dry?"
32	Introduction of other victims	**And others, two criminals, were being led along with him to be put to death.**
33a	Place identification	When they came to the place called "the Skull,"
b	Crucifixion	**they crucified him there**
		along with the criminals,
c		one on his right and
		one on his left.
34a	Jesus' response	**Jesus began to say:**
		"Father, forgive them,
		for they do not know what they are doing."
b	Response: division of his garments	**And they cast lots to divvy up his clothing among themselves.**
35a	Sympathetic observation	**And the people stood watching.**
b	Mockery as Messiah	**But the rulers mocked, saying,**
		"He saved others;
		let him save himself,
		if this one is God's Messiah, the elect one."

Continued on next page.

| 36 | Mockery as king of the Jews | **The soldiers made fun of him as well,** coming to him, offering sour wine, and |
| 37 | | saying, |

> "If you are the↩
> king of the Jews,
> save yourself!"

| 38 | Explanation for the mockery | **There was an inscription over him:** |

> "This one is the king of the Jews."

39a	Mockery as Messiah	**One of the criminals who was hanged [on a cross] began to rail against him,**↩ **saying,**
b		"Are you not the Messiah?
c		Save yourself and us!"

| 40 | Sympathetic response | **The other rebuked him and said,** |

> "Do you not fear God,
>   since you are under the same judgment?

41a	Confession	Indeed, we [have been judged] justly,
		for we are getting paid back for what we have done,
b		but this one has done nothing harmful."

| 42 | Request | **And he said,** |

> "Jesus, remember me when you come into your kingly power!"

| 43 | Jesus' response | **And he said to him,** |

> "Amen, I say to you, today, you will be with me in paradise!"

44a	Time reference	**It was already around the sixth hour,**
b	Sign in the heavens	**and darkness came over the whole land until the ninth hour.**
45a		When the sun's light failed,
b	Sign in the temple	**the curtain of the temple was split down the middle.**
46a	Jesus' response	**Jesus cried out with a great voice and said,**

> "Father, into your hands I entrust my spirit." (Ps 31:5)

| b | Death | When he said this, |
| | | **he expired.** |

| 47 | Sympathetic response | When the centurion saw what had happened, |
| | | **he began to glorify God, saying,** |

> "This man was really righteous."

48	Sympathetic response	When all the crowds who came together for this spectacle observed the↩ things that had happened,
		they returned beating their breasts.
49a	Sympathetic observation	**But all those who knew him stood from afar,**
b		**and so did the women who followed him from Galilee and saw these things.**

Structure and Literary Form

Luke presents Jesus' crucifixion and death in four sections, each containing a statement of Jesus:

1. On the way to the cross (23:26 – 31), with Jesus' lament over the mourning women (23:28 – 31)
2. The crucifixion (23:32 – 38), with Jesus' request to forgive the perpetrators (23:34)
3. The mockery (23:39 – 43), with Jesus' announcement to the repentant evildoer that he will be with him today in paradise (23:43)
4. His death (23:44 – 49), with Jesus' entrusting his spirit to the Father (23:46)

Each section also records the reactions of different groups to what is happening to Jesus. The bystanders lament as they follow Jesus to the site of the crucifixion; the executioners cast lots for his garments; his fellow victims respond differently to his plight; the centurion glorifies God after his death; the bystanders lament as they return home; and his acquaintances gaze at it all in silence. What is noteworthy is that women are specifically singled out from the crowds at the beginning and at the end of this section. The "daughters of Jerusalem" follow him to Golgotha bewailing his fate (23:27); the "women who followed him from Galilee" stand quietly at the end observing all that happened (23:49).

Exegetical Outline

➡ **I. On the way to the crucifixion (23:26 – 31)**

    A. Simon of Cyrene compelled to carry Jesus' cross (23:26)

    B. Women lament Jesus' fate (23:27)

    C. Jesus laments their fate (23:28 – 31)

II. Crucifixion (23:32 – 34)

    A. Introduction of two other crucifixion victims (23:32)

    B. Crucifixion of Jesus between two wrongdoers (23:33)

    C. Jesus' prayer to the Father to forgive (23:34a)

    D. Division of Jesus' garments among the soldiers (23:34b)

III. Mockery (23:35 – 43)

    A. Mockery of Jesus as the Messiah by the Jewish leaders (23:35)

    B. Mockery as king of the Jews by the Roman soldiers (23:36 – 38)

    C. Mockery as the Messiah by one of the wrongdoers (23:39)

    D. Defense of Jesus by the other wrongdoer (23:40 – 41)

    E. Request to be remembered by Jesus in his kingdom (23:42)

    F. Promise of being with Jesus in paradise (23:43)

IV. Jesus' death (23:44 – 49)

A. The sign of darkness over the land (23:44 – 45a)

B. The sign of the temple veil rent in two (23:45b)

C. Jesus' prayer entrusting himself to the Father (23:46)

D. Three reactions to what is witnessed (23:47 – 49)

1. Confession of the centurion (23:47)

2. Lament of the crowds (23:48)

3. Silence of Jesus' acquaintances and women followers (23:49)

Explanation of the Text

23:26 And as they led him away, they took hold of a certain Simon, a Cyrenian, who was coming from the countryside, and laid the cross on him to bear it behind Jesus (καὶ ὡς ἀπήγαγον αὐτόν, ἐπιλαβόμενοι Σίμωνά τινα Κυρηναῖον ἐρχόμενον ἀπ' ἀγροῦ ἐπέθηκαν αὐτῷ τὸν σταυρὸν φέρειν ὄπισθεν τοῦ Ἰησοῦ). The condemned person normally carried the crossbeam (*patibulum*) to the crucifixion site, where a vertical post (*stipes, staticulum*) had already been fixed in the ground.[1] Luke does not say why it was necessary for Simon to carry the cross, but first-century readers familiar with such things might surmise that the ordeal of scourging that normally preceded crucifixion (though Luke does not mention it) had so weakened Jesus that he was unable to carry it himself or was too slow. Luke eschews giving any grisly details of the tortures associated with crucifixion.[2] He simply presents the bare facts and prevents the reader from becoming a voyeur of this savage violence.

The soldiers would not carry the cross themselves because of the shame associated with it, and they grab someone of non-Roman origin to

shoulder it. Since Luke identifies Simon (a common Hebrew name) as coming from the countryside, he is not portrayed as a resident of Jerusalem and has not participated in the clamor for Jesus' crucifixion. He is possibly a pilgrim (like the Ethiopian eunuch, Acts 8:27 – 28) who came to the feast and lodged outside the city.[3] He is from Cyrene, the prosperous capital of the North African Roman province of Cyrenaica (present-day Libya). Luke mentions that people from Cyrene were present at Pentecost (Acts 2:10), that one of the early teachers and prophets was Lucius from Cyrene, and that the synagogue of the Cyrenians joined others in opposing Stephen (Acts 6:9).

Luke does not employ the term that appears in Mark and Matthew connoting that Simon was "impressed" (ἀγγαρεύω) into service. Instead, he uses a more general word that they laid (ἐπέθηκαν) the cross on him.[4] Luke also does not identify it as "*his* cross," that is, Jesus' cross (as in the Greek text of Matt 27:32; Mark 15:21), but simply as "*the* cross" (τὸν σταυρόν) and adds a distinctively Christian formula when he presents Simon carrying the cross "behind Jesus." Jesus taught that to

---

1. Plutarch, *Sera* 554B.

2. Contrast the graphic descriptions of the deaths of Jewish faithful in 2 Macc 6 – 7 and 4 Macc.

3. He is the third Simon mentioned in the gospel (5:3; 6:14; 7:40).

4. Evans, *St. Luke*, 861, claims that the Greek construction

requires the preposition "upon" (ἐπί) with the genitive or dative of the person to mean they laid the cross on him, but Luke uses the same construction meaning to lay an object (in the accusative) on someone (in the dative) in 4:40; 13:13; Acts 6:6; 8:19; 9:12; 13:3;15:28; 19:6; 28:8.

become his follower one must take up the cross daily and follow him (9:23; 14:27). Luke's wording ironically portrays Simon as a model disciple and reveals that carrying a cross may become a literal reality.

23:27 A large number of the people were following, and women were beating their breasts and wailing for him (ἠκολούθει δὲ αὐτῷ πολὺ πλῆθος τοῦ λαοῦ καὶ γυναικῶν αἳ ἐκόπτοντο καὶ ἐθρήνουν αὐτόν). Luke alone notes that "a large number of the people" (πολὺ πλῆθος τοῦ λαοῦ), residents of Jerusalem and pilgrims, lamented Jesus' fate as he was being led out to be crucified. "The people" (ὁ λαός) are the object of God's saving word in Jesus (1:17, 68, 77; 2:10) and the object of Jesus' preaching (19:48; 20:1). His popularity with the people (23:5), who regarded him as a prophet mighty in deed and word (24:19), prevented the leaders from immediately carrying out their intent to do away with him (19:47 – 48; 20:1 – 6, 19, 26, 45 – 46; 22:2). "The people" suddenly have switched allegiance in the mob scene before Pilate (23:13) and ardently cried for Jesus to be crucified (23:18, 21, 23).[5]

Luke records no instance of a woman being hostile to Jesus, and he singles out the mourning women amidst this crowd of onlookers. Like Peter, who wept after his denial of Jesus (22:62), they weep bitterly over what is about to happen to Jesus. The Jewish leaders, however, remain unmoved. They scoff at him when he is being crucified, while "the people" only stand by and watch (23:35). The people's grief over what is being done to Jesus ironically contrasts with the joyous hope voiced by Zechariah (1:68 – 69) and Anna (2:38) in the opening scenes.

23:28 – 30 Jesus turned to them and said, "Daughters of Jerusalem, do not weep for me, but weep for yourselves and for your children. Because behold, the days are coming when they will say, 'Blessed are the barren and the wombs that did not give birth and the breasts that did not nurse.' Then they will begin to say to the mountains, 'Fall on us!' and to the hills, 'Cover us!'" (στραφεὶς δὲ πρὸς αὐτὰς [ὁ] Ἰησοῦς εἶπεν· θυγατέρες Ἰερουσαλήμ, μὴ κλαίετε ἐπ᾽ ἐμέ· πλὴν ἐφ᾽ ἑαυτὰς κλαίετε καὶ ἐπὶ τὰ τέκνα ὑμῶν, ὅτι ἰδοὺ ἔρχονται ἡμέραι ἐν αἷς ἐροῦσιν· μακάριαι αἱ στεῖραι καὶ αἱ κοιλίαι αἳ οὐκ ἐγέννησαν καὶ μαστοὶ οἳ οὐκ ἔθρεψαν. τότε ἄρξονται λέγειν τοῖς ὄρεσιν· πέσετε ἐφ᾽ ἡμᾶς, καὶ τοῖς βουνοῖς· καλύψατε ἡμᾶς).

Jesus does not offer comfort to the women who openly bemoan his fate but heightens their pain with a prophetic warning about the fall of Jerusalem. What is now happening to him has been determined by God (9:31; 18:31; 22:22, 37; 24:25 – 26; 24:44, 46; Acts 2:23; 3:18; 4:25 – 28; 13:27 – 29). He goes to the cross knowingly and obediently, faithful to the mission given him according to God's redemptive will (9:22; 13:33; 17:25; 24:7, 26). He is not the one to be pitied; they are.

"Turn[ing] to them" (στραφεὶς δὲ πρὸς αὐτὰς) need not be a precursor to a rebuke (see its various results in 7:9, 44; 9:55; 10:23; 14:25). "Daughters of Jerusalem" recalls his ominous prophecy that Jerusalem kills the prophets and will face judgment (13:34 – 35). The term is not intended to present them as symbolic representatives of Jerusalem or Israel (Zech 12:10 – 14). Since innocent children will be among the victims in Jerusalem's looming destruction (19:44), Jesus directs his lament to these women.

5. See Jerome Neyrey, "Jesus' Address to the Women of Jerusalem (Lk. 23:27 – 31): A Prophetic Judgment Oracle," *NTS* 29 (1983): 75.

Mothers and their children will be innocent victims like him, and the suffering will be so terrible for the city that barren women, viewed throughout Scripture as reproached by God and unfortunate (see 1:25), will be consider "blessed" (μακάριαι). The barren woman at least "will not have the added agony of seeing her children suffer too."[6] This ironic beatitude complements the earlier woe directed to those who are pregnant and nursing during the "great calamity" (21:23).

Is this a prophetic oracle of doom over the city, or is it a woe of compassion, or perhaps a call to repentance?[7] Neyrey contends that the passage with its address (23:28), statement of crimes ("these things are done when the tree is green," 23:31), and pronouncement of a sentence or curse (23:29–31) matches the form of a prophetic oracle of judgment (see 13:33–35; 19:41–44).

The phrase "the days are coming" (ἔρχονται ἡμέραι) also fits a judgment context (see 17:22–37; 21:6, 22–24; Jer 7:32; 16:14), and the cry for the mountains and hills to fall on them and cover them (23:30) is either a call for a convulsion of nature to put them out of their misery or to hide them from God's wrath (see Hos 10:8; Rev 6:16; 9:6). What is clear is that those who do not flee to the hills when desolation approaches (21:21) will call to the mountains to fall on them when it arrives. If the reference in the next verse to the dry wood is to be connected to the image of fire, it may envision the conflagration from a fiery divine judgment striking a forest of dry, sapless trunks (see 3:17; Ezek 20:47).[8]

I take Jesus' response to the death wail of these women as a word of compassion that is similar to the lament he uttered when he entered the city and wept over it (19:41–44). To be sure, this lament expresses the inevitability of Jerusalem's destruction, which will be particularly catastrophic for pregnant mothers and those with young children. He has already warned that the inhabitants will fall by the edge of the sword and be led away captive and that the city will be trodden down by the Gentiles (21:20–24). Jerusalem's fate is sealed, and when these days arrive, innocent and guilty alike will suffer in the city's devastation.

Throughout Luke's passion narrative, Jesus is more concerned about what will happen to others than what will happen to him. At the Last Supper, Luke turns the spotlight off Jesus for a moment as Jesus shows his care for the plight of the disciples and their future mission (22:35–36). He is more absorbed by the predicament of his disciples after his death than he is by his own imminent death. The reference to his own fate in 22:37 is intended solely as a warning to his disciples that they can expect no better treatment than their Master receives. Jesus exudes divine love in his warning to Peter (22:31–34, 61), his tender reproof of Judas (22:48), his prayer for forgiveness for his executioners (23:34), and his offer of a reprieve to the criminal on the cross. This lament is uttered in the same spirit. Just as he wept over the city on his entrance (19:41–44), so now on his exit he expresses grief over the coming devastation that will consume the innocent.

23:31 For if these things are done when the tree is green, what will happen when the tree is dry? (ὅτι εἰ ἐν τῷ ὑγρῷ ξύλῳ ταῦτα ποιοῦσιν, ἐν τῷ ξηρῷ τί γένηται;). This proverb basically means that something far worse can be expected to happen to those deserving of punishment (see Prov 11:31), but it can have various applications. In the

6. Manson, *The Sayings of Jesus*, 343. See Isa 54:1.
7. The "for" (ὅτι) introduces the reason for the dire prediction that follows.
8. Neyrey, "Jesus' Address to the Women of Jerusalem," 79–83.

structure, "these things" (ταῦτα) refers to what is being done to Jesus ("do not weep for me") as "the green tree" (τῷ ὑγρῷ ξύλῳ, "moist wood"). The deliberative question "What will happen?" (τί γένηται) refers to Jerusalem's destruction in the coming days. My translation "if these things are done" takes the impersonal verb "they do" (ποιοῦσιν) as a substitute for the passive voice.[9] It is unclear who is the agent "doing these things." The ambiguity allows the reader to draw multiple conclusions about its meaning, which need not be mutually exclusive.

(1) If it refers to what the leaders of Jerusalem are doing to Jesus (see 13:34-35), then the dry wood (ξηρῷ) may refer to their future situation after having rejected both Jesus and his apostles (see 1 Pet 4:17). If Jerusalem deals in this way with one who came to save Israel, what can the people expect to receive from God for having killed him (see 20:9-18; 1 Thess 2:14-16)?

(2) If it is a circumlocution for God (see 6:38; 12:20, 48; 16:9), it would mean: *If God has not spared his innocent Son from such tribulation* [by permitting his crucifixion], *how much worse will it be for a sinful nation when God unleashes his righteous wrath upon it* [by permitting the Romans to destroy Jerusalem]."[10]

(3) If it refers to what the Romans are doing to Jesus, whom the governor declared to be innocent (23:4, 14, 22), it would mean: "What will they do to those who rebel against them and are guilty?" As one of the malefactors says on the cross, we are receiving the due reward of our deeds, but this man has done nothing wrong (23:41).

23:32 And others, two criminals, were being led along with him to be put to death (ἤγοντο δὲ καὶ ἕτεροι κακοῦργοι δύο σὺν αὐτῷ ἀναιρεθῆναι). If this statement is punctuated "and two other criminals were led" so as to include Jesus, it could be an ironic fulfillment of the Scripture cited in 22:37, "He was reckoned with the lawless." It is more likely that Luke is contrasting the innocent Jesus with these two criminals who are deserving of their punishment (23:41; though no human deserves crucifixion as punishment) and are to be crucified with him. My translation punctuates the clause to distinguish Jesus from the criminals.

Luke does not identify them as "rebels" (λῃσταί), as do Matthew (Matt 27:38) and Mark (Mark 14:27). The generic term "malefactors" or "evildoers" (κακοῦργοι) leaves their crimes unspecified, which prevents first-century readers from lumping Jesus together with violent insurrectionists, who were frequent victims of crucifixion.[11]

23:33 When they came to the place called "the Skull," they crucified him there along with the criminals, one on his right and one on his left (καὶ ὅτε ἦλθον ἐπὶ τὸν τόπον τὸν καλούμενον Κρανίον, ἐκεῖ ἐσταύρωσαν αὐτὸν καὶ τοὺς κακούργους, ὃν μὲν ἐκ δεξιῶν ὃν δὲ ἐξ ἀριστερῶν). According to Roman and Jewish law (Lev 24:14), execution was to take place outside the city. The Romans would have chosen a place near a gate serving a main route into the city, which would draw the most spectators. As the most humiliating and torturous death imaginable, it was intended to strike fear in the hearts of all and to deter others from committing acts that would bring this penalty.

Luke avoids the Aramaic place-name "Golgotha" and provides the Greek equivalent, "Skull"

---

9. M. Zerwick, *Biblical Greek Illustrated by Examples* (Rome: Pontifical Biblical Institute, 1963), §1.

10. Stein, *Luke*, 586.

11. See Martin Hengel, *Crucifixion* (trans. John Bowden;

Philadelphia: Fortress, 1977), 46-50. Josephus records that under Felix a day did not pass that he did not put to death brigands (*Ant.* 20.8.5 §161).

(Κρανίον), which would be the name for the region that included the crucifixion and the burial
site. Taylor concludes that the area

> was probably an oval-shaped disused quarry lo-
> cated west of the second wall, north of the first
> wall. Jesus may have been crucified in the south-
> ern part of this area, just outside the Gennath

Gate, and near the road going west, but at a site
visible also from the road north and buried some
200 m. away to the north, in a quieter part of Golgotha where there were tombs and gardens.[12]

Ironically, Jesus' crucifixion would not be the end,
and the place of the skull will become the place
where sin and death are conquered.

Crucifixion

In the New Testament world, crucifixion was to be public.

> Whenever we crucify the condemned, the most crowded roads are chosen,
> where the most people can see and be moved by this terror. For the penalties
> relate not so much to retribution as their exemplary effect. (Quintilian, *Decl.* 274;
> see also Josephus *J.W.* 5.11.2 §§450 – 51)

> The practice approved by most authorities has been to hang notorious brigands
> on a gallows in the place which they used to haunt, so that by the spectacle
> others may be deterred from the same crimes, and so that it may, when the
> penalty has been carried out, bring comfort to the relatives and kin of those
> killed in that place where the brigands committed their murders. (Justinian, *Di-
> gest* 48.19.28.15)

The methods of crucifixion were varied.

> Yonder I see crosses, not indeed of a single kind, but differently contrived by
> different peoples; some hang their victims with head toward the ground, some
> impale their private parts, others stretch out their arms on a fork-shaped gibbet.
> (Seneca, *Dial.* 6.20.3; see Josephus, *J.W.* 5.11.1 §451)

**23:34a Jesus began to say: "Father, forgive them,
for they do not know what they are doing"** (ὁ
δὲ Ἰησοῦς ἔλεγεν· πάτερ, ἄφες αὐτοῖς, οὐ γὰρ
οἴδασιν τί ποιοῦσιν). The translation interprets
the verb "began to say" (ἔλεγεν) as an inceptive
imperfect rather than an iterative. This prayer
is absent from early, diverse, and significant

manuscripts, which leads some to conclude that it
was not original to the text but inserted at a later
time by a scribe.[13] Those who argue against its
authenticity make the following arguments: (1) If
23:28 – 31 is a prophetic doom oracle, it conflicts
with a prayer for forgiveness. (2) It seems to interrupt the sequence of the soldiers crucifying him

12. Joan E. Taylor, "Golgotha: A Reconsideration of the
Evidence for the Sites of Jesus' Crucifixion and Burial," *NTS* 44
(1998): 201. See Josephus, *J.W.* 5.4.2 §146.

13. 𝔓75 ℵa vid B D* W Θ it a d syrs cop sa bo (mss) 38 0124
435 579 1241 Cyril.

(23:33) and then casting lots to divide his garments (23:34b). (3) Possibly, the prayer was modeled after Stephen's prayer that the sin of those stoning him not be held against them (Acts 7:60). With the influence of Isa 53:12, "he ... made intercession for the transgressors," later scribes may have thought that if Stephen spoke so compassionately, Jesus must have said something similar since he himself commanded this attitude in 6:28.

The external evidence that it was original to Luke is equally strong, and the internal evidence is persuasive.[14] (1) Each of the four sections of the crucifixion contains a saying of Jesus. If this saying were not original to Luke, this pattern would be disturbed. (2) The prayer does not interrupt the connection between 23:33 and 34b any more than does the statement in 23:33c about the two criminals being crucified on his right and left does. But Brown comments: "Indeed, it is quite effective to find in the midst of hostile actions by the crucifiers a prayer by Jesus for their forgiveness."[15] (3) The language and ideas are Lukan in character.[16] If it were a gloss inserted by a scribe modeling it on Stephen's prayer, one would expect the wording to be closer to that in Acts. It is more likely to find conceptual similarity without identical wording if it were original to Luke than if it were composed by a later copyist.[17] (4) Crump argues that Luke's theology of prayer leads one to "expect just such a prayer to be found at this point in the story."[18]

Jesus' prayer life is "mediatory," and his unique relationship to God as Father gives him the authority to mediate God's salvation.[19]

This prayer may have been omitted by a later copyist because he believed that Jesus would not have prayed for the forgiveness of the Jews since it appears to exonerate them from their guilt. Anti-Jewish polemic emerged early, and Codex Bezae (D) demonstrates a particular anti-Jewish bias in its readings.[20] The events of AD 66 – 70, 115 – 118, and 132 – 135, with the accompanying devastation of Jerusalem, may have suggested to those copying this text in a later era that Jesus' prayer had *not* been answered because God had allowed the city to suffer ruin not only once but three times (see 1 Thess 2:14 – 16).

It was normal for the one being executed to cry out for vengeance and to threaten the executioners (see Ps 69:22 – 28; 2 Macc 7:9, 14, 16 – 19, 34 – 36; 4 Macc. 9:15).[21] By praying that his persecutors be forgiven, Jesus models what he taught his disciples to do — to love their enemies and pray for those who abused them (6:27 – 28; see 11:4) — and how he pictures God as liberal in forgiveness (15:20 – 23).

Jesus says in 17:3 – 4, however, that his disciples are to forgive the brother "if he repents." This saying may be another reason why the passage was omitted. The copyists may have felt that since the Jews as a group had not repented but remained obdurate in their sin against Christ, they could not be

---

14. ℵ[c] A C D[b] L f[1] f[2] 28 33 565 700 (many minuscules) aur, b, c e f, ff[2] l, r[1] vg syr bo (mss) Marcion, Tatian, Hegesippus, Justin, Ireneaus, Clement of Alexandria, Origen, Eusebius.

15. Brown, *The Death of the Messiah*, 2:976.

16. Addressing God as "Father" (10:21; 11:2; 22:42; 23:46); the reference to ignorance as forgivable (Acts 3:17 – 19; 13:27; 17:30); the reference to what "they do" (6:11; 19:48); and the concern for forgiveness (6:28; 11:4).

17. Crump, *Jesus the Intercessor*, 84.

18. Ibid., 85.

19. Ibid., 96.

20. See George E. Rice, "The Anti-Judaic Bias of the West-

ern Text in the Gospel of Luke," *AUSS* 18 (1980): 51 – 57; "The Role of the Populace in the Passion Narrative of Luke in Codex Bezae," *AUSS* 19 (1981): 147 – 53. In Codex Bezae, the Jews participate in the arrest, the demand for crucifixion, and the mocking to save himself. See also Eldon J. Epp, *The Theological Tendency of Codex Bezae Cantabrigiensis in Acts* (SNTSMS 3; Cambridge: Cambridge Univ. Press, 1966), 41 – 64; and "The 'Ignorance Motif' in Acts and Anti-Judaic Tendencies in Codex Bezae," *HTR* 55 (1962): 51 – 62.

21. In *Mart. Isa.* 5:14, Isaiah is praised for neither crying aloud nor weeping when he was sawn in two (see 1 Pet 2:23).

forgiven. From the perspective of those Christians who were victims of Jewish persecution, they are no longer doing this in ignorance but know what they are doing (see Justin Martyr, *Dial.* 113.6). The prayer, however, is characteristic of Jesus' entire ministry in Luke. He forgives those who show no demonstrable sign of having repented, and it lays the foundation for the apostles' ministry (24:47).

The antecedent of "them" could be limited to the Roman soldiers carrying out orders to execute him. The "they" naturally refers to the soldiers since their actions, crucifying Jesus (v. 33) and casting lots for his clothes (v. 34b), surround the saying. They would not have known the Law and the Prophets and probably lacked any information about his ministry. Since Jesus charges the disciples to preach "repentance for the forgiveness of sins in his name to all the nations" (24:47), the prayer should not be interpreted as limited to one particular group involved in the crucifixion and imply that others might be excluded from forgiveness. The sin is universal — the disciples also belong to the category of the "lawless" (22:37) — and the prayer for God to forgive those who act from ignorance applies universally.

23:34b And they cast lots to divvy up his clothing among themselves (διαμεριζόμενοι δὲ τὰ ἱμάτια αὐτοῦ ἔβαλον κλήρους). The victim was stripped of all his clothing, which increased the public abasement.[22] Not only does the victim suffer from the excruciating pain, thirst, and the torment of insects burrowing into open wounds, but he must also endure the shame of jabs of spectators poking at his bodily parts and their mocking when he is unable to control his bodily functions. In the structure, the casting of lots is, in effect, a response to Jesus' prayer for forgiveness. It

epitomizes a world caught up with its petty greed and acquisitiveness.

23:35 And the people stood watching. But the rulers mocked, saying, "He saved others; let him save himself, if this one is God's Messiah, the elect one" (καὶ εἱστήκει ὁ λαὸς θεωρῶν. ἐξεμυκτήριζον δὲ καὶ οἱ ἄρχοντες λέγοντες· ἄλλους ἔσωσεν, σωσάτω ἑαυτόν, εἰ οὗτός ἐστιν ὁ Χριστὸς τοῦ θεοῦ ὁ ἐκλεκτός). Mockery normally accompanied crucifixion (see *Gen. Rab.* 65:22), and the mockery scene follows a chiastic pattern:

A The people (sympathetically) behold (23:35a)
  B The leaders mock, "Let him save himself, if this one is God's Messiah" (23:35b)
    C The soldiers mock, "If you are the king of the Jews" (23:36–37)
    C′ The *titulus* announcing: "This one is the king of the Jews" (23:38)
  B′ One evildoer taunts: "Are you not the Messiah? Save yourself and us" (23:39)
A′ The other evildoer expresses sympathy and faith (23:40–42).[23]

The dignity of the persons who deride Jesus on the cross is presented by Luke in descending order: the Jewish high priests and leaders, the soldiers, and one of the criminals being crucified. Their mockery drips with unintended irony. All taunt him to save himself. The scoffing of the Jewish leaders recalls their questions about his identity posed in the Jewish proceedings (22:67, 70). They do not know nor would they accept that the Christ must suffer (9:22; 17:25; 24:7, 26, 46) or that salvation will come through the demonstration of divine power in this powerless death. For them, the Messiah is by definition a winner, not a loser. They

---

22. The executioners may have left a loincloth on the victims out of deference to Jewish scruples about nakedness.

23. Weatherly, *Jewish Responsibility*, 82.

take for granted that God would not allow the elect Messiah to suffer so ignominiously; consequently "they turn up their nose at him" (ἐξεμυκτήριζον, the literal meaning of the verb). Such a humiliating death on a cross discredits any claim that he could save others.

He has saved others by healing them. The verb "to save" (σῴζω) is used when Jesus exorcizes demons from a man (8:36), heals a woman suffering from hemorrhages for twelve years (8:48), brings a synagogue ruler's daughter back to life (8:50), and heals a blind man (18:42). These were saved by faith. But what is more important, he came to seek and save the lost, and the cross would be the means to bring a different kind of salvation. He cannot save himself (see 9:24) because his mission is to give his life to save others. As the Son of God, Jesus remains obedient to God's will, which requires his death. He will not escape from death by his own power but will pass through death and be raised by God's power.

23:36–38 The soldiers made fun of him as well, coming to him, offering sour wine, and saying, "If you are the king of the Jews, save yourself!" There was an inscription over him: "This one is the king of the Jews" (ἐνέπαιξαν δὲ αὐτῷ καὶ οἱ στρατιῶται προσερχόμενοι, ὄξος προσφέροντες αὐτῷ καὶ λέγοντες· εἰ σὺ εἶ ὁ βασιλεὺς τῶν Ἰουδαίων, σῶσον σεαυτόν. ἦν δὲ καὶ ἐπιγραφὴ ἐπ᾽ αὐτῷ· ὁ βασιλεὺς τῶν Ἰουδαίων οὗτος). The soldiers' mockery of Jesus as "the king of the Jews" recalls the accusation against him before the Roman governor (23:2–3). The *titulus* over the cross explains why they would taunt him in this way. That this pitiable figure could be king even of such an inconsequential group as the Jews was laughable. The soldiers also take for granted

that no bona fide king would suffer so ingloriously and would not have the means to extricate himself from his predicament.

The "sour wine" (ὄξος) was made from water, egg, and vinegar; and Marcus Cato was said to have called for it when he was in a raging thirst or when his strength was failing. The Romans did not consider this drink to be intoxicating but more of a woman's drink.[24] The executioners would have given this to an exhausted Jesus not to dull the pain but to give him more strength so that his suffering would last longer.

23:39 One of the criminals who was hanged [on a cross] began to rail against him, saying, "Are you not the Messiah? Save yourself and us!" (εἷς δὲ τῶν κρεμασθέντων κακούργων ἐβλασφήμει αὐτὸν λέγων· οὐχὶ σὺ εἶ ὁ Χριστός; σῶσον σεαυτὸν καὶ ἡμᾶς). The climax of humiliation is for Jesus to be scorned by a companion in torment who is deserving of his punishment. One of the malefactors sharing the torment joins in the derision and rails against Jesus (ἐβλασφήμει) by picking up the taunt of the Jewish leaders.[25] Apparently, he is a Jew who understands what "Anointed One" means, and he baits Jesus to save himself "and us." He too expects that a true Messiah would use physical force to deliver himself and others from adversity. This taunt for Jesus to save himself is repeated for the third time and recalls Satan's onslaught in the desert (4:1–13).

23:40–41 The other rebuked him and said, "Do you not fear God, since you are under the same judgment? Indeed, we [have been judged] justly, for we are getting paid for what we have done, but this one has done nothing harmful" (ἀποκριθεὶς δὲ ὁ ἕτερος ἐπιτιμῶν αὐτῷ ἔφη· οὐδὲ φοβῇ σὺ

24. Wilhelm Michaelis, "σμύρνα, σμυρνίζω," *TDNT*, 7:458–59.

25. The verb "hanged" (κρεμασθέντων) appears in Deut 21:22–23 (LXX): "When someone is convicted of a crime punishable by death and is executed, and you hang him on a tree … for anyone hanged on a tree is under God's curse."

τὸν θεόν, ὅτι ἐν τῷ αὐτῷ κρίματι εἶ; καὶ ἡμεῖς μὲν δικαίως, ἄξια γὰρ ὧν ἐπράξαμεν ἀπολαμβάνομεν· οὗτος δὲ οὐδὲν ἄτοπον ἔπραξεν). In contrast to Mark's account, Jesus does not meet with total hostility as he dies on the cross. One of the criminals responds sympathetically and with faith. Tannehill notes: "Normally Jesus himself answers the objections and challenges which he encounters. Allowing the second criminal to step into the role gives him unusual prominence."[26]

This malefactor's rebuke of his companion implies that they also have been tried and condemned to crucifixion by the governor. He also makes an implicit confession: they were condemned justly for their crimes (see 15:21; 2 Macc 7:18). The evildoer must also be a Jew who understands what it means to "fear God." "Fearing God," who is the righteous Judge, is the basis of Jewish piety (see 18:2, 4; Sir 1:11 – 20) and the basis for expecting goodness from God: "Oh, how abundant is your goodness, which you have stored up for those who fear you and worked for those who take refuge in you, in the sight of the children of mankind!" (Ps 31:19 ESV). He confesses that they are dying justly and will also have to answer to God for their crimes, but he recognizes that Jesus is an innocent man.[27]

When one is staring death in the face, it is not the time to pile on someone else who has obviously done nothing worthy of death (see Acts 25:11) but the time to repent. He implies, however, that Jesus is someone close to God, and taunting him will bring divine chastisement. Psalm 31 figures prominently in the scene, and Jesus' response to this criminal's statement reveals that his fear of God will indeed bring abundant goodness from God.

The criminal's fear of God is different from that manifested by Adam in the garden of Eden ("paradise" in the LXX). Adam hid from God out of shame and disgrace for his sin (Gen 3:11). Such fear is similar to that of the servant who carelessly wrapped his mina in a handkerchief and did nothing with it because he feared his master as a harsh man (19:20 – 21).[28] This criminal, by contrast, fears God out of sorrow for his sins and boldly appeals to Jesus as one he trusts will show mercy to the likes of him.

23:42 And he said, "Jesus, remember me when you come into your kingly power!" (καὶ ἔλεγεν· Ἰησοῦ, μνήσθητί μου ὅταν ἔλθῃς εἰς τὴν βασιλείαν σου). This touching plea is one of the few instances in Luke where Jesus is addressed by his personal name, not as "Lord," "sir," or "teacher." He humbly asks that Jesus remember him when he comes into his kingly power (εἰς τὴν βασιλείαν).[29] Evans interprets this as a request for favorable judgment when Jesus exercises his sovereignty as King.[30] Unlike the criminal's colleague, he does not ask for earthly deliverance, but for salvation in the world to come.

This man was not at the Last Supper when Jesus announced that the Father had bestowed on him a kingdom and promised his loyal disciples that they would eat and drink at his table in his kingdom and sit on thrones (22:29 – 30; see 1:33). What would have led him to believe that this man being crucified next to him would ever exercise sovereign power? The only thing in the context to cause his sudden insight into Jesus is his intercessory prayer for forgiveness (23:34). The Father answers the prayer by revealing his Son to this criminal and opening the door "for his salvation."[31]

---

26. Tannehill, *Unity of Luke-Acts*, 126.

27. Literally, he has done nothing "out of place" (ἄτοπον).

28. David Liberto, "To Fear or Not to Fear? Christ as Sophos in Luke's Passion Narrative," *ExpTim* 114 (2003): 223.

29. "Remember me" (μνήσθητί μου) was a common funerary inscription in Palestine.

30. Evans, *St. Luke*, 873.

31. Crump, *Jesus the Intercessor*, 88.

According to *Ps. Sol.* 3:9 – 12, the sinner "will not be remembered when [God] looks after the righteous." Hearing Jesus' petition to the Father to forgive his executioners gave this criminal the temerity to make a bold petition. He addresses Jesus as if he were God, who remembers people in his covenant mercy (Ps 106:4; Luke 1:54, 72; Acts 10:31). His appeal is similar to the prayer of the toll collector in Jesus' parable. He beat his breast and pled for God to make atonement for him (18:13). If his hands were not nailed to a cross, this criminal would be beating his breast as well. His case seems even more hopeless, but he trusts that God will somehow make an atonement for him as well that will save him.

23:43 And he said to him, "Amen, I say to you, today, you will be with me in paradise!" (καὶ εἶπεν αὐτῷ· ἀμήν σοι λέγω, σήμερον μετ᾽ ἐμοῦ ἔσῃ ἐν τῷ παραδείσῳ). For the sixth time in Luke Jesus uses the phrase, "Amen, I say to you" (4:24; 12:37; 18:17, 29; 21:32), and each saying is related in the context to the reign of God and/or the final judgment. "Today" (σήμερον) is not to be taken with "I say to you" but is placed first in the clause for emphasis and requires a comma after it: "Today, you will be with me...." The word "today" is associated with salvation throughout the gospel of Luke. Salvation is not reserved for a distant future but is already present (see 2:11; 4:21; 5:26; 19:9). If the man expects favorable regard from Jesus in some distant future, Jesus corrects him. Salvation is available immediately.

"Paradise" (ἐν τῷ παραδείσῳ) originally referred to a garden or pleasure park such as a king would possess (2 Chr 33:20; Neh 2:8; Eccl 2:5; Song 4:12 – 13 LXX), but it was also used to refer to the primeval garden of Eden where Adam and Eve lived in God's bounty and loving care until their

disobedience led to their eviction (Gen 2:8 – 10; 13:10; Isa 51:3; Ezek 28:13; 31:8 – 9; Joel 2:3; Rev 2:7). Paul uses the term to refer to a region of heaven (2 Cor 12:4).

Jews had a wide variety of notions about the afterlife, as people do today. One stream of thought conceived of paradise as a transformed garden of Eden. It was the realm of the righteous dead, a counterpart to hell (*1 En.* 60:8, 23; 61:12; *Apoc. Ab.* 21:6; 4QEn^e 1 xxxvi 21). Paradise was opened up for Ezra (2 Esd 8:52) because he humbled himself and did not consider himself to be among the righteous (8:47). He also was not like those who "when they had opportunity to choose, they despised the Most High, and were contemptuous of his law, and abandoned his ways. Moreover, they have even trampled on his righteous ones, and said in their hearts that there is no God — though they knew well that they must die" (8:56 – 58). In this narrative Luke reveals his theological conviction that through his death Jesus opens the gates of paradise (see Rev 2:7; *T. Levi* 18:10).

Since Jesus promises that he will be "with" the criminal in paradise "today," it cannot be thought of as an intermediate abode. It is where Jesus is seated at God's right hand (22:69). Jesus is the first to enter paradise and makes it accessible to sinners. If paradise is the realm of the righteous dead, Jesus implies that this criminal will belong to the righteous dead. Caird comments, "Whatever he expected when he made his request, the promise of Jesus is all out of proportion to it."[32] Jesus implies that this man crucified with him is now acquitted even though he has no merit except his appeal to him. His assurance that he will be *with him* in paradise means that he also will be vindicated with him.

Jesus' assurance turns on its head a view found in the rabbinic literature that different levels exist

32. Caird, *Saint Luke*, 252.

in paradise and that persons will be assigned to a billet appropriate to their rank or achievements.[33] A late tradition in *Qoh. Rab.* 3:9 highlights the contrasting perspectives:

> R. Simeon b. Lakish was studying Torah as much as he required in a cave at Tiberias, and a potter used to prepare a drink of water for him every day. He used to come in feeling very tired, and take and drink it. On one occasion the man entered, sat down by the Rabbi and stayed with him a short while to rest. He said to him, "Master, do you remember that you and I used to go to school together; but whereas you were worthy [to devote yourself to the study of the Torah], I was not so worthy. Pray for me that my portion may be with you in the World to Come." He replied to him, "How can I pray for you since it will be your lot to go with your fellow-craftsmen? Because they do not allow a man to dwell except with his fellow-craftsmen."

Jesus, who is known as someone who "receives 'sinners'" (15:2), implies that no distinctions will exist in paradise. This criminal who confesses at the last minute and asks to be with him will be hosted by Jesus in the highest heaven.

23:44 It was already around the sixth hour, and darkness came over the whole land until the ninth hour (καὶ ἦν ἤδη ὡσεὶ ὥρα ἕκτη καὶ σκότος ἐγένετο ἐφ᾽ ὅλην τὴν γῆν ἕως ὥρας ἐνάτης). Herod demanded that Jesus perform some sign (23:8), and signs abound at Jesus' death. The one who came to bring light to those who sit

in darkness (1:78 – 79; Acts 26:18) is now himself engulfed in darkness. The darkness covers the whole land (ἐφ᾽ ὅλην τὴν γῆν; see 4:25; 21:23), not the whole earth. It is obviously remarkable that thick darkness occurs at noon (the sixth hour), and it can convey multiple meanings — such as the mourning of nature, a portent of judgment, or a cosmic sign that accompanied the death of great men and kings.[34] But it should be interpreted from the context of Luke. Since the darkness is reported as covering the land *before* his death, it mostly represents the enmity of Satan. It is still his "hour and the dominion of darkness" (22:53), and Jesus is in the grip of satanic forces.[35]

23:45 – 46 When the sun's light failed, the curtain of the temple was split down the middle. Jesus cried out with a great voice and said, "Father, into your hands I entrust my spirit." When he said this, he expired (τοῦ ἡλίου ἐκλιπόντος, ἐσχίσθη δὲ τὸ καταπέτασμα τοῦ ναοῦ μέσον. καὶ φωνήσας φωνῇ μεγάλῃ ὁ Ἰησοῦς εἶπεν· πάτερ, εἰς χεῖράς σου παρατίθεμαι τὸ πνεῦμά μου. τοῦτο δὲ εἰπὼν ἐξέπνευσεν). According to *m. Šeqal.* 8:5, the veil was "one handbreadth thick." Its length was forty cubits and its width twenty cubits. There were actually two curtains with a cubit space between them (*m. Yoma* 5:1). It could refer to the curtain separating the Holy Place (with the showbread, seven-branched candlestick, altar of incense) from the Most Holy Place, the dark chamber where only the high priest could enter on the Day of Atonement (Exod 26:31 – 33; Josephus,

---

33. *Sipre Deut.* 10 enumerates seven different groups of the righteous in paradise, each one higher than the other (see also *b. Ber.* 12b; *Lev. Rab.* 18:1; 27:1; *Exod. Rab.* 52:3; *Ruth Rab.* 3:4; *Midr. Ps.* 11:6).

34. Josephus cites a letter of Mark Anthony about the assassination of Caesar: "Our enemies and those of the empire overran Asia, sparing neither cities nor temples, and committed lawless deeds against men and gods, from which we believe the very sun turned away, as if it were loath to look upon the

foul deed against Caesar" (*Ant.* 14.12.3 §309).

35. Joseph Torchia, "The Death of a Righteous Man: Redactional Elements in Luke's Passion Narrative (23:44 – 56)," *IBS* 26 (2005): 67; J. Bradley Chance, *Jerusalem, the Temple, and the New Age in Luke-Acts* (Macon, GA: Mercer Univ. Press, 1988), 119. All three Synoptic Gospels identify the moment of Jesus' death occurring at the ninth hour, which means that Jesus dies during the time of the afternoon Tamid sacrifice, the daily whole offering for the forgiveness of sins.

J.W. 5.5.5 §219). Hebrews 9:3 identifies it as the second curtain: "Behind the second curtain was a room called the Most Holy Place."

Some argue, however, that the public nature of the event points to the outer curtain before the Holy Place that was publicly visible (Exod 26:36; Josephus, *J.W.* 5.5.4 §212). But no one at the crucifixion site would have been able to see the temple veil in the pitch darkness. It most likely does refer to the inner curtain between the Holy Place and the Most Holy Place. Priests could have reported this event at a later time. The passive voice "was split" (ἐσχίσθη) suggests a divine passive; it is God's doing.

The translation links the tearing of the veil to the sun's light failing (expressed by a genitive absolute, τοῦ ἡλίου ἐκλιπόντος). The verb "failed" (ἐκλιπόντος) can mean "eclipse" (BDAG). A natural solar eclipse would have been astronomically impossible during the full moon of the Passover (15 Nisan) and would have lasted no more than six minutes. The problem is avoided in some copies of Luke with the reading the sun "was darkened." Luke, however, uses the verb to mean "to fail" — referring to mammon in 16:9 and to faith in 22:32. Since Luke has already stated that darkness covered the land, why does he go on to say more? What does it mean that all this occurs *before* Jesus' death? It is not simply attributable to a tendency to multiply portents or to recall eschatological prophecies (Joel 2:31 [3:4]; Acts 2:20; Amos 8:9).[36] Luke ties the sun's ceasing to shine with the tearing of the veil, which implies that now God is behind this darkness.[37] These events are then tied to Jesus' final cry and death.

Luke does not interpret the darkness as an evil omen or as a token of God's wrath (Joel 3:15; Job

9:7). Plutarch uses similar language of the sun's light failing (along with great peals of thunder) in describing the disappearance of Romulus. Plutarch explains that he was "caught up into heaven, and was to be a benevolent god for them instead of a good king" (Plutarch, *Rom.* 6.27.6 – 8). Greco-Roman readers who knew of this account of the founding of Rome might interpret Jesus' death in this way as a similar "exodus."

Jewish readers, however, may have known a similar legend about the assumption of Enoch. The Lord sent darkness onto the earth, "and the angels hurried and grasped Enoch and carried him up the highest heaven, where the Lord received him." The people could not figure out how it happened, glorified God, and then all went to their homes (*2 En.* 67:1 – 2).

In the midst of the darkness, Jesus faces death calmly. God has declared him to be his beloved Son when the heavens opened before (3:22), and Jesus can trust God to care for him. His last prayer, "Father, into your hands I entrust my spirit," is the third "Father" prayer: before his crucifixion on the Mount of Olives (22:42), as he is being crucified (23:34), and now as he is about to die. Jesus quotes Ps 31:5 (30:6 LXX). Changing the future tense in the psalm from "I will entrust" (παραθήσομαι) to the present "I entrust" (παρατίθεμαι) gives these words greater immediacy.[38] Jesus also addresses God more intimately as "Father" (see 10:21; 11:2; 22:42; 23:34) instead of as "Lord, my faithful God."

Karris comments on this final prayer, "Instead of trying to save himself, Jesus gave himself trustingly into the hands of His Father. In this way, he was saved from the hands of his enemies. In this way, he proved himself to be the righteous one and son of God."[39] The Jewish leaders wanted "to

---

36. Contra Barnabas Lindars, *New Testament Apologetic* (Philadelphia: Westminster, 1961), 90.

37. See Dennis D. Sylva, "The Temple Curtain and Jesus' Death in the Gospel of Luke," *JBL* 105 (1986): 242 – 43, for

other options.

38. Torchia, "Death of a Righteous Man," 71.

39. Robert J. Karris, "Luke 23:47 and the Lucan View of Jesus' Death," 67.

lay hands on" Jesus (20:19) and got their wish; but in the end Jesus gives himself over to his Father's hands, who ultimately controls his destiny. He entrusts himself to the Father's saving power. The hand of God will rescue him from the hand of all who hate him (1:71) and who are enemies (1:74).

23:47 When the centurion saw what had happened, he began to glorify God, saying, "This man was really righteous"

(ἰδὼν δὲ ὁ ἑκατοντάρχης τὸ γενόμενον ἐδόξαζεν τὸν θεὸν λέγων· ὄντως ὁ ἄνθρωπος οὗτος δίκαιος ἦν). Luke records three reactions to Jesus' death based on how the different groups interpret what they have just seen. The first reaction comes from a centurion (ἑκατοντάρχης, lit., "a commander of one hundred"). Centurions were experienced soldiers responsible for the administration and discipline of their troops. They received much higher pay and had the prospect of social advancement (into the equestrian order) and therefore were judged to be particularly loyal to the higher authorities they served.

Even though the whole land is covered in darkness, the centurion saw "what had happened" (τὸ γενόμενον, which is singular). Herod wanted to see a sign performed by Jesus and saw nothing (9:7, 9; 23:8). The centurion's confession reveals that he saw something beyond surface appearances. One can only assume that Jesus' prayer that his executioners be forgiven and his tranquility and trust in God at the moment of death penetrated the flinty veneer of the centurion's callousness and evoked his praise and confession. The result is that Jesus'

life begins (2:14) and concludes (23:47) with the most unlikely persons praising God.[40] The centurion joins a medley of those who witness God's mighty salvific deeds worked through Jesus and praise God.[41]

He declares Jesus to be "really righteous" (ὄντως ... δίκαιος).[42] Some render the adjective as "innocent," which has the officer reiterating the verdict of Herod and Pilate and also that of the criminal.[43] Luke does not use the adjective elsewhere to refer to forensic innocence. In the immediate context, the adjective and its cognate adverb mean "justly" (23:41) and "righteous" (23:50). Joseph of Arimathea is also identified as "righteous," and the clarification that he was a member of the council but did not consent to their actions indicates that the adjective has a double meaning. He was righteous in the sense of his obedience to God and innocent of the plot to kill Jesus.

Luke may be playing on the duality of meaning in this word.[44] Jesus is guiltless (translating it "innocent" in English conceals its theological import). Luke does not present Jesus' dying as an innocent martyr but interprets his suffering as that of a suffering righteous one.[45] In Acts, the term becomes a messianic title for Jesus, "the Righteous One" (Acts 3:14 – 15; 7:52; 22:14; see Jer 23:5; 33:15). In the psalm Jesus has just uttered in his plea to God, the psalmist identifies himself as "righteous" (Ps 31:18 [30:19, LXX]). For auditors familiar with Scripture, identifying Jesus as truly righteous resonates with Ps 118:17 – 23, a portion of which was cited in 20:17, and it may offer another explanation

---

40. Crump, *Jesus the Intercessor*, 91 – 92.

41. Shepherds (2:20); a paralytic and the crowds (5:25 – 26); the crowd who witnessed the raising of a widow's son (7:16); a woman freed from her spirit of infirmity (13:13); a Samaritan leper (17:15); a blind man (18:43); see also Acts 4:21; 11:18; 21:20.

42. Doble, *The Paradox of Salvation*, 70 – 92.

43. So G. D. Kilpatrick, "A Theme of the Lucan Passion Story

and Luke xxiii.47," *JTS* 43 (1942): 34 – 36; Schmidt, "Luke's Innocent Jesus: A Scriptural Apologetic," 117 – 19; Marshall, *The Gospel of Luke*, 876; Danker, *Jesus and the New Age*, 242.

44. Neagoe, *The Trial of the Gospel*, 102 – 3; Torchia, "Death of a Righteous Man," 73.

45. Karris, "Luke 23:47 and the Lucan View of Jesus' Death," 67 – 68.

why in Luke the temple veil splits before Jesus' death:

> I will not die but live,
>> and will proclaim what the LORD has done.
>
> The LORD has chastened me severely,
>> but he has not given me over to death.
>
> Open for me the gates of the righteous;
>> I will enter and give thanks to the LORD.
>
> This is the gate of the LORD
>> through which the righteous may enter.
>
> I will give you thanks, for you answered me;
>> you have become my salvation.
>
> The stone the builders rejected
>> has become the cornerstone;
>
> the LORD has done this,
>> and it is marvelous in our eyes.

23:48 When all the crowds who came together for this spectacle observed the things that had happened, they returned beating their breasts (καὶ πάντες οἱ συμπαραγενόμενοι ὄχλοι ἐπὶ τὴν θεωρίαν ταύτην, θεωρήσαντες τὰ γενόμενα, τύπτοντες τὰ στήθη ὑπέστρεφον). The multitudes attending the Passover festival would have made for the possibility of a large crowd gathering to gawk at this grim spectacle.[46] The crowds also see what the centurion saw even though the whole land is covered in darkness. The difference is that "the things that had happened" (τὰ γενόμενα) is plural. Seeing Jesus' prayer evokes their repentance and is an answer to it. "Beating their breasts" can be taken as a sign of repentance (18:13) and serves as an inclusio of the crucifixion scene (see 23:27). It further attests from their perspective that Jesus did not deserve to die and that he belonged to no normal revolutionary movement. There was no violence, no rioting, no looting — only peaceful lament.

23:49 But all those who knew him stood from afar, and so did the women who followed him from Galilee and saw these things (εἰστήκεισαν δὲ πάντες οἱ γνωστοὶ αὐτῷ ἀπὸ μακρόθεν καὶ γυναῖκες αἱ συνακολουθοῦσαι αὐτῷ ἀπὸ τῆς Γαλιλαίας ὁρῶσαι ταῦτα). "The women who followed" translates a present, feminine participle (αἱ συνακολουθοῦσαι) and suggests ongoing activity. They are likely to include the women listed in 8:1 – 3, which means that they have been with him throughout the course of his ministry. They ventured with him to Jerusalem and stuck with him to the end, which, as it turns out, will not be the end but the crowning point of his redemptive activity. Their presence reveals that they not only received the word with joy; they are deeply rooted and in a time of testing do not fall away (8:13). The masculine "those who knew him" (οἱ γνωστοὶ αὐτῷ) are distinguished from the women. They could be anybody from relatives (2:43 – 44) to the seventy-two (10:1 – 17) to the 120 (Acts 1:13 – 15).

Their standing "from afar" (ἀπὸ μακρόθεν) may suggest their reluctance to approach the cross out of reverence for him. They also would want to distance themselves from the mockers and spectators. Luke may also see this as confirmation of Jesus as the suffering Righteous One who complains in Ps 38:11 (37:12 LXX): "My friends and companions avoid me because of my wounds; my neighbors stay far away." Unlike the centurion and the crowds, nothing is said about their reaction to what they have observed. They do not praise God, and they do not go home beating their breasts. It may explain why they are not identified as disciples. Disciples must prove themselves before they can be identified as disciples. Luke takes this issue up in Acts.

---

46. The noun "spectacle" (θεωρία) matches the verb "observed" (θεωρήσαντες) in Greek.

Theology in Application

1. Salvation through a Suffering Death

At the beginning of Luke's story, an angel announced to lowly shepherds the birth of "a Savior" (2:11). When Simeon lay eyes on Jesus in the temple, under the inspiration of the Spirit, he declared that he has seen God's "salvation" (2:30). It becomes clear that divine salvation does not come through military triumphs but through suffering. The cruelty, mockery, and sorrow of the crucifixion turn into conversion and vindication.

Jesus braves his suffering death calmly. Luke's depiction of his demeanor in the face of death would win the admiration of Greco-Roman auditors (see Plato, *Phaedo* 63e – 64a). He is not simply to be honored as a wise man who lived and died well. His death leads to salvation for others.

2. The Offer of Forgiveness of Sins

When Jesus benevolently asks that the perpetrators be forgiven, it implicitly also pronounces them guilty. They have done something that needs to be forgiven. What is forgiven is the sin, but forgiveness is not the same thing as reconciliation. The action of the soldiers and the taunts of the Jewish leaders after Jesus' gracious words demonstrate that his grace under dire circumstances has no immediate effect on them. It reveals that forgiveness is the preliminary stage that can lead to reconciliation, but it is not equivalent to the restoration of fellowship. This word of absolution makes reconciliation possible by removing the barriers that stand in the way.[47] The wrong done has been cancelled, but it does not guarantee that the wrongdoers will respond with repentance and glorifying God. Some will; others will not.

The crowds' mourning suggests that they are ready to repent for crying out for Jesus' death. The centurion's pronouncement reveals that he too is prepared to receive the reconciliation now available to all. Others, who taunt Jesus on the cross, remain hardened. Marcus states: "The crucifixion is the place where the mystery is unlocked or else finally rendered inscrutable; where either a door is opened for humanity, or one is slammed in its face."[48] Astoundingly, it is a criminal who is crucified with Jesus and one of the executioners, a Roman centurion, who enter through the door and see what is hidden from others.

3. Forgiveness and Reconciliation

The interaction with the evildoers illustrates how forgiveness and reconciliation work. There is always a divided response to the offer of forgiveness. One felon

47. This discussion applies the insights of Vincent Taylor (*Forgiveness and Reconciliation: A Study in New Testament Theology* [2nd ed.; London: Macmillan, 1956], 1 – 13) to this passage.

48. Joel Marcus, "Mark 4:10 – 12 and Marcan Epistemology," *JBL* 103 (1984): 574.

brushes it off with derision and remains alienated and hostile. The so-called "good thief" responds with repentance and seeks reconciliation. Brown is right in noting that the scene presents "the good Jesus" rather than "the good thief."[49] He was neither "good" nor a "thief" but a terrorist bandit. This account also has nothing to do with putting off repentance until the last hour. It was his first encounter with Jesus, and he does not hesitate to make an appeal to Jesus after he has heard his gracious words of forgiveness. The barrier is broken down by forgiveness. He then confesses his sins and boldly asks for redemption, and Jesus responds by offering reconciliation to be with him. This scene represents what God offers — at-one-ment — to humans through Jesus' death on the cross.

The passage also introduces the issue of sin and "ignorance." Sinning from a lack of information is different than sinning from presumption (Num 15:22 – 30). In Luke-Acts, ignorance is a sinful condition, but as a prelude to conversion it is an excuse. In Acts 3:17, 13:27 it is presented as a mitigating circumstance (see 1 Tim 1:12 – 13). According to Acts 17:30, God passes over the time of ignorance of Gentiles, who, from a Jewish perspective, do not know their spiritual left from their right, but now he calls all to repent. If it is fixed ignorance, it is then deliberate and particularly damnable. The execution of Jesus is not simply committed out of ignorance. This deed involves more than human blindness and evil (1 Cor 2:6 – 8; 2 Cor 3:14 – 17); it is the work of the power of darkness. The cross makes this spiritual ignorance inexcusable and defeats the diabolic forces.

4. The Response of Repentance

The response of the one wrongdoer further illustrates what repentance involves. (1) He demonstrates proper fear of God, recognizing that he will have to appear before the tribunal of God (Ps 2:11 – 12; Acts 10:34 – 35; Rev 11:18). In fearing God, he is like other characters who encounter the divine in Luke's story (1:12, 65; 2:9; 5:26; 7:16; Acts 2:43; 5:5,11; 9:31). But he is *not* like Cornelius, the centurion in Acts, who is described as fearing God but also as being a just man (Acts 9:22). The criminal is not just, yet God's salvation comes to both the just and unjust who demonstrate the proper fear of God.

(2) He demonstrates humility. He recognizes himself to be a sinner receiving his just punishment. Kodell writes that lowliness is the biblical posture of availability and openness to salvation. It signifies one's readiness to be raised by the hand of God (see 1 Sam 2:8, Job 29:12; Pss 72:12 – 13; 149:4; Isa 11:4; Zeph 2:3).[50] Mary acknowledges that God has regard for those of low degree and exalts them. The mighty are the self-sufficient and think that they can raise up themselves. Consequently, they do not consider themselves in need of salvation, do not plead for mercy, and do not repent.

49. Brown, *The Death of the Messiah*, 2:1013.   50. Kodell, "Luke's Theology of the Death of Jesus," 226.

This scene gives further evidence that Jesus' kingdom is populated with repentant outcasts.

(3) He demonstrates proper regard for Jesus. He recognizes Jesus' innocence; moreover, he prays to him as one would pray to God, "Remember me!" He assumes Jesus' royalty and asks for some kind of royal clemency. How absurd it must have seemed to an onlooker. He does not pray to God but to the man who is being crucified beside him. Evans comments:

> The statement proclaims the gospel of salvation in that the criminal is treated immediately as righteous, and it is Jesus, the messiah and judge to be, who from the cross determines that it is so.... As the innocent martyr Jesus himself belongs with the righteous in Paradise, but as their king; and he takes another with him to be amongst his companions — *with me*.[51]

(4) He demonstrates remarkable faith. In 17:20, Jesus said, "The reign of God does not come with observable [signs]." When this man makes his request of Jesus, there are no apparent grounds for any reasonable person to believe that Jesus would ever have any part of any kingdom. What kingdom could a man being hanged on a cross possibly have? Who would want to be with him? This wrongdoer, however, hears and sees what is hidden to most of the spectators and believes that the one who seems to be as powerless, as humiliated, and in as much torment as he is will reign after his death.

Despite the scoffers who claim that Jesus was a charlatan and a fool, this man trusts that Jesus' dying on the cross is only a prelude to kingly power and part of God's plan. He repents even though he is not able to demonstrate it in his actions. Repentance requires first of all a change of thinking. He trusts that Jesus will be merciful enough to lift him out of his shame and lead him into a glorious life to come. He therefore makes public his commitment by acknowledging him before others (see 12:8 – 9).

5. The Reward of Repentance

The promised reward seems all out of proportion to such a small act of repentance, but it reveals that salvation comes by grace. As Simon of Cyrene illustrated the disciples' requirement to carry the cross after Jesus, the repentant malefactor's faith illustrates the promise that the disciple who dies with him will be raised with him (2 Tim 2:11; see Rom 8:17).

Jesus' promise to the wrongdoer reveals what his death accomplishes for others. A maxim in rabbinic literature that states, "Repentance atones along with the day of death, and the day of death atones when there has been repentance" (*'Abot R. Nat.*

---

51. Evans, *St. Luke*, 874.

39), is amended here. The death of Jesus atones, and entry into paradise requires trust in and allegiance to Jesus. The reference to paradise cannot help but recall the story of Adam.

6. Paradise Regained

Luke is the only gospel to trace Jesus' genealogy back to Adam, the son of God (3:38). The reference to paradise here may reflect an Adam typology. Death in early Hebrew thought "involved a movement from the created realm to the realm of un-creation, or chaos."[52] But in Jesus' assurance, one does not return to the primordial chaos in death. One enters paradise with him. Brown comments: "By bringing this wrongdoer with him into paradise, Jesus is undoing the results of Adam's sin which barred access to the tree of life (Gen 3:24)."[53]

The first Adam lost paradise; the second Adam regains it and opens it up for others (Rom 5:12 – 21; 1 Cor 15:20 – 22). It is Jesus who is the final judge (Acts 10:42). He decides who will or will not be with him, and the sinner who confesses and expresses trust in him will share his destiny. Luke expresses theologically in a narrative what Paul states in prose in Rom 10:9: "If you declare with your mouth, 'Jesus is Lord,' and believe in your heart that God raised him from the dead, you will be saved."

7. The Death of the Righteous One for the Unrighteous

The centurion makes a profound theological announcement: "This man was really righteous"; that is, Jesus stood in the right relation to God. It recalls the righteous people introduced in the opening chapters of the gospel, Elizabeth and Zechariah (1:6) and Simeon (2:25). Declaring a crucified man to be righteous, however, requires a redefinition of righteousness. It may seem incongruous for a righteous and innocent man to meet such a cruel death, but it was entirely consistent with God's purposes for his Righteous One as outlined in Scripture: "After he has suffered, he will see the light of life and be satisfied; by his knowledge my righteous servant will justify many, and he will bear their iniquities" (Isa 53:11).

Jesus is the one who is truly righteous because of his obedience to God's salvific plan in his suffering and death: "For Christ also suffered once for sins, the righteous for the unrighteous, to bring you to God" (1 Pet 3:18). The declaration by the centurion and Jesus' emphatic statement that the criminal will be with him in paradise open the way to understanding that "through the obedience of the one man the many will be made righteous" (Rom 5:19).

---

52. Dominic Rudman, "The Crucifixion as *Chaoskampf*: A New Reading of the Passion Narrative in the Synoptic Gospels," *Bib* 84 (2003): 106.

53. Brown, *The Death of the Messiah*, 2:1011 – 12.

Luke 23:50 – 24:12

Literary Context

Luke records three episodes occurring on the third day after Jesus was crucified (24:1 – 12, 13 – 35, 36 – 49). In the first account, the tomb where Jesus was buried is empty and he is nowhere to be seen. Divine messengers interpret what the empty tomb means: he has been raised. In the next two accounts, Jesus appears to disciples, teaches them from Scripture, and then disappears from view.

The three accounts outline three steps in the process of how one comes to recognize Jesus as the risen Lord. The first step, emphasized in this passage, requires remembering Jesus' words and ministry. The second step requires reading his life and death in light of the divine plan for the Messiah laid out in the Scriptures, and it is emphasized in the conversation with the disciples on the road to Emmaus. The third step also appears in the Emmaus road episode, namely, the gathering of the Christian community in a fellowship meal where Jesus becomes present to disciples in word, the sharing of testimony, and the breaking of bread. The last episode emphasizes all three of these steps.

In the first two accounts, the individuals are disheartened and have no expectation that God would raise Jesus from the dead. The women dutifully attempt to carry out the task of attending to the corpse, failing to remember Jesus' promise that he would be raised. The disciples in the next scene return to their lodging in Emmaus in despair, quarreling about what has happened. They do not ignore the report of the women that Jesus was not in the tomb and had been raised from the dead, but they do not accept it as true. In the third scene, Jesus' disciples have gathered together after hearing more reports that Jesus has been raised.

All three scenes include perplexity on the part of his followers. Each mentions some error on their part: seeking the living among the dead (24:5), not recognizing him (24:16), and thinking he was an apparition (24:37). Each contains a rebuke for not remembering what he said when he was with them (24:6 – 7, 44) or not believing what the prophets have spoken (24:25 – 26, 44 – 46). Each scene then mentions the gathering of the community (24:9, 33, 36). The last two scenes mention a meal (24:30, 42 – 43). The episodes all end with disciples going forth to tell others or being commanded to do so (24:9, 33 – 34, 47 – 49). Encountering the resurrected Jesus is intended to create witnesses to the resurrection, which becomes a central theme of the preaching in Acts (2:23 – 24; 3:13 – 15; 5:30; 13:29 – 30).

VI. Jesus' Suffering and Death (22:1 – 23:49)
    F. Jesus on Trial (22:66 – 23:25)
    G. The Crucifixion of Jesus (23:26 – 49)
➡ **VII. Jesus' Resurrection and Ascension (23:50 – 24:53)**
    A. Jesus Dead and Buried, Raised and Living (23:50 – 24:12)
    B. Resurrection Encounter on the Road to Emmaus (24:13 – 35)

Main Idea

Failing to remember Jesus' words and promises leads to despair. Jesus was dead and buried, but his promise that he would be raised on the third day has been fulfilled.

Translation

Luke 23:50–24:12

23:50a	Character introduction	**And behold, [there was] a man by the name of Joseph,**
b		who was a member of the council,
c		a good and righteous man.
51a		**He did not agree with their purpose and action.**
b		**He was from the Judean town of Arimathea and**
c		**was waiting for the reign of God.**
52	Request	**This one went to Pilate and asked for Jesus' body.**
53	Burial	When he took [the body] down,
		he wrapped it in a linen cloth and placed it in a tomb cut out of the rock
		where no one had ever been 🌿
		laid.
54	Time reference	**It was the day of preparation,**
		and the Sabbath was beginning.
55	Character introduction	**The women who had come from Galilee followed him and observed the tomb 🌿**
		and how the body was placed.
56	Circumstance	After they returned,
		they prepared aromatic spices and perfumes,
		and on the Sabbath they rested
		according to the commandment.
24:1a	Circumstance	On the first day of the week, at early dawn,
b		**they came to the tomb bringing the spices that they had prepared.**

Continued on next page.

2	Discovery	**They found the stone rolled away from the tomb,**
3		but when they entered, **they did not find the body of the Lord Jesus.**
4a	Perplexity	And when they were at a loss concerning this,
b	Appearance of divine figures	**behold, two men stood before them in gleaming clothing.**
5a	Terror	When they became terrified and bowed their faces to the ground,
b	Questioning rebuke	**the men said to them,**

"Why do you seek the living among the dead?

6a	Assurance	*He is not here but*
		has been raised.
b	Questioning rebuke/ reminder	*Remember how he spoke to you [about this] while he was still in Galilee*

| 7 | | *that it is necessary for the Son of Man to be handed over to the hands of sinners and to be crucified, and* |

on the third day
to rise again."

8	Remembrance	**And they remembered his words.**
9	Exit/announcement	And when they returned from the tomb, **they announced all these things to the Eleven and all the rest.**
10a	Identification	Now **it was Mary Magdalene,**
		Joanna,
		Mary, James's mother, and
		the rest with them
b	Announcement	**who kept telling these things to the apostles.**
11	Disbelief	**And these words appeared to them as utter nonsense** **and they were refusing to believe them.**
12a	Discovery	**But Peter rose up and ran to the tomb,** and when he peered in, **he saw the linen cloths alone.**
b	Marveling	**He went away marveling to himself over what had happened.**

Structure and Literary Form

The structure contains two panels. The first panel reports details of Jesus' burial and his female followers observing it. The two panels are double-hinged by chronological notes about the approaching Sabbath that brings a cessation to human action, and the end of the Sabbath when humans spring into action. The second panel reports details of the discovery of the empty tomb by the women, two angels announcing the resurrection, and the women announcing the news to skeptical disciples. It concludes with a report of Peter's visit to the tomb that verifies the women's account.

Exegetical Outline

➡ **I. Introduction of Joseph of Arimathea (23:50 – 51)**

II. Burial of Jesus (23:52 – 53)

    A. Joseph's request of Pilate to bury the body (23:52)

    B. Burial in a tomb that had never been used (23:53)

III. Chronological notice about the beginning of the Sabbath (23:54)

IV. Introduction of the women (23:55 – 56)

    A. Had followed Jesus from Galilee and observed the burial (23:55a)

    B. Prepared spices for anointing after the Sabbath (23:56)

V. Chronological notice about the end of the Sabbath (24:1a)

VI. The empty tomb (24:1b – 3)

    A. Arrival at the tomb (24:1b)

    B. Discovery that the stone had been rolled away (24:2)

    C. Discovery that the body of the Lord Jesus was gone (24:3)

VII. The revelation of two angels to the women (24:4 – 8)

    A. Reproach for seeking the living among the dead (24:4 – 5)

    B. Reminder of Jesus' prophecy (24:6 – 7)

    C. Remembrance of Jesus' words (24:8)

VIII. Announcement of the women to the Eleven and all the rest (24:9 – 11)

IX. Peter's visit to the tomb (24:12)

Explanation of the Text

23:50 – 51 And behold, [there was] a man by the name of Joseph, who was a member of the council, a good and righteous man. He did not agree with their purpose and action. He was from the Judean town of Arimathea and was waiting for the reign of God (καὶ ἰδοὺ ἀνὴρ ὀνόματι Ἰωσὴφ βουλευτὴς ὑπάρχων [καὶ] ἀνὴρ ἀγαθὸς καὶ δίκαιος — οὗτος οὐκ ἦν συγκατατεθειμένος τῇ βουλῇ καὶ τῇ πράξει αὐτῶν — ἀπὸ Ἀριμαθαίας πόλεως τῶν Ἰουδαίων, ὃς προσεδέχετο τὴν βασιλείαν τοῦ θεοῦ). Luke offers no explanation why Joseph would take responsibility for burying the body of Jesus except his moral character: he is a righteous man. Describing him as "good and righteous" (ἀγαθὸς καὶ δίκαιος) and awaiting the reign

of God (προσεδέχετο τὴν βασιλείαν τοῦ θεοῦ) means that righteous Jews waiting for the fulfillment of the messianic promises appear in both the infancy and burial narratives (1:6; 2:25, 38).

Joseph is also identified as a member of the council, but as a righteous man he was not involved in their plotting (22:4 – 5) or decision (22:66 – 71). Luke does not clarify if he was absent from the proceedings or overtly opposed to their course of action. Identifying him as being from the Judean town of Arimathea, which could also be translated "a town of the Jews," reveals the divided response in Israel to Jesus. Not all Jews or even Jewish leaders are malevolent toward Jesus (see Gamaliel, Acts 5:33 – 39).

23:52 This one went to Pilate and asked for Jesus' body (οὗτος προσελθὼν τῷ Πιλάτῳ ᾐτήσατο τὸ σῶμα τοῦ Ἰησοῦ). The Romans normally forbade burial for people sentenced to death (Tacitus, *Ann.* 6.29). To be denied burial was universally regarded as the most humiliating indignity that could be done to the deceased because it meant that the corpse was left to be devoured by animals and birds of prey (1 Kgs 14:11, 21:24; 2 Kgs 9:34 – 37; Ps 79:2 – 3; Jer 7:33; 8:1, 2; 9:21 – 22; Ezek 29:5). Most victims of crucifixion were left to rot on the cross or given a dishonorable burial.

Jews, however, considered burying corpses to be a pious duty (Josephus, *Ag. Ap.* 2.29 §211). Tobit claims to walk "in the ways of truth and righteousness" (Tob 1:3) because "I would give my food to the hungry and my clothing to the naked; and if I saw the dead body of any of my people thrown out behind the wall of Nineveh, I would bury it" (Tob 1:17; see 2:7). The Hebrew Scriptures also declared that leaving a criminal's body to hang on a tree overnight defiled the land (Deut 21:22 – 23).

As a righteous man of means, Joseph performs an act of pious devotion by taking the initiative to bury Jesus (see Acts 8:2). He must also be a man of influence and impeccable reputation to be so bold as to request that the governor allow him to bury someone accused of sedition. As a council member, he would not be suspected of collusion with the victim. Pilate may have consented to allow him to bury the body of Jesus because he did not judge Jesus to be guilty of any of the charges brought against him.

23:53 When he took [the body] down, he wrapped it in a linen cloth and placed it in a tomb cut out of the rock where no one had ever been laid (καὶ καθελὼν ἐνετύλιξεν αὐτὸ σινδόνι, καὶ ἔθηκεν αὐτὸν ἐν μνήματι λαξευτῷ οὗ οὐκ ἦν οὐδεὶς οὔπω κείμενος). Joseph takes on the unpleasant task of removing the brutalized, bloody body from the cross and transporting it to the tomb. Presumably he has help, but others are not mentioned by Luke.[1] Jesus' burial by someone who is not part of his circle of followers makes clear that his death was real. The power of death has him in its grasp.

After the shameful death by crucifixion, Jesus receives some honor in being placed in a tomb that had never been used (expressed in Greek with a triple negative for emphasis).[2] The tomb is like the colt that had never been ridden, which Jesus borrowed to enter Jerusalem (19:30). The statement that the tomb has never been used needs clarification. Jews who could afford a tomb practiced secondary burial.[3] When the flesh had decomposed, the bones were carefully gathered up and placed in an ossuary box, the larger bones on the bottom and smaller ones on top. This practice allowed tombs to be reused, and they could have multiple occupants. The coffinless body would be placed in a niche cut horizontally into the wall of the tomb chamber or on a low bench.

Joseph wraps Jesus in a linen cloth (σινδόνι) because his clothing has already been confiscated, and it was regarded as disgraceful to be buried naked.

23:54 It was the day of preparation, and the Sabbath was beginning (καὶ ἡμέρα ἦν παρασκευῆς, καὶ σάββατον ἐπέφωσκεν). The literal rendering of the phrase translated the Sabbath "was beginning" is that it "was lighting up." This is strange because in Jewish time reckoning, the Sabbath began at

1. John 19:39 – 40 mentions that Nicodemus was also involved in the burial.

2. Jodi Magness ("Ossuaries and the Burial of Jesus and James," *JBL* 124 [2005]: 145) observes: "Had Joseph not offered Jesus a spot in his tomb … Jesus likely would have been disposed of in the manner of the poorer classes: in an individual trench grave dug into the ground."

3. The poor were buried in shallow graves.

sundown. It therefore may be a reference to the evening star or the lighting of the Sabbath candles.

"The day of preparation" refers to the day preceding the Sabbath (Thursday evening to Friday evening) in which everything (food and lights) must be prepared in advance so that work could be avoided on the Sabbath. If the Sabbath was beginning, Joseph had little time to do all that was necessary to bury Jesus. The time reference, then, may not be precise, or the women's preparation was permitted on the Sabbath as an emergency related to the burial of a corpse (*m. Šabb.* 23:5). They could prepare spices but could not carry them to the tomb on the Sabbath. The primary purpose of the time reference, however, is to explain why the women do not return to the tomb until three days later (counted as Friday evening, Saturday, and Sunday morning).

23:55 The women who had come from Galilee followed him and observed the tomb and how the body was placed (κατακολουθήσασαι δὲ αἱ γυναῖκες, αἵτινες ἦσαν συνεληλυθυῖαι ἐκ τῆς Γαλιλαίας αὐτῷ, ἐθεάσαντο τὸ μνημεῖον καὶ ὡς ἐτέθη τὸ σῶμα αὐτοῦ). The women stick it out to the bitter end and leave the crucifixion site sedately, unlike the inhabitants of Jerusalem, who departed the scene beating their breasts in grief. The women are said to follow "him" (αὐτῷ), which may refer to Joseph or Jesus. The latter is possible and might explain why the verb "to follow" is changed from "to follow with" (συνακολουθοῦσαι) in 23:49 to "to follow after" (κατακολουθήσασαι) here. They can no longer follow with or communicate with the dead Jesus.[4] The term for "tomb" (μνήμειον here and in 24:2) literally means "place of remembrance," but what is to be remembered is

not the burial site — it is not to become a shrine — but Jesus' words and deeds (24:6 – 7).

23:56 After they returned, they prepared aromatic spices and perfumes, and on the Sabbath they rested according to the commandment (ὑποστρέψασαι δὲ ἡτοίμασαν ἀρώματα καὶ μύρα. καὶ τὸ μὲν σάββατον ἡσύχασαν κατὰ τὴν ἐντολήν). Mark records that the women watched *where* Jesus was laid (Mark 15:47), but Luke records that they watched *how* the body was laid. That may explain why they prepare spices to anoint him. Obedience to the Sabbath laws prevented Jesus from being anointed as was customary when he was first laid in the tomb.

Luke presents Jesus' life as one that begins with his family following the prescriptions of the law (2:22 – 24) and ends with his followers doing the same.[5] After the Sabbath is over, the women last at the cross are the first at the tomb to attend to the hastily buried body.

24:1 – 3 On the first day of the week, at early dawn, they came to the tomb bringing the spices that they had prepared. They found the stone rolled away from the tomb, but when they entered, they did not find the body of the Lord Jesus (τῇ δὲ μιᾷ τῶν σαββάτων ὄρθρου βαθέως ἐπὶ τὸ μνῆμα ἦλθον φέρουσαι ἃ ἡτοίμασαν ἀρώματα. εὗρον δὲ τὸν λίθον ἀποκεκυλισμένον ἀπὸ τοῦ μνημείου, εἰσελθοῦσαι δὲ οὐχ εὗρον τὸ σῶμα τοῦ κυρίου Ἰησοῦ). The stone is rolled away from the tomb so that the women can peer in to see that Jesus is not there. The account emphasizes that they do not find Jesus' body, which they witnessed being laid in the tomb (23:55; 24:23). Luke reports this fact from the perspective of faith in Jesus as the risen Lord (see Acts 1:22; 4:33; 8:16; 11:17, 20;

---

4. Sjef Van Tilborg and Patrick Chatelion Counet, *Jesus' Appearances and Disappearances in Luke 24* (Biblical Interpretation Series; Leiden: Brill, 2000), 30.

5. Matera, *Passion Narratives and Gospel Theologies*, 180.

15:11; 16:31; 19:5, 13, 17; 20:21, 24, 35; 21:13; cf. 7:59; 15:26; 28:31). It is "the body of *the Lord* Jesus" (τὸ σῶμα τοῦ κυρίου Ἰησοῦ).[6] The disappearance of the body only causes perplexity (24:4) when one does not recognize him to be "the Lord."

24:4 And when they were at a loss concerning this, behold, two men stood before them in gleaming clothing (καὶ ἐγένετο ἐν τῷ ἀπορεῖσθαι αὐτὰς περὶ τούτου καὶ ἰδοὺ ἄνδρες δύο ἐπέστησαν αὐταῖς ἐν ἐσθῆτι ἀστραπτούσῃ). The significance of the empty tomb is not immediately obvious. What is beyond finite human minds to grasp on their own requires divine revelation to explain. Two men in resplendent clothes do not automatically signify angels to most moderns, since we are accustomed to portraying them as having wings. Only the seraphim, however, had wings and they numbered six (Isa 6:2). Cherubim had animal and human features, but the description of angels in the Bible is quite humanlike (Gen 18:2; 19:1 – 3). In 2 Macc 3:26, angels are described as "two young men … remarkably strong, gloriously beautiful, and splendidly dressed" (see also 2 Macc 3:36; Tob 5:4 – 5, 7, 10). Luke identifies these men specifically as angels in 24:23.

The description of their clothing gleaming in the darkness of the tomb suggests something out of the ordinary and harks back to the description of Jesus' clothing in the transfiguration (ἀστραπτούσῃ, see 9:29; 10:18; Acts 9:3; 22:6). It also corresponds to the apparel of the two men (angels) present at the ascension (Acts 1:10).[7] The phrase "they stood before them" (ἐπέστησαν αὐταῖς) is also used in 2:9 and Acts 12:7 for a sudden appearance of a supernatural being. The angel Gabriel appeared to interpret signs and events to chosen humans at the beginning of the story to explain what God was

about to do. Now angels appear at its close to explain what God has done. They come only to impart privileged information about divine workings: the conception of John and Jesus, Jesus' birth, and his resurrection. Since they speak in unison, they meet the criteria of two witnesses.

24:5 When they became terrified and bowed their faces to the ground, the men said to them, "Why do you seek the living among the dead?" (ἐμφόβων δὲ γενομένων αὐτῶν καὶ κλινουσῶν τὰ πρόσωπα εἰς τὴν γῆν εἶπαν πρὸς αὐτάς· τί ζητεῖτε τὸν ζῶντα μετὰ τῶν νεκρῶν;). The women are terrified in the presence of the divine beings and show their submission by bowing their faces to the ground. The angels do not offer a word of assurance, nor do they invite them to come and see the place where Jesus lay to prove that he is not here, as they do in Matt 28:6 and Mark 16:6.

Instead, the divine beings issue two mild rebukes. First, they question why the women are looking for the living among the dead. This question "noticeably diminishes the interest in the empty tomb as providing by itself direct or even inferential evidence for the fact of Jesus' resurrection."[8] The text emphasizes, "It is as a *living savior* that Jesus brings salvation."[9] There will be no lamentation at the tomb because the body is not there for loved ones to pay their last respects. There will be no joyful reunion because he has not been resuscitated back to life, as were the son of the widow of Nain (7:15) and the daughter of Jairus (8:54 – 55), to resume life as usual.

24:6 – 7 "He is not here but has been raised. Remember how he spoke to you [about this] while he was still in Galilee that it is necessary for the Son of Man to be handed over to the hands of sinners

---

6. The phrase is omitted by Bezae (D) and some Old Latin manuscripts.

7. Bock, *Luke*, 2:1890.

8. Schubert, "The Structure and Significance of Luke 24," 167 – 68.

9. Nave, *Repentance in Luke-Acts*, 28.

and to be crucified, and on the third day to rise again" (οὐκ ἔστιν ὧδε, ἀλλὰ ἠγέρθη. μνήσθητε ὡς ἐλάλησεν ὑμῖν ἔτι ὢν ἐν τῇ Γαλιλαίᾳ λέγων τὸν υἱὸν τοῦ ἀνθρώπου ὅτι δεῖ παραδοθῆναι εἰς χεῖρας ἀνθρώπων ἁμαρτωλῶν καὶ σταυρωθῆναι καὶ τῇ τρίτῃ ἡμέρᾳ ἀναστῆναι). The absence of Jesus' body from the tomb may at first be confusing, but remembering his prediction of what would happen to him quickly clears up the confusion. It can only mean that he has been resurrected. The charge to remember what he said (see 24:44) is therefore the second mild rebuke and recalls a collage of Jesus' prophecies about his death and resurrection (9:22, 44; 18:32 – 33). These women should have been expecting his resurrection since Jesus told them it would happen. This gentle reproof places them in "the inner circle of disciples with whom such a prediction had been shared."[10]

24:8 And they remembered his words (καὶ ἐμνήσθησαν τῶν ῥημάτων αὐτοῦ). When prompted by the angels, they remembered Jesus' words, and their report to the disciples reveals that they also believed. Like Mary at the beginning of the gospel (1:38), these women respond with faith. Remembering Jesus' words is vital both for faith (22:61; Acts 11:16; 20:35) and for understanding his death and resurrection.

24:9 – 10 And when they returned from the tomb, they announced all these things to the Eleven and all the rest. Now it was Mary Magdalene, Joanna, Mary, James's mother, and the rest with them who kept telling these things to the apostles (καὶ ὑποστρέψασαι ἀπὸ τοῦ μνημείου ἀπήγγειλαν ταῦτα πάντα τοῖς ἕνδεκα καὶ πᾶσιν τοῖς λοιποῖς. ἦσαν δὲ ἡ Μαγδαληνὴ Μαρία καὶ Ἰωάννα καὶ Μαρία ἡ Ἰακώβου καὶ αἱ λοιπαὶ σὺν αὐταῖς. ἔλεγον πρὸς τοὺς ἀποστόλους ταῦτα).

With the announcement of Jesus' resurrection the women can rise up from bowing down to the ground and go to tell others. They serve as eyewitnesses — traveling with him from Galilee, standing by at the cross, witnessing the burial, discovering the empty tomb, and hearing the announcement of his resurrection from the angels.

The women duly report what has transpired to "the Eleven," a reminder of the fracture in the disciples' band created by Judas's betrayal. The "twelve" are now "eleven," an incomplete number, but "all the rest" leaves hope that there are some who can replace the missing Judas (see Acts 1:15 – 26). The followers have not dispersed, and the unexpected news from the women and Peter's visit to the tomb will keep them from falling apart completely until Jesus appears to them.

The grammar and punctuation of vv. 9b – 10 are problematic, but Dussant spots a chiastic structure that helps to unlock the meaning.[11]

> A They reported all these things to the eleven
> > B and to all the rest.
> > > C Now it was Mary Magdalene,
> > > > D Joanna,
> > > C' Mary the mother of James,
> > B' and the rest of the women with them
> A' who kept telling these things to the apostles.

Joanna appears in the center of this structure, and it is the second reference to her in Luke (see 8:3). Bauckham argues that Luke does not redact Mark 16:1 – 8, since the verbal agreement is minimal, nor is he dependent on John. Literary reasons do not adequately explain the differences from Mark. Instead, it is more likely that Luke draws on another source for the account of the empty tomb, namely, from Joanna. This explains why he names her while Mark does not, and places her name in

---

10. Craddock, *Luke*, 282.
11. Louis Dussaut, "Le tryptyche des apparitions en Luc 24 (analyse structurelle)," *RB* 94 (1987): 168; see also Nolland, *Luke*, 3:1191; and Bauckham, *Gospel Women*, 187 – 88.

the center of the chiasm.[12] The verb "kept telling" (ἔλεγον) is read as an iterative imperfect and may mean that they had to keep insisting that their story was true, or, more likely, that they were all telling the same story.[13]

24:11 And these words appeared to them as utter nonsense and they were refusing to believe them (καὶ ἐφάνησαν ἐνώπιον αὐτῶν ὡσεὶ λῆρος τὰ ῥήματα ταῦτα, καὶ ἠπίστουν αὐταῖς). Jesus made the same predictions about his resurrection to the men, but they also apparently did not remember and "were refusing to believe" (ἠπίστουν, an iterative imperfect). They dismiss the women's report as "utter nonsense" (λῆρος), a unique term that was used to describe the delirious talk of the very sick.[14] Their reaction seems to be the precursor of Celsus's mockery that only half-frantic women had seen the resurrected Jesus in their crazed imaginations (Origen, *Cels.* 2.55).

Josephus writes that women were to be disqualified as witnesses on account of their giddiness and impetuosity (*Ant.* 4.8.15 §219), and such a story from women would automatically be viewed with suspicion (see John 4:41 – 42). Karris notes, however, "It is not their fault, but rather a sign of the denseness of human perception that the men do not believe them."[15] Jesus' own disciples are the first skeptics of the resurrection, and their unbelief highlights one of the key themes in the three resurrection scenes in Luke. How is unbelief and skepticism about Jesus' resurrection overcome?

24:12 But Peter rose up and ran to the tomb, and when he peered in, he saw the linen cloths alone. He went away marveling to himself over what had happened (ὁ δὲ Πέτρος ἀναστὰς ἔδραμεν ἐπὶ τὸ μνημεῖον καὶ παρακύψας βλέπει τὰ ὀθόνια μόνα, καὶ ἀπῆλθεν πρὸς ἑαυτὸν θαυμάζων τὸ γεγονός). After his denial of Jesus, Peter apparently has already "turned" (22:32) because he is back with his brother apostles. He takes the first step toward "strengthening" them by "rising up" (ἀναστάς) and going to the tomb to check things out for himself (see John 20:3 – 10).[16] He "peers in" (παρακύψας, not "stoops down")[17] and sees the linen cloths that were left behind. Since the linen cloths would be the only valuable thing to steal, and since it also would be unlikely that anyone would strip the body before stealing it, their presence discredits any suspicion that tomb raiders broke in and stole the body. This brief note provides another human witness to the fact that the tomb was empty.

Does going away "marveling" (θαυμάζων) imply that Peter believes? "Marveling" can be associated with doubt and unbelief (11:38; Acts 13:41), but Luke typically uses the verb to describe a positive response to a wondrous event (Luke 1:21, 63; 2:18, 33; 4:22; 8:25; 11:14; 20:26; Acts 2:7; 4:13). Peter's marveling should not be interpreted negatively, but Luke does not narrate him announcing the news to the other disciples; it is only implied in 24:24. The result is that the emphasis falls on the testimony of the women, who watched Jesus' burial, visited the tomb, and heard the announcement of the angels. Luke reports but also does not narrate Jesus' resurrection appearance to Peter (24:34).

---

12. Bauckham, *Gospel Women*, 192 – 93.

13. Van Tilborg and Counet, *Jesus' Appearances and Disappearances in Luke 24*, 244.

14. Plummer, *Luke*, 550.

15. Karris, *Luke: Artist and Theologian*, 115.

16. Codex Beza (D) and the Old Latin manuscripts omit 24:12 entirely, as it does the phrases the body "of the Lord Jesus" in 24:3, "he is not here but has been raised" in 24:6, and

"from the tomb" in 24:9. The strength of the manuscript tradition that includes 24:12 and the other phrases is much too strong to be rejected. The statement that some of us "went to the tomb" (24:24) cross-references 24:12 and provides strong internal evidence for its inclusion in the original text.

17. Frans Neirynck, "ΠΑΡΑΚΥΨΑΣ ΒΛΕΠΕΙ: Lc 24, 12 et Jn 20,5," *ETL* 53 (1977); 113 – 52.

Theology in Application

Luke does not write as an omniscient author who can narrate the resurrection. Like other New Testament writers, he reports only its aftermath (contrast the *Gospel of Peter* 9:35 – 10:42, which describes an angel waking Jesus, and Jesus sitting up, unraveling the grave clothes, and exiting the tomb). The reason that the canonical gospels do not describe this event is because the resurrection is not something open to a human witness. Jesus did not experience the corruption of death (Acts 2:31; 13:37) and was not raised to resume his life on earth but to move to a new kind of bodily existence. He entered into paradise (23:43) and into glory (24:26).[18] Humans cannot witness that. Minear writes: "So an angel brings the decisive word, thus protecting God from the prying gaze of human beings yet conveying to chosen witnesses an understanding of meanings hidden behind the events."[19]

The confession of the church is that the resurrection of Jesus is a unique event unparalleled in history. The resurrection is God's overruling the human verdict that condemned him to death (see Acts 2:23 – 24, 36). The resurrection is God's triumph over the designs of Satan. The resurrection demonstrates God's power over death, the last enemy (see Acts 2:24). Death could not hold the Son of God in its power, which means that the disciples' proclamation and deeds of power are carried out in the name of one whose power is greater than death, greater than Satan, greater than any earthly power (Acts 3:12 – 16; 4:7, 10, 33; 26:18). The preaching of the apostles in Acts also proclaims that Jesus' resurrection opens the way for the resurrection of others who believe in him (Acts 4:2).

Humans can only see the effects of the resurrection — the empty tomb and the linen cloths lying by themselves. The empty tomb may seem an ambiguous sign, but Bickerman shows that ancient readers would have been familiar with stories of the disappearance of a body from a tomb and would have been likely to interpret this detail religiously. The disappearance of a body in many ancient stories leads the mourners to assume that the gods took the body and that the deceased is now divine.

For example, in the earliest extant Greek novel, Chariton's *Chaereas and Callirhoe*, the heroine Callirhoe was prematurely buried, and pirates stole her comatose body from the tomb. When her husband, Chaereas, came to the tomb at the crack of dawn, "he found that the stones had been moved and the entrance was open. He was astonished at the sight and overcome by fearful perplexity at what had happened." He then found the tomb empty. Chaereas immediately assumed that his wife had been taken away to heaven by one of the gods and that he had been married to a goddess without knowing it (*Chaer.* 3.2 – 3).[20] The beloved disciple in the gospel of John saw

---

18. Fitzmyer, *Luke*, 2:1538 – 39.
19. Paul S. Minear, "Matthew 28:1 – 10," *Int* 38 (1984): 60.
20. Elias Bickermann, "Das leere Grab," *ZNW* 23 (1924):

281 – 92. See also Van Tilborg and Counet, *Jesus' Appearances and Disappearances in Luke 24*, 189 – 235.

the empty tomb and believed without the intervention of angels (John 20:8). Since Luke shows Jesus to be conceived of the Holy Spirit and born the Son of God, the reader might have expected something miraculous to occur at the end of his life. The empty tomb would have been a convincing pointer to Jesus' divinity.

Modern readers come to this text with assumptions quite different from those of the ancient readers. Van Tilborg and Counet assert, "our way of reading and understanding is completely different from that of the readers from the time in which these stories were a living reality."[21] The empty tomb is a sign that radical skeptics say proves nothing: the women took a wrong turn and went to the wrong tomb; disciples stole the body; Jesus only swooned on the cross and did not die and later revived; dogs dragged the body away. As with Jesus' conception and birth, humans are not left to draw their own conclusions. Their spiritual myopia will mislead them. That is why it is necessary for angels to announce the resurrection. The proof of Jesus' resurrection comes only to those who have faith and who know and remember the words of Jesus.

---

21. Van Tilborg and Counet, *Jesus' Appearances and Disappearances in Luke 24*, 230.

Luke 24:13 – 35

Literary Context

Luke connects this episode to the previous one by noting that it occurs on the same first day of the week. The Emmaus story bridges "the gap between the disbelieving apostles in the first part (24,1 – 12) and Jesus' appearance to the eleven when he 'opened their minds to the understanding of the Scriptures' in the third part (24,36 – 50.)"[1] It marks the debut of Jesus' appearances to his followers that continued for forty days (Acts 1:3).

This narrative brings together several Lukan motifs. It begins on a journey moving away from Jerusalem but ends with a journey back to Jerusalem after the man whom the two followers meet on the road opens their eyes. It highlights the second and third steps in removing the blinders that prevent one from recognizing Jesus as the risen Lord — reading Jesus' life and death in light of the Scriptures, and the gathering of the Christian community in a fellowship meal where Jesus becomes present in the breaking of bread. The passage also emphasizes the necessity of Jesus' death and the fulfillment of prophecy in the Scriptures and highlights hospitality and fellowship over a meal. It ends with the community gathered together with their gloom dispelled and their hopes rekindled.

VI. Jesus' Suffering and Death (22:1 – 23:49)
VII. Jesus' Resurrection and Ascension (23:50 – 24:53)
    A. Jesus Dead and Buried, Raised and Living (23:50 – 24:12)
→   **B. Resurrection Encounter on the Road to Emmaus (24:13 – 35)**
    C. Jesus' Appearance to the Disciples and His Ascension (24:36 – 53)

---

1. Gillman, "The Emmaus Story in Luke-Acts Revisited," 168.

Main Idea

It is through a knowledge of the Scriptures that we understand God's plan, and in the life of the gathered community of believers that the suffering Christ becomes known as the risen Christ.

Translation

Luke 24:13–35

24:13a	Circumstance	**Behold, two of them were going the same day to a village**
b		by the name of Emmaus sixty stadia from Jerusalem.
14	Confusion	**And they were conversing with one another concerning all the things that⤴ had happened.**
15a		It happened while they were conversing and disputing,
b	Appearance of Jesus	**Jesus himself drew near and began to go along with them.**
16	Lack of recognition	**Their eyes were seized** so as not to recognize him.
17a	Question	**He said to them,** *"What are these words that you are exchanging with one another while⤴ you walk?"*
b	Response	**They stopped in their tracks, looking glum.**
18	Question	**One of them named Cleopas answered him,** *"Are you the only stranger in Jerusalem who does not know what has⤴ happened there during these days?"*
19a	Question	**He said to them,** *"What things?"*
b	Recitation of events	**They responded,** *"The things concerning Jesus of Nazareth,* *who was a prophet mighty in deed and word⤴* *before God and all the people,*
20		*and how our chief priests and rulers both handed him over to be⤴* *condemned to death and* *crucified him.*
21a	Statement of hopes	*We were hoping that he was the one who was about to redeem Israel.*
b	Time reference	*Whereas in addition to these things, it is the third day since these things⤴ took place.*
22	Recitation of events	*Moreover, some of the women from our group astounded us.*

Continued on next page.

Continued from previous page.

23		When they were at the tomb early in the morning and

When they were at the tomb early in the morning and
                        did not find his body,
they came [back] and said they had seen a vision of angels
                                        who said that he↺
                                                was living.

24   *Certain ones of those with us went back to the tomb and*
                                found it just as the women had said,
            but they did not see him."

25   Rebuke   **He said to them,**
                "O foolish and slow of heart to believe in all that the prophets have spoken.
26   Question   *Was it not necessary for the Christ to   suffer these things and*
                                        enter into his glory?"

27   Interpretation of   Then, beginning with Moses and from all of the prophets,
     Scripture   **he interpreted for them the things concerning himself in all the Scriptures.**
28a Circumstance   **They drew near to the village where they had been headed,**
  b   **and he made as if he were going farther.**
29a Offer of hospitality   **But they prevailed upon him, saying,**
                "Stay with us,
                    because it is afternoon and the sunset approaches."

  b   **And he went in to stay with them.**

30   Meal   It happened while he reclined at table with them,
                   he took bread,
                        blessed it, and

                            breaking it
                        gave it to them.

31a Recognition   **Their eyes were opened,**
                      and they recognized him.
  b   Disappearance of Jesus   **And he vanished from their sight.**

32   Recognition   **They said to one another,**
                "Were our hearts not burning within us
                            as he spoke to us on the way
                            as he opened the Scriptures to us?"

33a Travel notice   **They rose up at that same hour and**
                      returned to Jerusalem and
  b   Gathering of community   **found the Eleven and those with them gathered together**
34   Announcement   **who were saying,**
                        "Truly, the Lord has been raised and appeared to Simon!"

35   Recitation of events   **They related the things that had happened on the road and**
                      how he was made known to them in the breaking of bread.

Structure and Literary Form

The structure fits a chiastic pattern:

A Journey from Jerusalem (24:13 – 14)
>   B Closed eyes (24:15 – 17)
>>   C Explanation without understanding (24:18 – 24)
>>>   D Suffering and glory (24:25 – 26)
>>   C´ Explanation with understanding (24:27)
>   B´ Opened eyes (24:28 – 32)
A´ Return to Jerusalem (24:33 – 35)

Exegetical Outline

→ **I. Setting of the encounter (24:13 – 16)**
II. Dialogue with Jesus on the road (24:17 – 27)
>   A. Jesus' query of his fellow travelers (24:17)
>   B. Recounting the facts of what had happened (24:18 – 24)
>   C. Interpretation of the facts from Scripture (24:25 – 27)

III. Hospitality in a meal (28:28 – 32)
>   A. Invitation to stay with them (24:28 – 29)
>   B. Recognition of Jesus through the fellowship meal (24:30 – 31)
>   C. Reflection on their experience (24:32)

IV. Sharing the experience with the gathered community (28:33 – 35)

Explanation of the Text

24:13 Behold, two of them were going the same day to a village by name of Emmaus sixty stadia from Jerusalem (καὶ ἰδοὺ δύο ἐξ αὐτῶν ἐν αὐτῇ τῇ ἡμέρᾳ ἦσαν πορευόμενοι εἰς κώμην ἀπέχουσαν σταδίους ἑξήκοντα ἀπὸ Ἰερουσαλήμ, ἧ ὄνομα Ἐμμαοῦς). The "two of them" who depart from Jerusalem presumably belong to "the rest" mentioned in 24:9. The reader is not told why they are traveling to Emmaus.[2] Since they identify Jesus as a "stranger" (24:18), they may be locals

2. While it is uncertain precisely where Emmaus is, Dillon (*From Eye-Witnesses to Ministers of the Word*, 86) argues that it is located in the environs of Jerusalem, "the locale of the paschal happenings at sacred history's focal point and the geographical symbol of its fulfillment-phase." Jesus is put to death in Jerusalem by divine necessity (Luke 13:33; 18:31; Acts 13:27); after he is raised by God, he appears in Jerusalem and its surroundings; and the disciples' witness will radiate from there.

A "stadion" (στάδιον) is 625 Roman feet (607 feet), and 60 stadia equal about seven miles. A textual variant reads 160 stadia, around nineteen miles. If the shorter distance is the correct reading, then a later scribe likely identified this Emmaus with Amwas, the Emmaus of 1 Macc 3:40, and added an extra hundred stadia as a correction. If the longer distance is original, the variant could be the result of a scribe adjusting the distance to something that is more likely to be walked in a day. Josephus (*J.W.* 7.6.6 §217) identifies the village of Ammaous as only thirty stadia from Jerusalem. If that is their destination, Luke's sixty stadia may refer to the round-trip distance.

now returning home.[3] Their departure from the city at the first opportunity, when the Sabbath is over, hints that the community of disciples is in danger of collapsing because of bitter disappointment, grief, and confusion. What starts out, however, "as a journey of despair away from Jerusalem … ends in a journey of joy back to Jerusalem."[4]

24:14–15 And they were conversing with one another concerning all the things that had happened. It happened while they were conversing and disputing, Jesus himself drew near and began to go along with them (καὶ αὐτοὶ ὡμίλουν πρὸς ἀλλήλους περὶ πάντων τῶν συμβεβηκότων τούτων. καὶ ἐγένετο ἐν τῷ ὁμιλεῖν αὐτοὺς καὶ συζητεῖν καὶ αὐτὸς Ἰησοῦς ἐγγίσας συνεπορεύετο αὐτοῖς). The two travelers try to digest what happened to Jesus as they walk, presumably asking themselves, "Where did things go so wrong?" The verb "disputing" (συζητεῖν) suggests that "Cleopas and his companion were not walking meditatively, on an Easter outing … but passionately discussing the events of Good Friday."[5] Jesus directly intercedes to clarify what has happened and to prevent the dissolution of his disciples' faith.

24:16 Their eyes were seized so as not to recognize him (οἱ δὲ ὀφθαλμοὶ αὐτῶν ἐκρατοῦντο τοῦ μὴ ἐπιγνῶναι αὐτόν). The disciples are walking both in a fog of doubt and in the presence of the risen Messiah at the same time. For Greco-Roman readers familiar with stories where gods take on human form and remain incognito, it would not be surprising for the resurrected Jesus to be temporarily unrecognizable.[6] But for Luke, their lack of recognition has theological significance. Their eyes were "seized" (ἐκρατοῦντο) may refer to their faithless frame of mind. Plevnik contends it refers to "their incomprehension of the mystery of Jesus who as the Christ had to pass through suffering 'all these things' to glory."[7]

The passive voice of the verb, however, suggests that the blindness is divinely imposed. Robinson argues that Luke takes for granted "the continuity between the risen and the earthly body of Jesus: Jesus looked the same after the Resurrection as he had done before and only a supernatural interposition could have prevented them from recognizing his features."[8] The eyes of these two people have been deliberately kept from recognizing Jesus until after the interpretation of the Scripture and their meal with him.

This blinding, however, does not remove their culpability. Their blocked vision continues a state that existed before Jesus' death. When Jesus warned his disciples that he would be betrayed into the hands of men, mocked and spat upon, flogged, and killed, as the prophets had written about the Son of Man (9:44–45; 18:31–34), the meaning of what he said "was hidden from them" (9:45; 18:34).[9] Their eyes will become unblocked only after they perceive that Jesus' death relates to God's plan still hidden to them in the Scriptures. Their bedimmed eyes will see when they understand that it was necessary for the Christ to suffer and then to enter his glory (24:26).

3. The verb form used in v. 18 (παροικεῖς) means "to dwell temporarily," "to sojourn."

4. Scobie, "A Canonical Approach to Interpreting Luke," 336.

5. Arnold Ehrhardt, "The Disciples of Emmaus," *NTS* 10 (1963–64): 186. So also Marshall, *The Gospel of Luke*, 893; Fitzmyer, *Luke*, 2:1563; and Stein, *Luke*, 610. Nolland, *Luke*, 3:1201, argues that this is a satanic blinding, which must be overcome by the victorious Jesus, but Satan makes no appearances in the resurrection narratives.

6. Nolland, *Luke*, 3:1201.

7. Joseph Plevnik, "The Eyewitnesses of the Risen Jesus in Luke 24," *CBQ* 49 (1987): 96.

8. B. P. Robinson, "The Place of the Emmaus Story in Luke-Acts," *NTS* 30 (1984): 484.

9. The verbs are perfect periphrastics (ἦν παρακεκαλυμμένον, 9:45; ἦν … κεκρυμμένον, 18:34).

24:17 He said to them, "What are these words that you are exchanging with one another while you walk?" They stopped in their tracks, looking glum (εἶπεν δὲ πρὸς αὐτούς· τίνες οἱ λόγοι οὗτοι οὓς ἀντιβάλλετε πρὸς ἀλλήλους περιπατοῦντες; καὶ ἐστάθησαν σκυθρωποί). Rather than appearing to large crowds, Jesus appears to these lone travelers and intrudes on their conversation with a leading question. The disciples are drowning in their own sorrows, bitter disappointment, and arguments. They supposed Jesus to be dead, but the women have reported that angels at the tomb said he was not! They also do not remember Jesus' words (24:6 – 7) and dismiss the women's report as "utter nonsense" (24:11). Having given up hope, they turn their backs on Jerusalem and head home dejected. They look like the gloomy-faced (σκυθρωποί) Pharisees when they are fasting (Matt 6:16) and take little notice of the fellow traveler until he speaks.

24:18 One of them named Cleopas answered him, "Are you the only stranger in Jerusalem who does not know what has happened there during these days?" (ἀποκριθεὶς δὲ εἷς ὀνόματι Κλεοπᾶς εἶπεν πρὸς αὐτόν· σὺ μόνος παροικεῖς Ἰερουσαλὴμ καὶ οὐκ ἔγνως τὰ γενόμενα ἐν αὐτῇ ἐν ταῖς ἡμέραις ταύταις;). Cleopas is the only one named and is mentioned only here in the Synoptic tradition.[10] Bauckham contends that Luke singles him out, as he did Joanna in the previous incident, because he is the source of this tradition.[11]

Cleopas's dejection surfaces in his acerbic response as he accuses this traveling companion of being a clueless outsider who missed what has just taken place in Jerusalem. The scene drips with irony. The readers get to see what human blindness looks like from God's perspective. They recognize that Jesus not only knows what has happened,

since everything has revolved around him; he is the only one in Jerusalem who knows its divine, eternal significance. Jesus' visit to Jerusalem was a divine "visitation," and the Jerusalem residents were the ones who were clueless (19:44).

24:19 He said to them, "What things?" They responded, "The things concerning Jesus of Nazareth, who was a prophet mighty in deed and word before God and all the people" (καὶ εἶπεν αὐτοῖς· ποῖα; οἱ δὲ εἶπαν αὐτῷ· τὰ περὶ Ἰησοῦ τοῦ Ναζαρηνοῦ, ὃς ἐγένετο ἀνὴρ προφήτης δυνατὸς ἐν ἔργῳ καὶ λόγῳ ἐναντίον τοῦ θεοῦ καὶ παντὸς τοῦ λαοῦ). Jesus' probing exposes the ignorance of the two about Jesus' true identity and how God's purposes were being worked out through his life and death. By identifying him as a prophet mighty in deed, like Moses (Acts 7:22), these two travelers reveal that their partial insight into Jesus is no better than that of the crowds who lauded him after he raised the widow's son in Nain: "A great prophet has been raised among us!" (7:16).

This acclamation, while true, misses the mark. It is not an adequate christological category for identifying who the resurrected Jesus is. These disciples apparently believe that the divine power that had been working in him had somehow fizzled (see 4:14, 36; 5:17; 6:19; 8:46; 10:13) so that he suffered the fate of all prophets who venture near Jerusalem (13:34). They recognize that Jesus was mighty in word (which refers to the content of his preaching, not his charismatic delivery), but they do not remember that his words prophesied his rejection, suffering, death, and resurrection.

24:20 And how our chief priests and rulers both handed him over to be condemned to death and crucified him (ὅπως τε παρέδωκαν αὐτὸν οἱ ἀρχιερεῖς καὶ οἱ ἄρχοντες ἡμῶν εἰς κρίμα

10. His name is the shortened form of Kleopatros, the masculine form of Cleopatra.

11. Bauckham, *Gospel Women*, 193.

θανάτου καὶ ἐσταύρωσαν αὐτόν). The men are like the women at the tomb, who needed to be prompted to remember what Jesus said in Galilee, "It is necessary for the Son of Man to be handed over to the hands of sinners and to be crucified, and on the third day to rise again" (24:6 – 7). Because of their loss of memory, they assume that the worst has happened. Their very own leaders betrayed him, and God's justice has not prevailed. What "consolation of Israel" (2:25) could come from a prophet crucified by the Romans and now dead and buried? The emphasis on Jesus' crucifixion is crucial. Jesus will draw the attention of these travelers to his suffering and entering into glory (24:26) as the decisive and pivotal moment in God's plan.[12]

24:21 We were hoping that he was the one who was about to redeem Israel. Whereas in addition to these things, it is the third day since these things took place (ἡμεῖς δὲ ἠλπίζομεν ὅτι αὐτός ἐστιν ὁ μέλλων λυτροῦσθαι τὸν Ἰσραήλ· ἀλλά γε καὶ σὺν πᾶσιν τούτοις τρίτην ταύτην ἡμέραν ἄγει ἀφ' οὗ ταῦτα ἐγένετο). The "third day" serves as a reminder to the reader that Jesus had previously predicted that he would be raised on the third day (9:22; 18:33; cf. 13:32). Apparently, "the third day" does not ring any bells for the travelers (24:6 – 8). With its arrival, the last ray of expectancy has faded.

"We were hoping" (ἠλπίζομεν, imperfect tense) recalls the expectancy of redemption in the infancy narratives. The recent history of Israel had been depressing as the nation for several centuries was trampled by various pagan oppressors. Israel had physically returned from Babylonian exile, but many believed that they remained in exile in their own land. Jesus offered them some hope that God's new order would soon arrive to set things

right. These disciples may have been among those who thought that when Jesus was about to enter Jerusalem, the reign of God was to appear immediately (19:11). They anticipated that he was "about to redeem Israel" (ὁ μέλλων λυτροῦσθαι τὸν Ἰσραήλ; see 1:68; 2:38), which they probably understood in terms of messianic liberation from Israel's enemies (1:71, 74). Their apocalyptic expectations embraced hopes for a national "ruler and deliverer" (see Acts 7:35), and these false hopes have also blinded them.

Such nationalistic fantasies were engraved on the coins minted during the briefly successful third revolt against Rome in AD 132 – 135 led by Simon Bar Kokhba. They had these inscriptions: (1) "Year One of the Redemption of Israel"; (2) "Year Two of the Freedom of Israel." This yearning from freedom appears as a lingering problem, since it resurfaces in Acts 1:6. Apparently, these disciples now believe that they have fallen victim to another failed prophet whose promises of deliverance were thwarted by the Romans (Acts 5:36 – 37).

"Redemption" must be denationalized and redefined through the interpretation of Scripture to mean spiritual redemption. Ultimate redemption awaits the end of time (21:28). What these disciples do not realize, which the reader does, is that the supposed ruin of all their hopes is actually their fulfillment. Israel will be redeemed, as the continuation of the story in Acts makes clear (Acts 2:30 – 36; 13:22 – 23; 28:20), but there will be a divided response. Some in Israel will reject the redemption offered by God through Jesus and be cut off from the people. Some who will accept it will be Gentiles (24:47; Acts 13:46 – 47; 28:28), and they will be grafted in to the people.

24:22 – 24 Moreover, some of the women from our group astounded us. When they were at the

tomb early in the morning and did not find his body, they came [back] and said they had seen a vision of angels who said that he was living. Certain ones of those with us went back to the tomb and found it just as the women had said, but they did not see him (ἀλλὰ καὶ γυναῖκές τινες ἐξ ἡμῶν ἐξέστησαν ἡμᾶς, γενόμεναι ὀρθριναὶ ἐπὶ τὸ μνημεῖον καὶ μὴ εὑροῦσαι τὸ σῶμα αὐτοῦ ἦλθον λέγουσαι καὶ ὀπτασίαν ἀγγέλων ἑωρακέναι, οἳ λέγουσιν αὐτὸν ζῆν. καὶ ἀπῆλθόν τινες τῶν σὺν ἡμῖν ἐπὶ τὸ μνημεῖον, καὶ εὗρον οὕτως καθὼς καὶ αἱ γυναῖκες εἶπον, αὐτὸν δὲ οὐκ εἶδον).

The only flicker of hope was the reported vision of angels by some women. They dismiss this astounding report as too fantastic. Since no one actually saw Jesus, these disciples remain distraught. The reports give ambiguous evidence for a pattern that they are not able to piece together in any meaningful way. Something more is required for them to believe. Stein argues, "By magnifying the disciples' incredulity, Luke magnified the miracle."[13] I would argue that their incredulity reveals that they need a word of interpretation before the reported facts can come to mean anything. As in the infancy narrative, heaven must intervene to reveal to befuddled humans what it all signifies. For these disciples, the heavenly interpreter is the resurrected Jesus himself, not an angel.

The details they recount of what happened confirm that the tomb was empty. The women found the tomb empty and other disciples discovered that it was true. But an empty tomb does not bring them to faith in the resurrection. It can lend itself to a variety of explanations.

24:25 He said to them, "O foolish and slow of heart to believe in all that the prophets have spoken" (καὶ αὐτὸς εἶπεν πρὸς αὐτούς· ὦ ἀνόητοι καὶ βραδεῖς τῇ καρδίᾳ τοῦ πιστεύειν ἐπὶ πᾶσιν

οἷς ἐλάλησαν οἱ προφῆται). "Slow of heart" (βραδεῖς τῇ καρδίᾳ) does not mean that they are mentally slow. As Green correctly points out, the phrase "calls attention to their failure to orient themselves fully around Jesus' teaching…. 'Heart' refers here as in the LXX to the inner commitments, the dispositions and attitudes, of a person that determine his or her life."[14] The inability of these two to believe is a moral failure, not an intellectual failure (see Hab 1:5; Acts 13:41).[15]

24:26 "Was it not necessary for the Christ to suffer these things and enter into his glory?" (οὐχὶ ταῦτα ἔδει παθεῖν τὸν Χριστὸν καὶ εἰσελθεῖν εἰς τὴν δόξαν αὐτοῦ;). The question is phrased in Greek to expect the answer "yes," but it is the last thing these disciples would ever conclude. What was to them a devastating disappointment that dashed their private hopes actually accomplished God's saving purposes. That the Christ must suffer becomes the hermeneutical key for understanding all Scripture and all that happened to Jesus (see Acts 17:3; 1 Pet 1:11). When Jesus referred to his suffering (9:22, 44; 17:24 – 25; 18:31 – 33; 22:22; 24:7), "he referred to himself not as the Messiah but as the mysterious Son of Man … or as the rejected prophet (13:33)."[16] Here, it becomes clear that "the Son of Man" is "the Christ," and "the Christ" is Jesus. Entering into glory marks God's overturning humankind's verdict on Jesus and his humiliation and the overthrow of the power of darkness.

24:27 Then, beginning with Moses and from all of the prophets, he interpreted for them the things concerning himself in all the Scriptures (καὶ ἀρξάμενος ἀπὸ Μωϋσέως καὶ ἀπὸ πάντων τῶν προφητῶν διερμήνευσεν αὐτοῖς ἐν πάσαις ταῖς γραφαῖς τὰ περὶ ἑαυτοῦ). Luke outlines the

13. Stein, *Luke*, 606.
14. Green, *The Gospel of Luke*, 848.
15. Johnson, *The Gospel of Luke*, 395.
16. Heil, *The Meal Scenes in Luke-Acts*, 204.

second step toward accepting the reality of Jesus' resurrection: understanding the Scriptures. Jesus does not overwhelm these two disciples by some spectacular revelation of himself that imposes faith on them. Instead, he interprets the Scriptures for them. They need to hear the Word of God to clear up the confusion of their own "words" (24:17). The parable of the rich man and Lazarus scores the point that if persons do not believe Moses and the prophets, they will not believe if someone is raised from the dead (16:29 – 31).

The gospel begins by recalling the promises to Israel in Scripture. Jesus began his ministry by citing Scripture and saying that it was fulfilled in him (4:16 – 21), and he now ends by showing how his ministry and death have fulfilled Scripture. In the narrative, Jesus has been shown to be a faithful interpreter of Scripture from the time he was twelve years old (2:46 – 47). Here he gives a captivating Bible study to which we are not privy. For Luke, "the Scriptures not only must 'open the mind' of the marveling disciples, but also the Scriptures in turn are themselves 'opened' by the living crucified one who is 'recalled to the disciples' presence 'in the breaking of the bread.'"[17] Luke does not identify any specific passages as proof texts. The whole narrative of God's dealings with Israel unlocks God's purposes that culminate in Jesus' crucifixion and resurrection.

24:28 – 29 They drew near to the village where they were headed, and he made as if he were going farther. But they prevailed upon him, saying, "Stay with us, because it is afternoon and the sunset approaches." And he went in to stay with them (καὶ ἤγγισαν εἰς τὴν κώμην οὗ ἐπορεύοντο,

καὶ αὐτὸς προσεποιήσατο πορρώτερον πορεύεσθαι. καὶ παρεβιάσαντο αὐτὸν λέγοντες· μεῖνον μεθ' ἡμῶν, ὅτι πρὸς ἑσπέραν ἐστὶν καὶ κέκλικεν ἤδη ἡ ἡμέρα. καὶ εἰσῆλθεν τοῦ μεῖναι σὺν αὐτοῖς).

Jesus does not simply pretend to go on down the road. He would have left them had they not prevailed on him to stay and accept their hospitality (see Acts 16:15; cf. Gen 19:2 – 3). It makes clear that "only those who desire his company will come to further realization of his identity."[18] The followers crave to hear more and emphatically invite him to stay with them (see Rev 3:20). Caring for the needs of this stranger with meal fellowship results in these men being changed profoundly by him (see Heb 13:2).

The phrase "it is afternoon and the sunset approaches" (πρὸς ἑσπέραν ἐστὶν καὶ κέκλικεν ἤδη ἡ ἡμέρα) is usually translated "it is getting toward evening, and the day is now nearly over" (NASB). My paraphrase attempts to avoid a potential misunderstanding about the meaning of "evening." Denaux demonstrates that the word "evening" was used in Jewish literature (LXX, Jewish Hellenistic authors, and later rabbinic writings) to refer to the period after noon, when the sun begins its decline and moves toward sunset.[19] Western readers, however, tend to understand "evening" as the time nearest to or after sunset. Denaux argues that this meal occurs around 3:00 p.m., the ninth hour, and the timing reflects Luke's allusive symbolism. It means that Jesus first appeared to these disciples at noonday, "the moment the sun is at its zenith, which would fit the biblical motif of God revealing his glory at this moment (cp. Gen 18; Acts 8, 26 – 40; 22,1 – 21; 26,1 – 23; Jn 4,1 – 45)."[20]

---

17. David P. Moessner, ""Reading Luke's Gospel as Ancient Hellenistic Narrative," 149.

18. Danker, *Jesus and the New Age*, 394.

19. Adelbert Denaux, "The Meaning of the Double Expression of Time in Luke 24, 29," in *Miracles and Imagery in Luke*

and John: Festschrift Ulrich Busse (BETL 218; ed. J. Verheyden, G. Van Belle, and J. G. Van der Watt; Leuven: Peeters, 2008), 67 – 88.

20. Ibid., 87.

The meal coincides with the evening sacrifice for the forgiveness of the sins of the people, with which the gospel narrative opened as Zechariah conducted the incense portion (1:8 – 23), and when Jesus died (23:44 – 46). The disciples "at that same hour" can travel back to Jerusalem and arrive before sunset, before the next day begins according to Hebrew reckoning. Jesus then appears to the gathered band. This understanding of the timing means that all of Jesus' appearances recorded in the gospel occur on the third day, the resurrection day.

24:30 It happened while he reclined at table with them, he took bread, blessed it, and breaking it gave it to them (καὶ ἐγένετο ἐν τῷ κατακλιθῆναι αὐτὸν μετ᾽ αὐτῶν λαβὼν τὸν ἄρτον εὐλόγησεν καὶ κλάσας ἐπεδίδου αὐτοῖς). In a role reversal, Jesus moves from guest to host by taking the bread, blessing it, breaking it, and giving it to them. Is this a reference to the Eucharist as so many interpreters assume? That supposition is unlikely for the following reasons. (1) Luke specifies that only the apostles were present at Jesus' Last Supper (22:14; presumably the Twelve, 22:30). These disciples are not identified as members of the Twelve and were not present at the Last Supper. Nothing would trigger some recognition of what Jesus did at that time.

(2) Why would this meal with these two disciples be intended to recall the Last Supper when the meal with the Eleven, who were present at that meal, does not (24:41 – 43)?

(3) Luke mentions the cup twice at the Last Supper (22:17, 20) but mentions only the breaking of bread here. The blessing and breaking of bread was common to every meal.

(4) Jesus speaks no words of interpretation about the bread.

(5) Luke understands that the revelation occurred to the disciples at Emmaus *in the course of the breaking of bread*, which is language for sharing a meal with them (Acts 2:42, 46). It is not that Jesus broke the bread in a distinctive way or uttered a distinctive prayer. It is not a single action by Jesus or their partaking the bread that opens their eyes.

While this meal may not hark back to the Last Supper, it is also not an ordinary meal, since no meals with Jesus were ordinary meals.[21] The meal has closer parallels to the miraculous feeding of the five thousand (9:12 – 17). The phrase that "the sunset approaches" (or "the day was nearly over") appears also in 9:12 when the disciples asked Jesus to send away the famished crowds. The same verb is used to describe the crowds reclining to eat (9:14 – 15) as is used for Jesus reclining (κατακλιθῆναι) with these disciples. Jesus' action of taking bread, blessing it, breaking it, and giving it to his companions appears in 9:16. The verb for giving the bread (ἐπεδίδου) is imperfect here, as it is in 9:16, whereas in the Last Supper Luke uses the aorist tense (ἔδωκεν; 22:19).

The miraculous meal with the five thousand appears sandwiched between questions about Jesus' identity (9:7 – 9, 18 – 20) and Jesus' first notice of his coming death and resurrection then follow (9:21 – 27). That miracle also led to the recognition of Jesus as the Christ (9:20). The Last Supper, by contrast, was not revelatory; the feeding of the five thousand was. Bock underscores the point:

> The table was a place where Jesus was heard and where his presence came across most intimately. This fact suggests that Jesus reveals himself in the midst of the basic moments of life. He is at home in the midst of our everyday activity.[22]

The meal after Jesus' exposition of the Scriptures on the road reveals that the proclamation

---

21. Robinson, "The Place of the Emmaus Story in Luke-Acts," 492.

22. Bock, *Luke* (NIVAC), 616.

of the Word is necessary for understanding, but it alone does not bring understanding. Understanding comes in the meal fellowship of the community and in welcoming and feeding strangers.[23] Meal fellowship alone also is insufficient. It needs to be accompanied by instruction related to Jesus.[24] Gillman notes: "The Emmaus meal together with the feeding of the eleven readily serves as a powerful symbol for the restored fellowship between Jesus and his disciples, a fellowship broken by Jesus' betrayal, denial and death, by the initial disbelief of the apostles and by the temporary 'blindness' of the Emmaus disciples."[25]

24:31 Their eyes were opened, and they recognized him. And he vanished from their sight (αὐτῶν δὲ διηνοίχθησαν οἱ ὀφθαλμοὶ καὶ ἐπέγνωσαν αὐτόν· καὶ αὐτὸς ἄφαντος ἐγένετο ἀπ᾽ αὐτῶν). Caring for the needs of the stranger leads to their eyes being opened (διηνοίχθησαν). This verb is in the passive voice, which again implies divine action (cf. 24:16). It means that "God is the revealer of the risen Christ."[26]

It is startling, however, that the moment they recognize Jesus he suddenly vanishes. Jesus' disappearance as soon as he is recognized may perplex the modern reader, but it does not confound the disciples. Ancient readers would have been more accustomed to divine beings "vanishing" (2 Macc 3:34). A similar vanishing act happened when the Spirit of the Lord snatched Philip away after the Ethiopian eunuch's baptism (Acts 8:39), and it did not mean that Philip was some diaphanous spirit. Jesus does not melt into thin air because he is an apparitional phantom. Disappearing from sight makes clear that his resurrection does not entail his continuing physical presence. He must enter into his glory, but believers can experience his presence through the study of Scripture and their fellowship meals that welcome strangers.

24:32 They said to one another, "Were our hearts not burning within us as he spoke to us on the way as he opened the Scriptures to us?" (καὶ εἶπαν πρὸς ἀλλήλους· οὐχὶ ἡ καρδία ἡμῶν καιομένη ἦν [ἐν ἡμῖν] ὡς ἐλάλει ἡμῖν ἐν τῇ ὁδῷ, ὡς διήνοιγεν ἡμῖν τὰς γραφάς;). Jesus has taught, exhorted, warned, and chastised his followers throughout the gospel, but they were not good at learning things at the time, let alone in advance. They seem to learn only in retrospect, and it is his teaching that they remember from this encounter (see 24:6 – 8). Their hearts change from being "slow" (24:25) to "burning," and they realize that their eyes had been closed, that they were blinded by false hopes, and that Jesus does bring the promised redemption of Israel. The burning of their hearts is only a foretaste of what is to come when the Holy Spirit is poured out on the disciples as tongues of fire (Acts 2:3).[27]

24:33 – 34 They rose up at that same hour and returned to Jerusalem and found the Eleven and those with them gathered together who were saying, "Truly, the Lord has been raised and appeared to Simon!" (καὶ ἀναστάντες αὐτῇ τῇ ὥρᾳ ὑπέστρεψαν εἰς Ἰερουσαλὴμ καὶ εὗρον ἠθροισμένους τοὺς ἕνδεκα καὶ τοὺς σὺν αὐτοῖς λέγοντας ὅτι ὄντως ἠγέρθη ὁ κύριος καὶ ὤφθη Σίμωνι). The disciples do not bask in the glories of their personal experience but join the community to share it. The words "at the same hour" mean they are able to return to Jerusalem before sunset

23. Poon, "Superabundant Table Fellowship," 230.

24. Dillon, *From Eye-Witnesses to Ministers of the Word*, 105.

25. Gillman, "The Emmaus Story in Luke-Acts Revisited," 169.

26. Liefeld and Pao, "Luke," 348.

27. The vocabulary differs, but the fiery passion that the psalmist and Jeremiah felt is similar (Ps 39:3; Jer 20:9).

and the beginning of the new day in Jewish time reckoning. What is important for Luke is that all of the resurrection appearances occur on the same day. The community of the Eleven, plus others, is "gathered together" (ἠθροισμένους). The passive voice and perfect tense of this verb may suggest that God has joined them together with permanent results.

The journey to Emmaus and back to Jerusalem mirrors the journey motif that dominates Luke. According to Robinson: "Whatever else he is doing in the Emmaus story, Luke is surely using the journey image of the Christian life, and indicating how the latter ought to be viewed — not as a solitary, melancholy progress, but as a following of Christ, in full assurance that he has not abandoned his own but will lead them through grief to glory."[28] The followers first moved away from where all the distressing action occurred and where danger still lay. But then they go back there after they encounter Christ on the way, reflect on the Scriptures, and share a meal with him. No longer are they racked by anxiety, confusion, and fear. Now they can face the dangers with resolve and with the assurance that God raised Jesus from the dead.

The table fellowship that is interrupted by Jesus' physical death can continue by virtue of his resurrection. Jesus, who is now physically absent, becomes spiritually present among the community of believers through the breaking of bread. Reflection on Jesus' words and the Scriptures and the meal fellowship can renew believers' resolve and confidence in the world in which they live.

What is surprising is that before the Emmaus companions speak, the gathered community reports news of Jesus' appearance to Simon. The two followers learn that they are not the only ones to have seen the risen Jesus. Luke does not narrate the appearance to Simon (see 1 Cor 15:3 – 5) and does not explain what happened that leads the group to accept Simon's account after they had dismissed the women's evidence. As the centurion declared that Jesus was "really" (ὄντως) righteous, so the disciples now declare that Jesus is "truly" (ὄντως) risen and is "the Lord." The two confessions are joined together in Peter's preaching in Acts 3:14 – 15.[29]

23:35 They related the things that had happened on the road and how he was made known to them in the breaking of bread (καὶ αὐτοὶ ἐξηγοῦντο τὰ ἐν τῇ ὁδῷ καὶ ὡς ἐγνώσθη αὐτοῖς ἐν τῇ κλάσει τοῦ ἄρτου). The opened eyes and burning hearts lead to opened mouths that proclaim the resurrection. The revelation about Jesus' resurrection does not come from extraordinary experiences but from the explication of Scripture and a meal.

28. Robinson, "The Place of the Emmaus Story in Luke-Acts," 482.

29. Dillon, *From Eye-Witnesses to Ministers of the Word*, 103.

Theology in Application

1. Experiencing the Resurrection of Jesus

The Emmaus disciples can supply the facts up to the crucifixion. Jesus from Nazareth was a prophet mighty in deed and word before God and the people (like Moses in Acts 7:22). He was betrayed to the chief priests and rulers, condemned to death, and crucified, and unconfirmed rumors have arisen about an empty tomb and a vision of angels.

A prophet mighty in deed and word inadequately expresses who Jesus is. If John is more than a prophet (7:26), Jesus is much more. Now he is the resurrected Lord. These disciples are unable to see that reality because their personal aspirations and expectations have prevented them from seeing past the scandal of the crucifixion. Cleopas unwittingly voices the basic obstacle to the belief in the women's report that Jesus had been raised: "We were hoping that he was the one who was about to redeem Israel," but he was "handed ... over to be condemned to death and [they] crucified him." Because they could not conceive of a Messiah crucified, dead, and buried, they could not accept that he had been raised by God, nor could they recognize him when they met him on the road. The problem is the scandal of the crucifixion.

The hope of the resurrection was central to the hope of Israel (Acts 23:6 – 9; 24:15, 21; 26:8), but these disciples did not anticipate Jesus' resurrection because their hopes were more mundane. They wanted more immediate gratification, a miraculous liberation of Israel now, without all the pain and suffering. Recognizing Jesus as the resurrected Christ required recognizing that Jesus had to die according to God's plan. God "brings to realization his salvific plan" through Jesus' suffering and death.[30] The hecklers' taunts ironically dramatized that he saved others through his death (23:35, 37, 39), and his teaching here makes clear that he enters into God's glory through his death. Entering into glory defines what it means for Jesus to have been raised. His status has changed from one derided and humiliated on the cross to one who is exalted in glory. He has become "the cornerstone" (20:17) and is "seated at the right hand of the power of God" (22:69) as Lord (Acts 2:36).

For these disciples, the report of an empty tomb and encounters with angels are inadequate to convey the reality and significance of the resurrection. Jesus' word alone rescues these travelers from their despair and leads them to see the truth by providing the scriptural basis for his suffering and how it relates to his resurrection to glory. The emphasis on the necessity of his death reappears: "Was it not necessary...?" (2:49; 4:43; 9:22; 17:25; 19:5; 22:37). The intelligibility of Jesus' death and resurrection depends on understanding Israel's Scriptures so that the mystery of God's working in the world becomes revealed. It is precisely how Mary came to

---

30. Fitzmyer, *Luke the Theologian*, 212.

understand the significance of the conception of Jesus (1:46 – 55). She interpreted what was happening to her in light of Israel's experience of God's power in the past and the promise to Abraham. Luke understands Scripture to be "a promise in search of fulfillment now imminent."[31]

Coleridge argues: "If memory does not come to birth, then the way to understanding and faith is blocked; and if that is so, then there will be no human recognition of God's visitation."[32] Remembering is the only way to interpret enigmatic signs. The idea that eyes were closed and then opened is parallel to what Paul describes in 1 Cor 2:6 – 16. God's wisdom is secret and hidden (1 Cor 2:7) and can only be comprehended through the Spirit of God by those who are spiritual (1 Cor 2:11 – 13). That is why people can read the same Scriptures but their minds remain veiled so that they cannot see the Christ of glory (2 Cor 3:12 – 18).

2. The Witness of the Scriptures

Luke conveys the basic Christian conviction about Jesus' death and resurrection in his narrative account that Paul rehearses in a creedal statement: "that Christ died for our sins *according to the Scriptures*, that he was buried, that he was raised on the third day *according to the Scriptures*" (1 Cor 15:3 – 4, emphasis added). Luke's narrative makes clear that these events can be understood and only understood from Scripture. Jesus' exposition causes the hearts of the Emmaus travelers to burn with dawning understanding. Full recognition occurs in the meal.

Many point out how the story of the Ethiopian eunuch (Acts 8:26 – 40) is a mirror image of this account. As Gillman notes: "The Emmaus companions were discussing the recent events about Jesus; the Ethiopian was reading from the prophet Isaiah. However, neither understood the significance of the matter at hand. In both cases, enlightenment comes from an unexpected stranger who joins the travelers."[33] The Emmaus disciples knew the events but did not know how to interpret them in light of the Scriptures or how they fulfilled "all that the prophets have spoken" (Luke 24:25). The Ethiopian knew the Scriptures but did not know the events to which the text applied (Acts 8:32 – 34).

Both accounts clarify that the Scriptures are to be interpreted in light of the good news of Jesus and that what happened to Jesus can be understood only in light of the Scriptures. The Scriptures help interpret the believers' reality and bring their hopes in line with God's wider plan. Philip represents disciples who have come to understand the Scriptures and their connections to what happened to Jesus and who now serve as interpreters for others. This development follows a pattern established in the infancy narrative. The strange events that are about to happen or have happened

31. Coleridge, *The Birth of the Lukan Narrative*, 94.
32. Ibid., 95.
33. Gillman, "The Emmaus Story in Luke-Acts Revisited," 169 – 70.

require a heavenly messenger to interpret them. Memory of the Scriptures is also required, and it pervades the prophecy and praise of Elizabeth, Mary, and Zechariah. Then, humble shepherds become the interpreters of what it means even to the mother of Jesus (2:16 – 20). The pattern is this:

1. Enigmatic events occur that humans cannot fathom.
2. Divine intervention makes sense of the events.
3. Scripture sheds light on how God works and what God has promised.
4. Humans become interpreters of the events for others.

Luke does not record Jesus' interpretative words, which presents an irony that the readers see who he is but do not hear what he says. The Emmaus travelers hear what he says but do not see who he is. This silence should provoke the reader to reread the narrative in Luke for clues and to reread the Scriptures looking for Christ. Reading Acts is also vital. One can assume that the Scriptures that Jesus emphasized were the ones the apostles used in their preaching.[34] The statement that Jesus interpreted Scripture to shed light on what it says about himself makes an implicit claim that Scripture points to a future hope that Jesus embodies. As Dillon puts it, "He alone is the definitive revelation of the whole Bible's meaning."[35]

This theological conviction that all Scripture is finally about Jesus is affirmed by the statement in 24:44. While the prophets may address issues that press upon their communities centuries before and mediate the Word of God to their situations, ultimately the Scriptures are about God's salvation drama that points beyond the immediate crises. The divine plan reaches its climax in Christ's death and resurrection, and it will reach its final resolution with Christ's return. The statement also implies that Jesus is the arbiter of its interpretation and how God's plan unfolds. The use of the past tense, "Was it not necessary?" (ἔδει), presents Jesus' suffering on the cross and entrance into glory "as stations on *an appointed course*."[36] The next stations waiting their fulfillment will be the disciples' mission to the world, the return of the Son of Man, the rescue of the elect, and the final judgment. Since the divine plot has been revealed in and by Jesus, his followers can discern where they are in the plot and how they must live.

---

34. This observation comes from correspondence with my editor, Verlyn Verbrugge.

35. Dillon, *From Eye-Witnesses to Ministers of the Word*, 205.
36. Ibid, 139.

Luke 24:36 – 53

Literary Context

Common threads run through the three resurrection appearances on the third day. In all these stories there is initial unbelief. The women were perplexed (24:4). The eleven disciples did not believe the report of the women and dismissed it as an idle tale (24:11). The disciples traveling to Emmaus were astounded but did not believe the report either (24:22 – 25). When Jesus now appears to the gathered disciples, they initially think it is an apparition from the spirit world. Even after Jesus invites them to handle him and see his scars, they are still disbelieving and wondering (24:40 – 41). The response to this disbelief emphasizes the fact that Jesus' suffering and death fulfill the Scriptures as something divinely ordained: "It was necessary" (24:7, 26, 44).

The appearances underscore the fact that the resurrected Jesus is the same one who was with them before in Galilee. He walks and talks with them, eats with them, and can be touched by them. The resurrection is a bodily resurrection. But the final scene emphasizes that Jesus has not simply been raised from the dead; rather, the one who was crucified in humiliation is exalted and ascends to glory to reign from heaven. Knight explains, "For the first readers of Luke, Jesus was the heavenly Lord whose presence was experienced whenever they met for worship. He was not a dead prophet but the living Lord whose installation as a heavenly being is symbolized by the ascension in the Gospel and celebrated in the gathered community."[1]

I have argued that Luke-Acts was intended to be one great work, and the connection of this section to the beginning of Acts should not be overlooked. Zwiep helpfully provides an outline of the macrostructure that shows the interrelationship.[2]

---

1. Knight, *Luke's Gospel*, 6.

2. Zwiep, *The Ascension of the Messiah in Lukan Christology*, 118.

I. The appearance of the risen Lord (Luke 24:36 – 43; Acts 1:1 – 3)

  A. Appearance of the risen Lord (Luke 24:36a)

    B. Proofs of the resurrection (Luke 24:36b – 39, 40 – 43)

      C. Mealtime setting (Luke 24:40 – 43)

  A′. Appearance of the risen Lord (Acts 1:3)

    B′. Proofs of the resurrection (Acts 1:3)

      C′. Mealtime setting (Acts 1:4)

II. The final instructions of the risen Lord (Luke 24:44 – 49; Acts 1:3 – 8)

  A. Fulfillment theme (Luke 24:44 – 46)

    B. Reference to passion and resurrection (Luke 24:46)

      C. Universal mission starting from Jerusalem (Luke 24:47)

        D. Motif of witness (Luke 24:48)

          E. Promise of the Spirit (Luke 24:49a)

            F. Command to stay in Jerusalem (Luke 24:49b)

              G. Empowerment with the Spirit (Luke 24:49c)

    B′. Reference to passion and resurrection (Acts 1:3)

          E′. Promise of the Spirit (Acts 1:4)

            F′. Command to stay in Jerusalem (Acts 1:4)

  A′. Fulfillment theme (Acts 1:5)

      C′. Universal mission starting from Jerusalem (Acts 1:8)

        D′. Motif of witness (Acts 1:8)

              G′. Empowerment with the Spirit (Acts 1:8)

III. The departure of the risen Lord (Luke 24:50 – 53; Acts 1:9 – 14)

  A. Localisation of the event (Luke 24:50)

    B. Action of Jesus (Luke 24:50)

      C. Departure of Jesus (Luke 24:51)

        D. Description of the ascension (Luke 24:51)

          E. The disciples' return to Jerusalem (Luke 24:52)

            F. Localisation (Luke 24:53)

              G. Communal life of worship and prayer (Luke 24:53)

    B′. Action of Jesus (Acts 1:9)

      C′. Departure of Jesus (Acts 1:9)

        D′. Description of the ascension (Acts 1:10 – 11)

          E′. The disciples' return to Jerusalem (Acts 1:12)

            F′. Localisation (Acts 1:13)

              G′. Communal life of worship and prayer (Acts 1:14)

Barrett unveils the significance of this linkage: "In Luke's thought, the end of the story of Jesus is the church; and the story of Jesus is the beginning of the church."[3]

---

3. C. K. Barrett, *Luke the Historian in Recent Study* (Philadelphia: Fortress, 1970), 57.

VII. Jesus' Resurrection and Ascension (23:50 – 24:53)
    A. Jesus Dead and Buried, Raised and Living (23:50 – 24:12)
    B. Resurrection Encounter on the Road to Emmaus (24:13 – 35)
→   **C. Jesus' Appearance to the Disciples and His Ascension (24:36 – 53)**

Main Idea

The community of disciples is restored and blessed through belief in the bodily resurrection of Jesus, understanding from the Scriptures the necessity of a suffering Messiah, and bearing witness to their faith.

Translation

Luke 24:36–53

24:36	Entrance/greeting	As they were speaking about these things,
		he himself stood in their midst and said to them,
		"Peace to you."
37	Fear reaction	**They were terrified and in a state of fear supposing that they were seeing a** ↺ **spirit.**
38	Question	**He said to them,**
		"Why are you troubled
		and why are doubts rising up in your hearts?
39a	Demonstration	*See my hands and my feet!*
		It is I myself!
		Touch me and see!
b	Explanation	*A spirit does not have flesh and bones as you can see that I have."*
40	Demonstration	And after saying this,
		he showed them his hands and feet.
41a	Disbelief	While they were in a state of disbelief from their joy and marveling,
b	Question	**he said to them,**
		"Do you have something here to eat?"
42	Response/action	**They gave him a piece of broiled fish,**
43	Demonstration	and **taking it he ate it before them.**

Continued on next page.

Continued from previous page.

44a	Reminder	**He said to them,**
		"These are my words that I spoke to you while I was still with you,
b	Statement of divine purpose from Scripture	that it is necessary for everything to be fulfilled
		that was written concerning me
		in the law of Moses, ↵
		the Prophets, and the Psalms."

45	Exposition of Scriptures	**Then he opened their minds to understand the Scriptures.**
46	Statement of divine purpose from Scripture	**And he said to them,**
		"Thus it stands written that the Christ should suffer and
		be raised from the dead on the ↵
		third day,

47a	Statement of divine purpose/ implicit command	and that repentance for the forgiveness of sins be ↵
		preached in his name
		to all the nations.

b	Location	Beginning from Jerusalem,
48		you are witnesses of these things.
49a	Promise	And behold, I am sending the promise of my Father upon you.
b	Command	You are to stay in the city
		until you are clothed with power from on high."

50a	Circumstance	**Then he led them out as far as Bethany,**
b	Blessing	and lifting up his hands,
		he blessed them.

51	Ascension	It happened that
		while he was blessing them,
		he parted from them and was being carried up into heaven.

52a	Worship	And when they worshiped him,
b	Circumstance	**they returned to Jerusalem with great joy**
53	Praise	**and were regularly in the temple praising God.**

Structure and Literary Form

This last unit of this gospel includes a farewell resurrection appearance that dispels doubt, a reiteration of the divine necessity of Jesus' suffering that is buttressed by scriptural proof, a commission for the disciples to be witnesses to all the nations, and a departure via an ascension into heaven. It divides into three units. In the first, Jesus appears to his disciples at a meal and proves that he is alive and that his resurrected body and crucified body are one and the same. In the second, he shows that his death and resurrection fulfill Scripture and gives his disciples a commission with the promise of divine power to fulfill it. In the last, he blesses them and is carried up into heaven, and the disciples respond with joy and worship of God.

Exegetical Outline

→ **I. Jesus' appearance to the disciples (24:36 – 43)**

II. Scriptural proof (24:44 – 45)

III. Commission (24:46 – 49)

IV. Ascension (24:50 – 53)

    A. Farewell blessing (24:50)

    B. Ascension (24:51)

    C. Worship (24:52)

    D. Praise in the temple (24:53)

Explanation of the Text

24:36 – 38 As they were speaking about these things, he himself stood in their midst and said to them, "Peace to you." They were terrified and in a state of fear supposing that they were seeing a spirit. He said to them, "Why are you troubled and why are doubts rising up in your hearts?" (ταῦτα δὲ αὐτῶν λαλούντων αὐτὸς ἔστη ἐν μέσῳ αὐτῶν καὶ λέγει αὐτοῖς· εἰρήνη ὑμῖν. πτοηθέντες δὲ καὶ ἔμφοβοι γενόμενοι ἐδόκουν πνεῦμα θεωρεῖν. καὶ εἶπεν αὐτοῖς· τί τεταραγμένοι ἐστέ καὶ διὰ τί διαλογισμοὶ ἀναβαίνουσιν ἐν τῇ καρδίᾳ ὑμῶν;). Jesus has an ethereal body that allows him to appear and disappear, but Luke has no interest in describing with what kind of body he was raised. It is probably because Luke does not know; consequently, neither can we.

Jesus' greeting of "peace to you" (εἰρήνη ὑμῖν) is essentially what he ordered his disciples to say to those who welcomed them on their missionary journey and then to eat whatever they might provide (10:5 – 7). Coming from Jesus, this greeting of peace packs more punch since he has come to guide our feet into the way of peace and actually brings peace to people's lives (1:79; 2:14, 29; 7:50; 8:48; 19:38, 42). But his way of peace is frightening since it requires self-sacrifice and even death.

Luke's gospel begins with a terrified Zechariah confronted by the angel Gabriel (1:12, 18 – 20) and ends with the disciples being terrified by Jesus' divine appearance. Like Zechariah, they must move from fear and doubt to faith and courage. Jesus knows their thoughts and gently rebukes them for their fright.

The disciples think they are seeing a disembodied "spirit."[4] Their doubts have to do with their misunderstanding of "the *corporeal nature* of the resurrection," not that Jesus was raised.[5] The resurrected Jesus is not a vaporous, shadowy

---

4. This fits one of the categories listed in Acts 23:8: "The Sadducees say that there is no resurrection, and that there are neither angels nor spirits, but the Pharisees believe all these things."

5. Brown, *Apostasy and Perseverance in the Theology of Luke*, 79.

apparition. Luke has emphasized that Jesus' body has disappeared from the tomb (24:3, 23), and this account seeks to prove that the resurrected Jesus is fully human, flesh and bones.

24:39 – 40 "See my hands and my feet! It is I myself! Touch me and see! A spirit does not have flesh and bones as you can see that I have." And after saying this, he showed them his hands and feet (ἴδετε τὰς χεῖράς μου καὶ τοὺς πόδας μου ὅτι ἐγώ εἰμι αὐτός· ψηλαφήσατέ με καὶ ἴδετε, ὅτι πνεῦμα σάρκα καὶ ὀστέα οὐκ ἔχει καθὼς ἐμὲ θεωρεῖτε ἔχοντα. καὶ τοῦτο εἰπὼν ἔδειξεν αὐτοῖς τὰς χεῖρας καὶ τοὺς πόδας). Luke's account seeks to show that Jesus' resurrection was a bodily resurrection (see 1 Cor 15). Jesus is not a specter, and the disciples do not experience a mirage. Touching him proves that he is not an airy ghost who can find no repose because of his violent death. Paul distinguishes the body of flesh and bones from the resurrection body, which is a spiritual body (1 Cor 15:44), but Luke's emphasis is that the Jesus who was with the disciples in Galilee and nailed to a cross is the same one who is risen. It is expressed in the emphatic "It is I myself" (ἐγώ εἰμι αὐτός).

Since Jesus does not mention the nail scars in his hands and feet (see John 20:20, 25, 27), showing his hands and feet may simply be a reference to his corporeality.[6] But Luke tones down the brutality associated with crucifixion, and it is more likely that he assumes his first readers would know that victims of crucifixion were normally nailed to the cross and that the wounds in his hands and feet would be visible. Luke leaves implicit that Jesus' resurrected body has not been transformed so that the disfigurement of his suffering has been erased.

24:41 – 43 While they were in a state of disbelief from their joy and marveling, he said to them, **"Do you have something here to eat?" They gave him a piece of broiled fish, and taking it he ate it before them** (ἔτι δὲ ἀπιστούντων αὐτῶν ἀπὸ τῆς χαρᾶς καὶ θαυμαζόντων εἶπεν αὐτοῖς· ἔχετέ τι βρώσιμον ἐνθάδε; οἱ δὲ ἐπέδωκαν αὐτῷ ἰχθύος ὀπτοῦ μέρος· καὶ λαβὼν ἐνώπιον αὐτῶν ἔφαγεν). The disciples are now plagued by a misunderstanding about the reports of Jesus' resurrection, and the ecstasy they experience when Jesus appears in their midst is so overwhelming that it does not quell their disbelief that he has been bodily raised. It requires the interpretation of the Word. Christianity is not simply a rapturous experience that sweeps over the soul and elates the believer. It involves the Word, which addresses the mind and heart.

This reference to eating is not a fellowship meal. By eating a piece of fish before them (see John 21:10), Jesus simply offers further proof that he is not a phantom on a walkabout from Hades. Incorporeal angels do not eat or drink and only pretend to do so (Tob 12:19; *T. Ab.* 4:9; Josephus, *Ant.* 1.9.2 §197; Philo, *Abraham* 118).[7] Nor do apparitions eat (Homer, *Od.* 11.219). Seeing Jesus eat augments their role as the eyewitnesses of the resurrection.[8]

24:44 – 45 He said to them, "These are my words that I spoke to you while I was still with you, that it is necessary for everything to be fulfilled that was written concerning me in the law of Moses, the Prophets, and the Psalms." Then he opened their minds to understand the Scriptures (εἶπεν δὲ πρὸς αὐτούς· οὗτοι οἱ λόγοι μου οὓς ἐλάλησα πρὸς ὑμᾶς ἔτι ὢν σὺν ὑμῖν, ὅτι δεῖ πληρωθῆναι πάντα τὰ γεγραμμένα ἐν τῷ νόμῳ Μωϋσέως καὶ τοῖς προφήταις καὶ ψαλμοῖς περὶ ἐμοῦ. τότε διήνοιξεν αὐτῶν τὸν νοῦν τοῦ συνιέναι τὰς γραφάς). When Jesus began his public ministry,

---

6. Johnson, *The Gospel of Luke*, 401.
7. Martin Goodman, "Do Angels Eat?" *JJS* 37 (1986): 160 – 70.

8. Johnson, *The Gospel of Luke*, 402.

he read the Scripture in the synagogue at Nazareth and announced its fulfillment (4:16–21). He ends his earthly ministry by showing how the Scriptures have been fulfilled. The disciples in Emmaus had their eyes opened (24:31); these disciples have their minds opened. Dillon concludes: "Only when the resurrected Christ demonstrated the fulfillment of prophecy in himself did puzzled Easter onlookers become prospective Easter witnesses (Luke 24:45–48)."[9]

Moses (the Pentateuch), the Prophets, and the Psalms may reflect a division of the Jewish Scriptures current at the time. The Psalms are named as the first book in the last division of sacred writings.[10] But it may be that Luke intends to highlight the Psalms as a key prophetic text outlining the necessity of a suffering Messiah. Dillon claims the Psalms are apt: "With their characteristic celebration of God's victories (and the righteous man's …) over human rebellion and wickedness, the Psalms offered prime attestation of the divine plan which brought about both suffering and the resurrection of Christ κατὰ τὸ ὡρισμένον."[11]

In 11Q5 27.2–11, David is described as "wise, and a light like the light of the sun," "discerning and perfect in all his paths before God and men." God "gave him a discerning and enlightened spirit," which enabled him to write the psalms and songs (numbered at 4,050). It concludes, "All these he spoke through (the spirit of) prophecy which had been given to him from before the Most High." In like manner, Luke cites the Psalms as prophetic literature, and David is specifically identified as a prophet in Acts 2:30 (see Luke 20:42). In Acts, the Psalms are regularly cited by the apostles as pointing to Jesus' suffering, resurrection, and exaltation (Acts 1:16, 20; 2:25, 30–35, 4:25; 13:33).

24:46 And he said to them, "Thus it stands written that the Christ should suffer and be raised from the dead on the third day" (καὶ εἶπεν αὐτοῖς ὅτι οὕτως γέγραπται παθεῖν τὸν χριστὸν καὶ ἀναστῆναι ἐκ νεκρῶν τῇ τρίτῃ ἡμέρᾳ). Jesus repeats what he has told the disciples before when he predicted his suffering and resurrection. What is significant is that the term "Son of Man," which was used in previous predictions of suffering and resurrection (9:22; 18:31–33; 24:7), is treated as synonymous with "the Christ" (Messiah).

24:47a-b And that repentance for the forgiveness of sins be preached in his name to all the nations (καὶ κηρυχθῆναι ἐπὶ τῷ ὀνόματι αὐτοῦ μετάνοιαν καὶ ἄφεσιν ἁμαρτιῶν εἰς πάντα τὰ ἔθνη). Jesus adds another dimension to what he declared to the disciples on the way to Emmaus about what the Scriptures reveal about his death. The Messiah was to suffer, die, and be raised, but the Scriptures also reveal that the message of repentance for the forgiveness of sins is to be taken to the rest of the world. Minear comments, "The fulfillment of one promise leads to the issuing of another, while all the promises are subordinated to a single goal, 'that repentance and forgiveness of sins is to be proclaimed in his name to all nations' (v. 47)."[12] "In his name" (ἐπὶ τῷ ὀνόματι αὐτοῦ) means "on the basis of his name."[13] This statement maps out the program for the next phase of the story, which continues in Acts.

A concordance quickly shows how prominent in Acts are the ideas of preaching, repentance, forgiveness of sins, "in Jesus' name," and "all the nations." The content of the preaching is about Jesus. The scope of the preaching is to all the nations. This creates the opportunity for repentance,

9. Dillon, "Previewing Luke's Project from His Prologue," 215–16.

10. David Flusser ("Wie in den Psalmen über mich geschrieben steht (Lk 24,44)," *Judaica* 48 [1992]: 40–42) notes that

4QMMT 3.17 refers to David and the Law and the Prophets.

11. Dillon, *From Eye-witnesses to Ministers of the Word*, 205.

12. Minear, *To Heal and to Reveal*, 132–33.

13. Marshall, *The Gospel of Luke*, 906.

which opens the door for the forgiveness of sins on the basis of Jesus' name — his death and resurrection. The disciples by their witness in Jerusalem are to provide new information to those who condemned the Christ out of their ignorance (Acts 3:17; 13:27). They are to press for a decision (Acts 2:38; 3:19; 5:31; 10:43; 13:38 – 39; 22:16; 26:18).

24:47c – 48 Beginning from Jerusalem, you are witnesses of these things (ἀρξάμενοι ἀπὸ Ἰερουσαλὴμ ὑμεῖς μάρτυρες τούτων). "Beginning from Jerusalem" (ἀρξάμενοι) is best taken as a masculine plural participle referring to "you are witnesses." From being the *goal* of Jesus' travels, Jerusalem now becomes the *starting point* for the testimony about him (Acts 1:8). This command fulfills another prophecy. Jerusalem is regarded as "the center of the nations" (Ezek 5:5; 38:12), and from there the word of the Lord shall go forth to the nations (Isa 2:3; Mic 4:2).

The story in Acts takes place in Jerusalem through chap. 7, but the apostles remain there and Jerusalem remains central even after the gospel expands into the world. Peter and John are sent from Jerusalem to Samaria to lay hands on those who accepted the word (Acts 8:14 – 17). Peter travels to Caesarea to meet the Roman centurion Cornelius but reports on what has happened to skeptics in Jerusalem (11:1 – 18). After every mission journey, Paul returns to Jerusalem (Acts 11:29 – 30; 15:2; 19:21; 20:16, 22; 21:13). Paul outlines his mission of proclaiming the gospel of Christ "by what I have said and done — by the power of signs and wonders, through the power of the Spirit of God. So from Jerusalem all the way around to Illyricum, I have fully proclaimed the gospel of Christ" (Rom 15:18 – 19).

The disciples move from being eyewitnesses to becoming ministers of the word (see 1:2). As witnesses, they no longer assume the passive role of observers but actively champion the gospel with their testimony (Acts 1:22; 20:21). Scobie remarks that Jesus' own journey motif reveals "the new Israel does not settle down to life in the land, but is sent forth, after Pentecost, upon a new series of journeys *from* Jerusalem and *from* the land."[14] Jesus leads them out to Bethany, and he will send the Spirit, who will lead them out even further.

24:49 And behold, I am sending the promise of my Father upon you. You are to stay in the city until you are clothed with power from on high (καὶ [ἰδοὺ] ἐγὼ ἀποστέλλω τὴν ἐπαγγελίαν τοῦ πατρός μου ἐφ' ὑμᾶς· ὑμεῖς δὲ καθίσατε ἐν τῇ πόλει ἕως οὗ ἐνδύσησθε ἐξ ὕψους δύναμιν). The disciples may not begin their journey yet. Nor should they skip town, as the disciples headed to Emmaus wanted to do. Despite Jerusalem's rejection of God's Messiah and their refusal to recognize the time of their visitation by God (19:44), the city will be the center of another divine visitation, this time by God's Spirit (Acts 1:8; 2:1 – 4), and the setting for God's renewal of Israel and the launching pad for the good news to be sent out into the world. Therefore, they must tarry in Jerusalem until they receive the "promise of my Father."

The assumption is that they will tarry together, not in isolation, and that they will have learned from Jesus' example to devote themselves to prayer (Acts 1:12 – 14). The opening scenes of Luke are filled with waiting people: Zechariah and Elizabeth, Mary, and Simeon and Anna. The gospel ends with waiting disciples, but the waiting is only to be temporary. Dillon notes, "The 'commission' is really only an appointment, and the Spirit is promised rather than bestowed; thus the actual inauguration of the mission, which is the very *raison d'être* of the Church, is saved for the second book."[15]

---

14. Scobie, "A Canonical Approach to Interpreting Luke," 342.

15. Dillon, *From Eye-Witnesses to Ministers of the Word*, 204.

Jesus does not specify what the "promise of the Father" is, and Luke must assume that the readers are familiar with Old Testament prophecies that speak of God's pouring out his Spirit (Isa 32:15; 44:3; Ezek 39:29; Joel 2:28 – 29). It is in Acts that the promise is fully identified as the Holy Spirit. Acts narrates the Holy Spirit's being poured out on the disciples so that they can begin to fulfill their charge (Acts 1:4 – 5; 2:2 – 4, 32 – 33). The same Holy Spirit that overshadowed Mary (Luke 1:35) and empowered Jesus will clothe them to fulfill their commission.

24:50 Then he led them out as far as Bethany, and lifting up his hands, he blessed them (ἐξήγαγεν δὲ αὐτοὺς [ἔξω] ἕως πρὸς Βηθανίαν, καὶ ἐπάρας τὰς χεῖρας αὐτοῦ εὐλόγησεν αὐτούς). Bethany is on the Mount of Olives (Acts 1:12). Luke gives no specific time marker in his gospel as to when the ascension will occur. In Acts 1:1 – 11, it occurs after forty days. It could be that he telescopes this event knowing that he will give further details in the opening of the second book.

Among the many explanations for the differences, Van Stempvoort is persuasive in arguing that the two accounts have different theological purposes.[16] The account in Luke is brief and appropriately worshipful, while the account in Acts examines more closely the disciples' response to the event. It answers such questions as: Why did Christ's earthly appearances end? Why did the end not come immediately? Departing on a cloud points to Jesus' future return on a cloud at the end (Luke 21:27).

At the conclusion of Sirach, the high priest Simeon II lifts his hands and blesses the whole congregation of Israelites, and the people bow in joyful worship (Sir 50:20 – 23). Hamm claims, "Like Simeon II for Ben Sira, Jesus was for Luke the culmination of Israel's life and worship."[17] Daube argues that Luke takes the reader back to the temple, where the story began with Zechariah in the temple during the Tamid service, the twice-daily sacrifice for the sins of the people. He maintains that Luke intends to show that "for the believers, the service from now on had a new meaning."[18] Brown claims, "It is not far-fetched to think that Luke has attached to the risen Jesus the fulfillment or replacement of the temple ritual."[19]

24:51 It happened that while he was blessing them, he parted from them and was being carried up into heaven (καὶ ἐγένετο ἐν τῷ εὐλογεῖν αὐτὸν αὐτοὺς διέστη ἀπ' αὐτῶν καὶ ἀνεφέρετο εἰς τὸν οὐρανόν). The phrase "was being carried up into heaven" (καὶ ἀνεφέρετο εἰς τὸν οὐρανόν) is absent from a small number of early texts,[20] but it is present in a wide variety of other witnesses and should be accepted. Jesus has already mentioned entering into his glory (24:26), and the preface to Acts describes his being taken up into heaven, using a different verb (ἀνελήμφθη; Acts 1:2). Had a copyist added the phrase in an attempt to harmonize the two accounts, one would expect that the same verb for "being taken up" would have been used rather than the more unusual verb that often means "to offer up" (ἀνεφέρετο). Also, the presence of this phrase in the original text

16. P. A. Van Stempvoort, "Interpretation of the Ascension in Luke and Acts," *NTS* 5 (1958): 30 – 42.

17. Hamm, "Tamid Service," 220.

18. David Daube, *The New Testament and Rabbinic Judaism* (New York: Arno, 1973), 234. Hamm ("Tamid Service," 219) claims that Sirach describes the Tamid service (so also Fearghus Ó Fearghail, "Sir 50,5 – 21: Yom Kippur or the Daily Whole-Offering?" *Bib* 59 [1978]: 301 – 16).

19. Brown, *The Birth of the Messiah*, 280 – 81.

20. ℵ* geo¹ D itᵃ, ᵇ, ᵈ, ᵉ, ff2, ʲ, ˡ. A copyist may have omitted the phrase because of a trick of the eye, since the next clause in v. 52 begins with the same four letters (καὶ αὐτοί). Or a redactor may have omitted it to eliminate the problem of the different timing of the ascension in Luke and Acts. In Luke, it appears to occur on the evening of Easter Sunday. In Acts 1:3 – 11, it occurs at the end of forty days with the disciples.

best explains the disciples' response of worship and praise (vv. 52 – 53). It is the proper reaction to witnessing a miracle.

Jesus' ascension has biblical models that would make it understandable to the witnesses. Enoch (Gen 5:24; Sir 44:16; Heb 11:5) and Elijah (2 Kgs 2:11; Sir 48:9; 1 Macc 2:58) were taken up (see also Ezra; 2 Esd 14:9), and there are also accounts of divine beings departing by ascending to heaven (Judg 13:20; Tob 12:20 – 21). It occurs in Greco-Roman literature (Euripedes, *Orest.* 1496; Livy, *Hist.* 1.16; Virgil, *Aen.* 9:657) as a confirmation of a person's divinity.[21] The difference is that these persons are taken up instead of dying. Jesus has died, was buried, and was raised from the dead by God, and now he is carried up to heaven.

24:52 – 53　And when they worshiped him, they returned to Jerusalem with great joy and were regularly in the temple praising God (καὶ αὐτοὶ προσκυνήσαντες αὐτὸν ὑπέστρεψαν εἰς Ἰερουσαλὴμ μετὰ χαρᾶς μεγάλης καὶ ἦσαν διὰ παντὸς ἐν τῷ ἱερῷ εὐλογοῦντες τὸν θεόν). The disciples' terror and doubts (24:37) have been replaced by faith that leads to worship. As a divine being, the worship of Jesus is appropriate and praising God is necessary. Hamm comments, "Luke is clear that worship of the God of Israel entails worship of the risen Jesus as Lord."[22] Satan had offered the kingdoms of the world if Jesus would worship him (4:5 – 8). Jesus refused with the response that one is to worship only God. Holmås contends, "In this way, the continuity is underlined between pious Israel and Jesus' disciples after the resurrection."[23] It also underscores the distinction between them and blind Israel (19:42, 44). They understand who Jesus is.

They worship "regularly" (διὰ παντός) in the temple, not "constantly" (see Acts 10:2 – 3). Their presence in the temple and the city is temporary (24:49, "until you are clothed with power from on high"). They await orders for their missionary task that is to begin in Jerusalem, and they do so in prayer. Verse 49 makes it clear that the temple is no longer central to salvation.

Theology in Application

1. Jesus' Bodily Resurrection

We are familiar today from novels and movies with stories of ghosts who come back from the dead. Ancient readers were also familiar with varieties of stories about those who appear to people after their deaths. There were accounts of disembodied spirits that looked as they did in life but appeared and disappeared at will and could not be touched, of corpses that temporarily came back to life, of heroes who came back to life and whose graves were known and revered, and of mortals who were translated into divine beings, often without death or whose death was in doubt, and appeared as they did in life or with completely cast-off bodies. Prince notes that Jesus' postresurrection appearances in Luke share some consistencies with these accounts of postmortem apparitions, but they also differ from them.[24]

21. Schweizer, *Luke*, 379.
22. Hamm, "Tamid Service," 230.
23. Holmås, " 'My House Shall Be a House of Prayer,' " 409.
24. Deborah Thompson Prince, "The 'Ghost' of Jesus: Luke 24 in Light of Ancient Narratives of Post-Mortem Apparitions," *JSNT* 29 (2007): 287 – 301.

That Jesus is dead and his tomb is known (23:46, 55) is consistent with stories of disembodied spirits, heroes, or reanimated corpses, but it is inconsistent with disappearance and translation traditions. Jesus' empty tomb (24:3, 6, 23 – 24) is consistent with stories about reanimated corpses but inconsistent with stories of disembodied spirits, heroes, and translation. Jesus' suddenly disappearing (24:31) and suddenly entering a room unseen (24:36) are consistent with stories of disembodied spirits but inconsistent with reanimated corpse traditions. The tactile inspection of Jesus' hands and feet to confirm his identity and to establish that he is flesh and bone (24:39) is consistent with the expectation that the appearance of the apparitions of resuscitated heroes is unchanged in death but inconsistent with stories about disembodied spirits. Eating in the disciples' presence (24:42 – 43) is consistent only with reanimated body traditions. Being taken bodily up to heaven (24:51) is consistent only with translation/apotheosis traditions and none of the others.

Prince argues from these comparisons that the purpose of the various details in the postresurrection accounts (the empty tomb, the ability to appear and disappear at will, the wounds that can be touched, eating to show that he has flesh and bones) "is an attempt to disorient the reader in order to reconfigure the traditions known to the author and reader in light of the disciples' extraordinary experience of the resurrected Jesus."[25] Jesus is not a reanimated corpse, a disembodied soul, or an apparition of a dead hero. The resurrected Jesus is the same one who had been with the disciples in Galilee, but resurrection is not resuscitation, rejuvenation, or regeneration. It is also not immortality of the soul. Jesus has not become a pale shade. The resurrection is a physical resurrection. Jesus' body does not lie moldering in the grave; death, the last enemy, has been fully conquered. Jesus' body and spirit have been raised to life. His resurrection is something vastly different and has no true parallel in human experience.

Showing the disciples that the scars of crucifixion remain after his resurrection does not only demonstrate that his resurrection is physical; it makes clear that the resurrection did not simply reverse an unfortunate tragedy that can now be forgotten. We proclaim Christ crucified (1 Cor 1:23; 2:2), not simply Christ glorified, and we boast in the cross of Christ our Lord (Gal 6:14). His suffering and death were a divine necessity tied to the forgiveness of sins that brings acquittal before God and an end to the enmity that separated us from God.

2. The Reality of the Resurrection for Dim-sighted Disciples

The doubt is not dispelled by what the disciples see with their very eyes and touch with their hands. Luke tells us that even after Jesus showed the disciples his hands and feet, "they were in a state of disbelief" (24:41). It seemed too good to be true. The eyes can be deceived. Two things convince them of its reality.

25. Ibid., 297.

First, Jesus teaches the necessity of his passion and prophecy of his resurrection in Scripture. The underlying conviction is that Old Testament prophecy concerning the Messiah is shrouded in mystery and that Jesus is the only one who can unlock this mystery. Fee's comments relating to Paul's discussion of how foolish a crucified Messiah looks from the vantage point of benighted human wisdom explains why Jesus himself must unveil the mystery of the Scripture for the disciples: "*Messiah* meant power, splendor, triumph; *crucifixion* meant weakness, humiliation, defeat."[26]

Humans, including the disciples who were with Jesus from the beginning, can only understand the eschatological meaning of his death and how it fits with the prophecies in Scripture with divine help. Jesus reveals that mystery through his definitive interpretation. He alone can open blind eyes and soften hardened hearts to open the way to understanding. In this context, Luke also affirms that the Old Testament can only be understood in relation to Jesus (see 2 Cor 3:12 – 18).

Second, the reception of divine power to obey the commission to become witnesses to the nations also confirms the reality of the resurrection. When the disciples go into the world with power and authority, they recognize that "Jesus is himself present in his power."[27] Jesus blessed them, but this blessing did not bring material blessings but provision to fulfill their commission. The surprising ending to the parable in 11:5 – 13 understands the Holy Spirit as God's greatest gift to those who ask!

3. The Import of the Ascension

(1) The ascension marks the point when the physically resurrected Jesus whom the disciples have known leaves them (see 5:35). It marks the conclusion of Jesus' life on earth, his earthly biography, and his entrance into celestial glory (24:26).[28] The ascension "rounds off an era of salvation history."[29] Christ's redeeming work has been completed (John 6:62; 17:4 – 11; Phil 2:5 – 11; Heb 1:3; 9:11 – 12), he is taken up in glory (1 Tim 3:16), and he reigns eternally from heaven (Luke 1:32 – 33).

(2) It is a visible event, in keeping with the physical resurrection, not the journey of a soul to heaven. Unlike Jesus' miraculous virginal conception and his resurrection, it is observable as a concrete display of his new status.[30] He is vindicated by God and taken home to God. But it is no less mysterious. It also requires heavenly messengers to explain it. Because they understand Jesus' departure to signify his vindication and exaltation, the disciples are not anguished but filled with joy.

(3) The ascension answers how it is that Jesus, declared Son of God in power (Rom 1:3 – 4), now sits on the right hand of God (Acts 2:33; Eph 1:20; Col 3:1; Heb 1:3; 8:1; 10:12; 12:2; 1 Pet 3:22), and it establishes a more intimate connection be-

26. Gordon Fee, *First Epistle to the Corinthians* (NICNT; Grand Rapids: Eerdmans, 1987), 75.

27. Dillon, *From Eye-Witnesses to Ministers of the Word*, 210.

28. Paul regarded the appearance of the Lord to him to be the *last* one, if "last of all" in 1 Cor 15:8 can be taken this way.

29. Zwiep, *The Ascension of the Messiah in Lukan Christology*, 171.

30. Franklin, *Christ the Lord: A Study in the Purpose and Theology of Luke-Acts*, 39.

tween heaven and earth. Jesus' resurrection does not entail simply his return to earthly existence. He is in heaven ("heaven" is repeated four times in Acts 1:10 – 11; see also Acts 3:21), and his presence there means that heaven is no longer inaccessible (Deut 30:12; Prov 30:4; Bar 3:29; see Rom 10:6 – 7). Jesus, who died like a criminal on a cross, now reigns as the living Lord from heaven. He moves from one sphere to another but does not abandon his disciples. He is seen by Stephen (Acts 7:55 – 56) and Paul (9:1 – 9; 22:14) and is present through his Spirit (16:7), but his "visible presence is not necessary for faith" for the rest who will not have this audio-visual experience.[31]

(4) The ascension is interpreted by Paul as indicative of his defeat of every power and authority (1 Cor 15:24; Col 2:15). He took captivity captive (Eph 4:8 KJV) and governs the whole universe from heaven and secures his followers from all cosmic threats.

(5) The ascension foreshadows Jesus' return to earth (Acts 1:11; Col 3:4). The curtain will reopen, and he will descend from heaven to bring universal restoration (1 Thess 4:17; 2 Thess 1:7; Rev 1:7). Zwiep comments, "the ascension is a confirmation of the certainty of the promise of the parousia. Jesus went up to heaven not to remain there forever, but to return on the Day of Judgment."[32]

(6) The ascension may mark the completion of Jesus' earthly work, but it also opens up a new era in which his work is continued through the mission of the disciples (Acts 1:1 – 8). The ascension opens the way for the sending of the Holy Spirit, who acts for God and Christ on earth and is not limited by the physical restraints that Jesus' humanity placed on him. He is beyond but not beyond reach through the Holy Spirit. Since the ascension marks the end of Christ's earthly ministry, it protects the church from frauds claiming to have witnessed an appearance of Jesus with ever new revelations. It also protects the church from the multitude of chimerical, fly-by-night teachers in the world who falsely claim to have authority and wisdom equal to Christ.

(7) The ascension should not be envisioned naturalistically as if Jesus had some divine jet pack that rocketed him to a distant location in the sky. The ascension is not like a scene from a science-fiction movie, which can then easily be dismissed as a fantasy that only a naïve child can believe. Luke describes something that is supernatural from an earthly perspective using spatial categories, which human experience, bound by space and time, can comprehend. Calvin recognized: "When Christ is said to be in heaven, we must not view him as dwelling among the spheres and numbering the stars," as if we needed to "build a cottage for him among the planets."[33] Oden avers, "It is doubtful that the language of descent and ascent in the New Testament ever really intended such a flat, unmetaphorical, literally three-story picture, even in the first century."[34] Jesus passes from this earthly sphere into a heavenly, divine sphere.

---

31. John F. Maile, "The Ascension in Luke-Acts," *TynBul* 37 (1986): 57 – 58.

32. Zwiep, *The Ascension of the Messiah in Lukan Christology*, 169.

33. John Calvin, *Second Defense of the Faith concerning the Sacraments in Answer to Joachim Westphal, Tracts and Treatises* (trans. Henry Beveridge; Grand Rapids: Eerdmans, 1958), 2:290.

34. Thomas C. Oden, *The Word of Life* (San Francisco: Harper, 1992), 508.

Theology of Luke

Bock maintains:

> Luke shows an interest in both history and theology, twin emphases evidenced not only in his attention to the time sequence of events and teachings, but in their topical and theological relationship as well. He writes as a theologian and a pastor, but is directed by the history which preceded him.[1]

Luke conveys aspects of theology through historical narrative and "sets himself to write the continuation of the biblical story, not only to defend the Christian movement, but above all to defend God's ways in the world."[2] The following are some of the key themes in Luke.

The Divine "Must"

Luke thinks in terms of "one unfolding plan in which important events are carefully prepared for and integrated with one another."[3] Showing how this plan unfolds may be what Luke means when he determined to write an "orderly" account (1:3). The outworking of the plan is determined by a divine "must." Cadbury observes, "There is a necessity about the course which Luke's story takes, a 'must,' to use Luke's own favorite auxiliary, rather than a mere predictive 'shall,' a necessity revealed by Old Testament prophecy or by visions."[4] The "must" covers all of Jesus' life and ministry. Jesus must be in his Father's house (2:49); he must "proclaim the good news of the reign of God," for he was sent for this purpose (4:43). This necessity also involves seeking out and saving the lost (19:5) and rejoicing over their recovery (15:32). As the Son of Man, he must undergo great suffering, and be killed, and on the third day be raised (9:22; see also 13:33; 17:25; 22:37; 24:7, 44; Acts 17:3). The "divine necessity" also involves a period of waiting before the end (21:9; Acts 1:16; 3:21). This interval gives time for the church's mission to the world to proclaim salvation in Jesus Christ, "for there is no other name under heaven given to mankind by which we must be saved" (Acts 4:12).

1. Darrell L. Bock, "Luke, Gospel of," *DJG*, 498.
2. Johnson, *The Gospel of Luke*, 10.
3. Giles, "The Church in the Gospel of Luke," 122.
4. Cadbury, *The Making of Luke-Acts*, 304.

(1) The divine necessity shows that the history of Jesus (through Acts) is rooted in God's plan. These are divinely authorized events. God's plan for the gathering of Israel and for the world's redemption is not something hidden, but the blueprint can be found in the prophetic foretelling of the Old Testament.

(2) It functions "as an imperative, a summons to obedience."[5] It is not like the "neutral power of fate." The plan of God is foreordained, but an individual's participation in it is not predetermined. Humans cannot sit back and passively wait for God to accomplish everything. The divine necessity has an imperatival aspect as God requires human action to respond.[6] For example, Cosgrove notes, "Jesus is no passive pawn of divine necessity in Luke's Gospel; he is the executor of that necessity."[7] Whereas in Mark 1:12, the Spirit "sent" Jesus into the wilderness where he was tempted by Satan, in Luke 4:1, Jesus initiates the temptation by venturing into the wilderness where he is led by the Spirit. Jesus also "sets his face" to go to Jerusalem, fully conscious of what awaits him there (9:51), and he will not be diverted from this purpose by threats (13:31 – 33).

(3) The imperatival aspect does not mean that everything is now left to human effort. Luke records God's miraculous interventions that guarantee that God's purposes will be accomplished. God remains in control of history.[8]

(4) The divine plan involves surprise reversals. Throughout Luke and Acts, those who receive healing and grace and who respond are not those one might expect would respond.

Universal Welcome to Outcasts, Sinners, and Gentiles

Luke emphasizes God's forgiveness (5:20) that results in a universal welcome to outcasts and sinners who are to be gathered into the people of God. In the temple, Simeon proclaims Jesus to be "your salvation, which you have prepared in the sight of all peoples, a light for revelation to the Gentiles and glory of your people Israel" (2:30 – 32, citing Isa 49:6; cf. 40:5). In describing John's preaching as an immersion of repentance for (or "on the basis of") the forgiveness of sins, Mark and Matthew quote only Isa 40:3 (Matt 3:3; Mark 1:3), "A voice of one calling: 'In the wilderness prepare the way for the Lord, make straight in the desert a highway for our God.'" Luke extends the quotation to include Isa 40:4 – 5: "every valley shall be filled, and every mountain and hill shall be brought low, and the crooked [roads] will be made straight, and the rough roads smooth; and all flesh shall see the salvation of God" (Luke 3:4 – 6). Luke shows that the way of the Lord leads to all flesh, to the Gentiles.

Hints of what will happen after Jesus' death, resurrection, and ascension appear in the first sermon at the synagogue in Nazareth (4:24 – 30). Jesus refers to the record

---

5. Cosgrove, "The Divine ΔΕΙ in Luke-Acts," 183, 189.
6. Ibid., 171.
7. Ibid., 180.
8. Ibid., 187.

of God's gracious acts to Gentiles: the widow of Zarephath helped by Elijah during a time of famine in Israel, and Naaman the Syrian, the only leper who was cleansed during the time of Elisha. The mention of the Gentiles who received God's help when Israel was bereft provoked the wrath of the synagogue. God's extension of mercy toward Gentiles remains a sore spot in Acts (see Acts 13:42 – 50; 22:21 – 23), but Luke's narrative makes it clear that they are recipients of God's grace. They are not worthy according to traditional Jewish criteria (Luke 7:4 – 6) but because of their faith. Jesus declares that the Gentile centurion, who never meets him in person, exhibits more faith than anyone else he has encountered in Israel (7:9).

Matthew's version of the parable of the lamp has it lit and set on a lampstand to give light for all those in the house (5:15). Luke repeats the parable twice (8:16; 11:33), but the lamp is placed on a lampstand so that "those who enter [may] see the light." This gospel puts no restrictions on who may enter. All are invited to do so. In Luke's version of the parable of the great banquet, the master commands his servants to scout the country roads and along the hedges and compel people to come in so that his house might be filled (14:23). In his final instructions to the disciples in the gospel, Jesus tells them that everything has happened according to the Scriptures and "that repentance for the forgiveness of sins be preached in his name to all the nations" (24:46 – 47; see Acts 1:8; 13:47). This theme is sounded again in the ending of Acts (Acts 28:28).

That Jesus will be concerned in his ministry with social outcasts becomes clear from his first public sermon. He proclaims good news to the poor, liberty to the captives, healing for the blind, and release for the oppressed (4:16 – 21). This group includes sinners. God's action to redeem (1:16, 78; 7:16) should evoke joy, and Luke's narrative is replete with the language of joy for those who respond to God's offer of forgiveness[9] and of praise to God for miraculous intervention (2:20; 4:15; 5:25 – 26; 7:16; 13:13; 17:15; 18:43; 23:47).

But not all respond warmly to Jesus' mission. When Jesus calls Levi, a tax collector, to follow him, he responds with a celebration banquet that includes a large crowd of tax collectors and others. The Pharisees voice a complaint that runs through the narrative, "Why do you eat and drink with tax collectors and sinners?" (cf. 15:1 – 2). Jesus' answer — "I have not come to call the righteous to repentance but sinners" (5:27 – 32) — sounds a key theme (see 19:10, "The Son of Man came to seek and to save the lost") and explains why he is dismissed as "a friend of tax collectors and sinners" (7:34).

Luke alone records the incident of a woman who crashes a dinner party at the house of Simon the Pharisee, in which he declares that her sins have been forgiven

---

9. The verb "rejoice" (χαίρω) appears twelve times (six times in Matt, twice in Mark). The noun joy (χαρά) appears eight times (six times in Matt, once in Mark). The noun "exultation" (ἀγαλλίασις) appears twice (absent from Matt and Mark) and the verb "exult" (ἀγαλλιάω) appears twice (once in Matt, not at all in Mark). The verb "to leap" (for joy) (σκιρτάω) appears three times (absent from Matt and Mark).

and chastises the Pharisee for his judgmental attitude (7:36 – 50). This incident shows that the Savior's coming will not be hailed by everyone. He will create a division within Israel (12:51 – 53), and those who reject God's purpose for themselves will be cut off (7:29 – 30). This division is illustrated by the parable of the Pharisee and the toll collector (18:9 – 14) and the account of the conversion of Zacchaeus, the rich, chief tax collector (19:1 – 10), which follows the very rich ruler's decision to decline Jesus' invitation to follow him (18:18 – 24). Division even occurs at the crucifixion. Luke is the only gospel to record the repentance of one of the criminals crucified with Jesus, but the other remains adamantly unrepentant (23:39 – 43).

The Samaritans are also to be gathered into the people of God, and they figure prominently in the gospel. After a Samaritan village rejects Jesus (9:51 – 56), their prospects look grim. The parable of the merciful Samaritan (10:25 – 37) and the story of the one leper of ten whom Jesus cleansed who returned to thank Jesus and give glory to God (17:11 – 19) bode well for their positive response to the gospel that is recorded in Acts 8:5 – 25.

Prayer

Luke is the evangelist of prayer. Nine references to Jesus' praying or teaching about prayer appear in Luke, seven of which are not recorded in the other gospels. Luke is the primary source both for knowledge of Jesus' prayer life and for instruction in prayer. Luke alone tells us that prayer was associated with many of the red-letter days in Jesus' life. Jesus was praying at his immersion when the heavens opened and the Holy Spirit descended on him and a voice from heaven announced, "You are my Son" (3:21 – 22). In 5:16, Jesus withdrew to the wilderness and prayed before his first clash with the Jewish leaders. Jesus prayed all night on the mountain prior to choosing his disciples (6:13 – 16). Only Luke tells us that Jesus was praying alone with his disciples when he asked them, "Who do you say I am?" and he made his first announcement of his passion (9:18 – 22).

At his transfiguration, Luke alone records that Jesus took Peter, James, and John up to the mountain to pray and tells us that the appearance of his face changed and his garment became dazzling white *as he was praying* (9:28 – 29). The face mirrors the inner state of a person, and this detail suggests that something transpired while he was praying. The event serves as a hinge between his ministry in Galilee and his journey to Jerusalem. In 9:51, he set his face to go to Jerusalem after Moses and Elijah conversed with him about his *exodos*, his departure (9:31), which was to be accomplished at Jerusalem. In 10:21 – 22, Jesus rejoiced at the return of the seventy from their mission and offered up a prayer of thanksgiving to God. Luke alone reports that Jesus was praying and the disciples requested him to teach them to pray, as John taught his disciples (11:1).

Luke also records unique parables related to prayer and its necessity: the parable of the friend who goes to his sleepy neighbor to request some bread for an unexpected guest who arrives at midnight (11:5 – 8), and the parable of the widow who badgers a wicked judge until she gets a judgment in her favor (18:1 – 8). He includes a parable that presents the contrasting prayers of a Pharisee and a tax collector in the temple (18:9 – 14). The Pharisee asks for nothing because he assumes that he needs nothing; the tax collector begs God for mercy because he recognizes that he has nothing and is nothing. At the Last Supper, Luke alone registers that *before* Jesus prophesies that Peter will deny him three times, he tells him that Satan had asked to sift him but he has prayed for him so that his faith would not fail (22:31 – 32). He then confidently commands him to strengthen his brothers after he turns. On the Mount of Olives, Luke emphasizes that Jesus exhorts his disciples to pray that they may not enter into temptation and prays this himself (22:40, 46). He presents Jesus as buoyed by his prayer and prepared for the upcoming battle. Luke alone also records Jesus' prayers to the Father on the cross (23:34, 46).

In the Lord's Prayer, "Jesus did not seek to teach us a prayer, but to teach us to pray — and that of course means at the same time to liberate us from anxious and superstitious use of formulas."[10] Prayer for Jesus is drawing near to the Father. All of the recorded prayers of Jesus begin with "Father." Other characteristics of prayer in Luke include the following:

- they are marked by thanksgiving and praise (2:37 – 38; 10:21 – 22)
- they intercede for others (10:1 – 2; 22:31 – 34)
- they contain a sense of urgency (11:9 – 13; 18:1 – 8)
- they include confession (18:9 – 14; 23:39 – 43)
- they open one up to learning God's will (9:28 – 31; 22:39 – 46)

Salvation

Giles states, "Luke is rightly called 'Evangelist' and only properly understood when we see that he wrote his Gospel to confront men with the ever present person and word of Jesus."[11] The coming of Jesus is the fulfillment of God's promise to rescue Israel and to bring salvation (1:46 – 55; 1:68 – 79; 2:9 – 14, 30 – 32).[12] The verb "to save" (σῴζω) is used not only for the cure of physical diseases but also for a person's spiritual restoration, since sickness is viewed as the outworking of evil (6:9; 7:50;

---

10. Gerhard Ebeling, *On Prayer* (trans. J. W. Leitch; Philadelphia: Fortress, 1966), 47.

11. Giles, "The Church in the Gospel of Luke," 122.

12. The word "savior" (σωτήρ) appears four times in Luke (1:47; 2:11) and Acts (5:31, 13:23) and only once in the other gospels (John 4:42). "Salvation" (ἡ σωτηρία) appears ten times in Luke (1:69, 71, 77; 19:9) and Acts (4:12, 7:25, 13: 26, 47; 16:17, 27:34) and only once in the other gospels (John 4:22, excluding the textual variant in Mark 16:9). "Salvation" (σωτήριος) occurs three times in Luke (2:30, 3:6) and Acts (28:28) and only twice (Eph. 6:17; Titus 2:11) in the rest of the New Testament.

8:12, 36, 48, 50; 9:24; 13:23; 17:19; 18:26, 42; 19:10; 23:35). The classic statement appears in 19:10: "The Son of Man came to seek and to save the lost."

A fundamental condition for salvation is repentance and faith. Words related to repentance are prominent in Luke, as are illustrations of repentance, such as the prodigal son who "came to himself" (15:17), and Zacchaeus, who announces his giving half of his goods to the poor and restitution to those he defrauded (19:8). Comparing Luke 5:32 with its parallels in Matt 9:13; Mark 2:17, Luke has the added phrase "I have not come to call the righteous to repentance but sinners." The gospel concludes with Jesus' declaring God's purpose as outlined in the Scriptures "that repentance for the forgiveness of sins be preached in his name to all the nations" (24:47). From Luke we learn that repentance is urged on all people with a sense of great urgency (13:3, 5). It is an attitude of life, not simply a onetime decision. It is linked to joy (15:1–2, 6–7, 9–10, 22–24, 32), because it looks to the future rather than bemoaning the past (22:32). It has ethical implications that should show up, for example, in one's attitude toward possessions and one's care for the poor. Being transformed by the gospel has social ramifications.

The stringent attitude toward wealth in Luke's gospel suggests that "Luke is primarily taken up with the rich members, their concerns, and the problems which they pose for the community."[13] It begins with the preaching of John the Baptist demanding that repentance means giving one of two cloaks to someone who has none, giving food (not extra food) to those who have nothing, and refraining from dishonest practices in a lust to get more and more (3:10–14; see also 14:12–14, 21). The beatitudes for the poor (6:20–22) are counterbalanced by a series of corresponding woes on the rich. In Luke's version of the interpretation of the parable of the sower, the thorns that choke the Word are "cares and riches and the pleasures of life" (8:14; see 21:34). The parallel in Mark 4:19 has "the worries of this life, the deceitfulness of wealth and the desires for other things." For Luke, it is not the "deceit" (NEB, "false glamour") of wealth but wealth itself that suffocates the fruit. In the extended explanation of the parable of the unrighteous agent who is commended for being prudent (16:1–13), possessions are identified as "Mammon." Green describes it as "an almost hypostasized power with respect to which one can never remain ambivalent, neutral or passive."[14] The Pharisees are condemned as "lovers of money," and they scoff at the idea that one cannot serve both God and Mammon (16:14–15). Wealth has a power that can make concern to acquire and retain it foremost in one's life. Jesus' teaching is clear: one cannot be devoted to making a profit and be equally devoted to God.

If some thought that riches were a sign of God's reward for godliness, the parable of the rich man and Lazarus debunks that myth (16:19–31). Those who gain the

---

13. Robert J. Karris, "Poor and Rich: The Lukan *Sitz im Leben*," in *Perspectives on Luke-Acts* (ed. C. H. Talbert; Danville, VA: Association of Baptist Professors of Religion, 1978), 124.

14. Joel B. Green, *The Theology of the Gospel of Luke* (Cambridge: Cambridge Univ. Press, 1995), 148.

world are sure to lose their soul in the process (9:25). Real treasure can only be stored in heaven (12:21–34) by sharing it with others in need (16:9–13). Jesus concedes how hard it is for those who have riches to enter the reign of God (18:24), but with God even this miracle is possible. Zacchaeus, the rich tax baron, becomes the model of one who enters the reign of God by prudently unloading his wealth in giving half of his goods to the poor and making fourfold restitution to those he has defrauded.

Luke records Jesus' rigorous demand that only those who renounce all that they have are able to be his disciples (14:33). He notes Simon, James, and John "*left everything*" to follow Jesus (5:11; contrast Mark 1:18, 20, where Peter and Andrew leave their nets and James and John leave their father). Levi also is portrayed as "*leaving everything*" to follow Jesus (5:28). Méndez-Moratella comments, "It is a Lukan feature to show the change of allegiance towards God via a change in attitude toward wealth."[15] Jesus tells the ruler to sell "*all*" that he has and give to the poor (18:22; see 12:33). The demand does not require "becoming financially indigent" but reveals that one has rightly mastered one's possessions and uses them in service to God."[16]

Jesus as Rejected Prophet

Important characters in the story of the birth of Jesus are filled with the Spirit: Elizabeth (1:41), Zechariah (1:67), Simeon (2:27), and Anna (2:36). It is the Spirit of prophecy that predicts John's and Jesus' future roles. The beginning of Jesus' ministry is marked by the Spirit's coming on him. At his baptism, the Spirit comes down on him bodily as a dove (3:22). In his inaugural sermon at Nazareth, Jesus quotes Isa 61:1 in 4:18, "the Spirit of the Lord is upon me," and he announces that "Scripture has been fulfilled" on that day (4:21). Moses predicted that God would raise up from the people a prophet like him and they must listen to him or be severed from the people (Acts 3:22–23; 7:37). God confirms that Jesus is this prophet at the transfiguration when the divine voice from the cloud orders the disciples, "Listen to him!" (9:35). But he is much more than a prophet. He is the chosen Son, and Moses and Elijah are overshadowed in more ways than one as they fade from view in this scene (9:33–36).

The admiring crowds recognize that in Jesus a great prophet has arisen among them because, like Moses (Acts 7:22), he is mighty in word and deed (7:16–17; 24:19). Even opponents recognize something prophetic about his ministry (7:39). Like a prophet, he utters woes (6:24–26; 11:42–52) and gives prophetic warnings and dire predictions about Jerusalem, using cosmic imagery (17:22–37; 21:5–36). As a prophet, however, Jesus is destined to be rejected just as the prophets of old were (4:24; 6:22–23; 11:47–50; Acts 7:52). The trend is set at Jesus' first public sermon in Nazareth. He identifies himself as a prophet who will not be accepted in his home country (4:24), and in doing so he uses a distinctive speech with the word "amen"

---

15. Méndez-Moratella, *The Paradigm of Conversion in Luke*, 91.   16. Ibid., 93.

(ἀμήν). "Amen" is the normal response to the speech of someone else, but Jesus uses it to validate his own speech beforehand, which reveals a prophetic consciousness.[17] He identifies himself with the work of Elijah and Elisha (4:25 – 27). The Nazareth synagogue validates his prophecy almost immediately by trying to kill him. When the Pharisees warn Jesus about Herod's desire to kill him, he says that he will be on his way because it is unthinkable for a prophet to be killed anywhere but Jerusalem, which is the city that murders the prophets and stones the messengers sent to her (13:32 – 35).

The glory of Jesus' mighty works and deeds are coupled with dire predictions of his death. At a seemingly climactic moment of success, when the crowds are extolling him as the second coming of one of the ancient prophets and Peter goes even further by identifying him as "the Messiah of God," Jesus immediately announces his suffering, rejection, and death (9:18 – 22). When everyone is astonished at the greatness of God that is working through him in his mighty deeds, Jesus again announces his betrayal (9:43 – 45). Even at the glorious moment of his transfiguration, his impending death surfaces when Moses and Elijah confer with him about his "exodus, which he was about to fulfill in Jerusalem" (9:30 – 31).[18]

The penalty for rejecting Jesus is horrifying. In various forms, Jesus prophesies the utter destruction of this generation and Jerusalem seven times in Luke (11:49 – 51; 13:1 – 9, 34 – 35; 19:41 – 44; 20:16; 21:20 – 24; 23:28 – 31). As the rejected stone (20:17), "Jesus will become the 'cornerstone' not of the temple in Jerusalem but of a new temple of God 'not made with hands' (Acts 7:48). With such traditional imagery Luke made clear that the locus of God's presence and the identification of God's people no longer were to be found in the house or city of national Judaism."[19]

The Geographical Movement of the Good News

Witherington notes that both Luke and Acts "bear some striking resemblance to the Greek κατὰ γένος style of arranging one's history, whereby the work proceeds along geographical as well as chronological lines." The prime example is the work of the historian Ephorus. He confined his discussion to events in a geographical or cultural region and developed the narrative chronologically. Witherington claims that "Ephorus's approach became standard for Greek historians after him" and that Luke adopted this method as well.[20]

In the gospel, the background and introduction to Jesus' ministry occurs in Jerusalem and Judea (1:5 – 4:13). It is followed by the account of Jesus' Galilean ministry (4:14 – 9:56). Then comes the long circuitous journey to Jerusalem, the so-called

---

17. Johnson, *The Gospel of Luke*, 80.

18. Tannehill, *Unity of Luke-Acts*, 98 – 99.

19. E. Earle Ellis, "Luke, Gospel according to," *ISBE*, 185.

20. Ben Witherington, III, *The Acts of the Apostles: A Socio-Rhetorical Commentary* (Grand Rapids: Eerdmans, 1998), 34.

travel narrative (9:51 – 19:44). The final chapters depict Jesus' ministry in Jerusalem and his death and resurrection (19:45 – 24:53).[21] The movement in Acts is recorded in summaries describing the progress (Acts 6:7; 9:31; 12:24; 16:5; 19:20; 28:30 – 31), which create six distinct panels: Jerusalem (Acts 1 – 8:1a); Judea and Samaria (Acts 8:1b – 40); Phoenicia and Syria (Acts 9:1 – 12:23); Asia Minor (Acts 12:25 – 16:4); Macedonia and Achaia (Acts 16:6 – 19:19); and Jerusalem to Rome (Acts 19:21 – 28:31).[22]

This method of arranging his history has theological ramifications. In Acts, the progress of the gospel to new regions is theologically significant as the fulfillment of Jesus' prophecy in Acts 1:8. It also marks how the gospel breaks through cultural barriers as it crosses over successfully from a Jewish milieu to a Gentile milieu. The inclusion of Gentiles in salvation is hinted at in various places in Luke (2:30 – 32; 4:25 – 27; 7:1 – 10; 8:39), and the geographical movement of the gospel is the only way "all flesh shall see the salvation of God" (3:6). Although Jerusalem is central in the gospel and Acts, the people of the world will not come trekking to Jerusalem to bask in its holy aura. The Christian missionaries will take the gospel to them — some going out to new lands they have never known, others going back to their homelands.

Jerusalem is literally pivotal in the history of Luke-Acts.[23] The last six chapters of the gospel and the first seven chapters of Acts take place in Jerusalem. Luke refers to it thirty-one times in the gospel and fifty-nine times in Acts. To compare, it is mentioned only thirty-five times in Matthew, Mark, and John combined. The action begins in the sanctuary of the temple in Jerusalem with a priest offering incense and being struck mute for doubting the angel Gabriel's announcement of what God is about to do. The gospel ends with the disciples rejoicing and blessing God in the temple in Jerusalem after witnessing the ministry of Jesus and his resurrection. The climax of the devil's tempting of Jesus occurs on the wing tip of the temple of Jerusalem (4:9 – 12).

Jesus is always on the move, but his primary destination is Jerusalem. Despite his awe-inspiring success in Capernaum, he strikes out into new territory because he *must* be on his way to proclaim the good news of God's reign in other towns (4:43). In the travel narrative, this centripetal movement toward Jerusalem is made explicit (9:51). He goes to Jerusalem "because it is impossible for a prophet to be killed outside of Jerusalem" (13:33). It is where his "exodus" will be accomplished (9:31). The result of his peripatetic ministry is that the message spread "throughout the province of Judea, beginning in Galilee" (Acts 10:37), but it culminates in Jerusalem.

Jerusalem does not become the permanent headquarters of the Christian way. In Acts, the gospel moves away from Jerusalem. Jesus prophesies that a time will come

---

21. G. W. Trompf, *The Idea of Historical Recurrence in Western Thought* (Berkeley: Univ. of California Press, 1979), 131.
22. James Moffatt, *An Introduction to the Literature of the*

New Testament (New York: Scribners, 1922), 284 – 85.
23. See Chance, *Jerusalem, the Temple and the New Age in Luke-Acts.*

when disciples must abandon Jerusalem when it is about to be destroyed (21:20 – 21). The implication is that the gospel is on the move and can have no holy headquarters. Its geographical center will shift like tectonic plates, as we are witnessing today.[24] In Stephen's sermon in Acts 7, he uses the tabernacle image to describe God as living in a tent, which provides no permanent place of worship. God does not have a resting place like a temple, a static edifice that is immovable (Acts 7:44 – 50), and it is not rigidly bound to any land. Likewise, the movement of God's Spirit cannot be rigidly bound to a land, a people, a culture. It will reach beyond Jerusalem to the ends of the earth.

24. See Philip Jenkins, *The Next Christendom: The Coming of Global Christianity* (rev. ed.; Oxford: Oxford Univ. Press, 2007); *The New Faces of Christianity: Believing the Bible in the* *Global South* (Oxford: Oxford Univ. Press, 2006); *God's Continent: Christianity, Islam and Europe's Religious Crisis* (Oxford: Oxford Univ. Press, 2007).

Scripture and Apocrypha Index

Leviticus

Proverbs

Luke

2 Corinthians

Galatians

Ephesians

Philippians

Index of Other Ancient Literature

Jewish War

Life

Philo

Against Flaccus

Allegorical Interpretation

On Abraham

On Rewards and Punishments

Subject Index

Author Index

We want to hear from you. Please send your comments about this book to us in care of zreview@zondervan.com. Thank you.

ZONDERVAN.com/
AUTHORTRACKER
follow your favorite authors